P9-DVP-901

Ducks, Geese & Swans of North America

Ducks, Geese

A completely new and expanded version of the
classic work by F. H. Kortright

& Swans of North America

by

FRANK C. BELLROSE

With the Assistance of
Glen C. Sanderson, Helen C. Schultz, and Arthur S. Hawkins

Illustrations by T. M. Shortt and Frank C. Bellrose, Jr.

A WILDLIFE MANAGEMENT INSTITUTE BOOK
SPONSORED JOINTLY WITH THE ILLINOIS NATURAL HISTORY SURVEY

Published by
STACKPOLE BOOKS

DUCKS, GEESE & SWANS OF NORTH AMERICA

Published by
STACKPOLE BOOKS
Cameron and Kelker Streets
Harrisburg, Pa. 17105

Second Edition, First Printing 1976
Second Edition, Second Printing, revised, 1978

Printed in the U.S.A.

Library of Congress Cataloging in Publication Data

Bellrose, Frank Chapman, 1916-
Ducks, geese & swans of North America.

"A Wildlife Management Institute book sponsored jointly with the Illinois Natural History Survey."
Bibliography: p.
1. Waterfowl—North America. 2. Birds—North America. I. Kortright, Francis H. The ducks, geese and swans of North America. II. Title.
QL696.A5B35 1976 598.4'1'097 75-33962
ISBN 0-8117-0535-8

To

C. R. "PINK" GUTERMUTH

and

LAURENCE R. JAHN

for their dedicated effort toward
maintaining the aquatic areas on which the
survival of America's waterfowl depends.

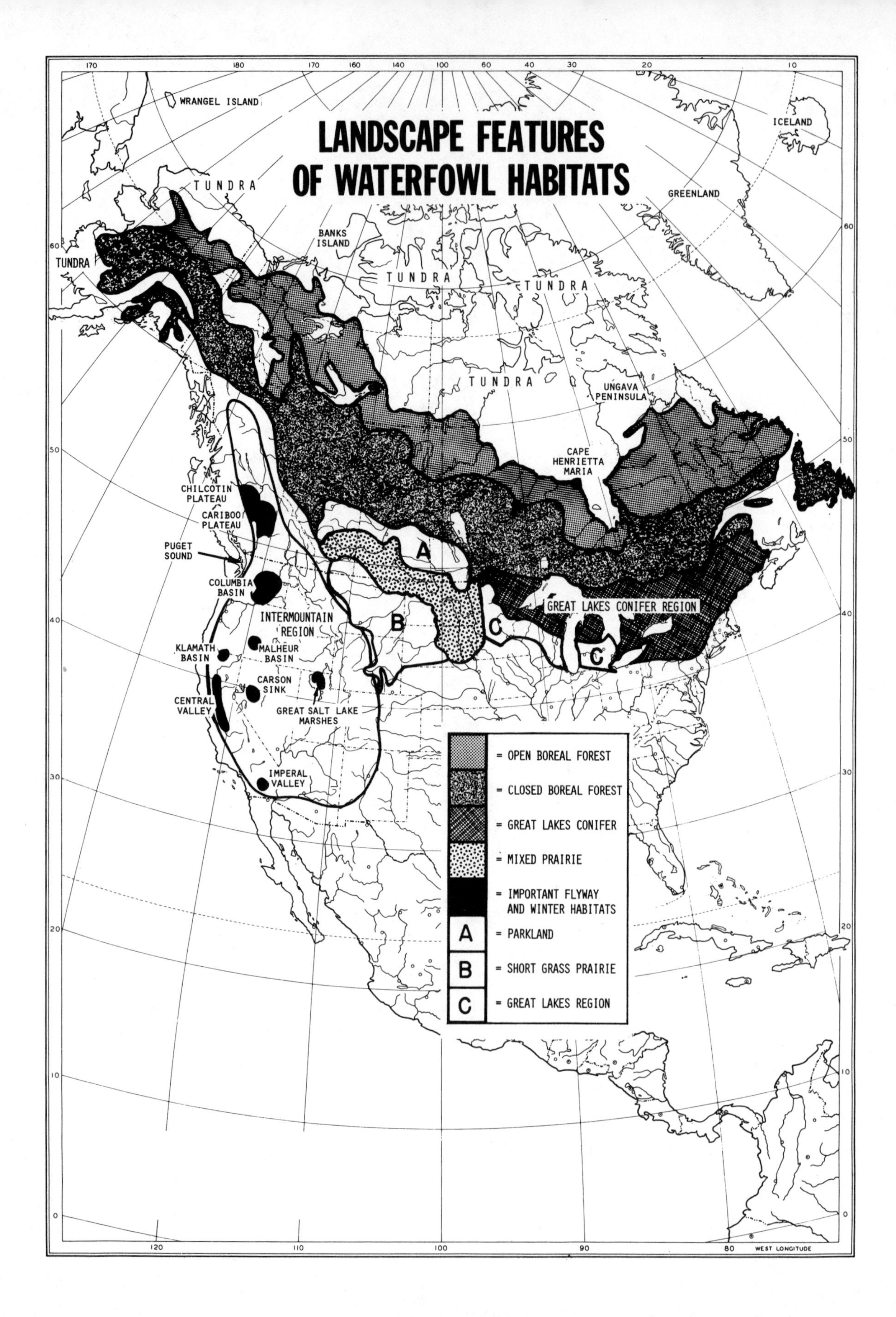

LANDSCAPE FEATURES OF WATERFOWL HABITATS
WRANGEL ISLAND
ICELAND
TUNDRA
GREENLAND
BANKS ISLAND
TUNDRA
TUNDRA
TUNDRA
TUNDRA
UNGAVA PENINSULA
CAPE HENRIETTA MARIA
CHILCOTIN PLATEAU
CARIBOO PLATEAU
PUGET SOUND
COLUMBIA BASIN
INTERMOUNTAIN REGION
GREAT LAKES CONIFER REGION
KLAMATH BASIN
MALHEUR BASIN
CARSON SINK
CENTRAL VALLEY
GREAT SALT LAKE MARSHES
IMPERAL VALLEY
A
B
C
C
= OPEN BOREAL FOREST
= CLOSED BOREAL FOREST
= GREAT LAKES CONIFER
= MIXED PRAIRIE
= IMPORTANT FLYWAY AND WINTER HABITATS
A = PARKLAND
B = SHORT GRASS PRAIRIE
C = GREAT LAKES REGION
WEST LONGITUDE

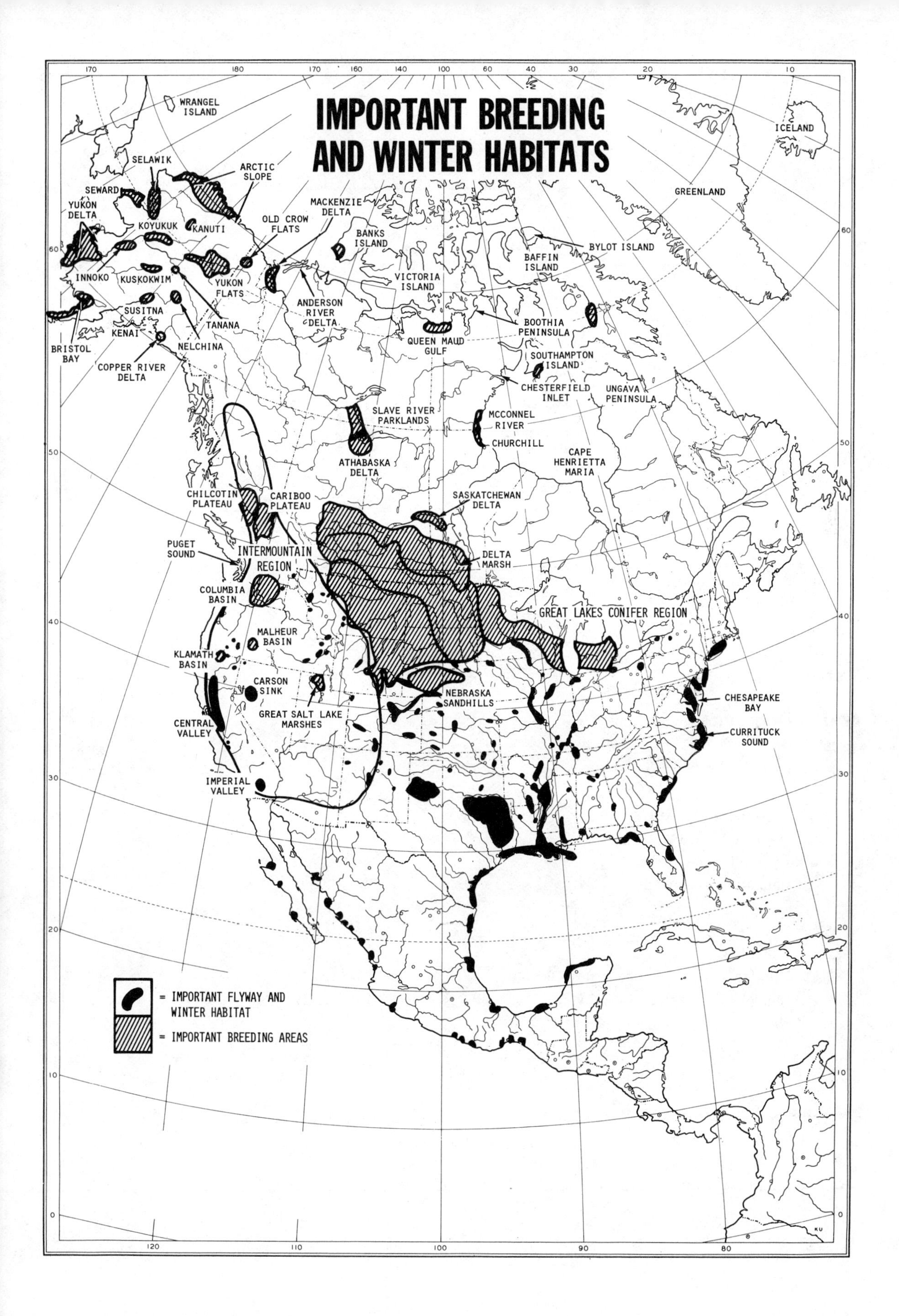
IMPORTANT BREEDING AND WINTER HABITATS
WRANGEL ISLAND
SELAWIK
ARCTIC SLOPE
SEWARD
YUKON DELTA
KOYUKUK
KANUTI
OLD CROW FLATS
MACKENZIE DELTA
BANKS ISLAND
ICELAND
GREENLAND
BYLOT ISLAND
BAFFIN ISLAND
INNOKO
KUSKOKWIM
YUKON FLATS
VICTORIA ISLAND
ANDERSON RIVER DELTA
SUSITNA
TANANA
KENAI
NELCHINA
BRISTOL BAY
COPPER RIVER DELTA
BOOTHIA PENINSULA
QUEEN MAUD GULF
SOUTHAMPTON ISLAND
CHESTERFIELD INLET
UNGAVA PENINSULA
SLAVE RIVER PARKLANDS
MCCONNEL RIVER
CHURCHILL
ATHABASKA DELTA
CAPE HENRIETTA MARIA
CHILCOTIN PLATEAU
CARIBOO PLATEAU
SASKATCHEWAN DELTA
PUGET SOUND
INTERMOUNTAIN REGION
DELTA MARSH
COLUMBIA BASIN
GREAT LAKES CONIFER REGION
MALHEUR BASIN
KLAMATH BASIN
CARSON SINK
NEBRASKA SANDHILLS
CHESAPEAKE BAY
GREAT SALT LAKE MARSHES
CENTRAL VALLEY
CURRITUCK SOUND
IMPERIAL VALLEY
= IMPORTANT FLYWAY AND WINTER HABITAT
= IMPORTANT BREEDING AREAS

CONTENTS

FOREWORD

Francis H. Kortright's classic work, *The Ducks, Geese and Swans of North America*, was first released in December 1942. Since that time it has undergone fourteen printings. Kortright's original book contained a wealth of information on waterfowl of the United States, Canada, and Mexico, but it arrived on the scene just as a ground swell of biological research on the ducks, geese, and swans was gathering momentum. Since publication of that work, modern aircraft, banding, telemetry, and computers are providing more efficient means for gathering, analyzing, and storing great volumes of new data on the various species of waterfowl. In the subsequent third of a century, knowledge of waterfowl habits, movements and migration routes, and populations has been refined using information assembled by federal and state wildlife agencies, by colleges and universities, and by private organizations.

To prepare a text to replace that of an established classic is an enormous responsibility. In selecting an author to undertake the updating of Kortright's work, the Wildlife Management Institute was faced with a narrow choice. The individual had to possess a rare breadth of practical experience, knowledge, and scholastic ability. Frank Bellrose, senior biologist of the Illinois Natural History Survey, met all of the desired qualifications, and no other authority is more highly respected by his professional associates.

This volume represents a summary of facts accumulated on waterfowl over several decades to place management of the resource on a firmer basis. It was on such information that the states in 1948 were grouped into four flyways—Pacific, Central, Mississippi and Atlantic—which in turn led to the establishment of the Flyway Councils in 1952. More than two decades of cooperative efforts through these administrative units emphasize their soundness for forging more effective management programs for waterfowl populations and their habitats. Much progress has been made, and more challenges await attention.

One of the most pressing challenges is to delineate management units for individual species, subspecies, and manageable populations on an international geographical basis. Bellrose's volume emphasizes the success of this approach with goose populations. It also lays part of the factual foundation for making more such delineations for other species or groups of species. Further research must provide the additional information required for this. Through continuing strong, cooperative working relationships to collect, evaluate, and exchange information, we firmly believe the foundation for waterfowl management can be improved. We hope this book helps stimulate the research and management efforts required to accomplish that objective.

But as important as this book may be to wildlife administrators and biologists, its value extends far beyond the scientific community. The information contained between its covers will prove of major interest to all naturalists, amateur ornithologists, and serious sportsmen concerned with the perpetuation of North America's waterfowl flights.

DANIEL A. POOLE, *President*
Wildlife Management Institute

PREFACE

Many times since C. R. "Pink" Gutermuth requested that I write this book, I have regretted my acceptance. It all started as I was departing the North American Wildlife Conference at Houston, Texas. That was in March 1968. While waiting for my car to appear at the door of the Shamrock Hotel, I passed the moments in conversation with Pink, then the Wildlife Management Institute's vice-president. During the conversation, I suggested that the Institute bring Kortright's *Ducks, Geese, and Swans of North America* up-to-date. I pointed out that it was a great book for waterfowlers in its day but that this day had passed; it ably covered the period of ornithological investigations, but appeared just as intensive waterfowl research was really getting under way.

Waterfowl research was in its infancy in the late 1930's and in the 1940's up to World War II, when it went into a state of abeyance for "the duration." Following the war, waterfowl studies by the federal and state agencies, by cooperative wildlife research units at several universities, and at other institutions figuratively exploded.

The three decades that followed the appearance of Kortright's book in 1942 have witnessed the flowering of waterfowl biology, both in research and in management. It probably represents that "golden age" in fact finding, for there were then the greater unknowns to be pursued with vigor by researchers who haunted continental wetlands from the cottonmouth-infested marshes of the Gulf Coast to the gale-swept tundras of the High Arctic.

However, investigations of waterfowl will never cease as long as civilized man holds sway over North America. Waterfowl are a highly dynamic group of birds; the habits of many species are in a constant state of flux as they attempt to adjust to man's activities, such as the "agricultural revolution" that has swept the continent. Some species, such as the scoters, have held, no doubt, to habits of centuries, but some races of Canada geese have adapted to man-dominated landscapes in a decade or two.

There is much more that we need to study: there is not a single species in which the population mechanisms are known thoroughly. In some species of waterfowl our lack of the simplest life history knowledge is scandalous. For example, much of the meager nesting information on the black and surf scoters dates back to the turn of the century.

In spite of many facets of waterfowl life history that still need to be unearthed, an impressive mass of facts and figures has been obtained on the habits and populations of many of these birds. There have been so many facts and figures to search out, to tabulate, and to present that this book took much, much longer than planned.

In fact, I had made so little a dent in the task the first year of working nights and weekends that I sought permission from Dr. George Sprugel, Jr., Chief of the Illinois Natural History Survey, to make the work a Survey project with the stipulation that there would be no personal remuneration from its publication. Dr. Sprugel kindly agreed, with the result that more time became available between other Survey activities.

Dr. Glen C. Sanderson, Head of the Section of Wildlife Research, also offered to assist. His administrative counsel and activities and his editorial supervision have proved invaluable. Helen C. Schultz, who edits many of the wildlife research papers, undertook the basic editorial work on the manuscript. In addition Arthur S. Hawkins, former Mississippi Flyway Representative, U.S. Fish and Wildlife Service, agreed to review the material for possible omissions of fact or commissions of error. I consider Art Hawkins to be one of the most knowledgeable waterfowl biologists in North America. He has studied waterfowl for as many years as I have—37 to be exact—but he has ranged far and wide. Art has astutely observed waterfowl in their habitats and their problems in almost every region of North America but the Arctic.

The greatest compensation to me for the "blood, sweat, and toil" that went into this book has been the wholehearted enthusiasm of every biologist who has been asked to help. Not one refused, even though in many instances it meant long hours of work to compile desired data. Often it meant providing information the investigator intended to publish, but the prevailing attitude was: "If it will help our waterfowl, here are my findings." There has never been a more unselfish and dedicated group of professionals.

I have tried to acknowledge the source of all information used, but with legions of persons contributing unpublished material, reports, and published material in a variety of forms, it will be a minor miracle if there is no oversight. For those I have missed, my deepest regrets for the oversight.

Havana, Illinois — FRANK C. BELLROSE

ACKNOWLEDGMENTS

More than one hundred waterfowl biologists made personal contributions of unpublished information. These and others who assisted in making material available are acknowledged here. Some of these individuals deserve special credit for their outstanding contributions as well as those who formed the unheralded "support force."

The support force was headed by Dr. Laurence R. Jahn, Vice-President, Wildlife Management Institute. Larry provided funds, cajoled, and prodded, but by and large was understanding of missed deadlines. Lianne Ruppel drew the maps and migration charts under the supervision of Lloyd LeMere, illustrator for the Illinois Natural History Survey. My son, Frank III, painted the pintail-gadwall replacement plate and the dust jacket, and made drawings of the Baikal teal and tufted duck. Carl Thompson, Illinois Natural History Survey, prepared the goose and duck migration corridor maps. Eleanore Wilson and Elizabeth McConaha typed two or more editions of each species account. Helen C. Schultz, Section of Wildlife Research, prepared the list of geographic names, verified the references, and checked the entire set of galleys. The references were typed by Pat Duzan. To my wife Esther I express my appreciation for her understanding and encouragement. James B. Trefethen, Director of Publications, and Kenneth J. Sabol, Administrative Assistant, Wildlife Management Institute, helped prepare the manuscript for publication and checked galley and page proof. Extensive editorial assistance was rendered to Stackpole Books by Blanche Nye Kinch, meriting thanks and special mention.

I am particularly indebted to the following U.S. Fish and Wildlife Service personnel: Richard S. Pospahala for making available data on breeding ground surveys, 1955-1974; James Salyer for making available weekly fall and spring censuses of waterfowl populations at National Wildlife Refuges; John Chattin for breeding, migration, and winter population data for the Pacific Flyway; James King, Calvin Lensink, and James Bartonek for Alaskan waterfowl nesting and population data; Walter Crissey and Henry M. Reeves for providing waterfowl banding records; David Trauger for information on the scaups, redhead, and canvasback; Lynn A. Greenwalt, Director, for permission to use data from Administrative Reports and Report No. 4, Flyway Habitat Management Unit Project; and Jessop B. Low for his enthusiastic support of student wildlife research.

Numerous biologists provided essential information to round out the distribution and abundance patterns of breeding waterfowl. They were: Karl Bednarik, Ohio; Richard Bishop, Iowa; Robert Jeffrey and Ellis Bowhay, Washington; Robert Jessen, Minnesota; Chester Kebbe, Oregon; Frank Kozlik, California; John Nagel, Utah; George Schildman, Nebraska; Marvin Schwilling, Kansas; Robert Stewart and Harold Kantrud, North Dakota; Michael Szymczak, Colorado; Dale Witt and Robert Eng, Montana; George Wrakestraw, Wyoming; R.T. Sterling, William Morris, and Ray D. Halladay, British Columbia.

An additional recognition to the authorities who prepared the special chapters: Dr. Milton W. Weller, University of Minnesota; Dr. Glen C. Sanderson, Illinois Natural History Survey; Arthur S. Hawkins, U. S. Fish and Wildlife Service.

Other authorities, including those cited in the text, who have made important contributions are:

C. Edward Addy, U. S. Fish and Wildlife Service
John W. Aldrich, U. S. National Museum
Robert Alison, Ontario Ministry of Natural Resources
Dale H. Arner, Mississippi State University
George C. Arthur, Illinois Department of Conservation
Kenneth Babcock, Missouri Department of Conservation
Edgar Bailey, U. S. Fish and Wildlife Service
Thomas Barry, Canadian Wildlife Service
Hugh Bateman, Louisiana Wildlife and Fisheries Commission
Karl Bednarik, Ohio Department of Natural Resources
Dirck Benson, New York Department of Environmental Conservation
Eric G. Bolen, Welder Wildlife Foundation
Eugene F. Bossenmaier, Manitoba Department of Mines, Resources and Environmental Management
Hugh Boyd, Canadian Wildlife Service
Patrick Brown, Iowa State University
Raymond J. Buller, U. S. Fish and Wildlife Service
Samuel M. Carney, U. S. Fish and Wildlife Service
F. Graham Cooch, Canadian Wildlife Service
Robert D. Crompton, Illinois Natural History Survey
Gerald E. Cummings, U. S. Fish and Wildlife Service
Christian Dau, University of Alaska
D. C. Dennis, Canadian Wildlife Service
Lemuel Due, Oklahoma Department of Wildlife Conservation
Alexander Dzubin, Canadian Wildlife Service
Warren Flock, University of Colorado
Leigh Fredrickson, University of Missouri
Angus Gavin, Ducks Unlimited-Canada
J. Bernard Gollop, Canadian Wildlife Service
Richard Graber, Illinois Natural History Survey
Ray D. Halladay, British Columbia Fish and Wildlife Branch
Henry A. Hansen, U. S. Fish and Wildlife Service
Rossalius C. Hanson, U. S. Fish and Wildlife Service
Donald W. Hayne, Institute of Statistics, North Carolina State University
Helen Hays, American Museum of Natural History
J. Douglas Heyland, Quebec Department of Tourism, Fish and Game
Richard Hunt, Wisconsin Department of Natural Resources
Mary Jackson, University of British Columbia
Robert Jones, Jr., U. S. Fish and Wildlife Service
David D. Kennedy, Illinois Department of Conservation
R. H. Kerbes, Canadian Wildlife Service
William Kiel, King Ranch
C. M. Kirkpatrick, Purdue University
J. Burton Lauckhart, Washington State Department of Game
Forrest B. Lee, U.S. Fish and Wildlife Service
William G. Leitch, Ducks Unlimited-Canada
Harry G. Lumsden, Ontario Ministry of Natural Resources
John J. Lynch, U.S. Fish and Wildlife Service
Rich McCamant, National Park Service
Charles MacInnes, Ontario Ministry of Natural Resources
Eldon McLuray, U.S. Fish and Wildlife Service
James R. March, Wisconsin Department of Natural Resources
Thomas Martin, U. S. Fish and Wildlife Service
Peter G. Mickelson, University of Michigan
Edward J. Mikula, Michigan Department of Natural Resources
Harvey Miller, U. S. Fish and Wildlife Service
William Morris, Canadian Wildlife Service
Duane Norman, U. S. Fish and Wildlife Service
Edward Oniel, U. S. Fish and Wildlife Service
Gary Pearson, U. S. Fish and Wildlife Service
Joseph M. Penkala, New Jersey Department of Environmental Protection
John P. Ryder, Lakehead University, Ontario
Douglas Schamel, University of Alaska
Peter E. K. Shepherd, Alaska Department of Fish and Game
Allen G. Smith, U. S. Fish and Wildlife Service
Paul F. Springer, U.S. Fish and Wildlife Service
R. T. Sterling, Ducks Unlimited-Canada
Vernon D. Stotts, Maryland Department of Natural Resources
Jerome H. Stoudt, U. S. Fish and Wildlife Service
Charles Stutzenbaker, Texas Parks and Wildlife Department
Daniel Timm, Alaska Department of Fish and Game
Richard Vaught, Missouri Department of Conservation
Clark Webster, Remington Farms
Charles F. Yocom, Humboldt State University

chapter 1

THE BASIS OF THIS BOOK

A good journalist identifies the source of information used in a news story. In this introductory chapter we seek to identify our sources of information, explain how it was obtained, evaluate its significance, and define some of the specialized terms used.

Sources of specific information are indicated by names and dates, which refer to papers listed in the *References* section of this book. Although most references are from publications, some are from unpublished reports and from theses. Another source is direct personal communication with authorities who have provided hitherto unreported information. In such cases, sources are indicated by full names with no accompanying dates.

Because certain kinds of information from authorities in the U. S. Fish and Wildlife Service appear in most species accounts, these sources are identified only under the appropriate topics discussed in this chapter.

WATERFOWL SURVEYS

Only a few decades ago, "abundant," "common," "scarce," and "rare" were the terms used to describe the size of waterfowl populations. But these descriptive terms imply different levels of magnitude to different people, who interpret abundance in light of their own experiences.

Numerical terms were first used to indicate the size of waterfowl populations during the mid-1930's. The U. S. Bureau of Biological Survey—forerunner of the U. S. Fish and Wildlife Service—commenced a January "inventory" of wintering waterfowl in the United States in 1935. During late summer of that year, a private foundation—More Game Birds in America—undertook a "wild duck census" of the breeding grounds in the Dakotas, Minnesota, and the Prairie Provinces of Canada.

In Leaflet BS-136, published in May 1939, the Bureau commented (p. 17): "Experience in the work has contributed greatly to the accuracy of the results, so that while coverage of the entire country is still far from complete, for comparative purposes it is felt that the data assembled are as nearly accurate as can be expected in an operation of such magnitude and complexity." In 1939, a grand total of 14,500,000 waterfowl were enumerated, and it was postulated that there were nearly 60 million waterfowl in the United States.

After their ground and aerial survey of waterfowl breeding grounds, More Game Birds in America (1935) concluded that, at a rough estimate, there were probably 65 million ducks on the continent as a whole during August 1935.

Today we look askance at the varied and cursory manner in which the initial surveys of waterfowl populations were made. A generation hence, water-

Figure 1-1. Transects and strata of annual aerial surveys of waterfowl breeding grounds by the U.S. Fish and Wildlife Service.

fowl investigators may view contemporary data with the same misgivings. Although enormous strides have been made in determining continental waterfowl populations in the four decades since 1935, the results are still less than perfect.

Over the last three decades waterfowl populations have been surveyed in North America twice each year: a May-June and a July survey of the breeding grounds and a midwinter survey of the winter grounds. The May-June surveys determine the number of ducks that return to the breeding grounds from their winter quarters. Surveys in July (brood counts) determine breeding success. These surveys are conducted by the U. S. Fish and Wildlife Service. The breeding ground surveys are made with the assistance of the Canadian Wildlife Service, Ducks Unlimited, and the conservation agencies of the Prairie Provinces and of certain states. The state conservation agencies of all states contribute greatly to the midwinter surveys.

Breeding Grounds

The breeding ground survey on an annual basis had its beginning in 1946, but it required several years for the "bugs" to be worked out. Today, for comparative purposes, the U. S. Fish and Wildlife Service uses data obtained in 1955 and thereafter on the breeding ground surveys.

At first, breeding ground surveys were undertaken largely by enumerating ducks observed from rural roads in the prairies; the use of aircraft was mostly restricted to roadless areas of the Far North. The increased use of aircraft in the prairies during the early 1950's greatly increased the scope of the surveys and assured a better distribution of transects.

A transect is usually an east-west strip 0.25 mile wide and up to 150 miles in length broken down into 18-mile segments. From an aircraft flying about 100 mph and 150 feet above the ground, the pilot counts ponds and ducks observed for 0.25 mile on his side of the plane. An observer follows the same procedure on the opposite side of the aircraft.

Transect lengths and intervals were established according to the quality and the distribution of wetlands—the greater their habitat potential for waterfowl, the greater the sampling frequency (fig. 1-1). For example, in high-density areas of the prairie, transects are 14 miles apart; in low-density areas, such as the boreal forest, they are from 30 to 60 miles apart (Hanson and Hawkins 1975). All transects total 50,000 linear miles and cover almost 2 percent of the total breeding habitat.

The region surveyed annually for breeding ducks covers the prairies, parklands, closed boreal forest, open boreal forest, and tundra stretching from the Dakotas on the southeast to the Bering Sea of Alaska on the northwest. The infertile, granite outcrop of the Precambrian Shield generally delimits the eastern border; the Rocky Mountains, except for Alaska, form the western border. In northern Manitoba and Saskatchewan, the survey area extends a short distance beyond the edge of the Precambrian Shield.

Although the use of aircraft increases the coverage of waterfowl breeding areas, it results in a proportion of ducks being overlooked. Among prairie-breeding species, about two-thirds are missed (Hanson and Hawkins 1975). However, the percentage missed varies by species and the amount of marsh cover. Consequently, each year ground crews "beat out" segments of transects by recording the numbers of waterfowl they observe to compare with the numbers recorded from the air within the same 24-hour period. Those missed in the aerial coverage result in a correction factor, called a visibility index, which ranges from 1.3 for scoters to about 10 for the diminutive difficult-to-see green-winged teal. The important mallard requires a correction of about three times the number counted from the air.

The more scattered the distribution of a species over the breeding grounds, the more likely that the transects do not adequately sample the population. Thus, a widely distributed species such as the mallard is unquestionably better sampled than the redhead or canvasback. Those species that predominate in the boreal forest and the Arctic are not as well sampled as those that frequent the prairies. Obviously, a slight change in the visibility index makes a large change in the final population figure. These figures are somewhat inflated by the assumption that for every lone male there is a female. Sex ratios show varying surpluses of males to females.

In spite of these built-in weaknesses of the breeding ground figures, they still make worthwhile comparison possible between species abundance, regional abundance, and yearly abundance. But it should be emphasized that the population figures that I have used so dogmatically are not exact but are subject to varying degrees of error. The problem in rounding figures is where to stop. If rounding errors are too gross, the parts do not equal the whole.

Since I started this project, the figures for breeding ground populations have changed twice. The original data contained no correction for visibility oversight. The second set of data was corrected by a visibility index factor that raised population totals several times. Further study resulted in a refinement of the strata (areas) and visibility indices that generally lowered population levels. The density of waterfowl on breeding grounds, as shown on a map accompanying each species account, is based upon the second set of population data corrected for overall change in status. The breeding ground figures in the text represent the third and the latest analysis of the data.

Richard Pospahala, U. S. Fish and Wildlife Service, provided the second and third analyses of breeding ground populations. We made our first analysis from breeding data reported annually by the U. S. Fish and Wildlife Service in their *Status Report* series. From this experience I can attest that Pospahala deserves much credit for his constant effort to improve the quality of the data, a most formidable task involving 20 species groups, 49 different strata, and 20 years. Although for most strata the compilation of breeding ground data covers a span of 20 years, 1955-74, for several strata the span is less.

We have grouped the stratified population figures for the breeding grounds according to ecological zones such as tundra, open boreal forest (taiga), closed boreal forest, parklands, mixed prairie, and shortgrass prairie associations. In addition, the importance of specialized zones is recognized: the river deltas of the Arctic and Subarctic, the Intermountain marshes, the marshes of the Great Lakes states, and others.

Supplementing the breeding ground data from the U. S. Fish and Wildlife Service are similar data from British Columbia and states where large numbers of ducks breed. Most of the western states contain impressive numbers of breeding waterfowl as do the Great Lakes states of Minnesota, Wisconsin, and Michigan. The authorities who provided this information are listed in the *Acknowledgments*.

The density of breeding waterfowl is shown on the distribution maps for the important species by spacing of "contour" lines. A density figure is given that represents the population of each space in each political division of the United States and Canada. A state, a province, or a territory is considered as a political division. Because of revised population data by the U. S. Fish and Wildlife Service after the maps were prepared, the maps do not always agree with the data in the text. For specific details the text should be consulted.

Winter Inventories

After World War II, the use of light aircraft to census waterfowl changed from a novelty to a necessity. This change resulted in better coverage of waterfowl winter grounds and more reliable yearly data. Even so, large numbers of ducks are not recorded. Many are overlooked because it is difficult to see them through the treetops of flooded swamps. Others are overlooked because they are too far from land, on large lakes, bays, sounds, and similar areas. Some are overlooked because they are in drainage ditches and small streams, easily missed from the air if the observers are not aware of their presence beforehand. Then, too, I believe that observers tend to underestimate large concentrations. Naturally, also, winter grounds south of the border are not as thoroughly surveyed as those within the United States; in fact, some have been surveyed either not at all or only once in a 25-year period.

The upshot is that figures derived from winter inventories are considerably below the level of the actual population of a given duck species. Generally, figures for breeding ground populations are several times higher than those for winter grounds. Because of the large visibility index used to correct the breeding population figures of some species, population levels derived from May-June surveys may sometimes be too high.

Winter surveys of waterfowl are of value in delineating their distribution at that time of the year, in yielding a rough index of yearly change, and in providing the only reliable year-to-year population data on geese. Because of the extensive use geese make of breeding grounds in the Arctic and Subarctic, it is impractical to survey these areas on a yearly basis. There are several reasons why goose populations on winter grounds can be inventoried much better than duck populations: they are more readily visible; they concentrate in well-known, well-defined winter areas; the winter areas are readily accessible to surveillance from aircraft; and, except for black brant, few geese winter south of the United States.

To obtain a better appraisal of goose populations in the Mississippi and Central flyways, the winter surveys on geese in these two flyways were changed in 1968, and subsequently, from early January to mid-December. We have treated these data as if they were obtained in early January.

Because midwinter surveys combine counts of eiders, scoters, and mergansers, we have used Audubon Christmas counts of these species and certain others to supplement the compilations of the U. S. Fish and Wildlife Service. We compiled the Christmas-period censuses of greater and lesser scaups, the sea ducks, and mergansers in the states and provinces flanking the Atlantic, the Pacific, and the Gulf coasts, and the Great Lakes for the years 1965, 1966, and 1968 (Audubon Field Notes 1966, 1967, 1969). In addition, all waterfowl were compiled for the United States and Canada as recorded on the 1972 Christmas bird counts (American Birds 1973).

Population figures from midwinter inventories were obtained for each state from 1955 through 1974 from the U. S. Fish and Wildlife Service's flyway representatives: C. Edward Addy, Atlantic; Arthur S. Hawkins, Mississippi; Raymond J. Buller, Central; and John E. Chattin, Pacific. Where the habitat for wintering waterfowl is extensively distributed within a state, the flyway representative and the state waterfowl biologist provided a breakdown of winter numbers according to regions of the state.

MIGRATION CORRIDORS

I developed the concept of migration corridors (figs. 1-2, 1-3) as a means of expressing the direction of passage and the geographic distribution of waterfowl between breeding and winter areas (Bellrose 1968, 1972). Flyways fail to define the passage of waterfowl because they cover too extensive an area and do not delineate movements of waterfowl that are lateral to a north-south direction. Conversely, migration routes are at most 10 miles wide and are only apparent when river valleys, seacoasts, and other significant landscape features are visible, so that the routes can be identified. Most waterfowl migrate at night. My radar observations indicate that nocturnally migrating waterfowl cover a broad front, with little suggestion that routes *per se* are being followed.

Flyway is a useful geographic term that conveniently designates four regions of the United States, just as we use New England, the Midwest, the Pacific Northwest, and similar regional terms. The flyways are useful political units in that they group together states with common borders whose waterfowl problems are similar. Waterfowl, too, show a greater affinity to a particular flyway than to the country as a whole. In some cases, where waterfowl migrations are north-south, their flights fit neatly into flyways. This pattern is most true of the black duck and many population units of geese.

The concept of migration corridors came about as a result of viewing waterfowl migration tracks on films made of radarscopes at numerous U. S. Weather Service stations scattered across the nation east of the Rocky Mountains (Bellrose 1968). I was struck by the rather consistent directional flow of waterfowl migrants night after night at the same location. The passage of migrants was seldom north-south, and at several sites there was a pronounced easterly component to the courses followed (Bellrose 1972). The directional information provided by Warren Flock for migrating waterfowl observed at several radar sites in the West assisted in the understanding of the complex directional passages in the Rocky Mountain region.

Waterfowl abundance in the breeding, migration, and winter seasons also tells us something about their passage across the United States. To this end, the peak number of each species recorded on weekly

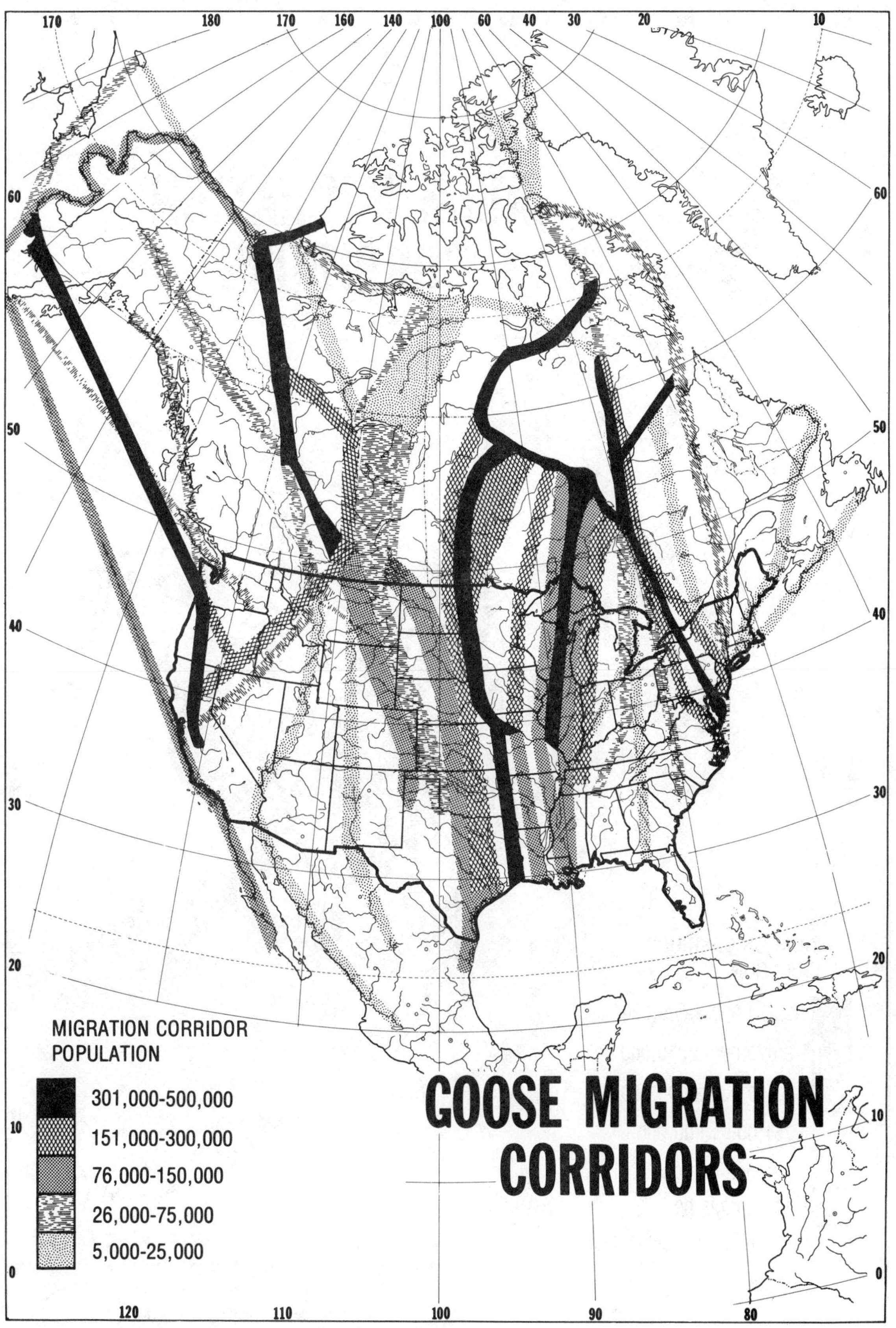

170
180
170
160
140
100
60
40
30
20
10
60
50
40
30
20
10
0
120
110
100
90
80
MIGRATION CORRIDOR
POPULATION
301,000-500,000
151,000-300,000
76,000-150,000
26,000-75,000
5,000-25,000
GOOSE MIGRATION
CORRIDORS

Figure 1-2.

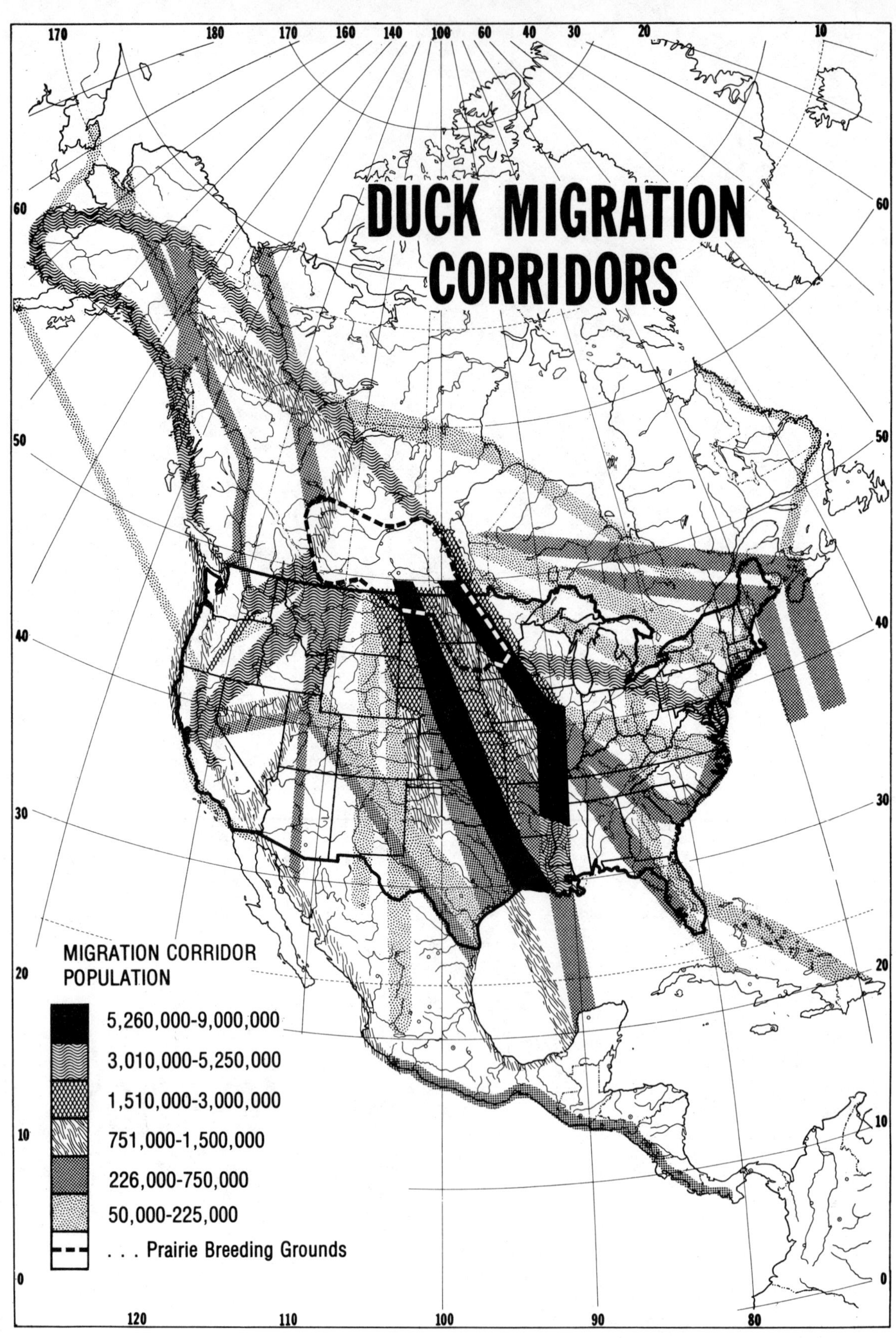
DUCK MIGRATION CORRIDORS
MIGRATION CORRIDOR POPULATION
5,260,000-9,000,000
3,010,000-5,250,000
1,510,000-3,000,000
751,000-1,500,000
226,000-750,000
50,000-225,000
. . . Prairie Breeding Grounds

Figure 1-3.

fall censuses on each important national wildlife refuge was averaged for 3 years: 1957, 1962, and 1967. The peak number was placed at the location of each refuge on a map for each species, along with fall census numbers from numerous states and with winter numbers drawn from midwinter inventories. The location of breeding populations in relation to abundance of a species on migration and on winter areas assisted in determining the magnitude of passage along the various migration corridors.

Band-recovery data provided by the U. S. Fish and Wildlife Service to Donald W. Hayne, Institute of Statistics, North Carolina State University, was most helpful in the corridor analysis. Dr. Hayne made a detailed statistical analysis of the geographic distribution of 10 species of ducks in relation to breeding population abundance. The recoveries were from the first season and involved preseason-banded mallards, pintails, gadwalls, wigeons, green-winged and blue-winged teals, northern shovelers, wood ducks, lesser scaups, and ring-necked ducks. This analysis was made for the Louisiana Wild Life and Fisheries Commission, who graciously made it available to me.

Band-recovery data of other species of waterfowl were made available to me by Walter Crissey and H. Milton Reeves of the U. S. Fish and Wildlife Service. In addition to these original analyses, numerous published papers and unpublished reports listed under references were used to determine migration patterns south of the breeding grounds.

Several hundred reports from pilots who observed geese in migration and radioed the information to the nearest FAA flight control station materially assisted in delineating the migration corridors of geese. Ground observations of the flight directions of diurnally migrating waterfowl also provided useful information.

John E. Chattin, Pacific Flyway Representative, U. S. Fish and Wildlife Service, played a major role in working out the complex migration corridors of the Pacific Coast and Rocky Mountain states.

Chronology of Migration

We have attempted to show the fall and spring migration across the breadth of the conterminous United States for most species of waterfowl. For this purpose the United States was divided into 18 regions as shown on the accompanying map (fig. 1-4). A standard or a coined name was applied to each region to identify it on the chronology graphs.

The data for composing the chronology of migration for each region were obtained from weekly waterfowl censuses made by refuge personnel on national wildlife refuges. To minimize the influence of any abnormal migration, the weekly populations of 3 different years spaced at 5-year intervals were summarized: 1957, 1962, and 1967. The percentages for each week were obtained by dividing the number censused each week by the number censused for the entire season (spring or fall).

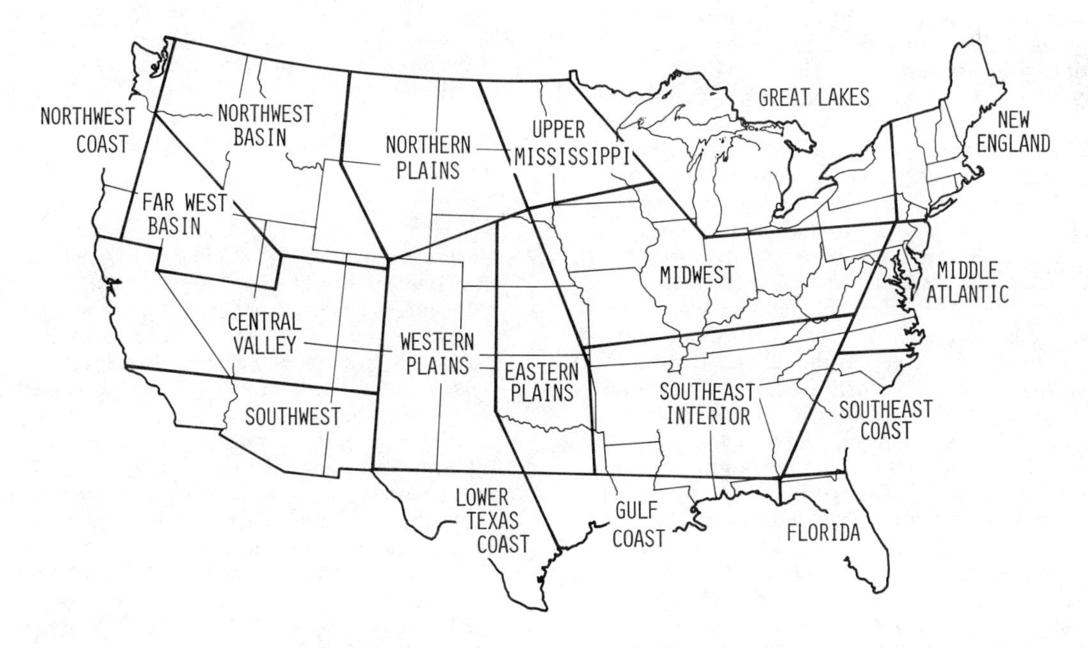

Figure 1-4. Eighteen regions of the United States selected for showing the chronology of migration based on weekly censuses at national wildlife refuges–1957, 1962, and 1967.

Although waterfowl populations on national wildlife refuges within a particular region do not always represent all waterfowl species within the region, we believe that in most instances they do. It is axiomatic that the larger the population frequenting the refuges of a region, the more reliable the graph depicting chronology of passage. Unfortunately, we have not shown the sample sizes on the graphs.

POPULATION DYNAMICS

Aspects of population dynamics—age ratios, sex ratios, and mortality rates—are important in discussions of the major game species of waterfowl.

Age Ratios

The proportion of adults to immatures in the fall and winter populations of waterfowl is an index to the reproductive success of the species the previous summer. The success or failure of the hunting season depends to a large extent upon the number of young fledged. Later chapters will show that over a period of years fall populations in the United States will be about equally composed of adults and immatures but that the proportion of these two age-classes in a population varies considerably from year to year.

Reasons for the yearly fluctuations in reproductive success are complex but hinge primarily on weather conditions. One of the more important factors is the availability of potholes, ponds, and sloughs on the prairies and parklands in the spring and summer. Temperature and precipitation at critical times affect success of the hatch and survival of the young. Temperature also affects the availability of animal food urgently needed by young waterfowl for growth and survival. In the Arctic, the disappearance of snow cover from tundra nest sites is essential. The extent to which nest areas remain blanketed with snow has a pronounced influence upon the degree of reproductive success experienced by brant, snow geese, and other waterfowl that breed in the Arctic.

The age ratios of waterfowl are usually measured by checking the proportion of immatures to adults in hunters' bags. Carney (1964) has worked out an ingenious but complex key to the feather pattern of wings that enables a trained observer to separate adults from immatures and males from females in practically all species of ducks. Each year, groups of waterfowl biologists gather after the hunting season in each flyway for a "wing bee." There they examine thousands of wings contributed by a solicited sample of hunters. The wings are sorted by species, age, and sex and the results tallied.

The findings of these "wing bees" are reported annually in *Administrative Reports* issued by the U. S. Fish and Wildlife Service. A report presents the current age and sex ratios in comparison with the 4 preceding years. Data for the mallard, black duck, pintail, green-winged teal, blue-winged teal, and wood duck extend back to 1961; for other species the data begin with 1966. For compiling data on age and sex ratios, we selected *Administrative Reports* prepared by Smart (1965), Croft and Carney (1971), and Sorensen et al. (1974).

Of course, the age and sex ratios obtained from waterfowl kills made by hunters are not the actual ratios in fall waterfowl populations. Immatures are more likely to be killed than adults. The degree of vulnerability of immatures to hunting varies with the species and to some extent from year to year.

Band data have been employed to correct for differences in vulnerability between adults and immatures (Bellrose et al. 1961). Over an 11-year period, immatures among mallards were 1.26 times more likely to be killed than adults (Smart 1965, Carney 1967, Sorensen and Carney 1972). The variation in vulnerability of immatures ranged from none in one year to a high of 1.58 in another year. Immature black ducks were 1.5 times more readily killed than adults (Geis et al. 1971). Immature pintails averaged 1.6 times more vulnerable to hunting than adults (Smith 1965, Sorensen et al. 1966). Immature wood ducks averaged 1.3 times more vulnerable, 1961-71 (Smart 1965, Carney 1967, Sorensen and Carney 1972); young green-winged teal 1.8 times (Moisan et al. 1967); young blue-winged teal 2.6 times (Martinson 1965, Sorensen 1966); and immature lesser scaups 1.3 times (David Trauger). Young canvasbacks were 1.6 times more readily killed than adults (Geis 1959). Where the data permitted, we corrected the age ratios derived from hunting to obtain a more valid index of the proportion of immatures in the fall populations. Over a period of years for the above species, the proportion of immatures in the fall populations in the United States was remarkably close to 1 to 1.

Sex Ratios

There is a surplus of males in every common game duck (Bellrose et al. 1961). Wild ducks are basically monogamous for the nesting season although a renesting hen may select a new mate. Therefore, at first thought, there seem to be extra males that serve no necessary reproductive function. But the details of courtship among ducks are so complex that ethologists are uncertain as to the role that surplus drakes may play in pair formation.

We reported that sex ratios in ducks appear to be slightly in favor of males from the time of hatch to the first breeding season; afterwards, males greatly exceed females (Bellrose et al. 1961). This finding is reiterated in the accounts of many species and is based upon the sex ratios of adults and of immatures obtained from tallying duck wings submitted by hunters and reported by Sorensen et al. (1974).

Because there are appreciably more males in the adult classes of ducks than among immatures, it is logical to assume that the greater the disparity in overall sex ratios, the greater the percentage of older drakes in the population. Certainly this conclusion would apply to a particular species if not among species.

The disparities in sex ratios among species are great; some are accountable, some not. Species of diving ducks have a greater spread in sex ratios than dabbling ducks. But the black-bellied whistling duck, like many geese, has a sex ratio that only slightly favors adult males, 52 to 48 (Bolen 1970). Whistling ducks and geese have lifelong pair bonds. This lifelong commitment suggests that where sexes remain together through the course of a year, they experience similar mortality rates, and thus sex ratios are similar.

As far as I can ascertain, the longer a species of duck is without a pair bond, the greater the disparity in its sex ratio. Mallards and wood ducks, for example, have one of the more balanced sex ratios among ducks that have sexual dimorphic plumages and are among the first to form pairs in the fall. Most other dabbling ducks have a greater excess of males, and a higher proportion form pair bonds later in the fall and winter. Diving ducks form pair bonds still later than do dabbling ducks; they also have a higher proportion of excess drakes, the lesser scaup topping the list. Since a large proportion of lesser scaups do not form pair bonds until the second year, the long period of unattachment combined with a reduced yearling class in the population appears accountable for the huge excess of males. We have too little knowledge of sex ratios in sea ducks, which do not nest before the second year, to know whether the age structures of their populations and their pair bond tenure falls into the pattern of other waterfowl.

The reasons for this apparent relationship between sex ratios and the duration of the pair bond are not entirely clear. They may relate in part to the lateness of the prenuptial molt, for there is a parallel between the time of initial pair formation and the completion of the molt. Generally, the species that are the first to assume their nuptial plumage in the fall are the first to initiate pair attachments (Weller 1965).

One basic reason for greater mortality of female ducks during the period they are separated from males is their greater exposure to predation and stress during the period of nesting and brood rearing. At the beginning of this period, males of most species of ducks leave their mates and settle on large lakes and marshes to undergo the molt. While incubating and rearing the young, the females lose considerable weight and are highly vulnerable to such predators as coyotes, foxes, and raccoons. Because breeding females usually molt in small marshes near the rearing grounds, they are probably exposed to more predation than the males, whose molt occurs earlier on larger bodies of water. Whether differential mortality persists after the period of the molt is unknown.

Mortality

Numerous studies have been made concerning the annual mortality rates of various species of waterfowl. The basis of these studies has been the subsequent yearly shrinkage in the number of recoveries from a group of birds banded in a particular calendar year. Most of the studies reported in this book employed the dynamic life table for analysis of data. More reliable and precise methods of analysis have been developed in recent years, but insufficient time has elapsed to permit their general use (Eberhardt 1969).

According to the analyses made to date, numerous species of immature ducks have a first-year mortality rate of 60 to 70 percent and a subsequent yearly rate of loss of 35 to 45 percent. Greater hunting losses among immatures appear to account for most of the difference in mortality rates between the two age-classes. Female ducks have an appreciably higher yearly mortality rate than males; higher nonhunting mortality, largely during the summer, accounts for the greater losses of females. In most species of ducks, hunters intentionally or unintentionally select slightly more males than females (Bellrose et al. 1961). However, canvasback females appear to suffer higher hunting losses than males (Geis 1959).

Changes in hunting regulations result in a change in yearly mortality rates. Geis et al. (1971) calculated that immature black ducks have a nonhunting mortality rate of 40 percent their first year but that the rate for adults is just slightly over 20 percent. For all age- and sex-classes of black ducks, Geis et al. (1971) concluded that hunting accounted for about half the total annual losses. Geis (1959) reached a similar conclusion about hunter-related losses in the canvasback.

Hunter losses compared with overall losses are somewhat different in the green-winged teal. Moisan et al. (1967) determined that immature greenwings experienced a mortality rate of 71 percent, 20 percent from hunting and 51 percent from nonhunting causes.

Realization of Reproductive Potential

Although age ratios in the fall express the ultimate outcome of the breeding season, we must understand the reproductive potential of each species and "leakage" of this potential at several stages of the breeding season. Only then can we realize the adversities that beset the reproductive capacity of a species. In some cases, management can either mitigate unusually severe losses or enhance reproduction by such activities as controlling predators, constructing nest islands, establishing dense nest cover, and other habitat manipulation.

Age. The age at which waterfowl breed affects the potential number of breeders in a population. There are varying proportions of nonbreeding birds in all species of waterfowl, even in those species in which yearlings are known to breed. This variation is particularly prevalent among the *Aythya* diving ducks: ring-necked duck, redhead, canvasback, and scaups. The proportion of these yearlings that breed appears to be highest in the ring-necked duck, lowest in the greater scaup, with the lesser scaup next, followed by the redhead and canvasback. There is some evidence that the late nesters have a larger proportion of nonbreeders than the early nesters. More and more evidence is appearing that availability of space on the breeding grounds also has a bearing upon the proportion of the yearlings that breed.

Nesting. We have tried to amass as much data on clutch sizes and nest success as we could find in published papers, unpublished reports, theses, and similar sources. Our object in summarizing a large mass of information on these topics was to provide as sound a basis as possible for evaluating breeding success, and to provide a baseline for future nest studies.

Where large numbers of studies were summarized, it was impractical to cite all the references. Most appear in the species accounts, dealing with some other facet of nesting. These and others not specifically referred to in the species accounts are listed in the *References* section.

Sample sizes throughout the book, unless specifically mentioned, are shown as numbers within parentheses. This method has been particularly useful for clutch sizes, nest successes, and brood sizes.

The range in clutch size may be misleading. Predators often remove so many eggs from a nest that some persistent hens are left incubating one or two eggs, far below the number laid. On the other hand, unusually large clutches are more than likely to contain eggs added by one or more intruding hens. Almost all species harbor some individuals that lay one or more eggs in nests of other hens of the same species, and some, particularly the redhead, lay eggs in the nests of other species.

A nest has been classed as successful if one egg hatches, but most successful nests hatch within one or two eggs of the average clutch size. The average number of eggs that fail to hatch is deducted from the average clutch size to provide an index of the number of young that leave the nest.

Unpublished studies of ducks nesting on the prairies of Canada in the late 1960's and early 1970's indicate that nest success is lower than it was one to three decades earlier, the period largely embraced by the findings reported in the species accounts in this book. The rise in nest destruction appears to stem from the loss of nest habitat and an increase in fox and raccoon numbers.

In recent years there has been a continuous clearing of aspen groves from lands adjacent to potholes in the Canadian parklands to create more arable land. Prior to the clearing, grassy and weedy openings in the aspen-willow groves provided nest sites for ducks. Now an increasing proportion of parkland-nesting waterfowl are restricted to a narrow band of nest cover around a pothole, where their exposure to predators is intensified. During this same period, raccoon numbers have appreciably increased, and in southern regions of the prairies and parklands they have become a serious menace.

Broods. Unknown numbers of broods are lost in their entirety throughout the brood period. Brood losses are especially large on overland treks that may occur first from an upland nest site to the water area, and perhaps later in moving across country from one pothole to another.

The attrition that occurs among broods as they grow from the downy stage to flight stage has been recorded for tens of thousands of broods. Usually, brood survival is recorded at three stages of growth: Class I, Class II, and Class III (fig. 1-5). Class I is the downy stage that covers the period from the hatch to the time body feathers begin to appear among the down. This stage varies with the species and latitude but usually covers a period of about 3 weeks. The Class II stage usually embraces the period from the start of the fourth week through the sixth week; during this stage the body (contour) feathers gradually replace all of the down plumage. Class III is the stage during which the young are fully feathered by the juvenile plumage, prior to flight. This stage of development covers a span of about 10 days (Gollop and Marshall 1954).

The growth rates of flight feathers vary with the ambient temperature. Smart (1965) found that the growth rate of primaries was more rapid in late-hatched than in early-hatched redheads. These feathers emerged from their sheaths when the late-hatched birds were 7 to 10 days younger than the early-hatched ones. The difference in development of flight feathers was also reflected in the age at first flight. However, the flight feathers in the late-hatched young were shorter than those in the early-hatched birds. The evidence points to a decrease in the secretion of thyroxine as temperatures increase.

Adult Dabbling Duck

Class I A, young are down-covered; 1-7 days of age

Class I B, young down-covered, but color fading; 8-13 days of age

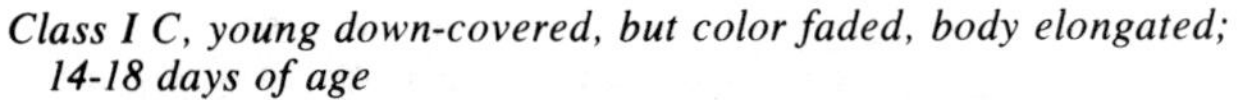

Class I C, young down-covered, but color faded, body elongated; 14-18 days of age

Class II A, first feathers appear, replacing down on sides and tail; 19-27 days of age

Class II B, over half of body covered with feathers; 28-36 days of age

Class II C, small amount of down remains, among feathers of back; 37-42 days of age

Class III, fully feathered but incapable of flight; 43-55 days of age, flying at 56-60 days

Figure 1-5. Plumage development of young waterfowl (after Gollop and Marshall 1954).

An increase in thyroxine stimulates feather growth, and this occurs as temperatures become cooler. Thus, it is apparent that environmental factors as well as inherent species differences may influence the rate of plumage development.

Vital Statistics

The length and wing measurements and weights are indices of the comparative size of a waterfowl species and can assist in its identification, grossly in the field and more precisely in the hand. Because there are appreciable size differences between the sex- and age-classes, these differences should be considered in species determination: males are larger than females and adults are larger than immatures. Adult males are invariably the largest, immature females invariably the smallest, and immature males are larger than adult females. The important point here is to recognize that the young-of-the-year are not fully grown during the fall hunting season. Unless otherwise noted, the lengths and weights given under the various species accounts were recorded from waterfowl shot during the hunting season. Length was determined by placing the bird on its back and measuring from the tip of its bill to the tip of its longest tail feather.

Wing measurements are used to assist the identification of the sex- and age-classes of wings submitted by hunters to the annual "wing bees." The wing measurements used here were provided by Samuel M. Carney, U. S. Fish and Wildlife Service. The wings were measured from the bend to the tip of the longest flight (primary) feather.

Weights are used to help define species and sex- and age-classes, but, more importantly, to measure the health of an individual bird. We hope that the average weight of a large number of individuals in each sex and age category will provide a weight standard by which to assess the physical condition of waterfowl.

It is apparent from our studies that a duck of normal weight can sustain a weight loss of about 40 percent before expiring. But temperature has some effect upon the weight threshold at death: the lower the temperature, the higher the weight.

Assessment of physical condition need not depend solely upon the base weights of each sex and age group. Within these groups there is a range in the skeletal size of individuals. By relating body weight to wing length, individual variation is further minimized and weight variances can be evaluated still more precisely.

chapter 2

CLASSIFICATION

Animals are classified into different groups that represent the current views of naturally evolved relationships. At the bottom of the hierarchy is the species, a biologically distinct entity because it is reproductively isolated and rarely mates with another species. One species of bird, for example, can recognize its own kind from other species.

Scientific names are used to identify a species anywhere in the world, to identify it in case it has more than one common name, and to relate it to those showing close ancestry within the same genus. Therefore, the scientific name of a species consists first of a capitalized generic name, followed by an uncapitalized specific name. Where races (subspecies) occur within a species, a third name is added to identify the particular geographical variant. Thus, *Branta canadensis* indicates a Canada goose, but *Branta canadensis minima* identifies the smallest race of Canada geese, the cackling goose. When the specific and subspecific (race) names are the same, the specific name is usually indicated by a single letter, for example, *Branta c. canadensis*.

The term subspecies or race is applied to a group of individuals of a species that show variation in size or plumage as a result of geographic or ecological isolation. A number of species of North American waterfowl have races, but the champion is the Canada goose with 11 presently recognized races that range in size from the mallard to almost as large as a swan.

The classification of waterfowl into particular genera and next into tribes is currently in a state of disarray. One reason is that the Committee on Classification and Nomenclature of the American Ornithologists' Union has not completed its current study of bird classification in North America. Until it does, differences in the groupings and arrangements proposed by several authorities will remain unresolved. Because it is obvious that the former classification (*Check-List of North American Birds*, Fifth Edition, 1957) adopted by the American Ornithologists' Union in 1957 is outdated, we have used Johnsgard's (1965) order of arrangement as representing the most valid classification available.

An arrangement of waterfowl species into genera and tribes involves studies of structure, plumage, physiology, habits, and courtship behavior. Delacour and Mayr (1945) used all of these characters in developing a new concept of relationship among species, genera, and tribes. Some of these authors' proposals were adopted by the American Ornithologists' Union when the Committee on Classification and Nomenclature revised the classification of birds in North America in 1957, but many waterfowl biologists believed that further change was warranted. Delacour (1954-1964) revised his earlier concepts of waterfowl classification in his classic volumes, *The Waterfowl of the World*.

Since then, Woolfenden (1961) has made a detailed analysis of the relationship of 10 postcranial bone structures as they concern relationships among most of the waterfowl genera in the world. On the basis of structural relationships, his proposed classification of tribes and genera was similar in many respects but different in a few cases from that of Delacour (1954-64).

Johnsgard (1960*a*, *b*, 1962, 1965) has conducted a long series of studies on the comparative courtship displays of waterfowl in relation to their classification. Using courtship behavior and habits as his primary criteria, Johnsgard (1965) grouped waterfowl somewhat differently from either Woolfenden's (1961) or Delacour's (1954-64) groupings.

Waterfowl, consisting of the swans, geese, and ducks, belong to one family, the Anatidae. Worldwide, there are about 145 species that are grouped into 11 tribes and 43 genera. North America can claim 43 waterfowl species that are native breeders and another 5 species that regularly visit it from Eurasian breeding grounds.

Authorities differ as to the genera into which the 43 species should be placed and as to the tribes that should include the genera. According to Johnsgard's (1965) grouping, there are 7 tribes and 15 genera of waterfowl in North America (fig. 2-1). In this book these are arranged phylogenetically, that is, from those deemed most primitive in their evolutionary development to those that are judged the most advanced.

WHISTLING DUCKS, SWANS, AND GEESE

The whistling (tree) ducks all belong to one genus, *Dendrocygna*, and one tribe, Dendrocygnini. There are eight species, largely in the Southern Hemisphere, but two species, the fulvous and black-bellied whistling ducks, occur in the United States. Their long legs, long necks, and their stance show gooselike affinities. As in swans and geese, the plumages of the sexes are similar, and both parents incubate and share the care of the young. Woolfenden (1961) pointed out bone structures that related the whistling ducks to the swans and geese rather than to the true ducks.

There are seven species of swans in the world, four of which frequent North America. The whistling and trumpeter breed here, the mute has become a feral species, and the whooper visits the Aleutian Islands. The large size and long necks give the swans a singular and majestic appearance. All swans are placed in the Tribe Anserini along with the true geese. This tribe is characterized by the similar plumage and voice of the sexes, one annual molt, lifelong pair bonds, simple courtship displays, sexual maturity at 2 or 3 years, and care of the young by both sexes.

Delacour and Mayr (1945) were of the opinion that swans all belonged in one genus, *Cygnus*. However, there are structural differences—a sternal loop of the trachea and a modified furculum in the trumpeter swan—that indicate that trumpeter and whistling swans should be placed in separate genera (Woolfenden 1961).

Geese have shorter necks and longer legs than swans. They graze extensively on uplands rather than feeding largely on aquatic plants as do swans. There are two genera, *Anser* and *Branta*, that embrace 14 species around the world, 6 species of which are North American. *Branta* are marked by black heads and necks, and, according to Woolfenden (1961), by structural differences.

The tribes embracing the whistling ducks, the swans, and the geese are placed in the Subfamily Anserinae because they are so distinct from other waterfowl: the sexes are of similar plumage, they have one molt, they mate for life, and both sexes care for their young. The remaining waterfowl in North America are placed in five tribes belonging to the Subfamily Anatinae. This subfamily is characterized by ducks that molt twice a year, that is, they possess eclipse and nuptial plumages; they have elaborate courtship displays; pair bonds are temporary and usually brief; and only the female incubates and rears the young.

OTHER DUCKS

The Tribe Anatini contains three genera and 40 species throughout the world. In North America there is but one genus, *Anas*, embracing 10 species of dabbling or puddle ducks, best represented by the ubiquitous mallard. Members of this group have their feet set farther forward than diving ducks, and in taking flight they bound directly upward. They customarily feed by "tipping up" so that their tails show above the water. Their hind toes lack the lobe of skin that is present in those of diving ducks.

Although a dabbling duck in general appearance, Delacour and Mayr (1945) placed the wood duck in the Tribe Cairinini, perching ducks. Perching ducks

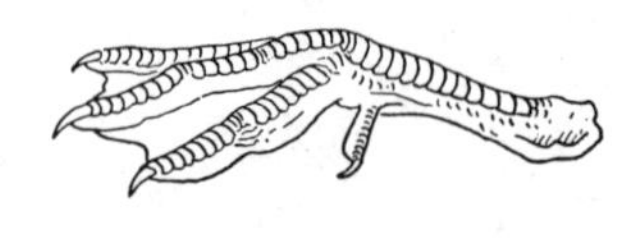

Typical bill and foot of a dabbling duck, showing hind toe without lobe

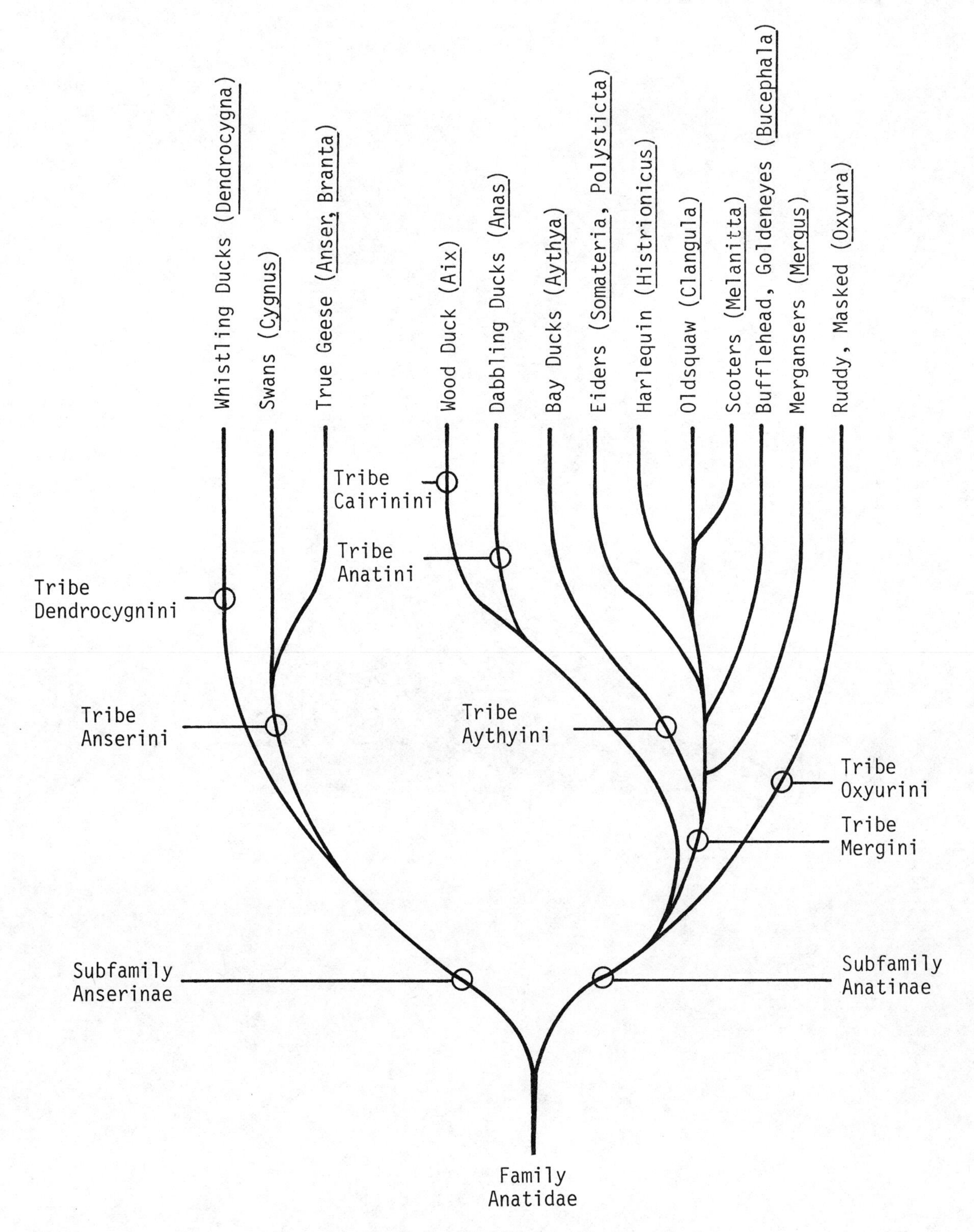

Figure 2-1. The family tree of North American waterfowl

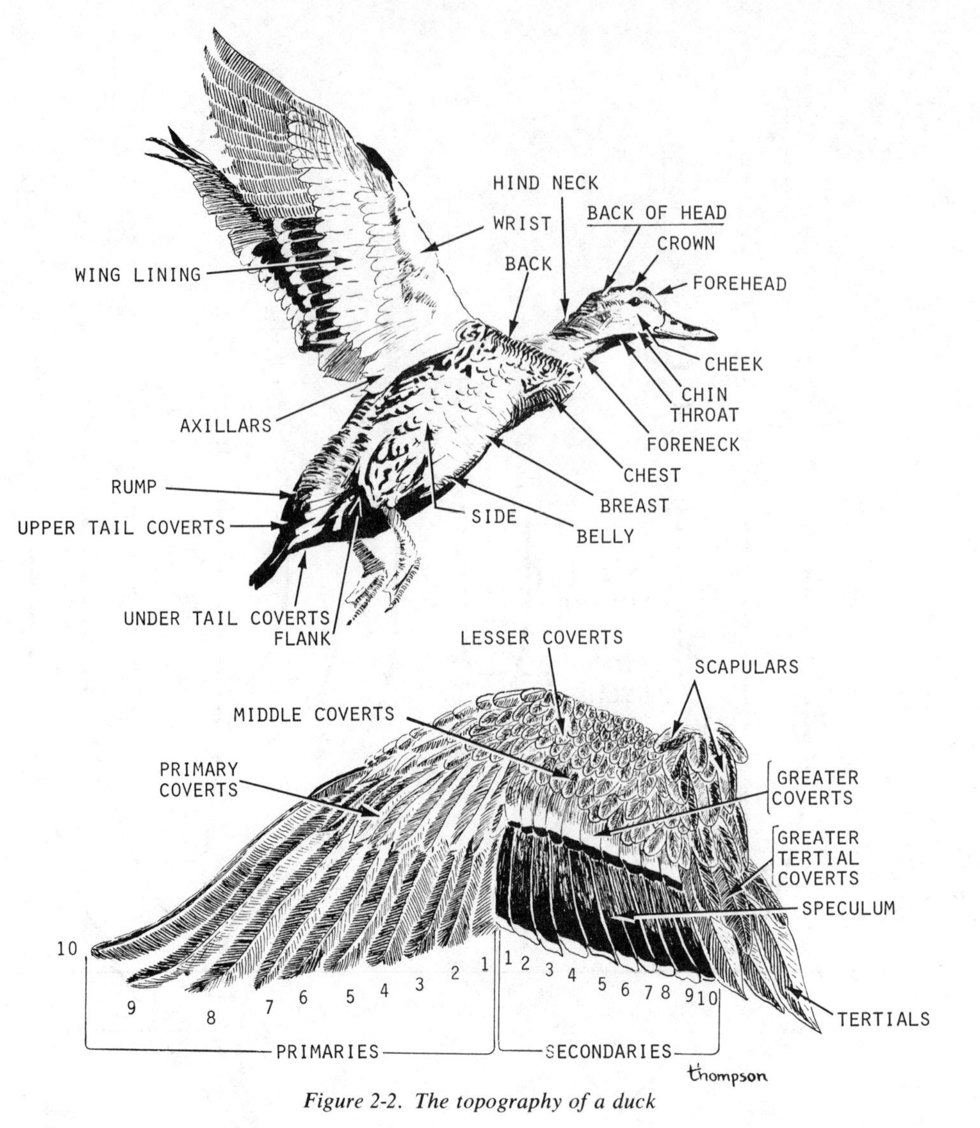

Figure 2-2. The topography of a duck

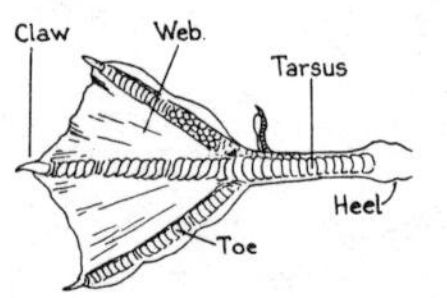

Typical foot

Typical bill

Under surface of wing

have legs farther forward than dabblers, sharp strong claws, well-developed hind toes, and broad wings. There are nine genera representing 13 species worldwide. Only one species, the wood duck, inhabits North America north of Mexico. The Muscovy duck, a resident of Mexico, is placed in this tribe.

The remaining ducks are all diving ducks that have their feet set far back on the body (a location that facilitates diving) and a lobe of skin on their hind toes. They are placed in three tribes embracing 12 extant genera around the world.

The Tribe Aythyini is represented by the bay ducks, or pochards. In North America all belong to one genus, *Aythya*, composed of the canvasback, redhead, ring-necked duck, and the scaups. The displays among the species are similar, and Woolfenden (1961) reported that the skeletal characters also show a close resemblance.

Members of the Tribe Mergini are called sea ducks, and although most of them frequent the sea during the winter, many also inhabit freshwater areas. There are seven extant genera and one extinct genus (represented by the Labrador duck). Species of this tribe do not breed until their second year, thereby differing,from the bay ducks. They have elaborate displays that bear little resemblance to those of other ducks. According to Delacour and Mayr (1945), the eiders, Harlequin, oldsquaw, and scoters resemble the goldeneyes and mergansers in both voice and display.

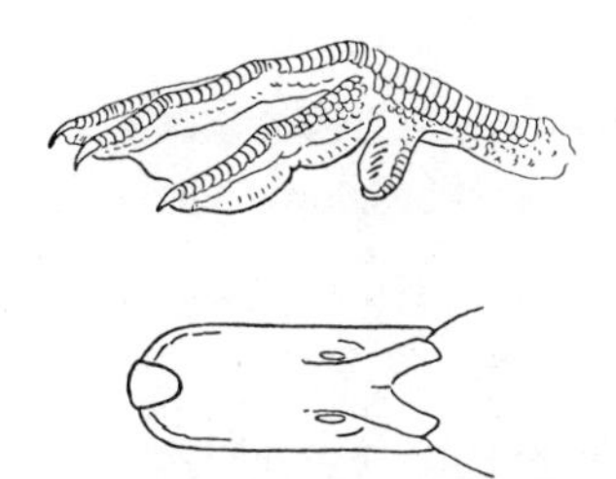

Typical bill and foot of a diving duck, showing hind toe with lobe

The Arctic eiders number four species and are placed in two genera, *Somateria* and *Polysticta*. Their syrinx is different from that of other sea ducks, the females resemble those of dabbling ducks, and the downy young lack the black cap typical of other sea ducks. Johnsgard (1960*b*) compared characteristics of sea duck genera with those of *Somateria* and *Polysticta* and found a 58 percent agreement with *Somateria* and a 68 percent agreement with *Polysticta* (Steller's eider). On the other hand, *Somateria* characters agreed with the puddle ducks (Anatini) in 45 percent of the items compared, whereas *Polysticta* agreed in 44 percent.

The Harlequin duck and the oldsquaw are each placed in a separate genus. Delacour and Mayr (1945) considered that Harlequins, oldsquaws, and goldeneyes were all related because of the dark gray and white pattern in the downy young. The three species of scoters are so similar in appearance as to be placed in one genus, *Melanitta*, although the black scoter (*M. nigra*) has a simple syrinx and the other two species both have a bulbous enlargement of the trachea.

The two goldeneyes and the bufflehead have similar plumage patterns and all three nest in tree cavities. Delacour and Mayr (1945) pointed out that, in general, the color pattern of female goldeneyes closely resembles that of female mergansers, as do the downy young.

All mergansers have long, slender, serrated bills that place them in a single genus, *Mergus*. Hybrids between the common goldeneye (*Bucephala clangula*) and the hooded merganser (*Mergus cucullatus*) in the United States and the smew (*Mergus albellus*) in Europe occur frequently, and suggest a close relationship between the mergansers and the goldeneyes.

Of the three genera of stiff-tailed ducks that form the Tribe Oxyurini, only one genus and two species frequent North America, the ruddy duck and the masked duck. This is the most distinct tribe among all ducks. Their tail feathers are long, stiff, and pointed; their legs are farther back on their bodies than in other ducks, making them more awkward on land. Their necks are short and thick. They lay the largest eggs among waterfowl, considering their size. They perform a bizarre courtship display, unique among waterfowl.

Topography of Waterfowl

In order to avoid long descriptive phrases, taxonomists have found it necessary to name various segments of a bird's plumage. Although we have tried to keep technical jargon to a minimum, there are times when it is advisable to use such terms to avoid verbiage. Technical words are essential in the description of plumages and the soft parts of waterfowl. In order to understand the descriptions of "birds at hand," it is recommended that the reader become familiar with the diagrams of a duck's plumage (fig. 2-2).

chapter 3

MOLTS AND PLUMAGES OF WATERFOWL

Milton W. Weller

A duck's survival after hatching and its success throughout life depend greatly on its protective layer of feathers. A major reason for the successful adaptation of ducks and geese to cold climates is the evolution of a plumage made up of dense feathers and an abundance of down. Different plumages have evolved to meet the needs of the bird at various stages of life from the time of hatch through the growth period until the bird reaches the definitive plumage by which we recognize adults. Thereafter, at least one annual shedding and replacement (a process known collectively as molt) is necessary because of wear. In addition, males of many species of ducks in the Northern Hemisphere annually assume a more colorful plumage prior to pair formation, and females may become duller and better camouflaged just before they nest.

Waterfowl share with some other waterbirds (grebes, loons, and coots) the unusual character of a complete, simultaneous wing molt that leaves them flightless. This molt occurs during the brood period of geese, the postbreeding period of male ducks, and after the brood-rearing period of most female ducks. Regrowth requires from 3 to 5 weeks, varying by species and probably by the bodily condition of the bird, but there are few direct measurements of this period. This molt demands considerable energy, and birds often feed and fatten before the flight feathers are shed. Ducks often desert the nesting grounds and seek out food-rich water areas where they are free from predation while flightless.

SOME TYPICAL PLUMAGES OF WATERFOWL

Although once considered unique, duck plumages have been reinterpreted by comparison with plumages of other birds. It now appears that plumages are homologous, differing mainly in duration, as shown in circular plumage diagrams (fig. 3-1). The terms employed here are those widely used and easily understood in relation to the life cycle of the bird. They follow a modification by Amadon (1966) of the basic system used by Dwight (1900). However, seasonal terms such as winter or autumn (as used in the color plates) and the terminology based on origin and evolution, suggested by Humphrey and Parkes (1959), will be used where pertinent.

Natal Plumage

Unlike newly hatched songbirds, which are naked (psilopaedic), newly hatched waterfowl are completely covered with downy feathers (ptilopaedic). Each down feather originates in a follicle that later will produce the definitive contour feather.

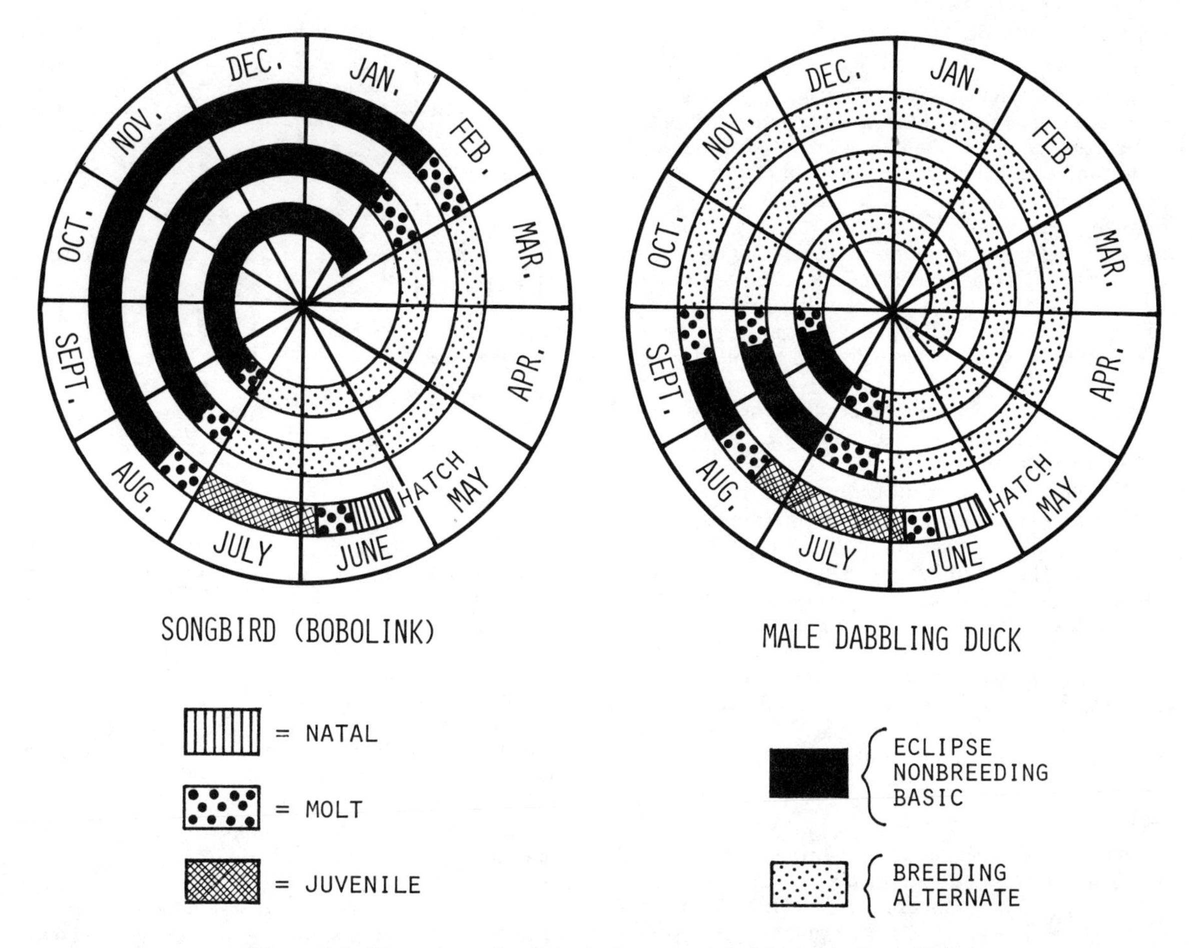

Figure 3-1. Chronology of molt in ducks compared with a typical songbird.

Juvenile Plumage

The natal down feathers are replaced in 2½ to 16 weeks, varying by species and area of the body. The resulting juvenile contour and flight feathers originate in the same feather follicles. In fact, natal down feathers are pushed out of their bases and, in some cases, remain attached to the shafts (rachises) of the new juvenile feathers. This phenomenon is most conspicuous on tail feathers because of their larger shafts. In this case, the growth pattern and severing of the two shafts produces a notch in each tail feather. These notches are used by wildlife biologists as a criterion of age. The juvenile plumage is completed and flight is attained from about 6 weeks (blue-winged teal) to 9 weeks (canvasbacks) in ducks, 6 to 7 weeks (lesser snow geese) to 8 to 9 weeks (Canada geese) in geese, and 14 to 16 weeks in swans. Juvenile feathers may be retained on some areas of the body well into winter or spring, and the juvenile wings are held until the next summer.

There is some evidence that feathers of late-hatched young redheads grow more rapidly than do those of early-hatched birds (Smart 1965). It was thought that young reared in high latitudes, such as the Arctic, might reach flight stage faster than those reared in temperate latitudes, but Schneider (1965) was unable to demonstrate this difference by comparing data from Alaska with data from the Prairie Pothole region. He suggested that age at flight attainment was similar in these two regions but that body feathers grew faster in the higher latitudes and hence birds became fully feathered at an earlier age. Faster growth of body feathers would have some protective advantage in a cold climate.

Prior to or concurrent with the growth of the first juvenile feathers, down develops from small feather follicles between those holding the natal down. This juvenile down is often less colorful and, along with fading of the natal down, reduces the contrasting color pattern found in older ducklings. The duration of the juvenile down is uncertain.

Immature Plumage

The males of most species of ducks have a partial to nearly complete body plumage that usually is similar in color to that of the juvenile plumage but in some cases is intermediate in color between the juvenile and adult plumages. It varies in males from a partial renewal of the head feathers and of a few body feathers in early fall (mallard) to a nearly complete but short-lived plumage (blue-winged teal) worn during fall migration and through early winter. The wing feathers are not shed in this molt but the notched juvenile tail feathers are replaced with pointed feathers characteristic of all adult plumages. Females also acquire an extensive postjuvenile plumage, but because differences in color or in patterns are more subtle, interpretation is even more difficult than in males.

The plumage of immatures has been considered homologous to nonbreeding ("eclipse") plumages of adults (Salomonsen 1949, Snyder and Lumsden 1951, Humphrey and Parkes 1959). Humphrey and Parkes (1959) termed it the "basic" plumage and assumed that it was a primitive plumage in evolution, which preceded the bright-colored breeding plumage that they termed "alternate." If they are correct, this immature plumage is a remnant of the first nonbreeding or eclipse plumage of ducks and is comparable to the first adultlike plumage of geese.

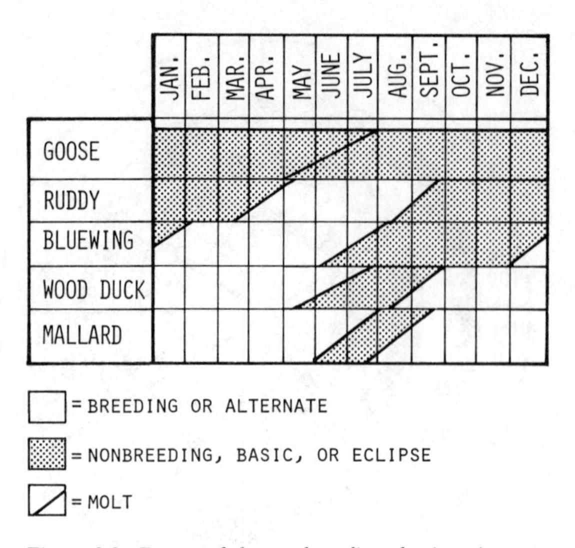

Figure 3-2. Extent of the nonbreeding, basic, winter, or eclipse plumage in adult male waterfowl of the Northern Hemisphere.

Adult Plumages

In birds like geese that have only one plumage per year, the term "adult" infers a definitive plumage by which the species is identified and in which breeding takes place. In cases where the plumage is superficially adultlike in appearance but the bird does not breed in it, the term "subadult" may be used. This single plumage is molted once annually in the postbreeding period prior to fall migration.

Ducks have at least two body plumages annually that may differ markedly in color by seasons (seasonal dichromatism) and sexes (sexual dichromatism)—well demonstrated in male ruddy ducks and mallards. But female dabbling and diving ducks, like female and male black ducks, are similar in color, and different plumages may be differentiated only by detailed study of feather patterns. The terms "breeding" and "nonbreeding" have been applied to these two plumages. In the ruddy duck, these plumages are also separated seasonally so that the breeding plumage occurs in summer and the nonbreeding or eclipse occurs as a winter plumage (fig. 3-2). This pattern is a logical one found regularly in songbirds (fig. 3-1), but plumages of most species of ducks are much more complex. The basic difference is that the period when males wear the dull nonbreeding plumage is shortened to the summer postbreeding flightless period. The dull plumage characteristic of the flightless period has become known as the eclipse or hiding plumage. Most male dabbling or diving ducks acquire this drab plumage after the breeding season. Blue-winged teal retain it well into early winter, but mallards and other dabbling and diving ducks lose it by late summer or early fall (fig. 3-2). Males then acquire a new breeding plumage and are seen in this plumage during the fall migration. In comparison, most songbirds fly southward in the dull nonbreeding plumage, which they, like ruddy ducks, retain until the next spring.

The situation in females is less clear-cut because plumage colors differ so little and it is difficult to relate slight color differences to function in the breeding cycle. It has been generally assumed that the pattern in adult females resembled that of ruddy ducks—females acquired the breeding plumage in spring prior to nesting and replaced this plumage with the nonbreeding plumage in the late-summer flightless period. Palmer (1972), based in part on Oring (1968), has suggested that females acquire the breeding plumage in late summer or fall, as do males, and retain most of it until spring. In the spring, their nonbreeding plumage develops in part before nesting (resulting in duller coloration and hence improved camouflage), and may then be completed after nesting. A nesting yearling gadwall female may have parts of three plumages: immature tertials, breeding tail, and nonbreeding body and back (Oring 1968). The plumage of nesting female yearling gadwalls involves an even greater evolutionary shift than occurs in males, with the winter nonbreeding plumage shifting forward in time to the prenesting period. Why such a difference should also have evolved in the female gadwall or other dabbling ducks whereas ruddy females retain a presumably primitive winter-summer pattern has not been explained. Certainly, much additional work needs to be done on these cycles.

At least one duck, the oldsquaw or long-tailed duck, seems to have more than two plumages a year. Although Palmer (1972) has referred to the extra one as a supplemental plumage, its function has yet to be determined, and the possibility exists that this plumage also is an ancestral one common in some component to plumages in other ducks.

PATTERNS OF MOLT IN VARIOUS GROUPS OF WATERFOWL

The pattern of molt is one of the major criteria for taxonomic groupings of waterfowl—the grouping of species that share certain characters. For example, only one species of waterfowl, the semipalmated goose (*Anseranas anseranas*) of Australia, has a serial rather than simultaneous wing molt. As a result, it is never flightless. This characteristic and other features result in its classification in a separate subfamily of the Family Anatidae, the Anseranatinae. The magpie goose has only one complete molt per year, and the sexes are colored alike.

Subfamily Anserinae (whistling ducks, swans, and geese)

The whistling or tree ducks (Tribe Dendrocygnini) and the geese and swans (Tribe Anserini) all seem to have similar molts and plumages. There is one plumage per year with a single complete annual molt involving the body and tail, and a concurrent simultaneous wing molt that renders them flightless during the postnesting period. Adults lack conspicuous sex-related differences in plumage color (sexual dichromatism). However, lesser snow geese are characterized by two color phases, the so-called "blue goose" (blue phase or morph) and the white phase "snow goose." The blue phase is genetically dominant over the white phase and is found mainly in the Eastern Arctic, whereas the white phase is characteristic of birds of the Western Arctic.

After the natal plumage, a juvenile plumage is acquired and much of it may be retained throughout the fall and winter. This juvenile plumage may be distinctively different in color, as in gray juvenile snow geese, or adultlike as in Canada geese. Thereafter, the juvenile plumage is replaced on the head, neck, and body by an adult-patterned plumage that can be termed "subadult." Whistling ducks retain the juvenile wings until after the first breeding season, which apparently occurs in their first year. In geese, which do not breed until 2 to 3 years of age, and in swans, which breed when they are 4 or 5, yearling nonbreeders molt during the breeding period of adults. The flight feathers are shed during the midst of the complete annual body molt. This new adult plumage then is retained a full year until the postbreeding period of the next summer.

Subfamily Anatinae (typical ducks and sheldgeese)

Plumages and molts of the typical ducks (Subfamily Anatinae) are much more complex, and patterns vary by subgroups (tribes) and geographic areas. In comparison with geese, their general pattern in the Northern Hemisphere is one of conspicuously colored males during the breeding season that assume a dull plumage afterwards (seasonal dichromatism). Females are drab-colored all year. There are two molts per year in adults of both sexes. There is at least one tail molt per year, which, like the wing molt, is associated with the postbreeding molt, but most species seem to molt some if not all tail feathers twice each year.

In South America and other southern continents, male ducks usually differ little in color from females, but, if they do, they lack the seasonal plumage change and are permanently dichromatic. However, they still seem to have two molts per year, as do northern ducks (Weller 1968).

Females in the prenesting period molt their down and a new, longer, and often darker down grows. This down covers and insulates eggs in the nest bowl.

Dabbling Ducks (Tribe Anatini). The first immature plumage of males is so similar to that of juvenile males or of hens that it has often been overlooked. Some species, like blue-winged teal, have a nearly complete plumage held for several months, whereas others, like the mallard, have a transient plumage restricted mostly to the head, breast, mantle, and tail (fig. 3-2). The definitive male breeding plumage is acquired early in fall in most species and precedes the fall and winter courtship period. It is held until the complete annual molt, which occurs after the breeding season. However, it is possible in fall to find molting birds with remnants of juvenile and the first nonbreeding plumage as well as new incoming breeding plumage. In subsequent years, the nonbreeding or eclipse plumage of most dabbling ducks is complete but is held only several weeks prior to and after the wing molt and late summer and the staging period that precedes migration (fig. 3-1).

Females develop their first nonbreeding plumage concurrently with that of males, then molt into the first breeding plumage. According to Oring (1968) and Palmer (1972), females seem to lose much of this plumage earlier than do males and start their molt into the nonbreeding plumage prior to nesting. This plumage varies in extent and color pattern by species, but it seems to renew worn feathers of the head, neck, scapulars, and sides. Female plumages become very worn after the brood period, when a complete molt in late summer places females in a neat, relatively bright new plumage that Palmer (1972) considers the breeding plumage.

Inland Diving Ducks (Tribe Aythyini). The pattern of plumage sequence in this group is similar to that of the dabbling ducks, but the immature plumage may cover more extensive areas of the body and may last longer. In redheads and canvasbacks, the immature plumage occurs mainly on the heads of males. After the juvenile plumage, females experience nearly continuous molt of the body plumage, which may involve three generations of feathers before nesting starts—the first nonbreeding plumage, the breeding plumage, and part of the second nonbreeding plumage.

In adult males, the late-summer eclipse plumage is held only until early fall, and the breeding plumage is present, as in dabblers, throughout the courtship and pair-formation periods of winter through the breeding season in early summer. There are some differences in timing among species, but the chronology is grossly related to the timing of nesting; canvasbacks precede the lesser scaup in acquisition of breeding plumage, pair formation, and nesting (Weller 1965). Gradual color changes in the eyes of at least female lesser scaup occur with age (Trauger 1974*a*).

Perching Ducks (Tribe Cairinini). The only North American representative of the dominantly tropical perching ducks is the wood duck. The molts in this species have been recently outlined by Palmer (1972). Present information suggests that the North American wood duck has a general pattern similar to that of dabbling ducks. Its early nonbreeding plumage is fleeting, and the female apparently nests while still in the breeding plumage.

Sea Ducks (Tribe Mergini). At least males, and probably both sexes, do not mature sexually until nearly 2 years of age. It is not surprising, therefore, to find that the definitive breeding plumage of males does not appear until the second fall of life prior to the winter courtship period.

Little is known of this group but the following pattern seems indicated: After the juvenile plumage, males have a fairly complete immature plumage that is like that of females but is distinguishable by the malelike colors and patterns in the juvenile wings. The soft parts (bills, eyes, feet) of young males take on malelike colors early but these parts show gradual maturation to completely adult forms. After this plumage the young males assume another, probably partial, henlike plumage that seems to be homologous with the breeding plumage in later life. It is retained until the complete annual molt of midsummer. There seems to be a nonbreeding or eclipse plumage of brief duration in late summer and early fall that is replaced in late fall by the male's first definitive breeding plumage at the age of 1 year and 3 or 4 months. Even this plumage is less distinctive than that of older birds.

Salomonsen (1949) suggested that oldsquaws regularly produce three generations of feathers each year and have at least four patterns at various seasons. Palmer (1972) regards the extra generation as a "supplemental" plumage.

The molt of female sea ducks is less well known because all their plumages are similar in color. Presumably, the molt pattern resembles that of females of other tribes that hold the first immature plumage until winter, when the first subadult breeding plumage is acquired.

Stifftails (Tribe Oxyurini). The ruddy duck is the only North American duck that resembles songbirds in having a typical bright summer plumage and a dull winter plumage. Because the dull plumage is long-lasting, the term "eclipse" (which means hiding) is not suitable. The young male molts from juvenile into complete immature plumage in December to January and into its first breeding plumage in March and April. The coloration of the immature plumage is like that of subsequent nonbreeding (winter) plumages. The breeding plumage is held until July or August, when both wing and body feathers are renewed. The male gradually assumes its winter-long nonbreeding or winter plumage. In this case, the winter nonbreeding plumage is dull like that of the female, whereas the mallard wears the bright breeding plumage most of the winter (fig. 3-2).

The molt of hens is less well known because there are no seasonal color differences, but the molt pattern seems to be the same in both sexes (Palmer 1972). There is some evidence that the flight feathers may be renewed when the new breeding plumage is acquired, so that the wings are molted twice a year in many members of this tribe.

chapter 4

MIGRATION

Most of the 775 species of birds in North America migrate, but because waterfowl are more visible than other species in migration, they epitomize this phenomenon to most people. And to most hunters waterfowl migration is an eagerly awaited event because of the drama they may witness from a blind and the success it may bring to them.

Only a few species of waterfowl are nonmigratory, best exemplified by the mottled and Florida ducks. Although both these species may fly 100 or more miles, their flights are random, with no directional or seasonal rhythm.

Segments of some migratory species do not migrate. For example, in the southern part of their breeding ranges, wood ducks and hooded mergansers are resident throughout the year. However, band recoveries from hunters show that some young and some of the adults fly northward 100 miles or more after the breeding season. Some groups of mallards and Canada geese migrate only short distances, or when winter conditions are favorable, not at all. Races of common eiders also belong to this quasi-migratory group.

As a whole, waterfowl make tremendously long migratory flights. Black brant that nest on Queen Maud Gulf in the central Canadian Arctic migrate along the continental coast to Baja California. Lesser snow geese and pintails that breed on Wrangel Island, Siberia, winter in the Central Valley of California. Pintails that have been banded in Alaska have been shot in Guatemala, almost 5,000 miles distant. Some of the blue-winged teal breeding in Alberta, Saskatchewan, Manitoba, and the Dakotas winter in Ecuador, south of the equator. There is indirect evidence that blue-winged teal leave New England and fly nonstop south over the Atlantic Ocean at least 1,600 miles to the Lesser Antilles, and possibly 2,500 miles to Guyana.

Other species of waterfowl also fly over vast stretches of ocean. Black brant departing the tip of the Alaska Peninsula fly almost 2,000 miles across the northeast corner of the Pacific Ocean before making landfall in northern California. Most of them then continue down the coast another 1,000 miles into Baja California. Pintails, American wigeons, and lesser scaups regularly winter in the Hawaiian Islands (Berger 1972); most of these birds come from Alaska, but a pintail banded on Oahu was recovered near Beringovaki, Russia. Several species of ducks, blue-winged teal in particular, migrate in large numbers 600 or more miles across the Gulf of Mexico to winter grounds in Central America.

In migrating over hostile environments, waterfowl fly continuously unless forced by exhaustion or adverse weather to land. Thus, there is every reason to believe that certain elements of the population in several species make nonstop flights of a minimum of 2,000 miles and possibly as much as 3,000 miles.

Even where there are suitable resting places, some waterfowl prefer to migrate nonstop to winter grounds. A large proportion of lesser snow geese that depart from the southern part of James Bay fly 1,600 miles nonstop to the coastal marshes of Louisiana.

Most waterfowl appear to migrate at speeds of 40 to 60 miles per hour and average about 50. A flight of 2,000 miles would, therefore, take 40 hours. In September I have seen flocks of Canada geese land in an almost complete state of exhaustion, having apparently flown 900 miles nonstop from James Bay to central Illinois. The short time that had elapsed between fledging of the young, their parents' acquisition of flight feathers, and their flight south probably contributed to their exhausted condition.

Migrating waterfowl fly from a few feet above the sea to over 20,000 feet above mean sea level. Apparently, the altitude of migration depends upon the terrain and the distance flown. The lowest migratory flights are those of sea ducks over the ocean. Waterfowl show no hesitancy in migrating sufficiently high to clear the loftiest ranges in the Rocky Mountains and sometimes reach altitudes of nearly 12,000 feet.

Of the extensive observation of bird migration that I have witnessed on radarscopes, shorebirds and lesser snow geese were most often at high altitudes. On radarscopes at both St. Louis, Missouri, and Lake Charles, Louisiana, I have witnessed snow geese at altitudes of slightly over 10,000 feet. At Lake Charles, the birds are at the end of a long migratory flight. I have one pilot report of a flock of snow geese near Alexandria, Louisiana, at the extreme altitude of 20,000 feet above the ground.

Canada geese in the Midwest migrate at lower altitudes, and usually not as far, as snow geese. Over 400 pilot reports of fall-migrating Canada geese, tabulated for the eastern half of the United States for 1960-69, revealed that most were flying 2,000 feet above the ground; 52 percent of the flocks were between 1,000 and 3,000 feet. Some flocks were as low as 500 feet and three flocks as high as 11,000 feet.

Although the spring records from 250 pilot reports indicate the largest number of geese were 2,500 feet above the ground, 500 feet higher than during the fall, the general altitudinal level was lower in the spring: 67 percent of the flocks were between 1,000 and 3,000 feet, and none were above 7,000 feet. At the site of observation in the spring, most flocks would not have migrated as far as in the fall. Here is another bit of evidence that the longer the migratory flight, the higher the altitude.

WHY WATERFOWL MIGRATE

Two questions that audiences have asked me countless times are: "Why do waterfowl migrate?" and "How do they find their way?" Both questions can be only partially answered at this time. The biological reason for waterfowl migration is survival. Most waterfowl would not survive if they did not migrate, for water areas—where the bulk of them breed—freeze over, making food unattainable. On the other hand, space and food supplies are insufficient to accommodate them on the winter grounds. The few resident species and individuals, such as wood ducks, mottled ducks, and the mallards that breed on winter areas exploit the habitat to its fullest. The inhospitality of each region—breeding area and winter area—at different times of the year dictate the seasonal movements to and from each region.

Individuals of numerous species migrate as short a distance as possible to find open water and food. As these conditions change during the winter or from year to year, so the migrants alter their winter areas to meet their needs. Examples are Arctic-breeding species that migrate only short distances to where seas remain open through the winter, such as: the emperor goose, four species of eiders, a scattering of dabbling ducks, both scaups, both goldeneyes, and the common and red-breasted mergansers. Population elements of the larger races of Canada geese and the mallard attempt to winter as far north as open water prevails and food can be obtained. Several hundred Canadas winter as far north as Newfoundland and up to 30,000 at Rochester, Minnesota. Small numbers of mallards usually manage to winter where waters remain open in Alberta, Saskatchewan, and North Dakota. But even more surprising are the mallards that winter in the interior of Alaska, where temperatures drop to −50° F (Gabrielson and Lincoln 1959).

In response to sources of food, the migratory habits of waterfowl are changing. Tens of thousands of Canada geese and mallards winter several hundreds of miles north of their former winter grounds as a result of the growing availability of both feed and cereal grains. During the last 5 years, an increasing number of snow geese have either wintered or attempted to winter in western Iowa and Missouri and eastern Nebraska. A few decades ago, none wintered north of coastal Louisiana and Texas.

When hurricanes opened up the densely vegetated coastal marshes in Louisiana, improving them for ducks, tens of thousands of ducks responded by wintering there rather than continuing across the Gulf of Mexico to Yucatan. Blue-winged and green-winged teal, shovelers, pintails, gadwalls, and wigeons all took advantage of the newly developed food resources.

It is evident, then, that food supplies determine where and when large segments of waterfowl migrate. Not so readily explained are large-scale movements among most species of waterfowl that occur before food supplies become a limiting factor.

The flights that occur before food shortages develop appear to be programmed in the endocrine system, probably going back eons in time when food shortages necessitated migration.

Literally hundreds of experiments have been conducted on the physiological factors responsible for bird migration, yet scientists still do not fully understand the complexities that govern the particular timing of migratory departures. This timing is caused by differences among species—differences that are particularly great among birds wintering in the north temperate, the tropical, and the south temperate zones. Because most waterfowl winter in the north temperate zone, the physiological state regulating their initiation of migration is probably more uniform than in most other bird families.

Regulators of the physiological state are both intrinsic and extrinsic. That means that factors within the bird itself enter into the timing mechanism as well as environmental factors. The length of night in comparison with day length (photoperiod) appears to be the key extrinsic factor that sets the intrinsic timing mechanism. Photoperiod operates through the influence of light upon the pituitary gland, which releases hormones that control the annual clock of the species. Once the annual clock is started by the increase in light, it needs to run the entire gamut of life activities—migration, courtship, breeding, and molt—before it can be reset.

An important corollary to the internal clock's stimulus of a migratory state is the deposition of fat. Many experiments have shown that birds must accumulate large reserves of fat before they are disposed to migrate. Fat provides the energy required to meet the needs of long flights. Fat is important because it provides twice the energy per unit of weight as does protein, as exemplified by the large flight muscles. When shortages of desirable foods exist, the length of time required to reach a readiness to migrate increases.

The endocrine cycle provides the evidence that explains why all individuals of a particular waterfowl species do not migrate at the same time. Fall migration in some species of ducks is extended over periods as long as 2 months. Nesting may be equally protracted. Hence, an early-nesting bird enters the molt before a late-nesting one, and, in turn, is ready to migrate early. Similarly, a duckling hatched 2 months earlier than its brethren would be prepared to migrate earlier by almost the same time span.

It's been said many times by many people that certain waterfowl migrate by "the clock." The early flights south in the fall and the late flights north in the spring certainly appear to fall within this connotation. However, weather conditions and food supplies, which become increasingly important as the fall progresses, may modify the immediate timing. The later the period of migration in the fall and the earlier in the spring, the greater the likelihood that weather and food supplies will influence the chronology of passage.

There is no simple relationship between weather factors and the initiation of migratory flights. Waterfowl migrate under a wide variety of weather conditions. In Illinois we observed arriving flights of ducks on 42 percent of a 66-day period, October 1-December 5, 1948-68 (Bellrose 1974). During any one fall in the 20-year period, ducks were detected arriving from a minimum of 17 percent to a maximum of 65 percent of the time. Numerous small flights of ducks probably arrived undetected. Indeed, radar surveillance suggests that there is some degree of migration in Illinois almost every night in November (Bellrose 1964).

Occasionally, a mass flight of waterfowl departs the breeding grounds. Conditions for these grand passages of ducks usually occur only once every few years. Although there were three grand passages in the falls of 1955 (October 31-November 3), 1956 (November 6-8), and 1957 (October 31-November 25), none occurred during the next 17 years (Bellrose and Sieh 1960).

Weather conditions responsible for initiating these massed movements were fairly strong winds that were partially or entirely favorable, falling snow, overcast skies, and falling temperatures. These conditions were associated with a low pressure in 2 years and a higher pressure the other year. They resulted in waterfowl departures during the day, rather than at sunset and at night, their customary time.

HOW WATERFOWL NAVIGATE

Waterfowl, like many other birds, have an ability to return to the same breeding, migration, and winter areas that they visited the previous year or years. Some species have more fixed homing patterns than others, as is evident when this trait is discussed in the species accounts. Perhaps species with poor homing records are as capable as those with good records but are simply more opportunistic in utilizing available habitats.

We found that mallards and black ducks had a strongly developed homing character that directed them during the fall migration to the same areas visited the previous fall (Bellrose and Crompton 1970). Homing of Canada geese back to the same winter grounds has been well documented (Hanson and Smith 1950, Vaught and Kirsch 1966, Grieb 1970, and others). Their return to the same breeding grounds is even more exact (Martin 1964, Sherwood 1965, Hanson and Eberhardt 1971). Because waterfowl need to utilize particular water areas, often several hundred miles apart, it is paramount to their survival that they reach these goals. Therefore, they need an accurate means of navigation, more precise than many land birds require.

In acquiring their navigational abilities, each species of waterfowl has evolved different usages of cues and different degrees of dependency on them, according to the distances and conditions under which each migrates. For example, mallards that migrate short distances show a different use of sun and star cues than do blue-winged teal, which migrate much farther (Bellrose 1963).

There can be little doubt that waterfowl make extensive use of the landscape in navigating across country. Over the years, I have observed hundreds of diurnally migrating flocks of waterfowl change directions by 35 to 45 degrees, from southeast to south, when they arrive at the Mississippi and Illinois rivers. Most flocks continue southward in flight, sometimes 100 miles or more to their particular "home" migration area. This home area represents the place where some members of the flock stopped the year before (Bellrose and Crompton 1970). Immatures in the flock learn the landscape cues on their maiden flights. This knowledge enables them in subsequent years to repeat the sequence of stopping places from breeding to winter areas. If it were not for such adaptive behavior, the dispersion now evident would not be as orderly.

The degree that waterfowl use landscape cues at night probably depends upon the visibility of the cues. We have empirical evidence that under low, heavy overcast at night, waterfowl often overshoot their home areas, necessitating a reverse migration after daylight or a return the next evening from some other water area.

On nights when bodies of water are visible, waterfowl use them to alter their direction of flight. While viewing an FAA radarscope near Chicago, Illinois, on the night of March 22, 1969, I observed a large Canada goose migration proceeding northward from southern Illinois. At the radar site most flocks were 20 to 35 miles west of Lake Michigan. The lake curves north-northwestward from its lower end. When flocks of migrating geese approached the lake's shoreline 30 miles north of the radar site, most of them turned in flight from north to east or northeast to pass out over the lake. We have other examples of waterfowl apparently using water areas to change directions at night, and Hochbaum (1955) discusses many instances of waterfowl use of landscape cues in diurnal migration.

Waterfowl migrate across trackless regions of the continent for distances up to several hundred miles where the landscape provides few, if any, cues. And they migrate on nights so dark from heavy, low clouds that the juxtaposition of land and water is apparent only at a few hundred feet, and when directly overhead. We have also held immature blue-winged teal in the fall until after other members of the species had departed Illinois. Band recoveries from these young teal indicated that without prior knowledge of the landscape and without the guidance of adult ducks, the young ones successfully migrated in directions taken by the species.

It is therefore evident that landscape alone is not a prerequisite for cross-country migration. From a series of experiments that we made over a decade ago, it was discovered that mallards and several other species of waterfowl used the position of the sun and stars to derive directional information (Bellrose 1958, 1963). An internal clock enables mallards to adjust for the changing position of the sun in the sky but not for the changing positions of the stars. Matthews (1963) determined that at night mallards used patterns of stars—not their relative positions to the horizon—to determine direction.

Thus, using landscape and celestial cues, waterfowl under clear skies would have no difficulty in navigating. However, radar surveillance of waterfowl migration disclosed that migratory flights occasionally occurred between cloud layers (Bellrose 1967). Although the dispersion of tracks on the radarscope was slightly greater under overcast than under clear skies, flight was still well oriented. Hence, the radar findings showed that some species of waterfowl are able to navigate directionally without references to landscape or celestial cues.

The two other environmental cues that waterfowl might use in navigation are wind and the earth's magnetic field. Evidence at this time favors the use of the earth's magnetic field for navigational purposes when other sources, easier to use, are unavailable.

Recent experiments with homing pigeons (Keeton 1971, 1972) and with gulls (Southern 1971) lend credence to the hypothesis proposed many years ago that migrating birds are able to use the earth's magnetic field for directional purposes. Although these experiments have not included waterfowl, it is evident that use of the earth's magnetic field by such diverse species as pigeons and gulls would place this source within the capability of waterfowl. Thus it appears that the earth's magnetic field may provide the missing link in the repertoire of navigational cues that migrating waterfowl resort to when they are unable to see the landscape or celestial bodies.

Field observations combined with empirical experiments lead me to believe that waterfowl use the available kinds of cues to different degrees. Such adaptive behavior may have evolved as a result of the demands placed upon each species by the distance between breeding and winter grounds and by the nature of the earth's surface over which the migration occurred. For example, the interior race of the Canada goose uses landscape cues to a greater degree than the lesser snow goose as they migrate through the Midwest. Similarly, mallards use landscape cues more assiduously than do blue-winged teal.

chapter 5

CONSERVATION OF WATERFOWL

Glen C. Sanderson

Waterfowl conservation embraces four distinct entities: habitat preservation and enhancement, the establishment of waterfowl regulations that permit the highest kill commensurate with the capability of the species to replace these losses, the control of disease, and propagation.

Of these four, habitat preservation and enhancement is the most important. Other depressing effects upon waterfowl abundance are transitory compared to the long-lasting effect that habitat destruction and deterioration have upon their populations. When waterfowl regulations miss their goal either by being too restrictive or too liberal, modern inventory methods detect the resultant changes in the populations within a short time and regulations can be adjusted accordingly. Although there are a number of diseases that man can do little to control, he can, if he wishes, exercise complete control of lead poisoning and a degree of control over botulism.

Only one species of waterfowl, the Labrador duck (*Camptorhynchus labradorius*), has become extinct in North America in historical times. It is reported that this species was not popular as food because of its fishy taste. However, it was easy to kill and its down was valuable commercially. Egg collectors may have been partially responsible for this sea duck disappearing from the waters of the northeastern United States and Canada by 1875. This duck became extinct so soon after it was discovered that we know very little about its habits and only a few specimens have been preserved. Over-exploitation by man may have been responsible for the extinction of the Labrador duck, but in the 20th century in North America man's regulated exploitation of waterfowl is not believed to be a major cause for the long-term decline of any species.

The principal reason for the drastic decline of ducks in the 20th century has been man's destruction of wetland habitats needed for breeding and feeding during migration periods and during the winter. Not only have millions of acres of wetlands been destroyed by drainage, filling, and inundation, but the quality of other millions of acres has deteriorated from siltation or other forms of pollution.

In some cases man has intentionally or unintentionally created wetland habitats or improved existing habitats for waterfowl. The U. S. Fish and Wildlife Service and conservation agencies of almost all states have accomplished a remarkable program of wetland acquisition, creation, and enhancement. State and federal programs in the late 1930's and the 1940's were concerned both with the restoration of previously drained marshes and the acquisition of existing wetlands. In recent years most of the emphasis has been on the acquisition of existing wetlands. By manipulating water levels through dams and levees, by constructing nest islands and nest sites, and by cultivating food resources, many federal and state wetland areas have been enhanced over pristine conditions.

The waterfowl hunters of North America have been largely responsible for the federal and state programs to acquire, restore, and improve wetlands for waterfowl. Funds for these programs have been derived from the so-called Duck Stamp, from the excise tax on sporting arms and ammunition, and from state hunting license fees. In addition, waterfowl hunters have donated $25 million to Ducks Unlimited, 1937-74, for the restoration and development of wetlands in Canada.

This chapter includes an appraisal of the distribution, abundance, and ecological characteristics of the wetlands in the United States together with the destructive and constructive forces that have affected their existence and a brief discussion of other management techniques. Separate chapters in this book discuss regulations and diseases.

WETLANDS

Distribution, Abundance, and Ecological Characteristics

The reader is referred to Sanderson and Bellrose (1969) for a more extensive discussion of wetlands and waterfowl.

United States. The original, natural wetlands, both freshwater and saltwater, of the United States have been estimated at 127 million acres. With a loss of about 52 million acres, there were in 1968 about 75 million acres of land in the United States too wet for crops or pasture—where drainage and flood control operations had not altered their original wet condition.

At that time, of the some 74.4 million acres being used in varying degrees by waterfowl, about 9 million acres were classed as high-quality wetlands, 13.5 million acres as of moderate value, 24 million as of low value, and 28 million acres as of negligible value.

Canada. The total area of the tundra and northern forests covers about 2.24 billion acres. Sanderson and Bellrose (1969:168-169) reported that waterfowl habitats in these biomes are stable and are unlikely to be seriously disturbed by man in the near future. The river deltas in the northern coniferous forests cover an area of about 35,648,000 acres. These areas are threatened by proposed dams and oil exploration. The Prairie Pothole Region of Canada covers an area of some 103,040,000 acres which up to the mid-1960's had suffered only minor losses, but since then has been under increasingly active destruction by drainage and clearing.

Lynch et al. (1963) reported that up to 1963 the wetlands of Canada had not sustained the extensive losses that had occurred in the United States. There were, however, serious isolated losses, such as the loss of 1.75 million acres of the delta of the Saskatchewan River. By the late 1960's Aus (1969) reported that the same land-use operations that have crippled the wetland resource in the United States were taking the same destructive toll of marshes across the Canadian waterfowl production prairies. Draining, filling, and clearing were accelerating in the Prairie Provinces. Although quantitative data were lacking, he saw drainage increase in intensity and sophistication each year. Expanding exports of grain created an increased demand for cropland acres, and the clearing of aspen woodlands and the filling and draining of wetlands were increasingly common on the prairie landscape of Canada. Aus (1969) further reported that 300,000 acres of land were cleared for farming in Saskatchewan alone during 1968. Drainage in the Minnedosa area of Manitoba, one of North America's important areas for producing canvasbacks, was especially severe.

Whitesell (1970:327-328) pointed out that data on drainage in the north country are hard to obtain and that the exact acreage drained is never as important as the total area affected. He reported that of the almost 3 million acres drained in the prairie provinces, half had been drained before 1930. He felt that these were barely minimal figures and that the loss of additional potholes will be even more critical for duck production during future periods of dry weather.

Tundra and Northern Forests. The tundra and northern forests contain millions of acres in lakes, marshes, and meadows that produce hundreds of thousands of ducks. Of special importance to waterfowl is the wide annual fluctuation in numbers of ducks recorded on northern marshes. These variations show an inverse correlation with the occurrence of small water areas on the northern Great Plains (Crissey 1969). Large numbers of ducks move farther north when drought dries up the multitudes of potholes and ponds on the northern plains. Most of the displaced ducks do not breed so the production of young on the more northern areas is similar to that occurring when fewer ducks are present; however, many of the adults survive to another breeding season.

Destruction of wetlands in the Far North has been limited up to now, with the only significant loss the previously mentioned 1.75 million acres on the delta of the Saskatchewan River. Proposed and potential hydroelectric projects menace several important wetlands in the Far North. Construction of the proposed Rampart Dam on the Yukon River of Alaska would have inundated 36,000 lakes and ponds, aggregating 760,000 acres of water. Also, 1.7 million acres of land for nest sites would have been flooded. About 500,000 ducks, representing 1.6 percent of the total continental breeding population, breed there (Smith et al. 1964*a*, Wellein and Lumsden 1964).

Great Plains. The area known as the northern prairie or Great Plains (Sanderson and Bellrose 1969 (fig. 5-1) extends from South Dakota north to the boreal forest of Saskatchwan and Alberta and is the most important breeding ground for ducks in North America. This area is known as the Prairie Pothole Region by waterfowl ecologists because of the thousands of small ponds or potholes dotting its surface. The area covers about 154 million acres in a northwest-southeast arc, about 1,000 miles long and 300 miles wide. The aspen parkland zone comprises the northern third of the region. Aspens occur on the grasslands from scattered clumps in the south to almost a closed forest in the north. This zone forms an ecotone of 54.4 million acres between the grass-

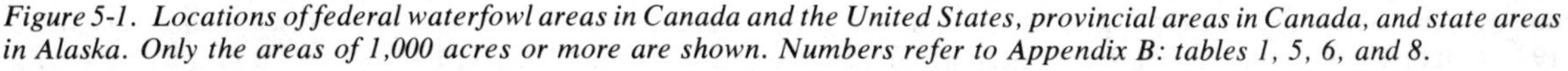
Figure 5-1. Locations of federal waterfowl areas in Canada and the United States, provincial areas in Canada, and state areas in Alaska. Only the areas of 1,000 acres or more are shown. Numbers refer to Appendix B: tables 1, 5, 6, and 8.

lands and the boreal forest. The grasslands, lying south of the aspen parklands, cover 64 million acres in Canada and 36,840,000 acres in the United States.

The potholes fill to different degrees with runoff water, especially in early spring, with the snow melt. Frozen soils, plus rapid and plentiful snow melt, produce an abundance of water areas for waterfowl (Harmon 1970). In years with little snowfall or unfrozen basins, or both, there is a scarcity of water to fill the potholes. When spring precipitation is also light, a large percentage of the potholes dry up before duck broods are flying (Smith et al. 1964*b*).

There may be as many as 6,661,400 (Lynch et al. 1963) to 10 million (Cooch 1969) water areas in prairie Canada. Estimating the total acreage of potholes is a difficult task. In 1951, one survey reported that the sum of all small water areas in the pothole region of the United States was 1.21 million potholes, aggregating 4.45 million acres (U. S. Fish and Wildlife Service 1953). Estimates for the Dakotas and Minnesota in 1968 were in excess of 3 million acres (Harmon 1970). The potholes cover some 300,000 square miles, with about 60,000 square miles in the United States, mostly in the Dakotas and in a significant section of western Minnesota (Harmon 1970).

The small water areas decline as the season progresses. For example, in one year in North Dakota, potholes declined from 664,000 in spring to 269,000 by late summer, a loss in water surface of 1.24 million acres (58 percent). Permanent water areas comprise 3.8 percent of Prairie Canada and semipermanent wetlands 7.7 percent; 23.3 percent of the wetlands are dry as often as they are wet; 56.1 percent is temporary waterfowl habitat; and 9.1 percent of the area is unsuited to waterfowl (Lynch et al. 1963).

Drought is the greatest single short-term disaster to hit breeding waterfowl. Breeding populations drop to low levels, and many individual waterfowl remaining in the Prairie Pothole Region fail to breed (Rogers 1964). Prairie ducks evolved with periodic drought and have adjusted their behavior to it. The periodic exposure of pothole basins to drying is essential for maintaining their productivity and for revitalizing plankton and aquatic and marsh vegetation (Jahn 1968). Therefore, even if it were possible, eliminating drought from the northern grasslands is not desirable from the standpoint of waterfowl production on a long-term basis.

The parklands have slightly higher annual rainfall, lower mean summer temperature, and lower rates of evaporation than the grasslands, and during droughts, are a more dependable area for duck production. They provide a wider range of cover, water, and nest and brood cover than the more intensively cultivated grasslands. During the droughts of the 1930's, late 1950's, and early 1960's the parklands demonstrated their greater stability. In May, the density of potholes in the parklands is twice the density in the grasslands, but by July the parklands usually have three times as many. In May, the total area of potholes in the grasslands is greater than it is in the parklands, but potholes in the grasslands go dry more frequently (Smith et al. 1964*b*).

The parklands also receive displaced ducks from the grasslands when drought causes the grassland potholes to become dry. When drought hits the parklands too, the ducks from the entire prairie region may move north to the tundra and northern forests, as was mentioned previously.

Originally, the Prairie Pothole Region of the United States covered 74 million acres in the Dakotas, Minnesota, northwestern Iowa, and portions of Montana. It now covers only 36 million acres. By 1950 about 50 percent had been lost to drainage or to cultivation of grasslands, or both (Schrader 1955, Harmon 1970). More than a million acres of potholes in the prairie states were drained between 1943 and 1961 (Briggs 1964). In the Dakotas and Minnesota, some 64,000 potholes—totaling 188,000 acres—were drained in 1949 and 1950 alone, and more than 2 percent of the remaining wetlands in these states were being drained each year (Schrader 1955). Private surveys made in the same states showed that about 125,000 acres of wetlands were drained from 1965 to 1968 in these three states alone (Harmon 1970).

The Prairie Pothole Region probably once produced 15 million ducks each year but now produces about one-third that number, with drainage the main reason for the difference. A second reason has been the destruction of upland nest cover by the more intensive cultivation of land adjacent to potholes and sloughs. The federal government subsidized widespread drainage without regard for its effects on waterfowl and other wildlife. The agricultural agencies in charge of the drainage programs erroneously maintained that the drainage done under their supervision was either beneficial or neutral in its effects on wildlife (Bureau of Sport Fisheries and Wildlife 1966).

At various times, the U. S. Department of Agriculture has altered drainage payments in an effort to reduce the loss of wetlands valuable for waterfowl, but even with the more restrictive regulations put into effect in the 1950's, wetlands valuable for waterfowl are still being lost. About 375,000 more acres will be lost prior to the year 2000 if the rate of drainage that occurred between 1954 and 1961 (an average of 9,885 acres per year) continues in the Dakotas and Minnesota.

So long as the U. S. Department of Agriculture provides any assistance, monetary or technical, for drainage in the primary waterfowl-producing zone of the United States, habitat will continue to be destroyed. A major shift from grains and row crops in the Prairie Pothole Region to grassland-livestock farming would eliminate much private drainage. The U. S. Department of Agriculture Conservation Reserve program helped provide a basis for such a shift in this region by establishing a large acreage of legumes and some permanent cover convertible to hay and grazing, and recommended that all federal assistance for drainage of surface water by tiles or open ditches be eliminated in the prairie wetland areas of Montana, North Dakota, South Dakota, Nebraska, and Minnesota as soon as legally possible. Some federal personnel concerned with the program expressed the opinion that the most effective single step to conserve waterfowl habitat would be the elimination of the federal drainage subsidy and recommended that agencies concerned with agriculture in this region promote a shift to grassland farming and beef production (Bureau of Sport Fisheries and Wildlife 1961).

In spite of all the studies and recommendations, Jahn (1966:2) wrote: "Objections of conservationists to habitat losses rest on one fundamental point. Public funds were and are being used in small watershed projects to destroy, as well as benefit, public values associated with private lands. Losses exceed gains. This conversion of wildland to cropland was and still is inconsistent with other Department of Agriculture programs aimed at converting existing cropland to non-crop uses. It also was and still is inconsistent with accelerated private and local, state, and federal governmental efforts to maintain and restore wetlands and other types of wildlife habitat. Planning agencies, in their comprehensive reports, have emphasized as major problems (1) deterioration of wildlife habitat and (2) maintenance of open space in rural-urban areas.

"Adverse effects of the watershed program on essential wildlife habitat largely relate to one predominant philosophy, namely 'give the local people what they want.' With public funds involved, that philosophy is seriously questioned. This concept is now being revised in some program phases, but needs modification in others."

Jahn suggested three approaches to handling small watersheds effectively: preservation of key wetlands, development of aquatic areas as an integral part of construction for flood control, and mitigation for wetlands damaged as a result of project developments.

Drainage of wetlands in the Prairie Pothole Region of Canada has not been as rapid as in the United States. Drainage in Canada began in the late 1800's and reached its first peak in the 1920's. During this period, settlers were encouraged to buy wetlands with a view to draining them for agriculture. Much of the drainage of the 1920's was sponsored by the Canadian government. Drainage declined during the droughts of the 1930's but increased again with the wet cycle and higher farm prices in the 1940's.

In Canada, the drainage resulting from activities of the Prairie Farm Rehabilitation Act (PFRA) is usually a by-product of flood control and irrigation projects, although some reclamation is undertaken under this act. In one reclamation project in Manitoba, 110,000 acres of marshes were drained from a total of 135,000 acres.

In Manitoba, little drainage is financed by the province, but in Saskatchewan the provincial government pays up to 50 percent of the cost for land reclamation on private lands and up to 100 percent on government land. In Alberta, the Water Resources Branch of the Provincial Department of Agriculture shares costs of drainage and flood control projects with towns, villages, counties, municipal districts, and drainage districts.

Up to 1960, wetland losses were greater in Saskatchewan than in Manitoba and Alberta. In Saskatchewan up to 1960, 841 registered ditches and drainage projects, licensed flood-irrigation projects, and large drained marshes and lakes involved nearly 200,000 acres. Unregistered drainage was substantial (Burwell and Sugden 1964).

Interior Wetlands. The geographic region embracing the Interior Wetlands is a vast region between the Appalachian Mountains and Rocky Mountains. The west half of this region embraces the Great Plains and the east half the deciduous forest. The north border in the west is the prairie pothole country; in the east it is the mixed boreal forest. From its northern border it stretches southward 1,000 to 1,500 miles to the coastal plain on the Gulf of Mexico. Most of this region is drained by the Mississippi River basin, but the Great Lakes via the St. Lawrence River drain the northeastern part.

The western part of the Great Plains receives less than 20 inches of annual rainfall. Evaporation is high from low humidity and strong winds. Thus, this area was never as well watered as the prairie pothole area.

Water areas of high value to waterfowl cover slightly over 2 million acres in this section. Some of these are artificial reservoirs, which, because of shallow water or juxtaposition to grain fields, are valuable to ducks and geese. State and federal conservation agencies own or manage 492,000 acres, 150,000 of which are open to public hunting.

Of the states in the western and southern Great Plains, Montana has the most wetland habitat—about 800,000 acres. Most of these water areas are valuable for nesting ducks, especially mallards, blue-winged teals, and gadwalls. About 252,000 acres are managed by the state or federal government (fig. 5-1, 5-2; appendix B: tables 1, 2, 3).

The Sandhills region of western Nebraska contains possibly 300,000 acres of small water areas

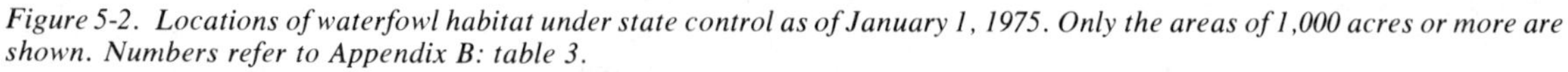
Figure 5-2. Locations of waterfowl habitat under state control as of January 1, 1975. Only the areas of 1,000 acres or more are shown. Numbers refer to Appendix B: table 3.

when precipitation is plentiful, and is the best area for breeding ducks south of the pothole country. Additional wetlands occur along the Platte River and in some of the large reservoirs. About 523,000 acres of wetlands occur in the entire state; 177,000 acres are managed by government agencies (appendix B: tables 1, 2, 3).

Kansas was blessed with two large marshes in the center of the state: the Cheyenne Bottoms north of Great Bend and the Salt Marshes south of there. To prevent possible drainage, the state acquired the 20,000-acre Cheyenne Bottoms (appendix B: table 3) and developed an adequate water control system by bringing water from the Arkansas River and discharging it back to the river. The U. S. Fish and Wildlife Service has acquired the Salt Marshes and is rehabilitating them for waterfowl. Including these areas and a few smaller natural marshes and artificial reservoirs of value for waterfowl, Kansas has 183,000 acres of wetlands.

Oklahoma has only about 72,000 acres of natural wetlands. The rest of the 400,000 acres of value to waterfowl consist of artificial reservoirs, lakes, and farm ponds.

Vast wetlands occur along the Gulf Coast of Texas, but inland shallow water areas are much more limited. In certain areas of the Staked Plains of west Texas, the landscape is dotted with small playa lakes aggregating 250,000 acres when local runoff fills their shallow basins. Playa basins tend to fill in spring and fall and to be dry in midsummer and midwinter. The playa lakes have few breeding waterfowl, but over a million visit them during migration and over 600,000 usually winter on them.

The Interlake area extends east from the prairies of Minnesota and southern Manitoba in an extensive forest area that encompasses most of the Great Lakes Basin. The forest is divided into two zones: (1) the northeast pines, and (2) the northeast hardwoods. Scattered through the forest are tens of thousands of lakes, most of them too deep to be classed as wetlands, and thousands of small marshes. Several large marshes occur near the Great Lakes.

Marshes in the Interlake area total 400,000 acres. One of the largest of these is the 32,000-acre Horicon Marsh (appendix B: tables 1, 3), an area restored from drainage in southeastern Wisconsin. The 26,000-acre Crex Meadows (appendix B: table 3) in northwestern Wisconsin represents a restoration of part of a much more extensive marsh that was drained for agriculture. A great loss to the wetlands of this area occurred in the late 19th century when the 400,000-acre Kankakee Marsh, in northern Indiana, was drained.

The marshes along the margins of the Great Lakes are largely intact from drainage. They aggregate 180,000 acres. The most extensive marshes, totaling 80,000 acres, occur along the north, west, and southwest shores of Lake Erie. Other large marshes are found at Lake St. Clair, Saginaw Bay, and Green Bay, all part of the Great Lakes.

The Great Lakes and Interlake marshes produce far fewer ducks per unit area than the wetlands on the northern Great Plains. Breeding waterfowl are restricted both in numbers and species composition. Mallards, black ducks, and blue-winged teals are the principal nesters.

In the northeastern pine forest, north and east of the Great Lakes in southern Ontario and Quebec, are countless thousands of lakes and smaller bodies of water. Most of the water areas are too deep to be valuable for wildlife. Where marshes, bogs, and shallow waters occur, they provide homes for the black duck, the eastern cousin of the mallard. Almost 300,000 black ducks breed in this vast forested area, where few wetlands have been drained or otherwise altered by man (Benson and Bellrose 1964).

The deciduous forest area of the Mississippi River basin encompasses most of the remaining wetlands in the Interior Region. There are almost 20 million acres of wooded and shrub swamps along the Mississippi River and its tributaries. Most of the wooded swamps are bottomlands subject only to seasonal flooding from adjacent streams; a few are in sumps, collecting water from local drainage.

The geologic delta of the Mississippi River, extending 500 miles from Cape Girardeau, Missouri, to New Orleans, Louisiana, embraces the bulk of the overflow lands of the Mississippi Basin. In places this prehistoric delta is several hundred miles wide. Arkansas, Louisiana, and Mississippi contain over three-fourths of this delta land.

The delta land has long produced bumper yields of cotton, and, in more recent year, rice and soybeans. Consequently, drainage levees and ditches have been extensively constructed, resulting in the loss of about two-thirds of the overflow timbered bottomland, seriously depleting the winter grounds for mallards and the breeding grounds for wood ducks.

North of the Mississippi Delta are about 1.1 million acres of overflow timbered bottomlands that provide habitat for breeding wood ducks and migrating mallards. Three hundred thousand acres along the upper Mississippi River, and 75,000 acres of bottomland lakes along the Illinois River are the largest segments of this habitat.

Because the Mississippi Basin is the area of greatest drainage activity in North America, state and federal conservation agencies have made valiant efforts here to acquire lands for waterfowl and other wildlife. Arkansas has led the way with almost 184,000 acres of timbered bottomland acquired for wildlife (appendix B: table 3). The U. S. Fish and Wildlife Service has also acquired about 133,000 acres in four refuges in Arkansas (appendix B: table 1).

The 8,000-acre Reelfoot National Wildlife Refuge in Tennessee; the 22,000-acre Mingo Swamp and the 6,000-acre Duck Creek Waterfowl Area in Missouri; and the 12,000-acre Yazoo Refuge in Mississippi are outstanding examples of southern swamps and lakes acquired in the lower Mississippi Basin for waterfowl (appendix B: tables 1, 3).

On the upper Mississippi River, two large refuges have been established by the federal government: the 195,000-acre Upper Mississippi River Wildlife and Fish Refuge and the 25,000-acre Mark Twain National Wildlife Refuge (appendix B: table 1).

Coastal Wetlands. Estuary has been defined as a "coastal area with more water than land on the ocean side and more land than water on the fast land side" (Latimer 1968:33). The complex of estuaries includes extensive bays, harbors, sounds, lagoons, and river mouths that are constantly flooded, sometimes deeply. Also included are tidal flats and semiupland marsh areas, salt and brackish water flats, marshes, and mangrove forests and salt brush, areas that may be flooded only by the highest moon and storm tides. Tidelands are the areas between the mean high water mark and the mean low water mark (Cottam 1968).

For our purposes, we find it convenient to separate the Atlantic Coast into three units: the New England states in the northeast; the Coastal Plain; and the coastal marshes and estuaries south of Long Island, New York.

The Atlantic Coast has about 32 million acres of wetlands habitat, 96 percent of it south of New Jersey. These coastal wetlands comprise more than one-third of all the wetlands in the United States. Only 4 million acres, or 12 percent, are considered of moderate to high value for waterfowl. The 29 million acres of inland freshwater areas consist of 14 million acres of marsh, 12 million acres of swamp, and 3 million acres of bog. Along the coast are 500,000 acres of freshwater marsh and 2.5 million acres of salt marsh (Addy 1964).

The New England coast is dissected by drowned river mouths bounded by a rocky coastline. Coastal marshes are few. About 13,000 acres of salt marsh and 55,000 acres of salt meadow, mostly in Massachusetts, and 25,000 additional acres of freshwater marsh occur along the coast.

Seaward from the coastal marshes of New England are 385,000 acres of estuaries; 91,000 acres of these are important to waterfowl. The limited habitat for waterfowl along the coast, in the marshes and bays, results in a dearth both of species and numbers. The brant; the white-winged, surf, and black scoters; the common eider; and the black duck are the species most abundant as migrants along the coast.

Inland in New England are about 60,000 acres of lakes and marshes of value to waterfowl, muskrat, and mink. The 300,000 acres in wooded and shrub swamps support only sparse populations of black ducks and wood ducks. Ninety thousand acres of bogs are too filled with vegetation to be of much value to waterfowl.

The Atlantic Coastal Plain lies between the Appalachian Mountains and the Atlantic Ocean on the east and the Gulf of Mexico on the south, and incudes all of Florida. The Coastal Plain contains many large swamps, the more famous being the Dismal Swamp of Virginia and North Carolina, and the Okefenokee of Georgia. Both of these are in sumps with poorly drained outlets. Numerous swamps occur along the sluggish streams that meander across the Coastal Plain from their source in the mountains of the Piedmont. These swamps provide nest habitat for the wood duck, egret, herons, ibises, and many other birds.

Drainage and flooding have taken their toll of coastal swamps. The Dismal Swamp once covered almost a million acres, but drainage has reduced it to only 384,000 acres. Extensive swamps along the lower course of the Santee and Cooper rivers in South Carolina were partly destroyed by flooding from hydroelectric development. Fortunately, most of the 400,000-acre Okefenokee Swamp has been spared; 378,000 acres were made a national wildlife refuge (appendix B: table 1).

Florida contains the largest acreage of swamps and freshwater marshes on the Atlantic Coast. The freshwater marshes are located primarily along the Indian River, around Lake Okeechobee, and the famous Everglades, which at one time covered several million acres. Large sections of the Everglades and the Okeechobee marshes have been drained; other marshes about Lake Okeechobee have been destroyed by water storage for irrigation. Sincock et al. (1964) reported that more than 10,000 acres of wetlands in Brevard and Indian River counties had been impounded with water for mosquito control. On the Gulf Coast side of the Everglades, a 500,000-acre mangrove swamp marks the only occurrence of this habitat in the United States. Part of it and much of the Everglades have been set aside as a 1,400,000-acre national park. Water control problems plague the park as a result of adjacent agricultural enterprises, but attempts have been made to at least partially solve these problems.

The 3 million acres of freshwater and saltwater marshes along the Atlantic Coast are relatively intact. In the 1930's, about 90 percent of the 625,000 acres of coastal marsh between Maine and Virginia were drained for mosquito control. This action failed to reduce the mosquito problem; happily, much of this area has reverted to wetland habitat as ditches have crumbled and filled. However, coastal marshes are slowly being lost. Schmidt (1966) reported that in a 10-year period (1954-1965), 45,000 acres of tidal marshes between Maine and Delaware were destroyed. About one-third of the loss was due to filling, resulting from dredging operations.

A most important restoration in the mid-1930's was that of 50,000-acre Lake Mattamuskeet in coastal North Carolina. The U. S. Fish and Wildlife Service acquired this defunct drainage enterprise early in their refuge program and readily restored it. Now it is the winter home of thousands of Canada geese, tens of thousands of ducks, and several thousand whistling swans.

Adjacent to many of the coastal marshes, on the ocean side, are about 5 million acres of estuaries along the Atlantic Coast and the Gulf Coast of Florida. Slightly over half of this area includes habitat of basic importance to marine life and wildlife, Walford (1968:81) stated: "In its totality the Great Atlantic Estuarine Zone stands unique in the world, unequalled anywhere for its length, breadth and productivity of valuable living resources."

Damage or destruction, or both, of estuaries have largely been by filling, the dredging of navigation channels, and pollution. In 10 of the Atlantic Coast states, containing 1.982 million acres of basic estuarine habitat. 149,000 acres (7.5 percent) have been lost to dredging and filling (Cottam 1968:233). Chapman (1968:97) reported that about 20 percent of Boca Ciega Bay, Florida, has been covered by waterfront lots.

Until recently, dredging and filling of Florida's bays was encouraged in order to foster the growth and economic development of the state. Of 796,000 acres of Florida estuaries less than 6 feet deep, about 60,000 acres (7.5 percent) have been dredged or filled. The filled areas are irretrievably lost and the dredged areas are too deep for bottom photosynthetic activity. Other serious damage comes from widespread siltation of nearby areas not actually destroyed (Marshall 1968:105-109).

Marine biologists have found that estuaries are the important spawning or nursery areas, or both, for many important marine fish and for shrimp. About 2 million diving ducks make their winter home on the estuaries of the Atlantic Coast (Addy 1964, Benson and Bellrose 1964, Sincock et al. 1964).

Along the Gulf Coast there are about 4.2 million acres of coastal marsh and over 5 million acres of estuaries adjacent to the Gulf of Mexico in the United States. Louisiana contains the largest area of marsh (3.514 million acres) and of estuary (3.545 million acres) of any state on the Gulf Coast. Texas is next, with 576,000 acres of coastal marsh and 1.344 million acres of estuaries along the Gulf Coast.

In recent years the Louisiana marshes have held more than two-thirds of the wintering waterfowl population of the Mississippi Flyway. Over 4 million ducks winter each year along the Louisiana coast alone.

The deep marshes of Louisiana extend westward into the deep-marsh rice belt east of Galveston Bay, Texas, covering about 520,000 acres flooded most of the year by either fresh or salt water. The saline marsh of 11,000 acres provides less waterfowl food plants (salt grass, bulrushes, spike rushes, widgeon grass, and similar plants) than do the fresh and brackish marshes. The marshes are heavily used by waterfowl, especially by lesser snow geese. Ducks are especially attracted to rice fields, which exceed marshes in acreage. Water management for rice also produces smartweeds, wild millet, and pondweeds, used along with waste rice as food by waterfowl. The shallow-marsh rice belt, found between fresh and tidal marshes, amounts to some 300,000 acres. The water is fresh to slightly brackish. The plants here are similar to those found in the deep marshes. The area is surrounded by about 2 million acres of rice land. Southwest of Galveston along the Gulf Coast to the Rio Grande River is a narrow saline marsh covering 500,000 acres. Adjacent to it are shallow bays that provide 750,000 acres of water attractive to pintails, redheads, and other ducks because of its shoalgrass and widgeon grass beds and animal foods.

The coastal marshes of Texas and adjacent rice fields and the coastal waters of the Gulf of Mexico accommodate up to 45 percent of the wintering ducks and 90 percent of the geese in the Central Flyway. The combined area covers 5 million acres, with an annual precipitation ranging from 52 inches on the upper coast to 24 inches in the lower reaches. These wetlands, and the nearby rice fields, winter about 2 million ducks and geese. The rice fields and the shallow bays provide the most stable wetland habitat. The marshes deteriorate as succession proceeds, and only when disturbance by man (fire, manipulation of water levels, herbicides), by nature (hurricanes), or by biological factors (muskrats and nutria) upsets succession do the marshes again become productive to waterfowl (Buller 1964, Chabreck 1960, Hawkins 1964, Sincock et al. 1964).

The Pacific Coast, unlike the Atlantic Coast, has no broad coastal plain, but rises abruptly to summits of several thousand feet in the Coast Range. True wetlands occur only where there are bays, representing drowned river mouths.

Less than 10,000 acres of salt marsh and salt flats occur around Puget Sound in northwest Washington, but about 50,000 acres of the Sound are sufficiently shallow to support aquatic plant life. Grays Harbor and Willapa Bay, farther down the coast of Washington, contain only about 7,000 acres of salt marsh and meadow. About 10,000 acres of shallow water are rated as excellent feeding grounds for ducks. Eelgrass is the principal food plant. American wigeons, pintails, green-winged teals, mallards, and black brants are the most common migrants. There are 193,800 acres in the estuaries on the Washington coast (Cottam 1968:233); 95,500 of these are considered valuable for marine life. Dredging and filling have destroyed 4,300 acres of estuarine habitat.

Tillamook and Coos bays are the only important estuaries on the Oregon coast and, with a few small estuaries, total 57,600 acres, of which 20,200 are basic to marine productivity. Only 2,000 acres of salt marsh occur. The beds of eelgrass and kelp in these waters are attractive to American wigeons, black brants, mallards, and pintails.

California at one time had 552,000 acres of estuaries, principally in San Francisco Bay and Monterey Bay. The only extensive coastal marshes on the Pacific Coast occur at the north and south ends of San Francisco Bay. Salt marshes cover about 100,000 acres and freshwater marshes about 5,000 acres. Salt flats cover 60,000 additional acres. The surface of San Francisco Bay has been reduced by 41 percent—from 435,200 acres in 1850 to 256,000 acres in 1968 (McBroom 1969:84).

The greatest threat facing marine life and wildlife on the Pacific Coast is the filling of salt flats, salt marshes, and shoal water areas of San Francisco Bay. This area has a total of 552,100 acres of estuaries. Of the 381,900 acres of primary importance to marine life, some 255,800 acres (67 percent) have been lost from filling and dredging (Cottam 1968:233). San Francisco Bay is important to black brants and to diving ducks. Most of the canvasbacks, lesser scaups, redheads, and ruddy ducks in the Pacific Flyway winter there (Chattin 1964).

Intermountain Wetlands. There are roughly 4 million acres, lying between the rugged ranges of the Rocky Mountains, in the expanses of level land in the valleys and basins that often contain extensive tracts of wetlands. They extend from the Cariboo Parklands in British Columbia to the Imperial Valley of California.

According to Chattin (1964:233), the acreage of quality waterfowl habitat in this region by states is: Washington, 450,000; Oregon, 600,000; Idaho, 520,000; Utah, 900,000; Arizona, 55,000; and California, 1.1 million. These figures include small amounts of coastal marshes in Washington, Oregon, and California.

The Cariboo Parklands, the Chilcotin Plateau, and the Rocky Mountain Trench in British Columbia contain many shallow lakes and innumerable ponds, essentially alkaline, which support breeding ducks of 10 to 20 per square mile. Both fresh and saline water marshes, aggregating about 75,000 acres, provide year-round benefits to ducks in western Washington and produce about 60,000 ducks for the fall flight.

In arid southeastern Oregon there are two excellent wetlands for waterfowl, Malheur and Summer lakes. When plentiful runoff from nearby mountains fills the lake basins, the area abounds in breeding mallards, gadwalls, cinnamon teals, and canvasbacks. At such times, Malheur has produced as many as 30,000 ducklings and Summer Lake 10,000 ducklings. Both areas are important concentration points for hundreds of thousands of migrating waterfowl. Malheur National Wildlife Refuge, encompassing 181,967 acres, is one of the largest waterfowl refuges in the United States (appendix B: table 1). Summer Lake, totaling 18,065 acres, is state owned (appendix B: table 3).

The Bear and Ogden rivers, on entering the Great Salt Lake, have created deltas highly valuable for breeding waterfowl. Man-made dikes and gates control water levels, thereby improving the marsh for ducks. On these 70,000 acres, from one to three ducklings are produced per acre, and densities of 60 to 80 nests per acre have been reported. More than 100,000 ducks have been fledged there. Important breeders are gadwall, cinnamon teal, redhead, mallard, and Canada goose.

More than 25,000 acres of high-quality breeding habitat for ducks occurs on the Tule and Lower Klamath lakes in northern California. About 50,000 ducklings are fledged—gadwalls, redheads, and mallards. Several million waterfowl rest and feed at these areas during migration, making this the greatest concentration point for waterfowl in North America. Both areas are federal refuges.

The most extensive marshes in the Intermountain region once occurred in the Sacramento-San Joaquin Valley of California. A survey in 1906 showed 3 million acres of wetlands. Sixty years later, agriculture had usurped all but about 450,000 acres of these fertile valley lands. Breeding ducks, largely mallards, are fairly abundant in the Sacramento-San Joaquin Valley, with about 60,000 young produced each year. About 4 million ducks and 700,000 geese arrive in the fall; most of them winter there but some move farther south into the Imperial Valley and Mexico.

Grays Lake, a 22,000-acre hardstem bulrush marsh in southeastern Idaho, has a moderate density of breeding ducks. About 40 nests per acre have been found on some edge segments, particularly mallards, pintails, redheads, and cinnamon and green-winged teals.

Even Nevada, an arid state, has wetland habitat productive of waterfowl. In the Carson Sink is the 24,203-acre Stillwater National Wildlife Refuge and 144,000-acre state-owned Stillwater Wildlife Area.

Return-flow irrigation water spread over alkaline soils creates a marsh habitat that produces 20,000 ducklings of mallards, redheads, and cinnamon teals (Jensen and Chattin 1964).

Federal Ownership

United States. In the United States, the federal wildlife refuge system began in 1903 with the establishment of the Pelican Island Refuge in Florida by Executive Order of President Theodore Roosevelt to protect a colony of brown pelicans and other colonial nesting birds (Salyer and Gillett 1964:499). By June 30, 1971, the system comprised 329 national wildlife refuges totaling 29,284,761.6 acres (Bureau of Sport Fisheries and Wildlife 1972:1). These refuges include areas for waterfowl, colonial birds, and big game. As of June 30, 1974, there were 289 national wildlife refuges consisting of 11,364,370 acres, including 6,854,700 acres in Alaska that provided substantial benefits to waterfowl. Also included were one National Antelope Refuge, one National Elk Refuge, one migratory bird refuge, and one fish and wildlife refuge (appendix B: tables 1, 4).

In 1962, the federal government actively managed approximately 1.5 million acres of shallow water and about 800,000 acres of marsh in the United States, exclusive of Alaska, and was preserving about 2.3 million acres of wetland in Alaska, mainly for waterfowl (Bureau of Sport Fisheries and Wildlife 1962:230).

In addition to the federal refuge system, the small wetlands preservation program was initiated in the north-central United States in 1961 (Nelson 1972). As of June 30, 1974, there were 116 designated waterfowl production areas totaling 1,370,766.2 acres, mostly in North Dakota, South Dakota, Minnesota, and Nebraska (appendix B: table 2). Most of these areas were protected by easements but about 27 percent were owned by the federal government. The areas owned by the government are open to hunting unless designated as closed. On the designated waterfowl production areas controlled under agreement, easement, or lease, hunting is controlled by the individual landowners. Also, management for waterfowl and other wildlife is not possible except on the areas owned by the government (Nelson 1972).

Canada. In Canada, most public lands are administered by the provinces; however, the federal government is empowered to establish migratory bird sanctuaries. These sanctuaries may be established on private or Crown (public) lands, but control of land use within the sanctuaries is limited to Crown lands. Most of the acreages are in large sanctuaries on Crown land in the Northwest Territories. These sanctuaries were established to provide control over mineral exploration and exploitation in the major breeding areas of arctic geese.

The federal government of Canada has acquired relatively few areas for the primary purpose of conserving waterfowl habitat (appendix B: table 5). Hunting is permitted in all the national wildlife areas except Big Creek, Iles de la Paix, Mississippi Lake, and part of Last Mountain Lake, which are all migratory bird sanctuaries. The federally owned areas in Canada acquired primarily for waterfowl total only 47,902 acres. In addition, more than 27 million acres in the Northwest Territories have been established as migratory bird sanctuaries on federal Crown lands (appendix B: table 5). No hunting is permitted on these areas.

State and Provincial Ownership

States. In 1870, California established the first state refuge for waterfowl—Lake Merritt in Oakland. At first the states placed primary emphasis on protection from hunting. This protection was intended to provide rest sites and supplementary foods, to delay migration for the improvement of local hunting, and to establish areas on which nonhunters could enjoy waterfowl. Other areas were closed to protect the birds from overshooting. Since 1935 the trend has been toward combination refuges and public shooting grounds. Hunting permitted on federal refuges is often managed by the state in cooperation with federal authorities. The states thus provide a service to hunters who pay part of the bill of restoring, preserving, and managing the game in the states (Sanderson and Bellrose 1969:179-180).

The 48 contiguous states control 2,023 waterfowl areas totaling 5,133,153 acres (appendix B: table 3). Approximately 87 percent of this acreage is open to hunting. Most of these areas are owned by the natural resource agencies in the various states. Included, however, are areas owned by other units of government—federal government, other agencies of state government, and various units of local government—and managed by the natural resource agencies of the states under leases of agreements. A few privately owned acres are also included where it was difficult or impossible to separate them from government ownership; however, these privately owned tracts form only minor parts of a few areas owned by units of government. Areas, regardless of size, owned by individuals or corporations and managed for waterfowl by the state natural resource agencies have been deliberately excluded. The intent was to include only areas owned by some unit of government, because it was felt that these areas were more likely to be maintained as waterfowl habitat in the foreseeable future than those privately owned.

West Virginia controls only one waterfowl area and Georgia two. Minnesota leads with 789 areas, followed by South Dakota with 351 and Iowa with 138. The total acreages for individual states range from a low of 1,273 acres in Rhode Island and 2,451 in West Virginia to a high of 1,594,720 acres in Florida. Other states each with more than 200,000 acres of state-controlled waterfowl habitat include Minnesota, Louisiana, Wisconsin, Nevada, and Washington (Appendix B: table 3).

In the contiguous 48 states, the federal and state governments control and manage for waterfowl approximately equal acreages—slightly more than 5 million acres by the states and about 5.9 million acres by the federal government (appendix B: table 4). The land under federal control includes 365,545 acquired acres and 900,000 additional acres of privately owned land as waterfowl production areas under agreement, easement, or lease (appendix B: table 2).

Provinces. In Canada, most of the provincial programs involve the establishment of sanctuaries or game preserves, many on privately owned land. Only recently have lands in Canada been acquired specifically for waterfowl, but several provincial game departments now have active programs to increase the acreage of waterfowl habitat under their control.

Provincial waterfowl acreages include Manitoba, 2,405,877 acres; British Columbia, 223, 227 acres; and Ontario, 48,960 acres. In several cases, these areas are less intensively managed than are waterfowl areas owned by the states. In total, the provinces own some 2.7 million acres (appendix B: table 6) of waterfowl habitat compared with less than 48,000 acres owned by the federal government in Canada (appendix B: table 5), excluding the migratory bird sanctuaries on federal Crown lands in the Northwest Territories.

Distribution of Governmentally Owned Waterfowl Habitat

The state and federal governments have 3.2 million acres of waterfowl habitat in the Atlantic Flyway, 3.3 million acres in the Mississippi, 2.8 million in the Central, and 1.6 million acres in the Pacific Flyway (appendix B: table 7).

The State of Alaska owns 657,958 acres of waterfowl habitat not including approximately a million acres of tidelands—critical habitat acres designated to protect waterfowl values—(appendix B: table 8). There are some 6.8 million acres of significant waterfowl habitat in eight federal refuges and wildlife ranges in Alaska (appendix B: table 8). Thus, Alaska has some 40 percent of the waterfowl habitat in government ownership in the United States (appendix B: table 4).

The provincially owned waterfowl areas in British Columbia, Manitoba, and Ontario are mostly located in the southern thirds of these provinces. Other provincial waterfowl areas are generally near the southern border of Canada. The federally owned waterfowl areas in Canada have a similar distribution except for the migratory bird sanctuaries in the Northwest Territories.

Crown (public) land comprises a substantial proportion of the Northwest Territories and Yukon Territory (95 percent or more). There are also substantial acreages of Crown lands in the provinces, especially in the northern portions of the larger provinces. For example, more than 80 percent of Quebec is publicly owned.

Private Ownership

State and federal lands are essential for managing the waterfowl resource, but must be supplemented by millions of acres of wetlands habitat on private farms and duck clubs and on land owned by private groups, individuals, and foundations (Sanderson and Bellrose 1969:181).

According to the Bureau of Sport Fisheries and Wildlife (1967), private duck clubs, state conservation agencies, and the Bureau of Sport Fisheries and Wildlife owned or controlled equal acreages of waterfowl habitat in the United States. Nearly 4,000 private duck clubs control a minimum of more than a million acres of wetland and upland in 12 of the 14 states (excluding Louisiana and Mississippi) in the Mississippi Flyway (Barclay and Bednarik 1968). Because many of the privately owned wetlands are not for sale, and, even if they were, agencies of the federal and state governments are not sufficiently funded to purchase them, other means must be sought to preserve these private properties.

The privately owned duck clubs are an example. Many are intensively managed for the benefit of waterfowl at unit costs far above the amount government agencies can afford. Also, the kill per unit of area is usually much lower than if the areas were open to public hunting. Often substantial acreages of privately owned areas are maintained as refuges. Thus, these private areas provide important benefits for waterfowl, shorebirds, migratory songbirds, and for various species of resident wildlife such as muskrats, beavers, raccoons, deer, and others on a year-round basis.

Many wetlands now in private hands will be maintained only so long as there is a hunting season on waterfowl. If it becomes necessary to close the waterfowl season permanently, or if the bag limits and seasons are reduced to the point that waterfowl hunting is no longer attractive, many of the best marshes and sloughs now in private duck clubs will quickly be converted from wetlands to corn and soybean fields or to factory sites.

Thus, state and federal governments should do all they can to help perpetuate private wetlands that have public values. Sound laws regarding harvest of wildlife will help, as will tax laws that encourage maintenance of wetlands. A tax law on wetlands similar to the forest-crop laws adopted by some states should help to preserve wetlands. By all means, all public subsidies for draining wetlands that have public values should be eliminated (Sanderson 1974).

In the United States the nonprofit Nature Conservancy obtains natural areas, including wetlands, as gifts, by purchase, and by assisting with the purchase. Initially its wetlands acquisitions were small; however, in 1967 the 11,290-acre St. Vincent Island and the 2,235-acre Mason Neck area were purchased and held for government agencies. Then in 1973 the Nature Conservancy obtained 49,097 acres within Virginia's Dismal Swamp. In addition, the Conservancy bought three tracts totaling 14,341 acres of the swamp in North Carolina (Nature Conservancy 1974:17).

A private organization such as the Nature Conservancy has a degree of flexibility seldom found in government. The Conservancy is proving to be a valuable tool in the preservation of natural areas; it can sometimes purchase available areas quietly and promptly and hold them until a government agency can obtain the necessary appropriations.

The National Audubon Society owns, operates, or maintains 49 sanctuaries, many of them containing wetland habitat, in 16 states (March 1974). The wetland habitat owned or leased by the Society totals more than 100,000 acres. Acquisitions are restricted principally to areas containing rare and endangered species of plants and animals or to strategic breeding areas (Anderson 1974).

Ducks Unlimited is a private nonprofit organization in the United States dedicated to preserving, restoring, and creating breeding habitat for waterfowl in Canada, and was incorporated in Washington, D. C., January 29, 1937. A companion Canadian corporation, Ducks Unlimited (Canada), was formed to construct the projects and handle the building program. To date (1974), the organization has spent over 25 million dollars to plan, build, and develop some 1,250 "duck factories" in Canada. DU has under lease about 1.7 million acres of prime wetland habitat with a shoreline of nearly 11,300 miles.

Citizens and governments in Canada have cooperated with DU by providing use of land, water rights, and other vital elements of conservation. Selected projects are planted with waterfowl food and cover plants and various areas are under active management. The objective is to ensure long-term benefits to wildfowl and other marsh inhabitants (Sanderson and Bellrose 1969:161-162, Ducks Unlimited 1974).

OTHER MANAGEMENT TECHNIQUES

The maintenance of natural and artificial wetlands and their improved management to enhance their attractiveness for nesting waterfowl and management schemes to prevent "burning out" of local breeding populations by overharvest will no doubt be the most important factors in maintaining relatively high waterfowl populations for many years. However, there are many other ways to aid waterfowl reproduction and survival. Those of a specific nature are applicable only to local situations and goals. General ones have wider applications.

Artificial Nest Structures

One of the most widely used programs has been the construction and placement of artificial nest structures to enhance natural reproduction of wild waterfowl. Although several species of wild waterfowl use nest houses, probably more houses have been built and put up for wood ducks than for all other species combined. The houses have undergone many changes in design in attempts to make them resistant to predators and more acceptable to wood ducks (Bellrose 1955, Bellrose et al. 1964, McGilvrey 1968, Bellrose and Crompton 1972). Artificial houses are readily accepted by wood ducks and supplement natural cavities. They provide virtually the only nest sites in some locations. Other species that have nested in houses put up for wood ducks, or in those erected for other species, include goldeneyes, hooded mergansers, and buffleheads, as cited under the respective species in this book.

Enough is known about the use of artificial houses in many parts of the wood duck's range to recognize its potential value as a management tool (Bellrose and McGilvrey 1966). However, these authors remind us that improvements are needed to deter small raccoons and rat snakes in the south, to provide a better liner than undercoat for galvanized-pipe houses, and to provide a vertical box that will deter use by starlings.

Bishop and Barratt (1970) placed 222 artificial nesting structures on 11 state-owned marshes in Iowa in 1964. Mallards utilized 26 percent of the structures the first year. Use averaged 33 percent for their 5-year study. They believed the ducks nesting in their structures were "normal wild mallards." Other species that used the structures were the redhead, blue-winged teal, gadwall, and Canada goose. Stenuphar (1974) also reported use of artificial nests by mallards.

Wild Canada geese also nest in man-made structures such as tubs, baskets, and platforms placed in trees and on various types of man-made supports (Yocom 1952, Craighead and Stockstad 1961, Rienecker 1971). Perhaps captive flocks of Canada geese, used to establish self-maintaining breeding flocks, have made the most extensive use of artificial nest structures. Use of this technique has increased since Hanson's (1965) rediscovery of the giant Canada goose (Brakhage 1965, 1966; Bishop and Howing 1972; Dill and Lee 1970).

Reestablishment and Establishment of Wild Populations

Various attempts have been made with a variety of techniques to reestablish local breeding populations that have been burned out by overshooting or that have disappeared because of deterioration of the habitat. The same techniques also are used to establish a species in suitable habitat in areas not previously occupied by the species.

Lee and Nelson (1966) summarized the early history of wood duck propagation. More recently, on the Arrowwood National Wildlife Refuge in east-central North Dakota, where wood duck nesting had not been recorded, 253 hand-reared ducklings 9 to 16 days of age were released in a half-acre enclosure from May to July 1968. The ducklings grew to flight stage and flew out of the pen; approximately 76 percent survived until migration began in late September. Nest houses were installed on the refuge in August. First-year band-recovery rates (4.7 percent) were comparable to the return rate for immature wild wood ducks. In 1969, homing female wood ducks made 16 nesting attempts and produced 175 ducklings. In 1970 there were 34 nesting attempts, and 311 ducklings were produced (Doty and Kruse 1972).

Pen-reared wood duck hens have been released to increase the nesting population (McGilvrey 1972). From 1967 through 1969, 67 such hens were released on the Patuxent Wildlife Research Center in Maryland. These hens were as successful as wild hens in hatching and rearing young and mortality was lower among the pen-reared hens (McGilvrey 1972). Before the release of these hens, about 100 young per year reached flight stage on the area; after the last release of hens in 1969, about 430 young reached flight stage.

Capen et al. (1974) found the most satisfactory technique for wood ducks was to release a wing-clipped hen and her ducklings together. The hens stayed with their broods and reared them successfully in the new areas. They knew that 8 of 87 female ducklings released returned to the release area to nest in later years.

Borden and Hochbaum (1966) reported that they established the gadwall as a breeding species in Massachusetts by liberating captive-reared immatures in late August and early September. The birds were hatched from eggs collected from captive ducks held at Delta, Manitoba, and were released on a private reserve of 45 acres of water and 25 acres of meadow and woods. A wild resident breeding population of redheads was established in New York and a Canada goose flock on the Delta Marsh through releases of pen-reared birds (Winthrop and Poole 1973).

Ward and Batt (1973) discussed several of the roles propagation can play in waterfowl conservation. Propagation measures can establish wild resident populations by releases of pen-raised birds, provide waterfowl (mostly mallards) for shooting preserves, insure the survival of rare and endangered species, serve as adjuncts to natural reproduction, provide birds for research purposes, for zoos, and for individuals who maintain private collections of waterfowl.

Because Flickinger et al. (1973) could not capture wild fulvous whistling ducks, they used 165 pen-reared immatures to study the movements of this species. Many of the released birds apparently joined wild ones as all of their marked ducks they observed were with wild flocks.

There have been many attempts to enhance wild populations of mallards through propagation and release of hand-reared birds. Brakhage (1953) reported that flight patterns of hand-reared mallards and redheads were not significantly different from those of wild-trapped mallards and redheads released at the same location. He found that both hand-reared mallards and redheads suffered much higher first-year mortality than wild-trapped birds. His birds were hatched from eggs collected in the wild and he warned that the possible adverse effects of removing eggs from the wild cannot be ignored, especially for diving ducks.

Hunt et al. (1958) reported the results of releasing over 10,000 hand-reared mallards produced from matings of domestic and wild mallards. Most of their stocked ducks were killed the first season after release. Therefore, releasing these birds during the prehunting season was essentially stocking for the gun. They concluded that improvement of existing wetlands to make them more attractive to breeding and migrating waterfowl was preferable to stocking these birds. Schladweiler and Tester (1972) reported similar results with hand-reared mallards released in the wild.

Each year some 6,500 five-week-old artificially propagated mallards are released on the 3,145-acre Remington Farms. After release, these ducks are fed to flight stage at three or four sites along 3 miles of tidewater shoreline and 26 man-made ponds. With a four-bird daily bag limit during the 1970-71 season, hunters averaged 2.8 ducks per day. Remington mallards comprised 85 to 90 percent of the annual harvest on this area during a 3-year period (Webster et al. 1972).

Lee and Kruse (1973) reported the release of 648 hand-reared wild-strain mallards at the Arrowwood National Wildlife Refuge, North Dakota. They placed the ducklings in an enclosed pond area at 25 to 45 days of age, and 97 percent of them reached flying stage and dispersed gradually to the wild. Only 11 percent were shot during the first year, and 33 percent of a possible 270 females returned the next year. The authors reported (p. 154): "The success of this release is attributed to the inherent capability of hand-reared, wild-strain mallards to revert to their wild behavior, and to the high survival to flight age and first fall migration afforded by the gentle release in a sanctuary area. Indications are that releases of this type under the described conditions can be used to increase the breeding population of mallards in a local area."

Eggs of Canada geese have been collected from nests, incubated artificially, the young transferred to the release sites, and then reared in brooders. Goslings were moved as much as 1,000 miles with little mortality. The geese were permitted to fly the same year they were hatched, but they remained at the release sites. The results of this program were termed excellent by Chabreck and Dupuie (1973).

Put and Take Shooting

Dickey (1957*a*) reported that game-farm mallards were increasing in popularity on shooting preserves. Of 549 shooting preserves listed in 1964, mallards were available on 143 (26.0 percent) (National Shooting Sports Foundation 1964). In 1974-75, mallards were available on 23.7 percent of 438 shooting preserves (*North American Shooting Preserve Directory*, 1974). In order to conform with federal regulations, mallards used on these preserves must be more than two generations removed from the wild (Dickey 1957*b*).

Kozicky and Madson (1966:71-101) described in detail the use of game-farm mallards on shooting preserves. They reported (p. 73) that although a successful preserve may offer only upland shooting, mallards alone are not enough to induce hunters to patronize a shooting preserve in sufficient numbers for its successful operation.

chapter 6

THE ROLE OF HUNTING REGULATIONS

Arthur S. Hawkins

In his classic work entitled *Game Management* (1933), Aldo Leopold proclaimed that "As long as game shortage prevails, the purpose of hunting controls is obviously to limit the kill of each species . . . to its productive capacity." Hunting regulations today, as in the past, attempt to balance supply and demand by limiting the harvest by hunters to the surplus of each kind of waterfowl. *Harvest*, as used herein, means waterfowl legally shot and retrieved (bagged) by hunters.

Surplus, as the name implies, is that portion of a population in excess of the number of breeders required to maintain the population at some desired level. The desired level, usually expressed as the number of breeders, is called the *population objective*. It can be no greater, in the long run, than the *carrying capacity* of the habitat. Population objectives must be adjusted occasionally to compensate for short-term effects of weather and long-term consequences of human impacts on both the birds and their habitats.

HUNTING REGULATIONS AS A MANAGEMENT TOOL

The purpose of regulations is to control the harvest, generally by changing season times and lengths, bag limits, and methods of hunting. During the early 1970's, the average annual harvest of ducks and geese was about 3.5 million in Canada and about 14.5 million in the United States. To this measured harvest of approximately 18 million birds must be added another 20 percent or so for crippling losses, a harvest and a crippling loss of unknown size in Mexico, and the indirect loss which occurs when waterfowl ingest spent shot and die from lead poisoning. Thus, legal hunting and related losses annually removed over 20 million waterfowl from the North American waterfowl population during the early 1970's.

DETERMINING THE SURPLUS

Determining either the size of the surplus or the number of breeders that should be maintained in any given year is no easy task. Such decisions rest heavily on the surveys described in Chapter 1. Population sizes must be known to permit estimation of surpluses. Knowing the impact of past regulations on the size of the kill is another prerequisite helpful in determining the allowable annual harvest.

Each waterfowl species has an inherent level of productivity. Each also differs in its vulnerability to hunting and natural or nonhunting mortality. Thus, the permissible harvest rate differs among species. The wide range of biological characteristics affecting the productivity and vulnerability of the various species are described in the species accounts.

Geese, swans, and several ducks, including the scaups, do not breed until they are at least 2 years old. At least one species—the wood duck—may, in southern latitudes, produce two broods in a single year.

Some species nest early in spring and have time for several renesting attempts should the first nest fail. Later nesting species often have time for only one nesting attempt. On the other hand, early nesters encounter more adverse weather conditions than late nesters. Waterfowl species also differ in the number of eggs laid; some lay twice as many as others. Some choose nest sites where plows and predators are constant threats, whereas others characteristically select more secure sites. Experienced hens are generally more successful in producing broods than first-year nesters. Production success, therefore, is highly variable among individuals, species, and years.

Experienced hunters know that some species, or age- and sex-classes of the same species, seem more wary than others. Some decoy well; others ignore decoys or duck calls. Some ducks are more prone to avoid gunshot by flying high, or beyond areas readily accessible to hunters; some frequent marshes and swamps where hunters can hide successfully, while others seek broad waters where concealment is more difficult. Differences in vulnerability resulting from one or more of these behavioral traits are reflected in band-recovery rates. They represent the proportion of banded waterfowl reported taken by hunters. Data derived from band recoveries provide pertinent information on the movements, mortality, and survival of sex and age groups of individual species.

This information is supplemented by data on the waterfowl harvest collected from hunters who submit name and address cards they receive when purchasing duck stamps at selected post offices. The total duck harvest by states is divided into species on the basis of wings returned for identification by cooperating hunters to collection points in each flyway. Similar surveys are conducted in Canada.

Canada requires every waterfowl hunter to obtain a federal migratory bird hunting permit. In 1973, a record 453,000 permits were sold. Every hunter in the United States, sixteen years of age or older, is required to have a federal hunting stamp, commonly called the "duck stamp," before he can legally hunt waterfowl. In the early 1970's the number of stamps sold averaged nearly 2.2 million annually. Mexico lacks similar requirements, thus its number of waterfowl hunters is unknown. The total number of waterfowl hunters in North America in recent years approached 3 million.

Through the Office of Migratory Bird Management of the U.S. Fish and Wildlife Service, information from waterfowl surveys and banding is analyzed carefully, often with the aid of computers. Printouts and a digest of preliminary findings are available by late July. Reviewers include waterfowl biologists employed by state, federal, and private organizations who serve together on technical committees of the flyway councils. The councils are briefed on the current situation affecting waterfowl and receive recommendations from their technical sections at annual meetings in late July and early August.

Flyway Councils

There are four flyway councils: the Atlantic, Mississippi, Central, and Pacific. They were conceived in 1951 at a meeting of the International Association of Game, Fish, and Conservation Commissioners to facilitate the management of waterfowl. Flyways are bio-administrative units, their boundaries representing compromises between biological and administrative considerations. Voting members of each council are the directors of state and provincial conservation departments or their designated representatives. They meet each year in late winter or spring and again in early August when consideration of hunting regulations is their primary concern. After receiving the recommendations of their technical sections, each council develops and adopts official recommendations on population objectives and hunting regulations. A basic premise is that hunting of migratory birds is prohibited unless an open season is established.

During the 1960's and early 1970's, procedures were initiated in setting annual waterfowl hunting seasons that involve a series of interrelated steps. Immediately after the August meeting in each flyway, two delegates from each council are dispatched to Washington to present the flyway's recommendations to the Director of the U. S. Fish and Wildlife Service at the annual meeting of his Waterfowl Advisory Committee. These delegates—eight in all, plus a chairman—also serve as members of the National Waterfowl Council that collectively represents the four flyways in matters of mutual concern. At a mid-August meeting, the views (on regulations) of other major national conservation organizations are presented; those groups represented include the National Audubon Society, the National Wildlife Federation, the Wildlife Management Institute, the Wildlife Society, Outdoor Writers of America, Ducks Unlimited, and the International Association of Game, Fish, and Conservation Commissioners. At this meeting the views of all participants are presented to the director. He also solicits the advice of staff members before deciding what harvest objectives and regulations seem most appropriate under conditions existing any given year. The director's recommendations on regulations require approval by the Secretary of the Interior and publication in the Federal Register before they become effective. A modification of this procedure in 1975 enables groups and individuals concerned about waterfowl, but not previously included in the regulations-setting process, to express their views for consideration along with those of other groups.

DISTRIBUTING THE HARVEST

Regulations are used to provide recreational opportunities and distribute and limit the size of the harvest. Both latitudinal and longitudinal dimensions are involved in the distribution process. In Alaska and northern Canada, the waterfowl hunting season must open in early September to permit some harvest before freeze-up, which may occur even before summer officially ends. Farther south, hunting seasons open within defined latitudinal belts that usually include entire states. Openings occur at progressively later dates, and closures occur when the maximum season length permitted by law has been attained. Before the final closure in Mexico in late February, some waterfowl have begun their northward migration. Thus, the hunting season is successively open in north-south bands for nearly half the year. This latitudinal system of hunting seasons, when synchronized with the time that the birds are most plentiful, is a potent tool used by most management agencies in distributing hunting opportunities and harvest.

Generally, the flyways have differing regulations designed to distribute recreational opportunities and harvest in relation to migrational patterns of the birds, hunting pressure exerted against them, or both. Flyway hunting regulations generally can be progressively more liberal as the proportion of migrating birds harvested by hunters decreases. This is in a flyway with least hunting pressure.

Zoning by management units within flyways—and in some cases, states—is yet another way to distribute the species composition, place, or time of the harvest. For example, two such units have been established to improve the management of mallard populations. One is the High Plains management unit west of the 100th meridian in the Central Flyway, and the second is the Columbia Basin management unit in the Pacific Flyway. In special cases, zones have been established in distinct regions within a state for specific management purposes. For example, Long Island's waterfowl hunting season differs from that of the rest of New York State.

In recent years, all states have been offered the option of a split season. In such a season hunting is successively opened and closed until the total number of days equals the number permitted had the season been uninterrupted. The two parts of the split need not be of equal length. Hunters living in latitudinally long states or those with major altitudinal differences usually choose a split season because it increases the likelihood of having hunting seasons open in various parts of the state when birds are present in peak numbers. Occasionally, the time of normal migration may be altered by unusual weather conditions. The passage of most waterfowl may then occur during the hiatus between the open seasons, much to the disappointment of hunters.

ANNUAL REGULATIONS

Waterfowl numbers may fluctuate annually in response to changing water conditions on the Canadian prairies, snow conditions in the Arctic, and other factors. Controlling the harvest by bag and possession limits, and by restrictions on times and places of hunting, is the only practical way waterfowl managers have found to compensate for these population changes.

Bag Limits

In 1933, when Leopold's *Game Management* appeared, the daily bag limit on ducks throughout the United States was 15 in the aggregate of all kinds, with not more than 30 allowed in possession. Wood ducks and eiders were fully protected. Four geese could be taken daily; 8 could be possessed. The brant limit was 8 daily and in possession. By 1935, the basic daily bag limit for most ducks had been decreased to 10 and remained there until 1944, when a bonus of 5 mallards, pintails, or wigeons, or any combination of 5 ducks of these species, was allowed. This regulation was followed by a daily limit of 10 again in 1945, 7 in 1946, and only 4 in 1947, the last year before the advent of management by flyways. Since then, there have been differential regulations among flyways. In the two easterly flyways, the daily limit was, with certain exceptions, 4 ducks from 1948 to 1958. The lowest limit ever permitted was only 2 ducks in all four flyways as drought ravaged the prairies in 1961 and 1962. Since then, a number of regulatory options have prevailed, including the point system described later in this chapter.

Wood ducks have consistently been given special protection since regulations were first applied. Canvasbacks and redheads have intermittently received special protection from the mid-1930's to 1958, and quite restrictive considerations since then. In two or more flyways, daily limits for mallards and black ducks have been reduced more years than not, starting in the early 1960's.

Length of Season

In 1930 a typical waterfowl hunting season in the northern United States opened September 16 and ended the last day of December, three and one-half months later. Waterfowl hunting in southern states continued until January 31. In response to the duck decline accompanying the drought-stricken 1930's, seasons were drastically shortened. In 1934, only 30 days of waterfowl hunting were permitted but the dates were spread over 2 months—5 days in succession followed by 2 rest days. Subsequently, further reductions were deemed necessary and from 1935 to 1937, federal regulations restricted hunting to 30 consecutive days. Hours of hunting were from 7 A.M to 4 P.M. In 1938, fifteen days were added to the season's length.

In 1940, a 2-month season was declared and the opening hour was returned to sunrise, although the 4 P.M. closing hour was retained. Hunters in 1942 were permitted a 70-day season from sunrise to sunset. The half-hour before sunrise was restored as the opening time in 1943, and the permissible opening day was advanced to September 25. During 1944 and 1945, the season was liberalized to 80 days, during the period between September 20 and January 20, with shooting permitted from a half-hour before sunrise to sunset. A year later the season's length was curtailed to 45 days between October 5 and January 6, and the hunting time reduced to a half-hour before sunrise to a half-hour before sunset. The last year before management by flyways was initiated, 1947, a brief 30-day season was granted between October 7 and January 3, with the closing hour restricted to 1 hour before sunset.

Thus, lengths of seasons, opening and closing dates, and opening and closing hours for waterfowl shooting were quite variable during the 1930's and 1940's. With the initiation of management by flyways in 1948, the variability became two-dimensional: among flyways and among years. Even within flyways, the season's length has not always been the same because states have sometimes been given the option of substituting days for ducks. For example, states could have longer seasons in exchange for a reduction of one duck in the daily bag. Under this arrangement from 1948 to 1974, the variance in season lengths ranged from 32 to 70 days in the Atlantic Flyway, 20 to 70 days in the Mississippi Flyway, 25 to 90 days in the Central Flyway, and 40 to 95 days in the Pacific Flyway. During the 1960's, hunting was not permitted before October 1 or after January 15. In 1962, the most restrictive year, the framework was October 12-December 30, except in the Pacific Flyway. Since 1971, the closing date in the United States has been January 20 except in the two western flyways, which have been permitted to open their seasons on the Saturday closest to October 1, and close on the Sunday nearest January 20. Opening and closing hours were inconsistent among years and flyways until 1966. In 1966, shooting hours for all except certain special or experimental seasons were standardized across the nation at a half-hour before sunrise to sunset.

Species Regulations

In 1918, the first regulatory announcement of the U.S. Department of Agriculture's Bureau of Biological Survey, now the U.S. Fish and Wildlife Service, exempted wood ducks and eiders from the aggregate duck bag limit of 25. Swans also were protected. In 1931, the same ducks and swans were still protected, but "snow geese in Florida and all States north thereof bordering on the Atlantic Ocean, Ross's goose [and] cackling goose . . ." were added to the protected list (U.S. Bur. Biol. Surv. 1931:2). In 1932, the species management concept was given impetus by an announcement stating: "It was found that certain species had not increased in numbers to the extent others had. It therefore became necessary to close the season entirely on ruddy ducks and buffleheads and to reduce the daily bag and possession limits on canvasbacks, redheads, greater and lesser scaup ducks, ring-necked ducks, shovelers, gadwalls, and blue-winged, green-winged, and cinnamon teals." In contrast, eider ducks increased in numbers sufficiently to justify an open season in 1932 with a limited bag (Sheldon and Grimes 1932).

Species regulations of recent years may not list any more kinds of waterfowl for special treatment than those of the early 1930's, but they are based on considerably better information than was available then. Modern fact-finding techniques date back only one to two decades and have been focused primarily on species that are most important in the harvest or otherwise require special attention.

A special September hunting season for blue-winged teal was initiated in 1965 as a 3-year experiment because this species had a low rate of harvest and migrated earlier than other ducks. Green-winged and cinnamon teal were also included because they mix with and are frequently difficult to distinguish from bluewings in some areas. Daily bag limits of 4 and possession limits of 8 teal were permitted. The experimental phase ended in 1967. Since 1969, September teal seasons have been offered on a regular basis to certain states of the Mississippi and Central flyways. Northern states generally have not been permitted the early season because of possible damage to locally nesting ducks. However, they have been permitted a bonus of 2 bluewings, in addition to the basic bag, during a 9-day period of the regular season.

In 1966, a special scaup-only season, with a daily limit of 5 birds and extending 15 days beyond the regular season length, was tested experimentally in two states. By 1968, sixteen states in the three easterly flyways participated in special scaup seasons on areas that are relatively free of other species. In

Minnesota and Wisconsin the special season was delayed until after most ring-necked ducks have departed, generally about November 1.

Other special regulations initiated or tested during the past decade include species-oriented duck seasons in the San Luis Valley of Colorado, the Columbia Basin, and western High Plains; a late black duck season in New England; and special seasons in certain states for hunting whistling swans and sea ducks. Concurrently, there were bag restrictions or complete closures on the wood duck, mallard, black duck, canvasback, redhead, Canada goose, white-fronted goose, brant, and swan. Also, different point values were applied to various species in states utilizing the point system for regulating harvests.

For canvasbacks and redheads, species similar in appearance, the harvest recently has been severely restricted by either complete or partial closures. The approach to harvest restriction, initiated in 1973, involves closing and posting high harvest areas to canvasback and redhead hunting and, additionally, allowing one of these two species in the bag in areas where canvasbacks and redheads occur infrequently.

Canada geese present fewer management problems. Each population can be managed as a unit. Most of the harvest occurs in predictably well-defined areas. Quotas have been set for some population units; the season ends when the quotas are reached. A tagging system has sometimes been used to distribute the harvest more widely. In the Horicon Marsh management area of Wisconsin, the season's limit for years has been one properly tagged Canada goose. Population goals are set for these managed flocks and the harvest is regulated until the goal is reached. Intensive harvest management for both geese and ducks seems destined to spread as more population units are identified and as demands for harvestable surpluses increase.

Point System

First tried experimentally, and more recently offered as an option in three of the four flyways, the point system of harvesting ducks has gained wide acceptance. Its chief virtue is that a conscientious hunter need not fear violating the law if he understands how this system works and complies with its rules. Under the point system, the daily limit is reached when the point value of the last bird taken, added to the sum of the point value of the other birds already taken that day, reaches or exceeds 100, or whatever the allowed point total may be. Duck species—and sometimes sexes of some species—are given high, low, or medium point values, depending on their relative population status and hunting vulnerability.

When the system is used properly, the hunter shoots a duck and retrieves and identifies it before shooting at another. Thus, he can carefully and leisurely identify each bird in hand and stop hunting when he reaches his limit. The system does not require the hunter to identify birds before shooting unless he is hunting in an area where one or more species (such as canvasback or redhead) is completely protected.

The attractive feature of the point system is its flexibility—it permits the hunter to conduct his hunting according to his skills and desires. By using skill and restraint he can avoid shooting at high-point birds, thereby being entitled to a larger bag limit than if he shoots high-point ducks. On the other hand, if his skill at identification on the wing is low or he wants to shoot nonselectively as opportunity permits, he can allow chance to determine the number of birds he can bag. Finally, if he cannot identify birds, even when he has them in hand, he can legally shoot two birds of any species provided he avoids areas where one or more species is completely protected.

As a technique for regulating harvest the point system depends on the willingness of hunters to abide by the rules. This is true to a large degree of all types of regulations, but perhaps more so for the point system. It offers each hunter not only unique opportunities and flexibility but also obligations for maintaining high standards for his conduct when afield. The point system is one regulatory system made available to improve management of individual species of waterfowl. Its ultimate success depends upon the knowledge and ethical constraints of hunters.

chapter 7

IDENTIFICATION

To be an effective waterfowl hunter, the correct identification of species is a "must." Under the point system of regulating the daily duck bag, it is absolutely necessary to identify ducks in the hand, and, of course, advantageous to recognize them in the field if only to avoid killing a "high point" bird.

Unfortunately, all too many hunters are poor at species recognition, particularly when the waterfowl are in flight. For example, tests among experienced waterfowl hunters in Wisconsin disclosed that 77 percent were successful in identifying correctly 166 flights representing 14 species (Evrard 1970). Novice hunters were able to identify only 52 percent of 129 waterfowl flights composed of 15 species. Tests of hunters elsewhere in the country show an equal or greater need for improvement in the skills of waterfowl identification.

Waterfowl identification is not easy; it requires effort. The more often a species is identified, the more readily will its characteristic flight and plumage patterns be recognized in the future. A continuing effort should be made by every hunter to identify every duck that comes within visual range. The old cliché that "practice makes perfect" aptly applies to the ability to identify waterfowl.

Because of a lack of time or the lack of a place to hunt, the average waterfowler pursues this activity from 5 to 6 days a year. Consequently, in such a brief span, the average hunter has little time to become knowledgeable in species identification. However, it costs little or nothing to practice waterfowl identification outside the hunting season. All a hunter needs is a good guide to species identification, a pair of binoculars, and a desire to learn.

I have often mused that waterfowlers could derive greater satisfaction from their sport if they became "duck watchers" throughout the year. In almost every locality within the United States some waterfowl are present throughout the year. The spring migration certainly offers a golden opportunity to observe waterfowl at close range and at a time when identification is facilitated by their full nuptial plumage.

Bird watchers find friendly competition in being the first to identify a bird, or to identify one at the greatest distance, or to see the most species. It seems to me that many hunters would enjoy the sport of waterfowling more, in season and out, if they would conduct a contest of species identification with their associates.

IDENTIFYING DUCKS IN FLIGHT

The old duck guide who spent a lifetime observing waterfowl could identify a familiar species about as far as he could see it. Slightly different nuances in behavior and appearance—depth of wing arc, wing beat, body conformation, and flock formation—provided him with the clues needed to name the species.

Most hunters and bird watchers need additional cues, for they have not watched waterfowl for the untold hours of one who has figuratively lived all his life with the denizens of the marsh. The next series of cues are provided by the arrangement and contrast of dark and light colors of the plumage. Often when light is poor because of early or late hours, or mist and overcast, plumage colors are not apparent or are not revealed in their customary tones. Then the amount and arrangement of dark and light plumage offers means of identification.

Under suitable light, colors of the plumage become evident and reveal further clues to identification. The first place to look for color clues in a flying duck is the wing. There are several reasons to pay particular attention to color markings on the wing. First, most wings have large areas of distinctive colors, and second, the somber body plumages of

SWANS

A. Whistling Swan. Adult. Sexes alike, juveniles grayer. Yellow spot at base of bill, when present, distinguishes it from trumpeter swan. (B) Head of juvenile.

C. Mute Swan. Adult. Sexes alike, juveniles grayer. Neck is S-curved and bill inclines downward. In other swans, neck is upright and bill is horizontal. Note that wing feathers are often raised to give a hooded appearance, and that there is a black knob at base of orange bill.

D. Trumpeter Swan. Adult. Sexes alike, juveniles gray. Best differentiated from whistling swans by its call, a trumpeting low note followed by a three higher notes. (E) Juvenile.

CANADA GEESE

A. Common Canada Goose. Adult. Sexes alike. Includes: Atlantic Canada goose, Todd's Canada goose.

B. Lesser Canada Goose. Adult. Sexes alike. Taverner's Canada goose is similar, but slightly darker.

C. Richardson's Canada Goose. Adult. Sexes alike.

D. Western Canada Goose. Adult. Sexes alike. Also called Great Basin Canada goose and Moffitt's Canada goose. Giant Canada goose is similar, but slightly lighter in color and is larger, with longer bill.

E. Cackling Canada Goose. Adult. Sexes and juveniles alike. Smallest and darkest race with short bill and neck. Aleutian Canada goose is similar. (F) Head. Occasionally, white cheek patches are divided by black throat. (G) Head and neck. White collar at base of neck.

H. Canada Goose wing, typical of the five subspecies.

Others: Dusky Canada goose and Vancouver Canada goose intermediate in size to other races, exceedingly dark, and restricted to northwest coast of North America.

Downy Young, see Plate No. 32.

Plate No. 2

SEA GEESE

A. Atlantic Brant (also called American Brant). (B) Wing. Adult. Sexes alike. Lacks white cheek patch of Canada geese. Adults possess incomplete white neck-ring. (C) Wing of juvenile.

D. Black Brant (also called Pacific Brant). (E) Wing. Adult. Sexes alike. Breast and belly much darker than in Atlantic race. Adults possess incomplete white neck-ring (C) Wing of juvenile.

F. Emperor Goose. (G) Wing. Adult. Sexes alike. Restricted almost entirely to coastal Alaska; a few stragglers reach California. Dark gray mottling completely covers head and neck of juvenile.

H. Barnacle Goose. (J). Wing. Adult. Sexes alike. Occasional stragglers from Greenland observed along the East Coast in flocks of brant or other geese.

Downy Young, see Plate No. 32.

Plate No. 4

TRUE GEESE

A. White-fronted Goose. (B) Wing. Adult. Sexes alike. White face patch and speckled breast and belly distinguish it from other geese. Found largely west of Mississippi River on Great Plains and in California.

C. White-fronted Goose. (D) Wing. Juvenile. Sexes alike. Lacks white facial disk and speckled belly of adults. Similar to juvenile blue goose.

E. Tule Goose, head of adult. A rare race of the white-fronted goose found in Central Valley of California. Facial disk shows staining by iron salts.

F. Blue Goose. (G) Wing. Adult. Sexes alike. A color phase of lesser snow goose, formerly considered a distinct species. Note white head and neck. Stains on head result from contact with iron salts during feeding. More abundant east of Mississippi River than white-phase of lesser snow goose. A few occasionally mingle with greater snow geese on Atlantic Coast.

H. Blue Goose. (J) Wing. Juvenile. Sexes alike. Similar to juvenile white-fronted goose except that legs and bill are purplish pink instead of yellow.

Downy Young, see Plate No. 32.

TRUE GEESE

A. Ross' Goose (formerly Ross's Goose). (B) Wing. Adult. Sexes alike. A diminutive and rare "snow" goose. In winter confined almost entirely to Central Valley, California. In recent years, some have been found among flocks of lesser snow geese in Great Plains. Rust spots on head result from contact with iron salts in soils where some geese feed.

C. Ross' Goose. (D) Wing. Juvenile. Sexes alike. Head and back grayer than those of adults. Shows more white, especially on wings, than juvenile snow goose.

E. Lesser Snow Goose. (F) Wing. Adult. Sexes alike. In flight, black wing tips contrast with white wing base and body. Gulls, white pelicans, and whooping cranes are other white birds with black wing tips.

G. Lesser Snow Goose. (H) Wing. Juvenile. Sexes alike. Similar to adults but noticeably grayer.

Greater Snow Goose not shown. Larger than white-phase lesser snow goose but otherwise almost identical. Confined to Atlantic Coast in winter, particularly Pea Island, North Carolina.

Downy Young, see Plate No. 32.

ECLIPSE AND NUPTIAL PLUMAGES*

A. Mallard. Adult female.

B. Mallard. Adult male in early stage of prenuptial molt. Represents plumage found in late August and early September.

C. Mallard. Adult male in slightly later stage of prenuptial molt.

D. Mallard. Adult male in late stage of prenuptial molt. Represents plumage found commonly in late September and early October.

E. Mallard. (F) Wing. Adult mallard in full nuptial plumage. Represents plumage found in late October.

*The change from eclipse to nuptial plumage in the mallard is unusually rapid. Nevertheless, there is much variation among individuals so that some birds are still in stage B while others are in stage E. Moreover, young males change from female-like plumage to their first nuptial plumage 2 to 8 weeks later than adult males undergo the prenuptial molt. As a consequence of individual variation among adults and juvenile mallards, the various transitional plumages occur over a greater time span than is indicated on Plate No. 6. For example, mallards like C may appear as late as mid-November. The periods given for the various stages of the transitional plumage of adult males apply only to the norm.

Downy Young, see Plate No. 33
Hybrids, see Plate No. 36.

Plate No. 6

Plate No. 7

BLACK DUCK*

A. Adult male. Yellow bill and U-shaped buff marking around vanes of breast feathers aid in distinguishing sex and age in a species exhibiting no pronounced differences in plumage.

B. Head of adult female. Dark marking on greenish bill and V-shaped buff marking on breast feathers serve to identify sex and age.

C. Wing of adult, both sexes. Note that purple speculum lacks pronounced white borders of mallard wing.

D. Juvenile. Note greenish bill and dull yellow feet. Breast feathers lack buff-colored U or V marking characteristic of adults.

E. Adult male in eclipse plumage. Note greenish bill and dull orange legs. Breast feathers are devoid of U-shaped buff marking.

F. Variations in color of feet are associated with sex and age differences among individuals.

*Black ducks become increasingly abundant from the Mississippi River to the Atlantic Coast, and few are found west of the Missouri River. In the Midwest, they often occur in flocks of mallards, where their darker color is in marked contrast to the brown plumage of mallard hens. The white underwings contrasting with the black bodies of birds in flight are noticeably different from those of the mallards.

Downy Young, see Plate No. 33.
Hybrids, see Plate No. 36.

MALLARD, MEXICAN DUCK, FLORIDA DUCK, MOTTLED DUCK

A. Mallard. Adult female. (B) Wing of adult mallard.

C. Mexican Duck (formerly New Mexican Duck). (D) Wing. Adult male. Note that wing is almost identical with that of mallard. Sexes and juveniles similar. Tail darker than that of female mallard—lacks white outer tail feathers. (E) Bill of female has black ridge shading to light olive-green, with minute amount of orange at base. Bill of male is light olive-green. Occurs in southwestern New Mexico, southeastern Arizona, and Central Uplands of Mexico.

F. Florida Duck. Sexes and juveniles similar. (G) Bill of adult female is dull orange, with black spots across the saddle. Body plumage is dusky, intermediate in color between plumages of black duck and mallard hen. Confined to Florida.

H. Mottled Duck. Sexes and juveniles similar. Almost as dark as black duck. Bill of male is plain olive-green; bill of female is orange with dark spots. Confined largely to coasts of Louisiana and Texas. (J) Wings of Florida and mottled ducks lack pronounced white bars found in front of mallard's speculum and are much shorter. Possess conspicuous white bars behind speculums, in contrast to narrow white band characteristic of black duck's speculum.

Downy Young, see Plate No. 33.

Plate No. 8

NUPTIAL PLUMAGES

A. American Wigeon (formerly Baldpate). (B) Wing. Adult male. A medium-sized duck with pronounced white shoulder patch and white belly. White to buff crown and green band behind eye are striking features at close range. Pronounced white patch between black tail and russet flank is conspicuous when drake is on water.

C. American Wigeon. (D) Wing. Adult female. Juveniles similar in fall. Head is lighter in tone than rest of body. Note that shoulder of wing is gray and speculum has more black than green.

E. European Wigeon (formerly Widgeon). (F) Wing. Adult male. Cinnamon head and rich buff crown, contrasting with gray back and sides, distinguish it from its American cousin with whom it associates. Although breeding in Eurasia, small numbers appear regularly along Atlantic Coast, less frequently along Pacific Coast, and rarely in the interior.

G. European Wigeon. (H) Wing. Adult female. Almost identical with American species except for rose-brown head and underwing dusky axillaries. Head of American female is grayer and axillaries are white.

Transitional Plumage, American Wigeon, see Plate No. 11.
Downy Young, see Plate No. 33.

Plate No. 10

NUPTIAL PLUMAGES

A. Pintail (formerly American Pintail). (B) Wing. Adult male. The slimmest, trimmest of all waterfowl, a veritable greyhound of the air. Long neck and tail and long pointed wings give it a buoyant appearance in flight. Narrow white stripe at back of speculum is conspicuous during flight. Frontal aspect of pintail at rest, with head held erect, is like a triangular sail of a toy boat.

C. Pintail. (D) Wing. Adult female. Juveniles similar in early fall. Lacks long central tail feathers of adult male, but tail still unusually long and pointed. Body plumage more gray-brown than that of female mallard; also lacks bright speculum of that species.

E. Gadwall. (F) Wing. Adult male. A nondescript duck at a distance but an elegant beauty at close range. Contrasting coloration includes brown head; gray breast, back, and sides; jet-black tail and tail coverts. Coloring accented by orangeish scapulars draped over folded wing. Like female mallard in flight except for white speculum and narrower wings.

G. Gadwall. (H) Wing. Adult female. Similar to hen mallard but lacks whitish outer tail feathers and displays small white speculum when in flight. Also, yellowish bill is narrower than that of mallard.

Transitional Plumages, see Plate No. 11.
Downy Young, see Plate No. 33.
Hybrids, see Plate No. 36

TRANSITIONAL PLUMAGES*

A. Pintail (formerly American Pintail). Adult male during early stage of prenuptial molt. Represents plumage found in late August and early September.

B. Pintail. Adult male during late stage of prenuptial molt. Represents plumage found in late September and early October.

C. Gadwall. Adult male during mid-stage of prenuptial molt. Represents plumage found in late September and early October.

D. Gadwall. Adult male during late stage of prenuptial molt. Represents plumage found in late Ocober and early November.

E. American Wigeon (formerly Baldpate). Adult male during mid-stage of prenuptial molt. Represents plumage found in September and early October.

F. American Wigeon. Adult male during late stage of prenuptial molt. Represents plumage found in late October and early November.

*The change from eclipse to nuptial plumage occurs as a result of the prenuptial molt. Individuals enter the molt at varying times during late summer and early fall, depending upon their chronology of breeding behavior. Because of the variation in breeding behavior (example: nonbreeding males are among the last to assume the eclipse plumage), plumages worn at any one time during the fall show a variety of transitional stages. Therefore, the time of the period given for each stage is only suggestive and applies to the norm and not to birds that molt exceptionally early or late. Juvenile males acquire nuptial plumages 2 to 8 weeks later than adults.

Nuptial Plumages:

Pintail, see Plate No. 10.
Gadwall, see Plate No. 10.
American Wigeon, see Plate No. 9.

Plate No. 12

NUPTIAL PLUMAGES

A. American Green-winged Teal. (B) Wing. Adult male. Smallest and one of the fastest flying ducks; zips low over marshes and mud flats, in flocks that wheel and dip much like shorebirds. White breast and belly and *lack* of blue patch on shoulder of wing distinguish it from blue-winged teal. Seen from a distance, on water, greenwing's most conspicuous features are buff lower tail coverts and vertical white "finger mark" between breast and sides; in flight, green speculum.

C. American Green-winged Teal. (D) Wing. Adult female. Juveniles similar early in fall. Body plumage a lighter shade of brown than that of blue-winged teal.

E. Eurasian Teal (formerly European Teal). (F) Wing. Adult male. Similar to American race but lacks white vertical stripe between breast and sides and possesses horizontal white bar above folded wing.

G. Eurasian Teal. (H) Wing. Adult female. Virtually identical with female American green-winged teal.

Transitional Plumage, Green-winged Teal, see Plate No. 14.
Downy Young, see Plate No. 33.

NUPTIAL PLUMAGES

A. Blue-winged Teal. (B) Wing. Adult male. Eclipse plumage, a nondescript mottled brown slightly darker than coloration of green-winged teal, is retained through much of fall. In late fall, crescent-shaped mark in front of eye becomes faintly visible. Males do not achieve full nuptial plumage, as shown here, until late winter. In fall, powder-blue shoulder patch is most distinguishable feature of bluewings in flight or at hand. Blue-gray head with white crescent, and white flank patch in front of tail, are conspicuous in spring.

C. Blue-winged Teal. (D) Wing. Adult female. Juveniles of both sexes similar. Mottled brown duck of small size. Pale blue patch on forewing is only distinguishing feature.

E. Cinnamon Teal.(F) Wing. Adult male. Found west of Great Plains, where it largely replaces blue-winged teal. Dull eclipse plumage retained through much of fall. Eyes become red when male is 8 weeks of age.

G. Cinnamon Teal. (H) Wing. Adult female. Juveniles of both sexes similar in fall, but red eyes distinguish males. Wing indistinguishable from wing of female blue-winged teal.

Transitional Plumages, see Plate No. 14.
Downy Young, see Plate No. 33.

TRANSITIONAL PLUMAGES*

A. American Green-winged Teal. Adult male during early prenuptial molt. Represents plumage found in late August and early September.

B. American Green-winged Teal. Adult male during late stage of prenuptial molt. Represents plumage found in early October.

C. Blue-winged Teal. Adult male during early stage of prenuptial molt. Represents plumage found through the fall.

D. Blue-winged Teal. Adult male during late stage of prenuptial molt. Represents plumage found in early winter.

E. Wood Duck. Adult male during late stage of prenuptial molt. Represents plumage found in September.

F. Cinnamon Teal. Adult male during early stage of prenuptial molt. Represents plumage found in early winter.

*The change from eclipse to nuptial plumage occurs as a result of the prenuptial molt. Individuals enter the molt at varying times during late summer and early fall, depending upon their chronology of breeding behavior. Because of variaion in breeding behavior (example: nonbreeding males are among the last to assume the eclipse plumage), plumages worn at any one time during the fall show a variety of transitional stages. Therefore, the time of the period given for each stage is only suggestive and applies to the norm and not to birds that molt exceptionally early or late. Juvenile males acquire nuptial plumages 2 to 8 weeks later than adults.

Nuptial Plumages:

Green-winged Teal, see Plate No. 12.
Blue-winged Teal, see Plate No. 13.
Wood Duck, see Plate No. 15.
Cinnamon Teal, see Plate No. 13.

Plate No. 14

NUPTIAL PLUMAGES

A. Northern Shoveler (formerly Shoveller). (B) Wing. Adult male. Retains female-like eclipse plumage through most of fall. Carries large spoon-shaped bill at downward angle while swimming or in flight. Pale blue wing patch similar to that of blue-winged teal.

C. Northern Shoveler. (D) Wing. Adult female. Juveniles of both sexes similar. Juveniles start to acquire nuptial plumage in late November.

E. Wood Duck. (F) Wing. Adult male. This Beau Brummel of waterfowl inhabits wooded swamps, streams, ponds, and lakes. Large crested head, broad wings, and large rectangular tail provide distinctive silhouette. At a distance, head and upper body appear black, belly is white and a white stripe borders trailing edge of wing. Adult and juvenile males acquire nuptial plumage in late summer and early fall.

G. Wood Duck. (H) Wing. Adult female. The white edging on the trailing edge of the female's wing is more conspicuous than in the male.

Transitional Plumages:

Northern Shoveler, see Plate No. 17.
Wood Duck, see PlateNo. 14.
Downy Young, see Plate No. 33.

Plate No. 16

NUPTIAL PLUMAGES

A. Redhead. (B) Wing. Adult male. A diving duck that inhabits vegetated lakes and marshes in the North, and shallow coastal bays on winter grounds. Gray, with black front and black hindquarters. Round red head distinguishable at suitable distances. Most likely confused with gray-backed scaups and canvasbacks in fall. Redhead has gray wing, scaup a white band on trailing edge of wing; canvasback has white extending from back halfway out on base of wing.

C. Redhead. (D) Wing. Adult female. Lacks white facial disk of scaup. Similar to ringneck female but head is rounder, and blue bill lacks white line at base.

E. Canvasback (formerly Canvas-back). (F) Wing. Adult male. Whitish back contrasts sharply with dark gray back of redhead and moderately gray backs of scaups. Red extends farther down on long neck than in shorter-necked rehead. Note that white extends from back halfway out on wings.

G. Canvasback. (H) Wing. Adult female. Sloping wedge-shaped head noticeably different from rounded head of redhead or heads of scaups.

Transitional Plumages, see Plate No. 17.
Downy Young, see Plate No. 34.

TRANSITIONAL PLUMAGES*

A. Northern Shoveler (formerly Shoveller). Adult male during early stage of prenuptial molt. Represents plumage found in October.

B. Northern Shoveler. Adult male during late stage of prenuptial molt. Represents plumage found in late November and December.

C. Canvasback (formerly Canvas-back). Adult male during late stage of prenuptial molt. Represents plumage found in early October.

D. Redhead. Adult male during stage of prenuptial molt. Represents plumage found in early October.

E. Lesser Scaup. Adult male during early stage of prenuptial molt. Represents plumage found in September.

F. Lesser Scaup. Adult male during mid-stage of prenuptial molt. Represents plumage found in early October.

*The change from eclipse to nuptial plumage occurs as a result of the prenuptial molt. Individuals enter the molt at varying times during late summer and early fall, depending upon their chronology of breeding behavior. Because of variation in breeding behavior (example: nonbreeding males are among the last to assume the eclipse plumage), plumages worn at any one time during the fall show a variety of transitional stages. Therefore, the time of the period given for each stage is only suggestive and applies to the norm and not to birds that molt exceptionally early or late. Juvenile males acquire nuptial plumages 2 to 8 weeks later than adults.

Nuptial Plumages:

Northern Shoveler, see Plate No. 15.

Canvasback and Redhead, see Plate No. 16.

Scaups, see Plate No. 19.

Plate No. 18

NUPTIAL PLUMAGES

A. Ring-necked Duck. (B) Wing. Adult male. Black back and black wings without white stripes distinguish it from gray-backed scaups, which also have white bars at trailing edge of wings. White triangle between gray side and black breast is clearly visible when ringneck is on water. Head pointed rather than rounded. Note two white rings around bill, one at base and another at tip.

C. Ring-necked Duck. (D) Wing. Adult female. A brown diving duck without white facial disks and white wing bands of female scaups; band at trailing edge of wing is gray. Similar to female redhead but eye-ring is white rather than buff; head is peaked rather than smoothly rounded; and ring at tip of bill is white rather than gray.

E. Bufflehead (formerly Buffle-head). (F) Wing. Adult male. The smallest diving duck, a miniature goldeneye with similar black and white plumage pattern but with larger white patch on head. Note large white wedge that extends from below eye across top of head, black back, white under-parts, and large white patch on wing. Hooded merganser also has large white head patch but darker body and wings, with less white visible when in flight or on water.

G. Bufflehead. (H) Wing. Adult female. Dusky brown with white dash behind eye and small white wing patch on trailing edge.

Transitional Plumages, see Plate No. 21.
Downy Young, see Plate No. 34.

NUPTIAL PLUMAGES

A. Greater Scaup. (B) Wing. Adult male. Best known as *big bluebill, broadbill.* Largely restricted to coastal bays from Maine to New Jersey, the Pacific Coast as far as San Francisco Bay, and the Great Lakes. May occasionally be found throughout the interior of the continent. Black coloration front and rear, gray midsection. Black-green head differs from smaller black-purple head of lesser scaup; also, white wing bar at rear of wing extends farther toward tip.

C. Greater Scaup. (D) Wing. Adult female. A dark brown duck with blue bill and white facial mask. White bar at rear of wing extends onto primaries; in lesser scaup, it is restricted to secondaries.

E. Lesser Scaup. (F) Wing. Adult male. Known as *bluebill* to hunters. The most abundant diving duck over most of North America. Black coloration front and rear, gray midsection. White bar at rear of wing confined to inner half of wing.

G. Lesser Scaup. (H) Wing. Adult female. Almost identical with greater scaup except for smaller size and shorter white bar at rear of wing. Note white facial disk encompassing blue bill.

Transitional Plumages, see Plate No. 17.
Downy Young, see Plate No. 34.

Plate No. 20

NUPTIAL PLUMAGES

A. Common Goldeneye (formerly American Golden-eye). (B) Wing. Adult male. Also known as *whistler* from resounding whistling sound produced by wings. A large, chunky, black and white duck with short neck and large puffy head. Head appears black at a distance, with circular white mark between bill and eye. At close range, head has greenish cast. Large white patch extending almost across base of black wing shows vividly during flight.

C. Common Goldeneye. (D) Wing. Adult female and juveniles. Note cinnamon-brown head, gray back, and white patch at base of wing. Yellow tip of bill (C.1) characterizes adult female from spring through breeding season and distinguishes common goldeneye from Barrow's goldeneye female which has all-yellow bill (G.1).

E. Barrow's Goldeneye (formerly Barrow's Golden-eye). (F) Wing. Adult male. Similar to common goldeneye, but white mark between eye and bill is crescent-shaped rather than round. Barrow's goldeneye at rest displays black scapulars (between back and wing) marked by a series of white dots; scapulars of common goldeneye are white with black hash marks. At close range, head is egg-shaped and purple-black rather than greenish and knobby as in common goldeneye.

G. Barrow's Goldeneye. (H) Wing. Adult female and juveniles similar. Resembles common goldeneye except for all-yellow bill of adult female during spring and breeding season. Less white on wing coverts.

Transitional Plumage, see Plate No. 21.
Downy Young, see Plate No. 34.

TRANSITIONAL PLUMAGES*

A. Ring-necked Duck. Adult male during mid-stage of prenuptial molt. Represents plumage found in early October.

B. Ring-necked Duck. Adult male during late stage of prenuptial molt. Represents plumage found in late October.

C. Common Goldeneye (formerly American Golden-eye). Adult male during early stage of prenuptial molt. Represents plumage found in September.

D. Barrow's Goldeneye (formerly Barrow's Golden-eye). Adult male during early stage of prenuptial molt. Represents plumage found in September.

E. Bufflehead (formerly Buffle-head). Adult male during early stage of prenuptial molt. Represents plumage found in September.

F. Harlequin. Adult male during early stage of prenuptial molt. Represents plumage found in early fall.

*The change from eclipse to nuptial plumage occurs as a result of the prenuptial molt. Individuals enter the molt at varying times during late summer and early fall, depending upon their chronology of breeding behavior. Because of the variation in breeding behavior (example: nonbreeding males are among the last to assume the eclipse plumage), plumages worn at any one time during the fall show a variety of transitional stages. Therefore, the time of the period given for each stage is only suggestive and applies to the norm and not to birds that molt exceptionally early or late. Juvenile males acquire nuptial plumages later than adults.

Nuptial Plumages:
Ring-necked Duck and Bufflehead, see Plate No. 18.
Common and Barrow's Goldeneye, see Plate No. 20.
Harlequin Duck, see Plate No. 23.

Plate No. 22

WINTER AND SPRING PLUMAGES*

A. Oldsquaw (formerly Old-squaw). (B) Wing. Adult male in winter plumage, November to April. Note exceedingly long central tail feathers. Pintail is only other duck to have elongated tail but, unlike oldsquaw, has brown head and white chest. In flight, oldsquaw presents a striking study in contrasting brown and white. Brown wings contrast vividly with white portions of body when bird is in flight. Found largely on Great Lakes and along both seacoasts.

C. Oldsquaw. (D) Wing. Adult female in winter plumage, November to April. Note brown collar, crown, and cheek mark, and white face.

E. Oldsquaw. (F) Wing. Adult male in summer plumage, May to August.

G. Oldsquaw. (H) Wing. Adult female in summer plumage, May to August.

*The oldsquaw is the most unusual of all ducks in wearing two diversely colored seasonal plumages in addition to the mid-summer eclipse plumage.

Downy Young, see Plate No. 34.

NUPTIAL PLUMAGES

A. Steller's Eider. (B) Wing. Adult male. Occurs along Aleutian Islands and Alaskan coast. Only eider with blue speculum. Note long, sickle-shaped tertials on inner wing and long black and white scapulars draped over folded wing.

C. Steller's Eider. (D) Wing. Adult female. Smallest and darkest of the four eider females found in North America, the only one with a blue, mallard-like speculum.

E. Harlequin Duck.* (F) Wing. Adult male. A gaudy and bizarre-appearing duck found almost exclusively in Pacific Northwest—on mountain streams in summer and along seacoast at other seasons. A few occur in winter from St. Lawrence Estuary to Long Island.

G. Harlequin Duck. (H) Wing. Adult female. Similar to females and juveniles of surf and white-winged scoters, but Harlequin is smaller and lacks white wing patch characteristic of white-winged scoter. (Heads of these scoters have two whitish marks, less distinct than triple white marks on Harlequin's head.)

*There are two races of Harlequin ducks in North America; one inhabits the Northeast Coast, the other the Pacific Northwest. The western race (J) shows a slight forward extension of the chestnut-colored stripe on the crown, compared with that exhibited by the eastern race (E).

Eastern Harlequin in transitional plumage, see Plate No. 21.
Downy Young, Steller's Eider, see Plate No. 34.
Downy Young, Harlequin Duck, see Plate No. 35.

Plate No. 24

COMMON EIDER*
NUPTIAL PLUMAGES

A. American Eider. (F) Wing. Adult male. A large black and white sea duck: white above, black below; wing has a triangular white patch. Note width and extension of bill process and long curved white tertials.

B. American Eider. (G) Wing. Adult female, Large-sized, heavily barred brown duck, with large sloping head.

C. Pacific Eider. (F) Wing. Adult male. Almost identical with American eider except for larger body size, narrower bill process, and black V-shaped mark on throat.

D. Pacific Eider. (G) Wing. Adult female. Identical with American eider except for bill process.

E. Northern Eider. (F) Wing. Identical with American eider except for bill process and less extensive green patches at back of head.

*There are four races of the common eider in North America and one in Europe. Unless the bird is in the hand, the most feasible way of determining the race is the locality of observation. Not shown is the Hudson Bay race, which has paler plumages.

Transitional Plumage, see Plate No. 29.
Downy Young, see Plate No. 34.

Plate No. 25

NUPTIAL PLUMAGES

A. King Eider. (B) Wing. Adult male. Has black back in contrast to white back of common eider, and also smaller white wing patch located on forepart of wing. Small numbers may be found in winter between St. Lawrence Estuary and Long Island. Most winter on Bering Sea.

C. King Eider. (D) Wing. Adult female. A large duck with rich brown coloring, marked with dark U's and V's rather than bars as in common eider.

E. Spectacled Eider. (F) Wing. Adult male. White spectacle on sea-green head distinguishes it from common eider, which it otherwise resembles. Restricted almost entirely to Bering Sea.

G. Spectacled Eider. (H) Wing. Adult female. Similar to female common eider except for lighter brown spectacle around eye.

Transitional Plumage, see Plate No. 29.
Downy Young, see Plate No. 34.

NUPTIAL PLUMAGES

A. Black Scoter (formerly American Scoter). (B) Wing. Adult male. A large, chunky, all-black sea duck, least common of the three scoters. Note yellow protuberance at base of bill and all-black feet.

C. Black Scoter. (D) Wing. Adult female. Light gray patch on side of head distinguishes it from other scoter females. Slight resemblance to ruddy duck in winter plumage, but scoter is larger.

E. White-winged Scoter. (F) Wing. Only black duck with white speculum. Most abundant scoter on Atlantic Coast and the one most likely to occur inland. Note pink feet and small white mark at eye.

G. White-winged Scoter. (H) Wing. A large, black-brown chunky duck with two indistinct whitish marks on side of head. Gleam of white speculum conspicuous during flight.

Downy Young, see Plate No. 35.

Plate No. 26

NUPTIAL AND JUVENILE PLUMAGES

A. Surf Scoter. (B) Wing. Adult male. All black except for two white patches on top of head, hence its nickname *skunkhead*. Most abundant scoter on Pacific Coast.

C. Surf Scoter. (D) Wing. Adult female. Dark gray-brown with two white facial marks. Similar to white-winged scoter female but lacks white wing patch.

E. White-winged Scoter. Juvenile. Note that two whitish marks on head are more distinct than in adult female.

F. Surf Scoter. Juvenile. White head marks more distinct than in adult female.

G. Black Scoter (formerly American Scoter). Juvenile. Lighter body plumage than that of adult, especially on breast and belly.

Downy Young, see Plate No. 35.

Plate No. 28

NUPTIAL PLUMAGES

A. Common Merganser (formerly American Merganser). (B) Wing. Adult male. Gooselike profile. Flies in a line low over water. Has steady, rapid, but shallow wingbeat. Similar in color pattern to goldeneyes, but long neck and body conformation dissimilar. At a distance, green head appears black.

C. Common Merganser. (D) Wing. Adult female and juveniles. Note gray back and reddish-brown head, white wing speculum. Almost identical with red-breasted merganser except that white throat patch is sharply delineated by reddish head and neck. In red-breasted female merganser, light throat merges indistinctly into color of head and neck.

E. Red-breasted Merganser. (F) Wing. Adult male. Tufted head, band of brown with black dots across chest, and gray sides distinguish it from male common merganser. Usually associated with salt water and Great Lakes; common merganser more frequently inhabits freshwater areas.

F. Red-breasted Merganser. (G) Wing. Adult female and juveniles. Note comparison with common merganser, under C.

Transitional Plumage, see Plate No. 29.
Downy Young, see Plate No. 35.

TRANSITIONAL PLUMAGES

A. Red-breasted Merganser. Adult male during mid-stage of prenuptial molt. Represents plumage found in October.

B. Common Merganser (formerly American Merganser). Adult male during mid-stage of prenuptial molt. Represents plumage found in October.

C. Hooded Merganser. Adult male from mid-stage to late stage of prenuptial molt. Represents plumage found in early October.

D. King Eider. Adult male during late stage of prenuptial molt.

E. American Eider. Adult male during late stage of prenuptial molt.

Nuptial Plumages:

Red-breasted Merganser, see Plate No. 28.
Common Merganser, see Plate No. 28.
Hooded Merganser, see Plate No. 30.
American Eider, see Plate No. 24.
King Eider, see Plate No. 25.

Plate No. 30

NUPTIAL PLUMAGES

A. Hooded Merganser. (B) Wing. Adult male. A medium-sized duck, appearing on water as a black duck with fanlike crest of white, white chest, and white finger mark on side. During flight, white crest is closed to a narrow ribbon, and black wings show white marks on shoulder and on inner trailing edge. Flight is low and swift, wingbeat rapid.

C. Hooded Merganser. (D) Wing. Adult female and juveniles similar. Note solid brown back, crested cinnamon-brown head and long narrow bill. Presents low profile on water.

ECLIPSE AND NUPTIAL PLUMAGES

E. Ruddy Duck. (H) Wing. Adult male in nuptial plumage. Most males complete full nuptial plumage during April. White face mark conspicuous at a distance, as is the fan-shaped tail often erected at a 45-degree angle.

F. Ruddy Duck. (H) Wing. Adult male in eclipse plumage, worn through fall and early winter. White face mark, small chunky body, swift low flight, and rapid wingbeat all aid in identification.

G. Ruddy Duck. (H) Wing. Adult female. Similar to male, but facial mark less distinct and bisected by brown stripe.

Transitional Plumage, Hooded Merganser, see Plate No. 29.
Downy Young, see Plate No. 35.

NUPTIAL PLUMAGES

A. Masked Duck. (B) Wing. Adult male. Similar to ruddy duck. Inhabits South America and West Indies and appears regularly in Mexico and along the Texas coast, occasionally in Florida, and rarely elsewhere.

C. Masked Duck. (D) Wing. Adult female.

E. Fulvous Whistling Duck (formerly Fulvous Tree Duck). (F) Wing. Adult. Sexes similar. Long neck and legs, broad wings rounded at tips present unusual appearance. Wingbeat slow, flight erratic, and flock formation irregular. Largely found in rice belt of Texas and Louisiana; small numbers regularly occur in southern Florida.

G. Black-bellied Whistling Duck (formerly Black-bellied Tree Duck). (H) Wing. Adult. Sexes similar. Black belly and large white patch on wing distinguish it from fulvous whistling duck. Found along lower coast of Texas and in Mexico.

Downy Young, see Plate No. 35

Plate No. 32

DOWNY YOUNG OF THE GEESE

A. Ross' Goose (formerly Ross's Goose) (after Blaauw).

B. Snow Goose (Greater and Lesser Snow Geese, identical).

C. Blue Goose.

D. White-fronted Goose (Tule Goose, similar).

E. Black Brant.

F. American Brant.

G. Emperor Goose.

H. Common Canada Goose (Lesser Canada Goose and Richardson's Goose, similar).

J. Western Canada Goose (Cackling Goose, similar).

Plate No. 33.

DOWNY YOUNG OF THE DABBLING DUCKS

A. Common Mallard.

B. Black Duck.

C. Mottled Duck (Florida Duck, similar).

D. Gadwall.

E. Pintail (formerly American Pintail).

F. American Wigeon (formerly Baldpate).

G. Blue-winged Teal.

H. Cinnamon Teal.

J. Green-winged Teal.

K. Northern Shoveler (formerly Shoveller).

L. Wood Duck.

Plate No. 34

DOWNY YOUNG OF THE DIVING DUCKS

A. Lesser Scaup.

B. Greater Scaup.

C. Canvasback (formerly Canvas-back).

D. Redhead.

E. Ring-necked Duck.

F. Bufflehead (formerly Buffle-head).

G. Common Goldeneye (formerly American Golden-eye).

H. Barrow's Goldeneye (formerly Barrow's Golden-eye).

J. Oldsquaw (formerly Old-squaw).

K. American Eider (Northern Eider, similar).

L. King Eider.

M. Pacific Eider.

N. Steller's Eider.

O. Spectacled Eider.

Plate No. 35

DOWNY YOUNG OF THE DIVING DUCKS
(Continued)

A. Eastern Harlequin Duck (Western Harlequin Duck, similar).

B. Black Scoter (formerly American Scoter).

C. Surf Scoter.

D. White-winged Scoter.

DOWNY YOUNG OF MERGANSERS AND OTHERS

E. Red-breated Merganser.

F. Common Merganser (formerly American Merganser).

G. Hooded Merganser.

H. Black-bellied Whistling Duck (formerly Black-bellied Tree Duck).

J. Fulvous Whistling Duck (formerly Fulvous Tree Duck).

K. Ruddy Duck.

HYBRIDS AND ALBINOS

A. Mallard-Black hybrid.

B. Mallard-Black hybrid.

C. Mallard-Pintail hybrid.

D. Mallard-Pintail hybrid.

E. Mallard-Gadwall hybrid (Brewer's Duck, after Audubon).

F. Hooded Merganser-Common Goldeneye hybrid.

G. Albino (Mallard).

H. Partial albino (Mallard).

Plate No. 36

females, immatures, and adults in eclipse plumage show little in the way of distinctive coloration. In all dabbling (puddle) ducks, there is a highly colored patch at the inner trailing edge of the wing, the so-called speculum, encompassing all or part of the secondary wing feathers. In many diving ducks this area of the wing is white, in others it is gray, a different color or shade from the rest of the wing. After noting the color of the speculum, the eye should move forward to perceive the color of the shoulder area. This area is basically one of four colors: white, blue, brown, or black.

The head is the next most likely feature to display a distinctive color. Note this color and the presence or absence of unusual facial markings, such as the green stripe from the eye to the back of the head in the American wigeon and the green-winged teal. Because the breast and belly are readily visible when waterfowl are in flight, the degree and conformation of white should be noticed. In a few ducks, no white is evident; in other species the white is margined with brown to form a distinct oval; and in still others these areas are completely white.

IDENTIFYING DUCKS ON THE WATER

On the water, ducks often appear slightly different from the way they are shown in many illustrations. To begin with, most resting ducks are shown with too much of the speculum color exposed to view. Most artists wish to display as much of the color markings as possible, so they tend to overemphasize the speculum as well as other wing markings. Yet when ducks fold their wings and the wings become partially covered by the side feathers, the speculums and other wing markings may either disappear completely or appear as narrow slots. The amount of color a resting duck may display varies somewhat among species, sexes, and individuals. For example, in the mallard the blue speculum shows much less frequently in the male than in the female. A sick or tired duck drops its wings more than a vital individual, thereby showing greater expanses of wing markings.

Some illustrations show diving ducks riding higher in the water than is normal. Consequently, the side and flank markings are overemphasized at the expense of the back markings. At a distance, this overemphasis makes considerable difference in the degree of black-white that is perceived. Usually, diving ducks are immersed to the level of their tails; sometimes their tails are awash. Their level of immersion does vary, however. The bodies of diving ducks are lowest in the water when the ducks are actively feeding, somewhat higher while they are resting, and highest during courtship displays. It is obvious that diving ducks can change their buoyancy at will through the amount of air in their air sacs.

IDENTIFYING WATERFOWL AT HAND

It should be possible to identify any male waterfowl in its nuptial (breeding) plumage by comparing it with the color illustrations in this book. The problem is that females of many species are similar, and early in the fall the immatures and males in full or partial eclipse plumage appear in varying degrees like females. Here, as with birds in flight, the wing markings offer the best clues for identification, because once acquired at the time of the late-summer wing molt, these markings for all practical purposes remain constant (fig. 8-1). There are differences between wings of males and females, as shown in the illustrations of this book. The subtle differences between wings of adults and immatures are so slight as to have no bearing on species identification.

Body plumage, especially early in the fall, may be confusing. Immatures in changing from the immature plumage to the nuptial (breeding) plumage, and adult males in changing from the eclipse to the nuptial plumage, exhibit various mixtures of plumages that are impossible to depict, but some phase of these changes is shown for most species.

If the immature and eclipse-plumaged ducks were not enough to add to the difficulties of species identification, there is the occasional hybrid or bird with aberrant plumage. Various plumages result from the cross mating of the same two species, but usually there are sufficient characters of each species to identify them.

Other water birds superficially resemble waterfowl, but their structural differences are such that taxonomists place them in other orders. These are the loons, the grebes, and the American coot. The loons and grebes are protected throughout the year by the Migratory Bird Treaty Act. Coots, or "mud hens" as they are commonly called, are closely related to the rails, and can be hunted during the open waterfowl season. A coot has a black head and neck, a soot-gray body with white undertail coverts, a white chickenlike bill with a black spot near the tip, and long greenish legs and feet that are lobed rather than webbed.

Escaped domestic ducks sometimes show up to confuse the hunter. These are usually the all-white Pekin duck, or the black Muscovy duck. The Muscovy is larger than the mallard and is black-bodied, with greenish or purplish iridescence on the black wings and back and a white wing patch. It is a native of Mexico and Central America.

Novice waterfowl hunters might well adopt the axiom of novice mushroom hunters who pick only those species that they know—usually the morel—and let all others go. Novice hunters should learn the appearance of the most abundant duck in their locality, usually the mallard, and confine their shots to it. A good way to help waterfowl conservation and avoid species with high points or special protection is the adage: "If in doubt, do without."

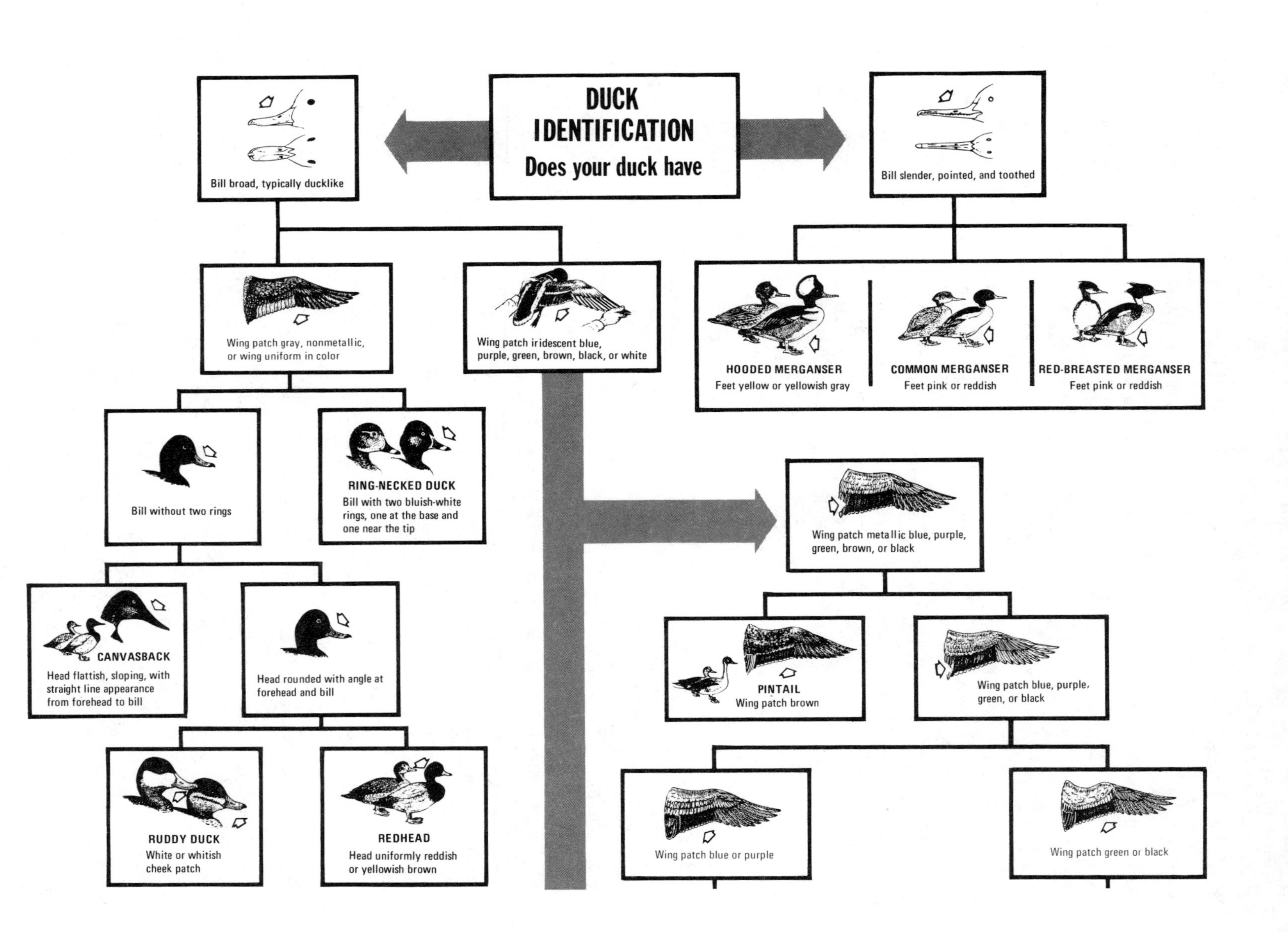
DUCK IDENTIFICATION
Does your duck have
Bill broad, typically ducklike
Bill slender, pointed, and toothed
Wing patch gray, nonmetallic, or wing uniform in color
Wing patch iridescent blue, purple, green, brown, black, or white
HOODED MERGANSER
Feet yellow or yellowish gray
COMMON MERGANSER
Feet pink or reddish
RED-BREASTED MERGANSER
Feet pink or reddish
Bill without two rings
RING-NECKED DUCK
Bill with two bluish-white rings, one at the base and one near the tip
Wing patch metallic blue, purple, green, brown, or black
CANVASBACK
Head flattish, sloping, with straight line appearance from forehead to bill
Head rounded with angle at forehead and bill
PINTAIL
Wing patch brown
Wing patch blue, purple, green, or black
RUDDY DUCK
White or whitish cheek patch
REDHEAD
Head uniformly reddish or yellowish brown
Wing patch blue or purple
Wing patch green or black

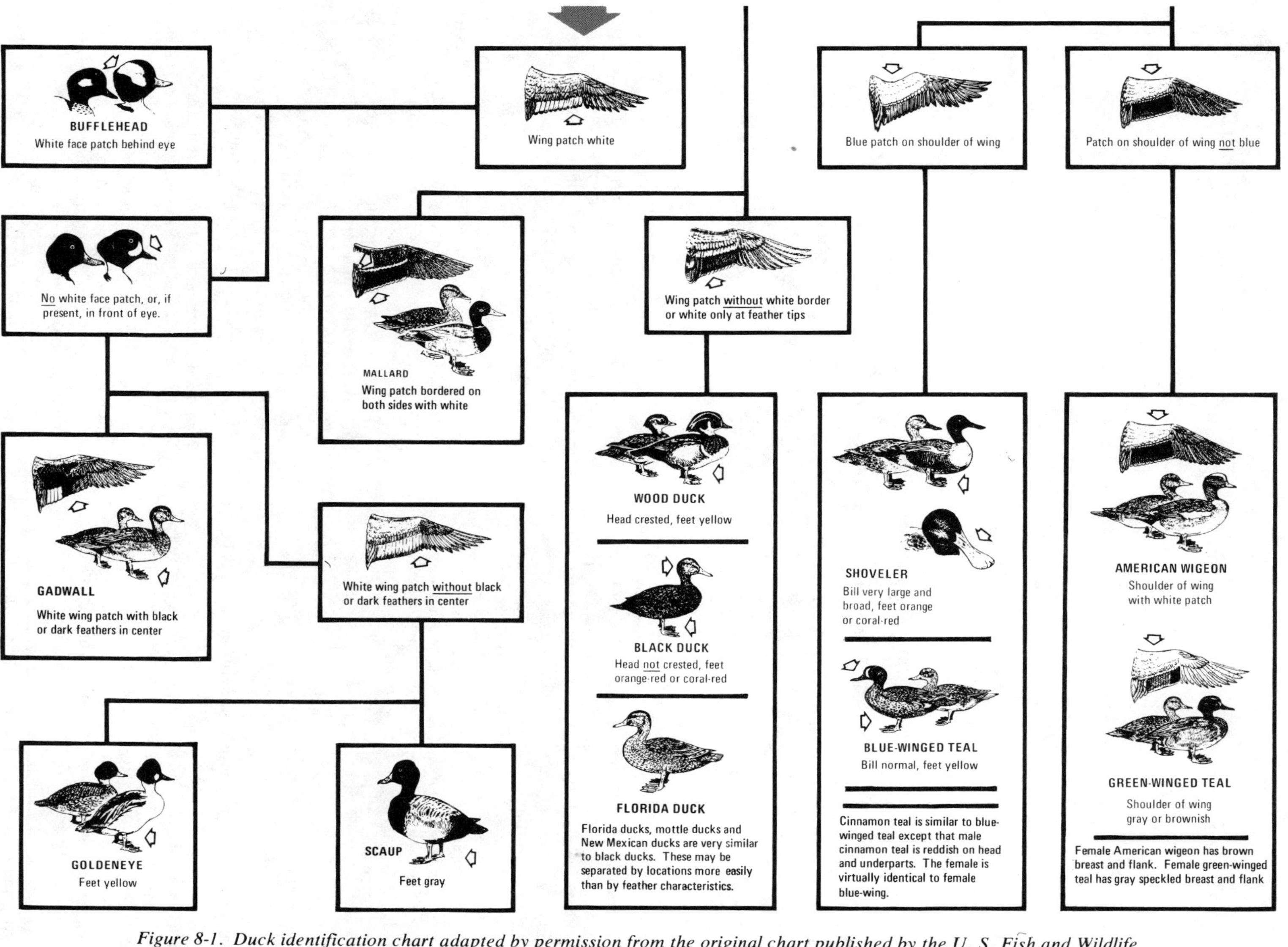

Figure 8-1. Duck identification chart adapted by permission from the original chart published by the U. S. Fish and Wildlife Service

chapter 8

MORTALITY AND DISEASE

Waterfowl die daily in tremendous numbers as a result of disease, but this mortality becomes apparent only when mass die-offs occur in a particular locality. One reason why the toll of disease is not highly visible is that predators—including man during the hunting season—eliminate the weakened birds before a terminal condition is reached. The carcasses of birds that die from illness do not last long; a host of organisms quickly erase their fragile remains from the landscape. I have marked numerous duck carcasses in the wild and have never ceased to be amazed at how quickly all traces vanish.

When a duck becomes ill, it leaves the company of its flock and seeks concealment in dense marsh or shoreline cover. As illness progresses, it crawls out of the water for the sanctuary of land. Amid dense cover these moribund birds sit quietly and usually go unnoticed by man.

It is only when an epidemic rages among waterfowl that we become aware of disease and become concerned. In epidemics, waterfowl die in such numbers that predators are able to eliminate only a small proportion of moribund birds, and carcasses litter the landscape.

Because predators have difficulty in capturing healthy adult waterfowl that are not breeding, I believe that most nonhunting losses result directly or indirectly from disease. Accidents, such as striking power lines, drowning in fishnets, and becoming engulfed in oil spills take their toll, but disease is by far the more important.

As shown by band-recovery rates, about half of the game ducks die each year. From 1955 through 1972, the continental breeding population of game ducks has averaged slightly over 40 million. For convenience, we assume that there are 40 million breeding birds and that they produce 40 million young that enter the fall population. (Age ratios indicate average fall populations composed equally of immature and old birds.) Hence, about 80 million game ducks are available for the hunting season. Kill data from the U.S. Fish and Wildlife Service show that from 1955 to 1973, hunters in the United States bagged an average of 10,733,000 ducks. In Canada, about 3.5 million game ducks are bagged yearly. The combined continental kill, excluding Mexico, is in the neighborhood of 14.5 million ducks. A standard figure used for crippling loss is 20 percent. Therefore, on this basis, hunters directly remove 20 million ducks, or about 50 percent of the number that die during the year. Nonhunting mortality—disease, predation, and accidents—accounts for a loss of 20 million. Disease directly or indirectly accounts for the largest proportion of nonhunting deaths.

DISEASES AFFECTING THE WATERFOWL POPULATION

The well-known diseases of waterfowl that frequently reach epidemic proportions are botulism, fowl cholera, duck virus enteritis (DVE), and lead poisoning. Diseases of lesser importance are aspergillosis, leucocytozoonosis and sarcosporidiosis.

The symptoms of many diseases afflicting waterfowl are similar. Even in the laboratory, pathologists may have difficulty identifying the etiological agent. Therefore, unless there is a massive outbreak, which provides numerous clues and abundant specimens, the cause of death among waterfowl usually remains undetected.

Botulism

Of all the diseases afflicting waterfowl, none has caused more massive or visible losses than botulism. Botulism is caused by a toxin produced by an anaerobic bacterium, *Clostridium botulinum*. Different strains of this bacterium produce different neurotoxins that have been labeled A through F. Type C has long been identified as the specific strain that produces the toxin responsible for waterfowl deaths.

Botulism toxin kills quickly, so waterfowl succumb in good weight. Because the birds do not eat while they are ill, bile stains the vent green, but so does lead poisoning. Sick birds have difficulty holding their heads erect, so the term "limber neck" is often applied when the causative agent is unknown. The nictitating membrane that sweeps across the eye ceases its rhythmic function. In spite of this syndrome, the only positive diagnosis of the disease involves infecting mice with blood serum from the sick bird. One half of the mice are treated by a botulism antitoxin, and, therefore, serve as controls. If the unprotected mice die within 6 days and those protected with antitoxin survive, botulism is clearly demonstrated.

When first noticed in Utah in 1910, this disease was called "western duck sickness," for the cause of death was a complete mystery. Subsequent study related the massed deaths to alkali lakes, thereby giving rise to the name "alkali poisoning." It was not until the studies of Kalmbach and Gunderson (1934) and others in the early 1930's that botulism was confirmed as the cause of "western duck sickness."

Although most prevalent in the West, botulism has occurred among waterfowl in many areas of North America, including states east of the Mississippi River. In 1910 it was reputed to have caused the deaths of millions of waterfowl in Utah and California. Years of quiescence appear to be followed by years of outbreak. The latest outbreaks occurred in the Central Valley of California in 1968 and 1969 and in the Tulare Basin in 1969. Deaths in the Central Valley were estimated at 250,000; the estimate for the Tulare Basin was 40,000 (Hunter et al. 1970). Without the corrective measures employed, the losses in 1968 and 1969 would have been much higher.

Botulism bacteria develop when high temperatures cause spores to germinate at the time there is a suitable nutrient medium and an environment devoid of oxygen. Hunter et al. (1970), from their recent studies in California, suggest that the nutrient medium consists almost entirely of animal matter. The demise of invertebrates and fly maggots feeding upon the decomposing carcasses of waterfowl provide the media for the growth of the bacterium. An airless environment is provided by the bodies of the invertebrates and maggots, where the toxin is stored from the metabolic activities of the bacterium. There was no evidence of free botulism toxin in the water or soils where botulism outbreaks occurred.

Hunter et al. (1970) found that outbreaks develop as a result of one or more of the following conditions: flooding of dry land during warm weather, resulting in the drowning of terrestrial invertebrates that then provide a nutrient medium for the bacterium; receding water levels that expose mud flats, causing the death of aquatic invertebrates that also provide a suitable medium; changes in water quality that result in the death of invertebrate fauna; and decaying animal carcasses that produce maggots. The greatest waterfowl losses in California occurred where tremendous numbers of toxic maggots developed in dead waterfowl. Maggots devouring the flesh of dead fish are another source of the toxin. It was this source of toxin that triggered a small outbreak of botulism in central Illinois in September 1974.

Once an outbreak of botulism occurs, it is of paramount importance that carcasses of waterfowl be removed and properly disposed of to reduce the fly maggot cycle. Every effort should be made to discourage waterfowl use of the infected area, either by scare tactics or by making the habitat less attractive by water manipulation. Draining the water entirely from the problem area or flooding it so that waterfowl no longer feed in the shallow areas inhabited by the toxin-producing bacteria are effective habitat measures.

Appreciable numbers of waterfowl ill from botulism can recover if given an opportunity. They need to be picked up and placed in pens that shield them from the sun, wind, and predators and provide them with fresh water. Further treatment depends upon the stage of the disease. Investigators recognize three stages: Class I birds readily walk, but they can not fly. They usually recover with "hospitalization" but without special treatment. Class II birds suffer a great degree of paralysis, have difficulty in walking, and usually "row" with their wings for propulsion. They require oral administrations of fresh water in order to recover. Class III victims are almost completely immobilized and require an intraperitoneal injection of antitoxin if they are to survive (Hunter et al. 1970).

Fowl Cholera

Fowl cholera is caused by a bacterium, *Pasteurella multocida*, that is commonly associated with poultry. Waterfowl losses from fowl cholera have numbered in the thousands, but this disease surfaces only at infrequent intervals and places. Domestic chickens and turkeys are believed to act as carriers of the disease, which is introduced into waterfowl through direct contact with the domestic birds and through contaminated soil, food, and water, or by contact with intermediate bird carriers. Once a duck has become infected, it acts as a carrier, disseminating the disease among its associates. Where waterfowl congregate in dense numbers, they are especially vulnerable to the rapid spread of this disease.

Birds commence dying of fowl cholera 4 to 9 days after exposure. At the onset it kills so rapidly that sick birds may not be evident. However, in the late stages of the disease, the virulence declines and sick birds may be observed for several days before they succumb.

Because of mucus in the respiratory tract, ill birds breathe with difficulty. A watery gray, yellow, or green diarrhea may or may not occur. The mucous membranes of the lungs and intestines and the fat of the abdomen may show spotty hemorrhages. The liver shows numerous pinhead spots of dead tissue, but the spleen is of normal appearance. Fowl typhoid is characterized by an enlarged spleen (Murray 1948). The only positive means of identifying fowl cholera is by finding bipolar staining organisms upon microscopic examination of the blood.

For a number of years after its diagnosis in the Texas Panhandle in 1944, fowl cholera took a heavy toll of ducks (Petrides and Bryant 1951). During the winter of 1947-48, it was estimated that 36,000 waterfowl succumbed from this disease. About 4,400 died during the winter of 1949-50. In the San Francisco Bay area an outbreak of fowl cholera resulted in serious losses (40,000 deaths) of ducks, geese, and coots during the winter of 1948-49. In the winter of 1965-66, the combined waterfowl losses to fowl cholera in California exceeded 70,000 birds (Rosen 1971).

It is difficult to relate eiders to poultry, but in June 1963, 200 breeding common eiders succumbed to fowl cholera at their nesting grounds on islands 6 miles east of Camden, Maine (Gershman et al. 1964). A sanitary program was initiated that appeared to halt the disease. It was theorized that the source of the infection came either from domestic poultry or refuse from ships.

An epidemic of fowl cholera caused a loss of 88,000 waterfowl in Chesapeake Bay during February 1970. Among those killed were 62,100 oldsquaws, 18,000 white-winged scoters, 2,500 buffleheads, 900 whistling swans, and 500 black scoters. The outbreak of this disease in Chesapeake Bay is understandable in view of the poultry industry on Maryland's east shore. Whistling swans, Canada geese, mallards, and black ducks feed in the farm fields, where they had a good opportunity to contact the disease. When the waterfowl returned to the bay, the disease may have spread from these carriers to the diving ducks.

During the spring of 1975, 20,000 to 25,000 waterfowl died of fowl cholera in eastern Nebraska (Gary Pearson). Thirty-seven percent were white-fronted geese, 21 percent mallards, 18 percent pintails, and smaller percentages of 14 other species.

Duck Virus Enteritis

Duck virus enteritis (DVE), also known as duck plague, first appeared in the Netherlands in 1923. It was first diagnosed in North America in 1967, at a commercial Pekin duck farm located near Eastport, Long Island, New York. Despite every effort to confine the disease to the original source of infection, it spread to nearby commercial duck farms, then to other confined waterfowl, and finally to wild waterfowl (U.S. Department of Agriculture 1969).

By 1969 it had been reported among captive and wild waterfowl in Suffolk, Cayuga, Chemung, and Dutchess counties in New York; Bucks, Dauphin, and Montgomery counties in Pennsylvania; and Prince Georges County, Maryland. Wild waterfowl that had been affected by 1969 included 15 mallards, 45 black ducks, a greater scaup, a bufflehead, and a Canada goose (Leibovitz 1969). Most of the dead waterfowl, including a feral mute swan, were found along the margins of creeks and rivers on Long Island.

Symptoms of DVE appear 3 to 7 days after exposure. Because of the rapid onset of death, the afflicted birds usually die in good weight. According to Leibovitz (1969), the specimens emit a dark brown tarry fluid from their bills when their heads are suspended downward. Their hearts have a red "paint-brush" striped effect as a result of hemorrhages in the coronary grooves. Hemorrhagic spots occur on the stomach walls and on the intestines. Both hemorrhagic and white spots appear on the liver. Free blood often fills the intestines and, occasionally, the body cavity. Leibovitz (1969) points out that with adequate clinical history and with necropsy findings, DVE can be diagnosed, but when information is incomplete, diagnosis must be based on isolation and identification of the virus.

After the appearance of DVE among wild waterfowl in the Long Island area in 1969 and minor outbreaks in Maryland and Pennsylvania, little was heard about it until mid-January 1973. Then, like a thunderbolt, this disease struck mallards wintering on the Lake Andes National Wildlife Refuge in southeastern South Dakota. By the time the disease had run its course in February, 28,845 dead ducks and 235 dead Canada geese had been collected. Total mortality was estimated at 40,000 to 43,000 ducks and 350 Canada geese. Personnel of the U.S. Fish and Wildlife Service took all possible precautions to reduce the transmission of the disease to other waterfowl populations and, once the disease had terminated, to disperse the waterfowl from Lake Andes.

Where DVE will appear next and what mortality it will cause are good questions. The virus is now present in wild waterfowl populations. A severe stress placed on local populations where carriers of DVE are present will doubtless result in an outbreak, the seriousness of which will depend upon many factors.

Sarcosporidiosis

Sarcocystis rileyi is a mysterious infection of muscles, particularly the large breast ones, in waterfowl. It is caused by a protozoan parasite. When the infestation is heavy, hunters frequently notice the cream wormlike cylindrical cysts under the skin on the large flight muscles. The elongated cysts are parallel to the muscle fibers and are divided into compartments that at maturity are filled with spores. Because of the wormy appearance, most hunters consider afflicted ducks unpalatable and discard them.

So far as is known, sarcosporidiosis is not fatal to waterfowl. However, because the large cysts replace muscle tissue, heavy infestations are believed to weaken the host. Up to the present time no scientist has been able to trace the path of infection from the source to the host and within the body to its resting place in muscle tissue. It is believed that the cysts rupture, releasing spores that are eventually carried by the blood stream to the intestines, where they are shed in the feces. The susceptible host picks up the spores, but how they reach the muscle tissue is unknown. The disease is not known to be transmitted from waterfowl to man. Moreover, thorough cooking should kill the spores.

Chabreck (1965) found sarcosporidiosis to be of common occurrence among ducks in Louisiana. Among 961 adult ducks of nine species that he examined, 35.7 percent showed some degree of infestation. However, among 552 immature ducks, this disease appeared in only 2 specimens (0.4 percent). Northern shoveler adults had the highest frequency of infestation, 78 percent, and gadwalls the lowest, with an incidence of 9 percent. Between these extremes, the incidence of the disease by percentage among other species was as follows: blue-winged teal, 48; green-winged teal, 47; pintail, 44; mallard, 27; American wigeon, 23; lesser scaup, 17; and mottled duck, 11 percent.

Aspergillosis

Aspergillosis is an infrequent fungus disease of waterfowl, but when it strikes, substantial losses may occur. The spores of *Aspergillus fumigatus*, the causative agent identified in deaths among wild waterfowl, is widely distributed in nature. Waterfowl usually come in contact with *Aspergillus* spores through contaminated food. Herman and Sladen (1958) found spores in soils on the Eastern Shore of Maryland but collected the spores most readily from cornstalks and other plants.

This fungus develops in the lungs and air sacs of birds. As a result, there is impaired breathing, the bills open and close convulsively, and the tails jerk spasmodically. In advanced stages, the fungus is visible to the unaided eye upon opening the body cavity. Early stages require microscopic preparation of the small "cheeselike" nodules visible in the lungs or other internal organs.

We found 89 wood ducks dead from this disease in September 1943 (Bellrose et al. 1945). From the number of sick birds observed, we estimated that of the 800 to 1,000 that were attracted to a pile of moldy corn, possibly 100 to 200 birds died. Presumably, the *Aspergillus* spores were present in the corn eaten by the wood ducks.

Neff (1955) reported that an outbreak of aspergillosis among mallards occurred late in January 1949 on two lakes near Boulder, Colorado. Losses were estimated at between 1,000 and 1,100 ducks from a possible 50,000 that were wintering there. Moldy corn distributed over the snow and used as a temporary source of food during a blizzard was considered the source of the infection.

At the Swan Lake National Wildlife Refuge, Chariton County, Missouri, about 2,000 Canada geese died from aspergillosis during the first 18 days of October 1966 (McDougle and Vaught 1968). There were about 75,000 geese on the refuge during this period. Spores of *Aspergillus* were isolated from grain heads of milo and corn grown on the refuge for goose food.

Near Riverdale, North Dakota, at least 177 mallards died from aspergillosis in late February 1968 (Pearson 1969). About 1,000 mallards frequented the area where the outbreak occurred.

Leucocytozoonosis

Of the blood parasites infecting waterfowl,

Leucocytozoon simondi in ducks and geese is most frequently the cause of significant losses. Leucocytozoonosis rarely kills adult birds but often virtually wipes out ducklings and goslings in a given locality.

Leucocytozoonosis is transmitted from infected to healthy waterfowl by two species of black flies of the genus *Simulium*. Waterfowl, particularly adults, that have survived the disease act as carriers and as reservoirs for overwintering parasites. Upon their return to breeding grounds in the spring, infected birds are available for newly emerged black flies to feed upon (Fallis and Trainer 1964).

This protozoan parasite, which invades the red blood cells of susceptible waterfowl, grows rapidly and reaches maturity in 48 hours. The destruction of the red blood cells produces anemia that may be sufficiently severe as to cause death. Afflicted waterfowl refuse to eat and have labored breathing and unsteady locomotion (Fallis and Trainer 1964). The severity of the infection within the host depends upon the number of parasites transmitted by black flies and the age of the susceptible ducklings (Trainer et al. 1962).

Where black flies and waterfowl occur together, there is a high incidence of this disease among the waterfowl. In northwest Wisconsin, Trainer et al. (1962) found *Leucocytozoon* present in mallards, black ducks, pintails, blue-winged teal, and wood ducks. It occurred in 17 percent of the adults and in 75 percent of the immatures tested. Levine and Hanson (1953) listed the occurrence of *Leucocytozoon* in 24 species of waterfowl, including 32 of 350 Canada geese that they examined.

Sherwood (1965) reported the probable loss, from this disease, of 500 Canada goose goslings at the Seney National Wildlife Refuge, Michigan, in early 1964. The goslings were 2 to 3 weeks old at the time of death. This loss represented 80 percent of the goslings hatched that year at Seney. In 1960, 690 of 790 goslings at the refuge died from leucocytozoonosis, and the low production of young in 1944, 1951, and 1955 was considered to be related to the abundance of black flies that transmitted this parasite.

LEAD POISONING

Most waterfowl that die from lead poisoning are never seen. Like birds afflicted with other diseases, unless there is a large die-off, scattered infected birds steadily disappear from the environment without man's being aware of their demise.

A mass die-off of waterfowl from lead poisoning or any other agent attracts the attention of man unless it occurs in remote areas beyond his surveillance. Occasionally, man's attention is focused on lead poisoning as a result of local die-offs of waterfowl. Actual records of waterfowl dying of this disease date back to the 1890's in the United States. Since then, numerous die-offs of many species of waterfowl from lead poisoning have been reported (Bellrose 1959, Mississippi Flyway Council 1965). Undoubtedly many outbreaks of this disease have occurred that have never reached the files of conservation agencies.

The importance of lead poisoning as a mortality factor in waterfowl does not lie in the losses incurred in mass die-offs that may or may not be observed, but in the day-to-day losses that pass unnoticed.

How do waterfowl biologists know that unrecorded day-to-day losses occur? First, from the lethality of lead. When ingested, lead shot is known to be highly toxic to waterfowl. Scores of experiments have been conducted with captive waterfowl of several species, and these experiments clearly demonstrate that even a single ingested shot pellet is likely to have a deleterious effect upon the well-being of the bird and may even cause its death. As the number of shot pellets swallowed increases, so does the mortality rate.

Laboratory experiments conducted by the Illinois Natural History Survey demonstrated that many factors affected the degree of toxicity from ingested lead. These factors were the sex, age, and size of the bird, and the kind of food consumed. Females were more susceptible to lead poisoning than males, except for a brief period prior to the breeding season. Adults were more affected by similar levels of lead shot than immatures. The larger the body size, the less the effect of ingested shot.

We feel that the kind of food consumed exerted an important influence on the toxic level of lead in ducks (Jordan and Bellrose 1951, Jordan 1968). Corn was at the high end of the toxicity spectrum, with commercial duck pellets at the low end. Native duck foods ranged between the two extremes, with quahog clams approaching duck pellets in their properties of alleviating lead toxicity.

In laboratory experiments, diets simulating those of mallards in the wild pointed to appreciable mortality from low doses of lead shot. Mortality was highest in females, lowest in males, and higher in adults than immatures until late winter, after which there was little age difference.

However, laboratory conditions protect sick ducks from predators and, to a degree, from the elements; moreover, the need to exercise is reduced. Therefore, it was decided to measure mortality under field conditions. To this end 6,000 wild mallards were trapped, fluoroscoped for ingested lead shot, and weighed. Samples aggregating 4,307 birds that met necessary criteria of health were banded and dosed with one, two, and four No. 6 shot pellets and were then returned to the wild. A suitable number of banded, lead-free birds were released as controls at the same time as the experimental birds.

Life tables were prepared for the 558 banded recoveries received over the next 4 years. This analysis indicated that mallard hens of mixed ages dosed with one No. 6 shot had a 22 percent greater shrinkage in number than did the population as a whole. Adult drake mallards that received one No. 6 shot had a shrinkage of 12.3 percent, but immature drakes that were similarly dosed lost only 4.2 percent more than the lead-free controls. The level of mortality in ducks that were given four lead shot was 41.3 percent for adults and 31.6 percent for immatures, over that of the lead-free controls (Bellrose 1959).

The mortality suffered by these lead-infected mallards provides information on the lethality of lead under natural conditions. It is still necessary to determine how often waterfowl swallow lead in their feeding activities. For this purpose, we inspected 36,145 waterfowl gizzards from numerous areas in the United States. These gizzards represented birds obtained during the open season, a time of year that is neither the lowest nor the highest for ingestion of lead.

Lead shot was found in 6.7 percent of all duck gizzards, 6.8 percent in mallards and from 11.8 to 14.2 percent in the bay diving ducks. Fortunately, 65 percent of those containing shot held one pellet, 15 percent two pellets, and only 7 percent contained more than six pellets.

A pellet in a gizzard represents about a 20-day period before the shot is passed or the bird dies. At a minimum, there are six 20-day periods during the year when waterfowl are very likely to pick up lead shot from the bottom of feeding areas.

On the basis of these findings, we conservatively concluded that 2 to 3 percent of the fall and winter waterfowl population falls victim to lead poisoning each year.

MISCELLANEOUS MORTALITY FACTORS

Waterfowl die from many other causes than the major ones previously discussed. Impaction of soybeans in crops of Canada geese, attributed to eating dry soybeans that swelled after water intake, has been reported by Hanson and Smith (1950) and Durant (1956). Page and Lynch (1961) studied a die-off of 15,000 to 20,000 mallards near Jonesboro, Arkansas, in January 1956. They believed that three different agents caused this mortality: lead poisoning, crop impaction, and a microbiological organism of low virulence that might have induced crop impaction.

Oil pollution is a constant threat to thousands, if not tens of thousands of waterfowl. Undoubtedly, untold numbers of eiders, scoters, and other sea ducks have been killed by oil slicks so far out to sea that their bodies never reached land. Even inland oil has caused the death of thousands of waterfowl. In the spring of 1960, Hunt and Cowan (1963) estimated that 12,000 ducks were killed by oil on the surface of the Detroit River.

The rupture of oil tanks at two different sites on the Minnesota River in the winter of 1962-63 sent 1 million gallons of petroleum oil and 2.5 million gallons of soya oil into the river. By the time of the spring thaw, the oil had moved into the upper Mississippi River as northward-migrating waterfowl were beginning to arrive (Public Health Service 1963). About 2,400 ducks were found disabled, but the actual number affected was much higher.

Oil causes waterfowl mortality in several ways. The birds drown because buoyancy is lost from their oil-matted feathers. They die of exposure in good weight because oil-coated feathers no longer provide insulation against the loss of body heat. Toxicity results from the ingestion of oil, adversely affecting kidney function.

At times, waterfowl contain a heavy load of helminth worms, and on other occasions, the infestation is light or moderate. For many years, parasitologists have been endeavoring to evaluate the effect of these parasites upon their hosts. Cornwell and Cowan (1963) attempted this evaluation for the canvasback. They concluded that intestinal worms probably result in limited mortality to the host except under conditions of severe stress, where parasite and host are in dire competition for nutrition.

There is too little knowledge of the role that nutrition plays in the expression of disease as a mortality factor. Few waterfowl die from starvation *per se*, but malnutrition is probably a very important factor in permitting disease organisms to overwhelm them. A review of the food habits of ducks reveals a wide diversity in items consumed by the same species in different localities. It is evident that waterfowl often feed upon items that are available but may not always represent the best nutrition. Considering some of the foods consumed, it appears that many times waterfowl are stuffing themselves with low-quality foods. In viewing the effect that various foods have on the health of captive waterfowl, the importance of nutrition is self-evident. From weighing many thousands of ducks and autopsying several hundred specimens, I have concluded that malnutrition is more widespread among waterfowl than is generally believed.

Fulvous Whistling Duck

Dendrocygna bicolor helva

Other Common Names: Fulvous tree duck, Mexican squealer, squealer
(In Mexico: pijía, serrano, pato silvón)

VITAL STATISTICS

Length:	Male, 17.7-18.5 inches, average 18.1 inches (7) Female, 16.0-18.3 inches, average 17.3 inches (15)
Wing:	7.9-9.3 inches
Weight:	Male, 1.1-1.9 pounds, average 1.72 pounds (7) Female, 1.2-1.9 pounds, average 1.49 pounds (15)

FIGURES IN PARENTHESES REPRESENT THE NUMBER OF SAMPLES RECORDED.

IDENTIFICATION

Field

The long-legged, long-necked fulvous whistling (tree) duck looks more like a goose than a duck. As in other whistling ducks, its broad wings are more rounded at the tips than those of other kinds of ducks. The flattened crown gives the head an odd profile and the short tail makes the body appear "dumpy." The slow wing beat and erratic flight, the long neck, and the feet trailing behind the tail, give it an ibis-like appearance in the air. Whistling ducks fly in irregular formations, quite unlike the trim flocks of other ducks. On land, they stand erect and walk with none of the waddle so characteristic of other ducks. The black-bellied whistling duck has a more erect stance than the fulvous (Rylander and Bolen 1974*a*).

The sexes have similar plumages. Immatures have similar but duller plumages than adults. In the adult, the head, chest, breast, and belly are tawny-brown; the back, dark brown. Ivory-edged side and flank feathers form a striking border between sides and back. A distinctive white "V" separates the brown-black tail from the dark-colored back.

The wings are brown-black except for the russet brown of the shoulder patches. At a distance the bird appears uniformly dark.

In flight they call incessantly, a two-note squealing whistle, *pee-chee*. The male utters the louder and higher whistle.

At Hand

The blue-gray bill of the fulvous whistling duck is about as long as the head; the legs and unusually large feet are also blue-gray. A black stripe extends along the hindneck from the brown crown to the back. The rest of the neck is white, with striations of tawny brown that the black-bellied duck lacks.

According to McCartney (1963), the female's plumage is slightly duller than the male's, and the black line on the hindneck is continuous from the crown; in males, this line is usually broken directly behind the head.

POPULATION STATUS

The status of the fulvous whistling duck in the United States is something of an enigma. For unknown reasons, its population appears to wax and wane in abundance.

McKay (1962) reported that although fulvous whistling ducks may have occurred in the Galveston, Texas, area as early as 1892, they did not begin breeding there until about 1916. They steadily increased in abundance, until in the late 1920's thousands were nesting in that area. Four thousand were found in Brazoria County, Texas, during the summer (Singleton 1953).

The first published record of fulvous whistling ducks in southwest Louisiana was November 30, 1916 (McCartney 1963). They were reported at Chenier au Tigre, Vermilion Parish, Louisiana, in May 1917, and again the next spring. By the fall of 1925 the number had risen to 2,000.

The first recorded breeding of this species in Louisiana occurred in the summer of 1939, when several nests were found in Acadia Parish (Lynch 1943). The number of fulvous whistling ducks in Louisiana has vacillated during the ensuing years. During mid-November 1949, 8,000 were found in southwest Louisiana and east Texas, but only small numbers were found there the next 2 years (McCartney 1963). In 1952, 3,000 fulvous whistling ducks magically appeared during the spring at the Locassine National Wildlife Refuge, near Lake Arthur, Louisiana.

Periodic waterfowl censuses in Louisiana, 1951-59, indicated that during the early 1950's, 4,000 to 5,000 fulvous whistling ducks were present after the summer breeding season, but that in the late 1950's, numbers were much lower (Smith 1961*a*). Peak fall numbers at the Locassine Refuge have ranged from 2,500 in 1957 to 500 in 1958 and 1959, up to 3,000 in 1960, and down to 1,500 in 1961 and 1962 (McCartney 1963).

In 1960 there were several thousand whistling ducks in each of three counties near Houston, Texas: Wharton, Chambers, and Brazoria (Flickinger and King 1972). By 1967, a drastic decline had occurred. Although Wharton County had the largest numbers in Texas, only 200 to 350 appeared on Flickinger and King's (1972) study area, 1967-71; small numbers (18 to 50) occurred in Chambers County and none in Brazoria County. Hugh Bateman noticed a similar decline in Louisiana. By the late 1960's, only a few thousand were censused in early fall, a time of peak numbers. Much of this regional decline was attributed by Flickinger and King (1972) to mortality caused by the eating of aldrin-treated rice seed sown in newly planted fields.

A resurgence in abundance of fulvous whistling ducks occurred in 1973. From aerial surveys of Louisiana coastal marshes during the fall, Hugh Bateman estimated a population of 8,000 to 10,000. Lacassine Refuge alone held 6,500. Unfortunately, the upsurge in Texas has not been as great. Charles Stutzenbaker estimated about 2,000 breeding birds in the rice belt of Texas in the summer of 1973.

Fulvous whistling ducks were reported in southern and central California in the late 1890's. Apparently, they were locally numerous into the 1920's, for Hoffman (1927) stated that they were common in the southern half of California. However, by the early 1960's, William Anderson (quoted by McCartney 1963) reported that there were only two small breeding colonies extant, one near Mendota, the other in the vicinity of the Salton Sea. He observed 500 near there on September 9, 1950, but by 1957, only 70 were counted.

After widespread dispersion of fulvous whistling ducks along the Atlantic Coast in the mid-1950's and early 1960's, small numbers began to remain in Florida throughout the year. When Howell (1932) wrote a book on Florida birds, fulvous whistling ducks had not been recorded in that state. Their first recorded appearance was at the Loxahatchee National Wildlife Refuge near Delray Beach during the winter of 1961-62, when 25 were observed. In early January 1967, 250 were present, declining to a summer population of 25 to 50. One nest was found. Fall populations gradually rose from 50 in early September to 125 through December. By February 1973, the number of whistling ducks wintering on Loxahatchee had risen to 3,500 (Thomas Martin). Only six remained into the summer.

DISTRIBUTION

The fulvous whistling duck has a unique distribution. As a species, possibly composed of two races, it inhabits Burma and India, skips the Arabian Peninsula, occupies a belt extending across central and down eastern Africa including Madagascar, dwells in two widely separated regions of South America, and, in North America, inhabits Mexico and parts of California, Texas, Louisiana, and Florida. Few birds have such isolated breeding populations that range over such a global expanse. Compounding the unique distribution is a lack of significant variation in plumage and size, which almost invariably develops with isolation. Somehow the fulvous whistling duck has managed to remain virtually the same over its vast range.

In North America this species inhabits the coastal plains of Mexico from the Yucatan Peninsula to the Rio Grande on the Gulf side and from the Gulf of Tehuantepec to the delta of the Rio Yaqui in Sonora on the Pacific side (Leopold 1959). It also occurs sparingly in the Southern Highlands.

Most fulvous whistling ducks depart their breeding range in the United States to winter in Mexico. Their range in the United States skirts the Gulf Coast from Brownsville, Texas, to Lafayette, Louisiana. They also appear to be colonizing Florida, but their breeding colonies in California are apparently fading.

Largest breeding numbers occur in the rice belt of east coastal Texas and west coastal Louisiana. The rice belt extends, roughly, from Victoria, Texas, to the Vermilion River in Louisiana. In Texas the rice lands extend 50 to 80 miles inland from the coastal marshes; in Louisiana they lie in a zone 15 to 70 miles wide north of the coastal marshes.

Fulvous whistling ducks in Louisiana were most abundant in Evangeline, Acadia, and Jefferson Davis parishes (McCartney 1963) and Wharton County is their most important area in Texas (Charles Stutzenbaker). There are two small breeding colonies in California, one in Fresno County, the other near the Salton Sea (William Anderson in McCartney 1963).

The fulvous whistling duck might well be called the wandering whistling duck, the common name used for an Australian form *(Dendrocygna arcuata)*. Prior to 1949 the only Atlantic Coast records of this duck were several from Florida and one from North Carolina (McCartney 1963). Then, in 1949, it was recorded from North Carolina, and in 1950 and 1951 from Florida. Starting in 1955 and extending over a decade, a succession of invasions occurred along the Atlantic Coast. Many whistling ducks were recorded from the tip of Florida to New Brunswick, and a few inland (McCartney 1963, Jones 1966, Munro 1967). Most of the ducks were reported during the fall and winter but a few appeared during spring and summer. The greatest influx on the Atlantic Seaboard occurred during the fall and winter of 1961-62 (the next largest number in 1960-61).

I believe that the invasions of whistling ducks along the Atlantic Seaboard originated from colonies in northern South America. Oceans pose no barrier to this species, as is demonstrated by its discontinuous range in India, Africa, and South America. Moreover, on October 25, 1964, Watson (1967) observed three fulvous whistling ducks swimming in the Sargasso Sea (lat. 23° N, long. 60° W) about 225 miles northeast of San Juan, Puerto Rico. A fulvous whistling duck was killed in Puerto Rico on December 21, 1960 (Biaggi and Rolle 1961). Whistling ducks also appeared frequently on islands in the Caribbean and on the Bahama Islands during the early 1960's. Previously, only two fulvous whistling duck specimens were known from the West Indies, one each in Cuba and Bermuda (Bond 1971).

The other alternative is that the Atlantic Coast birds originated from Texas and Louisiana. They have generally appeared on the Atlantic Seaboard after their departure from Louisiana and Texas, ostensibly for winter areas in Mexico, but instead some may have migrated eastward.

Migration Corridors

Fulvous whistling ducks breeding in southeast Texas and southwest Louisiana have a choice of two migration corridors: one along the rim of the Gulf to winter grounds in Mexico, the other across the west end of the Gulf.

McCartney (1963) presents several reasons for believing that the birds migrate across the Gulf. First, refuges on the lower Texas coast fail to show any increases in their local populations in the fall and spring. Second, he quotes Ralph Andrew's observation of 30 whistling ducks alighting between the jetties at Calcasieu Pass, Louisiana, at about 6 P.M. on April 22, 1961. This unusual site selected for resting before flying farther north suggests that they had just completed a long overwater flight. John J. Lynch's observation of five whistling ducks on the open Gulf 3 miles off High Island, Texas, December 11, 1962, suggests that the Gulf is not a barrier.

On the other hand, Eric Bolen and other Texas ornithologists frequently see migrating flocks of fulvous whistling ducks flying north along Padre Island in April. It seems probable that this species uses migration corridors across part of the western end of the Gulf as well as around it.

Winter Areas

Most fulvous whistling ducks leave Louisiana and Texas to winter, ostensibly, along the east coast of Mexico. Occasionally, small numbers of whistling ducks linger in Texas and Louisiana well into the winter, but rarely are many present after mid-January. The small numbers breeding in California are assumed to winter along the west coast of Mexico.

Biologists of the U.S. Fish and Wildlife Service, on many of their frequent surveys of wintering waterfowl in Mexico, have combined their counts of whistling duck species. However, the survey of the east coast of Mexico in January 1963 identified 841 fulvous whistling ducks and 34,643 black-bellied whistling ducks. Slightly over half of the fulvous whistling ducks were on the Alvarado Lagoon, 200 in lagoons near Tampico, 33 in the Tamaulipas Lagoon, and 150 in the Rio Grande Delta (McCartney 1963).

Aerial surveys of the west coast of Mexico made in January in 1952 and 1965 recorded fulvous and black-bellied whistling ducks separately. The survey of 1952 found 945 fulvous and 39,815 black-bellied whistling ducks. Almost all the fulvous ducks were in lagoons near Acapulco, Guerrero. The survey in 1965 recorded 39,315 whistling ducks, 21.1 percent fulvous and 78.9 percent black-bellied. The bulk of the fulvous whistling ducks (5,360) were recorded on the Sesecapa Marshes, near the Guatemala border. Almost 2,000 were found in the marshes south of Mazatlán, 500 near Culiacán, and 450 near Los Mochis.

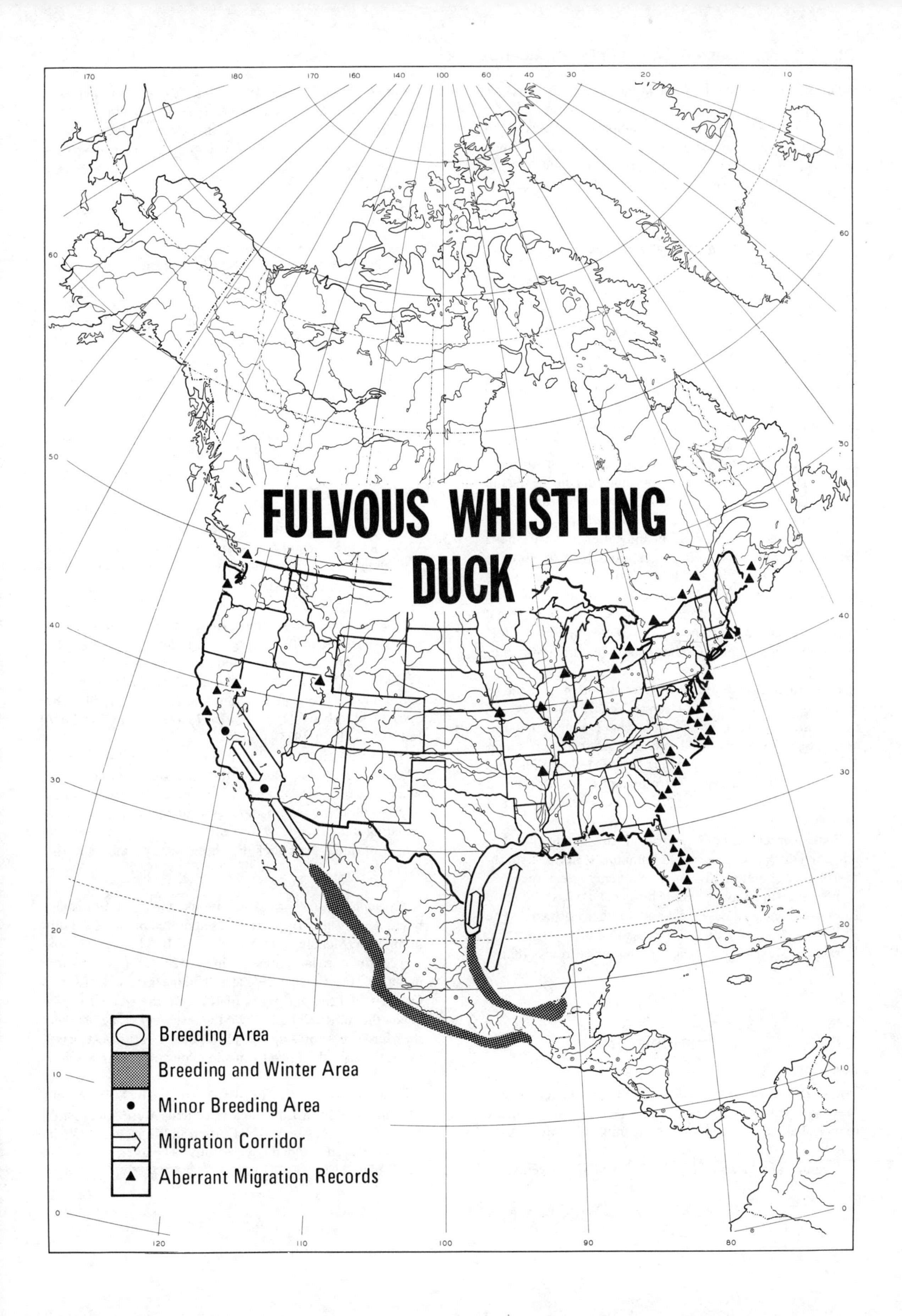
FULVOUS WHISTLING DUCK
Breeding Area
Breeding and Winter Area
Minor Breeding Area
Migration Corridor
Aberrant Migration Records

During the 1960's only a few hundred fulvous whistling ducks appeared in Florida during the winter months. However, in the early 1970's, their number dramatically increased to several thousand. The center of their abundance in Florida is the Loxahatchee National Wildlife Refuge, near Delray Beach, but they range up the east coast at least as far as Merritt Island.

MIGRATION BEHAVIOR

Fulvous whistling ducks apparently migrate by night and by day. A flock of about 20 on the night of November 2, 1962, flew into a football stadium, near Oak Grove, Louisiana (McCartney 1963). Observers on the Texas coast frequently see them migrating during the day (Eric Bolen).

They leave the rice fields of Louisiana for the coastal marshes through September and early October, reaching peak numbers at the Lacassine National Wildlife Refuge the third week in October (McCartney 1963). The Lacassine Refuge in coastal marshland appears to be their most important area of concentration in Louisiana during the fall and spring. A general exodus from the refuge occurs during the last week of October and extends through November into early December. From all indications, these ducks leave in migration for their winter grounds at this time.

Records made at the Lacassine Refuge show that whistling ducks return in late March or early April and increase in number through the month. At the Salton Sea National Wildlife Refuge in the Imperial Valley of southern California, they appear in late March and remain until mid-November.

Band recoveries indicate a diversity of movement. A whistling duck banded near Orange, Texas, was recovered near Iota, Louisiana, over 2 years later. One banded at Salton Sea, California, in March 1956 was recovered near Fulshear, Texas, in November 1957. At Avery Island, Louisiana, four recoveries were made from birds banded there, two a year later, one 2 years later, and the last, 3 years later.

Flickinger et al. (1973) released 165 banded fulvous whistling ducks, all pen-reared immatures, in three southeast Texas counties. Six band recoveries were received from over 50 miles away. Three birds moved east, two into Louisiana; one bird flew west and another northeast. The sixth flew from El Campo, Texas, to Lerdo de Tejada, Veracruz, Mexico, a distance of 665 miles in less than 7 weeks!

BREEDING

Behavior

Age, Pair Bond, and Homing. Fulvous whistling ducks breed at 1 year of age, perhaps late in the season. Yearling females held in captivity did not lay until July (McCartney 1963).

Meanley and Meanley (1958) observed a captive male 8 months old and a female 19 months old engage in spectacular postcopulatory displays over a period of 4 months. They saw a similar display in wild birds in May. Fulvous whistling ducks, like black-bellied whistling ducks, probably remain paired for life.

Nesting

Nest Sites. Over most of its range in Texas and Louisiana, the fulvous whistling duck prefers to nest in rice fields. Nests are placed on the low, contour levees as well as over water among the rice plants and weeds growing between levees (Meanley and Meanley 1959). Where rice fields do not occur, these ducks nest in dense vegetation, usually over water. At the Welder Wildlife Foundation Refuge, near Sinton, Texas, they nested in dense stands of *Paspalum*, and in cut-grasses, cattails, and other water-tolerant plants (Cottam and Glazener 1959).

Nests are usually constructed of the surrounding vegetation and are a few inches above the water. Some nests have canopies of vegetation over them and ramps of vegetation leading to the nest bowls. The nests are constructed as egg-laying proceeds, and sometimes early eggs fall through the flimsy floors into the water below (Cottam and Glazener 1959). Unlike most species of waterfowl, fulvous whistling ducks do not add down to their grass- and weed-lined bowl-shaped nests.

Clutch Size, Eggs, and Incubation. Clutches in Louisiana average 12 to 13 eggs, but dump nests of 21, 23, and 62 eggs have been reported (McCartney 1963). At the Welder Refuge in Texas, the clutch size ranged from 6 to 16 and averaged 9.6 eggs (Cottam and Glazener 1959). The eggs are bluntly ovate, 53.4 by 40.7 mm (212), and white to buff-white (Bent 1925).

The incubation period lasts 24 to 26 days (McCartney 1963). At the Welder Refuge, the eggs were left uncovered when not being incubated. Perhaps because of the high temperature, the parents appeared to spend little time incubating until shortly before the hatch. Flickinger (1975) has confirmed the belief that both parents incubate the eggs.

Chronology of Nesting. Fulvous ducks in Louisiana begin nesting as early as May 8, but more commonly about midmonth (Meanley and Meanley 1959). The nesting season continues to late August. Three of 20 clutches collected in the field (McCartney 1963) hatched the last week of June. One hatched the first week of July, six the second week, seven the third week, and two the last week. One hatched the third week of August. Initiation of early nests may await the growth of rice to an adequate concealing height.

Nest Success. Only 3 of 10 nests studied by Meanley and Meanley (1959) in Louisiana rice fields were successful. Nine of 17 nests observed by Cottam and Glazener (1959) in a Texas marsh hatched successfully. The average loss for these nine nests was 2.1 eggs.

Most of the nest destruction in rice fields was caused by farmers, who purposely destroyed nests or robbed them of eggs. Raccoons, opossums, skunks, and dogs were other sources of nest destruction (Meanley and Meanley 1959).

Rearing of Young

Like geese, both whistling duck parents assist in rearing their young. Most broods are reared in the flooded rice fields until the fields are drained for harvest, usually in late July or early August. Young unable to fly at this time probably suffer heavy mortality because of their exposure to predators. A young bird reared by Meanley and Meanley (1959) was able to fly when 63 days of age.

POSTBREEDING SEASON

Fulvous whistling ducks have no eclipse molt but appear to have a flightless period, for McCartney (1963) reported that birds held captive by John J. Lynch molted and were flightless during the second and third weeks of September. However, McCartney was unable to find any flightless adults in the wild.

In late August and early September, whistling ducks begin to gather in large ponds and flooded rice stubble. Aggregations of several hundred may occur in favored feeding areas. A month later they move to the coastal marshes of Louisiana, where they select extensive beds of maiden cane dotted with openings covered by water shield.

FOOD HABITS

Fulvous whistling ducks are noted for their nocturnal feeding in rice fields. Hasbrouck (1944:306) vividly describes such an event that occurred in May 1943 near Thornwell, Louisiana: "We reached the place before dusk and distributed ourselves along the low dykes or levees that divide the fields into paddies. Not a duck was to be seen or heard, and it was hard to believe what we were told, that in a few minutes the place would be swarming with them. 'Just wait a few minutes' was the admonition, and presently we could hear them before we could see them. On they came, in no particular formation as with ordinary ducks—singly, in pairs, in companies of a dozen or more, and in irregular groups, and in twenty minutes they were flying and squealing everywhere, hundreds of them."

A small sample of gizzards taken from whistling ducks collected in newly sown rice fields contained 78 percent rice (Meanley and Meanley 1959). However, in late summer and fall, rice appeared only as a trace among food items consumed; seeds, particularly millets, nutgrass, and *Paspalum* grass seeds, were important. Two gullets from whistling ducks collected from wet pastures in the spring were crammed with the seeds of knotgrass, signal grass, and Walter's millet. Seeds of water shield were the most important food item of 15 whistling ducks taken in coastal marshland.

Both the fulvous and wandering whistling ducks feed on aquatic vegetation obtained by swimming and diving. Others, such as the black-bellied and plumed whistling ducks, are grazers (Rylander and Bolen 1974*b*). Because of their differing food habits, these two types of whistling ducks developed differences in their skeletal structures to meet the needs of their respective environmental niches (Rylander and Bolen 1974*b*).

Black-Bellied Whistling Duck

Dendrocygna autumnalis autumnalis

Other Common Names: Black-bellied tree duck, cornfield duck
(In Mexico: pichichi, pato maizal)

VITAL STATISTICS

Length:	Male, 18.7-19.8 inches, average 19.4 inches (11) Female 18.5-20.0 inches, average 19.1 inches (10)
Wing:	Male, 9.2-9.8 inches, average 9.4 inches (11) Female, 9.0-9.7 inches, average 9.3 inches (10)
Weight:	Male, 1.50-2.00 pounds, average 1.80 pounds (35) Female, 1.44-2.25 pounds, average 1.85 pounds (37)

IDENTIFICATION

Black-bellied whistling ducks fly slowly in shapeless formations. In flight they resemble fulvous whistling ducks because of their long necks, trailing legs, and broad blunted wings, but they are more distinctly colored. The most noticeable coloration during flight is the contrasting black and white on the wings. The upper wing is white with a black band along the back margin to and around the tip; the underwing is solid black.

The most erect of all ducks, its posture and long legs give it a heronlike appearance. When the duck is at rest, the black belly and sides are the most noticeable features, followed by the red bill and the pink legs and feet. The breast and lower neck are cinnamon-brown; a black streak extends up the hindneck to the cinnamon-brown crown. The back is an even cinnamon brown, and the folded wing forms a large white sash between it and the black side. The sides of the head and upper neck are a dull pearl-gray; the undertail coverts are white, spotted with black.

The sexes are similar in appearance, but the females' black abdomens are more dully colored than those of males. Immatures, with no pronounced brown and black colorations, appear grayer than adults. The bills of these whistling ducks are dusky and their feet and legs are purplish gray. They are vociferous in flight, repeatedly uttering a whistling *pe-che-che*, which provides them with one of their local names.

POPULATION STATUS

Age Ratios

The age ratio in the fall population of black-bellied whistling ducks in 1963 was 1 adult to 3.9 young (Bolen 1967*a*), a much higher ratio than those found for other species of ducks. If such production prevails over a period of years, the species should prosper in Texas.

Sex Ratios

The sex ratios in black-bellied whistling ducks of all ages are more balanced than in other ducks (Bolen 1970). Sex ratios of 631 birds trapped during the spring, 1963-65, were 1:0.92, male to female (51.8 percent).

Mortality

Eric Bolen and Rich McCamant used band recoveries from hunters and recaptures of marked birds in nest houses to compute mortality rates. Both methods gave similar results, indicating that black-bellied whistling ducks breeding in Texas experienced an annual mortality rate of 45-52 percent. Females appear to have a slightly higher mortality rate than males.

DISTRIBUTION

The northern black-bellied whistling duck breeds from southern coastal Texas through coastal Mexico and Central America. A southern race breeds from Panama south into northern Argentina.

In 1974 about 3,000 bred in lower coastal Texas, the majority in the vicinity of Lake Mathis north of Corpus Christi (Eric Bolen). Others nest on the Santa Ana and Laguna Atascosa national wildlife refuges and on the King Ranch (Arthur Hawkins). They regularly occur as far north as Refugio County, and Charles Stutzenbaker has observed them irregularly in the spring as far afield as Fort Bend, Brazos, and Jefferson counties. Among the four species of ducks basically resident in Mexico, namely, fulvous and black-bellied whistling ducks, Muscovy duck, and Mexican duck, Leopold (1959) considered the black-bellied whistling duck to be by far the most abundant.

The aerial survey of the west coast of Mexico by the U. S. Fish and Wildlife Service in January 1952 revealed 39,815 black-bellied whistling ducks (Leopold 1959). Slightly over 34,000 were found in one area, the extensive mangrove swamps south of Mazatlán. An aerial survey of the same region by the Service in January 1965 identified 31,005 black-bellied whistling ducks. The largest concentration (13,800) was again south of Mazatlán, but this time large numbers were found elsewhere: 5,060 near Culiacán; 4,170 near Los Mochis; 2,425 at Nexpa Lagoon, south of Acapulco; and 2,185 at Mitla Lagoon, north of Acapulco.

On the east coast of Mexico, the aerial survey made by the U. S. Fish and Wildlife Service in 1963 found 34,643 black-bellied whistling ducks. The bulk of them (25,010) were in coastal lagoons within the state of Tabasco. About 7,000 were noted in lagoons near Tampico and 2,599 in lagoons near Alvarado.

Only a handful of both species of whistling ducks have been recorded on aerial surveys of the Interior Highlands. Leopold (1959) stated that the black-bellied whistling duck occasionally occurred in the Central Highlands.

MIGRATION BEHAVIOR

Leopold (1959) considered the black-bellied whistling duck in Mexico to be nonmigratory but acknowledged that there was some wandering by individuals and flocks. The small population breeding in Texas is migratory. Recoveries from birds banded by Bolen (1967*a*) at Lake Mathis, near Corpus Christi, were reported from 160 to 360 miles away in the Mexican state of Tamaulipas. One was from the Interior Highlands, near Hidalgo, San Luis Potosí. A later recovery concerned a second-year female trapped near Bluntzer, Texas, on April 8, 1968, and shot on December 20, 1969, near Pecan Island, Louisiana (Eric Bolen).

Over a 4-year period, 1962-65, black-bellied whistling ducks appeared between March 20 and April 12 (average, March 31) at the Santa Ana National Wildlife Refuge in the Rio Grande Valley, near McAllen, Texas, and at Lake Mathis, March 4-18 (Bolen 1967*a*). Over a 10-year period, 1956-65, they arrived at the Santa Ana Refuge between March 1 and April 12 (average, March 25).

BREEDING

Behavior

Age, Pair Bond, and Homing. Black-bellied whistling ducks breed during their first year of life. Pairing evidently occurs during the winter, for Bolen (1967*a*) believes that they are paired upon arrival in Texas in late March, indicating that young acquire mates their first winter. Bolen (1971) presents good evidence from banded birds that their pair

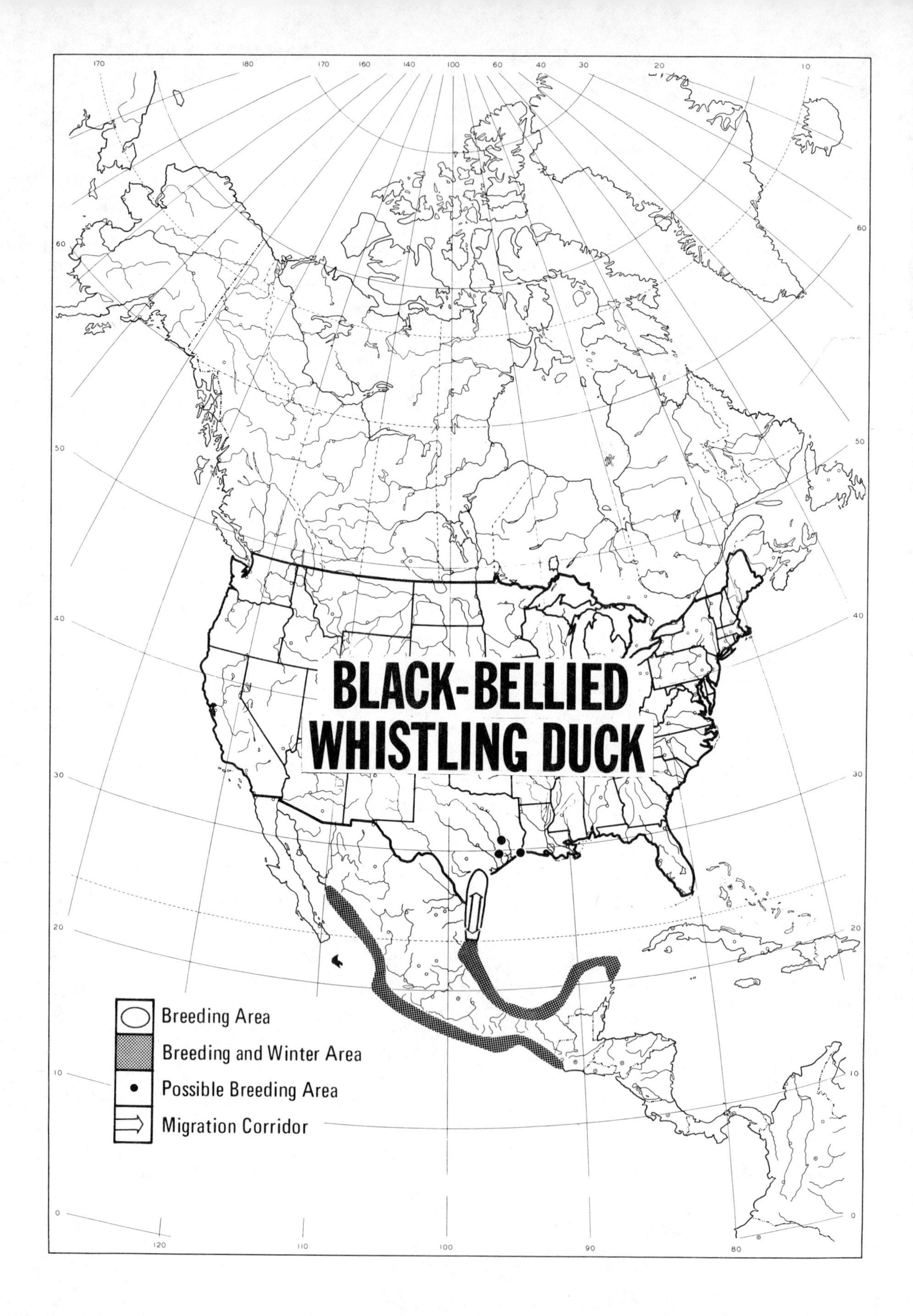
BLACK-BELLIED WHISTLING DUCK
Breeding Area
Breeding and Winter Area
Possible Breeding Area
Migration Corridor

bond is lifelong. He captured the same seven pairs in the same nest houses 2 years in a row. Subsequent studies by Eric Bolen and Rich McCamant have shown that 15 pairs remained as mates at least through a second year; two pairs remained together for 4 years. However, there are five instances where pair bonds dissolved as each member re-mated and nested again. One female renested the same season with a different male.

Males and females return with equal fidelity to their breeding areas. Of 31 banded adults that returned a second year to the area of banding, 42 percent were males and 58 percent females (Bolen 1971). Some ducklings of both sexes returned as yearlings to their natal area. Twenty-two percent of 107 incubating birds banded on their nests returned to the same area the second year (Bolen 1967*a*). Other marked birds were known to return but were not captured.

Nesting

Nest Sites. Black-bellied whistling ducks customarily nest in tree cavities. They also nest on the ground and in nest houses made especially for them (Bolen 1967*a*, *b*).

Bolen (1967*a*) found 45 percent of 83 occupied cavity nests in live oaks, 19 percent in ebony, 16 percent in willow, 13 percent in mesquite, and 1 percent in hackberry. The average entrance hole measured 7.0 by 12.5 inches (40), the smallest 4.0 by 4.75 inches. Cavities averaged 23 inches in depth and about 26 inches in diameter. Entrances averaged 8.7 feet above the ground or water. Eggs were laid directly on the bottoms of the cavities, often without benefit of nest material and always without down feathers.

Thirty-seven nest trees were on dry land and were a few to 1,000 yards from water, most of them between 500 and 1,000 yards. Seventeen trees stood in water from impoundment flooding, from a few to a range of 200 to 500 yards from land.

Most ground nests (7) were composed of dead grasses woven into shallow bowls about 7.5 inches in diameter (Bolen 1967*a*, Bolen et al. 1964). One nest was a bare depression in the ground. Nests were situated mostly in grazed brush pastures and were usually well hidden under low shrubs. Bolen (1967*a*) found a few nests in such odd sites as a chimney, a cotton gin exhaust pipe, and a pigeon loft.

Nest houses erected by Bolen (1967*b*) were made of wood and were 22 inches high in the front, 20 inches at the rear, 11 inches square, with a 5-inch circular entrance hole near the top. Several inches of sawdust and wood shavings were placed on the bottom. The houses were mounted on well pipe, with 36-inch conical sheet metal guards for protection against predators. Six hundred and twenty-two houses were inspected, 1964-75, by Eric Bolen and Rich McCamant, for nests of black-bellied whistling ducks. They found nests in 81.4 percent of the boxes erected for the use of these ducks, an unusually high rate of occupancy.

Clutch Size, Eggs, and Incubation. First complete clutches by single hens ranged in size from 9 to 18 eggs and averaged 13.4 eggs (58) (Bolen 1967*a*). Eggs are laid at the rate of one per day, usually between 5 P.M. and 7 P.M. Dump nests, in which eggs are laid by more than one hen, have held fantastic clutches—41, 52, 65, and, recently, 101 eggs (Eric Bolen).

The white, ovate eggs are similar to those of domestic poultry and measure 38.9 mm X 52.7 mm (Bolen 1967*a*). Incubation in four nests in the wild was 25, 27, 28, and 30 days. Incubator eggs hatched in 31 to 32 days. Both sexes incubate the eggs, a most unusual practice among waterfowl, but apparently occurring among all eight species of whistling ducks. Rich McCamant and Eric Bolen found that the removal of either of the incubating birds resulted in the abandonment of the nest. Thus, it is essential that both male and female be available through the incubation period.

Chronology of Nesting. Black-bellied whistling ducks commenced nesting 33 to 80 days (average, 56 days) after arriving on three different areas in lower coastal Texas (Bolen 1967*a*). First nests were started between April 25 and May 26 (average of 3 years, May 5). Attempts to nest were most frequent between mid-May and mid-June. Last nests were initiated August 18, 19, and 25, 1963-65. Thus, whistling ducks initiated nesting over a period of 102 to 117 days. In contrast, most northern prairie ducks initiate nests over a 70-day period.

Nest Success. Of 32 nests in natural cavities, 44 percent hatched (Bolen 1967*b*). Nest houses unprotected from predators had a nest success of 46 percent (13), but nest houses protected against climbing predators had an astounding 77 percent (44) of their nests hatch. Of four nests on the ground, only one hatched.

Eric Bolen and Rich McCamant noted a high nest success in houses: 75 percent of 279 incubated nests in houses hatched. The difference in success represents nests in which eggs were laid in dump nests but were not incubated. In 210 successful nests 63 percent of the eggs hatched, an average of 20.4 eggs of the 32.3 eggs laid. Dump nesting from more than one hen contributed to the large clutch sizes and the low rate of hatch.

Most nest failures were caused by desertion, raccoons, Texas rat snakes, and, in the pre-incubation period, golden-fronted woodpeckers.

Nest Failure. Rat snakes and raccoons caused most of the nest failures in natural cavities and unprotected nest houses (Bolen 1967*b*).

Renesting. Some black-bellied whistling ducks renest when their first nests are destroyed. At least 19 percent of 57 pairs that lost initial clutches renested (Delnicki and Bolen 1976). When two clutches were removed from renesting pairs, both pairs renested a second time. In three other instances, black-bellied whistling ducks renested even though their first nests hatched successfully. One pair renested 6 weeks after their first nest hatched, and another pair waited 8 weeks to renest.

Rearing of Young

Broods. Ducklings of the black-bellied whistling duck remain in their nest cavity 18 to 24 hours after hatching, then jump from the cavity entrance to the ground or the water (Bolen 1967*a*). Both parents escort the brood and remain with the young for at least 6 months, 4 months after flight is reached (Eric Bolen).

Development. An interesting study of the growth of black-bellied whistling ducks has been made by Cain (1970). He observed that wild ducks flew for the first time at 53 to 63 days of age. Although flying was possible for pen-reared birds when the first primary reached 69 mm (56 days for larger ducklings, 63 days for smaller ones), the primary did not reach maximum growth of 125 mm until the ducklings were about 100 days old. During the fifth to eleventh weeks of age, the heavier ducklings had longer flight feathers than the lighter ones. It was apparent that the faster-growing ducklings flew several days in advance of the slower-growing birds.

Class I ducklings were 1 day to 2 and 3 weeks old; Class II ducklings, 3 to 7 weeks old. They were completely feathered in Class III but flightless at 7 to 8 weeks (Cain 1970).

Survival. Bolen 1967*a*) reported that broods of black-bellied whistling ducks tended by both parents averaged 10.7 ducklings (15) the first week, 8.8 ducklings (17) for broods sighted during the second through fourth weeks, 10.3 ducklings (21) for those noted the fifth through seventh weeks, and 9.7 (45) for flying broods. Nine broods accompanied by only one parent averaged only 7.7 ducklings, an indication that brood mortality is higher when only one adult is in attendance.

POSTBREEDING SEASON

In pen-reared birds, the postjuvenile molt begins on the head and tail areas during the 13th to 14th week and is completed in the 34th to 35th week, when the young first assume adult body plumage (Cain 1970). The wing feathers are first molted when the birds are 19 months of age, leaving them flightless for 20 days. Like geese and swans, they have but one annual molt.

FOOD HABITS

According to Bolen and Forsyth (1967), soon after black-bellied whistling ducks arrived in the spring they flew to cattle feedlots to consume scattered grain. In May they branched out to feed in pastures, stripping Bermuda grass heads of their seed. When the sorghum harvest began in June, the birds started flights to the stubble fields to feed upon waste grain and continued to feed there through the summer and fall. On water areas, broods—and older ducks later in the season—utilized water star grass. Animal life, principally snails and insects, made up 9 percent of the items consumed.

Mute Swan

Cygnus olor

VITAL STATISTICS

Length:	Adult male and female, 56-60 inches
Wing:	Adult male, 23.3 inches Adult female, 21.7 inches
Weight:	Adult male, 25 pounds Adult female, 21 pounds

IDENTIFICATION

Field

Both sexes of adult mute swans, like all species of swans in the Northern Hemisphere, have white plumages and long necks. When the mute swan is in flight, the motion of the wings produces a unique whistling sound, sometimes audible up to 1 mile. At rest, the mute swan holds its neck in a graceful S-curve, with the bill pointed downward. The bill is orange except for the black base that extends to a fleshy knob on the forehead. The knob is less prominent in the female than in the male. In an aggressive display, the mute swan raises its wing feathers to form a hood over its back, the only swan in the Northern Hemisphere to do so.

The juvenile mute swan has a grayish-brown head, neck, and back, with a whitish breast and belly. The bill and feet are gray. A small frontal knob appears the second year, when the plumage is white and the bill is a dull orange. Adult physical characters are assumed the third year.

As their name implies, mute swans are silent most of the time. When irritated or alarmed, they hiss or make a snorting sound.

In all species of swans the male is referred to as the *cob*, the female as the *pen*, and the young, during the first year, are known as the *cygnets*.

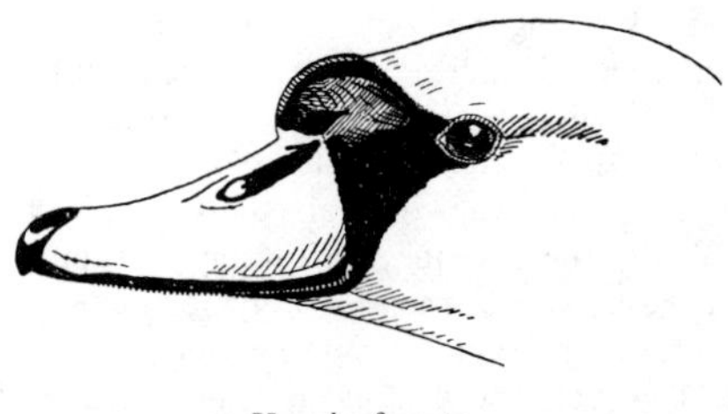

Head of mute swan

POPULATION STATUS

The mute swan is the common swan of country estates, city parks, and zoos. It has escaped confinement in several regions of the country, to establish sizable feral populations. There are at least 4,000 of these birds in the United States.

The mute swan population in Michigan stems from a single pair imported in 1919. A small flock built up near East Jordan, Michigan; after 1933, these birds had to fend for themselves (Wood and Gelston 1972). There were 47 in the mid-1940's, and 500 by 1974. Based upon the current rate of increase, 18 percent annually, the population of mute swans in Michigan is expected to reach 2,000 by 1980 (Edward Mikula).

Mortality

The mute swan population in Michigan suffers at least a 15 percent loss each year. Sources of mortality have been identified as collisions with overhead wires, lead poisoning, and shooting (Wood and Gelston 1972).

DISTRIBUTION

On the East Coast, the mute swan breeds from Massachusetts south into New Jersey; it is especially abundant on Long Island (Edward Addy). Those in Michigan are scattered as breeders over 11 counties in the northwestern part of the Lower Peninsula (Wood and Gelston 1972).

The East Coast swans fly short distances to coastal bays

for the winter. The Michigan swans convene for the winter in Traverse Bay, requiring flights of a few to 100 miles from breeding areas.

During Audubon Christmas counts in 1972 (*American Birds 1973)* 2,235 mute swans were seen along the Atlantic Seaboard, with numbers distributed as follows: New Hampshire, 2; Massachusetts; 287; Rhode Island, 249; Connecticut, 468; New York, 598; New Jersey, 436; Pennsylvania, 5; Delaware, 93; and Maryland, 97. The only large concentration in the Midwest (390) centered about Traverse Bay, Michigan. On the Pacific Coast, 86 mute swans were counted: 77 in British Columbia and 9 in Oregon.

Although some populations of mute swans native to other countries make extensive migratory flights, those in the United States do not appear to be truly migratory.

A southward passage of escaped mute swans is reported to have occurred from Cuyahoga Falls, Ohio, to the Ohio River near New Cumberland, West Virginia, a distance of about 65 miles (Hicks 1935). More remarkable is the return of four adult mute swans to Traverse Bay from central Illinois (Edward Mikula). These four were among the 40 captured in Michigan and transplanted to strip mine lakes near Canton, Illinois, in 1971. They were found back in Traverse Bay during the winter of 1971-72.

The mute swan is indigenous to Eurasia from Denmark and central Sweden east across northern Germany, central Russia, Asia Minor, and Turkestan to Mongolia and East Siberia. Wild mute swans in England disappeared prior to the 13th century because they were trapped and pinioned in such numbers as to become entirely semidomesticated. Until the 18th century, all swans were the property of the Crown. The mute swan is easily tamed and generally flourishes in association with civilization, in marked contrast to the trumpeter and whistling swans.

BREEDING

Pair Bond

Loose pair bonds among mute swans may develop as early as the spring of their first year, and, by spring of their second year, some pairs may even establish a nest territory (Wood and Gelston 1972). However, the first attempt to nest does not occur until the birds are 3 years old. According to Wood and Gelston (1972), most pair bonds are permanent, but remating does occur if one member of the pair dies. Separations occasionally occur and some males have resorted to polygamy.

The nest territory, which is vigorously defended against other swans, radiates out from the nest to embrace 4 to 10 acres and is reoccupied by the same pair in succeeding years (Wood and Gelston 1972). With the appearance of broods, territories are enlarged to provide the young with greater feeding areas.

Swans select their nest sites in March and early April in Michigan. A preferred site is a large clump of cattails or bulrushes surrounded by water; other desirable sites include small islands and narrow peninsulas, where the nests are placed at the water's edge (Wood and Gelston 1972).

Nests are constructed mostly of marsh and aquatic plants piled in an elliptical shape, 4 feet wide by 5.5 feet long. A shallow cavity 3 or 4 inches in depth provides the receptacle for 1 to 8 eggs (average, 4.5). The greenish-blue eggs, laid at intervals of 36 to 48 hours, are 74 mm by 112 mm (Wood and Gelston 1972).

The mute swan is unique among waterfowl of the Northern Hemisphere in that the male has been observed incubating in the absence of the female (Witherby et al. 1952, Wood and Gelston 1972). Incubation requires 36 to 38 days, and hatching can require 24 hours from the first to the last egg. The male will often care for the first hatched young while the female continues to incubate.

The broods, averaging 4.8 young, remain with the parents until late fall, when they are abandoned or forced away as the adults return to defend their nest territories (Wood and Gelston 1972). The young reach flight stage at 115 to 155 days.

POSTBREEDING SEASON

Wood and Gelston (1972) reported that among successful breeding swans the chronology of molt of the male differs from that of the female. The female begins to molt first, usually by July 12; the male delays his molt for about 45 days, until about the time the female regains flight. During this period, the defense of the young rests with the parent able to fly.

Nonbreeding subadult swans and unsuccessful breeders begin to molt their flight feathers in early July and regain them in 45 to 50 days.

FOOD HABITS

Submerged aquatic plants are the mainstay of the mute swan's diet. Insect larvae, aquatic insects, crustaceans, and fish are reported by Wood and Gelston (1972) to be important foods of young and molting birds.

The mute swans at Traverse Bay, Michigan, have been able to survive the winter because of artificial feeding. It was estimated that 20 tons of corn were fed to the swans in 1971, in addition to untold quantities of lettuce and bread.

Trumpeter Swan

Cygnus buccinator

VITAL STATISTICS

Length: Adult male, 56-62 inches, average 59 inches (9)
Adult female, 55-58 inches, average 57 inches (10)
Yearling male, 55-57 inches, average 57 inches (8)
Yearling female, 52-57 inches, average 55 inches (8)

Wing: Adult male, 24.3 inches (5)
Adult female, 24.5 inches (3)

Weight: Adult male, 21-38 pounds, average 27.9 pounds (7)
Adult female, 20-25 pounds, average 22.6 pounds (4)

Flightless, June 26-August 17
Adult male, 21.3-30.4 pounds, average 26.75 pounds (10)
Adult female, 20.2-23.3 pounds, average 21.5 pounds (11)
Yearling male, 22.2-28.3 pounds, average 25.4 pounds (8)
Yearling female, 15.2-24.3 pounds, average 21.2 pounds (8)

IDENTIFICATION

Field

Adult trumpeter swans have snowy all-white plumage, but the more subdued coloring of the immatures is a dull mouse-gray. Trumpeters have remarkably long necks—as long as their bodies—held outthrust during flight but proudly erect when attentively swimming and in a graceful semicurve the rest of the time. Trumpeters are usually content to associate in small flocks of 3 to 5, but, during the fall and winter, may come together in loose aggregations of 25 to 50.

Although the trumpeter is larger than the whistling swan, it is hard to tell them apart in the field. Perhaps the best way to distinguish them is by their voices. The trumpeter's call is more vociferous than that of the whistling swan and has been likened to the sonorous notes of a French horn. The whistling swan's call is a high-pitched, often quavering *oo-oo-oo*, accentuated in the middle. It is reminiscent of a flock of snow geese calling but is more melodious.

A yellow spot in front of the eye distinguishes some whistling swans when seen at close quarters. A dark spot means that the bird is either a whistling or a trumpeter swan. Many trumpeters, like whistling swans, have their white heads and upper necks stained a rusty color from contact with ferrous minerals in the soils of marsh bottoms during their search for food. Young trumpeters wear their gray plumage until late spring or early summer, but young whistling swans don their parents' white plumage by midwinter.

At Hand

The size advantage of the trumpeter over the whistling swan is readily apparent for most specimens in the hand, but there is a degree of overlap between small trumpeters and large whistling swans. Banko (1960) determined that any swan over 1 year old that measured 2 inches or more from the tip of the bill to the front of the nostril is probably a trumpeter; measurements less than 2 inches probably indicate whistling swans.

Dissection is the most infallible method of distinguishing the two species. A cross section of the sternum reveals that the windpipe of the trumpeter swan makes a vertical loop over a bony hump. This raised loop is absent in the whistling swan. The syrinx is also considerably larger in the trumpeter than in the whistling swan and is probably responsible for the trumpeter's deeper and more resonant tones.

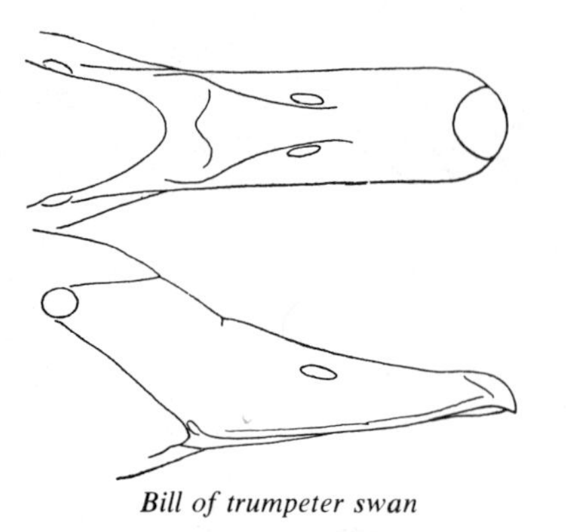

Bill of trumpeter swan

POPULATION STATUS

Not many years ago conservationists feared for the survival of the trumpeter swan, but in recent years its status has greatly improved, and it is no longer considered an endangered species.

In the 19th century, the trumpeter swan was believed to be fairly numerous and to occur over an extensive range in North America. According to Banko (1960:18) quoting MacFarlane (1905:754), "From 1853 to 1877 they [Hudson's Bay Company] sold a total of 17,671 [swan skins], or an average of nearly 707 a year." Sales of swan skins were high from 1853 to 1867 and low from 1870 to 1877. Most of the swan skins obtained by the Hudson's Bay Company were of trumpeters (Richardson *in* Swainson and Richardson 1832, quoted by Banko 1960:14).

The drastic decline in the swan population is clearly evidenced by the decreased numbers of skins sold yearly after 1870 by the Hudson's Bay Company. MacFarlane stated that only 57 swan skins were in the fur-sale offerings in London, 1888-97, and none appeared in 1897, 1900, 1902, and 1903.

In 1912, Forbush, an eminent ornithologist, wrote that the total extinction of the trumpeter swan was only years away. As late as 1925, Bent (1925) believed that the trumpeter belonged to a vanishing race and was making a last stand in the wilds of northern Canada. The only contemporary breeding record known to Bent—in the United States—was from Yellowstone National Park, where a few breeding birds were reported in 1919.

Later, a small colony of trumpeter swans were found on Red Rock Lakes in Centennial Valley, west of Yellowstone National Park. In 1932, this population numbered 26, that in Yellowstone National Park, 31, and those elsewhere in the United States, 12, bringing the total known population to 69 (Banko 1960). Thanks to the establishment of a national wildlife refuge at Red Rock Lakes in 1935, the small colony found there now numbers about 250 swans. In addition, there are about 65 trumpeters at Yellowstone and 600 elsewhere in the United States (Hansen 1973).

In the 20th century, trumpeter swans were first found breeding in Alaska in 1954 by Melvin A. Monson (Hansen et al. 1971). These swans were nesting at the confluence of the Bremner and Tasnuna rivers with the Copper River. Since then, breeding colonies have been found in several other areas of southeastern Alaska. An aerial survey in 1968 of known breeding areas in Alaska revealed 2,884 trumpeter swans, and it was believed that several hundred birds were either overlooked or were present in areas not surveyed.

The approximately 150 trumpeter swans that summer in Canada, added to those in the United States, indicate a North American population of 3,600 to 4,400 trumpeters at the end of the breeding season.

Mortality and Survival

Trumpeter swans have lived to be 29 years old in captivity, but in the wild, accidents and predators eliminate most birds long before old age is reached. Band recoveries from trumpeters have been inadequate to establish the mortality rate of these swans in the wild.

In spite of being legally protected throughout the year, trumpeter swans are killed by thoughtless shooters. Even in the restricted range of the Red Rock Refuge, swans have been shot in the nearby Island Park, Idaho, winter area. Shot pellets were found in the flesh of 15 of 103 nonbreeding trumpeters fluoroscoped at the refuge during the summer of 1956 (Banko 1960).

Between 1932 and 1954, trumpeter swan populations at Red Rock Lakes steadily increased from 26 to 380. However, during the next two decades, their numbers fluctuated between 150 and 300 (Page 1974). It is evident that the breeding habitat became saturated by the mid-1950's. The decline in numbers since then is probably due to a general reduction in the availability of submerged aquatic plants used as food. Temporary upward surges in numbers appear related to favorable weather conditions, resulting in a large production of cygnets.

DISTRIBUTION

Breeding Range

The largest numbers of summering trumpeter swans occur along the coast of the Gulf of Alaska between the delta of the Copper River and Yakutat Bay (Hansen et al. 1971). In 1968, 1,022 were counted there. Other numbers found in Alaska were: Gulkana Basin, 590; Tanana-Kantishna river valleys, 478; Cook Inlet-Susitna Basin, 419; Kenai Peninsula, 181; and Copper Canyon, 158.

There are slightly over 100 trumpeters in the Grande Prairie area of west-central Alberta, and a few can be found in the Cypress Hills of southern Alberta and Saskatchewan.

The Yellowstone-Centennial Valley (Red Rock Lakes) region of northwestern Wyoming and southwestern Montana provides the only important breeding area for this species in the contiguous United States. The peak population of 467 reached in 1954 has declined slightly since then.

Transplants of trumpeter swans have been made from

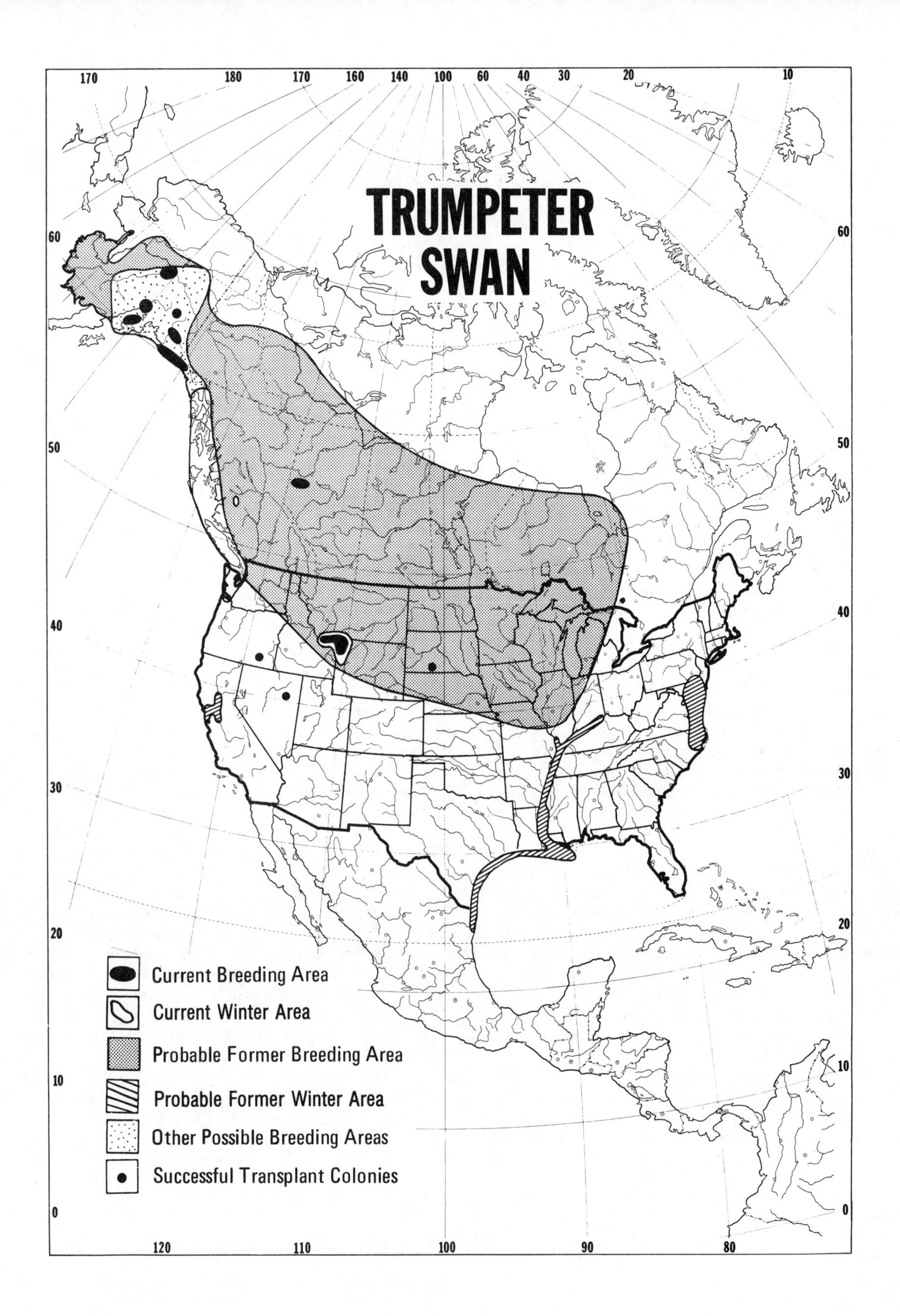

TRUMPETER
SWAN
Current Breeding Area
Current Winter Area
Probable Former Breeding Area
Probable Former Winter Area
Other Possible Breeding Areas
Successful Transplant Colonies

the national wildlife refuge at Red Rock Lakes to several other refuges: Malheur in Oregon, Ruby Lake in Nevada, Lacreek in South Dakota, and Turnbull in Washington. Small numbers of breeding swans occur on all four refuges. The most successful transplant—the one at Lacreek—has steadily increased from 15 swans in 1964 to 96 in 1972. Other transplants have been made in Delta, Manitoba, and Hennepin County, Minnesota.

Winter Areas

In spite of the severe winters in Yellowstone Park and the Centennial Valley, the trumpeter swans breeding there also winter there or in nearby areas. The most important winter ground is Henrys Fork of the Snake River, near Island Park, Idaho (Banko 1960), some 25 miles over the Centennial Mountains from Red Rock Lakes. From 257 to 419 trumpeter swans have been reported there during the course of several winters, 1950-57.

At Red Rock Refuge, 12 to 325 trumpeter swans have been found during various winters, 1951-57. Small numbers of trumpeters also winter in Jackson Hole, Wyoming, and the Madison River drainage in southwestern Montana.

Banko (1960) attributed the survival of the trumpeter swan in the Yellowstone area to its avoidance of extensive passage along heavily shot migration routes. Warm springs in the mountain valleys have enabled these swans to find open water (even when temperatures dropped to −30 F) on or adjacent to breeding areas. Without the fortuitous locations of these springs, breeding trumpeters would be forced to seek winter quarters considerable distances away.

Trumpeter swans breeding in Alaska winter along the Pacific Coast from the Alaska Peninsula to the mouth of the Columbia River. The first large number of wintering trumpeters was reported by Gabrielson (1946), who found over 300 birds on Prince of Wales Island and the Cleveland Peninsula on March 10, 1944.

The next important winter concentration of trumpeter swans was reported by Eklund (1946), who counted 134 individuals in Tweedsmuir Provincial Park in west-central British Columbia during February 1945. A census of trumpeters in 1969-70 on Vancouver Island and adjacent areas of mainland British Columbia revealed that 531 swans were wintering in that region (Hansen et al. 1971).

In the winter of 1970-71, Smith and Blood (1972) found 1,076 swans, considered all trumpeters, on Vancouver Island. On the same estuaries checked 2 different years, they found 341 trumpeters during the winter of 1968-69, and 782 during the winter of 1970-71, a remarkable increase.

Small numbers of trumpeters winter south of Vancouver along the Pacific Coast as far as Grays Harbor, Washington. From 50 to 75 have been found in recent winters on a small lake on the outskirts of Mount Vernon, Washington.

Band recoveries from the small population of trumpeter swans breeding in the Grande Prairie, Alberta, area indicate that these birds migrate into northern United States to winter. Some of them join with flocks of swans from Red Rock Lakes, Montana (Mackay 1957).

The present range of the trumpeter swan is only a vestige of the once vast region of North America that it frequented in both summer and winter. Its former breeding range extended from Washington, Idaho, Wyoming, Nebraska, northern Missouri, Illinois, and northwestern Indiana to west-central Alaska. It wintered on Chesapeake Bay and Currituck Sound, the lower Mississippi River valley, the coasts of Texas and Louisiana, the Sacramento Valley, the lower Columbia River, and the Pacific Coast from Puget Sound to Alaska.

BREEDING

Behavior

Age, Pair Bond, and Homing. Reports differ concerning the age at which trumpeters breed. At the Lacreek National Wildlife Refuge, where they had been newly introduced, trumpeters established pair bonds by the time they were 20 months old and nested the next year (Monnie 1966), but Banko (1960) concluded from his review of case histories that trumpeters may begin nesting as early as their fourth year or as late as their sixth year. Perhaps the density of territorial pairs accounts for some of the variation in the age at which breeding occurs.

Swans usually mate for life. If one of the pair is lost, the remaining spouse may subsequently remate. Trumpeter swans are no exception, for Hansen et al. (1971) reported that a marked female remated the next year after the loss of her mate.

Of six birds captured on their territories in 1971, Page (1974) recaptured three on the same territories in both 1972 and 1973.

Territory. Territorial behavior is strikingly evident among trumpeter swans; a mated pair vigorously defends the mating, nesting, and cygnet feeding grounds (Banko 1960). A pair selects its territory as soon as open water occurs in the spring, and some pairs defend their territories until late summer, when the cygnets are half grown.

At Red Rock Lakes Refuge, territories varied in size from 70 to 150 acres, according to the irregularity of the shoreline (Banko 1960). The greater the interspersion of marsh and open water, the smaller the territory. In Alaska, Hansen et al. (1971) found only one pair of territorial trumpeters on each small water area ranging from 6 to 128 acres. Only a few large lakes, 1 to 4 miles long, were occupied by two or three breeding pairs.

As breeding numbers increased at Red Rock Lakes, new territories were established in previously unoccupied, less suitable, habitat (Banko 1960). Existing territories were not made smaller to accommodate more breeders. Banko speculated that the new, less desirable territories may have accounted for the lower reproductive success that occurred as breeding swans became more numerous.

Nesting

Nest Sites. Trumpeter swans build their nests in extensive beds of marsh vegetation: sedges, bulrushes, cattails, and juncus in Montana and horsetail and sedges in Alaska. The nests are placed in water 1 to 3 feet deep. Ordinarily, the same nest site is used for several years.

To build the nest, the trumpeter uproots the marsh plants that immediately surround the nest site, thus leaving a ring of open water around the nest. At Red Rock Lakes, most of the nests are placed on muskrat houses (Banko 1960), but in Alaska, where there are no muskrats, the nests are built directly on the marsh bottom (Hansen et al. 1971).

Construction of the nest is a joint endeavor, the male usually bringing clumps of uprooted marsh plants while the female tucks the material in place. The nest mound reaches a diameter of 6 to 12 feet and an average height of 18 inches; the nest cavity varies from 10 to 16 inches in diameter and 4 to 8 inches in depth (Hansen et al. 1971).

Clutch Size, Eggs, and Incubation. The clutch size averaged 5.2 eggs (213) in Alaska and 4.65 eggs (457) at Red Rock Lakes. In Alaska, the clutch size varied from a low of 4.4 eggs in 1964 to a high of 5.7 in 1965, perhaps a result of early and late springs (Hansen et al. 1971). During 17 years at Red Rock Lakes, the clutch size varied from a low of 3.4 in 1967 to a high of 6.0 in 1947 (Page 1974). An early spring in 1972 with consequent early nesting may have resulted in the large clutch size of 5.39 eggs (33) that season. Individual clutches have ranged in size from 1 to 9 eggs.

The female trumpeter lays an egg every other day until the clutch is complete (Hansen et al. 1971). The off-white eggs soon take on a brownish stain from the nest material, and the shells have a granular texture. Eggs of trumpeter swans in Alaska measured 117.4 mm by 75.0 mm (146 eggs); those at Red Rock Refuge measured 110.9 mm by 72.4 mm (109).

Both parents are in attendance at the nest, but only the female incubates. The period of incubation varies from 33 to 37 days (Banko 1960, Hansen et al. 1971). Incubation normally started May 10-20 at Red Rock Lakes, Montana, and May 12 in southeast Alaska. Although these two breeding areas are far apart in latitude, this difference is offset by the 6,600-foot altitude of Red Rock Lakes compared with the near sea level of the lower Copper River, so that the chronology of nesting is similar.

Nest initiation at Red Rock Lakes spanned 11 days in 1949 and 16 days in 1952. Nest initiation in southeastern Alaska apparently extends over a longer period, 28 to 34 days, judging from the spread in dates of hatch.

Nest Success. Nests of trumpeter swans at Red Rock Refuge were seldom destroyed. Not a single egg in 61 nests observed in 1949, 1951, and 1955 was lost to predators (Banko 1960), and, in seven seasons, only 4 nests contained eggs that were destroyed by predators. The low production of cygnets at the refuge was caused by the failure of 34 percent (1951) to 49 percent (1949) of the eggs to hatch. In a later study of swan nests at Red Rock Lakes, 1971-73, Page (1974) found that eggs hatched in 76 percent of 101 nests. All failures were due to abandonment of nests, some of which had infertile eggs. Among all eggs laid, 54.5 percent hatched, 23.6 percent were infertile, 16.7 percent were fertile but failed to hatch, and either predators or an unknown fate accounted for 5.2 percent.

Of 138 nests studied in Alaska, 81 percent hatched at least one cygnet. Thirty-six percent of all eggs laid in both successful and destroyed nests failed to hatch. In successful nests, 19 percent of the eggs did not hatch (Hansen et al. 1971). Nest losses were attributed to bears, a wolverine, and desertion—possibly caused by human activity.

Rearing of Young

The female usually broods her newly hatched young on the nest for the first 24 hours—longer if the weather is inclement (Hansen et al. 1971). Both parents are solicitous of their young, the family forming a tightly knit group with the young actively swimming or feeding flanked by each parent.

Broods. During the first days of their lives, cygnets feed in shallow water along the margins of emergent vegetation, where they probe for aquatic insects, crustacea, and some aquatic plants. When they are a few weeks old, their diet changes to include more aquatic vegetation. The diet of cygnets 2 or 3 months old is similar to that of their parents (Banko 1960).

Some broods remain near their nest sites, while other families trudge to adjacent ponds or lakes, usually through marsh growth but sometimes across forested areas (Hansen et al. 1971).

Development. Trumpeter swans grow rapidly, from 7 to 8 ounces at hatch to 19 pounds in 8 to 10 weeks (Hansen et al. 1971). Because of their large size, there is considerable individual variation in development. Cygnets are fully feathered in 9 to 10 weeks but are unable to fly until 13 to 15 weeks of age in Alaska and 14 to 17 weeks in Montana.

Survival. The number of cygnets per brood at Red Rock Lakes averaged 3.17 (175) for a 12-year period, as few as 1.87 (15 broods) in 1954 to as many as 4.25 (14) in 1937 (Banko 1960). In general the brood size decreased as the numbers of mated pairs increased. In Alaska the brood size was recorded as 3.6 (251) in 1968 (Hansen et al. 1971).

In spite of the protection afforded the young by their parents, many are lost prior to flight. A loss of 15 to 20 percent during the first 8 weeks of life occurred on the breeding area at Copper River, Alaska (Hansen et al. 1971). On nearby Kenai Island, broods suffered losses, between hatching and flight, of 20, 29, and 23 percent, 1965-67. Broods totaling 31 cygnets in mid-June lost 14 (45 percent) of their numbers by the end of August (Banko 1960). Page (1974) found an enormous loss of entire swan broods at Red Rock Lakes, 1971-73. Of 264 cygnets hatched, only 72 survived to fledging, a mortality of 73 percent. These serious losses were attributed to early summer storms and a bacterial infection.

POSTBREEDING SEASON

Nonbreeding subadults and adults are the first swans to molt. The period of molt among individual nonbreeders occurs about the same time (Banko 1960, Hansen et al. 1971). Most nonbreeding birds in Alaska begin their molt in late June or early July. At Red Rock Lakes, the molt may be completed as early as June in some instances—but does not reach a peak until July.

Among breeding birds, it is rare for both mates to be flightless at the same time, and, although some paired birds may begin to molt as early as the nonbreeders, many delay a month or longer. The male of the pair usually molts first (Hansen et al. 1971, Page 1974). Because the molt of the parent birds is asynchronous, some birds are flightless until early September in Alaska and until October in Montana. Trumpeter swans are normally flightless for about 30 days (Hansen et al. 1971), but Banko (1960) cited two unusual records of 120 and 148 days.

FOOD HABITS

The meager information available on the diet of trumpeter swans indicates that a variety of marsh and aquatic plants compose the bulk of the food consumed. Where they occur, tubers of duck potato and sago pondweed are important items. The stems and leaves of sago and other pondweeds, white water buttercups, water milfoil, muskgrass, waterweed, and duckweed are taken in quantity. Seeds of yellow pond lily, water shield, and sedges are next in importance.

In feeding experiments at Red Rock Lakes, confined adult swans preferred waterweed over water milfoil, chara, various pondweeds, and water buttercup (Page 1974). Every day each bird consumed nearly 20 pounds of moist leafy aquatic vegetation.

Whooper Swan

Cygnus cygnus

The whooper swan resembles the trumpeter swan in size, appearance, and voice. In fact, Delacour (1954) considers these two swans to be of the same species, but most taxonomists continue to regard them as distinct species.

Whooper swans breed over an extensive region of Eurasia from Norway eastward through northern Russia to Kamchatka and the Commander Islands, Siberia, then south to central Russia, Turkestan, and northwest Mongolia.

The whooper swan was first recorded in North America by Wilke (1944), who obtained a specimen on St. Paul Island, Alaska, on December 7, 1941. Since then, Kenyon (1961, 1963) has recorded it on Amchitka Island in the outer Aleutians on several occasions. He observed 66 adult and 56 juvenile whoopers on Amchitka from February 13 to April 3, 1962, and believed that they stopped there regularly during their migration between nest and winter areas in Siberia.

Reports from the Aleutian Islands National Wildlife Refuge, 1967-69, indicated the presence of 400 whooper swans during the report periods of January-April and September-December each of those 3 years. By contrast, 30 to 100 whistling swans were estimated during the report period of January-April, 250 to 300 during the May-August period, and 140 to 250 during the September-December period. Because of the remoteness of the islands in the Aleutian Chain and the attendant problems of access to them, these figures represent only crude estimates by refuge personnel.

Whistling Swan

Cygnus columbianus

VITAL STATISTICS

Length:	Adult male, 48-57 inches, average 52 inches (30) Adult female, 47-58 inches, average 51.5 inches (39)
Wing:	Adult male, 19.7-22.4 inches, average 21.2 inches (8) Adult female, 19.9-22.1 inches, average 20.9 inches (15)
Weight:	Adult male, 12.0-18.6 pounds, average 16.0 pounds (42) Adult female, 10.5-18.3 pounds, average 13.9 pounds (63) Of 105 weighed in Utah, November-December, 1962-63: Adults, 17.3 pounds, immatures, 13.3 pounds

IDENTIFICATION

Field

The large size, the long, extended neck, equal in length to the body, and the all-white plumage of the adult whistling swan serve to distinguish it from the short-necked snow goose, with its black-tipped wings. The white pelican also has black wing tips.

In migratory flight, whistling swans form V's or oblique lines—usually in flocks of 25 to 100, rarely up to several hundred. Their wing beat is slow, steady, and shallow. In local movements, they fly low over the water, most often in lines.

When the whistling swan is at rest, the neck is straight or slightly curved toward its base, with a much slighter S-curve than the neck of the feral mute swan.

The head and upper neck are sometimes stained a rusty color from ferrous minerals in the marsh soils, encountered when the swan is grubbing for tubers of sago pondweed and other plants. When feeding, large flocks usually break up into family units of three to six. The black bill of the adult often has a yellow spot at its base. The legs and feet are black. The immatures are brownish gray, with darker heads and necks, and their pinkish, black-tipped bills become increasingly darker through the winter and spring. The feet and legs are flesh-colored. During the winter the gray body feathers of the immatures are gradually replaced by white; by March most of the gray is restricted to the head and neck.

At Hand

Most whistling swans are shorter in total length and wing length and weigh less than trumpeter swans. Other features distinguishing the two species are noted in the description of the trumpeter swan.

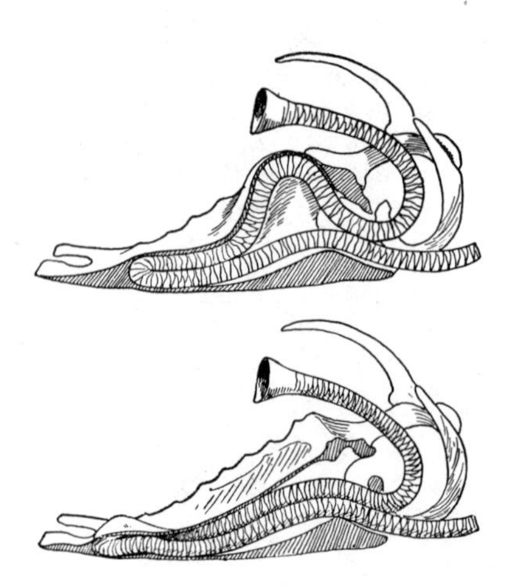

Above, windpipe of trumpeter swan; below, windpipe of whistling swan. Note difference of convolution of windpipe within the breastbone.

POPULATION STATUS

Winter surveys of whistling swans during the 1950's in the United States revealed an average population of 78,000. This figure increased to 98,000 during the 1960's and to 133,000 during 1970-74. The lowest population recorded from 1949 to 1974 was 49,000 in 1950, and the highest was 157,000 in January 1971. Although the number of swans found on winter surveys has varied considerably from year to year, there has been a slow increase in the continental population over the last 25 years.

Age Ratios

The brownish-gray plumage of the young and the white plumage of the adults make it possible to separate birds-of-the-year from older whistling swans during the fall and winter. On their principal winter grounds in the Atlantic and Pacific flyways, 1961-73, the proportion of young to old swans was 11.9 percent immatures for the Atlantic population and 18.5 percent for the Pacific population (Lynch and Voelzer 1974). A continent-wide production of young equal to 15 percent of the adult population may represent the reproductive potential of this species.

The probable reason for the consistently different age ratios for whistling swans in the two flyways is that the majority of the swans in the Atlantic Flyway come from breeding grounds in the Canadian Arctic, whereas those of the Pacific Flyway are from Alaskan breeding grounds. Weather conditions are more severe and variable during the summer in the Canadian Arctic than in the Alaskan Arctic.

DISTRIBUTION

Breeding Season

The whistling swan's breeding activities span most of the subarctic and arctic tundra from Bristol Bay, Alaska, north along the coast of the Bering Sea, the Arctic Ocean east to Baffin Island, and, recently, south to the northwest coast of Quebec (Heyland et al. 1970). In this vast tundra region there are extensive areas devoid of, or sparsely inhabited by, swans and a few areas with large breeding populations.

About 60,000 adults occur on Alaskan breeding areas and 30,000 on breeding areas in Canada. The breeding populations in Alaska have shown no upward trend from 1956 to 1971; therefore, if the winter surveys in the last decade truly reflect a continental increase, this increase has occurred on Canadian breeding areas.

James King has separated populations of whistling swans in Alaska into the following geographic units: Aleutian Islands, 500; Bristol Bay, 11,000; Yukon-Kuskokwim Delta, 40,000; Nunivak Island, 50; St. Lawrence Island, 100; Seward Peninsula, 1,000; Selawik-Noatak rivers, 2,000; and the Arctic Slope, 1,000.

Surveys made by Barry (1960) in the Canadian Arctic, from the 140° meridian east to the 90° meridian, place major populations of whistling swans in the following locations: Old Crow Flats, 200; Mackenzie Delta—Liverpool Bay area, 20,000; southwest Banks Island, 200; southeast Victoria Island and Prince Albert Peninsula, 300; Bathurst Inlet to Sherman Inlet, 300; and King William Island, 300. Macpherson and Manning (1959) estimated 200 additional swans on the Adelaide Peninsula.

Ornithological expeditions made during the last three decades in the eastern Canadian Arctic reported whistling swans nesting sparsely from Chesterfield Inlet and the Adelaide and southern Melville peninsulas eastward across Southampton Island and a part of Baffin Island. An aerial survey of Southampton Island in 1952 revealed 51 breeding swans. About 300 have been found in tundra ponds along the Hudson Bay coast of Manitoba (Pakulak and Littlefield 1968). Deducting the numbers reported for Alaska and western Arctic Canada from the known continental population suggests that about 5,000 adult swans occur in eastern Arctic Canada. An apparent southward extension of this breeding population onto the northeast coast of Hudson Bay in Quebec was reported by Heyland et al. (1970). They found 24 broods of cygnets during August 1966-68 and, in addition, 19 broodless pairs in 1967 and 1968 between lat. 59° 08′ N and 62° 15′ N.

Migration Corridors

From the Seward Peninsula of Alaska north along the Arctic Slope, whistling swans probably migrate east to the valley of the Mackenzie River, then south-southeastward down the valley to a major staging area at Athabasca Delta (Thomas Barry). To complete the Alaskan contingent of whistling swans bound for the Atlantic Flyway, 10,000 additional birds must be accounted for. These are believed to be a contribution from the Yukon Delta breeding area. Swans from the Mackenzie Delta-Liverpool Bay area also follow this migration corridor. Swans from the region of Queen Maud Gulf probably migrate to the Athabasca Delta from the north-northeast.

The population of 32,000 whistling swans found on the Athabasca Delta by Thomas Barry during an aerial survey on October 1, 1959, attests to the importance of the delta as a staging area. On the same survey, only 250 whistlers were found on Hay Lake in northwestern Alberta.

Farther north along the Mackenzie River valley from the Hay River to Norman Wells, Thomas Barry found 1,200 swans on September 27, 1963. On the preceding day, he found 760 swans on various reaches of Great Slave Lake. From Great Bear Lake to Yellowknife on Great Slave Lake, Barry counted 579 swans on September 28, 1963. His figures emphasize the importance of this migration corridor.

Two migration corridors extend from the delta of the Athabasca River. One goes south to the vicinity of Freezeout Lake, Montana, and the other southeast to a staging area in the vicinity of Whitewater Lake, Manitoba, and the Devils Lake region of North Dakota. At Goose Lake, southwest of Saskatoon, Saskatchewan, in the southeast corridor, Bernie Gollop estimated 20,000 swans the third week in October 1973. From northeastern North Dakota

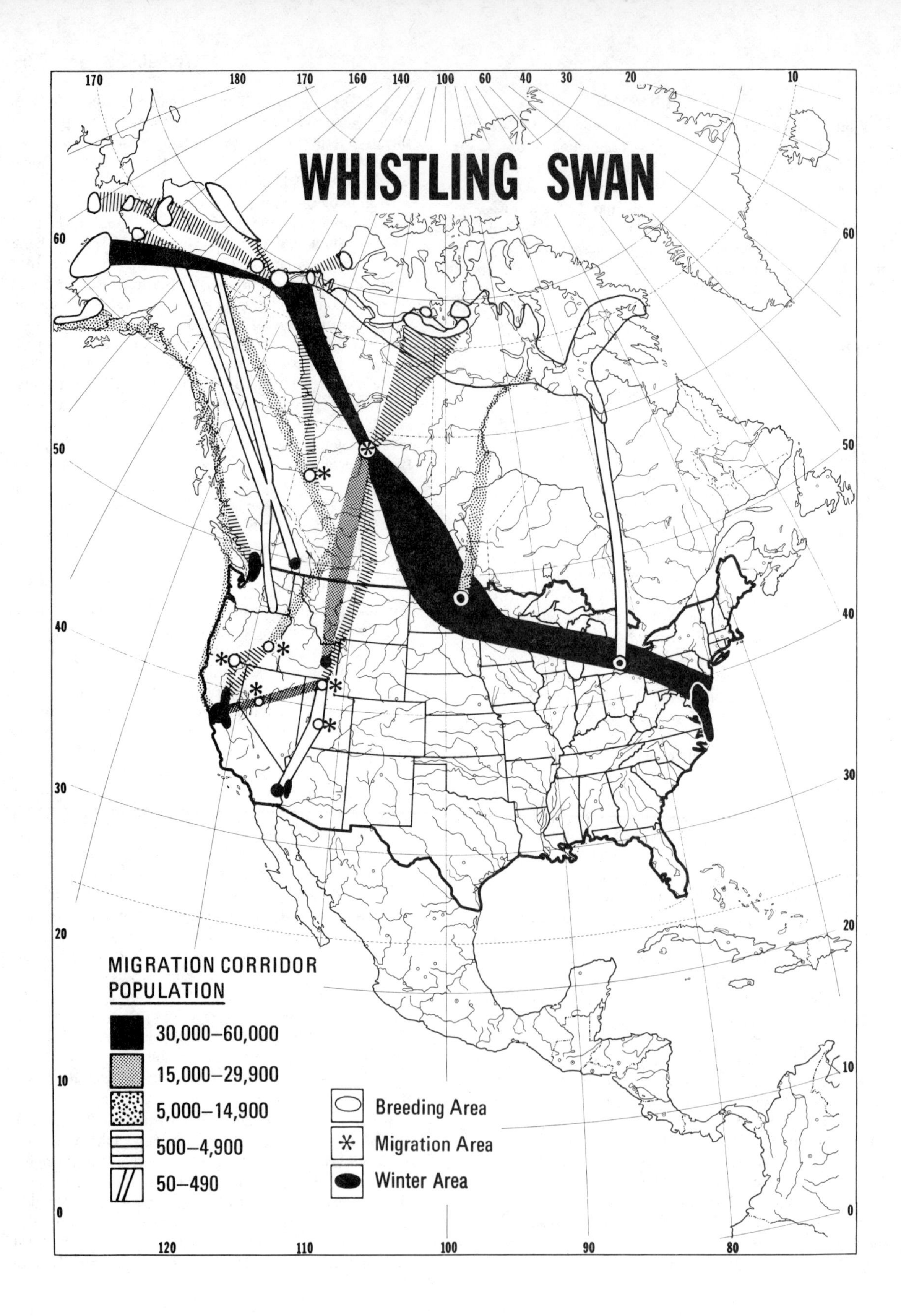
WHISTLING SWAN
MIGRATION CORRIDOR POPULATION
30,000–60,000
15,000–29,900
5,000–14,900
500–4,900
50–490
Breeding Area
Migration Area
Winter Area
170
180
170
160
140
100
60
40
30
20
10
60
50
40
30
20
10
0
120
110
100
90
80

WHISTLING SWAN

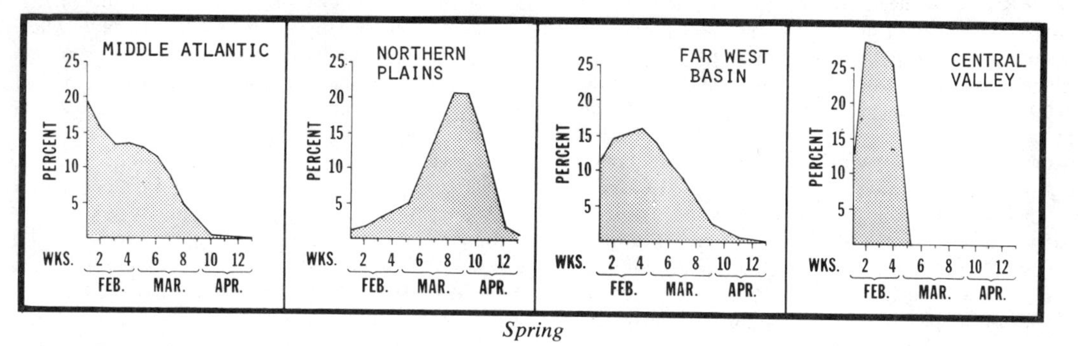

Spring

(For explanation of percentages shown see chapter 1 under heading Chronology of Migration.)

this corridor turns to a more easterly direction, passing over central Minnesota and Wisconsin to southeastern Michigan. Part of this migration corridor passes over the area of Twin Cities, Minnesota. At times large numbers are seen. For example, on November 8, 1973, Arthur Hawkins counted 630 swans in 10 flocks that passed over his home near White Bear Lake in 1 hour; they were on a course slightly south of due east. Small numbers consistently stop along the Mississippi River as far south of the Twin Cities as La Crosse, Wisconsin. Many flocks are observed passing east-southeastward through Wisconsin between Green Bay and Milwaukee. A thousand or more swans following this migration corridor pause during the fall at Lake St. Clair, Detroit River, and southwestern Lake Erie. Most, however, continue nonstop east-southeast to Chesapeake Bay.

On their return journey in the spring, 20,000 to 30,000 whistling swans visit the Lake Erie marshes of Ohio and Michigan, Lake St. Clair, and the Detroit River. Other thousands concentrate in Green Bay, at Horicon Marsh, and in the marshes of the Mississippi River near La Crosse, Wisconsin.

Swans nesting in northwest Quebec, Baffin Island, and Mansel Island apparently depart the migration area at western Lake Erie and move northward through James and eastern Hudson bays. Freeman (1970*b*) reported swans passing north over the Belcher Islands on May 17 and 24, 1959. Lumsden (1971) reported that each fall small numbers of swans migrate along the south coast of Hudson Bay and through James Bay. In 1971 he saw six pairs with 14 young, and 29 adults in eight flocks unaccompanied by young.

Another migration corridor apparently connects with the main eastern corridor in the Devils Lake region of North Dakota (Sladen 1973). This auxiliary corridor extends from there to the Hudson Bay coast near Churchill. The whistling swan is reported to be a fairly common migrant in the Churchill area (Jehl and Smith 1970). In 1955 many hundreds were seen 40 miles up the Churchill River between September 28 and early October.

Over 4,000 whistling swans have been found south and east of Edmonton, Alberta, on the corridor from the Athabasca Delta to Freezeout Lake, Montana. Dale Witt has reported that the number of swans at Freezeout Lake exceeds 10,000 during each fall and spring migration. Most of these swans, and others that have bypassed Freezeout Lake, continue south to the Great Salt Lake marshes of Utah, where as many as 25,000 congregate. About 3,000 swans winter on these marshes.

From 15,000 to 20,000 swans migrate from these Utah marshes west toward San Francisco Bay, and about 100 fly south-southwest to the Imperial Valley and the Colorado River valley of southeastern California. About 5,000 of the westbound swans settle at Carson Sink, Nevada, to winter there; the rest continue on to central California.

One migration corridor appears to extend from southeastern Alberta to Malheur Lake, Oregon, the Klamath Basin on the Oregon-California border, and the Sacramento River valley of California. John Chattin has observed flocks of swans, on a south-southwest course, passing over the Wallowa Mountains east of Troy, Oregon—these were some of the migrants that use this corridor. About 10,000 swans stop at Malheur and 5,000 in the Klamath Basin.

Probably the entire populations of 10,000 to 15,000 swans from the Aleutian Islands and Bristol Bay, Alaska, migrate south along the coast to Vancouver Island and points south. About 1,000 stop in the area of Puget Sound and others continue farther south—5,000 terminating their flight to winter along the lower Columbia River and in several small bays of the Oregon coast, a few hundred at Humboldt Bay, California, and the rest in the San Francisco Bay area. On a late fall afternoon Henry Hansen witnessed part of this coastal flight of whistling swans. At the Stikine River delta, near Wrangell, Alaska, he observed 5,100 to 5,200 whistlers descend to the flats during a snowstorm; they were gone the next morning.

How intensively swans use the two migration corridors that extend along the Tanana River and the upper Yukon River of Alaska through the interior of British Columbia to Idaho and western Washington is little known. Moderate numbers of whistling swans have been reported (Soper 1954) stopping at lakes near Whitehorse, Yukon Territory. Waterfowl censuses conducted in British Columbia during the early 1950's suggest that only a few thousand swans use these routes. The largest number of whistlers censused in the interior of the province was 1,200 on December 12, 1951.

Winter Areas

Only small numbers of whistling swans winter in the interior of the United States, and most of these appear to be misplaced birds. Fifty-one percent of the 123,000 (average) whistlers recorded on winter grounds, 1970-74, occurred in the Pacific Flyway, 48 percent in the Atlantic Flyway, and about 1 percent elsewhere.

The most important winter ground in the Atlantic Flyway is Chesapeake Bay, where each year about 40,000 congregate. Fourteen thousand more winter in an area extending from Back Bay, Virginia, through Lake Mattamuskeet and Pamlico Sound, North Carolina. A few swans are found scattered farther south along the coast as far as Georgia. Fewer than a hundred whistling swans winter north of Chesapeake Bay in Delaware and New Jersey.

Back of San Francisco Bay lie the delta marshes, which, next to Chesapeake Bay, winter more whistling swans than any other area. About 30,000 whistlers winter there, with 3,500 more in adjacent areas of the Central Valley. Elsewhere in California, about 400 winter in other bays, a few as far south as Morro Bay. About 1,500 swans manage to winter in the Klamath Basin on the California-Oregon border, while a scant hundred enjoy the warmth of the Imperial Valley-Colorado River area.

The arid Carson Sink of Nevada hosts almost 4,000 wintering swans, and despite the cold and ice, 2,600 remain on the Bear River marshes of Utah. About 5,000 winter in Oregon, mostly along the lower Columbia River and in several small coastal bays.

The numbers of whistling swans wintering in Washington average about 900, the largest number along the lower Columbia River; nearly 100 winter on Skagit Flats, about 100 in the Columbia Basin, and half that many on the coast.

Of the 400 whistling swans wintering in British Columbia, a few occur on the coast, but most are found inland from Kootenai Lake to Kamloops. Warm waters associated with the Snake River enable 200 whistling swans to remain in Idaho. A small number winter from the Aleutian Islands along the coast of the Gulf of Alaska.

On their fall flight across the Mississippi Flyway, 2,000 swans often stop to rest for a day or so about 1 mile off the eastern shore of Lake Michigan (Edward Mikula). Several hundred pause for 2 or 3 weeks in southeastern Michigan. Usually, a few hundred stay during the winter, but in some years none remain. In 1966 an unusually large number (1,500) wintered there. A few stragglers are occasionally found wintering in Minnesota and Wisconsin.

Rarely do whistling swans appear in winter south of their migration corridor extending from Devils Lake, North Dakota, to Chesapeake Bay. In some years, 5 to 55 are found in the Central Flyway, mostly in eastern Texas but a few in New Mexico. Missouri is the most consistent state in the Mississippi Flyway south of the migration corridor to harbor one or two stray whistling swans each year. Most of the stray singles are immatures lost from their family flock, but occasionally entire families appear. These errant swans are believed to have missed the landscape cues that are used to change their migration course, and instead of turning eastward or westward continued in their southerly flight until hospitable waters were reached. Some remain where they land for the winter, far from their compatriots, while others reorient to traditional winter areas.

MIGRATION BEHAVIOR

Whistling swans migrate as family units, with several families and probably some nonbreeding birds combining in a single flock. Flocks on the Yukon Delta averaged 61 individuals in September and 45 in October (Calvin Lensink).

During the fall migration, swans bound for the Atlantic Coast make some tremendous long-distance flights. Consequently, they fly both day and night. Not only are rest stops infrequent but also any one migration area is used by only a small segment of the population and is bypassed by the remainder of the migrants, who fly on to other areas. As a consequence of this leapfrog passage, the rest stops of a particular flock are even farther apart than those of the population as a whole, perhaps a thousand miles or more.

Reports from airplane pilots on the altitude of migrating whistling swans between Minneapolis and Washington, D. C., show the swans at heights ranging from 2,000 to 6,000 feet MSL (mean sea level). Most were at altitudes of 3,000 to 5,000 feet.

On the return flight in the spring, the Atlantic Coast swans progress more slowly and stop more frequently. Large numbers assemble at the west end of Lake Erie and in Wisconsin at Green Bay, Lake Winnebago, and the Mississippi River between Lake Pepin and La Crosse.

Small numbers drop out at numerous lakes across central Minnesota until the Devils Lake area of North Dakota is reached, where many thousands gather.

Stormy weather often forces migrating swans to seek temporary refuge on streams and reservoirs in the mountains of Pennsylvania. When swans encounter cloud tops too high to be surmounted and clouds so low that their bases envelop the tops of the Appalachian ridges, many birds seek temporary refuge on unlikely water areas.

For the most part, the swans of the Pacific Flyway have an easier time; they migrate shorter distances and their rest stops are closer together. Only those following the migration corridors through the interior of British Columbia are confronted with long flights between rest stops and over rugged terrain.

Chronology

Fall. Whistling swans leave major breeding grounds in Alaska in late September and early October. Gabrielson and Lincoln (1959) cited dates as early as September 14 and 19 and as late as October 14 and 16. Most swans leave the Yukon Delta by late September but some remain until freeze-up in October (Calvin Lensink). The proportion of the population that stays late is determined by the lateness of the spring—the later swans begin nesting, the later they leave in the fall.

Almost 1,800 swans had made their first move from their breeding grounds by September 12-14, 1963, when Thomas Barry surveyed numerous lakes between Great Bear and Great Slave lakes. On September 26-27 he found 2,500 in the same region. Over 1,500 swans had already arrived at Athabasca Delta on September 27, 1960, when Barry made an aerial survey of the area; the number had declined to 154 by October 4. An early freeze-up probably accounted for the 32,000 swans concentrated on the Athabasca Delta on October 1, 1959 (Thomas Barry).

Swans begin to arrive in central Alberta and Saskatchewan late in September, and usually rise to peak numbers by mid-October. From then until freeze-up, usually in early November, swans appear in only slightly diminished numbers; most of them do not continue their migration until their feeding areas begin to freeze over.

Censuses of whistling swans at Freezeout Lake, Montana, made by Dale Witt, 1963-69, revealed that the swans start arriving early in October, build up to peak numbers by the end of the month or early November, and depart rapidly thereafter, so that most are gone by mid-November.

Marshes adjoining the eastern shore of Great Salt Lake begin to receive whistling swans in mid-October. Peak numbers are reached by mid-November, with a large proportion of the population remaining until mid-December.

Whistlers begin arriving at the Malheur National Wildlife Refuge in Oregon about mid- and late November and remain abundant well into December. Not far away in the Klamath basins, where whistling swans winter, they do not arrive in substantial numbers until late November or early December. On their principal western winter grounds adjacent to San Francisco Bay, the swans are not present in great numbers until early December, and the numbers increase throughout the month.

The eastern contingent of swans passes across Minnesota, Wisconsin, and Michigan, largely during November 5-15, but smaller numbers predate and postdate that time period by about 2 weeks. Swans on Chesapeake Bay slowly increase in number through December and reach a peak in January. Twenty-five percent of the Chesapeake swans arrive in the month following the main flight (Chamberlain 1967).

Spring. With the first spring thaw, whistling swans begin to leave their winter quarters and push northward. Swans from Chesapeake Bay cross Pennsylvania to Lake Erie from the first week in March into early April, with the largest flights about mid-March. Large numbers pause a week or two before continuing their flight west. The first significant numbers reach central Michigan and the Mississippi River between La Crosse, Wisconsin, and Minneapolis the last week in March and remain 2 or 3 weeks. A few hardy individuals push into the Dakotas late in March, but the largest flights arrive about mid-April; most are gone by the end of the month, with only small numbers lingering to mid-May.

Swans begin leaving their central California winter grounds in mid-February, and within 3 weeks almost all have departed. By mid-March they are leaving the Klamath Basin, and by late March, the higher Malheur and Great Salt Lake basins. Their departure is rapid, so that by early April most have migrated north into Canada. The western population of whistling swans migrates earlier and more swiftly than its eastern counterpart.

Whistling swans move rapidly to the area of the Athabasca Delta, where Soper (1951) reported their arrival between mid-April and early May and their departure for more northern areas after 2 or 3 weeks. They have been reported in McKinley National Park, Alaska, on May 4 and migrating down the Yukon-Kuskokwim valleys about May 1 (Gabrielson and Lincoln 1959). Other arrival dates cited for Alaska are: Tanacross, April 23; Kantishna, May 4; Anaktuvuk Pass, May 20.

According to Calvin Lensink, the first swans reach their breeding grounds on the Yukon Delta in late April and almost all have arrived by mid-May. Porslid (1943) reported that they arrived on their Mackenzie Delta breeding grounds on May 9, 1932, and on May 15, 1933. A short distance to the east, at the Anderson River, Barry (1966) reported their arrival between May 13 and 18 over a 7-year period.

In the central Canadian Arctic, spring arrives later and so do swans. Migrating whistlers first reached Churchill, Manitoba, on Hudson Bay, May 24, 1968 (Littlefield and Pakulak 1969). At Cambridge Bay, Victoria Island, they arrived June 1, 1960 (Parmelee et al. 1967). Farther east at Perry River, they arrived on May 31 and on June 9 (Ryder 1967). June 4 was the date of their arrival at Adelaide Peninsula (Macpherson and Manning 1959).

A similar chronology of migration prevails in the eastern Canadian Arctic. A pair was observed migrating over the Belcher Islands, Hudson Bay, on May 17, and another pair on May 24, 1959 (Freeman 1970*b*). A 4-year average date of first arrivals on Southampton Island was May 26 (Barry 1956). The earliest arrivals on Baffin Island (Soper 1946) occurred on June 15.

BREEDING

Behavior

Age, Pair Bond, and Homing. Little is known about the age at which whistling swans pair and the age at which they nest. Considering the large proportion of the population in nonbreeding flocks, Calvin Lensink conjectures that few swans breed before their third summer, and probably most are older.

Flocks of whistling swans average 48 individuals when they arrive at the Yukon Delta in May (Calvin Lensink). Mated pairs shortly disperse over the delta tundra; nonbreeding birds remain in large flocks along coastal estuaries. In most years, 40 to 60 percent of the swans are paired and are occupying territories.

Nesting

In early years, nesting began soon after the arrival of the flocks on the outer delta, on May 20, but in late years, the date of nesting is delayed, perhaps until June 1. Inland from the coast, where the snow melts earlier, nesting occurs earlier also (Calvin Lensink). In a particular season, nest initiation is remarkably synchronous. Calvin Lensink reports that 75 percent or more of the nests hatch in a 3- or 4-day period.

Nest Sites. On the Yukon Delta, the greatest densities of nesting swans occur near the coast between Nelson Island and Romanzof. Calvin Lensink estimates that half of the nesting birds select sites on the main shore of a lake or pond, within 20 yards of water; 30 percent on small islands or points in lakes; and the remainder in a variety of locations: heath tundra up to 100 yards from water, hummocks in marshes or tidal meadows, and, more rarely, level stretches in marsh or meadow areas.

Swans frequently choose elevated hummocks, possibly because they provide a better view of the surrounding terrain. Hummocks and other high spots are the first areas free of snow, which may also influence their selection (Calvin Lensink).

Most of the swans' nests are in heath tundra, which not only dominates the nesting grounds but also provides most of the elevated sites used by swans. The nest is an elaborate platform, 12 to 18 inches high, composed of moss, grass, and sedges, and resembles a muskrat house surrounded by a moat (Calvin Lensink). In making the nest, the vegetation is plucked from around the nest site, creating a circle of open water up to 15 feet in diameter.

Clutch Size, Eggs, and Incubation. On the Yukon Delta, whistling swans laid an average of 4.26 eggs per clutch in 354 nests checked, 1963-71 (Lensink 1973). The average clutch size varied from a low of 3.30 in 1964 to a high of 4.95 in 1967. Differences in clutch size appear attributable to the lateness of the spring—the later the birds commenced nesting, the smaller the clutch.

Eggs of the whistling swan are noticeably smaller than those of the trumpeter swan. They average 107 mm (94 eggs) and are elliptical ovate in shape. At first creamy-white and nonglossy, the eggs acquire a brownish stain from the damp plant material of the nest (Bent 1925).

Probably only the female incubates, as is true of the trumpeter and most other swans. However, Witherby et al. (1952) reported that the male mute swan takes the female's place on the nest while she feeds, chiefly during the night. During nesting, paired swans are frequently separated from their mates for short intervals.

The best-known incubation period is one where the last egg was laid May 31 and hatched on July 1, a 31-day span (Calvin Lensink). Another nest examined on May 31 had been incubated fewer than 3 days when found, and hatched on June 29. The evidence at hand indicates that the incubation period of the whistler is several days shorter than that of the trumpeter.

Nest Success. Nest success is exceptionally high in the whistling swan—Calvin Lensink considers it to be over 90 percent. Only three nests examined by Calvin Lensink have been unsuccessful: one had infertile eggs, one was destroyed by gulls after human disturbance, and one was destroyed by a fox. A brood size of 3.28 in June and July, shortly after hatch, suggests that about one egg of the average clutch fails to hatch.

Yet in spite of apparent high nest success, production of young is low. From 1964 to 1973 only 13 percent of the mature adults in the Atlantic Flyway were accompanied by young (Lynch and Voelzer 1974). During the same 10-year period in the Pacific Flyway, 27 percent of the mature birds were accompanied by young. Thus, only about one-fourth of the pairs wintering along the Atlantic Coast and one-half of those in the Pacific Flyway succeeded in rearing young.

On aerial surveys of Alaskan breeding grounds, Lensink (1973) observed that territorial pairs of swans with broods ranged from 18.3 percent to 50.9 percent and averaged 36 percent, 1963-71. He attributed the reduction in the proportion of nesting swans to the low temperatures that caused the late breakup of ice on rivers, lakes, and ponds. Survival of young during migration was also highest in years with early springs. When summers are brief, a few young are unfledged and others have just acquired the power of flight prior to migration. Under such late development, the demands of flight may take a heavy toll of young.

Rearing of Young

Broods. Both parents guard the welfare of their young. On the Yukon Delta, broods stay within 100 to 400 yards of their nests for considerable periods of time (Calvin Lensink).

Development. Calvin Lensink provided growth curves of cygnets that showed males increasing from about 6 ounces at hatch to 12 pounds, 4 ounces in 70 days; females gained almost 11 pounds in the same period. The first brood noticed in 1969 was observed on June 20, and the first fledged brood was seen August 19—60 days later. In 1971, the first nests hatched on June 26, and the first young fledged September 4, a 70-day interval. Most cygnets probably reach flight stage in 60 to 70 days; some may require 75 days.

Survival. Broods suffer only slight losses during their growth period. Lensink recorded broods averaging 3.15 in July, 3.01 in August, 3.01 in September, and 2.70 in October, 1963-71. In 1970, he found broods that averaged 3.43 (47) in July, 3.45 (69) in August, and 3.34 (236) in September. In 1971, swan broods averaged 2.66 (41) in July, 2.61 (115) in August, and 2.52 (140) in September. Swan families on Atlantic Coast winter grounds averaged 1.92 young each in December, 1964-73 (Lynch and Voelzer 1974). On Pacific Flyway areas, the average was 2.32 young.

POSTBREEDING SEASON

On the Yukon Delta, adult swans seldom fly between July 1 and August 15, but Calvin Lensink reports that the actual loss of flight is difficult to determine because flying and flightless birds remain together. He estimates a flightless period of 35 to 40 days.

The date when the first flightless swans were observed on the Mackenzie Delta ranged from July 9 in 1958 to July 22 in 1962 (Barry 1966).

Nonbreeders, which remain in flocks of 3 to 15 during the breeding season, regain flight in late August and begin to congregate in sizable flocks along the coast or near large inland lakes. Families of swans begin to join these premigrant flocks about 85 days after the peak of hatching.

FOOD HABITS

Whistling swans feed largely on the leaves, stems, and tubers of aquatic and marsh plants. They usually feed in water so shallow that immersion of the head and neck is sufficient to enable them to obtain the desired food items. Sometimes, to reach food in deeper water, they tip up, so that only the tail protrudes above the surface.

On their principal eastern winter grounds in Chesapeake Bay, 76 percent of the swans frequented brackish estuarine bays, 9 percent salt estuarine bays, 8 percent fresh estuarine bays, 6 percent slightly brackish estuarine bays, and 1 percent other habitats (Stewart 1962). They feed on widgeon grass and sago and clasping leaf pondweeds in the brackish estuarine bays and wild celery and clasping leaf pondweed in the fresh estuarine bays.

Tubers and seeds of the sago pondweed were the exclusive diet of swans collected in the Great Salt Lake marshes (Sherwood 1960). Nagel (1965) also reported the dependence of area swans upon sago pondweed but observed that they fed upon corn in harvested fields when marshes were covered with ice.

Near Stockton, California, whistling swans fed on waste corn in both dry and flooded fields and upon unharvested potatoes (Tate and Tate 1966). In Illinois, they fed on waste corn in both dry and flooded fields.

In the winter of 1969-70, whistling swans on Chesapeake Bay departed from their long-standing tradition of feeding exclusively on aquatics and commenced a supplementary feeding on waste corn in fields on Maryland's Eastern Shore (Vernon Stotts). Since then swans, almost as extensively as Canada geese, have adopted field feeding in Maryland. They commonly fly as far as 10 to 15 miles inland to glean waste corn and soybeans and to browse upon shoots of winter wheat.

White-Fronted Goose

Anser albifrons frontalis

Other Common Names: Specklebelly, specklebelly brant, speck, laughing goose

VITAL STATISTICS*

Length: Adult male, 27-31 inches, average 29.1 inches (57)
Adult female, 26-29 inches, average 27.3 inches (51)
Immature male, 25-30 inches, average 28.0 inches (45)
Immature female, 25-28 inches, average 26.7 inches (57)

Wing: Adult male, average 17.3 inches (57)
Adult female, average 16.5 inches (51)
Immature male, average 16.5 inches (45)
Immature female, average 16.0 inches (57)

Weight: Adult male, 5.45-7.30 pounds, average 6.29 pounds (57)
Adult female 4.69-6.63 pounds, average 5.53 pounds (51)
Immature male, 4.58-6.63 pounds, average 5.63 pounds (45)
Immature female, 4.30-6.07 pounds, average 5.16 pounds (57)

*Data from livetrapped birds, Kindersley, Saskatchewan, October 10-12, 1964, by Alex Dzubin and Harvey Miller.

IDENTIFICATION

Field

White-fronted geese are brownish gray in appearance and, at a distance, show no distinguishing plumage characteristics. They tend to fly in large flocks and in V's like Canada geese. Far away in flight, their most distinguishing characteristic is their high-pitched laughing call, *kow-yow, kow-yow*. They are among the most vociferous of geese.

The dark brown to black blotches and irregular bars discernible at close range on the brownish breasts of adults have led many hunters to use the name "specklebelly." In adults, a white patch around the front of the brown head and neck is a further distinguishing mark giving rise to the appellation of "whitefront." At a distance, the immatures are virtually impossible to distinguish from immature lesser snow geese in the blue-phase. Near at hand, the yellow bill and legs of the immature whitefront are in contrast to the dark legs and bill of the immature "blue" goose.

At Hand

The bill of the white-fronted goose is pinkish in adults and yellowish in immatures and lacks the "grinning patch" of the snow goose. The legs of adults are orange and those of immatures are straw-yellow. The head, neck, and upper back of both adults and immatures are grayish brown, but the adults have a white face patch. In both age-classes, the lower back, rump, and tail are dark brown, the tail edged with white.

The chest and breast are ash-gray, lighter than the back in all ages, but only the adult whitefront has the dark brown to black blotches and bars on the breast. The belly and both upper and lower tail coverts are white. In the wings, the primaries are black, the secondaries black-brown, and the coverts buff-brown.

POPULATION STATUS

An average of 200,000 white-fronted geese have been found in North America on winter surveys, 1955-74, about 18,000 in Mexico and the remainder in the United States. Numbers in the United States have ranged from a low of 107,000 in 1968 to a high of 279,000 in 1970.

The Pacific Flyway component of the population has declined over the 20-year period 1955-74. This decline has been balanced by increased numbers in the midcontinent component. That segment of the midcontinent population wintering in Louisiana steadily increased from 1955 to

1970, then leveled off the next 4 years. Since 1968, the numbers wintering in the Central Flyway have shown a consistent upward trend.

Age Ratios

Populations of white-fronted geese on Gulf Coast winter grounds have contained an average of 39 percent young, 1959-71 (Lynch 1971), ranging from a high of 52 percent in 1959 to a low of 20 percent in 1961. Among winter populations of whitefronts in the Pacific Flyway, the average proportion of young was 36 percent, 1961-71; the largest percentage, 41 percent, occurred in 1968; the smallest, 28 percent, in 1970 (Lynch 1971).

Field counts of age-classes by Miller et al. (1968) in the area of Kindersley, Saskatchewan, indicate that 23 percent of the fall population there was composed of immatures during 1960-66. They also corrected the age-classes in hunters' bags for the greater vulnerability of young to the gun and determined that in Texas, 1962-64, 24 percent of the population was made up of immatures.

Mortality

Twenty-nine percent of the adult male whitefronts, 34 percent of the adult females, 45 percent of the immature males, and 44 percent of the immature females banded near Kindersley, Saskatchewan, died the first year after banding (Miller et al. 1968). The annual rate of mortality for all sex and age groups combined was 34 percent. According to Harvey Miller, the mortality rates have remained at about this same level during the years subsequent to their initial study (1961-64).

DISTRIBUTION

Races of the white-fronted goose are circumpolar in their breeding distribution except for a gap in the northeastern Canadian Arctic. A small population that breeds on the west-central coast of Greenland winters mainly in Ireland and to a lesser extent in England and Scotland. A few of these whitefronts from Greenland are occasionally found in eastern North America during migration and winter periods. There are two other races in North America, one abundant and the other—the tule goose—rare.

Breeding Range

There are approximately 250,000 white-fronted geese in Alaska after the breeding season (King and Lensink 1971). A fall population of this size indicates that about 100,000 are breeding birds. Lynch's (1971) data on productivity suggest that about 75,000 are immatures, 75,000 are subadults, and the remainder are potential breeders.

Band recoveries (Miller et al. 1968, Lensink 1969) indicate that most of the 200,000 whitefronts composing the early fall population in the Pacific Flyway originate from breeding grounds on the Yukon Delta. Only 10 percent of the whitefronts banded on the nearby Innoko-Iditarod breeding grounds have been recovered in the Pacific Flyway (Lensink 1969). The Yukon Delta is, therefore, the most important breeding ground for this species in North America, with a probable breeding population of 80,000.

About 90 percent of the white-fronted geese from the area of the Innoko and Iditarod rivers, and all those from breeding areas along the Selawik River east of Kotzebue Sound on the Arctic Slope and from interior areas of Alaska, migrate through the interior of North America.

James King has estimated the postbreeding population on the Arctic Slope to be nearly 54,000—5,800 breeders, 12,800 immatures, and 35,000 nonbreeders. Most of the nonbreeders that were molting had probably moved to the Arctic Slope from interior breeding grounds. Even though the estimated fall population of 250,000 in Alaska may be too low, it is apparent that the number of breeders in the interior is small. Interior breeding grounds are located on the Kobuk River, the Yukon Flats, the upper Koyukuk River, and the lower Tanana River.

In the western and central Canadian Arctic, Thomas Barry has estimated the population of white-fronted geese in the postbreeding season as follows: 40,000 in the Mackenzie Delta-Anderson River area; 1,400, Old Crow Flats; 1,800, Victoria Island; 10,000, Queen Maud Gulf; and 100 on King William Island. Breeding pairs and broods of whitefronts have also been found along the Thelon River, Northwest Territories (Kuyt 1962). Sterling banded 146 molting adults between Aberdeen and Beverly lakes on the Thelon River in 1964 and 1965 (Miller et al. 1968).

The population figures cited for Alaska and Canada leave few white-fronted geese unaccounted for in midcontinent. Therefore, only small numbers might be expected to nest elsewhere in the Canadian Arctic. During spring migration, 55 whitefronts were observed on the eastern shore of Sherman Basin, the Adelaide Peninsula, by Macpherson and Manning (1959). They found only one nest and speculated that these migrants nested farther north. Höhn (1968) reported that the whitefront was a comparatively rare spring migrant at Chesterfield Inlet on Hudson Bay. A few have been observed on Banks Island, but none have been known to nest there (Manning et al. 1956).

The Greenland white-fronted goose (*Anser albifrons flavirostris*) breeds on the west coast of Greenland between latitude 64° and 72° 30′ N (Salomonsen 1950-51). Except for rare occurrences along the east coast of North America, this population winters in the British Isles, particularly in Ireland. Fewer than 25 specimens of this race have been taken in North America over the last 100 years, largely in Massachusetts, New York, and New Jersey (Bent 1925, Nichols and Nichols 1946).

Migration Corridors

When fall comes, 200,000 (average) white-fronted geese depart the Yukon Delta, bound on a 2,000-mile flight across the Gulf of Alaska to make landfall near the mouth of the Columbia River. Occasionally, small numbers of white-

WHITE-FRONTED GOOSE

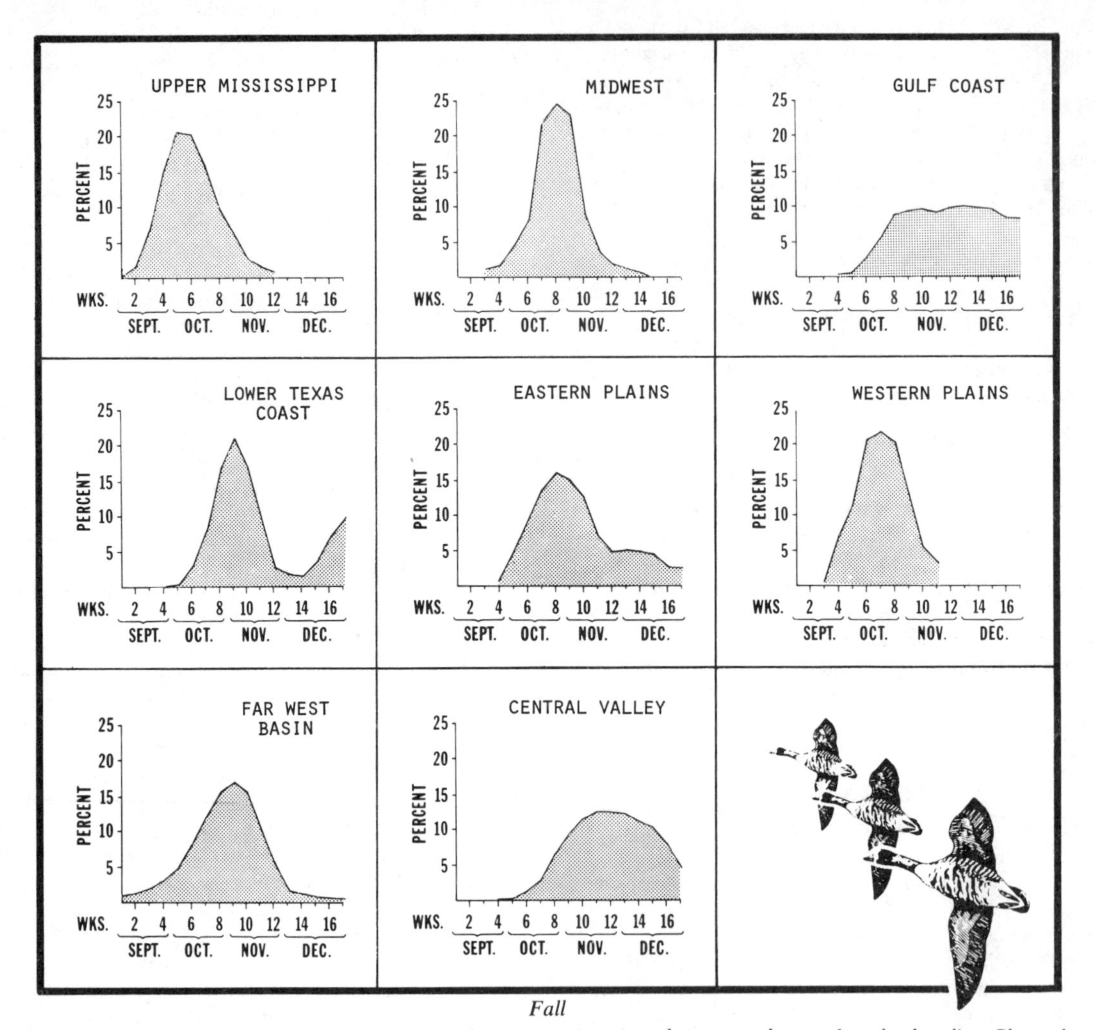

Fall

(For explanation of percentages shown in this and subsequent migration charts see chapter 1 under heading Chronology of Migration.)

fronts are driven ashore along the coast of southeast Alaska. A few hundred may stop briefly at Willapa Bay on the southwest coast of Washington, but most continue southeastward overland to Malheur and Summer lakes, Oregon, and the Klamath Basin in northern California.

The largest concentration of white-fronted geese in North America occurs in the Klamath Basin, where almost the entire population gathers in late October and early November. Most of them leave this area in 6 to 8 weeks for the Central Valley of California, but a few thousand continue to the Imperial Valley in southern California and along the west coast of Mexico almost to Guatemala.

The midcontinent population of white-fronted geese is made up of birds from breeding grounds in Alaska (other than the Yukon Delta) and from Arctic Canada and consists of two subpopulations: one from Alaska and the western Canadian Arctic, the other from the central Canadian Arctic (Miller et al. 1968). Most, if not all, of the western subpopulation stages in southeastern Alberta and southwestern Saskatchewan, forming the greatest concentration of this species in interior North America.

Recoveries from whitefronts banded in Alaska (Lensink 1969) show that only small numbers pause in migration in northwestern Alberta; most fly nonstop directly from

WHITE-FRONTED GOOSE

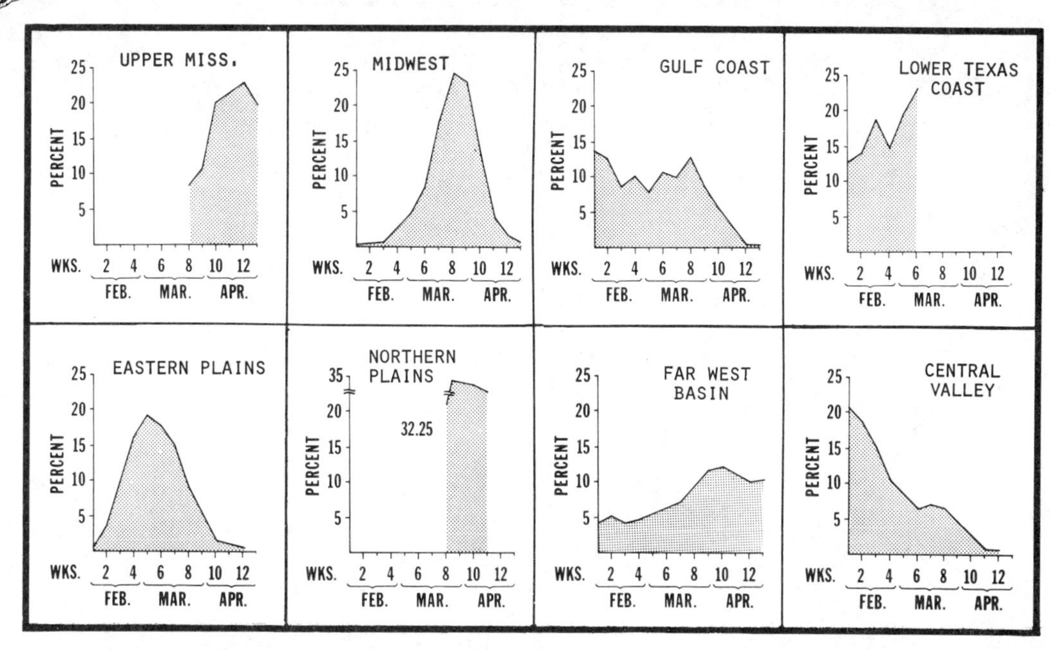

Spring

Alaska to the staging area in Alberta-Saskatchewan, 900 to 2,000 miles distant from their various breeding grounds. Similarly, whitefronts from the western Canadian Arctic seldom pause en route to this staging area. A few stop along the Mackenzie River.

From the Alberta-Saskatchewan staging area, centered about Kindersley, Saskatchewan, the migration corridor of the western subpopulation extends southeastward through Saskatchewan and then turns south through the eastern Great Plains of the United States to the Gulf Coast of western Louisiana and eastern Texas (Miller at al. 1968, Lensink 1969), and then south along the coasts of Texas and Mexico.

Birds of the eastern subpopulation of whitefronts appear to migrate directly south from their breeding grounds adjacent to Queen Maud Gulf and the Thelon River. A few thousand stop at the Saskatchewan River delta, west-central Manitoba, and Oak and Whitewater lakes in southwestern Manitoba (Larche 1970). About 25,000 frequent the national wildlife refuges on the Souris River, North Dakota, but bandings (Lensink 1969) there suggest that these geese originate about equally from the eastern and western subpopulations.

Band recoveries from the eastern subpopulation are 6.0 times more numerous in western Louisiana than in eastern Texas. On the other hand, band recoveries from the western subpopulation are 4.6 times more numerous in Texas than in Louisiana (calculated from Lensink 1969). Thus, most of the eastern subpopulation winters in western Louisiana, and most of the western subpopulation winters in Texas and Mexico.

Winter Areas

The principal winter ground for white-fronted geese in the Pacific Flyway lies in the Central Valley of California, where about 136,000 concentrate. Four thousand additional whitefronts winter at the opposite ends of California—2,000 in the Klamath Basin and 2,000 in the Imperial Valley. About 125 are found in Oregon, and only occasionally are a few found in Washington.

About 7,400 whitefronts winter along the west coast of Mexico, distributed as follows: 1,000 near Ciudad Obregón, 2,300 near Los Mochis, 1,700 on Santa Maria Bay, 2,000 on Ensenada del Pabellon, and fewer than 500 from there south to Guatemala.

The whitefront population that winters in midcontinent has averaged about 75,000, 1955-72. Of these, 64,000 are in the United States and 10,500 in Mexico. The coastal marshes of western Louisiana hold 26,000; the coast of Texas, 38,000; the east coast of Mexico, 4,500; and the interior lakes and reservoirs of Mexico, 6,000.

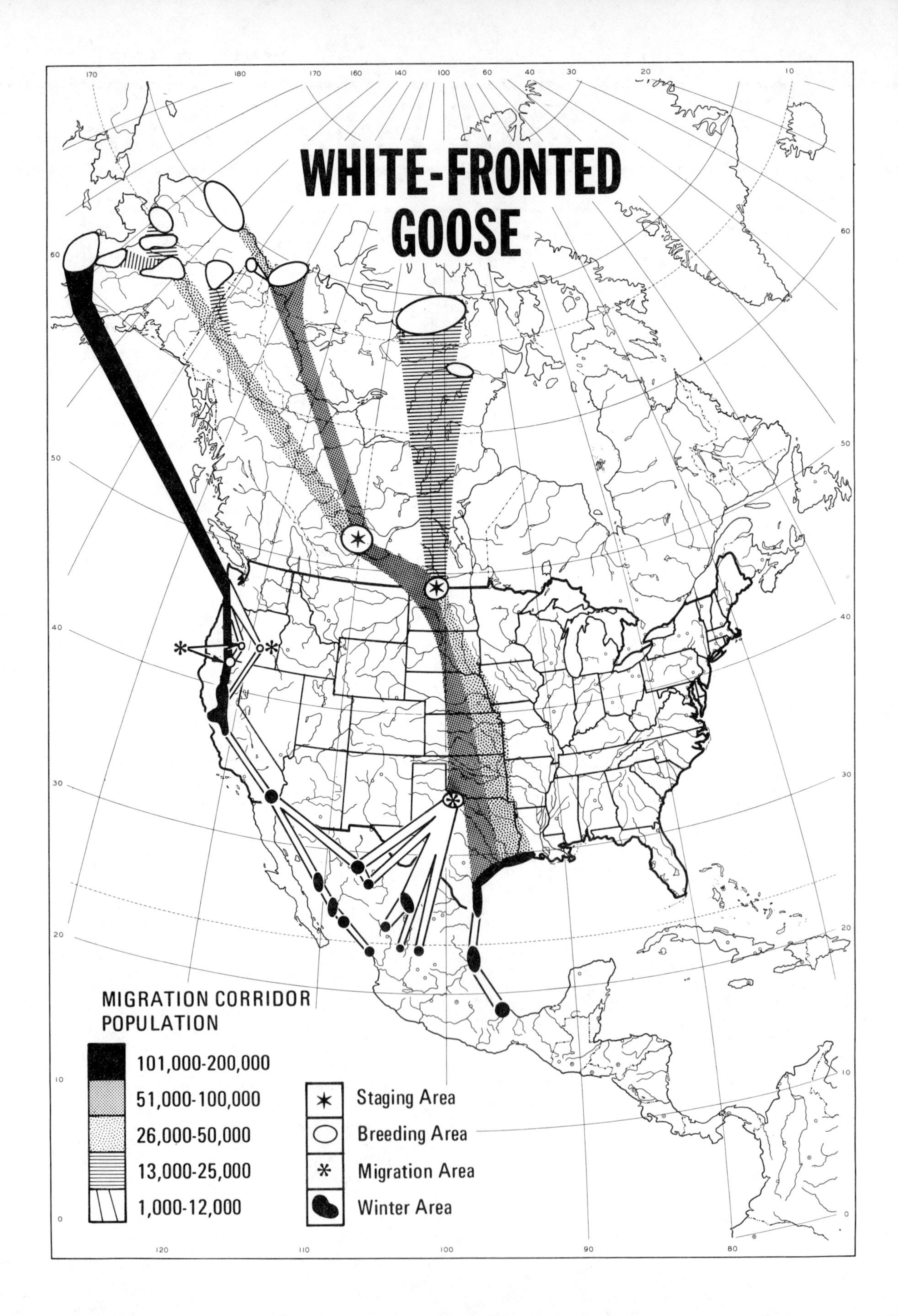

WHITE-FRONTED GOOSE
MIGRATION CORRIDOR POPULATION
101,000-200,000
51,000-100,000
26,000-50,000
13,000-25,000
1,000-12,000
Staging Area
Breeding Area
Migration Area
Winter Area

Along the Texas coast, about 30,000 concentrate between Galveston Bay and Corpus Christi; 6,000 congregate in east Texas; and the remainder are distributed from Corpus Christi to Mexico. The east coast of Mexico has the following concentrations of white-fronted geese: delta of the Rio Grande River, 900; lagoons near Tampico, 1,400; lagoons south of Veracruz, 1,700; and several hundred as far south as the state of Tabasco.

Major areas of concentration in the Northern Highlands of Mexico are: Laguna de Babicora, 1,500; Laguna de Santiaguillo, 1,300; and Laguna de los Mexicanos, 600. The largest number of recoveries in Mexico from whitefronts banded in Saskatchewan and the Central Flyway has been reported in the state of Zacatecas. Apparently there have been no aerial surveys in this state.

Bandings of whitefronts at Tule Lake, California, indicate a small number of recoveries in the Mexican states of Chihuahua and Durango. Since the previously reported populations on lagoons in the Northern Highlands are in these states, these areas apparently contain birds from both the Pacific and Central flyways.

MIGRATION BEHAVIOR

Chronology

Fall. Because most whitefronts fly from the breeding grounds to the staging areas without stopping—other geese make intermediate stops—they are the first geese to appear on southern areas. Flocks have reached their staging area in Saskatchewan as early as August 27 (Barry 1966), and nonbreeders have departed their breeding grounds on the Anderson Delta by August 15-20. From that time on, there is a steady exodus until all are gone by early October. Small numbers have frequented the Athabasca Delta during September 8-21 (Soper 1951).

According to Gabrielson and Lincoln (1959), evidence of fall migration in Alaska has appeared as early as August 6 on Nunivak Island and by September 4 at Craig, in the extreme southeast Panhandle. A concentration of 100,000 migrants was recorded near Cordova on September 5. Late records for Alaskan migrants are: September 12 at the Kobuk River; October 7-8, St. Michael, Yukon Delta; October 18, St. George Island; and November 8, Craig.

By the first week in September, 10,000 white-fronted geese are already present in the Klamath Basin, California. The population there steadily increases each week to peak numbers the last week in October and then steadily declines as birds leave for the Central Valley of California.

At the staging area near Kindersley, Saskatchewan, whitefronts arrive in early September and depart by mid-October (Miller and Dzubin 1965). Peak populations of 25,000 to 50,000 birds are reached the last week of September.

A few whitefronts appear in North Dakota as early as the first week in September, but it is September 15-21 before several thousand are found. Peak numbers are reached the first week in October, and then their abundance gradually declines throughout the remainder of October, but small numbers of stragglers stay until late November.

Whitefronts appear on winter grounds in Louisiana and Texas the last week of September, and the population reaches its winter level 4 weeks later.

The chronology of band recoveries, reported by Miller et al. (1968), suggests the following sequence of passage in the midcontinent population: Alberta, arrival in early September, peak in late September, departure in mid-October; Saskatchewan, arrival in mid-September, peak in early October, departure in late October; Texas, appreciable numbers present when the season opens during the last part of October; and Mexico, one recovery in early October, recoveries at a low level through January but slight increases the last 10 days of October and the first 10 days of December and January.

Spring. White-fronted geese begin leaving their winter grounds in Louisiana and Texas in early February and continue their straggling departure through most of March. They begin to appear in sizable numbers in Oklahoma and Kansas in mid-February, and large numbers remain until the third week in March; small numbers linger until late April.

In the Nebraska section of the Missouri River, the first sizable contingent of whitefronts arrives in mid-March; most of them stay only 2 to 3 weeks before heading north. They arrive in North Dakota in late March and sizable numbers remain throughout April. Large numbers arrive in the area of Kindersley, Saskatchewan, about April 20, remaining until the first week in May (Barry 1966). They arrive in the Athabasca Delta from late April to mid-May (Soper 1951). First arrivals on the Mackenzie Delta were noted on May 14 and May 31 in two different years (Porslid 1943). On the nesting grounds of the Anderson Delta, whitefronts arrived May 12-17 over a 6-year span (Barry 1966). They did not arrive on their breeding grounds at the Perry River until June 1, 1963 and 1964 (Ryder 1967).

On the Pacific Coast the spring exodus from the Central Valley of California to the Klamath Basin is very gradual, starting in early February and continuing through March. Peak numbers are not reached in the Klamath Basin until late March, and many whitefronts linger there through April and frequently as late as mid-May.

Whitefronts have been observed migrating over southeastern Alaska on April 21, 24, and 27 in different years (Gabrielson and Lincoln 1959). First appearances on the Yukon Delta have been recorded on April 17, 23, 25, and 27 in different years. On Norton Sound they have been seen May 5, at Kotzebue Sound on May 1, and at Kobuk River on May 10. Dates of arrival at Point Barrow range from April 30 to May 20. At Anaktuvuk Pass, Irving (1960) observed whitefronts passing over on May 9, 13, 15, 16, 18, and 21 in various years, apparently headed for their nearby breeding grounds on the Arctic Slope. In east-central Alaska, near Fairbanks, the date of first arrivals averaged April 27, 1948-55.

BREEDING

Behavior

According to Barry (1966), whitefronts first breed at 3 years of age unless, as in other geese, particularly favorable nest conditions induce some 2-year-olds to breed. Both Hanson et al. (1956) and Barry (1966) reported unusual instances of adults paired with, but not breeding with, yearlings.

The whitefronts' family ties persist longer than in other geese. Barry (1966) found that yearlings remained with their parents even during the nesting activities of the adults. The yearlings moved away a short distance when they began to molt, a few days prior to the brood period of their parents.

Homing. About 57 percent of the downy young banded by Barry (1966) were recaptured the subsequent year on the same breeding area. The second year he captured 44 percent of the banded young, but none the third year. Barry speculated that when the whitefronts reached breeding age, they left their natal area to nest elsewhere in the same general region. Because of variations in the snow melt, Barry (1966) doubted that the same nest site was occupied from year to year. Only 5.7 percent of the banded adults were recaptured on the same area in subsequent years, but he believed that other banded birds probably nested in the general vicinity of their previous nests.

Territory. Unlike many geese breeding in the Arctic, white-fronted geese do not nest in colonies. Because they are solitary breeders, they are not militant territorialists (Barry 1966). Barry reported that most of the territorial defense against predators and human intruders is provided by the nonbreeding yearlings. They fly out to meet the intruding party and attempt, usually successfully, to lure any animal away from the nest site.

Nesting

Calvin Lensink reports that among all the waterfowl on the Yukon Delta, white-fronted geese occupy the most extensive breeding habitat. Nesting occurs on both tidal flats and upland areas. The whitefronts typically nest in tall grass bordering tidal sloughs or in sedge marshes and, less often, in grass-covered pingos or the margins of tundra hummocks. Infrequently they nest on heath tundra, sometimes as far as 50 to 100 yards from water. On the Anderson River-Liverpool Bay breeding area, they spread over the coastal plains to nest beside rivers, tributary streams, and countless lakes, nesting farther inland than the black brant or the lesser snow goose (Barry 1966).

The female selects a shallow depression, building the nest from nearby plant material as the eggs are laid (Barry 1966). Small amounts of down are added as the clutch progresses, but the nests of whitefronts contain less down than those of other geese that nest in the Arctic.

Chronology of Nesting. First nest of the white-fronted goose on the Anderson River in 1961 was initiated on May 26 (Barry 1966), but the first hatch that year was not recorded until July 3. Nests were started over a 10-day period. In 1963 and 1962, first hatches occurred on June 29 and June 30. Mickelson (1973) reported that on the Yukon Delta, the whitefronts were the first waterfowl to nest, with a short nest initiation period of 10 days in late May 1969 and 1970, and in late May or early June, 1971 and 1972.

Clutch Size, Eggs, and Incubation. Reported clutch sizes ranged from 5 to 7 on the Anderson Delta (Barry 1966) and 2 to 10, averaging 4.75 (301), on the Yukon Delta (Calvin Lensink). During 1964-71, the smallest average clutch was 3.7 (1971) and the largest was 5.3 (1970).

The eggs are elliptical ovate to elongate ovate, 79.0 mm by 52.5 mm (109), and are creamy white to light buff (Bent 1925). As most goose eggs do, they usually acquire a brown stain from the nest material.

Incubation is solely by the female, and, as it progresses, she spends an increasing amount of time on the nest. The average incubation period on the nest area at the Anderson River was 23 days (Barry 1966). Four nests in Alaska hatched 23 to 25 days after incubation started (Calvin Lensink).

The young leave the nest within 24 hours and are led to the nearest water. On the nest area at the Anderson River, the nearest water was usually a small slough margined with sedges (Barry 1966). The male assumes the dominant role in brood life, the female the secondary role.

Nest Success. White-fronted geese nest in dispersed fashion over the tundra or in the taiga. Their nests are difficult to locate, and few have been studied. Mickelson (1973) has made the most intensive study to date on the nesting of this species. Over a 4-year period, he found 77 white-fronted goose nests on the Onumtuk area, Yukon Delta. Sixty-five nests were successful (84.4 percent), and in these nests an average of 4.08 eggs hatched, 0.53 egg less than the incubated clutch. Prorated for nest failures, each breeding pair produced 3.4 young. The greatest nest loss resulted from predators; most of the destruction was caused by parasitic jaegers or glaucous gulls during the incubation period. The proportion of adults with young to mature adults in December populations of white-fronted geese provides an index to hatching success. Lynch (1971) found that 68 percent of the adults were accompanied by young birds in populations wintering on the Gulf of Mexico, 1961-71. The highest proportion of parents among the potential breeders was 96.5 percent in 1963; the lowest, 36.5 percent in 1961.

Among populations of white-fronted geese in the Pacific Flyway, 57 percent of the mature adults, 1961-71, were parents (Lynch 1971). The highest proportion of parents was 75 percent (1961), the lowest was 43 percent (1964).

The extreme variation in the yearly proportion of mature adults that were apparently successful in rearing young suggests variations in the influence of Arctic weather conditions on nest success. Predation on waterfowl nests in the Arctic is light and, overall, fairly constant from year to year, so that the large fluctuations in numbers of successful breeding pairs are apparently attributable to weather.

The black markings on the breast of white-fronted geese are variable.

Rearing of Young

Broods. The young become dry and are ready to leave their nests 24 hours after hatching (Barry 1966). Upon being led to the nearest water, usually a small slough with a margin of thick sedges in which to hide, the males become the more watchful parents. On the Anderson River, during the first week, broods remained well hidden in cover before becoming increasingly venturesome and wandering considerable distances. Barry believes that broods suffer their heaviest losses at this stage, as the young easily become separated from their parents.

Development. Young whitefronts, according to Barry (1966), grow as rapidly as young snow geese and are able to fly at the same age—about 45 days. At Anderson River the first young flew on August 9. On the Yukon Delta, Mickelson (1973) reported that young whitefronts required 55 to 65 days to reach flight stage, longer than brant, cackling, and emperor geese. The family bond among white-fronted geese is both strong and persistent. Whitefronts remain in families during the fall, winter, and spring, and into the nest season. During the fall, Miller and Dzubin (1965) observed that when families were separated by livetrapping and were released separately, they reformed their original family groups.

Survival. Little is known about brood survival in relation to age in whitefronts. Scott (1948) recorded an average of 4.4 goslings in Class I in 13 broods on the Yukon Delta, Alaska. Families of whitefronts tallied on their winter grounds on the Gulf Coast during December averaged 2.5 young, 1959-71 (Lynch 1971). There was little yearly variation in young per family; the largest average brood size was 2.9 (1966), the smallest was 2.0 (1961). In the Pacific Flyway, December families of whitefronts averaged 2.4 young (Lynch 1971); the largest families, 3.1, were recorded in 1960, and the smallest, 2.2, in 1970.

POSTBREEDING SEASON

On their breeding area at the Anderson River, Barry (1966) reported that, like other geese, the first molters are the yearlings and older subadults that gather in numbers up to 20,000 on traditional areas. Their molt begins about June 25, regardless of previous weather conditions. They regain flight in about 35 days (about August 1). Some adult breeders may complete their wing molt as early as August 10, when the young also first begin to fly. By August 20, evening flights of family groups are a common sight, and, by August 25, most of the geese have dispersed from their molt areas (Barry 1966). On the Yukon Delta, Mickelson (1973) reported that adults with broods began to molt when the broods were 3 weeks old, in the third week of July, and replaced their flight feathers in about 4 weeks.

FOOD HABITS

White-fronted geese in California feed extensively on the seeds of rice, water grass, milo, and barley (McFarland and George 1966). The consumption of rice seed in Sacramento Valley was 7 times greater than that of water grass, the consumption of water grass was 1.5 times greater than that of milo, which in turn was over 10 times greater than that of barley. Feeding tests among penned geese of several species, including whitefronts, showed a 2:1 preference of rice over water grass; water grass was preferred 5-6:1 over milo, alkali bulrush, and safflower, and 9:1 over barley.

In the rice belt of the Texas coast, rice constituted the bulk of the food eaten by three species of geese, including whitefronts (Glazener 1946). On the central and south coasts of Texas, the same species consumed corn, salt grass, sorghum, and a variety of other plants. Seeds were eaten in most instances, but the stems and blades of salt grass were consumed also.

Tule Goose

Anser albifrons gambelli

VITAL STATISTICS

Length:	Male, 31.9 inches (15) Female, 29.7 inches (13)
Wing:	Male, 17.4-18.9 inches, average 17.76 inches (17) Female, 16.1-17.4 inches, average 16.65 inches (12)
Weight:	Male, 7.00 pounds (19) Female, 6.75 pounds (4)

IDENTIFICATION

Field

Although the tule goose is a larger and darker edition of the white-fronted goose, few observers are knowledgeable enough to identify the tule goose in the wild. Tule geese occur in flocks of 5 to 25, fewer than the number in most flocks of whitefronts. Tule geese are also reputed to be less wary and to fly lower than the smaller race.

At Hand

Size is the most important criterion for distinguishing tule geese from white-fronted specimens. Tule geese are longer, weigh more, and have longer wings, bills, and legs, and larger feet, than whitefronts. Table 1 provides data on the comparative sizes of the two races.

In addition to the difference in size, tule geese are noticeably browner than whitefronts. The head and neck are dark brown. Most specimens examined by Wilbur (1966) showed a blackish-brown "cap" above the eye.

The tule goose is one of the most enigmatic waterfowl in the world—its very existence has been a question mark. Its status has been uncertain ever since Swarth and Bryant (1917) described it as a larger race of the white-fronted goose. Hartlaub (1852) first described the tule goose over a century ago from three specimens taken in Texas; it was considered the white-fronted goose of North America until Swarth and Bryant (1917) presented evidence that two distinct races existed in California.

POPULATION STATUS

No one knows how abundant the tule goose was in the past. In recent years, only small numbers of this race have been reported from three localized areas in California. During the winter of 1964-65, U. S. Game Agent Tom Harper (Wilbur 1966) estimated that there were 250 tule geese among the 2,000 white-fronted geese in the Suisun marshes, near Fairfield, California; he observed even fewer tule geese in the Suisun area in 1965-66.

Wilbur (1966) identified 40 tule geese among 179 whitefronts bagged by hunters on the Sacramento National Wildlife Refuge, near Willows, California, during the winter of 1965-66. At least 21 were bagged there in 1966-67 (Wilbur and Yocom 1972). Four were taken in Solano County, California, in December 1954, one was shot near Los Banos in the winter of 1965-66, and two were killed at the Tule Lake National Wildlife Refuge in November 1965.

Although its true status is a mystery, it is believed to be a rare and endangered species. Because it flies lower and is less wary than the whitefront, it probably suffers heavier losses from gunning.

DISTRIBUTION

The tule goose is known with certainty only on its winter ground in California. When it migrates from there, for all practical purposes it disappears into the limbo of the Arctic. At one time Gavin (1947) believed that he found this race nesting near the mouth of the Perry River, Northwest

Comparison of Size Between Tule and White-fronted Geese.

	Tule Goose		White-fronted Goose	
	Male	Female	Male	Female
Length (inches)	31.9 (15)	29.7 (13)	28.6 (102)	27.3 (108)
Weight (pounds)	7.0 (19)	6.75 (4)	6.0 (102)	5.3 (108)
Range		6.63-7.0	4.58-7.30	4.30-6.63
Wing (mm)	451 (17)	423 (12)	410 (18)	388 (15)
Range	441-480	410-441	391-441	362-405
Bill (culmen, mm)	58 (17)	55 (12)	50 (20)	47 (17)
Range	55-62	49-59	47-57	46-54
Leg (tarsus, mm)	82 (4)	78 (3)	76 (20)	71 (17)
Range	79-86	44-55	68-82	66-75

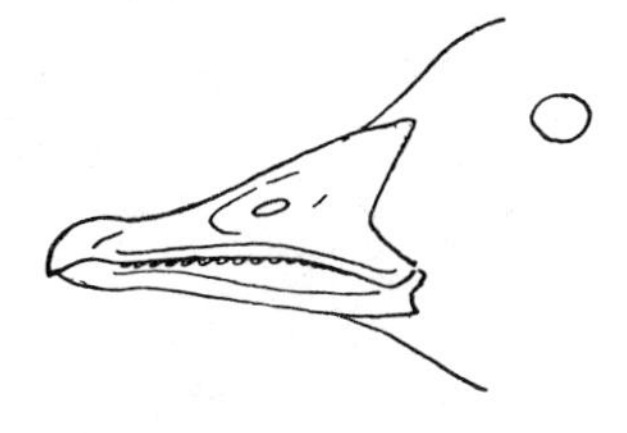

Comparative bill sizes: left, white-fronted goose; right, tule goose.

Territories, Canada, but subsequent investigation by Hanson et al. (1956) found only the smaller race.

There is inconclusive evidence that at least some tule geese nest on the Old Crow Flats, Yukon Territory, Canada. Elgas (1970) captured several goslings there that he raised to maturity. The measurements and plumage color reported by him indicated that his captives belonged to the race of the tule goose. However, his finding needs to be confirmed by additional specimens from the area.

The three small areas of California where the tule goose is known to winter are the Butte Creek basin, near Marysville; the Sacramento Refuge, near Willows; and the Suisun marshes, near Fairfield.

Lesser Snow Goose

Anser c. caerulescens

Other Common Names: Blue goose, wavie, brant

VITAL STATISTICS

Length:	Adult male, 28-31 inches, average 29 inches (32) Adult female, 27-29 inches, average 28 inches (36) Immature male, 27-29 inches, average 28 inches (36) Immature female, 25-28 inches, average 27 inches (35)
Wing:	Adult male, 17.7 inches (32) Adult female, 16.9 inches (36) Immature male, 16.7 inches (36) Immature female, 16.1 inches (35)
Weight:	Adult male, 6.06 pounds (534) Adult female, 5.50 pounds (483) Subadult male, 5.75 pounds (249) Subadult female, 5.38 pounds (270) Immature male, 4.81 pounds (888) Immature female, 4.44 pounds (687)

IDENTIFICATION

The lesser snow goose has two color phases: a dark plumage (the so-called blue goose) and a white plumage (the snow goose). Until Cooch (1961) presented unquestionable evidence that the blue and lesser snow geese were simply color phases of the same race, the two color phases were considered to indicate separate races.

Field

Geese in both dark and white phases regularly appear together east of the Great Plains. West of the eastern Great Plains, the dark or blue-phase is rare. Lesser snow geese migrate in large flocks of from 100 to 1,000 birds.

Snow geese fly in a peculiar undulating fashion: individual members of a flock fly at staggered heights, rising and descending slightly, giving rise to their pseudonym: wavie. They fly more rapidly than Canada geese, with a faster wingbeat. In flight, the flocks form U's, oblique lines, √'s, and irregular masses, seldom flying in the well-formed V's of Canada geese.

When geese in the white-phase are in flight, the white bodies and inner wings contrast with the black outer wing tips. Only the white-plumaged pelican has a similar appearance in the air. These geese are the most vociferous of all waterfowl, and the incessant clamor of a large flock about to take flight or land can be heard a mile or more. Their call is a varying high-pitched yelp, *ou, ou*, somewhat similar to the bark of a fox terrier.

At Hand

Blue-phase. The sexes are similar in appearance. The adults have white heads (sometimes partially stained a rusty hue) and white upper necks, with slate-gray bodies, whitish tail coverts, and varying amounts of white on their bellies; the pearl-gray wing coverts contrast with the black primaries. Their bills are pink, with black "grinning patches"; the feet and legs are rose-red.

The drably colored immature is almost entirely brownish gray, slightly lighter below, with medium gray wing coverts, and a white chin spot. The legs, feet, and bill are grayish brown. Immature blue geese resemble immature white-fronted geese, except that the latter have yellow legs and bills.

White-phase. The sexes are similar in appearance. Adult snow geese are completely white except for black wing tips. Occasionally the head has a rusty stain from feeding where ferrous minerals occur in bottom soils. The feet and legs are rosy red, and the bill is pink with a black "grinning patch."

The immature snow goose, less strikingly appareled than the adult, is sooty gray on the top of the head, the back of the neck, the back, and the wing coverts but is mostly white below; the wing tips are black, as in adults. The bill, legs, and feet are grayish brown.

POPULATION STATUS

The population of lesser snow geese wintering in the United States averaged 1,277,000 during 1955-74, with 28,000 in Mexico. During 1955-70, there has been 1 white-phase goose for 1.3 blue-phase geese in midcontinent where the two color phases intermingle. The blue-phase has predominated in the Mississippi Flyway 6 to 1 and the white-phase in the Central Flyway 4 to 1.

Recently there has been a gradual trend toward a greater intermingling of blue and white phases on the winter grounds. On three consecutive 5-year periods (1955 to 1970) the proportion of blue-phase to white-phase geese in the Mississippi Flyway has declined from 9.5:1 to 5.9:1 to 4.2:1 as more white-phase geese entered the winter grounds of the blue-phase. Conversely, in the Central Flyway, blue geese have encroached upon the winter grounds of the white geese. There, the ratio of white to blue has changed by 5-year periods, 1955 to 1970, on the order of 8.3:1 to 7.5:1 to 2.0:1.

At one time the winter grounds of the blue goose were largely restricted to southeast Louisiana, with the snow goose predominating in western Louisiana and Texas, but, in the last two decades, there appears to be a trend in midcontinental areas toward a more uniform distribution of the color phases.

From 1955 to 1974 there have been decided shifts in the overall proportion of blue-phase to white-phase snow geese in mid-America. Between 1955 and 1959, the proportion was 1.24 blue-phase to 1.0 white-phase. It increased to 1.49:1.0 in 1960-64 but declined to 1.20:1.0 in 1965-69.

Cooch (1963) documented the increasing proportion of blue-phase geese in the eastern Arctic up to 1961 and predicted their continued increase over the white-phase at the rate of 2 percent per year. He attributed the increase of the blue-phase to the less severe weather in the Arctic, which favored the production of blue-phase goslings over white-phase ones.

Although snow cover in Arctic lands began to increase as early as the 1940's, the pace apparently quickened in the 1960's, and increased further in the early 1970's. More severe weather in the Arctic in recent years may have favored the white-phase birds over the blue-phase birds.

Winter surveys of lesser snow geese numbers in the Mississippi and Central flyways combined show an upward trend of 47 percent from 1955 to 1975. Until 1968 there was also an upward trend in the Pacific Flyway, but from that year on, numbers have fallen to a lower level, hovering about the 440,000 mark. During the 5-year period prior to 1968, the population averaged 520,000. The prolonged depression in the Pacific Flyway population probably stems from the decline in breeding numbers at Wrangel Island, Siberia. In recent years extensive snow cover has prevailed there throughout the summer, inhibiting breeding.

Age Ratios

For many years Lynch (1971) and then Lynch and Voelzer (1974) recorded the proportion of young in December populations of lesser snow geese, based upon the observed age differences in plumage. From 1950 to 1973, an average of 29.7 percent of the snow geese wintering along the Gulf of Mexico were immatures. The proportion of young in this wintering population varied from 6 percent in 1954 to 54 percent in 1955.

Among wintering lesser snow geese in the Pacific Flyway, 1956-73, Lynch (1971) and Lynch and Voelzer (1974) reported an average of 27 percent young, ranging from 5 percent in 1965 to 49 percent in 1966. In both populations, the year of lowest production was followed by the year of greatest production.

Combining the average age ratios for the Gulf of Mexico population and the Pacific Flyway population, 1956-73, indicates a proportion of 28 percent young in winter populations of lesser snow geese.

The proportion of immature lesser snow geese in fall populations appears related to weather conditions on their Arctic breeding grounds (Lynch and Voelzer 1974). The weather appears to have become harsher during the 1960's and early 1970's, because immatures in midcontinent populations have shown a downward trend. From 1950 to 1960 immatures composed 35 percent of the December population, declined to 25 percent during 1961-65, remained at about that level (26 percent) during 1966-70, and declined further to 22 percent, 1971-73.

Pacific Flyway populations of snow geese do not show as great a decline in the proportion of immatures: 31.1 percent, 1956-60; 21.7 percent, 1961-65; 30.8 percent, 1966-70; and 24.1 percent, 1970-73. The midcontinental population of lesser snow geese is derived almost entirely from the eastern Arctic and Subarctic, and the Pacific Flyway population is derived from the western Arctic, Banks Island to Wrangel Island.

The area of ice and snow in the Northern Hemisphere suddenly increased by 12 percent in 1971 and the increase has persisted (Lynch and Voelzer 1974). Weather before and during the breeding of snow geese has apparently been more unfavorable in the eastern Canadian Arctic than in the western Arctic.

Sex Ratios

Hanson et al. (1972) reported the sex composition of blue and snow geese cannon-trapped at two national wildlife refuges in the upper Midwest, 1964-69. Among immatures of both color phases there were 52.4 percent males; among subadults and adults there were 52.2 percent males. The white-phase geese had more balanced sex ratios than the blue-phase geese.

Mortality

Cooch (1958) calculated annual mortality rates of snow goose populations as 50 percent for immatures, 25 percent for subadults and other nonbreeders, and 30 percent for adults. Yearly mortality rates for adults varied from 25 to 36 percent; rates in other groups remained remarkably constant from year to year.

In-season and postseason bandings of lesser snow geese at Tule Lake, California, 1953-60, revealed similar rates of annual mortality (Rienecker 1965): immatures, 55 percent; adult males, 25 percent; and adult females, 26 percent. Eighty-five percent of the total losses of immatures were caused by hunting, compared with 62 percent for adult males and 31 percent for adult females.

DISTRIBUTION

Breeding Range

The breeding range of lesser snow geese has changed dramatically in the last 2 decades, with new colonies and dynamic growth at several locations along the *west side* of Hudson Bay.

Centered on the McConnell River delta along the west coast of Hudson Bay is the most vital colony of all. When it was first discovered by Angus Gavin in 1941, it numbered 14,000 (Cooch 1963). By 1961 its numbers had increased to 35,000, and 8 years later it numbered at least 100,000 (Hanson et al. 1972). When photographed from the air by Kerbes (1975) in June 1973, it numbered 520,000 birds and extended between the Tha-Anne and Maguse rivers. About 390,000 were breeding birds, and 24 percent were in blue plumage.

Colonies on Baffin Island barely remained the largest. Kerbes (1975) calculated 595,000 (446,000 breeders) from sample counts of aerial photos taken in 1973. Back in 1955, Cooch estimated 400,000 lesser snows grouped in four large and two small colonies. At that time he determined that 72 percent were of the blue-phase variety; 18 years later, Kerbes determined that blue-phase birds composed 73 percent of the population.

Between the Baffin Island colonies and those on the west side of Hudson Bay lie three colonies on Southampton Island; most are at Boas River (Kerbes 1975). These totaled 208,000 in 1973 as determined by sample counts of aerial photos. Three-quarters were breeders and 24 percent were blue-phased.

Nesting of lesser snow geese at Cape Henrietta Maria was first discovered in 1947 when a few were photographed from the air (Hanson et al. 1972). When Harry Lumsden investigated this colony in 1957, he estimated that it contained 17,300 birds. By 1968 the colony was estimated to number 40,000 geese. Aerial photos taken in 1973 by the Canadian Wildlife Service indicated that it had grown to 79,000 birds (61,500 breeders) and was composed of 73 percent blue-phase geese (Kerbes 1975).

Snow geese began nesting around La Pérouse Bay, near Cape Churchill, between 1951 and 1958. Fifteen nests were recorded there in 1956. By 1966 the colony included 5,300 birds (Hanson et al. 1972). Canadian Wildlife Service photographs indicated a population of 8,000 in 1973 (6,000 breeders) of which blue-phase birds composed 26 percent (Kerbes 1975).

Hanson et al. (1972) found small numbers of broods scattered along the west coast of James Bay from the Albany River to Cape Henrietta Maria, and from there to the Seal River along the southwest and west coasts of Hudson Bay. Others, too, have observed nesting of small numbers of snow geese breeding at long distances from the main colonies: Macpherson and Manning (1959) found them nesting on the southeast side of Sherman Basin near the Kaleet River on the Adelaide Peninsula, and Parmelee et al. (1967) estimated 1,500 near the coast of southeastern Victoria Island, Northwest Territories, Canada. In the entire eastern Arctic in 1973, Kerbes (1975) determined there were 1,410,000 lesser snow geese in five widely separated areas. Blue-phase birds composed 43 percent of the total.

In the central Arctic, between Bathurst Inlet and Sherman Basin, Ryder (1969) in 1965 estimated that there were 8,430 nesting lesser snow geese in 16 scattered colonies and 1,470 nonbreeding birds. He found that 5 percent were blue-phase geese.

The largest nesting colony of lesser snow geese in the western Canadian Arctic, located inland along the Egg River on Banks Island, has grown in recent years to number over 200,000 breeding birds in 1973 (Thomas Barry). Only a small number of blue-phase geese occur as far west as this colony.

About 7,500 lesser snow geese breed near the delta of the Anderson River, Northwest Territories, Canada, and, 150 miles to the west, about 5,500 birds nest on Kendall Island, part of the Mackenzie Delta (Thomas Barry).

Only a few lesser snow geese breed in Alaska. In 1966, King (1970) observed 19 broods of snow geese and 343 molting nonbreeding birds on the Arctic Slope between Point Barrow and the Colville River—about half of the actual population summering there. The broods were widely scattered on lakes 2 to 3 miles from the coast.

At Wrangel Island, Siberia, the breeding population of lesser snow geese has declined catastrophically since Uspenski (1965) estimated 200,000 occupied nests (400,000 birds) in 1960. Kistchinski (1973) reported that several years ago there were 60,000 pairs of snow geese breeding there. According to F. Graham Cooch, the latest word is that after several years of negligible production, the population has dwindled to a remnant of its former size. The tremendous reduction in this colony appears to stem from protracted snow cover that has prevented most, if not all, birds from nesting.

Migration Corridors

Fall. The lesser snow goose is primarily a migrant in mid-America and the Pacific Flyway. However, from 800 to 1,400 blue-phase birds migrate to Chesapeake Bay, Currituck Sound, and adjacent waters of the Atlantic Coast. Their migration corridor extends south from James Bay across western New York and central Pennsylvania. Prior to the winter of 1934-35, this goose was considered an accidental visitor to the Atlantic Flyway (Cottam 1935), but since then it has appeared there regularly, although in low numbers.

Lesser snow geese from the eastern Arctic breeding grounds gather in tremendous numbers in the south end of James Bay and in lesser numbers along the west coast. Lumsden (1971) made two aerial surveys of this region on October 4-6 and 15-18, 1971. He estimated 304,000 on the first census and 331,000 on the second one. The largest concentration—some 179,000—occurred in southeast James Bay between Eastmain River and Moosonee. Northward along the west coast of James Bay, the geese were distributed as follows: Moosonee to Fort Albany, 64,000; Fort Albany to Attawapiskat River, 80,000; and Attawapiskat to Cape Henrietta Maria, 63,000 (October 4-6 for the last area, which had 8,000 on October 15-18).

At the lower end of James Bay, Lumsden (1971) found on his two October surveys that the blue-phase element composed 94 to 95 percent of the lesser snow populations. In the region of Fort Albany, they formed 90 to 93 percent; at Attawapiskat from 77 to 86 percent; and below Cape Henrietta Maria from 67 to 73 percent.

The comparatively low proportion of the white-phase component in the James Bay populations of lesser snow geese indicates that white-phase geese must be predominant on the fall staging areas on the southwest coast of Hudson Bay. Doubtlessly, the proportion of white-phase birds increases rapidly from Cape Henrietta Maria to York Factory.

A series of corridors extends from the southeast coast of James Bay through Michigan and Wisconsin, merging into large corridors along the lower Mississippi River and terminating in the coastal marshes of eastern Louisiana. In recent decades about 300,000 lesser snow geese have followed these corridors from James Bay to the Louisiana coast.

The westerly corridors extend from the southwest coast of Hudson Bay across western Ontario and central Manitoba to merge between the James River in North Dakota and the Missouri River in northwest Missouri. A single large corridor extends from there to the coastal marshes in western Louisiana and east Texas. In the early 1970's, about 800,000 geese were using the westerly corridors in mid-America.

Small numbers of the lesser snow geese that migrate via the easterly migration corridors consistently linger along their routes. From 1,000 to 4,000 delay their fall passage in Michigan, Wisconsin, and Indiana. Approximately 15,000 remain a few weeks in the Illinois River valley and nearly as many in the Mississippi River valley between Moline and Alton, Illinois. Almost all the others fly nonstop for 1,500 miles along the easterly migration corridors to Louisiana. About once every 10 years unusually large numbers of lesser snow geese stop in migration among the easterly states of the Mississippi Flyway.

The lesser snow geese following the westerly migration corridors through the midcontinent interrupt their fall passage more frequently to rest and feed than those following the easterly corridors. In the last 5 years, at least 120,000 have stopped annually at the Sand Lake National Wildlife Refuge, near Aberdeen, South Dakota; 200,000 at the De Soto National Wildlife Refuge, just north of Omaha, Nebraska; and 175,000 at the Squaw Creek National Wildlife Refuge, north of St. Joseph, Missouri (Gerald Cummings).

The Mackenzie Delta is the major staging area for lesser snow geese in the western Canadian Arctic. A migration corridor followed by over 150,000 geese extends up the Mackenzie River to near the mouth of the Liard River, with a major branch to the areas of Hay Lake and Grande Prairie in northwest Alberta and a minor branch to the Athabasca Delta. These geese move on to important resting and feeding areas in southeastern Alberta and southwestern Saskatchewan.

In the vicinity of Freezeout Lake, west of Great Falls, Montana, the migration corridors diverge, one turning southwest for the Klamath Basin of northern California, one south-southwest for Carson Sink, Nevada, and one directly south to the Bear River marshes of Utah.

Most of the snow geese that breed on Wrangel Island, Siberia, migrate along several corridors off or along the coast of southeast Alaska and British Columbia. The largest corridor is believed to extend from Bristol Bay, Alaska, across the Gulf of Alaska to make landfall near the mouth of the Columbia River, and then on to Klamath Basin, California, and Summer Lake, Oregon. The coastal corridor is much smaller than the offshore corridors; a few thousand snow geese on the route pause at the Stikine Delta, near Wrangell, Alaska, before reaching their winter grounds on the Fraser River delta, British Columbia, and Puget Sound, Washington.

Almost 90,000 lesser snow geese were recorded in the area of Hay Lake, Alberta, on October 2, 1959, by Thomas Barry. A day earlier he found only 20,000 in the area of the Athabasca Delta. As many as 106,000 snow geese have been found in southeast Alberta (October 10, 1963), and up to 36,000 have been found in southwest Saskatchewan.

The largest number of snow geese observed in the fall at Freezeout Lake, Montana, has been 50,000, but the usual number is between 10,000 and 20,000 (Dale Witt). The Bear River marshes of Utah harbor about 12,000 migrants. Almost 100,000 lesser snows gather in October at Summer Lake, Oregon, and 300,000 additional snows are found 75 miles to the southwest in the Klamath Basin. Practically all of these geese eventually migrate to the Central Valley of California.

Spring. Many lesser snow geese shift migration cor-

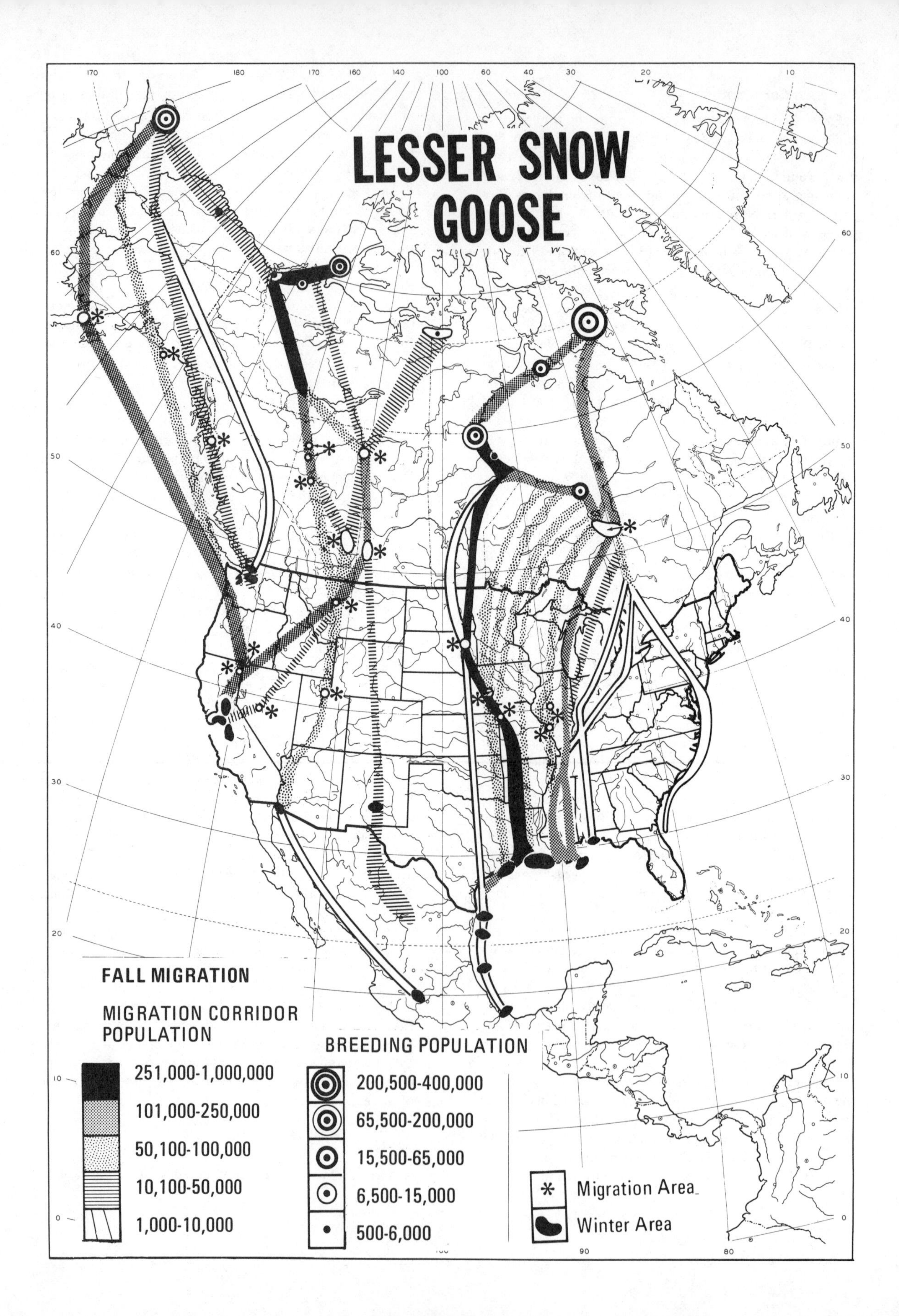
LESSER SNOW GOOSE
FALL MIGRATION
MIGRATION CORRIDOR POPULATION
251,000-1,000,000
101,000-250,000
50,100-100,000
10,100-50,000
1,000-10,000
BREEDING POPULATION
200,500-400,000
65,500-200,000
15,500-65,000
6,500-15,000
500-6,000
Migration Area
Winter Area

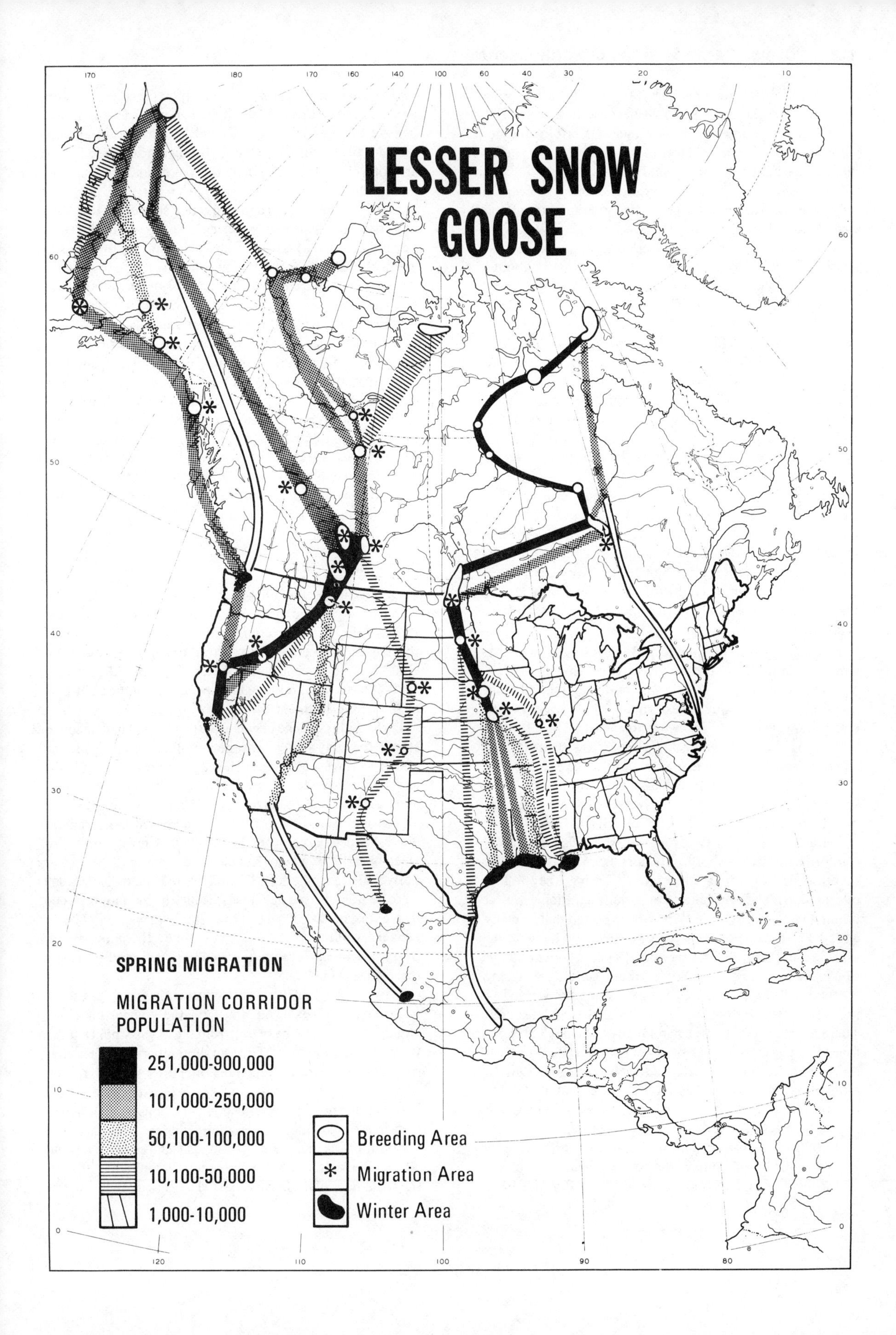
LESSER SNOW GOOSE
SPRING MIGRATION
MIGRATION CORRIDOR POPULATION
251,000-900,000
101,000-250,000
50,100-100,000
10,100-50,000
1,000-10,000
Breeding Area
Migration Area
Winter Area

ridors between fall and spring, but the details of the spring migration are not as well known because of a paucity of band recoveries and population data. Therefore, the description of migration corridors in the spring is more speculative, especially for Canada and Alaska.

The most notable shift in migration corridors occurs in mid-America. Lesser snow geese that migrate through the eastern part of the Mississippi Flyway in the fall swing west to rendezvous with the western contingent along the Missouri River in northwest Missouri. By easy stages, about 1 million snow geese advance up the Missouri Valley as snow and ice melt. Below Sioux City, Iowa, they leave the Missouri Valley to pass on to the vicinity of the Sand Lake National Wildlife Refuge, South Dakota. From there they move up to the Devils Lake region of North Dakota, then to Portage Plains west of Winnipeg, Manitoba. From these two areas, the snow geese depart almost en masse east-northeast for James Bay. Baillie (1955) reported large numbers passing east-northeast over Lake St. Joseph at Rat Rapids, Ontario, and 25 to 50 miles farther north at Pickle Crow, Mud Lake, and Spruce River.

The bulk of the snow geese in the spring return to their eastern Arctic nesting grounds via the west coast of James and Hudson bays. On May 19, 1973, an aerial survey disclosed over 1,400,000 distributed thusly: 325,000 along the west side of James Bay, north of Fort Albany; 300,000 on the southwest coast of Hudson Bay between Fort Severn and Winisk; and 810,000 in the vicinity of York Factory (Harry Lumsden).

A population of approximately 25,000 lesser snow geese, wintering in north-central Mexico and south-central New Mexico, apparently migrate nonstop during the fall from the staging area in southwestern Saskatchewan. In the spring, however, they first swing northeast to Two Buttes, Colorado (Michael Szymczak), where 3,000 to 4,000 stop, and then north to Alliance, Nebraska (George Schildman), where 15,000 pause before heading northwest for Saskatchewan. Most of the geese in this group apparently breed adjacent to Queen Maud Gulf (Barry 1966).

In the fall, the majority of the snow geese that migrate to California utilize offshore corridors from Alaska to the mouth of the Columbia River; in the spring, they follow interior corridors. This pattern of spring migration was first pointed out to me by Dale Witt, who reported that as many as 350,000 snow geese congregate at Freezeout Lake, Montana, in the spring, about three-fourths of the entire population in the Pacific Flyway. Witt further reported that spring trapping of 1,000 snow geese at Freezeout Lake yielded 11 recoveries from birds banded on Wrangel Island, Siberia. There have been only three band recoveries in fall in Montana from geese banded at Wrangel Island (Dale Witt), yet there were 465 for California and 196 for Oregon, 1961-66 (John Chattin). Consequently, it is apparent that large numbers of snow geese breeding on Wrangel Island migrate in a counter-clockwise fashion fall to spring.

A study of the spring migration of snow geese, made by Kozlik et al. (1959), contains the best information available on the location of their migration corridors after they head north from Freezeout Lake. From reports received of snow geese that were dyed at Tule Lake in northern California, I believe that most Wrangel Island geese migrate along a corridor from southern Alberta through the Grande Prairie area of west-central Alberta to the Yukon and Tanana river valleys in Alaska. From there, the corridor probably branches out to Norton and Kotzebue sounds on the Alaskan coast and then crosses Bering Strait to Wrangel Island. Several color-marked geese observed only in this coastal area, of the entire coast between Puget Sound and the Alaska Peninsula, suggest that the interior corridor divides at Grande Prairie, Alberta, with a side branch across the Rocky Mountains to the coast near Juneau, Alaska.

Many more snow geese are observed in interior Alaska during the spring than during the fall (Gabrielson and Lincoln 1959, Irving 1960, James King), lending further credence to a larger return passage along interior corridors. Irving (1960) reported consistent passage of snow geese through Anaktuvuk Pass in the spring but rarely in the fall. The snow geese that utilize the coastal route in the spring apparently remain closer to shore than in the fall, for in the spring, greater numbers of them stop at the deltas of the Stikine, Copper, and Susitna rivers.

Winter Areas

During the period 1970-74, there were about 1,100,000 lesser snow geese in the midcontinent at the start of winter. Prior to the 1970's, a comparatively small proportion of these geese wintered north of traditional areas along the Gulf Coast in Louisiana and Texas. But unpredictably, in 1970-71 large numbers began to spend at least the early part of the winter in the Midwest.

Perhaps this change began with the few that had begun to stop in the early 1950's near the mouth of the Illinois River and in northwest Missouri. The population wintering in the lower Illinois Valley increased to 2,000 by the late 1950's, and by the late 1960's became stabilized at 10,000 to 15,000. The group in northwest Missouri increased more rapidly but remained largely below the 25,000 level until mid-December 1970, when 133,000 were recorded.

By mid-December of 1972 and 1973, as many as 185,000 were being censused in Kansas; 16,000 in Oklahoma; 5,000 in Nebraska; 40,000 in southwest Iowa; and 115,000 in western Missouri. At the same time, the numbers in Louisiana those 2 years averaged 380,000, and in Texas there were 435,000.

Prior to the 1970's, the wintering snow geese in Louisiana and Texas remained on the coastal marshes, largely restricted to the region from the Mississippi Delta to Corpus Christi, Texas. Then large numbers of geese that wintered in eastern Louisiana marshes shifted to the western part of the state and north into the rice fields. Many thousands in Texas also left the coastal marshes to feed in the rice stubble, lying immediately to the north.

South of the rice field district that ends near Victoria, Texas, the wintering snow geese number about 10,000 for the remainder of the Texas coast. They are even less abundant along the east coast of Mexico: only 1,400 are found at Laguna Madre; 1,000 on lagoons near Tampico; and 200 south of Veracruz.

Most of the 23,000 snow geese that wintered in the interior of Mexico, 1958-64, were located at several lakes in the state of Chihuahua; the most important sites were Laguna de Babicora, 13,500 geese; Laguna de los Mexicanos, 3,200; and Laguna Bustillos, 1,300. An average of 2,500 geese have been found on Laguna de Santiaguillo near the center of the state of Durango.

Since 1968, a steady increase has occurred in the number of snow geese wintering at the Bosque del Apache National Wildlife Refuge on the Rio Grande River south of Socorro, New Mexico. They numbered 12,000 in January 1972, an increase of 9,000 in 4 years. This buildup has probably occurred at the expense of the winter grounds in the interior of Mexico.

The rapidly shifting patterns of distribution among wintering snow geese make it extremely difficult to pinpoint their winter distribution in mid-America. Their distribution in the Pacific Flyway has remained more traditional.

Over 90 percent of the 450,000 lesser snow geese that frequent the Pacific Flyway (1955-74) winter in California, 14,000 in the Imperial Valley and almost all the rest—some 400,000—in the Central Valley. By far the largest number of these (330,000) are found in the valley of the Sacramento River.

The area of Puget Sound winters about 21,000 snow geese, and a few hundred remain in southern British Columbia. About 200 winter in Oregon, 500 along the Colorado River in Arizona, and almost 4,000 in the Carson Sink area of Nevada. A few errant individuals winter in Idaho, Montana, and Utah but none winter in Wyoming and Colorado.

Fewer than 300 snow geese winter along the west coast of Mexico, but it is likely that the 1,000 to 1,500 that often winter on Lago de Chapala, near Guadalajara, are Pacific Coast birds.

MIGRATION BEHAVIOR

Lesser snow geese migrate in unusually large flocks—flocks of 100 to 1,000 are common—made up of many family units. They usually start their migration after sunset but continue their flight both night and day. Their speed of passage for 23 different flights was timed at 50 miles per hour.

Radar has fairly often recorded migrating snow geese at altitudes as high as 5,000 to 10,000 feet, but their usual passage is sustained between 2,000 and 3,000 feet (mean sea level). Aircraft pilots have reported them fairly often at 5,000 to 6,000 feet, infrequently at 11,000 to 12,000 feet, and on one occasion at the astonishing altitude of 20,000 feet!

Chronology

Fall. Nonbreeding snow geese are the first to fly and to begin to leave molt areas on Banks Island by mid-August for the northwestern edge of the Mackenzie Delta (Barry 1966). Early in September they are joined by the adults with their young. The main departure from the western Canadian Arctic occurs September 15-20, but, in 1966, departure was delayed until October 12.

Other records from this region indicate that snow geese departed Banks Island by the end of August and passed over Tuktoyaktuk during the first week in September (McEwen 1958). Porslid (1943) observed them migrating westward along the edge of the Mackenzie Delta on September 10, 1933.

In the eastern Canadian Arctic, Soper (1946) reported that lesser snow geese left Baffin Island on September 16, 1928, with large-scale departures occurring September 24-29. Macpherson and McLaren (1959) observed them leaving Baffin Island September 1-3. Geese, undoubtedly from Baffin Island, were observed to pass over the Belcher Islands, in southeastern Hudson Bay, on August 25, and in larger numbers on September 1 (Freeman 1970*b*). Fay (1961) observed snow geese from Wrangel Island, Siberia, passing over St. Lawrence Island, Alaska, between August 20 and September 20.

Reports from Stirrett (1954) indicate that snow geese began to arrive in southern James Bay about September 10 and continued their influx until the population reached a peak by October 18. They remained there in large numbers until late October or early November, depending upon time of freeze-up. However, small numbers of geese continually left the staging areas in southern James Bay and the southwestern coast of Hudson Bay from mid-September through October prior to the mass departure.

Geese migrating from James Bay to eastern Louisiana fly almost nonstop so that by November 1, two-thirds of the wintering population have reached their destination and by November 15, about 90 percent are there. Snow geese continue to arrive in west Louisiana and coastal Texas in early October, but the peak is delayed until December because large segments of the population linger for several weeks at Sand Lake, South Dakota, and the Missouri River in Iowa and Missouri.

Snow geese begin to arrive at Sand Lake late in September, reach peak numbers by the end of the month, and are largely gone by late November. In the Midwest, a few small flocks appear in early October, and peak numbers are reached the last half of that month. Fairly large numbers prolong their stay until late November.

Small numbers of snow geese arrive on their great concentration grounds in southeast Alberta and southwest Saskatchewan in early September. Numbers rapidly increase until mid-October, and most are gone by early November. At Freezeout Lake, Montana, small numbers arrive late in September, peak numbers are usually reached the first week in November, and most have departed by the end of that month. The chronology of passage into the Bear River marshes of Utah parallels that at Freezeout Lake.

By mid-September an advance contingent of several hundred lesser snows has already reached the Klamath Basin of northern California. By mid-October there are

85,000, and a peak of 250,000 by mid-November is followed soon thereafter by a rapid exodus to winter grounds in the Central Valley of California. While some migrants are arriving at Klamath Basin, others are assembling in the Central Valley so that over 150,000 are already present there prior to the influx from the Klamath Basin the third week in November.

Spring. When the melting of icebound lakes and sloughs and the diminishing snow cover expose areas of bare land, lesser snow geese move north. They are more of one mind and in a greater hurry than in the fall. Sometimes winter does not retreat quickly enough, particularly in the Dakotas, and the geese overfly ice-covered lakes and snow-covered fields only to turn back. Occasionally, a late blizzard forces them to retreat temporarily, but they push ever northward with the faintest hint of spring.

In late February or early March the midcontinent group of over half a million birds leaves the Gulf Coast for northwest Missouri. There they reach peak numbers in mid-March; by the end of March over 90 percent have resumed their northward flight. At Sand Lake, in northeastern South Dakota, they begin to appear by mid-March, but large numbers do not arrive until a week later and peak numbers not until the second week in April.

The first spring migrants appear west of Winnipeg early in April and large numbers arrive near the middle of the month (Soper 1942). They reach James Bay in late April and early May. Baillie (1955) described a spectacular flight midway between Winnipeg and James Bay on May 4-6, 1942. He noticed a few migrating flocks thereafter until May 17.

Migrating snow geese passed over the Belcher Islands in Hudson Bay on May 10, 1959, and on May 20 and 25, 1960 (Freeman 1970*b*). They reached Churchill, Manitoba, on May 20, 1965 (Littlefield and Pakulak 1969). At McConnell River, Northwest Territories, they arrived May 23, 1960, and May 29, 1959, with peak numbers on May 28-29 and June 1 (MacInnes 1962). On their breeding grounds on Southampton Island, lesser snow geese were recorded as arriving on May 29, 1953 (Barry 1956), June 2, 1940, and June 8, 1939 (Manning 1942).

Lesser snow geese wintering in the Imperial and Central valleys of California begin their northward trek in early February. All but the laggards have moved farther north by early March. They remain about a month in the vicinity of Klamath Basin and Malheur Refuge before departing in mid-April for southeastern Alberta. At this stage of migration, they follow the snow clearance by a week or so (Barry 1966). However, north of the agricultural zone these geese migrate more quickly so that in subarctic areas they pass the snow-melt line.

The first flocks reach central Alberta by April 20, where they feed in grain fields until early May (Barry 1966). Some flocks arrive at Hay Lake, in northwestern Alberta, the first week in May. The earliest arrival noted at the Athabasca Delta occurred on April 27, 1932 (Soper 1951), and the latest northward flight observed was on May 22, 1933.

Recorded dates of first arrivals of snow geese on the Mackenzie Delta were May 9, 1927, and May 10, 1932, and the last migrants appeared on May 22 (Porslid 1943). A short distance to the east (150 miles) at the delta of the Anderson River, Barry (1966) reported the dates of early arrivals to be May 15, 1963, and May 19, 1960, with late arrivals occurring on May 26, 1962, and June 9, 1959.

In 1953, snow geese arrived at the large breeding area on Banks Island between May 16 and June 18, with a peak on May 29 (Manning et al. 1956). In 1955, they arrived at almost identical times, May 17 and June 14, with the largest number of arrivals occurring on May 30 (McEwen 1958). The first arrivals at the Perry River breeding area occurred on June 1, 1964, and June 3, 1963 (Ryder 1967).

The snow geese that migrated to far-off Wrangel Island to breed arrived in interior Alaska as follows: Fairbanks, May 5-May 18, average date May 11, 1952-56 (Rowinski 1958); Fort Yukon, May 12, 1950, and May 6, 1951 (Gabrielson and Lincoln 1959); and Anaktuvuk Pass, May 20, 1949, and May 14, 1953 (Irving 1960). Those that migrated along the coast were earlier: March 30-April 17 at Stikine Delta, April 25 at Susitna Delta, and April 29 on the Yukon Delta (Gabrielson and Lincoln 1959). They have been reported passing St. Lawrence Island on May 20-29 (Fay 1961). Dates of first arrivals on Wrangel Island were May 21, 1963 and 1964, and May 22, 1957 (Uspenski 1965). Mass influx followed first arrivals by 3 days in 1957, 4 days in 1963, and 14 days in 1964.

The first intrepid arrivals are usually adult geese, but yearling birds may accompany some adults—most of the yearlings arrive 1 to 2 weeks later (Barry 1966). In migration, the male invariably leads his mate in flight, the opposite of ducks, where the female leads.

BREEDING

Behavior

Pair Bond. Pairing probably occurs on the breeding grounds among 2-year-old birds. Cooch (1958) concluded that although lesser snow geese reach sexual maturity at 2 years of age, the majority do not breed until their third year and in some seasons not until their fourth year. Barry (1966) concurred that most snow geese nest for the first time when in their third summer, but that in particularly favorable seasons, some 2-year-olds may breed. Mating apparently occurs during northward migration, particularly at rest stops immediately preceding their last passage to their nesting grounds. The yearlings do not return to their specific natal colony site but remain on nearby water areas.

Homing. Barry (1966) found that during their second year only 17 percent of the geese banded as young returned to their nesting colony but that 51 percent appeared there in their third season. One of nine banded adult hens that returned to breed in the colony on Southampton Island used the same nest site (Cooch 1958); the others nested within 300 feet of their original sites.

When lesser snow geese return to their nesting colonies, the ground is covered by snow except for ridgetops and other windswept areas. As the snow melts, flocks break up into small groups and then into pairs (Barry 1966). Each pair occupies an area of bare ground that is vigorously defended. Prior to incubation, a male on his territory attacks intruding males, his mate intruding females.

Territory. Territories vary greatly in size with the demands upon space. Where the area of bare ground is limited by delayed snow melt, pressure on territory size is tremendous. Territories are smaller in the interior of a nesting colony; they steadily decrease in size as incubation progresses.

At Boas River on Southampton Island, Cooch (1958) found that territories ranged in size from 18 to 38 square yards per goose and that the geese would tolerate densities as high as one nest per 6 square yards—an avian "inner city." Barry (1966) reported that nests were as little as 10 to 15 feet apart in dense areas in the central part of a colony at Anderson Delta but that along a ridge 100 to 200 feet wide they averaged about 50 feet apart. Nest density at the McConnell River colony was 323 square yards per nest, 15 per acre (Harvey 1971). On Wrangel Island, Uspenski (1965) reported an average density of 12.5 nests per acre (range, 4.9 to 25.9).

Nesting

Lesser snow geese usually locate their nesting colonies on low grassy tundra plains—within a few miles of the sea, along broad shallow rivers near the coast, and on islands in shallow lakes 10 to 80 miles inland. All of the colonies along Hudson Bay are near the coast, as are those on the Anderson River delta and Kendall Island. The small colonies south of Queen Maud Gulf are on islands in shallow lakes; the large colony on Banks Island is located on both sides of the Egg River, about 16 miles from the west coast. The principal colony on Wrangel Island is in the valley of the Tundovaya River (Uspenski 1965).

Nest Sites. The nest of the lesser snow goose is a built-up scrape requiring several years to reach final form (Cooch 1958). Beginning nests are little more than scrapes in moss or gravel that are enlarged by the females as eggs are laid, the eggs being covered with material from the depressions. Moss, willows, and grass are added to old nests to form fairly substantial raised structures. The female deposits a small amount of down in the bowl of the nest, some with the first egg but most with the third and fourth egg (Barry 1966).

Clutch Size, Eggs, and Incubation. The eggs of the lesser snow goose are elliptical ovate, measure 80.5 by 53.0 mm (83 specimens), and are white, later becoming stained a yellowish hue from the nest material.

Cooch (1958) found that females usually laid an egg a day for the first three eggs, skipped a day, and then completed their clutches. An average of 1.3 days per egg laid was found for snow geese studied by Ryder (1970*a*), who reported an interval of 2.4 days to complete a clutch of two eggs to 9.8 days to complete a clutch of seven.

Clutches vary in size from 2 to 10 eggs, but only a small proportion of the nests contain more than 5. For six regional nest studies of the snow goose, the average clutch size was 3.90 (3,514), the largest was 4.42 for Southampton Island (Cooch 1958), and the lowest was 3.2 for Wrangel Island in 1965 (Uspenski 1965). In years of normal weather, clutch size on Wrangel Island was 5-6 eggs, but the late spring in 1964 accounted for the small clutch size that year. The smallest average clutch size in eight seasons at Anderson Delta, 3.2, occurred when the snow melt was delayed the longest (Barry 1966). The largest clutch size, 4.3, occurred with one of the earliest snow melts.

Dump nesting is rare. The largest dump nest found at the Anderson Delta contained 16 eggs (Barry 1966). Dump nesting occurs when a pair of snow geese are evicted from their nest territory by other pairs. Many small clutches probably occur because nests are destroyed during the laying period and the remaining ova developed are deposited in new nests. Lesser snow geese are determinate layers—they have no ability to renest once the developed ova have been passed or resorbed. Each day that a snow goose delays initiating her clutch, the smaller the clutch will be (Cooch 1958).

When the last egg is laid, the female begins incubation. The male guards the nest site from other snow geese and from predators, charging intruders with outstretched wings and neck and calling defiantly. The female leaves the nest only briefly in the early stages of incubation and seldom if at all in the later stages. A female observed by Cooch (1958) remained on her nest continually during 72 hours of observation. Such devotion to duty causes adult females to lose 25 percent of their spring weight by the time of hatching (Cooch 1958).

At the nesting colony near the McConnell River, Harvey (1971) observed more than 20 dead females on or near their nests; the weight loss of four was 43 percent, which suggests starvation as the cause of death. McEwen (1958) also reported finding dead geese after 2 days of strong winds and rain during the period of hatching.

The incubation period averaged 23.1 days for 201 nests observed by Cooch (1958); Ryder (1970*a*) reported 22.4 days of incubation for 48 nests, ranging from 19 to 24 days, and a period of 1.4 days for the eggs in a single nest to hatch.

Chronology of Nesting. When snow conditions allow, snow geese begin to nest within a few days after their arrival on the breeding grounds. Soper (1946) reported that laying started on Baffin Island June 20, 1929, and reached a peak on July 3. In 6 years, 1952-57, at Southampton Island, the earliest date of laying the first egg was June 4, 1952, the latest, June 16, 1957, and the average, June 10 (Cooch 1958); the average date that the last egg was laid was June 23. At Perry River, peak nesting occurred during July 14-17, 1949 (Hanson et al. 1956). Later, at the same place, Ryder (1967) found that egg-laying started on June 4, 1963, and June 7, 1964.

Geese at the McConnell River colony initiated laying on May 28, 1960, and June 1, 1959 (MacInnes 1962). Barry (1966) reported that over a 6-year period at Anderson Delta, snow geese commenced laying between May 23 (1961) and June 11 (1959), with an average date of May 31. On Banks Island, laying was started by June 6, 1955 (McEwen 1958). The initiation of laying on Wrangel Island varied from May 26, 1957, to June 10, 1958, and over a 6-year period the average date was June 3 (Uspenski 1965). Mass laying was underway only a few days later.

The evidence at hand indicates that laying in the nesting colonies of the western and southern Arctic begins a week or more sooner than in the colonies of the eastern Arctic.

Nest Success. Lesser snow geese are extremely successful nesters except during years of unusually severe weather. During the 8 years of his study at Anderson River, Barry (1966) found that only 6.2 percent of 3,929 nests failed completely. At the Karrak Lake colony, Ryder (1971*a*) determined that all but 13.8 percent of 124 nests failed to hatch at least one egg. On Wrangel Island, Uspenski (1965) reported that 12.9 percent of 741 nests observed were unoccupied at the time of discovery.

Cooch (1958), including both successful and unsuccessful nests on Southampton Island, noted a high of 4.1 hatched eggs per nest in 1952 and a low of 3.1 eggs in 1957. Excluding complete failures, he found a range from a high of 4.2 hatched eggs per successful nest in 1952 to a low of 3.6 in 1956. Egg loss in successful nests amounted to 6 percent. An apparent egg loss of 3 percent occurred among successful nests studied by Barry (1966) at Anderson Delta. Ryder (1970*a*) reported that 31 percent of all eggs laid in both successful and unsuccessful nests at Karrak Lake failed to hatch. Harvey (1971) observed that at the McConnell River colony, egg loss during the incubation period amounted to 20 percent and resulted almost entirely from the abandonment or destruction of complete nests, usually occurring immediately prior to hatch. Only 1 egg in 327 disappeared from nests that hatched successfully.

Barry (1966) found a relationship between nest success and snow cover; the earlier that snow cover exposed bare soil, the greater the subsequent hatch. In 1964 at Wrangel Island, Uspenski (1965) observed that late-melting snow caused many mature birds to forego nesting. The largest proportion of nonbreeding geese occurred where snow was late in melting and nest density was at its lowest. For each day that nest initiation was delayed, there was a corresponding decrease in the number of eggs that hatched (Cooch 1958); desertion accounted for the largest share of these losses.

Reasons for the desertion of large numbers of nests late in incubation are unknown, but Harvey (1971) postulated that hunger caused incubating birds to abandon their nests.

When pairs leave their nests, the eggs are exposed to predation by herring and glaucous gulls and by parasitic jaegers. The attendance of the parent birds protects the eggs from such depredations. At the colony on Banks Island, McEwen (1958) considered the Arctic fox to be the most serious predator on the eggs of snow geese, but he believed that adverse weather was the most important factor controlling production.

Lynch (1971) calculated the productivity of lesser snow geese by observing parents with goslings in December populations. From 1950 to 1971, 57 percent of the mature breeders that appeared on the Gulf Coast had young. Successful breeders ranged from a low of 10 percent in 1954 to a high of 97 percent in 1959. In the Pacific Flyway, mature adults were successful in rearing young an average of 46 percent of the time, with a low of 6 percent in 1965 and a high of 79 percent in 1960 (Lynch 1971).

The thread of evidence among all the nest studies on lesser snow geese indicates that the great variations in the hatch are caused by weather. A late melt of snow cover, with a consequent delay in nesting, is particularly detrimental. The flooding of nests is of local importance (Cooch 1958).

Rearing of Young

Broods. Both parents guard the brood, but only the female broods the young. Brooding steadily decreases in frequency as the young mature and ceases when they are 2 to 3 weeks old (Cooch 1958). The parents lead the broods from the nesting grounds during the first days of life, apparently in a search for food. Broods have been found as far as 30 miles from their nest areas. Many families of lesser snow geese tend to group in packs and move together.

Development. With long daylight hours in which to feed, young snow geese grow rapidly. Cooch (1958) reported that goslings weighed 2.5 ounces when hatched and within 90 days weighed over 80 ounces. The young were completely fledged in 45 days but short flights were made as early as 35 days (Cooch 1958). The first flights of young geese at Southampton Island, 1952-57, occurred August 15, and the latest initial flights occurred on August 25.

Survival. Losses among broods are highest during their first week of life. Cooch (1958) recorded a 15 percent shrinkage in brood size between the date of hatch and the end of the first week. Between the first and twelfth week an additional 14 percent of the goslings were lost. Broods of lesser snow geese at Southampton Island averaged 3.5 (141) the first week and 3.0 (140) the twelfth week.

In their first week of life at Banks Island, broods averaged 3.3 (419) goslings (McEwen 1958). Broods at McConnell River averaged 3.5 (143) early in life, only slightly below clutch size (Harvey 1971). At Wrangel Island in

1964, broods about 1 week old averaged 2.7 (33) goslings (Uspenski 1965).

After some removal of immatures by hunters, Lynch (1971) found an average survival in December, 1956-71, of 2.0 goslings per successful family for those snow geese that winter along the Gulf of Mexico. The number of young per "December brood" ranged from a low of 1.6 in 1971 to a high of 2.5 in 1959 and 1966. Geese wintering in the Pacific Flyway during the same period averaged 2.1 goslings per successful family, ranging from 1.7 in 1967 to 2.6 in 1966.

POSTBREEDING SEASON

The first snow geese to molt are the yearlings, followed by 2-year-olds and those mature breeders that failed to nest successfully, and then by the successful breeders. At Southampton Island, the molt of subadults started about July 8, 1952-57, and the last ones entered the molt as late as July 23 (Cooch 1958). Subadults at the Anderson Delta began to molt about July 1 (Barry 1966).

At Southampton Island, the successful breeders commenced their molt about July 26, with tardy individuals delaying until August 5. Thus, these birds molted 13 to 18 days later than the nonbreeding ones. Barry (1966) reported that the molt of successful nesters at the Anderson Delta occurred about 2.5 weeks after the young had hatched; the molt appeared to be regulated by the timing of nesting, which in turn is determined by weather conditions in spring.

Molting snow geese are able to fly again about 24 days after losing their flight feathers (Cooch 1958, Barry 1966); breeding adults regain their powers of flight either a few days before or by the time the goslings are able to fly. Families at Southampton Island are, therefore, able to take flight together between August 15 and 25.

FOOD HABITS

The varied food habits of snow geese have become revolutionized in recent years by agriculture. As evidenced by the cutting edges on their mandibles, the birds had evolved over the centuries an effective tool for clipping the rootstocks of bulrushes and marsh grasses.

On the coastal marshes of Louisiana and in the Arctic, snow geese still feed the way they did centuries ago. A major staging area in the Arctic is the Mackenzie Delta, where they first feed on sedges, grasses, and horsetails and later, inland, on cranberry, curlewberry, salmonberry, and cotton grass tubers (Barry 1966). On James Bay, the principal foods of these geese are horsetails, prairie and common three-square bulrushes, and sedges (Stirrett 1954).

On the Louisiana coastal marshes, lesser snow geese feed largely on the roots and tubers of Olney's, salt-marsh, and three-square bulrushes and on the rootstocks of cordgrass and cattail (McIlhenny 1932). For several decades it has been known that a wet cover burn is the best way to attract multitudes of snow geese to a particular marsh area. The burn makes it easier for the geese to grub for roots of marsh plants and encourages the growth of the succulent green shoots that the birds relish (Hoffpauer 1968).

Several decades ago in California, snow geese began to shift from marsh plants to food produced by agriculture. Their use of agricultural plants spread through the West, then the Midwest, Texas, and, recently, into the pasturelands and rice fields of Louisiana.

In California, these birds feed upon the grains of barley, wheat, and rice and graze upon the green shoots of pasture grasses and the cereal grains. These crops are important sources of food for snow geese almost everywhere in the West. The tubers and rootstocks of bulrushes and cattails are utilized at Bear River marshes, Utah; Klamath Basin, California; and Summer Lake, Oregon. Snow geese on the Bear River marshes feed almost exclusively on the succulent tips of shoots and the tubers of alkali bulrush, and in the wheat and barley fields of Utah they seek the young shoots of volunteer grain and weeds rather than the kernels of waste grain (Nagel 1969). Snow geese in the Midwest frequent mechanically picked cornfields for waste grain and supplement their diet by grazing on shoots of winter wheat. Increasing numbers of geese are delaying their southward migration in the Midwest to feast on waste corn. In the early 1970's, several hundred thousand snow geese lingered along the Missouri River in Iowa, Nebraska, Missouri, and Kansas into January. In both Texas and Louisiana, many thousands now winter just to the north of the coastal marshes, where they feed on pasture grasses and in rice fields.

Greater Snow Goose

Anser caerulescens atlantica

Other Common Names: Wavie, brant

VITAL STATISTICS

Length:	Adult male, 28-33 inches, average 31 inches (20) Adult female, 28-32 inches, average 30 inches (20) Immature male, 28-32 inches, average 30 inches (65) Immature female, 25-30 inches, average 28 inches (64)
Wing:	Adult male, 18.4 inches (23) Adult female, 17.7 inches (23) Immature male, 17.5 inches (74) Immature female, 16.9 inches (69)
Weight:	Male, 7.44 pounds (19) Female, 6.12 pounds (12)

IDENTIFICATION

The greater snow goose is a slightly larger edition of the white-phase of the lesser snow goose. No color dimorphism has been discovered in this race. In the field it is virtually impossible to tell these two races apart. In the hand, the larger size and longer bill of the greater snow goose may distinguish it from its smaller counterpart.

According to J. D. Heyland, the bill lengths (exposed culmen) of the greater snow goose are as follows: adult males, 65.5 mm (23); adult females, 64.4 mm (23); juvenile males, 64.5 mm (74); juvenile females, 61.1 mm (69). Corresponding measurements for the lesser snow goose are: adult males, 56.2 mm (32); adult females, 53.3 mm (36); juvenile males, 55.9 mm (36); juvenile females, 52.6 mm (35) (Trauger et al. 1971).

Occasionally on the Atlantic Coast a lone lesser snow goose in the blue-phase is observed with a flock of greater snows. The difference in size between the two varieties may then be discernible in the field.

POPULATION STATUS

The breeding grounds of the greater snow goose are so remote that its status has mainly been determined from winter surveys. The winter population, 1955-74, averaged 54,000. The two population extremes of 29,500 and 95,000 were recorded in 1970 and 1974.

On October 24, 1969, J. D. Heyland censused 73,585 greater snow geese on the St. Lawrence River, with 6,000 additional geese in Delaware. On May 14 of that year there were 89,580 on the St. Lawrence. On October 27, 1970, Heyland censused 111,330 on the river at a time when 9,000 additional geese were already in Delaware. The subsequent winter survey revealed only 48,500. It is evident, then, that varying numbers of greater snow geese have been overlooked on their winter grounds, which include vast stretches of coastal waters. Thus, the population is probably from 50 to 100 percent larger than the average of 54,000 recorded on the winter surveys.

Fall populations (representing almost the entire continental population of greater snow geese) on the St. Lawrence River below Quebec City have increased remarkably since 1900. The number of geese stopping there was estimated to be 2,000 to 3,000 in 1900; 5,000 to 6,000 in 1921; 10,000 in 1937; 20,000 in 1941; 30,000 in 1951; 47,500 in 1958 (Godfrey 1966); and 111,330 in 1970 (J. D. Heyland). Winter inventory figures, 1955-74, show a 74 percent increase during the 20-year period. Except for an unusually low level in 1970, the upward trend has been fairly consistent.

Age Ratios

On the average, young snow geese made up 23.7 percent

of the December populations in 1956-71 (Lynch 1972). The proportion of young was far below this level in 1958, 1961, 1965, 1967, 1968, and 1971 but was considerably above average in 1956, 1957, 1959, 1960, 1963, 1966, and 1970.

DISTRIBUTION

The breeding, migration, and winter areas of the greater snow goose are all restricted to a small section of Greenland, several Arctic islands in the extreme northeastern part of Canada, a narrow migration corridor through eastern Canada, and the northeastern United States to the middle Atlantic Coast.

Breeding Season

The greater snow goose nests in such far northern regions of the Arctic that its breeding grounds are seldom inventoried. The largest and best-known breeding grounds are on Bylot Island, off the northeast coast of Baffin Island, Northwest Territories, Canada. About 15,000 greater snow geese nested on Bylot Island in 1957, in small scattered colonies with 25 to 300 nests (Lemieux 1959).

Northern Ellesmere Island, particularly the Fosheim Peninsula, probably supports the second largest number of breeding greater snow geese. Parmelee and MacDonald (1960) reported that greater snow geese were common summer residents on the Fosheim Peninsula, and Tener (1963) reported 2,320 adults on Ellesmere Island in 1961, 1,090 of which were on the Fosheim Peninsula. A breeding population of 1,047 adults occurred on adjacent Axel Heiberg Island (Tener 1963). These breeding areas are almost as far north as land extends into the Arctic Ocean and are less than 800 miles from the North Pole.

The greater snow goose is one of the few North American birds that nest in Greenland. It breeds in small scattered colonies near Thule and between Robertson and MacCormick bays (Salomonsen 1950-51). Heyland and Boyd (1970) surveyed the region of these two bays in July 1969 and found about 500 adults at the head of MacCormick Bay. They speculated that there were no more than 1,000 greater snow geese in all of Greenland.

Small numbers of greater snow geese have also been known to breed on islands in the northeastern Canadian Arctic—Devon, Somerset, and the northern part of Baffin (Parmelee and MacDonald 1960). In the aerial survey of 18 islands in the Queen Elizabeth group, Tener (1963) found 57 snow geese on Bathurst Island, 5 on Melville, 5 on Cornwallis, 2 on Prince Patrick, and a flock on Devon. Although Tener could not be certain of their race, he inferred from their far northern location that they were greater snow geese.

Migration Corridors

The migration corridor used by greater snow geese in passage from their breeding grounds to their migration stop between Rivière du Loup and Quebec City is largely conjectural. According to White and Lewis (1937), large numbers of these geese stopped in migration on lakes at the headwaters on the Manikuagan River, about 75 miles west of the Labrador border and almost midway between Ungava Bay and the St. Lawrence Estuary. The geese have been observed in spring passing down the St. Lawrence River past Murray Bay, so somewhere east of there they turn northward to strike, perhaps, the Manikuagan River.

There are spring migration records of greater snow geese at Winchester, New Hampshire; Lenox, Massachusetts; Ossining, New York; Union, Boonton, and Troy Meadows, New Jersey; and Upper Darby, Pennsylvania. These observations fall along a fairly well defined corridor between Quebec City and Delaware Bay.

Apparently, in both fall and spring migration the entire greater snow goose population stops at the St. Lawrence River, centering on Cape Tourmente, 40 miles below Quebec City. From there they migrate directly across country to arrive at the New Jersey coast near Atlantic City and at Delaware Bay near Dover, Delaware. The majority eventually pass farther south to winter on the coast of Virginia and North Carolina.

Winter Areas

The largest number of greater snow geese, about 30,000 (1958-72), winter in Currituck and Pamlico sounds of North Carolina, particularly in the area of Pea Island. About 19,000 birds spend the winter in Virginia, largely at Back Bay. Most of the 700 snow geese that winter in Maryland are on Chincoteague Bay, and the 670 in Delaware are located on or near the Bombay Hook National Wildlife Refuge. Slightly over 5,000 (1958-72) snow geese winter in New Jersey along the lower coast and on Delaware Bay near Fortescue.

Fewer than 100 move south of North Carolina in winter, and most of these are on the South Carolina coast. A few strays may occasionally appear north of New Jersey.

MIGRATION BEHAVIOR

The scarcity of records of this goose in passage suggests that it usually migrates at altitudes above 2,000 feet. Spring flocks vary in size from 35 to 400. According to White and Lewis (1937), flocks that departed the area of the St. Lawrence River in the spring contained several hundred birds and were much larger than flocks that arrived in the fall. Departure of greater snow geese from the area of Cape Tourmente in the fall generally took place by day but sometimes occurred at night (White and Lewis 1937).

Chronology

Fall. Parmelee and MacDonald (1960) reported that flocks of snow geese departed the Fosheim Peninsula on August 20 and 23, 1955; within a few days most of the geese had gone. In 1954, none were noted after August 20. Some nonbreeders take flight from their far northern nesting

SNOW GOOSE *

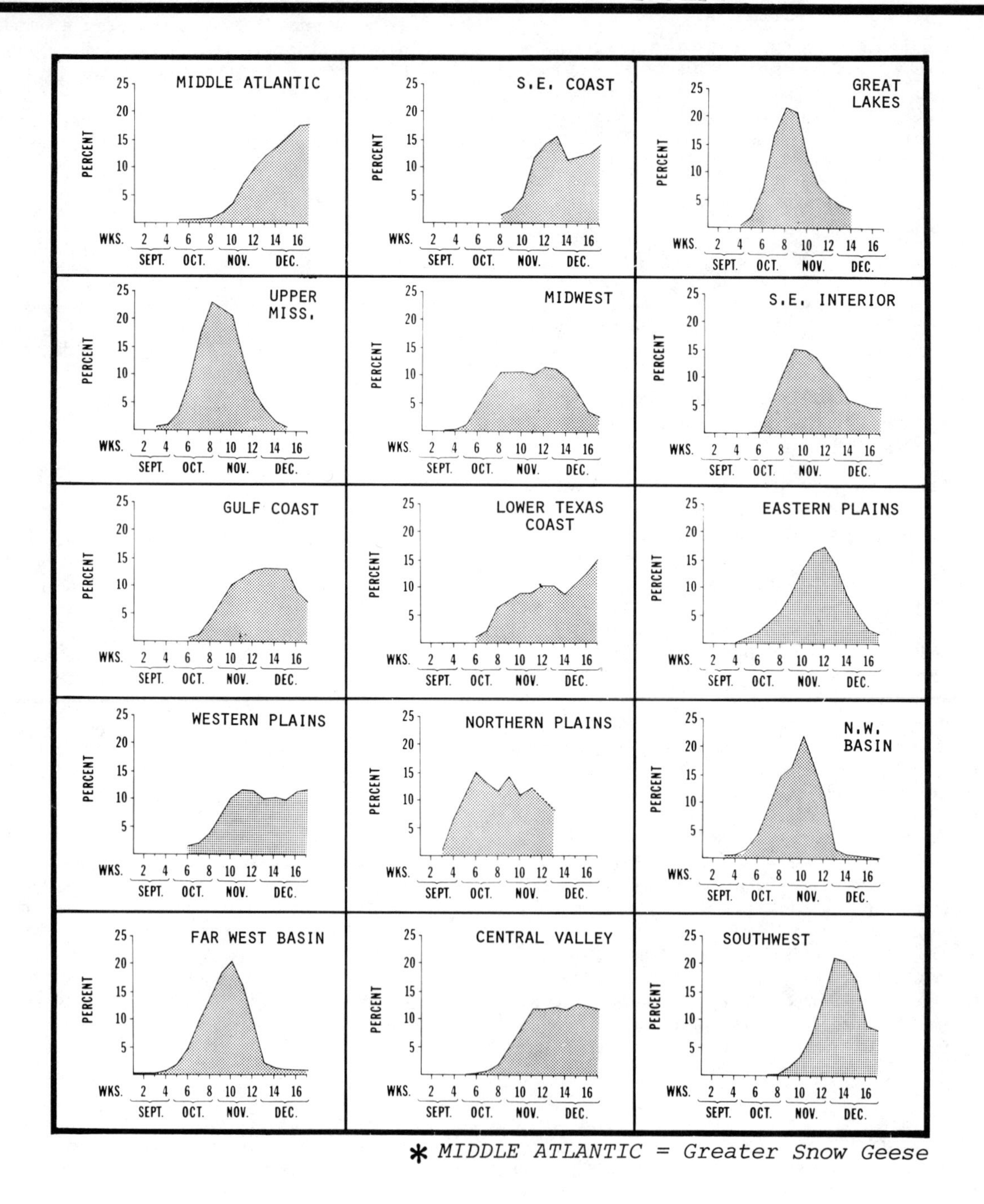

* *MIDDLE ATLANTIC = Greater Snow Geese*

Fall

* SNOW GOOSE

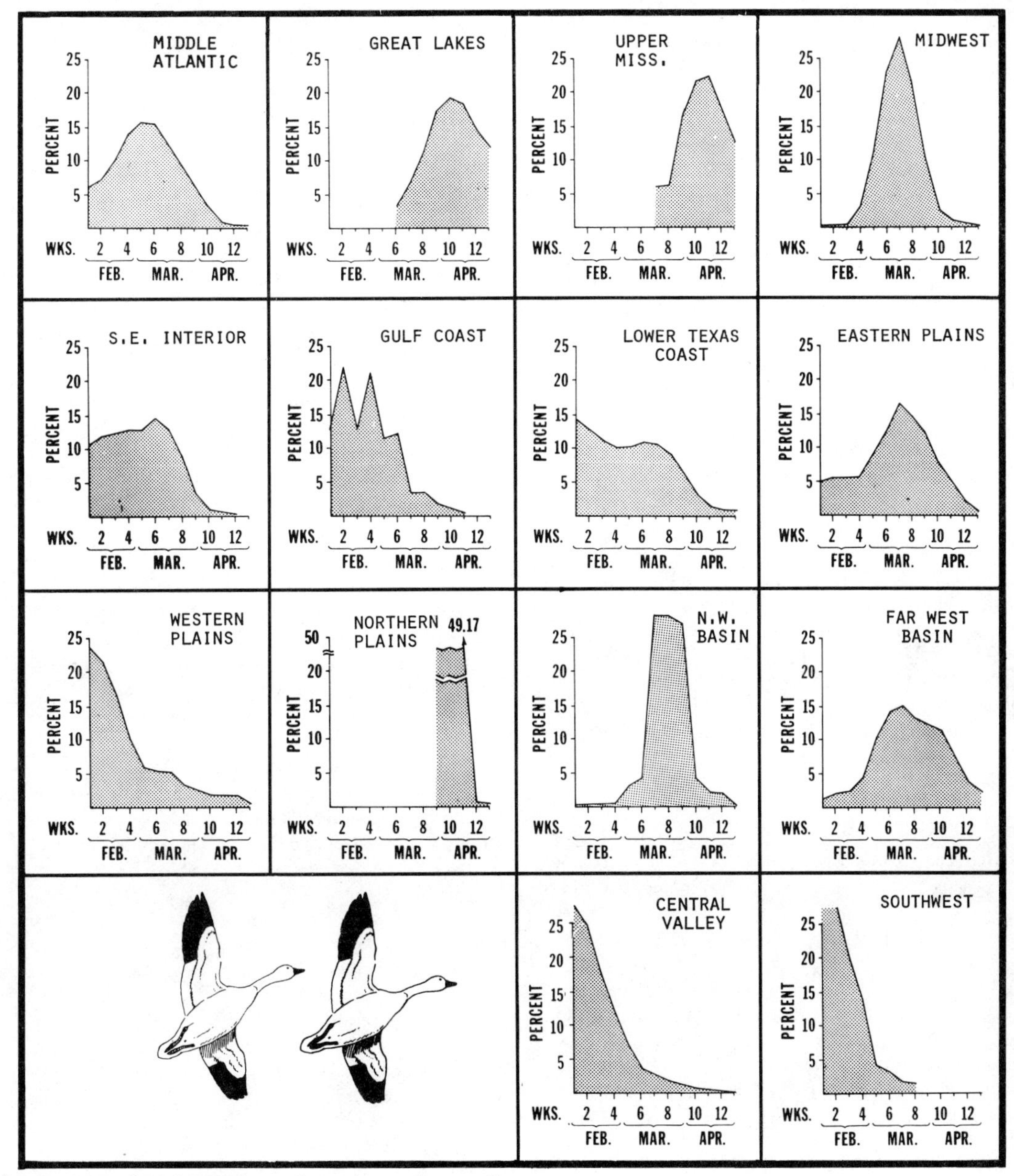

* *MIDDLE ATLANTIC = Greater Snow Geese*

Spring

grounds in August—before all goslings are fledged. Salomonsen (1950-51) reported that snow geese left Greenland before mid-September, as soon as the molt was complete and the young had fledged.

White and Lewis (1937) observed that snow geese began to arrive on the St. Lawrence River, below Quebec City, about September 12, and that flocks continued to arrive steadily, increasing the population, for the next month. The first arrivals were adults; family groups arrived later. After October 10, young birds made up a large part of the population. Most of the geese remained on the St. Lawrence River until freeze-up, sometime between November 15 and 30.

A few hundred greater snows—the vanguard—appear on Delaware Bay in late September. Sizable contingents reach their winter grounds early in November, but most of the population does not arrive until the third week of that month. The chronology of arrivals and departures at Delaware Bay varies considerably from year to year, depending upon freezing of shoal water areas there and on the St. Lawrence River.

Spring. Snow geese commence to leave their winter grounds in North Carolina and in the Back Bay area of Virginia for Delaware Bay about mid-February but, in some years, delay large departures until well into March. They remain in Delaware Bay into April. Records of snow geese in passage between Delaware Bay and the St. Lawrence River occur between April 6 and 16. White and Lewis (1937) reported that greater snow geese began to arrive on the St. Lawrence River the last of March or early in April and remained until about May 20.

The first glimpse of greater snow geese on Bylot Island in 1957 occurred on May 30, and the number of local birds increased rapidly (Lemieux 1959). At Fosheim Peninsula, Ellesmere Island, they arrived from their winter grounds in late May or early June (Parmelee and MacDonald 1960). In the Thule District of Greenland, the snow geese arrived in early June (Salomonsen 1950-51).

BREEDING

Breeding adults separate from flocks of nonbreeding birds along the coast, and, as pairs, move inland to nesting grounds. On Bylot Island, the greater snows nest 0.25 to 2 miles from the coast, principally on well-drained westward slopes but also on hilltops where vegetation occurs (Lemieux 1959). They do not always use the same colony sites each year—probably the deciding factor is the distribution of snow cover.

Lemieux (1959) found colonies of greater snow geese on Bylot Island about 1 mile apart along a 15-mile stretch of coast. Some of the nests were only 15 to 20 feet apart. In another area on Bylot Island, nests were widely separated on knolls and hillcrests (Drury 1961).

Nesting

The nests are scrapes, with pieces of the surrounding vegetation added, and are lined with down. An egg is laid each day, except for the frequent lapse of a day after the third egg (Lemieux 1959).

Clutch Size, Eggs, and Incubation. The average clutch size of snow geese on Bylot Island in 1957 was 4.6 eggs (118), with a range of 2 to 9. The clutches initiated earliest averaged 6.5. The number of eggs laid diminished in proportion to the number of days initiation was delayed. For example, a delay of 4 days caused the clutch size to decline to 4.0 (Lemieux 1959). Eggs removed from nests were not replaced, which indicated that there is no compensation for eggs lost or destroyed.

The eggs of the greater snow goose are elliptical ovate, 81.2 mm in length by 53.4 mm in width (123).

The female incubates while the male stands guard at a particular spot within a few feet of the nest. Lemieux (1959) observed both sexes defending the small territory around the nest from intrusion by other snow geese.

Of 18 nests for which incubation was determined, 8 nests hatched in 23 days, 6 nests in 24 days, and 4 in 25 days (Lemieux 1959).

Chronology of Nesting. On Bylot Island, 1957, egg-laying started in the earliest nests on June 8, and the last egg was laid in late nests on June 20. Egg-laying was at a peak between June 12 and 17 (Lemieux 1959). The hatch in 56 nests occurred between July 8 and 13; two nests hatched later.

Nest Success. In 1957 the fate of 52 nests on Bylot Island was determined. Thirty-five of these nests hatched successfully, although eight of them lost eggs. Thirteen of the unsuccessful nests were deserted and four were destroyed by predators (the Arctic fox). Scattered nests have been found by other ornithological expeditions to Bylot and Ellesmere islands.

Far more important than predators in limiting production of young is the failure of a large proportion of the population to breed in certain years. In 1953, snow geese were abundant nesters on the Fosheim Peninsula; in 1954 there were few nests. Again in 1955, almost the entire population in this region failed to nest (Parmelee and MacDonald 1960). A near failure in the production of young snow geese in 1954 was also reported for Bylot Island by Drury (1961). He attributed the low production of young to the late snow melt coincident with the low ebb in the lemming population that channeled fox predation to their nests.

On an aerial survey of Ellesmere and Axel Heiberg islands in 1961, Tener (1963) found over 3,000 snow geese, almost all of which appeared to be without goslings. Later, Lynch (1972) confirmed that the production of young by greater snow geese was almost negligible in 1961, the lowest in a 16-year record, 1956-71.

Spring arrived about 2 weeks late in 1961 and was unusually cold and wet, leading Tener (1963) to postulate that these conditions caused the failure in breeding. The failure of large numbers of greater snow geese to breed on

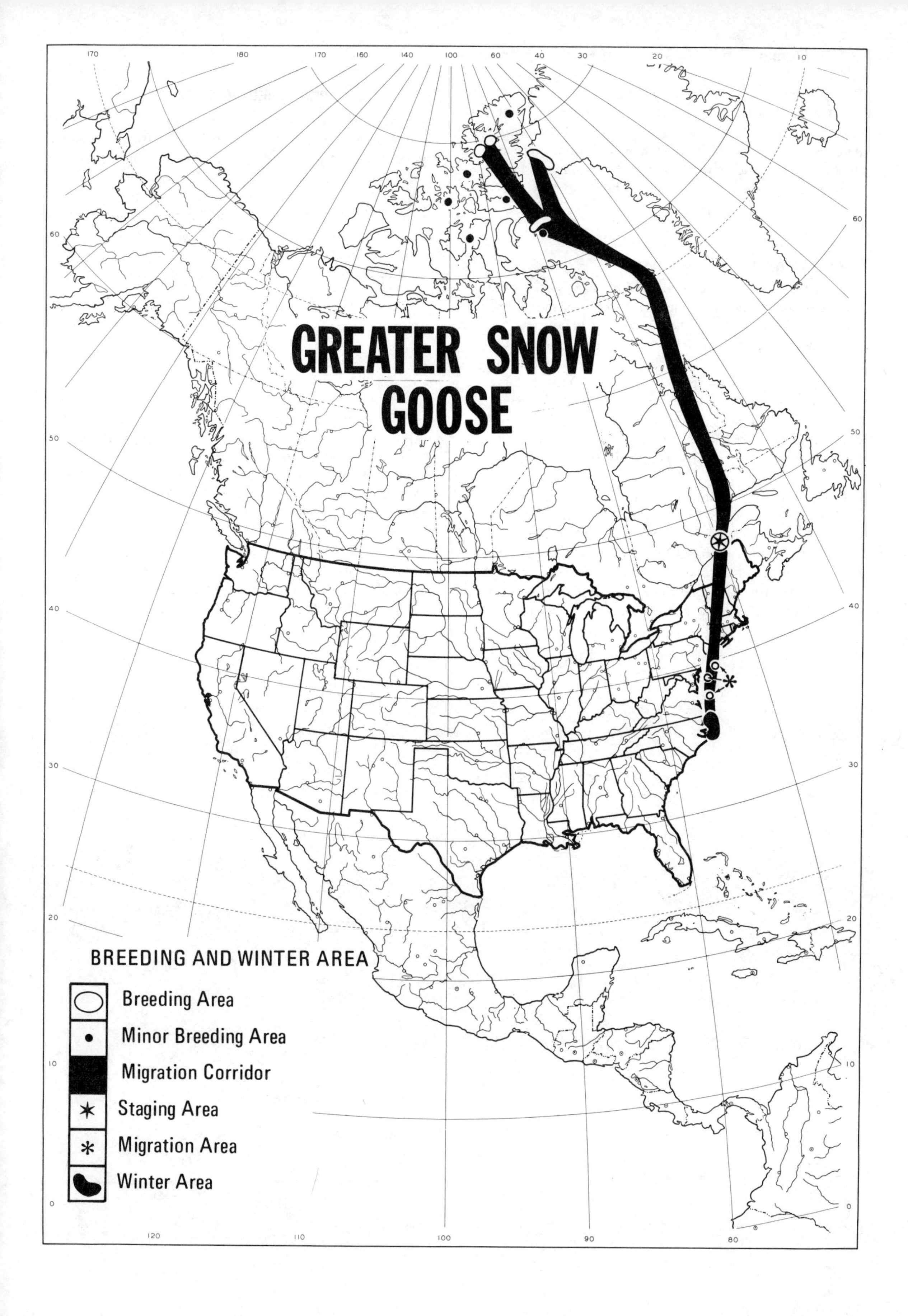
GREATER SNOW
GOOSE
BREEDING AND WINTER AREA
Breeding Area
Minor Breeding Area
Migration Corridor
Staging Area
Migration Area
Winter Area

Fosheim Peninsula in 1954 and 1955 puzzled Parmelee and MacDonald (1960). They reported that the spring thaw, although late in 1955, had occurred early in 1954. Whatever the cause, they concluded that when conditions were favorable, snow geese on the Fosheim Peninsula form loose colonies and produce many young; otherwise, only a few widely dispersed pairs nest.

Rearing of Young

Lemieux (1959) reported that as soon as the young were dry the broods dispersed inland to the base of the mountains several miles distant. They fed almost 24 hours a day. When the young geese reached a large size, the broods commenced to move slowly back toward the coast, flocks forming as broods converged, so that by August 20 large flocks were seen all along the southwest coast of Bylot Island. The young began to fly about August 20, approximately 6 weeks after hatching. On the Fosheim Peninsula, young were fledged as early as August 18 and as late as August 26.

The number of immatures identified per family in December, 1958-71, was 2.23 (Lynch 1972). The smallest-sized broods averaged 1.53 in 1961 and 1.65 in 1967; the largest-sized broods averaged 2.99 in 1956 and 2.89 in 1970. The loss among immatures is slightly greater than among adults, between breeding and winter grounds, so that brood size in December is smaller than earlier in the year.

POSTBREEDING SEASON

The earliest observation of flightless subadults occurred on July 14 (Lemieux 1959) and the first flying subadults were seen on August 6. Breeding adults began to molt their flight feathers about July 25, soon after the young hatched. The first ones regained flight by August 16 but some were still flightless on August 25. The flightless period lasts for about 22 days. Nonbreeding snow geese on the Fosheim Peninsula began to molt in early July, breeding birds in late July or early August (Parmelee and MacDonald 1960).

FOOD HABITS

At their area of great concentration on the St. Lawrence River below Quebec City, greater snow geese fed on the rootstocks and shoots of the common three-square bulrush, and, in the spring, they resorted also to nearby fields (White and Lewis 1937). Favorite foods of this species on the South Atlantic Coast are the rootstocks and shoots of three species of bulrushes: common three-square, Olney's, and salt-marsh. A second choice is the rootstocks and shoots of salt-marsh cordgrass. In recent years snow geese have also started to feed in agricultural fields adjacent to Back Bay, Virginia, and Currituck Sound, North Carolina.

Ross' Goose

Anser rossii

Other Common Names: Little wavie, warty-nosed wavie, horned wavie

VITAL STATISTICS

Length:	Adult male, 24-26 inches, average 25 inches (47)
	Adult female, 22-24 inches, average 23 inches (32)
	Immature male, 22-25 inches, average 24 inches (44)
	Immature female, 21-23 inches, average 22 inches (36)
Wing:	Adult male, 15.5 inches (47)
	Adult female, 14.8 inches (32)
	Immature male, 14.7 inches (44)
	Immature female, 14.2 inches (36)
Weight:	Adult male, 4.00 pounds (47)
	Adult female, 3.56 pounds (32)
	Immature male, 3.50 pounds (44)
	Immature female, 3.25 pounds (36)

IDENTIFICATION

Field

A small white goose with black wing tips in adults of both sexes, the Ross' goose can be confused only with the snow goose. Its smaller body size, shorter neck, more rapid wing beat, and more highly pitched call distinguish it from the snow goose. The juvenile Ross' goose is pale gray, noticeably lighter in color than the juvenile snow goose.

At Hand

The short stubby bill (the exposed culmen averages 1.6 inches in adult Ross' geese as compared with 2.2 inches in lesser snow geese) is without the black tomia that form the "grinning patch" in lesser snow geese. Many Ross' geese display warty protuberances between the nostrils and the base of the upper bill. The feet and legs of adult Ross' geese are rose-pink; those of lesser snow geese are scarlet.

Juvenile Ross' geese are light gray on the back of the head, the neck, and the back, and are white below. The gray is paler than in juvenile lesser snow geese and is not as extensive. The legs of juveniles are dark gray with tan webs and toes.

POPULATION STATUS

Until the late 1950's the population status of the Ross' goose was obscured by the difficulty in surveying its remote breeding area in the Canadian Arctic during summer and by its habit of intermixing with lesser snow geese on migration and winter areas. Then it was discovered that in late winter the Ross' goose tended to become isolated from the lesser snow goose on the winter grounds even though both species wintered in the San Joaquin Valley, California (John Chattin).

Since 1956, surveys in late February have provided reasonably reliable figures on the continental population of this goose. The average population of Ross' geese, 1956-74, was 23,400. The highest population recorded was 38,980 in 1968, and the lowest, 7,925, occurred in 1957.

Within the last 25 years, there has been a great upsurge in numbers of Ross' geese. Hanson et al. (1956) found 1,951 Ross' geese in the region south of Queen Maud Gulf in July 1949. A survey of the same area in 1960 by Barry (1960) revealed 9,000 Ross' geese. Only 5 years later, July 1965, Ryder (1969) reported 32,086 Ross' geese in the same area.

Those surveys of winter grounds that were considered reliable also reflect the increase in the number of Ross' geese. From 1956 to 1960, the population in California averaged 13,000. During the next 5 years, 1961-65, it averaged 28,100, and during the succeeding 7 years, 1966-74, the average was 27,000.

Population data that are especially reliable are available for one biological year, 1964-65, at the three most important zones of activity of the Ross' goose. During the fall of 1964, Dzubin (1965) estimated that there were 34,300 Ross' geese on migration areas in Alberta and Saskatchewan. In February 1965, 31,880 were estimated to be on the winter grounds, and in July 1965, 32,086 were found on their principal breeding grounds adjacent to Queen Maud Gulf (Ryder 1969).

DISTRIBUTION

Breeding Range

The breeding location of the Ross' goose remained a mystery until June 1938, when Gavin (1947) found a nesting colony of about 100 birds 14 miles southeast of the Perry River delta. Hanson et al. (1956) discovered a second nesting colony of 260 pairs about 25 miles south of the Perry River delta on June 28, 1949.

A survey of the lowlands adjacent to the Queen Maud Gulf was made in July 1965-67 by Ryder (1969). He found 35 nesting colonies with 30,037 breeding and 2,049 nonbreeding birds. Although most Ross' geese nest in central Arctic Canada, small numbers have been found elsewhere.

Evidence of the breeding of Ross' geese at the Boas River in Southampton Island, Northwest Territories, was found by Cooch (1954) and confirmed by Barry and Eisenhart (1958). A few were found breeding near the mouth of the McConnell River by MacInnes and Cooch (1963). Although several Ross' geese have been observed during the breeding season on Banks Island (Manning et al. 1956, Barry 1960), none have been found nesting there.

Migration Corridors

The first stage in the migration of Ross' geese takes them from their breeding grounds adjacent to Queen Maud Gulf to the Athabasca Delta. Until 1960, most of the geese migrated from the delta to the area centering on Sullivan Lake, 110 miles southeast of Edmonton, Alberta (Dzubin 1965). However, during the early 1960's, an increasingly greater proportion of these geese stopped in the area between Macklin and Kindersley in southeastern Saskatchewan.

From eastern Alberta and western Saskatchewan, Ross' geese migrate to the vicinity of Great Falls-Freezeout Lake, Montana. A few hundred stop here, but most alter their flight direction to a more westerly course that takes them to the Klamath Basin in northern California. From there, they depart for the Sacramento Valley of California and, ultimately, the San Joaquin Valley (Dzubin 1965).

Winter Areas

The bulk of the Ross' geese winter in the lower San Joaquin Valley centering on the Merced National Wildlife Refuge, Merced County, California. However, appreciable numbers winter in the Sacramento Valley, and a few stragglers occasionally winter as far north as the Klamath Basin. Rarely, small numbers of Ross' geese are found as far south as the Imperial Valley.

Extralimital Records

Because of the overall rarity of the Ross' goose, its extralimital records have attracted more than the customary attention accorded to misplaced waterfowl. Most extralimital records have occurred in the Central Flyway, particularly in eastern New Mexico, Nebraska, Texas, and Oklahoma. Surveys made countrywide in January revealed 50 Ross' geese in eastern New Mexico in 1969, 20 in 1970, 100 in 1971, and none in 1972. Two were found in Oklahoma in January 1969 and two in Texas in 1971.

Small numbers of Ross' geese were trapped along with larger numbers of lesser snow geese, in northwestern Nebraska in the springs of 1963 and 1964 (Sweet and Robertson 1966). During the fall of 1961 these diminutive geese were observed with flocks of lesser snow geese in South Dakota and with flocks of small Canada geese in Oklahoma and Texas (MacInnes and Cooch 1963). Almost every fall, moderate numbers of Ross' geese are observed among the 40,000 to 100,000 lesser snow geese that stop at the Squaw Creek National Wildlife Refuge in northwestern Missouri (Harold Burgess). For areas east of the Missouri River there are records from Minnesota, Wisconsin, Illinois, and North Carolina.

Where Ross' geese, lesser snow geese, and Canada geese associate, whether on breeding areas or on major staging areas, it is likely that departing flocks of one species attract individuals of other species to accompany them. Consequently, areas frequented in winter by geese from the Alberta-Saskatchewan staging area are liable to have some Ross' geese also.

MIGRATION BEHAVIOR

Chronology

Fall. The Ross' goose and the white-fronted goose are the first geese to depart their Arctic breeding grounds. Ross' geese begin appearing in the Athabasca Delta early in September, with most flocks arriving the last 2 weeks of the month. They also have about the same schedule of arrival in southeast Alberta and southwest Saskatchewan—first arrivals occur during the first week in September and the major influx takes place the third week (Dzubin 1965). Departures from the Alberta-Saskatchewan staging area begin after the first week in October and have been largely completed by mid-October.

By the first week in October, Ross' geese have reached Freezeout Lake, Montana, with numbers increasing to late

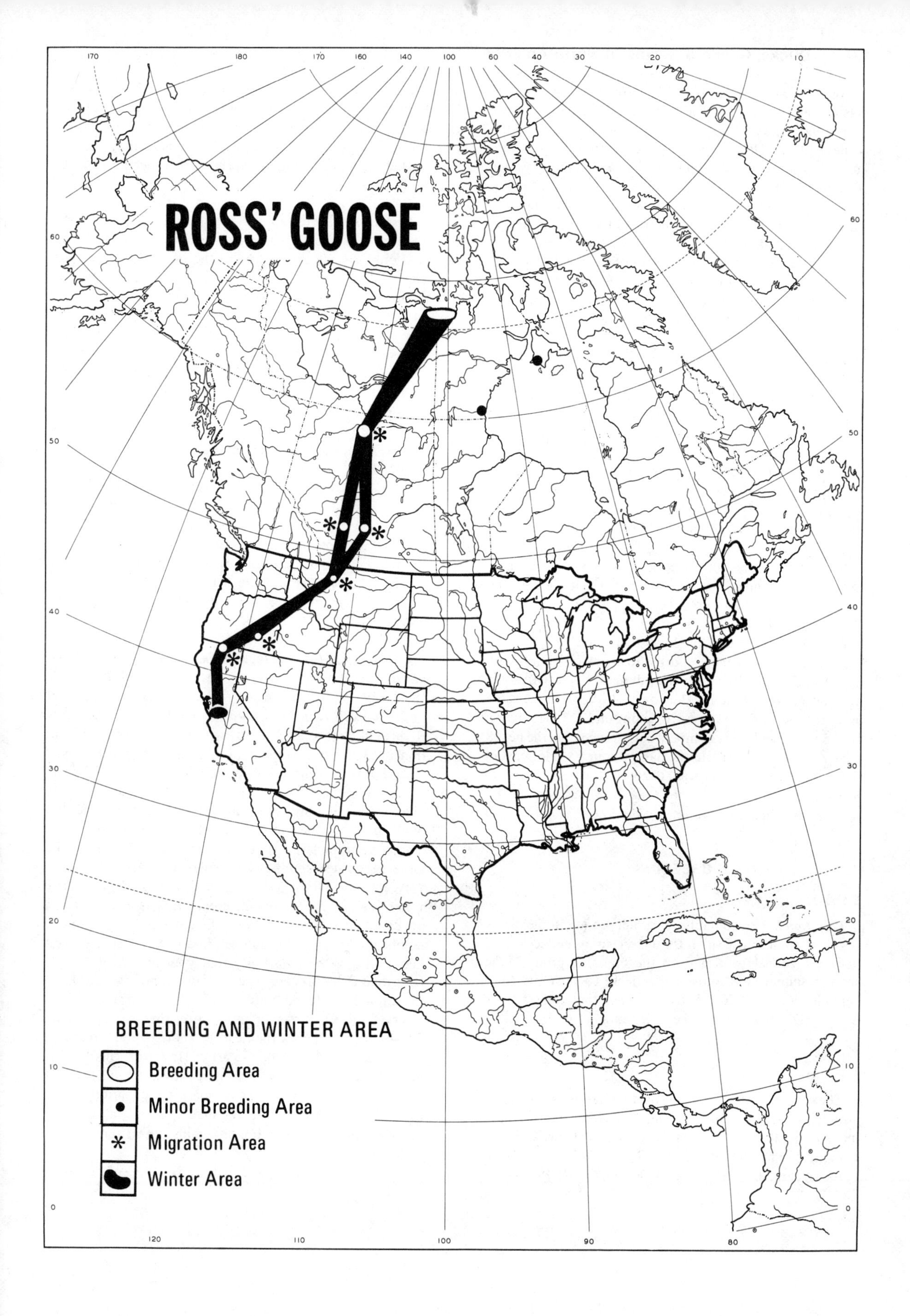
ROSS' GOOSE
BREEDING AND WINTER AREA
Breeding Area
Minor Breeding Area
Migration Area
Winter Area

October or early November. They arrive in the Klamath Basin, California, about mid-October and remain a month before moving southward 200 miles into the Sacramento Valley. In mid-December, these geese move still farther south to their winter grounds in the San Joaquin Valley (Dzubin 1965).

The calculations of Prevett and MacInnes (1972) placed the numbers of Ross' geese wintering along the Louisiana and Texas coasts at 441 during the winter of 1967-68, at 1,135 the next winter, and as 1,030 in 1969-70. About half of these were estimated to have come from the snow goose nesting colonies along the west coast of Hudson Bay and the other half from Queen Maud Gulf.

Spring. Late in February or early in March, Ross' geese begin to move north through the Sacramento Valley to the Klamath Basin. They pause there 2 to 4 weeks before migrating to the area of the Malheur National Wildlife Refuge in Oregon, where they usually appear late in March or early April.

They reach the area of Freezeout Lake, Montana, in late April and arrive in southeastern Alberta about the same time (Dzubin 1965). According to Soper (1951), they reach the Athabasca Delta about mid-May and leave about the end of the month.

Ryder (1967) analyzed the spring passage of Ross' geese in relation to temperature. He concluded that they arrived at each of their major spring stops behind the advance of the 32° F isotherm, thus assuring that the snow and ice had started to melt, making food available.

Ross' geese have been reported to arrive on their breeding grounds at the Perry River on June 6, 1949, with some arriving as late as June 18 (Hanson et al. 1956). In the same area, they were observed arriving on June 1, 1964, and on June 5, 1963, with peak numbers being reached in the next 3 days (Ryder 1967). At Karrak Lake, about 50 miles east of the Perry River, Ryder (1970*a*) observed the first arrivals of Ross' geese on May 30, 1966, June 4, 1968, and June 10, 1967; peak numbers were reached the next 3 to 4 days.

BREEDING

Behavior

Pair Bond. Presumably, the pair bond in the Ross' goose is similar to that in the lesser snow goose—loose pairs are probably formed on the breeding grounds the second summer and most pairs begin to nest the third summer. Ryder (1970*a*) found evidence that some female Ross' geese breed at the age of 2 years.

Nesting

The geese arrive on their nesting grounds in family groups, and the yearlings remain with their parents until incubation starts. They then leave the nest territories to congregate on communal areas (Ryder 1967).

In 5 years, 1963-64, 1966-68, Ryder (1967, 1970*a*) observed that Ross' geese began nesting within a week of their arrival, a shorter span than is usual among other geese that nest in the Arctic. The geese nested in small colonies on islands in shallow tundra lakes, where they were afforded some protection from predators, especially the Arctic fox.

Nest Sites. Preferred nest sites were adjacent to rocks or patches of birch. Open areas, despite their availability, held only a small proportion of the nests (Ryder 1970*a*). The average distance from a nest to its nearest neighbor in a colony that Ryder studied on Karrak Lake was 15 feet. The successful nests tended to be slightly farther apart than the unsuccessful ones. Preferred nest sites were used first and determined the initial distance between nearest nests. Geese that nested later used less suitable sites interspaced among the first occupied sites, resulting in more crowded conditions.

Nest initiation ranged from as early as June 4, 1964, to as late as June 19, 1967, and spanned a period of 7 to 12 days (Ryder 1967, 1970*a*).

Nests are composed of materials immediately surrounding the nest site: moss, dead leaves and twigs from birch and willow trees, grass, and old droppings. Ryder (1967) reported that the outer diameter of nests varied from 10 to 28 inches, the inner diameter from 4 to 9 inches, and the depth of the nest receptacle from 1.5 to 4.5 inches. The receptacle is lined with down that is added largely after the last egg is laid.

Clutch Size, Eggs, and Incubation. The eggs of the Ross' goose are white and measure 73.1 mm by 47.5 mm (52) (Ryder 1971*b*). The female lays an egg at an average interval of 1.3 days (Ryder 1970*a*). At Arlone Lake, on the Perry River, clutches averaged 3.6 eggs (1,675) prior to incubation and 3.5 eggs after incubation (Ryder 1967). All nests at Karrak Lake averaged 3.7 eggs (597), but successful nests averaged 3.9 eggs per clutch. Ryder (1970*a*) believes that older birds lay more eggs than younger breeders and that older birds are the more successful nesters, thereby accounting for the larger clutch size in successful nests. The largest recorded clutches contained six eggs.

According to Ryder (1970*a*), the clutch size decreased by 1.3, 1.4, and 1.9 eggs in 3 different years as nest initiation occurred progressively later. Occurrence of a greater number of incomplete clutches late in the period of nest initiation and the possibility that younger breeders nest later than older breeders are considered possible explanations for the reduced clutch size.

The female begins incubation after the last egg is laid. She frequently leaves the nest for short periods to obtain the meager food available nearby. However, this food is not sufficient to maintain her energy level, for she loses 44 percent of her body weight during the incubation period (Ryder 1970*b*). Meanwhile, the male remains on their nest territory, prepared to defend it against intrusion by other members of the species.

Eggs hatch after being incubated an average of 22 days, a

few as early as 19 days, and one clutch as late as 25 days (Ryder 1970*a*). It requires 1.3 days for all eggs in a single clutch to hatch. The young leave the nest a few hours after they are hatched.

Nest Success. Unless there is a disaster from violent storms during the period of nesting, nest success in the Ross' goose is high. At Arlone Lake, Hanson et al. (1956) reported only six nest failures in 260 nests found in 1949. At the same place, Ryder (1967) found that nest success was 97 percent in 1963 and 86 percent in 1964. In 3 years at Karrak Lake, nest success ranged from 67 percent in 1968 to 88 percent in 1967 (Ryder 1970*a*). Among the 597 successful nests at Karrak Lake, 88 percent of the 1,791 eggs laid hatched.

Nest Failure. The loss or abandonment of complete nests resulted largely from predation by gulls and jaegers upon eggs. The lower rate of nest success at Karrak Lake in 1968 was attributed to the large proportion of inexperienced geese that were nesting for the first time. Although the failure of some eggs in successful nests to hatch was due to a variety of reasons, the principal cause was predation.

Rearing of Young

Broods. Both sexes zealously guard the young. When approached by an intruder the female leads the young away while the male stands guard with outspread wings and mouth agape (Ryder 1967).

Family units leave the nesting grounds a few days after the hatch occurs and move to other island lakes and watercourses. Some family units move as far as the estuary, about 50 miles downstream. Families combine, so that 3 weeks after the hatch, aggregations may total 200 birds (Ryder 1967).

According to Ryder (1967), a drop in brood size among the downy young is caused by abandonment and predation. He observed glaucous gulls snatching young Ross' geese off the water and devouring them.

Development. At hatching, goslings weigh 2.3 ounces; at 4 weeks of age they weigh 32.1 ounces, a fourteenfold increase. As pointed out by Ryder (1969), the young must grow rapidly to be able to fly by the time freezing starts, 40 to 45 days after they hatch.

POSTBREEDING SEASON

The first Ross' geese to enter the molt are the subadults and nonbreeding adults who leave the nest area at the start of incubation. This group becomes flightless by the middle of July. Breeding birds do not lose their flight feathers until July 20-25, 15 to 20 days after the peak of hatch (Ryder 1967). They are flightless about 3 to 4 weeks. By the time the parents have regained flight, the young have started to fly.

FOOD HABITS

On their major migration area of concentration in Alberta and Saskatchewan, Ross' geese feed on waste grain in wheat and barley fields (Dzubin 1965). In the fall they use the larger lakes for resting, and in the spring they frequent the smaller runoff ponds, flying to the fields early in the morning and late in the afternoon.

In the Klamath Basin they feed largely upon barley, in the Sacramento Valley largely upon rice, and on their winter grounds in the San Joaquin Valley they utilize green grass (John Chattin).

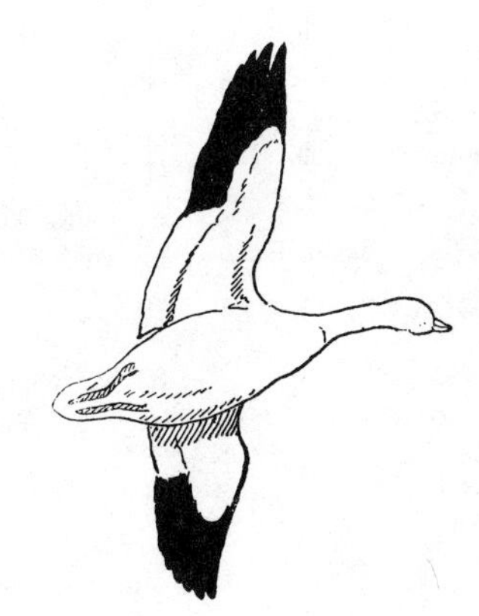

Emperor Goose

Anser canagicus

VITAL STATISTICS

Length:	Adult male, 26-28 inches, average 27 inches (7) Adult female, 26-28 inches, average 27 inches (8)
Wing:	Adult male, 15.0-15.7 inches Adult female, 13.8-15.2 inches
Weight:	Adult male, 6.12 pounds (5) Adult female, 6.25 pounds (4)

IDENTIFICATION

Field

The emperor goose is a moderate-sized goose, with a short thick neck, short bill, heavy body, and comparatively short wings, requiring rapid strokes to maintain flight. Its flight is comparatively slow and it flies low over the water, often just skimming the waves. Eisenhauer and Frazer (1972) report that the black brant are faster in flight, usually occur in larger flocks, and alter their position more frequently.

At a distance the emperor appears similar in plumage to the "blue" goose, but the throat and lower neck of the adult emperor are black and the remainder of the head and neck is white. The undertail coverts of both adult and immature emperor geese are bluish gray whereas those of blue geese are white. The white tail contrasts sharply with the dark bluish-gray body. As may be seen on land, the legs of the emperor goose are yellow; those of the blue goose are pink. The infrequent but distinctive call of the emperor is a piercing *kla-ga, kla-ga, kla-ga*.

At Hand

Many ornithologists rate the emperor goose as the most beautiful goose in the world. The bluish-gray feathers of the back are edged with black and then distally with white. The white edgings of the feathers form wavy bands across the back, sides, and flanks but are less in evidence on the darker chest and breast.

The white head of the adult is often stained a rusty hue from feeding where concentrations of iron oxide occur in tidal ponds. The short pink bill lacks the black "grinning patch" present in the bills of snow geese.

Except for the white wavy barring on the back, sides, and flanks, immature emperor geese are quite dark. The bill and feet are black; the head, neck, and chest are black-brown. The head and upper neck of the immature become largely white by late October but are flecked by a scattering of dark feathers.

POPULATION STATUS

The fall population of emperor geese in Alaska is estimated to be 150,000 (King and Lensink 1971). Probably 60,000 to 75,000 of the postbreeding population are mature breeders. These figures represent the entire population in North America and the bulk of the population in the entire world. A smaller proportion of the breeding population occurs adjacent to the Bering Sea in the Union of Soviet Socialist Republics.

DISTRIBUTION

The entire population of the emperor goose is, with minor exceptions, restricted to the region of the Bering Sea. Its principal breeding and winter ranges encompass the opposite ends of this sea.

Breeding Season

James King estimates that over 90 percent of the emperors in Alaska breed on the Yukon Delta. According to King, approximately 1,000 nest near Shishmaref on the Seward Peninsula. He estimates that 200 breed on Nunivak Island, 500 along the eastern shore of Kuskokwim Bay, and small numbers near Kivalina on the Chukchi Sea. Although the emperor was formerly known to breed on St. Lawrence Island, its occurrence there has not been substantiated in recent years. Fay (1961) considered that less than one-tenth of the 10,000 to 20,000 emperors summering on St. Lawrence Island nested there.

In the USSR, the emperor goose is one of the rarest and least known of waterfowl (Kistchinski 1971). It breeds along the shores of the Gulf of Anadyr and the Chukot Peninsula westward to Amguyema Lagoon.

Migration Corridors

Most emperor geese apparently migrate from their breeding grounds on the Yukon Delta across Bristol Bay to Port Moller and Izembek Bay near the tip of the Alaska Peninsula. Large flocks are reported by Robert Jones, Jr., (Headley 1967) to pass northeastward in the spring along the tip of the Alaska Peninsula to the Izembek Bay-Port Moller area, where they turn north to head across Bristol Bay. On May 18, 1958, near Port Moller, McKinney (1959) observed a flock pass northward out to sea. At times in the fall, Izembek Bay has contained from 50,000 to 120,000 emperors, practically the entire population in North America. From Izembek Bay, they gradually move westward along the Aleutian Chain as far as the outermost island, Attu.

On the west side of the Bering Sea, emperors migrate over the Kamchatka and Commander islands on their way to winter grounds in the Kamchatka Peninsula (Dement'ev and Gladkov 1967).

Winter Areas

Except for 2,000 to 3,000 emperor geese that winter along the coast of Kodiak Island, most of the remaining population winters from Port Moller west along the entire Aleutian chain of islands. In addition, the emperor goose is

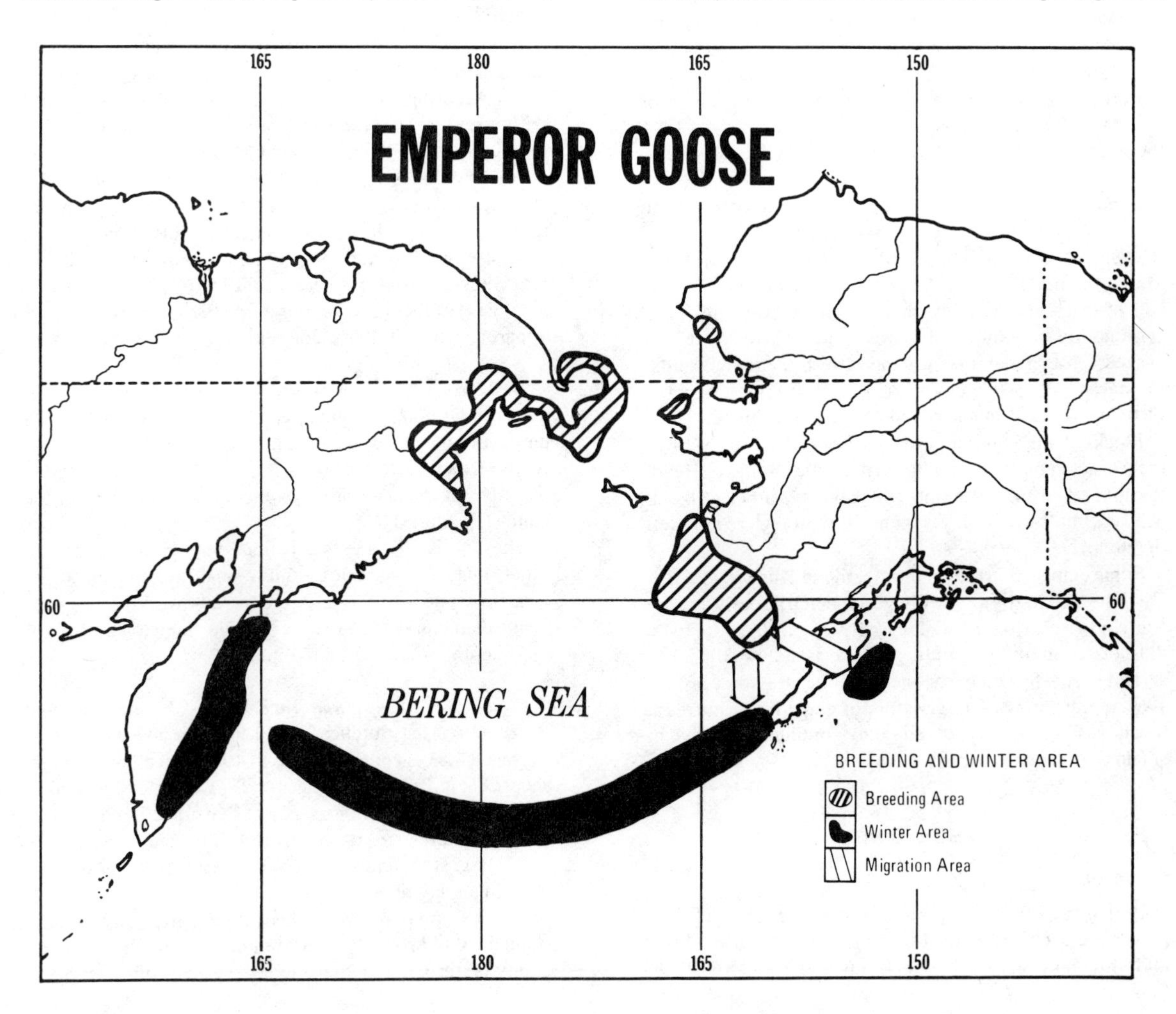

a rare but rather consistent winter visitor to the Pacific Northwest. The areas where it has been reported most regularly are the Oregon coast, Humboldt Bay, the Klamath Basin, and the Sacramento Valley in California (Wilbur and Yocom 1972). A few have been observed as far south as Los Angeles County. They have been infrequent visitors on the coast of British Columbia (Godfrey 1966) and the southeast coast of Alaska (Gabrielson and Lincoln 1959).

MIGRATION BEHAVIOR

Chronology

Fall. Emperor geese begin arriving in small numbers at Port Moller and Izembek Bay during late August (Headley 1967). A large influx of these geese arrived at Izembek Bay between September 24 and 29, 1966. Large numbers remained through October.

In 1965, Lensink (Headley 1967) recorded the first arrivals at Amchitka Island on October 12. The main flight arrived there on October 19 and thereafter emperors were common. At that island in 1957, Kenyon (1961) reported the first flock on October 16. On an aerial survey around the island on November 19, he saw 500 to 700 geese.

Farther out on the Aleutians, at Attu Island, emperor geese usually do not appear until late December. In 1944 the main flight arrived on December 20 (Wilson 1948).

Spring. Emperors leave the island area of Attu-Agattu by mid-March, migrating eastward along the Aleutians (Headley 1967). Kenyon (1961) reported that by early March the population at Amchitka had declined to about half of that found in midwinter. It continued to decrease through March until April 21 when the last flock was observed. On an aerial survey of the eastern Aleutian Islands, on March 3-4, 1960, Kenyon found 12,500 emperors, most of them around Umnak Island and Unalaska Island.

Flocks of migrating emperor geese appear along the tip of the Alaska Peninsula early in April, (Robert Jones *in* Headley 1967). During that month, 40,000 may gather at Izembek Bay but, by mid-May, all but a few stragglers have left the area.

Some emperors arrive in the vicinity of Kuskokwim Bay the first week in April. They have appeared as early as May 5 at Hooper Bay on the Kolomak River, but Brandt (1943) did not see them there until May 15. Headley (1967) observed only a few emperors near Hooper Bay on May 23, 1966, a late spring. A large influx of emperors occurred a few days later, May 28-29, and they continued to arrive in smaller numbers into early June.

BREEDING

Behavior

Both aggressive behavior and courtship behavior of emperors were observed by McKinney (1959) during April and May in the area of Izembek Bay and Port Moller. On April 10, he observed a prolonged fight between two birds, and on May 10, he observed a pair making precopulatory neck-dipping movements. By the time emperor geese arrive on their nesting grounds on the Yukon Delta in May, they have mated and are ready to begin nesting (Headley 1967).

Age, Pair Bond, and Homing. The age at which emperor geese breed is unknown but, considering the large numbers of nonbreeders, most emperors probably do not nest until they are 3 years old. Headley (1967) believes that the initial pair bond is formed among subadults either during spring migration or on the breeding grounds. They probably mate for life.

Eisenhauer et al. (1971) reported that many nest sites at Kokechik Bay had been used in previous years. They found one site that had been used at least 3 years by emperors.

Nesting

Emperor geese tend to nest slightly inland from the nest areas of the black brant, on the coastal fringe (Calvin Lensink). According to James King, almost all emperors nest within several hundred yards of tidewater, which may extend up to 30 or 40 miles inland along tidal streams. They nest on tidal grasslands, lowland pingo tundra, and sedge marshes. In their study area on Kokechik Bay, Eisenhauer and Frazer (1972) found the highest density of nests, 0.24 per acre, in lowland pingo tundra. In this tundra at Kokechik Bay, nests were from 25 to 650 feet apart—average, 195 feet (Eisenhauer et al. 1971). Emperor geese apparently nest in loose colonies.

Nest Sites. Emperors prefer to nest on an elevated site near a tidal pond. Eisenhauer et al. (1971) found that 78 percent of the nest sites were less than 30 feet from water. At the Kolomak River on the Yukon Delta, 15 of 28 nests were beside ponds, with 2 as distant as 75 feet from the water (Headley 1967).

The nest is a scrape that is lined with grass, sedges, or other adjacent vegetation, and a small amount of down. Eisenhauer et al. (1971) reported the following dimensions: inside diameter, 85 to 210 mm; outside diameter, 135 to 410 mm; depth of cup, 33 to 135 mm.

Clutch Size, Eggs, and Incubation. Eisenhauer and Frazer (1972) list clutches for 710 emperor goose nests that averaged 4.83 eggs. From 1963 to 1970, 250 clutches averaged 4.86; in 1971 the average for 257 was 4.54 eggs; and in 1972 there were 5.16 eggs per clutch for 203 nests. Extremes in clutch size ranged from 1 to 12, but at least three of the largest clutches appeared to result from more than one female laying in the same nest.

The eggs are pure white when laid but gradually become stained a dull brown from nest material. The shells have a grainy texture, unlike the smooth eggshells of other geese that nest in the Arctic (Eisenhauer et al. 1971). The eggs are elliptical ovate, measuring 80.2 by 52.2 mm (295).

Four of eight nests studied by Headley (1967) hatched in 24 days, the others in 25 to 27 days. Eisenhauer and Frazer (1972) found that the incubation period for 18 nests ranged from 23 to 27 days, hatching at almost an equal rate each of the 5 days.

Chronology of Nesting. In 1966 Headley (1967) found that emperors began nesting a few days after arriving on their breeding grounds on the Yukon Delta. Egg-laying started in 2 of 21 nests on May 30 and other laying started daily through June 9. In 1971, egg-laying started May 22-24 and reached the peak of initiation May 31-June 8; the last nests were started June 15-17 (Eisenhauer et al. 1971). The chronology of nest initiation in 1972 was virtually the same as in 1971 (Eisenhauer and Frazer 1972). In both years, the onset of laying extended over a span of about 24 days.

Perhaps the more moderate climate of the Yukon enables emperor geese to initiate laying over a longer period of time than is possible for geese nesting in the Canadian Arctic. Even so, there is no evidence that renesting occurs among emperors.

Nest Success. Emperor geese have an unusually high nest success, amounting to 86.2 percent for 427 nests. Eisenhauer and Frazer (1972) found a nest success of 81.6 percent (124) in 1971, and 90.9 percent (151) in 1972. On a different area in the Yukon Delta, Mickelson (1973) determined a success of 88.9 percent for 81 nests. Of 28 nests studied by Headley (1967), 21 hatched.

On the Onumtuk area, an average of 4.21 eggs hatched in successful nests, a loss of only 0.42 egg from incubated clutch size (Mickelson 1973). At Kokechik Bay, Eisenhauer and Frazer (1972) observed that there was a loss of 0.6 egg from the 5.35 of preincubated clutches to the 4.75 in clutches shortly before hatch. Viability of eggs was excellent; only 16 of 629 (2.5 percent) were infertile or addled.

Nest destruction was caused almost entirely by predators, believed to be parasitic jaegers and glaucous gulls.

Rearing of Young

Broods. Frazer (1972) observed a high degree of integrity among emperor goose broods, but he did note two instances of adoptions of young from other broods.

As with other geese, both parents are solicitous of their young, the male assuming the principal role of guarding them from predators. Families move first to the coast, where they feed for a few days before moving to the larger rivers. There they join many nonbreeders for the annual molt. Some families move as far as 5 miles from their nest sites to the molt area (Eisenhauer et al. 1971).

Development. Although young emperors grow rapidly, they still require 50 to 60 days to attain flight (Mickelson 1973). Those hatched the first week in July become fledged by the third or fourth week in August. However, some flightless young were seen during the first week in September, which is the first week of the waterfowl hunting season in Alaska.

Survival. According to Mickelson (1973), Class I broods of emperor geese averaged 3.93 goslings (73), Class II broods contained 3.95 goslings (43), and Class III broods held 3.29 young (139). A loss of 16 percent from Class I to flight and of 22 percent from the brood size at hatch is evidence of exceptionally low mortality among waterfowl.

The glaucous gull is considered to be the principal predator on goslings, but young goslings are also menaced by jaegers (Headley 1967). A glaucous gull was observed to kill a young 3-pound emperor, but usually only smaller goslings are victims.

The young attempt to escape the attacks of gulls by diving while their parents ward off the swoops of the attackers. If the goslings remain near their parents and are old enough to dive completely under water, the assaults by glaucous gulls are usually repulsed (Headley 1967). Goslings are most vulnerable to predation by gulls when they become separated from their parents or when they are on land.

POSTBREEDING SEASON

Nonbreeding emperor geese are the first to enter the wing molt, beginning about the first week in July and flying again by August (Headley 1967). The paired adults enter wing molt when the young are 20 to 25 days old and regain their flight feathers by the time the young are fledged (Headley 1967). According to Mickelson (1973), emperor geese with broods began losing their flight feathers in the third week of July and regained them in the third week of August.

On St. Lawrence Island, Fay (1961) observed 10,000 to 20,000 nonbreeding adult emperor geese during the summer. During the wing molt they congregated in large flocks along the south coast. The Eskimos were seen capturing flightless birds between June 17 and August 7 and a few as late as August 15. Only 10 geese in a flock of 5,000 were capable of sustained flight on July 21, 1960.

In the USSR, adult emperors begin to molt as soon as broods appear (Dement'ev and Gladkov 1967). Their body molt begins when replacement of flight feathers occurs in late July or early August. The young molt the black feathers of the head and upper neck in October (Headley 1967), so that by the end of the month they are similar in appearance to adults except for traces of black feathers in their otherwise white heads and necks.

Emperor geese remain in family groups throughout the late-summer molt, the fall migration, and into the winter. According to Headley (1967), the immatures leave their parents either on winter areas or during spring migration.

FOOD HABITS

The emperor is a sea goose in habit if not in name. Because it spends most of its life, except for the breeding season, in shallow waters adjacent to or connected with the sea, its food habits reflect this habitat. Eelgrass composed the exclusive contents of 17 crops from geese collected in October and November at Izembek Bay (Headley 1967). Crops and gizzards from geese collected on Adak Island contained sea lettuce almost entirely, except for one goose that had fed exclusively on barnacles (Headley 1967). At Amchitka Island, Kenyon (1961) observed emperors feeding on kelp beds washed ashore and exposed at low tide.

An earlier study of the foods present in the gizzards of 33 emperor geese, collected largely during the summer (Cottam and Knappen 1939), disclosed that algae, primarily sea lettuce, were of first importance. Tender shoots of sedges and grasses were second in importance, followed closely by eelgrass. A variety of animal foods comprised 8.4 percent of the contents of the gizzards.

On their breeding grounds, emperor geese are mainly grazers, feeding principally upon the leaves of sedges and, to a slight extent, upon green algae and crowberries (Headley 1967).

Canada Goose

Branta canadensis

Other Common Names: Honker, Canada

VITAL STATISTICS

Race	Age & Sex Group	Length (inches)	Weight (lb)	Bill Length (mm)	Wing (mm)	Tail (mm)	Tarsus (mm)	Reference
Atlantic	Ad. male		8.8(4,175)	56(7)	466.3(7)	143(7)	70.8(7)	Aldrich (1946)
B. c. canadensis	Ad. female		7.6(3,452)	53.9(7)	465.0(7)	147.3(7)	85.9(7)	Clark Webster
	Imm. male		7.5(3,406)					
	Imm. female		6.8(3,444)					
Interior	Ad. male	36.2(25)	9.2(128)	55.5(18)	509.9(43)	151.8(20)	89.1(9)	Hanson (1965)
B. c. interior	Ad. female	33.5(25)	7.7(121)	49.9(19)	479.1(43)	146.1(20)	83.6(10)	Raveling (1968a)
	Imm. male	34.8(25)	7.8(116)	53.5(127)	484.2(139)	128.8(111)		David Kennedy
	Imm. female	32.4(18)	6.8(139)	50.2(109)	459.8(123)	122.2(98)		
Dusky	Ad. male		9.9(134)	46.5(214)	478.7(79)	143.5(79)	92.3(80)	Chapman (1970)
B. c. occidentalis	Ad. female		8.3(98)	44.4(199)	450.2(61)	137.4(60)	85.9(61)	
	Imm. male		8.8(436)	46.9(368)	462.3(48)	129.7(48)	91.2(47)	
	Imm. female		7.6(366)	44.6(350)	440.4(52)	124.4(47)	86.3(52)	
Vancouver	Ad. male			51.9(18)		168(6)	93.9(18)	Daniel Timm
B. c. fulva	Ad. female			48.8(13)		142(8)	88.7(13)	
	Imm. male							
	Imm. female							
Giant	Ad. male		12.5(28)	60.7(27)	525.8(35)	162.4(24)		Hanson (1965)
B. c. maxima	Ad female		11.1(25)	57.3(26)	495.6(32)	154.0(22)		
	Imm. male		10.6(29)	60.3(65)	498.6(48)	146.0(21)		
	Imm. female		8.9(18)	56.5(48)	478.3(23)	138.3(11)		
Western	Male	37.1(19)	9.9(10)	56(18)	518(20)	152(17)	100(18)	Yocom (1972)
B. c. moffitti	Female	34.5(19)	8.2(9)	52(20)	478(20)	146(20)	93(19)	Aldrich (1946)
Taverner's	Male	29.8(2)	5.9(2)	37.9(21)		136(26)	76.8(22)	Yocom (1972)
B. c. taverneri	Female	26.7(4)	4.7(4)	36.9(17)		122(10)	71.5(15)	Daniel Timm
Richardson's	Male			33.7(6)	377.8(6)	123.7(6)	70.3(6)	Aldrich (1946)
B. c. hutchinsii	Female			31.6(7)	365.5(7)	116.6(7)	67.4(7)	
Lesser	Ad. male		6.1(184)	44.2(184)	445.5(184)		81.8(184)	Grieb (1970)
B. c. parvipes	Ad. female		5.4(194)	42.4(194)	422.1(194)		77.0(194)	
	Imm. male		5.5(125)	43.4(125)	418.5(125)		80.8(125)	
	Imm. female		4.8(151)	41.3(151)	397.1(151)		75.0(151)	
Aleutian	Ad. male			34.7(39)	385.0(37)	122.0(8)	81.0(39)	John Aldrich
B. c. leucopareia	Ad. female			32.5(21)	369.0(20)	120.0(9)	75.0(21)	
Cackling	Male		3.4(28)	27.3(4)	363.8(4)	113.3(4)	66.9(4)	Aldrich (1946)
B. c. minima	Female		2.8(17)	28.2(11)	353.5(11)	104.2(11)	65.7(11)	Kortright (1942)

IDENTIFICATION

To most North Americans the word "goose" conjures up the Canada goose, and most are familiar with its clear resonant honking call and black-stockinged head and neck and white cheek patch. Although most people can readily identify the species, *Branta canadensis*, the 11 recognized races pose varying degrees of difficulty. At times professional biologists resort to the terms "large," "medium," and "small" to identify birds where there is a mixing of races in winter populations. To compound the problem, the existing racial classification leaves much to be desired, because many birds fail to fit the "pigeonholes" defined by their describers. Ornithologists have considered these variations to be clines of integration between racial groups.

However, a number of years ago it became apparent to Harold C. Hanson of the Illinois Natural History Survey that there were many more races than were currently recognized. Since then, he has been working diligently to delineate the numerous races that develop as a result of ecological or geographical isolation on their breeding grounds. The various races on breeding grounds mix together on migration and winter areas. For example, Hanson (1965) found that six, possibly seven, races of Canada geese occur on the Squaw Creek National Wildlife Refuge in Missouri. Hansen (1968) reported that seven races winter on the Pacific Coast. Until all the races of Canada geese have been delineated, reported, reviewed, and evaluated, those enumerated here will suffice to demonstrate the tremendous morphological range of a single species, some almost as large as a swan to others barely larger than a mallard.

Field

Fortunately, for identification purposes all sex- and age-classes of Canada geese are alike, eliminating the difficulties inherent among ducks as a result of age and sex differences in plumage. Canada goose flocks are noted for their V-formation flight, though sometimes they fly in trailing lines. The larger the race, the longer the call, the lower the pitch, and the more sonorous the quality. Giant Canada geese call less frequently than other races but have the most prolonged call at the lowest pitch; diminutive cackling geese call the most frequently, have the highest pitch, and the briefest notes. Phonetics range from the resonant *uh-whonk* of the larger-sized races to the yelping high-pitched *unc* of the smaller ones. The larger the race the slower the flight, the slower and more measured the wing beat, and the shallower the wing arc. Giant and western Canada geese, the large ones, are prone to fly in small family-sized flocks; other races occur in migration in flocks that range from several score up to a thousand or more.

Size can be misleading in the field unless other waterfowl are present to provide a means of comparison. But because the races do vary so much in size, matching individual Canada geese against the size of a snow goose or a mallard, for example, helps to identify the race. Moreover, the place where it is found further restricts the number of possibilities, thus increasing the chances of correctly identifying it.

As shown by data under vital statistics, races steadily decline in size as follows: giant, western, Vancouver, dusky, interior, Atlantic, lesser, Taverner's, Aleutian, Richardson's, and cackling. The giant has the longest neck in proportion to body size, the cackling goose the shortest neck. Although color of the wings and body varies considerably among individuals of a single race, there are differences among races that further assist identification. The lightest-colored races are the giant and western; increasingly darker are the Richardson's, lesser, Taverner's, interior, and Vancouver. Darkest of all are the medium-sized dusky and the tiny cackling goose, both of the Pacific Northwest.

At Hand

Canada geese have a distinctive appearance that might conceivably be confused only with the brants, marine species almost entirely confined to the seacoasts. All races of Canada geese have the following in common: black bill, legs, and feet; black head and neck with a white cheek patch that usually covers the throat; gray-brown to dark brown back and wings; sides and breast a mouse-gray to dark brown, a lighter shade than the back in all but the Pacific Coast races; white belly, flank, and undertail coverts; and black tail and rump separated by a white V-bar formed by the white uppertail coverts.

Several races of Canada geese stand out because of size or plumage or distribution: giant, western, Atlantic, interior, Vancouver, dusky, Aleutian, and cackling. Of all these races, the most individualistic is probably the diminutive cackler. Other races may require careful measurement of bill (culmen), folded wing, central tail feathers, and tarsus for racial identification. These are given under vital statistics and should be used when identification of a race is in doubt.

POPULATION STATUS

The increase in the population of the Canada goose during the last three decades is one of the more spectacular accomplishments of wildlife management, rivaling the comeback of the white-tailed deer and the wild turkey. Winter inventory data show that the number of Canadas has almost doubled in the United States between 1955 and 1974. In 1974, there were 2,141,000 Canadas after most of the hunting seasons had been completed, and about 3 million on September 1, prior to hunting.

During the 20-year period 1955-74, the populations in the Atlantic, Mississippi, and Central flyways increased by 138.6 percent, 169.5 percent, and 70.6 percent, respectively. But the combined population of all races of Canada geese in the Pacific Flyway declined 10.2 percent.

The increase that has occurred is even more spectacular when information is available for the years preceding 1955. Hanson and Smith (1950) showed that 76,700 Canada geese were inventoried in the Mississippi Flyway during the winter of 1943-44; this population rose to 662,600 in 1973-74. In the Atlantic Flyway, Addy and Heyland (1968) reported 179,000 Canada geese in January of 1948; this population contained 760,000 in the winter of 1973-74. Small geese wintering in the Central Flyway are divided into an eastern and western segment. Grieb (1968) showed that the eastern segment increased from 6,000 in 1948 to almost 30,000 in 1966, an average annual rate of more than 21 percent. The western segment rose from 15,000 in 1948 to 66,000 in 1966, an average annual rate of 19 percent.

At one time the giant Canada goose was considered to be extinct (Delacour 1954). But Hanson (1965), in an exciting discovery, found this large race extant and numerous at Rochester, Minnesota, in January 1962. He surveyed the number of giant Canadas in North America in 1962-63 and determined that 54,600 were present in the wild and under confinement. Giant Canada geese are most amenable to management: they are readily propagated under confinement; they take readily to artificial nest structures; and their nest success and brood survival are high even on areas subject to considerable human disturbance.

Age Ratios

Age ratios express not only nest and brood success but the proportion of the population actually breeding. Because yearling Canada geese do not breed and only limited numbers of 2-year-olds breed, the age structure of the population affects the proportion of young found in fall populations.

Hanson and Smith (1950) calculated over a 7-year period that first-year birds composed 53 percent of the Canada geese in populations at Horseshoe Lake. Grieb (1970), studying small Canadas in southeastern Colorado, concluded that first-year immatures formed 40 percent of the populations, 1950-64. Only 23 percent of the fall population of dusky Canada geese migrating into Oregon were first-year birds (Chapman et al. 1969).

Sex Ratios

Sex ratios in Canada geese vary with the sampling method, the region, and the differential hunting pressure on a particular sex. Nevertheless, most data indicate a fairly even proportion of the sexes among the several age groups.

Among 157 goslings of the giant Canada geese examined by Sherwood (1965) on the refuge at Seney, Michigan, the sexes were almost evenly divided. Martin (1964) found that males made up 52.5 percent of 1,130 flightless immature western Canada geese trapped on the wildlife area at Ogden Bay, Utah. Males composed 52.4 percent of 1,801 goslings of dusky Canadas trapped on the Copper River delta (Chapman et al. 1969). This evidence suggests that early in life males survive slightly better than females.

The next stage in life at which sex ratios have been taken is during the first fall and winter of the young. In 1940-46, 54.6 percent of the immatures trapped at Horseshoe Lake, Illinois, were males (Hanson and Smith 1950). However, at Swan Lake National Wildlife Refuge in central Missouri, Vaught and Kirsch (1966) found that males composed only 48.2 percent of 10,664 trapped immatures. Chapman et al. (1969) concluded from the higher mortality rates among males that they composed 49.3 percent of the yearlings and 46.3 percent of the adults.

Hanson and Smith (1950) found 58 percent males among 2,213 adult Canadas trapped at Horseshoe Lake, 1940-46. At Swan Lake, Missouri, Vaught and Kirsch (1966) tallied 53.5 percent males among 7,741 trapped adults. In southeastern Colorado, Rutherford (1970) reported 50.6 percent males among 8,828 small Canadas of all ages. Among 11,057 flightless yearling and older geese captured on the Ungava Peninsula, Quebec, Heyland and Garrard (1974) recorded 49.6 percent males.

On the other hand, Sherwood (1965) found that males composed only 43.2 percent of 1,189 yearling and adult giant Canadas trapped at Seney, Michigan. At Trimble, Missouri, Brakhage (1965) also reported that there were more females than males among breeding geese. The low proportion of males in breeding populations at Seney and Trimble undoubtedly explains why a high proportion of yearling males pair with older females. Brakhage (1965) observed that 42 percent of the yearling males at Trimble were paired, compared with 14 percent of the yearling females. At Seney, Sherwood (1965) noted that some 2-year-old females were paired with yearling males and others were unpaired; he believed that more would have been paired if more older males had been available.

Mortality

Because of the numerous discrete populations among Canada geese, there are wide variations in the mortality rates stemming from the degree of shooting pressure on a particular population. The adjacent table presents mortality rates for several races of Canada geese in one or more regions.

Annual mortality rates, averaged for all years, ranged from 32 to 52 percent. They were highest for immatures experiencing their first hunting season, ranging from 39 to 65 percent. These rates were 1.2 to 2.2 times higher than annual mortality rates for the surviving birds in subsequent years. In most instances, males suffered higher annual mortality as a result of higher shooting losses than females, but an exception occurred at Ogden Bay, where the rate for females was slightly higher. The differential mortality rate between the sexes indicates that most populations probably contain more females than males. In dimorphic ducks, females have the higher mortality and compose the smaller proportion of the sexes.

DISTRIBUTION

Canada geese have a strong propensity to home to particular migration and winter grounds, resulting in highly localized populations. A specific migrating or wintering

Annual Mortality Rates, Canada Geese

Race	Area Banded	Banding Year	Age-Class Class at Banding	Sex	First Year	Sub-sequent Years	All Years	Reference
B. c. interior	Illinois	1940-47	Imm.		65.4		52.0	Hanson & Smith (1950)
B. c. interior	Missouri	1950-60	Imm.	M	62.6	35.4	49.5	Vaught & Kirsch (1966)
			Imm.	F	53.1	24.4	35.4	
B. c. maxima	Ohio	1968	Imm.		37.0		28.4	Cummings (1973)
			Ad.		22.9			
B. c. maxima	Michigan	1962-64					35.0	Sherwood (1965)
B. c. maxima	Minnesota	1961-66	Ad.				45.8	Gulden & Johnson (1968)
B. c. parvipes	Colorado	1951-64		M	38.9	41.7	41.0	Grieb (1970)
				F	33.5	37.1	37.1	
	Canada	1961-64	Imm.		38.9	49.4	37.8	
B. c. hutchinsii	South Dakota	1951-66	Imm.				51.0	Grieb (1970)
			Ad.				32.0	
B. c. moffitti	Bear River, Utah	1937-41	Imm.		53.0	38.0		Martin (1964)
		1946-49	Imm.	M	47.0	40.0		
		1952-58	Imm.	F	47.0	36.0		
	Ogden Bay, Utah	1952-58	Imm.	M	63.0	46.0		
			Imm.	F	65.0	50.0		
B. c. moffitti	Washington	1950-60	Imm.		40	30		Hanson & Eberhardt (1971)
B. c. fulva	Alaska	1956-65	Ad.				33.5	Chapman et al. (1969)
B. c. occidentalis	Alaska	1952-59	Imm.	M	58.8	38.8		Chapman et al. (1969)
			Imm.	F	53.5	32.1		
B. c. minima	Alaska	1949-54	Imm.		46.0	35.9		Nelson & Hansen (1959)
			Ad.				31.9	
B. c. taverneri	Alaska	1948-58	Imm.		45.6		27.1	Timm (1974)
			Ad.		22.5		25.4	

group may include from one to several races. Because of the cohesion demonstrated by populations of Canada geese on winter grounds, wildlife biologists have found it convenient to refer to particular units by their geographic affiliations (Hansen and Nelson 1964). The adjacent figure delineates the geographic ranges of 12 generally recognized populations across the breadth of North America.

North Atlantic Population

The North Atlantic population of Canadas inhabits the Atlantic coastal region from northern Labrador to Nags Head, North Carolina, and, at present, is composed largely of the Atlantic race, *B. c. canadensis*. This population numbers about 35,000 in winter.

Breeding Range. Its breeding range extends through the Labrador Peninsula east of the height of land from Hopes Advance Bay to the north shore of the St. Lawrence and includes Newfoundland (Todd 1963).

Migration Corridor. A single migration corridor extends down the Labrador coast to the Maritimes, where it picks up birds from Newfoundland. It continues along the coast of New England, across Long Island down the New Jersey shore, and along coastal Maryland to Pea Island National Wildlife Refuge, North Carolina.

Winter Areas. It winters along the coast from southeast Newfoundland through the Maritimes, New England, Long Island, and New Jersey. Almost 1,000 winter in Newfoundland; 5,000 in the Maritimes; 200 in Maine; 1,600 in New Hampshire; 7,000 in Massachusetts; 750 in Connecticut and Rhode Island; 3,000 in Long Island and coastal New York; 3,000 in New Jersey; an unknown number in the Delmarva Peninsula; and 10,000 at Pea Island, North Carolina.

Mid-Atlantic Population

The Mid-Atlantic population of Canada geese contains about 650,000 birds after the hunting season, making it the largest unit on the continent. The range of this population extends through the Ungava Peninsula, along the east shore of Hudson and James bays south across New York and eastern Pennsylvania to Chesapeake Bay, and North and South Carolina. Most of these birds belong to the interior race, but some members of the Atlantic race drift down the Atlantic Coast to the Delmarva Peninsula, and small numbers of giant Canada geese migrate from Ohio.

Breeding Range. The principal breeding grounds of this population lie in the tundra zone of the Ungava Peninsula, Quebec (Addy and Heyland 1968). Two noted areas of concentrated nesting occur on strips of tundra 15 to 30 miles wide, one along the west shore of Ungava Bay between the Payne and George rivers and the other along the shore of Hudson Bay between Port Harrison and Kovik Bay. South of the tundra, breeding geese decrease in density through the boreal forest to about the 50th parallel (Kaczynski and Chamberlain 1968). About 10,000 breeding birds inhabit the Belcher Islands.

In addition to the breeding Canadas, the Ungava Peninsula is the scene of a large number of nonbreeding molting geese from the Tennessee Valley and Mississippi Valley populations (Heyland and Garrard 1974). Small numbers appear from as far west as the range of the Eastern Prairie population.

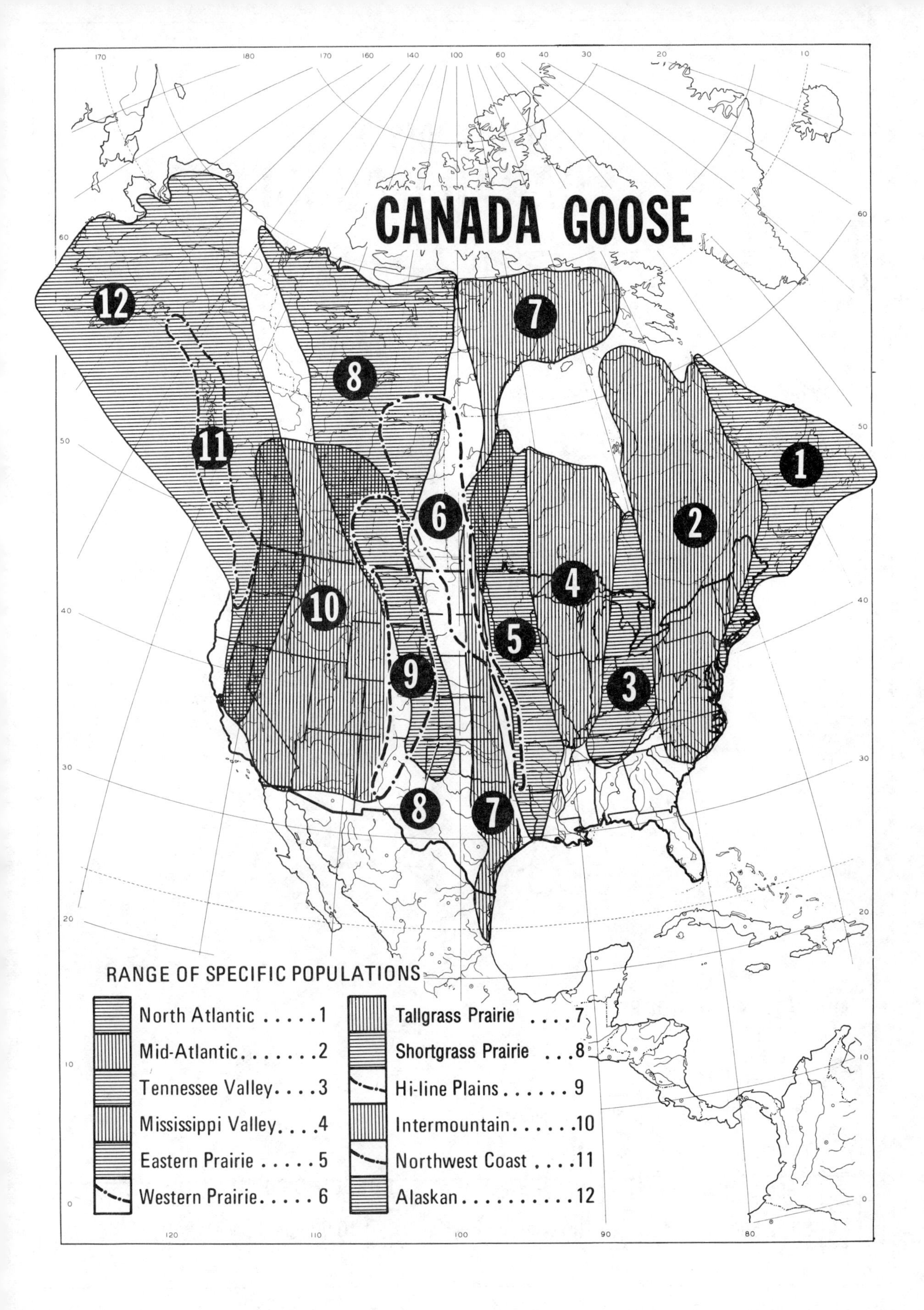

CANADA GOOSE
RANGE OF SPECIFIC POPULATIONS
North Atlantic 1
Mid-Atlantic. 2
Tennessee Valley. . . . 3
Mississippi Valley. . . . 4
Eastern Prairie 5
Western Prairie. 6
Tallgrass Prairie 7
Shortgrass Prairie . . . 8
Hi-line Plains 9
Intermountain. 10
Northwest Coast 11
Alaskan 12

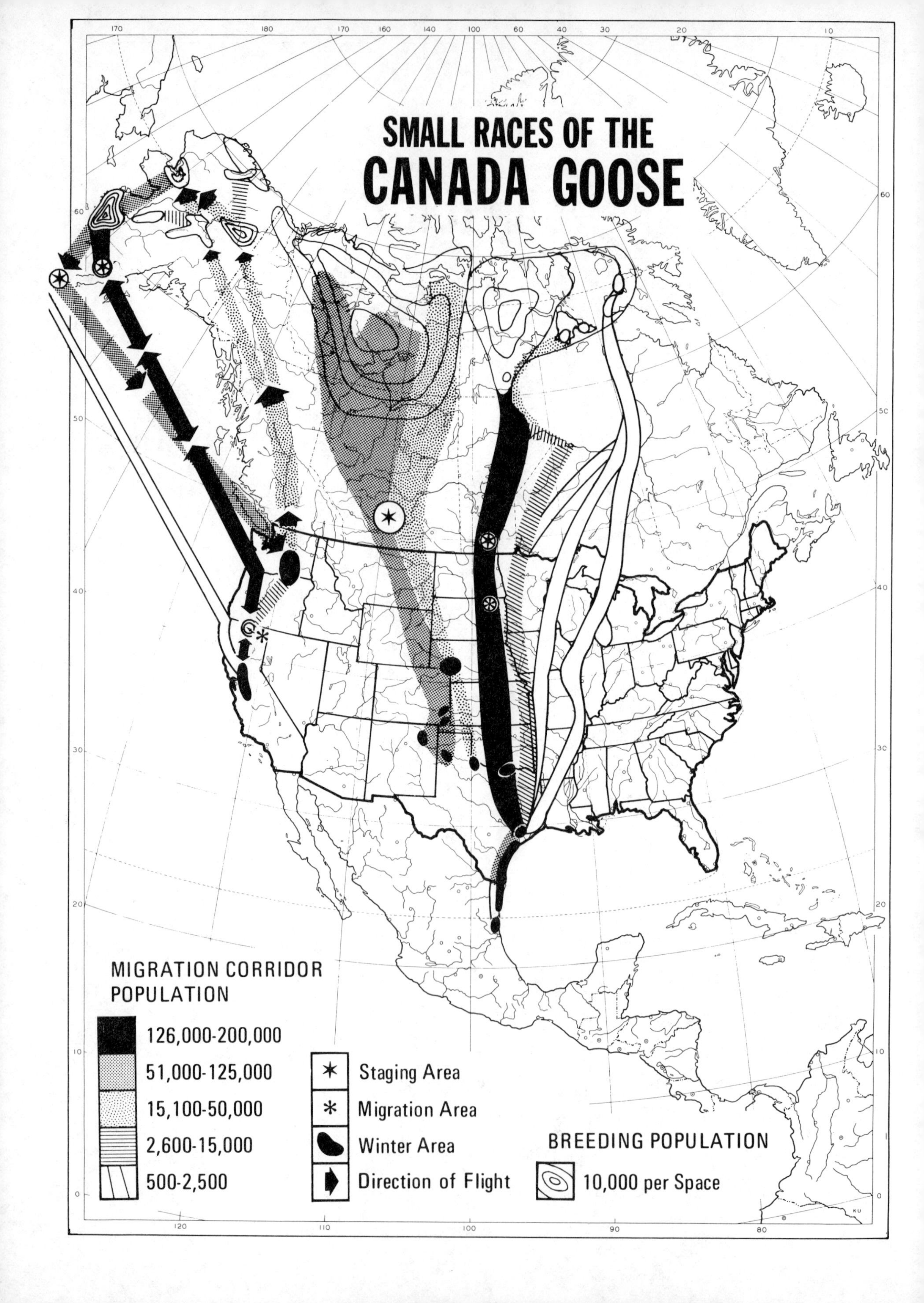
SMALL RACES OF THE
CANADA GOOSE
MIGRATION CORRIDOR
POPULATION
126,000-200,000
51,000-125,000
15,100-50,000
2,600-15,000
500-2,500
Staging Area
Migration Area
Winter Area
Direction of Flight
BREEDING POPULATION
10,000 per Space

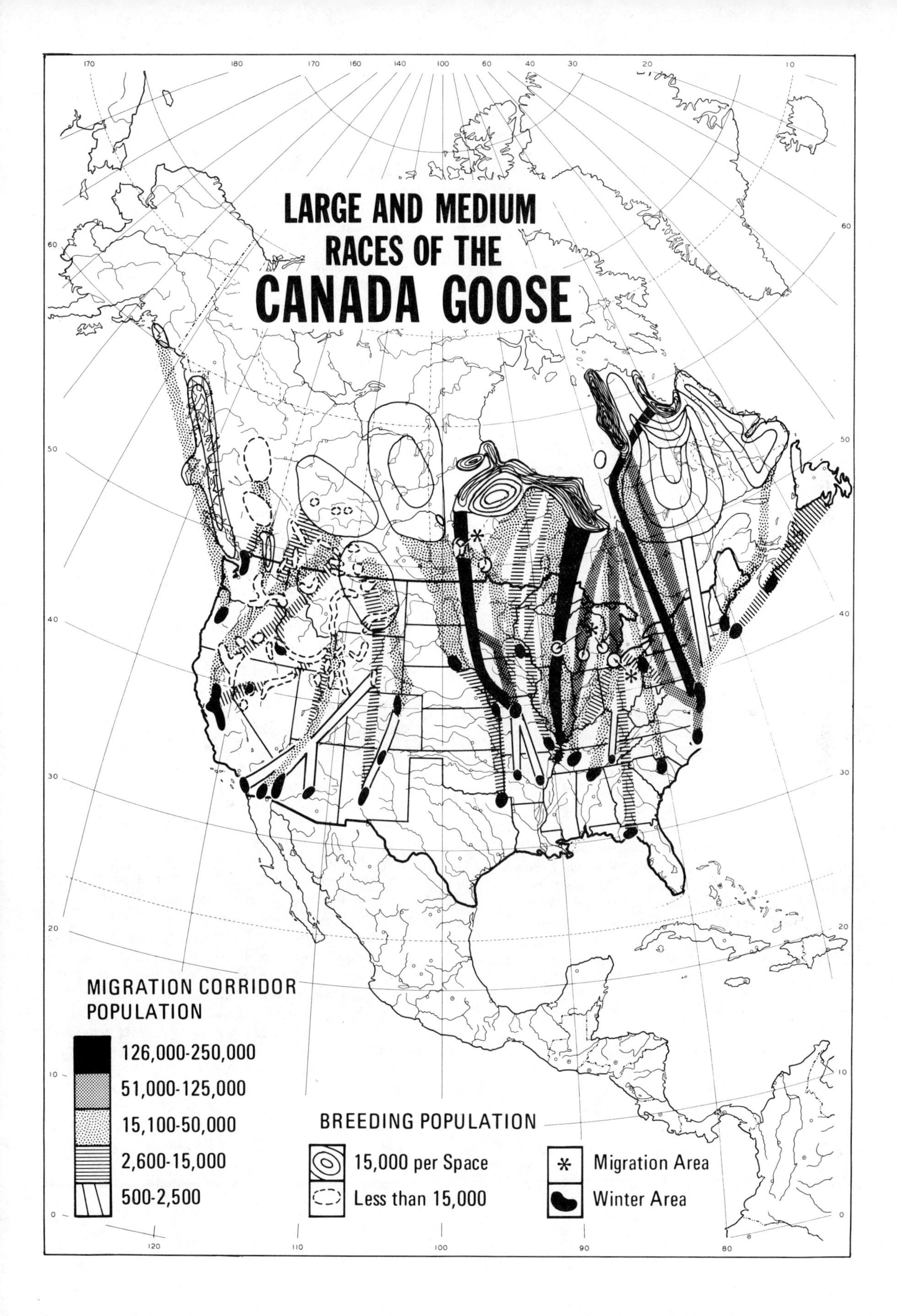
LARGE AND MEDIUM RACES OF THE
CANADA GOOSE
MIGRATION CORRIDOR POPULATION
126,000-250,000
51,000-125,000
15,100-50,000
2,600-15,000
500-2,500
BREEDING POPULATION
15,000 per Space
Less than 15,000
Migration Area
Winter Area

Migration Corridors. The most heavily used migration corridor extends along the east shore of Hudson and James bays, south across central New York and eastern Pennsylvania to the east shore of Maryland, and thence to northeastern North Carolina. Other corridors in the interior, east of Hudson and James bays, are followed by smaller numbers of geese to the same winter grounds (Heyland and Garrard 1974).

Winter Areas. At one time (1948-52), the principal winter ground for this population centered on the refuge at Lake Mattamuskeet, North Carolina (Addy and Heyland 1968). An increment to the total population went to Maryland in 1953, and North Carolina began to lose wintering birds to Delaware-Maryland in 1965. During the period 1970-75, the Mid-Atlantic Canadas wintered as follows: central and western New York, 8,000; western Pennsylvania, 26,000; Delaware and Maryland (Delmarva Peninsula), 537,000; coastal Virginia, 60,000; North Carolina, 58,000; and South Carolina, 10,500. The tremendous concentrations using the Delmarva Peninsula feed on waste corn in the harvested fields and rest on Delaware and Chesapeake bays.

Tennessee Valley Population

The range of the Tennessee Valley population extends from Akimiski Island and the southeast coast of James Bay south across Lake Huron to southeastern Michigan, and on to major winter grounds that include the Tennessee Valley from Knoxville, Tennessee, on the east to the Kentucky line on the west (Cummings 1973). The interior and the giant are two principal races of this population. In midwinter the Tennessee Valley population numbers approximately 130,000 birds, about 20,000 of which are giants.

The Tennessee Valley population originated as a result of the Wheeler National Wildlife Refuge and the state Scottsboro Wildlife Management Area, both in northern Alabama (Hankla and Rudolph 1968). In the early 1940's there were fewer than 500 Canada geese in all of Alabama and occasionally a few thousand in Tennessee. By 1950 there were 7,600 geese wintering in Alabama, largely at Wheeler, but there were still only 2,100 in Tennessee. The winter population in Alabama rose to 60,000 in 1964; at that time there were 49,000 in Tennessee. By January 1974 the wintering numbers in Alabama had declined to 22,800 and in Tennessee to 40,900.

Breeding Range. The breeding range of the Tennessee Valley population apparently encompasses the muskeg bog extending as far back as 120 miles from the east coast of James Bay and as far north as, and including, Akimiski Island (Cummings 1973). A part of the Mississippi Valley population also nests in this region, but its breeding range is more extensive, continuing farther north to the south shore of Hudson Bay (Hanson and Smith 1950).

Migration Corridors. Two migration corridors extend southward from the southeast coast of James Bay. One leads to the Shiawassee National Wildlife Refuge southwest of Saginaw, Michigan; the other to Lake St. Clair, the Jack Miner Bird Sanctuary in Ontario, and the Lake Erie marshes between Toledo and Port Clinton, Ohio (Cummings 1973). From these points of concentration, the migration corridors swing south-southwest to the national wildlife refuges near Decatur, Alabama (Wheeler) and Paris, Tennessee (Tennessee and Cross Creeks), and to state refuges such as Hiawassee in Tennessee and Scottsboro in Alabama.

Winter Areas. The Tennessee Valley population was distributed in mid-December, 1969-74, as follows: Ontario, 23,000; eastern Michigan, 11,000; Ohio, 26,000; Indiana, 3,000; Kentucky, 500; Tennessee, 37,000; and Alabama, 27,000 (Hanson 1974).

Florida Population

Most of the Canadas in this population breed along the south coast of Baffin Island, with the possible addition of some birds from the northwestern part of the Ungava Peninsula. Their migration corridor extends along the east coast of Hudson Bay and along the Ontario-Quebec border through central Ohio to the Florida Panhandle (Graham Cooch). In the early 1950's as many as 28,000 honkers used this migration corridor, but by the mid-1970's, only 1,000-2,000 continued as far south as Florida. It is likely that part of this population now stops farther north and winters with segments of the Tennessee Valley population.

Mississippi Valley Population

Canada geese of the Mississippi Valley population originate in the extensive muskeg bog lying between the west coast of James Bay and the southwest coast of Hudson Bay. Their range extends southward to encompass western Michigan and Indiana, all of Wisconsin and Illinois, western Kentucky and Tennessee, and southeast Missouri (Hanson and Smith 1950).

Almost all the geese in the Mississippi Valley population are of the interior race, numbering nearly 300,00 birds in midwinter. In addition, about 8,000 giant Canadas are a part of this regional population.

Prior to the establishment of the Horseshoe Lake Refuge in the southern tip of Illinois in 1927, geese of this population are considered to have wintered largely along the Mississippi River between Cape Girardeau, Missouri, and Baton Rouge, Louisiana (Hanson and Smith 1950). During the winter of 1928-29, this newly created refuge held 1,000 to 1,900 geese. By 1932-33 the population had risen to 30,000. It fluctuated about this level until the winter of 1948-49, when numbers in southern Illinois zoomed to 90,000. By the mid-1950's southern Illinois and adjacent areas in Kentucky were wintering almost 200,000 Canadas and by the early 1970's almost 300,000.

Breeding Range. The breeding grounds of the Mississippi Valley population, as originally delineated by Hanson and Smith (1950), were between the Kinoje River and Severn River watersheds to the west of James Bay and south of Hudson Bay. The northern terminus was pinpointed by Vaught and Arthur (1965), who found that the separation between the breeding grounds of the Mississippi Valley population and the Eastern Prairie population occurred about 25 miles east of Port Nelson, Manitoba. As described by Hanson and Smith (1950), the breeding grounds cover a tremendous area of muskeg roughly triangular in shape lying between the west coast of James Bay and the south coast of Hudson Bay, a region underlain by sedimentary rocks of the Paleozoic era. They outline seven production centers between the Albany and Severn rivers, the important ones lying within 25 to 60 miles of the coast of James Bay. Two production centers along the Winisk and Severn rivers are located 50 to 100 miles inland from the southwest coast of Hudson Bay. The south-central portion of Akimiski Island is also considered an important production area.

Migration Corridors. Migration corridors of the Mississippi Valley population originate from the west shore of James Bay and the south shore of Hudson Bay. They sweep down each side of Lake Michigan to terminate in southern Illinois. The migration corridor extending through western Michigan is followed by about 90,000 geese. Part of this flight—up to 30,000 geese—stops temporarily at the Swan Creek marsh near Fennville, Michigan, and about 5,000 geese pause at several state refuges in northwest Indiana before continuing on to winter in southern Illinois. Almost 200,000 follow a migration corridor across the east end of Lake Superior and through eastern Wisconsin, where most stop at Horicon Marsh, 50 miles northwest of Milwaukee. After spending from 4 to 10 weeks there, October into early December, they continue their flight to winter grounds in southern Illinois.

Winter Areas. During mid-December, 1969-73, an average of 321,000 Canada geese in the Mississippi Valley population were distributed as follows: Wisconsin, 21,000; southwestern Michigan, 8,000; northwestern Indiana, 8,000; Illinois, 238,000; Ballard County, Kentucky, 25,000; southeast Missouri, 12,000; and Reelfoot Lake, Tennessee, 9,000 (Hanson 1974).

Eastern Prairie Population

The range of the Eastern Prairie population extends from 25 miles east of York Factory and 80 miles north of Churchill on Hudson Bay almost directly south through western Ontario and Manitoba, Minnesota, Iowa, Missouri, and Arkansas to the coast of western Louisiana (Vaught and Kirsch 1966). Prior to 1941, the bulk of this population was reputed to winter in southwestern Louisiana and southeastern Texas. But when I visited this region in February 1942 with Robert H. Smith and John J. Lynch of the U. S. Fish and Wildlife Service, we could locate only a few thousand birds.

At present, the Swan Lake National Wildlife Refuge near Brunswick, Missouri, is the principal winter area with 166,000 geese in mid-December 1973 (Hanson 1974). The first geese—only 150—were recorded there in 1938, but not until 1941, when 800 frequented the area, did they begin to appear consistently in appreciable numbers (Vaught and Kirsch 1966). Fall populations rapidly rose so that by 1955 there were 133,000 at the peak but still only 30,000 during winter.

During mid-December, 1969-73, there were 180,000 geese in the Eastern Prairie population, including 27,000 giant Canadas. Most of this population is composed of the interior race, with varying numbers of "small" Canadas in addition to the giant race.

Breeding Range. Geese of the Eastern Prairie population breed primarily from the Machichi River, 20 miles east of York Factory near the coast of Hudson Bay, to about 80 miles north of Churchill (Vaught and Arthur 1965, Vaught and Kirsch 1966). Their breeding ground in the interior, ranging through the boreal forest northeastward from Lake Winnipeg to Hudson Bay, is sparsely populated but becomes increasingly populous the nearer the bay.

The small Canada geese that migrate into the region of the Eastern Prairie population probably originate from the coastal tundra immediately to the north of the range of the interior race. This origin will be further delineated under the Tallgrass Prairie population. Giant Canada geese that become a part of the Eastern Prairie population either breed in southwestern Manitoba or as local flocks within the southerly range of the Eastern Prairie geese. The region between Lake Winnipeg and Lake Winnipegosis in Manitoba is especially noted for productivity of giant Canadas (Hanson 1965).

Migration Corridors. As shown by band recoveries (Vaught and Kirsch 1966), the bulk of the Eastern Prairie population leaves the Hudson Bay Coast between Churchill and York Factory. The geese start southwestward, but when they reach the Interlakes region of Manitoba, they turn south to pass through western Minnesota and eastern North and South Dakota. As many as 50,000 stop at Minnesota's Lac qui Parle refuge on the upper Minnesota River. The largest migration corridor runs along the border of those states, then turns slightly southeastward to the Swan Lake area of north-central Missouri, where in the early 1970's about 90 percent of the geese wintered. Slightly over 1,000 continue to follow migration routes into Arkansas and southwest Louisiana.

Most of the giant Canadas migrate from their breeding grounds in the Interlake district of Manitoba southeastward to Silver Lake, Rochester, Minnesota, where they spend the winter (Hanson 1965).

Winter Areas. The Swan Lake National Wildlife Refuge in north-central Missouri is the center of wintering Canada geese of the Eastern Prairie population. During mid-December, 1969-73, more than 125,000 wintered there. About 1,200 wintered in Iowa; 25,000 in Minnesota; 1,500 in Arkansas; and 1,200 in Louisiana (Hanson 1974). Included in these figures are giant Canada geese, representing 18,000 of the 25,000 found wintering in Minnesota. Most of the giant Canadas in that state winter at Rochester, most of the interior race at Lac qui Parle.

Western Prairie Population

The range of this comparatively small population has been delineated by Vaught and Kirsch (1966). Its breeding grounds include the countless lakes scattered across the boreal forest of northwestern Manitoba and northern Saskatchewan. Geese of this population migrate into the Missouri River valley of the Dakotas, then down that river to Squaw Creek National Wildlife Refuge in northwest Missouri, with small numbers continuing on to northeast Texas. Most of these birds belong to the interior race, but an unknown number are giant Canadas and members of other races (Vaught and Kirsch 1966). The abundance of small Canadas has been mentioned previously. This admixture of races totals about 40,000 geese.

Breeding Range. Vaught and Kirsch (1966) reported the southern edge of the breeding grounds to be Dauphin, Manitoba, and Yorkton, Saskatchewan, the northern border to extend into the Northwest Territories, the eastern border about the 100th parallel, and the western border to be near the Alberta line.

Migration Corridor. The bulk of this population migrates from the breeding grounds to the Saskatchewan Delta and then south to the Missouri River and the Missouri Coteau, near Bismarck. The geese collect in large numbers at Lake Andes and the Fort Randall Reservoir in southeastern South Dakota, where most of them winter. Others continue along the Missouri River to Squaw Creek in northwest Missouri, where a large contingent winters, and others continue to the Gambell Refuge, near Paris, Texas, and to southeast coastal Texas.

Winter Areas. About 28,000 Canada geese wintered during 1970-74 at Lake Andes and on the Fort Randall Reservoir in southeast South Dakota. An average of 10,000 geese occur from Squaw Creek in northwest Missouri south to the state-owned Schell-Osage and Montrose waterfowl areas in the west-central part of the state. Nearly 2,000 of this number are small Canada geese (Kenneth Babcock). Several thousand more winter in eastern Texas.

Tallgrass Prairie Population

The range of the Tallgrass Prairie population is the longest among Canada geese; it extends from north of the Arctic Circle to south of the Tropic of Cancer. From Baffin Island, and the northern and western shores of Hudson Bay, the migration corridor of these geese extends diagonally across Manitoba, then due south through the eastern Great Plains to the Texas coast. Most of them winter there but several thousand continue along the coast as far south as Tampico, Mexico. The distribution of this population and that of the Shortgrass Prairie population has been reported by Marquardt (1962), Rutherford (1965), MacInnes (1963), and Grieb (1970).

Several races of Canada geese—Richardson's, lesser, and giant—have been associated with this population. During January 1970-74, the population averaged 135,000 geese.

Breeding Range. According to MacInnes (1963), the breeding range of Canada geese in the eastern Canadian Arctic is extensive, embracing some 30 degrees of longitude and 10 degrees of latitude. The breeding area starts on the west coast of Hudson Bay at the 60th parallel, extends northeastward along the coast to include Southampton Island and the west-central part of Baffin Island, then west across the top of the Melville Peninsula, the base of the Boothia Peninsula, including King William Island, as far west as the 102° meridian, and then south to Hudson Bay. In the vicinity of the 102° meridian and Queen Maud Gulf, there is a slight overlap with breeding birds of the Shortgrass Prairie population. In this vast region much of the breeding distribution is unknown. What is known suggests that breeding birds are largely confined to the deltas of tundra streams.

Migration Corridors. From staging areas along the west coasts of Hudson and James Bays, fall migrants of the Tallgrass Prairie population move south across western Ontario and eastern Manitoba. Small Canadas nesting on Baffin Island migrate along the east coast of Hudson Bay to the west coast of James Bay. There the corridor splits into three subcorridors: The one farthest east passes south-southwestward from James Bay, by Sault Sainte Marie and the west side of Lake Michigan, and south-southwesterly across Illinois and Arkansas to southeastern Texas. A second subcorridor crosses the western end of Lake Superior on a southwesterly course to western Missouri and then passes south to Texas. The third subcorridor swings west-southwest to northwestern Minnesota, where it flanks the major corridor of other small Canadas migrating from the west-central coast of Hudson Bay.

That part of the population breeding from Southampton Island westward across the northeastern part of the District of Keewatin constitutes over 85 percent of the Tallgrass population. These geese follow a migration corridor south-southeastward across Manitoba to a migration area in the southern part of that province and the Devils Lake region of North Dakota. About 15,000 stop to rest and feed in Manitoba and 25,000 at Devils Lake; 20,000 additional geese stop in the area of Lake Ashtabula and the Arrowwood Refuge in east-central North Dakota (Rutherford 1965 and updated). Farther south, the Sand Lake National Wildlife Refuge in northeastern South Dakota is an important feeding area for up to 50,000 geese. Six hundred miles to the south, at the state wildlife area of Cheyenne Bottoms and the Quivira National Wildlife Refuge in south-central Kansas, about 55,000 halt their migration to rest and feed. Slightly over 100 miles to the south, 25,000 stop at the Salt Plains National Wildlife Refuge in northern Oklahoma, and many winter there. The Tishomingo and Hagerman national wildlife refuges on Lake Texoma offer resting places for 30,000 during the fall. From there they move largely nonstop across Texas to the coast west of Houston. The majority winter there, but others move along the coast, wintering at scattered localities all the way to Tampico, Mexico.

Winter Areas. A problem arises in reporting the distribution of Canada geese that winter on the Great Plains, because current populations are changing rapidly from year to year. For example, in the last half of the 1960's, an average of 50,000 Canada geese wintered in Kansas and Oklahoma, but during the first half of the 1970's this number rose to 140,000. Yet the population in Texas between these two periods decreased by only 6,000, down to 111,000. Although most of the 75,000 Canada geese wintering in Kansas are still found on the Kirwin and Quivira national wildlife refuges and on the state wildlife area of Cheyenne Bottoms, Marvin Schwilling informs me that they have started to build up impressive numbers on over a dozen artificial reservoirs, listed in descending order of use: Hazelton, Cheney, Glen Elder, Elk City, Milford, Lovewell, John Redmond, Webster, Fall River, Toronto, Council Grove, Marion, and Wilson. According to Schwilling, about one-third of the wintering Canada geese are of the giant race.

The two important winter areas for Oklahoma's 60,000 Canadas are the Salt Plains and Tishomingo national wildlife refuges, but, as in Kansas, artificial reservoirs are laying claim to increasing numbers. The important winter areas of the 60,000 geese composing the Tallgrass Prairie population in Texas are the Hagerman National Wildlife Reguge, 15,000; coastal Texas, 40,000; and coastal Mexico, less than 5,000.

Shortgrass Prairie Population

As implied by its designation, the Shortgrass Prairie population of Canada geese occupies the western Great Plains, a region of sparse precipitation. It ranges from the western Canadian Arctic, south and southeastward across Saskatchewan and Alberta to winter grounds that stretch from western Nebraska through eastern Colorado, to the northeast corner of New Mexico, and to the Texas Panhandle. This population consists of two branches: an eastern segment that winters in the eastern panhandle of Texas and a western segment that winters in Colorado, in the western panhandle of Texas, and in northeastern New Mexico.

The most important single winter ground for this population is in the vicinity of Two Buttes Reservoir in southeastern Colorado. Grieb (1970) determined that the lesser race (*B. c. parvipes*) composed 90 to 95 percent of the Canadas of this reservoir, with the Richardson's (*B. c. hutchinsii*) and western (*B. c. moffitti*) races each representing from 5 to 10 percent. Like all the previously discussed populations of geese, this one has steadily increased from at least 1948 to the mid-1970's (Grieb 1970 and updated). During midwinter, 1970-74, the two segments combined averaged 125,000.

Breeding Range. This population of Canada geese breeds from Victoria Island and the Mackenzie Delta south into northern Alberta and Saskatchewan. Small Canada geese have been reported nesting by Parmelee et al. (1967) on Jenny Lind Island and throughout southeastern Victoria Island in the central Canadian Arctic. These small Canadas are not found north of latitude 70° 31′ in eastern Victoria Island, but in the south they sparsely inhabit a strip extending 60 miles inland from the coast, where Barry (1960) observed 2,000. Twelve—possibly more—pairs of geese nested within 1 square mile on Jenny Lind Island. Smith (1973) recorded Canada geese as uncommon along the coast of western Victoria Island. Manning et al. (1956) did not find this species on several visits to Banks Island. On the mainland, the principal breeding area extends from Queen Maud Gulf west to the Mackenzie River and southward across tundra and open boreal forest of the District of Mackenzie into the closed boreal forest of northern Alberta and Saskatchewan (Grieb 1970).

Porslid (1943) stated that the Canada goose was a common summer resident on the Mackenzie Delta. Soper (1957) reported that pairs were scattered throughout the region of the Slave River delta. Earlier, Soper (1951) found them as summer residents on the higher terrain of Wood Buffalo Park, northern Alberta, but they were much more abundant in migration. Aerial surveys of this vast region by the U. S. Fish and Wildlife Service indicated densities of 0.03 to 0.56 per square mile. Thomas Barry described the western segment of the population as scattered nesters in the Mackenzie Drainage, using stream banks, islands, and beaver ponds (Grieb 1970). He believed that the eastern segment nested along the Arctic Coast. In the region of Queen Maud Gulf, Bathurst to Sherman inlets (therefore including both the Tallgrass and Shortgrass Prairie populations), he estimated 20,000 Canada geese (Barry 1960). One-fourth of this total consisted of a large race of nonbreeding geese; the rest were breeding small geese.

Migration Corridors. Grieb (1970) presented band-recovery data indicating that the eastern segment migrates south from the region of Dease Strait and Queen Maud Gulf to a staging area between Kindersley, Saskatchewan, and Hanna, Alberta. There, this segment is joined by birds of the western segment, migrating down the Mackenzie Drainage. This staging area is also noted for its concentrations of snow geese and white-fronted geese. The eastern segment of Canadas migrates from this staging area southeastward across eastern Montana to the North Platte River near Ogallala, Nebraska. According to Hinz (1974), increasing numbers of these geese are stopping on the Yellowstone River in eastern Montana, from 194 in 1959 to 16,000 in 1973. About 20,000 stop on the North Platte River and many continue on to ranchlands near Vernon, Texas, where most of them winter.

The western segment migrates from the Alberta-Saskatchewan staging area southeastward across central Montana and eastern Wyoming to winter grounds in southeast Colorado, Buffalo Lake, Texas, and lakes in northeast New Mexico.

Winter Areas. Geese of the eastern segment that winter on the North Platte River, Nebraska, number about 12,000. A few hundred winter on the Washita National Wildlife Refuge in western Oklahoma and about 25,000 winter near Vernon, Texas. The bulk of the western segment of the Shortgrass Prairie population, about 95,000, winters in southeast Colorado, centering about the Two Buttes Reservoir. About 30,000 winter on the Buffalo Lake and Muleshoe national wildlife refuges southwest of Amarillo, Texas, and almost 5,000 winter in northeast New Mexico.

Highline Population

The population of large Canada geese that inhabits the Highline Plains is identified by the name of its chosen region. Its entire range extends from central-west Saskatchewan and central-east Alberta south across central Montana, Wyoming, and Colorado into central New Mexico (Rutherford 1965). As a result of diverse transplants establishing new breeding flocks, two races appear to be involved—giant and western. The population in January 1970-74 included about 53,000 birds.

Breeding Range. The breeding range includes the Cypress Hills and plains region of Alberta and western Saskatchewan, the ponds, marshes, and reservoirs of Montana and Wyoming east of the Rocky Mountains, and the Yellowstone and Bighorn rivers in Montana and Wyoming. Because of numerous reservoirs and stockponds that have been recently constructed in this region, there has been a remarkable proliferation of breeding flocks into many new water areas.

Migration Corridor. Canada geese of this group migrate a short distance southward from central Wyoming, through the plains immediately east of the front range in Colorado, and as far as the Bosque del Apache National Wildlife Refuge, New Mexico (Rutherford 1965). Some winter as far north as southeastern Wyoming, many more in north-central Colorado.

Winter Areas. In recent years about 10,000 geese of this population have wintered along the North Platte River in southeastern Wyoming. However, the largest winter concentrations occur in the reservoirs east of the front range in northern Colorado. Only a few geese wintered there prior to 1960, when 660 remained on an area closed to hunting near Fort Collins (Grieb 1968). By 1967 nearly 10,000 wintered there, and by 1975 the population had increased to 30,000. About 5,000 have continued to winter on the Bosque del Apache Refuge in New Mexico.

Intermountain Population

Consisting solely of the western (Great Basin) Canada goose, the Intermountain population occupies the marshes and stream channels interspersed among the mountain ranges and basins of the Far West. The entire range of this population extends from central British Columbia east to central Alberta on the north to southern California and Arizona on the south. Data supplied by John Chattin indicate that the fall population numbers slightly over 100,000 geese, the winter population about 82,000, similar to the 120,000 estimated by Yocom (1965) decades earlier.

Breeding Range. Intermountain Canada geese have a discontinuous breeding distribution resulting from the mountain ranges and the arid basins among which scattered water areas provide breeding habitat. Important breeding areas include the Chilcotin and Cariboo plateaus; the upper Columbia and Okanagan valleys of British Columbia; the Columbia Basin of Washington; the Flathead Valley of Montana; the Snake River of southern Idaho; the upper Snake River and upper Green River in western Wyoming; the Yampa River in northwestern Colorado; Bear River, Ogden Bay, and other marshes flanking the east side of Great Salt Lake, Utah; the Carson Sink marshes of Nevada; and the Klamath Basin and Honey Lake region of Northern California.

Migration Corridors. Many geese from the various segments of this population have been banded, providing detailed information on the complex migration corridors that lead from mountain valleys to lower altitudes and latitudes. Many segments are only partially migratory and others migrate short distances. In the Northwest, migration corridors tend to funnel birds into the Columbia Basin of Washington, some continuing to the Central Valley of California. Farther east, geese collect along the Snake River in southern Idaho, and some move on southwest to Carson Sink, Nevada, and the Central Valley. Migration corridors from the complex of breeding areas in northeast Utah and western Wyoming lead to the Imperial Valley and the lower Colorado River of southern California and to Roosevelt Lake and the Salt River valley near Phoenix, Arizona.

Winter Areas. The more important concentrations of western Canada geese during winter in the Intermountain region are the following: 20,000 in the Columbia Basin, Washington and Oregon; 10,000 in Harney Basin, Oregon;

12,000 in the Snake River plain of southern Idaho; 6,000 in the Carson Sink, Nevada; 10,000 at Honey Lake, 15,000 in the Central Valley, and 14,000 in the Imperial Valley, California; and 2,500 each in the lower Colorado River and Salt River valleys of Arizona. Surprising numbers of geese persist in wintering in northern valleys where swift currents keep waters open and snowfall is sufficiently low to permit grazing: 2,800 in western Montana, 400 in western Wyoming, 2,700 in Utah, and 500 in western Colorado.

Northwest Coast Population

The range of the Northwest Coast population extends from the Copper River delta, Alaska, south through the Alexander Archipelago and Vancouver Island to the Willamette Valley of Oregon. It is largely composed of two races: the dusky and the Vancouver Canada geese, but several other races also occur on the winter grounds. About 125,000 geese belong to this population. King and Lensink (1971) estimate a fall population of 80,000 Vancouver geese in southeast Alaska, and about 7,000 are believed to breed in British Columbia. Inventories on the winter ground of the dusky goose in western Oregon averaged 16,600 during 1960-67 (Chapman et al. 1969). Several hundred to several thousand winter along the southwest coast of Washington and the northwest coast of California. The fall flight in 1966 was calculated at 35,000 birds (Chapman et al. 1969).

During two winters, 1965-66 and 1966-67, Chapman et al. (1969) determined that 96 and 99 percent of the geese taken in the center of the population's winter range were dusky geese, with small numbers of cackling and one medium-sized goose, plus two Aleutians and two western geese. Since then, the number of nondusky geese in the Willamette Valley has greatly increased.

Breeding Range. According to Hansen (1962), the dusky goose breeds along the southeast Alaskan coast for 275 miles between Cook Inlet and Bering Glacier; the center of its abundance is the Copper River delta near Cordova, Alaska. Vancouver Canada geese breed from Glacier Bay through the Alexander Archipelago of Alaska, the Queen Charlotte Islands, and Vancouver Island. The summer population of the dusky goose is about 20,000. According to R. T. Sterling, William Morris, and Ray Halladay, there are about 7,000 Vancouver geese on their breeding grounds on Vancouver Island and on the Queen Charlotte Islands in British Columbia. King and Lensink (1971) estimated 80,000 Vancouver geese in fall in southeast Alaska.

Migration Corridors. Band recoveries and population distribution (Hansen 1962, Chapman et al. 1969) ably delineate the migration corridor of this species. The dusky geese migrate from the area of Cordova, Alaska, across the Gulf of Alaska; some stop at the Queen Charlotte Islands and at Vancouver Island but most make landfall in southwest Washington. They follow the Columbia River inland to Portland, where they turn south to follow the Willamette Valley 75 or more miles to winter grounds in Polk, Linn, and Benton counties. Small numbers of Vancouver geese also migrate to the Willamette Valley, but they appear to occupy a winter ground in Yamhill County, 50 miles north of the principal winter area of the dusky (Hansen 1962).

Winter Areas. Hansen (1962) deduced from band recoveries that the Vancouver race was largely nonmigratory; 62 percent of the recovered birds banded at Glacier Bay had traveled no farther than 100 miles, and 20 percent had exceeded that distance by no more than 50 miles. Only 17 percent were recovered from the coast of Washington and the Willamette Valley.

Almost a third of the 20,000 dusky geese wintering in Oregon are found in Benton County, 28 percent in Lane County, and 18 percent in Polk County. A few hundred winter along the northern California coast, a few hundred to a few thousand in southwest coastal Washington, and Hansen (1962) reported 1,000 to 1,500 wintering regularly off the islands of Prince Edward Sound.

Alaskan Population

The Alaskan population of Canada geese ranges over the entire state except for the southeast coast occupied by the Northwest Coast population. Most of the Alaskan population migrates to the interior of Washington, northeast Oregon, and the Central Valley of California. Three races of Canada geese are members of this population: cackling, Taverner's, and Aleutian. The entire population prior to the hunting season numbers about 250,000 birds.

Breeding Range. Breeding cackling geese are confined to a 10-mile-wide strip of coastal tundra between the Kuskokwim and Yukon rivers (Nelson and Hansen 1959). Previously, the breeding range of this species may have been more extensive, reputedly including the Bering Sea coast as far as Wainwright and westward along the coast of the Alaska Peninsula. King and Lensink (1971) have reported that approximately 150,000 cacklers compose the late-summer population on the Yukon Delta.

Taverner's Canada geese breed throughout the interior of Alaska, including the upper regions of the Yukon Delta. The fall population of this species numbers about 100,000 (King and Lensink 1971). The endangered Aleutian goose numbered slightly over 1,200 birds in the fall of 1976 (Paul Springer). Once it nested in the outer two-thirds of the Aleutian Islands as well as in the Commander and Kurile islands. In recent years it has bred only at tiny Buldir Island, near the tip of the Aleutian Chain. The introduction of the Arctic fox, 1910-30, into most of the Aleutian Islands apparently resulted in such high nest losses that the Aleutian goose was extirpated as a breeding bird from all but fox-free Buldir Island (Byrd and Springer 1976).

Migration Corridors. On the basis of band recoveries,

Nelson and Hansen (1959) were able to trace the migration corridor used by cackling geese. After leaving the Yukon Delta, a part of the population stops at Bristol Bay before heading south-southeast across the Gulf of Alaska to make landfall near the mouth of the Columbia River. There they turn inland to enter the Klamath Basin in northern California, a major rest stop and feeding area for almost the entire population, before they proceed to their winter grounds in the Central Valley of California. A few hundred cacklers reach the Izembek Bay and the eastern Aleutians, but Robert Jones, Jr., reports that almost the entire population crosses the Alaska Peninsula at Ugashik Lakes.

At least 70,000 of the 100,000 Taverner's geese gather in the fall at Izembek Bay at the tip of the Alaska Peninsula. They feed along with 200,000 black brant on the luxuriant beds of eelgrass in the bay. Robert Jones, Jr., reports that both the geese and the brant depart across the sea on a course of about 113°. The geese depart sporadically, but the brant leave en masse.

Robert Jeffrey has observed the Taverner's geese making landfall at Skagit Bay in northwestern Washington. A few thousand stop there but the majority continue over the Cascade Range to Soap Lake in central Washington. Under low, heavy cloud cover, migrating geese have been observed passing through the Skykomish Pass. From Soap Lake, the geese spread out over the Columbia Basin and into adjacent areas of Oregon, south of the Columbia River.

About 80 percent of the Taverner's population migrates into the Columbia Basin, and the remainder migrate from the mouth of the Columbia River through the Willamette Valley of Oregon to the Klamath Basin and eventually to the Central Valley of California.

The Taverner's goose is the only Canada goose that migrates north along an entirely different migration corridor in the spring from that which it does in the fall. Visual observations and radar sightings in the spring indicate that the bulk of these birds return to interior Alaska via the Okanagan Valley of British Columbia, the Fraser Valley, Nechako Plateau, and the Yukon Basin. Thus, these geese have adapted an elliptical counter-clockwise passage between fall and spring, probably to obtain new sources of food in the spring. The snow geese of the Pacific Flyway also make a similar seasonal change in migration corridors.

Robert D. Jones, Jr., reports that during the fall some Aleutian geese migrate eastward along the Aleutian Chain for almost 1,000 miles to Izembek Bay. Recent evidence indicates that these geese probably migrate across the Gulf of Alaska to the northern California coast and then turn inland to winter in the Central Valley of California. From 200 to 900 have been observed both spring and fall at Castle Rock, near Crescent City, California (Byrd and Springer 1976). Recoveries in the Central Valley, 1975-76, from Aleutians banded at Buldir Island indicate that most of them winter there. However, a recovery from Imperial County, California, and another from Mohave County, Arizona, suggest that some of these geese winter at extreme limits of the winter range of western Canada geese.

Winter Areas. Almost 98 percent of the 135,000 cackling geese found on January surveys winter in California. About 39 percent winter in the San Joaquin Valley, 25 percent in the San Francisco Bay area, and 34 percent in the Sacramento Valley. Slightly over 3,000 cacklers winter in Oregon and about 240 in Washington.

During the past 20 years, nearly 80,000 Taverner's Canada geese have been inventoried after the end of the hunting seasons. Over 85 percent of these have been found in the Columbia Basin of Washington and in adjacent areas of north-central Oregon. Most of the remainder, slightly over 10,000, winter in the Central Valley of California.

MIGRATION BEHAVIOR

Canada geese migrate in flocks that are highly variable in size depending upon the race, region, and season. Small geese tend to migrate in larger flocks than large geese, and late-season flights are apt to contain larger flocks than early flights. Seventy-four flocks of interior Canada geese migrating through central Illinois varied in size from 23 to 300 and averaged 96. An unusually large flock of 1,200 was not included in this figure.

According to Raveling (1969), large flocks of geese on the winter grounds are composed of subflocks, which in turn are composed of families. Families are considered to be two or more geese resulting from a pair bond and progeny-sibling relationships. Some families Raveling observed included yearlings as well as immatures, but yearlings were not as strongly bound to their parents as the younger birds. When families were disrupted by trapping and marking, flock members reunited in a matter of minutes to 7.5 days. From Raveling's (1969) studies of marked and telemetered geese on winter grounds, it is logical to assume that flocks in migration are composed of similar units.

Raveling (1970) also observed that large families dominate smaller families that dominate pairs that dominate single birds. Ganders dominate family units. I suppose this same relationship occurs in flocks during a migratory flight; the lead bird, therefore, is probably the gander of the largest family. Although some reports indicate that the point goose changes position during a migratory flight, we have never seen such a change when following many flocks many miles by car and plane.

The altitude at which Canada geese migrate varies greatly with weather conditions and, apparently, the distance between points of departure and arrival. Under low, heavy overcast, geese may migrate only a few hundred feet above the ground. But with fair skies, a few have been recorded by pilots at an altitude of over 8,000 feet. Several hundred reports from pilots, received by the traffic control centers of the Federal Aviation Administration, indicate that most flocks of geese observed during fall migration were flying at an altitude of 2,000 feet; 64 percent were at heights between 750 and 3,500 feet. During spring migration, maximum altitudes were not as great: fewer were over

4,000 feet above ground level and the highest was at 7,000 feet. Seventy-seven percent of the flocks were sighted at altitudes between 750 and 3,000 feet.

Chronology

Canada geese are paradoxical in many ways about their chronology of migration. Numerous populations are prone to leave breeding areas in late summer or early fall, long before weather conditions would seem to dictate, and yet birds of these same populations return to their Subarctic or Arctic breeding grounds while snow covers the ground and the first open water is just appearing. On the other hand, populations of giant Canada geese and some of the western Canadas are notorious for their late fall departures from breeding areas (Hanson 1965, Sherwood 1965, Arneson 1970).

Fall. Cackling geese leave their breeding grounds on the Yukon Delta as single families or small flocks and move leisurely down the coast to a staging area on Bristol Bay at the base of the Alaska Peninsula (Nelson and Hansen 1959). In early October they leave this staging area for their long flight to Klamath Basin, California, where they arrive in two waves—October 15-20 and October 25-30. They remain at Klamath until late November, then move into the Sacramento Valley. In late December and early January they shift still farther south into the San Joaquin Valley.

Across the Arctic at an almost identical latitude, 61° on Hudson Bay, MacInnes (1963) reported that a peak southward departure occurred on September 1. On Subarctic staging areas south of Hudson Bay in Manitoba, Canada geese achieve peak numbers about September 20. In the northern two-thirds of their migration corridor (the Dakotas, Nebraska, and the northern half of Oklahoma) they first arrive on September 22, reach peak numbers on October 15, and the last geese depart about November 10. From central Oklahoma to central Texas, the Canadas first arrive in early October and reach peak numbers in mid-November, with many thousands wintering in the area. On their principal winter grounds, along the Texas coast, they first arrive October 10 and achieve maximum numbers about December 15.

Canada geese of the Mid-Atlantic population begin to leave their breeding grounds on the Ungava Peninsula by mid-September (Heyland and Garrard 1974). They arrive in southern Quebec during October 11-20, judging from the recovery of bands. This same period also produces most of the recoveries in New York and Pennsylvania. Many recoveries occur in Delaware and Maryland the first day of the hunting season, usually November 1, indicating that appreciable numbers of geese are already present on their principal winter grounds. Numbers of band recoveries remain consistently high through November and December.

From censuses at several national wildlife refuges, Cummings (1973) traces the southward passage of the Tennessee Valley population. These geese arrive at the Shiawassee Refuge, near Saginaw, Michigan, by September 15 and reach maximum levels about mid-November. The last departures occur by Christmas. The chronology of passage is similar at the Ottawa National Wildlife Refuge, near Toledo, Ohio. On the main winter refuges located near Paris, Tennessee, and Wheeler, Alabama, geese arrive in mid-September, as early as their arrival at Shiawassee 500 to 600 miles to the north. At the two winter refuges in Tennessee and Alabama, numbers of geese steadily increase through October, November, and December.

Canada geese of the Mississippi Valley population migrate from the south coasts of Hudson Bay and the northwest coast of James Bay from early September through October. The first migrating flocks reach Horicon Marsh, Wisconsin, during the first week of September, with the population rapidly building up to 200,000 by mid-October. A small proportion of the early flights bypass Horicon and continue on to refuges in southern Illinois, where numbers gradually increase from September into late November. Then, in late November or early December, the freezing of Horicon Marsh, combined with a heavy snowfall, results in a mass departure of 100,000 or more geese to southern Illinois.

Canada geese of the Eastern Prairie population start their migration from the southwest coast of Hudson Bay in early September (Vaught and Kirsch 1966). Band recoveries indicate an extensive passage through northern Manitoba through September and the first 10 days of October. Geese begin to appear at the terminus of their fall flight—the Swan Lake Refuge in north-central Missouri—in mid-September, with numbers rapidly increasing to maximum levels by November 10.

Spring. For the farmer, the rancher, the city dweller, and the Cree Indian, the northward flight of Canada geese symbolizes spring. And rightly so, for they move northward as rapidly as melting snow unearths food and melting ice provides drinking water. Because the isotherm of 35 degrees produces these conditions, their northward progress has been associated with it.

Thus, Canada geese begin to leave their winter grounds in mild temperature zones as early as mid-January. In moderate zones of warmth, they leave about mid-February, and in the more frigid zones they do not begin to move northward until early March. Just as the alternate cold and warm fronts battle over the unsteady progress of spring, the first northward movements of Canada geese are equally unsteady. A heavy snowfall or a blast of cold air stops the migrants in their tracks and, occasionally, sends them into retreat.

Not all Canada goose families are of like mind when it comes to pressing their way northward against the snow and ice barriers. Many families are content to remain on winter grounds for up to 2 months after the first departures

CANADA GOOSE

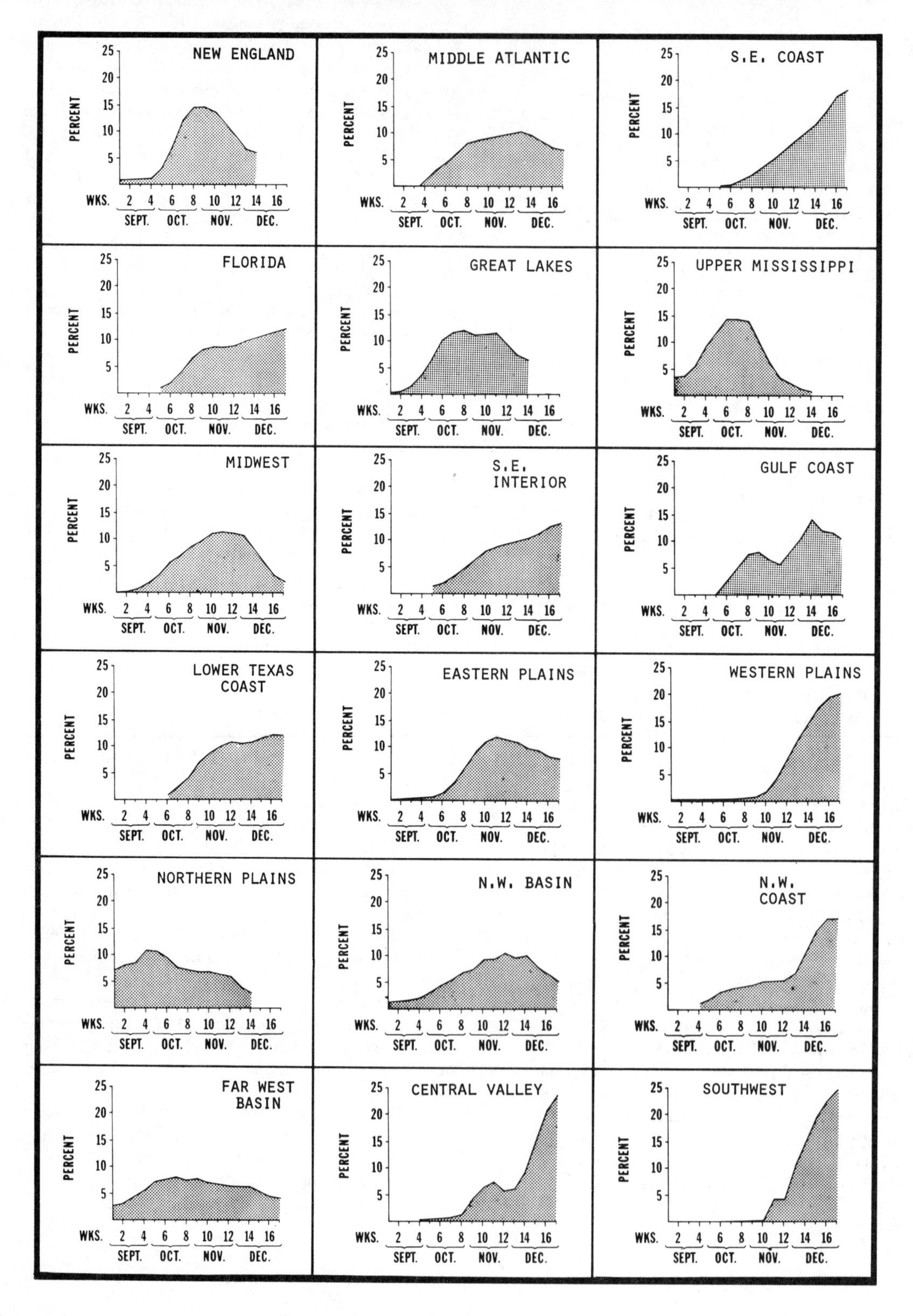

Fall

CANADA GOOSE

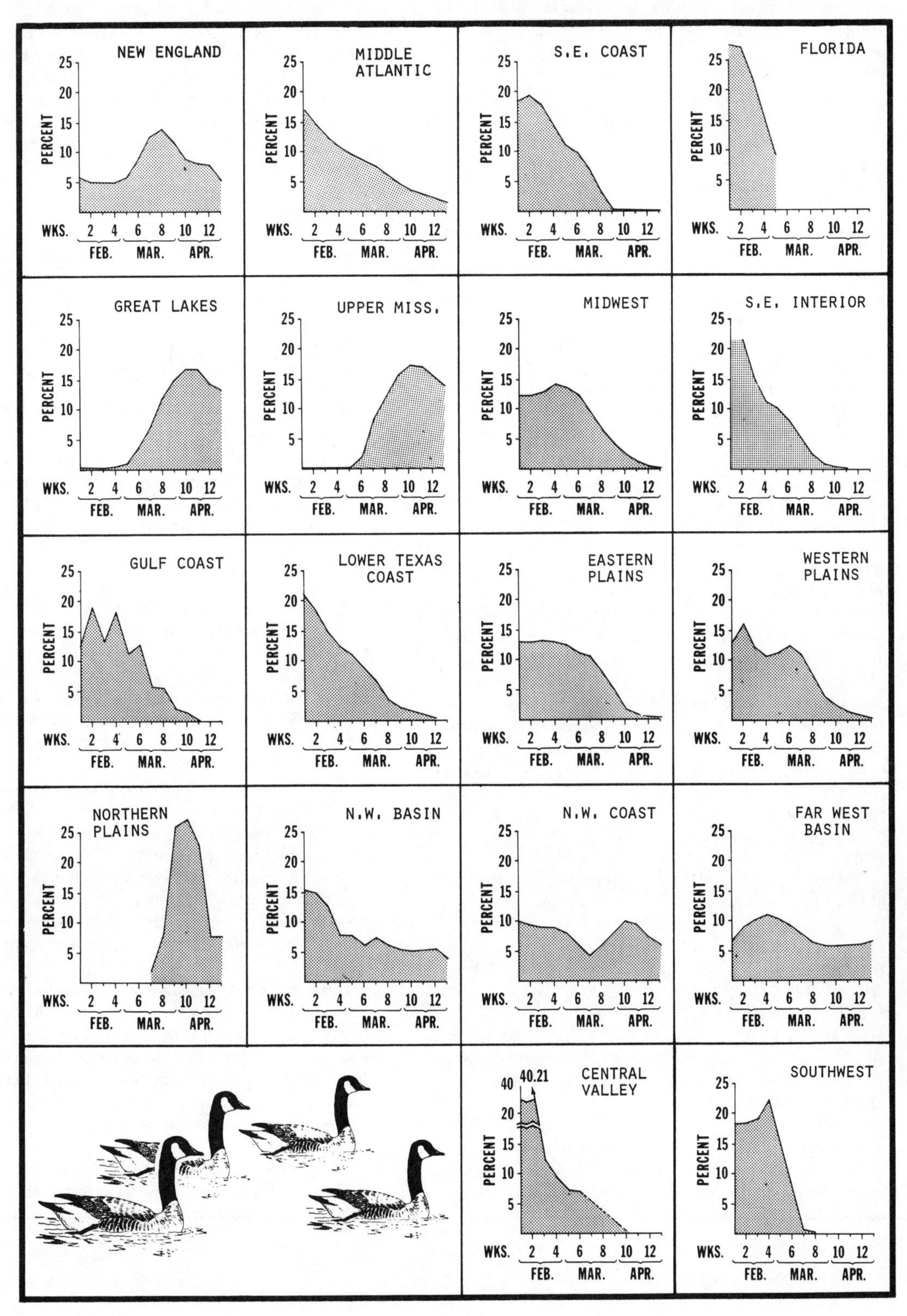

Spring

to the north. Although the first geese north move in 50- to 100-mile steps at a time, the late migrants tend to travel in longer leaps and, accordingly, make up for some of the time lost by lingering overlong on the winter areas.

Because of the vagaries of spring, and the latitudinal and altitudinal range in their breeding grounds, Canada geese arrive at their summer homes on a wide range of dates. For example, over a 21-year period, giant Canada geese arrived at Seney Refuge, northern Michigan, from as early as March 1 to as late as March 29 (Sherwood 1965). The main flight arrives about 3 weeks after the first arrivals and small numbers trickle in for 2 more weeks.

Interior Canada geese arrive on their nest area along the Kinoje River (near the southwest coast of James Bay) about mid-April (Lumsden 1969). The large flights into and over the area occur during the last week of April. At Churchill, Manitoba, Pakulak (1969) recorded Canada geese arriving during the last 8 days of April in 1966 and 1968 and the first week of May in 1967. Major flights arrived May 11-13, 1965 and 1968, and May 21, 1967.

Farther up the Hudson Bay coast on the delta of the McConnell River, MacInnes (1963) observed first arrivals of the Tallgrass Prairie population on May 20, with peak numbers on June 1. The bulk of these birds had arrived on their Dakota migration areas April 15 and had departed by May 15.

In the eastern Arctic, Freeman (1970*b*) observed the first Canada geese in the Belcher Islands, southeast Hudson Bay, on April 30 and during the first half of May. On southwest Baffin Island, two races of geese appeared from mid-May to June in slightly increasing numbers (Macpherson and McLaren 1959). The first Canada geese appeared on Adelaide Peninsula on June 10 and continued to arrive for the next 10 days (Macpherson and Manning 1959).

Canada geese arrive in the Athabasca Delta region between April 15 and 25 (Soper 1951). Farther north on the Slave River delta, they arrive during the last week of April (Soper 1957). Five hundred miles to the northeast at Karrak Lake (45 miles inland from Queen Maud Gulf), Ryder (1971*a*) observed the first Canada geese during May 27-June 1, 1966-68. At Cambridge Bay, Victoria Island, Canada geese arrive as early as May 22 (Parmelee et al. 1967).

Irving (1960) observed the first Taverner's Canada geese at Old Crow, northwest Yukon Territory, on May 6, and the migratory flights continued during May and into early June. At Anaktuvuk Pass, Alaska, the earliest geese arrived May 11-22, 1949-54, and at Kobuk, in the northwestern part of the state, May 19 (Irving 1960). Gabrielson and Lincoln (1959) cited the following early records of Taverner's geese in the interior of Alaska: April 5, McGrath; April 8, Flat; April 24, College; April 27, Tanacross; April 30, upper Kuskokwim River; May 1, Beaver Mountains; and May 14, Tolugak Lake.

Cackling geese, confined exclusively to the Yukon Delta as breeding birds, arrive a few at a time in early May but build up rapidly to peak numbers either by mid-May in normal springs or late May when spring is delayed (Mickelson 1973).

BREEDING

Behavior

Age. A few yearling geese have attempted to nest, but none has hatched a clutch successfully (Hall and McGilvrey 1971, Mickelson 1973). Some 2-year-olds nest. Craighead and Stockstad (1964) found that between 27 and 36 percent of the wild 2-year-old geese marked in the Flathead Valley, Montana, nested for the first time, and all of the 3-year-olds nested. Martin (1964), studying marked Canada geese at the Ogden Bay Wildlife Area, Utah, reported that 33 percent of the 2-year-old females nested and probably all of the 3-year-olds.

In southeast Alberta, Surrendi (1970) found that only one of five 2-year-olds nested, but he concluded that a higher proportion might have nested had competition for nest sites been less. The availability of nest territories may well explain differences in the proportion of 2-year-olds that nest. As shown by Brakhage (1965), 2-year-old females nest later than older birds, not reaching their peak until the fourth week of the nesting season, whereas 3-year-old birds peaked during the third week and 4-year-olds during the second week. At Ogden Bay, Utah, birds marked as adults nested 1 to 2 weeks earlier than 2-year-olds (Martin 1964).

MacInnes et al. (1974) noted that, for unknown reasons, some marked geese that had nested previously failed to nest. Minimum estimates of nonbreeding adults ranged from 6 to 22 percent, with the maximum number placed at 18 to 41 percent.

Pair Bond. Pairing occurs among some yearlings after their return to northern summer areas that may or may not be their natal areas. In northwest Missouri, Brakhage (1965) determined that 42 percent of the yearling males paired, but, somewhat surprisingly, only 14 percent of the females. Such sexual imbalance suggests that there was a shortage of males in this particular population. Although displaced 100 miles when young, 80 percent of the yearling females that returned to their transplanted home formed pair bonds (Surrendi 1970). Sherwood (1965) observed that when old geese returned to their breeding areas without mates, pair bonds might be established in a matter of hours. But among yearlings, weeks or even months of association might occur before attachment. Once formed, pair relationship remains steadfast throughout life, but when separated by death, the survivor seeks a new mate.

Homing. Most Canada geese return to their breeding grounds as family units, but shortly after their arrival yearlings leave their parents. Depending upon the race, the nest area, and individual traits, the yearlings remain in the vicinity of their parents or strike out for "fresh fields." Some return after the wing molt to rejoin their parents, who have completed their task of brood rearing (Martin 1964, Sherwood 1965).

From studies of marked geese at Ogden Bay, Dey (1966) concluded that Canada geese nest in the same area of a marsh year after year; moreover, they prefer the same vegetative cover and a nest foundation similar to their initial one. However, if earlier nest sites are unavailable because of high water, snow cover, or destruction of muskrat houses, the pair resorts to a nearby site.

Even 7- to 8-week-old geese, transplanted 100 miles from Brooks to near Hanna, Alberta, demonstrated a strong return to their new home. Surrendi (1970) found that 58 percent of the anticipated yearling females returned, though only a scant 39 percent of the males returned. A year later, about 85 percent of the initial sightings of females were within a mile of their former release site; the males had a 32 percent return. Two yearling males were observed 25 miles distant from their "home" lake, and two 2-year-olds were 60 miles away.

Territory. Pairs of Canada geese break away from the flock that carried them back to their breeding grounds, as each pair seeks to lay claim to a bit of earth. Among breeding birds, the territories claimed will contain the nests, but for some strange reason not all geese that defend territories attempt to nest. Aggressive calls and displays of both male and female usually serve to turn trespassing pairs aside without the necessity of physical combat (Collias and Jahn 1959, Martin 1964, Sherwood 1965). The male is the more aggressive of the two, often pursuing an invading bird into the air.

The size of the defended site varies greatly with the density of the breeding population, the age of the birds, the nature of the surrounding cover, the chronology of breeding, and subtle factors not readily apparent. For example, Sherwood (1965) found that the same pair of geese occupied the same nest site in 1963 and 1964, yet their 1964 territory was only half the size of the one they occupied the preceding year. But he also believed that returning breeders had a proprietary stake in their preceding year's territory that other geese recognized and rarely challenged.

Ewaschuk and Boag (1972) believe that both vegetative cover and the level of aggressiveness of the male influence the size of the territory. Several investigators have observed that the most aggressive ganders maintained the largest territories (Dow 1943, Wood 1965, Brakhage 1965). Large territories are rarely vacated and include not only the nest site but food and water as well. Small territories often lack adequate food and water. As a result, the gander temporarily leaves the territory and thus makes it more difficult for the pair to retain it (Ewaschuk and Boag 1972).

Nesting

Nest Sites. Canada geese have a greater diversity of nest sites than all other species of waterfowl. They nest in dense marshes, on islands, on cliffs, on elevated platforms in trees, in muskeg, and on tundra. The western and giant races of Canada geese seem to be especially versatile. The western race has been found nesting in marshes on mats of bulrushes and on the tops of muskrat houses (Williams and Marshall 1937, Dow 1943, Martin 1964), on haystacks (Dow 1943, Steel et al. 1957, Arneson 1970), on cliffs and on abandoned heron and osprey nests (Geis 1956), on dikes and ditch banks (Williams and Marshall 1937, Naylor 1953, Miller and Collins 1953), but most of all on islands. The islands may be in natural lakes, reservoirs, streams, or rivers; they may cover a fraction of an acre or several hundred acres. Less often the nest islands may be located in canyons or in the middle of rapids.

Both the western and giant Canada geese have taken readily to elevated man-made structures. Yocom (1952) was the first to report the adoption by Canada geese of such unusual nest sites as galvanized washtubs, wicker baskets, and other devices placed in trees. Craighead and Stockstad (1961) erected wood platforms for nesting geese in the Flathead Valley of Montana. They found 107 aerial nests of geese, 49 on aerial platforms and 58 in natural elevated sites; 13 percent of all aerial platforms erected were used by nesting geese. At Honey Lake Wildlife Area, California, Rienecker (1971) experimented with various artificial platforms. Platform occupancy by geese increased from 15 percent the first year to 53 percent the fourth year. He concluded that the ideal platform should be 3 to 4 feet in size and located 50 to 300 feet from shore in an area containing more geese than the natural habitat can accommodate. Giant Canada geese in northwest Missouri readily accepted washtubs placed on posts and dead trees, at a height of 1 to 20 feet above the water (Brakhage 1965). He filled the tubs—22 inches in diameter and 10 inches in depth—with sawdust topped with straw. Over a 3-year period, 1961-64, 51 female geese selected tub sites 79 percent of the time and ground sites 21 percent.

In the pothole muskeg of the Kinoje Lake region, near Moosonee, Ontario, Raveling and Lumsden (1967) reported that Canada geese preferred to nest on islets 5 to 25 feet in diameter and supporting trees less than 2 feet high. Other sites included the shores of creeks and the hummocks in marshes. Preferred lakes were less than 5 acres in size. Most of the nests were situated 6 to 12 inches above the ice layer. Eight hundred miles to the northwest, where the McConnell River enters Hudson Bay, MacInnes (1962) found small Canada geese nesting on wet tundra flats dotted with ponds. He reported (1960) that preferred sites were hummocky sphagnum-covered islets between 1.5 to 15 feet in diameter and extending barely 1.5 feet above the summer water level.

Similarly, cackling geese on the pond-studded tundra of the coastal Yukon Delta selected islets for 81 percent of their nest sites (Mickelson 1973). The islets averaged 5 by 11 feet in size and 8 inches in height. Sixteen percent of the geese nested on small peninsulas extending into tundra ponds, but only 3 percent placed their nests on the mainland shore.

A female Canada leads her mate on a search for a particular nest site, which often includes a look at previously used scrapes. However else the site might vary, standard prerequisites are proximity to water, cover for the nest itself, and an exposed view for the incubating bird. Most nests are located within a few feet of water and about 90 percent are within 50 yards, but Klopman (1958) found one 300 yards distant.

If females do not use old scrapes, new ones are wallowed out in the earth. Hollows are rounded out on mats of bulrushes or the domes of muskrat houses. Usually the females reach out from the saucer-shaped depressions to gather vegetation for the bases and rims. Nest improvement continues as laying progresses. Down is plucked from the breast for the nest lining with the laying of the third or fourth egg. More down is added until incubation commences.

Dimensions of 30 nests of the giant Canada goose ranged on the outside from 17 to 48 inches, inside from 9 to 11 inches, and in depth from 3 to 6 inches (Kossack 1950). Western Canada goose nests measured by Williams and Nelson (1943) ranged from 15 to 37 inches in diameter on the outside, 6 to 13 inches on the inside, and 2 to 5 inches in depth. Brandt (1943) reported that 8 nests of the tiny cackling goose ranged from 11 to 14 inches on outside diameters, 9 to 11 inches on inside diameters, and 3.5 to 4.5 inches in depth.

Clutch Size. Thirty-four studies of 11,786 Canada goose nests, including several races, show an average clutch size of 5.14 eggs. Completed clutches range from 1 to 12 eggs, but those containing more than 8 eggs probably represent dump laying by intruding females. Almost 90 percent of the clutches contain four to seven eggs.

Average clutches are largest for the western Canadas, an average of 5.34 eggs (6,366 nests). There are records of 5.22 eggs per clutch for the giant Canadas (2,982 nests). Farther north, interior Canadas average 4.57 eggs (522 nests). And in the Arctic, small Canada geese average 4.27 eggs (430 nests) on the McConnell River delta (MacInnes et al. 1974). An identical clutch size, 4.27, was found by Mickelson (1973) for cackling geese (1,038 nests) on the Yukon Delta.

MacInnes et al. (1974) found significant changes in clutch size from year to year in the frequency of six- and three-egg clutches but a constancy in the frequency of four- and five-egg clutches. Because year-to-year changes were similar for two different Canada goose races and populations at McConnell River and Churchill, the authors concluded (p. 693) that "events during April and early May must be critical to determination of the size of clutches laid in late May and June." They found that age of the breeding birds had no detectable effect upon clutch size. However, Brakhage (1965) observed an increase in clutch size as age increased: from 4.5 for 2-year-olds to 5.9 for 5-year and older birds.

Eggs. As might be expected from the vast range in size among the races of Canada geese, there is a considerable range in egg sizes. Eggs of the giant Canada goose measure 90.1 by 60.1 mm (Hanson 1965); the western race, 87.2 by 59.1 mm (Williams and Nelson 1943); the interior race, 84.6 by 58.3 mm (Hanson 1965); and the diminutive cackler race, 74.0 by 49.4 mm (Mickelson 1973). The ellipitcal ovate eggs are dull creamy white at first but become glossy and stained from nest materials during incubation.

Egg-laying begins shortly after nest construction starts. Mickelson (1973) observed that among cackling geese, egg-laying began within 24 hours after nest construction was initiated. Both Kossack (1950) and Brakhage (1965) reported that giant Canada geese laid an egg, on the average, every 1.5 days. At Dowling Lake, Alberta, Vermeer (1970*a*) recorded an interval of 1.87 days per egg laid. In the Arctic, laying is more compressed: at McConnell River, MacInnes (1962) recorded an egg per day, with a day skipped after the fourth egg; on the Yukon Delta, Mickelson (1973) found the deposition rate to be an egg a day, with an occasional day missed either between the third and fourth or the fourth and fifth eggs.

Incubation. While the male stands guard a short distance from the nest, the female incubates. Usually she leaves the nest twice daily for a short rest break, early in the morning and late in the afternoon (Collias and Jahn 1959, Brakhage 1965, Sherwood 1965). The male accompanies his mate on these excursions and alertly watches as she feeds, drinks, bathes, and preens.

Female giant Canada geese incubate for 25 to 30 days, with the average in various studies ranging from 26 to 28 days (Kossack 1950, Collias and Jahn 1959, Brakhage 1965). Western Canada geese incubate for an average of 28 days (Dow 1943, Hanson and Browning 1959). In southeastern Alberta, Vermeer (1970*a*) found that incubation ranged from 25 to 28 days and averaged 26.8 days (21 nests). Cackling geese on the Yukon Delta were observed by Mickelson (1973) to incubate for 24 to 30 days and averaged 26 days (45 nests).

Chronology of Nesting. Except for the great horned owl and a few other bird species, the Canada goose is the very first bird to nest in the spring. It is certainly the earliest of the waterfowl. In the high mountain valleys of the West and in the Subarctic and Arctic, the geese arrive while the land is clothed in snow and with the ice-covered marshes, ponds, and lakes just commencing to thaw. As soon as snow leaves the nest sites and ice retreats from the rest and feeding sites, Canadas begin to nest. A late-season snow storm has been seen to blanket many an incubating bird.

Because of low latitude and altitude, the earliest-nesting Canadas are the giant race nesting in the Midwest. In northwest Missouri, Brakhage (1965) found first eggs being laid March 15-20. At Horicon Marsh, Wisconsin, the first eggs are laid about April 4 (Collias and Jahn 1959). Three hundred and fifty miles to the north by latitude, at Lake Kinoje, Ontario, the dates of first eggs ranged from April 20 to May 3 in 3 years (Raveling and Lumsden 1967, Lumsden and Raveling 1968, Lumsden 1969). Another 500 miles to the north by latitude at Cape Churchill, Manitoba, Canada geese started to lay their first eggs as early as May 19, 1965, as late as June 2, 1969, and on May 30, 1970 (MacInnes et al. 1974). At McConnell River, 130 miles north of Churchill, a smaller race of geese initiated early egg-laying on

June 1, 1966, and late egg-laying on June 9, 1969 (MacInnes et al. 1974).

The northern plains warm up earlier than other regions of equal latitude. Consequently, Canada geese are found initiating nesting at Lac qui Parle in southwestern Minnesota as early as March 28 (Benson 1973), at South Saskatchewan River, Saskatchewan, on April 4 (Caldwell 1967), and in southeast Alberta, March 28 (Vermeer 1970*a*).

Western Canada geese nest at a wide variety of altitudes, from a few hundred feet above sea level along the Columbia River in Washington to over 7,000 feet in the Yellowstone Plateau. Consequently, within short linear distances, there are wide divergences in the time of nest initiation. Local weather conditions of snow and temperature also play a role, graphically illustrated by Dimmick's (1968) report for Jackson Hole, Wyoming. Although only 60 miles apart and 300 feet higher in elevation, goose nests in the lower valley hatch before those in the northern part are initiated. Heavier snowfall that takes longer to melt is held accountable.

The earliest nests in the West start the first days of March at Honey Lake, California (Dow 1943, Naylor 1953); March 2 and 11, Tule Lake, California (Miller and Collins 1953, Rienecker and Anderson 1960); early March, Columbia River, Washington (Hanson and Eberhardt 1971); March 15, Flathead Valley, Montana (Geis 1956); March 20, 26, and 28 at Ogden Bay and Bear River marshes, Utah (Williams and Marshall 1937, Dey 1966); March 24 and April 3, Jackson Hole, Wyoming (Dimmick 1968); April 8 and 10, Grays Lake, Idaho (Steel et al. 1957); and early April in south-central British Columbia (Munro 1960).

Dusky geese on the Copper River delta, Alaska, commence laying their first eggs on May 10 (Trainer 1959). On the Yukon Delta over a 4-year period, Mickelson (1973) found that cackling geese began laying within the interval of May 20 (1969) to June 1 (1972).

At the lower altitudes and latitude, where Canada geese begin to nest early in March, the span of nest initiation extends over a period of 50 to 60 days. But most nests are started over a period about two-thirds that long, with comparatively few late nesters or renesters during the last 20 days. Where nesting commences 1 month later, April 1-15, nest initiation lasts 20 to 30 days. When it does not start until mid-May, its duration is 10 to 20 days. On the Yukon Delta, Mickelson (1973) recorded nest starts over a period of 16 days in 1972 and up to 34 days in 1969, but 80 percent occurred within periods of 7 and 10 days. At Cape Churchill, Manitoba, first eggs were laid over an average span of 10 days, 1965-70; at McConnell River during the same period, the average was 9 days (MacInnes et al. 1974).

Nest Success. Although extremes in nest success of 21.4 percent (Craighead and Craighead 1949) and 88.5 percent (Pakulak 1969) have been recorded, most studies show a nest success similar to the average of 70.1 percent for 11,865 nests. In eight studies of the giant Canada goose, 69.3 percent of 2,484 nests hatched. In 14 investigations of the western Canada, 69.2 percent of 6,724 nests hatched. Studies of the interior Canada goose nesting at Kinoje, Ontario (Raveling and Lumsden 1967, 1968, Lumsden 1969), and at Churchill, Manitoba (Pakulak 1969), disclosed that 81.2 percent of 425 nests hatched successfully. Small Canada geese breeding on the McConnell River, Northwest Territories, hatched 88.5 percent of 418 nests (MacInnes et al. 1974). A race breeding in southeast Alberta hatched 54.2 percent of 384 nests (Vermeer 1970*a*, Ewaschuk and Boag 1972). Dusky Canada geese breeding on the Copper River delta, Alaska, had a success rate of 76.3 percent for 519 nests (Trainer 1959). On the Yukon Delta, 68.2 percent of 911 nests of the cackling goose were successful (Mickelson 1973). The establishment of artificial nest platforms has increased the success of the hatch among giant and western Canada geese. In northwest Missouri, 73.2 percent of 179 giant Canadas nesting in raised washtubs were successful compared with 46.7 percent of those nesting on the ground (Brakhage 1965). Western Canadas in the Flathead Valley of Montana averaged 3.63 young per pair in 42 platform nests and 3.06 young per pair for 1,113 ground nests (Craighead and Stockstad 1961). At the Honey Lake Wildlife area, California, Rienecker (1971) reported the astounding success of 98.1 percent of 104 Canada goose nests built on platforms. Earlier studies of marsh-nesting geese at Honey Lake indicated nest successes of 56.9 percent (Dow 1943), 68.3 percent (Naylor 1953), and 69.2 percent (Anderson 1965).

In the 5,959 successful Canada goose nests for which data on unhatched eggs are available, clutch size averaged 5.31 eggs, slightly higher than the overall average of 5.14 eggs. Most studies reported that the nests with the larger clutches tended to be the more successful. An average of 0.60 egg failed to hatch in successful nests (11.3 percent of the eggs laid). Thus about 4.7 goslings left each successful nest, although a few dead goslings were infrequently found at the nest sites.

Hanson and Eberhardt (1971) made an intensive study of the fate of 1,625 Canada goose eggs that failed to hatch. Of this number, 24 percent were infertile, 18 percent were broken or missing, and 58 percent contained dead embryos (32 percent at 1 week of development, 6 percent at 2 weeks, 8 percent at 3 weeks, and 12 percent at 4 weeks). Fifty dead goslings were found at the sites of 2,688 successful nests.

Nest Failure. Because of its extensive breeding range, there are many causes of nest failure in the Canada goose. Nest losses can be broadly grouped under three categories: desertion, destruction by predators, and destruction by other natural agents. In 17 studies, nest destruction by predators caused 48.2 percent of the losses reported for 2,488 nests failing to hatch, desertion caused 42.6 percent, and destruction by other natural agents (mainly flooding) 9.2 percent.

Predators varied from skunks, coyotes, crows, and magpies in the southern breeding areas to Arctic and red foxes, ravens, jaegers, and herring gulls in the northern areas. Desertions may occur because of harassment by predators, human activity, stressful weather, or intraspecific strife.

Ewaschuk and Boag (1972) observed that undue harassment of an incubating female—particularly in the absence of her mate—by nearby nesting pairs or nonterritorial pairs led to desertion. They found that as the number of nesting pairs increased on an island in Dowling Lake, Alberta, the percentage of successful nests markedly declined. Earlier, Collias and Jahn (1959) and Weigand et al. (1968) reported a similar relationship between crowding and nest desertion among captive breeding flocks of Canada geese.

Renesting. The reduction in the period of nest initiation between the Midwest and the Arctic decreases the opportunity for Canada geese to renest. In northwest Missouri, 10 of 30 pairs that lost clutches during laying continued to lay in new sites nearby, 7 renested after an interval of 5 to 22 days depending upon the number of eggs laid, and 13 made no further attempt to lay (Brakhage 1965). Only one female renested whose loss occurred during incubation, and that loss was only 5 days after incubation started.

In Phillips County, Montana, Atwater (1959) observed 12 marked pairs whose nests were destroyed: two females renested, one twice. Geis (1956) reported that 416 pairs in the Flathead Valley of Montana produced 479 nests, suggesting a renesting effort of 13 percent. Hanson and Eberhardt (1971) believed that a substantial number of geese that deserted their nests early in the season renested 1 to 2 weeks later on islands in the Columbia River, near Hanford, Washington. Rienecker and Anderson (1960) believed that renesting contributed importantly to the production of young at Tule and Lower Klamath lakes.

However, both Martin (1964) and Dey (1966) reported that renesting was not significant among Canada geese breeding at Ogden Bay, Utah. At the Seney Refuge in northern Michigan, Sherwood (1965) observed no evidence of renesting among marked geese, but a few late-hatched broods suggested the possibility of limited renesting. Steel et al. (1957) considered that renesting was unlikely at Grays Lake, Idaho. Neither MacInnes et al. (1974) in 10 years at McConnell River nor Mickelson (1973) in 4 years on the Yukon Delta found evidence of renesting among the small races of Canada geese in the Arctic.

Rearing of Young

Broods. Both parents escort their young from the time they leave the nest, from several to 24 hours after hatching, through the brood period. Broods remain within a few miles of their nest sites on western and midwestern marshes, but on some of the western rivers they drift downstream many miles from island or canyon nest sites to favorable feeding meadows. Even more lengthy journeys are made down the rivers draining the west side of James Bay.

Female Canadas brood their young at night and frequently during the day throughout the first week, less often thereafter (Collias and Jahn 1959). Males defend small areas around their broods from intrusion by other geese. Nevertheless, in some of the more densely occupied nesting grounds, particularly in the West, the mixing of broods is prevalent (Williams and Marshall 1938, Naylor 1953, Geis 1956). According to Brakhage (1965), broods started to amalgamate after the goslings were 5 to 7 days old. He observed one group that contained 110 goslings and 21 adult and subadult geese. Sherwood (1965) reported that mixing of broods occurred because at first neither the parents nor the goslings could recognize each other. When the young were 2 to 3 weeks old, the parents could recognize them and brood mixing halted. Goslings were unable to recognize their parents or broodmates before they were 5 to 6 weeks of age.

Development. At Seney Refuge, Michigan, goslings of giant Canadas attained flight at about 71 to 73 days, 1963-65 (Sherwood 1965). Goslings of the western Canada goose in California reached flight at ages ranging from 49 to 56 days (Moffitt 1931) and in British Columbia at 63 days. According to Hanson (1965), goslings of the interior race became fledged in about 63 days at Akimiski Island, James Bay. On the McConnell River delta, the small Richardson's goose attained flight at 52 to 60 days (Charles MacInnes). Cackling goose goslings became fledged in the extraordinarily brief time of 40 to 46 days (Mickelson 1973).

Survival. Where Canada goose broods are mixed, attrition becomes difficult to assess because, with age, the broods often become larger rather than smaller. However, by comparing numbers of young reaching flight stage with the numbers of breeding pairs, the ultimate achievement of the breeding effort may be deduced.

Geis (1956), in the Flathead Valley of Montana, found an average of 2.72 goslings reaching flight stage for 416 nesting pairs, a loss of 18.8 percent of the young from hatch. She reported that mortality was important in only a few areas where overland movements or low water levels made young especially vulnerable to predators. At Ogden Bay, Utah, 1956-58, Martin (1964) observed a decline of 7 percent from hatch to flight, at which time there was an average of four young per breeding pair. During the subsequent 2 years at the same place, Dey (1966) reported a loss of 9.3 percent in goslings from hatch to flight, with an average of 3.9 fledged young per nesting pair. In Jackson Hole, Wyoming, Dimmick (1968) observed that a group of broods totaling 26 goslings lost one member in 9 days.

At times, the loss of goslings among breeding geese at the Seney National Wildlife Refuge, Michigan, is unusually high. In 1964, Sherwood (1965) estimated a loss of 84 percent in goslings, either directly from black flies or indirectly from *Leucocytozoon*, a blood parasite carried by them. Fortunately, such enormous outbreaks of black flies do not occur every year, and in 1963 and 1964, Sherwood (1965) found that gosling mortality averaged 22 percent and 28 percent.

During their intensive study of western Canada geese on the Columbia River, Washington, Hanson and Eberhardt (1971) observed that a 4 percent decrease in brood size occurred the first week of life. On their McConnell River study area, MacInnes et al. (1974) reported that from 7 to 26 percent of the eggs or young goslings disappeared between the last observation before the hatch and the family groups observed on summer feeding areas a week later; once broods reached the feeding areas, survival was high.

Seldom did cackling goose broods mix on the Yukon Delta, where Mickelson (1973) considered brood size in relation to age a good index to survival. There, brood size declined from about 4 goslings at hatch to 3.7 at flight stage, a 13.0 percent reduction. The greatest loss in the number of young occurred during the first 10 days of life.

With the exception of unusual losses of goslings noted at Seney, all investigators have noted an exceedingly high rate of survival to flight. Many of the early losses often occur on the trek from nest site to feeding area. An average of 4.7 goslings left 5,959 successful nests, and the evidence is that an average 4.0 reached the flight stage. About 70 percent of the breeding pairs are successful, resulting in a net production of approximately 2.8 young per breeding pair.

POSTBREEDING SEASON

Nonbreeding yearlings, adults who have not nested, and those whose nests have been destroyed are the first to molt. After the yearlings return with their parents to their natal areas in the spring, they break family ties and usually move on to other areas for the wing molt, some moving only a few miles but others migrating hundreds of miles to the north.

Arneson (1970), studying western Canadas nesting in southwest Wyoming, observed that marked yearlings molted on or near their natal areas. In Jackson Hole, most of the nonbreeding and unsuccessful nesting geese left in mid-June for their molt area at Turbid Lake, 50 to 75 miles to the north in Yellowstone Park (Dimmick 1968). Many yearlings, 2-year-olds, and unsuccessful breeders leave Ogden Bay to molt at the Bear River National Wildlife Refuge, only 25 miles to the north (Martin 1964). Others apparently go farther north: marked geese from Ogden have been seen at Red Rock Lakes and Minidoka national wildlife refuges in southwestern Montana and south-central Idaho. Hunting season recoveries have also been received of yearlings and 2-year-olds in Alberta, Idaho, Montana, and Washington, suggesting that they represented birds migrating far afield before or after the wing molt. At Hanford, Washington, Hanson and Eberhardt (1971) reported that yearlings and other subadults continued on to northern Canada in the spring, returning to join the local flock in the autumn after the wing molt.

One of the more spectacular molting areas for several races of Canada geese is the Beverly and Aberdeen lakes region of the Thelon River, 250 to 350 miles west of Chesterfield Inlet on Hudson Bay (Kuyt 1962, 1966; Sterling and Dzubin 1967). There, upwards of 30,000 "large" Canada geese undergo the wing molt in a region devoid of breeding geese (Sterling and Dzubin 1967). Flightless geese captured in the Thelon River area had been previously banded at many diverse localities: near Malta and Monida, Montana; Soda Springs, Idaho; Yoder, Wyoming; Alderdale, Washington; Redmond Lake, Utah; Lewellen, Nebraska; Rochester, Minnesota; Oak Point, Manitoba; Lake Andes, South Dakota; Swan Lake and Squaw Creek refuges, Missouri; Holla Bend National Wildlife Refuge, Arkansas; Two Buttes, Colorado; and Canton, Illinois. Most of these recoveries were members of the giant and western races but also included birds of the interior, lesser, and Richardson's races. Birds of the giant and western races migrated from 1,000 to 2,000 miles north of their natal areas to molt in the Thelon River region.

Appreciable numbers of nonbreeding interior Canada geese continue northeastward beyond their natal areas in the muskeg bog on the west side of James Bay to undergo the wing molt in the Ungava Peninsula of Quebec (Heyland and Garrard 1974). Yet in subsequent years they leave the Ungava Peninsula to the breeding Atlantic race and return to their ancestral breeding grounds on the southwest side of Hudson Bay and the west side of James Bay.

Those Canada geese that have young to raise, molt on the brood-rearing marshes. In southern areas the goslings are about a month old before their parents begin to lose their flight feathers. Canadas nesting in the Arctic begin to molt within 1 to 2 weeks after their young hatch.

At the Seney Refuge, in northern Michigan, breeding adults start their wing molt June 10-20, about 10 days later than nonbreeders (Sherwood 1965). Steel et al. (1957) reported that at Grays Lake, Idaho, the molt of flight feathers commences shortly after June 10, 3 weeks after the peak of the hatch. According to Williams (1967), the shed primaries of Canada geese appear on Utah breeding marshes between May 18 and 23, about a month after goslings are hatched. On the molt areas near the Thelon River, geese begin to shed their flight feathers in late June and start flying by July 16 (Sterling and Dzubin 1967). Breeding Canadas on the McConnell River delta begin their wing molt soon after the goslings hatch; 3 weeks into the rearing period adults have already partially regrown their flight feathers (MacInnes 1966). Cackling geese on the Yukon Delta begin molting flight feathers in the second week of July when the goslings are 1 to 2 weeks of age (Mickelson 1973).

The adult molters regain their flight feathers about the time their young reach flight stage. According to Hanson (1965), the wing molt in the interior race in the area of James Bay is 32 days, when the primaries have reached 85 percent of their growth. The flightless period of western Canadas in Jackson Hole covers a span of 5 weeks (Dimmick 1968). A breeding population in Utah has a flightless period of 6 weeks, less for an individual (Williams 1967). The molting population in the Thelon River area is flightless for about 25 days, not exceeding 30 days (Sterling and Dzubin 1967). On the Yukon Delta the wing molt takes 3 to 4 weeks (Mickelson 1973).

FOOD HABITS

More than any other waterfowl in North America, the Canada goose has benefited from the agricultural products of man. Because of their ability to take advantage of feed grain and cereal foods on their migration and winter grounds, Canada geese have greatly increased in number during the last three decades. Today, there are probably more of them than when the Pilgrims landed in Massachusetts.

Much of the feed grains, cereals, and green forage available as food for Canada geese is grown on state and federal refuges that are managed primarily for them. There are more than 70,000 acres of croplands providing food for Canada geese on refuges in the Mississippi Flyway alone (Arthur 1968).

Canada geese browse on the leaves of clovers and grasses and consume cultivated grains. At refuges in southern Illinois, Arthur (1968) determined that the order of preference among browse plants was: ladino, alsike, and red clovers, bird's-foot trefoil, barley, wheat, rye, alfalfa, brome, orchard grass, and bluegrasses, creeping red and Kentucky fescues, and timothy. Omitting weed seeds, grain preferences were as follows: German proso and foxtail millets, corn, oats, buckwheat, grain sorghums, and soybeans. Bell and Klimstra (1970) studied the feeding activities of geese on the Crab Orchard National Wildlife Refuge in southern Illinois. Cornfields attracted 41 percent of the birds, small grains 24 percent, pasture 22 percent, soybeans 9 percent, and wheat stubble and lespedeza fields 4 percent.

In southeastern Colorado, green winter wheat fields provide choice food for wintering geese (Rutherford 1970). Sorghum grains are also important foods there. At Rochester, Minnesota, waste corn in harvested fields is the primary source of food throughout the winter for the many thousands of giant Canadas (Gulden and Johnson 1968).

Canada geese on the Atlantic Flyway have largely forsaken aquatic plants for upland crops (Addy and Heyland 1968). The availability and quality of agricultural foods determine the locations of primary concentrations of geese. Grain fields to be attractive to geese need to be large and open with an undisturbed body of water nearby that is large enough to provide a feeling of security.

Although agricultural crops are unquestionably the mainstay of Canada geese on their migration and winter grounds, food habits studies reveal that many geese do consume natural foods. Yelverton and Quay (1959) found that two-thirds of the contents of Canada goose stomachs at Lake Mattamuskeet, North Carolina, contained roots, stems, and seeds of the spike rush and the roots, rhizomes, and seeds of the American bulrush. Native grasses accounted for 11 percent and corn kernels for 22 percent of the measured volume of foods from 263 gizzards and 31 crops.

Korschgen (1955) examined 184 stomachs from Canada geese collected in Missouri and determined that the principal foods were wild millet, 36 percent; smartweed seeds, 10.1 percent; cut-grasses, 10.2 percent; spike rushes, 8.3 percent; winter wheat, 6.1 percent; corn, 5.5 percent; nutgrasses, 4.8 percent; and soybeans, 3.2 percent.

Barnacle Goose

Branta leucopsis

IDENTIFICATION

This rare species is a moderate-sized goose with a black chest, neck, and crown but a cream-white face. The expanse of black from the neck over the back and top of the head gives the face a hooded appearance. The upper back is black shading posteriorly to silver-gray. The breast, sides, and flanks are a pale gray; the belly, undertail coverts, and rump are white, contrasting markedly with the large black tail. The relatively long legs are black and so is the short bill. Immatures are similar to adults in appearance.

DISTRIBUTION

The barnacle goose is so rare in North America that it is unlikely to be encountered in the wild. Since the turn of the century, there have been fewer than 20 records of this goose in North America. Its infrequent appearances have been limited to the East: Labrador; Kingsville, Ontario; three locations in Quebec; Massachusetts; Long Island, New York; Vermont; Ohio; and Shiawasee Refuge, Michigan.

Barnacle geese breed along the northeast coast of Greenland, and on Spitsbergen, Novaya Zemlya, and adjacent Vaigach Island (Boyd 1961). The Greenland geese winter in Ireland and the Inner and Outer Hebrides of Scotland. Those from Spitsbergen winter largely in the Solway Firth (on the border between England and Scotland), and those from Novaya Zemlya winter in the Netherlands and Germany.

The world population of barnacle geese in 1959-60 was estimated at only 30,000 (Boyd 1961), with winter populations as follows: 11,000 in the Netherlands, 8,600 in Germany, 7,100 in Scotland, and 2,800 in Ireland.

Atlantic Brant

Branta bernicla hrota

Other Common Names: Sea goose, brant goose, white-bellied brant

VITAL STATISTICS

Length:	Adult male, 22-26 inches, average 24 (3) Adult female, 22-24 inches, average 23 (12)
Wing:	Male, 11.9 inches Female, 11.2 inches
Weight:*	Adult male, 3.4 pounds (301) Adult female, 3.1 pounds (263) Immature male, 3.0 pounds (112) Immature female, 2.7 pounds (125)

*From Penkala (1975).

IDENTIFICATION

Field

The brant in flight appears more like a duck than a goose because of its relatively small size, rapid wing beat, and short neck. It is the swiftest of all geese in flight. It flies in irregular masses or in trailing or abreast lines, usually close to the water. At a distance, the Atlantic brant appears almost black except for the white breast, belly, and upper-tail coverts. The white posterior contrasts with the dark anterior to create the illusion of a foreshortened torso.

At rest on the water, the birds appear very dark except for the white sides and, at close hand, a white lip-shaped mark on each side of the upper neck. When facing a strong wind, they often tilt their heads and necks forward about 25 degrees. On other occasions they hold their heads low, so that their necks appear short.

The Atlantic brant is confined almost exclusively to the Atlantic Coast. Only rarely do black brant appear among flocks of the eastern race.

At Hand

The sexes are similar in appearance in both races of

Left, Atlantic brant; right, black brant

brant. The immatures show no white on the neck until midwinter, but the adult has a white crescent on each side of the upper neck. The dark brown greater and middle wing coverts of the immatures are tipped with white, thus differing, until the first wing molt, from the solid dark brown coverts of the adults. In both races, the bill, head, neck, and chest are black and the back and wings are dark brown. The tail coverts form a white band at the base of the black tail. The legs and feet are black.

The breast and belly of the Atlantic brant are white and are sharply defined by the black chest. The sides and flanks are white barred with gray-brown, becoming more sharply defined posteriorly. The black brant differs in having a black breast and a black belly as far back as its legs.

POPULATION STATUS

During 1955-74, the winter population of Atlantic brant averaged 177,000, ranging from a maximum of 266,000 in 1961 to a minimum of 42,000 in 1973, evidence of a severe decline since 1961. A high kill of 70,000 during the 1971-72 season, over twice the customary number (Penkala et al. 1975), combined with an almost complete failure to produce young in 1972, precipitated the decline from 151,000 in 1971 to the low level of 42,000 in 1973. A favorable breeding season the next year brought the population back to 87,600 in 1974 and it remained at that level in 1975.

The severe fluctuations in the abundance of Atlantic brant appear to stem from the vagaries of weather on their Arctic breeding grounds. Important breeding grounds for this species lie farther north than for any other waterfowl. Lynch and Voelzer (1974:40) state: "The recent worsening of weather in Arctic Canada offers a credible explanation for the general decline in reproductive success that began in 1961 among Atlantic Brant and associated species."

The population of this brant decreased alarmingly in the early 1930's, attributed at that time to a calamitous reduction in its principal food, eelgrass (Lincoln 1950). Numbers at Barnegat Bay, New Jersey, declined from 28,800 in the winter of 1927-28 to 1,980 by the winter of 1932-33. The population along the Atlantic Coast during the winter of 1933-34 was only 10 percent of that in 1930-31 (Cottam et al. 1944). The brant changed its food habits to include sea lettuce and upland grazing, and the eelgrass began a partial recovery in the 1940's. As a consequence, the brant population increased steadily in the late 1930's and early 1940's to regain much of its former status.

The early 1930's were not the only times of great depression in brant numbers. Phillips (1932:446) cited a scarcity in brant at Monomoy, Massachusetts, between 1863 and 1909: in 1865, 1877-86, 1895, 1900, 1903, and 1906-09. The journal of the Monomoy Brant Club noted in 1882: "We feel more and more every year that if things continue for a few years more and the birds grow fewer and fewer every year, in ten years there will not be birds enough to render Brant shooting a sport at all."

Age Ratios

According to Penkala et al. (1975), there was an average of 0.65 immature per adult (39 percent) from 1961 to 1972 in the Atlantic brant populations of New Jersey. In the fall of 1973, there were 1.94 (66 percent) immatures per adult, but in 1974 the ratio declined to 0.14 (12 percent) immature per adult. With a closed season, the population remained stable.

Mortality

Band analysis showed mortality rates of 20 percent and 45 percent for adults and immatures (Penkala et al. 1975). These rates are almost identical to those derived for the black brant.

DISTRIBUTION

The three races of brant are circumpolar in their breeding, occurring along the coasts of the Arctic Ocean and extending southward into connecting bays and seas. The validity of a fourth race, Lawrence's brant, has not been satisfactorily established. The Atlantic brant is one of the few birds bridging Europe and North America, for it migrates from breeding grounds in northern Greenland to both England and the United States. Some birds banded on Ellesmere Island by J. D. Heyland have been recovered in Ireland.

Breeding Range

The Atlantic brant vies with, and perhaps surpasses, the greater snow goose for the honor of being the northernmost breeding bird in the world. In Greenland, it nests along the entire north coast as far as Thule on the northwest coast (Salomonsen 1950-51). It was reported by Dement'ev and Gladkov (1967) to nest as far east as Franz Josef Land, USSR. It nests as far west as Prince Patrick Island (Handley 1950) and as far south as Southampton Island (Bray 1943, Barry 1962). It has also been known to breed on Ellesmere Island (Parmelee and MacDonald 1960), Baffin Island (Soper 1946), Bylot Island (Heyland 1970), and on tiny islands in Queen Maud Gulf, Canada, near the mouth of the Perry River (Gavin 1947, Hanson et al. 1956). Tener (1963) observed four scattered flocks, totaling 205 birds, on Bathurst Island on June 21 and 27, 1960, but no evidence of nesting was found.

Black brant nest along with Atlantic brant on Prince Patrick Island and on islets of Queen Maud Gulf. Although Gavin (1947) reported thousands of the Atlantic race nesting along Queen Maud Gulf, Hanson et al. (1956) found only one Atlantic brant in a nesting colony of black brant at the Perry River delta.

An aerial survey of the coast of Queen Maud Gulf by Barry (1960) in 1960 revealed 1,500 Atlantic brant and 3,500 black brant. He also observed 2,000 brant of uncertain racial identity on King William Island, but he believed that they were probably Atlantic brant. Recently Maltby-

Prevett et al. (1975) found nesting colonies in the High Arctic at Okse Bay, Ellesmere Island; Bracebridge Inlet, Bathurst Island; Surprise and South fiords, Axel Heiberg Island; 12 sites on Melville Island; 6 sites on Prince Patrick Island; and 1 site on Eglinton Island. They are also known to nest on the islands of Ellef Ringnes, Meighen, and east Devon (Hugh Boyd).

Manning et al. (1956) examined 66 brant collected in the Arctic from Alaska to Greenland and concluded that 12 specimens showed color intergradation between the Atlantic and black brant races. The Lawrence brant, based entirely upon three specimens in the American Museum of Natural History (Delacour and Zimmer 1952), is probably not a valid race but is an intergrade between the Atlantic and black brant.

Migration Corridors

Several decades ago, Lewis (1937) described two migration routes for the Atlantic brant. One passed across the Labrador Peninsula from Ungava Bay to the St. Lawrence Estuary, and the other passed across southern Quebec from James Bay to the St. Lawrence Estuary at Seven Islands. From that point, one route continued south across New England to Long Island Sound, whereas the other route followed the coastline of New Brunswick and New England to the same destination.

Although a small proportion of the Atlantic brant population still appears to follow the coastal route, I believe that the bulk of the population migrates directly overland from James Bay to the New York City area. In 1972, J. D. Heyland could find no evidence that brant stopped in sizable numbers at their former gathering place at Seven Islands on the St. Lawrence. In the New York City region, brant are regularly seen migrating inland, chiefly along the Hudson Valley, but occasionally they are reported by hawk watchers along the ridges (Bull 1964).

James Bay is a most important fall staging area for these high-Arctic nesting geese. In mid-September of 1971, J. D. Heyland estimated about 60,000 Atlantic brant along the east coast of James Bay near Fort George. On the other side of James Bay, near Ekwan Point, Harry Lumsden observed about 42,000 brant on October 19 and 20, 1973. Each of these assemblages in its respective year accounted for almost half of the brant censused later on January surveys.

A small flight of Atlantic brant appears to follow the coastal route to the St. Lawrence Estuary. C. E. Addy told me that each fall and spring from 15,000 to 20,000 brant gather near Grand Manan Island, off the coast of Maine and New Brunswick. About 500 appear during the spring on Chaleur Bay, on the north shore of New Brunswick. A provincial game officer reported to J. D. Heyland that perhaps 20,000 brant stop both spring and fall along the coast of the Gaspé Peninsula between the towns of Gaspé and Matapedia. This contingent probably crosses Quebec from James Bay to the south shore of the Gaspé Peninsula and Northumberland Strait and then passes along the New England coast.

It is apparent that Atlantic brant breeding in the eastern Queen Elizabeth Islands of the Canadian High Arctic migrate eastward across Greenland to Iceland and Ireland (Maltby-Prevett et al. 1975). Four birds banded on Ellesmere Island were shot or found dead in Ireland, and one in coastal France. Twenty-three of 289 brant marked with yellow neck collars in 1974 were observed in September of that year off the coast of southwest Iceland. One bird was from a colony on Axel Heiberg Island, the others from colonies on Melville Island. No marked birds have been found in the United States.

Winter Areas

The Atlantic brant winters along the Atlantic Coast from Massachusetts to South Carolina but is most abundant along the coast of New Jersey, where 150,000 winter (1958-72). The second largest winter population, almost 25,000, occurs among the bays of Long Island, New York. About 3,500 winter on Delaware Bay, and 1,500 winter along the coast of Maryland and the northeastern shore of Chesapeake Bay. Most of the 8,000 that winter in Virginia are concentrated in Back Bay. Only a few hundred Atlantic brant reach Currituck and Pamlico sounds, North Carolina, where once they were an abundant bird. Rarely are small numbers found as far south as coastal South Carolina. Some years as many as 1,000 have wintered near Monomoy Island, Massachusetts, but the average in recent years, 1958-72, has been only 200. Between 10,000 and 14,000 Atlantic brant winter along the northern coast of Ireland. These are believed to originate from breeding colonies in Greenland and the High Arctic of North America (Maltby-Prevett 1975).

MIGRATION BEHAVIOR

Lewis (1937) reported that Atlantic brant left their concentration point at Seven Islands on the Gulf of St. Lawrence in the evening, spiraling upward to a great height before starting northward. On Long Island, Cottam (1933) observed a flock of brant departing during the day, circling upward and heading northeastward in a long, irregular line. During the same day, April 9, 1933, six other flocks passed in migration at high altitudes.

Eighty-three percent of 155 brant flocks at Seven Islands averaged 17 birds per flock, 12 percent averaged 67, and 5 percent averaged 129 (Lewis 1937). Most of these flocks arrived at Seven Islands in the morning and none arrived between sunset and sunrise.

Chronology

Fall. Atlantic brant, like most other Arctic geese, leave their breeding grounds in late summer. Departures from Greenland occur in September and early October; at these times large flocks have been observed following the outer skerries along the northwest coast (Salomonsen 1950-51).

Atlantic brant were reported to leave Queen Maud Gulf about September 1 (Gavin 1947). The fall migration of brant from Prince Patrick Island started about August 1, the last Atlantic brant were observed on August 31, and the last black brant were seen on August 30 (Handley 1950).

Twomey observed flocks of brant passing Churchill, Manitoba, on September 5 and 10, 1936 (Lewis 1937). They passed Fort Chimo, Ungava Bay, in late September and early October. At Charlton Island, in southern James Bay, 2,000 arrived about October 1. Flocks were observed passing over Wells River, Vermont, on October 21 and 26 (Lewis 1937). At the Brigantine National Wildlife Refuge, New Jersey, brant arrived in numbers in early October, the main flight occurred in late October, and the last flight took place in early November. Stewart (1962) placed the bulk of the fall migration of these birds in the Chesapeake Bay region between October 25 and December 10.

Spring. The spring migration of brant at Chesapeake Bay is at its greatest intensity between February 20 and April 10. At the Brigantine National Wildlife Refuge, near Atlantic City, the main departure of brant occurs between the last of March and late April, but a few remain until June. The arrival of brant at Monomoy, Massachusetts, was reported to begin early in March, with the largest numbers occurring between March 25 and April 20 (Phillips 1932). Brant arrived at Seven Islands on the Gulf of St. Lawrence about mid-April and remained into June (Lewis 1937).

At Rupert House near the southern end of James Bay, Atlantic brant were reported arriving from the south about May 1 and departing northward near the end of the month (Lewis 1937). They migrated past Fort George on the northeast coast of James Bay about mid-May. Brant reached Fort Chimo near Ungava Bay May 20 to June 20 (Bent 1925). They were recorded at Churchill, Manitoba, on Hudson Bay, June 13 (Littlefield and Pakulak 1969), and, 300 miles farther north at Chesterfield Inlet, brant appeared on June 8, 10, and 13 (Höhn 1968).

Atlantic brant arrived on their breeding grounds on Baffin Island on June 7, with peak arrivals June 15-24 (Soper 1946). The first arrivals on Southampton Island occurred on June 8, 1953 and 1956, and June 7, 1957 (Barry 1962). In 1953, arrivals continued until June 13; the birds arrived in small flocks, seldom larger than 20 birds (Barry 1956).

Brant arrive at Scoresby Sound, Greenland, in mid-May and at areas farther north during late May and early June (Salomonsen 1950-51). They reach extreme northern Greenland as early as June 11 (Peary Land) and 17 (Hall Land). Those migrating to Prince Patrick Island have about the same distance to fly as those nesting in northern Greenland. The first Atlantic brant observed by Handley (1950) on Prince Patrick Island arrived June 17, but black brant had arrived on June 12 and 15.

BREEDING

Behavior

Atlantic brant apparently return to breed in the same general region each year. Barry (1962) reported that even during the poor breeding conditions in 1957, he recaptured 38 percent of the adult birds banded the previous summer.

Brant arrive paired on the breeding grounds although they remain in flocks until the snow melts from their nest area (Barry 1962). They mate for life unless one of the pair is lost. Most do not breed until they are 3 years old.

Territories are established in areas free of snow on tidal flats dotted with innumerable sedge-covered islets, 2 to 3 yards in diameter. The Atlantic brant occupies a zone lower in elevation and closer to the sea than other geese that nest in the eastern Arctic. The territories are defended by both sexes prior to incubation and by the male thereafter until the eggs hatch. The few yearlings still in family groups are tolerated on territorial margins for the first few days of incubation and are then driven away. Yearling brant and other nonbreeders gather in undefended communal grounds (Barry 1962).

Nesting

Nest Sites. The female selects the nest site and builds the nest, which initially is a depression formed in the soggy earth; sedges then are molded around the scrape, and down is added as egg-laying and incubation progress. The nests of brant contain much more down than those of other waterfowl in the eastern Arctic (Barry 1962). Barry reported the following averages: depth of nest, 2.3 inches; inside diameter of down, 7.4 inches; outside diameter of down, 12.0 inches; and the outside of the entire nest, 18.0 inches.

Nests of the Atlantic brant are usually close to the edge of water. Barry (1962) reported that at two colonies on Southampton Island, the nests averaged 1 to 5 yards from the water's edge and only 7 to 18 inches above it. The average distance between nests in optimum habitat on the island was 37 yards, 1.65 nests per acre. However, many brant pairs choose an independent life, for numerous isolated nests have been found by Arctic expeditions.

Chronology of Nesting. Egg-laying began June 16, 1953; on June 20, 1956; and June 23 in 1957 on Southampton Island (Barry 1962), 7 to 16 days after arrival. Snow covered 40 percent of the ground during the shortest interval between arrival and nesting and 94 percent of the ground during the longest interval. In Greenland, egg-laying started immediately after arrival and eggs were found from June 14 to July 8 (Salomonsen 1950-51).

Clutch Size, Eggs, and Incubation. The eggs of Atlantic brant are creamy white, tending toward pale olive as incubation progresses (Barry 1962). They are ovate, 72.9 mm by 47.2 mm (521). The brant lays a determinate clutch of 4 to 6 eggs, with an average of 4.5, but egg losses resulted in an average clutch of only 3.9 eggs in 835 nests (Barry 1962). Over one-third of the brant laid an egg each day until their clutches were complete; most of the others skipped a day after the second egg was laid. In general, Atlantic brant do not renest, but when eggs are lost during laying they may build a second nest to receive the remaining eggs developed in the ovary. Dump nesting does not occur in normal years and is rare even in late seasons (Barry 1962). Resorption of yolk predominates over the dumping of eggs, which reduces the waste and loss of energy that nesting brant in the Arctic can ill afford.

The female brant performs all the chores of incubation, beginning with the last egg laid. She leaves the nest for a short time late in the afternoon to feed nearby while the male remains on guard at the nest. Barry (1962) reported that incubation averaged 24 days, with variations from 22 to 26 days.

The young usually leave the nest within 48 hours after the first egg pips. They are led by the parents to tidal flats and pools to feed upon marine invertebrates, mosquito larvae, and sedges (brant grass) (Barry 1962).

Nest Success. Nests of Atlantic brant studied by Barry (1962) suffered an egg loss of 27 percent. Herring gulls were responsible for half of this loss and desertion was the next most important cause. The Arctic fox was not a serious predator where water barriers prevented it from reaching brant nests; however, on a small nest area not isolated by water, Arctic foxes destroyed 16 nests. At Prince Patrick Island, all brant nests found were already destroyed by dogs or foxes (Handley 1950).

Rearing of Young

Broods. The male Atlantic brant assumes the leading role in shepherding the brood, and the female follows closely (Barry 1962). The young grow rapidly from 1.6 ounces at hatch to 11 to 14 ounces at 2 weeks to slightly over 2 pounds at 32 days. They are probably capable of flight at 45 to 50 days of age. The necessity for such rapid growth and early flight is evident from Barry's finding of 21 young brant that appeared to have been frozen in the ice the previous fall because they missed flight stage by about 5 days.

There are no records of brood sizes for Atlantic brant in the Arctic, but on their winter grounds the average number of young per family was 2.3, 1969-71 (Lynch 1972).

POSTBREEDING SEASON

Subadults are the first brant to molt (Barry 1962). They begin to molt their body feathers in late June and become flightless consistently between July 15 and 19. On Southampton Island, they regain their flight feathers and their black body plumage by August (Barry 1962).

The timing of molt among breeding adults varies according to the date of the onset of incubation. Molt begins approximately 14 days after the young are hatched (Barry 1962). The flightless period of nonbreeding and unsuccessful adults occurs between those of the subadults and the successful breeders. At Perry River, the peak of the flightless period occurred about June 10 (Gavin 1947).

The early molters start their southward flight in the latter part of August. Although adults with young are flying by late August or early September, they delay migration until mid-September; a few wait until mid-October.

FOOD HABITS

The Atlantic brant was forced to alter its food habits drastically during the 1930's as a result of the almost complete disappearance of its principal food, eelgrass. Prior to 1932, the analysis of stomach contents revealed that 85 percent were composed of eelgrass and 12 percent of widgeon grass (Cottam et al. 1944). Stomach contents examined during 1932-41 showed that eelgrass made up only 9 percent of the food of Atlantic brant, widgeon grass 16 percent, and algae, mainly sea lettuce, the remainder.

In 1972-74, Penkala (1975) examined the stomachs of 801 Atlantic brant collected along the New Jersey coast. The most important food consumed was sea lettuce, followed by eelgrass, widgeon grass, and salt-marsh grass. A change in food habits from sea lettuce to salt-marsh grass did not appear to have an adverse effect upon the weights of these birds.

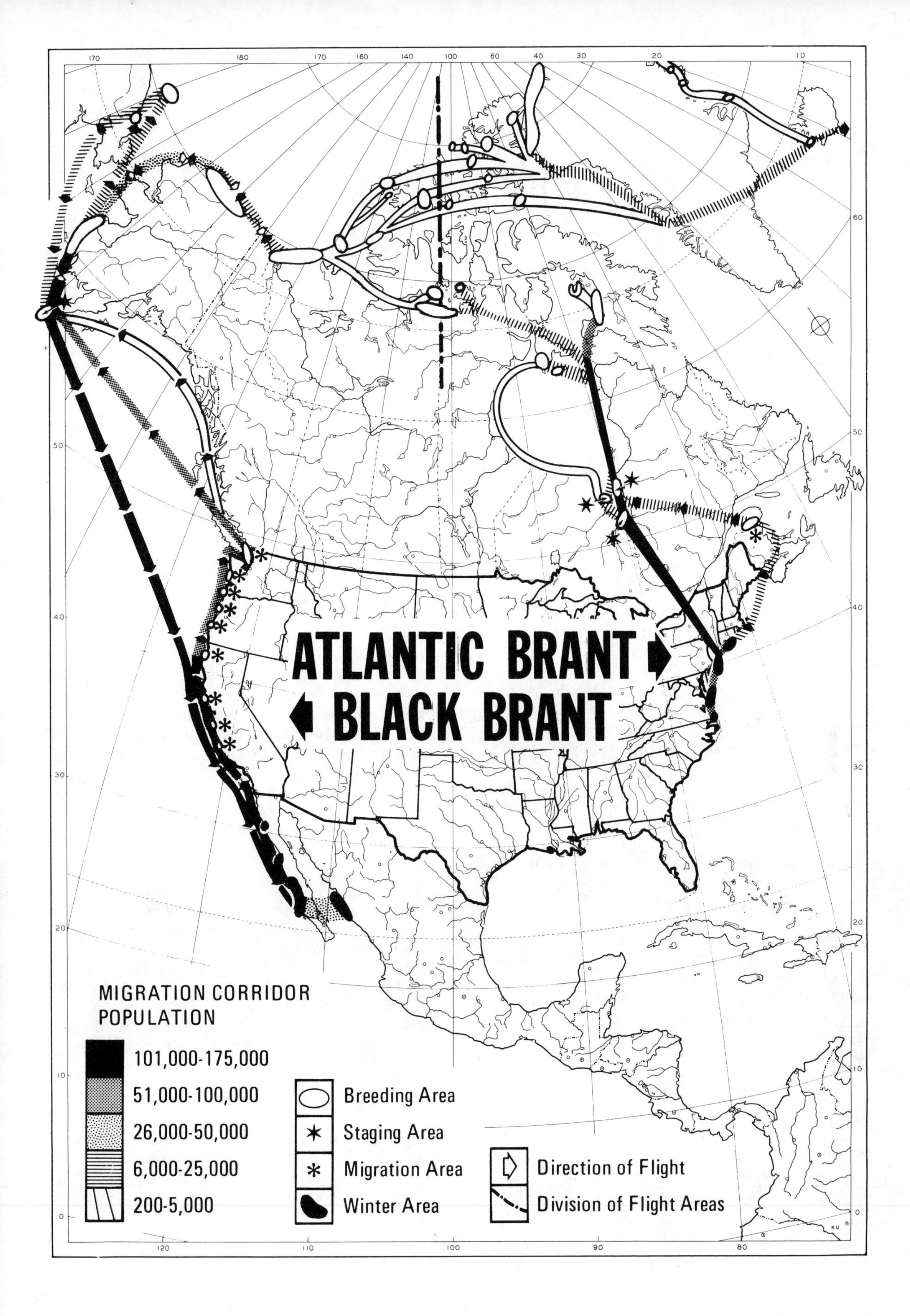
ATLANTIC BRANT
BLACK BRANT
MIGRATION CORRIDOR
POPULATION
101,000-175,000
51,000-100,000
26,000-50,000
6,000-25,000
200-5,000
Breeding Area
Staging Area
Migration Area
Winter Area
Direction of Flight
Division of Flight Areas

Black Brant

Branta bernicla nigricans

Other Common Name: Pacific brant

VITAL STATISTICS

Length:	Adult male, 24-26 inches, average 25 inches (23) Adult female, 22-25 inches, average 23 inches (12)
Wing:	Male, 12.1 inches (12) Female, 11.6 inches (6)
Weight:	Adult male, 3.19 pounds (189) Adult female, 2.88 pounds (181)

IDENTIFICATION

Field

The black brant is similar in appearance to the Atlantic brant, except that the breast and belly of the black brant are a uniform dusky brown as far back as the legs, instead of white as in the Atlantic race. The sides and flanks of adult black brants are strongly barred gray and white; the immatures appear entirely dark except for the white undertail coverts. The white neck mark of the adults is larger, encircles the neck, and therefore is more noticeable than in the Atlantic race. The black brant is one of the darkest of waterfowl and only casually might be confused with cormorants or scoters.

At Hand

The short bill, sloping forehead, black plumage, black bill and feet, and a long wing in relation to body length distinguish the black brant from other waterfowl. Immatures can be distinguished from adults by the light gray edging of the wing coverts.

POPULATION STATUS

Winter surveys indicate that population levels of black brant have remained relatively stable at approximately 140,000 along the Pacific Coast, 1951-74 (Smith and Jensen 1970 and updated), in marked contrast to fluctuating population levels of the Atlantic brant. Except for 1959, the numbers of black brant have remained above 100,000 birds. The unusually low population of 68,500 recorded in 1959 does not suggest a drastic decline from the preceding year, followed by a rebound in 1960—but rather that large numbers of birds were overlooked during the census of 1959.

Earlier censuses (Moffitt 1943) revealed an average population of 58,000 along the California coast during a 12-year period, 1930-42. There were 43,800 brant in California in 1952 (Leopold and Smith 1953). Since then, a shift in winter areas has caused a drastic decline in the numbers of brant wintering in California.

Mortality

Hansen and Nelson (1957) computed the yearly rate of mortality from 8,804 black brant banded on the Yukon Delta, Alaska, 1949-54. They found that immatures suffered a mortality of 45 percent during the first year of life. Adult brant lost 22 percent of their numbers during the first year after banding. The bag of brant in 1955-56 was determined to be 21 percent of the population, and the total hunting loss, including crippling, was 26 percent.

DISTRIBUTION

Although the black brant breeds as far as the delta of the Lena River in Siberia and winters as far as Japan, the numbers frequenting Asia are small. Most brants are indigenous to the western coast of North America, where they range from the central Canadian Arctic all the way around Alaska and south to Baja California.

Breeding Range

The largest breeding grounds of the black brant are located on the outer Yukon-Kuskokwim Delta. Spencer et al. (1951) and Hansen and Nelson (1957) have noted the importance of this area to brant. James King estimated in 1968 that breeders, nonbreeders, and young on this area totaled 150,000, which suggests a breeding population of about 75,000 birds. The estimate by James King of a combined fall population of 35,000 brant along the coast of the North Slope of Alaska between Wainwright and the Colville River indicates a breeding population there of about 17,000. Only small numbers of brant nest elsewhere in Alaska, principally on the coast of Kotzebue Sound.

Populations of black brant in late summer in the Canadian Arctic were determined by Barry (1960) as follows: Mackenzie Delta, 200; Liverpool Bay, 3,000; Banks Island, over 9,000; southeast Victoria Island and Prince Albert Peninsula, 3,000; and the coast and adjacent islands of Queen Maud Gulf, 3,000. Tener's (1963) survey of the Queen Elizabeth Islands disclosed 250 black brant at the head of Bay Fiord, Ellesmere Island, and 14 on the east side of Cornwallis Island. These locations are unusually far east for this race and greatly overlap the range of the Atlantic brant. Both black brant and Atlantic brant have nested in the same general area of Prince Patrick Island, but Handley (1950) saw no more than 100 brant there.

On Wrangel Island, off the coast of Siberia, Uspenski (1965) estimated 1,000 to 2,000 pairs of nesting black brant, and at least 10,000 molting, nonbreeding birds. Band recoveries indicate that most of the black brant breeding in Siberia migrate to North America rather than to Asia. Japan is the only Asian country known to winter small numbers of black brant (Einarsen 1965).

Migration Corridors

Fall. All evidence points to the fall passage of black brant from their most distant eastern Canadian breeding grounds westward along the Arctic Coast around Alaska to gather at Izembek Bay near the tip of the Alaska Peninsula. There they are probably joined by most of the black brant breeding in Siberia. About 250,000 brant concentrate at the Izembek National Wildlife Range in the fall (Robert Jones, Jr.) and depart en masse on a true course of 113°. I believe that most of them pass over the Pacific Ocean west of the Gulf of Alaska and make landfall in northern California. South of Humboldt Bay, California, their passage is often observed offshore from ships or from promontories that jut into the ocean (Einarsen 1965). "Possibly most of the flocks do not stop on land until they arrive in California . . ." (Hansen and Nelson 1957:240).

Only small numbers of brant are found in the fall along the shore of the Gulf of Alaska and the coasts of British Columbia. Larger numbers occur at Puget Sound, and still larger numbers in the bays of California. However, most of the fall population migrates directly to Baja California, where many flocks barely arrive before heading back north along the California coast.

Spring. Peak populations of black brant develop along the Pacific Coast of the United States and British Columbia during late winter and early spring in their gradual northward passage from Baja California. In California, the following bays are important concentration points: Morro, Bolinas, Tomales, Drake's, and Humboldt; in Oregon, Coos, Yaquina, Tillamook, and Netarts bays; in Washington, Willapa Bay, Grays Harbor, and the Puget Sound area, particularly Padilla and Samish bays, and Boundary Bay in extreme southwest British Columbia.

In January, only small numbers of brant occur on Humboldt Bay, but appreciable numbers begin to appear in February, and the peak numbers of 20,000 to 40,000 gather there throughout most of March and April (Denson and Murrell 1962).

Censuses of black brant between Anacortes, Washington, and Sea Island, British Columbia, were made during the springs of 1958 and 1959 by E. W. Taylor of British Columbia. Brant populations there rose from 2,300 on March 15 to 14,100 by April 7, 1958, and from 2,700 on March 18 to 23,600 on April 8, 1959. These data emphasize the great importance of the spring passage to local brant populations on the West Coast.

It is evident that a much greater proportion of black brant migrants are found in the more northerly reaches of the Pacific Coast in the spring than during the fall passage. Consequently, the flight of the migrants to Izembek Bay in spring is much shorter and across a lesser expanse of open sea than it is in the fall. The migration corridor in spring differs in another respect from that in the fall—at least a small segment of the population passes through the interior of Alaska via the Yukon Basin (Cade 1955, Irving 1960).

Winter Areas

Prior to 1958, about 50 percent of the black brant observed on January surveys were in Baja California, 35 percent in California, and 15 percent in Washington and Oregon. Numbers in California, Washington, and Oregon have all declined, most drastically in California. Beginning in 1959, the numbers of brant observed in Mexico in midwinter have steadily increased, largely at the expense of California, where January populations have dwindled to a few hundred birds. Before 1959, black brant wintering in Mexico were observed only on the coast of Baja California, where they averaged 81,400, 1951-58, and 106,500, 1959-69 (Smith and Jensen 1970). The striking increase in abundance of brant on the mainland coast of Mexico from only 1,400 in 1949 to 41,300 in 1967 signals a major shift in winter grounds.

About 100 brant winter in British Columbia and surprisingly, several thousand brant brave the rigors of winter in the vicinity of the Izembek National Wildlife Range, Alaska (Robert Jones, Jr.).

MIGRATION BEHAVIOR

Chronology

Fall. Although the black brant depart Izembek Bay almost all at once in the fall, their return in the spring is more gradual and peak numbers are from one-third to one-half lower than in the fall. On several occasions in May, small flocks of about 20 birds each have been observed migrating across the Gulf of Alaska less than 20 feet above its surface (Einarsen 1965). These brant make a final flight from Izembek Bay to nest areas 1,000 to 2,000 miles away in only 3 to 6 days (Barry 1966).

Black brant begin arriving at Izembek Bay about August 25 (Jones 1964) and depart in late October or early November. Some appear off the California coast as early as October 8-15, with a later flight occurring November 10-20 (Moffitt 1941). They begin to appear in the bays of the Oregon coast about mid-November, but the greatest influx occurs from December into February (Batterson 1968). Dates reported for first arrivals in British Columbia are November 11 and December 27, with mid-March or April peaks (Einarsen 1965). The latest spring departures from British Columbia have been as early as April 15 to as late as June 14.

Spring. Black brant migrating in spring arrive at Izembek Bay in late April and early May. Most of them stay about 3 weeks. Some have reached their breeding grounds on the Yukon Delta by May 12, and the population increases to maximum numbers by the last week of the month (Mickelson 1973). Small numbers of brant migrating in the interior have appeared at Anaktuvuk Pass, Alaska, on May 27 and at Old Crow, Yukon, Canada, on May 25 (Irving 1960). Over a 5-year period, brant reached their breeding grounds on the Anderson River delta, Canada, between May 23 and May 28 (Barry 1966). On breeding areas farther east, black brant have appeared on Banks Island on June 2 (Manning et al. 1956), southeast Victoria Island on June 8 (Parmelee et al. 1967), the delta of the Perry River on June 16 (Hanson et al. 1956), and Adelaide Peninsula on June 14 (Macpherson and Manning 1959). The flight of 2,500 miles from the Yukon Delta to the Adelaide Peninsula in 1 month attests to the rapidity of passage along Arctic shores.

Behavior

Most black brant breed when they are 3 years old, but good seasons encourage perhaps 10 percent of the 2-year-old birds to nest (Barry 1966). Pairing takes place during a long association of subadults, perhaps 1 or 2 years before sexual maturity. Barry observed three-bird courtship chases among yearlings just before and after the annual molt. However, courtship activity has been known to occur on the winter grounds between mid-January and April (Einarsen 1965). Brant apparently remain mated for life unless one of the spouses is lost.

Homing. Brant have a great ability and a strong desire to return to the same nest area each year. Barry (1966) reported that 40 percent of the adults neck-banded at the Anderson River delta returned 1 year later. Only 6 of the 10,000 brant banded as immatures on the Yukon Delta were recaptured at the Anderson Delta, and only 3 of the 3,000 brant banded at the Anderson Delta were recaptured as nesters in Alaska (Barry 1966), thus demonstrating a remarkable affinity for their original nest areas.

Territory. A few days after arrival on their breeding grounds, pairs leave their flocks to fly over nest habitat, the female in the lead (Barry 1966). Flocks of breeding birds decline rapidly in size as more and more pairs leave to establish nest territories. The size of a territory varies greatly depending upon habitat and competition. Barry (1966) cited extremes of a single territory several hundred yards across centering on a small lone hummock, contrasted with a 40- by 20-foot hummock that held seven brant nests and two snow goose nests. Black brant tend to nest in colonies. On the Kashunuk study area on the Yukon Delta during a 4-year period, 1961-64, the number of brant nests per acre ranged from 0.96 to 1.44 (Shepherd 1964). At Onumtuk, Mickelson (1973) observed two colonies that contained over 1,000 nests per square mile, almost two nests per acre.

Nesting

Nest Sites. Calvin Lensink reports that black brant on the Yukon Delta are confined either to the extreme coastal rim or to the areas along major estuaries flanked by tidal meadows. He describes their nest areas as "giving the impression of a poorly maintained lawn." Nests on the delta were most frequently established on small islets or on the shores of tidal ponds, but sometimes as far as 30 yards from the nearest water. The nests were placed in either a short sedge or, more rarely, in clumps of wild rye.

On their nesting grounds on the Anderson Delta, Barry (1966) found their nests on grassy hummocks surrounded by tidal flats. Over a 3-year period, nests in any one year averaged 3 to 7 inches above the high tide line or above standing water. In 1959 the nests were located an average of 20 feet from both standing water and snow cover.

The nests of black brant are placed in depressions or scrapes, as described for the Atlantic brant. Down is more abundant in the nests of black brant than in those of any other species, including eider ducks, and appears to have the same quality as that of the eider (Calvin Lensink). Cottam et al. (1944) described the brant nest as the most beautiful of all waterfowl nests, with a grass foundation and a symmetrical ring of pure down, 14 to 18 inches in diameter. They described the down feathers as powder-blue, slate, and steel-gray, forming an "admirable setting for the four or five eggs, which are faintly glossy white or soft ivory'' (Cottam et al. 1944:51).

Clutch Size, Eggs, and Incubation. Peter Shepherd and Calvin Lensink found an average of 3.52 eggs (1,877) per nest, 1961-71, on the Yukon Delta. Mickelson (1973) reported an average incubated clutch of 3.63 eggs (58). On the Anderson River delta, Barry (1966) reported an average of 3.92 eggs in 700 black brant nests. Clutch sizes varied from 1 to 10, with the largest number of nests containing 4 eggs. Large clutches are rare and represent the use of a nest by more than one pair.

Calvin Lensink observed an incubation period of 23 to 25 days (12) for black brant nesting on the Yukon Delta. Mickelson (1973) found that the incubation period for seven nests ranged from 22 to 25 days. At Anderson Delta, Barry (1966) reported an average incubation period of 24 days. The female alone incubates; the male stands guard nearby during the entire time, except for feeding excursions. The male escorts his mate from the nest to feed, and the female covers the eggs with down before she leaves.

Black brant, like other waterfowl that nest in the Arctic, do not renest if a nest is destroyed after completion of the clutch. They are determinate layers and build a second nest only to lay the remaining eggs of an incomplete clutch that has been destroyed (Barry 1966).

Chronology of Nesting. On the Yukon Delta, most of the breeders begin nesting about mid-May, but this date may vary as much as 2 weeks depending upon the time of the ice breakup in the spring (Calvin Lensink). At Igiak Bay (Kokechik Bay) egg-laying commenced May 26 and 27, 1971-72 (Eisenhauer et al. 1971, Eisenhauer and Frazer 1972). New nests were started up to June 13 and 11, respectively, a span of 18 and 15 days. On the Onumtuk area, egg-laying started May 19 in both 1969 and 1970, but, because of the lateness of spring in 1971 and 1972, it did not start until the first week of June (Mickelson 1973). The first nests of brant at their colony on the Anderson Delta were initiated as early as June 2, 1961, and as late as June 13, 1959, with June 6 as an 8-year average; nest initiation embraced a 10-day period. At Perry River most black brant began incubation about June 23, but a few began as late as July 7 (Hanson et al. 1956). In 1960, the brant on Victoria Island started egg-laying on June 9 and continued to mid-June, in one case as late as June 18 (Parmelee et al. 1967).

Nest Success. Studies determining the success of black brant nests on the Yukon Delta have been made by Shepherd (1964), Mickelson (1973), Eisenhauer et al. (1971), and Calvin Lensink. Of the 821 nests that they have documented, 73.7 percent hatched successfully. Mickelson (1973) reported that 2.93 eggs (58) hatched per successful nest, 0.7 egg less than the 3.63 incubated. But Class I broods averaging 3.2 goslings indicate that a better hatch of eggs generally occurs.

On the Onumtuk study area, glaucous gulls were responsible for the destruction of numerous brant nests during laying and the first half of the nest period (Mickelson 1973). A storm tide in 1963 destroyed many of the brant nests that Calvin Lensink had under observation. This catastrophe has not recurred, and, according to Lensink, the Eskimos could not recall an earlier instance. He considers that on the Yukon Delta, predators cause serious nest losses only in unusual situations. He cites two study plots where foxes often destroy nearly all the brant nests, but nests on many other plots remain undisturbed. Island sites are safer than peninsular and shore sites.

A violent storm of wind and snow resulted in the abandonment of most brant nests on the Anderson Delta in 1964 (Barry 1966). Otherwise, the success of the hatch was high, with only a small percentage of the eggs failing to hatch because of infertility, desertion, and predation.

In 1937, most nests of black brant on the lower Mackenzie Delta were flooded, and subsequently only a few pairs were observed to nest (Einarsen 1965). However, flood losses appear to be relatively infrequent and are usually local.

Rearing of Young

The time from the pipping of eggs to the drying of young, usually 24 to 48 hours, may be extended to 72 hours during stormy weather (Barry 1966). When they are dry, the young are led from the nest by the male, who now assumes the dominant role in family life. The male heads the procession, the female brings up the rear, and the young are sandwiched in between as the family makes its way to open water. The parents then establish a small territory around their swimming brood. Although the territory becomes smaller as the brood matures, it persists as flocks form for the fall migration (Barry 1966).

These geese are still in family units when they arrive at the staging area at Izembek Bay late in August, but by the time they leave, 2 months later, the family units have dissolved (Jones and Jones 1966). Band recoveries show that immatures generally winter farther south than the adults (Hansen and Nelson 1957), a further indication of the separation of young from their parents during the fall. Young black brant establish their independence much sooner than the young of many other species of geese.

Development. Young brant can swim as soon as they can walk, dive when 2 days old, and by 10 days can maintain themselves without brooding (Barry 1966). By the time they are 40 to 45 days old, the young are able to fly—at Anderson Delta the approximate date of first flight is August 15, but the date varies with the chronology of nesting.

Survival. Brood sizes determined by several biologists on the Yukon Delta over a number of years show the following attrition with age: Class I, 3.22 (517); Class II, 2.41 (410); and Class III, 2.30 (109). Brood counts of brant are difficult to make because of the propensity of families to band together in flocks as the young increase in age. Brood size declined by 30 percent from hatching to flight, attributed on the Onumtuk area to predation by glaucous gulls (Mickelson 1973).

POSTBREEDING SEASON

The molt of nonbreeding black brant at Anderson Delta started about July 4 and was so consistent from year to year that Barry (1966) believed it was controlled by day length. He reported that among breeding birds at Anderson Delta the molt began approximately 2 weeks after their eggs hatched; the dates varied yearly—from July 9, 1958, to July 22, 1962—depending upon the date incubation started. The flightless period of adult molting brant lasted about 3 weeks, enabling them to regain flight a few days before their young could fly (Barry 1966).

Black brant usually depart their breeding grounds in the Arctic in late August or early September, with specific dates as follows: Banks Island, August 28, 1953; August 31, 1952 (Manning et al. 1956); southeastern Victoria Island, August 28, 1960 (Parmelee et al. 1967); Adelaide Peninsula, September 7, 1957 (Macpherson and Manning 1959); and Prince Patrick Island, August 30, 1949 (Handley 1950).

FOOD HABITS

The distribution of black brant outside the breeding season is intrinsically related to the distribution of eelgrass, which is by far the black brant's most important food (Cottam et al. 1944). When eelgrass is scarce or unavailable, brant resort to rockgrass and sea lettuce.

The extensive, luxuriant eelgrass beds at Izembek Bay, Alaska, attract a tremendous concentration of black brant each spring and fall. All along the Pacific Coast from Izembek Bay to lower Baja California, the large concentrations of brant occur on those bays with the most extensive beds of eelgrass.

When disease ravaged the eelgrass beds along the California coast in the early 1940's, brant sought food in such unlikely places as pastures and golf courses, where they clipped grass for food (Moffitt and Cottam 1941). Even today, when eelgrass beds become scarce in Oregon bays during the spring, brant leave bay waters several times a day for adjacent meadowlands (Batterson 1968); flocks of thousands gather there to graze upon grass "like a herd of sheep."

Wood Duck

Aix sponsa

Other Common Names: Woodie, summer duck, acorn duck, swamp duck, squealer.

VITAL STATISTICS

Length: Adult male, 18.8-21.2 inches, average 20.0 inches (15)
Adult female, 18.5-20.1 inches, average 19.5 inches (5)
Immature male, 15.9-18.5 inches, average 17.4 inches (14)
Immature female, 15.1-17.8 inches, average 16.5 inches (8)

Wing: Adult male, 8.9 inches (37)
Adult female, 8.6 inches (54)
Immature male, 8.6 inches (50)
Immature female, 8.4 inches (60)

Weight: Adult male, 1.2-1.9 pounds, average 1.50 pounds (84)
Adult female, 1.1-1.9 pounds, average 1.48 pounds (60)
Immature male, 1.1-1.8 pounds, average 1.47 pounds (45)
Immature female, 1.0-1.8 pounds, average 1.35 pounds (47)

IDENTIFICATION

Field

Wood ducks are inhabitants of creeks, rivers, floodplain lakes, swamps, and beaver ponds. The loud, squealing *wee-e-e-e-k, wee-e-e-e-k* call by the hen is often the first indication of the presence of these birds as they beat hasty retreats through the trees. No other duck has a call as distinctive as that of the hen wood duck, and, once learned, it is usually remembered. The male's call is a goldfinch-like *twee, twee* uttered so softly that it is rarely heard.

Over much of the year, wood ducks occur in pairs or in flocks of 4 to 15, but hundreds may gather at fall and winter roost sites. Their flight is only moderately swift, but they are adept at twisting and turning as they adroitly thread their way through the branches of trees. Perhaps they have this ability because their wings are proportionately broader than those of other ducks.

Their crested heads, broad wings, and large rectangular tails create an unusual conformation. They bob their heads up and down in flight like no other duck. Flying wood ducks are most frequently confused with wigeons because of their similar size and white bellies. However, the short, broad wings of wood ducks contrast noticeably with the longer, narrower wings of wigeons. Moreover, single white stripes on the back edges of the dark wings of wood ducks show up well during flight. Wigeons show white on their shoulders. Because of long crown feathers, the heads of wood ducks appear larger, and because their tails are rectangular rather than wedge-shaped as in wigeons, they too appear larger.

When the wood duck drake is at rest on the water or perched on a log, its gaudy colors are apparent. The crested head has many hues of purple and green, with two white parallel lines extending from the base of the bill and from the back of the eye to the rear of the crest. The white of the chin and throat sweeps upward in U-like prongs onto the sides of the head. The red eyes and red at the base of the bill complete the vivid head color. The burgundy chest, flecked with white, is separated from the bronze sides by "fingers" of black and white. The glossy purplish black of the back and tail is in marked contrast to the white of the breast and belly.

The wood duck hen is more attractively colored than the mottled brown hens so typical of other dabbling ducks. Pronounced white rings surround the eyes and trail behind, like exclamation marks, on the sooty-gray, slightly crested head. The white chin and throat are discernible at considerable distances. The chest, sides, and flanks are gray-brown, with disconnected lines of white dashes. The belly is white.

On the water, wood ducks ride higher and more buoyantly than other ducks, as evidenced by their tails jauntily inclined an inch or more above the surface.

At Hand

The resplendent nuptial plumage of the drake wood

duck, giving it the title of most beautiful duck in North America if not in the world, can be truly appreciated only at close hand. Hues change constantly with changes in light refraction, adding still greater variety to the many iridescent colors.

At close hand the crest is iridescent green in front to purplish in the rear, with a touch of burgundy behind each eye; the sides of the head are purple, blue-green, and bronze set with red eyelids and irises. The short bill has a black tip and ridge, white on the sides, and a red base bordered with a narrow yellow line.

The bronze sides are vermiculated with fine black lines, the upper feathers are broadly tipped with black, and there is a white border along the green, purple, and bronze back and rump. Dark burgundy flanks add a bright patch of color near the base of the tail. The feet and legs are a dull straw-yellow.

Up close, the hen woodie displays additional characteristics. The crest is brown, glossed with green, the bill is a dark blue-gray, and the eyes are brown-black. The back is an olive-brown with a shimmer of iridescent green and the undertail coverts are white, like the belly.

The wings provide a means of distinguishing sex and age groups. The tertials in males are purple or black, in females bronze-green. The steel-blue secondaries are edged with single white bars in the males; in the females the white bars are broader and are shaped like teardrops.

The tertials in adult males are black and deep purple and tend to be square; those in immatures are brown and wispy, with more rounded tips. In adults of both sexes, the distal greater coverts are purple edged with black and are square in shape; those of immatures are brownish, rounded, and wispy. Among females, the greater tertial coverts, the color of an oil slick, extend 0.4 inch or more beyond the greater secondary coverts in adults but are shorter in immatures.

Birds in juvenile plumages resemble adult females, but their bellies are a streaked mottled brown rather than white. Males display the two white prongs extending upward on the sides of the heads. Young females may or may not show white eye-rings, depending upon age. Adult males in eclipse plumage can be distinguished from immatures by their red eyes and the red coloration on their bills, characters not lost in the molt.

POPULATION STATUS

Historical

Passage of the Migratory Bird Treaty Act between the United States and Canada in 1918 may have saved the wood duck from near extinction. Prior to this act, waterfowl seasons usually extended from September to April, bag limits were either nonexistent or so large as to be meaningless, market hunting abounded, and enforcement was almost unknown. Because the wood duck's haunts coincided with the areas of greatest hunting activity, the wood duck was hunted over a longer period than that experienced by other ducks. Thus, it suffered the heaviest losses. The Migratory Bird Treaty Act made it possible to give the wood duck complete protection and reduced hunting seasons to fall and early winter.

In the early 1900's, ornithologists and conservationists were so alarmed by the virtual disappearance of wood ducks that they voiced fears of extinction. For example, Grinnell (1901:142) stated: "Being shot at all seasons of the year they [wood ducks] are becoming very scarce and are likely to be exterminated before long."

Slightly over a decade after enactment of the Migratory Bird Treaty Act, Phillips and Lincoln (1930:296) could report: "Once greatly reduced by summer shooting, especially in our Northern States, this fine duck has recovered everywhere with protection." The greatly curtailed hunting seasons in the 1930's appear to have also aided the wood duck by reducing hunters afield and attendant illegal kills. By 1941 the wood duck had sufficiently increased in number to permit one in the bag in 14 states.

Wood ducks continued to increase in abundance through the 1940's but suffered population reverses in the Mississippi Flyway during the mid-1950's. From the mid-1960's on, the woodie has ranked second or third in the bags of hunters in both the Atlantic and Mississippi flyways. The comeback of the wood duck is a tribute to man's concern for waterfowl.

Current

Population estimates of adults after the breeding season are based upon the known hunting kill divided by the rate of harvest from band recoveries. Kimball (1970, 1971, 1972) has reported on the calculated populations of wood ducks in the eastern United States and Ontario, 1964-71. The average adult population during this period was 1,365,000 with a low of 1,100,00 in 1967 and a high of 1,694,000 in 1966.

Because weather conditions are more stable in the eastern United States than in the northern prairies and the Arctic, there is less annual fluctuation in numbers of wood ducks than among species nesting in those regions.

However, the steady clearing and drainage of swamps and overflow river bottomlands during the last two decades has adversely affected wood duck populations. The clearing of bottomland hardwoods destroys nest, brood, and winter habitats. The loss of these lands has been particularly severe in the Delta country of the Mississippi Basin: western Tennessee, Mississippi, eastern Arkansas, and Louisiana. The acreage of bottomland hardwoods in eastern Arkansas alone declined from 4,301,000 acres in 1940 to 1,799,000 acres in 1970 (Holder 1971). Most of the cleared land has been replaced by soybean fields. The increase in numbers of wood ducks in Ontario from the 1940's into the early 60's was attributed to restrictive hunting regulations and to an improvement in the breeding habitat from an increase in beaver ponds and in cavities excavated by pileated woodpeckers (Cringan 1971). For unknown reasons, the wood duck also extended its breeding range farther west on the Great Plains during the 1950's and 1960's.

Age Ratios

Immature wood ducks in the United States were 1.37 times more likely to be killed by hunters than were adults, 1960-71 (Martinson & Henny 1966, Kimball 1972). The yearly range in vulnerability was between 1.17 and 1.68.

Age data corrected for selectivity bias indicate that during 1960-71 there were 1.22 young per 1.0 adult in the preseason fall populations. The production of young per adult was lowest in 1966 (0.93) and highest in 1965 (1.65). Wood ducks outproduce other species of ducks, and this is why they have been able to recover from near extinction and to maintain population levels in spite of heavy hunting losses.

Sex Ratios

Except for the mallard and the black duck, wood ducks appear to have more balanced sex ratios than other species. The most cogent data on the sex ratios of this species are derived from winter bandings. On the numerous and widely distributed areas where woodies have been banded during the winter, 1967-69, the male:female sex ratio of 5,504 birds was 1.0:0.76, or 56.8 percent males (Henny 1970). At that rate there is one extra drake for every four hens.

Mortality

Recoveries from prehunt bandings of wood ducks made in eastern United States suggest the following annual mortality rates: for immatures—60 percent for 1962 bandings, 64 percent for 1968-69 bandings, and 60 percent for 1969-70 bandings; for adults—50, 54, and 54 percent, respectively, for the same years (Kimball 1970, 1971).

Wood ducks banded during the summer in New England suffered an annual mortality loss of 76.7 percent among immatures and 62.8 percent among adults (Grice and Rogers 1965). Still higher mortality rates occurred among wood ducks banded during the summer in Ontario: 82 percent of the immatures banded during 1954-63 and 81 percent of those banded in 1964-65 were lost, and adults lost 41 percent of their number each year during 1954-63 and 56 percent during 1964-65 (Cringan 1971). Bandings of wood ducks during late summer at Lac qui Parle, Minnesota, 1963-68, indicated a mortality rate of 59 percent among immatures and 53 percent for adults (Benson 1970).

Our abundant information on mortality rates in the wood duck shows that it experiences the highest yearly loss of any species for which data are adequate. Fortunately, its productivity rate is also very high.

If we assume an overall annual mortality of 60 percent for 124 flying young in September and of 52 percent for 100 adults, the survival would be 98 adults the following September. It is obvious that at the average current rate of mortality and productivity, the species is barely holding its own. Because of habitat destruction, it may be declining so slightly per year as not to be evident in these imprecise population data.

DISTRIBUTION

There are three largely distinct wood duck populations in North America: Atlantic, Interior, and Pacific. The range of the Atlantic population includes southern Quebec, southeastern Ontario, the Maritime Provinces, and the states of the Atlantic Flyway. The Interior population ranges over the states of the Mississippi Flyway and the eastern half of the eastern states in the Central Flyway. The Pacific population's range includes southern British Columbia; parts of western Idaho, Montana, and Washington; Oregon; and California.

There is some overlap in the Atlantic and Interior populations at the extremes of their ranges. About 75 percent of the wood ducks banded in Ontario are associated with the Atlantic population and 25 percent with the Interior (Cringan 1971). Small numbers of the Interior population migrate into the Carolinas and Florida, and, similarly, small numbers of the Atlantic population migrate into Alabama and Mississippi. The Pacific population is separated from the Interior population by the western three-fourths of the Great Plains and most of the Rocky Mountains.

Breeding Range

Wood ducks breed throughout their range from near the southern tip of Florida to northern Nova Scotia, then west across southern Quebec and Ontario. In Quebec, woodies breed south of the St. Lawrence River between Montreal and Quebec, and along the Ottawa River between Ottawa and Montreal. They are regular breeders in Ontario south of a line from North Bay to Sault Ste. Marie, and occasionally as far as 100 miles to the north (Harry Lumsden). Sporadic breeding of wood ducks also occurs in southwestern Manitoba, probably in the Interlake region and possibly as far northwest as the Saskatchewan Delta (Arthur Hawkins, Godfrey 1966).

In the Great Plains states the wood duck breeds as far west as the Missouri River in the Dakotas (Robert Stewart). George Schildman reports that the wood duck breeds in the eastern third of Nebraska as far west as Hastings in the south and Springview in the north. According to Marvin Schwilling, the wood duck breeds in the eastern three-fourths of Kansas although the principal breeding is confined to the eastern third of the state.

Sutton (1967) records wood ducks almost as far west as the panhandle in northern Oklahoma; southward, the records are more confined to the eastern half of the state, with most in the eastern third. Charles Stutzenbaker reports that most of the wood ducks in Texas breed as far west as a line from Denton in the north to Victoria in the south. Sporadic breeding occurs farther west in the state to a line from Wichita Falls in the north to Corpus Christi in the south. The most southerly record is a nest found at Lake Corpus Christi by Bolen and Cottam (1967), who also reported a nest near Bloomington, Texas, 70 miles to the northeast.

The Pacific population breeds from northern Vancouver Island, part of Queen Charlotte Islands, and southeastern

British Columbia (Godfrey 1966) into the panhandle region of Idaho (Burleigh 1972), where it spills over into the Flathead and Bitterroot valleys of Montana (Dale Witt). Wood ducks breed in northeast and northern Washington, largely west of the Columbia River, and on lakes in the Puget Sound region (Yocom 1951). Wood ducks in Oregon are rare breeders east of the Cascade Mountains; the majority breed west of the Cascades and they are particularly abundant in the Willamette River valley and on Sauvie Island in the Columbia River below Portland (John Chattin).

According to Naylor (1960), wood ducks breeding in California are distributed sparsely over much of the state north of the Tehachapi Mountains. He reported that the most concentrated breeding occurs in Shasta and Plumas counties; the Butte Sink near Gridley; along the Feather River in Butte, Sutter, and Yuba counties; and along stretches of the Cosumnes, Mokelumne, Tuolumne, Merced, San Joaquin, and Kings rivers on the western slope of the Sierra Nevada mountains. A few breeding pairs occupy each of the many north coastal streams.

Because of their secretive habits, wood ducks are the most difficult of all species of ducks to census throughout the year. They make good use of overhanging woody vegetation to remain hidden until approached closely. I have flown over swamps without seeing a single bird, only later to observe thousands leave on an evening feeding flight. They are indeed the bobwhite quail of the duck tribe.

Therefore, conventional aerial inventories of waterfowl populations are inadequate for the wood duck, and other means must be used to determine its relative abundance. The distribution of breeding wood duck populations presented here is based upon rough estimates made for each state as of May 1965 by Sutherland (1971) and supplemented by data from other informants. Although these figures are not exact, they are, in my opinion, reasonable approximations of breeding numbers in the various states and provinces.

As discussed under migration, a late-summer dispersal by some adult and young wood ducks places them in different states and provinces during the hunting season. Therefore, breeding populations determined from state banding and kill ratios are often distorted. Ontario's population appears to be especially high because of northward preseason influxes of birds.

Wood Duck Breeding Populations (largely from Sutherland 1971)

ATLANTIC POPULATION	
Ontario	169,500 ***a***
Quebec	33,100 ***b***
Nova Scotia	1,500 ***b***
New Brunswick	5,900 ***b***
Maine	17,000
Vermont	15,000
New Hampshire	25,000
Massachusetts	25,000
New York	40,000
Rhode Island	2,000
Connecticut	8,000
Pennsylvania	23,000
New Jersey	18,000
West Virginia	2,000
Delaware	5,000
Maryland	11,000
Virginia	10,000
North Carolina	40,000
South Carolina	40,000
Georgia	30,000
Florida	60,000
Total	581,000
INTERIOR POPULATION	
Ontario	56,500 ***a***
Minnesota	89,000
Wisconsin	70,000
Michigan	40,000
Iowa	30,000
Illinois	60,000
Indiana	40,000
Ohio	40,000
Missouri	29,000
Kentucky	12,000
Tennessee	13,000
Arkansas	34,000
Mississippi	44,000
Alabama	28,000
Louisiana	31,000
North Dakota	13,100 ***b***
South Dakota	5,700 ***b***
Nebraska	4,000
Kansas	5,000
Oklahoma	5,000
Texas	16,000
Total	665,100
PACIFIC POPULATION	
British Columbia	3,000 ***c***
Washington	14,500 ***d***
Oregon	18,000
Idaho	1,000
Montana	500 ***e***
California	26,000
Total	63,000

a Cringan (1971).
b Don W. Hayne.
c R. T. Sterling, William Morris, and Ray Halladay.
d Jeffrey and Bowhay (1972).
e Dale Witt.

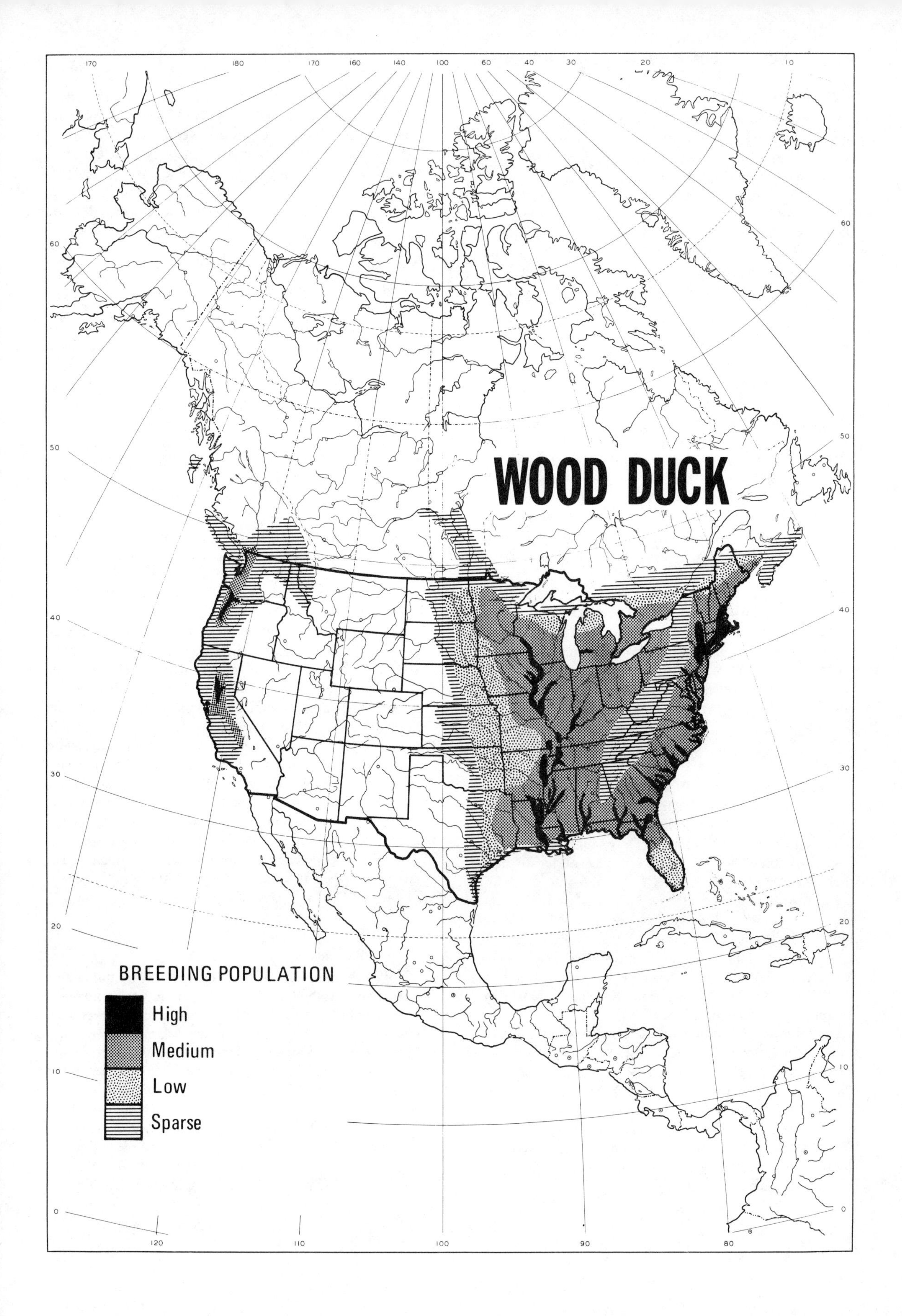
WOOD DUCK
BREEDING POPULATION
High
Medium
Low
Sparse

Migration Corridors

Because one-third or more of the breeding range contains within it the entire winter quarters for wood ducks, migration corridors are short and not well defined. Band recoveries indicate that the Atlantic and Pacific populations have the better delineated migration corridors.

The Atlantic corridor extends along the coast, and about 100 miles inland, from New Brunswick to North Carolina. There it broadens to 150 miles to include the Piedmont and the Coastal Plain of the Carolinas and Georgia (Grice and Rogers 1965). However, about 18 percent of the Atlantic population migrates to interior areas, particularly Alabama, Mississippi, and Louisiana (based upon analyses by Don W. Hayne).

The interior corridors extend, mainly, in a north-south alignment across the east-west expanse of the wood ducks' breeding range, although many breeding populations also fan out in south-southeast and south-southwest directions. These diversities in passage are most noted among populations in the eastern and western extremities of the interior range. Bandings in Ohio indicate that almost 30 percent of those wood ducks migrate to the Carolinas to winter, 25 percent migrate to Georgia and Florida, 20 percent to Alabama and Mississippi, and another 20 percent to Louisiana. By contrast, bandings in Minnesota suggest that about 85 percent of their wood ducks winter in eastern Texas, Louisiana, and Arkansas; 11 percent in Mississippi and Alabama; and 4 percent in the Carolinas and Florida.

The Pacific corridor funnels wood ducks from southern British Columbia through western Washington to the lower Columbia River, the Willamette River valley, and into the Sacramento River valley and its associated drainage (John Chattin, Naylor 1960).

Winter Areas

Although small numbers of wood ducks occasionally winter north into southern Ontario, most of them winter from Maryland south along the Atlantic Coastal Plain and the Piedmont and into Florida. Only small numbers of wood ducks breeding from North Carolina southward migrate still farther south.

The distribution of winter populations has been computed, based upon a 60 percent survival of the fall populations to mid-January, in relation to the breeding sources of the wood duck in the kill of each state (determined by Don W. Hayne). On this basis 158,000 wood ducks winter in North Carolina; 235,000 in South Carolina; 190,000 in Georgia; and 200,000 in Florida.

The Interior population winters almost entirely south of a line from Columbus, Ohio, to St. Louis, Missouri, to Wichita, Kansas. Most winter in the Deep South and eastern Texas. Calculated wood duck populations for this region in January are as follows: Alabama, 45,000; Mississippi, 125,000; Arkansas, 150,000; Louisiana, 465,000; and Texas, 115,000. A few woodies winter in scattered areas through southern Michigan, Wisconsin, Minnesota, northern Indiana, Illinois, and Iowa.

Small numbers of wood ducks winter from southwestern British Columbia through western Washington and Oregon. However, most of the birds breeding north of California migrate into the Sacramento Valley and adjacent areas for the winter. Naylor (1960) estimated that at least 90 percent of the Pacific population (about 55,000) wintered in California; small numbers wintered as far south as Mexico.

MIGRATION BEHAVIOR

Before the southward migration occurs, some wood ducks migrate northward. Throughout their breeding range south of Canada, small numbers of both adults and recently fledged young fan out from their breeding and natal areas to new "fields." In southern regions, this dispersal is more likely to be lateral than northerly, but north of the Mason-Dixon line the reverse is true. (These findings are derived from a band analysis by Don W. Hayne.)

Over the entire range of the wood duck, 3.2 percent of the adults and 2.1 percent of the banded young flew north to other states. Ontario received 8.7 percent of the adults and 2.7 percent of the immatures in its fall population from breeding areas to the south, some as far away as Indiana, West Virginia, and South Carolina. However, the greatest influx was from Quebec: 40.4 percent of the adults and 23.7 percent of the immatures taken in Ontario during the fall were from that province. Yet no Ontario wood ducks have appeared in Quebec.

Prior to the fall migration, wood ducks from Louisiana, largely immatures, migrated to Alabama, Arkansas, Mississippi, Oklahoma, Texas, and Wisconsin. Thirteen percent of the wood ducks in Florida flew to Alabama.

Most of this late-summer dispersal involves adult and immature drakes and some immature females. Available evidence suggests that these birds return in subsequent years to the areas from which they initiated their fall migration (Bellrose 1958). Therefore, although most females return to their natal areas to nest, some pioneering into new areas probably develops from the late-summer dispersal of immature females. Probably because of this premigration dispersal, wood ducks are found during the fall migration in all states, albeit in small numbers in the western Great Plains and Rocky Mountain regions.

Chronology

Fall. Wood ducks in the Atlantic Flyway population begin to depart the New England states in late September, their numbers gradually decreasing to mid-November, when most are gone. In the Middle Atlantic states, numbers rise and fall as flights from farther away arrive and depart, although many migrants remain all winter in the southern part of the region. Wood duck numbers in the South Atlantic region and Florida rise steadily from September through December as an ingress occurs from farther north.

Wood ducks of the Mississippi Flyway begin to depart the Great Lakes region in late September, with a continu-

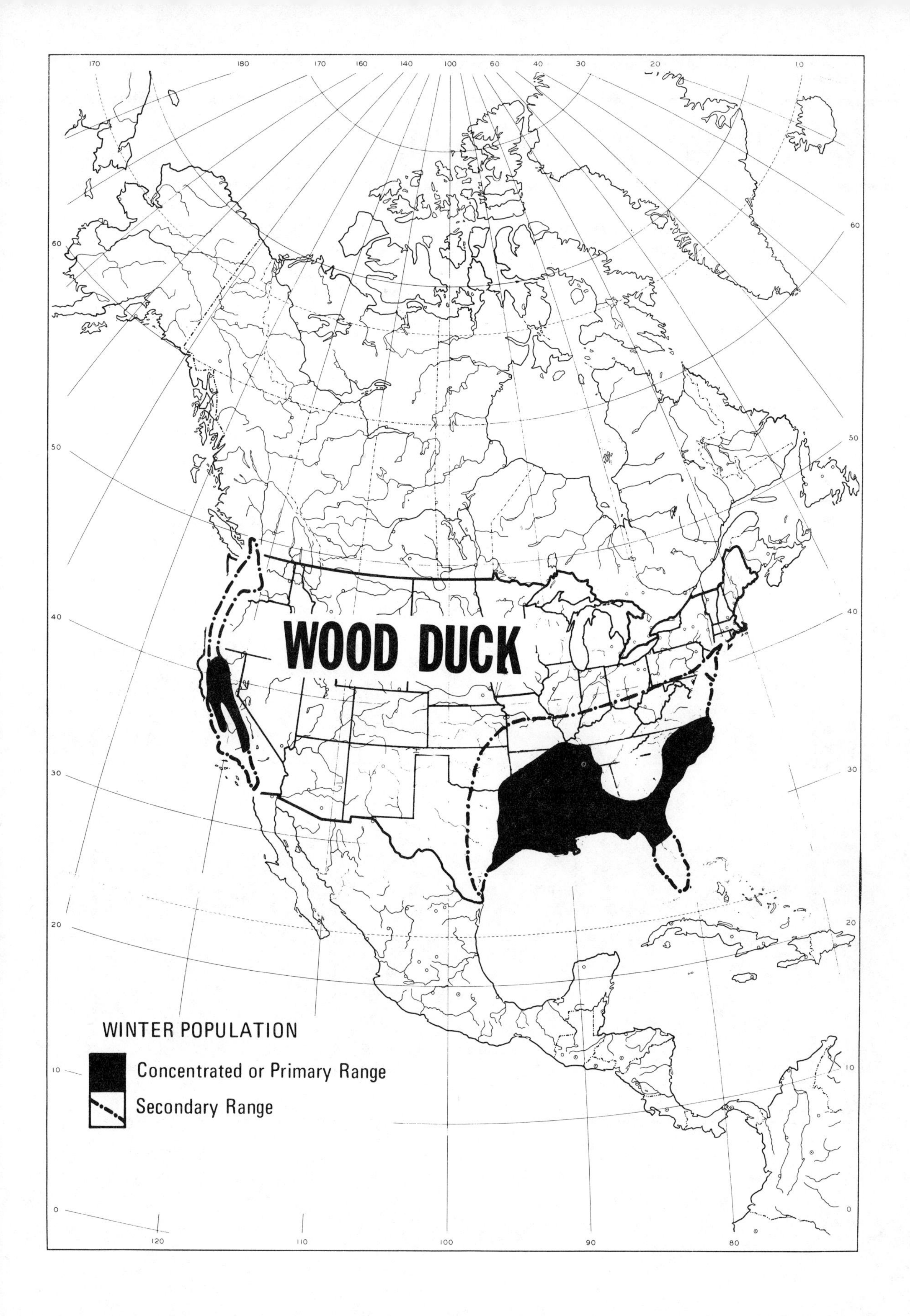
WOOD DUCK
WINTER POPULATION
Concentrated or Primary Range
Secondary Range

WOOD DUCK

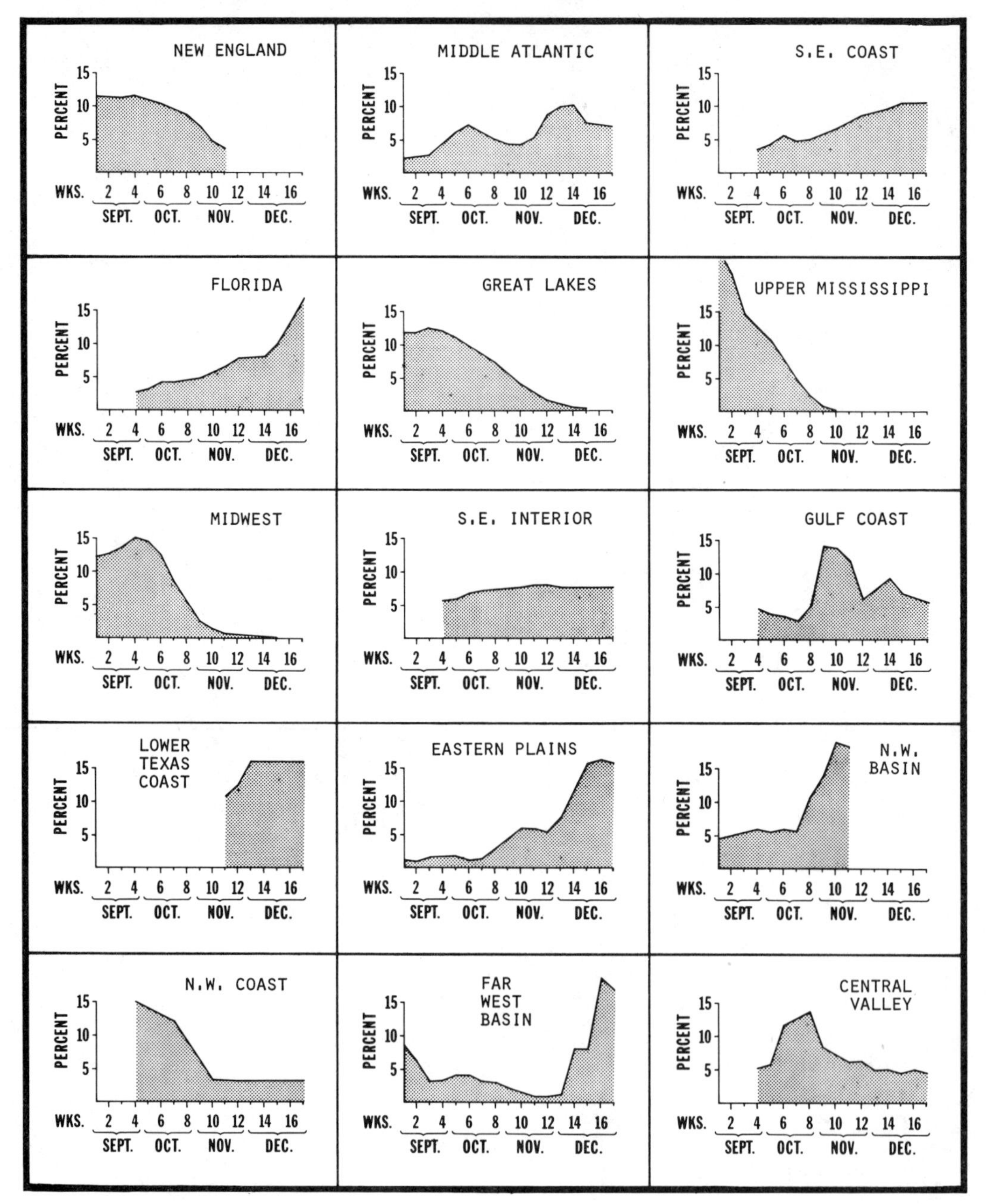

Fall

WOOD DUCK

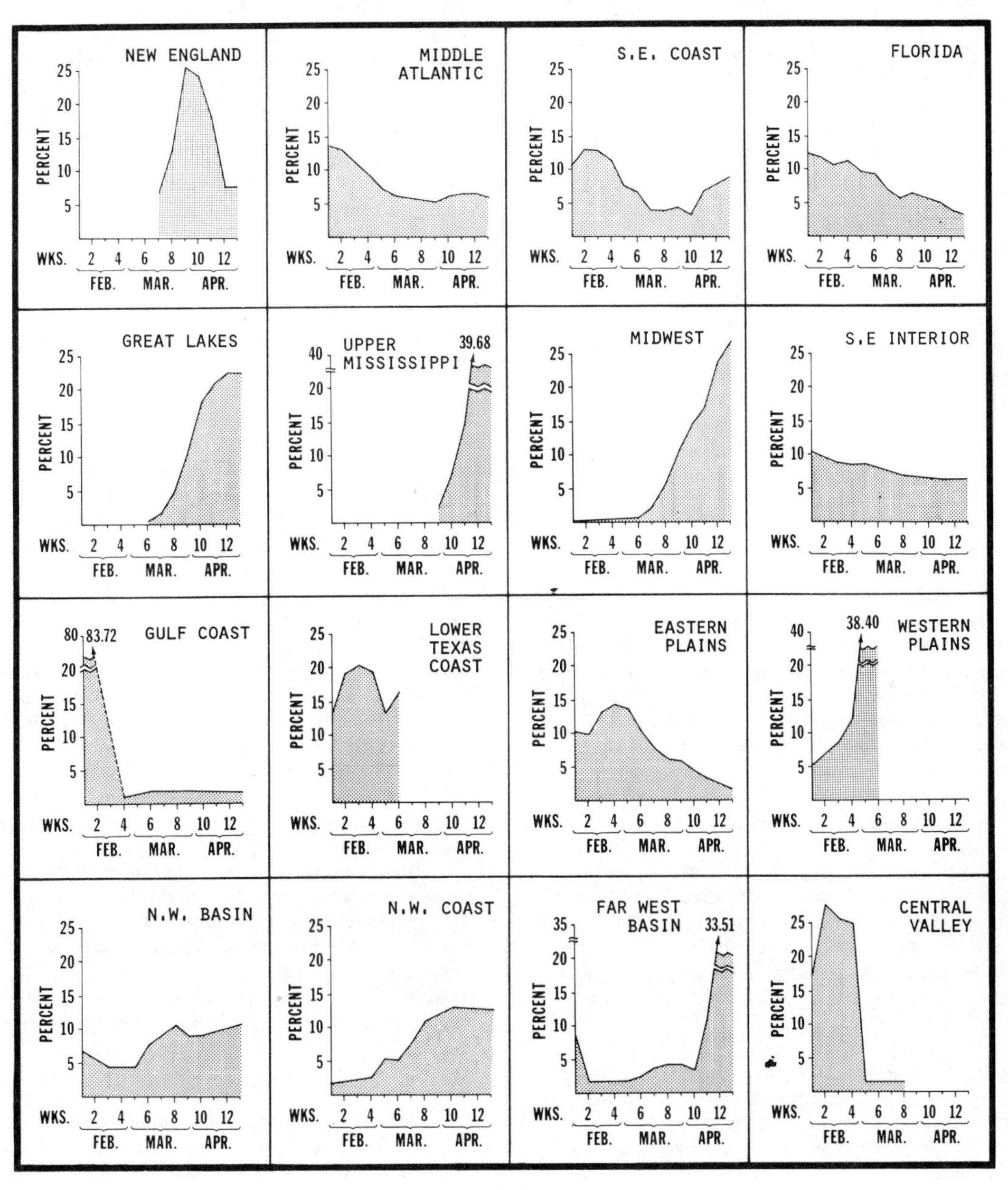

Spring

ing exodus through October and November. The birds arriving from farther north increase the Midwest population slightly in late September as they join the local birds in their southerly departures during October and early November.

Although censuses in the South show no remarkable seasonal change through the fall, there is, of course, a steady increase in this region during the fall as woodies depart the Midwest to winter there.

Spring. Waterfowl censuses taken on the winter grounds during late winter and spring reflect two activities: (1) indigenous wood ducks leave concentration areas to nest locally, and (2) migrants fly north to their breeding grounds. These simultaneous activities confuse the picture of migration chronology, especially along the mid- and South Atlantic Coast.

Wood ducks begin to arrive in the Midwest in early March, but it is midmonth before appreciable numbers are present. Birds continue to arrive in impressive numbers through April. Although woodies appear in the Great Lakes region in mid-March, large numbers are not present until April and migrants continue to arrive throughout the month. They first reach Minnesota in early April and a large ingress continues through that month.

BREEDING

Behavior

Age, Pair Bond. Most wood duck hens breed as yearlings. In Illinois, Robert Crompton has found sizable numbers of marked ducklings returning to nest their first year, but a small proportion do not return to nest until their second year. At Great Meadows, Massachusetts, 1951-56, 2 to 24 percent of the returning wood ducks were 2-year-olds found nesting for the first time (Grice and Rogers 1965). The second-year nesters may reflect latent sexual maturity as a result of late hatching.

Some pair bonds are formed as early as late October, and pairing continues through the fall and winter. By late February, probably 90 percent of the hens have mates. We see only a few unattached hens in Illinois when the birds arrive in the spring. Drake woodies remain with their mates longer than most ducks, usually until the eggs are pipped. However, late-nesting hens lose their mates at earlier stages of incubation.

Homing. Wood ducks have a phenomenal ability to return to the same breeding area year after year. In Mason County, Illinois, we found 49.1 percent of the adult females and 6.5 percent of the immature females returning to the same nest area the subsequent year (Bellrose et al. 1964). Considering the high annual mortality rate, this homing rate represents almost every living adult hen and a moderate proportion of the yearlings.

In Massachusetts, 43 percent of the adult hens returned a second year to the same nest areas (Grice and Rogers 1965). About 23 percent of the immature hens returned, which, considering their mortality loss in past years, indicates a rate of return up to 61 percent.

Near Raleigh, North Carolina, 14 of 30 (47 percent) banded hens returned to the same groups of nest houses the second year (Hester 1965). At the Noxubee National Wildlife Refuge near Starkville, Mississippi, an extraordinary 76 percent of Baker's (1971) banded adult hens returned in 1969, but only 48 percent returned in 1970. The disparity between the two percentages probably stemmed from differences in yearly mortality. An average of 58 percent of the nesting hens returned to the Mingo National Wildlife Refuge near Puxico, Missouri (Hansen 1971). Between 1967 and 1970, the rate of return ranged from 49 to 72 percent; the differences were attributed to hunting losses the previous falls. Forty-eight percent of the nesting hens banded during 1967-70 returned to the same area to nest in a subsequent year. Of 94 hens marked on nests in 1970 at Big Lake, Arkansas, Brown (1973*a*) recaptured 68 and another one was killed during the following nesting season for a return rate of 73.4 percent.

At Arrowwood National Wildlife Refuge, north of Jamestown, North Dakota, Doty and Kruse (1970) raised and released wood ducks where they were unknown as breeding birds. Fifteen percent of the 100 young hens released in the fall of 1968 returned the next year to nest in houses. Of 40 young hens trapped in 1969, 28 percent were captured on nests in 1970.

Drake wood ducks lack the great proclivity of hens for returning to their breeding or natal areas. At Great Meadows, Massachusetts, Grice and Rogers (1965) bait-trapped 210 males, only 19 (9 percent) of which had been banded there in previous years, compared with 48 percent of the 217 females that had been banded previously. Doty and Kruse (1972) noted that 3 of 93 pen-released drakes returned the following year and an additional one the next year.

The low homing of wood duck drakes is thought to occur because the male follows his mate to her former breeding area. Drakes that pair early in the fall undoubtedly often do so with local hens, and so both return to their native area. There is also evidence that unmated drakes return to their natal areas. Most of the late-summer dispersal involves drakes; they may pair with hens north of their former breeding areas. Killing one of a pair during the hunting season must end many pair bonds. Undoubtedly most remaining spouses later form new pair bonds on the winter grounds, probably diverting drakes to new areas.

Home Range. Unlike most other dabbling ducks, woodies do not have a stable home range. They do have a home base of sorts, but it is quite flexible in its dimensions and boundaries. Perhaps this flexibility stems from the rapid rise and fall of floodwaters, so typical of the wooded swamps and river bottomlands occupied during the breeding season. Because of the fluctuating water levels in many breeding areas, pairs move about a great deal in an effort to accommodate their needs as to cover, water depth, and food sources.

Perhaps wood duck pairs do not recognize definite home range boundaries because their wooded habitat limits their visual range. Neither do they have fixed waiting sites, as many prairie-nesting ducks do, but swim over extensive acreages, utilizing a variety of floating logs, stumps, and bank sites for resting. When a hen leaves her nest for feeding, she calls vociferously upon landing in the water area near the nest site. Often her mate is at a distance but if he hears her, he flies to her side. The unusually loud calls of wood duck hens are probably necessary under the visual restrictions of their habitat.

As pairs swim about, they frequently come in contact with other pairs and with single drakes. Mated drakes keep other drakes from approaching within several feet of their spouses. Thus, each pair of woodies has a small, mobile "territory" revolving around the hen for a brief period prior to nesting. Whatever the means, a spacing on water areas evolves among many pairs of woodies. But, occasionally, two and even three pairs remain associated into the early stages of incubation in what I believe is an attachment between mother and daughter(s). We often see two or three pairs flying together from water to nest woods. The attachment of yearlings to adult pairs appears to be the means by which yearlings find their way from local waiting areas to their upland nesting areas where they hatched the previous year (Bellrose et al. 1964).

Nesting

In central Illinois there is considerable variation between the time wood ducks return and the time they start looking for nest sites. Pairs that return in late February or early March often wait 2 or 3 weeks before searching for cavities or nest houses. On the other hand, when abnormally cold weather delays their arrival until late March, woodies begin to look for nest sites within a day or two after arrival (Frank Bellrose, Robert Crompton).

Nest Sites. The male follows the female in the search for a nest site. They leave their water area shortly after daybreak, fly to wooded areas adjacent to or, rarely, more than a mile away. There they spend an hour to several hours looking for and entering cavities. On cloudy days they remain in the woods longer—often until noon—than on clear days.

A pair of woodies usually flies first to one of the larger trees, landing on a broad horizontal limb about midway up the crown. From such a vantage point, the female cranes her neck looking for a cavity. She flies to many that are too small for entrance, not to mention others that are too shallow or unsuitable in some other way. The male waits on the same perch or flies closer to the cavity his mate is inspecting; only rarely does he enter a cavity. Unless the hen returns to the cavity occupied the previous year, she prospects for cavities for several days before finding an acceptable one.

We found in Mason County, Illinois, that wood ducks prefer natural cavities with these dimensions: entrance, 10 to 19 square inches; depth, 10 to 19 inches; cavity volume, 500 to 2,999 cubic inches; and base area, 40 to 49 square inches. Cavities 30 feet or more above the ground are preferred to lower ones (Bellrose et al. 1964), although we have found occupied cavities as high as 65 feet above the ground and as low as 2 feet.

Cavities deemed suitable for wood ducks occurred at the rate of one per 4.8 acres in black oak woodlots of Mason County, Illinois (Bellrose et al. 1964). On the Mingo National Wildlife Refuge in southeast Missouri, Weier (1966) found 2.5 cavities per acre in uncut pin oak-overage oak timber and 1.2 per acre in lumbered tracts. On the Piedmont National Wildlife Refuge in Georgia, Almand (1965) reported one suitable cavity for 3.7 acres of hardwood bottomland timber. The number of suitable cavities in the virgin floodplain timber of the St. John River in central New Brunswick is exceptional—2.2 per acre (Prince 1968). In the bottomland forest of the Mississippi River, below Muscatine, Iowa, Dreis and Hendrickson (1952) found one suitable cavity per 23.6 acres. At the Yazoo National Wildlife Refuge, Mississippi, one suitable cavity per 4 acres of timber was found (Strange et al. 1971).

Tree species important in producing desirable cavities in floodplain forests, listed in descending order of importance, are bald cypress, sycamore, silver maple, black ash, sour gum, and black willow. On upland areas black oak, red oak, white oak, blackjack oak, bur oak, and basswood are important (Hansen 1966). The best cavity-producing trees found in both lowland and upland areas are American elm, sweet gum, and red maple.

Bellrose et al. (1964) found that natural cavities in black oak upland woods in central Illinois were occupied by wood ducks at the rate of 37 percent (631) over a 6-year period (50.7 percent, 1938-39; 33.3 percent, 1958-61). Grice and Rogers (1965) reported that in Massachusetts about half of the available cavities (22) were used by woodies. At the Piedmont Refuge in central Georgia, Almand (1965) found that about 40 percent (22) of the suitable cavities were occupied by wood ducks.

At Mingo Refuge, Missouri, Weier (1966) found no cavities used among the 109 checked on his study area. He located six wood duck nests in natural cavities outside the area. On the Yazoo Refuge, 27 cavities suitable for wood ducks were unoccupied (Strange et al. 1971). I believe that large numbers of apparently suitable cavities are not used by wood ducks because high predation limits local populations.

Clutch Size. The wide range of clutch sizes in wood duck nests is caused by predation and dump nesting. Often a squirrel or other predator removes part of a clutch without causing the female to desert the remainder, which may number no more than six eggs. On the other hand, several hens may lay in the same nest, producing clutches of 40 or more eggs. We have known four hens to lay in the same nest during 1 day, and Grice and Rogers (1965) reported the involvement of five hens at a single nest.

A nest with over 15 eggs is generally conceded to be a dump nest, with more than one female contributing eggs (Grice and Rogers 1965, Jones and Leopold 1967, Morse and Wight 1969, Hansen 1971). However, some clutches under 15 contain one or two dumped eggs, and sometimes a single duck lays more than 15 eggs. The clutch size in normal nests averaged 12.2 eggs (820) but has ranged in different areas from 10.4 to 14.7. Clutches in dump nests averaged 21.2 eggs; the lowest average, 16.3 eggs (120), occurred in Oregon (Morse and Wight 1969), and the highest, 28.5 eggs, in Mississippi (Cunningham 1969).

Morse and Wight (1969) concluded that dump nesting among wood ducks in Oregon was a common occurrence and did not appear related to competition among hens for nest sites. Nevertheless, Cunningham (1969) observed that as the number of breeding pairs increased from 150 to 260 to 375 on the Yazoo Refuge, 1966-68, the number of dump nests rose from 0 to 21 to 98.

The size of clutches in normal and dump nests in central Illinois declined as the season progressed. Dump nests had 16.7 eggs (216) prior to April 15, 16.0 (133) eggs April 15-30, 13.8 eggs (114) May 1-15, 11.9 eggs (53) May 16-31, and 9.7 eggs (12) June 1-15 (Frank Bellrose, Robert Crompton). Normal clutches declined as follows: 12.3 eggs (102) prior to April 15, 11.6 eggs (78) April 15-30, 10.7 eggs (80) May 1-15. No dump nests were detected after May 15.

Eggs. Eggs are customarily laid at the rate of one a day, usually early in the morning. Leopold (1951) noted that only 13 "egg days" were skipped out of 297. The eggs are elliptical ovate, 38.8 by 51.1 mm, dull white, very similar in appearance to the eggs of poultry.

The hen covers her first eggs either with litter found at the bottom of the nest cavity or with sawdust placed in the bottom of a nest house. This covering results in a slight mound. However, before she starts to lay, she rounds out the bottom material into a saucerlike depression. After the sixth or seventh egg she adds a few down feathers and then continues to add small amounts of down every day until the clutch nears completion, when she deposits large amounts of down plucked from her breast. Leopold (1951) believed that the plucking of down was the reason some females spend the last two or three nights on their nests during egg-laying. He found about 200 cubic inches of down in early nests but often less than 100 cubic inches in renests.

Incubation. We observed that wood duck hens incubate their eggs 28 to 37 days, the average about 30 days (Bellrose 1955). Many other investigators have reported similar incubation periods, but Breckenridge (1956) reported one nest in which incubation lasted only 25 days. Under semiconfinement, a male wood duck whose spouse had deserted her nest was observed incubating eggs during the night for almost a week (Rollin 1957). Making the situation more bizarre, the male was in eclipse molt and flightless.

The female customarily leaves the nest twice daily, early in the morning and late in the evening, for about an hour each time. The duration of her rest breaks often depends upon temperature and stage of incubation—less time is taken on cold days and late in incubation (Breckenridge 1956). Upon leaving the nest the hen covers her eggs with the mat of down. Rarely, two hens have been found side by side incubating the same nest (Bellrose 1943, Fuller and Bolen 1963).

Some dump nests, strangely, are never incubated nor is there even an indication with the laying of the first egg that the nests ever will be incubated. In these cases the eggs are not covered by any material (powdered wood, leaves, sawdust) nor is down added to the nests, and the eggs are either scattered or randomly arranged. During 4 years, 1958-61, we found that 2 to 10 percent of the dump nests (372) under observation were not incubated.

Comparing the number of breeding woodies on our Quiver Creek study area with the number of nests has led us to conclude that most, if not all, parasitic birds later have their own nests—they lay eggs that they incubate. However, the energy expended in promiscuous laying may curtail their ability to renest.

Chronology of Nesting. Wood ducks' nesting chronology varies greatly between southern and northern areas within their breeding range. Even though the Yazoo National Wildlife Refuge is slightly over 200 miles north of the Gulf Coast in Mississippi, wood ducks begin nesting there the first of February, reach peak nest initiation between mid-March and mid-April, and start their last nests in late June (Cunningham 1969).

About 500 miles north of the Gulf Coast, wood ducks began nesting at the Mingo National Wildlife Refuge, Missouri, between February 16 and March 7, 1966-69 (Hansen 1971). They reached peak nest initiation March 8-28 and started their last nests June 12-20. Almost 800 miles north of the Gulf Coast in Mason County, Illinois, wood ducks initiate their first nests as early as March 18 or as late as April 2, depending upon the temperature (Frank Bellrose, Robert Crompton). Peak nest initiation during a 16-year period was between April 17 and May 2. Most nests are started no later than June 25, but in over 1,000 nestings we have found a few that were initiated in early July.

About 1,100 miles north of the Gulf Coast, in central Morrison County, Minnesota, the first woodie nests were started April 10-22, 1964-66, the peak occurred April 15-25, in 1966, and last nests were started June 8-13 (Fiedler 1966). Still farther north and west at the Arrowwood National Wildlife Refuge in central North Dakota, wood ducks commenced nesting April 19, 1970, and April 21, 1969 (Doty and Kruse 1972).

Thus, in a span of about 1,000 miles, initiation of the first wood duck nests was spread over a period of about 80 days. However, with few exceptions, the last nests were started about the same time in late June. Therefore, nest initiation that spans about 140 days in the south is reduced to about 60 days in the north.

Yearling wood ducks in central Illinois begin to nest about 2 weeks later than adults (Bellrose et al. 1964). At

Great Meadows, Massachusetts, Grice and Rogers (1965) reported that woodies nesting during the first half of the season were predominantly adults, whereas those nesting during the last half were largely yearlings. A similar situation prevailed at the Noxubee Refuge, Mississippi (Baker 1971). Woodie adults at the Mingo Refuge, Missouri, started nesting March 28, 1967-69, on the average, and yearlings April 27 (Hansen 1971).

Nest Success. We found that 49.2 percent (118) of the wood ducks nesting in natural cavities in central Illinois in 1938-40 were successful, but only 39.9 percent (158) were successful in 1958-61. An increase in raccoon numbers leading to intensified depredation on wood duck nests caused the lower nest success in 1958-61.

At St. John River, New Brunswick, 52 percent (23) of the wood duck nests in natural cavities hatched (Prince 1965). On the Piedmont Refuge, Georgia, 55 percent (9) of the nests were successful (Almand 1965). In southeast Missouri on the Mingo Refuge, Weier (1966) noted that 2 of 6 woodie nests in cavities hatched, and Hansen (1971) reported that only 1 of 14 nests hatched.

Including 474 successful normal and dump nests that we studied, an average of 2 eggs out of 13.5 failed to hatch. About 70 percent of the unhatched eggs (927) contained dead embryos, and the remainder appeared infertile. Late in the season we occasionally found entire clutches that were infertile.

Nest Failure. Of the 155 nest failures found among wood duck nests in natural cavities in central Illinois, fox squirrels were responsible for 37 percent. Raccoons caused 33 percent of the failures; desertion caused 18 percent; bull snakes, 5 percent; wind damage, 5 percent, and birds, 2 percent (Bellrose et al. 1964). There is a noteworthy difference between fox squirrel and raccoon destruction in two periods, 1938-40 and 1958-61. During the first period, fox squirrels caused 48 percent of the losses and raccoons caused 8 percent. However, raccoon predation rose to 48 percent during the second period, and squirrel depredations declined to 30 percent. Raccoons started a great expansion in numbers about 1943 in Illinois and elsewhere. They have maintained their high population levels since the mid-1940's, posing a continuing threat to nest success of wood ducks.

Raccoons were the principal destroyers of wood duck nests in natural cavities along the St. John River, New Brunswick (Prince 1965), despoiling over twice as many nests as the gray squirrel, the next most important nest predator.

Renesting. Because of their propensity to renest, wood ducks are able to maintain a high level of productivity (as shown by age ratios) in spite of high nest losses. We and other investigators (Bellrose 1955, Hester 1965, Grice and Rogers 1965, McGilvrey 1966*a*, Odom 1971, Baker 1971, and Hansen 1971) have found numerous wood ducks renesting once and sometimes twice.

Destruction of nests during incubation prompts most renesting, but evidence is growing that woodies sometimes renest even after their first nests hatch successfully. Hester (1965) was the first to report this phenomenon. He found that four hens that had hatched broods nested again, and three were successful a second time. Hansen (1971) in particular has additional information on this topic. At the Mingo Refuge he observed 12 instances of second nestings after earlier hatchings had occurred. Although second nestings that follow initial nest successes probably occur most often because broods are destroyed prior to flight, Hansen (1971) discovered that marked young of seven first broods survived to flight stage even though their mothers renested. Brown (1973*a*) at Big Lake, Arkansas, found that 27 wood duck hens hatched two broods in 1970 and 1971. Members of at least 16 of the first broods hatched survived to flight stage. Three hens that hatched two clutches the first year also repeated this performance the second year. Hence, some wood duck hens contribute two broods to the fall population, the only duck known to do so.

In central Illinois the interval before renesting averaged 13 days (Bellrose 1955). Woodies in Massachusetts delayed renesting 0.33 day for each day of incubation, after the first, up to the day of nest loss (Grice and Rogers 1965). Although one enterprising hen started to nest again only 5 days after nest loss, all others waited at least 11 days. At the Mingo Refuge, none renested sooner than 9 days (Hansen 1971). Those that hatched broods at Mingo and renested waited from 22 to 40 days (average, 31 days). Near Raleigh, North Carolina, four females initiated second nests 28 to 89 days after losing their first nests (Hester 1965).

Wood ducks renesting because of earlier nest destruction change nest locations. We have observed in Illinois that renesting hens moved 0.25 to 4.8 miles from their initial nest sites.

Nest Houses

Thousands of nest houses have been erected for wood ducks during the last three decades. Countless houses have been placed, with no follow-up studies to determine their use and safety as nest sites for woodies. However, as the accompanying table shows, biologists in numerous areas have examined many hundreds of nest houses in an effort to evaluate their importance to the welfare of wood ducks.

Unless nest houses are safer from predation than natural cavities, they contribute little or nothing to the benefit of the bird. In fact, because successful predators learn that houses provide a potential meal, many systematically visit vulnerable houses for this purpose. Consequently, poorly protected houses suffer greater nest losses than natural cavities (Bellrose et al. 1964).

In an effort to limit predation upon wood duck nests in houses, many different types of houses and methods of erection have evolved. There are three basic models: vertical wood, vertical metal cylinder, and horizontal metal cylinder. We developed the first two types (Bellrose 1955)

Use of Nest Houses by Wood Ducks and Nest Success in Numerous Areas.

Place	Number of House Years	Nests			House Type			Reference
			Percent					
		Number	Use	Hatch	Wood	Protected Wood	Metal	
Alabama	98	9	9	—	X			Bryan (1945)
Arkansas	254	341	134	95		X	X	Brown (1973*a*)
California	388	164	42	76		X		Naylor (1960)
California	89	86	97	51			X	Jones & Leopold (1967)
Connecticut	6,225	4,102	66	91	X	X		Beckley (1962)
Georgia Piedmont	194	67	35	69		X		Odom (1971)
Illinois	3,218	1,579	49	36	X			Bellrose et al. (1964)
Illinois	1,427	574	40	73			X	Bellrose et al. (1964)
Iowa, Lake Odessa	26	18	69	—	X			Dreis & Hendrickson (1952)
Iowa, Burlington	398	281	71	94	X			Leopold (1966)
Louisiana	1,229	416	34	73	X			Smith (1961*b*)
Louisiana	130	79	61	77		X		Louisiana Tech Club (1972)
Maryland	70	27	39	—			X	McGilvrey & Uhler (1971)
Maryland	944	315	33	—			X[a]	McGilvrey & Uhler (1971)
Massachusetts	483	415	86	66	X	X		Grice & Rogers (1965)
Minnesota, central	64	27	42	81	X	X		Fiedler (1966)
Minnesota, northern	612	68	11	—	X			Johnson (1970)
Mississippi, Yazoo	392	496	151	65		X		Cunningham (1969)
Mississippi, Noxubee	309	126	41	78		X		Baker (1971)
Mississippi (general)	2,475	1,747	71	68		X		Strong (1973)
Missouri, Mingo	550	182	33	74			X	Hansen (1971)
New York	135	30	22	80	X	X		Klein (1955)
Ohio, 1967-74	26,084	7,363	28	68			X	Bednarik et al. (1974)
Oregon	319	202	63	74		X		Morse & Wight (1969)
Pennsylvania	141	71	50	32	X			Decker (1959)
Pennsylvania	78	24	31	67		X		Decker (1959)
Rhode Island	92	66	72	—	X			Cronan (1957*a*)
Rhode Island	95	50	53	—		X		Cronan (1957*a*)
Vermont	242	183	77	80	X			Miller (1952)

[a] Horizontal-positioned cylindrical houses.

and McGilvrey and Uhler (1971) developed the third. These types are shown in accompanying illustrations.

The predator that poses the greatest threat to nesting wood ducks over their range is the raccoon. Locally, fox squirrels, rat snakes, other snakes, and starlings are important predators. By making houses with elliptical entrances, 4 inches horizontally by 3 inches vertically, raccoons 10 pounds and over have been prevented from gaining access to nests (Bellrose 1955). The tunnel guard extensions developed by Grice and Rogers (1965) on wood houses are also effective. Unfortunately, south of the Mason-Dixon line, raccoons weigh less than 10 pounds and gain entrance through any holes that wood ducks can enter.

To prevent small raccoons from entering wood duck houses, it is necessary to place the houses on brackets in trees or to place conical or other devices around the posts on which houses are erected (Webster and Uhler 1964). Grice and Rogers (1965) have demonstrated the value of placing wood duck houses on posts in marshes or other water areas where water levels do not rise above them. However, it has been discovered that raccoons can climb posts, steel or otherwise, and therefore houses placed on posts must be given protective shields.

Fox squirrel depredations can almost be eliminated by using metal cylindrical nest houses or by placing houses on posts in water. Where fox squirrels abound, as in upland oak woodlots, they can be almost as great a threat to wood duck nests as raccoons.

The use of metal houses in Illinois reduced predation by bull snakes. But in Louisiana the gray rat snake readily entered metal wood duck houses and was the single most important cause of nest loss (Smith 1961*b*). Its near relative, the black rat snake, was also the greatest cause of nest destruction at the Mingo Refuge in southeast Missouri

METAL NEST BOX

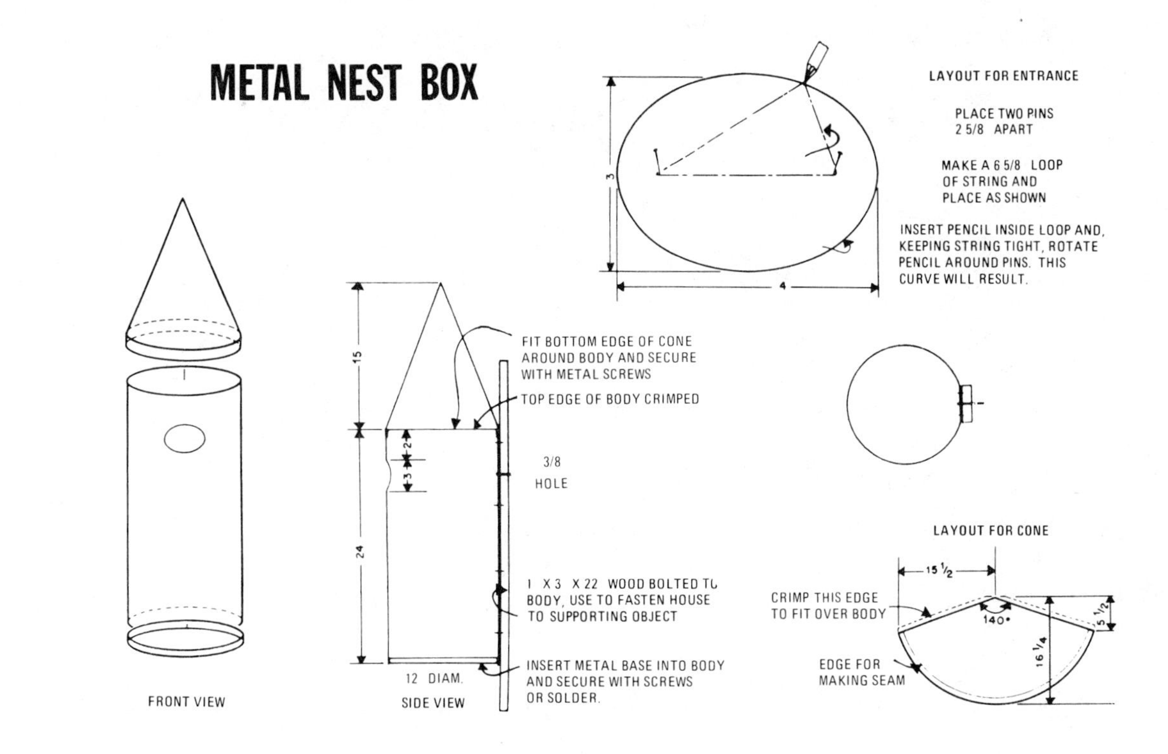

NOTE: ALL MEASUREMENTS ARE IN INCHES

WOOD NEST BOX

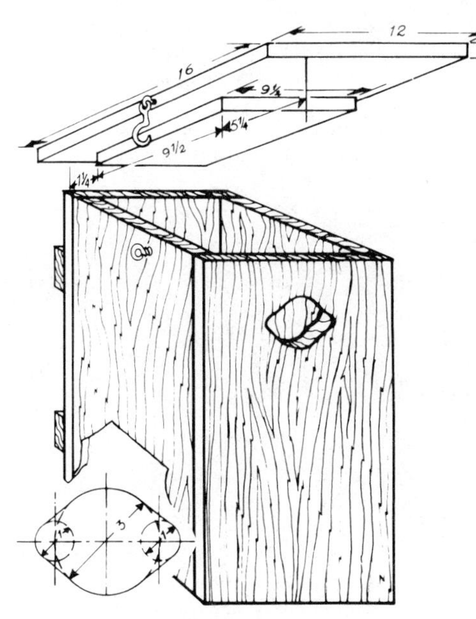

CONSTRUCTION DETAIL

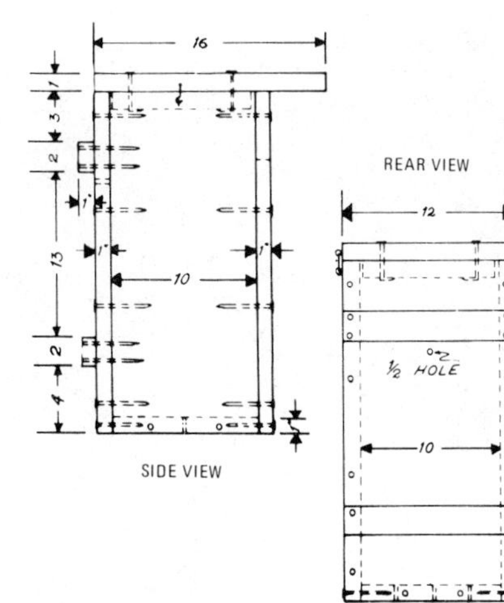

SIDE VIEW

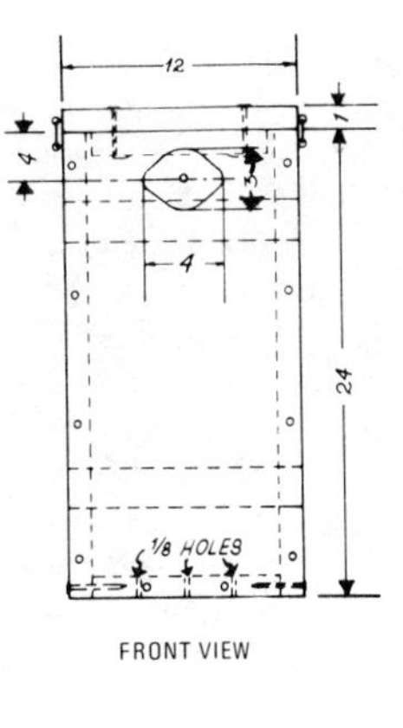

FRONT VIEW

Wood duck house in horizontal position on post in pond. The large opening discourages use by starlings.

(Hansen 1971), accounting for the loss of 25 percent of all wood duck nests. These snakes do not hesitate to swim and have been found in swamps a mile or more from the nearest shore. Because of their length and their ability to swim and climb, they are difficult predators to combat. At the present time, inverted conical shields of an adequate diameter, placed on posts, are the only feasible means.

Where other types of predators have been controlled at nest houses, starlings have become a serious threat to wood duck nests in some places. In 1963, starlings usurped an astounding 24 percent of the nests in which woodies were either laying or incubating on our Quiver Creek study area, Illinois (Robert Crompton). Starlings are especially troublesome where nest houses are placed in open areas (McGilvrey and Uhler 1971). Similarly, the denser the timber in Illinois, the fewer starlings—and wood ducks, to a lesser extent—use the houses.

At the Patuxent Research Center, McGilvrey and Uhler (1971) developed a horizontal cylindrical house, erected on posts, that wood ducks accepted but starlings disliked. Vertical houses had a 39 percent use by wood ducks and 46 percent use by starlings. Horizontal houses had only a 5 percent use by starlings but a 33 percent occupancy by woodies.

Seldom will a situation develop, as it did near Marysville, California, in which wood ducks become their own worst enemies. A local nesting colony increased to such an extent that nest interference among pairs became so great as to substantially reduce nest success (Jones and Leopold 1967).

Management Suggestions

No one type of nest house or placement meets all the requirements imposed by the diversity of habitat and predators. Consequently, each nest house program needs to be designed with local conditions in mind. However, certain generalizations are warranted.

1. Initially, wood houses are more acceptable to wood ducks than metal houses, but, because of greater nest success, metal houses in a few years may have the higher occupancy rate. Rough-cut lumber is best for wood houses, but when smooth wood is used a "ladder" of ¼-inch-mesh hardware cloth should be attached inside so that the day-old duckling may climb out. Vertical metal houses should be provided with either a hardware cloth ladder inside or with a car undercoat material sprayed or troweled inside to permit ducklings to exit.

2. Houses should be made as predator-proof as possible or should be mounted in such a way as to prevent predators from entering. North of the Mason-Dixon line, both wood and metal houses should have elliptical "coon-proof" entrances. Where starlings are likely to be a problem, and houses can be placed on posts in marshes and water areas, horizontal cylindrical houses are recommended. Houses vulnerable to raccoons and placed on posts should be provided with inverted metal cones of adequate diameter, or, instead, the bases of vertical metal houses can be centered on steel pipes.

3. All nest houses should be provided with 3 to 4 inches of sawdust, wood chips or shavings, a necessity for the nest base and for covering the eggs during laying.

4. Houses placed in groups of 2 to 4 per acre ultimately have the highest use because of homing of successful nesters and the association of young birds with homing adults. However, the grouping of houses increases their exposure to predation. Without adequate protection from predators, grouped houses can be a disaster to nesting wood ducks.

Unprotected houses should be spaced no closer than one per 10 acres.

5. Wood ducks use nest houses on poles in water at a higher rate than those in woods. In woods, the nearer the water the better, but up to 0.25 mile is fine, 0.5 mile satisfactory, and 1 mile a possibility. The more open and parklike the woods, the better for wood ducks and, unfortunately, for starlings. But dense woodland deters starlings more than wood ducks. Houses in trees should be placed 12 to 20 feet above the ground, where the canopy is open and does not overhang the entrance.

Rearing of Young

The hen broods her young about 24 hours before she calls them from the nest site. She usually calls 2 to 4 hours after sunrise and after she has scanned the landscape several times for danger. When she is sure there are no intruders, the female flies to a nearby limb, the ground, or water, and calls to her ducklings. They respond with peeping calls and immediately begin to spring upward toward the nest entrance. At the peak of the first jump they cling to the wall and then spring upward again, as often as necessary to reach the opening. At the entrance, each duckling pauses momentarily before springing outward to the water or ground below. Sometimes the jump is over 60 feet, but they land unhurt.

Usually the hen waits until the last peeping duckling has left the nest cavity. On land, she then sets out for water, with the brood a black pod trailing a foot or two behind. She pauses in the shade of overhanging cover and scoots across open areas with head depressed and neck outthrust. Depending upon the distance and the hazards, it may take the hen and her brood several hours or the entire day to reach a water haven. Many broods hatched at a distance from water never reach it. Broods leaving nests on a bluff overlooking the Mississippi River in Burlington, Iowa, lost 33 percent of their members before reaching the river (Leopold 1951).

Even after arriving on water areas, hen woodies are likely to keep moving their broods. McGilvrey (1969) observed a marked hen move her brood seven times through four different impoundments during a 47-day period. Near Raleigh, North Carolina. Hardister et al. (1965) observed that hens led their young from their open-water nest pond to a vegetated millpond 1.5 miles away. Before some broods reached flight, they were found 4 miles away on a different watershed. However, in Ohio, Stewart (1958) observed wood duck broods on water areas near their nest sites for the first 2 weeks, after which they moved to new areas; one brood moved 3.5 miles to a congregation site.

Stewart (1958) reported that when the young were about 6 weeks of age, the females started spending more time away from them but did not completely abandon their young. At Patuxent, McGilvrey (1969) observed that brood bonds often began to break up after the fifth week. Late-hatched broods were usually deserted by the hens when the young were about a month old.

Development. Wood duck ducklings begin to lose their downy plumage at 2 to 3 weeks of age as the juvenile tail feathers start to appear. Until then, they are placed in the Class I category. With the appearance of body feathers, at about 3 weeks, the ducklings enter the Class II phase, where they remain until all down is replaced by body feathers when the ducklings are about 6 weeks old.

From the time the ducklings are fully feathered until they can fly at 8 to 10 weeks of age, they are placed in the Class III stage of development. During this phase, the males begin to show the white hornlike marks on the sides of their heads, but the females do not exhibit their white eye-rings for another month.

Almost immediately after completing their juvenile plumage, wood ducks molt into their adult plumage, at an earlier age than other ducks. By the time they are 4 months old, some male ducklings in Illinois have already acquired their first nuptial plumage. In central Illinois, we have trapped young male woodies in full plumage as early as August 9, but some young captured as late as mid-October have parts of their juvenile plumage.

Survival. Overhanging wooded vegetation from willows, swamp privet, buttonbush, or emergent herbaceous vegetation provided by American lotus, pond or water lilies, marsh smartweed, and similar plants are essential to brood prosperity. Even so, there is a sharp decline in brood size the first few days of life. About 11 ducklings leave the average successful nest, yet Class I broods average only 6.9 (202), a 37 percent decrease. Class II broods average 5.7 (127) ducklings and Class III broods 5.4 (52) young, suggesting a loss of 22 percent between the downy and flying stages, and about half of those leaving the nest.

Recapture of marked ducklings in Massachusetts indicated that 47 percent survived to flight stage (Grice and Rogers 1965). Early-hatched broods had a 66 percent survival, midseason broods 42 percent, and late-season broods only 22 percent. At the Patuxent Research Center, near Laurel, Maryland, broods suffered a 47 percent loss during the first 6 weeks of life (McGilvrey 1969). Fifty-six percent of marked ducklings at the Noxubee National Wildlife Refuge, Mississippi, survived to fly (Baker 1971). At Big Lake, Arkansas, Brown (1973*a*) determined that 52 percent of the ducklings marked in 1970 survived to flight. However, in 1971, only 27.1 percent survived to the flight stage.

Survival of large broods of wood ducks appears proportionately similar to that of small broods, according to a study of Heusmann (1972). He recaptured almost identical percentages of ducklings hatched from large dump nests and from smaller normal nests.

POSTBREEDING SEASON

As females begin to incubate, some males fly to small communal roosts to spend the night. In central Illinois, these roosts increase in number through May until the eclipse molt starts in early June. During the eclipse molt, wood ducks seek swamps, wooded ponds, and marshes where cover is abundant and dense. Few are seen, in proportion to the numbers molting.

Two to 3 weeks after the body molt begins, the drakes lose their flight feathers for about 3 weeks. There is much individual variation in the timing of the eclipse molt. Robert Crompton in central Illinois has trapped adult drakes still in full plumage as late as early August and flightless ones as late as September 29. Some drakes regain their nuptial plumage by mid-September, but most regain it between then and mid-October.

In southeast Missouri, from mid-July into September, Hartowicz (1965) observed steadily increasing numbers of wood ducks flying to roosts. At first this seasonal increase probably represented drakes that had renewed their flight feathers and later represented flying young and both drakes and hens that had regained flight.

The nocturnal roosting of wood ducks has been documented in many areas of eastern United States. It commonly occurs in the northern states from midsummer until the birds depart in migration. On the Mississippi River in northern Iowa, the numbers of wood ducks observed flying to roosts increased sharply from late August to late September but then declined steadily through October (Hein and Haugen 1966). In Louisiana, such flights were observed from mid-July through February (Tabberer et al. 1972).

Roost flights commence shortly before sunset, reach a peak after sunset, and continue until dark. As days shorten in the fall, woodies tend to fly later after sunset (Hester and Quay 1961, Tabberer et al. 1972).

FOOD HABITS

Ducklings

Early in life ducklings feed almost entirely on animal life, changing to plant food as they grow older. At a lake in east Tennessee, Hocutt and Dimmick (1971) found a steady decline in the amount of animal food taken by ducklings up to 6 weeks of age, by which time they were feeding almost entirely on vegetable matter. Their early diet consisted largely of adult and immature stages of terrestrial and flying insects. Among aquatic insects, pupa and newly emerged imagos of midges were the most important. Floating masses of sago pondweed provided tubers that made this species important as food.

At the Noxubee Refuge, Mississippi, animal foods, particularly mayfly and dragonfly nymphs, made up 85 percent of the foods taken by ducklings up to 6 weeks of age (Baker 1971). Surprisingly, tiny fish made up 15 percent of the foods consumed. Although 15 percent of the diet consisted of plant items, ducklings over 4 weeks of age took a higher proportion of plant food than younger ducklings. Algae, watermeal, water shield, and duckweed were the plants consumed.

Older Birds

Acorns are the favored foods of more wood ducks in more places than any other plant food—from New Hampshire to South Carolina to Mississippi to Wisconsin. At the Noxubee Refuge, an average of 5.3 acorns were found in each wood duck gullet, compared with 5.4 acorns per mallard (Hall 1965). Little other food was found in the crops and gizzards.

Woodies prefer to find their acorns in shallow flooded swamps and overflow bottomlands. But if the ground is devoid of undergrowth, they may seek acorns on the ground, in groves of pin and white oaks. When acorns are lacking they turn to the most available and palatable foods at hand. In many swamps, these foods are seeds of bald cypress, hickories, buttonbush, arrow arum, and bur reed.

When mulberries and wild grapes are ripe, Robert Crompton and I have often observed wood ducks feeding on them. The mulberries are gleaned from the water or ground, but woodies fly into trees where grapevines are twined and snatch the grapes from arboreal perches.

Where harvested cornfields are close to habitats lacking an abundance of desired foods, wood ducks utilize waste corn. They fly to the fields early in the morning or near dusk to pick up scattered corn kernels or to rip kernels from fallen ears. We have seen scattered pairs and small flocks in the spring, and up to several thousand in the fall, feeding on waste grain in wheat and corn stubble in the Illinois Valley. In feeding in these fields, pintails departed the rest lakes first, late in the afternoon, then mallards, and lastly wood ducks. They were prone to depart for field feeding about the time mallards commenced to return.

European Wigeon

Anas penelope

Other Common Name: Redhead wigeon

VITAL STATISTICS

Length:	Male, 18.2-20.5 inches, average 19.3 inches (15) Female, 16.5-19.5 inches, average 17.9 inches (7)
Wing:	Male, 7.4-7.8 inches, average 7.6 inches Female, 6.9-7.6 inches, average 7.2 inches
Weight:	Male, 1.2-2.1 pounds, average 1.6 pounds (12) Female, 1.1-1.8 pounds, average 1.4 pounds (5)

IDENTIFICATION

Field

The European wigeon is most often found as a lone bird in the company of a flock of American wigeons, and, more rarely, mallards or pintails. The drake's bright russet-red head, topped with a cream stripe, and its gray back and sides distinguish it from its American cousin.

The white shoulder patch, green speculum, and white belly displayed by the European wigeon when in flight resemble those of the American wigeon, but the latter's underwings are paler than the mottled gray ones of its European counterpart.

Most females and immature-plumaged birds of the two species are so similar as to cause unreliable identification in the field. But adult hen European wigeons have two color phases: gray and red. Hens in the reddish plumage have russet-brown heads, necks, chests, backs, sides, and flanks, with a much redder tinge than in female American wigeons.

At Hand

At close range, it can be seen that the russet-red head and neck of the drake are flecked with black speckles, the bill is blue-gray with a black tip, and the feet and legs are blue-gray. Fine dusky vermiculations on white give the back, scapulars, and sides of the male's nuptial plumage their gray coloration.

Adult hens and immatures can best be distinguished from American wigeons by their axillars. These are finely speckled with dark gray in the European species and almost pure white in the American one.

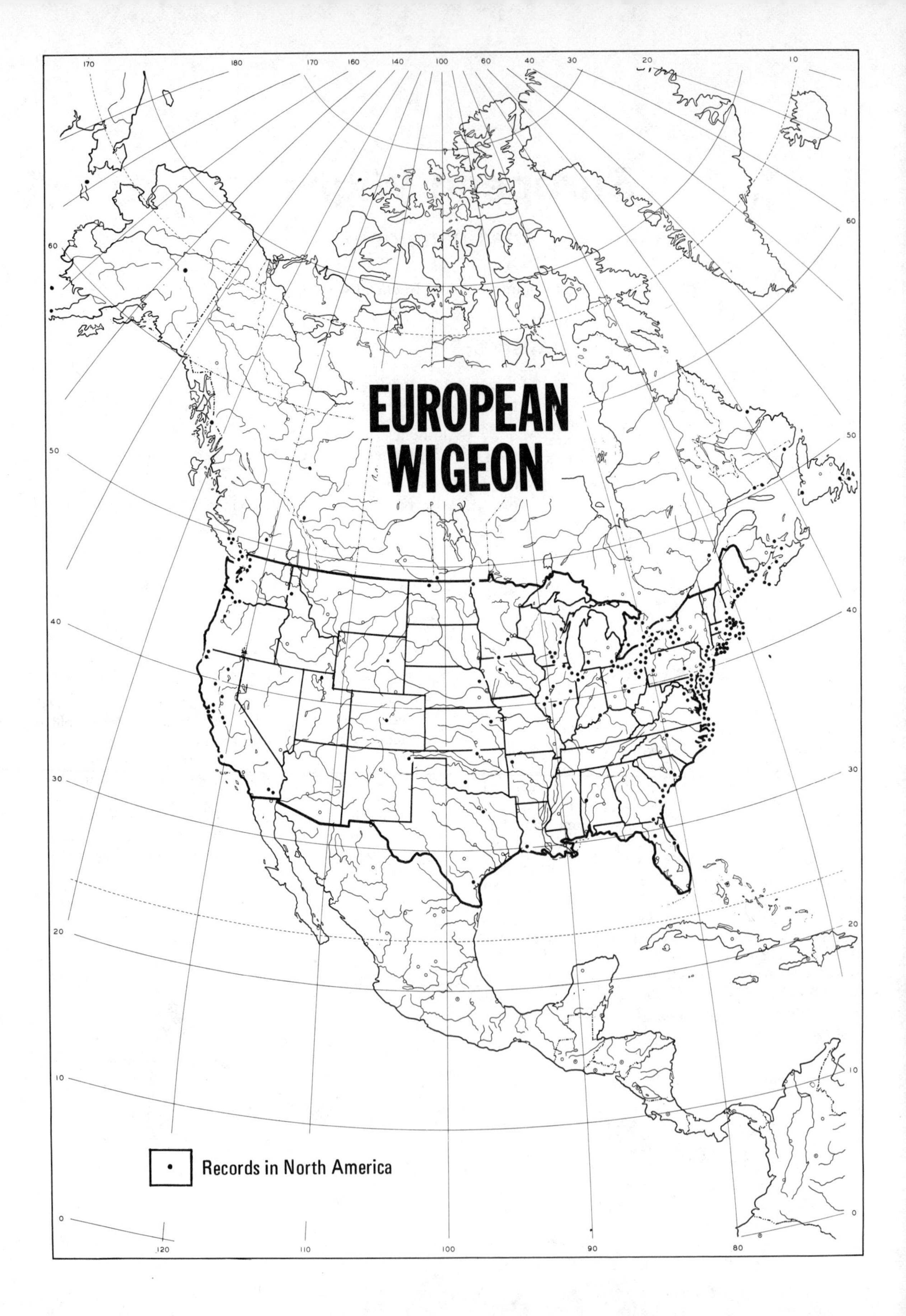
EUROPEAN
WIGEON
Records in North America

DISTRIBUTION

The European wigeon does not breed in North America but it is a regular visitor to both coasts. Except for Greenland, Canada, and Alaska, its breeding range spans the Northern Hemisphere, largely between latitudes 48° and 71° N.

The recoveries on the Atlantic Coast of a number of European wigeons banded in Iceland suggest that this is the source of the birds that frequent eastern North America. Pacific Coast birds probably originate from breeding grounds in eastern Siberia, particularly the Kamchatka Peninsula.

Hasbrouck (1944) summarized most of the records of the European wigeon in North America from 1842 to about 1940. He listed 520 records by regions: 274, Atlantic Coast; 165, the interior; and 81, Pacific Coast. On both the Atlantic and Pacific coasts, 91 percent of the records occurred between October 1 and March 1, but in the interior only 21 percent fell within this period—79 percent occurred between April 1 and September 30. Hasbrouck incorrectly believed that the late spring records in the interior represented birds migrating to breeding grounds in the boreal forest of Canada. Numerous additional reports of the European wigeon have appeared since Hasbrouck's (1944) summary.

Audubon Christmas bird counts in 1972 (American Birds 1973) revealed 33 European wigeons and 188,000 American wigeons south of Canada. The European wigeons were distributed as follows: Massachusetts, 1; New York, 3; New Jersey, 1; Florida, 2; Washington, 12; Oregon, 16; and California, 5. In addition, 12 were found in British Columbia and 9 at Adak, Alaska. The affinity of the European wigeon for the coasts, especially the Pacific, is evident.

About three-fourths of the observers of European wigeons report only one bird, with two, three, and four being progressively less common. Flock sightings have been rare. Hasbrouck (1944) listed flocks of 21 and 20 to 30 and Kenyon (1961) observed flocks of 11 and 13 on Amchitka Island in the Aleutians.

According to reports from the Aleutian Islands National Wildlife Refuge, about 1,000 European wigeons have been present during May-September each year, 1967-69. During the fall, 75 to 250 have been reported each year.

American Wigeon

Anas americana

Other Common Names: Baldpate, gray duck

VITAL STATISTICS

Length:	Adult male, 18.4-23.0 inches, average 20.3 inches (56) Adult female, 17.7-20.3 inches, average 19.0 inches (17) Immature male, 16.8-21.2 inches, average 18.6 inches (45) Immature female, 16.8-18.5 inches, average 17.3 inches (16)
Wing:	Adult male, 10.4 inches (61) Adult female, 9.7 inches (34) Immature male, 10.1 inches (62) Immature female, 9.6 inches (74)
Weight:	Adult male, 1.3-2.4 pounds, average 1.81 pounds (84) Adult female, 1.2-2.3 pounds, average 1.69 pounds (68) Immature male, 0.7-2.5 pounds, average 1.75 pounds (358) Immature female, 0.9-2.1 pounds, average 1.56 pounds (373)

IDENTIFICATION

Field

Wigeons fly rapidly with fairly deep wing beats, in compact flocks; their flight is more erratic than that of all other dabbling ducks except the teals. They have medium-sized bodies, short bills, proportionately narrow wings, and moderately long, wedge-shaped tails.

The most distinctive feature of the wigeon in flight is the white rectangular shoulder patch of the drake; the patch is indistinct in the hen and in immatures. In both sexes, the elliptical white belly is sharply outlined by the brown chest and sides; the gadwall and wood duck display similar white underparts.

The frequent call of the drake wigeon in flight is composed of three whistling, piping notes—the middle note higher than the others. Only the pintail has a similar whistling call, but its call is briefer and is evenly pitched.

When the drake is at rest, the white crown of the full-plumaged bird provides a distinctive mark and also gives the bird its common name: baldpate. A green band extends from the eye to the back of the head. The pinkish-brown breast and sides are separated from the black undertail coverts by white flank feathers. The white wing patch, so noticeable in flight, may appear as a narrow elliptical mark or be completely hidden by scapular and side feathers.

The gray head of the adult hen and of immatures contrasts with the brownish chest and sides. At close range, the bluish, black-tipped bill is apparent in all wigeons, regardless of plumage.

At Hand

The white shoulder patch of the drake is separated from the speculum by a black stripe, followed by a greenish stripe in the otherwise black speculum. The white patch on the wing of the immature drake is smaller than in the adult, and only a trace of green appears in the black speculum.

Hens of both age groups display an indistinct gray-tinged shoulder patch, formed by the brownish, gray-tipped lesser and middle covert feathers. The lesser and middle coverts conceal much of the whitish greater coverts, which are margined with black. Sometimes a tinge of green occurs in the dark speculum, which is black in the adult hen and fuscous in the immature.

In the adult drake, the pinkish-brown back and side feathers are marked by fine, wavy black lines; the chest is plain pinkish brown. Hens and young drakes have gray-brown backs with rust-colored sides and chests.

The heads and necks of wigeons in all plumages are buff streaked with black except for the white crown and green head stripe of the adult drake. The feet and legs of both sexes are blue-gray.

Some adult drakes begin to show traces of eclipse plumage early in June; by late July, the number in eclipse plumage is at its peak. At this stage, drakes resemble hens. By mid-October many drakes have regained most of their nuptial plumage. However, there is great variation among individuals, and we have observed adult drakes that still wore 10 to 30 percent of their eclipse plumage in January; not until mid-February were all in full plumage.

Immature hens and drakes have similar plumages, resembling that of the hen, which persist through much of the fall. Immatures are slow to acquire their complete nuptial plumage, for about half of several hundred young that we examined during January still retained 10 to 50 percent of their juvenile feathers.

POPULATION STATUS

The wigeon breeding population in North America, 1955-73, averaged 3,139,000 with a low of 2,222,000 in 1963 and a high of 3,752,000 in 1970, a variation of 41 percent. Breeding numbers were below average from 1961 to 1969. Surveys of both breeding ground and winter populations reflect a slight overall decrease in numbers during the past 19 years. Wintering populations have increased dramatically in the Mississippi Flyway (Louisiana), remained about the same in the Central Flyway, and have shown pronounced declines in both the Atlantic and Pacific flyways.

Age ratios, corrected for hunting vulnerability, suggest that about 3,296,000 immatures reach flight stage in an average year. Therefore, the early fall population of wigeons in North America is believed to number nearly 6,500,000 birds.

Age Ratios

The age ratios of wigeons in hunters' bags across the United States averaged 1.60 immatures per adult, 1966-73. Recent banding data indicated that immatures were 1.52 times more vulnerable to hunting than adults. Correcting the age ratios in the kill for hunting bias suggests that during early fall, 1966-70, there were 105 immatures for every 100 adults in wigeon populations in the United States.

Sex Ratios

Visual counts of wigeons during the spring at various locations across North America indicated that 54.6 percent were drakes (Bellrose et al. 1961). In the bags of hunters, 1966-73, 69.5 percent of the adults and 51.9 percent of the immature wigeons were drakes. Inasmuch as bandings on the breeding grounds disclosed no significant selection of drakes by hunters (Bellrose et al. 1961), the sex ratio in the bag should be a reasonably accurate indicator of the sex ratio in nature. An equal proportion of both age-classes among prebreeding wigeons would imply a population containing 60.7 percent drakes, or about three drakes for every two hens.

DISTRIBUTION

There are three species of wigeons: one in South America, the Chiloe wigeon; one in Eurasia, the European wigeon; and one in North America, the American wigeon. The Chiloe (southern) wigeon inhabits the southern one-third of South America, from southern Brazil, northern Argentina, and central Chile to Tierra del Fuego. The European wigeon breeds in Iceland and northern Eurasia, largely north of 48° latitude almost to the Arctic Ocean. It winters from central Eurasia south nearly to the equator in west and east Africa, Jordan, Iraq, all of India, Burma, southern China, and Japan; small numbers occur regularly in North America. The American wigeon breeds from the tundra of North America south through the Dakotas and the Intermountain marshes into Wyoming, Utah, and Oregon. It winters from New England and British Columbia south to Central America and the West Indies.

Breeding Range

Wigeons nest in abundance farther north than any other dabbling duck except the pintail. Almost 9 percent (270,000) of the more than 3 million wigeons breeding in the average year nest in Alaska, 13 percent (400,000) in the contiguous states, and 78 percent in Canada. Saskatchewan leads other Canadian provinces, with 880,000 breeders, Alberta is a close second with 856,000, and Manitoba trails with 211,000; about 568,000 breed in the Northwest Territories.

The highest density of breeding wigeons, 16.6 per square mile, occurs on the Mackenzie Delta and Old Crow Flats. The Yukon Flats have 9.4 per square mile, and other Alaskan areas have 0.7 to 4.8 wigeons per square mile. The tundra coastal areas have about one-third as many per square mile as the interior wetlands.

The large river deltas between Great Slave Lake and Lake Winnipeg harbor about 145,000 wigeons, 7.3 per square mile. The parklands, on the average, support about the same density—7.4 per square mile—but because of their vast area the breeding numbers amount to almost 680,000. Although lakes abound in the boreal forest, wigeons do not find conditions to their liking, for there are only 1.3 per square mile in the open (taiga) boreal zone and 1.66 in the closed boreal zone as far east as Ontario. In the western Ontario zone there is only 0.1 wigeon per square mile.

The mixed prairie region of southwestern Canada and north-central United States supports a variable breeding population from year to year. Over a 19-year period it averages 3.1 per square mile and aggregates 560,000 birds. The shortgrass prairie is home to 2.5 wigeons per square mile (357,000).

Outside the mixed grass and shortgrass regions of the United States (the Dakotas and Montana), where about 315,000 wigeons breed, 50,000 occur in the Intermountain marshes northward from northern California, central Utah, and southern Wyoming. From 60,000 to 80,000 breed in the mountain valleys and plateaus of British Columbia. Minnesota, with about 38,000 wigeons, is as far east as large numbers breed. A few small isolated breeding colonies occur in eastern Ontario, southwestern Quebec, and New Brunswick (Godfrey 1966). In the United States, limited nesting has occurred in the Sandhills and in the Rainwater Basin of Nebraska (George Schildman), the Cheyenne Bottoms of Kansas (Marvin Schwilling), the North Park tract and the San Luis Valley of Colorado (Michael Szymczak), four counties in Wisconsin (Jahn and Hunt 1964), and the Lake Erie marshes of Ohio (Bednarik 1970).

Migration Corridors

The yearly local abundance of wigeons varies more than for many dabbling ducks, which suggests that part of the population occasionally changes its migration patterns. On many migration and winter areas, numbers of wigeons have fluctuated with changes in food supplies. The greatest single change in their migration pattern was recorded in Louisiana. During the mid-1950's, peak concentrations of wigeons on Louisiana coastal marshes in fall numbered about 100,000. From 1957 on, the numbers of wigeons steadily increased to a fall population of 1,062,000 in 1970 (Richard Yancey, Hugh Bateman). This dramatic increase in numbers of wigeons and other dabbling ducks was brought about by hurricanes, which created more open-water ponds among the dense emergent vegetation of the extensive coastal marsh.

Over a 15-year period, the peak population of wigeons in fall in Louisiana has averaged 426,000, with an average wintering population of 292,000. The difference of 134,000 suggests that considerable numbers of these ducks cross the Gulf to Yucatan, more than sporadic aerial surveys have reported.

Almost 95 percent of the recoveries from wigeons banded in Alaska have occurred in states of the Pacific Flyway, largely in Washington, Oregon, and California (King and Lensink 1971). Most wigeons migrate from Alaska to Puget Sound along the coastal corridor. However, bandings of wigeons on the Yukon Flats breeding area indicate that important corridors also exist through the interior of British Columbia and through Alberta. Virtually all of the wigeons breeding in British Columbia migrate directly southward to winter areas in Washington, Oregon, and California.

About 80 percent of the wigeons breeding in Alberta migrate to the Pacific Flyway, largely to Oregon and to California (Lensink 1964). Saskatchewan contributes 25 percent of its wigeon population to this flyway, most of which migrate directly to California, many via the Bear River marshes of Utah.

The Central Flyway receives about 3 percent of the wigeons breeding in Alaska, an unknown proportion of those nesting in the Northwest Territories, about 12 percent of Alberta's breeding birds, 28 percent of Saskatchewan's, and 22.5 percent of Manitoba's breeding population.

Migration corridors through the Central Flyway lead to the Panhandle, the southeast coast of Texas, and the southwest coast of Louisiana. The Missouri River migration corridor, bordering both the Central and Mississippi flyways, is probably followed by most of the wigeons wintering in Louisiana and Yucatan.

Many of the wigeons entering the Mississippi Flyway, aside from those that enter Louisiana, are bound for winter areas in the Atlantic Flyway, but some migration corridors in the Mississippi Flyway lead to two other important winter areas—eastern Arkansas and western Tennessee. Other corridors pass on to the Atlantic Coast.

Recoveries from bandings in Alaska (King and Lensink 1971) indicate that only 1.9 percent of the Alaskan wigeons enter the Mississippi Flyway (most enter Louisiana) and 0.3 percent reach the Atlantic Flyway. For Alberta wigeons (Lensink 1964), the respective percentages are 7.4 percent and 1.7 percent. The Mississippi Flyway is followed by 36 percent of the wigeons from Saskatchewan and 57 percent of those from Manitoba. Eleven percent from Saskatchewan and 20 percent from Manitoba enter the Atlantic Flyway.

Winter Areas

The Central Valley of California and the coastal marshes of Louisiana are the two principal winter grounds for wigeons. About 700,000 winter in the Central Valley and 300,000 in Louisiana. The third most important winter ground lies in the Texas Panhandle, which hosts 150,000. Puget Sound in Washington and the valley of the Willamette River in Oregon each winter over 50,000 wigeons, and the valley of the lower Columbia River, bordering those two states, harbors 60,000 more. Other important winter areas in the Pacific Flyway include: the Imperial Valley of southern California with 55,000; the coast of Mexico, 75,000; the Columbia Basin of Washington-Oregon, 45,000; the Fraser River delta of British Columbia, 25,000; and the numerous small coastal bays and the several large ones between Grays Harbor, Washington, and San Diego Bay, California, 40,000. Wigeons occur in considerable numbers along the west coast of Mexico as far south as the Gulf of Tehuantepec and in lesser numbers in Guatemala (Saunders et al. 1950).

Western Tennessee and eastern Arkansas winter the largest numbers of wigeons in the Mississippi River basin, from 25,000 to 30,000 each. On the Atlantic Coast, the marshes of South Carolina support almost 60,000 wigeons, the largest number in the East. In the early 1960's,

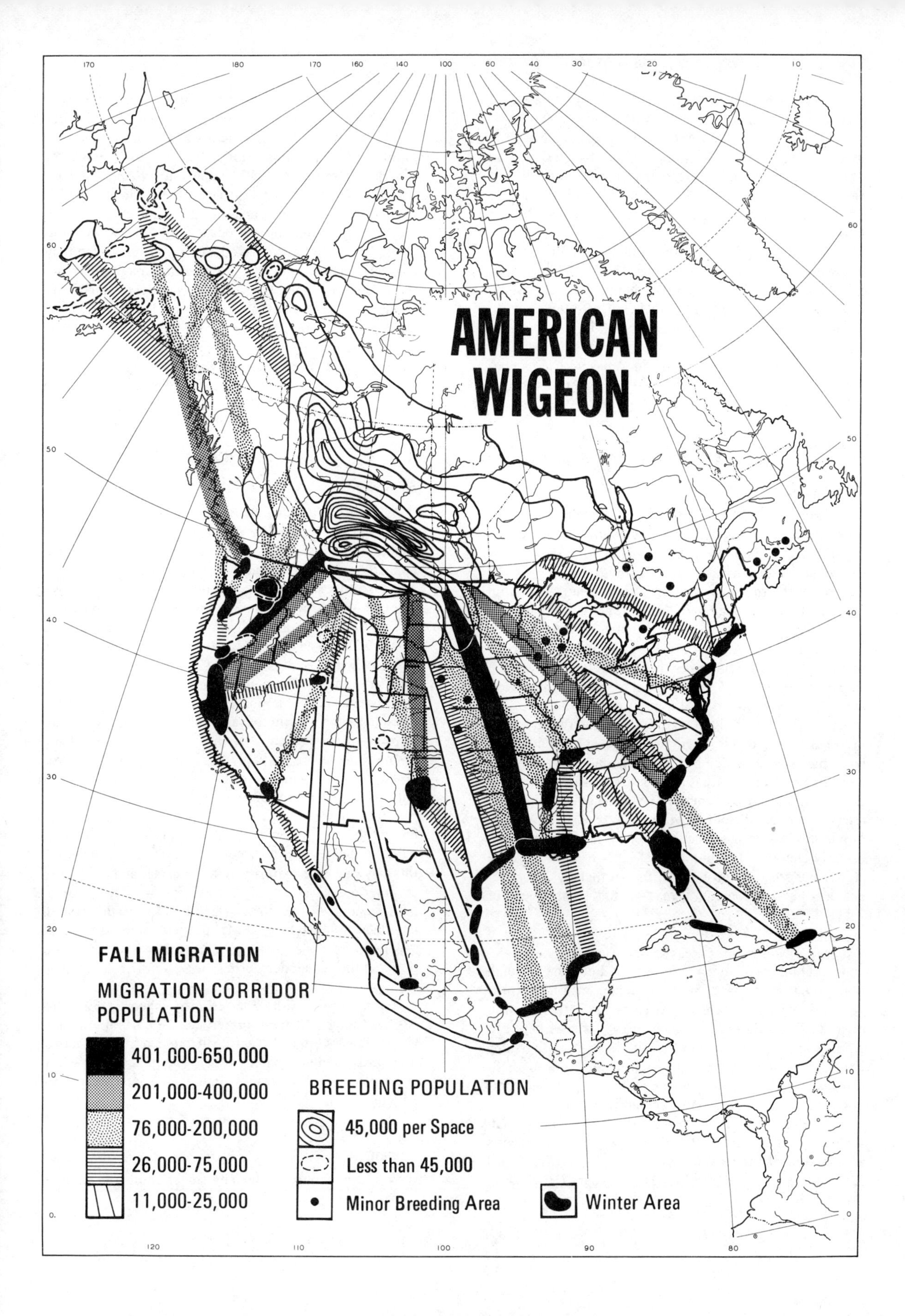
AMERICAN WIGEON
FALL MIGRATION
MIGRATION CORRIDOR POPULATION
401,000-650,000
201,000-400,000
76,000-200,000
26,000-75,000
11,000-25,000
BREEDING POPULATION
45,000 per Space
Less than 45,000
Minor Breeding Area
Winter Area

Chesapeake Bay had the largest wintering population of wigeons north of South Carolina, with about 20,000. However, in the late 1960's and early 1970's, many of these birds shifted farther south to Currituck Sound, North Carolina, where the population has increased from 7,000 to 29,000. Small numbers of wigeons winter as far up the coast as Connecticut. Florida has a wintering population of about 20,000.

Some wigeons pass beyond Florida to winter in Cuba, Hispaniola, Jamaica, and the Lesser Antilles. The Dominican Republic winters the largest number, about 45,000. Wigeons also migrate across the Gulf of Mexico from Louisiana and Texas to winter largely in the Yucatan Peninsula. About 115,000 wigeons winter on the east coast of Mexico, 85,000 in the lagoons of Tabasco, Campeche, and Yucatan. Small numbers migrate as far south as British Honduras.

MIGRATION BEHAVIOR

Chronology

Fall. Next to the blue-winged teal and pintail, the wigeon is the earliest duck to migrate southward. Wigeons begin to move south into adjacent states from their major Canadian breeding areas as early as mid-August.

In the northern plains, the population remains high until mid-October, then begins to decline rapidly, so that most ducks have departed by mid-November. While wigeons from Canadian and Alaskan areas are filtering into northern states all through September, other wigeons are leaving staging areas in these states for intermediate migration areas to the southwest, south, and southeast.

The intermediate migration areas, lying between breeding and winter grounds, begin to receive small numbers of wigeons in early September and large numbers a month later. In most of these areas peak numbers are reached late in October and late November. The intermediate migration areas are largely devoid of wigeons.

Winter areas begin to acquire wigeons late in September or early October. The numbers of birds usually increase slowly but steadily through the fall so that by early December the winter areas have their full complement of wigeons.

Spring. Most winter areas show a slow but steady decline in numbers of wigeons from early February through March, with a few tardy birds remaining well into April. Wigeons begin to appear in most intermediate migration areas early in March and reach peak numbers between April 1 and 15, thereafter declining abruptly. In states immediately south of their principal breeding grounds in Canada, wigeons begin to arrive early in April, and their numbers rapidly increase throughout that month.

Wigeons arrive on their breeding grounds later than mallards and pintails. At Delta, Manitoba, the first wigeons appeared during the periods April 5-12 in 5 years, April 13-20 in 7 years, and April 21-28 in 3 years (Hochbaum 1955). At Redvers, in southeastern Saskatchewan, most of the wigeons arrived May 1-15; they averaged 2 weeks earlier at Lousana, Alberta, which is farther north and west (Smith 1971). At Brooks, Alberta, the first wigeons arrived as early as March 23 (1955) and as late as April 5 (1954).

At Yellowknife, Northwest Territories, Canada, the first wigeons appeared between April 25 and May 3, 1962-64, but the major influx did not occur until May 5-15 (Murdy 1964). Wigeons have arrived at various places on the Yukon Delta on May 4-9 (Gabrielson and Lincoln 1959) and on the Yukon Flats in 1962, May 3. However, wigeons did not appear at Anaktuvuk Pass in the Brooks Range of northern Alaska until May 13, 1953; May 20, 1950; and May 24, 1949 (Irving 1960). At Old Crow, Yukon Territories, Canada, Irving (1960) observed wigeons migrating in flocks of 20 to 30 on May 17-19 and in small flocks throughout June.

BREEDING

Behavior

Age, Pair Bond, and Homing. Wigeons begin to form pair bonds in November on their Texas winter grounds (Soutiere et al. 1972). As many as one-fourth of the hens appeared to be associated with drakes during November and December, with the proportion steadily increasing through March, when about 80 percent of the hens were paired. Courting groups in Texas were observed as early as January 21 and as late as March 13 (Soutiere et al. 1972).

Many wigeons, however, wait until they reach more northern areas before pairing. At Delta, Manitoba, Sowls (1955) reported numerous courting parties in April and considered the wigeon the last of the puddle ducks to pair. In view of the late molt of the juvenile plumage, many young wigeons are probably late in pairing. Weller (1965) noted that display and pairing in ducks seemed correlated with the development of breeding plumage.

Although some wigeons are late in establishing pair bonds, there is no evidence that many hens remain unpaired. Apparently, most hens breed their first year, but this may vary with maturity of the yearlings and availability of water areas.

For many wigeons, the pair bond is of short duration. In an Idaho study (Oring 1964), 60 percent of the drakes separated from their hens during the first week of incubation and the remainder during the second week.

Home Range. Pothole selection by wigeons at Lousana, Alberta, indicated their preferences for semipermanent water areas of 0.6 to 1.0 acre, surrounded by hayfields or ungrazed woodland (Smith 1971). The quantity of willow and aspen wholly or partially rimming the potholes was not a factor in pothole selection.

Nesting

Nest Sites. Wigeons usually select an upland nest site from a few yards to as many as 400 yards from water. On islands in Lake Newell, Alberta, they nested an average of 36 yards from water, farther than any other species (Vermeer 1970*b*). In the pothole region near Caron, Saskatchewan, most nests were 16 to 50 yards from water—none closer than 6 yards—and were usually located in clumps of buckbrush (William Leitch). Nests averaged 24 yards from water on the plains of southeastern Alberta and were most often found in extensive stands of juncus (Keith 1961). Clumps of greasewood were used for nesting at Freezeout Lake, Montana (Ellig 1955).

The nest is in a slight depression lined with grass or other nearby herbaceous vegetation and with light gray down.

Clutch Size, Eggs, and Incubation. The average clutch size for 179 nests was 8.5. The largest average clutch size reported was 9.5 (45 nests) in the Flathead Valley of Montana (Girard 1941). In Alberta, the average clutch size was 7.6 eggs (18) for nests in the parklands (Smith 1971) and 8.9 eggs (20) for nests on the plains (Keith 1961). At Redvers, Saskatchewan, wigeons laid 9.0 (40) eggs per nest; in Alaska the average was 7.3 eggs (19).

The eggs are ovate, creamy white, and measure 53.9 by 38.3 mm (Bent 1923). Wigeons incubate their eggs 23 days (Hochbaum 1944) or 24 to 25 days (Delacour 1956).

Chronology of Nesting. In southeastern Alberta, wigeons began to nest May 11, two weeks later than mallards (Keith 1961). Wigeons began nesting on May 18, slightly over a week after arriving at Yellowknife, Northwest Territories, but nesting did not reach a peak until June 15 (Murdy 1964). They have been found nesting May 10 at Minto Lakes and May 23 on the Yukon Flats, Alaska (Lensink 1954, Rowinski 1958), about 2 weeks after their arrival.

As far apart as Brooks, Alberta, and Minto Lakes, Alaska, wigeons initiated nesting over a period of 50 days; at Yellowknife, the average span was only 28 days.

Nest Success. The nests of wigeons are notoriously difficult to find, partially explaining why only 142 nests have been observed in the numerous studies made on nesting waterfowl. Of the nests studied, 56 percent hatched successfully. Success has ranged from 75 percent in the Flathead Valley of Montana to 57 percent for several localities in Alaska, 43 percent at Redvers, Saskatchewan, 39 percent at Brooks, and 33 percent at Lake Newell, Alberta.

We have no definitive information on the renesting propensity of the wigeon. Information gained by Smith (1971) on his Lousana, Alberta, study area suggested that a considerable number of wigeons renest. He reported that 39 percent of the wigeon hens successfully produced broods, 1953-65, compared with only 31 percent of the mallards, which are noted renesters.

Nest Failure. Crows, skunks, and ground squirrels were apparently responsible for most nest destruction among the wigeon nests studied (Keith 1961, Kalmbach 1937, William Leitch, Smith 1971, Stoudt 1971).

Rearing of Young

Broods. Marked wigeon broods in South Dakota were more sedentary than most other species studied, venturing less than 0.2 mile from their home water areas in over a month (Evans et al. 1952). They preferred the larger potholes, 2.5 to 4.0 acres, to the smaller ones, 0.5 to 2.5 acres. Broods near Lousana, Alberta, also favored the larger potholes of 2.1 to 5.0 acres to those of 0.6 to 1.0 acre (Smith 1971).

The hen accompanies her brood until the young ones are either full grown or almost so. Wigeon hens were commonly observed accompanying Class II broods, but similarly aged young were often seen without escorting hens (Beard 1964).

Development. The development of duckling wigeons parallels that of mallards until a late stage of Class II is reached; then growth accelerates so that the birds reach flying stage earlier than mallards (Gollop and Marshall 1954). Flight stage in this species was reached in 47 days in South Dakota (Evans et al. 1952); 45 to 48 days in Manitoba (Hochbaum 1944); 44 days at Yukon Flats, Alaska (Lensink 1954), and 37 days at Minto Lakes, Alaska (Hooper 1951).

Survival. Brood counts of wigeons do not mirror the losses suffered by the flightless young, for they show no reduction with age. Class I broods averaged 6.3 (1,564), Class II broods averaged 6.8 (993), and Class III broods 6.5 (283). Although these brood counts were from many different regions, most of them were consistent in showing an increase in number with age.

The gain in brood size indicates that some broods combine with others. Combinations of young from different broods occur among all species but are of minor occurrence among other dabbling ducks.

POSTBREEDING SEASON

Drakes desert their hens shortly after incubation begins and move to large marshes for their eclipse molt. Drake wigeons in Idaho left their hens on June 22, showed the first eclipse plumage by July 11, and became flightless by July 29 (Oring 1964). At Delta Marsh, Manitoba, large numbers of drake wigeons arrived for the eclipse molt between mid-June and early July and many flightless birds were observed July 25 (Hochbaum 1944).

Several hundred drake wigeons moved into the Pel and Kutawagan marshes, 75 miles north of Regina, Saskatchewan, in mid-July (Sterling 1966). At that time, the earliest molting pintails were regaining flight as the number of wigeons increased. On July 9, 1953, large numbers of drake

AMERICAN WIGEON

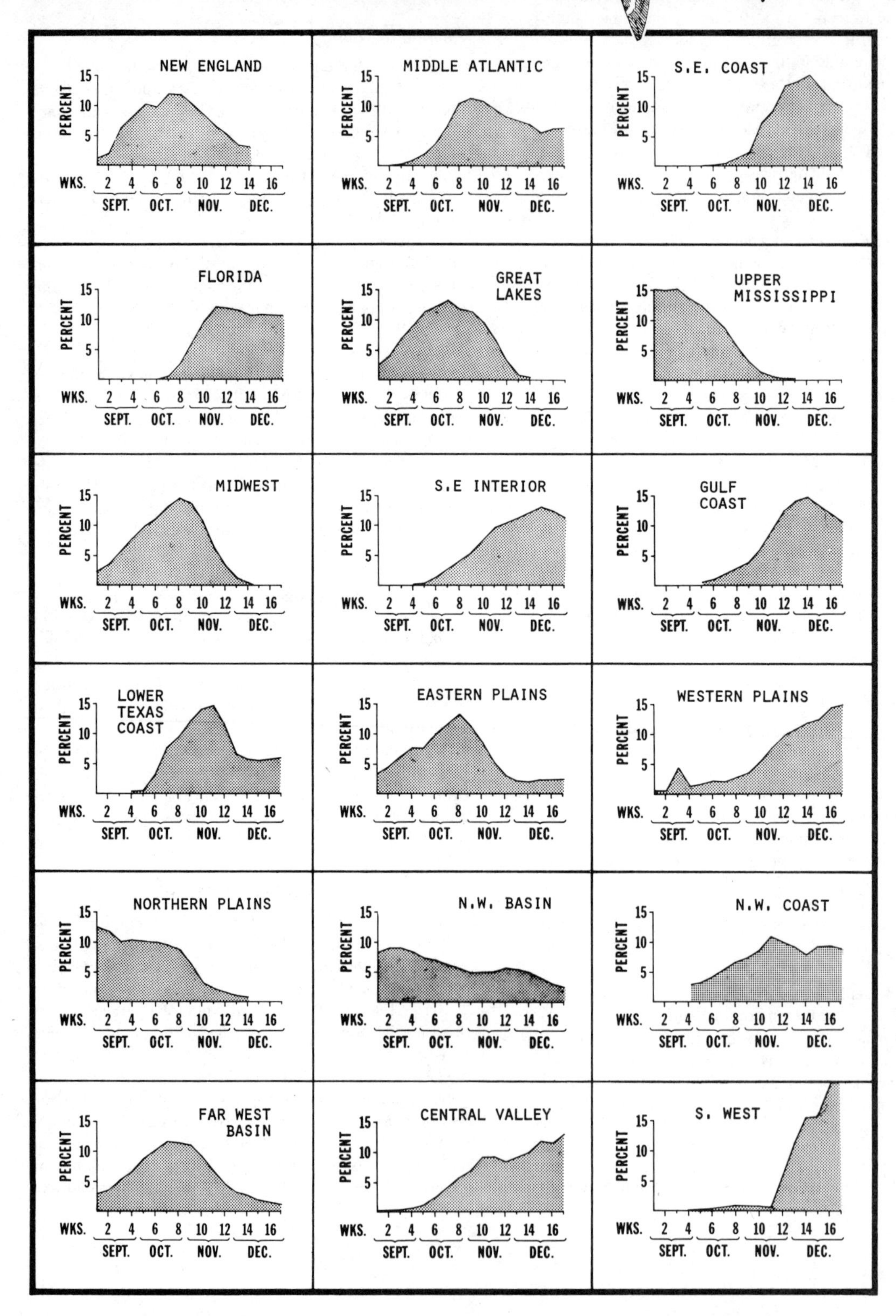

Fall

AMERICAN WIGEON

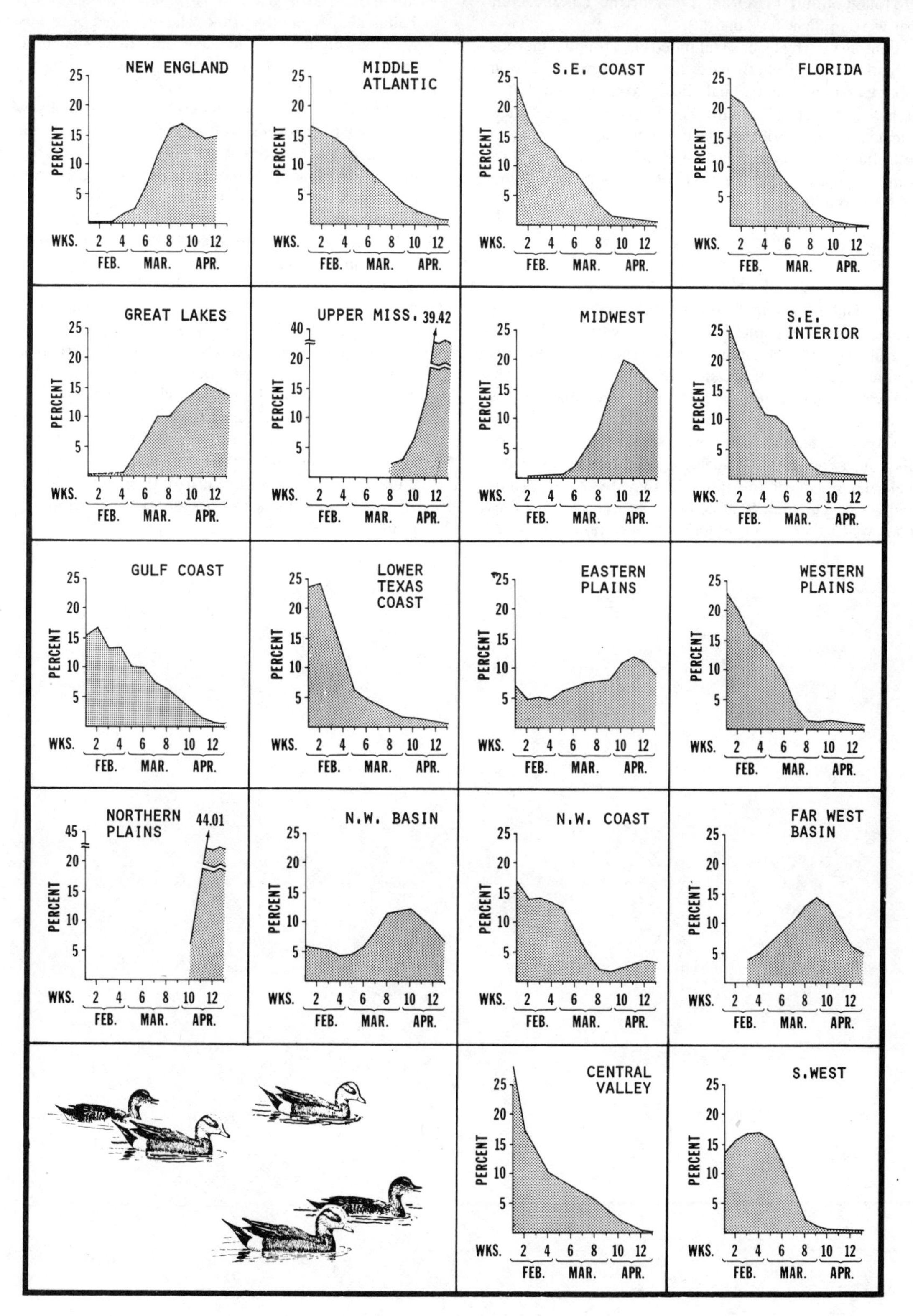

Spring

wigeons at the Pel Marsh were already flightless (Henry Reeves).

On the Yukon Flats, Alaska, many flightless wigeons were found on July 1 (Lensink 1964); on the Yukon Delta, most were in flight on August 3.

Aerial surveys by Ducks Unlimited have found hundreds of flightless wigeons between August 6 and August 25, on Upper Cummins, Canoe, and Kazan lakes in central Saskatchewan (William Leitch). The lateness of their molt indicates that many of these birds were probably hens. At the Delta Marsh, there was a large influx of wigeon hens during August (Hochbaum 1944). Wigeons remain flightless for about 35 days.

FOOD HABITS

Most dabbling ducks feed primarily upon the seeds of aquatic and marsh plants, mast, or cultivated grains, but not the wigeon. The individualistic wigeons prefer the stems and leafy parts of aquatic plants to their seeds and, in the West, even graze on the leafy parts of upland grasses and clovers.

In coastal estuaries, wigeons consume eelgrass, widgeon grass, bushy pondweed, and muskgrass. In the freshwater lakes and ponds of the interior, they feed on various pondweeds, coontail, wild celery, and even filamentous algae. When their favorite aquatic vegetation is lacking, they seek the seeds of rice cut-grass, wild millet, smartweed, and buttonbush.

For many years, wigeons have been feeding intensively upon the waste grain in sorghum fields of the Texas Panhandle. Recently, some wigeons have been observed feeding with mallards on waste corn in harvested fields of the Midwest. Wigeons are obviously adapting to new foods, but more slowly than mallards.

The wigeon's adoption of new foods is especially evident in the West. According to J. Burton Lauckhart, there were no wigeons in western Washington about 1900, but after timber was cleared for the development of grass pastures, the wigeon resorted to pasture grasses for food and has become the most abundant species of duck in that region.

In their utilization of green foods, wigeons have sometimes caused considerable damage to cultivated crops in California (Biehn 1951). They have fed on lettuce, alfalfa, clover, pasture grasses, and young fall-planted barley, causing consternation among local farmers.

Wigeons frequently gather where coots and redheads are diving for the succulent foliage of aquatic plants. As a diving bird pops to the surface with a bit of material in its bill, a wigeon may promptly relieve it of part of its fare. It is amazing how tolerant coots and redheads are to this thievery by wigeons. This trait on the part of wigeons has doubtlessly developed because of their lack of diving ability, but Arthur Hawkins once observed them diving with redheads in shallow water.

Gadwall

Anas strepera

Other Common Names: Gray duck, gray mallard

VITAL STATISTICS

Length:	Adult male, 19.5-22.5 inches, average 20.9 inches (20) Adult female, 18.2-20.2 inches, average 19.2 inches (14) Immature male, 18.5-21.7 inches, average 20.0 inches (27) Immature female, 18.0-19.5 inches, average 18.8 inches (13)
Wing:	Adult male, 10.7 inches (22) Adult female, 10.1 inches (6) Immature male, 10.5 inches (58) Immature female, 9.8 inches (56)
Weight:	Adult male, 1.6-2.3 pounds, average 2.13 pounds (37) Adult female, 1.4-2.3 pounds, average 1.84 pounds (45) Immature male, 1.3-2.3 pounds, average 1.89 pounds (204) Immature female, 1.1-2.1 pounds, average 1.71 pounds (200)

IDENTIFICATION

Field

At a distance, both sexes of the gadwall resemble the hen mallard in drab plumage and body shape. Gadwalls also resemble wigeons, with which they often associate on feeding grounds. Flocks of gadwalls are usually smaller than those of mallards and wigeons, and a flock that appears to be composed entirely of mallard hens is most likely to be a flock of gadwalls. Rarely, if ever, do mallard hens associate in flocks south of their breeding grounds.

At closer range, the body plumage of the adult drake appears gray, the head is brown, and the upper and lower tail coverts are black. The black lower tail coverts form a distinguishing mark that is visible at a surprising distance. At short distances, the light gray tertials form a noticeable gray patch at the rear of the folded wing. And at close range, the long tawny-orange scapulars, overlying the folded wing, create a bright spot. The bill of the adult drake is dark in contrast to the yellowish bill of the drake mallard.

When the gadwall is in flight, the partially white speculum (seldom visible otherwise) becomes the most distinctive feature. The amount of white in the rear wing patch is greatest in adult drakes and least in immature hens. The wing of the gadwall shows less white than the wing of the wigeon and the white areas are located on the rear of the wing instead of on the front, as in the wigeon.

In proportion to its length, the wing of the gadwall is slightly narrower than the mallard's and broader than the wigeon's, which possibly explains why the gadwall's wing beat is faster than the mallard's but slower than the wigeon's. The gadwall has a slimmer, trimmer appearance in the air than the mallard, but less so than the pintail.

In both sexes when on the wing, the white breast and belly are sharply defined by the darker chest, side, and flank feathers, as in the wood duck, wigeon, and green-winged teal.

The call of the female gadwall is a quack similar to, but less strident, than that of a mallard. Males are quieter, but utter a loud *kack, kack* when alarmed.

At Hand

In all plumages, the wing provides the best cues for identification. The inner area of the speculum has a white patch, and the outer area contains either a gray patch (immatures) or a black patch (adults). Forward of the speculum, the greater coverts show varying amounts of black, most pronounced in adult drakes and least in immature hens. Drakes show chestnut feathers on the shoulder—more noticeable in adults than in immatures. Hens usually show a trace of chestnut, barely discernible among immatures.

The bill of the gadwall is narrower, in proportion to its length, than those of other dabbling ducks—it is gray-black in drakes and dusky yellow with black dots on the lower edge in hens. Feet and legs are a dull orange in drakes, paler in hens.

The chest, flanks, sides, and back of the adult male are in varying shades of gray disposed in wavy lines except on the chest, which has crescent-shaped markings. The ash-brown tail contrasts with the black rump and upper and lower tail coverts.

The female gadwall has a dusky brown head, neck, and back. Most of these body feathers are broadly edged with buff. The chest, sides, and flanks are gray-brown; the breast and belly are white.

During the eclipse plumage, male gadwalls resemble hens, but most have attained full nuptial plumage by early November. Immatures also resemble hens through much of the fall, not acquiring full nuptial plumage until late winter or early spring.

POPULATION STATUS

During the past two decades, the numbers of gadwalls on breeding ground surveys and in winter inventories have risen dramatically. At a time when most other duck species are either declining or barely holding their own, it is gratifying to behold a rather steady rise in gadwall numbers since the late 1950's. According to the population trend from breeding ground surveys, numbers have almost doubled. Winter numbers in the United States have nearly quadrupled, but part of this increase may have stemmed from the improved winter habitat in Louisiana, which may have retained a proportion of the population that formerly wintered in southeast coastal Mexico. Both the Mississippi (Louisiana) and the Central flyways have shared in this gadwall bonanza. On the Pacific Flyway, the gadwall population has fluctuated but shows no definite trend. In the Atlantic Flyway, however, January surveys show a steady downward trend in numbers since 1960.

For unknown reasons, the gadwall appears to go through long-term "cycles" of abundance and scarcity. Discussing the gadwall in the Camrose, Alberta, region, Farley (1932:19) stated: "Formerly an abundant summer resident, now quite scarce. The gadwall, at the beginning of the century, was one of the most plentiful of ducks. In 1907, and several years following, more gadwalls were shot in the Camrose country than all other ducks together. . . . About 1920 there was a perceptible decrease in their numbers, and this has continued up to the present time. During the past year, in all my travels I have not seen a dozen individuals."

Kiel et al. (1972) compared an 1890 account of waterfowl in Manitoba with the present situation and remarked: "The gadwall, now a fairly common nester throughout Manitoba's pothole area, was listed with the wood duck as a rare resident, except along the border. . . . The gadwall represents perhaps the biggest change in species ranks between the two periods."

Gadwall populations in the regions of North America where their annual status has been determined have averaged 1,432,000, 1955-74. An unusually large number—210,000—breed in the Intermountain marshes, the tallgrass prairie and other places outside the principal contiguous breeding grounds.

Age Ratios

The age of gadwalls tallied from hunters' bags, 1966-73, averages 1.6 immatures per adult. Because the greater vulnerability of the young to shooting has not been measured, I am assuming that the young are 1.5 times more vulnerable than adults. A correcting factor of 1.5 suggests that there are 1.1 immatures per adult in the average fall population.

Sex Ratios

There were 2.21 males per female (68.8 percent) among adult gadwalls in the bags of hunters, 1966-73. Among immatures, the sex ratio was 1.1 males per female (52.4 percent). Banding data that reflect selectivity of sexes by hunters are unavailable but males are probably a little more vulnerable to hunting than hens.

The reasonable assumption that breeding populations of gadwalls are composed half of yearling birds and half of older birds suggests a possible ratio of three males per two females (60 percent). Visual counts taken in the spring suggest a lower proportion of males, 52.8 percent (Bellrose et al. 1961). The actual proportion is probably somewhere between 53 and 60 percent.

Mortality

In a study of mortality, based on banding of gadwalls in marshes adjacent to Great Salt Lake, Utah, Gates (1962) found that immatures suffered a first-year loss of 67 percent and that adults had an annual mortality rate of 52 percent. A fall population composed equally of adults and immatures would suffer an annual loss of about 60 percent.

DISTRIBUTION

The gadwall occurs over much of the middle latitudes of the Northern Hemisphere as a single race. It breeds largely between 40° and 60° latitude and winters largely between 20° and 40° latitude in both North America and Eurasia. A race, now extinct, formerly occurred on Washington Island, 1,000 miles south of the Hawaiian Islands, in the Pacific Ocean.

Breeding Range

In North America, the gadwall reaches its greatest breeding numbers, nearly 800,000 (4.1 per square mile), in the mixed prairie of the Dakotas and the Prairie Provinces: 256,000 in North Dakota (6.3 per square mile); 237,000 in Saskatchewan (5.0); 108,000 in South Dakota (4.4); 104,000 in Alberta (4.2); and 22,000 in Manitoba (4.8).

The parklands of the Prairie Provinces harbored an average of 394,000 (4.3 per square mile) breeding gadwalls, 1955-74, and was second in importance to the mixed grasslands. Breeding numbers in Alberta parklands were the most dense (6.8 birds per square mile); those in Manitoba parklands were the lowest (1.9 gadwalls per square mile). Saskatchewan parklands average about 3.6 gadwalls per square mile.

The shortgrass plains association—extending west from the Missouri River in the Dakotas through Montana, the southwest corner of Saskatchewan, and the southern tenth of Alberta—was populated by nearly 200,000 (1.4 per square mile) breeding gadwalls, 1955-74: 3.0 per square mile in southwestern Saskatchewan, 1.5 in Alberta and Montana, 1.0 in western South Dakota, and 0.4 in western North Dakota. Twenty thousand more breed in the Sandhills of Nebraska, about 3,000 in western Minnesota, and about 50 as far south as the Cheyenne Bottoms, Kansas.

Except for an average of 19,000 (2.8 per square mile) breeding on the delta of the Saskatchewan River and 2,100 (1.3 per square mile) on the Athabasca Delta, only a few thousand nest north of the parklands in the boreal forest of Canada. From 6,000 to 19,000 gadwalls breed in the Cariboo Parklands and the Okanagan Valley of British Columbia.

Almost 175,000 gadwalls breed in the Intermountain marshes of the western states. The largest number, about 65,000, nest in marshes adjacent to Great Salt Lake, Utah. Other important breeding areas are the Klamath Basin (California-Oregon border), 12,000; the Central Valley of California, 6,500; Carson Sink, Nevada, 4,500; Oregon, 13,000; the Columbia Basin, Washington, 3,500; Idaho, 30,000; Wyoming, 27,000; Colorado, 8,500 (5,000 of these in the San Luis Valley).

Apparently because of the moderating influence of the Japanese current, small numbers of gadwalls nest along the coast of the Alaskan Panhandle and on the Alaska Peninsula (James Bartonek).

Gadwalls were first reported breeding along the East Coast in 1939. Since then, Henny and Holgersen (1973) report that they have rapidly extended their breeding range to include more than 30 locations in the East, over 1,200 miles from their main breeding range in the West. Breeding locations are associated with the freshwater impoundments created on the brackish marshes of national wildlife refuges and state wildlife management areas.

Other isolated breeding colonies of gadwalls have been reported at Horicon Marsh and Green Bay, Wisconsin (Jahn and Hunt 1964); Luther Marsh and Lake St. Clair, Ontario (Godfrey 1966); the Lake Erie marshes, Ohio (Bednarik 1970); and Montezuma Marsh, New York (Cummings 1963). A colony of breeding gadwalls was established near Concord, Massachusetts, by introducing flightless young from Delta, Manitoba (Borden and Hochbaum 1966).

Migration Corridors

Most of the comparatively small numbers of gadwalls that migrate to the Atlantic Coast select the marshes of South Carolina. To reach these marshes, most gadwalls apparently migrate through the Reelfoot Lake-Tennessee Valley area of Tennessee, where 60,000 may congregate during the fall. Oddly, band recoveries in South Carolina are predominantly from gadwalls banded far to the west on breeding grounds in Alberta.

Thousands of gadwalls are occasionally observed in nonstop passage during the fall along the Mississippi River in Illinois, most of them probably bound for the Tennessee areas. From this important area of concentration, gadwalls also depart for Florida; Mobile Bay, Alabama; and Louisiana.

Over three-fourths of the gadwall population of North America reaches Louisiana during the fall. From the mid-1960's to the early 1970's, peak gadwall numbers in Louisiana in the fall have reached the 1 million to 1.5 million mark. Yet, in recent years the winter populations have averaged 500,000 less than peak fall numbers. Although hunters usually kill about 125,000, many thousands must cross the Gulf of Mexico to Yucatan and other nearby areas of Mexico. Because winter surveys of that region do not report that many, it seems likely that large numbers have been overlooked because of the extensive and distant region surveyed.

To reach Louisiana, most gadwalls apparently follow the midplains migration corridor. Large concentrations appear in fall along this corridor: 80,000 at the Lacreek, South Dakota, and Valentine, Nebraska, national wildlife refuges; 45,000 in central Kansas, most on the Great Bend Wildlife Area. Other migration corridors in the eastern Great Plains and along the Missouri River funnel additional tens of thousands of gadwalls into Louisiana.

Gadwalls wintering along the Gulf Coast north of Tampico, Mexico, arrive there from Alberta and Saskatchewan breeding grounds via the west plains migration corridor. Some birds wintering there have come directly south from breeding grounds in the Dakotas.

In addition to their own considerable production of gadwalls, the marshes of Great Salt Lake receive at least comparable numbers from breeding grounds in Alberta and Saskatchewan. From the Great Salt Lake Basin, migration corridors radiate out to the Texas coast, the west coast of Mexico, the Imperial Valley, Carson Sink, and the San Joaquin Valley.

California contributes greatly to its fall population of gadwalls, but, in addition, receives almost as many from Alberta via several migration corridors. Most of the gadwalls breeding in British Columbia, Washington, and Oregon winter in the Central Valley of California.

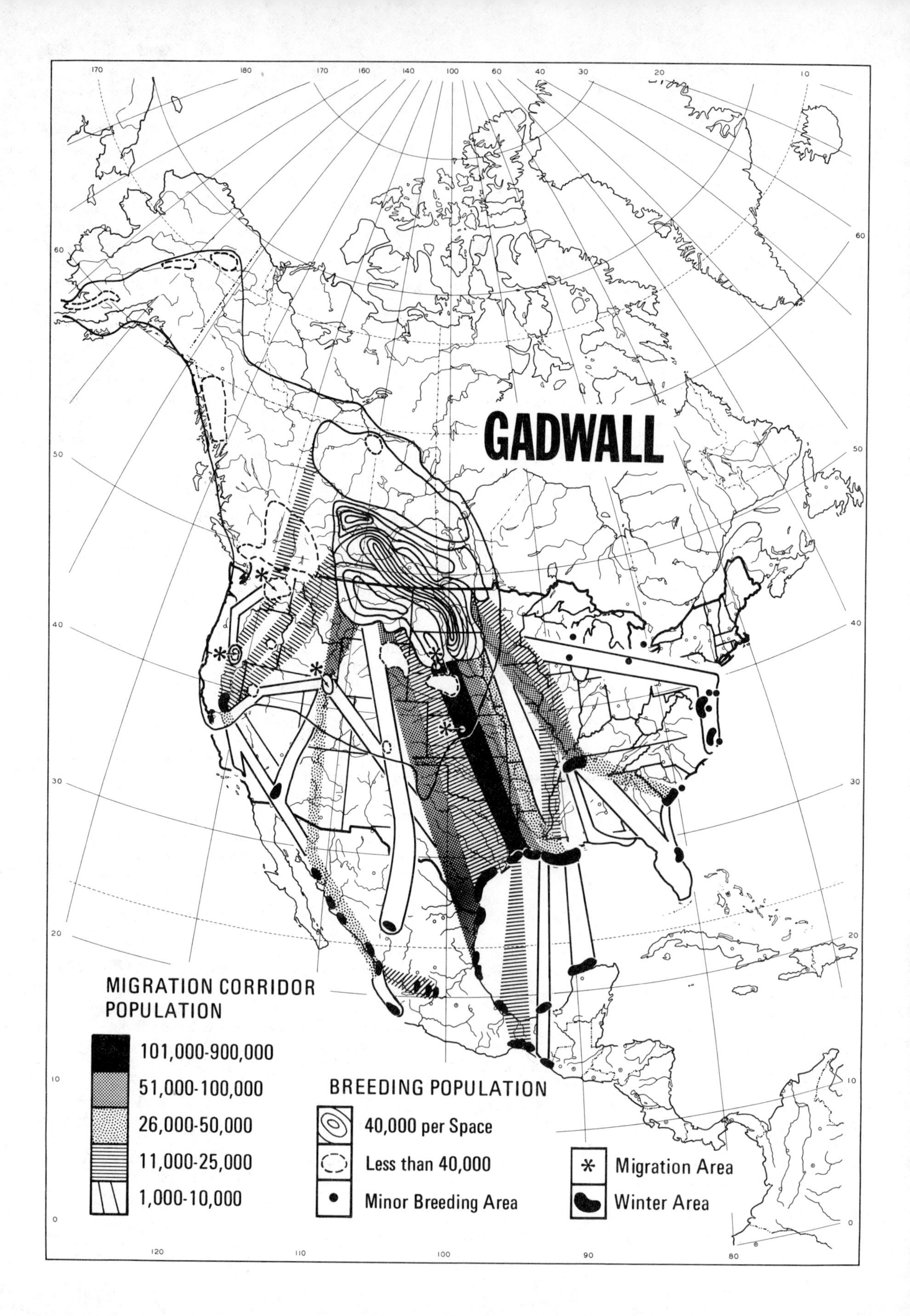

GADWALL
MIGRATION CORRIDOR POPULATION
101,000-900,000
51,000-100,000
26,000-50,000
11,000-25,000
1,000-10,000
BREEDING POPULATION
40,000 per Space
Less than 40,000
Minor Breeding Area
Migration Area
Winter Area

Winter Areas

About 1,000 gadwalls winter in Chesapeake Bay and only a few winter north of there. Three-fourths of the 40,000 that winter in the Atlantic Flyway occur in South Carolina; and Georgia and Florida each winter about 2,500.

Primarily because of Louisiana, the Mississippi Flyway winters the bulk of the gadwalls found in North America. The numbers on January surveys in Louisiana rose from 127,000 in 1955 to 1,152,000 in 1965 (Hugh Bateman). Since then, the numbers of gadwalls in Louisiana have fluctuated from 570,000 (1972) to 938,000 (1969). Much of the increase in wintering populations of gadwalls in Louisiana is attributed to the opening up of dense stands of marsh vegetation by hurricane action. Arkansas with a population of gadwalls averaging 25,000, Tennessee with 10,000, and Alabama with 8,000 are other important winter areas in the Mississippi Flyway.

Slightly over a thousand gadwalls winter north of Texas in the Central Flyway. About 30,000 winter along the Texas coast, over half between Sabine Lake and Galveston Bay, and 25,000 more winter in the interior of the state. Along the east coast of Mexico, about 35,000 have been found on winter surveys. The largest concentrations occur in lagoons near Tampico.

In the interior of Mexico, almost 2,000 gadwalls winter in the Northern Highlands and 12,000 in the Southern Highlands, mostly west of Mexico City and centering on Lago de Chapala. Gadwalls numbering 28,000 winter along the west coast of Mexico as far south as Guatemala. Over half occur in the marshes north of Tuxpan.

About four percent of the gadwalls in North America winter in the Pacific Flyway (average, 37,000). Of this number, 28,000 winter in California, mostly in the San Joaquin Valley. At times, gadwalls migrating along this flyway go astray. Yocom (1964) reported that 100 to 200 gadwalls appeared during the winter of 1959-60 on Kwajalein in the Marshall Islands, about midway between Hawaii and New Guinea. The extinct island race that once developed on Washington Island in the mid-Pacific probably resulted from wayward gadwalls that became stranded far from their usual haunts.

MIGRATION BEHAVIOR

Gadwalls migrate mostly at night in small to moderate-sized flocks. Only when blizzards drive ducks from the Great Plains are gadwalls commonly observed migrating during the daytime. Under these conditions, C. E. Shanks (Bellrose and Sieh 1960:31) observed an exceptionally large passage of gadwalls on November 7, 1956, at the Fountain Grove Wildlife Area in north-central Missouri:

"At about this same time [12:30 P.M] flocks of gadwalls began coming in to land 100 to 150 yards out from my blind, drinking, and immediately taking to the air. According to my counts there were, on the average, 75 gadwalls landing in this area every 2 minutes. However, since they were departing so quickly there were never more than 200-300 birds on the water at any one time. It is interesting to note that they all landed exactly in the same spot. This gadwall flight continued in this manner for approximately 2 hours, which, figuring 75 every 2 minutes, calculates to 4,500 birds landing during this 2 hour period.

"During this same period there were just as many low flying flights which passed on without stopping so that I feel it is safe to say that 9,000-10,000 gadwalls came by this particular spot between 12:30 and 2:30 p.m. This gadwall flight seemed to stop as suddenly as it started, and was replaced by an even heavier flight of mallards. . . ."

Chronology

Fall. Gadwalls begin to leave their breeding grounds in Canada in early September and move south into nearby areas of the Great Plains. Later departures tend to be southeastward. The Dakotas and Minnesota are bereft of gadwalls by the end of October. About this time, large numbers appear in Michigan, Wisconsin, Iowa, and Illinois, where they remain until late November.

Gadwalls wintering at Chesapeake also arrive about the end of October. Those wintering in South Carolina, Florida, Louisiana, and Texas arrive later, the first week in November in any abundance, with numbers increasing throughout the month.

Gadwall passage in the High Plains region is 3 weeks in advance of their passage in the east plains at similar latitudes, perhaps because of the higher altitude.

So many gadwalls nest in the basins and valleys of the Rocky Mountains that local populations mark the influx from prairie breeding areas, which show a steady decline in population from September through November. However, at Klamath Basin marshes in northern California, a large influx occurred through October, then exited through November.

Gadwalls migrate into California's Central Valley in early October, but not in sizable numbers until late in the month.

Spring. Gadwalls gradually begin to leave major winter areas in February. The tempo of departures accelerates during March, but not until late April are most of the gadwalls gone from their winter homes.

They reach the Midwest and the Great Lakes states about mid-March and increase in number for the next several weeks. In the southern Great Plains, appreciable numbers of gadwalls appear by the third week in March, with numbers rising for the next month.

Although a pronounced departure of gadwalls from the Central Valley of California occurs in February, large numbers do not appear in the Klamath Basin until late March. They arrive in the Great Salt Lake Basin, Utah, and the Columbia Basin, Washington, about mid-March, with numbers either increasing or at a high level through April.

Gadwalls arrive on the northern Great Plains of the United States about April 1, and throughout that month

GADWALL

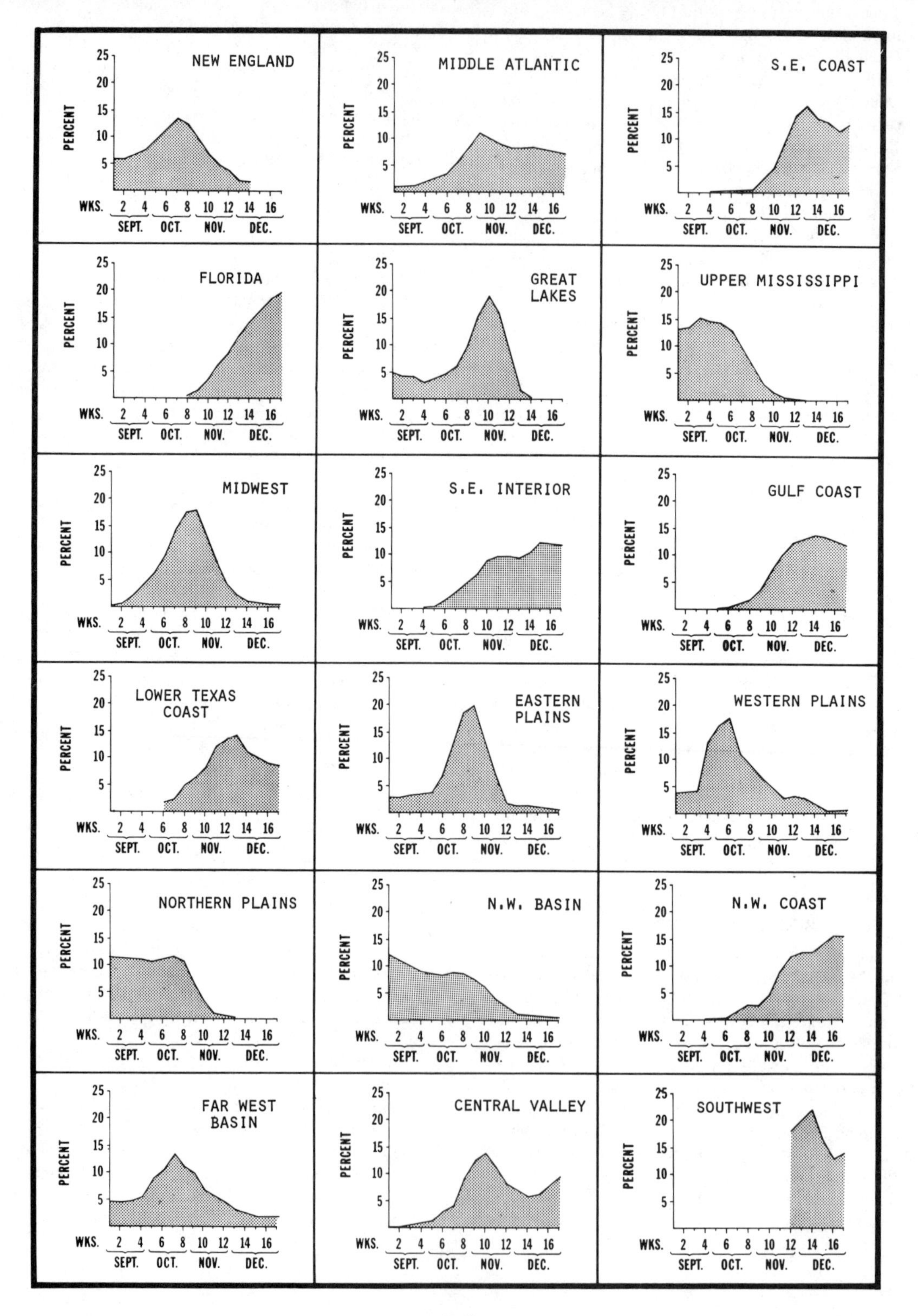

Fall

GADWALL

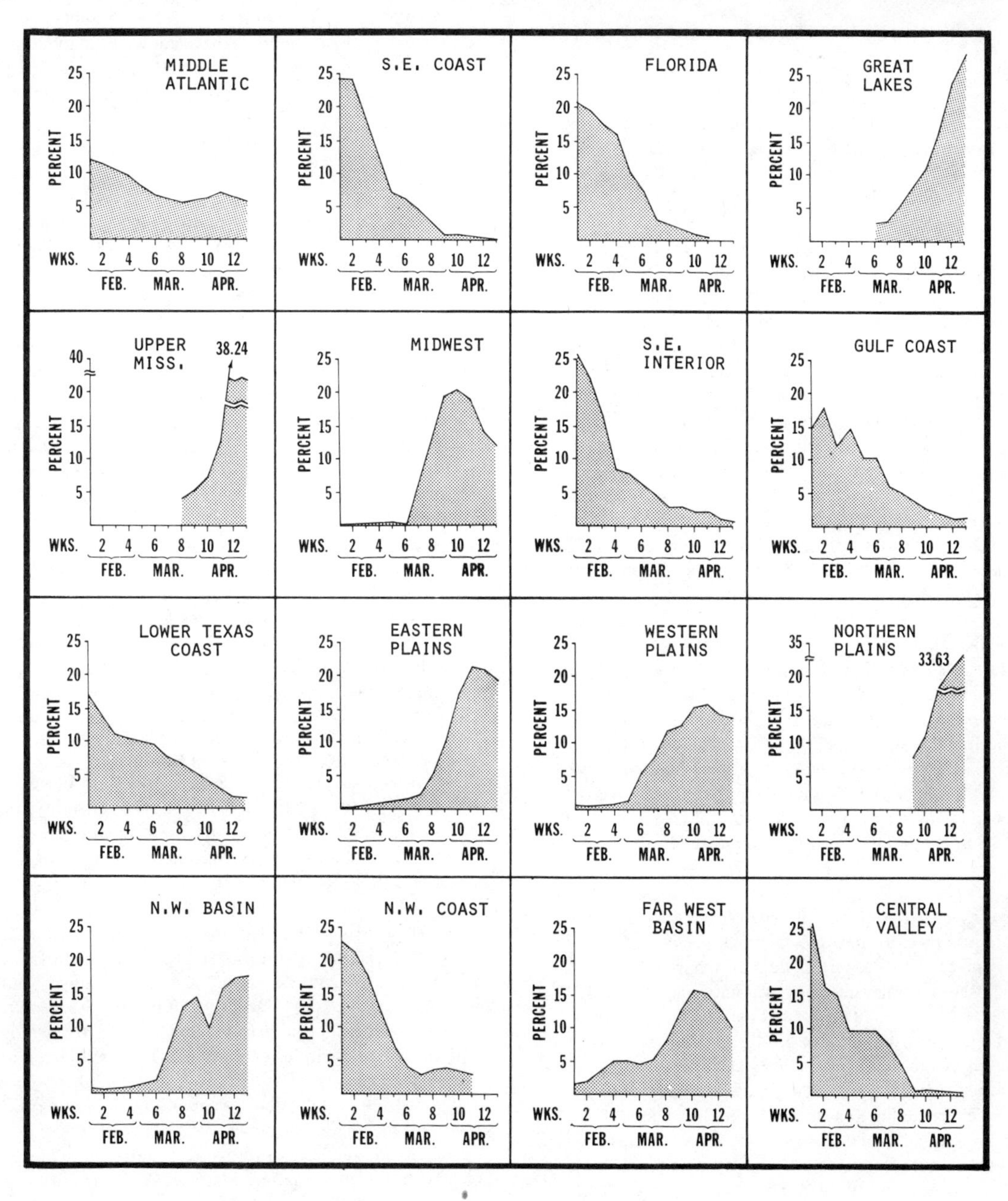

Spring

their population continues to grow with arrivals from the southeast and the south.

BREEDING

Behavior

Age, Pair Bond, and Homing. Although most gadwalls breed as yearlings, some late-hatched young of the previous summer are probably not sufficiently mature to do so. Oring (1969) noted that yearling males are less likely to breed than older birds. The initiation of the pair bond in gadwalls has not been studied, but it probably begins by midfall in mature birds and by midwinter in immatures. Courtship flights observed in the spring probably most often involve yearling females and older males.

The duration of the pair bond is highly variable. A few endure through the incubation period, but most dissolve during the first 2 weeks of nesting (Oring 1969). However, in studying radio-equipped gadwalls in North Dakota, Gilmer et al. (1973) concluded that the gadwalls they observed exhibited strong pair bonds, with mated pairs remaining together almost constantly during the nest period. An uncommonly faithful gadwall drake may accompany a hen and brood for a short time after hatching, as Chura (1962) observed at the Bear River Refuge in Utah. At the Camas Refuge in Idaho, the first separations of drakes from their hens occurred on June 14 and the drakes commenced their eclipse molt on June 22 (Oring 1964).

At Delta Marsh, Manitoba, Sowls (1955) found that at least 37 percent of the adult female gadwalls that remained alive returned to nest in the same area. The homing of yearling females was only 12 percent. Gates (1962) observed that 29 percent of the nesting hens banded previously on the Ogden Bay Wildlife Area, Utah, returned the next year. Considering a mortality rate of 52 percent, at least 60 percent of the hens still alive returned to the same nest area.

Home Range. As flocks of recently arrived gadwalls separate into pairs for nesting, each pair selects a favored loafing and feeding site. At Ogden Bay marsh, Utah, 11 days elapsed from the time of arrival until pairs separated themselves on loafing sites (Gates 1962). From these sites, pairs range from 100 yards to 3 miles in their search for suitable places to nest (Gates 1962, Duebbert 1966). The home range, which encompasses loafing, feeding, and nest sites, varied from 34 to 87 acres at Ogden Bay (Gates 1962). Where an unusual concentration of nests occurred on an island in a North Dakota marsh, many pairs had home ranges of several hundred acres because of the long distances between loafing areas and the nest island (Duebbert 1966).

Although home ranges may overlap, pairs seldom visit the same areas on the home range at identical times (Gates 1962). Duebbert (1966) observed that gadwalls, unlike most other puddle ducks, most often loafed on open water sites rather than on shoreline sites. He believed that gadwall territories were mobile and revolved around the hens. However, he noted that three-bird pursuit flights were more frequent where nesting was crowded than where it was dispersed. In spite of the numerous conflicts between pairs nesting close together, these gadwalls adapted themselves to the crowded conditions and nested successfully. Few other ducks have this adaptability in their inherent drive towards isolation during the nest period.

Nesting

The gadwall is one of the last ducks to arrive in numbers on breeding areas in the spring, yet in North Dakota and Utah it was 23 to 28 days before they began to lay, a much longer interval than for mallards and pintails.

Nest Sites. Pairs searching for nest sites fly low over the surrounding meadow and upland areas, landing where the vegetation is relatively short. The hen, sometimes followed by her drake, investigates the higher clumps of vegetation for desirable cover and nest-building material and suitable soil for scrapes. A gadwall hen began building a nest in a scrape 3 days after Duebbert (1966) prepared it. Where present, small islands are the favorite nest sites. Dikes in marshes, fields, and meadows are other preferred sites. Gadwalls are less inclined than most other ducks to nest over water in marshes.

On islands and dikes in marshes, gadwall nests are usually within a few feet of water. However, on islands in Lake Newell, Alberta, gadwall nests averaged 80 feet from water (Vermeer 1970*b*), farther than for all other species except the wigeon. In general, most nests are located on upland areas less than 100 yards from water, although nests several hundred yards from water are known to occur.

As with most upland nesting ducks, the gadwall's choice of vegetation for nesting depends upon availability, density, and height. Whitetop was preferred on the Delta Marsh, Manitoba (Sowls 1955); juncus, near Brooks, Alberta (Keith 1961); buckbrush, at Caron Potholes, Saskatchewan (William Leitch); nettle, at Klamath Basin, California (Miller and Collins 1954); greasewood, at Freezeout Lake, Montana (Ellig 1955); alfalfa and summer-fallow fields of various weeds, at Lower Souris Refuge, North Dakota (Martz 1967); upland grasses, nettle, and other weeds, at Ogden Bay, Utah (Gates 1962); willows and weeds, at Bear River marshes, Utah (Williams and Marshall 1938*b*). Nettle was preferred to all other weeds.

Gadwalls seek tall, dense vegetation for nesting more than do other dabbling ducks. When a choice was made between mowed and unmowed vegetation, gadwalls clearly preferred the latter (Martz 1967, Page and Cassel 1971, Oetting and Cassel 1971).

Clutch Size, Eggs, and Incubation. Gadwalls usually lay from 5 to 13 eggs per nest, but dump nests may contain as many as 20 eggs. The average clutch size, 10.04 (2,545), ranged on various areas studied from 8 to 11 eggs.

The eggs of gadwalls are ovate and creamy white and measure 39.7 by 55.3 mm (Bent 1923). The hen incubates the eggs for 24 to 27 days, average 25.7 (8) (Oring 1969). The average period of hatch for eggs incubated artificially was 24 days. Incubation periods vary according to the degree of chilling to which the eggs are subjected under natural conditions of incubation.

Chronology of Nesting. South to Pea Island, North Carolina, gadwall nests did not reach the peak of hatch until the last 3 weeks of June (Parnell and Quay 1965). Similar dates of hatch prevailed in the grasslands of Merced County, California (Anderson 1956).

At Klamath Basin, California, gadwalls began hatching about mid-June and continued until mid-August (Rienecker and Anderson 1960). Gadwalls began nesting at Ogden Bay, Utah, about mid-May and continued to initiate nesting until mid-July (Gates 1962). In the area of Waubay, South Dakota, gadwalls commenced nesting about May 20 and peaked in their initiation of nesting in late June (Evans and Black 1956). Most gadwalls at Delta Marsh, Manitoba, began their nest efforts the last 2 weeks in May, with peak activity during the first 2 weeks of June (Sowls 1955). Near Brooks, Alberta, gadwalls started nesting in late May (Keith 1961).

Although the breeding range of the gadwall extends over 1,400 miles of latitude and several thousand feet of altitude, the periods of nesting are remarkably similar throughout its range.

Nest Success. The gadwall excels all other species of dabbling ducks in nest success. In studies made at numerous areas throughout its range, nest success has amounted to an astounding 67.5 percent (2,173). Where the fate of 100 or more nests has been determined on a specific study area, success has varied from 52 percent at Ogden Bay, Utah (Gates 1962), to 90 percent at Klamath Basin, California (Miller and Collins 1954).

The remarkably high nest success of the gadwall probably results from its late nesting and its propensity to nest on islands and in thick, tall vegetation. Predators usually prey more actively on early nests and tend to avoid the dense vegetation, particularly nettles, that gadwalls often prefer.

Several studies have demonstrated that gadwall nests in unmowed nest cover are significantly more successful than those in mowed cover (Martz 1967, Page and Cassel 1971, Oetting and Cassel 1971). Similarly, gadwalls nesting on ungrazed lands were more successful than those nesting on grazed lands (Kirsch 1969).

Hatchability was exceptionally high in successful nests of gadwalls. In 1,889 nests containing hatched eggs, only 0.98 egg per nest failed to hatch, ranging from 0.65 egg per nest at Klamath Basin (Miller and Collins 1954) to 1.6 eggs per nest at Lower Souris, North Dakota (Duebbert 1966). About two-thirds of the unhatched eggs contained dead embryos and one-third were infertile.

Nest Failure. Most of the losses of gadwall nests were attributed primarily to mammalian predators and secondarily to avian ones. Among the mammalian predators, striped skunks were listed most often, with coyotes second in importance. Foxes, badgers, ground squirrels, and raccoons were of lesser importance as predators. Avian predators were identified as crows, magpies, ravens, and California and ring-billed gulls.

Egg losses to California and ring-billed gulls were negligible at Honey Lake, California (Anderson 1965), and nonexistent on islands in Miquelon Lakes, Alberta (Vermeer 1968). But at Farmington Bay, Utah, California gulls destroyed 18.6 percent of the gadwall eggs laid (Odin 1957).

Renesting. Many gadwalls will renest if their first nest is destroyed. At Ogden Bay, Utah, Gates (1962) reported that 74 percent of his marked hens whose first nests were destroyed nested again, 27 percent renested after losing their second clutch, and 25 percent renested even after the third incubated clutch was lost. Near Brooks, Alberta, 82 percent of the gadwalls that lost their initial nests tried again (Keith 1961). At Delta Marsh, 4 of 16 marked hens renested (Sowls 1955). However, renesting was considered a negligible factor in the productivity of gadwalls at Lower Souris, North Dakota (Duebbert 1966).

Gates (1962) observed that three hens continued to lay when incomplete clutches were destroyed: one persistent hen laid 22 eggs in 22 days; a second, 17 eggs in 17 days; and the third, 12 eggs in 12 days. Another hen that lost 10 unincubated eggs began laying again after an interval of 3 days. Hens whose nests were destroyed during the incubation period waited longer to start a new clutch. The ability of gadwall hens to renest declined as the stage of incubation lengthened (Gates 1962).

Renesting hens moved their nest location when a nest was destroyed. At Delta Marsh, renests were 45 to 600 yards (average, 320) from earlier nest sites (Sowls 1955). At Ogden Bay, hens moved 110 to 525 yards (average, 241) to establish new nests (Gates 1962).

Clutch sizes in gadwall renests were smaller than in initial nests. Clutch size declined from 9.7 (3) to 7.7 (3) at Delta Marsh (Sowls 1955) and from 10.7 (19) to 7.8 (24) at Ogden Bay (Gates 1962). Hatching success in renests was similar to that in initial nests.

Rearing of Young

Broods. The female gadwall leads the young to favorable feeding grounds, usually some distance from the nest site. Duebbert (1966) observed hens leading their broods across 500 yards of open water the same day they left their nests. One favored feeding area, containing an abundance of plant and animal foods, was 300 yards from nest sites. At Ogden Bay, gadwall broods traveled 0.26 to 1.15 miles (average, 0.56) from their upland nest areas to deepwater marshes and the margins of impoundments (Gates 1962).

Development. Young gadwalls reached flying stage in

48 to 52 days in South Dakota (Gollop and Marshall 1954). A careful study at Delta Marsh in Manitoba (Oring 1968) disclosed that 2 percent of captive young gadwalls flew at 48 days and 2 percent at 49 days, 10 percent at 50 days, 50 percent at 51 days, 12 percent at 53 days, 22 percent at 56 days, and 2 percent at 63 days. Late-hatched young flew in fewer days than those hatched early in the season.

Survival. Gadwall broods commence life with an average of 6.87 young per brood (3,891). The average for Class II broods is 6.10 ducklings (5,035), a decline of 11 percent. However, like wigeons, Class III gadwall broods are slightly larger, numbering 6.28 young (2,545), suggesting that hens with broods adopt orphaned or deserted young.

Because of their physiological readiness for the wing molt, hen gadwalls and wigeons are more prone to desert unfledged late broods than unfledged early broods. Dabbling duck hens that nest earlier would not be as sorely pressed by the forthcoming wing molt.

Although gadwall broods appear to lose few ducklings, entire broods may be wiped out by certain gulls. California gulls consumed all of the gadwall ducklings hatched on islands where both species nested (Vermeer 1968). A lack of nearby brood cover in this particular area made the ducklings unusually vulnerable to the gulls.

POSTBREEDING SEASON

As soon as drakes desert their incubating mates, they begin to socialize with other drakes in similar circumstances. Duebbert (1966) reported that at Lower Souris, North Dakota, practically all drakes were gathered in flocks by July 1. The body feathers are molted first. As the molt advances toward the complete loss of wing feathers, the drakes become more secretive and wary. Because of their ability to hide in marsh vegetation, Duebbert did not see many males after July 15.

The first gadwalls to enter the molt are those yearling and older males that were thwarted early in their courtship activities (Oring 1969). Early-breeding males start the molt syndrome next, followed by late-breeding males. The last drakes to begin molting are those that were active sexually but were unable to secure mates. Early-nesting and then late-nesting hens follow the drakes into the molt cycle.

At Delta Marsh, Manitoba, Oring (1969) noted the first flightless gadwalls on July 23, when 10 to 15 percent were in that condition. The wing molt among drakes developed rapidly; by August 5, fifty percent were flightless. As early as mid-August, drakes were beginning to fly again. Gadwall hens began to molt in mid-August, about 6 weeks after their young hatched (Oring 1968). An unusually late wing molt among hens occurred in October of 1962 and 1964 in the coastal marshes of Louisiana (Chabreck 1966)—these birds were 1,000 to 2,000 miles south of their normal breeding and molt areas.

Captive gadwalls, both adult drakes and hens, completely renewed their wing feathers in 35 to 40 days but were capable of flight as early as 25 days (Oring 1968).

FOOD HABITS

Gadwalls seek shallow marshes and ponds abounding in underwater aquatic plants: pondweeds, naiads, widgeon grass, coontail, muskgrass, eelgrass, and filamentous algae. Like wigeons, they often prefer the succulent stems and leaves to seeds. The two species frequent the same habitats and often feed together on the same plant beds, but gadwalls, unlike wigeons, rarely graze on grass pastures or frequent upland grain fields. Exceptions do occur, and in central Washington, gadwalls were known to feed extensively on cultivated oats (Yocom 1951).

Sago pondweed, widgeon grass, salt grass, hardstem bulrush seeds, horned pondweed, and spike rush in that order were the preferred foods of gadwalls at Ogden Bay marsh, Utah (Gates 1957). This list probably typifies their food habits on Great Plains and Intermountain marshes.

In the Midwest, where preferred aquatic plants are often absent from duck marshes, gadwalls feed upon the seeds of millets, marsh smartweed, other smartweeds, and buttonbush (Korschgen 1955, Anderson 1959, Rawls 1954). I have often observed them feeding upon filamentous green algae in the absence of other food plants, and algae has been found frequently in the gizzards of gadwalls from Illinois, Tennessee, and South Carolina.

On important winter grounds in South Carolina, the seeds of soft-stem bulrush, the vegetative parts of the southern naiad, and leafy pondweed are principal food items (McGilvrey 1966*b*). At Chesapeake Bay, gadwalls in the brackish estuarine areas fed largely upon widgeon grass and, to a lesser extent, upon eelgrass, muskgrass, and clasping leaf pondweed (Stewart 1962). Where waters were fresher, southern naiads were highly utilized with smaller amounts of leafy pondweed and red algae.

Baikal Teal

Anas formosa

IDENTIFICATION

This bizarre-appearing teal is larger than our native teals and is a straggler to Alaska from Asia. The male's variegated head displays a black crown and hindneck and two buff patches, a circular one in front of the eye and a lance-shaped one behind the eye, extending onto the neck. Behind the lanceolate patch, a scimitar-shaped one of metallic green, margined by a white line, adorns the head and upper neck. The sides and breast are similar to those of the green-winged teal: the chest is buff dotted with black spots; the gray sides and flanks are barred with fine, wavy black lines; and a white fingerlike mark extends from in front of the folded wing to the white belly. Long scapulars striped with black, chestnut, and buff drape over the rear of the folded wing. The wing is brown, and the green speculum is edged with white in back and with a bar of red-brown in front.

Except in size, the female Baikal teal greatly resembles the female green-winged teal. Two distinguishing marks of the Baikal female are the pronounced whitish spot on the cheek at the base of the bill and the brown-red bar edging the forward margin of the green speculum.

DISTRIBUTION

Baikal teal breed in East Siberia as far west as the middle course of the Angara River and the lower course of the Nizhnyaya Tunguska River and on the tundra between the Yenisei and Pyasina rivers. In the Yenisei River basin, they range as far north as 70° latitude, but farther east they seldom appear north of the open boreal forest-tundra as far as the Anadyr Range. The southern border extends through the Kamchatka Peninsula to Sakhalin Island and west to Lake Baikal. They winter from southern Siberia through Korea, Japan, Mongolia, and eastern China.

Strays from eastern Siberia wander into Alaska. Gabrielson and Lincoln (1959) cited the following records: a male taken at Wainwright, September 2, 1921; two males collected on May 23 and 25, 1931, 80 miles northwest of Nome; a pair in breeding plumage, St. Lawrence Island, July 23, 1937; and a pair and a male at Wales, Alaska, June 8, 1942, and June 24, 1944, respectively. Maher (1960) observed a pair at Cape Sabine, Alaska, May 29, 1959, and cited a possible breeding record for Hooper Bay, Yukon Delta, in June 1959. Four Baikal teal were noted in nonbreeding plumage on St. Paul Island, Bering Sea, September 9, 1961, one of which was collected (Sladen 1966). Two other immature males were taken later, September 21 and October 8, 1961.

A few records of the Baikal teal in the conterminous United States are given by Sykes (1961): Currituck County, North Carolina, February 19, 1912; Contra Costa County, California, December 13, 1931; and one seen on the Scioto River, Delaware County, Ohio, April 1973. An immature male was collected at Ladner, British Columbia, December 20, 1957 (Hatter 1960). It is possible that some of these birds escaped from aviaries.

American Green-Winged Teal

Anas crecca carolinensis

Other Common Names: Greenwing, green-winged teal, common teal

VITAL STATISTICS

Length:	Adult male, 13.7-15.5 inches, average 14.7 inches (47) Adult female, 13.0-14.5 inches, average 13.9 inches (28) Immature male, 12.1-15.2 inches, average 13.8 inches (51) Immature female, 12.1-14.0 inches, average 13.4 inches (22)
Wing:	Adult male, 7.3 inches (86) Adult female, 7.0 inches (51) Immature male, 7.2 inches (66) Immature female, 6.9 inches (71)
Weight:	Adult male, 0.5-1.1 pounds, average 0.71 pound (113) Adult female, 0.4-1.1 pounds, average 0.68 pound (79) Immature male, 0.3-1.1 pounds, average 0.72 pound (332) Immature female, 0.3-0.9 pound, average 0.64 pound (265)

IDENTIFICATION

Field

The smallest of ducks, the green-winged teal is one of the fastest fliers, and, where abundant, occurs in larger flocks than similar species. In the marshes of the semi-arid West as well as on major winter grounds, flocks of several hundred greenwings are common; elsewhere they frequently occur in flocks of 50 to 100.

Greenwings in flight have a wing beat almost as fast as diving ducks, but their wings are longer and narrower in proportion to the body. They often dart about in flight like shorebirds. As they twist and turn in the air the white flash of their bellies distinguishes them from the brown-bellied blue-winged teal. But early in the fall, the bellies of immature greenwings are suffused with brown and are not distinctive. The green speculum usually is evident against the otherwise brown-gray wing and may provide the only color readily visible in flight. In some lights, the speculum appears dark, but its white or buff borders are readily visible.

On the water there is little to distinguish hens, immatures, and eclipse-plumaged drakes from blue-winged teal in the same plumages. The plumages of these greenwings have a gray-brown tone compared with the darker brown of the blue-winged teal. In mixed flocks viewed from an aircraft, the gray-brown plumage of the green-winged teal is noticeably lighter than the chocolate-brown plumage of the blue-winged teal. The first conspicuous mark early in the fall in male green-winged teal is the buffy undertail coverts. At a distance the undertail appears as a light spot, especially noticeable against the darker body plumage.

During the fall, both immature and adult drake greenwings are molting from henlike plumages into brighter breeding plumages. Full breeding plumage may be assumed as early as mid-October by some adults and as late as mid-December by late-hatched immatures.

The head is the last visible area to acquire breeding plumage. Drakes in full breeding plumage are distinguished while at rest by the chestnut-red head with a dark green stripe sweeping backward from the eye. A vertical white stripe extends from the breast to the shoulder, and, at a distance, is the most noticeable field mark. The green speculum is usually visible, but at times it is covered by the flank feathers.

At Hand

Green-winged teal are the size of pigeons and both sexes have white breasts and bellies. The male in breeding plumage is extremely colorful. In addition to the cinnamon-red head and green eye-stripe, the chest is pink-brown speckled with black; the back, sides, and flanks are vermiculated gray, separated from the chest by a white bar; the undertail coverts are buff on the outside, black in the center; the uppertail coverts are black and so is the bill; and the legs and feet are gray.

Female green-winged teal are mottled brown and the sides of the head and throat are paler than the crown; a dark brown line extends from the bill through the eye. The back and rump are a shade darker and less mottled than the breast, sides, and flanks. Black speckles on the blue-black bill distinguish females from males in all plumages; the legs and feet are a light gray.

Early in the fall both adult and immature males resemble females. As the fall progresses, the bright colors of the male breeding plumage gradually appear until even the head assumes its full color. The V-notched gray-brown tail feathers are the last vestige of immature plumage to be shed.

The wings provide a means of separating sex and age groups. Wing coverts of adult males are gray, the greater coverts tipped with buff-brown. The coverts of adult females are slightly browner, the lesser and middle ones with a light halo margin, the outer greater coverts tipped with white, the inner ones with buff. The green part of the speculum, in relation to the black, is slightly smaller in the female than in the male.

The wings (coverts, primaries, tertials) of immature greenwings are a shade browner than those of adult females. The two outermost tertials are edged with white, bordered by a clearly marked black streak on the outermost one in the male and by an indistinct dusky line in the female. The outer tertials in the adult female are indistinctly edged with buff.

POPULATION STATUS

Because of its small size and its predilection for emergent vegetation, the green-winged teal is overlooked a great deal more frequently on aerial surveys than any other common duck. Comparisons of simultaneous ground and aerial counts have been used to determine visibility indices for various regions and habitats in order to adjust the data from aerial surveys. Of necessity, especially larger correction factors have been applied to the breeding ground figures obtained from aerial surveys. Large correction factors result in greater unreliability of the data. It is in this context that the population status and distribution data are presented.

Like all species, the numbers of green-winged teal on the breeding grounds fluctuate from year to year, a reflection of the productivity and mortality of the previous season. In spite of these yearly fluctuations, there is a pronounced upward trend for the period 1955-74; this trend is particularly evident after 1959.

Winter surveys across the United States during the same period also show a valid upward trend in numbers of green-winged teal. Although all four flyways show upward trends in numbers of green-winged teal, the magnitude of increase among flyways varies. The trend is lowest for the Pacific Flyway, higher for the Atlantic Flyway, and still higher—and about equally so—for the Mississippi and Central Flyways.

The green-winged teal has undoubtedly prospered at a time that many other species have not. Perhaps this healthy condition of the greenwing's population relates to the large proportion that breed north of the agricultural lands of Canada. Because so many breed in the wetlands of the boreal forest, populations of this species have not suffered the attrition resulting from habitat loss experienced by species more confined to the prairies of Canada.

Annual inventories of breeding populations, conducted by the U.S. Fish and Wildlife Service, average 1,992,000 for 1955-74. Perhaps 200,000 nest elsewhere through the boreal forest of Ontario and Quebec and the Intermountain valleys of the West and Northwest. Even so, this number is far below the 3,225,000 adults estimated as the average preseason population by Moisan et al. (1967), who used band and kill data to arrive at this figure.

Age Ratios

The proportion of immature to adult green-winged teal found in hunters' bags across the United States, 1961-73, was 1.69. Banding data analyzed by Moisan et al. (1967) indicated that immature greenwings are 1.23 times more readily killed by hunters than are adults. Hence, the fall population of greenwings contains about 1.37 young for each adult.

Sex Ratios

Among adult greenwings taken by hunters in the United States, males have predominated by 2.26:1 (69.3 percent). In immatures, the sex ratios have been more even, 0.9 male per female (47.4 percent). Assuming that immatures are one-third more abundant in the fall population than adults, the sex ratio for the species is 56.6 percent male. Because of hunter selectivity for drakes, the sex ratio is probably more even than that shown by hunters' kill.

Mortality

Preseason bandings of green-winged teal indicate an annual mortality rate of 62.8 percent for immatures and of 58.5 percent for adults (Moisan et al. 1967). Hence, about 60 percent of the fall population is lost within the year. The data cited here on mortality and productivity approach a balance between the two population forces.

DISTRIBUTION

The three races of green-winged teal encircle the northern hemisphere during summer and extend in winter to northern South America, central Africa, southern India, Burma, and the Philippines. In North America, the race *Anas crecca carolinensis* occurs across the continent, but it is joined in the Aleutian Islands by *A. c. nimia*, which apparently remains there throughout the year. Across Eurasia, *A. c. crecca* has exclusive domain but occasionally strays into the United States.

Breeding Range

The North American green-winged teal breeds from the Aleutian Islands, northern Alaska, Mackenzie River delta, northern Saskatchewan, Manitoba, Ontario, Quebec, and Labrador south to central California, central Utah, southern Colorado, central Nebraska, central Kansas, southern Minnesota, Wisconsin, Ontario, Quebec, Newfoundland, and the Maritime Provinces.

Although small in size, the greenwing is hardy; and, except for the pintail and the wigeon, it is the most abundant dabbling duck on Arctic breeding grounds. Over 160,000 greenwings occur in Alaska during summer. They are most abundant on the Yukon Flats, where the population numbers 58,000 (5.4 per square mile). Other important Alaskan breeding grounds are: Tanana-Kuskokwim basins, 32,000 (3.5 per square mile); Yukon Delta, 35,000 (1.3 per square mile); Innoko Basin, 8,500 (2.5 per square mile); Seward Peninsula-Kotzebue Bay marshes, 11,000 (1.2 per square mile); and Bristol Bay marshes, 7,400 (0.75 per square mile). Although the Copper Delta is a small area, a density of 1.9 green-winged teal per square mile attests to its high quality.

In Arctic Canada, green-winged teal populations are calculated at 20,000: 14,000 (2.7 per square mile) are found on the Mackenzie Delta and 4,700 (2.4 per square mile) on Old Crow Flats. Subarctic deltas support 122,000 greenwings (6.1 per square mile), with 83,000 in the Slave River parklands and about 20,000 each on deltas of the Athabasca and Saskatchewan rivers, 2.3 and 2.9 per square mile.

Water areas in the open boreal forest shelter slightly over 100,000 greenwings (0.55 per square mile), and about 900,000 (2.1 per square mile) reside in the western closed boreal forest. The number of greenwings nesting in the closed boreal forest of eastern Canada (Ontario, Quebec, and the Maritimes) is problematical. Based upon the number that migrate into the United States from this region (band recoveries, kills, and winter populations), a rough estimate is 250,000.

Like many ducks, greenwings are abundant in the Canadian parklands, where 335,000 (3.7 per square mile) breed. As is also true of many other species, the density of greenwing populations is greatest in the parklands of Alberta (5.6 per square mile), least in those of Manitoba (1.9 per square mile), and intermediate in Saskatchewan (3.1 per square mile).

Like most other ducks, greenwings are both more numerous and more dense in the mixed prairie association (230,000 or 1.3 per square mile) than in the shortgrass association (120,000 or 0.8 per square mile). In the shortgrass areas of Montana, greenwings reach their greatest abundance of 70,000 but with a density of only 1.0 per square mile. Although they are less abundant in southern Alberta (11,000) and southwestern Saskatchewan (16,000), densities average respectively 0.8 and 1.4 per square mile. There are about 27,000 greenwings west of the Missouri River in the Dakotas, where they average 0.6 per square mile.

Because the mixed prairie association in south-central Saskatchewan is so vast, greenwings there number 93,000 but have a density of only 2.5 per square mile. However, in southwest Manitoba there is a density of 3.7 per square mile even though the population numbers a mere 33,000. Greenwings number 46,000 (1.9 per square mile) in central Alberta and 36,000 (0.55 per square mile) in eastern North and South Dakota.

Perhaps 55,000 greenwings breed in the Intermountain valleys of the United States and British Columbia: 32,000 about Great Salt Lake, Utah; 12,000 in British Columbia; 3,500 in Washington, three-fourths in the Columbia Basin; 3,300 throughout the mountain ranges of Colorado; 2,500 in Idaho and western Montana; and 1,200 in Oregon. Almost 10,000 nest in the Great Lakes states, roughly two-thirds in Minnesota, one-third in Wisconsin, and a few in Michigan and northwestern Ohio. Small numbers have been found nesting as far south as the Cheyenne Bottoms Wildlife Area, Kansas (Marvin Schwilling), and Burford Lake in northwestern New Mexico (Huey and Travis 1961) and as far east as the Montezuma Refuge in New York (Cummings 1963).

Migration Corridors

About 85 percent of the 350,000 green-winged teal adults and young originating on Alaskan breeding grounds migrate along two corridors to British Columbia, Washington, Oregon, and California. Waterfowl censuses in British Columbia suggest that the coastal corridor is used by four times as many greenwings as the interior corridor. The remaining 15 percent migrate through the plains of Alberta and the United States to Texas (one-third) and Louisiana (two-thirds).

The 900,000 greenwings from the Northwest Territories of Canada divide about equally between the Pacific Flyway and the Central Flyway, including Louisiana. About 60 percent of those entering the Central Flyway head for Texas and 40 percent for Louisiana. Comparatively small numbers migrate to areas east of the Great Plains.

Forty percent of Alberta's fall population of 1,600,000 greenwings migrate to the Pacific Coast states; 15 percent to the Rocky Mountain states farther east; 30 percent to the Central Flyway, with Texas and Louisiana, the principal recipients, sharing almost equally; and 15 percent to the Mississippi Flyway states, largely Minnesota and Iowa.

Of the 950,000 greenwings that originate in Saskatchewan, 15 percent migrate to California via Utah, about 9

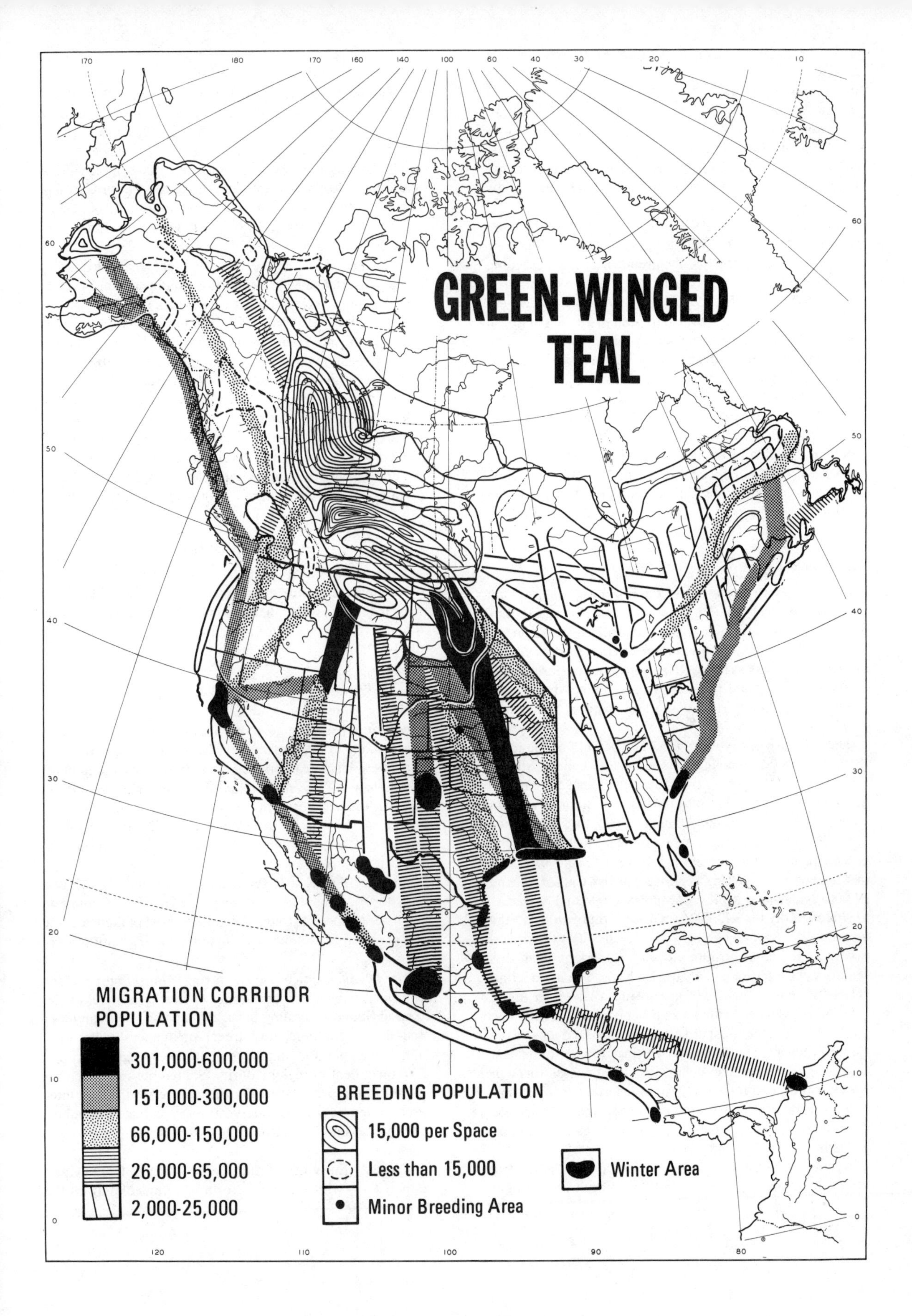

GREEN-WINGED TEAL
MIGRATION CORRIDOR POPULATION
301,000-600,000
151,000-300,000
66,000-150,000
26,000-65,000
2,000-25,000
BREEDING POPULATION
15,000 per Space
Less than 15,000
Minor Breeding Area
Winter Area

percent migrate to the eastern Rocky Mountains, and 47 percent to the Great Plains states—about one-third to Texas and two-thirds to Louisiana. Mississippi Flyway states, mostly Minnesota, Iowa, Illinois, and Arkansas, receive 22 percent. Only 7 percent of Saskatchewan's greenwings make their way to Ontario, Quebec, New York, and South Carolina.

About two-thirds of Manitoba's 240,000 greenwings move into states of the Mississippi Flyway and here we include Louisiana. Most of the greenwings from breeding grounds west of Manitoba reach Louisiana across the eastern Great Plains, but the bulk of Manitoba's Louisiana-bound greenwings follow the Mississippi River migration corridor. Twenty percent of the greenwings from Manitoba migrate almost due south across the eastern Great Plains to Texas and about 8 percent move east or southeast to such diverse regions as Ontario and Florida.

Probably 90 percent of the green-winged teal migrating into the Atlantic Flyway originate from breeding grounds in Ontario, Quebec, Labrador, Newfoundland, and the Maritimes. Only small numbers from Manitoba and Saskatchewan reach winter areas in South Carolina and Florida.

Winter Areas

In addition to their vast breeding range, American green-winged teal have an extensive winter range. Small numbers are sometimes found as far north as Alaska on the Pacific Coast and Newfoundland on the Atlantic, with moderate numbers as far south as northern South America. In the interior, small numbers of greenwings have been found as far north as Montana, South Dakota, Minnesota, and Michigan.

The Mississippi Flyway winters 55 percent of the more than 1,200,000 greenwings found in the United States. Some 600,000 (95 percent) of these winter in the coastal marshes and rice fields of Louisiana; Arkansas winters 15,000, Mississippi 5,000, Alabama 4,000, and Tennessee 3,000. The Pacific Flyway is second in importance for the greenwing in winter, accounting for about 280,000: 21,000 in Washington; 10,000 in Oregon; 225,000 in California; and 24,000 divided among Nevada, Idaho, Utah, and Arizona.

Undoubtedly the 123,000 greenwings that winter on the west coast of Mexico belong to the Pacific Flyway population. Largest concentrations occur in lagoons near Los Mochis (39,000), near Culiacán (62,000), and near Mazatlán (11,000). Some of the 43,000 greenwings that winter in the Interior Highlands of Mexico probably pass through the Pacific Flyway, but most are considered to be ducks of the Central Flyway. The 13,000 greenwings found on the east coast of Mexico are also believed to have passed through states of the Central Flyway. Although most of the greenwings on the east coast winter between the Rio Grande Delta and Tampico, small numbers occur as far south as Yucatan.

About 198,000 greenwings winter in states of the Central Flyway. Texas leads with 184,000, about 40 percent (75,000) along the coast, the rest in the interior—almost 100,000 in the Panhandle region. New Mexico harbors about 10,000 greenwings; Oklahoma 1,700; Kansas 1,200; and Nebraska 100.

The Atlantic Flyway winters about 77,000 green-winged teal, about 70 percent (55,000) along the South Carolina coast. North Carolina shelters 9,500; Florida 4,500; Georgia 3,500; Chesapeake Bay 1,500; Delaware 1,200; and New Jersey 1,600.

Occasionally, some green-winged teal leave Florida for Cuba. In aerial surveys of the West Indies during six winters, Walter Crissey found greenwings in Cuba only twice: 5,000 in 1954 and 100 in 1959. The only other greenwings found in this area were also observed in 1959, 120 on the Bahama Islands and 30 in the Dominican Republic.

An aerial survey of waterfowl winter areas in Central and South America, conducted by Glover and Chamberlain (1960) in January 1960, revealed a surprisingly large number of green-winged teal. Although they found but 900 in Central America, there were 40,000 in northern South America, practically all of them on the Magdalena River delta and upstream marshes in northwestern Colombia.

MIGRATION BEHAVIOR

Green-winged teal migrate in larger flocks than do most other ducks. At times as many as several hundred teal may band together. Although they sometimes migrate diurnally, most of their migratory flights are made at night.

Chronology

Fall. Gabrielson and Lincoln (1959) reported that greenwings leave the northern part of their Alaskan breeding grounds in September. On the Yukon Delta, 1970-72, they were last seen between August 21 and September 5 (Mickelson 1973). At Mount McKinley National Park, Alaska, the last observation occurred on September 24.

Fall arrivals in the Alaskan Panhandle have been reported at Craig on August 10, and at Tracy Arm on September 26.

At the Athabasca River delta, in Canada's Northwest Territories, Soper (1951) found greenwings fairly common from September 8 through the month, most of them leaving the area before October 10 but some staying until freeze-up.

The fall migration of the greenwing in most regions of the continent is a protracted affair. In northern areas of the United States, migrating birds appear in early September and flights continue until freeze-up, generally between mid-November and mid-December. They begin migrating into most central regions during September and often remain through December. On their more southerly winter areas, a few greenwings arrive as early as late September, but most do not appear until late November.

Spring. Early in February, green-winged teal begin to depart their winter grounds for areas immediately to the north. As in the fall, the migration period is protracted—departures continue through April. In midway areas greenwings begin to arrive early in March, with peak numbers in early April and the migration extending another month. They begin to arrive on their southern breeding grounds in early April, and numbers increase steadily until mid-May.

At Delta Marsh, Manitoba, the earliest greenwings arrived between April 5 and 12 in 5 years; April 13 and 20 in 7 years; and April 21 and 28 in 3 years (Hochbaum 1955). Near Yellowknife on Great Slave Lake, Canada, greenwings over a 3-year period arrived between April 25 and May 4, with a major influx between May 5 and 15 (Murdy 1964).

Green-winged teal arrived on the Yukon Delta from May 12 to May 23, 1969-72 (Mickelson 1973). Elsewhere in Alaska they have been noted at College on April 27, Mount McKinley National Park on May 17, and on the Porcupine River on May 18 (Gabrielson and Lincoln 1959). On the Mackenzie Delta, Porslid (1943) reported greenwings on May 18 and 25.

BREEDING

Behavior

Most green-winged teal breed as yearlings, as indicated by the large proportion of young to old birds in the fall population. Little is known about their establishment of pair bonds, their homing propensities, or their home ranges.

McKinney (1965) studied the courtship displays of captive green-winged teal. He observed social courtship from the first week in February until mid-June and once on a mild day in early October. He considers that in the wild, courtship continues through the fall, winter, and spring. At the Rockefeller Refuge, Louisiana, in mid-March, virtually all green-winged teal were paired. McKinney (1965) believes that courting groups observed in Manitoba during April represented males gathering around females that were weakly paired.

Nesting

The nests of green-winged teal are so difficult to find that only a few have been studied—and these have been found during searches for all waterfowl nests in the area.

Nest Sites. These small teal are largely upland nesters, locating their nests 2 to 300 feet from water, an average of 95 feet. They utilize available cover but favor unusually dense stands of grass, weeds, and brush. Near Brooks, Alberta, Keith (1961) found most nests in beds of *Juncus*, and in western Montana most nests were located under greasewood bushes (Ellig 1955).

On the Yukon Delta, Alaska, Christian Dau observed a pair of greenwings searching for a nest site on May 27, 1972. The male waited where the pair landed in tall grass while the female made several exploratory excursions through the grass before selecting a site. When she returned to her waiting mate, the pair departed. On June 14, the nest contained a completed clutch of 7 eggs. When approaching her nest, the hen customarily landed 10 to 15 feet away and walked to it, but, when leaving, she always flew directly from the nest after first covering her eggs.

Clutch Size, Eggs, and Incubation. The green-winged teal lays from 5 to 16 eggs, average 8.6 (91). The eggs are dull white, cream, or pale olive-buff, ovate in shape, and measure 45.8 by 34.2 mm (Bent 1923). Bent (1923) and Delacour (1956) give the incubation period as 21 to 23 days.

Chronology of Nesting. One instance in North Dakota, green-winged teal initiated nesting on April 20 (Page and Cassel 1971). At Yellowknife, Northwest Territories, Canada, the span of nest initiation varied from 28 to 34 days within the period May 29-July 1 (Murdy 1964). At Minto Lakes, Alaska, greenwings commenced nesting as early as June 1 and as late as July 20 (Rowinski 1958), with a span of 33 days. At Anaktuvuk Pass, Alaska, nesting began on June 5 (Irving 1960).

Nest Success. We know the fate of only 104 greenwing nests—only 32 (31 percent) hatched successfully. This unusually low nest success may not be typical of the species. The lowest nest success, 2 of 24 nests, occurred near Lousana, Alberta (Smith 1971), and the highest success, 11 of 15 nests, was reported from western Montana (Girard 1941).

Little is known about the renesting potential of green-winged teal. Keith (1961) determined that 15 pairs on his study area near Brooks, Alberta, produced 21 nests. Among 10 species of ducks studied, the greenwing, with 1.4 nests per pair, was about midway between the mallard (2.15 nests per pair) and the redhead (0.45).

Nest Failure. Skunks, other mammals, crows, and magpies are the principal known agents of nest destruction.

Rearing of Young

Broods. Drake green-winged teal desert their hens during early stages of egg incubation, leaving their mates the task of rearing the young. Hens lead their day-old ducklings to nearby ponds, sloughs, and marshes.

Development. At Yellowknife, Northwestern Territories, most young greenwings commenced flying between July 22 and August 12, about 35 days after hatching (Murdy 1964). At Minto Lakes, Alaska, dates of hatch and flight dates indicated a fledging period of 34 days (Hooper 1951). Similar data for the Yukon Flats, Alaska, also indicated a 34-day fledging period (Lensink 1954). Young greenwings have the fastest growth rate of all ducks.

Survival. In the downy stage (Class I), green-winged

GREEN-WINGED TEAL

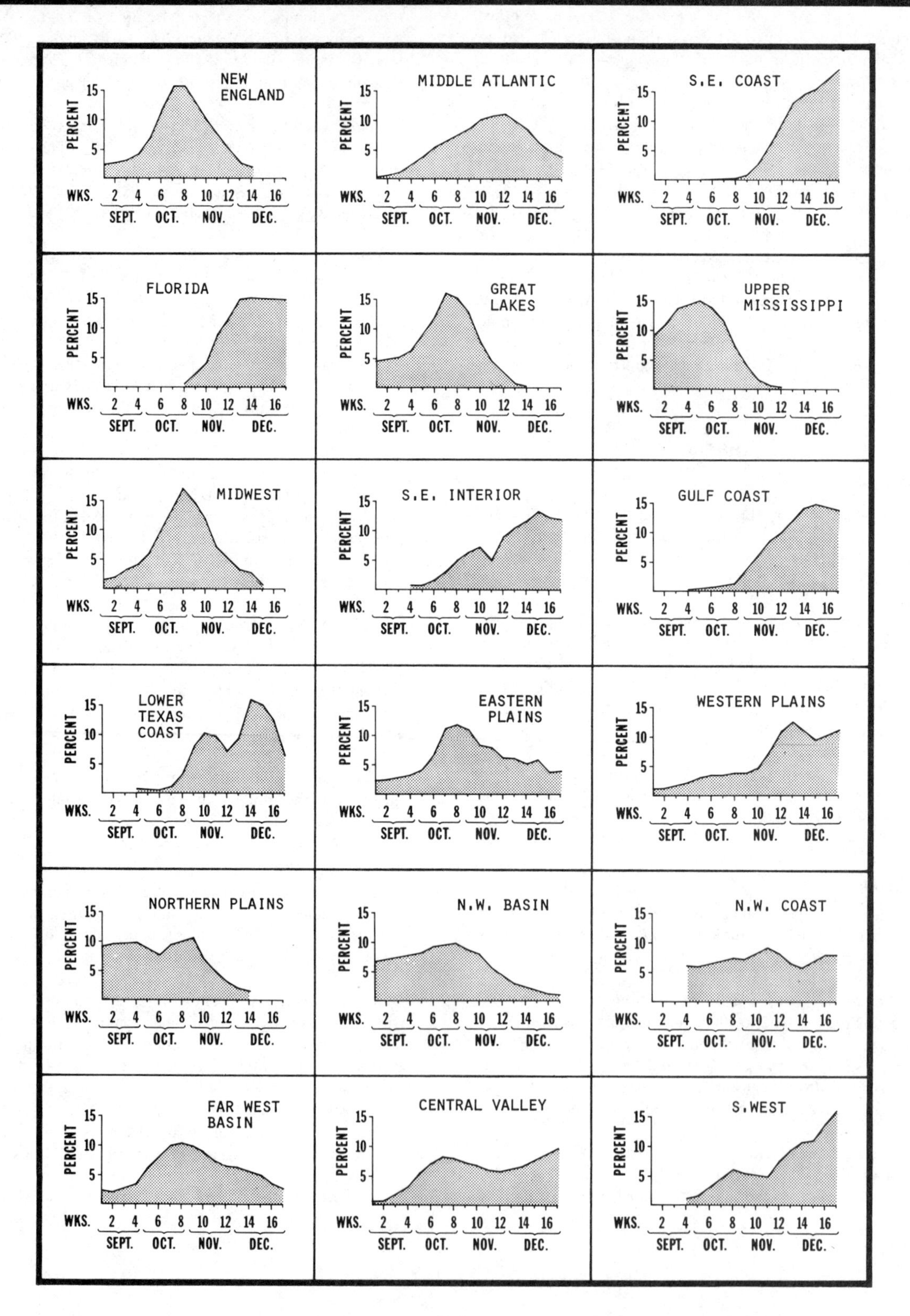

Fall

GREEN-WINGED TEAL

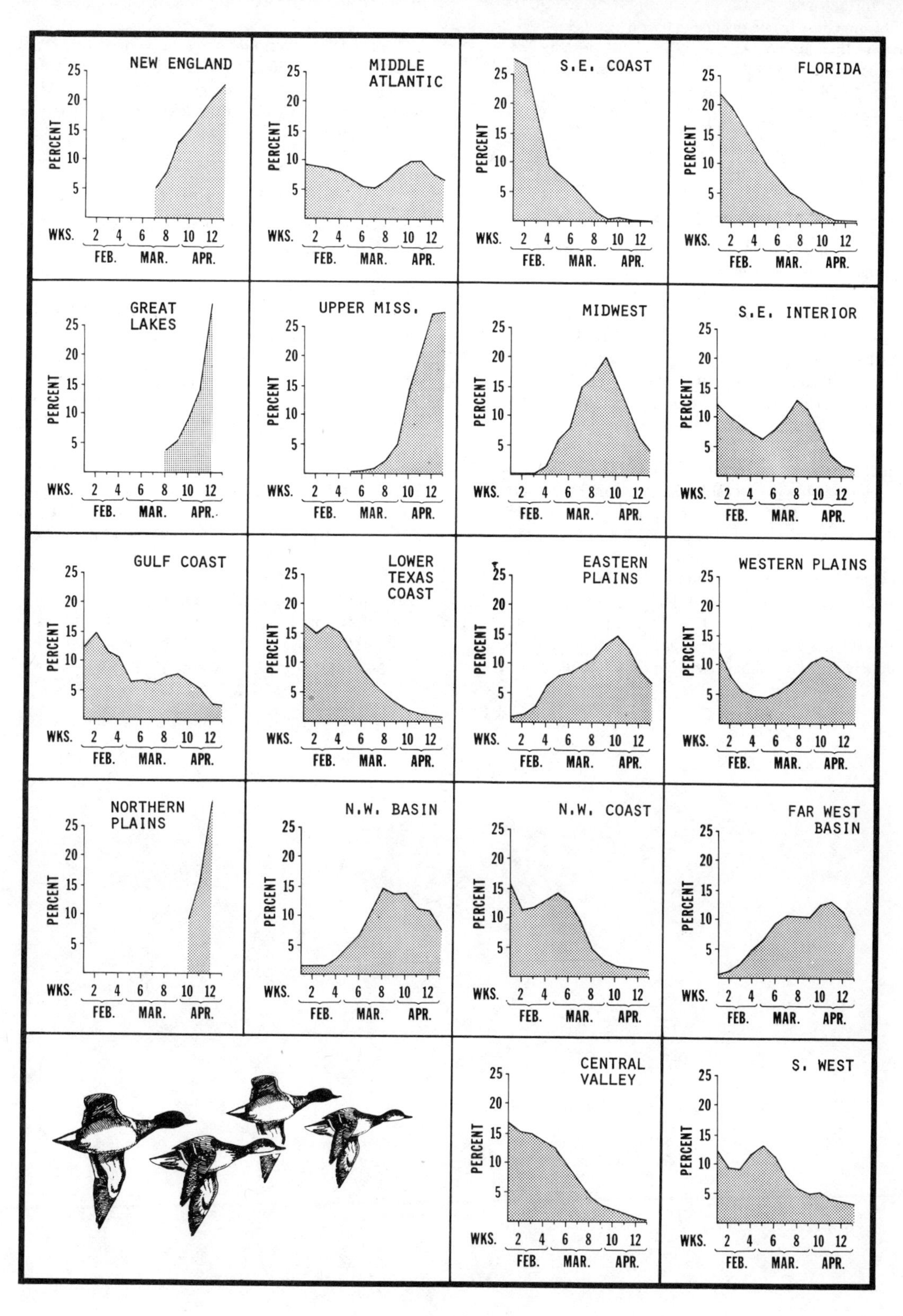

Spring

teal broods average 7.0 young (177). By the time they have reached Class II, broods average 5.7 young (214), a decrease of 19 percent. Class III broods average 5.4 ducklings (128), a further decline of 5 percent and a decline of 23 percent from Class I. The decline in brood size is lower for greenwings than for most species of ducks. A nest success of 31 percent and a brood size of 5.4 yields 0.88 flying young per adult, a number appreciably lower than that indicated by age ratios.

POSTBREEDING SEASON

After deserting their hens, drake green-winged teal move to large marshes or lakes preparatory to the wing molt. In Idaho, the earliest drake desertion of hens occurred on June 12; they entered the eclipse molt on July 3, and the first flightless drakes were noted on July 11 (Oring 1964).

At Delta Marsh, green-winged teal drakes arrive from considerable distances between mid-June and early July for molting (Hochbaum 1944). Some hens arrive later, for more flightless hens are observed in August than during the breeding season.

A noted area for molting greenwings is the Pel-Kutawagan marshes in central Saskatchewan. There, during July 9-24, 1955-58, Sterling (1966) captured 4,316 flightless adult greenwings, second in abundance to the pintail. On the coast of Hudson Bay, near Fort Severn, George Arthur captured 32 flightless adult drakes and 5 flightless adult hens between July 3 and August 17, 1955.

On aerial surveys by Ducks Unlimited, conducted north of the parklands between the Athabasca River and the Saskatchewan Delta, William Leitch reported thousands of green-winged teal on Niska Lake, August 25, 1940. He estimated 20 per acre on Macallum Lake, August 24, 1941; 500 per mile for 8 miles of Gipsy Lake shoreline, August 20, 1947; and 300 per mile of shoreline on Canoe Lake, August 24, 1950.

Occasionally, even female green-winged teal make extended premolt flights. Four adult flightless hens were captured near Puxico, Missouri, on September 25, 1963 (Rogers 1967), at least 500 miles south of their nearest breeding area.

FOOD HABITS

The green-winged teal more than any other duck prefers to seek food on mud flats. Where mud flats are lacking, they prefer the shallowest of marshes or temporarily flooded agricultural lands.

On mud flats, greenwings pick up seeds of moist soil plants (nutgrasses, millets, smartweeds, water hemp) deposited in previous years, as well as insects and mollusca. Green-winged and blue-winged teal have similar food habits and are often found feeding together. Greenwings seem to favor mud flats and the seeds of moist soil plants, and bluewings show a predilection for ponds and marshes supporting beds of pondweeds and other submerged aquatic vegetation.

Greenwings appear to prefer the small seeds of nutgrasses, millets, water hemp, and sedges to larger seeds, but, when necessary, they have utilized corn, wheat, barley, and buttonbush seeds.

In marshes, sloughs, and ponds, greenwings select the seeds of bulrushes, pondweeds, and spike rushes. To a lesser extent they feed upon the vegetative parts of muskgrass, pondweeds, widgeon grass, and duckweeds.

Eurasian Green-Winged Teal

Anas crecca crecca

Other Common Names: European teal, Eurasian teal, common teal, whistler teal (Russian)

VITAL STATISTICS

Length:	Male, 14.2-15.6 inches, average 15 inches (8)
	Female, 12.7-13.7 inches, average 13.2 inches (3)
Wing:	Male, 6.9-7.6 inches, average 7.2 inches
	Female, 6.8-7.1 inches, average 7.0 inches

IDENTIFICATION

The Eurasian green-winged teal is a rare visitor to eastern North America. Seldom, therefore, is one likely to be seen in the field. At best, only the adult drakes of the Eurasian green-winged teal and the American green-winged teal can be separately identified; those in eclipse plumage, the females, and the immatures are so nearly identical as to be indistinguishable.

Principal differences in adult drakes are: the Eurasian green-winged teal displays a highly visible horizontal white line between the gray flanks and back; a cream line extends in a half-circle from the bill, above the green eye swatch, to the back of the head. The American green-winged teal has a vertical white band extending across the gray side.

The Aleutian teal (*Anas crecca nimia*) has been established as a race of the Eurasian green-winged teal. The two are identical in appearance but the Aleutian teal is slightly larger.

DISTRIBUTION

The Eurasian green-winged teal breeds across Europe and Asia, from Iceland, Finland, and to 70° north latitude in Russia and Siberia east to the Bering Sea and south to southern France, northern Italy, Romania, northern Iran, northwest Mongolia and Manchuria, and Japan. It winters along the coasts of Europe from Norway to the Black Sea; in Africa, in Nigeria and Kenya; and also in Iran, India, Burma, much of China, Formosa, Korea, and the Philippines.

Because it covers so vast an area in both Europe and Asia, Bull (1964) proposed that its common name be changed to Eurasian teal, certainly more appropriate geographically than the formerly used European designation.

In over a century, fewer than 50 records of the Eurasian green-winged teal have been reported in North America. All but five have been along the Atlantic Seaboard from Hamilton Inlet, Labrador, to Charleston, South Carolina.

Most reports of this teal have come from Long Island, New York, and northeastern New Jersey (Bull 1964), perhaps in part because of the large number of bird watchers there. West of the Atlantic Seaboard, it was observed two different years near Lexington, Virginia, once at Lake Cayuga, New York, once in northwestern Pennsylvania, and once at Buckeye Lake, east of Columbus, Ohio. On the 1972 Audubon Christmas bird count, three were reported south of Canada: one in New Jersey, one in Delaware, and one in North Carolina (American Birds 1973). In addition, two were reported at Vancouver Island, British Columbia.

Seldom has more than one Eurasian green-winged teal been sighted, and it is usually with a small flock of American green-winged teal.

The Aleutian teal (with the exception of a few stragglers to British Columbia) is confined to the Aleutian Islands throughout the year. Gabrielson and Lincoln (1959) quoted Murie as reporting it to be the most abundant dabbling duck. They also stated that Frank Beals found it common to plentiful at all seasons of the year from Unimak to Amchitka.

There is a pronounced difference between the proportions of Aleutian teal and American green-winged teal on Izembek and Aleutian Islands wildlife refuges. The Izembek National Wildlife Range is near the tip of the Alaska Peninsula, beyond which stretch the Aleutians for 1,100 miles. Refuge reports, 1967-69, indicate that on Izembek, Aleutian teal have ranged in number from 50 to 100, while American green-winged teal have ranged from 1,500 to 4,000. But on the Aleutian Islands Refuge, Aleutian teal have numbered 85,000 to 100,000—greenwings, 500 to 8,500. The proportion of Aleutian to American green-winged teal is 1:36 at Izembek, 20:1 in the Aleutians. The data for the Aleutian Islands represent rough approximations of waterfowl populations rather than the actual numbers.

Mallard

Anas platyrhynchos platyrhynchos

Other Common Names: Greenhead (drake); gray duck (hen); susie (hen)

VITAL STATISTICS

Length: Adult male, 20.4-27.5 inches, average 24.7 inches (101)
Adult female, 21.7-24.7 inches, average 23.1 inches (11)
Immature male, 18.4-26.0 inches, average 22.3 inches (87)
Immature female, 19.8-21.5 inches, average 20.4 inches (5)

Wing: Adult male, 11.4 inches (1,392)
Adult female, 10.6 inches (590)
Immature male, 11.0 inches (996)
Immature female, 10.4 inches (750)

Weight: Adult male, 1.5-3.8 pounds, average 2.75 pounds (1,809)
Adult female, 1.2-3.8 pounds, average 2.44 pounds (1,417)
Immature male, 1.2-3.6 pounds, average 2.63 pounds (3,186)
Immature female, 1.1-3.7 pounds, average 2.31 pounds (2,402)

Comparison of Vital Statistics

Female mallards at 135 days of age.*

Measurement (inches or pounds)	Wild	Game Farm
Length	21.6 (14)	22.1 (30)
Wing	10.5 (30)	10.5 (30)
Bill	2.15 (14)	1.96 (30)
Tarsus	1.76 (14)	1.81 (30)
Weight	2.38 (14)	2.65 (30)

*Greenwood (1972)

Note: Game-farm mallards have longer bodies, longer tarsi, and shorter bills and weigh more than wild mallards.

IDENTIFICATION

Field

Flocks are well formed, usually in V's or U's and with 40 to 60 members but often as many as several hundred; flocks tend to be larger than those of other species. The wing beat is slower than in other ducks, with a shallower stroke largely below the horizontal plane of the body.

The wing of the mallard is broad in proportion to its length; only the wood duck among dabbling ducks has a broader wing. The broad wing and the relatively short tail create the impression that the wings are set far back on the body.

The green head, brown chest, violet-blue speculum, and white outer tail feathers characterize the drake in one or more flight attitudes; only the violet speculum distinguishes the somber brownish hen in flight. Her whitish outer tail feathers are splotched with brown and are therefore inconspicuous. The white underwings flash with each wing stroke in both sexes, contrasting with the darker outer margins of the primaries.

At rest, the mallard's large size and stocky build are apparent. The drake's white neck-ring, separating the green head from the chestnut-brown chest, contrasts with the gray sides, brownish back, black rump, and black upper- and undertail coverts. A dark line formed by the folded wings and extending from the neck to the tail, separating the gray sides from the gray scapulars, is noticeable at distances up to 75 yards.

The blue speculum is seldom evident in resting drakes but, oddly, appears in a small proportion of resting hens.

The mallard is the most vociferous of game ducks. Its calls are especially noticeable during the fall, when other species are inclined to be quiet. The mallard has a variety of quacks that set the standard of comparison with other species, and for hunters attempting to call ducks.

At Hand

The violet-blue speculum bordered by a pronounced white stripe at the front and back identifies the mallard in any plumage. The bill is yellow to yellowish green in the drakes and orange splotched with black in the hen. Legs and feet are coral-red in the adult drake, yellowish orange in the immature drake, and less vividly colored in the respective age-classes of the hen.

Hens are straw-brown, streaked with dark brown, more heavily on the back than on the belly. The crown of the head is dark brown with a dark brown stripe through the eye. The remainder of the head and neck is lighter brown than the upper body. The overall appearance is of a mottled brown duck similar in color to the hen northern shoveler and gadwall.

The drakes enter the eclipse molt in June, and from then until late September they resemble the hens. A few adult drakes still show traces of their eclipse plumage in November. The plumage of the immature is similar to that of the hen. Early-hatched young begin to acquire their first nuptial plumage in late August, and by mid-October they closely resemble adults. Some late-hatched drakes may resemble hens as late as mid-November. A few green feathers on the cheek distinguish late-molting adult and immature drakes from hens.

POPULATION STATUS

The mallard is the number one duck in the United States, in North America, and in the Northern Hemisphere. It reaches its zenith of abundance in mid-America, between the Appalachian and Rocky Mountains. In the heartland of its breeding range—annually surveyed by the U. S. Fish and Wildlife Service—an average 20-year (1955-74) population in May was 8,700,000. According to Pospahala et al. (1974), this figure represents about 84 percent of the estimated population of breeding mallards. Numbers of breeding mallards have ranged from a high of 12,690,000 in 1958 to a low of 5,837,000 in 1965.

During 1955-59 and 1970-73, mallard numbers exceeded the 20-year average; during 1960-69 they were below the average. The trend in mallard populations, 1955-74, from both breeding ground surveys and January inventories is similar—down slightly over 20 percent. Because the two high population periods so greatly exceeded the low period, the trend line does not fit well, but perhaps it is significant that the second high was 2,400,000 lower than the earlier one in 1958.

The 20-year trends of winter numbers in the four flyways are different. Both the Atlantic and Mississippi flyways show proportionately large declines in numbers. Wintering mallards in the Central Flyway have shown only an insignificant decline in numbers, and the Pacific Flyway shows a slight upward trend.

Age Ratios

The proportion of immature to adult mallards in hunters' bags, 1961-73, averaged 1.23:1. During this period, immatures were 1.36 times more readily killed by hunters than were adults (Anderson et al. 1970). A correction of the combined age ratios for vulnerability to the gun disclosed that fall populations of mallards in the United States were composed of 0.9 immature per adult. However, computing the average age ratios (corrected for vulnerability) on the basis of each year, 1961-72, results in 1.03 immatures per adult. These data suggest that the average fall population is composed about equally of immatures and adults.

Sex Ratios

The sex ratio in mallards has been determined from the kill and from visual counts of drakes and hens. Hunters intentionally and perhaps unintentionally select for drakes. Banding data, 1967-69, showed that adult males were 1.31 times more readily bagged than adult females; and the corresponding rate for immature males over immature hens was 1.28 (Anderson et al. 1970). Sex ratios of mallards found in hunters' bags across the United States, 1966-73, when corrected for selectivity, showed that 62.3 percent of the adults in the fall population and 50.7 percent of the immatures were drakes. If immatures and adults are in equal proportions, about 57 percent of the mallard population in the fall is made up of drakes.

Visual counts of the sexes during the spring have shown that drakes composed 52.6 percent of the population (Bellrose et al. 1961). Similar tallies on breeding marshes have recorded the percentage of drakes as 51.1.

By any means of appraisal, the mallard has the most balanced sex ratios of all the common game ducks. The margin of surplus drakes in mallard populations is small but appears to be increasing. From 1966 to 1969, adult drakes composed 59 percent of the kill corrected for their vulnerability; from 1970 to 1974, adult drakes composed 64 percent of the kill. This change suggests that the "health" of mallard populations in recent years is below normal.

Mortality

The killing of mallards by hunters replaces some natural losses, but, in general, the more ducks hunters kill the greater the overall mortality (Hickey 1952). Consequently, depending largely upon shooting pressure, mortality rates vary annually by age-classes and by regions, but differing rates between sex-classes are more affected by the greater nonhunting losses suffered by hens than by drakes.

The death rate of mallards in the United States, determined from winter bandings, 1950-64, was 37.8 percent for drakes and 43.9 percent for hens (Martinson 1966). (Preseason bandings would indicate higher mortality rates.) Since recovery rates the first hunting season after banding were 27 percent higher for drakes than for hens, the above percentages illustrate the greater natural mortality of hens. Mallard bandings in Illinois also indicated that hens have a higher mortality rate than drakes—46.7 percent to 41.8 percent (Bellrose and Chase 1950).

Where losses from hunting are low in the western half of the Central Flyway, the annual mortality rate for mallard drakes was 25.5 percent, for hens 27.2 percent (Funk et al. 1971). In the eastern half of the Central Flyway, where shooting pressure is greater, the annual mortality rate for drakes was 27.2 percent and for hens was 38.2 percent.

Summer bandings of mallards in Minnesota, 1958-61, indicated that 71 percent of the immatures and 56 percent of the adults meet death each year (Lee et al. 1964). Mallards banded on various breeding grounds had a mortality rate of 68 percent among immatures and 50 percent among adults (Hickey 1952). Seventy percent of the young mallards banded during the summer, 1938-50, at Delta, Manitoba, died during their first year (Brakhage 1953).

The death rate in mallards, derived from preseason bandings in two regions of Washington, points up the effect of regional differences in shooting pressure. At Yakima, in the central part of the state, the annual mortality rate was 57 percent; at Skagit Flats in the northwestern corner of the state, it was 79 percent (Lauckhart 1956). Considering the high annual mortality of both adults and immatures, the mallard has experienced a loss equal to or exceeding 50 percent a year. Therefore, mallards must produce more than one flying young per adult to maintain any given population level. In years when production of young falls below this level, the mallard population declines, and in years when it is above this level, the population increases.

DISTRIBUTION

The mallard is the most abundant and widely distributed duck in the Northern Hemisphere, ranging from the Arctic to the subtropics in Europe, Asia, and North America. The same race occurs throughout its range except for Greenland, where a local race has been recognized. Most forms of domestic ducks owe their origin to the mallard.

Breeding Season

The mallard has the most extensive breeding range of any duck in North America, encompassing the northern one-third of the United States northwestward to the shores of the Bering Sea. However, within this broad range, it has marked areas of preference, reaching its greatest density in the southern regions of Saskatchewan, Alberta, and Manitoba. Crissey (1969) calculated that between 1955 and 1964, 54 percent of the continental mallards bred there. As he and others have pointed out, this is a region of rapidly changing water abundance; about half of the ponds present in May in the prairie parklands are gone by July (Pospahala et al. 1974). And in one year (1955), May ponds numbered over 7,100,000; in another year (1968), they numbered only 1,583,000.

As May ponds change in number, so, roughly, does the mallard breeding population (Pospahala et al. 1974). When numbers of May ponds decline, a larger proportion of mallards overfly the prairies to the lakes of the boreal forest. Unfortunately, the areas north of the prairie parklands are less favorable for mallard reproduction, and the overall productivity of the population declines.

Omitting the Arctic, mallards form about 28 percent of the ducks found on areas surveyed annually (Pospahala et al. 1974). The prairie parklands of south-central Canada support a 20-year average of 17.6 mallards per square mile (4,694,000), the highest of any extensive region. The parkland portion embraces a population of 2,500,000, for a density of 27.3 mallards per square mile, whereas the mixed praire portion holds 2,196,000—a density of 12.5 per square mile.

The subarctic deltas are small but favorable areas. All three (Saskatchewan, Athabasca, Slave) have a 20-year average of 17.2 per square mile, adding up to a population of 347,000. The Athabasca Delta is particularly outstanding with 66.7 mallards per square mile. Such a high population no doubt stems from a large influx of prairie-hatched mallards when ponds farther south are too few.

Meadows, bogs, and marshes of the closed boreal forest west of Ontario contain an average of 4.4 mallards per square mile. This vast region holds 1,857,000 mallards, but a sizable proportion are the result of overflights of the prairie in drought seasons. Pospahala et al. (1974) estimate that 300,000 mallards occupy the boreal forest of eastern Ontario and western Quebec.

The open boreal forest in Canada, north of the closed forest and south and west of the tundra, supports 1.1 mallards per square mile for an average population of 208,000. At the northwestern edge of the open boreal forest are two pockets of wetlands: the Mackenzie Delta and Old Crow Flats. Combined, they summer an average of 38,000 mallards, 5.5. per square mile.

Although 165,000 mallards are distributed throughout Alaska, they are most numerous in the areas of the Yukon Flats, the Yukon Delta, the Tanana-Kuskokwim district, Bristol Bay, and the Innoko River. On the small Copper River delta, mallard numbers are most dense—14.1 per square mile—followed by Yukon Flats at 4.6, Tanana-Kuskokwim at 4.3, Innoko at 3.1, Bristol Bay at 1.2, and Yukon Delta at 1.1.

South and west of the mixed prairie lies the shortgrass region, extending westward from the Missouri River in the Dakotas to include Montana, southwestern Saskatchewan, and southern Alberta. An average of 980,000 mallards breed in this region, a density of 6.8 per square mile. Southern Alberta has a density of 12.7 per square mile, southwestern Saskatchewan 13.5, northern Montana 7.9, and other areas from 3.5 to 5.5 per square mile.

Mallards breed through the moutain ranges of the West from the Yukon Territory as far south as the White Mountains of southern Arizona. This region embraces a population of 950,000, about half in British Columbia, where the Cariboo and Chilcotin plateaus afford excellent breeding conditions. Other populations are distributed as follows: California, 140,000; Washington, 62,000; Utah, 55,000; Oregon, Idaho, and Colorado, 50,000 each; western Wyoming, 34,000; Nevada, 15,000; and western Montana, 12,000.

Mallards breed through the southern Great Plains as far south as southern Texas, where they come into contact with Mexican ducks. The most important breeding grounds in this region are: eastern Wyoming, 110,000; the Sandhills area of central and western Nebraska, 70,000; and the Rainwater Basin of southeastern Nebraska, 6,000. Slightly over 200 nest in the Cheyenne Bottoms of central Kansas.

The Great Lakes states contain about 300,000 breeding mallards distributed thusly: Minnesota, 133,000; Wisconsin, 122,000; Michigan, 47,000; and the Lake Erie marshes, Ohio, about 600. According to Pospahala et al. (1974), 40,000 breed in the Chesapeake Bay and western mid-Atlantic area and almost 24,000 in northeastern United States.

Migration Corridors

Mallards migrate along numerous migration corridors between breeding and winter areas. The corridor with the highest density, followed by 2 million mallards, extends from southeastern Saskatchewan to northwestern Illinois and then south to Tennessee, eastern Arkansas, and Mississippi. A second high-density corridor, with 1.5 million mallards, parallels the upper Missouri River and extends to the area of Stuttgart, Arkansas.

Two important corridors cross the Great Plains: one extends to eastern Kansas and on to east Texas and coastal Louisiana; the other extends to western Nebraska, eastern Colorado, and the Texas Panhandle.

The most important migration corridor in the Far West extends from Alberta to the Columbia Basin of Washington and Oregon. The second largest corridor extends from Alberta to the Snake River near Boise, Idaho. Other corridors lead to the Snake River in eastern Idaho and the Klamath Basin in northern California. From these winter areas, some mallards continue along several corridors to reach the Central Valley of California, and a few continue on into Mexico.

Only small numbers of mallards frequent the Atlantic Flyway north of Long Island, New York, most of these from local breeding populations (Anderson and Henny 1972). From Long Island south, most of the mallards originate from breeding grounds in Ontario. Migration corridors from the lake states to Chesapeake Bay and from the Midwest to South Carolina are used by mallards breeding in the eastern Great Plains region.

Winter Areas

Mallards winter throughout most of the United States and along the West Coast as far north as the Alaska Peninsula, and westward along the Aleutian Chain. They have been found in interior Alaska north to the Arctic Circle, where warm springs provide open water (Gabrielson and Lincoln 1959:146).

If uncensused areas winter about the same concentrations of mallards as the few censused areas, then approximately 33,000 mallards winter in Alaska (Hansen 1956). The largest concentrations have occurred near Petersburg and Ketchikan in the Alexander Archipelago, where 10,000 winter; 2,000 winter at Kodiak.

About 12,000 mallards (9-year average) have been found wintering in British Columbia, largely along the coast. Elswhere in Canada, 5,000 to 10,000 mallards usually winter in Alberta, near Calgary and Edmonton, but in other areas most attempts to remain through the winter have been unsuccessful (William Leitch).

About 1,970,000 mallards were recorded in the Pacific Flyway, 1954-70. The largest concentration of some 750,000 occurred in the Columbia River basin of south-central Washington and north-central Oregon. Fifty thousand wintered around Puget Sound in northwest Washington and 90,000 in the Willamette River valley of western Oregon.

A spectacular buildup of wintering mallards has developed in the Columbia Basin since the mid-1940's. Commencing with only 86,000 mallards in the entire state of Washington in 1947 (Yocom 1951), the number steadily rose to 730,000 in 1960 and has remained at about that level. The additional food sources resulting from the recent establishment of irrigated grain farms attracted this large wintering population.

About 350,000 mallards winter in the Snake River valley near Boise, Idaho, with an additional 90,000 farther east between Twin Falls and American Falls. In California, the marshes of the Central Valley and of San Francisco Bay winter about 410,000 mallards with 75,000 scattered elsewhere in the state. A few thousand winter in extreme southern California, with small numbers extending into Mexico.

Surprisingly, about 60,000 mallards are able to find sufficient open water to spend the winter at six locations in western Montana (Dale Witt). About 3,600 are able to winter in mountain valleys of western Wyoming and 13,000 among the mountains of western Colorado.

Almost 2 million mallards winter in the Central Flyway, all the way from the Missouri River in eastern Montana to the Rio Grande River in New Mexico. Some mallards pass south of the border, for about 2,900 winter in the Interior Highlands of Mexico.

During the 1960's, Kansas became the most important

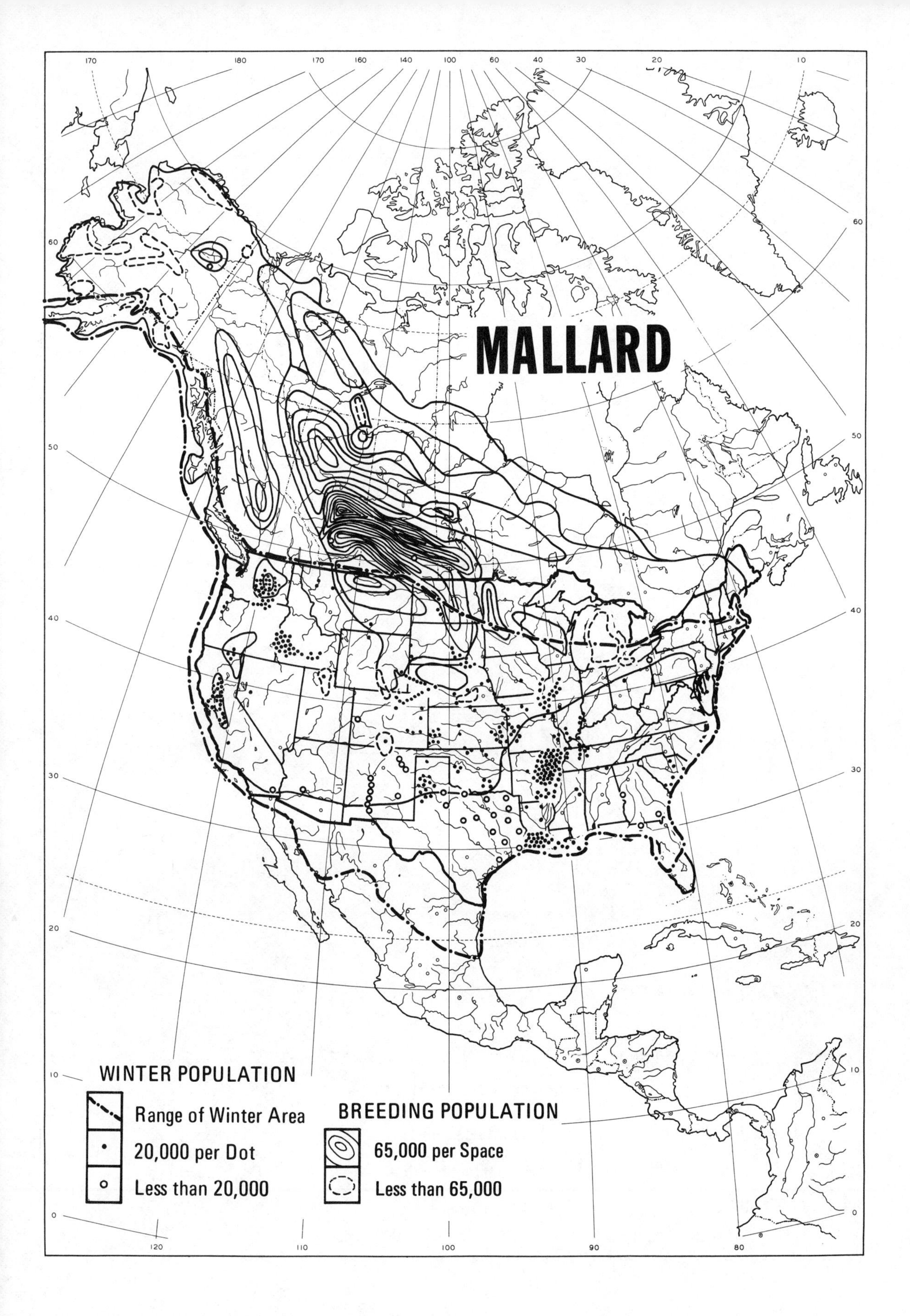
MALLARD
WINTER POPULATION
Range of Winter Area
20,000 per Dot
Less than 20,000
BREEDING POPULATION
65,000 per Space
Less than 65,000

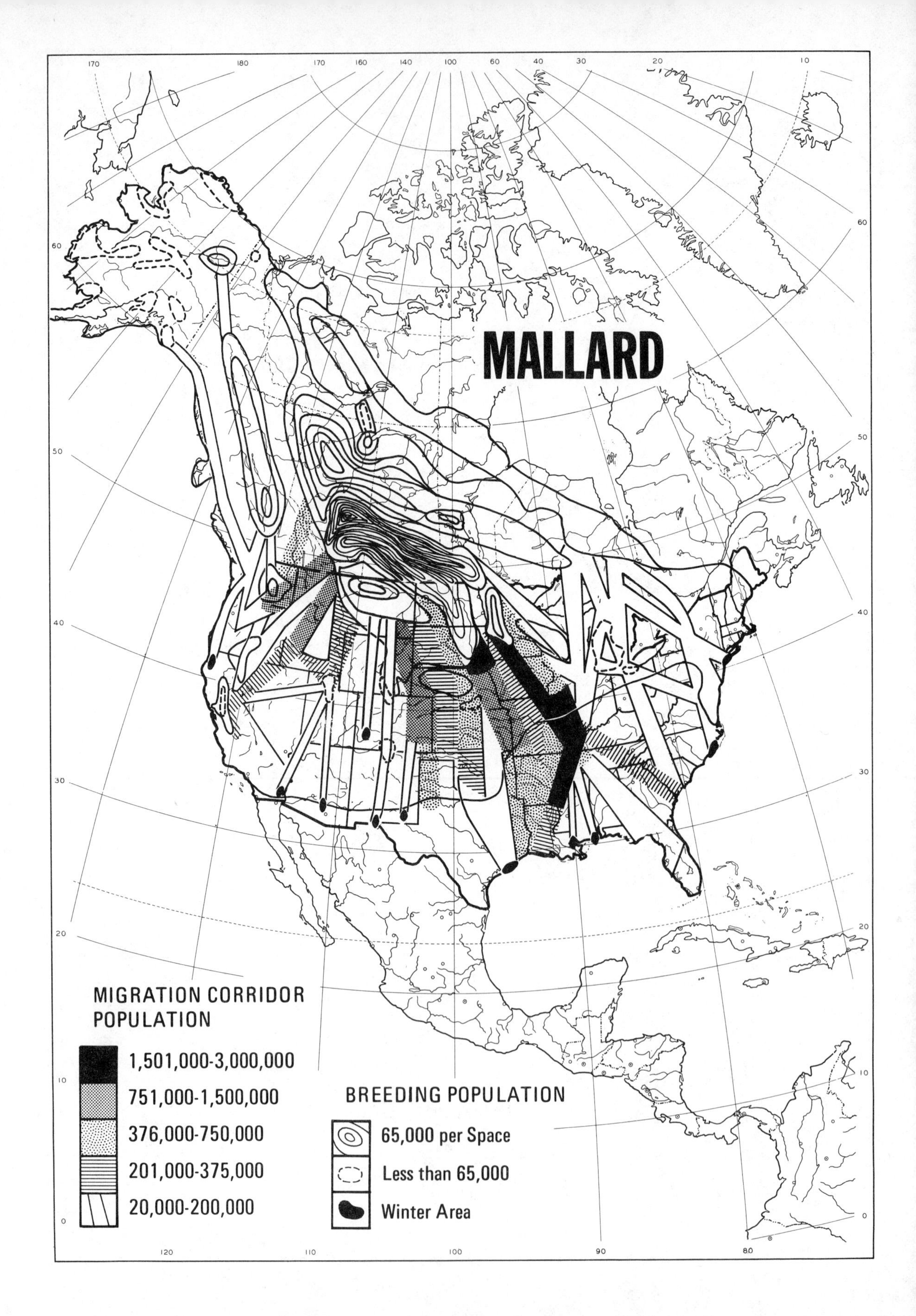
MALLARD
MIGRATION CORRIDOR POPULATION
1,501,000-3,000,000
751,000-1,500,000
376,000-750,000
201,000-375,000
20,000-200,000
BREEDING POPULATION
65,000 per Space
Less than 65,000
Winter Area

state in the Central Flyway for wintering mallards, with an average of 525,000. In 1955, only 144,000 mallards wintered there, but the creation of state and federal refuge areas and the available waste grain in nearby fields resulted in a steady increase in the number of wintering birds through the late 1950's.

Texas is the second most important state for wintering mallards in the Central Flyway, with an average of 420,000; some 300,000 of these are associated with the playa lakes and sorghum fields of the Panhandle. Most of the remaining mallards occur in east Texas, with only 15,000 frequenting the Gulf Coast.

Eastern Colorado winters nearly 300,000 mallards, about two-thirds in the basin of the South Platte River and one-third in the Arkansas River basin. Again, fields of sorghum and corn provide waste grain enabling large concentrations to develop where waters remain at least partly open.

Of the 250,000 mallards wintering in Nebraska, almost half concentrate along the North Platte River. An additional 25,000 congregate along the South Platte River, and about 50,000 along the Platte River east of Ogallala. The remainder are found on various reservoirs, mostly in the south-central part of the state.

Large impoundments on the Missouri River in South Dakota created open water areas that wintered an average of 200,000 mallards in the 1960's. The largest concentrations occurred in the area of Fort Randall Dam and Lake Andes. An additional 30,000 mallards usually winter about several warm springs adjacent to the Black Hills.

Open water along the North Platte and Bighorn rivers in Wyoming makes it possible for 35,000 ducks to winter in the southeastern and north-central areas of that state. Farther north, in eastern Montana, 65,000 mallards find open water and waste grain along the Bighorn, Yellowstone, and Missouri rivers. Only a few thousand mallards winter in North Dakota, mostly below the Garrison Dam on the Missouri River.

The Mississippi Flyway is aptly called the mallard flyway, for over 3,100,000 have been recorded on winter surveys, 1960-70, more than in any other flyway. The heart of this winter ground extends through the ancient Mississippi River delta lying between Cape Girardeau, Missouri, and the Gulf of Mexico.

In the remnants of the once vast overflow swamps, mallards still find sustenance in acorns, but because of extensive drainage and clearing of timber they have had to seek substitute foods in the waste grains of rice and soybean fields. Almost 1,500,000 mallards find a winter home in this delta country, particularly in Arkansas, where 1,100,000 congregate. The rice belt and adjacent coastal marshes of Louisiana, between Lafayette and the Sabine River, winter about 400,000 mallards.

As many as 1,200,000 mallards winter in the Midwest, where they feed on waste corn in combined fields when lakes and marshes become frozen. Because springs and currents create open water areas along the Mississippi River from Muscatine, Iowa, to Alton, Illinois, and in the Illinois River valley, about 500,000 remain during the winter until snow covers the waste corn too deeply. In January the mallard population elsewhere in Iowa, Illinois, and Missouri, together with Indiana and Ohio, numbers 350,000. As many as 50,000 mallards may attempt to winter in Minnesota, Wisconsin, and Michigan.

The Atlantic Flyway attracts a comparatively small proportion of the continental mallard population, for only about 200,000 winter there. Over half (110,000) winter in southeastern South Carolina. About 40,000 winter in the Chesapeake Bay region, and a similar number from there along the coast north to Massachusetts. Only a few hundred mallards brave the rigors of winter in Maine, Vermont, and New Hampshire, and, at the other end of the line, Florida is host to only 7,000.

MIGRATION BEHAVIOR

Chronology

Fall. Among dabbling ducks, the mallard and the black duck are the latest fall migrants. Many mallards appear reluctant to migrate any farther south than necessary to obtain food. The last big flight south may not leave the Canadian prairies until mid-November, and a sizable population remains in the northern tier of states through November.

Mallards are found in southward migration at times throughout the winter, depending upon the difficulty of finding waste grain buried under the snow. Mallards have been forced by snow and cold to leave central Illinois as late as mid-February, only to return by March 1.

In the northern tier of states, local breeding populations of mallards are not appreciably augmented by more northerly birds until early October; peak numbers are reached in early November from which a gradual decline ensues.

Small numbers of mallards arrive in the intermediate migration areas in early September, but numbers remain low until early October. From that time on, migrants arrive steadily until peak populations are reached either in late November or early December. On southern winter grounds, mallards begin to arrive early in October, with additional arrivals steadily swelling the population through November and a large part of December.

The mallard has the most prolonged fall migration of any duck, extending as it does from late summer to early winter. Consequently, there are no sharp peaks in population trends, but instead, rather gentle slopes.

Spring. The mallard and the pintail vie with each other in the northward race back to the breeding grounds. Sometimes one is ahead, sometimes the other. The leaders race spring itself, often foraging ahead to be forced into temporary retreat by late winter blizzards.

Mallards start to leave their winter grounds in the South by early February. A steady stream of departures continues through February and March. By April, only small numbers of these ducks remain on winter areas in the southern states.

They winter, too, on intermediate migration areas that are more noted for migratory than for winter populations. Departures from most of these areas occur during February and March and continue later in April than on winter grounds. In the Midwest, wintering mallards are joined by migrating mallards, beginning the last week in February, and numbers continue to rise steadily throughout March. A rapid decrease follows through April, and only a few are left by the end of the month.

On northern breeding areas within the United States, numbers of mallards begin to arrive between mid- and late March. Arrivals rapidly increase the population through most of April, but late in the month a decline occurs as many birds move to more northern breeding grounds in Canada.

Mallards arrive at the larger sloughs and marshes on the breeding grounds as soon as open water occurs. The first mallards arrived at Delta, Manitoba, early in April; the average date for the arrival of the main flight was April 18 (Sowls 1955). At Redvers, Saskatchewan, most mallards arrived April 1-20, whereas farther west and north at Lousana, Alberta, the date of arrival was earlier, March 25-April 15. For Brooks, Alberta, Keith (1961) reported a 10-day spread in arrival, the average date being March 27.

Farther north, mallards arrived at the Saskatchewan River delta, April 5, 1959 (Townsend 1966), and at Yellowknife on Great Slave Lake, April 23-May 4, 1962-64 (Murdy 1964). On the Yukon Flats, Alaska, the first spring mallards arrived May 3, 1962, and at Anaktuvuk Pass in the Brooks Range, May 13-20, 1949-54 (Irving 1960).

BREEDING

Behavior

Age, Pair Bond, and Homing. Although most mallards breed late in their first year, probably some late-maturing young do not. Especially in those years when drought reduces water areas on the prairies, it is probable that a large proportion of the mallards that fail to breed are yearlings. Certainly the older birds are favored in establishing home ranges and finding nest sites. When the nest habitat is crowded, it is doubtless the later-nesting yearlings that are most excluded.

Mallards begin to establish loose pair bonds as early as August, according to Barclay (1970), who estimated that one-third of the mallards on the Winous Point marsh, Ohio, were paired by early September and that 75 percent were paired by late October. In Louisiana, 90 percent of the mallard hens were associated with drakes during January (Weller 1965). In central New York, Johnsgard (1960*a*) observed pairing of mallards in mid-October; pairing rapidly accelerated thereafter until by early January 80 percent of the flock had mated.

Aerial courtship flights and displays, performed by small numbers of mallards during spring migration, indicate that a few hens remain unattached until the breeding grounds are reached. Later courtship flights on the breeding grounds evidently involve hens that are seeking new mates after the loss of their first nests (Sowls 1955).

The pair bond in mallards begins to weaken with the beginning of incubation. Ten of 13 pairs observed in Idaho (Oring 1964) separated on the first day of incubation. One pair stayed together into the first week of incubation, another into the second week, and the third until the eggs were pipped. Barclay (1970) believed that hens, not drakes, were the deserters, because the hens' association with their waiting sites deteriorated more quickly than that of drakes.

Dzubin (1955) observed that mallard drakes in Manitoba remained in the vicinity of their nests up to the 16th day of incubation. On rare occasions he observed drakes accompanying a hen and brood.

At the Delta Marsh, Manitoba, Sowls (1955) found that 13 percent of 15 adult mallard hens and 5 percent of 20 immature hens returned to nest in the same marsh the year after banding. Forty-two percent of 24 banded adult mallard hens at Lake Champlain, Vermont, returned subsequently to nest (Coulter and Miller 1968). Because finding nests and retrapping mallard hens are difficult tasks, the figures on homing are probably low for this species.

Until recently, evidence suggested that mallard drakes did not return to their natal or breeding areas. It was believed that drakes mated with hens on the winter grounds and returned to the hens' home areas. However, Barclay (1970) found that two of seven marked drake mallards returned the following spring to the same marsh at Winous Point, Ohio.

Home Range. After flocks arrive on the larger water areas, they begin to break up as pairs disperse to potholes and other small water areas. Here a spacing occurs between breeding pairs, as each pair establishes a home range (Sowls 1955, Dzubin 1955) with a central core area or "territory" embracing one or more waiting sites. The waiting site is usually a bare shore surrounded by standing vegetation.

The home ranges of mallards differ greatly in size, depending upon habitat and population density. In Manitoba, the home ranges of mallards exceeded 700 acres (Dzubin 1955); the central core area was much smaller.

Spacing between breeding pairs develops as a result of defensive behavior expressed in three-bird flights, attempted rape flights, drake-to-drake conflicts, and chasing (Barclay 1970). Of all defensive behavior, the pursuit of an intruding pair by the drake intruded upon (resulting in a three-bird flight) is the most common.

Spacing regulates the number of mallards that a breeding ground can accommodate. When drought reduces the abundance of ponds on the prairie parkland breeding grounds, space requirements reduce the number of mallards (and other ducks) that can be accommodated. Pospahala et al. (1974) believe that spacing mechanisms cause varying proportions of mallards to overfly their former breeding grounds when ponds decline in abundance. They concluded that spacing resulting in a northward overflight from prime breeding areas is an important density-dependent factor in regulating the density of the total population.

Nesting

Nest Sites. Within a few days of selecting a particular pothole or section of slough for feeding and resting, the mallard pair, with the hen in the lead, flies low over the surrounding land on evening reconnaissance. These evening flights are believed to lead to the selection of the nest site.

Mallards are catholic in their selection of nest sites. They prefer upland to marsh, but the distance from the water varies greatly with the habitat. Sites on levees, small islands, or where potholes are numerous, often limit maximum distances from water to a few feet or a few yards.

Most studies indicate that nests are located within 100 yards of water. Girard (1941) found mallard nests as far as 500 yards from water, the greatest distance reported. In the western Intermountain valleys, mallard nests are confined largely to marshes, and many are built in marsh growth over water (Wingfield 1951, Miller and Collins 1953). However, when choice nest cover is at a distance from water areas, mallards (and other ducks) may fly as far as 3 to 5 miles to reach it (Duebbert 1969). In a retired crop production field of 125 acres, South Dakota, Duebbert (1969) found 61 duck nests; 24 were mallard nests. Yet there were only 17 pairs of mallards inhabiting potholes in a 4-square-mile block surrounding the crop field. Apparently, other mallards came from outside the 4-square-mile block to nest in the field. According to Dzubin and Gollop (1972), the more dense the breeding population, the greater the distance that mallards nested from prairie ponds.

The female mallard forms a nest bowl or scrape in old plant litter or in the moist earth. The depressions are 7 to 8 inches in diameter and 1 to 2 inches deep and are lined with successive layers of fragments from nearby vegetation as laying progresses. The interval between construction of the scrape and egg-laying has been reported variously as 1 to 3 days (Coulter and Miller 1968) and 6 days (Sowls 1955).

Down is added sparingly to the nest until just prior to completion of the clutch, when the hen plucks large amounts of down from her breast to form a fluffy ring. When absent from the nest, the hen covers her eggs with the down lining.

Mallards utilize many types of nest cover, as a result of the innumerable habitats in which they breed. Dense vegetation about 24 inches high appears to be the primary requirement, regardless of other cover qualities. On Canadian prairies and parklands, grassy areas or buckbrush clumps are the favorite sites (Smith and Stoudt 1968). In southeastern Alberta, *Juncus* communities are heavily used (Keith 1961). Whitetop is the preferred nest cover at the Delta Marsh, Manitoba.

In agricultural areas, hayfields are often preferred by nesting mallards, as shown by studies in North Dakota (Salyer 1962), South Dakota (Duebbert 1969), Minnesota (Moyle et al. 1964), Wisconsin (Labisky 1957, Gates 1965), and Manitoba (Milonski 1958).

In the 125-acre retired crop field in South Dakota, mentioned previously, Duebbert (1969) found a variety of plants: wheat grass, many forbs, sweet clover, and alfalfa. Ducks showed a strong preference for the sweet clover: one-half of the mallard nests and one-fourth of all duck nests were placed in it. Arthur Hawkins considered sweet clover to be the preferred nest cover for mallards in Manitoba.

Mallards nesting on many Intermountain marshes prefer hardstem bulrushes to other marsh plants (Wingfield 1951, Hunt and Naylor 1955), but on drier sites saltbush ranks high. At Greenfield (Freezeout) Lake, Montana, greasewood clumps were favored (Ellig 1955). Across the country in Vermont, mallards nested under clusters of American yew and white cedar, among fallen logs and limbs, in hollow tree trunks, and tree crotches (Coulter and Miller 1968). On occasion, shallow cattail marshes contained the highest nest densities of mallards that Arthur Hawkins found in Manitoba.

Mallards have readily accepted as nest sites artificial cone-shaped baskets lined with grass and erected on pipes (Bishop and Barratt 1970). Thirty-three percent of the baskets placed in Iowa marshes were used. The preferred baskets were those placed 3 to 4 feet above the water in areas free of heavy vegetation.

On a 19-acre island in Lake Albert, South Dakota, Drewien and Fredrickson (1970) found an unusually dense concentration of mallard nests. In 1967 there were 37 nests on the island and 28 the next year. Most nests were confined to a 9-acre tract, where they ranged from 7 to 150 feet apart and averaged 34 feet.

Clutch Size, Eggs, and Incubation. The hen usually lays one egg a day, most often in the morning, until the clutch is complete. The drake follows the hen from a waiting site, flying low over the terrain until within a few yards of the nest. At that point, the hen drops to earth and the drake continues in flight back to its activity center. Laying may last from a few minutes to an hour. Some hens apparently do not rejoin their mates immediately but remain at the nest site for extended periods (Coulter and Miller 1968).

The eggs are ovate, measure 57.8 by 41.6 mm, and vary in color from grayish buff to greenish buff (Bent 1923).

An average of 9.0 eggs were laid in 5,170 mallard nests. Studies that included over 100 nests reported clutches that ranged from a low average of 6.8 eggs at Lousana, Alberta (Smith 1971), to highs of 9.6 eggs at Ogden Bay, Utah (Fuller 1953), and Maine-Vermont (Coulter and Miller 1968). Individual clutches have ranged from 1 to 18 eggs.

One reason for variations in clutch size is the period during which the nest is started. Dzubin and Gollop (1972) reported that mallards at Roseneath, Manitoba, had an average clutch size of 8.6 eggs (111) prior to May 25 and 7.2 eggs (55) after that date. Likewise, at Kindersley, Sas-

MALLARD

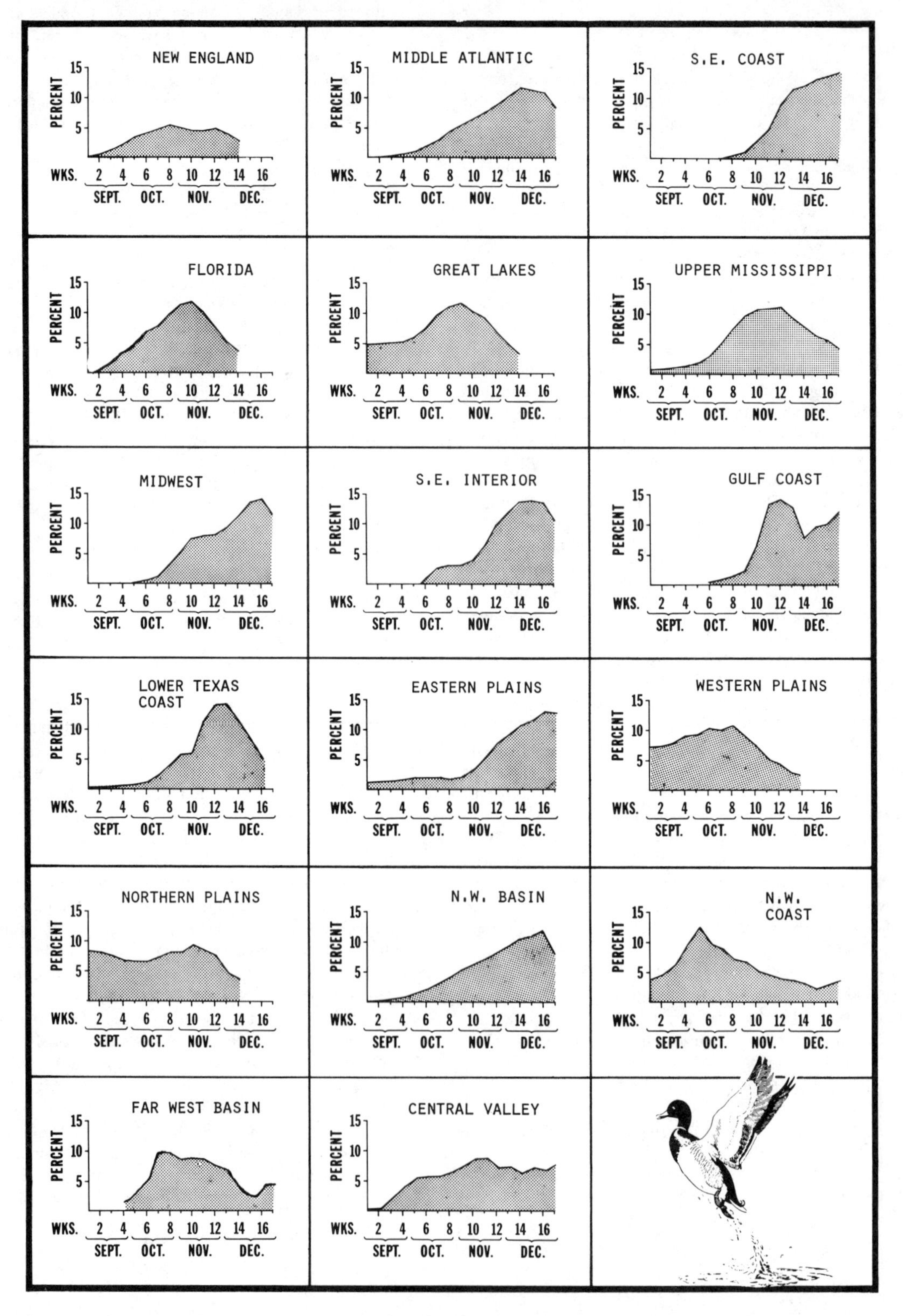

Fall

MALLARD

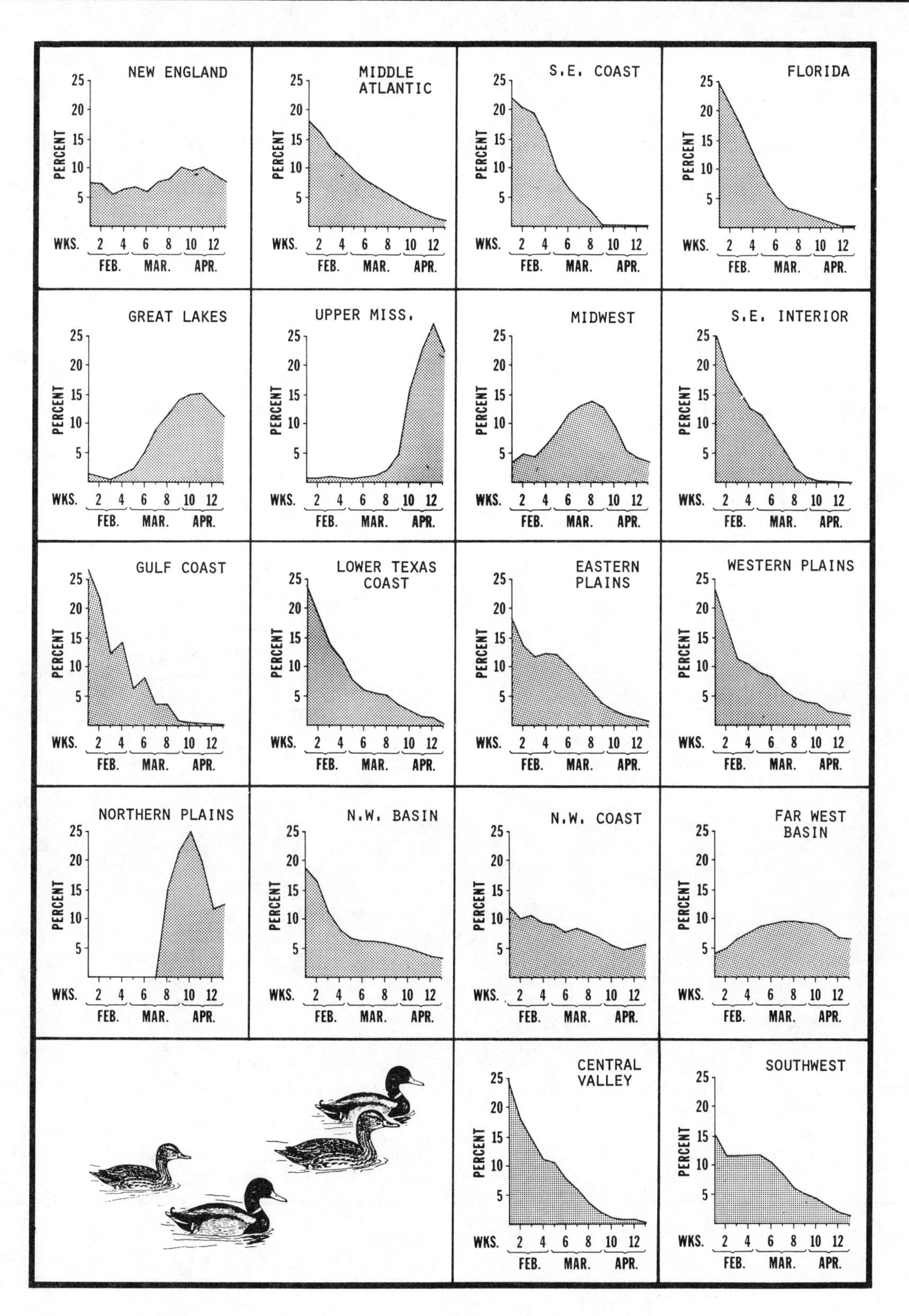

Spring

katchewan, they found an average of 9.1 eggs per clutch (529) prior to May 15 and 7.7 eggs (98) afterwards.

Renesting hens are considered to lay fewer eggs than they did initially. Fifteen marked renesting mallards laid an average of 9.6 eggs; their first nests averaged 10.6 (Coulter and Miller 1968). Keith (1961) determined that initial clutches contained 9.6 eggs and second clutches 8.1 eggs.

Mallards ordinarily incubate their eggs from 26 to 30 days, with a 28-day average (Girard 1941). Under artificial incubation, mallard eggs took 24.6 days to pip and 1 more day to hatch (Forest Lee). Hens have been known to incubate infertile or dead eggs for 49 days (Sowls 1955).

Chronology of Nesting. The mallard begins to nest between April 10 and April 30 over vast reaches of its breeding range. Timing is remarkably similar in such diverse locations as California (Sacramento Valley, Tule Lake), Utah (Ogden Bay), Montana (Flathead Valley), South Dakota (Waubay Hills), Wisconsin (Horicon), New York (Howland Island), Vermont (Lake Champlain), Manitoba (Delta), Saskatchewan (Redvers, Saskatchewan Delta), and Alberta (Lousana, Lake Newell, and Brooks). The peak of nest initiation occurs in most of these areas between May 5 and May 20.

In the more northern areas, such as the Athabasca Delta in northeast Alberta, and Yellowknife, Northwest Territories, Canada, mallards do not start to nest until May 10, but nest initiation quickly reaches a climax between May 20 and May 30. Mallards have been reported nesting as early as May 11 on the Yukon Flats, Alaska, with a maximum of nest initiation between May 20 and June 5. At Minto Lakes, near Fairbanks, Alaska, a few mallards have started nesting by May 23, but most nesting does not begin until early June.

Except in the Far North, mallards initiate nesting over a span of about 60 days. Nest initiation has continued for over 30 days at Yellowknife, Northwest Territories; 55 days on the delta of the Saskatchewan River; 65 days in southern Saskatchewan, southern Manitoba, Minnesota, and California; 70 days in Wisconsin, Utah, and southern Alberta; 75 days in central Washington; and 80 days in northeast South Dakota.

Low temperatures in the spring may delay mallard nesting by as much as 2 weeks (Yocom 1950, Sowls 1955, Evans and Black 1956, Townsend 1966, Dzubin and Gollop 1972). Sowls (1955) indicated that when nest initiation was delayed, the period of nesting was extended equally. However, the yearly differences in the span of nesting observed by Evans and Black (1956) and Yocom and Hansen (1960) were attributed to environmental conditions.

Evans and Black (1956) considered that a rapid drop in water levels retarded late-season nesting in the mallard and that a long nest season occurred only when water conditions were favorable. They attributed a short nest season in 1953 to a high initial nest success with correspondingly fewer late renests. Yocom and Hansen (1960) concluded that cold, dry springs in Washington discouraged many mallards from renesting when their first attempts were unsuccessful. The yearly span of nest initiation in any single area varies according to how much late renesting occurs.

Nest Success. The known fate of 7,728 mallard nests, as determined from many studies in a variety of nest habitats, indicates that 45.9 percent of the nests were successful. Nest success was highest for mallards nesting in the mixed prairie of the Dakotas and the Prairie Provinces, where 60.5 percent of 1,035 nests were successful.

In the parklands, where mallards reached their greatest breeding density, only 31.2 percent of 3,028 nests hatched. Nest studies in the Intermountain marshes of western United States point to a success of 54.2 percent for 2,718 nests. Mallards nesting in the Great Lakes states experienced the poorest success, 24.8 percent for the 478 nests studied.

Among individual areas, the greatest success was reported at Ogden Bay, Utah, where 74.8 percent of 114 mallard nests (Fuller 1953) and 65.7 percent of 321 nests (Wingfield 1951) hatched. The lowest success was reported by Anderson (1956) in the San Joaquin Valley, where only 12.7 percent of 510 nests hatched.

An average of 0.56 egg has failed to hatch in each successful nest (1,229). Hence, about 8.4 ducklings have left the average successful mallard nest.

Nest Failure. The causes of nest losses in mallards are legion and vary greatly with the nest habitat. In the Canadian parklands, crows and magpies were the principal destroyers of nests, followed by skunks, ground squirrels, foxes, and coyotes. Plowing, burning, and flooding often caused large losses among early-nesting mallards, particularly those selecting stubble fields (Arthur Hawkins).

On the northern prairies, skunks, foxes, other mammals, and crows committed most of the depredations on mallard nests (Kalmbach 1937, Girard 1941, Reeves et al. 1955, Keith 1961). In eastern North Dakota, Sargeant (1972) found that the red fox preyed heavily on nesting hen mallards and hens of other species—blue-winged teal, pintail, northern shoveler, gadwall, green-winged teal, and American wigeon.

Mallards nesting in areas where agriculture was intensive—as in Minnesota, Nebraska, and Wisconsin—suffered heavy losses directly from hayfield mowing and indirectly from exposure of nests to predators. Trampling by cattle and burning caused other nest destruction (Labisky 1957, Moyle et al. 1964, Gates 1965, Evans and Wolfe 1967).

In the marshes adjacent to the Great Salt Lake of Utah, the most important enemies of nesting mallards were California gulls and skunks (Wingfield 1951, Nelson and Klett 1952, Odin 1957). In California, a wide variety of mammals were responsible for most of the destruction of mallard nests (Hunt and Naylor 1955, Anderson 1956, 1957, 1960, 1965; Rienecker and Anderson 1960). Striped skunks were identified most often as the culprits, but Norway rats, coyotes, raccoons, and opossums also caused extensive nest losses.

Desertion of nests by the hens accounts for 10 to 15 percent of the nest loss in mallards. Why hens desert their nests is usually undetermined, but harassment by predators is considered the most likely cause.

Nest success during drought years declined hardly at all at Redvers, Saskatchewan, but was reduced by one-half at Lousana, Alberta, although at both places, the reason for the loss in productivity was the same—fewer pairs attempted to nest (Stoudt 1971, Smith 1971). At Redvers, mallard broods declined from 15 per square mile in predrought years, 1952-58, to 4 per square mile during drought years, 1959-63. At Lousana, the decline was from 18 to 8 broods per square mile.

Renesting. An unknown, probably varying, number of mallard hens attempt to renest when their first efforts fail. At Lake Champlain, Vermont, renesting was attempted by 57 percent of 30 marked hens whose nests were destroyed (Coulter and Miller 1968). The older hens were more likely to renest than the younger ones. The interval between nest loss and renesting was highly variable. One hen started laying again 4 days after her nest was destroyed, another waited 15 days, and the average for 15 hens was 12.5 days.

Two-thirds of the renesting mallards at Lake Champlain selected new nest sites within 100 yards of the original ones, and one-fourth chose sites between 100 and 200 yards from their previous nest attempts. One hen moved to the next closest island, which was within the 401- to 1,000-yard zone.

Near Brooks, Alberta, 82 pairs of mallards made 176 nest efforts that resulted in the eventual success of 49 percent of the hens (Keith 1961). At Roseneath, Manitoba, Dzubin and Gollop (1972) estimated that 50 percent of the mallard hens that lost their initial clutches renested. They calculated that 40 percent of these hens fledged broods and that nests established late in the season were 7 percent more successful than early nests. Dzubin and Gollop (1972) found fewer hens, 30 percent, renesting at Kindersley, Saskatchewan, but 55 percent of them fledged broods. At Kindersley, early nests were 16 percent more successful than late nests.

An extensive nest study at Redvers, in the southeastern corner of Saskatchewan, 1952-60, indicated that nest success for the mallard was 33 percent but that renesting raised the success rate to 48 percent (Stoudt 1971). Renests appeared to be as successful as initial nests. In their study of mallard populations, Pospahala et al. (1974) concluded that late nesting and renesting were greatest when midsummer water conditions were good.

Rearing of Young

Broods. As soon as the ducklings are dry, within the first 12 hours of hatching, the hen mallard leads them to water, a few feet to several hundred yards away and, rarely, 1 mile or more. On occasion, the hen may return to brood her young at the nest for a day or more (de Vos 1964).

In order to find proper food and cover, the hen often takes her brood to more than one body of water, or to distant reaches of large marshes and lakes. Near Minnedosa, Manitoba, where potholes abound, mallard broods remained no longer than 20 days in a single pothole; the average was only 7 days (Evans et al. 1952). Two broods moved a distance of 0.48 mile in 38 days. However, under drought conditions, Salyer (1962) observed a marked mallard brood 2 miles from its nest site. At Kindersley, Saskatchewan, Dzubin and Gollop (1972) recorded hens moving broods as far as 3 miles in 1 week and 5 miles in 9 days. A drying slough resulted in 18 of 123 marked ducklings moving 1.6 miles to a pothole. At Minnedosa, Manitoba, mallard broods remained for an average of 7 days on the same pond. Mallard hens sometimes lead their broods across extensive areas when water levels fall, and perhaps for better food supplies, but certainly many movements are inexplicable.

Evans and Black (1956) found that mallard broods in the Waubay Hills of South Dakota preferred deep marshes and open water areas and were seldom seen on temporary shallow marshes. Broods in eastern Montana sought to move from bare ponds to those with emergent vegetation, from small to larger ponds, and to ponds with the most stable water level (Berg 1956). At Redvers, Saskatchewan, in the Canadian parklands, mallard broods frequented potholes 0.6 to 1.0 acre most extensively, those 0.1 to 0.5 acre less so, and larger ponds least (Stoudt 1971); but at Lousana, Alberta, they favored potholes 0.1 to 0.5 acre most and those 0.6 to 1.0 acre least (Smith 1971).

Flooded whitetop, sedge, and hardstem bulrush beds provide the favorite cover for mallard broods. However, mallards are more tolerant of open water and bare shores than all other dabbling ducks except the pintail.

Development. Mallard ducklings in South Dakota remained in the downy stage (Class I) for about 18 days (Gollop and Marshall 1954). The first body feathers appeared on the side (Class II) about the 25th day and persisted to the 46th day, when feathers completely covered the head and body (Class III). The young could fly when they were 52 to 60 days old. At Delta, Manitoba, Hochbaum (1944) reported flight in 49 to 60 days.

The flight stage was reached more rapidly in Alaska. Mallards on the Yukon Flats attained flight in 42 days (Lensink 1954) and 43 days (Rueter 1955). At Minto Lakes, Hooper (1951) reported flight in 40 days. However, under confined conditions in Alaska, young mallards did not fly until 61 to 64 days (Schneider 1965), but this figure is suspect because of the confinement and the artificial diet.

Survival. The average number of ducklings in Class I broods was 6.6 (2,103); in Class II broods, 6.1 (1,587); and in Class III broods, 5.9 (1,169). These averages indicate only a small loss of individual ducklings during the growth period: 8 percent between Classes I and II and 3.3 percent between Classes II and III. The number of broods lost entirely is unknown, but at Kindersley, Saskatchewan, it was quite high. Dzubin and Gollop (1972) determined that over a 3-year period only 48 percent of the broods reached a water area. This figure is probably below average because of the unusually long distance—more than 200 yards—that broods had to travel from nest sites to water. Additional broods—58 percent—disappeared on the Kindersley study area after reaching water (Dzubin and Gollop 1972).

Hence, from the 197 clutches that hatched, only 55 broods reached flight stage, an average of 0.5 immature per adult mallard in the September population. However, Dzubin and Gollop's (1972) calculation of 1.2 immatures per adult in September on their Roseneath, Manitoba, study area more likely typifies mallard productivity as a whole. For, as discussed under age ratios, mallard immatures average 0.9 to 1.0 per adult in the fall population in the United States.

POSTBREEDING SEASON

Mallard drakes begin to leave their home ranges about mid-May and to collect in large marshes for their eclipse molt. At Delta, Manitoba, bands of drakes in ragged plumage began appearing by May 15, with numbers increasing to form large flocks of several hundred to several thousand by early June (Hochbaum 1944). On Whitewater Lake in southwestern Manitoba, groups of mallard drakes assembled on May 21 and 28, 2 different years (Bossenmaier and Marshall 1958). By mid-July, about 10,000 mallards had gathered for the molt.

Bands of mallard drakes in nuptial plumage were observed by Munro (1943) in British Columbia from May 21 to June 7, yet on June 9, he observed a drake already in nearly full eclipse plumage. In southeastern Idaho, drakes in eclipse plumage first appeared on June 15 (Oring 1964). At Delta, Hochbaum (1944) observed flightless mallards in full eclipse by mid-June. Differences in chronology of molt appear related to age and breeding activity. Hochbaum (1944) found that in captive ducks, the first to enter the eclipse were the earliest-mated drakes and the last were the nonbreeding drakes.

Flightless drake mallards have first appeared at Whitewater Lake about mid-June, in Idaho on June 28, and on the Yukon Flats, Alaska, June 15. The first flying drakes were observed at Whitewater on July 24, 1950, a late spring when the first flightless birds were seen on June 22 (Gene Bossenmaier). Hochbaum (1944) believed that most individual ducks are flightless for 3 to 4 weeks.

Some hen mallards, apparently unsuccessful nesters, join drakes early in June on molt areas in large marshes. Successful hens stay with their broods until the young can fly, then molt on the rearing area or move to larger marshes to molt.

On a large marsh near Swift Current, Saskatchewan, the proportion of drakes and hens was reversed; several hundred flightless drake mallards were captured on July 7, 1957, and over 100 flightless hens were captured on August 3, less than 1 month later (Henry M. Reeves). Between July 9 and July 24, 1955-58, Sterling (1966) captured 1,698 flightless mallards, 65 miles north of Regina, Saskatchewan, most of them during the early part of the period. At Whitewater Lake, Manitoba, most mallards were renewing flight feathers by the fourth week in July. At the Delta Marsh, Hochbaum (1944) observed many mallards, again on the wing, starting to fly to stubble fields in early August; by midmonth, most drakes were flying again.

Flying young and hens also gravitate to the large marshes initially inhabitated by molting drakes, so that by early September the waters of the large marshes are teeming with thousands, if not tens of thousands, of mallards. Many thousands of these ducks fly to nearby wheat stubble fields to feed upon grain until their departure in migration.

Because drakes and hens molt at different times and in different places and the flightless hens are separated from their flying young, it is doubtful that many family members reassemble for the fall migration. Some mallard broodmates may stay together, but others obviously disperse and become attached to flocks bound for different migration winter areas (Martinson and Hawkins 1968).

FOOD HABITS

Natural

Mallards are highly adaptable in their use of the natural and domestic foods available in the localities they visit. Since they frequent many varied habitats, the native food plants taken are numerous and diverse. Only the most important ones are listed here.

At Swan Lake, British Columbia, mallards fed primarily on the seeds of bulrushes and pondweeds (Munro 1939*a*). They consumed seeds of wild millet, beaked sedge, and reed canary grass in the Columbia Basin of Washington (Yocom 1951). Pondweed seeds, spike rush, bulrush and sedge seeds, along with eelgrass, were important foods at Humboldt Bay, California (Yocom and Keller 1961).

Mallards in Illinois (Anderson 1959) fed largely on rice cut-grass, coontail, and seeds of wild millet and marsh smartweed. In adjacent Missouri, the three principal foods were smartweed, millet seeds, and oak acorns (Korschgen 1955). Acorns were important in both Arkansas (Wright 1961) and Tennessee (Rawls 1954), but the remainder of the foods were different. Wild millet and other grasses predominated in Arkansas, but seeds of smartweeds, buttonbush, and bald cypress, and minute duckweed plants predominated in Tennessee. Louisiana mallards consumed seeds of Jamaica saw grass, jungle rice, spike rush, brownseed paspalum, and wild millet (Dillon 1959).

Blue mussels made up 45 percent of the mallard's food in Rhode Island, the only place where animal life was important in the diet (Cronan and Halla 1968). The foods of mallards differed sharply between the freshwater estuarine marshes and the brackish water marshes of Chesapeake

Bay (Stewart 1962). Seeds of smartweeds, soft-stem and three-square bulrushes, and bur reeds were the predominant foods consumed on freshwater marshes. On brackish marshes, the important foods were seeds of widgeon grass, pondweeds, and smartweeds, and the leaves and stems of submerged aquatic plants.

The stems and leaves of pondweeds, widgeon grass, and bushy pondweed, along with bulrush seeds, were staple items in the food of mallards in North Carolina (Quay and Critcher 1965). In South Carolina, mallards relished seeds of rice cut-grass, Hydrochloa, sweet gum, buttonbush, and swamp smartweed (McGilvrey 1966*b*).

Cultivated

More than any other duck, mallards have been able to utilize agricultural fields for feeding. On the northern breeding grounds, mallards feed in wheat and barley stubble; then, upon moving southward into central areas, they feed upon waste corn, sorghum, or barley; when they reach southern areas, they utilize rice, soybeans, and peas.

In North Dakota, mallards preferred wheat to barley and barley to oats (Bossenmaier and Marshall 1958). At Whitewater Lake, Manitoba, they liked durum wheat and then barley, but at The Pas, Manitoba, the order of preference was barley, oats, and wheat. Their first choice in Alberta was peas, then barley, wheat, and oats.

Irrigated lands in the Pacific Northwest enable hundreds of thousands of mallards to feed upon waste grain in harvested fields of corn, wheat, and barley. Many feeding areas are in semi-arid regions and others are north of where the mallard formerly wintered (John Chattin).

From Nebraska south through eastern Colorado, most of Kansas and Oklahoma to the Panhandle of Texas, mallards rely on waste corn and sorghum for sustenance. In the Midwest, they resort almost exclusively to combined or mechanically picked cornfields. Rarely do they select soybeans and then only when the beans have been softened by moisture.

Rice is the most important domestic food for mallards in Arkansas, Louisiana, and the Sacramento Valley of California. Soybeans rank a poor second and are usually eaten only when inundated by water or when birds are hard pressed for food. Mallards in the Chesapeake Bay area utilize corn extensively (Stewart 1962) but less so where they winter in South Carolina (Kerwin and Webb 1972). About daybreak and again in late afternoon, mallards wing their way to upland grain fields. The afternoon flight is invariably the larger. With light snow, severe cold, or overcast, mallards often abandon their normal schedule and feed extensively in upland fields during midday. The distance flown to fields depends upon their proximity to rest lakes and upon weather conditions. Under poor visibility or severe cold, mallards rarely fly more than 1 mile. Otherwise, they frequently fly 25 miles one way, and, rarely, up to 40 miles when the occasion demands.

When natural plant foods are readily available in Illinois, mallards do not resort to cornfields until marsh foods are covered with ice, indicating that native foods in water are preferred to corn on dry land.

Field feeding by mallards is at present a double-edged sword: it assists in their survival, and yet because of their depredation on crops the hand of many a northern prairie farmer is turned against them. The problem stems from the necessity of swathing spring-planted wheat and barley to permit even ripening of the grains prior to threshing by combines. During the time the grain is in swaths, it is highly vulnerable to consumption and damage by waterfowl, particularly mallards and pintails. This problem is accentuated when rains delay combining, resulting in prolonged feeding and an almost equal loss caused by the trampling of seed heads.

The problem of crop depredation is greatest in the Prairie Provinces of Canada, followed by the Dakotas. Conservation agencies have been attempting to minimize the economic loss to individual wheat and barley farmers by several means: underwriting crop insurance, growing crops specifically for waterfowl so as to lure them from extensive field feeding, the intensive use of a subsidized crop, and using automatic scare devices to frighten waterfowl from farm fields.

All three programs are costly and each at times fails to meet the demands of a local situation. Nevertheless, it is necessary for waterfowl management to reduce the seriousness of this problem if one reason for the drainage of wetlands is to be minimized.

An entirely different aspect of the problem of field feeding on migration and winter grounds concerns the mallard's future welfare. The use of waste corn, sorghum, rice, and other grains in harvested fields on migration and winter areas has unquestionably increased the mallard's survival by reducing nonhunting mortality. As drainage and pollution reduced the quantity of natural food resources, the use of combines to harvest crops fortuitously provided a substitute food source for mallards.

Unfortunately for mallards and other field-feeding waterfowl, combines are constantly being improved to reduce the field loss of grain. Plant scientists too are at work breeding better strains of crops that lodge less and therefore are harvested more efficiently. Extensive fall plowing of grain stubble in the Midwest is a relatively new cultural practice that has greatly reduced the availability of waste grain.

The future of food supplies for migrating and wintering mallards gives grounds for concern. The time is fast approaching when mallards will be forced to rely more and more heavily on natural foods. A continued drainage of marshes and swamps, their filling, and their deterioration from silt pollution will further reduce natural food resources, placing the present level of mallard numbers in great jeopardy.

Mexican Duck

Anas platyrhynchos diazi

IDENTIFICATION

Drakes and hens of this species are similarly colored and resemble the hen mallard, but are slightly darker than the hen mallard and considerably lighter than the black duck. The fuscous-brown tail of the Mexican duck lacks the white outer tail feathers characteristic of the mallard. The tail, especially, appears darker than that of the hen mallard. The black and white bars that border both front and back of the greenish-blue speculum distinguish the Mexican duck from the black, mottled, and Florida ducks, which lack the white border in front of the blue speculum.

The sexes can best be distinguished by the color of the bill. The male has an olive-green bill; the bill of the female has a black saddle shading to light olive-green, with a minute amount of orange at the base.

At one time, this species was believed to include a northern and a southern race. After an intensive study of specimens, Aldrich and Baer (1970) concluded that only one race existed. They considered the Mexican duck a distinct species because of its reproductive isolation from the mallard in areas where both occurred. This contention is further supported by the observation of Bevill (1970) near Rodeo, New Mexico. In an area frequented by both mallards and Mexican ducks, he observed 26 mated Mexican duck hens. All but one hen mated with drakes of their own species; the one exception mated with a mallard drake that did not acquire nuptial plumage until early May, an unusually late date for the species.

POPULATION STATUS

Winter surveys of waterfowl populations in Mexico by various personnel of the U. S. Fish and Wildlife Service provide the best data on the status of this species. An average population of 4,400 was recorded during 1957-63. In 1964 the survey recorded 7,720; and in 1965, 7,442 were sighted on the aerial reconnaissance. All of the surveys cited included the lakes in the Interior Highlands of Mexico. It was not until January 1970 that the lakes in the Interior Highlands were again included in the survey. On that aerial reconnaissance, 14,760 Mexican ducks were recorded, the largest number ever observed (Hanson and Smith 1970).

In the semi-arid land inhabited by the Mexican duck, the availability of water during the nest and brood season must be crucial to the production of young. During favorable years for surface water, the Mexican duck population no doubt increases greatly to decline markedly when shallow waters disappear. Thus, the wide variations in the numbers of Mexican ducks found on winter surveys may reflect the favorable as well as unfavorable conditions of the previous breeding seasons.

In spite of the relatively large number of Mexican ducks found in 1970, the future for this species is not bright. Long-term changes in the population are perhaps most influenced by the accelerated conversion of wetlands to cropland and rangeland. The disturbance of its habitat by people and livestock is so extensive that its survival is probably in jeopardy (Aldrich and Baer 1970).

DISTRIBUTION

The Mexican duck ranges in the Interior Highlands of Mexico from the Trans-Mexican volcanic belt south of Mexico City north to southeastern Arizona and in the Rio Grande Valley north to Albuquerque, New Mexico.

Breeding Range

In the United States this species nests in only a few localities along the Rio Grande River and in the San Simon Valley near Rodeo, New Mexico (Bevill 1970). A brood and several adults were observed 16 miles south-southeast of Alpine, Texas, on June 18, 1969 (Ohlendorf and Patton 1971).

Small dispersed populations breed in Mexico in the sparsely watered highlands of the states of Chihuahua, Durango, Aguascalientes, Jalisco, Michoacán, Mexico, Puebla, and Tlaxcala (Aldrich and Baer 1970, Johnsgard 1961). From May 6 to May 29, 1966, only 120 Mexican ducks were observed by Aldrich and Bear (1970) in 14 of 43 areas inspected in Mexico.

Winter Areas

Despite the importance of the state of Chihuahua for

breeding Mexican ducks, few winter there. The average number observed on January surveys, 1960-65, was 170. The largest number, 547, was noted in 1965. Even in 1970, when almost 15,000 were found in Mexico, only 85 were observed in Chihuahua.

The largest numbers of Mexican ducks in winter have been reported from the state of Jalisco, particularly from Lago de Chapala. In 1970, there were 5,000 on this lake alone and 3,375 near Tepatitlán, 50 miles to the north. The adjacent states of Michoacán and Guanajuato harbor most of the other wintering Mexican ducks. The vast majority of the Mexican ducks that breed in the north apparently migrate southward for varying distances up to 600 miles (Johnsgard 1961).

BREEDING

Little is known about the breeding activities of Mexican ducks. Their nests are well hidden, for even where broods are frequently observed, nests have rarely been found. Bevill (1970) observed courtship behavior in December and considered pair bonds to be well established in January. They began to disintegrate in early June as home ranges were abandoned and flocks began to form.

In New Mexico, Lindsey (1946) found three nests of this species at the San Simon marsh on April 30 and May 15 and one nest at Bosque del Apache National Wildlife Refuge on June 25. The nests were located in meadows of salt grass, sedge, and rushes. Arched runways led through the vegetation to the nests. One nest, composed of compacted grass fragments and lined with down, measured 12 by 9 inches on the outside and 8 by 5.5 inches inside the down bowl. The clutches ranged from 4 to 9 eggs, with an average of 6.4 (8). The eggs were a "water green" in color and averaged 56.8 by 41.2 mm (23). All three nests at the marsh failed to hatch because of desertion. One unusual observation concerned a hen that was seen to carry one of her eggs from the nest. Near Rodeo, New Mexico, the earliest egg-laying began about April 10, 1968-69 (Bevill 1970). Nests were located as close to water as suitable grass cover permitted; three nests were within 70 feet of water, and the farthest were 200 feet distant. All three nests were successful in 1968, and three of six were successful in 1969. One of several renesting efforts was successful, hatching in late June.

Aldrich and Baer (1970) found two nests near Julimes, Chihuahua, Mexico, May 9-27. Another nest, containing four eggs, was reported near Maravatío, Michoacán, on July 8. Downy young were collected on July 12 at Laguna del Carmen, Puebla, and on August 3 at Lago de Chapala, Jalisco.

Florida Duck

Anas fulvigula fulvigula

Other Common Name: Florida mallard

VITAL STATISTICS

Length: Adults, average 23 inches (41)

Weight: Adult male, heaviest, 2.81 pounds, average 2.25 pounds (30)
Adult female, heaviest, 2.50 pounds; average 2.12 pounds (11)

IDENTIFICATION

The Florida duck is darker than the hen mallard and slightly lighter than the black duck. The body plumages of both sexes are a mottled fuscous-brown, but the male has a brilliant yellow bill with a black spot at the base and the female has a dull orange bill with black spots across the saddle. Thus, the sexes in this species can best be distinguished by bill color.

The cheeks and neck of the Florida duck are lightly streaked; those of the black duck and hen mallard are heavily streaked. The speculum of the Florida duck often has a more greenish hue than that of the mallard or black duck. Usually, the speculum is not bordered by white as it is in the mallard, although a narrow white border sometimes occurs behind the speculum.

POPULATION STATUS

The kill of Florida ducks has averaged 17,290 for the period 1960-70, fluctuating from 13,000 to 26,000 with no apparent upward or downward trend.

If hunters kill about one-third of the Florida duck population each year, as Stieglitz and Wilson (1968) assumed, there is an early fall population of 50,000. On this same basis, the preseason population has varied between 39,000 and 78,000, 1960-70.

Age Ratios

The proportion of immature to adult Florida ducks in hunters' bags during the years 1966-73 has averaged 1.89:1 or 65.4 percent immature; this percentage has not been corrected for the greater vulnerability of immatures to the gun. This ratio is higher than that for uncorrected age ratios of mallards, 1.23:1, during the same period.

DISTRIBUTION

The Florida duck is nonmigratory and makes his year-round home in the Florida peninsula, south of a line extending from Cedar Key to Gainesville to Daytona Beach (Chamberlain 1960). The counties of Hendry, Lee, Charlotte, and Glades harbor over 60 percent of the population.

BREEDING

Behavior

Age, Pair Bond, and Homing. Paired Florida ducks have been observed during all months of the year (Stieglitz and Wilson 1968). Small flocks of 4 to 15, perhaps immatures not yet paired, are more commonly noted in late fall and early winter and single pairs are seen from February to October. Pair attachment is much more prolonged than it is in the mallard and may persist throughout the year except for the brood period.

Nesting

Nest Sites. Florida ducks preferred to nest on small islands in the Merritt Island area of Florida. Of 117 nests, 114 were on islets and 3 were on levees (Stieglitz and Wilson 1968). Three of five nests studied by Beckwith and Hosford (1956) were in tomato fields. Over half of the nests on Merritt Island were located in paspalum grass, almost one-fifth in broom sedge, and others in wax myrtle shrubs

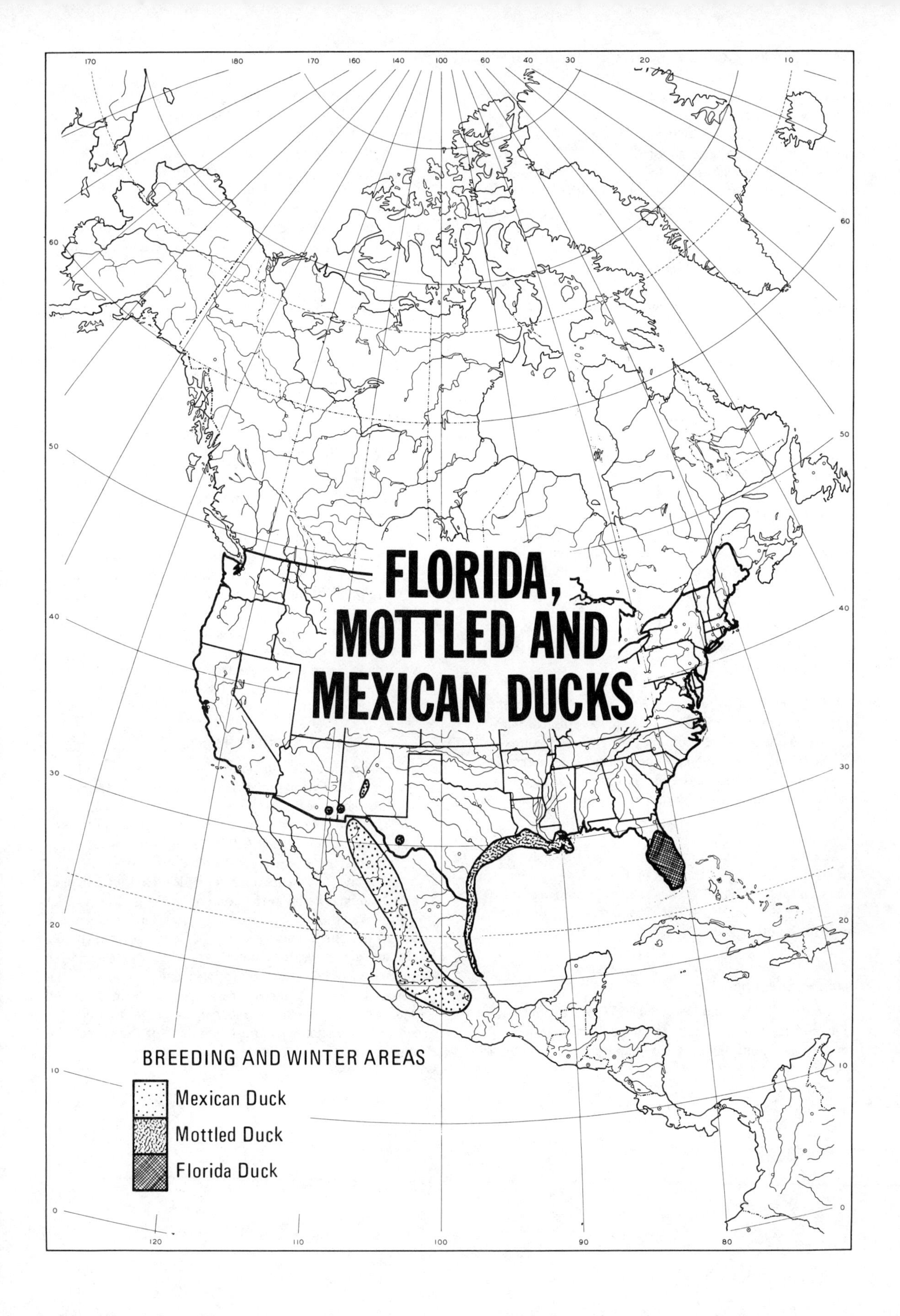
FLORIDA, MOTTLED AND MEXICAN DUCKS
BREEDING AND WINTER AREAS
Mexican Duck
Mottled Duck
Florida Duck

and scrub palmetto. Height of cover ranged from 6 to 96 inches and averaged 34 inches (Stieglitz and Wilson 1968). Nests were as close as 6 feet and as distant as 79 feet from water, with an average of about 28.

Nest density on one islet was 1.2 active nests per acre, and through the entire nest period at another islet there were 23 nests per acre. Three nests were found within a 15-foot circle.

The Florida duck builds her nest by excavating a scrape 2 to 3 inches deep and 6 to 8 inches in diameter and lining the bowl with grasses and other nearby plants. She adds a lining of down after the fifth egg has been laid.

Chronology of Nesting. Although Merritt Island Florida ducks started their nests as early as February 11 and as late as July 17, over two-thirds of the nests were initiated between March 1 and April 15 (Stieglitz and Wilson 1968). Nest initiation spanned a period of 80 days in 1966 (midpoint, March 29) and 125 days in 1967 (midpoint, April 3). Hatching started in late March and peaked the last 2 weeks of April; only a few nests hatched later than June.

Clutch Size, Eggs, and Incubation. Clutch size at Merritt Island varied from 5 to 13 eggs and averaged 9.5 eggs (78). Early clutches averaged 10.1 eggs and late ones 8.9 eggs (Stieglitz and Wilson 1968). Eggs were usually laid at the rate of one per day.

The smooth-shelled eggs are ovate to elliptical ovate, measure 57 by 44 mm (52), and vary in color from creamy white to greenish white (Bent 1923). The incubation period is 25 to 26 days.

Nest Success. Stieglitz and Wilson (1968) determined the fate of 93 nests—74 percent were successful. All 3 nests on dikes were destroyed, but 69 of the 90 nests on islets were successful. Ninety-six percent of the eggs in the successful nests hatched; most of the unhatched eggs were infertile but some disappeared and in others the embryos died.

Nest Failure. Raccoons probably destroyed the nests on dikes. The cause of the loss of almost half the nests on islets was unknown but was believed to be human pilfering. Avian predators, probably fish crows, were responsible for most of the other losses.

Rearing of Young

Broods. LaHart and Cornwell (1971), during the course of capturing Florida duck broods by nightlighting, observed their habits and preferred habitats. The most productive habitat for broods occurred in the brackish water marshes of Merritt Island on the east coast of Florida and Sanibel Island on the west coast. Needlerush, salt grass, and cordgrass were the predominant emergents and spiny naiad and widgeon grass the submergents. Broods were less than half as abundant in freshwater as in brackish marshes, and about half as abundant in saltwater as in freshwater marshes. Broods were observed feeding largely on animal matter, particularly on almost emergent mayflies.

Survival. Florida duck broods declined in size from 7.06 (134) at Class I to 6.2 (27) at Class II and to 4.4 (20) at Class III age (LaHart and Cornwell 1971). This decline represents a 52 percent reduction in brood size from the 9.1 ducklings that hatched in successful nests.

POSTBREEDING SEASON

The males leave their mates during the late stages of incubation and gather with others where food, water, and cover conditions are favorable. At Merritt Island, Johnson (1973) found flightless Florida ducks of both sexes during the month of August. Flightless hens were alone, but flightless males were in small groups. The flightless ducks frequented shallow water impoundments of slightly over 500 acres, containing an abundance of salt grass and mangrove. Near Lake Okeechobee, Beckwith and Hosford (1956) noted an absence of adult birds in late July and early August, indicating that they were probably in seclusion for the wing molt. Some hand-reared young entered the wing molt in July. The flightless period lasts about 4 weeks.

FOOD HABITS

The Florida duck consumes a wide variety of food, considering its restricted range. The items consumed vary with season, water areas, and water levels. Beckwith and Hosford (1956) found over 75 species of plants in the contents of 144 gizzards. Stieglitz (1972) found a pronounced difference in food habits between Florida ducks from the coastal marshes and those from the Everglades. He found 36 plant and 34 animal items in the contents of 85 gizzards.

Preferred foods vary with the habitat. On interior freshwater marshes, smartweeds, beak rushes, paspalum grasses, saw grass, and nutgrasses are important. Ducks on coastal marshes utilize spring naiad, shoalgrass, salt grass, muskgrass, and widgeon grass. During fall and winter, vegetable matter composes most of the food contents, but in summer almost one-third of the items consumed are animal foods.

Mottled Duck

Anas fulvigula maculosa

Other Common Names: Black duck, summer duck, mallard hen

VITAL STATISTICS

Length: Males, 19.8-24.0 inches, average 22.4 inches (205)
Females, 17.5-23.4 inches, average 20.9 inches (208)

Weight: Males, heaviest, 3.19 pounds; average, 2.50 pounds (214)
Females, heaviest, 2.81 pounds; average 2.31 pounds (152)

IDENTIFICATION

The mottled duck is a large duck with mottled fuscous-brown plumage that appears black at a distance. Like the black duck, which it resembles, the male and female are almost identical in appearance. In the hand, the plumage appears darker than that of the hen mallard but browner than the plumage of the black duck. The wing is noticeably smaller than the wing of the black duck.

The blue-green speculum of the mottled duck is bordered in front by a single black bar rather than a black and a white bar as in the mallard. The white bar behind the speculum is more pronounced in the mottled duck than in the black duck. Drakes can best be distinguished from hens by the color of the bill: The hen has dark spots or blotches on an orange bill; the drake's bill is plain olive-green.

Compared with the Florida duck, the mottled duck's plumage is slightly darker, the streaking on the cheeks and neck is more pronounced, and the green speculum has a more bluish cast.

POPULATION STATUS

Populations of mottled ducks fluctuate with changing water conditions along the Gulf Coast. When droughts occur, their numbers decline markedly only to rebound when wet seasons return (Singleton 1968). Favorable breeding conditions result in an early fall population of 200,000 to 250,000 mottled ducks in the United States and Mexico, indicating a breeding population of 100,000 to 125,000 (Hugh Bateman, Charles Stutzenbaker).

Mottled ducks in Louisiana appear to have increased in number in the late 1960's and early 1970's as a result of improvement in coastal marshes and an extension of their breeding range (Hugh Bateman). Recent hurricanes have created many new ponds in the otherwise dense marsh vegetation. The greater interspersion of ponds and marshes has made for better breeding habitats. Mottled ducks have also increasingly exploited the rice fields for nesting, thereby extending their range northward.

Age Ratios. The proportion of immatures to adults in hunters' bags averaged 1.26:1 during 1966-73. This figure was uncorrected for the greater vulnerability of immatures to shooting. It is almost the same as the uncorrected proportion of immature to adult mallards (1.20:1) found in the United States during those same years.

DISTRIBUTION

Mottled ducks inhabit the Gulf Coast from the Pearl River marshes on the Mississippi-Louisiana border to the Alvarado Lagoon near Veracruz, Mexico. In the United States, they range through the extensive coastal marshes, the adjacent rice fields, pastures, and farmlands in a band 30 to 80 miles wide.

The primary breeding range in Louisiana lies in the great marsh of 3,859,000 acres that borders the Gulf Coast. According to Hugh Bateman, 39 percent inhabit the 1,222,000 acres of freshwater marsh; 32 percent utilize the 652,000 acres of marsh intermediate between fresh and brackish water; 19 percent are found in the 1,186,000 acres of brackish marsh; and 1 percent frequent the 799,000 acres of saline marsh. About a million acres of agricultural land, largely in rice, are used by 9 percent of the mottled ducks in Louisiana.

Early fall populations of 75,000 to 120,000 occur in

Louisiana (Hugh Bateman) and 60,000 to 100,000 in Texas (Charles Stutzenbaker). The highest breeding densities in Texas have been recorded between Sabine Lake and Galveston Bay (Singleton 1953). From that area to Corpus Christi, breeding densities gradually decline and then increase slightly between Corpus Christi and Brownsville.

Preferred habitats in Texas are the slightly brackish and freshwater marshes on the upper Gulf Coast, the rice fields, the shallow marshes along the southern coast of Texas, and the ponds in row crop agricultural lands (Singleton 1968). Small numbers of mottled ducks breed in Mexico, most of them in marshes immediately south of the mouth of the Rio Grande. On an aerial survey in January 1970, Hanson and Smith (1970) observed 1,800 in Mexico, with numbers decreasing rapidly along the coast from the Rio Grande to Tampico. They saw only two mottled ducks south of Tampico in the Alvarado Lagoon near Veracruz.

Although mottled ducks are nonmigratory, sizable numbers move inland from the coastal marshes to the rice fields during harvest in September and October. Afterwards, the population concentrates on the coastal marshes for the winter (Hugh Bateman, Charles Stutzenbaker).

MIGRATION BEHAVIOR

Shifts in abundance of mottled ducks occur within their range, and a few individuals have been reported as far as 250 miles from their sites of banding. Frequent surveys during the course of a year by Hugh Bateman show that population abundance fluctuates between southeast and southwest Louisiana.

Some mottled ducks banded in east Texas by Charles Stutzenbaker have shown a propensity to move eastward into Louisiana, but most birds do not venture far from their natal areas. Numerous recoveries have been obtained of mottled ducks banded as ducklings and killed within 1 mile of their points of capture 1 to 3 years after banding.

BREEDING

Behavior

Mottled ducks in Louisiana were observed in courting groups from September through November, with courting activity declining during December (Weeks 1969). The average group contained six individuals, males predominating 1.5 to 1.

Age, Pair Bond, and Homing. Immature birds probably pair by midwinter, for by that time Weeks (1969) found that 90 percent of all mottled ducks he observed were in pairs. Many adults pair earlier, for half of all ducks observed in September were already paired. From observations in Texas, Charles Stutzenbaker believes that the pair bond remains intact until about the time the eggs hatch; by the end of July, fewer than 10 percent of the birds are still paired.

Because mottled ducks are nonmigratory, most hens are assumed to nest near their natal areas. Molting males have been recaptured at the same marsh during successive years, illustrating a return to a specific area (Charles Stutzenbaker).

Home Range. Three-bird chases, resulting in dispersal of breeding pairs, were observed in Louisiana as early as February 17 and as late as June 14 (Weeks 1969). The home ranges of four ducks covered areas from 105 to 327 acres. From waiting sites, pairs made low exploratory flights over the surrounding marsh, apparently searching for nest sites.

During incubation, the male waits for his mate at a particular place within their home range. He often flies out to the incubating hen, who then joins him in the air for a flight to their feeding area (Charles Stutzenbaker). Occasionally, the hen leaves the nest to fly to the waiting area.

These feeding and rest breaks for the incubating hen occur twice daily, early in the morning and late in the evening. On their return flight, the hen leading, they fly about 200 feet above the marsh until they are near the nest, then dip to within a few feet of the ground. The female drops out of the air while the male continues to fly low for several hundred yards before rising abruptly and returning to his waiting area (Charles Stutzenbaker).

Nesting

Nest Sites. Mottled ducks prefer to nest in cordgrass meadows at the edge of the coastal marsh, but they also nest in open prairie meadows and in fallow rice fields (Charles Stutzenbaker). Nest sites are usually slightly higher than the surrounding terrain and within 500 feet of water in ditches, marshes, ponds, or bayous, although some are as far as 1 mile from water. The nest is usually located in a clump of cordgrass so dense that the nest bowl is actually several inches above the ground, which in wet years may be covered by several inches of water. Some mottled ducks build nests directly on the ground.

The nests are well concealed with overhead cover of grasses or baccharis bush. Nest cover in unburned cordgrass meadows can be as high as 2 to 3 feet. Usually, nests are scattered over an extensive area, but in one Texas marsh, one nest per 10 acres was found (Charles Stutzenbaker). On rare occasions, nests have been located only 30 feet apart.

Clutch Size, Eggs, and Incubation. A study of over 200 nests of mottled ducks in Texas showed early clutches ranging from 8 to 13 eggs, with an average of 10 (Charles Stutzenbaker). Late nests (renests) averaged 8 eggs. The eggs are ovate to elliptical ovate, 54.9 by 40.5 mm, and cream-white to greenish white. Nests in the wild are incubated 25 to 27 days, an average of 26 days (Charles Stutzenbaker).

Chronology of Nesting. A few mottled ducks may commence nesting in February, but most of them begin to nest in early March, with nest initiation continuing at a diminishing rate until late June and, rarely, beyond. Most unusual was a newly hatched brood observed on December 25 by U. S. Game Agent Gustav J. Nun.

Nest Success. The nest success of the mottled duck is extremely precarious—only 25 percent of over 200 nests (Charles Stutzenbaker) and about 28 percent of 108 nests Singleton (1953) were successful. Of the eggs that reached the hatching stage, 95 percent hatched.

Nest Failure. Raccoons are primarily responsible for the high rate of nest destruction (Stutzenbaker). Flooding, trampling by cattle, farm dogs, and human activities are other reasons for nest loss.

Renesting. Charles Stutzenbaker believes that only extensive renesting by the mottled duck enables it to survive despite the high nest losses. One hen laid 34 eggs in five nesting attempts before achieving success (Singleton 1953). There are several instances of three attempts to renest.

Rearing of Young

Broods. The hen mottled duck leads her brood to the nearest water—a pond in the marsh, a ditch, a bayou—when the ducklings are dry, usually less than 24 hours old. Brooding is frequent the first 3 days—young hatched by a domestic hen sought the hen for warmth several times hourly (Singleton 1953). Early in life, the ducklings feed avidly upon water insects.

Development. Young mottled ducks are capable of limited flight at 60 days, but most of them probably do not fly until they are 70 days of age (Charles Stutzenbaker).

Survival. Broods of Class I young average 9.8 ducklings (28). By the time broods are approaching flight as Class III young, the average is 6.3 (44), a decrease of 36 percent.

POSTBREEDING SEASON

As females complete incubation, the deserting males gather with others of their sex in secluded water areas. Large numbers enter the flightless period of postnuptial molt in late July, and males in this condition are found in progressively smaller numbers to mid-September (Charles Stutzenbaker). Some hens become flightless in August, and others are in this stage of the molt through September. By October 1, practically all adults are again on the wing.

With the ability of young and old to fly, concentrations of up to 3,000 mottled ducks form during September and October in areas where food is plentiful (Singleton 1968). This period is the only time during the year when large aggregations occur. By November, the larger concentrations have broken up into flocks of 5 to 25 ducks, and, shortly, even these flocks break up into pairs.

FOOD HABITS

The contents of 32 stomachs suggest that the mottled duck, in contrast to the mallard, feeds heavily on animal life (Singleton 1953). Over half of the food contents consisted of animals, mostly insects, fish, snails, and crayfish. Among plants, the seeds of wild millet, rice, delta duck potato, spike rush, and pondweeds were important foods.

Black Duck

Anas rubripes

Other Common Names: Black mallard, red leg

VITAL STATISTICS

Length:*	Adult male, 21.6-24.2 inches, average 22.5 inches (43) Adult female, 20.0-23.7 inches, average 20.8 inches (21) Immature male, 21.6-23.7 inches, average 22.4 inches (10) Immature female, 19.0-23.5 inches, average 20.0 inches (41)
Wing:	Adult male, 11.4 inches (195) Adult female, 10.7 inches (113) Immature male, 11.1 inches (454) Immature female, 10.4 inches (304)
Weight:*	Adult male, 2.5-3.4 pounds, average 2.76 pounds (346) Adult female, 2.3-3.3 pounds, average 2.45 pounds (224) Immature male, 2.3-3.4 pounds, average 2.64 pounds (657) Immature female, 2.0-3.2 pounds, average 2.39 pounds (598)

*Length data and part of the weight data from Karl Bednarik

IDENTIFICATION

Field

The black duck closely resembles the mallard in size, body conformation, and flight characteristics, but its plumage is much darker than that of the hen mallard, to which it bears a superficial resemblance. It is the only common duck in eastern North America in which the sexes are almost identical in appearance. The Florida duck and the mottled duck, both near relatives of the black duck, have sexes of similar plumage, but their range is restricted to Florida, Louisiana, and Texas.

If visibility is good, the contrast between the lighter brown head and the brown-black body of the black duck is noticeable. In the paler-hued hen mallard, there is little contrast between head and body. Moreover, the white coloration in the tail feathers and the band of white bordering the violet-blue speculum of the mallard are absent in the black duck.

In flight, the white underwings of the black duck flash in vivid contrast to the brown-black body.

Where both species occur, black ducks are frequently found in flocks of mallards. However, progressively farther eastward in the black duck's range, the greater the likelihood for this species to be observed in pure flocks. Flocks of black ducks, usually numbering from 5 to 25 individuals, are generally smaller than flocks of mallards.

At Hand

The sooty-brown plumage of both sexes is considerably darker than the mottled straw-brown plumage of the hen mallard. The speculum of the black duck is also a darker blue and is bordered by black, sometimes margined with a faint white line much less pronounced than the white stripes bordering the mallard's paler blue speculum.

Sex and age in the black duck can be determined to a large extent by the color of the bill and legs. The adult drake has a bright yellow bill and coral legs. The adult hen has an olive-green bill with black mottling; her legs are a dull carmine. The immature male has a plain olive-green bill, without the darkened center, and yellowish-red legs. The colors of fleshy parts fade with death.

Hybrids between mallards and black ducks exhibit a variety of plumages. Some "black ducks" show only traces of green on the sides of their heads and traces of white bordering their blue speculums but otherwise appear very much like the pure form. Other specimens, like drake mallards, may have green heads but possess dark body feathers and lack the white neck-rings.

The following data on the proportion of mallard-black duck hybrids to black ducks are based upon their composition in hunters' bags as determined from wing collections by the U. S. Fish and Wildlife Service, 1963-70. One of every 33 "black ducks" in the Atlantic Flyway shows plumage characteristics of both the mallard and the black duck. One of every 22 "black ducks" in the Mississippi Flyway shows plumage patterns typical of each species. Johnsgard (1967) concluded after a detailed study of mallard-black duck hybrids that a hybridization rate of about 4 percent results from chance contact between the two species.

POPULATION STATUS

For a number of reasons it is difficult to determine the continental population of the black duck from surveys of breeding and winter grounds. Therefore, Geis et al. (1971) used the average annual kill and the rate of band recovery to calculate that the preseason population of this species during the 1950's averaged 3,738,000.

Other methods of calculation yield other figures, probably less valid but more useful for determining population trends. From data on the winter population, plus the kill for the preceding fall, Geis et al. (1971) determined that populations of 1,311,000 during 1952-54 declined to 1,146,000 during 1955-58, and to 804,000 during 1959-62. Winter inventory data, 1955-74, show an almost continuous steady decline—amounting to slightly over 40 percent—in both the Atlantic and Mississippi flyways during this 20-year period. The reasons for this drastic decline in black duck numbers is unclear; it is not related to a comparable loss of breeding habitat.

Age Ratios

The proportion of immatures to mature black ducks in hunters' bags in the United States averaged 1.48 immatures per adult for 1961-71 (Smart 1965, Sorensen and Carney 1972). However, because immatures are 1.2 times more vulnerable to hunting than adults (Geis et al. 1971), the true proportion in fall populations in the United States averaged 1.2 immatures per adult, 1961-71.

Sex Ratios

The sexes of black ducks are similar, yet there was an average of 1.48 drakes per hen in the kill (Sorensen and Carney 1972). The proportions of each sex that were banded, compared with their recoveries the first fall, indicate that male black ducks in the United States are 1.2 times more readily shot than females. Therefore, the proportion of drakes in the fall population is approximately 1.23 per hen (55 percent).

Mortality

Geis et al. (1971) calculated that 65 percent of immature black ducks die during their first year of life and 40 percent are lost each subsequent year. Adult females have a mortality rate approximately 25 percent greater than that of adult males. Geis and his colleagues determined that hunting accounted for half of all mortality among immatures and adults of both sexes. They further determined that although increased shooting pressure resulted in increased mortality, it was not proportionate—some mortality from shooting replaced nonhunting mortality. The compensation of hunting losses for nonhunting losses was greater among immatures than among adults. Geis et al. (1971) concluded that with no shooting losses, a yearly mortality of 40 percent among immatures and of 22 percent among adults would still occur.

DISTRIBUTION

The black duck is confined to eastern North America, largely east of the Great Plains and south of the tundra. North of Long Island and east of Ohio, it replaces the mallard as the most abundant dabbling duck and becomes its ecological equivalent in many habitats.

Breeding Range

With minor exceptions, the black duck breeds in scattered numbers across the northern tier of states west to about the Mississippi River and north through Ontario and extreme northeastern Manitoba to Hudson Bay. It breeds as far north in Quebec and Labrador as the open boreal forest extends. On the Atlantic Coast, the black duck nests in coastal marshes as far south as Cape Hatteras, North Carolina. In the United States, the black duck probably reaches its highest breeding density in the coastal marshes and is particularly abundant in the marshes adjacent to the eastern shore of Chesapeake Bay.

In Canada, the highest breeding densities of black ducks occur in the region of mixed forests, embracing the Great Lakes, St. Lawrence, and Acadian areas (Reed 1968); breeding densities in Newfoundland are low. Brackish tidal marshes and barrier ponds make up the important breeding habitat in Nova Scotia and Prince Edward Island. In New Brunswick, floodplains of rivers (especially the St. John), are the principal breeding areas, but some inland lakes are of local importance. The highest known breeding densities in Quebec are along the St. Lawrence River and its major tributaries. Over the vast boreal forest of Quebec with its countless lakes, ponds, and streams, nest densities are low. The lakes and ponds dotting the Canadian Shield in Ontario provide an extensive but sparsely populated area, with breeding density declining from east to west.

On aerial surveys in the boreal forest of Quebec and eastern Ontario, Kaczynski and Chamberlain (1968) observed 0.15 to 0.45 black duck per square mile, an average of 0.29. This figure, adjusted to allow for the proportion overlooked from the air (×3), indicates a black duck breeding population of 0.87 per square mile over much of its northern range.

Migration Corridors

After breeding, many black ducks move north to Hudson Bay and west into Manitoba and eastern Saskatchewan. Because of the premigration movement westward, several migration corridors have a southeasterly slant in the northern states. Most migration corridors, however, extend along a north-south axis and converge funnel-like from north to south (Bellrose and Crompton 1970).

About two-thirds of the black ducks utilize corridors extending through the Atlantic Flyway; the remainder follow corridors in the Mississippi Flyway. The single most important corridor extends along the Atlantic Coast from the Maritime Provinces to Florida. Other corridors cross the eastern states to enable the more westerly breeding black ducks to reach important winter grounds on the coast.

In general, the black duck's migration corridors are poorly defined partly because of the short distance traveled and partly because of the conterminous and overlapping breeding areas and winter grounds.

Winter Areas

About 33,000 hardy black ducks winter in Canada, largely along the coast, Lake Erie, and the St. Lawrence River. The Maritimes harbor the greatest numbers, but almost 1,000 have wintered as far north as Newfoundland. Along the Atlantic Coast of the United States, black ducks winter all the way from the Canadian border to Cape Canaveral, Florida. However, almost two-thirds (220,000) of these are concentrated between Long Island and North Carolina. As many as 70,000 black ducks winter north of Long Island and 50,000 south of Virginia.

In the interior of the United States, the largest numbers of black ducks are found wintering in the Lake Erie marshes of Ohio and the valley of the Tennessee River. Other areas of concentration are the large river valleys in Ohio; Lake St. Clair and the Detroit River, Michigan; the lower Wabash River, Indiana; and the upper Illinois River valley and the region between the Ohio and Mississippi rivers in Illinois.

MIGRATION BEHAVIOR

Black ducks tend to return to the same marshes in fall and winter that they visited the previous year (Addy 1953, Martin 1960, Bellrose and Crompton 1970). Martin (1960) reported that 48 percent of all males recovered in years after banding were from the vicinity of the banding station; the figure for hens was 37 percent. Although all ducks exhibit some degree of homing to specific migration and winter areas, this trait appears most pronounced in the black duck. Their attachment to a particular winter ground is so strong that when tidal feeding grounds have become frozen in New England, some black ducks have starved rather than migrate farther southward.

Chronology

Fall. Black ducks migrate into areas of New England early in the fall, beginning in late September and reaching peak numbers by mid-October; their passage into Michigan, Wisconsin, and Minnesota occurs 2 weeks later than in the Northeast.

They evidently are in no hurry to migrate farther southward, for in the middle states they do not appear in abundance until mid-November. The small numbers that winter in the southern states do not make a significant appearance until late November and early December. It is apparent that black ducks are a hardy lot, and most of them delay their southward migration until marshes freeze over.

Spring. The spring migration northward is a gradual affair starting in early February in the southern states and in mid-February in the middle states. Steady departures continue into early April. Populations of black ducks in the lake states begin to show an influx from farther south in mid-March and continue to increase throughout the month, with numbers not appreciably declining until mid-April. Black duck populations in New England show little change during the spring as ingress and egress apparently balance.

Black ducks appear in the northern part of their range almost as soon as the ice begins to melt. According to Wright (1954), they appeared at the following locations on the dates given: St. John Estuary, April 11; St. Lawrence Estuary, April 15; Hamilton Inlet, Labrador, May 2; and Makkovik Bay, Labrador, May 26.

BREEDING

Behavior

Age, Pair Bond, and Homing. Black ducks breed late in their first year of life. However, Vernon Stotts has found that from 6 to 10 percent of the hens do not breed as yearlings. He suspects that these are birds hatched late the previous summer. Stotts and Davis (1960) believed that immatures begin pairing in December or January when females are 6 or 7 months old. Immature males probably start pairing when 1 or 2 months older.

Adult birds begin pair formation in early September and

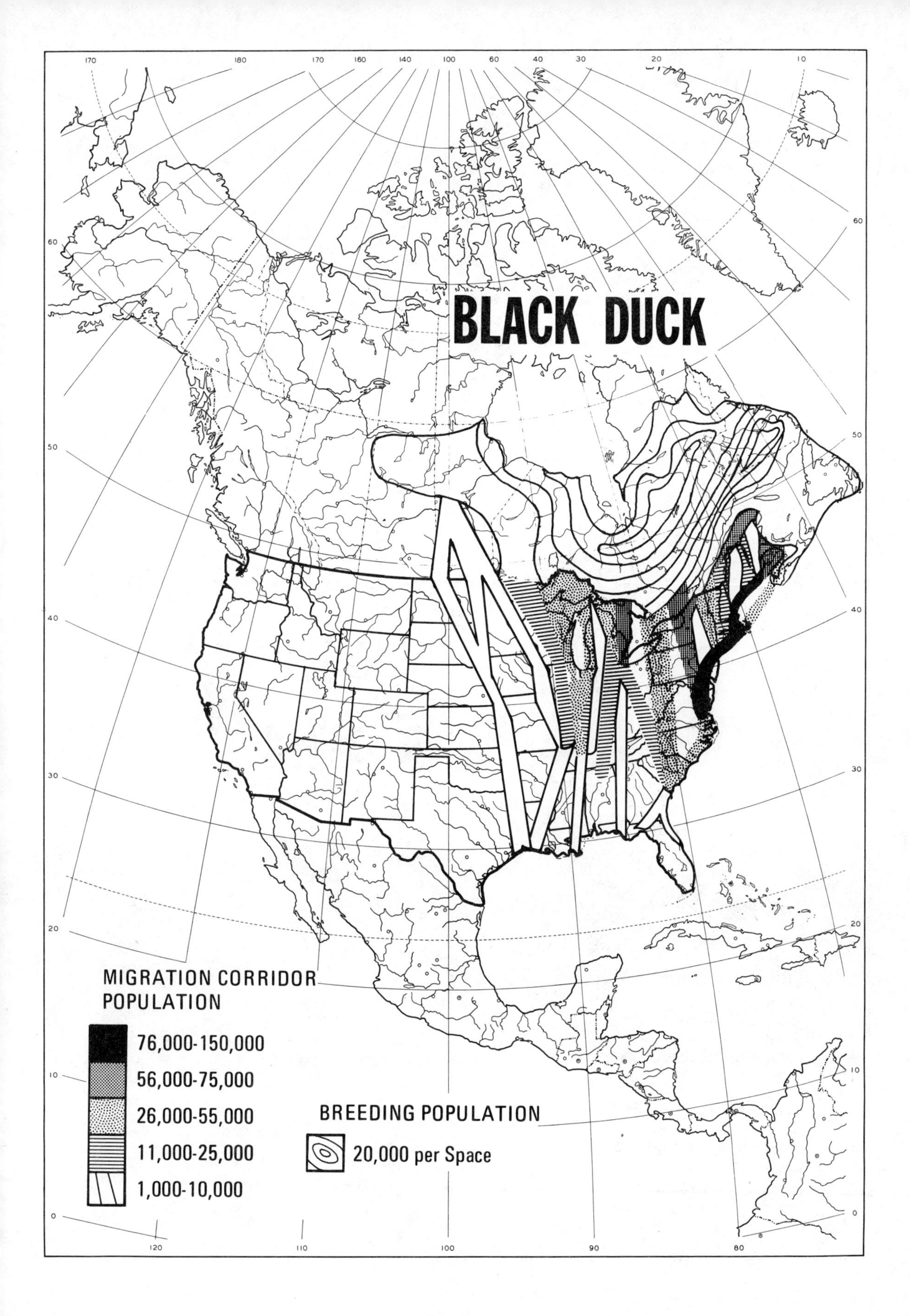
BLACK DUCK
MIGRATION CORRIDOR POPULATION
76,000-150,000
56,000-75,000
26,000-55,000
11,000-25,000
1,000-10,000
BREEDING POPULATION
20,000 per Space

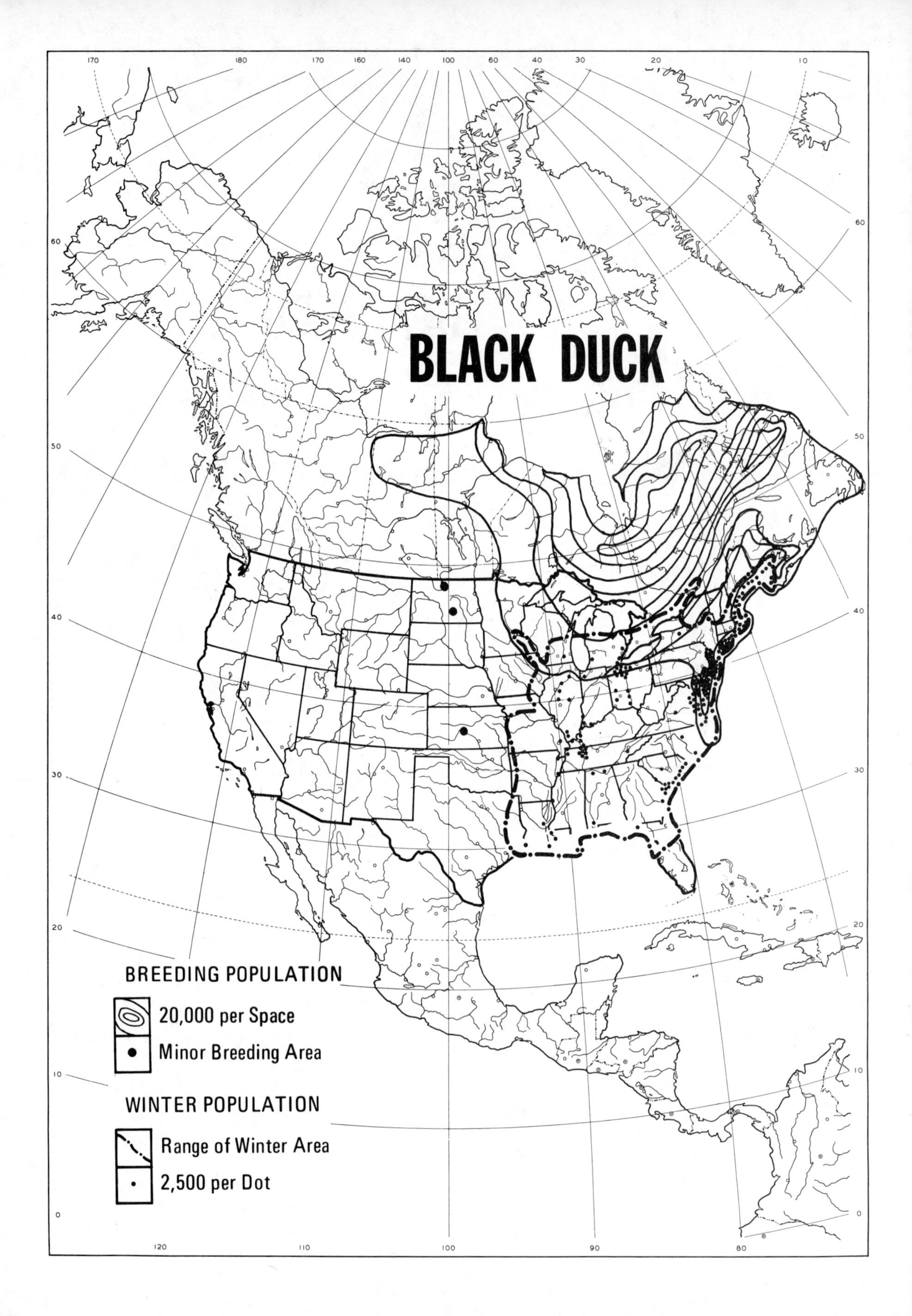
BLACK DUCK
BREEDING POPULATION
20,000 per Space
Minor Breeding Area
WINTER POPULATION
Range of Winter Area
2,500 per Dot

attachments proceed rapidly thereafter; probably most are paired by mid-December. Johnsgard (1960*a*) reported that among black ducks of all ages, sexual displays reached a high frequency in mid-October and continued at a high level to mid-February. In new York, 80 percent of the birds he observed were paired by mid-January and almost all by April. During April and early May, Stotts and Davis (1960) found that 88 percent of the black ducks at Chesapeake Bay were paired. Barclay (1970) estimated that one-third of the black ducks at Winous Point marsh, Ohio, were paired by early September and three-fourths by late October.

Male black ducks remained with their mates for an average of 14 days after the incubation of first clutches began; some stayed for as long as 22 days and others for as few as 7 days (Stotts and Davis 1960). Drakes remained in attendance on renesting females for an average of 9 days, with a range of 4 to 16 days. However, on occasion the pair bond in black ducks may be more enduring. Barclay (1970) observed a marked pair of black ducks in the spring of 1969 that was still paired the following November. In Maryland, Stotts and Davis (1960) observed small numbers of paired black ducks through the entire summer. Probably some of the hens that remained with their mates were unsuccessful nesters.

At least 25 percent of marked hens returned to their former nest areas at Lake Champlain, most to within 100 yards of previous nest sites (Coulter and Miller 1968). On an island in the St. Lawrence Estuary, 4 of 24 marked hens returned the next year and 2 appeared the third year (Reed 1968). All subsequent nests were within 1,000 feet of the initial nest sites. One female used the same site under a cabin for 3 years.

Home Range. Nesting pairs of black ducks range over diversified habitat including waiting sites, nest sites, and feeding areas. Defensive behavior, centering on three-bird flights, results in some degree of isolation for breeding pairs (Barclay 1970). This type of behavior in black ducks has been most prevalent in large marshes and least observed on islands, where density of nests is greater (Reed 1968).

The home ranges of black ducks in New England are up to 5 square miles in size (Coulter and Miller 1968). The heart of the home range has been termed "the activity center," which embraces the waiting site (Barclay 1970). The waiting site is usually an area of shoreline open on one side with a vegetative screen on the other. A pair spends much of its preincubation time in the activity center, where the male waits for his mate during the early stages of incubation. At Winous Point, Ohio, activity centers averaged 1.5 acres in size.

On large marshes in New England, the drake usually waits on the nearest open water, sometimes 0.25 mile from the nest site (Coulter and Miller 1968). However, the mates of some hens nesting on islands in Lake Champlain used waiting sites more than 2 miles away.

Nesting

On their breeding grounds along the St. John River in New Brunswick, Wright (1954) found a 9-day lapse between the arrival of black ducks and the laying of the first egg. The interval between arrival and laying was 2 to 3 weeks on the St. Lawrence Estuary (Reed 1968).

Nest Sites. Black ducks nest in a variety of habitats, depending upon the cover available. On the east shore of Chesapeake Bay, 65 percent nested in upland areas, 17 percent in marshes, and 19 percent in old duck blinds (Stotts and Davis 1960). Most of the nests in upland areas were in wooded tracts.

Wright (1954) reported that in the St. John Estuary, New Brunswick, black ducks began nesting when the river was at flood. Consequently, they nested either on the ground in the cultivated and wooded uplands back of the flood zone or in cavities and crotches of large trees in the extensive flooded lowlands. A comparison of cavities used by wood ducks, goldeneyes, and black ducks in this region indicated that those selected by black ducks were larger, shallower, and more bucketlike than those used by the other species (Prince 1968). Black ducks also made extensive use of stumps and dead snags for nest sites in flooded timber at the Montezuma National Wildlife Refuge, New York (Cowardin et al. 1967).

On islands of the Kennebec River, Maine, two-thirds of the black ducks nested under live conifers and one-fifth in blueberry patches (Coulter and Miller 1968). On islands in Lake Champlain, 21 percent of the black ducks placed their nests in new herbaceous growth—chiefly nettle—20 percent in low dead herbaceous plants, 15 percent among fallen logs and limbs and dead treetops, and 14 percent under live conifers. In northern bogs, preferred nest sites were in the sweet gale-leatherleaf-sedge zone.

Nests in the St. Lawrence Estuary were located primarily in clumps of grass and secondarily under shrubs and trees (Reed 1968). A few ducks even nested in rock crevices. In many parts of their range, black ducks have a proclivity for nesting on wooded islands, where densities are unusually high. However, Coulter and Miller (1968) pointed out that black ducks favored islands that were near sedge meadows; nearby meadows without sedge cover had little or no use. Black ducks nesting in the Lake Erie marshes make extensive use of dikes and muskrat houses for nest sites (Barclay 1970).

The female selects the nest site and begins to form the nest basin 3 or 4 days before the first egg is laid (Stotts and Davis 1960). She usually digs a scrape, using both feet and her bill, and lines it with adjacent plant material. In Maryland, most nests were constructed of pine needles (Stotts and Davis 1960); tree nests in New Brunswick were made of punk and bark (Wright 1954). Small amounts of down are added after several eggs are laid, but most of the down is added just as the clutch is completed.

Clutch Size, Eggs, and Incubation. Black ducks lay an average of 9.3 eggs (1,189), most clutches ranging from 7 to

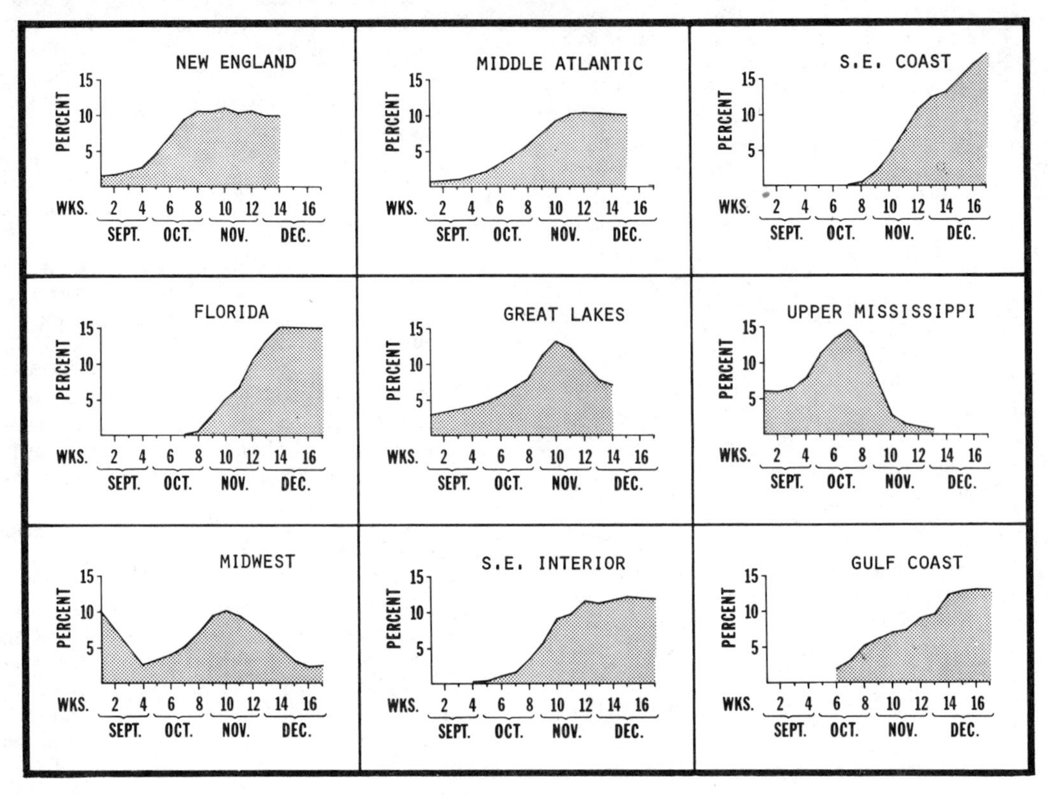

Fall

12 eggs but with extremes of 1 and 17. Clutch size declines as the nest season progresses, early clutches averaging about 11 eggs and late ones about 8. In Maryland, marked hens that renested laid one egg less than in their initial clutches (Stotts and Davis 1960); in New England, Coulter and Miller (1968) found a decrease of only 0.7 egg in renests. The age of the prospective parents had no significant influence on clutch size (Stotts and Davis 1960, Coulter and Miller 1968).

Black duck eggs are in varied shades of white, cream-white, or pale buff-green, with smooth shells. They are ovate to elliptical ovate and measure 59.4 by 43.2 mm (82) (Bent 1923).

The length of the incubation period among black ducks varies considerably. Much of the variation results from the attentiveness of the hen and the ambient temperature. In 51 clutches in Maryland, incubation ranged from 23 to 33 days with an average of 26 days (Stotts and Davis 1960). Hens flushed from the nest 1 to 7 times required 25.5 days to hatch their eggs but hens flushed 8 to 17 times needed 27 days to complete the hatch. On the St. Lawrence Estuary, where temperatures are lower than in Maryland, 19 clutches averaged 29 days of incubation (Reed 1969).

Chronology of Nesting. The first black duck egg laid in Maryland, on average, was on March 19, the peak of initial egg-laying was reached during April 12-25, and the initial eggs of the last clutches were deposited on the average on June 20 (Stotts and Davis 1960). At Lake Champlain, the average date for the laying of the first egg was April 6, and the last clutches were started on June 14-15 (Coulter and Miller 1968).

On the St. John River, New Brunswick, the first egg was laid on April 6, a peak was reached in May, and the few attempts to renest continued into July (Wright 1954). On the St. Lawrence Estuary, black ducks started laying during April 12-25 and the last clutches were begun June 7-20 (Reed 1968). Black ducks in the Lake Erie marshes of Ohio begin to nest about mid-March and continue to initiate nests into early June (Barclay 1970).

The period of nest initiation extends over a 90-day interval at Chesapeake Bay, Maryland, and lasts about 80 days

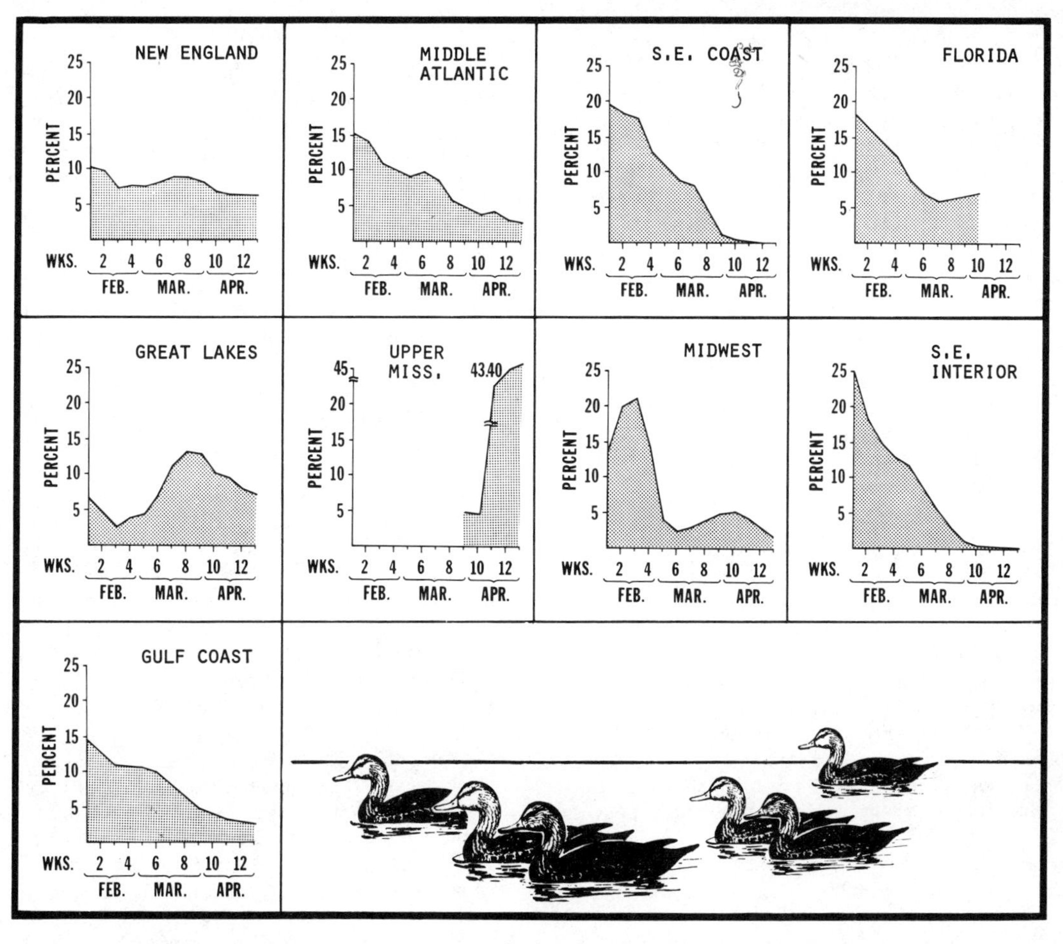

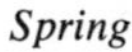
Spring

in New England and 70 days on the St. Lawrence Estuary. Although the dates when nesting was initiated advanced from south to north, laying was terminated at almost the same time regardless of latitude.

Nest Success. Nest success of the black duck averages about 42 percent (842). Stotts and Davis (1960) reported a success rate of 38 percent (574) in the Chesapeake Bay area of Maryland. About 6 percent of the eggs in successful nests failed to hatch, but less than 1 percent of the unhatched eggs were infertile. Renesting black ducks in the Chesapeake area were not as successful as the first nesters—their rate of hatch was about 9 percent lower. Reed's (1968) studies on the St. Lawrence Estuary revealed a success rate of 49 percent (268).

Nest Failure. Many factors contribute to the loss of black duck nests. In Maryland, nests were deserted because of tidal flooding and human activities, including mowing; about half the nests were destroyed, largely by crows, mammals, and humans. Raccoons killed three incubating hens on their nests (Stotts and Davis 1960). About 9 percent of the nests studied on the St. Lawrence Estuary were deserted, but 41 percent were destroyed by predators—crows and gulls (Reed 1968). Over the southern breeding range of the black duck, the raccoon is the most important predator.

Renesting. When nests are destroyed, some black ducks lay a second clutch and, rarely, a third clutch. At Chesapeake Bay, a minimum of 16 percent of the black ducks that lost nests or young broods renested (Stotts 1968). In New England, about 33 percent of the black ducks renested when their first nests were destroyed (Coulter and Miller 1968). Two hens each laid three clutches in one season. Older hens are more likely to renest than yearlings. Almost half (49 percent) of 51 hens 2 years of age or older renested, but only 1 of 7 yearlings (14 percent) renested.

Black ducks in Maryland renested 13 to 26 days (average, 18) after losing clutches they had incubated for an average of 18 days (Stotts 1968). In New England, the time from the loss of the first nest to the first egg deposited in a new nest ranged from 5 to 15 days and averaged 13 days (Coulter and Miller 1968). Those New England renests were usually within 100 yards of their first nest sites, but several were 400 to 1,000 yards distant, and two were between 1,000 and 1,760 yards away. A surprisingly high 77 percent of the renests (30) hatched.

Renesting is most important to the production of the black duck where seasonal breeding chronology is of sufficient duration to permit renests. In Maryland, for example, where nest success is 38 percent, Stotts (1968) believed that about 62 percent of the birds produced broods.

Rearing of Young

Broods. Hens nesting in upland habitat often lead their broods many hundreds of yards overland to the nearest water. In New Brunswick, journeys of 2 miles have been recorded (Wright 1954). Near Sudbury, Ontario, Young (1967) recorded two broods of black ducks traveling across at least 1 mile of rough terrain to reach another lake. The brood area selected by the female embraces a wide variety of habitats: sedge, cattail, and bulrush marshes; beaver ponds; alder-fringed streams; and swamp loosestrife bogs.

Development. The hen usually remains with her brood until the young have reached flight stage, a period of 58 to 63 days (Gollop and Marshall 1954). At first, the young remain tightly clustered under the close guidance of their mother's soft quacks (Beard 1964). As the ducklings become older, the hen permits them to separate into groups of twos, threes, and fours and to range at greater distances when feeding. When danger threatens, she is still able to call her brood together and direct their course. By the age of 5 weeks, the ducklings rarely assemble as a full brood and are less responsive to their mother's call. Sometimes black duck hens were still seen in company with fully feathered but flightless young, but Beard (1964) observed other groups of similar age that were unattended by adults.

Survival. The number of ducklings per brood changes from 7.5 (171) in Class I broods to 6.2 (125) in Class II broods to 6.7 (149) in Class III broods. The slight gain in size of Class III broods over Class II broods indicates a breakup of some broods and the association of the unattached ducklings with other broods as they approach flying stage. Despite the addition of stray ducklings, broods in Class III are 11 percent smaller than those in Class I, and represent a 23 percent reduction over the number of ducklings leaving successful nests.

POSTBREEDING SEASON

According to Wright (1954), the first female black ducks in southern New Brunswick separate from their broods about July 11. From then to after September 15, flightless hens are found in the marshes. In late May, male black ducks begin to congregate in the larger marshes for the wing molt, where they are adept at hiding in the available cover. The earliest date for the molt is June 23. When they regain their flight feathers, the males concentrate at traditional staging areas prior to the fall migration (Wright 1954). They are later joined by adult hens, probably the unsuccessful nesters, and then by the young, and last by the successful hens.

Molting areas are located on tidal marshes and estuaries all along the Atlantic Coast from Ungava to Chesapeake bays. Far from the Atlantic, black ducks select favorable tidal flats along Hudson and James bays.

Between June 27 and September 2, Manning and Macpherson (1952) observed 1,723 black ducks along the east coast of James Bay. Manning (1946) failed to find the species along the east coast of Hudson Bay, yet black ducks are very abundant on the southwest coast of the bay.

Near Cape Henrietta Maria, Peck (1972) considered the black duck to be the second most abundant species, with flightless males noted in late June. Farther up the coast of Hudson Bay, from Shagamu River 60 miles south of Fort Severn to the Seal River 20 miles north of Churchill, George Arthur and Richard Vaught observed about 75,000 black ducks. Of this number, 60,000 to 70,000 were between Fort Severn and the Kettle River; 1,700 between Fort Severn and the Shagamu River; and 5,000 to 6,000 between Churchill and the Seal River. Their surveys covered different sections of the Hudson Bay coast during each of three summers: 1955, 1956, and 1961. All through July most of the black ducks were flightless, and those collected were adult males. During the first week in August most of the black ducks appeared to have regained their flight feathers.

During the postbreeding period, black ducks wander far and wide, reaching areas hundreds of miles beyond their breeding range. They have been found on the Thelon River and Athabasca Delta in the Subarctic and all across the Canadian Plains into Alberta (Wright 1954).

FOOD HABITS

Black ducks exhibit great diversity in the food items they consume, due to the multitude of habitats they frequent. Along the Atlantic Coast, they are equally at home on salt, brackish, and freshwater marshes. Inland, black ducks resort to marshes, lakes, water impoundments, beaver ponds, and rivers.

Eelgrass, widgeon grass, and species of animal life are

the more important foods on estuaries. Animal foods, which are utilized more by black ducks than by mallards, become increasingly important to black ducks during winter. Among the animal foods taken, periwinkles, blue mussels, and various snails predominate. In Illinois, black ducks often feed upon gizzard shad, especially about openings in the ice where shad collect and become moribund.

Birds on coastal marshes eat the seeds of sedges, various bulrushes, wild rice, bur reed, and pickerelweed. Marshes in the interior provide black ducks with seeds from pondweeds, yellow pond lily, smartweeds, and millets, and the leafy segments of coontail. In more swampy areas, acorns and the seeds of buttonbush, bald cypress, and tupelo gum are extensively utilized.

Where waste corn is available in harvested fields near water areas frequented by black ducks, it is an important food source for them, particularly in late fall and winter. They leave their rest areas at daybreak and shortly before sunset to fly up to 25 miles in an effort to find sufficient waste corn.

Pintail

Anas acuta acuta

Other Common Names: Sprig, sprigtail, spike, spiketail

VITAL STATISTICS

Length:	Adult male, 23.6-30.1 inches, average 25.2 inches (26) Adult female, 20.6-24.8 inches, average 21.4 inches (15) Immature male, 21.7-26.9 inches, average 23.9 inches (7) Immature female, 20.0-22.5 inches, average 20.4 inches (17)
Wing:	Adult male, 10.7 inches (45) Adult female, 10.1 inches (27) Immature male, 10.5 inches (30) Immature female, 9.8 inches (31)
Weight:	Adult male, 1.4-3.2 pounds, average 2.26 pounds (390) Adult female, 1.3-2.6 pounds, average 1.91 pounds (166) Immature male, 1.1-2.9 pounds, average 2.09 pounds (760) Immature female, 1.1-2.6 pounds, average 1.76 pounds (526)

IDENTIFICATION

Field

Because of its trim appearance and swift flight, the pintail has been aptly called "the greyhound of the air." Pintails are long, slender ducks with long, narrow wings that are more gull-like in shape than those of other ducks; the wing tips move over a higher, more extended arc with a more rapid beat than in the mallard. The length of the tapered body makes the wings appear to be centered, in contrast to those of other dabbling ducks, which appear to be positioned farther back.

Because of his long neck and long tail, the pintail drake in full nuptial plumage is 3 to 4 inches longer than the mallard drake, yet weighs almost one-fifth less. The hen pintail is about the same length as the hen mallard but also weighs one-fifth less, pointing up the comparative slenderness of the pintail. The length of the neck in relation to that of the torso is greater in the pintail than in any other duck and is similar to that of many geese. The tail, made especially long by the central tail feathers in drakes, is one-fourth of the drake's total length. In early fall some drakes in nuptial plumage have not yet developed their long tail feathers. I have observed immature pintail drakes in late November with the central tail feathers only half of their ultimate length.

In late summer and early fall, the plumages of immature and many adult drake pintails are similar to those of hens. A sprinkling of drakes migrating south early in September show partial nuptial plumages with white breasts and bellies. However, those in more somber plumage molt into their nuptial plumage rapidly, and by early October about half of the males are recognizable. In another 2 weeks, almost all drakes can be distinguished from hens by their white underparts.

Pintails on the water are elegant; they float higher than most dabblers, and the males, with brown heads erect on slender white necks and with long tails jauntily swept upward, create scenes of poignant beauty. Frontal views of the white-necked drakes bring to mind flotillas of toy sailing ships.

In full nuptial plumage, the black scapulars in drakes form an eye-shaped patch just above the gray sides over the closed wing. The back is also gray; the black upper and lower tail coverts stand out against the white flanks and belly.

Hen pintails are a mottled brown, similar in color to female mallards, gadwalls, shovelers, and the two teals.

The noniridescent brown or brown-green speculum, bordered in front with buff and in the rear with white, is sometimes but not always visible when the hen is at rest. When the pintail is in flight, the speculum (iridescent black and green or green in males) is helpful in identifying both sexes.

The male pintail has a distinctive short whistled note, most often heard in the spring.

At Hand

The drake pintail in breeding plumage has a chocolate-brown head, with the white foreneck extending upward, as a stripe, onto the back of the head. The back of the neck, vermiculated with black, appears gray, and so do the back and sides. The pair of long central tail feathers are black, the others are gray margined by white.

The upper body feathers of the female pintail are dark brown, and the head and lower body feathers, noticeably lighter, are buff or gray, spotted with tan or fuscous, giving the bird a streaked appearance. Except in size, female pintails are similar to female blue-winged teal. The bills of both sexes are about the length of their heads, blue-gray in color, black along the central ridge in the male and blotched with black in the female. Fuller (1953) observed that female ducklings developed black spots on their bills when 5 weeks of age and that the number and size of the spots increased to form blotches as the ducklings became older. The legs and feet of both sexes are slate-gray.

The iridescent green or green-black of the male speculum and the dull brown or bronze, sometimes tinged with green, of the female speculum are among the indicators of sex and age groups in pintails. The coverts of adult males are ash-gray; those of immatures are ash-gray tipped with a minute edging of pale buff or light gray. Female wing coverts are dark brown, broadly edged with pale buff in adults and thinly edged in immatures.

POPULATION STATUS

The pintail is either the second or third most abundant duck in North America, vying with the scaups in a seesaw battle for these positions. In some years, production of young favors one of these two species more than the other, which places the favored species second in rank to the mallard. Pintails are the most abundant duck in the Pacific Flyway and are second to the mallard in the Central Flyway.

During 1955-73, the average number of pintails on major breeding grounds in North America was estimated at 6,193,000. Extremely large breeding populations of 9,300,000 and 10,140,000 occurred in 1955 and 1956. The populations declined to a low of 4 to 5 million during 1961-65 and recovered partially in the early 1970's. The trend in breeding numbers over the 19-year period (1955-73) was down 24 percent, but omitting the unusually high years of 1955 and 1956, the trend was upward by 10 percent.

Winter surveys, 1955-73, showed an upward trend of 15 percent in pintail numbers in the United States. During this same period, the number of pintails wintering in the Atlantic and Central flyways showed decreases of 80 and 23 percent. The Mississippi (including Louisiana) and Pacific flyways had increases of 44 and 40 percent. The increase in the Mississippi Flyway and the decrease in the Central Flyway were mainly caused by a shift in wintering populations between Texas and Louisiana during 1963-69.

Age Ratios

The proportion of immature to adult pintails sampled from hunters' bags, 1961-73, averaged 1.39:1. Assuming that pintails are vulnerable to the gun at the same ratio as many other ducks, immatures are 1.5 times more readily shot than adults. Consequently, the average for the fall pintail population would be about 0.93 immature per adult.

Sex Ratios

Adult drake pintails outnumbered hens in hunters' bags, 1966-73, by 2.19:1 (68.6 percent drakes). On the other hand, immature drakes were only slightly more abundant than immature hens, 1.13:1 (53.0 percent). Because the average fall population is composed of about equal age-classes, sex ratios would be 1.66:1 (62.4 percent drakes). Probably, a slight selection of drakes by hunters somewhat biases this figure upward. This bias is indicated by visual sex ratios taken in the spring, which averaged 59.4 percent drakes (Bellrose et al. 1961). Thus, there are about three drakes for every two hens.

Mortality

Pintails banded as flightless young or flying immatures in Minnesota suffered first-year mortality of 90 percent (Lee et al. 1964). This unusually high mortality rate suggests abnormally high losses among flightless young. The subsequent yearly mortality averaged 57 percent. Among adult pintails banded in Minnesota, the yearly mortality rate averaged 58 percent. At Delta Marsh, Manitoba, wild-trapped pintails experienced a first-year mortality of 66 percent, and hand-reared birds lost 89 percent of their number the first year (Brakhage 1953).

Band recoveries from flightless adult drake pintails captured in July in south-central Saskatchewan showed an average annual mortality rate of 43 percent (Sterling 1966). Pintails banded in California prior to the hunting season (Kozlik 1972) had a mortality rate of 46 percent the first year and 35 percent the second. Clearly, the pintail has a lower mortality rate than most other game ducks.

DISTRIBUTION

A single race of pintails inhabits the Northern Hemisphere, ranging farther over the earth's surface than any other species of waterfowl. It is circumpolar in its breeding range, nesting across northern Siberia, Russia, the Scandinavian Peninsula, Iceland, a few areas in Greenland, the central Canadian Arctic, and Alaska. In Eurasia, pintails nest as far south as southern Europe, central Siberia in the west and southern Siberia in the east. Their range in North America extends to the Great Lakes, central Kansas, southern Colorado, northwestern New Mexico, and southern California.

Pintails winter as far south as the Philippines, Borneo, Malaysia, India, Ceylon, Pakistan, Central Africa, West Indies, Colombia, and, in the mid- and south Pacific Ocean, the Hawaiian Islands, Palmyra Island, and the Marshall Islands.

Breeding Range

Breeding pintails cover a vast area of North America, with small numbers crossing the Bering Sea to nest in eastern Siberia. They are by far the most abundant dabbling duck breeding in the Arctic, outnumbered only by the scaups, which are divers.

Northern Areas. Over one million pintails breed in the Arctic—an unknown number in eastern Siberia, 180,000 in Arctic Canada, and 1,040,000 in Alaska (King and Lensink 1971). In favorable habitat in Alaska and the Canadian Arctic, breeding pintails average 13 per square mile. Over one-fourth of the pintails nesting in Alaska occur on the Yukon Delta and almost one-fifth on the Yukon Flats. Even in the harsh environment of the Arctic Slope, 120,000 pintails have been found in summer (King and Lensink 1971).

The largest numbers of breeding pintails in Arctic Canada occur on the Mackenzie Delta—about 100,000 (23 per square mile). Substantially the same density occurs on Old Crow Flats, a smaller area that accommodates almost 50,000 pintails during the summer. Along the Arctic Coast, east of the Mackenzie Delta to the Anderson River delta, 40,000 additional pintails breed at a density of only 4.5 per square mile.

In spite of their proclivity for the Arctic, fewer pintails are found on the subarctic deltas of Canada than mallards. Pintails total 125,000 (6.3 per square mile) on subarctic deltas but are particularly abundant on the Athabasca Delta, where they number 62,000 (38.1 per square mile).

Pintails breed in small numbers in the central Arctic and rarely in the eastern Arctic of Canada. On an aerial reconnaissance of the Arctic Coast between Bathurst and Sherman inlets, Barry (1960) found 2,000 summering pintails, but the number breeding there is unknown. Hanson et al. (1956) considered that pintails nested occasionally in the area of Queen Maud Gulf.

Although pintails were observed on Banks Island during the breeding season, no nests were found (Manning et al. 1956). A similar situation prevailed in the vicinity of southeast Victoria Island (Parmelee et al. 1967). Several pintails were found in summer on Adelaide Peninsula by Macpherson and Manning (1959), but again there was no evidence of nesting.

At Chesterfield Inlet, on the northwest shore of Hudson Bay, Höhn (1968) reported that pintails were fairly common and nested there. Macpherson and McLaren (1959) saw five pintails of both sexes on the Foxe Peninsula of Baffin Island but found no evidence of their breeding. On Southampton Island, Bray (1943) observed small numbers of pintails; again no nests or broods were observed. However, far to the north at latitude 80° 49′ on Ellesmere Island, a brood of pintails were observed on July 13, 1966 (Maher and Nettleship 1968).

Manning (1946) believed that pintails bred in considerable numbers in the Povungnituk region on the east side of Hudson Bay as well as on the Sleeper and King George islands, where he collected a downy young. Eklund (1956) found a pintail brood near Lake Aigneau in southern Ungava Peninsula, Quebec. In the same region on the False and Koksoak rivers near Ungava Bay, Gabrielson and Wright (1951) observed numerous pintails.

Near the mouth of the Roggan River, on the northeast shore of James Bay, Manning and Macpherson (1952) saw a pintail brood but only a few adults along the east shore of James Bay between Long Point and Cape Jones. Small numbers of pintails were observed and a nest was found on the Belcher Islands in southeastern Hudson Bay by Freeman (1970*b*).

Although the mallard is the most abundant duck in North America, the pintail outnumbers it in the Arctic, is comparable in number in the mixed prairie association, and is only slightly less numerous in the shortgrass prairie. However, in the parklands, the boreal forest, and the subarctic deltas, mallards outnumber pintails by a wide margin.

The mixed praire region supports about 2,154,000 pintails (11.9 per square mile). They are most abundant in Saskatchewan (888,000; 20.4 per square mile) and most dense in Alberta (570,000; 23.2 per square mile). Densities were less in North Dakota, 10.3 per square mile (population 422,000); Manitoba, 9.2 per square mile (42,000); and South Dakota, 7.3 per square mile (181,000).

The parklands support almost 1,100,000 (11.7 per square mile) pintails. Their density throughout the parklands is exceptionally similar, 11.0 to 14.7 per square mile, except in Manitoba, only 5.4 per square mile.

In the shortgrass prairie area, breeding pintails number about 785,000 (5.4 per square mile). They are most abundant in northern Montana (243,000; 7.4 per square mile), southwestern Saskatchewan (181,000; 16.0 per square mile), and southern Alberta (207,000; 15.6 per square mile). They occur in limited numbers in western North Dakota (77,000; 2.8 per square mile), South Dakota (50,000; 2.5 per square mile), and southern Montana (46,000; 1.1 per square mile).

About 780,000 pintails nest in the marshes and meadows of the boreal forest almost equally between the open and closed associations. In Alberta the density is 1.2 pintails per square mile. Densities of 0.27 in Saskatchewan, 0.18 in Manitoba, and 0.04 in Ontario point to a marked decline in numbers from west to east.

The relatively small number of pintails that breed in Quebec appear restricted to the region of the St. Lawrence River and the coasts of James and Hudson bays (Todd 1963). The pintail is rare or absent from vast regions of the interior of Quebec and is a rare breeder in Labrador. Between 26,000 and 42,000 are considered to breed in British Columbia.

Other Areas. Almost 190,000 pintails nest in areas outside the northern plains of the United States. Approximately 60,000 of these breed in Utah, mostly in the marshes adjacent to the Great Salt Lake. Other important nest areas are the Nebraska Sandhills (35,000), the plains of Wyoming (26,000), California (20,000), western Minnesota (13,000), Idaho (13,000), Colorado (7,000; two-thirds in the San Luis Valley), Nevada (5,000), the Columbia Basin, Washington (4,700), and eastern Oregon (4,400).

A few hundred pintails breed in Wisconsin and on the Cheyenne Bottoms Wildlife Area of Kansas. Small numbers have been known to breed at Burford Lake, northwestern New Mexico (Huey and Travis 1961), the Texas Panhandle (Hawkins 1945), and Lake St. Clair and Saginaw Bay, Michigan (Edward Mikula).

Migration Corridors

"California, here I come" is a refrain that applies to migrating pintails as well as to homesick Californians. Over half of the pintails in North America migrate to California. About three-fourths spend the winter there but the remainder prolong their flight to winter along the west coast of Mexico, with small numbers continuing as far south as northern South America. Almost 85 percent of the pintails from Alaska migrate directly or indirectly to California.

There appears to be an important corridor across the corner of the Pacific Ocean from near the tip of the Alaska Peninsula to the Klamath Basin in northern California. About 75,000 pintails that gather on the Izembek National Wildlife Range and other pintails from nearby concentration areas on the Alaska Peninsula and the Aleutian Islands (fall peak 15,000 pintails) probably migrate along this corridor directly to California. I believe that the pintails that Yocom (1947) observed migrating over the Pacific Ocean 465 miles west of Cape Blanco, Oregon, represented birds slightly off course from this corridor. The pintails that Yocom (1954) reported flying over or at rest on Crater Lake, Oregon, an unnatural habitat for them, were believed to be tired birds that dropped out after completing their long flight across the northeast corner of the Pacific Ocean.

Another migration corridor extends from the base of the Alaska Peninsula along the Pacific Coast to Puget Sound. Smaller migration corridors extend from the interior of Alaska through the interior of British Columbia and to northern Alberta.

Slightly over two-thirds of the pintails from breeding grounds in Alberta migrate to California, most of them directly, but several hundred thousand via the Great Salt Lake marshes of Utah. Almost half of the pintails from Saskatchewan breeding grounds also migrate to California, largely by way of the Great Salt Lake Basin. In addition, pintails from the marshes adjacent to Great Salt Lake migrate directly south to the coast of Mexico and southeast to the vicinity of the Rio Grande Delta.

Texas receives about 40 percent of its pintails from Saskatchewan, 16 percent from Alberta, 14 percent from North Dakota, 8 percent from South Dakota, and 5 percent each from Alaska, District of Mackenzie, and Manitoba. Over 300,000 migrate south along a corridor from Saskatchewan to the Texas Panhandle. If the weather is favorable, over half of this number may winter there, but during harsh winters considerably fewer pintails are present. Those that continue south fly 1,000 additional miles to winter in central Mexico.

Other migration corridors are followed by pintails from Saskatchewan to the Gulf Coast of Texas and western Louisiana. The largest of these, followed by probably 800,000 birds, crosses the eastern plains from Saskatchewan to the east coast of Texas and west coast of Louisiana. The Missouri River migration corridor is used by about 350,000 pintails to reach eastern coastal Louisiana. Almost one-third of the pintails that reach Louisiana come from Saskatchewan, 17 percent from North Dakota, 13 percent from Alberta, 12 percent from South Dakota, 8 percent from Manitoba, and smaller percentages from other areas.

About 300,000 pintails use the Mississippi migration corridor. Thirty percent of these come from Saskatchewan, 20 percent from Manitoba, 17 percent from North Dakota, 15 percent from South Dakota, 10 percent from Alberta, and lesser numbers from other areas. In Illinois, this corridor turns in the fall from southeast to south, with a subcorridor branching eastward to South Carolina.

East of a line from Lake Michigan to the Mississippi River delta, pintails are relatively uncommon. As few as 200,000 frequent this region in fall. About one-fourth of these pintails originate from eastern breeding areas in New Brunswick, Quebec, Ontario, and the District of Keewatin; about two-thirds come from breeding areas on the northern prairies, particularly Saskatchewan, the Dakotas, and Manitoba; and about 8 percent are derived from Alaska and the District of Mackenzie.

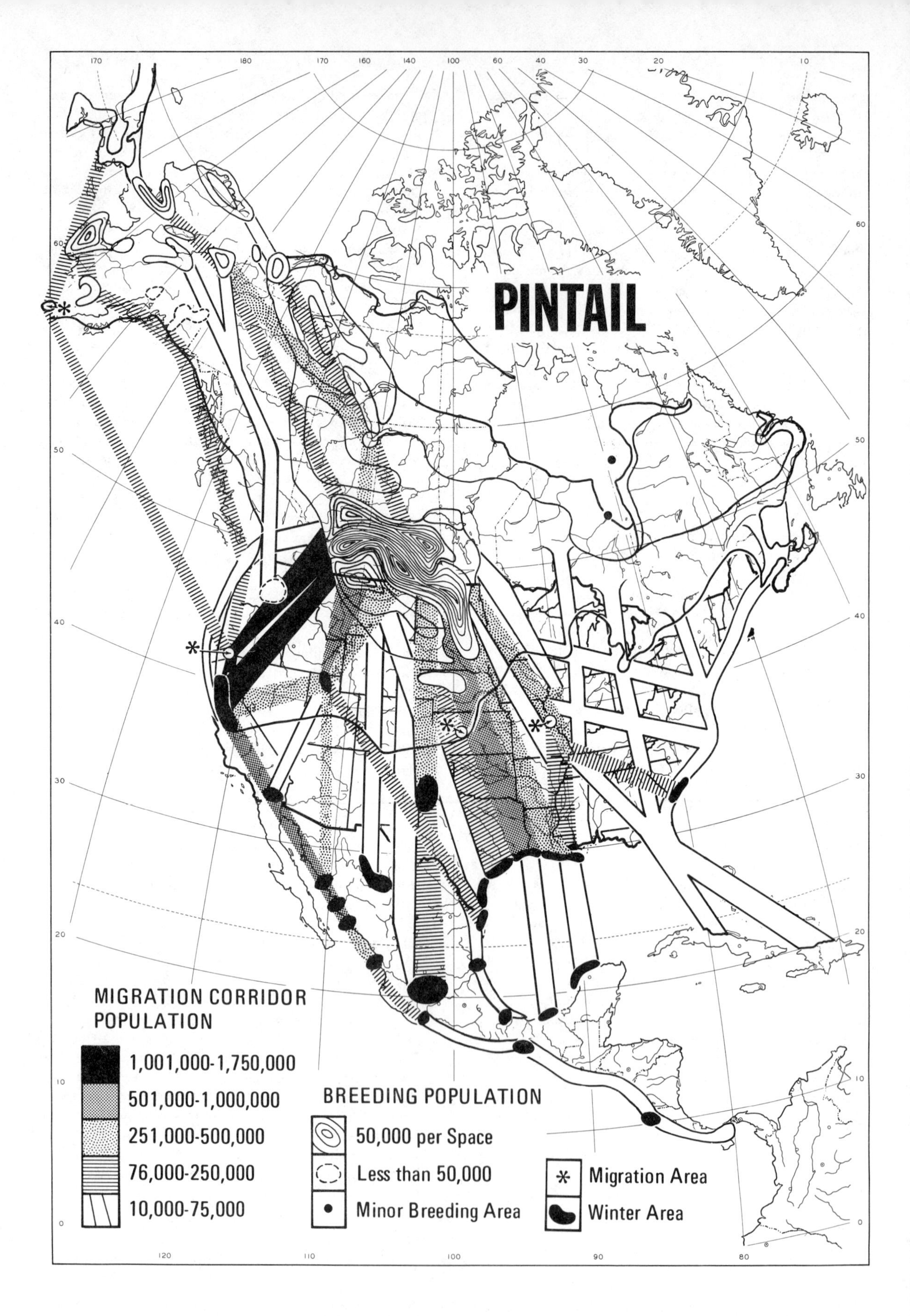
PINTAIL
MIGRATION CORRIDOR POPULATION
1,001,000-1,750,000
501,000-1,000,000
251,000-500,000
76,000-250,000
10,000-75,000
BREEDING POPULATION
50,000 per Space
Less than 50,000
Minor Breeding Area
Migration Area
Winter Area

As migration corridors progressively funnel pintails from the Midwest to the Altantic Coast, the proportion of birds from prairie breeding grounds steadily increases from New England to Florida. From 25,000 to 50,000 pintails pass through Florida to Cuba and other islands of the West Indies.

Winter Areas

Although small numbers of pintails winter as far north as the Aleutian Islands and the Alaskan Panhandle (Gabrielson and Lincoln 1959), they prefer the mild temperatures of the Central Valley of California, the coasts of Mexico, and the coastal marshes of Louisiana.

In the Pacific Flyway, Puget Sound, Washington, attracts the first sizable contingent of wintering pintails, 30,000; and over the Cascade Range in the Columbia Basin, another 20,000 find conditions mild enough for a winter sojourn. Sixty-five thousand winter on the lower Columbia River and Willamette Valley in Oregon.

Almost 2 million pintails winter in California: 1 million in the Sacramento Valley; 600,000 in the delta marshes near San Francisco Bay; 250,000 in the San Joaquin Valley; 60,000 in the Imperial Valley; and 30,000 along the south coast. Forty-eight thousand pintails winter farther inland on Intermountain marshes: 17,000 in Idaho; 11,000 in Utah; 10,000 in Nevada; and a similar number in Arizona.

About 625,000 pintails spend the winter along the west coast of Mexico. Large concentrations of 300,000 pintails occur near Los Mochis and 210,000 near Culiacán. As many as 15,000 winter in lagoons adjacent to the Gulf of Tehuantepec.

In their waterfowl survey of Central and South America, Glover and Chamberlain (1960) estimated 1,900 pintails on the Gulf of Nicoya, Costa Rica, and 300 on the Magdalena River delta, Colombia. Arthur Hawkins observed 100 pintails on Pozo de Agua, Costa Rica, January 4, 1969. Saunders et al. (1950) reported that the pintail is a common migrant and winter resident in Guatemala, and is most abundant on coastal waters during migration.

Of the 900,000 pintails that winter in the Central Flyway, almost two-thirds are found in Texas, about equally divided between the coast and the Panhandle. Mexico is second in importance with 275,000 wintering pintails, 30 percent of the flyway population. About 15,000 winter in the Northern Highlands and 140,000 between Guadalajara and Mexico City. Slightly over 120,000 pintails choose to winter along the east coast of Mexico, from the Rio Grande to Yucatan. The largest concentrations are: 40,000 on the Rio Grande Delta and Laguna Madre; 12,000 on Tampico Lagoon; 20,000 on lagoons in the state of Tabasco; and 40,000 on lagoons in Campeche and Yucatan.

Smaller numbers winter elsewhere in the Central Flyway. The Pecos and Rio Grande valleys in New Mexico harbor 30,000 pintails. Over 2,000 winter in Oklahoma, 800 in Kansas, an equal number in Colorado, and a few as far north as South Dakota.

Slightly over 800,000 pintails winter in the Mississippi Flyway, 90 percent in Louisiana. Because a large proportion of pintails migrating to Louisiana cross the eastern Great Plains, it is perhaps more logical to consider them as Central Flyway birds. Pintails wintering in Louisiana averaged only 23,000 below the peak fall level during a 15-year period. However, in certain years, winter numbers were several hundred thousand below peak fall populations, suggesting large variations in the numbers of pintails that cross the Gulf of Mexico from Louisiana to Yucatan. Large yearly variations in the numbers of pintails wintering in Yucatan appear to substantiate this supposition.

Although small numbers of pintails winter as far north as Iowa and Michigan, most of those found north of Louisiana are in Arkansas, with 55,000. Tennessee, Mississippi, and Alabama are next in importance, each with 6,000 to 8,000 pintails in winter.

Almost 200,000 pintails frequent winter grounds in the Atlantic Flyway. About 35,000 of them have migrated through Florida to the West Indies, particularly Cuba and Hispaniola. The largest number, 87,000, winter in South Carolina. North Carolina hosts 35,000 and Florida harbors 22,000. A few wander as far north as New England, but usually only 20,000 winter north of North Carolina, and over half of these are on Chesapeake Bay.

MIGRATION BEHAVIOR

Some pintails have a greater proclivity for wandering and pioneering new areas than perhaps any other species. A pintail from Utah was found on Palmyra Island, over 1,000 miles south of Honolulu, Hawaii (Lincoln 1943). Small numbers that regularly migrate to Hawaii are probably from Alaska. A banded pintail from Iceland reached Quebec (Lewis 1933), and two banded in Labrador were later found in England.

When drought strikes the northern prairies and parklands, drastically reducing the number of potholes, individual ducks of many species overfly this region to reach waters of the boreal forest and the subarctic and arctic deltas (Hansen and McKnight 1964). However, the pintail exceeds all other species in the numbers that move northward when drought areas develop.

Smith (1970) found that the proportion of pintails migrat-

PINTAIL

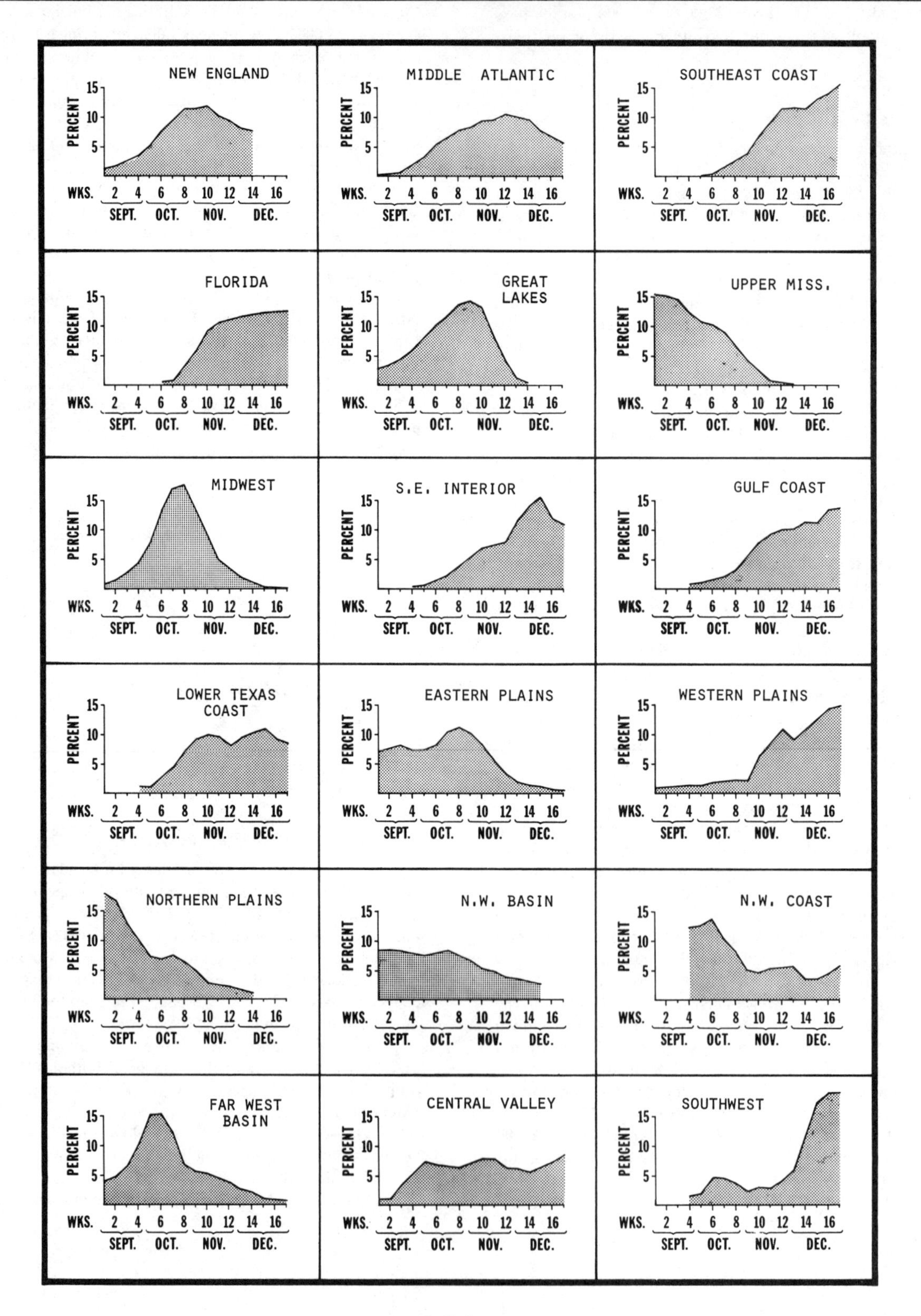

Fall

PINTAIL

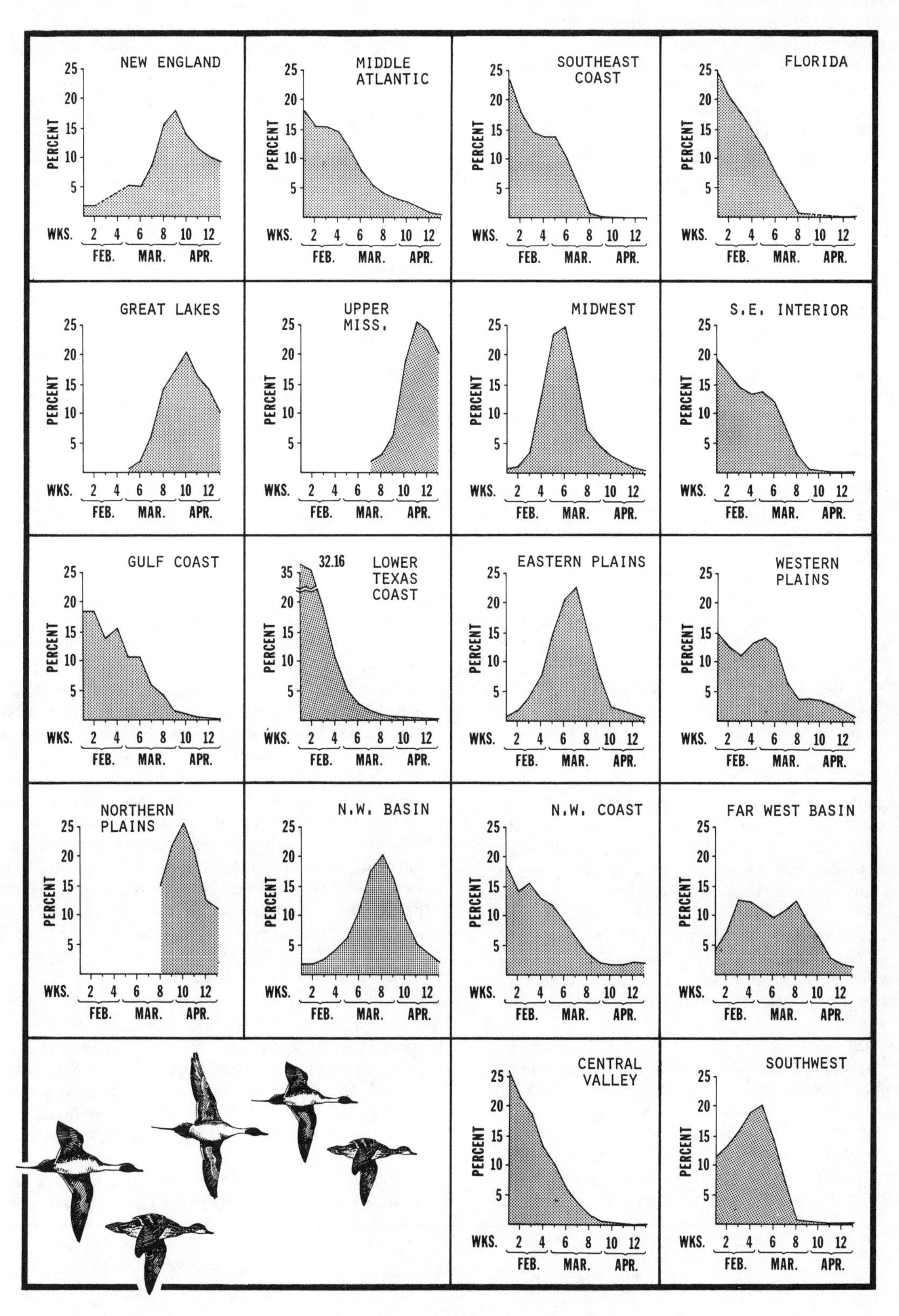

Spring

ing to northern areas varied directly with the availability of small water areas on the prairies. When pintails shifted northward, the production of young declined in proportion to the numbers that moved north, either because the displaced birds were less successful in their unfamiliar range or they made no attempt to nest.

Some of the pintail overflight of prairie areas extends as far as eastern Siberia (Henny 1973). Pintails banded in the interior of North America have been found most often on Siberian river deltas during the years when prairie water areas were fewest. Henny (1973) concluded, however, that a small portion of the pintails that winter in western United States nest in eastern Siberia each year, regardless of water conditions on the prairies.

We have evidence that some of the pintails migrating into the Pacific Flyway during the fall return to their breeding areas in the spring via the Central Flyway. Low's (1949) data on California bandings of pintails show some recoveries in the Central Flyway during the same migration season.

Biweekly waterfowl censuses in Louisiana (Smith 1961*a*) indicated that in 5 to 9 years, 1951-59, pintails were most abundant January 1 or later in the winter. Since the pintail is an early migrant, this information suggests a winter influx into Louisiana from areas to the west or southwest.

Pintail population estimates made weekly at national wildlife refuges fall and spring for 3 years were compiled. Peak numbers were 81 percent lower in the spring than in the fall in the Pacific Flyway and 33 percent lower in the Mississippi Flyway; conversely, peak numbers in spring in the Central Flyway were 24 percent higher than those in the fall. This change is added evidence of a counter-clockwise passage on the part of some pintails, fall to spring, that leads from the Pacific to the Central Flyway and possibly as far east as the western part of the Mississippi Flyway.

Chronology

The pintail is the most paradoxical of ducks in its seasonal migration—it is one of the first ducks to migrate south in the fall, yet one of the first ducks to migrate north in the spring. It tends to have a more protracted fall passage and a shorter spring passage than other species.

Fall. During September, pintails are in migration the length of the North American continent. While some are leaving their Arctic breeding grounds in Alaska, others are arriving on their winter grounds in California, Texas, and Louisiana.

Although departing Alaska in August and September, pintails have been found there (north to south) as late as September 2, Demarcation Point; September 7, Point Barrow; September 14, Kobuk River; October 9, Nunivak Island; October 24, Dutch Harbor; October 23, Cordova; and November 4, Craig (Gabrielson and Lincoln 1959).

Soper (1951) reported that large numbers of pintails remained in the region of the Athabasca Delta, northern Alberta, through the third week of September and moderate numbers until the second week of October.

Although the marshes about Great Salt Lake, Utah, are the recipients of an influx of thousands of premolt adult drakes in late June, most pintails begin to arrive there in August, reach peak numbers in September, and gradually depart through November.

California, the greatest migration and winter area for pintails in the world, already has 700,000 to over 1 million by mid-September (Kozlik 1972). In the Klamath Basin of northern California, peak numbers occur from late September to late October, with a continuing decline through November and December. Peak numbers of several million pintails reach the Sacramento Valley and delta marshes in early October and remain throughout the winter. In southern California, the Imperial Valley has a modest ingress of pintails in late September, but the main influx occurs in early December.

Pintails in the northern Great Plains region of the United States are at their greatest abundance the first week in September. From then on there is a gradual exodus throughout the fall, terminating in late November. In the central Great Plains region, they are abundant through September and early October, increase in number in late October and early November, and steadily decline through November and early December. Although small populations of pintails are on the southern plains through September and October, the main influx commences in mid-November and continues to mid-December.

Small numbers of pintails arrive on Gulf Coast marshes and lagoons of Louisiana and Texas in September. The number of arrivals accelerates through October and early November, and smaller numbers add to the total through December.

The passage of pintails through the Great Lakes states and the Midwest forms a "normal curve"—from a bare beginning the first week in September, numbers steadily rise to peaks in late October and early November and then subside to mid-December, when few remain.

Pintails arrive in the New Jersey-Chesapeake Bay area 2 to 3 weeks earlier than at points south of there along the Atlantic Coast. Although small numbers appear in September, significant numbers are not present until mid-October and peak numbers until late November. Their fall passage into South Carolina, Georgia, and Florida is similar. Small numbers begin arriving in mid-October, and the population continually rises until peak wintering populations are reached in late December.

Spring. Wherever their winter grounds, the stirring of spring starts the pintails northward often before the ice and snow have retreated from the marshes that are their destinations. They commence to leave their winter quarters in late January or early February and the northward push continues through March, rapidly depleting wintering populations.

The numbers arriving in middle latitudes reach peaks from mid- to late March, with populations rapidly diminishing by early April. On the Northern Plains of the United States, pintails arrive in early April and peak populations are quickly reached by midmonth, before large numbers migrate still farther north.

Pintails usually arrive at Delta Marsh, Manitoba, in early April but occasionally as early as March 20 or as late as April 19 (Sowls 1955). Near Brooks, Alberta, their average date of arrival was March 25, with variations from March 22 to April 1 in 4 years (Keith 1961). At Yellowknife, Northwest Territories, pintails arrived between April 25 and May 4 over a 3-year period; major influxes occurred April 30-May 15 (Murdy 1964).

Pintails were recorded on May 14 at Churchill, Manitoba, on Hudson Bay (Littlefield and Pakulak 1969) and on May 28 from Belcher Islands in the bay (Freeman 1970*b*). In the Eastern Arctic, pintails appeared on Southampton Island on June 3 (Barry 1956) and on Adelaide Peninsula, June 25 (Macpherson and Manning 1959). They arrived in the central Arctic at the Perry River region on June 2 and 15 (Ryder 1967) and June 10-30 (Hanson et al. 1956), on Jenny Lind Island and Victoria Island June 14 and 18 (Parmelee et al. 1967), and on Banks Island, May 18 (Manning et al. 1956).

On the Mackenzie Delta, the first spring arrivals occurred on May 10, 1932, and May 17, 1934 (Porslid 1943). They reached Old Crow, Yukon Territory, May 7-17 (Irving 1960) and Anaktuvuk Pass, Alaska, May 13.

Earliest dates of arrival on the Yukon Delta over a 4-year span occurred between May 8 and May 20 (Mickelson 1973). Pintails arrived at Selawik, May 12, 1955. In the far interior, they have been seen on the Yukon Flats on April 21 (Lensink 1954). Their arrival in the Fairbanks area, 1948-55, varied from April 21 to April 30 and averaged April 26 (Rowinski 1958).

BREEDING

Behavior

Age, Pair Bond, and Homing. When conditions are favorable, probably most pintails breed their first year. However, when prairie water areas are scarce, a large proportion of the pintails that do not attempt to nest are undoubtedly yearlings.

Smith (1968) observed that drakes and hens tended to flock separately during the fall, a period when he observed no pairing. By mid-December flocks began to contain a greater mixture of the sexes. But Arthur Hawkins and William Kiel observed that flocks of separate sexes are numerous as late as mid-January. On the Texas coast during December and January, Weller (1965) found that 87 percent of the female pintails were paired. Courtship among pintails in the same area was observed most frequently by Smith (1968) between mid-December and April. Courtship continues during spring migration and in the early days on the breeding grounds.

At Delta Marsh, Manitoba, Sowls (1955) observed that drake pintails deserted their spouses a few days after incubation started. In Idaho, Oring (1964) reported that drakes left their mates the first dayof incubation. Pintail drakes are poor husbands at best, and, as is true of most ducks, are fathers in name only.

Where habitats are fairly stable, as at Delta Marsh, pintails may home as well as any duck. Of the hens Sowls (1955) marked there, 39 percent of the adults and 13 percent of the immatures returned in a subsequent year to nest. However, because of the unstable water conditions in prairie pothole districts, and the sensitive response of pintails to these conditions, they may completely abandon home areas when habitats deteriorate. A corollary to their abandonment of unsatisfactory winter areas is their tendency to pioneer new breeding habitats. For example, newly flooded lands north of Winnipeg, Manitoba, were immediately utilized by breeding pintails (Hochbaum and Bossenmaier 1972). The key was the large acreage of new nest habitat and the elastic response of the pintail to the favorable habitat.

Home Range. Flocks of pintails are often the first ducks noticed returning to breeding grounds in early spring, concentrating wherever ice-covered shallow waters have opened. From the open waters of sloughs and lakes, pairs soon appear fanning out over the potholes in the morning and evening, the flocks diminishing in size as pairs take up residence on the smaller bodies of water.

With the laying of eggs, pursuit flights become prevalent, as mated drake pintails chase hens of other mated pairs (Smith 1968). This behavior tends to space females at some distance apart during the period of egg-laying. Smith (1968) considered that although the pursuit flights were sexually motivated, they indirectly resulted in a greater spacing among the nesting birds.

Nesting

Winter is reluctantly giving way to spring when the first pintails begin to nest. A late snowstorm may temporarily cover the backs of incubating birds, and some desert under these stressful conditions.

Nest Sites. Pintails, more than other ducks, select open areas for their nests where vegetation is either low or sparse. In fact, the nest is sometimes located on bare earth, as in stubble fields. Scrapes are dug by the hen 4 days before the first egg is laid (Sowls 1955). Egg-laying usually occurs within 4 hours of sunrise, customarily at the rate of one per day. Fifteen nests measured on the Yukon Delta (Brandt 1943) were: height, 3 to 7 inches; scrape depth, 2.75 to 6 inches; inside diameter, 7 to 8.5 inches; outside diameter, 7.5 to 14 inches.

Pintails tend to locate their nests farther from water than other ground-nesting ducks, sometimes a mile or more but most often within 100 yards; the average is about 40 yards. On islands, levees, and complexes of potholes, nest sites are of necessity close to water. Because of the restricted upland habitat at Ogden Bay, Utah, Fuller (1953) found no nests (91) farther than 100 yards from water; 80 percent were within 25 yards, but only one was located over water.

Vegetation at the nest site varied greatly with geography. At Ogden Bay, pintails preferred juncus, bassia, and spike rush beds (Fuller 1953). A few miles away, at the Bear River marshes, pintails selected willows, hardstem bulrushes, and weeds (Williams and Marshall 1938*b*). Pintails at Tule Lake, California, used weedy patches of nettles and mustard for nesting (Miller and Collins 1954).

At Delta Marsh, Manitoba, most pintail nests were in extensive stands of whitetop and bluegrasses (Sowls 1955). At Caron, Saskatchewan, William Leitch found almost all nests in clumps of buckbrush. At Redvers, Saskatchewan, most nests were found in grassland areas, followed by buckbrush clumps (Stoudt 1971). Near Brooks, Alberta, pintail nests were placed in juncus beds, mixed prairie grasses, and burned weed areas (Keith 1961).

More than other species of waterfowl, pintails nest in farmland habitats (Milonski 1958). Stubble fields were the sites most frequently chosen, followed by roadsides, hayfields, pastures, fallow fields, field edges, and fields of growing grain.

Clutch Size, Eggs, and Incubation. Pintail nests have been found with 3 to 14 eggs in completed clutches, the average being 7.76 eggs (1,276 nests). Eggs range in color from gray-buff to pale olive-green and measure 53.6 by 38.2 mm. Fuller (1953) found that incubation began with the laying of the last egg and continued for 22 to 23 days, all eggs in any one clutch hatching within a span of 8 hours.

Chronology of Nesting. In a vast region—South Dakota to Utah and California and north to the Delta marshes, Manitoba; Redvers, Saskatchewan; and Brooks, Alberta—nesting commences at almost the same time, early April to midmonth. However, cold weather just prior to nesting may delay initiation by as much as 2 weeks (Sowls 1955). At Redvers, Saskatchewan, snow and below-freezing temperatures occurred from the end of April through the first week of May in 1954, delaying pintail nesting from April 10-30 to May 10, when they started nesting immediately upon their arrival (Smith 1971). Peak nest initiation over the northern prairies occurs May 1-15, and the last nests are started June 15-July 12.

Beyond the plains and parklands, pintails nest later. At Yellowknife, Northwest Territories, first nests were started as early as May 7, 1964, and as late as May 21, 1961 (Murdy 1964). Last nests were initiated in 2 years on June 6 and 8. On the Yukon Flats, pintails began to nest May 8-18, and at Minto Lakes, near Fairbanks, Alaska, from April 27 to May 11.

At Hooper Bay on the Yukon Delta, Conover (1926) found incomplete clutches on May 25 and new nests as late as July 10. According to Irving (1960), pintails commenced nesting in the vicinity of Anaktuvuk Pass, Alaska, from May 20 to June 10.

The span of nest initiation depends upon local temperature and water conditions and the individual pintails's physiology and renesting propensity. In the Intermountain marshes of Utah and California, the span of initiation has ranged from 61 to 82 days, and on the northern prairies from 54 to 83 days. At Yellowknife, Northwest Territories, nest initiation was limited to 31 days. It was curtailed to 39 days at Minto Lakes, near Fairbanks, and 35 days near Selawik, Alaska.

At Portage Plains, Manitoba, nest initiation during 1956 and 1957 extended over 54 days for the pintail and 59 days for the mallard (Milonski 1958).

Nest Success. The pintail's nest success is moderate. Studies of nesting on many areas from California and Utah to Alaska show that 55 percent of 1,452 nests hatched successfully. Nest success on Intermountain marshes has averaged 67.0 percent (974); in the Dakotas, 52.4 percent (63); in Manitoba, 32.3 percent (31); in Saskatchewan, 40.2 percent (157); in Alberta, 43.7 percent (176), and in Alaska, 67.9 percent (28).

Successful nests contain few unhatched eggs. An average of 0.90 egg failed to hatch per successful nest (range, 0.46 to 1.33). Failure of eggs to hatch was attributed about equally to infertility and dead embryos.

Nest Failure. Perhaps because pintails nest early and in more open sites than other species of ducks, they suffer greater nest losses from bird predation. Both birds and mammals were about equally responsible for nest destruction. Crows accounted for over half of the nests destroyed, magpies and gulls about one-sixth each. Skunks primarily, and ground squirrels secondarily, were the principal mammalian predators. Minor nest losses were caused by coyotes, foxes, and badgers. In recent years, raccoons have become an important agent of nest destruction in the prairies and southern parklands.

Nest losses due to predators are related in part to the degree of nest concealment. In a study of California gull predation on waterfowl nests, Odin (1957) rated the loss of well-concealed pintail nests at 7.7 percent, partially concealed nests at 26.7 percent, and poorly concealed nests at 46.2 percent. In analyzing the loss of pintail nests at Ogden Bay, Fuller (1953) found that 21 percent of the nests lost were well concealed but a whopping 79 percent were poorly concealed.

Nests are especially vulnerable to farming operations because pintails like to nest in stubble fields. Milonski's (1958) study of pintails nesting on the Portage Plains, Manitoba, disclosed that farming operations directly destroyed 57 percent of all pintail nests in 1956 and 41 percent of all nests in 1957. Largest losses were caused by cultivation, followed by disking, mowing, plowing, and harrowing.

In North Dakota, great numbers of nesting pintails select grain stubble fields, and nearly all of their nests are plowed under in spring fieldwork (Merrill Hammond *in* Milonski 1958). Burning of stubble fields in the spring often destroyed many pintail nests.

Renesting. Some pintails renest when their initial nests are destroyed. At Delta, Manitoba, 30 percent of 62 marked pintail hens renested, one even after losing her brood (Sowls 1955). Two pintail hens had sufficient energy to renest again after destruction of their second nests. Clutch sizes in Sowls' study averaged 8.6 (13) for initial nests, 6.6 (13) for first renests, and 7.5 (2) for second renests. Near Brooks, Alberta, initial pintail clutches averaged 7.2 eggs and renest clutches 6.2 (Keith 1961). The interval between the loss of a nest and the start of laying a new clutch was 16 days. Pintails renested an average of 282 yards from initial nest sites at Delta (Sowls 1955).

Sowls (1955) considered that the pintail at Delta was a more persisitent renester than the mallard, shoveler, gadwall, and blue-winged teal, but Smith (1971) considered that pintails at Lousana, Alberta, were less likely to renest than the other early nesters, mallards and canvasbacks. Differences in the renesting propensities of pintails on the two areas may be related to the stable habitat conditions at Delta and the variable conditions at Lousana. The renesting potential in pintails doubtlessly varies with the availability of water areas.

Rearing of Young

Broods. Hen pintails lead their broods farther overland from nest site to water area than other prairie ducks, and frequently from one pond to another. At Delta Marsh, Manitoba, Sowls (1955) observed a hen move her brood 800 yards the first 24 hours of life. However, three other broods remained within 500 yards of the nest sites until they learned to fly. Evans et al. (1952) found that pintail broods did not occupy a single pothole for more than 14 days. Three marked broods were observed to move 0.78 mile in 71 days. On the Minnedosa pothole area, pintail broods were considered to be the greatest transients, followed by canvasbacks, mallards, redheads, blue-winged teals, wigeons, and ruddy ducks.

Seldom does a male pintail deign to appear with a brood, but on one occasion Fuller (1953) observed a drake accompanying a hen and her brood. This unusual drake appeared solicitous of the brood's welfare and entered into defensive postures.

Development. In South Dakota, Gollop and Marshall (1954) found that pintail broods reached flight stage in 46 to 57 days. In southern Manitoba, pintail young attained flight in 42 days. In Alaska, young pintails at Yukon Flats were flying after 36 days (Lensink 1964) and at Minto Lakes after 43 days (Hooper 1951).

Survival. From a hatch of 6.86 ducklings per successful nest, mortality reduces Class I broods to 5.89 (1,342). Class II broods are further reduced 4.4 percent to 5.63, and Class III broods an additional 7.3 percent to 5.22—the number of young reaching flight. Entire broods are frequently destroyed by predators or are lost because water areas dry up. Also, 25 to 35 percent of the breeding hens are deprived of broods because of nest losses. Production per hen is also diluted by excess males that play no known role in the production picture. Consequently, it is understandable that fall age ratios indicate about one immature per adult.

POSTBREEDING SEASON

Some pintails perform one of the greatest premolt migrations in the world. According to Jessop Low, tens of thousands of adult drakes appear in full nuptial dress on the marshes at the north end of Great Salt Lake, Utah, between June 1 and 10. They begin to molt into their eclipse plumage 2 weeks after arrival. Most are flightless by July 10 and regain their flight feathers early in August. Sowls (1955) noted that pintails required about 4 weeks to renew their flight feathers. Each year pintails congregate in the same areas, which are somewhat isolated from those of local birds. The molting pintails are more wary than the local pintails. Their numbers suggest that they originate from breeding areas hundreds of miles to the north, probably in Alberta.

Thousands of pintails also move into the Camas Refuge lakes of northeastern Idaho during late July and early August just prior to entering the wing molt (Oring 1964). An aerial survey on August 10 revealed that nearly half of 52,000 ducks were flightless and that flightless pintails greatly outnumbered other flightless ducks. Because molting pintails were so much more abundant than local breeding populations, Oring (1964) concluded that they migrated from considerable distances.

Sterling (1966) banded 13,980 flightless adult drake pintails, July 9-24, 1955-58, at Pel and Kutawagan marshes, 65 miles north of Regina, Saskatchewan. In the year after their initial banding, he captured 242 that returned to the marshes for the eclipse molt. The number of pintails returning to molt was 27 times greater than chance would warrant.

From band recoveries during the hunting season, Sterling (1966) found that early-molting male pintails also migrated early, the opposite of late-molting birds. The first postbreeding pintail drakes began to concentrate on the Pel-Kutawagan marshes as early as mid-May. Although the first flightless drake was noted as early as June 17, the majority became flightless early in July with the peak about mid-July. At this time, the early-molting drakes were just regaining flight. By late July, hen pintails began to gather in the marsh for their wing molt. On July 9, 1958, Sterling (1966) captured a much larger proportion of flightless hens than was customary for the season. He believed that these were hens that failed to nest successfully, because production of young was exceptionally low that year. The proportion of male to female birds on the molt area provides good evidence as to relative nesting success in a given season.

On the coast of Hudson Bay, near Fort Severn, George Arthur found several hundred flightless adult drake pintails between July 11 and August 5, 1955. A few flightless adult hens were captured in late July. Hanson et al. (1956) observed that on the Perry River, pintails were first flightless on July 8, with peak numbers in midmonth, and the last on July 21. Large flocks of molting pintails were noticed on the Mackenzie Delta the first week in August (Porslid 1943). Male pintails on the Yukon Delta were observed flocking on June 6 and by July 5 were well along in their eclipse molt; most appeared to regain flight by August 1 (Conover 1926).

FOOD HABITS

When their wing molt is completed, pintails on the northern Great Plains start to feed in grain stubble fields and continue this type of feeding from August until the time they depart southward. Along with mallards, pintails utilize the grains of wheat, barley, and oats, often doing considerable crop damage when the fields are swathed. Swathing of grain prior to combining permits ripening of those heads of grain that are not ripe when cut. If combining of swathed grain is delayed by wet weather, damage by pintails and mallards can be staggering to local farmers. The amount of grain eaten by thousands of ducks can be sizable, but, when the grain is wet, the loss from trampling far exceeds the loss from consumption. Crop damage by waterfowl in the Prairie Provinces of Canada is a serious problem in waterfowl management because it results in a greater incentive to drain wetlands.

Whether wheat or barley is preferred is a moot point on the Great Plains. Some observations suggest one, some the other (Bossenmaier and Marshall 1958). In the southern Great Plains, the ducks consume waste sorghum grains as well as those of wheat.

On their winter grounds in California, pintails make extensive use of barley and rice grains. Because cereals and natural foods are available to pintails on state and federal waterfowl refuges, the problem of crop damage in California has been largely ameliorated. Pintails are able to feed upon foods in refuge areas until after the grain crops on private lands have been harvested. Then the birds are welcome to feed upon waste grain on private lands because of the hunting they provide.

Pintails, unlike mallards, make little use of waste corn in the Midwest. However, they join with mallards in feeding upon waste rice in the coastal fields of southeast Texas and southwest Louisiana.

Even where they make the greatest use of cereal grains, in the northern Great Plains and in California, pintails also have an appetite for natural foods. For example, at Pel Lake, Saskatchewan, the seeds of alkali and hardstem bulrushes and sago pondweed composed over 50 percent of the pintails' diet; insects and Cladocera made up most of the remainder (Keith and Stanislawski 1960). At Swan Lake, British Columbia, pintails fed largely on bulrush seeds, followed by muskgrass spores and branches (Munro 1939*a*).

Sauvie Island on the Columbia River, below Portland, Oregon, is an important pintail area. Principal food items there are buckwheats, smartweeds, grass vegetation, and seeds (Trainer 1965).

In central Washington, seeds of the following plants were important: oats, smartweed, bulrushes, and salt grass (Yocom 1951). At Humboldt Bay, California, pintails fed on barley, prairie bulrush, spike rush, widgeon grass, and, surprisingly, 11 percent on clams (Yocom and Keller 1961). The food of pintails in Utah during the fall was principally composed of sago and horned pondweeds and prairie and hardstem bulrushes (Fuller 1953).

Pintails in the Midwest as well as in many other areas feed extensively on the seeds of moist soil plants. Gizzards analyzed in Missouri (Korschgen 1955) and Illinois (Anderson 1959) show that millets, nutgrasses, smartweeds, rice cut-grass, and water hemp are preferred foods. Catahoula Lake in east-central Louisiana is famed for its large number of pintails; they concentrate there largely to feed upon chufa and other nutgrasses.

In the coastal marshes of Louisiana, pintails consume seeds of several grasses: fall panicum, brownseed paspalum, Walter's and duck millets (Glasgow and Bardwell 1965). From 20,000 to 150,000 pintails winter on Laguna Madre along the lower Texas coast where few aquatic plants grow because of its saline waters; there, pintails subsist almost exclusively on shoalgrass (McMahan 1970).

A wide variety of foods are taken by pintails along the Atlantic Coast, depending upon the habitat frequented. In Rhode Island, pondweed, three-square bulrush, and bur reed seeds were most important (Cronan and Halla 1968). Pintails wintering on Chesapeake Bay chose seeds of smartweeds, millets, corn and panic grasses (Stewart 1962). North Carolina pintails fed primarily upon the vegetative parts of pondweeds and widgeon grass and secondarily on pondweed and bulrush seed (Quay and Critcher 1965). Those wintering in coastal South Carolina utilized bulrush, widgeon grass, and tall redtop (McGilvrey 1966*b*).

Blue-Winged Teal

Anas discors

Other Common Names: Bluewing, summer teal, white-faced teal

VITAL STATISTICS

Length: Adult male, 15.0-16.2 inches, average 15.6 inches (32)
Adult female, 14.7-15.5 inches, average 14.3 inches (20)
Immature male, 14.0-16.2 inches, average 15.4 inches (28)
Immature female, 14.1-15.7 inches, average 14.8 inches (30)

Wing: Adult male, 7.37 inches (50)
Adult female, 7.09 inches (31)
Immature male, 7.28 inches (49)
Immature female, 7.02 inches (59)

Weight: Adult male, 0.7-1.2 pounds, average 1.02 pounds (35)
Adult female, 0.5-1.1 pounds, average 0.83 pound (129)
Immature male, 0.5-1.2 pounds, average 1.01 pounds (146)
Immature female, 0.5-1.1 pounds, average 0.86 pound (315)

IDENTIFICATION

Field

The most distinguishing feature of the flying blue-winged teal is the large gray-blue patch on the wing. This patch may appear whitish under bright reflected light or may not show up at all under poor light. The cinnamon teal and the shoveler have similar blue shoulder patches. However, the cinnamon teal is confined largely to the area west of the Great Plains, where the blue-winged teal is rare, and the shoveler, even in flight, can be distinguished by its huge spoon-shaped bill.

Blue-winged and cinnamon teals resemble each other in the fall when adults are still in their drab eclipse plumages and the young still in their juvenile plumages. Females of the two species are indistinguishable in all plumages. When the heads of adult male bluewings in nuptial plumage begin to show single white crescents, any time from mid-November through December, adult drakes can be identified with certainty, but it is late winter before immature males begin to show these distinguishing marks. Full nuptial plumage is usually not reached by immatures until late February or early March.

When the drake is arrayed in full nuptial plumage (early winter for the adult, late winter for the immature), the white facial crescent contrasting with the steel-blue head and neck is a unique feature. The tan chest and sides sprinkled with dark brown polka dots offer other clues of identification when the drake is at rest. The blue shoulder patches are hidden by the brown feathers when the wings are folded. On the water, the bluewing male exhibits a white patch in front of the black tail and its coverts, in contrast to the similarly placed buff patch in the green-winged teal.

In flight, blue-winged teal show brownish underparts; they do not reveal the glimpses of white breasts and bellies that the twisting-turning torsos of green-winged teal provide. Bluewings are more vociferous than greenwings, and their frequently uttered *keck, keck, keck* calls are part of the mélange of sounds associated with bird-rich marshes. Hens quack similar to mallards, but more softly and rapidly.

At Hand

Because of the late fall molt in the adult male from eclipse to nuptial plumage and the still later change in the immature male, they resemble hens through most of the fall. Bluewing hens are small—among dabbling ducks only green-wings are smaller. They have mottled brown plumage closely resembling the plumages of many other dabbling duck hens. The gray-blue shoulder patches, brighter in the males, are the only really distinctive color marks.

Bluewing hens, and drakes in similar fall plumage, have dark brown backs and slightly paler brown underparts. Adult hens have pale bellies suffused with brown; immatures are more heavily streaked on their breasts and bellies. The bills of bluewings are almost as long as their heads, blue-black in adult males, dusky in females and margined with yellow marked with black spots. According to Dane (1965), the size of the black spots is an indicator of age: the longest bill spot during the first year of life averaged 5.9 mm (range, 3 to 11 mm); in hens 2 years old and older the longest bill spots averaged 20.3 mm (range, 9 to 32.5 mm).

The wing of the adult shows a green speculum, brighter and more iridescent in the male and blacker in the female. A white stripe between the blue shoulder and green speculum is noticeable in the male wing but is absent in that of the female.

The ages of female blue-winged teal can often be detected by the presence or absence of white inverted V-marks on the greater coverts (Dane 1965). The absence of white V's on the otherwise brown feathers indicates birds in their first year; the presence of good to perfect V's indicates birds older than one year.

POPULATION STATUS

Next to the mallard, the scaups, and the pintail, the blue-winged teal is the most abundant duck in North America. During 1955-74, their average breeding population numbered 5,069,000.

Breeding ground surveys by the U.S. Fish and Wildlife Service revealed populations to be above average in 1955-59, 1966, and 1970-74, and below average in 1960-65 and 1967-69. Because of these large-scale fluctuations in numbers, the basic trend is not consistently displayed. Although the trend may not be significant, it does show a 20 percent decline in numbers through the 20-year period.

Most blue-winged teal winter south of the United States and are not inventoried. The numbers that remain in the United States are variable, depending upon food and weather conditions, and therefore, January surveys of those wintering in the States do not indicate the status of the bluewing population.

Age Ratios

The proportion of immature to adult blue-winged teal (includes small numbers of cinnamon teal) found in hunters' bags in the United States is 2.09 to 1.00 for a 13-year average, 1961-72. However, immature teal, on the average, are 2.58 times more vulnerable to hunting than are adults (Martinson 1966, Sorenson 1966). Correction of the age ratios found in hunters' bags for the bias created by the selection of immatures suggests that fall populations of blue-winged teal contain about 0.81 young per adult, a production figure lower than those of most other game species.

If we assume that hunting selectivity remained the same through the years (which it rarely does), the highest production was 1.30 young per adult in 1969 and the lowest was 0.54 in 1962. Thus, the amplitude of production was almost three times the lowest points, depending upon habitat and weather conditions.

Sex Ratios

In hunters' bags, bluewing drakes outnumbered hens 1.04 to 1, or 51 percent drakes, 1966-73. Among immatures, hunters took more hens than drakes, 1 to 0.86, or 46.3 percent drakes. Comparative band-recovery rates between the sex-classes suggest that there is no selection among adults and that among immatures there is a slight selection for males (1.17 to 1). The evidence from hunting samples indicates that the sexes are about even in fall populations. However, visual observations of bluewing sex ratios in the spring show that males compose about 59.3 percent of the population (Bellrose et al. 1961). In view of the higher mortality rate for adult hens than for drakes and the early fall departure of adult drakes from the Prairie Provinces, the spring sex ratios are likely to provide the more valid appraisal.

Mortality

Band recoveries from blue-winged teal provide indices of their mortality rates. Bluewings banded in the Prairie Provinces had the following annual mortality rates (Geis et al. 1963): adult males, 41.7 percent; adult females, 52.7 percent; immatures, 71.7 percent (first year); adults and immatures combined, 64.3 percent.

Bluewings banded in the Dakotas and Minnesota had higher mortality rates than bluewings banded in Canada: 67.8 percent for adults and immatures combined. Recoveries from bandings of all age- and sex-classes of bluewings in Illinois showed an annual mortality rate of 57 percent (Bellrose and Chase 1950).

In spite of low hunting losses, bluewings have a higher annual mortality than other dabbling ducks. Perhaps the high nonhunting losses occur because of the bluewings' lengthy overwater flights to South America.

DISTRIBUTION

Two races of blue-winged teal are recognized by ornithologists. The nominate race *(Anas discors discors)* inhabits that part of the breeding range west of the Appalachian Mountains. Those nesting along the Atlantic Seaboard from New Brunswick to Pea Island, North Carolina, were proposed as a separate race *(Anas discors orphna)* by Stewart and Aldrich (1956) and accepted as a valid race by the nomenclature committee of the American Ornithologists' Union (1957).

Breeding Range

The blue-winged teal is primarily a bird of the northern prairies and parklands, with numbers rapidly diminishing northward, so that fewer than 100 (probably nonbreeders) reach the Canadian Arctic and only a few hundred occur in Alaska.

The bluewing is the most abundant breeding duck on the mixed prairie grasslands of the Dakotas and the Prairie Provinces of Canada, followed closely by the mallard and the pintail. In this vegetation zone there is an average of 2,400,000 breeding bluewings, with a density of 13.3 per square mile. The highest density, 36.7 per square mile, occurs in southwest Manitoba and lessens westward and southward. To the west, Saskatchewan has a density in the mixed prairie association of 11 per square mile and Alberta has 7.7 per square mile. Southward, North Dakota and South Dakota have densities of 17.8 and 19.1 per square mile.

Although the parklands contain a higher density of breeding bluewings (16.4 per square mile) than the mixed prairie, their smaller area results in decreased breeding numbers—1,500,000. As in the mixed prairie, density was highest in southwest Manitoba, 19.3 per square mile, tapering off westward to 18.0 per square mile in eastern Saskatchewan, 11.4 in western Saskatchewan, and 16.2 in Alberta.

Northward, the deltas of the Saskatchewan and Athabasca rivers hold about the same density of breeding bluewings, 11.8 and 12.5 per square mile, but the larger area of the Saskatchewan Delta accommodates a population of 85,000 and the Athabasca Delta scarcely 19,000.

Because of the vastness of the closed boreal forest association with its attendant lakes, marshes, and meadows, about 590,000 bluewings breed there, but the density is low, 1.3 per square mile. Unlike breeding density on the prairies, that in the closed boreal forest generally improves from east to west: 0.2 per square mile in western Ontario, 0.6 per square mile in Manitoba, 0.4 in eastern Saskatchewan, but 1.2 in the west, and 1.3 per square mile in Alberta. A crude estimate places the numbers of breeding bluewings in eastern Ontario and Quebec at 25,000. Few bluewings occur as far north as the open boreal forest association, where surveys indicate a population of 5,000. About 800 bluewings reach Alaska to breed in the Susitna River delta, the Copper River delta, and the Seward Peninsula.

To the south and west of the mixed prairie lies the shortgrass prairie association, a more arid region. In this landscape about 465,000 bluewings breed, 3.0 per square mile. Because of the more abundant ponds, bluewings are most dense, 6.2 per square mile, in southwest Saskatchewan, followed by 4.9 per square mile in South Dakota, 3.0 per square mile in Montana north of the Missouri River but only 1.3 south of there, and 2.3 per square mile in western North Dakota. Thirty thousand, at an unknown density, breed in the plains region of Wyoming.

Wetlands in the former tallgrass prairie or deciduous woods associations, or both, harbor breeding populations of the following sizes: about 140,000 in the Sandhills and 30,000 in the southeasterly Rainwater Basin, Nebraska; 145,000 in Minnesota; 60,000 in Iowa; 90,000 in Wisconsin; 35,000 in Michigan; and 100 in Ohio.

From the Rocky Mountains west to the Cascade Mountains, the bluewing is largely and sometimes exclusively replaced by the cinnamon. Nevertheless, appreciable numbers of bluewings breed in the Intermountain marshes of this region: 120,000 in British Columbia; 17,000 in Washington; 11,000 in Utah; 4,000 in Colorado; 3,400 in western Montana; 1,200 each in California and Idaho; and 1,000 in Oregon.

In certain years when habitat conditions are particularly good, bluewings breed by the hundreds in marshes and rain ponds along the Gulf Coast of Louisiana and Texas. In 1958, a year after the coast of Louisiana was struck by a hurricane, large numbers of bluewings nested in the coastal marshes (Smith 1961*a*). William Kiel reported that Hurricane Beulah deluged the south Texas coast with 20 inches of rain in September 1967. The resulting rainwater ponds induced 200 pairs of bluewings to nest on the King Ranch in the spring of 1968. Kiel actually counted 119 broods, on an aerial survey, and estimated several times that number along the Texas coast between the Nueces and Rio Grande rivers. In the spring of 1969, when water conditions were normal, he found only two blue-winged teal broods.

Ponds created by high floods in the spring of 1973 induced numerous blue-winged teal to nest in southern Illinois, where none had been known to nest previously (David Kennedy). The number of blue-winged teal breeding on the Cheyenne Bottoms Wildlife Area in central Kansas varied, depending upon habitat conditions, from 814 in 1968 to 2,800 in 1969 to 600 in 1970 (Marvin Schwilling).

The varying response of blue-winged teal to unusual water conditions far south of their primary breeding grounds is amazing. Although some other species exhibit this same behavior, none do it on such a grand scale as the blue-winged teal.

Even rough figures on the breeding numbers of blue-winged teal along the Atlantic Seaboard are lacking. A review of scattered breeding records of bluewings in this region (Parnell and Quay 1965) and our own perusal of reports from national wildlife refuges leads to the conclusion that they are not abundant, perhaps 10,000 to 25,000 at most.

Migration Corridors

The blue-winged teal has the most complex migration pattern of all ducks in North America. In late summer many immatures and even some adults move north from their southern breeding grounds in Montana and North and

South Dakota to the Prairie Provinces of Canada. From countless staging areas widely dispersed over the northern Great Plains, bluewings fan out far and wide. Most fly long distances in migration before stopping, and apparently because of these long flights, few really large concentrations of migrants are found north of their winter grounds.

The lack of great fall concentrations, so characteristic of most other species, makes the plotting of migration corridors more speculative than with other common ducks. Adding to the problem is the paucity of data on the abundance of bluewings on their principal winter grounds in Central and South America. Further compounding the difficulty are the vast stretches of the Atlantic Ocean, the Gulf of Mexico, and the Caribbean Sea, crossed with the barest of traces.

A sizable segment of blue-winged teal—more than other prairie-nesting ducks—migrates directly eastward, some as far as New Brunswick and Maine. Even teal banded as far west as Alberta have been recovered there (Sharp 1972). At various points the eastward-bound bluewings alter flight direction to more southerly courses and eventually head out over the Atlantic Ocean for the West Indies and South America.

The bluewings migrating through southeastern Canada and northeastern United States tend, more than others, to winter in eastern Venezuela and Guyana. Just as teal migration corridors cross the United States from west to east, these corridors terminate from west to east across Central and South America.

Although the continent east of the Rocky Mountains is blanketed by many migration corridors, only two are outstanding for the blue-winged teal. One leads from Manitoba and Minnesota to Florida; the other extends from Saskatchewan south-southeast across the eastern Great Plains to east Texas and Louisiana.

Probably because the blue-winged teal has an ecological equivalent—the cinnamon teal—in the Pacific Flyway, bluewings are rare migrants there. Band recoveries indicate that only small numbers migrate from Alberta and Saskatchewan to the mid-Central Valley of California, and probably from there to the west coast of Mexico. Along this coast, bluewings increase in number. Progressively southward, the migration corridors increase in volume of use from west to east.

Band recoveries of bluewings have been obtained from below the equator in Brazil and Peru, the farthest south of any duck in the Western Hemisphere. Stoudt (1949) recorded the flight of a banded bluewing from Oak Lake, Manitoba, to Lima, Peru, a distance of over 4,000 miles! He also reported the amazing 3,800-mile flight of an immature bird from the Athabasca Delta to Maracaibo, Venezuela, made in 1 month, an average of 125 miles per day.

Winter Areas

Blue-winged teal winter farther south in greater numbers than any other duck in North America—most of them in northern South America. Until 1957, fewer than 25,000 wintered in the United States, mainly in Florida. However, the hurricane that opened up the extensive coastal marshes of Louisiana in June 1957 apparently resulted in over 100,000 bluewings remaining there through the winter of 1957-58 (Smith 1961*a*).

Since 1957, the blue-winged teal has become an important winter resident in Louisiana. Winter surveys, 1960-74, have found an average of 190,000, with 650 more in the nearby states of Arkansas, Mississippi, and Alabama. Bluewings also began to stop in coastal Texas in greater numbers. An average of 8,750 have wintered there during the past decade; earlier, only a few hundred—or none—had remained.

Other important states for wintering bluewings are Florida, with almost 11,000, and South Carolina, with 5,000. Small numbers have been found on winter surveys in Georgia, North Carolina, Missouri, Tennessee, Oklahoma, and New Mexico.

About 266,000 blue-winged teal have been estimated on winter surveys in Mexico: 127,000 along the east coast, 105,000 along the west coast, and 34,000 in the interior. The largest concentrations along the east coast occur on the Tabasco lagoons (55,000) and the Campeche and Yucatan lagoons (48,000). On the west coast, the largest concentrations were found in lagoons near Culiacán (14,000), in lagoons between Mazatlán and Tuxpan (26,000), in lagoons north and south of Acapulco de Juárez (13,000), and in lagoons from Tehuantepec to the Guatemala border (40,000). Most of the blue-winged teal in the interior of Mexico winter in lakes and marshes between Guadalajara and Mexico City.

The only survey of part of the extensive winter grounds of waterfowl in Central America and northern South America was made in January 1960 by Glover and Chamberlain (1960). They calculated that there were 16,000 bluewings in lagoons along the west coast of Central America: 7,500 adjacent to the Gulf of Fonseca at the Honduras-Nicaragua border; 2,500 on Lago de Managua, Nicaragua; and 5,700 on marshes of the Gulf of Nicoya, Costa Rica. In marshes on or near the coasts of Colombia and Venezuela, Glover and Chamberlain (1960) calculated 313,000 bluewings, only 17,000 of which were in Venezuela in marshes adjacent to the southwest shore of Lago de Maracaibo. They did not survey marshes in eastern Venezuela or in Guyana, from which large numbers of bands are received.

Most of the 296,000 bluewings found in Colombia were in the marshes and lagoons at the delta of the Magdalena River and in the marshes farther upstream. Small numbers of band recoveries have been received from Ecuador, Peru, and Brazil.

Aerial surveys of waterfowl on certain islands of the West Indies, made by Walter Crissey during 1951-55, suggest that no more than 50,000 bluewings winter there. He found an average of 20,000 bluewings in Cuba, 5,000 in the Dominican Republic, 4,000 on the Bahama Islands, and 1,500 in Haiti.

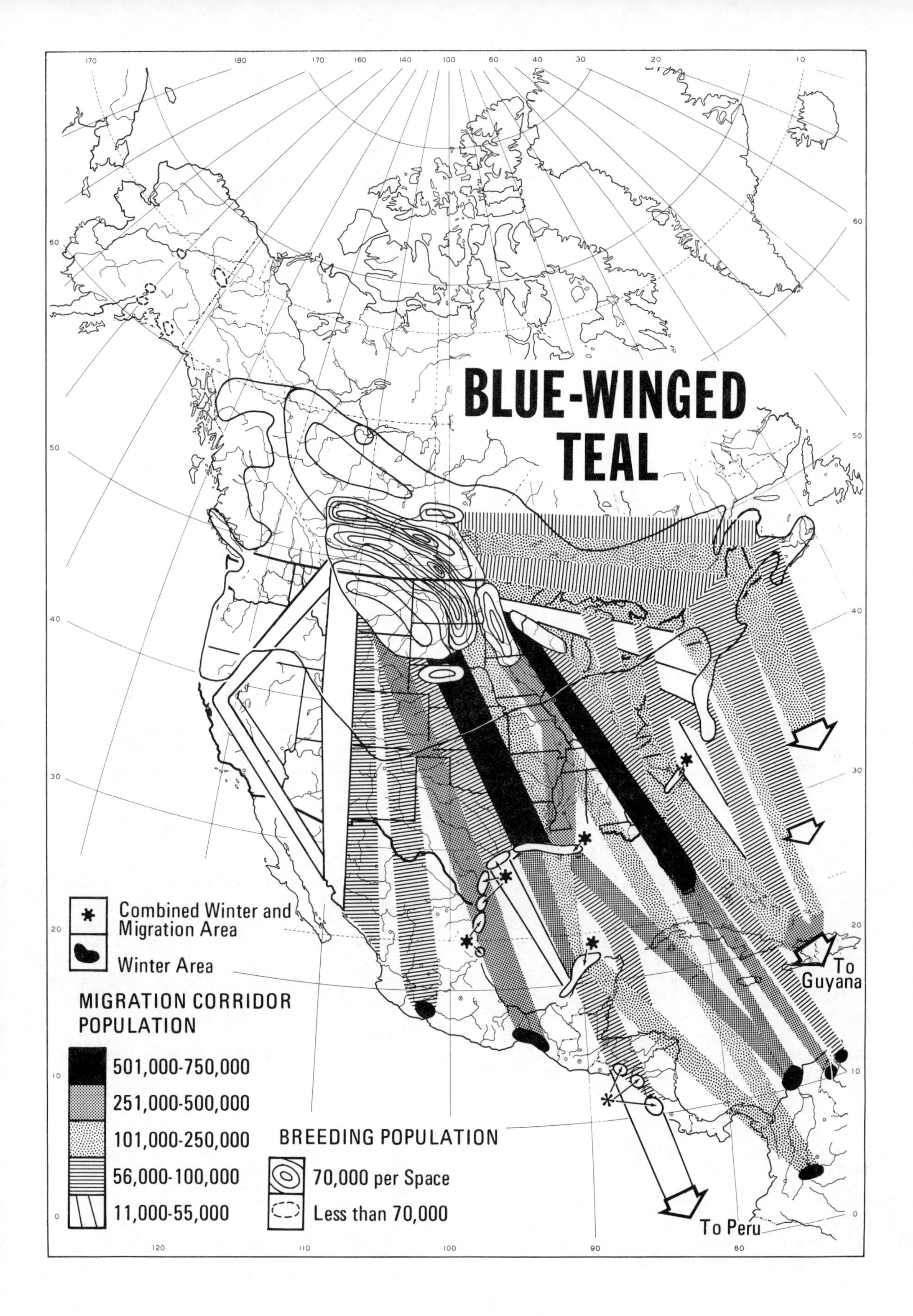
BLUE-WINGED TEAL
Combined Winter and Migration Area
Winter Area
MIGRATION CORRIDOR POPULATION
501,000-750,000
251,000-500,000
101,000-250,000
56,000-100,000
11,000-55,000
BREEDING POPULATION
70,000 per Space
Less than 70,000
To Guyana
To Peru

MIGRATION BEHAVIOR

Blue-winged teal are generally the first ducks south in the fall and the last ones north in the spring. It seems hardly possible that the birds could have nested and molted by the time they appear on migration areas in late July and early August.

Compared with other dabbling ducks, blue-winged teal make exceedingly long flights, many over vast expanses of water, between feeding and rest areas. I have talked to fishermen who found flocks of bluewings riding the swells of the Gulf of Mexico, south of the Mississippi Delta. When frightened, they headed southward over the Gulf, no doubt on their way to Yucatan.

Because of their long flights, bluewings are sometimes observed migrating during the day, not having reached their goal by sunup. However, all of the many departures that I have seen occurred between sunset and dark.

More than other ducks, bluewings differ in chronology of migration between the sexes. Banding records and kill data show that adult drake bluewings depart the breeding grounds well in advance of the adult hens and immatures. Most bluewing flocks after mid-September are composed largely of adult hens and immatures.

Chronology

Fall. The graphs do not adequately depict the late summer migration of blue-winged teal because censuses were not taken prior to September. All of the northern regions experience a steady decline in their bluewing populations from early September until early November, when only a few remain.

Blue-winged teal in the central migration areas are only slightly behind the departure schedules of bluewings in the more northern regions. They tend to remain in appreciable numbers through September, then diminish rapidly during October, with small numbers remaining into December.

On southern areas in Florida, Louisiana, and Texas—where many bluewings winter—large numbers appear in September (Chamberlain 1960, Smith 1961). Local populations increase as the season advances, with seasonal and yearly variations in the numbers of bluewings departing for other winter grounds farther south. In some years (1957-58, 1958-59, 1959-60, 1960-61, 1962-63, 1967-68), almost as many bluewings wintered in Louisiana as were found at the peak of fall migration. In other years (1963-64, 1964-65, 1965-66, 1968-69, 1969-70, 1970-71), only a small proportion of the fall population remained over winter (Hugh Bateman). Bluewings censused in east-central Florida, 1948-58, declined 35 percent from mid-October into December, increased in numbers from January through February, and declined 33 percent from February to mid-March (Chamberlain 1960).

Spring. In February, bluewings migrating northward from Central and South America start to augment populations wintering in Texas and Louisiana. Their numbers increase through March, with populations declining through April but small numbers remaining into May.

Migration areas immediately north of the winter grounds begin to receive appreciable numbers of bluewings about mid-March. Numbers increase until mid-April and then dwindle as populations move northward. On their principal breeding grounds in the United States, bluewings begin to arrive in late March, with a tremendous surge boosting numbers upward through April. It is usually late April before the first wave of bluewings arrive on the Canadian prairies and mid-May before the last migrants arrive.

BREEDING

Behavior

Age, Pair Bond, and Homing. From his study of the breeding of blue-winged teal at Delta Marsh, Manitoba, Dane (1965) concluded that almost all yearlings nest.

Among hand-reared birds, Dane (1965) found that association of juveniles 4 to 9 weeks of age increased the likelihood of their subsequent pairing. He observed that the onset of courtship among immatures started in late January or early February as the drakes began to acquire their nuptial plumage. On areas south of the breeding grounds, bluewings are more active in courtship during the spring migration than most other ducks. About 60 percent of the first spring arrivals in northwest Iowa were paired (Glover 1956), and by the time they arrived in the region of Minnedosa, Manitoba, all were mated (McHenry 1971). In mid-January 1974, Arthur Hawkins observed courtship and paired birds among bluewings on the lower Texas coast.

Unlike pintails, the pair bond in blue-winged teal is very strong. In Idaho, most drakes did not desert their hens until the third week of incubation (Oring 1964). Pair bonds of bluewings in northwest Iowa were terminated between the 11th and 19th day of incubation; the average was 14 days (Strohmeyer 1967). Renesting hens retained their original mates for the same length of time as those nesting only once. Consequently, McHenry (1971) believed that the duration of the pair bond in bluewings was related more to the lateness of the season than to the period of incubation. At Minnedosa he observed that most drakes forsook their hens during the last 2 weeks in June regardless of the stage of incubation. He (1971) noted that as incubation progressed, the female remained on her nest longer and the drake became less consistent in occupying his loafing site, ranging more widely and becoming less aggressive toward intruding drakes.

Bluewings are poor homers but great pioneers. Of the five prairie-breeding ducks studied by Sowls (1955), bluewings had the lowest rate of return—14 percent of 58 banded adult hens and none of 30 banded juveniles. McHenry (1971) trapped and marked 16 incubating hens in southwest Manitoba; none returned the following year. He also released 200 hatchery-reared bluewings in 1968 and none were found on the area in 1969.

Blue-winged teal are obviously more flexible in their homing proclivity than many species. Apparently they are footloose in their ability to pursue changing water patterns on the prairie. This flexibility enables the bluewing to make some adjustments to drought conditions when they occur. The heart of the blue-winged teal breeding range coincides with the region most affected by drought. Shallow waters are fast disappearing by the time these late nesters are ready to breed. Their ability to breed in Louisiana, Texas, Kansas, Illinois, and elsewhere when unusually favorable habitat conditions develop indicates their adaptability in meeting the challenges of their environment.

Home Range. McHenry's (1971) studies of paired blue-winged teal at Minnedosa, Manitoba, led him to conclude that drakes defended a mobile area about the hen rather than a specific area. Flight pursuit of intruding males is less common in bluewings than in many other prairie ducks, which probably accounts for their small home ranges.

Dzubin (1955) studied the home ranges of three species of ducks in the Minnedosa area and observed that a bluewing's home range covered 250 acres, a mallard's 700 acres, and a canvasback's 1,300 acres. Later, in the same area, McHenry (1971) calculated that bluewing home ranges averaged 17 acres (41), with extremes of 1.4 and 78.6 acres. Evans and Black (1956) in northeastern South Dakota found that 11 bluewing home ranges averaged 89 acres (1 was 256 acres).

McHenry (1971) considered that the pattern of water distribution was more important than breeding density in determining home range size. Increasing the breeding population on his study area by releasing hatchery-reared birds failed to reduce the size of home ranges. Fewer and more widely scattered water areas resulted in larger home ranges than where water areas were small and more numerous. McHenry (1971) concluded that in the Minnedosa area, nest cover was more important than availability of water in limiting the size of breeding populations.

Nesting

Behavior. Almost immediately after establishing waiting sites, females followed by their mates fly low over the surrounding terrain, prospecting for possible nest sites. McHenry (1971) observed that searching pairs periodically dropped into the grass, walked about, and then resumed flight. One pair explored 160 acres or more, over several days, before selecting a nest site. Most nest-building and egg-laying occurs between 7:00 and 10:00 A.M.

Nest Sites. Bluewings favor grass for nest sites; where prevalent, bluegrass is preferred. Hayfields are used extensively for nesting in the Midwest (Labisky 1957). Buckbrush is second to grasslands on the northern prairies, and sedge meadows are locally important.

Nests have been found near the water's edge and as far away as 1 mile; numerous nest studies list average distances ranging from 71 to 661 feet, with a general average of 125 feet. Two active nests were found within 10 yards of each other (Glover 1956), but most were over 50 yards apart.

Egg-laying often starts when the nest is barely a scrape in the ground. Plant material, usually grass, but always vegetation that is within reach, is used to line the nest bowl. Down feathers are customarily added after four or more eggs are deposited and their number dramatically increases as laying nears completion.

Glover (1956) measured 186 bluewing nests and found these average dimensions of the nest bowl: outside diameter, 7.7 inches; inside diameter, 5.3 inches; depth, 2.2 inches; and thickness, 0.8 inch.

Clutch Size, Eggs, and Incubation. Blue-winged teal lay one egg a day until the clutch is complete. Strohmeyer (1967) found that 350 eggs were laid in 358 days by various teal. Clutches of 6 to 15 eggs have been found, averaging 9.8 in 1,735 nests. Regional means ranged from 8 to 11 eggs. The later bluewings initiated laying, the smaller the clutch size. At Delta, Manitoba, Sowls (1955) found 10.6 eggs in clutches completed before June 15 and 8.8 eggs after that date. A later study (Dane 1966) in the same area showed that early clutches ranged from 10 to 12 eggs but that clutches started after June 4 steadily declined, as the season progressed, from 10 to 7 eggs. Clutch size also varied with age of the laying hen: yearlings 10.5 eggs and older birds 11.4 eggs (Dane 1965). Initial nests of blue-winged teal in Iowa averaged 10.7 eggs, first renests 9.2 eggs, and second renests 8.3 eggs (Strohmeyer 1967). Apparently, late clutches are smaller because they represent renests.

The smooth-shelled eggs are creamy tan in color, elliptical ovate in shape, and measure 33.9 mm by 47.1 mm (Glover 1956).

Incubation periods in the wild averaged 24.2 days, with a range of 23 to 27 days (Dane 1966). Dane's and Strohmeyer's (1967) evidence indicates that bluewings begin to incubate several hours before the last egg is laid. For conformity, the date of the last egg laid is used for calculating incubation periods.

Chronology of Nesting. Because of late arrival on breeding areas, bluewings are among the last dabbling ducks to nest. Unlike gadwalls, after their arrival they do not tarry long before beginning to seek nest sites. Many begin to nest within 1 week.

The earliest initiation of nesting occurred on April 24, Iowa (Strohmeyer 1967); April 25, South Dakota (Evans and Black 1956); May 9, Delta Marsh, Manitoba (Sowls 1955); May 5, Redvers, Saskatchewan (Stoudt 1971); and May 22, Brooks, Alberta (Keith 1961). Nest activity by bluewings rises rapidly, with peak nest initiation commencing within 2 to 3 weeks—in most areas this is the last week in May. Few nests are started after mid-July. Dane (1965) found that at Delta Marsh, yearlings begin nesting 4 days later than older hens.

BLUE-WINGED TEAL

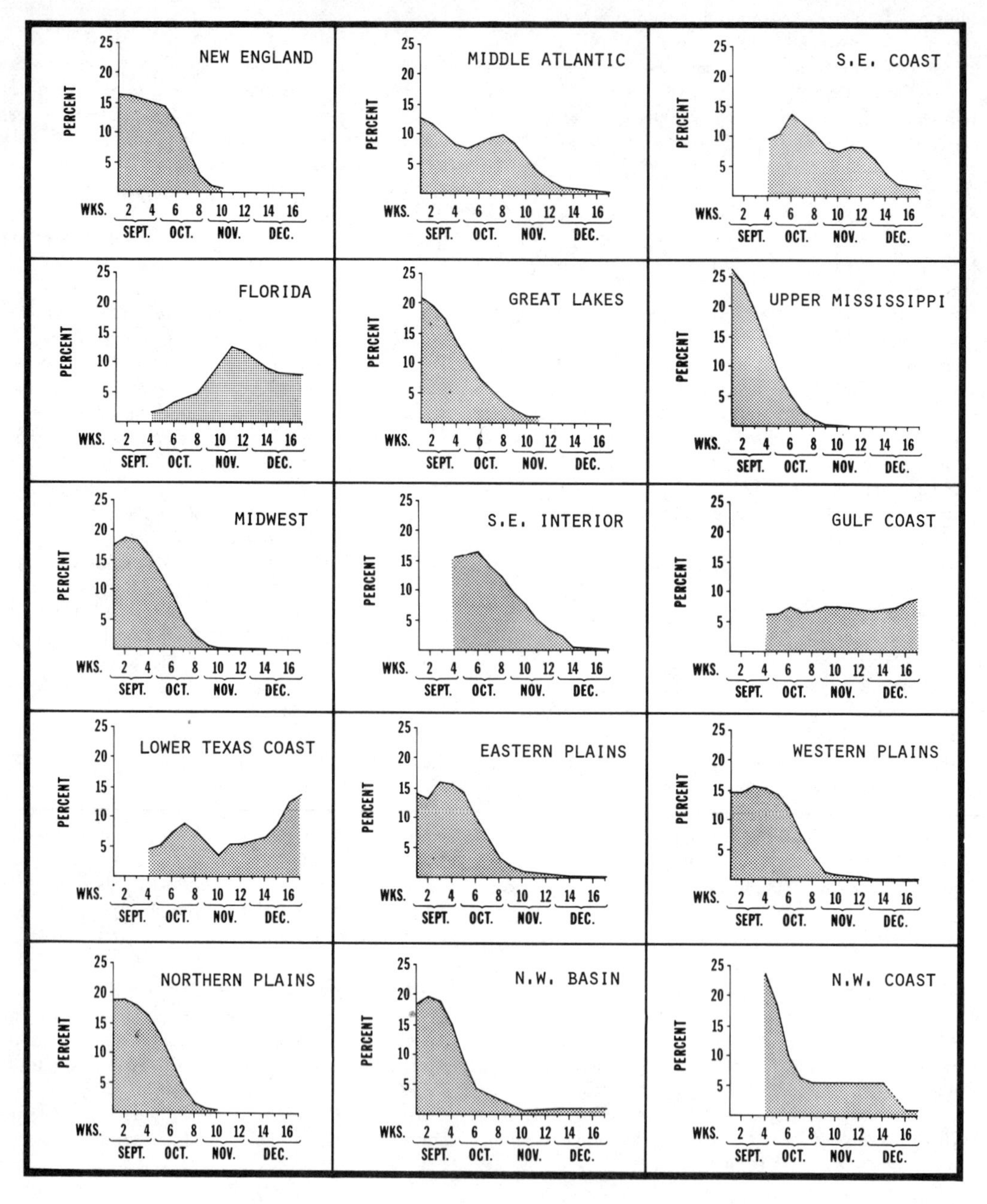

Fall

BLUE-WINGED TEAL

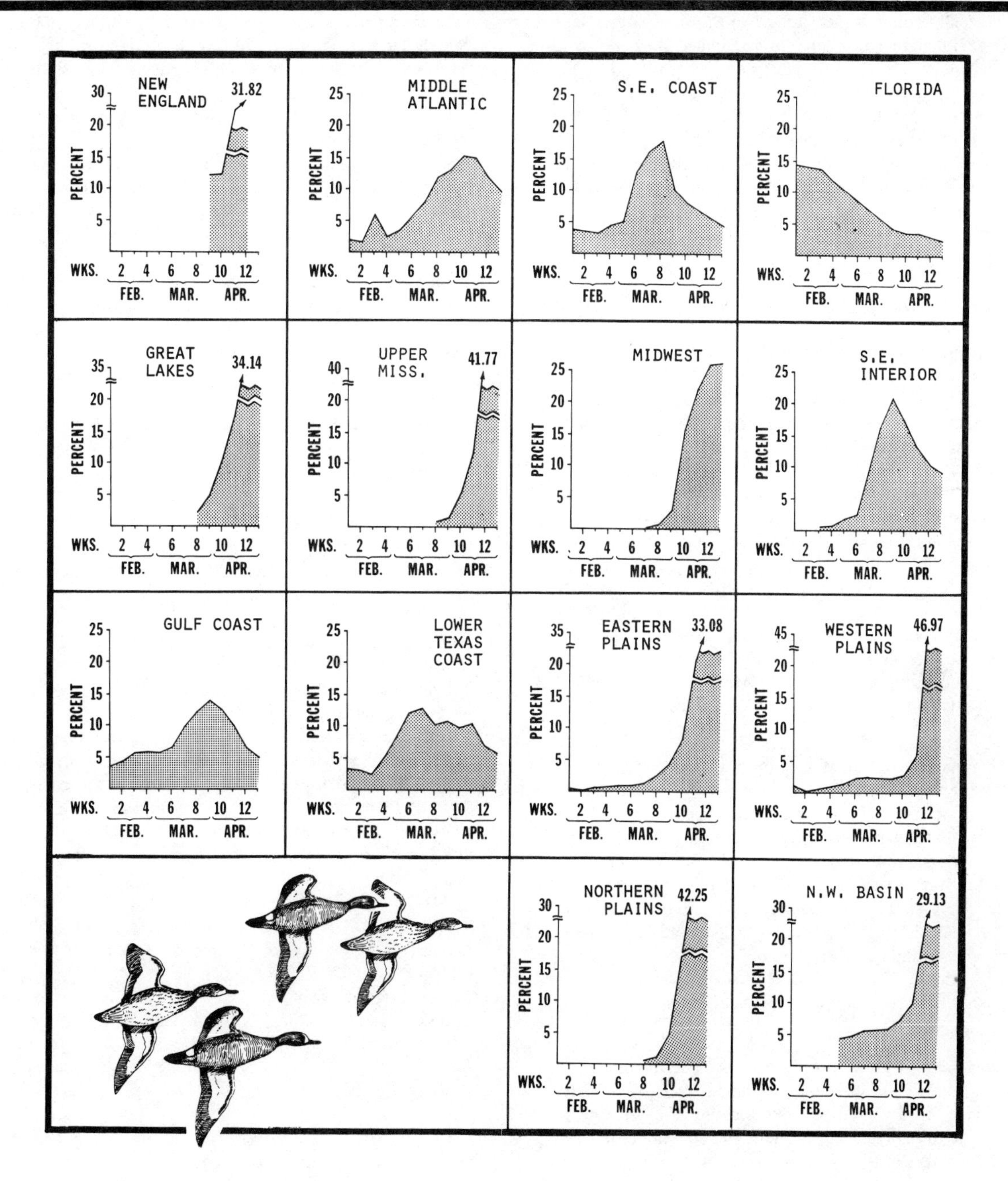

Spring

Chronology of nesting varies from year to year as a result of weather conditions. At Delta Marsh, Sowls (1955) observed that bluewing nesting was delayed a week in 1950 by abnormally cold weather. Later, in the same area, Dane (1966) noted that nest initiation declined during a cold wave, May 21-24, 1963. A cold wave on May 9-11, 1966, slowed the nesting activity of bluewings in the area of Minnedosa, Manitoba; the peak occurred on May 22, 2 weeks later than in 1965 (Strohmeyer 1967).

The span in nest initiation among bluewings varies more from year to year than it does with latitude, possibly because of their midcontinental range. Most studies show that the starting of nests extends over a period of 50 to 77 days.

Nest Success. Although the bluewing is one of the more abundant ducks in North America, its nest success is amazingly poor. Studies made in many areas, over a period of years, indicate that only 35 percent of 2,533 nests have been successful. On the study area at Ruthven, Iowa, nest success has ranged from 60 percent, 1932-36 (Bennett 1938), to 21 percent, 1948-49 (Glover 1956), to 13 percent, 1964-66 (Strohmeyer 1967). The low rate of success in 1964-68 was attributed by Strohmeyer (1967) to an overall density of 1.5 nests per acre (5 per acre on one-third of the most heavily used pasture) that encouraged predators by high rewards for their search efforts.

Nest success on other areas, each involving over 100 nests, was as follows: Brooks, Alberta, 42 percent (Keith 1961); Lousana, Alberta, 32 percent (Smith 1971); Redvers, Saskatchewan, 41 percent (Stoudt 1971); several areas in Minnesota, 35 percent (Moyle et al. 1964); and Flathead Valley, Montana, 72 percent (Girard 1941).

Nest Failure. Almost half (47.5 percent) of the nest failures of blue-winged teal were caused by mammals. Striped and spotted skunks were responsible for two-thirds of these losses. Other culprits were ground squirrels, foxes and coyotes, mink, weasels, raccoons, and badgers.

All nest losses caused by birds (18 percent) were attributed to either crows or magpies. Farm activities—mowing of hayfields, burning of meadows and stubble fields, plowing, fence-building, and the trampling of nests by grazing cattle—caused 12 percent of the losses. Flooding caused 4 percent and unknown factors the remainder.

Renesting. Strohmeyer (1967) has made the most thorough study of the bluewing's propensity to renest. He concluded that when nests were lost during egg-laying, at least one-third of the yearling hens and one-half or more of the older hens renested. However, only 20 percent of the hens that lost incubated clutches attempted to renest. Almost 40 percent of the hens whose first renests were destroyed tried again, 43 percent of those whose second nests were destroyed tried a third time and 33 percent of those that lost third nests tried a fourth time. The net result was that 18 percent of the nests known to hatch were renests. Strohmeyer determined that the young from renests survived as well as early-hatched broods.

Sowls (1955) considered the bluewing to be the poorest renester among five species of ducks he studied at Delta Marsh. Near Brooks, Alberta, Keith (1961) calculated that 55 percent of the unsuccessful bluewing hens renested, 100 percent of the unsuccessful mallard hens, 82 percent of the gadwalls, 75 percent of the shovelers, but only 39 percent of the lesser scaups renested.

Up to a loss of the first six eggs, blue-winged teal continued to lay additional eggs, with no interruption (Strohmeyer 1967), but after the destruction of nests with eight or more eggs, some time elapsed before new nests were started. As the number of eggs laid and the days of incubation increase, so does the interval before renesting. After 1 day of incubation the interval averages 6 days; after 10 days of incubation it averages 7.5 days. Hens that lost nests during their last week of incubation did not renest.

Forty-four renesting bluewings selected sites an average of 596 feet from their destroyed nests, with a maximum distance of 2,223 feet (Strohmeyer 1967). Five renests observed by Sowls (1955) averaged 810 feet from earlier nest sites.

Rearing of Young

Broods. Blue winged teal broods often travel overland 100 to 1,600 yards from their nest sites to sloughs or ponds selected by their mothers for brood rearing. The minimal long-distance record for a marked teal brood is 2.25 miles (Evans and Black 1956).

Once ensconced on a brood area, bluewings are more likely to remain there than many other species. Evans and Black (1956) reported that blue-winged teal broods spent an average of 11 days on one pothole before leaving for another, pintails spent 5 days, mallards 7 days, and wigeons 20 days. Perhaps because invertebrate food for ducklings is more available as the season advances, late-brooded species play "musical chairs" less often than early-brooded ones.

At Redvers, Saskatchewan, blue-winged teal, mallard, and pintail broods most often occupied ponds 0.5 to 1.0 acre in size, yet in July only 12 percent of the ponds were of this size (Stoudt 1971). A similar preference was noted at Lousana, Alberta (Smith 1971). There, they also preferred semipermanent potholes, often as deep as 3 feet, ringed with emergent vegetation and located in hayfields. Stockponds were favored by both bluewings and mallards at Redvers.

Development. Blue-winged teal in South Dakota reached flying age in 35 to 44 days (Gollop and Marshall 1954). In northwestern Iowa, young teal 6 weeks of age had begun to fly (Bennett 1938). Hatchery-reared bluewings could make soft landings at 41 days and maneuver slightly in the air at 43 days (Dane 1965).

Survival. Class I broods are amazingly large for a

species that averages only 9.8 eggs per clutch—8.4 (3,039). We have no records of any common duck with broods of such large size. (A small sample of mottled duck broods averaged 9.8 in Class I.) The large size of Class I broods indicates remarkable fertility and hatchability among successful nests. Class II broods average 7.9 (3,061) young, and Class III average 7.51 (2,924). The attrition in bluewing broods is comparable to that in many other ducks: 6.5 percent lost from Class I to Class II and 4.6 percent lost from Class II to Class III. Consequently, at flight, blue-winged teal broods average 7.5 birds, the largest number of young per brood to reach flight stage among all North American ducks. This high survival of young undoubtedly helps to compensate for their below-average nest success. A nest success of 35 percent, no renests, and 7.5 young at flight results in a production of 1.3 young per adult—a figure higher than is indicated by fall age ratios.

POSTBREEDING SEASON

As drake blue-winged teal begin to wander from their breeding home ranges during the last half of June and early July, hostility ceases and they begin to group with other males. They are preparing for the eclipse molt, during which they will be flightless from 26 to 36 days (McHenry 1971).

Before becoming flightless, the bright plumage of the male is replaced by a more mottled plumage, similar to that of the hen. During the flightless period the teal remain among extensive beds of cattails, bulrushes, and other emergent vegetation.

At Minnedosa, Manitoba, McHenry (1971) reported that most bluewings were flightless between July 10 and August 10. In this pothole area, many bluewings remain on their breeding grounds for the wing molt rather than moving to larger marshes. Yet many hundreds of teal gather for the wing molt on Whitewater Lake, less than 100 miles south of Minnedosa. Vast numbers of bluewings concentrate in large marshes for the wing molt. At the Pel-Kutawagan marshes, north of Regina, Saskatchewan, Sterling (1966) captured 3,683 flightless bluewings during the third week of July. They were third in abundance, below the pintail and green-winged teal but above the mallard.

Small numbers of blue-winged teal breed on and about Freezeout Lake, Montana. But, according to Dale Witt, 5,000 to 10,000 bluewings move onto the lake for the eclipse molt.

Blue-winged teal apparently move into the Camas Refuge, Idaho, to join local birds in molting. Oring (1964) reported first eclipse-plumaged drakes on July 6 and first flightless ones on July 12. An aerial reconnaissance on August 10 revealed many flightless teals of two species.

FOOD HABITS

Blue-winged and green-winged teal are often observed feeding together in the same marsh habitats or mud flat areas. However, there are minor differences in the diet of these two species. One-fourth of the food consumed by bluewings consists of animal life, a much greater proportion than is taken by the vegetarian greenwings.

Bluewings also feed more heavily on the vegetative parts of aquatic plants: filamentous algae, muskgrass, duckweeds, the foliage of widgeon grass, coontail, and pondweeds. Greenwings tend to prefer the seeds. However, where sedge meadows and bulrush marshes occur, bluewings feed heavily on the seeds of these plants.

The plants that grow on mud flats—nutgrasses, smartweeds, millets, water hemp, and rice cut-grass—provide seeds that are avidly consumed by bluewings. These plant beds need to be flooded to make the seeds readily available, but residual seeds, deposited in past years, are often gleaned from mud flats.

Cinnamon Teal

Anas cyanoptera septentrionalium

Other Common Names: Red teal, red-breasted teal

VITAL STATISTICS

Length:	Male, 15.3-17.0 inches, average 16.0 inches (18) Female, 14.5-16.3 inches, average 15.5 inches (10)
Wing:	Adult male, 7.56 inches (42) Adult female, 7.22 inches (40) Immature male, 7.45 inches (34) Immature female, 7.09 inches (38)
Weight:	Male, 0.62-1.10 pounds, average 0.75 pound (13) Female, 0.62-1.10 pounds, average 0.78 pound (11)

IDENTIFICATION

Field

The brilliantly colored breeding plumage of the drake cinnamon teal renders him unique among waterfowl. When the male is awing during spring and early summer, the cinnamon-red head and body and powder-blue wing shoulders create striking contrasts in color. From midsummer through fall, however, he remains cloaked in his eclipse plumage of mottled brown, only slightly redder than the mottled brown hen and the blue-winged teal.

The female cinnamon teal is so like the blue-winged teal hen that they can not be separated in the field.

Cinnamon teal occur in small flocks, often only three to five, more frequently than do other teals. Their fast, low, darting flight is a common sight during the summer and early fall over Intermountain marshes. When the bird is at rest, the flank feathers usually conceal the blue shoulder patches on the wing.

The calls of the cinnamon teal are similar to those of the blue-winged teal: the female utters a harsh *karrr, karrr, karrr;* the male, a low whistled *peep.*

At Hand

The distinctive red eye of the male cinnamon teal, evident at about 2 months of age, distinguishes him not only from the female of the species but also from male blue-winged teal, whose eyes are not red (Spencer 1953).

The drake cinnamon teal is a small bird with yellow feet and legs and a black bill. The vivid cinnamon-red color of the head, neck, breast, and belly identifies the drake in nuptial plumage. The iridescent green speculum is separated from the powder-blue shoulder patch by a white stripe. The back, rump, uppertail coverts, and tail are a dull brown; the undertail coverts are black.

Adult drakes start to molt into their eclipse plumage in late June and by late July most closely resemble their hens. They retain this plumage through the fall. In Utah, Spencer (1953) observed several males of unknown age that had partially cinnamon-red plumages in mid-January. He reported that captive males did not completely assume breeding plumage until mid-March.

Female and immature cinnamon teal closely resemble their counterparts in the blue-winged teal except for minor differences. Bills of cinnamon teal are slightly longer, averaging 46 to 50 mm (Spencer 1953), and their foreheads slope more gradually to the tops of their slightly flattened heads; the foreheads of bluewings rise more abruptly. The blue shoulder patch of the cinnamon teal has a chalky tone in contrast to a waxy appearance, as in the blue-winged teal, and the wings of cinnamon teal average slightly longer than those of bluewings.

POPULATION STATUS

A breeding population of about 260,000 cinnamon teal has been inventoried in the western states and British Columbia. During the period 1960-72, breeding numbers in Utah and California fluctuated over a range of 50 percent, but there was little similarity in the fluctuations in numbers between the two states and no evidence of a trend.

Age Ratios

Although small numbers of blue-winged teal are bagged in the Pacific Flyway, the bulk of the "bluewings" taken are cinnamon teal. Therefore, we have used the combined kill data for these species in the Pacific Flyway, 1966-73, as representing the cinnamon species. Uncorrected age ratios obtained from hunters' bags revealed 1.5 immatures per adult. If corrected by the immatures' probable greater vulnerability to hunting, the data suggest a balanced composition between adults and immatures in fall populations. Uncorrected age ratios varied from a high of 2.5 immatures per adult in 1970 to a low of 0.6 per adult in 1973.

Sex Ratios

Adult male cinnamon teal in hunters' bags outnumbered female adults 1.3 to 1.0 (56 percent), but immature females were more numerous than immature males by a margin of 1.33 to 1.0 (57 percent). The unusually low ratio for males suggests that many immature males depart for winter grounds earlier than immature females.

Mortality

First-year mortality rates computed from data derived from preseason bandings of cinnamon teal in California (Kozlik 1972) amounted to 71 percent, suggesting that most of the banded birds were immatures. Second-year rates amounted to 54 percent, about the expected rate for adults.

DISTRIBUTION

There are five races of the cinnamon teal in the Western Hemisphere; four races breed in South America and one in North America (Delacour 1956).

Breeding Range

Some 150,000 of the approximately 260,000 to 300,000 cinnamon teal breeding in North America nest in Utah, many of them favoring the marshes bordering east and north shores of Great Salt Lake. About 93 percent of the two species of "blue-winged" teals breeding in Utah are cinnamon teal and 7 percent the blue-winged variety (John Nagel).

Next in importance to Utah is Oregon with about 20,000 breeders, the largest number in the Malheur Lake-Summer Lake region (Chester Kebbe). Cinnamon teal comprise about 95 percent of the "blue-winged" complex.

An average of 25,000 teals breed in California, 95 percent cinnamon and 5 percent blue-winged (Frank Kozlik). Most of the bluewings are confined to the northeast corner of the state, but a few have been found at Lake Earl in northwestern California (Johnson and Yocom 1966). About 9,000 teal nest in the Sacramento Valley; 4,500 in the San Joaquin Valley; 5,000 in the northeast part of the state and 4,000 in the Klamath Basin. In recent years the blue-winged teal have expanded their breeding range and numbers in northern California (Wheeler 1965).

All but 2,500 of the 23,000 composing the blue-winged teal group in Washington breed east of the Cascade Range. Thirty percent of these teal are cinnamons (Yocom and Hansen 1960), indicating a breeding population of about 6,000.

About 11,000 cinnamon teal breed in Nevada, largely in the Carson Sink. Nevada is an exclusive cinnamon domain, for few, if any, bluewings are known to nest there.

Population records from national wildlife refuges in Idaho indicate that about 70 percent of the 4,000 breeding blue-winged teal complex are cinnamon. Western Montana hosts about 4,000 teal of the blue-winged group but only about 15 percent are cinnamon (Dale Witt). Very few cinnamon teal breed east of the Rocky Mountains in Montana.

West of the Bighorn Mountains in Wyoming, cinnamon teal compose 30 percent of the nesting teal population (George Wrakestraw). East of there, where most of the state's 35,000 teal nest, only 1 percent are cinnamons. A rough calculation indicates 2,600 cinnamon teal west of the Bighorn Mountains-North Platte River axis and 300 east of there.

Colorado has a breeding population of almost 9,000 teal belonging to the blue-winged group, of which 5,000 are cinnamon. Slightly over half of Colorado's teal nest in the San Luis Valley, where cinnamons compose 73 percent of the population. About 1,000 teal breed along the South Platte River on the western plains of Colorado; only 10 percent of these are cinnamon. Small numbers of cinnamon teal breed in New Mexico at Burford Lake (Huey and Travis 1961) and at Bosque del Apache and Bitter Lake national wildlife refuges.

The cinnamon teal is a rare and an irregular breeder in the western panhandle region of Nebraska (George Schildman). Only one brood has been observed on the Cheyenne Bottoms in central Kansas during 1963-74 (Marvin Schwilling), and a few cinnamon teal have been found in the Texas Panhandle in summer, but no nests or broods (Hawkins 1945).

A few cinnamons have strayed east to breed as far as central North Dakota (Robert Stewart, Harold Kantrud) and the Waubay Hills of South Dakota (Evans and Black 1956).

North of the United States, cinnamon teal nest only in southern British Columbia and southwestern Alberta. From 6,000 to 10,000 are estimated to breed in British Columbia, most in the Cariboo-Chilcotin parklands. Allen

Smith considered the cinnamon teal a common breeder as far north as Lethbridge, Alberta. Stragglers are occasionally seen during summer in Saskatchewan and Manitoba.

According to Leopold (1959), small numbers of cinnamon teal breed in the highlands of Baja California, and as far south in Mexico as Jalisco in the west and Tamaulipas in the east.

Migration Corridors

Because of its restricted breeding range and the closeness of the breeding grounds to the winter grounds, migration corridors for the cinnamon teal are not well delineated. Teal from breeding grounds in the Northwest appear to funnel through the Central Valley of California to Mexico.

Marshes about the Great Salt Lake are staging areas for those cinnamon teal breeding in the valleys of the north-central Rocky Mountains. From these marshes most of the teal migrate almost directly to winter grounds in central Mexico. However, there are also migration corridors from Great Salt Lake to the Central Valley and to the Imperial Valley of California.

During migration a few vagrant cinnamon teal are sometimes found east of their normal range. Teal banded in California have been reported from Oklahoma, Arkansas, Texas, and Louisiana, and banded teal from Nevada have been found in Oklahoma and Louisiana. Occasionally a cinnamon teal appears in the Midwest or farther east, usually in the company of blue-winged teal and most often in spring. No doubt these strays become attached to flocks of blue-winged teal on their mutual winter grounds and become, at least temporarily, a part of the bluewings' traditional migration pattern.

Winter Areas

Of the 500,000 to 600,000 cinnamon teal estimated to be on marshes in the western United States in late summer, all but five to six thousand migrate to winter grounds in Mexico and Central America.

About 5,000 cinnamon teal, representing 95 percent of the number wintering in the United States, remain in California. Most (2,500) winter in the San Joaquin Valley, with an additional 1,500 in the Sacramento and Delta marshes. Usually, fewer than 100 winter in Nevada, Idaho, Oregon, Utah, and Arizona. From 25 to 50 have been found in winter on the Santa Ana and Laguna Atascosa national wildlife refuges near Brownsville, Texas.

Band recoveries occur throughout much of Mexico, the vast majority (80 percent) along the west coast from Guaymas to Guadalajara and then eastward in a broad belt across the Southern Highlands to Veracruz.

Recoveries from cinnamon teal banded in Utah, California, Nevada, and Oregon have been reported from Colombia, indicating that small numbers venture at least that far south to winter.

MIGRATION BEHAVIOR

Cinnamon teal migrate in smaller flocks (usually 10 to 25) than most species of dabbling ducks. Although they have been observed in diurnal migration (Spencer 1953), they usually migrate at night. Spencer (1953) observed that adult males were the first to depart Great Salt Lake marshes and that few were found there after mid-September.

Chronology

Fall. Like their close relatives, the blue-winged teal, cinnamon teal depart their breeding grounds in late summer and early fall for winter habitats. Over most of their Intermountain breeding marshes, numbers steadily decline through September until few remain by the end of October.

The Imperial Valley of southern California sustains an increasing influx of cinnamon teal from late September to late October. For the next 2 months, small numbers regularly depart the valley for Mexico, leaving a residual population that remains throughout the winter. On the lower Gulf Coast of Texas, migrants appear in late November and linger there about 1 month before the majority take wing for Mexico.

Spring. Cinnamon teal begin to appear on the higher Intermountain marshes between early March and early April. Populations continue to increase gradually through April, with numbers subsiding on the more southern breeding areas as the ducks that breed farther north move on. By mid-May, most cinnamon teal are well established on their breeding grounds.

BREEDING

Behavior

Age, Pair Bond, and Homing. Most yearling cinnamon teal breed. Captive birds observed by Spencer (1953) commenced courtship activities leading to pairing in late February as the breeding plumage neared completion. When spring migrants arrive in Utah, many have already chosen their mates, but pairing continues to early May. Nuptial courtship continues to late June, or to the time the males begin to enter the eclipse molt.

Oring (1964) reported that 25 percent of the cinnamon drakes he observed deserted their hens in the second week of incubation, 63 percent during the third week, and the rest (12 percent) remained in attendance until the eggs were pipped.

Home Range. At Ogden Bay, Utah, core areas of home ranges were rarely over 30 square yards (Spencer 1953). A choice loafing site consisted of old muskrat houses or logs or small points of land and was occupied by the drake when

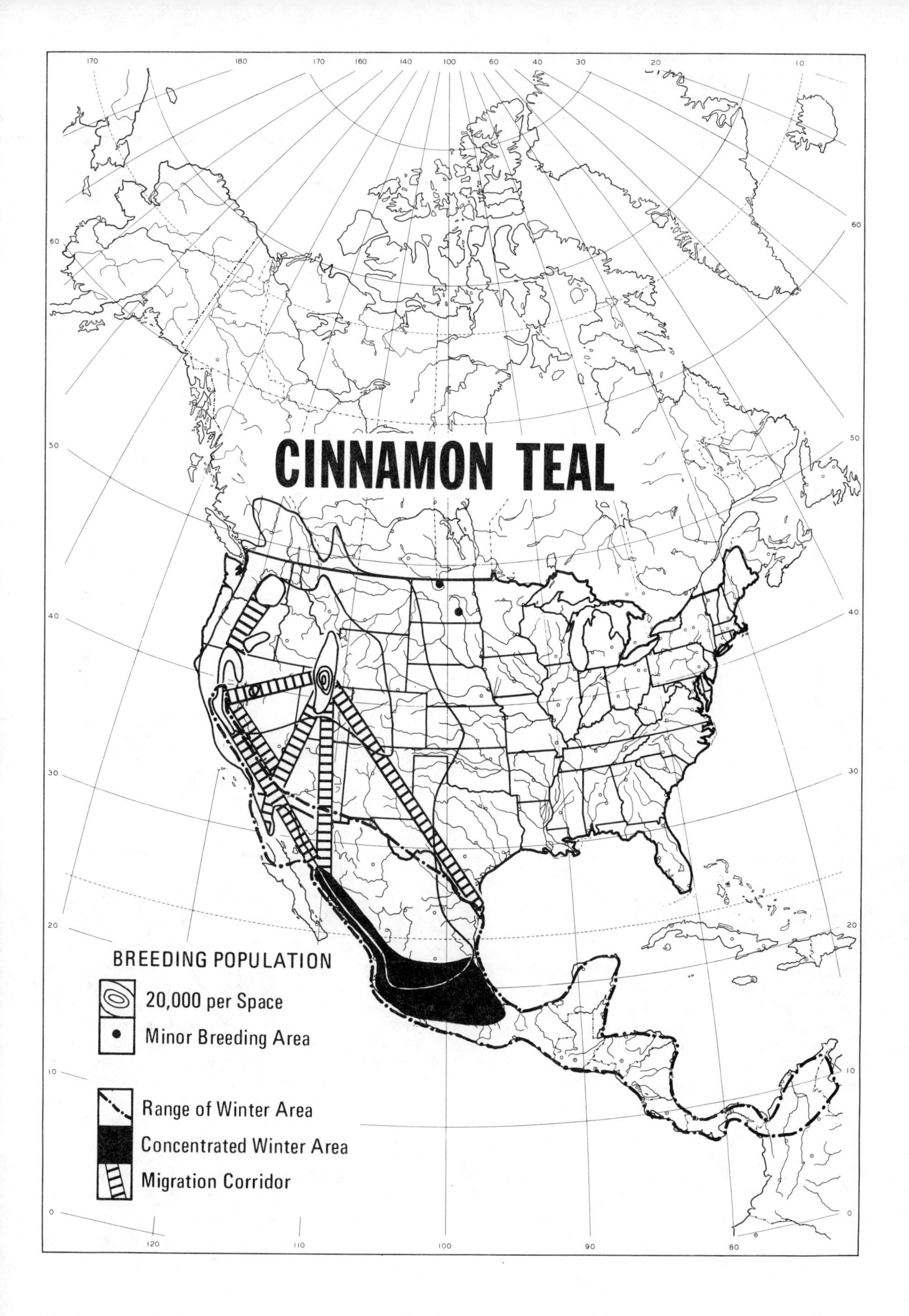

CINNAMON TEAL
BREEDING POPULATION
20,000 per Space
Minor Breeding Area
Range of Winter Area
Concentrated Winter Area
Migration Corridor

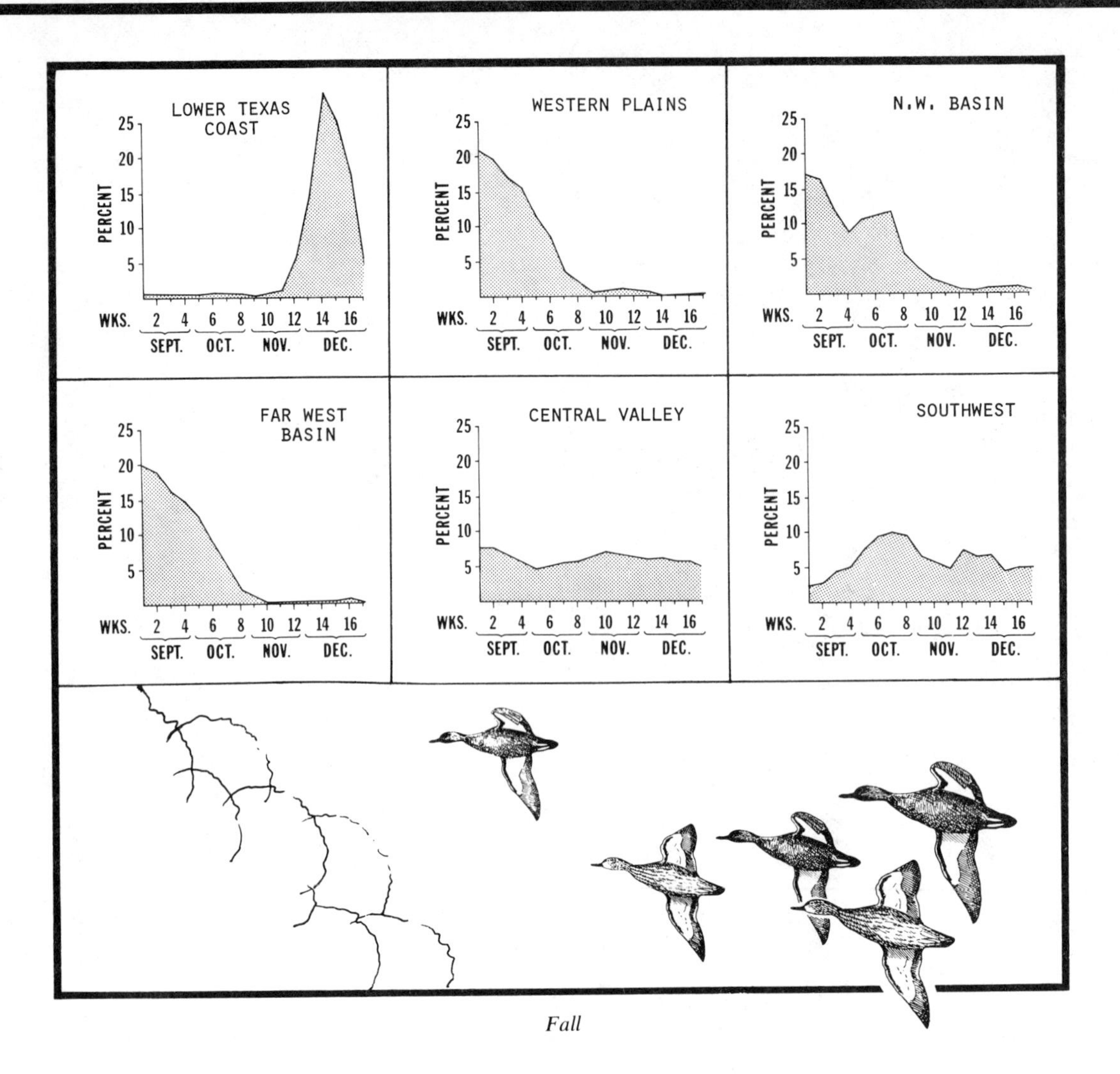

Fall

the hen was on the nest. The hen usually joined the drake during her respite from incubation but flew elsewhere to feed. Canals adjacent to levees are favored activity centers for cinnamon teal breeding in many western marshes.

The nest site is usually within 100 yards of the waiting site. Where nest density is high on many Intermountain marshes, home ranges are small. Marked pairs were found only a little over 0.25 mile from their activity centers after their nests had been destroyed (Spencer 1953). Three cinnamon teal nests were located in a 3-foot triangle of salt grass, suggesting that home ranges may overlap, without undue friction, at points distant from activity centers.

Nesting

Nest Sites. Pairs make reconnaissance flights over marsh areas to choose the general area of the nest site, then the hen goes on foot to select the exact spot (Spencer 1953). Most nest sites are within 75 yards of water but have varied from being over water to 220 yards distant from water.

Dense cover is a more important prerequisite for the nest site than the type of vegetation. In many western marshes, teal favor salt grass beds, but at Knudson's Marsh, Utah, they preferred hardstem and Olney's bulrush (Wingfield 1951). Hardstem bulrush was extensively used for nest cover at the Bear River Refuge, although over twice as many cinnamon teal selected beds of salt grass (Williams and Marshall 1938*b*).

Spencer (1953) observed that nest density was greater where salt grass beds were broken up by clumps of cattails, bulrushes, or tall weeds. Among spike rushes and bulrushes, nests were often found under the mat of dead stems from the previous year, the females entering through access tunnels under the matted vegetation.

Unless nest bowls are located in dense, matted vegetation, the bowl is excavated in the earth and is usually lined with dead grasses and other plant stems available at the site. Down is added as the clutch nears completion and during early incubation.

Nest bowls measured by Spencer (1953) averaged 7.2 inches in diameter (6.5 to 8.2) and 2.7 inches in depth (2.2 to 3.2).

Clutch Size, Eggs, and Incubation. Hens usually laid eggs between 8:00 and 10:00 A.M. at daily intervals; early in the season the first several eggs were sometimes deposited at 1- to 3-day intervals (Spencer 1953). Clutch size ranged from 4 to 16, averaging 8.85 eggs (1,368). Various nest studies have reported average clutch sizes of 7.2 to 11.6 eggs. Early and late clutches were smaller than midseason ones (Spencer 1953).

Redheads parasitized 38 percent of 59 cinnamon teal nests in 1949 and 22 percent of 170 nests in 1950 (Spencer 1953). One teal nest also contained shoveler eggs.

The pale pinkish-buff eggs are ovate in shape and measure 34.6 by 46.4 mm. Within 24 hours of laying the last egg, the hen begins incubation and spends 21 to 25 days at this task (Spencer 1953).

Chronology of Nesting. In the western United States, cinnamon teal have initiated egg-laying between April 11 and May 18. Peak nest initiation has varied from May 24 to June 26, and last nests have been started as early as June 5 and as late as July 25. Variations in chronology of nesting were due to variations in temperature, the result of latitude, altitude, and yearly changes.

The span of time in which nests were initiated in any one area varied from 50 to 92 days and averaged 68 days.

Nest Success. The histories of 1,700 cinnamon teal nests have been followed by investigators in Utah, California, Idaho, and Montana. Fifty-one percent of these nests hatched one or more eggs successfully.

The number of unhatched eggs per successful nest varied from less than one to more than five in various studies. The average was 1.9 eggs, indicating that the successful nests hatched 6.9 ducklings. Eighty-four percent of the egg failures reported occurred because the embryos died and 16 percent because of infertility.

Nest Failure. About 20 percent of the unsuccessful nests were deserted, probably because of adverse weather and molestation by predators. Flooding demolished a few nests, but most nests were destroyed by predators. In California, mammals were responsible for most nest destruction. At Ogden Bay, Utah, California gulls destroyed 29.7 percent and skunks 8.1 percent of the eggs laid in cinnamon teal nests (Spencer 1953). Several incubating birds were killed by minks and weasels.

Renesting. In Lassen County, California, 6 of 48 cinnamon teal hens renested after their nests were destroyed (Hunt and Anderson 1966). One determined hen renested twice. Five and 6 days elapsed between the loss of unincubated eggs and the start of new nests. First clutches averaged 10 eggs (16) and second clutches 8.3 eggs (6).

Rearing of Young

Broods. Of the many species of ducks nesting on Ogden Bay, Utah, Spencer (1953) considered cinnamon teal to be the best mothers. They kept their broods near escape cover, and at the first sign of danger the young slipped out of sight while the female diverted attention by feigning injury.

Small ditches, canals, and ponds where submerged aquatics flourish and adjacent emergent vegetation is plentiful are favored rearing sites. Spencer (1953) observed that broods were larger where juxtaposition of good nest cover and rearing cover occurred.

Development. Spencer (1953) hand-reared several young cinnamon teal and observed that juvenile feathering was nearly complete at 6 weeks. By 7 weeks the young were capable of flight and the eyes of the males were changing from brown to red.

Survival. Downy young of cinnamon teal (Class I) averaged 7.65 per brood (158). By the time broods reached Class II development, their numbers had dwindled by 18 percent to an average of 6.83 (94). A further decline of 27 percent between Classes II and III resulted in broods of 5.58 young (95) just prior to flight.

FOOD HABITS

Cinnamon teal inhabit small, shallow water areas rich in submerged aquatics and surrounded by marsh plants. Bulrush seeds, particularly those of the alkali bulrush, pondweed seeds and leaves, and salt grass seeds are consumed in greatest quantity (Munro 1939*a*, Martin et al. 1951, Spencer 1953), supplemented by small amounts of animal life, mostly insects and mollusks.

Northern Shoveler

Anas clypeata

Other Common Names: Shoveler, spoonbill, spoony

VITAL STATISTICS

Length:	Adult male, 19.0-20.2 inches, average 19.4 inches (24) Adult female, 18.0-20.0 inches, average 18.7 inches (13) Immature male, 18.5-19.5 inches, average 19.2 inches (11) Immature female, 17.1-18.5 inches, average 17.8 inches (22)
Wing:	Adult male, 9.6 inches (114) Adult female, 9.0 inches (58) Immature male, 9.3 inches (72) Immature female, 8.8 inches (78)
Weight:	Adult male, 1.1-1.8 pounds, average 1.5 pounds (21) Adult female, 1.1-1.7 pounds, average 1.4 pounds (20) Immature male, 1.0-1.8 pounds, average 1.4 pounds (89) Immature female, 0.7-1.6 pounds, average 1.3 pounds (118)

IDENTIFICATION

Field

The most impressive diagnostic character of the shoveler is its extraordinarily large bill, usually angled downward 30 to 45 degrees in flight and at rest. The bill is not much longer than the head, but its breadth and spoon-shaped tip make it unique in size among waterfowl. Although the northern shoveler's gray-blue shoulder patch is similar to that of the blue-winged teal, it is not apparent in some plumages.

Shovelers usually occur in small flocks of 5 to 10. They fly swiftly but more slowly than teal. In flight, they have a humpbacked, blocky appearance, totally unlike other dabbling ducks. When they spring into the air, their white outer tail feathers are prominently displayed, like those of mallards. At a casual glance, shovelers are often mistaken for mallards. Because of their mallardlike appearance and poor flavor, they are often called "neighbor's mallards." (Hunters pass them off to their neighbors as mallards—a good way to lose a neighbor!)

During the fall, when hunters view waterfowl, the mottled brown coloration of most shovelers makes them resemble hen mallards. At this time, immatures are still in their juvenile plumage and adult males have not yet molted their eclipse plumage to assume nuptial plumage. As the fall season progresses, more and more shoveler drakes begin to show white chests and breasts, a chestnut darkening of the bellies and sides, white flank spots, and, lastly, a greening of the gray-brown heads. By late November, about 10 percent of the drakes are in full nuptial plumage. I have observed small numbers of shovelers with green heads as early as the first week in November and others that did not attain full nuptial plumage until early February.

In full nuptial plumage, the drake shoveler is strikingly colored. A green head and neck are separated from a chestnut belly and sides by a white chest and breast. White stripes (formed by white scapulars) extend from the upper white breast along the margin of the gray-brown back. When the shoveler springs into the air, the pronounced black "peninsula" on the back attracts the eye so strongly that often the blue shoulder patch on the wing is overlooked.

When shovelers are on the water, their blue shoulder patches are usually hidden by the scapulars. At best, the patches show only as narrow slits. Shovelers appear to ride in the water "down at the bow." The green heads of nuptial drakes are darker than those of mallards and, under poor light, often appear black. Single white flank spots are most noticeable in front of the black undertail coverts.

At Hand

The shoveler is a middle-sized duck, about halfway between a blue-winged teal and a mallard. Its large bill is 2.50 to 2.75 inches in length and steadily widens from ⅝-inch at its base to 1.25 inches near the tip. The bill is black in males and olive-green, speckled with small black dots, in females. The feet and legs are orange in both sexes, but redder in males and duller in immatures.

The wing of the adult male shows a bright gray-blue shoulder patch separated from a brilliant green speculum by a tapered white stripe. The tertials are long, pointed, and black, with a white midrib. In the immature male, the blue wing patch is much duller, and the green speculum and first tertials are edged with white. The blue shoulder patch of the immature female is barely discernible; the wing coverts are brown, slightly dusted with pale blue.

POPULATION STATUS

With a breeding population that averages 1,885,000, shovelers are one-third as abundant as pintails and one-fifth as abundant as mallards. Most hunters are happy that the situation is not the reverse. But the shoveler has increased during the past 20 years whereas the mallard and pintail have declined.

Both breeding ground surveys and January inventories show a fluctuating but rather consistent rise in shoveler numbers from 1955 to 1974. The trend toward higher populations is most pronounced in the Central Flyway, followed in order by the Pacific and Mississippi flyways. There is a slight downward trend in the Atlantic Flyway, but the yearly fluctuations are so pronounced that this trend may not be significant. Certainly the shoveler has not prospered in the Atlantic Flyway.

Age Ratios

When breeding populations of shovelers were high, 1966-73, the number of immatures bagged per adult was 1.91 to 1. Among dabbling ducks, this is the highest proportion of immatures recorded in hunters' bags, second to the blue-winged teal.

Because of a lack of suitable band data, I am assuming that the greater vulnerability of immature shovelers to hunting is similar to that of blue-winged teal (2.58 immatures to 1 adult). Therefore, the actual proportion of immature shovelers in the fall population, 1966-73, was 0.74 to each adult. The uncorrected proportion of immatures per adult shoveler was at its lowest in 1968 (1.17 to 1) and at its highest in 1969 (3.03 to 1), a change of 61 percent in productivity in only 1 year.

Sex Ratios

Shovelers bagged by hunters had these average sex ratios, 1966-73: among adults, 1.96 males to each female (66.2 percent); among immatures, 1.10 males per female (52.4 percent). A spring population composed equally of immature and adult shovelers would contain 59 percent drakes. Sex ratios taken visually during the spring on numerous marshes in the United States show a composition of 60 percent drakes (Bellrose et al. 1961).

Mortality

Information on mortality in shovelers is scanty. Immatures from a small sample banded in Minnesota suffered an annual loss of 71 percent; adults, 61 percent (Lee et al. 1964).

DISTRIBUTION

The shoveler is one of the most cosmopolitan of ducks, occurring extensively in both the Northern and Southern hemispheres. The northern species breeds in North America, Europe, and Asia and winters in the Hawaiian Islands, Central America, West Indies, tropical Africa, Iran, India, southeast Asia, Philippines, Formosa, and Japan. Three other species breed in southern South America, southern Africa, Australia, and New Zealand.

Breeding Range

The shoveler in North America reaches its greatest breeding numbers—818,000 (4.5 per square mile)—in the mixed prairie association. It is most abundant in Saskatchewan, with breeding numbers of 283,000 (6.0 per square mile), and most dense (6.7 per square mile) in Alberta, with a population of 163,000. The mixed prairie in Manitoba supports a density of 5.7 per square mile (26,000 shovelers) compared with 4.7 per square mile in the Dakotas (305,000 shovelers).

North of the mixed prairie association lie the parklands, second in importance for breeding shovelers. Slightly over 500,000 of these ducks nest in the parklands, an average of 5.5 per square mile. As in the mixed prairie, Alberta supports the greatest density of shovelers, with 6.5 per square mile, a population of 173,000. Saskatchewan, with its larger area of parklands, is populated by 293,000 shovelers (5.5 per square mile). Manitoba's parklands contain only 34,000 (2.3 per square mile).

The shortgrass prairies are populated by 204,000 shovelers (1.4 per square mile), with largest numbers in southwestern Saskatchewan and southern Alberta and lowest numbers in southern Montana.

In the tallgrass prairie zone of Nebraska, 32,000 shovelers breed in the Sandhills district and 5,000 more in the Rainwater Basin. Wetlands in the tallgrass prairie and deciduous forest regions in Minnesota are home to 15,000 shovelers. About 5,000 breed in Wisconsin, but only a few breed in Michigan at Saginaw Bay and Lake St. Clair.

Almost 75,000 shovelers breed in the Intermountain marshes of the Rocky Mountains, from central British Columbia to southern Colorado. The largest number, some

35,000, breed in the marshes adjacent to the Great Salt Lake. Other important areas are Wyoming, 16,000; British Columbia, 6,000; California, 5,700; Washington, 4,500; Colorado, 3,600; Oregon, 2,300; Nevada, 1,500; western Montana, 1,500; and Idaho, 1,000.

North of the parklands the breeding density of shovelers greatly declines. Water and marsh areas in the closed boreal forest are inhabited by 245,000 shovelers, only 0.8 of a bird per square mile. In the open boreal forest farther north, breeding numbers decline to 5,000 (0.3 per square mile). On subarctic deltas, shovelers number 55,000 (2.8 per square mile). The Athabasca Delta has a population of only 22,600 shovelers, but, because of its quality, harbors 13.9 per square mile. In contrast, the larger area of the Saskatchewan River delta contains a slightly larger number of shovelers, but, prorated for its size, a mere 3.7 shovelers per square mile.

Old Crow Flats, the Mackenzie Delta, and the Eskimo Lakes area in Arctic Canada support 5,800 shovelers (0.84 per square mile). Shovelers are somewhat more abundant in Alaska, with a population of 41,500 (0.52 per square mile). Most of these, about 31,500, breed in the interior of Alaska, but 10,000 are scattered along the coast, in marshes and on tundra, from the Copper River delta to Kotzebue Bay.

The southern border of the range is marked by nestings in the San Joaquin Valley, California; Burford Lake, New Mexico (Huey and Travis 1961); and the Cheyenne Bottoms, Kansas (Marvin Schwilling). The eastern periphery includes nestings in the Lake Erie marshes, Ohio (Bednarik 1970); the Montezuma Marsh, New York (Cummings 1963); Dunnville, Ottawa, and Kingston, Ontario; Lake St. Peter and Lake St. Francis, Quebec; Sackville, New Brunswick; and Prince Edward Island (Godfrey 1966).

Migration Corridors

During migration, less than 3 percent of the shoveler population frequents the United States east of the Mississippi River. Most shovelers that visit the Atlantic Coast appear to follow the Mississippi migration corridor to western Tennessee, where the majority turn east-southeastward to terminate migration in coastal South Carolina. Several thousand continue southeast to Florida, Cuba, and the West Indies. Farther north, a migration corridor is followed eastward by several thousand shovelers from Manitoba to north-central New York and then south-southeast to coastal New Jersey, Delaware, and Maryland. Another corridor followed by 1,000 to 2,000 shovelers extends east-southeast from the Dakotas across central Wisconsin and southern Michigan to the Lake Erie marshes and thence over the Appalachian Mountains to Chesapeake Bay.

From the plains of Canada there are two outstanding divergent passages of shovelers, one to northern California, the other to coastal Louisiana. About 300,000 shovelers migrate to Louisiana along three corridors, the principal one through the eastern plains. As many as 2,000 of these ducks cross the Gulf of Mexico to winter in Yucatan and Honduras. Most of the Louisiana-bound shovelers were raised in the Dakotas and Saskatchewan.

Over 500,000 shovelers migrate into California, the bulk from Alberta but one-fifth from Saskatchewan. Most of those hatched in Alaska and the Northwest Territories of Canada eventually reach California. Although 260,000 shovelers winter in California, almost as many continue south in migration to various marshes and lagoons along the west coast of Mexico.

Utopia for shovelers in the West is the Klamath Basin, particularly Upper Klamath Lake in southern Oregon. On October 29, 1968, John Chattin, Duane Norman, and I estimated 200,000 shovelers on the relatively deep, murky waters of this lake nestled amid the forested slopes of the Cascade Range. And this is not unusual! In September 1965, Edward Oniel estimated 195,000 shovelers there, and 130,000 again in October 1966. Lower Klamath Lake has held from 16,000 to 62,000 during various falls, and nearby Tule Lake an average of 30,000. Populations of 150,000 shovelers appear in the Sacramento Valley, 80,000 in the area of San Francisco Bay, and 120,000 in the valley of the San Joaquin River (Frank Kozlik).

The Salt Lake marshes not only produce thousands of shovelers but also receive as many as 50,000 during the fall, half from Alberta and half from Saskatchewan. From the Salt Lake Basin, migration corridors lead to the Imperial Valley of California, Arizona, Mexico, and the Rio Grande Delta.

Winter Areas

California, with a wintering population of 260,000 shovelers, ranks slightly ahead of Louisiana, with 235,000. About half of the California shovelers winter in the San Joaquin Valley, almost one-fourth in the Sacramento Valley and a like number in San Francisco Bay and its adjacent marshes. Several thousand shovelers also winter in the bays on California's southwest coast and in the Salton Sea area.

About two-thirds of the shovelers that winter in Louisiana are found in the coastal marshes from Marsh Island to Sabine Lake. Mexico is also a noted winter area for shovelers, but three-fourths of the 260,000 found there are restricted to marshes and lagoons along the west coast. Over 100,000 shovelers congregate in Laguna del Caimanero and Laguna de Agua Brava between Mazatlán and Tuxpan on Mexico's west coast. As many as 40,000 winter as far south as Laguna de la Joya in the state of Chiapas.

Only a few thousand shovelers winter south of Mexico as far as Panama. Glover and Chamberlain (1960) found small numbers of shovelers on the Gulf of Fonseca, Honduras, and Lago de Nicaragua, Nicaragua. In the Tempisque Basin, above the Gulf of Nicoya, Costa Rica, Arthur Hawkins in 1969 observed only 200 shovelers.

On Mexico's east coast, 12,500 shovelers winter between the Rio Grande Delta and Tampico. South of there, only a few thousand have been found as far as the lagoons

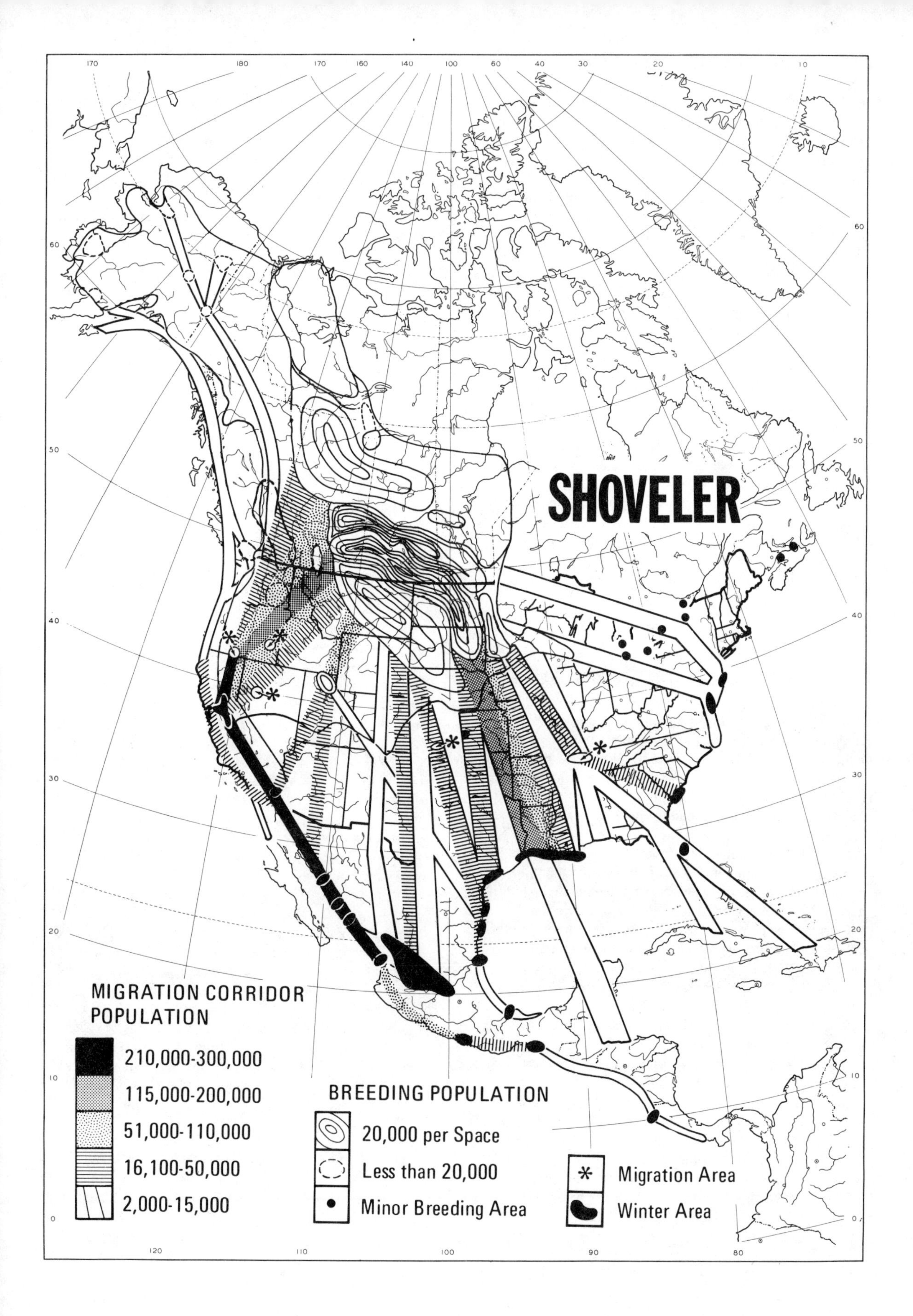
SHOVELER
MIGRATION CORRIDOR POPULATION
210,000-300,000
115,000-200,000
51,000-110,000
16,100-50,000
2,000-15,000
BREEDING POPULATION
20,000 per Space
Less than 20,000
Minor Breeding Area
Migration Area
Winter Area

on the northwest coast of Yucatan. The interior of Mexico harbors about 50,000 shovelers in winter—10,000 in the Northern Highlands centering on Chihuahua and 40,000 in the Central Highlands, largely between Guadalajara and Mexico City.

Populations of shovelers in Cuba and Hispaniola vary yearly from a few hundred to a few thousand. In 1951, Walter Crissey observed 1,500 in the Dominican Republic and 500 in Cuba.

Along the Atlantic Coast, 20,000 shovelers have been recorded on winter surveys. About 2,000 of these were in Florida, 15,000 in South Carolina, and 3,000 scattered in small flocks from there as far north as Long Island. About 17,000 shovelers winter north of Louisiana in the Mississippi Flyway, all but a few hundred south of Missouri and Kentucky. Occasionally, small numbers have been found in winter as far north as Iowa and Minnesota.

The Central Flyway winters only 54,000 shovelers, over 90 percent of them in coastal Texas but an occasional few as far north as Nebraska and South Dakota. About 15,000 shovelers are found outside of California, in the Pacific Flyway: 3,000 each in Nevada, Utah, and Oregon, and half that many in Washington. A few hundred shovelers winter along the southern coast of British Columbia.

MIGRATION BEHAVIOR

Chronology

Fall. Shovelers are early migrants, not as early as bluewings but on a par with wigeons. Except for southern California, the chronology of migration in shovelers and wigeons is quite similar. Numbers on the northern Great Plains remain fairly constant from September 1 through October, then decline precipitously. However, migrants begin to arrive in midmigration areas in late September, reach peak abundance about mid-October, and, in most places, taper to small numbers by late November; some may linger throughout the winter.

A few shovelers appear on important winter grounds in September, but numbers do not increase as rapidly as on midmigration areas, peak numbers not being reached until mid- to late November.

Fairly stable populations of shovelers occur early in the fall on northern Great Plains areas, even though areas farther south continue to accumulate birds. Apparently, egress is balanced by ingress from more northern areas.

Spring. Shovelers have an unusually protracted spring migration. Although some hardy individuals depart their winter areas in February, large numbers remain there well into April and small numbers into May.

Migration areas north of the principal winter grounds begin to acquire sizable numbers early in March, and populations steadily increase through most of April. Shovelers begin to arrive in the northern Great Plains states in late March, with constant influxes of new birds enlarging populations through all of April.

At Delta Marsh, Manitoba, shovelers first arrived, 1939-50, as follows: earliest, April 12; latest, May 9; and average, April 21 (Sowls 1955). In southeastern Saskatchewan, they arrived May 1-15 (Stoudt 1971). Near Brooks, Alberta, 1953-56, first arrivals averaged April 7 but varied by 8 days (Keith 1961).

May 8 was the average date of arrival, 1962-64, for shovelers at Yellowknife, Northwest Territories, 800 miles north of Brooks (Murdy 1964). Major influxes these 3 years occurred May 12-14.

Arrivals in Alaska occurred May 11-16 on the Yukon Delta (Gabrielson and Lincoln 1959) and April 28-May 8 (average, May 3), 1948-55, at Fairbanks (Rowinski 1958). At the time shovelers are arriving in Alaska, some tardy birds are still on winter areas in Texas and Louisiana.

BREEDING

Behavior

Age, Pair Bond, and Homing. Most shovelers breed when they are about 1 year old. As with other species that are late in acquiring their nuptial plumage, they do not establish pair bonds until the winter season. On spring migration areas, courtship of a hen by a coterie of drakes is a common occurrence. Poston (1969) considered that pair bonds were still weak when shovelers arrived on their breeding grounds in southwestern Alberta. McKinney (1967) observed captive birds and reported that pair bonds were formed from November to May.

Drakes vary in the length of time they remain with their mates after incubation begins. Some desert on the first day of incubation, others stay for 2 or more weeks, and a few are faithful until the hatch (Oring 1964).

Shovelers return to the same nest area to a greater degree than blue-winged teal. At Delta Marsh, Manitoba, 42 percent of the shovelers marked on the nest one year returned a subsequent year (Sowls 1955). In view of their high annual mortality, this homing rate represents almost all the shoveler hens that might still be alive. One shoveler hen returned to the same area 3 years. Only 8 percent of the yearlings returned.

On an area east of Calgary, Alberta, 15 percent of the adult hens marked by Poston (1969) returned the next year, about a third of the number expected. Only 4 of 116 marked juvenile hens returned. Perhaps some of the marked birds returned to nearby areas, for 2 years later Poston observed two more adult hens and one marked as a juvenile.

Drakes homed, also. Two of 19 marked adult drakes and one of 134 marked juvenile drakes returned the next year. It is perhaps significant that all three drakes were unpaired when they returned. Since most shovelers pair at a distance from their breeding areas, the paired drakes would follow their spouses to the breeding areas of the hens.

Home Range. Shovelers return to the larger sloughs on their breeding grounds in small flocks that break up as paired birds disperse over the available nearby ponds. As time for nesting nears, each pair becomes increasingly confined to a specific area (Poston 1969). The home range contains a waiting or "core" area, several peripheral ponds, and a nest site. McKinney (1967) observed captive males involved in hostile encounters throughout May and the first 3 weeks of June. Clearly defined territories could be observed after 1 or 2 weeks.

Eight home ranges surveyed by Poston (1969) covered from 20 to 128 acres (average, 76 acres). Parts of most home ranges overlapped and some were completely within boundaries of others. Nest cover, use of peripheral ponds, and occupancy of waiting areas were all shared, but only one pair at a time occupied the waiting area. Also, only one pair at a time occupied the core area, and they spent 60 to 90 percent of their total time there. Although the pair bond might disintegrate, most males remained in the home ranges until the eggs hatched (Poston 1969).

Nesting

Girard (1939) observed that shovelers spent 6 to 8 days selecting a nest site and constructing the nest, usually a scrape in the ground lined first with grasses and then with down. Captive female shovelers increased their time in nest cover 1 to 4 days preceding the laying of the first egg (McKinney 1967). Pairs selected nest sites where friction was minimal with other pairs.

Nest Sites. Grasses of many kinds form the vegetative substrate that shovelers prefer for nest sites. Shortgrasses were preferred to tallgrasses in the Flathead Valley of Montana (Girard 1939). When sufficient grass cover is not available, shovelers utilize hayfields, meadows, and, rarely, marshes of bulrushes. In some western wetlands, salt grass is used extensively. Unlike the gadwall, the shoveler seldom chooses weedy patches, and unlike the mallard, it does not like to nest in or adjacent to woody vegetation, such as clumps of buckbrush and willows.

Only small numbers of shovelers nest within a few feet of water; those that do are usually on levees or islands. A few may nest as far as 1 mile from the nearest pond, but most shovelers nest 75 to 200 feet from their waiting areas.

Clutch Size, Eggs, and Incubation. Shovelers lay one egg almost every day (occasionally they skip a day) until the clutch is complete. Clutch size ranges from 5 to 14, with an average of 9.4 eggs per nest (585 nests). Keith (1961) reported that nests that were started near Brooks, Alberta, before June 1 averaged 10.7 eggs per clutch; June 1-15, 10 eggs; and after June 15, 9.4 eggs.

The eggs are elliptical ovate, 52.2 by 37mm, the color varying from pale olive-buff to pale green-gray (Bent 1923). According to Bent, shovelers' eggs are almost identical to those of mallards and pintails in color and smooth texture but not in size or shape.

Although Girard (1939) stated that the incubation period of the shoveler is about 28 days, I suspect that this represents the maximum. Delacour (1956) gave it as 23 to 25 days, which appears to be the more logical figure.

Chronology of Nesting. Shovelers are intermediate nesters, midway between the early-nesting mallards and pintails and the late-nesting blue-winged teals, gadwalls, and scaups. At the Klamath Basin in northern California, they have initiated earliest nests on April 15 and 26 (2 years), with peak initiation May 15-22, and last nests on June 15.

At Delta Marsh, shovelers commenced nesting May 2, reached peak activity May 13-19, 1949, and May 27-June 2, 1950, and started last nests about July 4 (Sowls 1955). Some shovelers delayed nesting in 1950 because of cold weather early in May. In southwestern Saskatchewan, shovelers began nesting about April 15, 1955, peaked about May 14, and started no nests after June 25 (Reeves et al. 1955).

Near Calgary, Alberta, shovelers initiated nesting on May 9 and started last nests on June 19 (Poston 1969). Near Brooks, Alberta, the midpoint in nest initiation ranged from April 24 in 1957 to May 18 in 1953 (Keith 1961).

On the Yukon Flats, Alaska, shovelers started nesting May 8-18, 1953 and 1954, and reached peak initiation activity May 26 and June 10, respectively (Lensink 1954).

The span of nest initiation in the shoveler has been timed by various investigators at 41 to 73 days, with 60 days the average.

Nest Success. Shovelers have a relatively high nest success. An overall appraisal from many nest studies scattered across the range of the shoveler indicates that 59 percent of the nests (575) hatch. Studies including 24 or more nests reported nest success as follows: 50 percent, Lousana, Alberta (Smith 1971); 42 percent, Brooks, Alberta (Keith 1961); 47 percent, Redvers, Saskatchewan (Stoudt 1971); 70 percent, Flathead Valley, Montana (Girard 1941); 64 percent, Lower Souris, North Dakota (Kalmbach 1937); 50 percent, Stutsman County, North Dakota (Oetting and Cassel 1971); 90 percent, Tule Lake, California (Miller and Collins 1954); 50 percent, Honey Lake, California (Hunt and Naylor 1955); 62 percent, Bear River, Utah (Williams and Marshall 1938*b*); and 60 percent, Ogden Bay, Utah (Fuller 1953).

In 295 successful nests for which records are available, 0.68 of an egg per nest failed to hatch. About one-fourth of the unhatched eggs were judged infertile and three-fourths contained dead embryos.

Nest Failure. Mammals destroyed almost twice as many shoveler nests as did birds. Of those identified, skunks were responsible for 85 percent of the destruction, and ground squirrels for the remainder. Crows and magpies caused three-fourths, and gulls one-fourth, of the nest losses attributed to birds.

Where shovelers nested near California gull colonies on the Farmington Bay Refuge, Utah, gulls took 13 percent of their eggs (Odin 1957). The gulls did not pilfer from five

SHOVELER

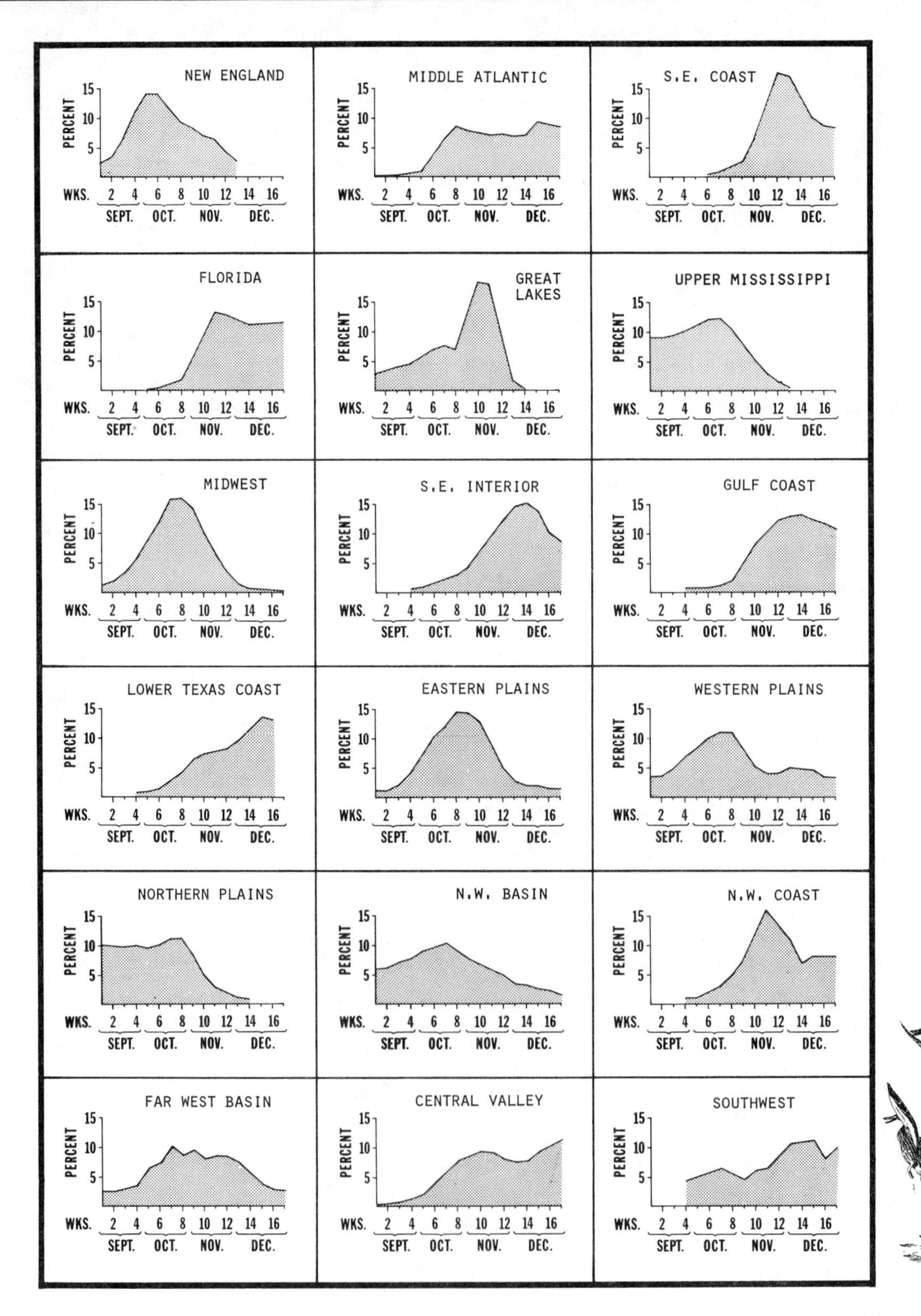

Fall

SHOVELER

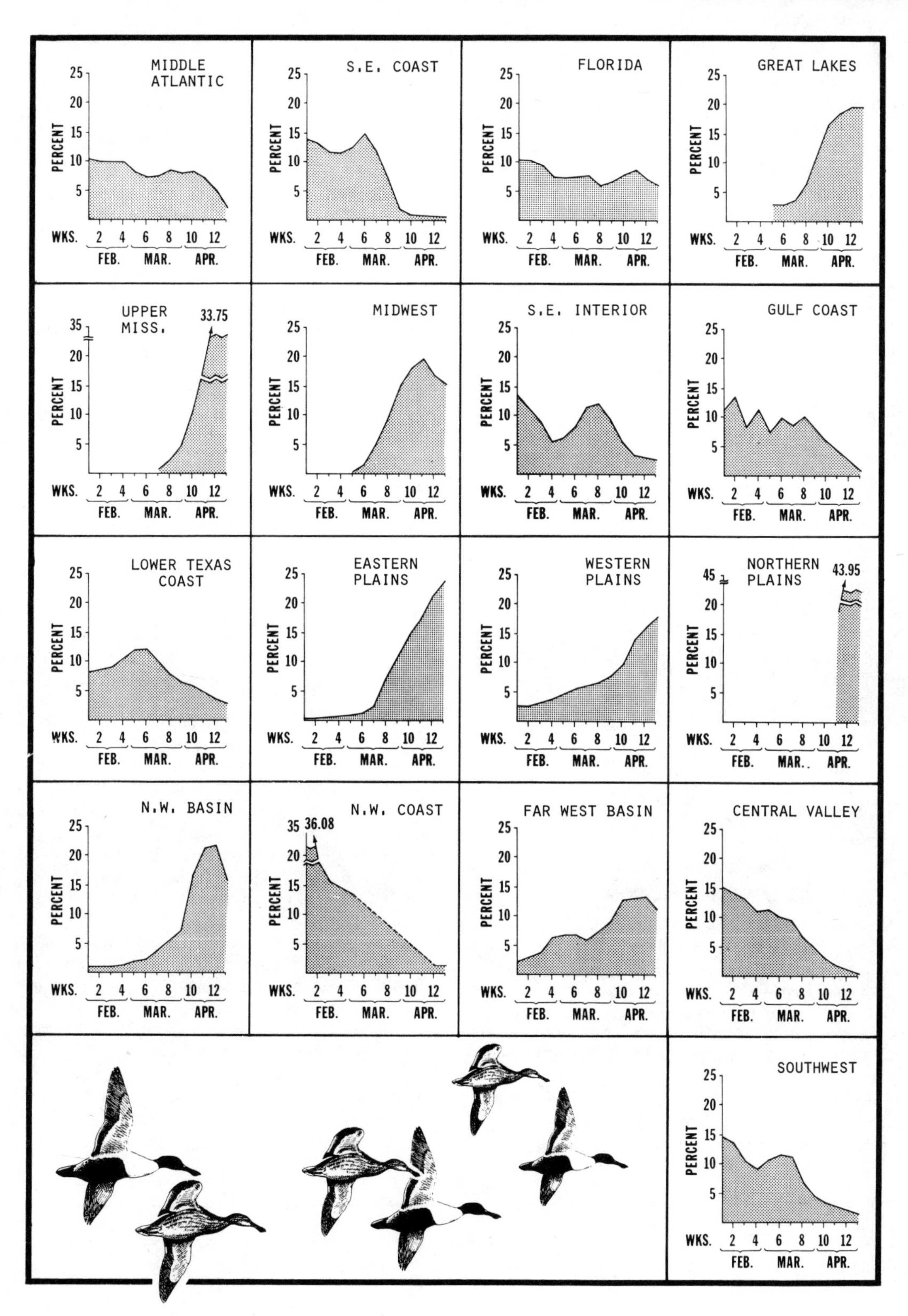

Spring

well-concealed nests but destroyed one of nine nests with fair concealment and one of three that were poorly concealed.

Renesting. Some shovelers renest when initial nests are destroyed. At Delta Marsh, Manitoba, 21 percent of 33 marked shoveler hens renested—one exceptional hen renested twice (Sowls 1955). On Keith's (1961) study area near Brooks, Alberta, 75 percent of the shovelers whose nests were destroyed renested. This success rate compares favorably with that of blue-winged teal (55 percent), gadwalls (82 percent), and mallards (100 percent).

Sowls (1955) found that shoveler hens moved 135 to 765 yards (average, 355) to renest. In two initial nests clutch size averaged 12; in the renests, the average was 8.5 eggs.

Rearing of Young

Broods. Poston (1969) observed that marked shoveler hens led their broods from the nests to the ponds used earlier as waiting sites. Broods seldom remained on any ponds longer than 7 to 10 days. One hen moved her brood 1 mile through a series of ponds in 29 days. Another hen took her brood from the waiting pond to another one, 0.5 mile away, in 12 days.

Development. Young shovelers reach flight stage in various areas at the following ages: 47-54 days, South Dakota (Gollop and Marshall 1954); 52-66 days, Delta Marsh, Manitoba (Hochbaum 1944); 38-39 days, Yukon Flats, Alaska (Lensink 1954); and 36 days, Minto Lakes, Alaska (Hooper 1951). Ducklings apparently grow faster in Alaska than farther south because longer days permit them to consume greater quantities of food.

Survival. Successful nests hatch 8.7 eggs, yet Class I broods contain only 6.8 ducklings (259), representing a considerable loss the first few days of life. Class II broods number 6.5 ducklings (151), down 4 percent, and Class III broods contain 5.9 ducklings (80), a 22 percent loss from those that left the nest.

POSTBREEDING SEASON

Drake shovelers near Calgary, Alberta, began to show a change to the eclipse plumage in early June (Poston 1969). By mid-June various stages of body molt were apparent among all drakes, and they began to leave the area for large lakes and the wing molt. By mid-July, all drakes had departed. On four large lakes within 15 miles of his study area, Poston (1969) observed as many as 2,500 shovelers during late July and August.

At the Camas National Wildlife Refuge in Idaho, Oring (1964) did not notice flightless shovelers until July 27, but at Fort Yukon, Alaska, the first flightless molters were seen on June 26 (Hansen 1956). Sterling (1966) trapped 315 flightless adult drakes July 9-24, at the Pel-Kutawagan marshes north of Regina, Saskatchewan. Shovelers are flightless about 35 days.

FOOD HABITS

The shoveler, which feeds actively in both deep and shallow waters, has the most unusual feeding habits of any duck. In deep water it apparently feeds on surface plankton. I have often watched shovelers feeding on the surface of lakes devoid of aquatic vegetation. A steady stream of water is taken in by the tip of the bill and jetted out at its base. From a tower, I have seen clear paths in the wake of their feeding passage through green waters rich in phytoplankton. Occasionally, a pair of shovelers rotate their bodies head to head, apparently stirring up the plankton-laden waters and straining them through the lamellae of their bills. Arthur Hawkins has frequently observed several dozen birds in a tight cell rotating as a "pin wheel," stirring up the surface water of a lake. Many such cells may dot the surface of the lake when feeding is at its peaks in the early morning and in the evening.

From 100,000 to 200,000 shovelers concentrate in the fall on the deep waters of Upper Klamath Lake in southern Oregon (Edward Oniel). This large lake is rich in zooplankton but poor in aquatic vegetation. Surface feeding by the shovelers in the absence of aquatic plants points to the zooplankton as the food source that attracts this tremendous number of birds. They also are prone to gather in sizable numbers on sewage lagoons.

Because of the microscopic size of plankton and its fast digestibility, it does not show up adequately in food habits studies, in which examination of gizzards is the usual procedure.

In shallow waters, shovelers usually feed by partially or fully immersing their heads. As they slowly move forward, their bills sweep from side to side, apparently just skimming the surface of bottom soils.

General food habits studies show that about one-fourth of the shoveler's diet is macroscopic animal life, particularly fingernail clams, water boatmen, aquatic beetles, and midge and caddis fly larvae. Small amounts of copepods and ostracods, representatives of zooplankton, have also been found (Martin et al. 1951).

Marshes and vegetated lakes contribute seeds of pondweeds and bulrushes to the diet of shovelers. Overflow river lakes in the Mississippi River basin provide these ducks with the seeds of nutgrasses, millets, smartweeds, rice cut-grass, and buttonbush (Anderson 1959, Korschgen 1955). At Reelfoot Lake, Tennessee, seeds of bald cypress, water willow, smartweeds, and buttonbush are important foods (Rawls 1954). In coastal South Carolina, seeds of panic grass, bulrushes, and spike rush are heavily utilized (McGilvrey 1966*b*).

Canvasback

Aythya valisineria

Other Common Name: Can

VITAL STATISTICS

Length:*	Adult male, 20.0-21.9 inches, average 20.73 inches (44)
	Adult female, 18.8-20.4 inches, average 19.81 inches (15)
	Immature male, 19.8-21.2 inches, average 20.48 inches (9)
	Immature female, 19.2-20.1 inches, average 19.67 inches (9)
Wing:	Adult male, 10.39 inches (13)
	Adult female, 9.01 inches (12)
	Immature male, 9.09 inches (13)
	Immature female, 8.75 inches (29)
Weight:	Adult male, 1.9-3.5 pounds, average 2.76 pounds (191)
	Adult female, 2.0-3.4 pounds, average 2.55 pounds (54)
	Immature male, 2.3-3.3 pounds, average 2.75 pounds (57)
	Immature female, 2.1-3.1 pounds, average 2.53 pounds (35)

*Measurements of living birds taken by David Trauger.

IDENTIFICATION

Field

Canvasbacks are about the same size as mallards but are chunkier. They are the fastest flying of the large ducks but are probably no faster than the smaller scaups, buffleheads, ruddies, and teals. Their flight is direct, without the dipping and weaving displayed by scaups and ring-necked ducks. Cans usually scale down from altitude to decoy, whereas scaups tend to dart in from lower atltitudes.

Flocks of canvasbacks frequently number 5 to 30 and are more often found in larger flocks than redheads. In prolonged flight, the flocks form a well-shaped "V." The wing beats of canvasbacks are more rapid than in redheads and mallards but are slower than in scaups. The wing arcs appear deeper than those of mallards but shallower than those of scaups.

The white back and belly and inner white half of the wings of males combine in flight to form the greatest expanse of white exhibited by any duck.

At rest, the canvasback presents a unique profile, with its wedge-shaped head sloping upward from the tip of a long black bill to the back of the crown. The neck is longer and stouter than in other diving ducks and the head is more erect. The white back and the chestnut-red head of the nuptial-plumaged male are visible at a considerable distance. Under brilliant sunlight, especially in the spring, the gray backs of scaups may also appear white at a distance.

In the full eclipse plumage (not all drakes molt all body feathers), drakes have cinnamon-brown heads and chests, with dusky gray backs, sides and flanks. Most have molted back into their bright nuptial plumage by late October.

The female canvasback has a buffy brown head and neck shading into a darker brown chest and foreback. The immature male is similarly colored early in the fall, a time when its back and sides as well as those of the female are still brownish. From early winter on through spring, the back and sides of the hen can is a dusky gray. The immature male begins to acquire a chestnut head and neck and a white back in mid-October, but it is usually late December before full plumage is attained.

At Hand

In the nuptial-plumaged male, a black band 2 to 3 inches

wide encircles the upper body below the chestnut-red neck. Behind the black band, the white back appears gray from fine black-brown vermiculations. The wing coverts are even more densely vermiculated, giving them a darker appearance. In the folded wings, long, heavily vermiculated scapulars extend back to the blackish-brown tail and overlie the black rump. The white breast, side, flank, and belly are in places lightly vermiculated. The eyes are red and the feet gray-blue.

Dzubin (1959) reports that by the time ducklings are 30 days old, gray vermiculations begin to appear on the scapulars of males. After the 45th day, males also begin to have darker heads than females. The eye color in males starts to change from olive-yellow to red when they are 10 to 12 weeks of age (Hochbaum 1944).

The female canvasback has a light brown head and neck, merging into a darker brown chest and foreback. Early in the fall the sides, flanks, and back are a dull brown from the eclipse plumage, but as the season progresses, the back becomes grayer. By January the back is blotched with patches of light and dark gray, giving it a mottled appearance throughout the spring. The degree of blotching varies with the individual.

The wings of male canvasbacks in nuptial plumage are unique. Nearly all of the wing feathers but the primaries are white, with dusky vermiculations, and the primaries are blackish brown. The secondaries are pearl-gray at the base, lightly vermiculated with dusky near the tips.

Adult females have brown wing coverts, well flecked with white near the end of each covert. Coverts over tertials are smooth and relatively broad. The wings of immature males are similar, but the flecking tends to be more dispersed and the tertial coverts are ragged and narrow. The wing coverts of female immatures are usually not flecked, or only lightly so, and the tertial coverts are ragged and narrow.

POPULATION STATUS

The canvasback, like the redhead, has not fared well in recent years; in fact, its status is even more precarious than that of the redhead. Both canvasbacks and redheads were first given special protection by completely closing the season on them in 1936 and 1937. From 1958 to 1973, some forms of restrictive regulations have governed the hunting of canvasbacks. The season was closed in 1960-63, only one or two were permitted in the bag from 1964 through 1971, and the season was again closed in 1972. Particular areas were closed to canvasback hunting in 1973 and 1974.

Of all the extensively distributed game ducks in North America, the canvasback is the least abundant. Population surveys, 1955-74, over its major breeding range (omitting Intermountain marshes and peripheral areas) reveal an average of 560,000. Yearly breeding numbers have ranged from a low of 386,000 in 1962 to a high of 713,000 in 1958, a change of 46 percent.

Both the breeding ground surveys and January inventories show a downward trend in canvasback numbers for the 20-year period 1955-74. For most species of ducks, breeding ground data are considered the better indices of yearly changes in abundance, but the January inventory figures are deemed the more valid for canvasbacks. These data show a decline of 53 percent in the numbers of canvasbacks wintering in the United States during the 1955-74 period. In the Atlantic, Mississippi, and Pacific flyways the decline is about the same, but in the Central Flyway wintering numbers show no significant trend.

Age Ratios

From 1966 to 1973, age ratios of canvasbacks in hunters' bags showed a ratio of 1 adult to 1.62 immatures. Ratios ranged in these 7 years from 0.84 immature per adult in 1968 to 1.89 immatures in 1967, a fluctuation of 66 percent in productivity. Band data from Geis (1959) indicate that immatures are more likely to be shot than adults on the order of 1.57 to 1.0. If this bias is roughly representative of hunter selectivity, then annual production amounts to 1.03 young per adult in fall populations.

Sex Ratios

As with other *Aythya*, canvasback populations have many more males than females. Visual counts during spring at several points of concentration across the United States point to 1.94 drakes (66.4 percent) for each hen (Bellrose et al. 1961). Sex ratios taken in Wisconsin during the spring by Jahn and Hunt (1964) show a slightly lower proportion of drakes: 1.7 to 1.0 (63 percent). The 27 percent higher annual mortality rate suffered by females accounts for the disparity in sex ratios (Geis 1959). Although Olson (1965) observed that female cans were more vulnerable than males to hunting under several types of conditions, hunting is not the sole reason for the sex ratio differential.

The proportion of females in canvasback populations has unfortunately declined in recent years. Sex ratio data obtained in the winter of 1972-73 at Chesapeake Bay indicated that female canvasbacks composed only 20 percent of the population. At most, 25 to 30 percent of the 1974 canvasback population may be females, compared with an earlier percentage of 30 to 35 (Trauger 1974*b*). The larger the proportion of hens in a duck population, the older the age structure of the population (Bellrose et al. 1961). Hence, there is a further indication that production of young in canvasbacks has fallen off. Moreover, the small proportion of females reduces the potential number of breeders in a population of 560,000 to 140,000 pairs.

Mortality and Survival

Summer bandings (1953-57) of canvasbacks in Manitoba and Saskatchewan revealed an annual mortality rate of 77 percent for immatures and 52 percent for adults (Geis 1959). Summer bandings in Minnesota yielded similar results. Immatures suffered a yearly mortality of 71 percent and adults 58 percent (Lee et al. 1964).

Canvasbacks banded on their Louisiana winter grounds suffered a 35 percent annual mortality rate among males and a 48 percent rate among females (Geis 1959). Among three species banded on Chesapeake Bay by Longwell and Stotts (1959), canvasbacks had a slightly lower mortality rate (38 percent) than either redheads (44 percent) or lesser scaups (42 percent).

To maintain a stable population with an assumed mortality rate of 75 percent for immatures and 45 percent for adults would require the production of 1.2 flying young per adult. Canvasback breeding efforts in the late 1960's and early 1970's appear to be below this level.

DISTRIBUTION

Canvasbacks are more prone to breed in the Arctic and Subarctic than redheads and less prone to breed in the Intermountain marshes of the West. On the northern prairies and parklands, they compete for similar nest sites. There, canvasbacks come out second best because of the redheads' semiparasitic habit of laying eggs in their competitors' nests.

The European equivalent of the canvasback is the European pochard, *Aythya ferina*. They breed across the British Isles, the Netherlands, Belgium, France, Denmark, Germany, Russia, and east as far as central Siberia. Their winter grounds include southern Europe, northern Africa, Iran, India, China, and Japan.

Breeding Range

Both canvasbacks and redheads find the parklands of Canada desirable breeding grounds—190,000 canvasbacks (2.1 per square mile) versus 200,000 redheads. Except for a higher density in southwest Manitoba, the distribution of canvasbacks is remarkably uniform across the parklands of Saskatchewan and Alberta. The 4,000-square-mile pothole district of Minnedosa, Manitoba, has exceeded 10 canvasbacks per square mile since waterfowl surveys were initiated in 1947 (Trauger and Stoudt 1974). This area harbors about 10 percent of the total continental breeding population of canvasbacks. The deltas of the Subarctic support a large number of canvasbacks per square mile; the Saskatchewan Delta has 4.4 (30,000 total) and the Athabasca Delta has 10.6 (17,000 total). The Mackenzie Delta in the Arctic has a density of 1.0 per square mile (5,000 total). Old Crow Flats, a fossil delta in the Yukon Territory, supports 4.0 cans per square mile, for a total population of 7,800. A sizable proportion of canvasbacks on the delta areas are probably nonbreeders, especially when water areas are in short supply on the prairies.

Canvasbacks occur in summer on all of the important breeding grounds in Alaska except those on the Arctic Slope. Of the 61,000 found in Alaska, 58,000 are in the interior, 2,300 on central coastal wetlands, and 180 on marshes of the southeast coast. The largest breeding population, 42,000 (a density of 3.9 per square mile), occurs on the Yukon Flats. The only other important breeding ground is the Tanana-Kuskokwim district, supporting 16,000 (a density of 1.7 per square mile).

About 132,000 canvasbacks are found on marshes of large lakes scattered through the boreal forest of northwestern Canada. Because of the vast forest and water areas, the density is only 0.22 per square mile. Except for an area of the boreal forest just north of the parklands in western Saskatchewan where the density is high, 0.42 per square mile, and western Ontario where it is low, 0.05 per square mile, the distribution is remarkably uniform.

South of the parklands on the mixed prairie of Canada and the Dakotas, canvasbacks number about 100,000, 0.6 per square mile. In this vegetation zone they are only about half as abundant as redheads, their principal competitors. Through the Dakotas, cans decline in density from 0.7 per square mile in the north to 0.2 in the south. About 35,000 breed in the mixed prairie area of North and South Dakota. On the drier shortgrass prairie area of western Dakotas, Montana, southwestern Saskatchewan, and southern Alberta, breeding canvasbacks number about 13,500 (0.09 per square mile), half the number of the redhead population.

Fewer than 10,000 canvasbacks breed in the Intermountain region; redheads are 20 to 25 times more abundant. Almost 3,000 canvasbacks occur in British Columbia; 1,000 in Wyoming and Oregon; 900 in Nevada; and 500 each in Idaho and Washington. Small numbers are found in the following areas: San Luis Valley and North Park, Colorado; Flathead Valley, Montana; and the Great Salt Lake Basin, Utah.

Important peripheral areas to the prairie breeding grounds include the Sandhills of Nebraska with slightly over 1,000 and western Minnesota with 3,000. A few pairs have nested in Wisconsin (Jahn and Hunt 1964) and on the Ontario side of Lake St. Clair (Godfrey 1966).

Migration Corridors

From their prairie breeding grounds and staging areas, most canvasbacks diverge toward either the Atlantic or Pacific coasts. Their passage to the Chesapeake Bay area in particular is by far the largest and follows a two-pronged migration corridor. The corridor originates in southeast Saskatchewan, extends southeastward into Minnesota, and then divides. One branch leads to the Mississippi River near La Crosse, Wisconsin, the other branch to the Mississippi River between Fort Madison and Keokuk, Iowa. Most of the La Crosse canvasbacks turn eastward, some to stop briefly at the Lake St. Clair area of Michigan, while others continue nonstop across the Appalachian Mountains to Chesapeake Bay. The bulk of the canvasbacks departing the Keokuk Pool also appear to head east for Chesapeake Bay, but other flight corridors extend southeastward to Florida and south to Louisiana.

Over the years there have been reversals in the magnitude of the canvasback flight down these two branches.

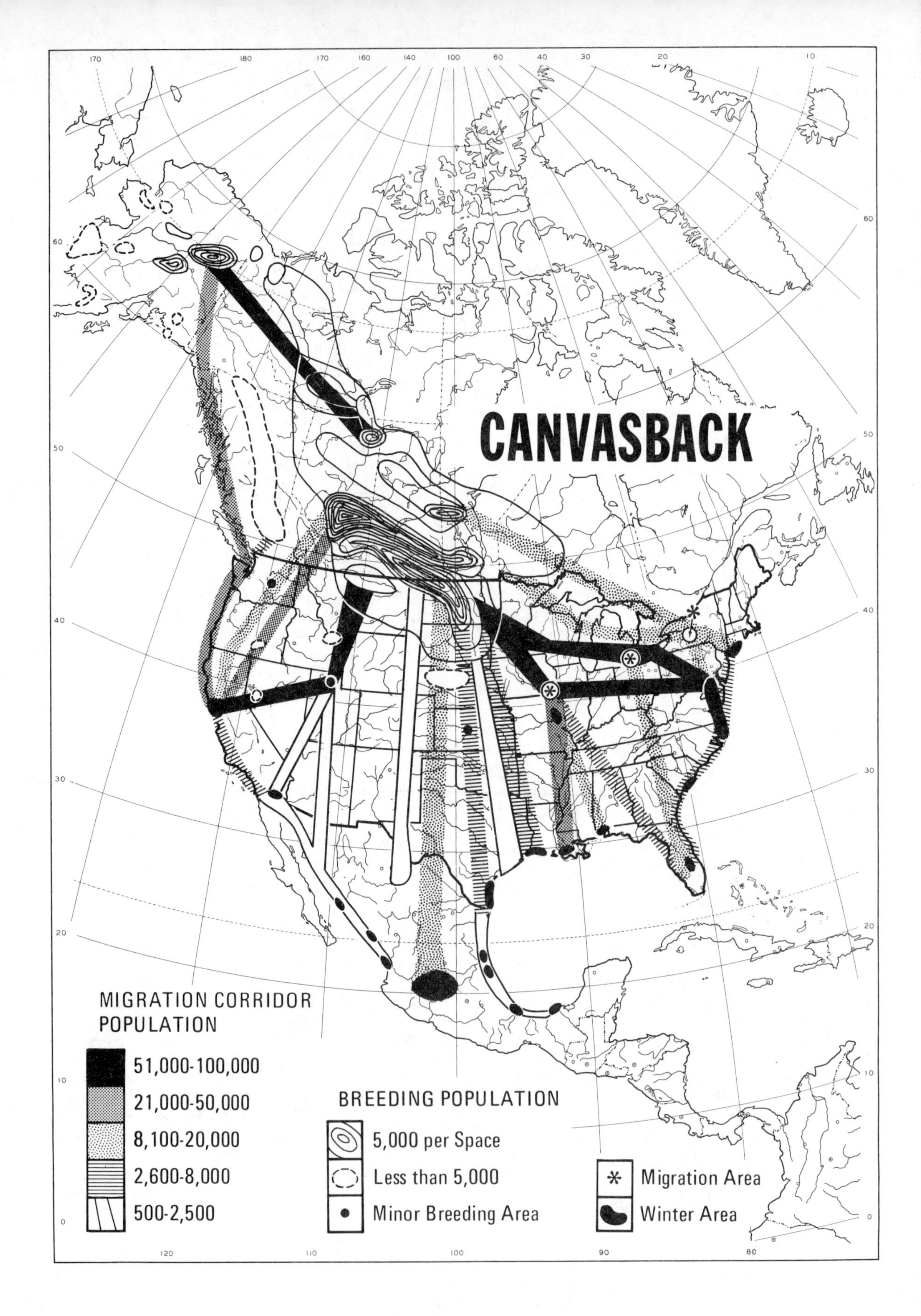
CANVASBACK
MIGRATION CORRIDOR POPULATION
51,000-100,000
21,000-50,000
8,100-20,000
2,600-8,000
500-2,500
BREEDING POPULATION
5,000 per Space
Less than 5,000
Minor Breeding Area
Migration Area
Winter Area

In the 1950's, the main point of concentration for the northern branch comprised Lake St. Clair, the Detroit River, and western Lake Erie. The average peak population in the area, 1954-58, was 260,000. During this same period, the south branch including both the Illinois and Mississippi valleys, was followed by only 25,000 canvasbacks. Beginning in the mid-1960's, the numbers following the south branch began to increase at the expense of those following the north branch. This increase culminated in 1970, with a peak fall population of 170,000 on the Keokuk Pool of the Mississippi River. At that time, the number of cans stopping in the La Crosse area was less than 15,000, and there were not many more in the Lake St. Clair area (Edward Mikula). Then in 1971 the canvasbacks began to increase in number in the La Crosse area and decline on the Keokuk area. Peak fall populations in 1973 amounted to over 100,000 at La Crosse and 65,000 at Keokuk (David Trauger). At Lake St. Clair and the adjacent area, cans numbered at least 45,000.

The number of canvasbacks observed along the north shore of Lake Erie as far east as Long Point that formerly resided in the Lake St. Clair area is undetermined, but late in November large numbers of canvasbacks have been found by the Canadian Wildlife Service in the Long Point area. For example, on November 22, 1972, the service estimated 70,000 to 80,000. Some of these birds move farther eastward to the Central Lakes of New York, but most migrate southeastward to Chesapeake Bay.

Migration corridors farther north are followed by cans bound for the Niagara River, the Central Lakes, and Lake Ontario. On November 29, 1973, the Canadian Wildlife Service estimated 18,000 in the northeastern end of Lake Ontario. Estimates in earlier years on the New York side of the lake varied from 1,000 to 7,000 (Benson et al. 1960). A large proportion of canvasbacks winter on these areas, but others, if the weather is severe, pass southward to Chesapeake Bay.

Most canvasbacks that reach Chesapeake Bay remain there for the winter, but some move south to Currituck Sound, North Carolina, and a few migrate along the coast as far south as Florida (Longwell and Stotts 1959, Stewart et al. 1958). However, most of those that reach Florida arrive by migration corridors extending southward from Lake Erie and south-southeastward from the Keokuk Pool.

Canvasbacks that reach both eastern Arkansas and Louisiana migrate along a corridor stretching due south from the Keokuk Pool to the Gulf Coast. Relatively small populations of canvasbacks pass along migration corridors from central North Dakota to western Louisiana and eastern Texas.

Winter Areas

About half of the 290,000 canvasbacks found on January surveys, 1960-71, winter in the Atlantic Flyway, slightly over a fourth in the Pacific Flyway, and the remaining quarter in between, including Mexico. The largest number of canvasbacks, 95,000, winter on Chesapeake Bay; the second largest number, 60,000, spend the winter months on San Francisco Bay.

Along the Atlantic Flyway, canvasbacks winter regularly from Vermont to Lake Okeechobee, Florida. About 2,600 winter on Long Island and slightly over 500 occur north of there (Benson et al. 1960). In inland New York, 4,000 winter in the Central Lakes district and 6,000 on the Niagara River and Lake Ontario. Omitting Chesapeake Bay, the numbers of cans wintering along the Atlantic Coast from Long Island to Florida are 5,500 in New Jersey (Raritan and Barnegat bays); 2,300 in Delaware; 10,000 in Virginia (Rappahannock and James rivers); 15,000 in North Carolina (principally Currituck Sound); 3,600 in South Carolina; and 1,000 in Georgia. Most of Florida's 7,500 canvasbacks winter inland, particularly on Lake Istokpoga and lakes in Polk and Osceola counties (Chamberlain 1960). A few winter on Tampa Bay. Apparently 10 canvasbacks overshot Florida and landed in Cuba in 1953, where they were observed by Walter Crissey, the only ones he ever encountered on aerial surveys of the West Indies.

In addition to San Francisco Bay, canvasbacks winter in many other bays along the Pacific Coast from British Columbia to the state of Jalisco, Mexico. Important concentrations occur at Puget Sound, Grays Harbor, and Willapa Bay, Washington, 2,500; Coos, Alsea, and Tillamook bays, Oregon, 3,000; and Lake Earl and Humboldt Bay, California, 3,000. The Mexican coast from Obregón to Cuyutlán winters 630 and only 170 winter in British Columbia. In interior areas of the Pacific Flyway 1,000 canvasbacks winter in the Columbia Basin, Washington; 2,000 in reservoirs of the Snake River (particularly Minidoka) in southern Idaho; 1,000 in the Carson Sink area of Nevada; 200 in Utah; 300 in Arizona; 1,000 in the Central Valley and 3,000 in the Imperial Valley, California.

The Mississippi Flyway winters canvasbacks all the way from Wisconsin and Michigan to the Louisiana coast. Nearly 15,000 of the 40,000 in this flyway winter in Louisiana, most at Six Mile and Wax lakes, near Morgan City. The 4,400 wintering in Mississippi occur largely on Lake Sardis and on bays of the Gulf Coast, and most of Alabama's 2,300 are on Mobile Bay. A large proportion of the 4,000 cans wintering in Arkansas are located on fish-farm ponds in the eastern third of the state. The 2,500 in Tennessee and 450 in Kentucky are largely on Kentucky Lake. Most of the 6,500 canvasbacks wintering in Illinois occur on the Mississippi River above Alton. Michigan winters 5,400 canvasbacks, largely on Lake St. Clair and the Detroit River, and Ohio has 500 wintering cans on Sandusky Bay, Lake Erie.

Probably most of the 4,500 canvasbacks found on Mexico's east coast and the 12,000 in the Northern and Central Highlands have passed through the Central Flyway. They are included with the meager 11,500 wintering in the Central Flyway region of the United States. Texas winters 9,400, about half scattered along the coast and the rest inland, mostly in the Panhandle. Almost 2,000 winter in eastern New Mexico (most on Bitter Lake National

Wildlife Refuge) and there are 200 in Oklahoma and a few in Kansas.

Along the east coast of Mexico, wintering canvasbacks number 400 at Laguna Madre, 1,900 at Tampico Lagoon, 1,800 at Tamiahua Lagoon, 325 at Alvarado lagoons, and fewer than 100 in the Yucatan Peninsula. Most of the 450 canvasbacks in the Northern Highlands of Mexico are on Laguna de Santiaguillo, north of Durango. The 11,500 canvasbacks in the Central Highlands occur largely on the lakes or lagoons of Chapala, Sayula, Pátzcuaro, and Yuriria.

The number of canvasbacks using the migration corridor from southwestern Manitoba to the lower Texas coast is small compared with that of redheads. However, many more canvasbacks than redheads pass directly south from prairie breeding areas to the Northern and Southern Highlands in the interior of Mexico.

In the Pacific Flyway, the key concentration points between breeding and winter grounds are the marshes adjacent to Great Salt Lake, Utah. There, an average of 90,000 canvasbacks gather during the fall, 1962-68 (John Nagel). Somewhat smaller concentrations of 25,000 occur at Malheur Lake and Klamath Basin, and 15,000 at Carson Sink, Nevada.

Bandings on breeding ground areas (Lensink 1964) suggest that most of the canvasbacks concentrating in Utah and Nevada originate in Alberta, with probably small numbers from Alaska and Saskatchewan. From these areas, the bulk of the population migrates to San Francisco Bay, with small numbers moving to the Imperial Valley and the west coast of Mexico.

Part of the migration of canvasbacks through the Malheur Lake area was observed by Eldon McLuray on October 2, 1968. He observed the arrival of over 4,000 from the northeast. About half alighted on the lake; the others continued their migratory flight to the southwest. The next day only 300 remained—all the others that paused at Malheur the previous day had departed during the night.

California not only receives canvasbacks from the western prairie breeding grounds via the marshes of the Great Salt Lake and Carson Sink but also 90 percent of those produced in Alaska (Lensink 1964). They evidently enter the Pacific Flyway by flying down the coast of British Columbia to Puget Sound, where some disperse inland.

MIGRATION BEHAVIOR

Although the breeding grounds of the canvasback and redhead overlap in the parklands of Canada, these species have evolved migration corridors that are followed by vastly different proportions of the two species. This difference in migration corridors probably stems from different winter ground requirements: cans are limited to less brackish water areas than the highly saline ones that are attractive to redheads. The numbers of redheads wintering on Apalachee Bay, Florida, and the Laguna Madre, Texas and Mexico, indicate that redheads are more tolerant of saline waters than are canvasbacks.

Population data suggest that certain elements in the canvasback population change migration corridors from year to year; Stewart et al. (1958) noted an inverse relationship in numbers between the mid-Atlantic and the Mississippi Valley regions and between the Mississippi Valley and Great Lakes regions. We have noticed similar inverse changes in abundance between the Great Salt Lake marshes in Utah, Malheur Lake in southeastern Oregon, and the Klamath Basin marshes in northern California.

Young from the same brood of canvasbacks may migrate southward as members of different flocks. Martinson and Hawkins (1968) reported on a small number of recoveries indicating differences among broodmates in time and geography of migration.

Chronology

Fall. Over most of the United States, canvasbacks migrate south either about the same time as scaups or slightly later. But in the eastern Great Plains the chronology of passage is slightly earlier.

Canvasbacks begin to move into the northern Great Plains states in early September. Numbers slowly build up to late October, followed by rapid departures in early November. The eastern contingent arrives in the Great Lakes states in early October, reaches peak numbers in early November, and declines rapidly to wintering numbers by the end of the month. Canvasbacks reach central New York in late October, and large numbers are present through November and December (Benson et al. 1960). However, on Lake Ontario they do not appear in abundance until late November and reach maximum numbers in late December or early January.

Canvasbacks appear on their Chesapeake Bay winter grounds in late October and steadily increase in numbers through November and December. Farther down the coast, they appear 2 to 3 weeks later, but in Florida they arrive as early as at Chesapeake Bay.

On their major concentration points in the Midwest, the La Crosse area and the Keokuk Pool (both on the Mississippi River), the chronology of migration is different. At La Crosse, Wisconsin, canvasbacks arrive in numbers the third week in October. They reach peak numbers the first of November and departures occur over the next 2 weeks. They arrive at the Keokuk Pool in late October and increase to peak numbers by the middle of November. Large numbers remain there until forced out by the freeze-up near mid-December. They reach Tennessee and Arkansas waters in late October, with a continuous rise in numbers to January.

Cans arrive on their winter grounds adjacent to the central Gulf Coast in late November. Farther south on the lower Texas coast, however, they arrive almost a month earlier. This earlier arrival in Texas probably results from their more rapid passage across the Great Plains, where habitats attractive to canvasbacks are sparse.

The marshes of the several basins and valleys in the western mountains are close to important canvasback breeding grounds. Therefore, it is not surprising that migrants appear in these areas in early October and reach maximum numbers in late October or early November. They arrive on winter grounds in central California in late October, and numbers steadily increase through November and December. On winter grounds in southern California, cans do not appear until late November and rapidly increase in number through December.

Spring. Canvasbacks, like other *Aythya*, begin departing many of their winter areas in early February as water areas open up farther north. Unlike scaups and redheads, once on their way, they do not tarry as long on migration areas. On most winter areas, there is a steady but gradual departure lasting almost to mid-April, but canvasbacks appear to depart en masse from Florida the third week in March.

On lakes midway to their breeding grounds, canvasbacks appear in small numbers in late February, with populations rapidly increasing through March. In most of these areas, populations decline rapidly the last half of April. Cans begin to arrive on the southern margins of their breeding grounds in the Great Plains in early April and oncoming migrants rapidly swell their abundance through April.

They appear at the Delta Marsh, Manitoba, variously between April 12 and 23, depending upon the spring thaw (Hochbaum 1944). After the first week in May, few but residents remain. On pothole breeding grounds near Minnedosa, Manitoba, Olson (1964) reported that canvasback pairs arrived suddenly, with maximum numbers reached on May 9 and 10.

At Yellowknife, Northwest Territories, Murdy (1964) observed the first canvasbacks on May 6-14, 1962-64, with the major influx on May 11-19. May 15 was their first date of arrival on Yukon Flats, Alaska, in 1954 (Hansen 1956).

BREEDING

Behavior

Age. From observations of the composition of canvasback populations at Delta Marsh, Manitoba, Hochbaum (1944) considered that most yearling hens nested. Olson (1964) found 2 yearling hens among 15 breeding birds; both yearlings were late layers. A study in 1973 by David Trauger indicates that a number of yearling canvasbacks do not breed when habitat conditions are adverse. He found no attended nests among 12 marked yearling hens, but 6 of 10 intensively observed yearling hens may have nested, and 1 of these may even have renested. Trauger has found that the urge to breed is weaker in yearlings than in adults.

Pair Bond. Weller (1965) observed only a small proportion of canvasbacks paired from December into March. During March-April, he observed that 41 percent of the females in Iowa were paired. At Lake Christina, Minnesota, no pairs were observed among the earliest arrivals the first week in April; by April 9, 10 percent were paired, and by April 16, 65 percent of the total population was in pairs (Smith 1946). Courtship activities at Delta Marsh, Manitoba, were at their peak in late April and early May, and Hochbaum observed that most canvasbacks were in pairs by mid-May. Among early migrants arriving in late March at Malheur Lake, Oregon, Erickson (1948) reported about 50 percent were already paired, and the proportion of pairs in the population steadily increased to 85 percent by April 23-26.

Hochbaum (1944) noted at Delta Marsh that males deserted their mates shortly after incubation commenced. According to Erickson (1948), canvasback drakes at Malheur Lake left their regular waiting areas within a week after incubation started but tended to remain in the same general area. Dzubin (1955) reported that drakes often remained in the vicinity of the nests until the 10th day of incubation—rarely to the 18th day.

Homing. According to David Trauger, canvasbacks exhibit a strong propensity to return to the same breeding area. Of 12 adult hens he marked in the spring of 1972 in the Minnedosa pothole area, 9 (75 percent) came back during the spring of 1973; among 50 marked young, 12 (24 percent) returned. When yearly mortality rates are considered, a surprising number of adult hens survived to return, and, quite likely, all of the yearlings alive homed to their natal area. A considerably larger proportion of canvasbacks than redheads marked at the same time returned (Trauger). Homing by lesser scaups to the Minnedosa area was at a level between the two.

Home Range. From observing the daily movements of marked canvasbacks in the pothole area of Minnedosa, Manitoba, Dzubin (1955) concluded that the home range of a breeding pair included a number of potholes, only a few of which were heavily utilized. Certain ones were used as waiting sites, others for nesting, and still others for feeding. Several pairs of canvasbacks may use parts of the same home range. One waiting pothole, occupied by a marked drake, was also used by three other pairs and an unmated drake. At times a drake may defend an area of about 15 feet around his mate, but at other times he ignores nearby drakes. The area in a drake's home range may exceed 1,300 acres.

A preliminary analysis of marked canvasbacks on the same area by David Trauger almost 20 years later led him to similar conclusions and to some extensions of Dzubin's conclusions: (1) Activity centers of many pairs overlap without creating a significant amount of either interspecific or intraspecific interaction. (2) The home range includes a large number and diversity of potholes, but only a comparatively few are used for feeding, resting, and nesting. (3) Activity centers of both canvasbacks and redheads encompass greater areas for yearlings than for adults. (4) Canvasback females have larger home ranges than redhead females.

Nesting

Nest Sites. Canvasbacks nest in diverse habitats: large marshes, ponds, sloughs, and potholes. Cans and redheads are almost equally abundant in some pothole habitats, but redheads are several times more abundant on large marshes (Olson 1964). At Delta Marsh, for example, redheads have been about four times more numerous than cans.

Canvasback pairs occupy the larger and deeper permanent ponds for feeding, resting, and courting but use the smaller, shallower, and less enduring ponds for nesting (Trauger and Stoudt 1974). These ponds are usually less than an acre in size and are encircled by bands of cattails and bulrushes. Brood ponds are intermediate in size betwen those used for feeding and for nesting but contain considerable marsh vegetation.

Erickson (1948) observed female cans searching through marsh vegetation during several periods of each day prior to nest-building. The male remained on the waiting area but joined his mate in flight when the searching extended to nest cover at a distance. He either dropped into the marsh with her or returned to his waiting area. At Delta Marsh, hens spend a week exploring bulrush beds before selecting nest sites (Hochbaum 1944). Laying followed the beginning of nest-building by 2 or 3 days, and construction continued along with egg-laying at the rate of one a day.

At Malheur Lake, Erickson reported that nest sites preferred by canvasbacks were difficult to determine because nests were found in various types of vegetation and water depths. One nest was found on land. Most nests were located either in pure stands of hardstem bulrush or in bulrush mixed with cattail or bur reed or sedge. He concluded that the most important factor in choosing a nest site was the degree of interspersion between emergent plants and water.

In prairie pothole areas, cattails were used for most nest sites, perhaps because this species is the most abundant overwater nest cover (Olson 1964). At Lousana, Alberta, 29 percent of the canvasback nests were among flooded willows (Smith 1971); at Redvers, Saskatchewan, 9 percent were among willows (Stoudt 1971). Sedges, too, ranked as important plant sites for nests. On the Saskatchewan Delta, Townsend (1966) found most nests in phragmites cane.

Canvasbacks usually nest over water 6 to 24 inches in depth, but when water recedes in prairie potholes their nests may become stranded on dry land. In 1959, Olson (1964) found 7 of 68 nests on land; with improved water conditions in 1968, only 1 of 54 nests was located on dry ground.

Clutch Size, Eggs, and Incubation. Determining the clutch size in canvasback nests is complicated by the effect of redhead parasitism on the number of host eggs. When redheads lay in can nests, host clutches are reduced in size. Erickson (1948) reported 9.9 (7) eggs in unparasitized canvasback nests but 7.7 (47) in parasitized nests. Weller (1959) found a clutch of 8 eggs in a normal can nest but 6.6 (38) eggs in parasitized nests. On larger marshes, where canvasback nests are heavily parasitized by redheads, host eggs averaged a mere 5.2 (13) but eggs of the intruding redheads averaged 12.9 (Olson 1964). Hochbaum (1944) found an average of 10 canvasback eggs and 3.7 redhead eggs in 38 nests. In a number of studies encompassing 519 canvasback nests, the average clutch size in parasitized and nonparasitized nests was 7.9 eggs. Apparently, clutches in nonparasitized nests range from 7 to 12 and average about 9.5 eggs. In the Minnedosa pothole district, from 1962 to 1972, redheads parasitized 57 percent of the canvasback nests (Trauger and Stoudt 1974). Female canvasbacks seldom lay eggs in the nests of other species but commonly parasitize the nests of other canvasback hens (Olson 1964).

Hochbaum (1944) described the canvasback egg as large and green, with a smooth shell, and the redhead egg as smaller and cream or buff in color. Canvasback eggs measured by Hochbaum averaged 63.7 by 44.6 mm (103), and redhead eggs averaged 58.8 by 43.2 mm (43). One hundred canvasback eggs measured by Erickson (1948) were 64.4 by 44.9 mm and were described as ovate to elliptical ovate in shape.

Erickson (1948) reported that canvasback hens began to incubate during the laying of the last two or three eggs of their clutches and continued for 24 to 29 days (average, 25 days). Under artificial incubation, Hochbaum (1944) reported that eggs hatched between 23 and 29 days (average, 24 days).

Chronology of Nesting. Over their breeding range, canvasbacks begin to nest about the same time, late April or early May. Even in the Subarctic, canvasbacks nest almost as early as in the northern prairies. At Yellowknife, Northwest Territories, nests were initiated May 11-22, 1961-64, and the last nest was initiated between May 29 and June 3 (Murdy 1964). On the Yukon Flats, Alaska, nests were started between May 9 and 20, 1953-56 (Hansen 1956).

In its principal breeding range, nest initiation is at its maximum during May 10-25, with few nests started after mid-June. At Delta Marsh, Hochbaum (1944) noticed that in 3 years cans began laying at the same time, May 5, but in one unusually early spring they started sooner, on April 25 or 26.

The span of nest initiation decreases as latitude increases: 63 days at Malheur Lake, Oregon (Erickson 1948); 60 days at Minnedosa, Manitoba (Stoudt 1965); 56 days at the Saskatchewan River delta (Townsend 1966); and 14 days at Yellowknife (Murdy 1964).

Nest Success. Canvasback nest success varies dramatically from year to year and among nest areas. In many studies ranging from Oregon to Alaska, success of 1,715 nests has averaged 46.2 percent.

Nesting of the canvasback has been studied most intensively in the pothole district of Minnedosa, Manitoba. In 1953, Kiel (1954) observed that 77 percent of 77 nests were successful. Olson (1964) reported 21 percent of 131 nests to be successful, 1959-61. And Stoudt (1965), in the same area, found 45 percent of 707 nests successful, 1961-65, the success rate varying from 32 percent in 1961 to 57 percent in 1964. However, catastrophic nest losses occurred in 1973 (Trauger and Stoudt 1974), when only 3 (2.7 percent) of 111 nests hatched in the Minnedosa area. Receding water levels in small potholes exposed can nests to unusually heavy predation by raccoons and skunks.

At the same time that nest success was alarmingly low in the Minnedosa potholes, Stoudt (1973) reported that 62 percent of 21 nests were successful in the area of Redvers, Saskatchewan. This rate compares favorably with his earlier (1952-65) records in that area, when 65 percent of 233 canvasback nests hatched (Stoudt 1971).

Nest Failure. The recent raccoon invasion into the southern part of the northern prairie breeding grounds presents a new agent of waterfowl nest destruction. These adaptable mammals have wreaked havoc particularly among nesting canvasbacks and redheads. Not until 1949 were juvenile raccoons first recorded on the Delta Marsh, Manitoba (Sowls 1949). Since then raccoons have established themselves as important denizens of the area.

Raccoons first appeared in the area of Minnedosa, Manitoba, in 1954 (Olson 1964), and since the 1960's they have become common inhabitants there. In 1973, Stoudt (1973) reported that they were responsible for 60 percent of all canvasback nests destroyed in the Minnedosa potholes.

At Redvers, Saskatchewan, Stoudt (1971) observed both the first raccoon and the first nest destruction by this mammal in 1960. From 1952 to 1965, Stoudt found that raccoons were responsible for only 5 of 104 canvasback nests destroyed there, but in 1973, raccoon depredations accounted for 4 of 6 nests that failed to hatch.

Skunks are the second most important mammalian predator upon can nests in the prairie breeding grounds. They are especially destructive in years when water recedes from marginal marsh cover, leaving the can nests stranded on dry ground, or when low water at the beginning of the nesting season necessitates placing nests out of the water. Coyotes, foxes, minks, and weasels are other mammals that occasionally prey upon canvasback nests.

Crows and magpies accounted for 30 percent of the 104 canvasback nests destroyed in the Redvers area, 1952-65 (Stoudt 1971) and caused most of the 40 percent loss attributed to bird predators at Lousana, Alberta (Smith 1971). At Malheur Lake, Oregon, ravens were the only important predator on canvasback nests, being responsible for 24 percent of all failures (Erickson 1948).

Desertion in canvasback nests looms as a far greater cause of nest loss than in most other species. Hens desert their nests for a variety of reasons, but the most important ones are flooding and intrusions by parasitic laying redheads and other canvasbacks. Heavy rains on small potholes or wind tides on large marshes often raise the water faster than the hens are able to build up the nest platforms. At Redvers, 1952-65, flooding accounted for 16 percent of all nests lost, and 22 percent of the canvasback nest losses at Minnedosa in 1963 and 20 percent in 1965 were also caused by flooding (Stoudt 1965).

The intrusion by parasitic laying redheads is a principal cause of canvasback nest desertion. Nest parasitism caused 64 percent of 42 nest failures at Malheur Lake (Erickson 1948). An average of 7.3 eggs hatched in unparasitized canvasback nests, but the average in parasitized nests that were successful was only 6.0 eggs.

Olson (1964) determined that 15 percent of the canvasback nests he studied in 1959 and 14 percent of those he studied in 1960 were deserted. He attributed these desertions to parasitic egg-laying by both redheads and canvasbacks.

Renesting. The proportion of canvasbacks renesting varies greatly from year to year, apparently depending upon the cause of nest destruction, the stage of incubation, and the current quality of the habitat. Weller and Ward (1959) reported that two of seven marked hens renested. Among five marked female cans intensively observed by Trauger (1973), two renested at least once and three at least twice. Stoudt (1965) reported that at Minnedosa there was little renesting by canvasbacks in 1961 and 1962 and a small amount of renesting in 1963 and 1964, but an astounding 70 percent of the pairs present renested in 1965. This tremendous renesting effort occurred after an almost complete desertion of nests because of rain, snow, and cold temperatures between May 23 and 26; incubation had just started on about half of the nests, and eggs were still being deposited in the others. Thus, probably 20 percent of the incubating hens—and almost all of those still laying—renested.

Considerable renesting is also shown by other data. On his study area at Brooks, Alberta, Keith (1961) observed that 10 pairs of canvasbacks produced 20 nests. Smith (1971) reported only 36 percent nest success, 1953-65, at Lousana, Alberta, yet 62 percent of the females produced broods.

Rearing of Young

Broods. Female canvasbacks guide their charges through the large marshes, and, in pothole districts, to ponds providing needed aquatic animal foods. As Evans et al. (1952) observed at Minnedosa, Manitoba, they are, next to the pintail, the most mobile of duck broods, seldom spending more than 7 days on the same pothole. Canvasback broods seek the most open, the largest, and the deepest potholes for their development. At Redvers, Saskatchewan, Stoudt (1971) found twice as many broods in potholes 5 to 10 acres in size as in potholes of 2 to 5 acres.

Hochbaum (1944) observed that canvasback mothers abandoned their broods at various ages, depending upon the lateness of the season. Those with early-hatched broods remained in attendance until the young were almost ready to fly; late-hatched young were deserted when only 2 to 3 weeks old. Few broods are observed with their mothers after the first week in August at the Delta Marsh.

CANVASBACK

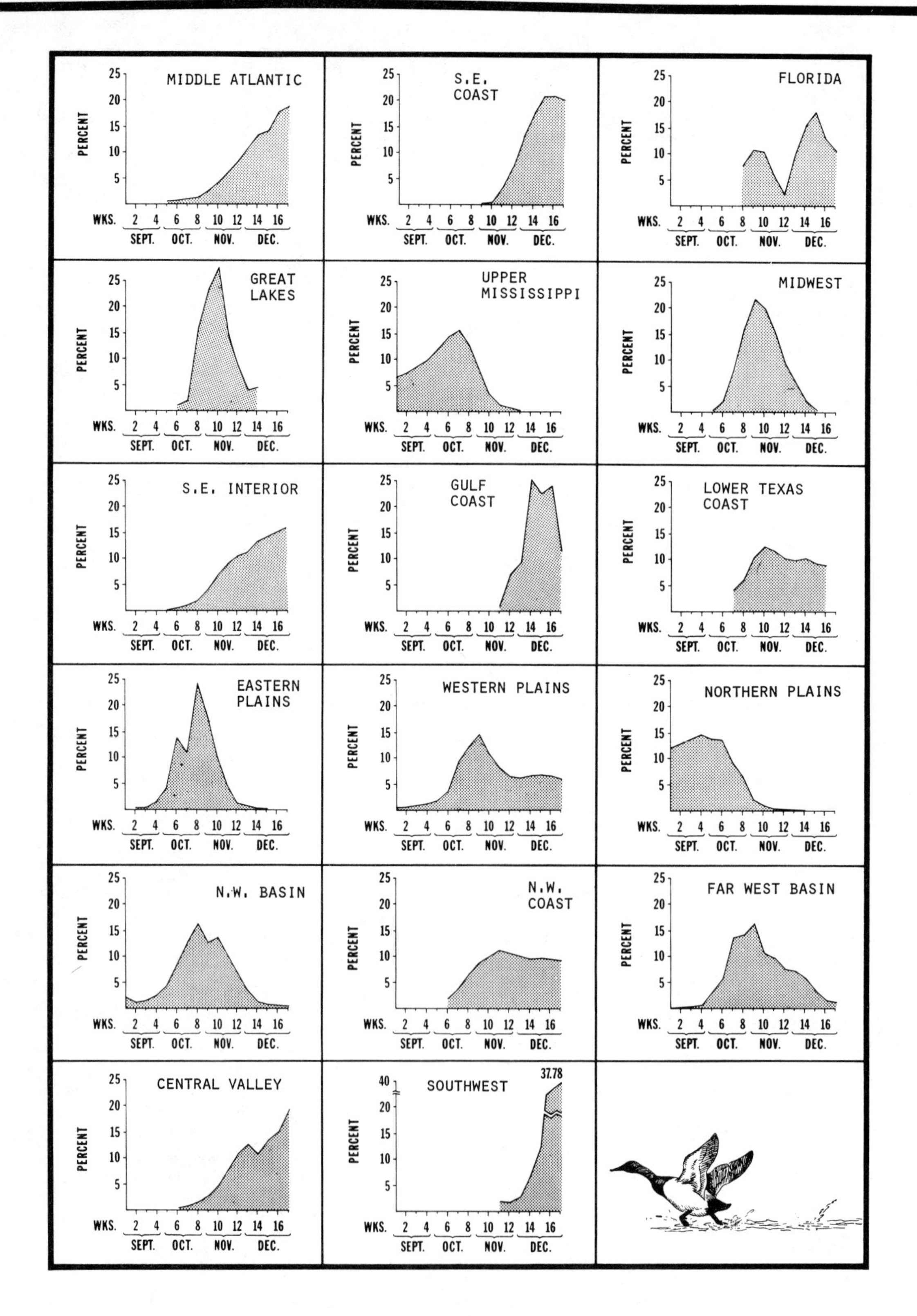

Fall

CANVASBACK

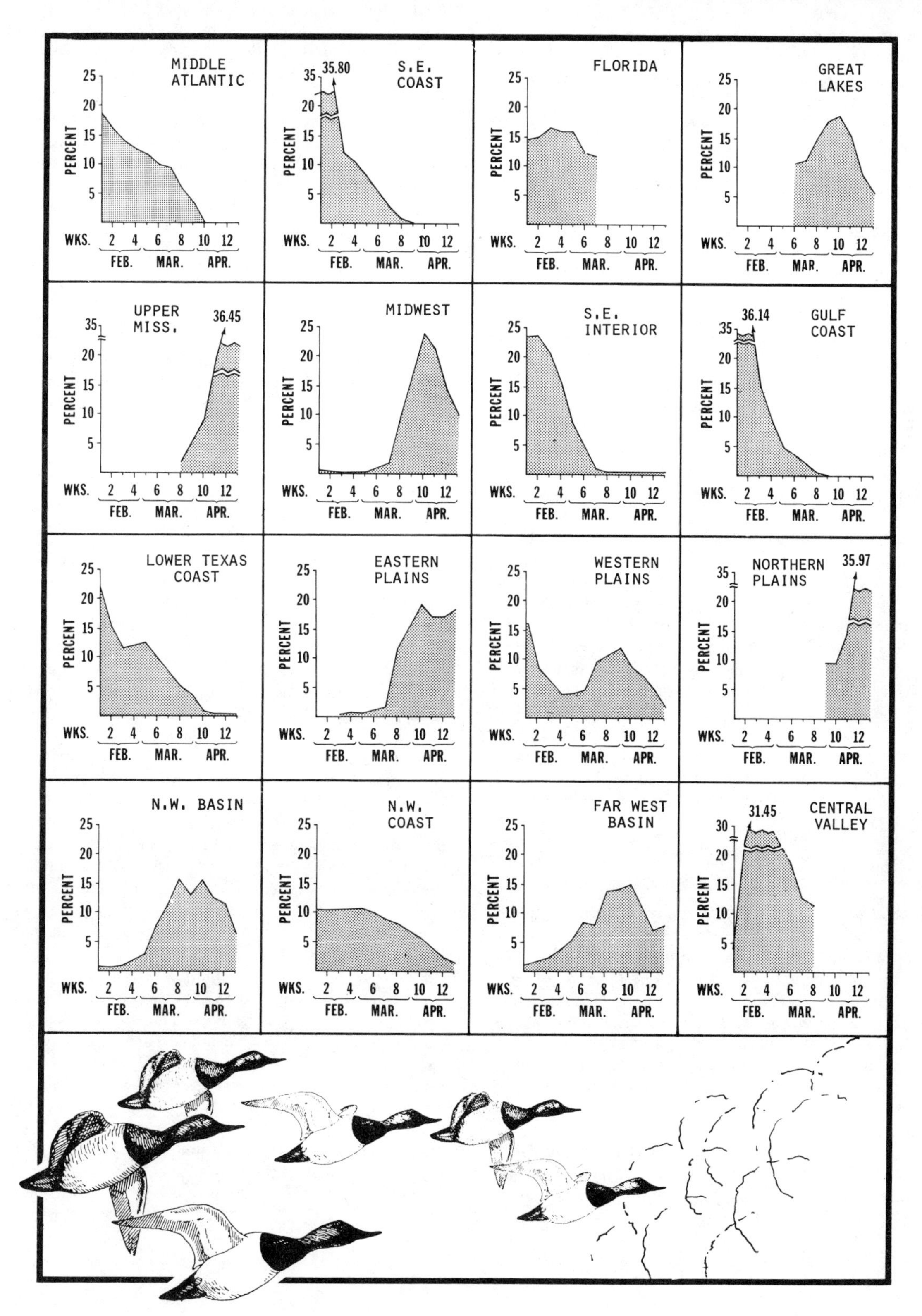
MIDDLE ATLANTIC
S.E. COAST
35.80
FLORIDA
GREAT LAKES
UPPER MISS.
36.45
MIDWEST
S.E. INTERIOR
GULF COAST
36.14
LOWER TEXAS COAST
EASTERN PLAINS
WESTERN PLAINS
NORTHERN PLAINS
35.97
N.W. BASIN
N.W. COAST
FAR WEST BASIN
CENTRAL VALLEY
31.45
PERCENT
WKS.
FEB.
MAR.
APR.

Development. The growth and development of young canvasbacks has been studied intensively by Dzubin (1959). He observed that Class I stage (from a ball of fluff to gawky downy) occurred the first 25 days; Class II stage (first body feathers to last down) lasted from 26 to 53 days; and Class III stage (fully feathered but flightless) from 54 to 65 days. During the Class I interval, hens on the water are 1.7 to 3.1 times longer than ducklings. They are 1.2 to 1.4 times longer during the Class II interval, and decrease to 1.1 times in the Class III stage. At Minnedosa, Manitoba, flight stage was reached in 56 to 68 days (Dzubin 1959). The first flying young canvasbacks were noted there on August 1, with peak numbers during August 14-20 (Evans et al. 1952). On the Yukon Flats, Alaska, the first fledged canvasbacks were noticed on August 20, 1953, some 56 days after the first brood was observed (Hansen 1956).

Survival. About 7.2 canvasback eggs hatch in the average successful nest. The average size of Class I broods is 6.33 (866), indicating a loss of 13 percent up to the 12-day midpoint in this age group. During the Class II interval, broods average 5.90 (866), a reduction of 7 percent; and Class III broods average 5.31 (312), a loss of 10 percent from the previous age-class. From the time it leaves the nest until about 2 months later when flight is attained, a brood loses about a fourth of its members.

Probably only rarely are entire broods of canvasbacks lost. At Redvers, 1952-65, Stoudt (1971) determined that 61 percent of the breeding females produced broods as compared with a 65 percent nest success. About 47 percent of the canvasback hens produced broods on the Delta Marsh and Minnedosa potholes in 1960 (Olson 1964).

On this basis, we assume that 55 percent of the canvasback hens are successful in rearing 5.3 young to flight stage. Thus, for all hens, successful and unsuccessful, the average would be 2.9 flying young. But the breeding females represent only 34 percent of all adult canvasbacks (2.9 males to 1 female). Therefore, the proportion of young raised to flight age, per adult, is 1 to 1. This ratio agrees almost precisely with the computed age ratios in fall canvasback populations.

POSTBREEDING SEASON

Hochbaum (1944) reported that small bands of male canvasbacks began to gather during the last of May at Delta Marsh, Manitoba. By mid-June the numbers of males in these flocks had greatly increased, and by the end of the month, rafts of males numbered 200 to 1,000. Small numbers of females appeared in late June and July, but Hochbaum (1944) did not see more than 5 percent at any time. In late July, the canvasbacks moved from the marsh to the open waters of Lake Manitoba, where they apparently underwent their molt of wing feathers, leaving them flightless.

Almost 200 miles north-northwest of Delta Marsh lies Swan Lake, a noted concentration area for molting canvasbacks, redheads, and scaups. According to Bergman (1973), canvasbacks steadily increase from fewer than 100 in late May to 1,000 or more in late July. During this period 95 percent are adult males, but by the end of August there are 15 to 20 percent females in the flocks, which range up to 200 individuals. He observed flightless canvasbacks from early August to mid-September.

Hochbaum (1944) considered that yearling drake canvasbacks experienced a complete eclipse plumage but that old birds lost only part of their nuptial plumage even though, like the others, they passed through the flightless state. Early-molting drakes began to lose their bright plumage in early June; Hochbaum considered these to be the earliest-mated drakes. He observed the earliest flightless drake at Delta Marsh on June 30, but the peak of the flightless period was not reached until late July and lasted to late August. The earliest flightless adult female was observed by Hochbaum (1944) on July 20, but most did not reach this state until August. He saw a female with primaries too short for flight as late as October 9. Female canvasbacks were much more dispersed than males during the molt and tended to remain on or in the vicinity of breeding marshes rather than to collect in sizable flocks on large lakes. They were flightless from 3 to 4 weeks (Hochbaum 1944).

FOOD HABITS

Canvasbacks are not as fastidiously inclined to feed upon plants as are redheads. When plants are lacking from a favored rest site, they readily partake of many forms of animal life, if available. Formerly associated with wild celery because of their fondness for this plant in the Great Lakes states and Chesapeake Bay, its depletion has forced canvasbacks to utilize other foods more heavily. What effect this forced change in diet has had upon their survival is unknown.

An early analysis of food habits from canvasback gizzards collected in 26 states and 5 provinces showed that plants composed 80 percent of the contents and animals comprised 20 percent (Cottam 1939). Pondweeds, particularly sago, formed 30 percent of the food items, with wild celery at 9 percent, delta duck potato at 8 percent, bulrush seeds at 6 percent, and other species in lesser amounts. Mollusks composed 9 percent, insects (mostly caddis flies and midges) 8 percent, and fishes 2 percent of the animal foods taken.

At one time on their principal winter grounds in Chesapeake Bay, canvasbacks fed largely on the following plants: wild celery, widgeon grass, eelgrass, and sago and clasping leaf pondweeds; their main animal foods were Baltic clams, other bivalve mollusks, and mud crabs (Stewart 1962). In recent years there has been a continuous decline in the aquatic plant beds of Chesapeake Bay (Perry 1974), primarily because of increased turbidity and secondarily because of lessened salinity. Accordingly, there has been a change in the canvasbacks' diet. Where once they fed on eelgrass and widgeon grass, two small clams—*Rangia* and *Macoma*—are now utilized as food (Perry 1975). Currituck Sound, North Carolina, is also a noted winter ground for canvasbacks, and only pondweeds and widgeon grass were important foods there (Quay and Critcher 1965).

At Humboldt Bay, California, Yocom and Keller (1961) reported that sago pondweed, widgeon grass, and clams were the favored canvasback foods. Canvasbacks at Reelfoot Lake, Tennessee, relied largely upon sago and leafy pondweeds and insects for food (Rawls 1954). Gizzards from Missouri canvasbacks contained mainly leafy and sago pondweeds and the seeds of bulrushes (Korschgen 1955).

Longleaf and sago pondweeds, duck potato, coontail, and midge larvae were the principal foods consumed by canvasbacks collected largely in the Illinois Valley, 1938-40 (Anderson 1959). A bountiful supply of these plants, with the addition of wild celery, resulted in a peak abundance of 110,000 canvasbacks at Peoria Lake in the Illinois Valley in 1953. When these plants almost entirely disappeared from Peoria Lake and other lakes in the Illinois Valley, commencing in 1954, canvasback populations declined drastically.

Subsequently, canvasback numbers increased on the Keokuk Pool, Mississippi River, with fall populations peaking at over 100,000 from 1969 to 1971 followed by a decline to 75,000 in 1974. At this important concentration point for canvasbacks, Thompson (1973) reported that the principal foods are fingernail clams, snails, and mayfly nymphs. The seeds of plants are of minor importance, but among these, pondweeds are the most frequently consumed. As at Chesapeake Bay, this change in the abundance of plants has resulted in the adoption of molluscan foods.

Bartonek and Hickey (1969) found that during the summer, adult female and immature canvasbacks fed almost entirely upon animal life—the larvae of caddis flies and midges and the nymphs of mayflies. In contrast, adult males fed almost entirely upon vegetable matter—pondweed tubers and seeds and muskgrass oogonia and vegetative parts. During the fall, canvasbacks of both sexes and all ages (collected in southwest Manitoba) had consumed pondweed tubers and seeds and the vegetative parts of muskgrass.

Redhead

Aythya americana

Other Common Name: Pochard

VITAL STATISTICS

Length:	Male, 18.1-21.7 inches, average 20.0 inches (42)
	Female, 18.0-20.5 inches, average 19.0 inches (29)
Wing:	Adult male, average 9.16 inches (29)
	Adult female, average 8.79 inches (21)
	Immature male, average 9.01 inches (16)
	Immature female, average 8.64 inches (11)
Weight:	Adult male, 2.1-3.2 pounds, average 2.44 pounds (105)
	Adult female, 1.5-2.9 pounds, average 2.14 pounds (87)
	Immature male, 1.4-3.0 pounds, average 2.11 pounds (201)
	Immature female, 1.4-2.8 pounds, average 1.91 pounds (186)

IDENTIFICATION

Field

Although slightly smaller than the mallard, the redhead in flight has about the same body conformation and arrangements of color patterns. Experienced waterfowlers mistake single pairs or a few redheads for mallards more often than for any other species. The arc of the wing beat is shallow, like the mallard's, rather than deep, like the scaup's. In rate of wing beat and in speed of flight, the redhead is faster than the mallard but is slower than the scaup and the canvasback.

The redhead usually occurs as singles, pairs, and in flocks of 5 to 15, which are smaller than the flocks of scaups and canvasbacks. But on a few favored winter grounds, where it is unusually abundant, it occurs in rafts of hundreds, if not thousands. Birds in flight form tight, wedge-shaped flocks. The broad band of light gray that extends across the rear of the dusky gray wing and out on the primaries distinguishes this species from the scaups, whose single white bands are on the trailing edges of their wings, and from the canvasback, with its white back and the whitish inner half of the wing. The wing pattern is slightly lighter in tone in redheads than in female ring-necked ducks and much lighter than in male ring-necked ducks.

At a distance on the water, the male redhead presents dark fore-quarters, a gray back, and black rear-quarters. The gray back is noticeably darker than the scaup's and much darker than the canvasback's. Even when the red coloration of the head is not discernible, the head appears of a lighter cast than the black chest. At moderate range, the red head of the male in nuptial plumage is readily apparent, and at close range the circular powder-puff shape of the head is quite distinctive. The male redhead, especially in the spring, is more prone than other divers, except the canvasback, to keep its head partially to fully raised while swimming.

Redheads in female and immature plumages are a tawny-brown, and, while waterborne, no other color is discernible. Actually, the side of the head is a lighter brown, the chin is whitish, and when the hen is in flight, the white belly is noticeable. Female scaups and ringnecks appear darker brown than redheads in similar plumages. Canvasback hens have gray backs and brownish heads that are distinctively sloped.

The male redhead is more vociferous than other diving ducks. His call resembles the *me-ow* of a cat.

At Hand

The drake in nuptial plumage is readily distinguished by its round chestnut-red head and upper neck, its black lower neck and chest, its gray back formed by dense dusky gray vermiculations, its white belly, and its black tail and tail coverts. The long bill is blue-gray, tipped with black. The feet are slate-gray and the eyes are yellow. The canvasback drake is similar in appearance but the head is wedge-shaped, the chestnut red covers the entire neck, and the back is whitish. The female common and red-breasted mergansers have cinnamon-brown heads and gray backs, but their bills, heads, and bodies are shaped differently.

It takes a sharp eye to distinguish female and immature redheads from ring-necked ducks of the same sex and age. The principal differences lie in the size of the body, in the shape of the head—the redhead's is round and that of the ringneck slopes from a slight bulge at the back—in the lack of a white eye-ring in the redhead, and in the black tip of the ringneck's bill, margined by a transverse white line. The bills of the scaups are entirely blue, and white facial patches usually surround them.

By early October, adult drakes have molted their dull brown eclipse plumage sufficiently to regain their red heads. However, brown feathers may still mottle the black chests and gray backs (Weller 1957). Usually, full nuptial plumage is acquired by November. Juveniles retain their femalelike brown plumage through most of the fall but in late November acquire their red heads and are usually in full nuptial plumage by late January.

The wings of female and immature redheads and canvasbacks are similar (Carney 1964). Overall, they are brown-gray, but the contrast between the dark secondary coverts and the pearl-gray secondaries is greater among redheads of all ages and sex groups than among female and immature canvasbacks, whose secondaries are a dusky gray. The upper wings of adult male canvasbacks are vermiculated gray, unique among all ducks.

Adult male redheads have dusky gray greater coverts that are lightly to heavily flecked and broadly rounded over the tertials. The greater coverts in immature males are brown-gray, usually indistinctly tipped with white; over the tertials they are either narrow and ragged, or, as new plumage appears during the fall, grayish and flecked. The lesser and middle coverts are faintly flecked.

Female redheads have plain brown-gray wing coverts; in adults the greaters are smooth and rounded over the tertials; in immatures they are narrow and ragged.

POPULATION STATUS

Over the period 1955-74, redhead breeding populations on their principal prairie breeding grounds have averaged 649,000. Breeding numbers have ranged from a low of 387,000 in 1963 to a high of 927,000 in 1965, a variation of 68 percent.

The status of the redhead has been so precarious in the 1960's and early 1970's as to merit some form of special protection. The killing of redheads was illegal from 1960 through 1963. One or two were permitted in the bag up to 1972 and 1973, when one redhead was permitted in the bag in the Pacific Flyway and the season was closed in the other flyways.

Age Ratios

Immature redheads appear in hunters' bags in much greater numbers than do adults. Unfortunately, this fact does not indicate a high production of young. Banding data show that immature redheads suffer a high rate of hunting loss. The recovery rate from bandings in Canada, 1946-54, was 3.48 times greater for immature than for adult redheads (Bellrose et al. 1961); the corresponding figure for Minnesota was 3.40 (Lee et al. 1964). However, a lower ratio of losses—two immatures per adult—is indicated by annual mortality data. I consider this rate of vulnerability to be the most likely one.

Because immatures are so highly vulnerable to the gun, the proportion of 1.96 immatures per adult in hunters' bags, 1966-73, is higher than the proportion of immatures in fall populations. The use of 2.0 to correct existing age-ratio data in redheads suggests an average of 0.98 young per adult in fall populations, 1966-73.

Sex Ratios

Visually determined sex ratios of redheads in numerous areas of the United States in spring disclosed that drakes composed 60.2 percent (1.50:1) of the populations sampled (Bellrose et al. 1961). A later study in Wisconsin by Jahn and Hunt (1964) revealed 63.9 percent drakes (1.78:1) in spring redhead populations. These data indicate a third more drakes than hens. Thus, when the production of young per hen is prorated against adults, the productivity ratio is lowered.

Mortality and Survival

All of the studies on mortality in the redhead show that this species experiences a high annual loss. Hickey (1952) reported that immature redheads banded in Utah, 1926-35, had a first-year mortality rate of 87 percent; that of adults was 54 percent.

Redheads banded in northeastern California, 1948-59, showed an annual mortality rate of 79 percent for immatures and 41 percent for adults (Rienecker 1968). Locally raised redheads in Minnesota suffered a mortality rate of 82 percent as immatures and 39 percent as adults (Lee et al. 1964). First-year mortality rates of immature redheads at Delta Marsh were calculated to be 80 percent (Brakhage 1953) and 85 percent (Weller and Ward 1959), with a subsequent yearly mortality of 55 percent.

The evidence suggests that a minimum of 80 percent of the immature redheads succumbed during their first year of life and that a 40 percent loss of adults occurs. In order to maintain a stable population when suffering such high mortality, redheads need to produce 1.6 flying young per adult. Hickey (1952) concluded that each pair of redheads needed to produce 3.6 young as of September 1. In recent years the production of young, as determined from age ratios in hunters' bags, has fallen below this level.

DISTRIBUTION

Breeding Range

Redheads are a breeding bird of the northern prairies and associated parklands and the Intermountain marshes of the West. The greatest concentration of redheads in North America occurs in the marshes adjacent to the east and north sides of Great Salt Lake. The bulk of Utah's 130,000 redheads breed there, a density of 355 birds per square mile of wetlands.

Other important breeding grounds in the West are: Malheur Basin, Oregon, 15,000; Columbia Basin, Washington, 7,000; Carson Sink, Nevada, 10,000; Klamath Basin, California, 11,000; southeast Idaho, 8,000; British Columbia, particularly the Cariboo and Chilcotin region, 7,000; Intermountain marshes of western Montana, 6,000; Colorado, 3,000, two-thirds in the San Luis Valley; and Wyoming, 1,000.

Perhaps 5,000 additional redheads breed elsewhere through the Pacific Flyway. Small numbers breed in the Suisun Marsh and throughout the Central Valley of California, and as far south as east-central Arizona (Fleming 1959). Minor breeding populations occur in the Ruby Mountains of eastern Nevada, in marshes in south-central Utah, and formerly at Burford Lake, New Mexico (Huey and Travis 1961). The highland region of northeastern Washington supports about 1,000 breeding redheads.

Although the redhead breeds in marshes throughout the northern boreal forest of Canada as far as Great Slave Lake, it is abundant in this region only on the deltas of the Athabasca and Saskatchewan rivers. Breeding numbers are calculated on the Athabasca Delta as 18,000 (11 per square mile) and 36,000 on the Saskatchewan Delta (5.3 per square mile). Over the remainder of the closed boreal forest, the redhead population is estimated at 122,000 (0.29 per square mile); it is most abundant in this zone in northern Alberta and west-central Saskatchewan.

The parklands provide the most extensive favorable habitat for breeding redheads; estimated breeding numbers are 200,000 (about 2.2 per square mile). With the exception of a low density (1.5 per square mile) in the parklands of southeastern Saskatchewan, the breeding density is quite similar all through the parklands from the Minnedosa potholes in southwestern Manitoba to Edmonton, Alberta.

The mixed prairie zone, south of the parklands, supports a redhead breeding population of 235,000, slightly larger than the population in the parklands, but then it covers an area almost twice as large and accordingly the density is much lower (1.3 per square mile). The density of redheads across the mixed prairies in Canada averages 1.0 per square mile, but in this zone in North Dakota the density is 2.6 per square mile.

South and west of the mixed prairie, the shortgrass prairie zone harbors about 27,000 redheads (0.18 per square mile).

In the southern plains of the United States, the Nebraska Sandhills contain a redhead population of nearly 4,500, and about 60 nest on the Cheyenne Bottoms Wildlife Area in central Kansas.

Minnesota is the only lake state with a sizable breeding population of redheads—30,000. Wisconsin's population is estimated at 1,300, and a few redheads are reported as breeding at Lake St. Clair and at Saginaw Bay in Michigan. About 200 breed in Clay and Palo Alto counties, Iowa (Weller 1964). A few breed as far east as the Lake Erie marshes of Ohio and the Montezuma Refuge, New York.

There are a few scattered nesting colonies of redheads in Alaska. Yearly populations average 93 on the Tanana breeding ground, 48 on the Innoko, and 30 on the Yukon Delta.

Migration Corridors

Redheads have an exceptionally significant migration corridor extending across the eastern Great Plains from southwestern Manitoba to the lower Texas coast. Over a third of all redheads in North America follow this corridor. Another important migration corridor to the lower Texas coast originates in southeastern Idaho. Apparently, a large proportion of the redheads from the important breeding grounds in the Great Salt Lake Basin move north into Idaho prior to the fall migration. From this staging area, migration corridors radiate out in several directions in addition to the direction of the Texas coast. One corridor passes directly south to the Mexican coast at Obregón and then south along the coast to Guatemala. A third corridor extends south-southwest to the Imperial Valley, and a fourth to the San Francisco Bay area.

If local recoveries made in Utah and Idaho are omitted, recoveries of redheads raised and banded in Utah disclose that 28 percent were from Texas, 6 percent from Arizona, 26 percent from Mexico, and 13 percent from California (Lensink 1964).

According to Lensink's analysis of bandings, a comparatively small proportion of redheads from Alberta migrate into the Pacific Flyway, and none from breeding grounds farther east. Probably 90 percent of the redheads in the Pacific Flyway originate from within the flyway and British Columbia. About 17 percent of the redhead production in British Columbia reaches Texas; the rest migrate into the Pacific coastal states and Mexico.

There is a pronounced migration eastward from the northern prairies across Minnesota, Wisconsin, and Michigan to southeastern Michigan and Lake Erie (Weller 1964). Peak fall populations of redheads, 1954-56, averaged 50,000 in Minnesota; 22,000 in Wisconsin; and 80,000 in Michigan. Censuses made by the Canadian Wildlife Service reveal a large population of redheads in some years in Lake Erie at Long Point, Ontario; 80,000 to 136,000 in 1966; 76,000 in 1967; 71,000 in 1969 (D. G. Dennis).

From the large areas of redhead concentration on Lake St. Clair and Lake Erie, two migration corridors radiate: one to Chesapeake Bay, the second to Florida. Band recoveries trace the migration corridors across Minnesota, Wisconsin, Michigan, and on to Chesapeake Bay

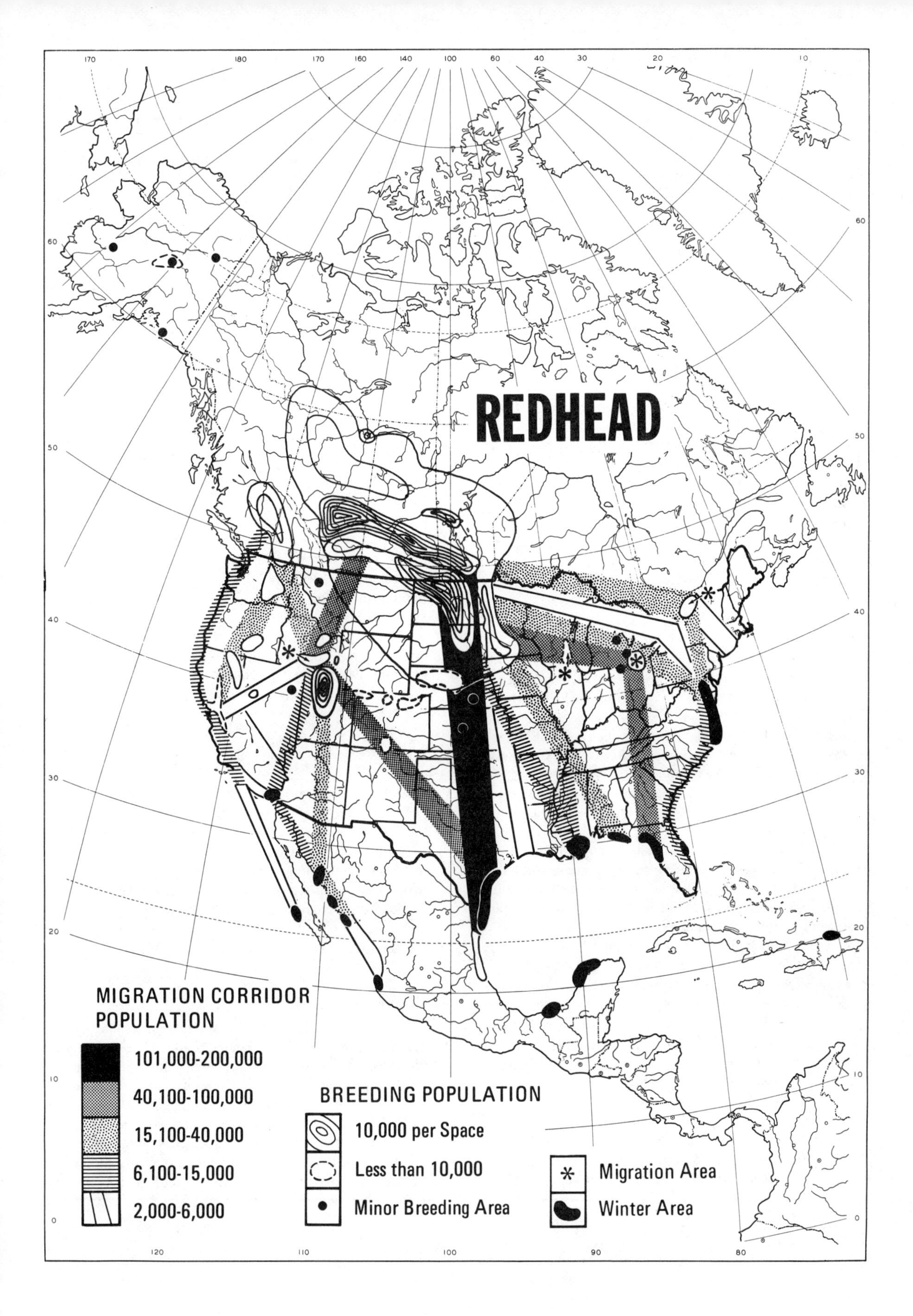

REDHEAD
MIGRATION CORRIDOR POPULATION
101,000-200,000
40,100-100,000
15,100-40,000
6,100-15,000
2,000-6,000
BREEDING POPULATION
10,000 per Space
Less than 10,000
Minor Breeding Area
Migration Area
Winter Area

(Longwell and Stotts 1959, Weller 1964). However, few band recoveries mark the significant migration corridor from Lake Erie to Apalachee Bay, Florida, a region scarce in waterfowl habitat. The number of redheads that winter in Chesapeake Bay and related waters is considerably smaller than that reported for Lakes St. Clair and Erie. Redhead populations on Chesapeake Bay in the fall are similar to those found on the January surveys (Vernon Stotts). Hence, a large part of the redheads from Lake Erie must pass directly south, as indicated by radar, to Florida.

As shown by bandings of redheads on Chesapeake Bay, moderate numbers move down the coast into North Carolina, but only small numbers continue as far south as Florida (Longwell and Stotts 1959). A third migration corridor extends to the Florida panhandle from the Mississippi River in the Midwest.

Bandings in central New York provide recoveries indicating that these redheads migrate eastward from Manitoba along migration corridors through Ontario and Michigan (Benson and DeGraff 1968). A sizable kill of redheads in Ontario also confirms the importance of their passage through that province.

Migration corridors that in part follow the courses of the Mississippi and Missouri rivers through the Midwest are used by redheads that winter off the Chandeleur Islands, Louisiana.

Winter Areas

Eighty percent of the 590,000 redheads censused in North America on January surveys, 1955-74, were found along the coast of the Gulf of Mexico from Apalachee Bay, Florida, to the tip of the Yucatan Peninsula. The largest concentrations were found on the Laguna Madre of Texas (300,000), the Laguna Madre of Mexico (60,000), and Apalachee Bay, Florida (50,000).

Winter areas for other redheads along the Gulf Coast are: Florida panhandle, 15,000; Mobile Bay, Alabama, 700; Chandeleur Islands between Biloxi, Mississippi, and the Mississippi Delta, Louisiana, 20,000; Matagorda and San Antonio bays, Texas, 20,000; Tamiahua Lagoon, south of Tampico, Mexico, 1,200; Alvarado lagoons, 200; Tabasco lagoons, 350; and Yucatan lagoons, 700. About 2,000 winter in the Texas Panhandle.

Next to the Gulf Coast, the largest numbers of redheads, about 60,000, winter along the Atlantic Coast. Chesapeake Bay with slightly over 30,000 has the largest concentration, followed by Cape Canaveral, Florida, with 15,000; Currituck and Albemarle sounds, North Carolina, 6,000; the Finger Lakes district, New York, 5,000; and a few as far north as Rhode Island and occasionally Massachusetts. But only 300 redheads are found in winter on the South Carolina-Georgia coast. On several surveys of the West Indies, Walter Crissey recorded them only once: he found 100 in 1953 in the Dominican Republic. Through the years about 2,000 redheads bound for the Atlantic Coast manage to persist through the winter on the Detroit River and Lake St. Clair, Michigan.

In addition to those wintering along the Chandeleur Islands, slightly over 2,000 redheads from the Mississippi migration corridor winter in the interior: Wisconsin, 50; Kentucky, 75; Missouri, 300; Tennessee, 600; and Arkansas, 1,200.

North of the Gulf Coast in the plains, an average of 7 redheads have been found wintering in Nebraska, 100 in Kansas, and 200 in Oklahoma. Nearly 800 winter in New Mexico and 450 in the Interior Highlands of Mexico.

About 37,000 redheads winter in the Pacific Flyway, 70 percent in Mexico. The largest concentration on the west coast of Mexico is 17,000 on Topolobampo and Santa Maria bays, south of Los Mochis. A sizable concentration of 3,200 occurs farther up the coast near Obregón. Small concentrations of a few hundred each are found south of Los Mochis near Culiacán, near Manzanillo, and 1,200 within a short distance of the Guatemala border. About 450 redheads winter on Laguna San Ignacio and San Quintin Bay, Baja California.

Surprisingly, the largest numbers of redheads wintering in the Pacific Flyway of the United States are found in Idaho (4,100); most of them are either on the Snake River in the southeast or in the northern tip of the panhandle. California is second with 2,900 redheads, almost half of them in the Imperial Valley. The Flathead Valley and nearby areas in western Montana winter the astonishing number of 1,800. Arizona's 1,100 wintering redheads are largely confined to the Colorado River on its western border. Small populations winter all along the Pacific Coast: 400 in the bays of the California coast; 150 in the bays of Oregon; 300 in Puget Sound, Washington; and a few in southern British Columbia. Fewer than 200 winter in Utah but Nevada hosts about 500.

MIGRATION BEHAVIOR

At least a part of the redhead population appears to change winter grounds some years. Comparing the numbers of redheads found on January surveys, 1955-74, in Florida with the numbers found in Texas, the two most important winter areas, suggests that population increases in one area are accompanied by decreases in the other area. The degree of change between the two areas is not always commensurate, and, in a few winters, populations rose or fell simultaneously at both areas.

Chronology

Fall. Redheads are the only members of the *Aythya* that nest commonly in the United States. Consequently, at the onset of migration in September, numbers of them are already present among duck populations found on the northeast prairies, the northwest plains, and the mountain basins. Except for these local populations of redheads the chronology of migration of this species is remarkably similar to that of the scaups, ring-necked ducks, and canvasbacks. In some regions, migrating redheads arrive and depart slightly earlier than canvasbacks.

Redheads begin to appear on migration areas adjacent to their breeding grounds in September, reach peak numbers by mid-October, and are largely gone by late November. Practically all have migrated from their major breeding grounds in the United States by mid-November.

Small numbers of redheads begin to reach their various winter grounds at about the same time, late October. Their numbers increase through November, and, in some regions, into December. In several winter areas—the southeast coast, the lower Texas coast, and the Imperial Valley—the population decline during December probably represents a continuing passage to more distant winter areas.

Spring. As soon as the ice begins to recede from lakes and marshes in the Midwest, in the central Great Plains, and in the higher valleys and basins in the West, the vanguards of redheads appear. Once started, the exodus of redheads from winter areas proceeds at a rapid pace; by mid-March the areas are deserted.

In areas intermediate between winter and breeding ranges, redheads spend 4 to 6 weeks, from about mid-March into late April, before continuing on to breeding areas. They reach breeding areas on the northern prairies in the United States in early April, and numbers rapidly increase through the month.

Near Brooks, Alberta, Keith (1961) noted first arrivals April 7-13, 1953-56, an average of April 11. Redheads arrived in the Minnedosa, Manitoba, area in mid-April in 1959 and 1961, but not until early May in 1960 (Olson 1964). Peak numbers were reached May 16, 1959; May 30, 1960; and May 12, 1961.

BREEDING

Behavior

Age, Pair Bond, and Homing. It is apparent that yearling redhead hens breed, but the proportion of yearling breeders and how much this proportion may vary with the availability of nest habitat are unknown factors. Keith (1961) found only 0.45 nest per pair of redheads, the lowest figure for all species on his Alberta study area. Weller (1959) compared the number of breeding pairs with the number of nests and concluded that only half attempted to nest. Obviously, many redhead hens do not breed. Considering the known latent sexual development in yearlings, it is likely that yearlings constitute the largest segment of nonbreeding redheads. Many redheads nest so late that their young are barely able to fly by freeze-up. Consequently, late-hatched young are the ones most likely to be sexually immature the next summer.

According to Weller (1965), redheads probably begin to pair in late winter. Many are paired by the time they reach Illinois in March, but courtship activity is common throughout the month and well into April. The peak of pair formation occurs in late April. Once incubation begins, males begin to desert their mates. Hochbaum (1944) considered that male desertion occurred shortly after incubation began, but one exceptional male remained for 3 days after the hatching of a brood. Oring (1964) reported that five of six drakes deserted their hens the first day of incubation; the sixth remained into the second week.

Four hens from 539 hand-reared redheads of both sexes released at Delta Marsh by Weller and Ward (1959) returned. In another release of 305 redheads at Lacreek National Wildlife Refuge, South Dakota, at least six hens returned the next spring. Although the known return rate is low, first-year mortality rates of 86 percent for the Delta release and 76 percent for the Lacreek release greatly reduced the numbers of birds available for homing.

In spite of their record for homing, redheads vie with ruddy ducks and blue-winged teal for recognition as pioneers. They successfully pioneered a newly developed marshland at Fish Springs, an isolated water area of north-central Utah (McKnight 1974). The number of redheads increased from two broods in 1960 to 146 young in 1964 and 960 in 1968. Ruddy ducks nested there for the first time in 1963; after 4 years, 180 young per year were being produced.

Home Range. Lokemoen (1966) followed marked breeding redheads in the Flathead Valley of Montana to determine their home range requirements. He found that several pairs maintained close association on waiting site potholes, with movements to nearby potholes where they nested. Two nests on one pothole were about 100 feet apart. Pairs moved 50 to 670 yards, averaging 180 yards, from waiting site potholes to nest site potholes. The level of tolerance between breeding pairs appeared to be high, and thus the space requirements for a pair of redheads appear to be small.

Nesting

Nest Sites. Redheads nest in the emergent vegetation of large marshes and the larger, deeper potholes of the prairies and parklands. Most nest sites are over water in dense stands of plants but are sometimes on islands (Vermeer 1970*b*) or on dry land. Keith (1961) reported that half of the redhead nests that he found were on land and all nests averaged 4 feet from water. Wingfield (1951) reported that most nests in the Bear River marshes were within 40 feet of open water and few were beyond 70 feet but that late in the nesting season many nests were built on dry land some distance from water. Lokemoen (1966) found that redhead nests averaged 7.5 feet from open water. Low (1945) observed in Iowa that nests were placed over water averaging 11 inches in depth and that 85 percent were placed within 50 yards of open water. At the Fish Springs National Wildlife Refuge, Utah, 72 percent of 69 redhead nests were on dry ground, although an average of 7 feet from water (McKnight 1974). The farthest distance from water that a nest has been discovered is 872 feet (Lokemoen and Duebbert 1973).

REDHEAD

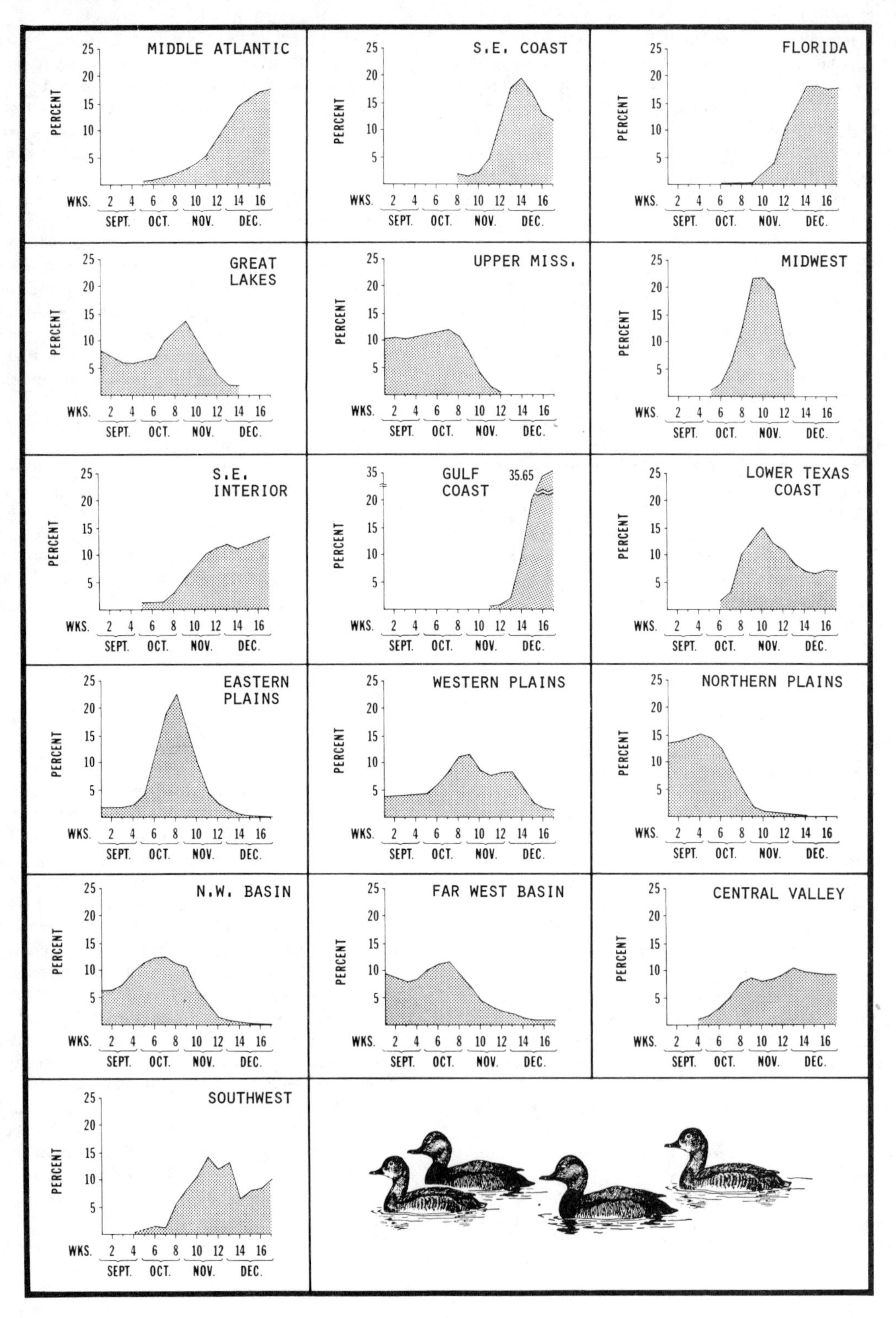

Fall

REDHEAD

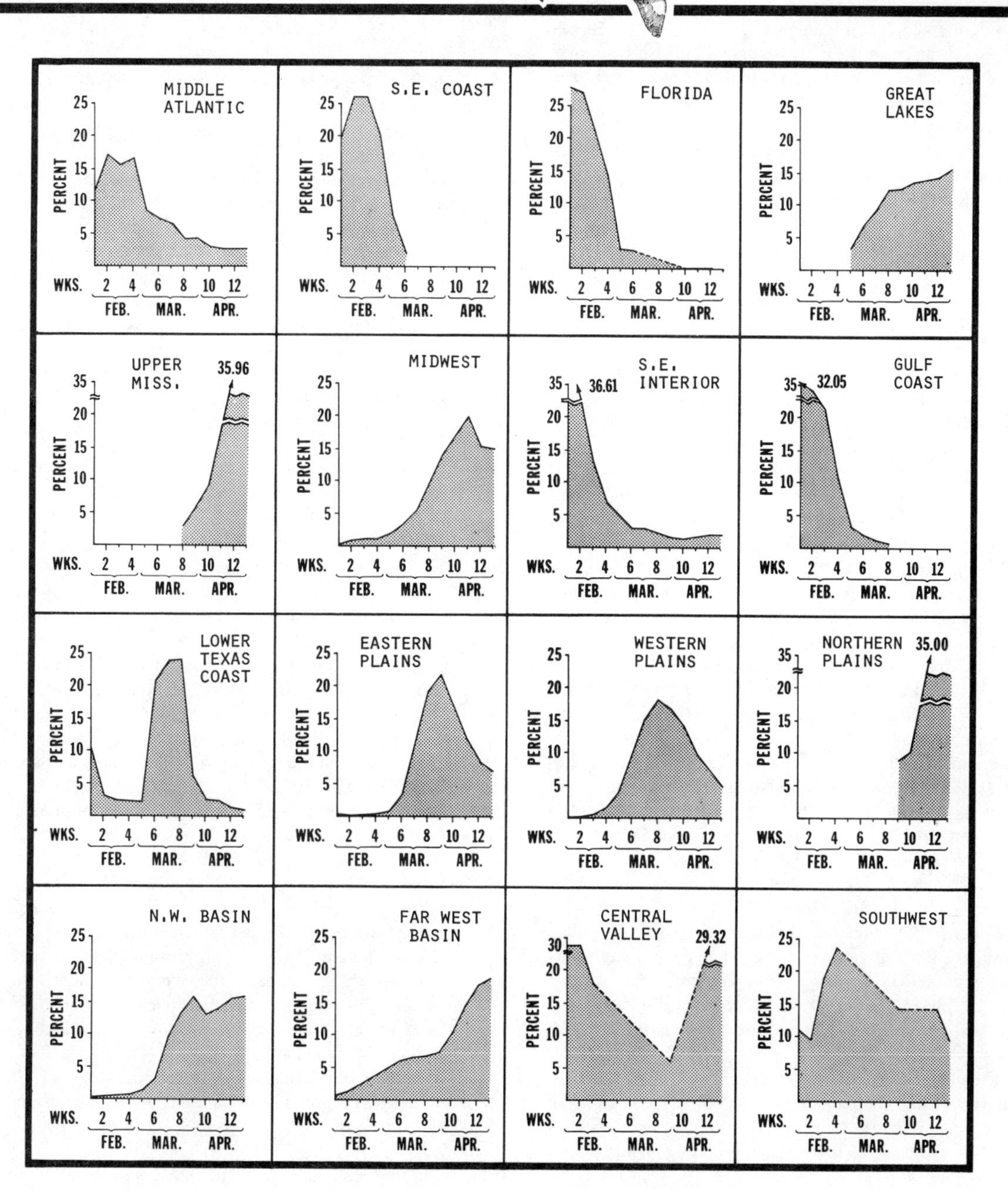

Spring

Many species of ducks select a wide variety of cover types for nesting, seeking only a growth form that provides concealment. The redhead, however, has more stringent site requirements. Many nest studies reveal that redheads have a strong preference for hardstem bulrush beds over other types of vegetation, with cattails a second choice and sedges a third. However, McKnight (1974) believed that a high protein food supply was more important than nest cover as an inducement to breed at Fish Springs. Redheads usually begin to build nests immediately prior to egg-laying and concurrently with it. Down is added to the nest near the completion of laying.

Clutch Size. It is more difficult to determine normal clutch sizes in the redhead than in any other duck because of the large proportion of hens that lay eggs in the nests of other redheads and even in the nests of other species.

In his classic study on the parasitic behavior of the redhead, Weller (1959) recognized three types of egg-laying by different hens: (1) normal; (2) semiparasitic—laying in other nests and also incubating their own clutches; and (3) parasitic—laying only in other nests. He considered that late nests with small clutches may be the first clutches of semiparasitic hens. Both Weller (1959) and Olson (1964) observed that the intensity of parasitic laying paralleled that of normal nesting activity and, therefore, is intrinsically related to the redhead's degree of nesting effort.

On the Bear River marshes, Utah, in 1950, redheads laid eggs in 70 percent of the mallard nests and in 79 percent of the cinnamon teal nests (Wingfield 1951). In 1955 on the same area, redhead eggs were deposited in 68 percent of the mallard nests and in 53 percent of those belonging to cinnamon teal (Weller 1959). Because of similar nest requirements, the redhead over its breeding range victimizes canvasback nests more than those of any other species, in direct proportion to the abundance of redheads (Olson 1964). Nest parasitism was heavy where redheads greatly outnumbered canvasbacks but was light where canvasbacks were the more numerous.

Weller (1959) calculated that parasitic redheads laid an average of 10.8 eggs. An average of 11.1 eggs per clutch has been recorded in 1,309 nests representing many areas. Studies embracing over 50 nests each have shown average clutch sizes of 12.5 (Williams and Marshall 1938*b*); 9.75 (Low 1945); 11.4 (Erickson 1948); 13.5 (Wingfield 1951); 9.4 (Steel et al. 1956); 10.1 (Rienecker and Anderson 1960); and 10.1 (Lokemoen 1966). Illustrative of the extensive dump nesting indulged in by redheads are the numerous clutches containing 19 to 39 eggs reported by Williams and Marshall (1938*b*).

Eggs are usually laid at the rate of one a day, but Low (1945) noted that 1 to 3 days were skipped before a clutch was completed.

Eggs and Incubation. Redhead eggs are a glossy, pale olive-buff and are ovate to elliptical ovate. Measurements of 237 eggs averaged 60.2 by 43.4 mm (Low 1945). Low determined that the incubation period in five clutches was 24 days and in one clutch was 28 days.

Chronology of Nesting. Redheads begin to nest late in the season, and their nesting activity, although lacking intensity, is prolonged into midsummer. Olson (1964) reported them to be on their breeding areas about a month before commencing to nest. In the southeastern part of their breeding range, redheads started to nest between May 5 and July 16 (Low 1945). At Delta Marsh, Manitoba, the first laying began on May 6, the last on July 23, 1952-54 (Weller 1959). Near Brooks, Alberta, May 16 was the midpoint in the initiation of redhead nests with the span extending from early May to late June (Keith 1961).

In Intermountain marshes the first eggs are laid during the following periods: Bear River marshes, Utah, May 2-July 11 (Wingfield 1951); Klamath Basin, California, April 29-July 8 (Rienecker and Anderson 1960); and Flathead Valley, Montana, April 26-June 26 (Lokemoen 1966).

The span of nest initiation for redheads ranges from 61 to 78 days. Three widely separated areas had spans ranging from 70 to 72 days. Perhaps because of the intermediate latitude of the redhead's range, the nesting span has less variation than those of many species.

Nest Success. Numerous studies of redheads, embracing 1,054 nests, indicate that some eggs in 52 percent of the nests hatched. The highest reported nest success of 85 percent occurred at Grays Lake, Idaho (Steel et al. 1956); the lowest, 15 percent, was in the Flathead Valley of Montana (Lokemoen 1966), where dump nesting and desertion were the principal reasons for failure. In many other areas nest success was similar to the overall average.

Redheads have an unusually large number of unhatched eggs among successful nests. In studies that reported 661 successful nests, an average of 5.4 eggs failed to hatch for each nest. Many eggs were dislodged from the nest and were found floating beside it. About a fourth of the eggs left in the nest were infertile and three-fourths contained dead embryos. The unusually high proportion of eggs with dead embryos probably indicates the extent to which intruder hens laid eggs after the host hen began to incubate. An average clutch of 11.1 eggs yields about 5.7 ducklings at hatching. Thus, the parasitic egg-laying trait so well developed in the redhead leads to a great wastage of eggs. From 44 to 77 percent of the redhead eggs laid in host nests studied by Weller (1959) were deposited after incubation began.

But the redhead's parasitic habit gains an unknown number of recruits from its eggs hatched by other species. According to Olson (1964), about 50 percent of the redheads produced on pothole habitats in Manitoba were reared in canvasback broods. Although canvasbacks appear to be the principal victims of the redhead's parasitism, mallards, blue-winged and cinnamon teals, lesser scaups, and ruddy ducks are also victimized. Lokemoen (1966) observed that of 57 redhead eggs laid in the nests of four other species, 14 percent hatched.

Nest Failure. The redhead appears to be its own worst enemy. Of the nests failing to hatch, 37 percent (136) were deserted, many because of the intrusion of parasitic females. In 131 nests where the cause of nest destruction was identified, mammals accounted for 42 percent, birds 27 percent, and flooding 30 percent. Skunks and raccoons were the principal mammal offenders identified. Skunks apparently destroyed redhead nests that were either built on dry land or where the water receded from the nest sites. Recent reports from the prairie breeding grounds indicate that the raccoon is a more important predator of redhead and canvasback nests on those areas than during earlier studies.

Raccoons are relatively recent arrivals on the prairie pothole scene (Kiel et al. 1972). Manitoba fur buyers received no raccoon pelts between 1924 and 1946. From 1947 to 1953, they purchased an average of 61 per year. This figure rose to an average yearly take of 663 pelts, 1959-63. This phenomenal increase of raccoons on important breeding grounds for redheads, canvasbacks, and ruddy ducks poses a serious threat to the future of these ducks. Water is no barrier to raccoons as it is to skunks. Consequently a new dimension has been added to the predation faced by marsh-nesting ducks.

Crows, magpies, and California gulls accounted for the bird destruction of redhead nests. Crows and magpies confined their depredations to the prairies, gulls to the Intermountain marshes. In addition to the nest studies summarized here, (Odin 1957) specifically studied the effect of California gulls on duck nests at Farmington Bay, Utah. He found that gulls destroyed 29 percent of the poorly concealed redhead nests but none of the well-concealed ones.

A sudden rise in water level accounted for 21 percent of the destroyed redhead nests in the Ruthven, Iowa, area (Low 1945) and for 24 of 28 nests destroyed in the Klamath Basin (Rienecker and Anderson 1960).

Low water levels in ponds on the prairie breeding grounds apparently produce a psychological deterrent to breeding by redheads. David Trauger observed many pairs in the Minnedosa pothole district of Manitoba in 1973, but only a few adults and not a single marked yearling attempted to nest. None was known to be successful. The prevailing drought lowered water levels in deep ponds, resulting in a ring of bare earth between the water and marsh vegetation on the potholes—an unattractive prospect for nesting redheads.

Renesting. Low (1945) in northwest Iowa considered that redhead nests started late in June were probably renests and amounted to 10 percent of the total nesting effort. In northwest Montana, Lokemoen (1966) believed that 15 percent of 138 nests were renests. Weller (1959), on the contrary, felt that renesting was unlikely because peak nesting in June would be followed by a renesting peak in July—and he found no new nests after June. Their late schedule of nesting in Canada would preclude any significant degree of renesting.

Rearing of Young

Broods. Just before the hatch, the hen redhead utters a low *kuk-kuk-kuk*, a call that imprints the young to follow the hen after hatching (Weller 1959). The ducklings remain in the nest from 3 to 18 hours after hatching, but usually only long enough for the down to dry (Low 1945). The hen redhead is reputed to be a poor mother, deserting her young at an early age. On the Delta Marsh, Weller (1959) observed a redhead brood without an accompanying hen on June 22-30, and by August 15-21, 11 of 12 broods were motherless. Redhead hens in Iowa were more attentive. Low (1945) observed that most broods were led by hens until 8 weeks of age. Large-scale desertions did not take place until August 8-15.

In the prairie potholes of South Dakota, redhead broods were found by Evans and Black (1956) to frequent open water areas 94 percent and deep marshes 6 percent of the time. Marked broods showed a mobility about midway between wide-ranging pintails and sedentary ruddy duck broods (Evans et al. 1952). They averaged 0.009 mile per day. However, Low (1945) found ducklings, just a week out of their nest, some 2 miles away in a different body of water. He observed broods cross a 40-acre water area several times daily.

Development. According to Low (1945), juvenile redheads in Iowa flapped across the water at 56 days and flew at 70 to 84 days of age. At Delta Marsh, Manitoba, Hochbaum (1944) observed that hand-reared juveniles required 63 to 77 days to learn to fly, but Weller (1957) noted that wild-reared birds required fewer days, 56 to 73. Near Minnedosa, Manitoba, Evans et al. (1952) observed that a redhead brood reached Class II stage at the age of 28 days, Class III at the age of 49 days, and flight stage at 56 days.

Survival. Extensive brood counts across the redhead's breeding range have revealed a Class I size of 6.2 (1,925), which is higher than the calculation of 5.7 ducklings per brood at hatch. These counts suggest that the figure derived from the data on unhatched eggs per nest was too high at 5.4. Class II broods averaged 5.9 (1,105), a decrease of a mere 4.8 percent, and Class III averaged 5.6 ducklings, a decrease of 10 percent from Class I. Although female redheads desert their broods early in life, both Low (1945) and Evans et al. (1952) observed that the broods remained as units until they could fly. Thus, the data probably reflect the number of redheads reaching flight stage per successful female and also demonstrate a survival of ducklings on a par with other species in spite of the female redhead's low level of attentiveness.

In view of the high mortality rates in the redhead, Hickey (1952) concluded that to maintain a stable population, each pair would need to produce 3.6 young as of September 1. However, only 52 percent of those that nest are successful, and there is little recruitment from renesting. Moreover, in some years perhaps fewer than half of the hens even attempt to nest. Thus, the production of young per hen may vary from 2.7 flying young per female to perhaps as low as 1.3. Because there are one-third more drakes than hens, the production ratio of adults to immatures becomes 1:1.08 as a high and 1:0.52 as a low. Age ratios, 1966-73, disclosed an estimated 0.98 young per adult in the fall population.

POSTBREEDING SEASON

Recoveries of summer-banded redheads indicate that some adults and young migrate northward after the nesting season (Low 1945, Weller 1964). The adult males leave their nest marshes on the prairies in late June and July for the wing molt; large numbers move northward to a string of lakes between the edge of the Laurentian Shield and the parklands from the Saskatchewan Delta to the Athabasca Delta.

Hochbaum (1944) first described the postbreeding concentration of redheads, canvasbacks, and lesser scaups in some of these northern lakes. On an aerial survey, August 14-17, 1939, he observed large concentrations of flightless drakes of these three species on Swan, Kawinaw, and Belanger lakes near The Pas, Manitoba. Subsequent survey flights by personnel of Ducks Unlimited have found many thousands concentrated during August and early September on Lakes Macallum, Kazan, Niska, Upper and Lower Cummins, Little Clarke, and Waterhen.

On Long Island Bay, a part of Lake Winnipegosis, Manitoba, Bergman (1973) observed that numerous adult male redheads commenced arriving there between mid- and late July. Numbers continued to increase through the first half of August in 1970 and during the entire month in 1969 to reach 10,000 or more. Adult males, which comprised more than 90 percent of this population in 1970, apparently gathered there for the wing molt. Populations declined in early September as some of the molters regained flight and departed. A second influx followed in late September and the first half of October as redheads moved in from other molt areas. Peak populations of 18,000 and 20,000, 1969-70, were reached immediately prior to fall departure in late October.

Weller (1957) reported that the body plumage of yearling males becomes dull in late June as they begin to enter the eclipse molt. They become flightless in July and August and renew their wing and body feathers in August and September. Flight feathers are fully renewed and hardened in 5 to 6 weeks.

FOOD HABITS

Redheads are more prevalent feeders in marshes, sloughs, and ponds than other divers. Like ring-necked ducks, they tend to feed in waters only a few feet deep, sometimes so shallow that they do not need to dive. In such instances they feed like dabblers, either tipping up or immersing their heads to glean bottom soils.

In keeping with the habitats they frequent, redheads feed more extensively on aquatic plants and less on animal life than other diving ducks. The foods taken by redheads, as determined from gizzards collected in 26 states and 5 provinces, consisted of 90 percent plant and 10 percent animal life (Cottam 1939). Pondweed seeds, tubers, and leaves composed almost a third of the foods consumed. Muskgrass and other algae formed slightly over a fifth of the food items. Bulrush seeds, wild celery, duckweeds, water lily seeds, and coontail were other important aquatic plants in their diet.

Pondweeds were also the single most important group of plants found in the redhead's diet in many areas across the continent: Currituck Sound, North Carolina, 76 percent (Quay and Critcher 1965); Chesapeake Bay, 50 to 75 percent by occurrence (Stewart 1962); Tennessee, 27 percent (Rawls 1954); Missouri, 21 percent (Korschgen 1955); and Illinois, 33 percent (Anderson 1959). Sago, widgeon grass, naiads, longleaf, and leafy were the principal pondweeds consumed. Coontail was an important item at Reelfoot Lake, Tennessee, and in Illinois.

On the redheads' principal winter ground on the Laguna Madre, Texas, shoalgrass composed 84 percent and widgeon grass 10 percent of the food consumed (McMahan 1970). Animal foods made up a mere 2.1 percent. At Apalachee Bay, Florida, another important winter area for redheads, shoalgrass comprised 85 percent of the food taken and animal foods 14 percent.

In southwestern Manitoba in the fall, redheads fed almost exclusively on muskgrass plant structures (Bartonek and Hickey 1969). Adult male and female redheads on their Manitoba breeding grounds fed more on animal than on plant life during the spring and summer. Caddis flies and midges were the principal animal foods taken, and pondweed winter buds formed the bulk of the plant items. Bartonek and Hickey (1969) found that juvenile redheads fed about equally on plants and animals. Their favorite plant foods were muskgrass oogonia and whitetop grass seeds; favorite animal foods were caddis flies, water fleas, and pond snails.

Ring-Necked Duck

Aythya collaris

Other Common Names: Ring-billed duck, ringbill, blackjack

VITAL STATISTICS

Length:	Adult male, 16.1-18.3 inches, average 17.2 inches (71) Adult female, 15.6-17.5 inches, average 16.6 inches (54) Immature male, 16.1-18.1 inches, average 17.0 inches (39) Immature female, 15.6-17.5 inches, average 16.4 inches (38)
Wing:	Adult male, 7.99 inches (94) Adult female, 7.64 inches (72) Immature male, 7.96 inches (60) Immature female, 7.52 inches (54)
Weight:	Adult male, 1.3-2.0 pounds, average 1.64 pounds (47) Adult female, 1.2-2.0 pounds, average 1.48 pounds (30) Immature male, 1.2-2.0 pounds, average 1.56 pounds (70) Immature female, 1.1-2.0 pounds, average 1.50 pounds (65)

IDENTIFICATION

Field

Ring-necked ducks bear a superficial resemblance to scaups but are more likely to frequent marshes, wooded ponds, bottomland lakes, and open areas in swamps. They occur in smaller flocks than scaups, usually no more than 20, and fly in compact wedges. Like all members of this genus, they fly swiftly and their wing beats are rapid. Perhaps because of the habitat they occupy, ringnecks dart about more, like teal, than do other divers.

The uniformly dark wings of the ringneck distinguish it in flight from the scaups, which have single white bars on their wings. On the water, the black back of the adult male ringneck appears noticeably darker than the gray backs of the scaups; the contrast between back and side is greater in the ringneck. The male in full plumage displays a white triangle in front of the wing. Despite its small size, this white triangle shows up surprisingly well at a distance, delineated by the black breast, back, and wing, and the gray sides. The black head appears angular rather than rounded.

Female ringnecks are brownish with white bellies, thus resembling scaups, but they lack the distinct white facial patches and white wing bars of the scaups. The single white bars across the blue bills of both sexes are noticeable at close range. In general appearance, female ringnecks resemble female redheads, although the ringnecks are smaller.

Ringnecks seldom call during the fall. Mendall (1958) described the female's call as a soft "purring growl," low-pitched during courtship display and when curious or mildly disturbed but shorter and higher pitched when frightened.

At Hand

The ring-necked duck is inappropriately named, for the chestnut-brown ring on the black neck of the male in nuptial plumage is barely discernible even in the hand. The transverse white bar separating the black bill tip from the gray-blue bill is much more apparent. Moreover, the base of the bill in the male is bordered by a white line, but, as pointed out by Mendall (1958), this white line is lacking in the female and is shown incorrectly in the color plate of this book. The black head and neck of the male show purplish reflections, and the long partially raised feathers of the crown give the head its angular shape. Although less conspicuous in the female, the angular head shape provides the best means of distinguishing the female ringneck from the almost identical but round-headed female redhead. The whitish eye-ring, more pronounced in the ringneck, is also a means of separating females in the two species. The white bar on the bill of the female ringneck is much less distinct than the white patches displayed by female scaups but is more conspicuous than in the female redhead. The feet and legs are gray-blue, as in the scaups, the redhead, and the canvasback. Most adult hens in both ring-necked ducks and redheads have small white feathers on the napes of their necks (Arthur Hawkins).

Males in eclipse plumage resemble females but are slightly darker. Only faint traces of the white bill markings and brown neck-rings persist. By early October, except for brownish heads and necks, adult males have regained their nuptial plumage, which is virtually completed early in November (Mendall 1958). Immature male ringnecks assume their nuptial plumage by mid-November.

The wings are brown-black in males and dark brown in females. The secondaries in both sexes are pearl-gray, dusky near the tips, and edged faintly with white. In males the tertials are pointed and green-black; in females they are rounded and green-brown. Middle coverts are broadly rounded and smooth in adults and narrow, square-tipped, and usually rough in immatures.

POPULATION STATUS

Prior to the 1930's the ring-necked duck was uncommon in the Northeast but became an increasingly abundant migrant between 1930 and 1935 (Mendall 1958). During the next two decades, it became established as a breeding bird over an extensive region of the Northeast. After pioneering new areas, breeding populations rapidly increased in numbers but then became stabilized as habitats apparently approached saturation levels.

Although drought is not as serious a problem for ringnecks as it is for prairie-nesting ducks, ringneck numbers wax and wane according to production, which is adversely affected by floods, low temperature, and other inclement weather. Favorable hunting conditions and regulations also may result in excessive kills in some years, so that fewer ringnecks return to breed.

Annual inventories (1955-73) indicate that an average of 460,000 ringnecks occupy the principal breeding grounds. Annual populations have ranged from a low of 152,000 in 1957 to a high of 744,000 in 1971. Winter inventory data, 1955-74, show large oscillations in abundance but no significant trend over the 20-year period. Among the four flyways, numbers have declined in the Atlantic, increased in the Mississippi, and remained about the same in the Central and Pacific.

Age Ratios

The proportion of adults to immatures in hunters' bags, 1966-73, was 1:2.08, almost the same as the ratio for redheads. The highest proportion of young (1:2.55) occurred in 1967 and the lowest (1:1.62) in 1968, a range of 64 percent. Meager banding data suggest that immatures are more readily shot by hunters than adults on the order of 1.20:1. This ratio may be too low, for immature scaups and redheads have a higher vulnerability ratio. However poor it may be, using it as a correction factor indicates that the fall population contains 1.7 immatures per adult, the highest ratio among all ducks.

Sex Ratios

Among adult ringnecks in hunters' bags, 1966-73, 64.3 percent were males; among immatures, the percentage of males was 51.2. Spring sex ratios recorded visually in many areas of the United States indicated that populations of ring-necked ducks contained 61.4 percent males (Bellrose et al. 1961). Mendall (1958) recorded 62 percent drakes on breeding grounds in Maine, 58 percent in New Brunswick. In Wisconsin, Jahn and Hunt (1964) found that drakes comprised 62.4 percent of the spring populations. Thus, there are about 5 surplus drakes for every 10 hens at the beginning of the breeding season.

Mortality

Smith (1963) calculated annual mortality rates for ring-necked ducks from winter and spring bandings. In those states where shooting pressure was the heaviest, annual mortality among males was also the highest: with a direct band recovery rate of 8.8 percent, mortality was 53 percent; 6.2 percent recovery, mortality 43 percent; 4.8 percent recovery, mortality 39 percent; and 2.5 percent recovery, mortality 28 percent.

Among hens, the relationship between band recoveries and mortality was not so close, probably because females suffered large nonhunting mortality during the nest and brood seasons prior to the first band recoveries. A comparison of direct band recoveries with annual mortality rates for four groups of states combined by similar shooting rates yielded the following percentages for females: 7.4 percent band recovery, mortality 56 percent; 5.5 percent, mortality 65 percent; 4.9 percent, mortality 45 percent; 4.6 percent, mortality 43 percent.

Because of high hunting losses, immature ringnecks banded in Minnesota suffered a first-year mortality of 77 percent. Females banded in Louisiana, 1929-41, had an annual mortality rate of 54 percent, males 43 percent.

DISTRIBUTION

Breeding Range

The ring-necked duck reaches its largest breeding numbers of 265,000 (0.66 per square mile) in the closed boreal forest of the District of Mackenzie and northern Alberta, Saskatchewan, and Manitoba. It is somewhat less abundant in the closed boreal forest to the east, numbering 50,000 (0.20 per square mile) in Ontario. Its abundance also fades to the northward in the open boreal forest, where about 70,000 (0.34 per square mile) occur. Barely 1,500 reach the Mackenzie Delta and only 100 the interior of Alaska.

The ringneck is not only averse to the Arctic but also exhibits little liking for the grasslands. It falls to its lowest breeding density (0.03 per square mile) in the shortgrass association of Montana and southern Alberta, where it numbers a scant 4,600. In the mixed prairie north of the shortgrass prairie, it is slightly more abundant, numbering 16,000 (0.11 per square mile). It again increases in abundance northward in the parklands, where almost 40,000 (0.30 per square mile) breed.

Because of the high quality marsh habitat in a limited area, ringnecks reach their greatest breeding density, 3.6 per square mile (72,000), on the Saskatchewan River delta, the Athabasca River delta, and the Slave River parklands.

The largest numbers of ringnecks breeding in the United States occur in the Great Lakes states. Of the approximately 25,000 found in that region, Minnesota and Michigan each have 10,000 and Wisconsin harbors 6,500. Most of the Michigan population is confined to the Upper Peninsula, but small numbers nest in the upper part of the Lower Peninsula.

A breeding population of slightly under 30,000 occupies the mountain valleys and basins from northeast California to slightly north of the 56° parallel in British Columbia. About 93 percent of this population occurs in British Columbia, 5 percent in the northern highlands and the Columbia Basin of Washington, and 2 percent east of the Cascade Mountains in Oregon and in northeastern California.

Breeding populations of ring-necked ducks in the Northeast are not regularly surveyed from aircraft. Consequently, their numbers can only be crudely determined by other means. These rough estimates suggest that about 2,500 ringnecks breed in Newfoundland, 2,000 in Nova Scotia, 1,000 in Prince Edward Island, 3,500 in New Brunswick, and 12,000 in Quebec. In northeastern United States, Sutherland (1971) calculated breeding numbers to be 6,000 in Maine, and 1,000 in both New Hampshire and New York (the Adirondacks).

A few small isolated breeding colonies of ringnecks occur elsewhere, in North Park and the San Luis Valley of Colorado, the White Mountains of Arizona, and, formerly, Pymatuning Lake, Pennsylvania.

Migration Corridors

There is a pronounced eastward passage of ring-necked ducks from their breeding grounds in the Prairie Provinces of Canada to Ontario and the eastern United States. Band recoveries suggest that about a third of the ringnecks from Alberta and one-twentieth of those from Saskatchewan visit Ontario prior to migrating farther south. Almost half of those bred in Ontario end up in Florida. Ringnecks from Maine, New Brunswick, and other breeding grounds in the Northeast migrate in a corridor along the coast to winter grounds in South Carolina and Florida. But the bulk of Florida's ringnecks are received almost equally from Ontario, Manitoba, and the District of Mackenzie. The most important migration corridor to Florida passes south-southeastward through Wisconsin, Indiana, Tennessee, and Georgia.

The largest fall concentrations occur in Minnesota, Wisconsin, and the Upper Peninsula of Michigan, where surveys in 1954-56 placed peak estimates at 180,000. On October 24, 1968, 88,000 were estimated to be on Nett Lake in northern Minnesota; 25,000 on the Rice Lake National Wildlife Refuge; 10,000 in Squaw Lake, Itasca County; and 17,000 elsehwere in the state (Benson 1969).

Wisconsin and the Upper Peninsula of Michigan are frequented by about three-fourths as many ringnecks as are found in Minnesota. Although both Minnesota and Wisconsin produce many ringnecks, the bulk of their fall populations appears to be derived from the District of Mackenzie, Saskatchewan, and Manitoba.

One of the three largest migration corridors extends southeastward across Minnesota to the Mississippi River in southern Iowa and from there south to southern Louisiana. Another corridor, almost as large, extends south-southeastward from southeastern Manitoba to western Louisiana and the east coast of Texas. Louisiana hosts the largest number of wintering ringnecks and receives over half of its birds from Manitoba, a fifth from the District of Mackenzie, and a tenth from Alberta. Almost half of the ringnecks visiting Texas are from Alberta, a fifth from Mackenzie, and over a tenth from Saskatchewan.

Only small numbers of ringnecks appear west of the eastern Great Plains. Between 1,000 and 2,000 follow migration corridors south from Saskatchewan to New Mexico and the Northern Highlands of Mexico. California winters about half of the ringnecks in the Pacific states. Almost 70 percent of these birds are derived from British Columbia, 15 percent from Saskatchewan, 9 percent from Alberta, and 6 percent from Washington.

Winter Areas

Ninety-two percent of the 300,000 ring-necked ducks found on January surveys winter in the eastern half of the continent: 44 percent in the Atlantic Flyway and 48 percent in the Mississippi Flyway. Including Mexico, about 5 percent winter in the Central Flyway and 3 percent in the Pacific.

Along the Atlantic Coast, ringnecks winter in small numbers from New Jersey to North Carolina, and with the exception of Georgia, in increasing numbers from there into Florida. Over half winter in Florida, particularly in the Lake Okeechobee area, where about 35,000 concentrate. On winter survey flights in the West Indies, Walter Crissey

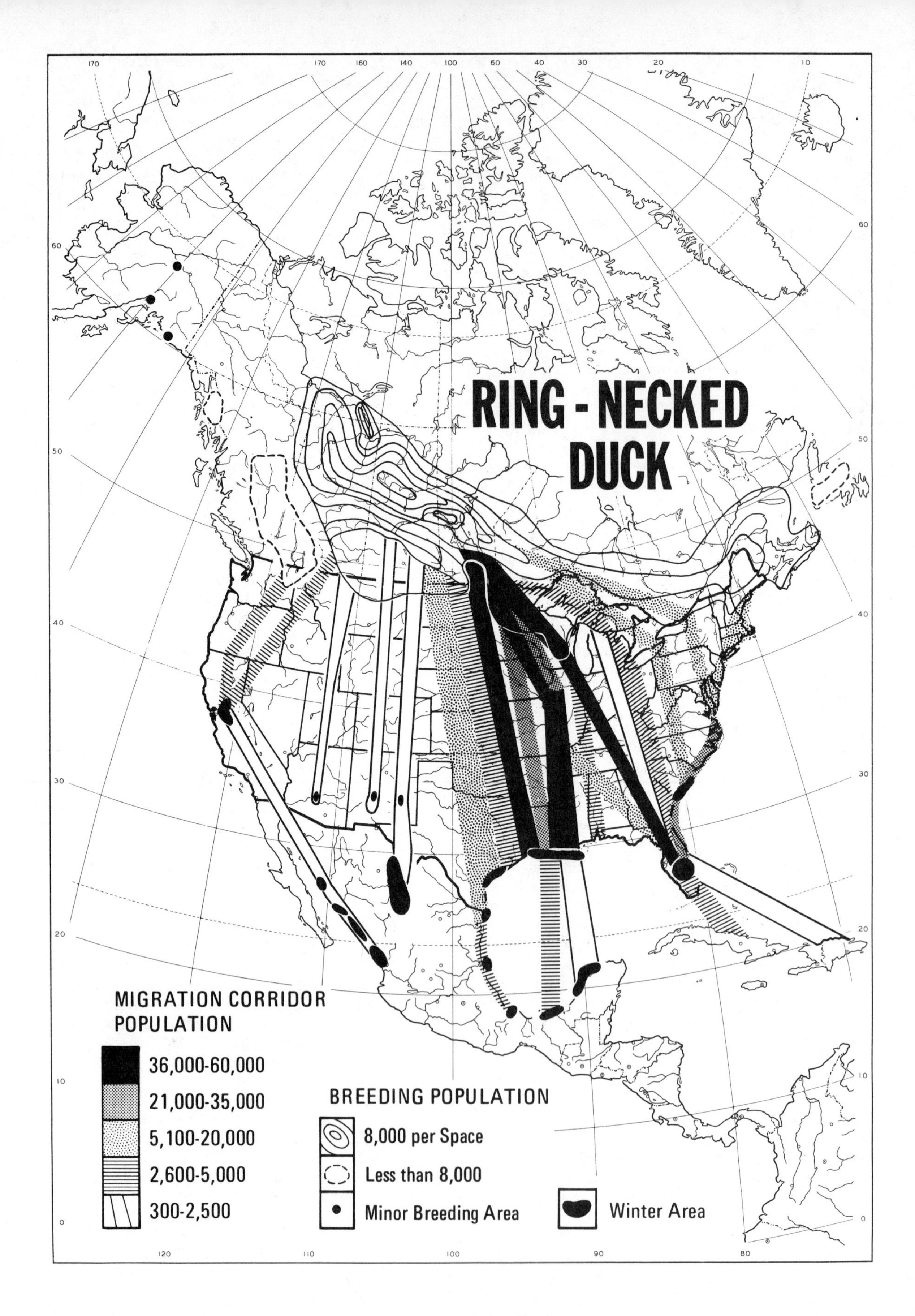
RING - NECKED
DUCK
MIGRATION CORRIDOR
POPULATION
36,000-60,000
21,000-35,000
5,100-20,000
2,600-5,000
300-2,500
BREEDING POPULATION
8,000 per Space
Less than 8,000
Minor Breeding Area
Winter Area

observed 15,000 ring-necked ducks in Cuba and 5,500 in the Dominican Republic.

A few of the 110,000 ringnecks found wintering in the Mississippi Flyway occur as far north as Minnesota, but large numbers are found only from Tennessee to Louisiana. Two-thirds (73,000) make Louisiana their winter home; there they find both the flooded swamps and the freshwater marshes to their liking.

Slightly over 10,000 ringnecks winter along the Gulf Coast from east Texas to Yucatan. Even these low densities dwindle from Corpus Christi south to Veracruz. A greater abundance (3,600) in Tabasco and Yucatan suggests that these ringnecks may cross the Gulf from Louisiana. About 200 are found in the Northern Highlands of Mexico, but over 1,000 elect to winter farther north in New Mexico.

About 6,000 ringnecks winter in scattered flocks along the Pacific Coast from British Columbia to Guatemala, over a third of them confined to the Central Valley of California. Fewer than 300 have been found along the west coast of Mexico, but some as far as San Marcos. Saunders et al. (1950) recorded this species in Guatemala, at Lake Petén and on interior highland lakes.

It is apparent that many ringnecks are missed on winter surveys, particularly in the Central and Pacific flyways. The kill of ringnecks, 1962-68, averaged almost 35,000 in the Central Flyway and about 24,000 in the Pacific Flyway. Obviously, the winter populations of ringnecks in these two flyways are several times greater than those recorded.

MIGRATION BEHAVIOR

Ring-necked ducks migrate in flocks of 20 to 60 birds, usually in a "train" formation. Their fall departure from a Maine lake is graphically described by Mendall (1958:162-3): "In the mid-forenoon on the twenty-first [October] the birds were generally in 2 large groups. They were very restless and fed intermittently, often rising and circling the marsh fairly high in flocks of 25 to 50. Between feeding they rafted together in the open water in numbers larger than usual, oblivious to the rapidly increasing wind. About half an hour before sunset, approximately 75 birds rose from the largest of the resting flocks, circled the lake twice at an elevation well in excess of 500 feet, rose even higher, then disappeared beyond the valley in a straight line, heading due southwest. Within the next 15 minutes 3 more flocks of 40, 30, and 45 birds each, rose from the lake, behaving about like the first group, and disappeared at a height which I estimated at between 600 and 1,000 feet in the same southwest course."

Their passage into eastern North Dakota and western Minnesota commences early in September, reaches peak numbers by mid-October, and is all but complete by mid-November. Farther east, from central Minnesota through Michigan, the migration pattern is similar but the timing is about 2 weeks later. And farther south in the Midwest there is another lag of 2 weeks, with peak numbers about mid-November. South of the Midwest, ringnecks begin to arrive on their winter grounds in Arkansas and Louisiana in mid-October, with numbers increasing for the next 4 to 6 weeks.

The rinkneck's chronology of passage through the eastern and the high Great Plains is similar: arrive in September, reach peak numbers by late October, steadily egress to mid-December, and reach winter grounds in Texas from late October into December.

Chronology

Fall. Ring-necked ducks are midseason migrants, not as early as many species and not as late as others. Wide variations in their departures from breeding grounds in the Northeast could not be correlated with variations in weather, but early successful nesting seasons resulted in early movements from breeding marshes (Mendall 1958).

In strictly migration areas, ringnecks have a less variable migration profile than most other ducks, as though they are less influenced by local weather than by their own internal synchrony of behavioral activity. They begin to arrive on the Middle Atlantic coast in early October, reach peak numbers late in November, and decline through December to wintering levels. Late in October they arrive on the southeast Atlantic Seaboard and in Florida, with numbers steadily rising through November to peak winter populations in December.

In the mountain valleys and basins of northwest United States, ringnecks appear in late September, reach peak numbers in early November, and gradually depart through December for winter grounds in the Central Valley of California. Migrants reach the valley early in October and steadily increase in number through December. On the northwest coast, where only small numbers winter, peak populations occur late in November.

Spring. Wherever they may winter, ring-necked ducks begin to leave their winter grounds early in February. Their departures continue at a steady pace through March, but it is late April before the last tardy ringnecks leave. They reach midmigration areas early in March and peak numbers early in April, with small numbers lingering into May. On northern migration areas that are also southern extensions of the breeding grounds, ringnecks begin to arrive from mid- to late March, with populations steadily increasing through April.

BREEDING

Behavior

Age, Pair Bond, and Homing. All evidence indicates that most ring-necked ducks breed when they are 1 year old. Some pair bonds are established as early as October, but in Maine, Mendall (1958) has observed many unpaired birds arriving in early spring flights. He reported that among early-nesting ringnecks, males remain with their mates until the fourth week of incubation and in some instances until the days of hatching. However, among

RING-NECKED DUCK

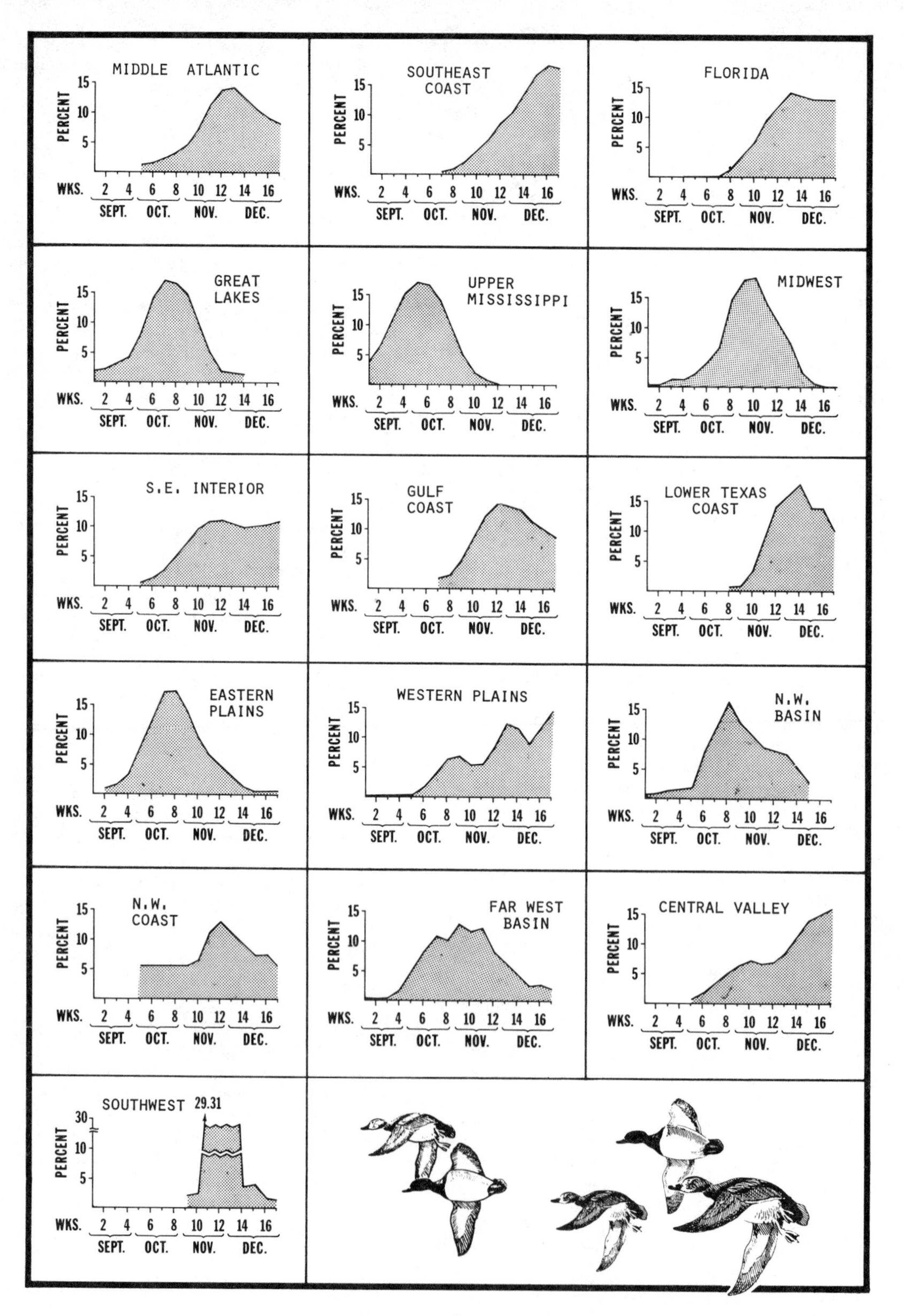

Fall

RING-NECKED DUCK

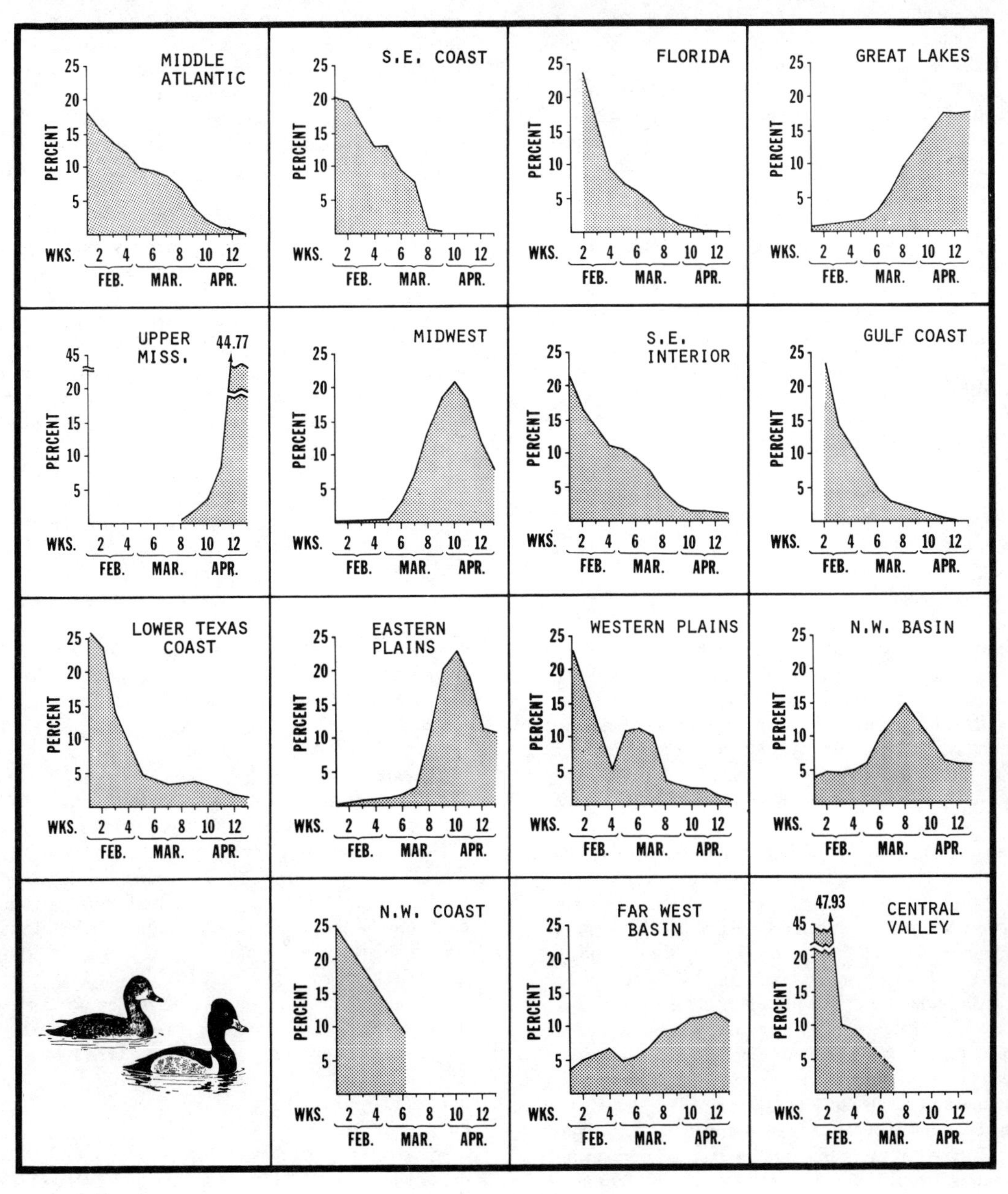

Spring

late-nesting birds, drakes desert their hens early during the incubation period, usually by the second week. On the other hand, some drakes may accompany unsuccessful hens, which make only one nest effort, to molt areas.

Banded juvenile and adult females both returned in subsequent years to nest on their same breeding grounds (Mendall 1958). Although the banding sample was small, 22 nests located on or within a few feet of a previous year's successful nest also suggested homing. Coulter and Miller (1968) reported that 3 of 10 banded ringneck hens returned to nest in the same area.

Home Range. On Maine breeding grounds, Mendall (1958) observed a spacing of pairs but very little aggression between them. The spacing was most evident just prior to laying but largely disappeared by the time incubation began. On various areas, maximum densities of breeding pairs ranged from one pair per 6 acres to one pair per 23 acres. Mendall concluded that their more modest home range requirements and lack of aggression enable ringnecks to nest in higher densities than do other ducks in northeastern United States.

Nesting

Nest Sites. Unlike most dabbling ducks, which nest in areas adjacent to marshland, ring-necked ducks nest in marshes, particularly favoring those at least partially surrounded by wooded vegetation. The female, followed by the male, swims along the border of marsh growth, probing and further investigating leads of water (Mendall 1958). The female alone explores clumps or beds of marsh vegetation while the male waits in open water. Early-breeding birds, interrupted by cold weather, may delay laying a week or more after selecting the nest site. Late-arriving hens may start laying within a few days of finding a nest site.

Almost half (47.9 percent) of the ring-necked duck nests (518) Mendall (1958) found in Maine were on islets of floating marsh plants, 38.4 percent were in clumps of marsh vegetation, 9.1 percent on solid islands, and 4.6 percent in miscellaneous sites. By far the largest proportion of nests (69.3 percent of 411) were an association of sedge, sweet gale, and leather leaf. Ten percent were in sedges associated with various plants other than the above. Sedge was also the cover plant chosen by 79 percent of the ringnecks found nesting in the Saskatchewan River delta, Saskatchewan (Townsend 1966). Much of this sedge was floating on a mat of decayed vegetation; 46 percent of the nests (46 nests) were on this floating mat, 26 percent on semifloating material, and 28 percent on a solid footing.

Most nest sites of ring-necked ducks are within a few feet of small openings in sedge marshes, but in both Maine and the Saskatchewan Delta, nests averaged slightly over 80 feet from a water expanse sufficiently large for the ducks to land and take flight.

According to Mendall (1958), egg-laying and nest-building occur almost simultaneously. A few flattened plants provide the base for the first eggs, but not until about the sixth egg does the nest assume a cup shape. Some down is then added, the eggs are covered for the first time, and overhead plants are occasionally woven to form a canopy. Most, but not all, nests contain a large amount of down during incubation. In Mendall's (1958) study, inside measurements of the nest cup ranged from 5 to 7 inches in diameter and 2 to 4 inches in depth.

Ringnecks often nest close together. In Maine, Mendall (1958) found two active nests on a floating islet of vegetation 10 by 15 feet and six nests on a 0.25-acre island.

Clutch Size, Eggs, and Incubation. Eggs are laid usually in midmorning at the rate of one per day, the laying visits lasting from 15 minutes to 3 hours (Mendall 1958). Clutch size was remarkably similar (9.0 to 9.3 eggs) in Minnesota (Moyle et al. 1964), Maine (Mendall 1958), and Redvers, Saskatchewan (Stoudt 1971). Clutches were slightly smaller, 8.4 eggs, on the Saskatchewan Delta (Townsend 1966) and in California, 7.9 eggs (Hunt and Anderson 1966). Overall, they averaged 9.0 eggs (535 nests) and ranged from 5 to 14 eggs. Renests averaged 7 eggs in Maine compared with 9 eggs for initial nests, and renests averaged 7.8 in California compared with 7.9 eggs in first nests.

Eggs of ring-necked ducks are elliptical, 57.5 by 39.8 mm in size, and are colored in various shades of olive-buff (Bent 1923). Incubation periods range from 25 to 29 days, averaging 26 days (Mendall 1958), and incubation usually begins the day the last egg is laid. Hens usually leave their nests in the early morning and late afternoon hours. Males fly to join their mates when the hens leave their nests if the distance is over 100 yards; if closer, they swim to meet their mates.

Chronology of Nesting. Ringnecks begin to nest in early May in Maine (Mendall 1958), northern Wisconsin (Jahn and Hunt 1964), and the Saskatchewan River delta (Townsend 1966), and in mid-June at Yellowknife, Northwest Territories (Murdy 1964). Peak nest initiation occurred May 23 in Maine, May 25 in northern Wisconsin, and early June in the Saskatchewan Delta. The last nests are started about July 3 in Maine, June 22 in Wisconsin, July 3 in the Saskatchewan Delta, and July 24 at Yellowknife.

The span of nest initiation comprises approximately 60 days in Maine, 56 days in northern Wisconsin, 55 days on the Saskatchewan Delta, and 30 days (12 to 44 days) in Yellowknife, where the ringneck is reaching the northern limit of its range.

Nest Success. Studies on the nest success of the ring-necked duck have been limited to four areas of North America: Maine (Mendall 1958), western Minnesota (Lee et al. 1964), Redvers, Saskatchewan (Stoudt 1971), and the Saskatchewan Delta (Townsend 1966). On these areas, the overall nest success amounted to 67 percent (642 nests), ranging from 38 percent at Redvers to 80 percent on the Saskatchewan Delta. In Maine, where the most extensive study occurred, success was 69 percent (522 nests). There,

83 percent of the nests on floating islets were successful, 62 percent of those on open marsh, 53 percent on solid islands, 28 percent on floating logs, and 33 percent in woods or dry meadow areas.

An average of 0.5 egg failed to hatch in 329 initial nests that were successful (Mendall 1958). The fate of 164 unhatched eggs resulted from infertility (42.3 percent), dead embryos (27.3 percent), predation (12.4 percent), displacement (7.2 percent), and disappearance (10.8 percent).

Nest Failure. Nest losses in Maine are due to predation (79 percent), flooding (16 percent), and desertion (5 percent) (Mendall 1958). Minks caused 30 percent of the predator losses, crows and ravens 22 percent, and raccoons 19 percent. At Redvers, Saskatchewan, crows and magpies accounted for 44 percent of the ringneck nest losses, and skunks for 32 percent (Stoudt 1971).

Renesting. Some ring-necked ducks renest when their first nests are destroyed. Mendall (1958) believed that at least half of the hens that suffer nest losses will attempt to renest. Coulter and Miller (1968) reported that when many ringneck nests in a small area in Maine were lost, pairs gathered in flocks and made no effort to nest again. When scattered nest losses occurred, however, 8 of 18 hens (31 percent) renested. Eight of 10 marked hens in northern California were known to renest (Hunt and Anderson 1966).

Both Mendall (1958) and Coulter and Miller (1968) reported that renest intervals ranged from 6 to 10 days in Maine. The span between nest attempts in northern California varied from 8 to 21 days (Hunt and Anderson 1966). One remarkable female renested twice at intervals of 17 and 11 days!

In Maine, renesting hens selected new sites 300 to 1,760 yards from their first nests (Mendall 1958, Coulter and Miller 1968). In California, renests averaged 591 yards from sites of the first nests (Hunt and Anderson 1966).

Clutch sizes in renests averaged 7.0 eggs in Maine, 2 less than in initial clutches, and 7.8 in California, only a 0.1 egg reduction from first clutches. Sixty-one percent of the Maine renests were successful, compared with 70 percent of the initial nests.

Rearing of Young

Broods. After the hatch, the female continues to brood her young for 12 to 20 hours, and, if the immediate area lacks dry sites, she may return at intervals during the first 4 or 5 days to brood them on the nest (Mendall 1958). Although the young begin to dive when only a few days old, they feed largely by dabbling on the surface; when about half grown, they dive for food almost entirely (Beard 1964). During the morning, ringneck broods spend almost 100 minutes feeding and about half that long sleeping. Where loafing mounds are scarce at the Seney National Wildlife Refuge, ringneck hens and their broods sometimes appropriate sites occupied by wigeon broods.

Mendall (1958) observed that most ringneck hens remain with their broods until flight stage. Even some flightless hens have been found still accompanying their young. When he once disturbed broods on a water area, five of the six fled on foot to another slough 0.5 mile away. Although broods of goldeneye frequently combine, as do broods of common eider and broods of common merganser, there is no evidence that ringneck broods do so (Mendall 1958).

Development. According to Mendall (1958), young ring-necked ducks remain in the down (Class I) stage about 16 days. Body feathers appear among the down successively along the sides, flanks, head, breast, and belly until the body is completely feathered in slightly over 5 weeks (Class II). The Class III stage extends from about 5.5 weeks to the flying stage—7 to 8 weeks.

Survival. From a hatch of about 8.5 eggs in successful nests, 7.81 ducklings (863) survive in Class I broods, a loss of 8.1 percent. Ducklings in Class II broods average 6.09 (585), and those in Class III broods 5.45 (213). Broods that escape complete annihilation undergo a 36 percent mortality from hatch to flight.

POSTBREEDING SEASON

Drakes begin to gather in flocks in Maine by the second week in June, earlier in a year of early nesting (Mendall 1958). Males in noticeable numbers leave the small breeding lakes and marshes in late June, and practically all are gone by mid-July. However, long before they abandon their hens, the drakes' nuptial plumage begins to fade, so that well in advance of the flightless stage they are almost as drab as the hens.

Most males move to a relatively few key areas in each region to undergo the wing molt. Erskine (1972*a*) reports on postbreeding concentrations of ring-necked ducks on two areas of Cape Breton Island, Nova Scotia, 1960-70. These areas supported an abundance of emergent cover plants in the form of sedges, bulrushes, and cattails, and many aquatic food plants such as various pondweeds, cow lilies, and bladderworts. Earliest influxes of males occurred in late June, peak numbers from late July to mid-August, and latest arrivals in early September. Flightless males were observed between July 30 and August 24, but during all observation periods many birds were able to fly, indicating a wide individual variation in timing of the wing molt.

In Maine, Mendall (1958) observed the earliest flightless male on July 28 and the latest on September 5, with the largest number between August 10 and 20. The earliest flightless female was noted on August 11, the latest October 2, and peak numbers September 5-15, almost a month later than the dates for males. The flightless period lasts 3 to 4 weeks.

FOOD HABITS

Ring-necked ducks feed in shallower water than other

diving ducks, usually less than 6 feet. When the water is only a foot or so deep, as in flooded fields in the spring, I have occasionally observed them tipping up for food rather than diving. This behavior is a rarity.

Ducklings feed upon animal life during their first few days of existence (Mendall 1958, Beard 1953), consuming such items as adult and immature insects, freshwater sponges, and tiny snails. Vegetable matter, consisting of bulrush and sedge seeds, is added to their diet when they are over 2 weeks of age.

On winter grounds in the southeast, ringnecks feed largely upon the seeds of water shield, pondweeds, sedges, and smartweeds, and upon leafy structures of coontail, pondweeds, and duckweeds (Cottam 1939, Kerwin and Webb 1972). Birds taken from the estuarian bays of Maryland fed primarily upon the leaves, stems, and rootstalks of pondweeds, and secondarily upon snails (Stewart 1962). In the northeast, during the fall, ringnecks depend upon the tubers of water bulrush, the seeds of other bulrushes, and the seeds of spike rushes, bur reeds, and pondweeds (Mendall 1958). Animal food, largely snails, made up 11 percent of the food items identified.

At Reelfoot Lake, Tennessee, seeds of pondweeds, coontail, spatterdock, buttonbush, hackberry, and bald cypress and the leafy structures of duckweeds were important foods (Rawls 1954). Snails, clams, and insects made up almost a third of the items found in fall-collected gizzards.

Snails, fingernail clams, and midge and mayfly larvae comprised almost a fourth of the food items consumed by ringnecks in Illinois (Anderson 1959). Leafy particles of coontail, corn, and the seeds of pondweeds and smartweeds made up the bulk of the vegetable matter consumed. In Missouri, however, ringnecks fed only slightly on animal life, and utilized the seeds of smartweeds, bulrushes, pondweeds, millets, and acorns for food (Korschgen 1955).

Cottam's (1939) statement that wild rice is probably a major food for ring-necked ducks in the north-central states is borne out by field observations. Ring-necked ducks reach their largest fall populations in Minnesota, and there they concentrate on lakes containing extensive beds of wild rice.

Tufted Duck

Aythya fuligula

IDENTIFICATION

The tufted duck is a straggler in North America from Eurasia. When observed on this continent, it is usually with a flock of scaups, although in appearance it resembles the ring-necked duck. In the male, the principal difference is the tuft of feathers that falls behind the head, like a lock of hair on a schoolboy's crown that fails to lie down. Unlike the scaup, it has a black back; and unlike the ringneck, it has white sides rather than gray. Like the ringneck, it has a white triangular niche between the black folded wing and the black chest. The bluish bill, like the ringneck's, has a white stripe behind the black tip but differs in not having the white margin at the base. It also resembles the ringneck in having black upperparts and white breast and belly. In flight, the tufted duck displays a white stripe at the back of the inner wing, like the scaups; the inner wing of the ring-necked duck is black.

The female tufted duck is similar in appearance to female scaups but is black-brown with a smaller patch of white at the base of the bill. At the back of the head, there is a slight protuberance of feathers, much abbreviated from the male's long dangling tuft. In both sexes the eyes are yellow, the feet blue-gray.

DISTRIBUTION

Tufted ducks breed across Eurasia from Iceland and the British Isles east across Russia and Siberia to the Kamchatka Peninsula and the Commander Islands. Their range extends from a short distance north of the Arctic Circle south to Germany, Yugoslavia, southern Russia, and northwest Mongolia, more or less along the 50th parallel. They winter as far south as the Mediterranean Sea, Saudi Arabia, the Persian Gulf, southern India, Thailand, and the Philippines.

As might be expected from its proximity to the Kamchatka Peninsula, the tufted duck appears fairly regularly in the Aleutian Islands. Two pairs were observed on Attu Island, May 23-24 (Wilson 1948). Byrd et al. (1974) recorded up to six tufted ducks every month of the year on Adak Island but found no evidence of breeding. They cited records of 21 birds on Amchitka Island in late May and June 1968, two males in July 1971, and up to eight birds during June-August in 1972. The tufted duck has been reported on the Pribilof Islands on several occasions.

Increasing numbers of tufted ducks are being reported in the conterminous United States. When Gochfeld (1968) summarized records of their occurrence up to 1967, he listed only a few: a specimen taken in Alameda County, California, 1949; one reported near Portland, Oregon, 1961; an immature male, Vancouver, British Columbia, November 1961; a pair at Falmouth, Massachusetts, January-February 1963; a male at New York City, February 18-April 1, 1966; and a male near Laramie, Wyoming, April 10, 1966.

A male tufted duck was observed at Seattle, Washington, from early January until March 1970 (Audubon Field Notes 1970).

Records of 11 tufted ducks in North America outside Alaska are as follows: one male, October 13-November 20 and December 31, Vancouver; four singles, February-March, Victoria; singles at Harrison Lake and Iona Island—all in British Columbia; a male near Palo Alto, California, February 4-March 7; a male at Falmouth, Massachusetts, December 5-20; and one near New London, Connecticut, January 11-February 7; two near New York City, February-March; one at Oakdale, Long Island, February 8; one at Lakehurst, New Jersey, December 26; and one on Lake Ontario, April 8-10 (American Birds 1971).

There were two observations of tufted ducks listed in 1972: a female at Golden Gate Park, San Francisco, California, February 15-March 3; and a male at Bayhead, New Jersey, February 21 (American Birds 1972).

Greater Scaup

Aythya marila mariloides

Other Common Names: Broadbill, bluebill

VITAL STATISTICS

Length:	Male, 16.5-20.2 inches, average 18.6 inches (35) Female, 15.5-18.7 inches, average 17.0 inches (18)
Wing:	Adult female, 8.45 inches (31) Immature male, 8.64 inches (24) Immature female, 8.34 inches (31)
Weight:	Adult male, 1.9-3.0 pounds, average 2.32 (44) Adult female, 1.6-2.8 pounds, average 2.15 (23) Immature male, 1.8-2.5 pounds, average 2.18 (40) Immature female, 1.8-2.6 pounds, average 2.17 (29)

IDENTIFICATION

Field

Greater scaups are most often found on the large bays, sounds, and inlets on the Atlantic and Pacific coasts. Although they tend to frequent extensive marine habitats whereas lesser scaups favor inland freshwater areas, small numbers of greater scaups associate with lesser scaups almost everywhere in the interior of the United States, especially on the Great Lakes.

Where greater and lesser scaups associate, the larger size of the greater is evident. They are more robust than lesser scaups, weighing about one-fifth more in relation to their body length. The more rounded, larger, green-tinted heads of male greater scaups contrast with the blacker, more domed, and proportionately smaller heads of the lessers. When greater scaups are in flight, the single white stripes at the back of the wings extend about halfway out on the primaries; in lessers, the stripes are restricted to the secondaries.

At a distance on the water, greater and lesser scaups appear identical: the males have black heads, necks, and chests separated by gray backs from the black rumps and tails; the females are brown, with single white oval patches around the bills.

At Hand

The blue bill of the greater scaup is broader than that of

Pair on left, greater scaup. Pair on right, lesser scaup. Showing differences in extension of white stripe on wing.

the lesser and slightly thicker at the base; its black nail is also broader. The side and flank feathers in the drake are whiter during the fall than those of the lesser; and the larger size and heavier weight are apparent. The white of the secondaries is present on the outer vane of the inner six primaries. The white secondaries and primaries are tipped with black or black-brown.

The differences between immature and adult plumages, and in adult drakes molting out of the eclipse plumage into nuptial plumage, are similar to those described for the lesser scaup.

POPULATION STATUS

Surveys in the Yukon Delta and other coastal breeding grounds reveal that the greater scaup breeding population, 1957-73, numbered about 515,000 in Alaska. Breeding numbers have varied from year to year on a magnitude comparable to those for other species. In 1965, a breeding population of only 301,000 was recorded, contrasting with a high of 660,000 in 1958, a differencc of 54 percent.

Age Ratios

The ratios of adults to immatures in hunters' bags averaged 1:1.38 for greater scaups and 1:1.65 for lesser scaups, 1966-73, suggesting that lessers are slightly more productive than greaters. However, mortality is probably lower in greater scaups than in lessers, for, in proportion to population size, the greater scaups experience fewer hunting losses.

The highest production recorded was 1.97 young per adult in 1966 and the lowest was 0.92 young for each adult in 1970, a reduction of 47 percent.

DISTRIBUTION

The greater scaup breeds on the tundra and in the boreal forest zones from Iceland eastward across northern Scandinavia, northern Russia, northern Siberia, and the western Arctic in North America. Curiously, it is absent from Greenland and the Canadian Arctic north and east of Hudson Bay. Two races are recognized: *Aythya marila marila* of Eurasia and *A. m. mariloides* of North America.

Breeding Range

Greater scaups breed almost entirely in the Arctic and Subarctic from Hudson Bay at Churchill, Manitoba, west to the northern part of the Alaskan Panhandle, north of the Bering Sea and the Arctic Ocean and east as far as Liverpool Bay.

In the open boreal forest (taiga), nesting by greater scaups is largely restricted to islands in large lakes. Almost all of the scaups present throughout most of the open and closed boreal forest are lessers.

Probably three-fourths of the greater scaups in North America breed in Alaska. This breeding population is estimated at 550,000, with a calculated guess that 200,000 additional greater scaups occur in Canada.

About 90 percent of the scaups breeding along the Bering Sea coast of Alaska from the Aleutian Islands through Kotzebue Sound are greaters (King and Lensink 1971). The largest breeding ground in this region is the Yukon Delta, with a scaup population of 303,000 (11.4 per square mile). Other areas in descending order of scaup numbers are: Bristol Bay, 87,000 (8.8 per square mile); Kotzebue Sound, 80,000 (14.9 per square mile); Seward Peninsula, 45,000 (11.7 per square mile); and the Arctic Slope, 14,600 (0.6 per square mile).

Gabrielson and Lincoln (1959) considered the greater to be the indigenous scaup on the Alaska Peninsula and the Aleutian Islands. They reported fair numbers of greaters breeding in the vicinity of Copper Center and along the Chulitna and Kvichak rivers.

In the open boreal forest of interior Alaska, dotted in places with tens of thousands of muskeg ponds, King and Lensink (1971) report that less than 10 percent of the breeding scaups are greaters. An example of the preponderance of lessers in interior Alaska is shown by banding records. At Tetlin and Fort Yukon, 8,347 lessers were captured—but only 40 greater scaups (Hansen 1961). Breeding surveys in interior Alaska reveal a total scaup population of 600,000. Probably 30,000 to 60,000 of these are greaters.

Scaups closely observed by David Trauger on the coastal strip of tundra from the Mackenzie Delta to Liverpool Bay were all greaters. Barry (1960) estimated 2,000 scaups in this area. He did not observe them east of Liverpool Bay even though his surveys extended to northern Baffin Island. However, south of Queen Maud Gulf along the Ellice River, Bromley (1973) found an isolated pair of breeding greater scaups.

Both the greater and lesser scaups frequent the Mackenzie Delta (Porslid 1943). Undoubtedly, greaters predominate on the outer tundra portion of the delta and lessers on the inner willow-clad part. Surveys by the U. S. Fish and Wildlife Service indicate that the scaup population on the Mackenzie Delta numbers 100,000, half of which we assume to be greaters.

Slightly over 100 miles west of the Mackenzie Delta lie the Old Crow Flats, a vast muskeg bog. Scaup populations there were calculated at 67,000, and Irving (1960) believed that lessers exceeded greaters by more than 10 to 1.

Southeast of the Mackenzie Delta stretches a vast land of tundra partially covered with stands of willow and spruce, called the open boreal forest. Many large lakes, hundreds of small lakes, and tens of thousands of muskeg ponds dot the landscape. This is where the scaup breeding population is at its greatest density, 9.1 per square mile, for a total population of 1,700,000. David Trauger, in the company of Thomas Barry, has made surveys through much of this region and in the closed boreal forest to the south. Only on the barrenlike islands of large lakes has he observed greater scaups breeding. The muskeg ponds were inhabited by lesser scaups.

Even on Great Slave Lake, where David Trauger found the largest number of breeding greater scaups, he discovered lesser scaups breeding along the inlets and forested inshore islands and greaters restricted to the tundralike offshore islands. The greaters' propensity for nesting on islands in large lakes is illustrated by the presence of a small breeding colony on Little George Island in Lake Winnipeg, far south of their documented breeding range (Vermeer et al. 1972).

Soper (1951) found no evidence that greater scaups bred in the Athabasca Delta, but he believed that they occurred there during the spring and fall migration. On the other hand, he classified lesser scaups as abundant and well distributed. Again according to Soper (1957), greater scaups are seldom seen in the Slave River delta but the lesser scaups are fairly common.

Although the deltas of the Athabasca and Slave rivers held only a scattering of greater scaups, Soper (1954) found them abundant on large lakes in the southern Yukon. They were the most abundant waterfowl in June, composing 25 percent of the total, but few were found in July. Apparently, most of the greaters observed in the Yukon were tardy nonbreeding migrants.

A few small breeding colonies of greater scaups have been discovered in eastern Canada. Manning and Macpherson (1952) reported collecting breeding birds at Moar Bay and Pointe au Huard on the east side of James Bay. They have also been reported breeding at Anticosti Island and on the Magdalen Islands and the lower end of Ungava Bay, near Fort Chimo, Quebec (Todd 1963).

Migration Corridors

Because most greater scaups breed in Alaska and northwestern Canada and winter on the Atlantic Coast, the principal migration corridors connecting the two regions extend in an east-southeast direction.

Band-recovery maps (Aldrich 1949 et al, Hansen 1960), population data, and kill data were used to determine the probable course of the migration corridors. Dirck Benson provided other band information and reports on visual observations of scaup flights across New York (Bellrose 1968).

Greater scaups either make extensive flights across the boreal forests of Canada before reaching the Great Lakes or else few are seen or shot in this sparsely populated region. In the Great Lakes region, they concentrate on Lakes Huron and Ontario. Dirck Benson reported that a cluster of recoveries from greater scaups banded on Long Island Sound occurred at Lake St. Francis (on the St. Lawrence River near Montreal) and along the west coast of James Bay. Lumsden (1971), who observed part of this population, estimated 25,000 scaups in rafts in James Bay on October 18, 1971.

Most greater scaups appear to use an offshore migration corridor between Alaska and the coasts of Washington and Oregon (Aldrich 1949 et al.). However, Soper's (1954) observations of large numbers of apparent migrants on lakes in southwest Yukon Territory suggest an interior migration corridor from Alaskan breeding grounds via the Fraser River valley to Puget Sound. Since possibly 5,000 to 10,000 greater scaups winter along the southeast coast of Alaska and British Columbia, there probably is a limited inshore migration corridor.

Winter Areas

Greater scaups winter along the Atlantic and Pacific coasts, the Great Lakes, and along the coast of the Gulf of Mexico. The accompanying table shows the number and distribution of greater scaups in the United States.

The January surveys indicate that slightly over 60 percent of the greater scaups winter on the Atlantic Coast, nearly 20 percent on the Pacific Coast, and the remainder in the interior. Almost half of the greater scaups on the Atlantic Coast winter in the vicinity of Long Island and the nearby shores of Massachusetts, Rhode Island, Connecticut, and New Jersey. Greater scaups decline sharply in abundance south of Chesapeake Bay, and only a few thousand winter in Florida, so important to lesser scaups.

On the Pacific Coast, greaters winter all the way from the Alaska Peninsula to Baja California. Gabrielson and Lincoln (1959) considered the wintering scaups of southeastern Alaska to be greaters. Winter surveys of these waters, 1953-57, revealed 5,400 scaups: 2,000 in the Kodiak Island area; 1,400 in the vicinity of Petersburg; and 2,000 in the Ketchikan region.

About 95 percent of the 6,000 scaups found wintering on the coast of British Columbia are greaters, and Puget Sound and Grays Harbor in Washington winter about 15,000. Most of the 36,000 greaters that winter in California concentrate in San Francisco Bay, but small numbers occur south of there in Morro and San Diego bays.

Audubon Christmas censuses and January inventories provide information on the greater scaups wintering in the Great Lakes region. A computed average of 25,000 greaters is distributed as follows: 6,000 around the shores of Lake Ontario; nearly 1,000 around Lake Erie; 8,000 along the west side of Lake Michigan, most near Milwaukee; and, in January, about 13,000 in Michigan (a large proportion of the Michigan scaups are believed to be greaters).

Although the proportion of greaters reaching Louisiana constitutes only 6.6 percent of the total scaup population, a wintering population of at least 900,000 scaups suggests that about 60,000 of these are greaters.

MIGRATION BEHAVIOR

Chronology

Little is known about the chronology of passage of greater scaups. In general it appears to coincide with that of lesser scaups. If there is a difference between the two species in chronology of migration, I suspect that the greaters would be later in the fall and earlier in the spring.

Fall. The departures of greater scaups from breeding

The Proportion of Greater versus Lesser Scaups in Hunters' Bags and Winter Numbers of Greater Scaups as Computed from January Surveys Compared with Population Figures Derived from Audubon Christmas Censuses.

Region	Percent of Greaters Among Scaups Bagged *a*	Number of Wintering Greater Scaups	
		U.S.F.W.S. *b*	Audubon *c*
ATLANTIC FLYWAY			
Maine-Massachusetts	60.3	12,338	8,132
Rhode Island-New York	75.3	93,592	80,080
New Jersey-Virginia	38.7	58,939	15,403
North Carolina-Georgia	13.5	6,023	323
Florida	9.1	28,400	153
Total	46.1	199,292	104,091
MISSISSIPPI FLYWAY			
Minnesota	5.3	2	0
Wisconsin	13.7	1,209	8,035
Michigan	29.7	3,990	21
Ohio	19.3	246	645
Illinois	8.3	183	51
Louisiana	6.6	57,511	1
Total	13.7	63,141	8,753
CENTRAL FLYWAY			
Texas	1.4	599	11
Total	2.3	1,026	—
PACIFIC FLYWAY			
Washington	41.0	15,012	2,347
Oregon	35.3	2,798	129
California	40.0	36,182	8,377
Total	37.7	53,992	10,853

a Proportion of greater to lesser scaups in hunters' bags (1967-69) from data provided by Sam Carney, U.S. Fish and Wildlife Service.

b January surveys of all scaups prorated by the two species in hunters' bags of regions shown. Surveys were conducted by state conservation agencies and the U.S. Fish and Wildlife Service.

c Audubon Christmas censuses, 1966, 1967, and 1969 (less comprehensive than the January surveys).

grounds on the Yukon Delta have been recorded by Mickelson (1973) over the period 1969-72 as July 10, 29, 21, and September 6. The July dates certainly represent their departures to possible nearby areas for the wing molt.

Gabrielson and Lincoln (1959) recorded late departures from Alaskan breeding grounds on September 9 at Nushagak River and September 11 at Koyukuk River. Migrants were observed arriving at Craig and Wrangell in southeast Alaska on September 25 and October 5. According to Munro (1941), the first fall migrants appeared in Okanagan Valley, British Columbia, in early October, reached peak abundance in early November, and departed by the end of the month. Although a similar sequence occurred along the coast, variable numbers spent the winter there. At Humboldt Bay, California, both greater and lesser scaups are reported to be the first ducks to arrive in the fall and the last to leave in the spring (Denson and Bentley 1962).

Greater scaups have been known to travel en masse to winter areas. A flight of 75,000 arrived on Long Island, New York, on October 24, 1929 (Bull 1964). Dirck Benson reports the occasional passage of large flights of scaups (presumably greaters) over central New York on a southeast course.

Spring. Mickelson (1973) observed the earliest greater scaups on the Yukon Delta on May 18, 1969 and 1970, May 27, 1971, and May 28, 1972. At Anaktuvuk Pass, Alaska, Irving (1960) recorded the earliest greaters on May 14-24, 1949-53. Gabrielson and Lincoln (1959) reported them arriving on the Seward Peninsula on May 11 and at Kobuk Delta on June 1. At Selawik, in 1955, the first greater scaups were seen May 18 (Shepherd 1955). Greaters were observed at Craig as late as May 22, and on Kasaan Bay, May 28. Migrating scaups were reported at Umiat on the Arctic Slope June 4-6.

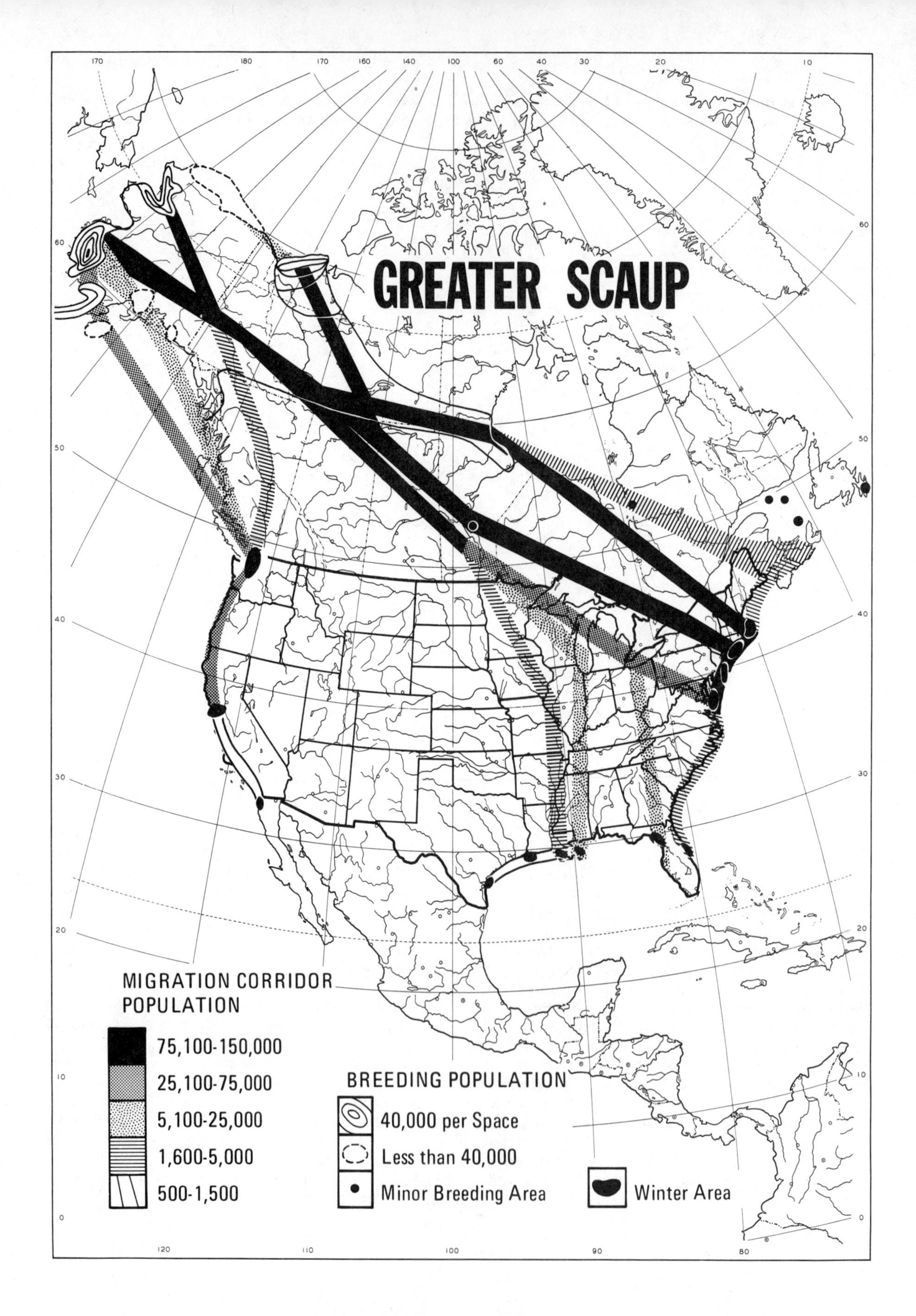
GREATER SCAUP
MIGRATION CORRIDOR POPULATION
75,100-150,000
25,100-75,000
5,100-25,000
1,600-5,000
500-1,500
BREEDING POPULATION
40,000 per Space
Less than 40,000
Minor Breeding Area
Winter Area

BREEDING

Behavior

Age, Pair Bond, and Homing. All the female greater scaups that David Trauger captured on nests at Great Slave Lake had yellow eyes, indicating birds 2 years of age or older. Most nonbreeding hens observed offshore had brown eyes, indicating year-old birds. These observations led Trauger to believe that yearling greater scaups are less likely to breed than yearling lessers. Conover (1926) reported that on the Yukon Delta, greater scaup drakes began to leave their mates by June 10, when small flocks composed entirely of males began to appear. After July 1, the drakes disappeared from the area, ostensibly for the wing molt. The homing ability of greater scaups has not been studied, but their limited, discontinuous breeding areas, at long distances from winter grounds, suggest a strong degree of homing among both adults and yearlings.

Home Range. The closeness of nests and the intraspecific egg parasitism found by Weller et al. (1969) indicate that greater scaups have ill-defined and overlapping home ranges. Two greater scaup nests found on an island in Great Slave Lake were only 7 feet apart. Laying by more than one female in the same nest occurred in a clutch of 22 eggs and in two clutches of 16 eggs each.

Nesting

Nest Sites. On their most important breeding ground in North America, the Yukon Delta, Brandt (1943) found greater scaups nesting solely on the marshy, lowland tundra. Their nest sites were on slight rises near tundra ponds, extremely close to the water—their favorite element. They scoop out bowl-shaped depressions that are lined with mats of grass. Some have added a little down to their nest bowls by the start of incubation, but by the time the nests are completed, all of them contain considerable amounts of down.

Greater scaups on both the tundra of the Yukon Delta and on islands in Great Slave Lake, and on Little George Island, Lake Winnipeg (Vermeer et al. 1972), selected the preceding year's growth of tall grass for nest sites. However, Weller et al. (1969) at Great Slave Lake found nests in a crevice of rock, under overhanging shrubs, and under a prostrate bough of a spruce tree. Most of the scaups nested in open sites that permitted good visibility and easy access to water. On the rocky islands, nests were placed 1 to 50 feet from water, an average of 19 feet (28 nests).

Clutch Size, Eggs, and Incubation. On islands in Great Slave Lake, 1968-73, Trauger and Bromley (1975) found that 93 incubated nests of the greater scaup averaged 9.0 eggs, with a range from 4 to 21. The average clutch was 8.5 eggs when seven intraspecifically parasitized nests that contained over 12 eggs each were omitted from the calculation. On the Yukon Delta, Brandt (1943) observed clutches of 6 to 11 eggs (50), but most numbered 6 to 8. He described the eggs as elliptical ovate, 2.50 by 1.66 inches, with a glassy surface of brownish olive-buff. The incubation period is 23 to 27 days, according to Delacour (1959), and 26 to 28 days as given by Dement'ev and Gladkov (1967).

Chronology of Nesting. On the Yukon Delta, Brandt (1943) found a greater scaup nest with fresh eggs on June 6 and three more nests on June 12. The peak in nest initiation occurred about mid-June, and the last unincubated clutch was found on June 24.

At Selawik, Alaska, the backdating of 67 greater scaup broods to the times of hatch indicated that hatching occurred from July 16 to August 8, with the peak on July 21 and 22 (Shepherd 1955). Allowing 35 days for the laying and incubation of eggs points to June 16 and 17 as the peak of nest initiation, with a range of June 11 to July 3.

Nest Success. At Selawik, Alaska, only 25 percent of 16 greater scaup nests hatched successfully (Shepherd 1955). Nine of 20 greater scaup nests at Minto Lakes hatched, 9 were destroyed, and 2 were deserted (Kirkpatrick and Buckley 1954).

Rearing of Young

Survival. Greater scaup broods in Alaska average 6.8 ducklings (69) in Class I and 6.3 (29) in Class II. If an average clutch consists of 8.5 eggs, there is a 20 percent loss of ducklings from successfully hatched nests up to the Class I age. A further loss of 6 percent occurs by the time the ducklings reach the Class II age. Mortality is apparently low among flightless ducklings.

POSTBREEDING SEASON

At Selawik, Alaska, Shepherd (1955) observed the first molting adult greater scaups on July 3 and determined that the wing molt was completed by August 16. On southern Yamal, USSR, first flightless greater scaups were noted on July 19, and some drakes were still flightless as late as August 25 (Dement'ev and Gladkov 1967). Billard and Humphrey (1972) made an extraordinary quantitative study of the body molt in greater scaups. They found that males molt intensively during November and December and again in March as they acquire further nuptial plumage. The molt in March is more pronounced among immatures than among adults. Females begin molting into their nuptial plumage in late winter; the molt is especially intense during late March and April, so that the nuptial plumage is essentially complete by May. Immature females molt less intensively but over a longer period than adult females.

FOOD HABITS

Greater scaups feed upon both plant and animal life, but in most areas clams constitute the principal items of diet.

Studies conducted in the area of Long Island Sound, where the largest concentrations of greater scaups in North America winter, demonstrate the importance of mollusks. Gizzards of greater scaups collected from the bays and inlets of Rhode Island contained 43 percent unidentified clams, 17 percent soft-shell clams, 13 percent eastern mud clams, and 9 percent dwarf surf clams (Cronan and Halla 1968). Mollusks, particularly blue mussels and dwarf surf clams, composed over 80 percent of the greaters' food on the Connecticut coast; sea lettuce constituted 3.6 percent, and unidentified plant food an additional 3.0 percent (Cronan 1957*b*).

In the salt estuarine inlets of Chesapeake Bay, also, mollusks predominate in the diet of greater scaups (Stewart 1962). However, in the fresh estuarine inlets, leaves, stems, and rootstalks of wild celery and the seeds of pondweeds are taken most frequently, with mollusks a secondary choice.

The diet of greater scaups on Apalachee Bay, Florida, is almost exclusively animal: greedy dove shell, 35 percent; variable nassa, 26 percent; Atlantic nautilus, 20 percent; and mud crab, 14 percent (Stieglitz 1967). Over 90 percent of the food of greaters taken from Humboldt Bay, California, consists of mollusks, with eelgrass comprising 4 percent (Yocom and Keller 1961). On saltwater areas of British Columbia, the diet of greater scaups consisted almost exclusively of mollusks (Munro 1941). In freshwater areas, muskgrass and other aquatic plants greatly exceeded the consumption of animal life.

Cottam (1939) reported on the food habits of greater scaups collected in 25 states, Alaska, and 7 Canadian provinces, probably representing more freshwater than marine areas. He found that 53 percent of the gizzards contained animal material and 47 percent plant material. Mollusks made up 39 percent of all food items, insects 7 percent, pondweed 19 percent, and muskgrass 5 percent.

Lesser Scaup

Aythya affinis

Other Common Name: Bluebill

VITAL STATISTICS

Length:	Adult male, 15.8-17.9 inches, average 17.0 inches (163) Adult female, 15.2-17.5 inches, average 16.5 inches (101) Immature male, 15.8-17.9 inches, average 16.9 inches (67) Immature female, 15.2-17.5 inches, average 16.3 inches (63)
Wing:	Adult male, 8.2 inches (381) Adult female, 8.0 inches (184) Immature male, 8.1 inches (206) Immature female, 7.8 inches (105)
Weight:	Adult male, 1.1-2.4 pounds, average 1.82 (177) Adult female, 1.0-2.1 pounds, average 1.65 (44) Immature male, 1.1-2.1 pounds, average 1.71 (190) Immature female, 1.0-2.1 pounds, average 1.62 (124)

IDENTIFICATION

Field

On favored feeding grounds lesser scaups may mass in rafts numbering from the hundreds into the thousands. During the fall and winter, they haunt the open water of large lakes, bays, and sounds but during the spring they frequent ponds and other small bodies of water as well.

Sitting on the water, usually rising and falling with the waves, the male shows black fore and aft and light gray in between. The head, neck, and breast appear black, as do the tail, rump, and upper and lower tail coverts. The pale gray sides show more white than the back, the amount of white dependent upon the degree of submergence of the body. When the male is actively feeding, the body is usually submerged so the tail rides on the surface, and, therefore, not as much white shows as when the body floats with the tail about an inch above the surface. The scaup's body rides at the higher levels during periods of rest, of alertness to danger, and courtship displays.

Since males outnumber the brown females about 3 to 1, gray backs predominate over brown. At a distance, scaups are most likely to be confused with canvasbacks, ring-necked ducks, redheads, and goldeneyes in that order. The backs of scaups are darker than the white backs of canvasbacks and lighter than the dark gray backs of redheads; the backs of ring-necked ducks and goldeneyes are black.

The gray backs of scaups become lighter from fall to spring as molt gradually replaces back feathers, and, thus, scaups appear more and more like canvasbacks. Particularly in strong light in the spring,the backs of scaups appear almost white. When these conditions occur, look for the distinctive sloping profile and reddish head characteristic of canvasbacks. In fact, all of the diving ducks have distinctively shaped heads, a great asset for identification of birds at rest or in the hand.

At rest, lessers can be separated from greater scaups by their smaller size, black-purple heads rather than dark green, and less rounded heads. Observing the two species together on Puget Sound, I was surprised by how readily they could be distinguished in the field.

The female scaup is brown and shows little other color on the water, except for a white oval patch around the bill. At close range the blue bills of both sexes are visible, giving rise among hunters to the scaup's common name, bluebill.

Scaups have rapid wing beats and fly fast in compact flocks of 25 to 50 birds. The most important identification mark in flight is a white band along the back of the wing. In lesser scaups the white stripe extends across the rear of the secondaries to the bend in the wing. But in greater scaups the white extends past the secondaries onto the primaries. The length of the white band provides the only usable cue for distinguishing these two species in flight.

Female scaups are silent much of the time, but when they

call, they utter a soft, purring *br-r-r-r-rp*. They are most prone to call when in flight. When alarmed, they utter a loud, harsh *scaup*.

At Hand

The male's black head shows a purplish cast. Back feathers are a light gray with broad, heavy vermiculations of sooty black. The vermiculations on the sides and flanks are olive-brown and not as broad as those on the back; they contrast with the white breast and upper belly; the lower belly is sooty black shading to a deeper black on the under-tail coverts.

The female's head, neck, and chest are fuscous brown; the back, rump, and white-flecked scapulars are dark brown. The white oval facial patch fades during the breeding season and in fall may be an indistinct buff or only partially present at the sides of the bill; by spring the patch again shows white and is complete above the bill.

In both sexes, the bill is blue-gray with a black nail, but the lesser scaup has a narrower bill and a narrower nail than the greater scaup. The feet are blue-gray, with dark webs.

Early males begin to assume the eclipse plumage in late June, but in some males it is still a month away. In eclipse plumage, the back is brown, the head brown-black, and the belly mottled with brown. Immature males are a darker brown than immature females, and the male has a white facial patch around the bill, lacking in the young female. By mid-October, adult males are well advanced in their assumption of the nuptial plumage even though traces of the eclipse are still evident. Most immature males still have much of their basic plumage at this time, but by December have the general appearance of adults. The notched V's in the tail feathers of immatures are still retained.

Trauger (1974*a*) found that eye color in females varies with age: olive-brown in yearlings, olive-yellow but variable in 2-year-olds, and yellow in females 3 years old and older.

The white stripe in the wing is formed by a white speculum bordered on the trailing edge with a quarter-inch brown stripe, creating a narrower white wing patch than in the goldeneye. Inner primaries are light brown becoming dark brown toward the tips and the outer primaries.

Sex and age can be distinguished in wings by the brown coverts, which are flecked with white in males and are almost entirely plain brown in females. Some middle covert feathers in females may show small flecks concentrated near the edge, in contrast to large recessed flecks in males. Tertials with rounded tips and greater coverts that are broadly rounded characterize adult scaups; the tertials and greater coverts of immatures are pointed. A large proportion of the lesser scaups that we trapped in April still retained the V-notched tail feathers of the immature plumage.

POPULATION STATUS

In the summer, the combined numbers of greater and lesser scaups form a population larger than that of any species but the mallard. From 1955 to 1975, scaup breeding populations have averaged 6,900,000, ranging from a high of 9,097,000 in 1959 to a low of 5,086,000 in 1965. During this 20-year period, scaup breeding populations have shown no significant trend in numbers. The 43 percent differential in the size of breeding populations is less than other common species experience. The reason for the more moderate yearly changes in scaup populations probably stems from the greater stability of its breeding habitat. A larger proportion of the scaup population breeds in the Arctic and Subarctic than of populations of other common game ducks more associated with prairie breeding grounds subject to drought.

Age Ratios

The proportion of adults to immatures in hunters' bags has ranged from 1:1.3 (1968) to 1:2.3 (1966), averaging 1:1.65 over a period of 8 years. The greater vulnerability of immatures than adults to the gun has been determined by David Trauger from the bandings of 4,055 immatures and 903 adults in the Yellowknife area, Northwest Territories.

Trauger determined that immatures were 1.3 times more vulnerable than adults during 1960-63, 2.0 times more vulnerable during 1966-69, and, among a group marked with nasal disks, 1966-69, the vulnerability of immatures rose to 2.4 times that of adults. The greater vulnerability of all immature groups averaged 1.94. Using this figure as a correction for hunting bias indicates that immature lesser scaups are outnumbered by adults in the fall population on the order of 0.85:1.

Considering the low proportion of yearling and 2-year-old females that succeed in rearing broods (Trauger 1971), the number of immatures in the fall population is surprisingly high.

Sex Ratios

Practically all data on sex ratios in ducks indicate that among the common game ducks the lesser scaup has the largest surplus of drakes. Large samples of scaups tallied according to sex during the spring from many regions of the continent revealed that 70 percent of the population was drakes, or 2.4 drakes per hen (Bellrose et al. 1961). This proportion of supernumerary drakes was approached only by the canvasback, with a ratio of 1.9 drakes per hen.

More recent studies continue to point up the large proportion of drakes among lesser scaups. Jahn and Hunt (1964) reported that 64.6 percent of 4,756 scaups whose sex was recorded during spring in Wisconsin, 1941-50, were drakes (1.9:1). On one of the principal scaup winter grounds off the coast of Louisiana, Harmon (1962) took aerial photos of rafts containing 1,018 birds and found that 81.3 percent were males, a ratio of 4.36:1. At Yellowknife, Northwest Territories, Trauger (1971) reported a sex ratio of 1.4 males per female (58.5 percent) during the prebreeding period.

The large proportion of drakes in scaup populations suggests that the overall population is basically an old-aged one, made up of a high proportion of 2-year and older birds, especially in the drake class. Trauger (1971) reported a direct band-recovery rate of 6.1 percent for young males, 5.5 for young females; for adult males the rate was only 0.7 percent, compared with 3.4 percent for adult females.

Mortality

Smith (1963) provided some pertinent information concerning mortality rates in lesser scaup populations. Summer bandings on breeding areas indicated that immatures have annual mortality rates of 68 to 71 percent, 69 percent in Alaska bandings, where adult males experienced a rate of only 32 percent. From recoveries of bandings made in winter and spring in eight states, Smith (1963) calculated annual mortality rates of 38 to 52 percent for adult males and 49 to 60 percent for females. The posthunting banding of lesser scaups at Chesapeake Bay, Maryland, by Longwell and Stotts (1959) provided an average yearly mortality rate of 42 percent for adults.

DISTRIBUTION

Breeding Range

The lesser scaup has one of the more extensive breeding ranges of North American ducks. Its principal range extends from Minnesota west to northeastern California, north to the Bering Sea, and east as far as the Laurentian Shield in the Northwest Territories.

The greatest density of breeding lesser scaups occurs in the interior of Alaska, where there are 19.2 scaups per square mile for a total population of 600,000. Both the greatest number and the greatest density occur on the Yukon Flats—324,000 (30 per square mile). Other important areas are Tanana, 175,000 (18.9 per square mile); Koyukuk, 43,000 (10.4 per square mile); Nelchina, 38,000 (9.7 per square mile); and Innoko, 24,000 (7.1 per square mile). Over 90 percent of these scaups are lessers (King and Lensink 1971). Small numbers of lessers breed on the Yukon Delta and elsewhere along the coast of the Bering Sea but King and Lensink (1971) consider about 90 percent of the scaups in the area to be greaters.

Probably a few lessers reach the Arctic Ocean from the Mackenzie River delta to Liverpool Bay, but most of the scaups in this area are greaters (David Trauger). The forested part of the Mackenzie Delta and Old Crow Flats in northwestern Yukon Territory appear to be heavily populated by lesser scaups. Old Crow has a scaup density similar to that of the Yukon Flats, 34 per square mile, a total population of 67,000.

The greatest density of breeding scaups anywhere, 41.6 per square mile (42,000 population), occurs in the Slave River parklands and extends alongside the north arm of Great Slave Lake past Yellowknife to Rae. According to Ross Hanson who has flown over this area numerous times, the boreal forest in the Slave River parklands is interspersed by countless meadows of grass and sedge dotted with thousands of ponds, apparently forming a lush habitat for lesser scaups.

Both the Saskatchewan and Athabasca deltas have the same scaup density, 17.5 per square mile, yielding a combined population of almost 150,000. Next to the river deltas in Canada, the open boreal forest, with 9.1 scaups per square mile (population of 1,700,000), has the highest density in summer. Because of the vast areas in the closed boreal forest east to Ontario, the scaup population there is calculated to be 1,900,000 (4.5 per square mile).

The parklands have a scaup density of 5.5 birds per square mile for a population of 500,000. Breeding density is considerably less south of the parklands in the mixed prairie, for there scaups number about 340,000, a density of 2.0 per square mile. They are even less abundant in the shortgrass prairie, with a population of almost 100,000 and a density of 0.67 per square mile. About 41,000 scaups breed in the Sandhills of Nebraska.

The Intermountain marshes of British Columbia and the United States have a lesser scaup breeding population of about 90,000, distributed as follows: British Columbia, 50,000; Washington (largely the Columbia Basin), 7,000; Utah (largely the marshes adjacent to Great Salt Lake), 5,000; Idaho, 3,000; Wyoming, 3,000; Oregon, 500; a few hundred in Colorado (San Luis Valley, North Park, and the Fort Collins-Boulder area); and Arizona (a few in the White Mountains, Fleming 1959).

The scaup is a rare breeder in the lake states. They have been found nesting in the northwestern counties of Minnesota (Lee et al. 1964) and in Dodge County, Wisconsin (Jahn and Hunt 1964).

A few small scattered colonies of breeding lesser scaups have been reported from eastern Canada: Lake St. Clair and Luther Marsh in southeastern Ontario; Toronto Island; the mouth of the Nottawasaga River; and Moar Bay, midway up the east side of James Bay (Godfrey 1966).

Migration Corridors

Most lesser scaups breed in the extreme northwestern part of the continent, yet most winter in the eastern half of the continent. Consequently, the fall flow of migration is southeastward, with a central axis extending from the Yukon Flats, Alaska, to Florida.

The largest migration corridor, followed by close to 500,000 scaups, stretches from the Yukon Flats to the Athabasca Delta to Lakes Winnipegosis and Manitoba, northwestern Minnesota, and the Keokuk Pool (Mississippi River, Burlington to Keokuk , Iowa). George Arthur for numerous years has watched many of the 250,000 that congregate there at one time during November depart along two basic courses, south and south-southeast. An extrapolation of the south-southeast course leads to Apalachee Bay, Florida, the south one to southeast Louisiana.

At times, mass flights of scaups occur along this cor-

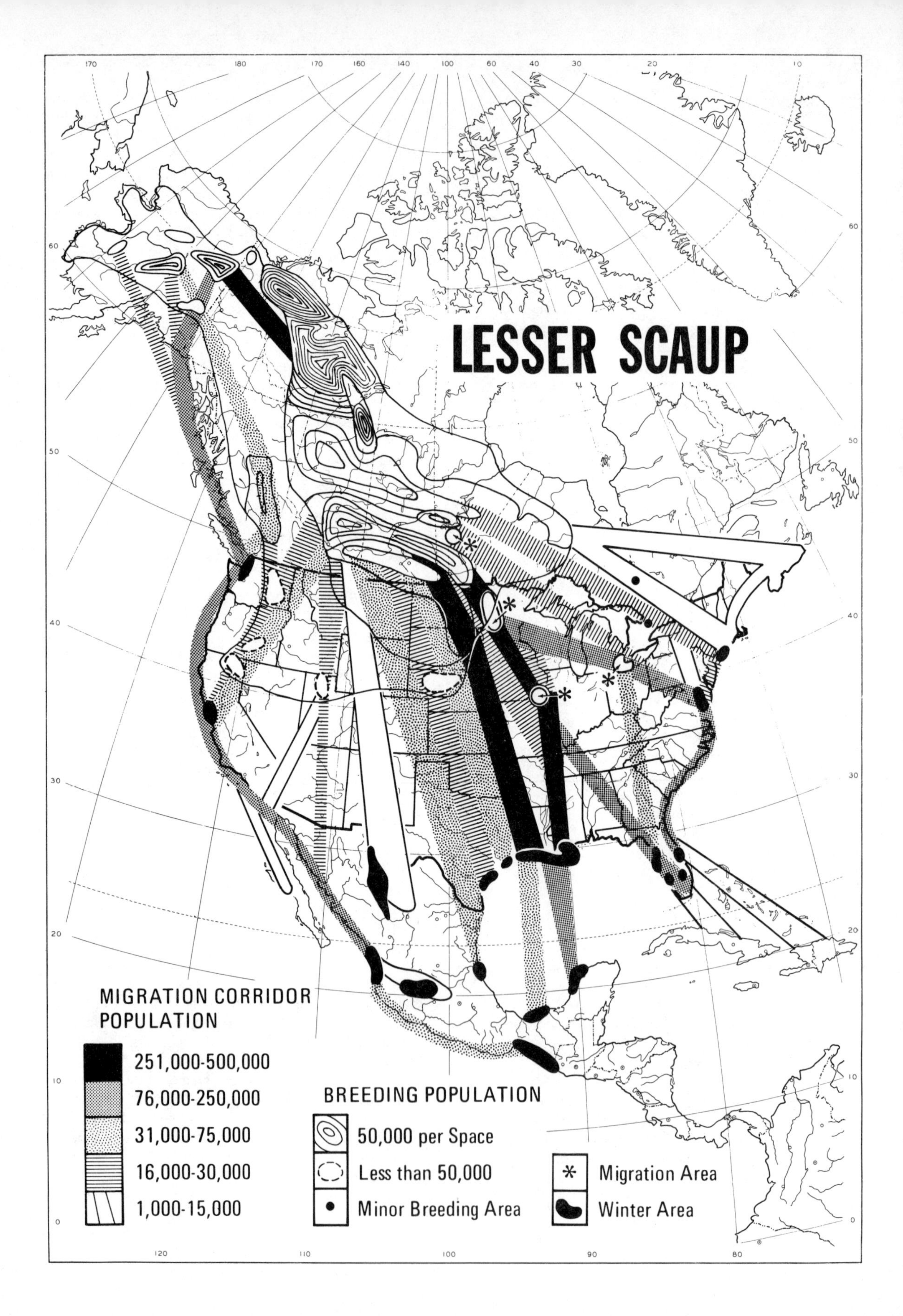
LESSER SCAUP
MIGRATION CORRIDOR POPULATION
251,000-500,000
76,000-250,000
31,000-75,000
16,000-30,000
1,000-15,000
BREEDING POPULATION
50,000 per Space
Less than 50,000
Minor Breeding Area
Migration Area
Winter Area

ridor. One such flight, reported by Hochbaum (1955), passed over the southern end of Lake Manitoba. At the peak of the 3-day flight, it was estimated that 100,000 ducks, mostly lesser scaups, passed over in one hour, November 6, 1947.

Band recoveries, points of scaup concentrations, and observations of courses taken by migrating flocks indicate that nearly 100,000 birds follow a corridor east-southeast from northwest Minnesota to Lake St. Clair, Michigan, to Chesapeake Bay, Maryland. Band recoveries suggest that 49 percent of the scaup population in Maryland originates in the District of Mackenzie, 40 percent in Alberta, and 11 percent in Alaska (Don Hayne).

Migration corridors followed by lesser scaups to Long Island Sound and southern New England pass east-southeastward through Ontario. Band recoveries suggest that 29 percent of the scaups passing through Ontario are from Alberta, 18 percent from Saskatchewan, 16 percent from the District of Mackenzie, 13 percent each from Alaska and Montana, and 11 percent from Manitoba.

The second largest corridor of passage extends from southeastern Saskatchewan to southwestern Louisiana, encompassing the Missouri River along the Iowa border. Louisiana, the most important winter ground, thus receives part of the scaups that use migration corridors along the Missouri and Mississippi rivers as well as smaller numbers from other migration corridors. About 30 percent of Louisiana's scaups originate from the District of Mackenzie, 23 percent from Saskatchewan, 21 percent from Alberta, 10 percent from Alaska, 8 percent from Manitoba, and smaller proportions elsewhere.

Three migration corridors of varying intensity cross the Great Plains in a south-southeast direction to the coasts of Texas and Mexico. About 60 percent of the scaups in Texas come equally from Saskatchewan and Alberta breeding grounds, 17 percent from the District of Mackenzie, 14 percent from Alaska, and 7 percent from Manitoba.

Probably no more than 300,000 lesser scaups frequent areas west of the Great Plains. Most of them follow a coastal corridor from Alaska to Guatemala, with intersecting corridors from British Columbia and Alberta. Banding data suggest that nearly half of the scaups in California originate in British Columbia, 27 percent in Alberta, 22 percent in Alaska, and 2 percent in Saskatchewan. However, 63 percent of those in Washington come from Alaska and only 27 percent from British Columbia.

Winter Areas

Although the largest number of greater scaups winter in the Atlantic Flyway, the largest number of lesser scaups winter in the Mississippi Flyway. Of the lesser scaups found wintering in the United States, almost 60 percent occur in the Mississippi Flyway (870,000), 31 percent in the Atlantic Flyway (455,000), 6 percent in the Pacific Flyway (85,000), and 3 percent in the Central Flyway (44,000).

An additional 297,000 scaups found in Mexico on winter surveys are assumed to be of the lesser species. A few greater scaups, no more than trace numbers, have been reported from Mexico. Winter surveys in the West Indies by Walter Crissey and others revealed an average of 7,500 scaups, 1951-55 and 1959. The bulk of these were in Cuba, others in the Dominican Republic.

A few lesser scaups are reported on Audubon Christmas bird censuses in Quebec, Ontario, and British Columbia, but most of the scaups wintering in these provinces are of the greater species.

The largest number of lesser scaups wintering in the Atlantic Flyway, like many people, select Florida. Almost 285,000 are recorded there on winter surveys. The largest concentrations are in the northern section of the Indian River, the Banana River, and the bays and estuaries of Charlotte and Lee counties, with smaller numbers on Lakes Okeechobee, Kissimmee, and Apopka (Chamberlain 1960).

About 95,000 lesser scaups are found in the bays and estuaries from Long Island to North Carolina, almost two-thirds of these on Chesapeake Bay. The bays of New Jersey accommodate about 50,000. The coasts of the Carolinas and Georgia are frequented by almost 40,000 lesser scaups, about one-fifth of these in North Carolina and two-fifths each in South Carolina and Georgia. Long Island Sound and the coasts of Rhode Island and Connecticut harbor mostly greater scaups, but about 30,000 lessers consort with their larger relatives. New England inlets and bays winter about 8,000 lessers compared with 12,000 greaters.

Over 90 percent of the lesser scaups wintering in the Mississippi Flyway occur in Louisiana. They concentrate in Lakes Ponchartrain and Borgne, the waters in and adjacent to the coastal marsh, and the open waters of the Gulf. The average peak fall population of scaups in Louisiana numbered 217,000 more birds over a 15-year period than were recorded on the January surveys (Hugh Bateman). The unaccounted-for birds were either farther out on the Gulf or were entirely across the Gulf, on the Tabasco, Campeche, and Yucatan lagoons—probably both, as 120,000 scaups winter in that region of the Yucatan Peninsula, and tremendous offshore rafts have been reported.

About 17,000 scaups winter from Mobile Bay west along the coast of Mississippi to Louisiana. Eastern Arkansas winters nearly 12,000 in fishponds and other impoundments; Tennessee winters 3,800, Kentucky 1,500 and Missouri 2,400. The Great Lakes enable fairly large numbers of lesser scaups to winter far to the north: 2,000 in Illinois; 7,600 in Wisconsin; 9,500 in Michigan; and 1,000 in Ohio.

With the exception of 200 scaups in Kansas and 1,300 in Oklahoma, practically all of the birds in the Central Flyway winter in Texas and along the east coast of Mexico as far south as the Alvarado lagoons. This coastal population numbers almost 100,000 birds. Largest concentrations occur in Galveston Bay (30,000), and in the Tamiahua Lagoon (32,000) south of Tampico, Mexico. Other important lagoons are Alvarado with 6,000 and Tampico and Tamaulipas with 5,000 each. The 4,200 scaups found in the Interior Highlands of Mexico probably migrated there along migration corridors in both the Central and Pacific flyways.

Almost 200,000 lesser scaups have been found in winter along the Pacific Coast from British Columbia to Central America. The major areas of concentration from north to south are Washington (mostly Puget Sound), 22,000; Oregon (various bays along the coast), 5,000; California, 48,500 (north coast 500; San Francisco Bay area 35,000; south coast 3,000; Imperial Valley 8,000; Central Valley 2,000); and Mexico, 120,000 (Baja Peninsula 900; Obregón to Mazatlán 17,500; Mazatlán to Acapulco 43,000; Acapulco to Guatemala 58,000).

Saunders et al. (1950) cited records of lesser scaups on inland lakes of Guatemala. They observed as many as 750 in a single day, their records extending from January 29 to as late as May 1, 2. Lesser scaups banded in Alaska have been recovered in Panama, some banded in Alberta were recovered in Salvador and Jamaica, and lesser scaups banded in Saskatchewan were recovered in Honduras.

Elsewhere in the Pacific Flyway, several thousand scaups winter in the basins of the Rocky Mountains: 3,300 in Idaho (largely along the Snake River), 330 in Nevada, and 300 in Utah.

MIGRATION BEHAVIOR

During the fall migration, lesser scaups fly long distances between areas of concentration on large bodies of water. These areas are in most cases 500 to 1,000 miles apart. For example, George Arthur and I have frequently observed tens of thousands of scaups departing the Mississippi River at Keokuk, Iowa, in a 2-hour period prior to darkness, headed on courses for the Louisiana coast or Apalachee Bay, Florida. Most of them pass nonstop directly to these two winter areas.

In the spring, scaups are more prone in their early stages of migration to cover shorter distances between rest sites than during the fall. They stop at many small bodies of water that they fly over in the fall. Moreover, the first flocks north in the spring proceed as the ice retreats, indicating northward passage in short spurts.

All of the many scaup departures that I have witnessed from the Illinois and Mississippi valleys have occurred in late afternoon, most often between sunset and dark, but their arrivals have varied from daybreak to midday. This pattern suggests that these birds flew all night and through varying numbers of hours during the morning to reach their destinations at varying times. Most flocks counted in migratory flight number 20 to 50 birds.

Chronology

Fall. On most migration areas the chronology of scaup passage during the fall is slightly behind that of redhead and ring-necked ducks but slightly ahead of that of canvasbacks. However, all four species are strikingly similar in their period and intensity of migration.

The earliest migrants south of their breeding grounds were recorded in the Alaskan Panhandle on September 7 and 25 (Gabrielson and Lincoln 1959).

The last scaups were noticed at Anaktuvuk Pass, Alaska, on September 10 (Irving 1960). Scaup were last recorded on the Mackenzie Delta on September 28 (Porslid 1943), but Soper (1957) reported them up to mid-October on the Slave River delta, Northwest Territories.

Aerial surveys of lakes and marshes in southern Manitoba, 1968-69, showed small numbers of scaups during September and large numbers from early October to November 6 (Larche 1970). The time of peak numbers varied with the individual area through this time span.

The rapid passage of lesser scaups, occasioned by long flights through various migration regions of the United States to winter quarters, is illustrated in the migration charts. There is a remarkable similarity of the chronology of arrival in many regions located at different latitudes.

In most regions of the United States, scaups begin to appear about mid-October and reach peak numbers about mid-November. On the Northwest Plains, a sizable local population is present through September but is greatly augmented by migrants arriving through October. Although scaups arrive on important winter grounds (Middle Atlantic, Florida, the south Gulf Coast, lower Texas coast, the northwest coast) in late October, their numbers continue to mount steadily through November and into December. Increases in populations occur on winter areas even as populations are building on the more northern migration areas, but the ingress into winter areas accelerates as departures from migration areas increase between mid-November and mid-December.

Spring. Scaups have the most protracted migration of all ducks during the spring. Some start northward as soon as the ice begins to retreat from lakes to the north of their winter grounds; others may not leave until May. Small flocks of males are often found on migration areas in late May.

Weekly censuses on national wildlife refuges where the scaups winter show a gradual exodus from those areas starting in early February and continuing through April. On migration areas, small numbers of scaups begin to arrive in February, but it is late March before large numbers appear and not until mid-April is there a flood tide of migrants.

Scaups arrive on north-central and northwest plains areas of the United States, where small numbers remain to breed, in early April, but with numbers rapidly increasing throughout the month. It is evident that as the scaups proceed northward they tend more and more to compress their chronology of passage.

The first scaups normally arrive at Delta Marsh, Manitoba, on April 14 (Rogers 1962). In the area of Brooks, Alberta, Keith (1961) recorded them as arriving April 9-16 during a 4-year period. At Yellowknife, Northwest Territories, where Murdy (1964) reported arrivals over a 3-year period, first arrivals were recorded May 8-15, numerous arrivals May 13-17, and major influxes May 14-26. Lesser scaups arrived May 23 at Churchill, Manitoba (Littlefield and Pakulak 1969); May 15, Old Crow, Yukon (Irving 1960); and May 28 and June 6 on the Mackenzie Delta (Porslid 1943). Dates of arrivals in Alaska are May 18, Fort Yukon (Hansen 1956) and May 14, 19, 24 during three springs, Anaktuvuk Pass (Irving 1960). When some migrants were still in the Midwest, other scaups were on their breeding grounds in Alaska and northern Canada.

BREEDING

Behavior

Age. Although small numbers of yearling lesser scaup females nest successfully their first year, most do not do so until their second year, and a few perhaps not until their third year (Trauger 1971). For many years, lesser scaups were considered to reach sexual maturity in their second year (Bent 1923), but then McKnight and Buss (1962) reported that 11 of 15 yearlings collected showed evidence of ovulation. In an intensive study of age in relation to breeding, Trauger (1971) found that even though some yearling females attempted to nest, fewer than 15 percent produced broods. The second summer 27 percent of the hens were successful, but 3- and 4-year-old birds were the most successful—more than 40 percent of them produced broods.

As shown by the large numbers of nonbreeding male lesser scaups found in flocks during late spring and early summer, it is unlikely that yearling males breed. It is also probable that a sizable proportion of 2-year-old males do not mate.

Pair Bond. Lesser scaups begin to pair on their winter grounds in December, when Weller (1965) observed 4 to 9 percent of the hens accompanied by drakes. By March-April, on their spring migration through Iowa, the proportion of females with mates had risen to 56 percent. Trauger (1971) observed that all females, including yearlings, were paired in mid-May when they arrived on their breeding grounds at Yellowknife, Northwest Territories. On a breeding area in east-central Washington, Gehrman (1951) observed courtship behavior from the time of their arrival in late March until mid-April. He observed that males remained on waiting sites for 3 to 9 days after females began to incubate. Rogers (1962) reported that pair bonds dissolved during the first 2 weeks in July at Erickson, Manitoba.

At Yellowknife, Trauger (1971) found that after July 1, breeding pairs declined rapidly in number as pair bonds weakened. When the females began incubation, their mates remained no longer than 7 to 10 days on the area. No pairs were recorded after July 15.

Homing. Trauger (1971) reported that on his Yellowknife study area, 1967-69, 20 percent of 330 marked adult females returned in a subsequent year and 12 percent of 626 marked immature females appeared the following year. The proportionate difference between the return rate of yearlings and that of older birds was ascribed to differences in their rates of mortality. Bandings of lesser scaups near Tetlin, Alaska, showed that a large percentage of the females returned the following year (McKnight and Buss 1962).

Although many female scaups return to their natal or breeding areas, males rarely do. Not one of 557 marked immature male scaups was observed by Trauger (1971) the following year. Only one of 37 marked adult males was observed the next year, and it appeared to be unmated. Adult females usually appeared earlier in the spring than yearlings.

Home Range. Lesser scaups have a large but ill-defined home range, possibly because of their extensive use of open water in the prenest period. Gehrman (1951) observed that as flocks dispersed into pairs, individual pairs became identified with a particular unit of a lake. Areas occupied early had stumps, logs, boulders, or beaches important as loafing sites, but later pairs relied solely on open water. In favorable locations, several pairs associated in harmony, except that a small area around each hen was defended by the male from other drakes.

Throughout the nest period at Yellowknife, Northwest Territories, pairs had a definite temporal pattern in their spatial distribution (Trauger 1971). In early morning they were dispersed, but by late afternoon they became associated in loose groups on the larger ponds.

Nesting

Lesser scaups are more prone than other diving ducks to nest on upland areas adjacent to lakes, sloughs, marshes, and potholes. On his Lousana, Alberta, study area, Smith (1971) found that they preferred permanent potholes, 10 feet or more in depth and 2.1 to 5.0 acres in size, partially surrounded by trees, and located in ungrazed grasslands. These potholes are larger, deeper, and more stable than those preferred by dabbling ducks.

Nest Sites. The female selects the nest, walking into grassy areas near the shore or flying to distant upland areas. The male accompanies his mate on these forays and often is followed by a second male. At first the nest consists of only a few meager plant stems or a shallow depression in which eggs are laid (Gehrman 1951). As additional eggs are laid, the nest rim is built up of surrounding vegetation, and frequently some down is added, mostly during incubation. However, not all nests contain down feathers, and even those that do, contain less down than most other duck nests.

Scaups selected sedges over other vegetation for their nest sites at Lousana, Alberta (Smith 1971), and the Saskatchewan Delta (Townsend 1966). Eighty-five percent of the nests in the Delta marshes were on floating or semifloating mats of vegetation. Near Brooks, Alberta, they chose extensive juncus beds for nest sites, with mixed prairie a second choice (Keith 1961). In eastern Washington, most

LESSER SCAUP

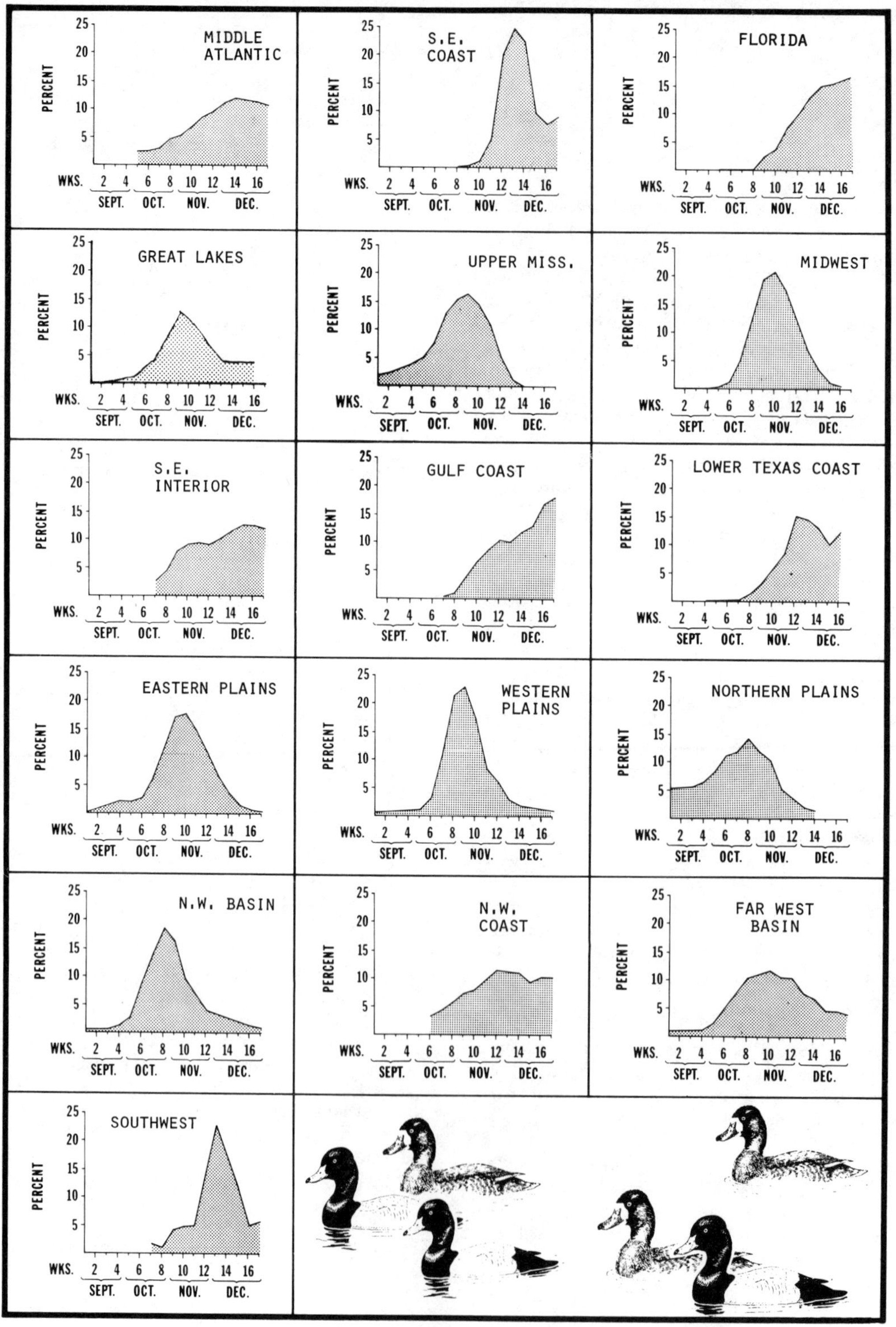

Fall

LESSER SCAUP

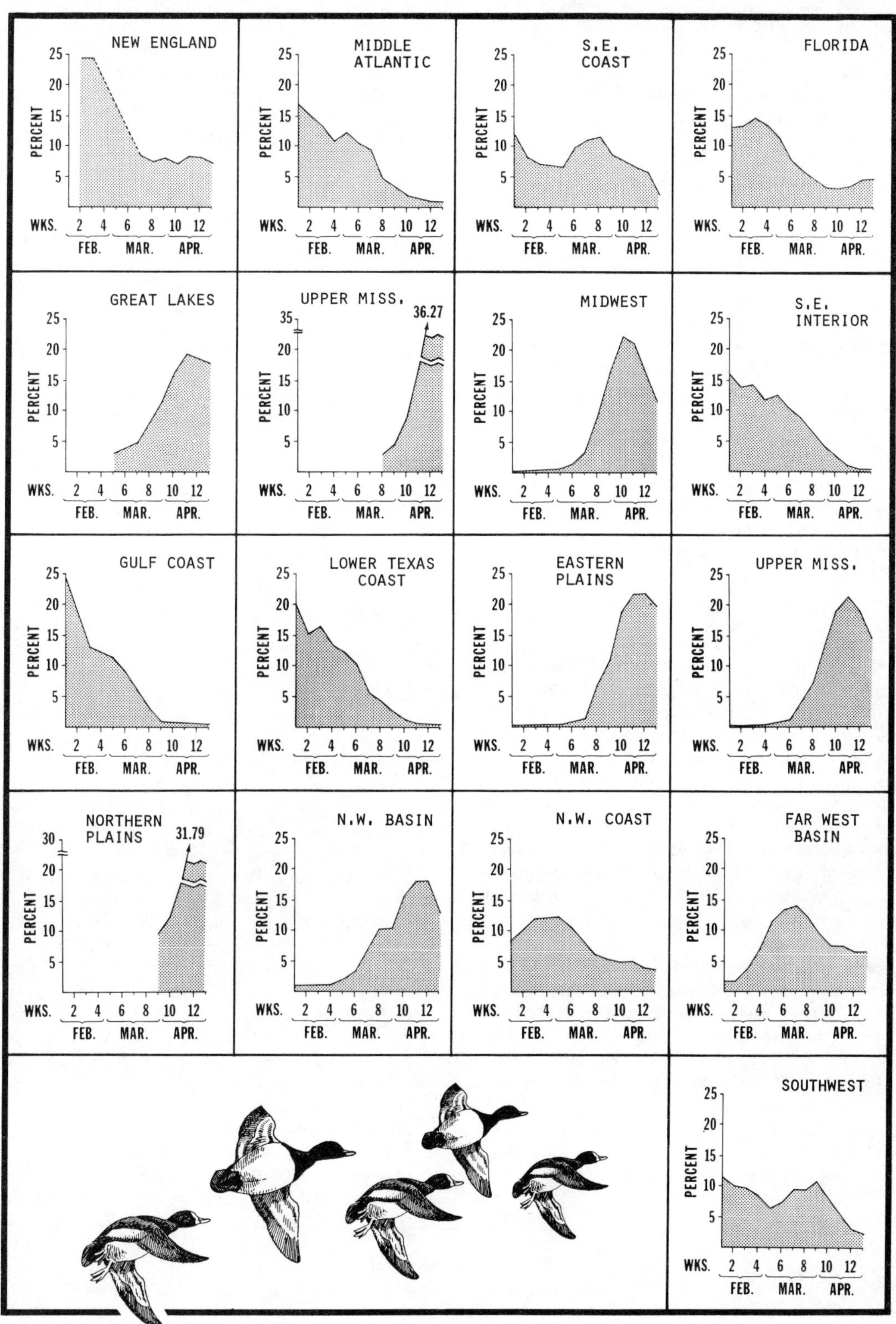

Spring

nests were located in reed canary grass, but Gehrman (1951) found others in such strange sites as a strawberry patch and an alfalfa field.

Vermeer (1970*b*) reported that lesser scaups were the most abundant nesting ducks on islands in lakes of the parklands and boreal forest. He found 5.3, 6.1, and 23.7 scaup nests per acre on islands in three lakes. Islands were also important sites for nests in the Saskatchewan Delta (Townsend 1966), Freezeout (Greenfield) Lake, Montana (Ellig 1955), and Klamath Basin, California (Miller and Collins 1954).

The location of nests in relation to water varies greatly, depending upon the habitat. On the Saskatchewan Delta marshes, 85 percent of the nests were on floating or semi-floating mats of vegetation and only 15 percent on a solid foundation. In southeastern Alberta, scaup nests averaged 39 feet from water, more than half within 15 feet (Keith 1961). Because of receding water levels in the pothole area of Erickson, Manitoba, nests averaged 109 and 125 feet in 1958 and 1959, with maximums of 600 and 900 feet (Rogers 1964). In 1957 and 1960, when water levels were more normal, nests averaged 7 and 21 feet from water, with the greatest distances 35 and 45 feet. On islands in Lake Newell, Alberta, scaup nests averaged 35 feet from water and wigeon nests 108 feet (Vermeer 1970*b*). Scaup nests studied by Gehrman (1951) were as far as 475 and 590 yards from water, although over half the nests were less than 20 yards away. In the Klamath Basin marshes, Miller and Collins (1954) found no scaup nests over water but all were within 50 yards of it.

Clutch Size, Eggs, and Incubation. The average clutch size for 880 scaup nests observed in over 10 breeding areas is 9.0 eggs. On individual study areas, the clutch sizes ranged from 8.3 (40) to 10.5 (59). Two hens contributed to a clutch of 14 eggs reported by Gehrman (1951)—9 eggs by the resident, 5 eggs by the intruder. Townsend (1966) observed that the average clutch size decreased by one egg for every 10.3 days of the nest season.

The eggs are elliptical ovate to oval, 57.1 by 39.7 mm (88), and a distinctive dark olive-buff (Bent 1923). Gehrman (1951) recorded similar measurements, 57.0 by 39.4 mm, for 145 eggs. According to Vermeer (1968), the female incubates 21 to 27 days and averages 24.8 days (18).

Chronology of Nesting. The lesser scaup is among the last ducks to nest. Starting dates vary with geography and year depending upon seasonal temperatures, but there is little range in the time of peak nesting activity. At Yellowknife, Northwest Territories, the first nests are initiated almost 3 weeks after the first arrivals and before the appearance of late arrivals (Trauger 1971).

Egg-laying was initiated as early as May 18 in the Klamath Basin, California (Rienecker and Anderson 1960); May 11, Freezeout Lake, Montana (Ellig 1955); May 21, Brooks, Alberta (Keith 1961); May 16, Saskatchewan Delta (Townsend 1966); May 18-26, 1967-70, Yellowknife (Trauger 1971); and May 21-June 3, 1953-56, Fort Yukon, Alaska (Hansen 1956). Peak nest initiation occurred about June 6, Klamath Basin; June 6, Freezeout Lake; May 31, Brooks; June 6, Saskatchewan Delta; June 7-13, Yellowknife; and June 19-20, Fort Yukon. The last nests were started July 13, Klamath Basin; July 11, Freezeout Lake; June 21, Brooks; June 27, Saskatchewan Delta; and June 25-July 3, Yellowknife. The span of nest initiation was 61 days at Freezeout Lake, Montana; 56 days in the Klamath Basin; 42 days, Saskatchewan Delta; 31 days at Brooks; and 32 to 38 days at Yellowknife.

Nest Success. About 43 percent of lesser scaup nests (1,055) were successful in studies made from California to Alaska. Success involving 50 or more nests ranged as follows: 14 percent in the Erickson, Manitoba, region (Rogers 1964); 25 percent near Brooks, Alberta (Keith 1961); 26 percent at Minto Lakes, Alaska (Rowinski 1958); 41 percent in the Redvers, Saskatchewan, area (Stoudt 1971); 47 percent in the Lousana, Alberta, area (Smith 1971); 48 percent in Saskatchewan and Alberta (Kalmbach 1937); 67 percent in the Saskatchewan Delta (Townsend 1966), and 90 percent on islands in Miquelon Lakes, Alberta (Vermeer 1968).

Reasons for the lowest and the highest nest success deserve elaboration. In the pothole region near Erickson, Manitoba, Rogers (1964) reported that scaup nest success ranged from 3.8 to 12.5 percent in three dry seasons but was 50 percent during a wet season. Nest success was low in the dry years because of heavy nest predation by skunks. Moreover, at the peak of the drought in 1959, receding water levels in the potholes deterred breeding, so that only 8 percent of the pairs nested compared with 60 to 68 percent in other years.

On two islands in Miquelon Lakes, Alberta, nesting California and ring-billed gulls may have discouraged crows and other nest predators, resulting in an unusually high nest success of 90 percent (Vermeer 1968). However, these gulls preyed so heavily upon the ducklings that none reached flight stage.

Various studies recording the fate of eggs in 228 successful nests reported that 0.67 egg per nest failed to hatch. On the unhatched eggs, 61 percent were infertile, and the others contained dead embryos. Thus, the average number of hatched eggs per successful nest is 8.33

Nest Failure. In studies of nest destruction, two-thirds of the predaceous losses of scaup nests were attributed to mammals and one-third to birds. Skunks were responsible for about 90 percent of the identified mammal losses, and other destruction was attributed to ground squirrels and weasels. Crows and magpies were the only avian predators identified. Rogers (1964) believed that high nest destruction occurred among scaups because of their tendency to nest near water late in the season, a time that juvenile skunks became active foragers in the same areas near water.

Renesting. Hunt and Anderson (1966) found that in Lassen County, California, 5 of 31 marked scaups renested once, 2 renested twice, and 1 renested three times. The scaups moved their renest sites an average of 464 yards from initial ones. Clutch size in first nests averaged 10.6, 8.8 eggs in first renests, 7.5 eggs in second renests, and 7 eggs in the sole third renest. The number of days between nestings ranged from 5 to 21.

Keith (1961) concluded that 39 percent of the scaup hens near Brooks, Alberta, renested, for he found 245 nests although there were only 190 pairs on his study area. Initial nests contained 10.6 eggs and presumed renests, 8.4 eggs. However, near Erickson, Manitoba, Rogers (1964) found no evidence of renesting, perhaps because of low water and generally poor conditions for nesting.

Production. During the predrought years of 1953-58, 16 percent of 558 pairs on a study area at Lousana, Alberta, produced broods (Smith 1971). During the drought years, 1959-63, 410 pairs produced 14 broods (3 percent). Recovery of the habitat from drought, 1964-65, resulted in 82 pairs producing 12 broods (15 percent).

On the Yellowknife study area, 1967-70, 29 to 41 percent of the pairs produced broods (Trauger 1971). Over a 4-year-period, a total of 636 breeding pairs produced 224 broods, a success rate of 35 percent, or 2.3 Class I ducklings per breeding pair. On the same area, 1962-64, 26 percent of 1,082 breeding pairs produced broods (Murdy 1964).

One-third of the scaup pairs in southeastern Alberta, 1953-57, were ultimately successful in producing broods (Keith 1961). There, as well as at Lousana, Alberta, scaups were considerably less successful than other species. Their rate of success at Yellowknife was less than those of all common species (100 or more breeding pairs, 1962-64) except mallards and pintails (Murdy 1964).

Rearing of Young

Broods. Lesser scaup hens often desert their young while they are still in the down stage, and most of the broods are on their own by the age of 4 to 5 weeks (Gehrman 1951). Deserted downy young may join other broods, so that one female may escort two or three broods, or, on the other hand, two or three hens with their broods may combine. Gehrman observed that females whose nests hatched early remained with their broods longer than those whose broods hatched late, but one female was observed with a brood as late as September 8.

Development. Young lesser scaups reach flight stage in 47-plus days in South Dakota (Gollop and Marshall 1954) and in 50 days in Manitoba (Rogers 1962). At Yellowknife, Northwest Territories, hatch and fledging dates of lesser scaups were 47 days apart (Murdy 1964). On the Yukon Flats, Alaska, dates of first broods observed and of first flying young span periods of 45 and 47 days (Lensink 1964).

Survival. Downy (Class I) broods average 6.98 ducklings (1,874), a decline of 16 percent from the 8.33 eggs hatched per successful nest. Because broods combine, the size of older broods is probably not a reliable measure of mortality prior to flight. Counts of Class II and III brood sizes, amounting to 6.83 (611) and 6.89 (73) ducklings, respectively, further suggest the addition of ducklings to older broods.

Munro's (1941) observations of scaup broods in British Columbia led him to conclude that the number of young surviving to late summer is higher than in other species. According to Gehrman (1951), mortality among young scaups appeared to be negligible in eastern Washington.

POSTBREEDING SEASON

In eastern Washington, Gehrman (1951) observed that some nonbreeding males began to show traces of the eclipse plumage as early as mid-June. Mated males began to reach this stage 2 weeks later, even though still paired. A large proportion of the males left the study lake before mid-July to molt elsewhere.

On the Yellowknife study area, Northwest Territories, Trauger (1971) noticed a constant exodus of males throughout the breeding season. Unmated males departed first, in early June, followed by breeding males in late June and early July. Small numbers of males remained on the area to complete the wing molt in late July and early August.

At Tetlin, Alaska, McKnight and Buss (1962) reported that lesser scaups normally begin the wing molt about mid-July and complete it by late August. During the first 2 weeks of this period, adult males make up most of the flightless birds, but early in August nonbreeding females compose almost half of the molters. They considered that the individual flightless period lasted 2 to 3 weeks, but this seems unusually brief.

In preparation for the wing molt, tens of thousands of lesser scaups migrate to the myriad lakes lying between the Athabasca Delta and Saskatchewan Delta in Canada's boreal forest. For many years these lakes have been surveyed in August and September by Ducks Unlimited. Data supplied by William Leitch from these aerial surveys show the presence of large numbers of flightless scaups: hundreds on Canoe, thousands on Macallum, several thousand on Upper Cummins Lake, August 25, 1940; about half of the 12,000 scaups were flightless on Macallum Lake, September 4, 1963; 10 per acre on Kazan Lake, August 6, 1946, but very few of 2,200 were flightless on August 28, 1954; 400 flightless scaups per acre on Niska Lake, and 400 per mile of shoreline on Garson Lake, August 19, 1947, but most of 34,000 observed there on August 25, 1957, could fly; 2,000 scaups per mile of shoreline on Gordon Lake and 8,000 to 10,000 on Methy Lake were flightless on September 9, 1962; yet, 3,800 on Canoe Lake could fly, September 4, 1962, as could 1,000 scaups per mile of shoreline on Macallum Lake, the same day; 3,000 to 4,000 scaups per mile of Macallum Lake were fliers on September 9, 1962.

Many more thousands of scaups are listed for other times and other lakes, but the reports fail to indicate the stage of the wing molt.

FOOD HABITS

Lesser scaups feed by diving in waters of diverse depths. I have observed them feeding in the spring in roadside ponds, farm ponds, and flooded fields only a few feet deep. By way of contrast, I have watched them feeding 5 to 10 miles offshore in the Gulf of Mexico in waters 15 to 40 feet deep. More commonly they feed in water 10 to 25 feet deep. With the exception of the sea ducks, they feed in deeper waters than do other diving species.

In most areas lesser scaups feed primarily on animal life, but in a few areas plant seeds or leafy structures are more important. At Currituck Sound, North Carolina, the seeds and foliage of pondweeds and widgeon grass made up over three-fourths of the scaup's diet, with animal foods forming only a trace (Quay and Critcher 1965). The principal foods of this species in coastal South Carolina were seeds of panic grasses, smartweeds, and bulrushes; animal matter composed less than 1 percent (Kerwin and Webb 1972). Muskgrass, bulrush, and smartweed seeds were important items consumed by scaups in Missouri, with animal foods composing only 11 percent (Korschgen 1955).

Plant foods comprised 60 percent and animal foods 40 percent of the contents of lesser scaup gizzards from several regions of the United States (Cottam 1939). However, almost half of these gizzards were collected in April from eastern Wisconsin, where aquatic plants were abundant. Seeds and vegetative parts of pondweeds, widgeon grass, and wild celery, the seeds of wild rice and bulrushes were the more important plant foods. Snails, clams, and aquatic insects were the animal foods most often consumed.

Other studies of food habits show animal life to be more important than plant life in scaup diets. Off the Louisiana coast, where a half to over a million scaups winter, 99.8 percent of the food consisted of surf clams (Harmon 1962). Scaups wintering on the Laguna Madre of Texas fed one-third more on animal foods (snails, clams, crabs) than on shoalgrass, the only plant food.

Almost two-thirds of the lesser scaup's diet from areas of Louisiana's coastal marsh was animal food (Rogers and Korschgen 1966), mostly fish, crayfish, freshwater shrimp, water boatmen, and midges. Along the Connecticut coast of Long Island Sound, plants composed 38 percent and animal foods 62 percent of the material found in lesser scaup gizzards (Cronan 1957*b*). Sea lettuce and salt-marsh bulrush seeds were the plant foods, and clams made up 85 percent of the animal food consumed. At Humboldt Bay on the northern coast of California, the principal foods of lesser scaups were clams, 45 percent; unidentified mollusca, 9 percent; unidentified crustaceans, 5 percent; unidentified plant parts, 35 percent; and wheat (undoubtedly bait), 5 percent (Yocom and Keller 1961).

Food habits of the lesser scaup on the Keokuk Pool of the Mississippi River, between Keokuk and Burlington, Iowa, have been studied by Rogers and Korschgen (1966), Thompson (1973), and Anderson (1959). This is one of the most important areas of concentration of lesser scaups in the interior of the United States during fall and spring migration, and therefore it is especially important to determine the foods required to support several hundred thousand scaups. Animal foods occurred in 90 percent of the ducks studied by Rogers and Korschgen and in 94 percent of those examined by Thompson. In the 18 years between the two studies, the important animal food changed from snails in 1948 (snails a minimum of 92 percent of occurrence, clams no more than 38) to clams in 1966-67 (snails a minimum of 68 percent of occurrence, clams a minimum of 92). Mayfly larvae occurred in 15 percent of the gizzards in 1948 and 13 percent in 1966-67. Anderson's (1959) studies showed that animals composed 90 percent of the food items taken by scaups, snails accounting for 48 percent and clams 39 percent of all animal foods.

About 90 percent of the summer foods of the lesser scaup on its breeding grounds in southwestern Manitoba are of animal origin (Rogers and Korschgen 1966, Bartonek and Hickey 1969). Scuds (amphipods), midges, water boatmen, and caddis flies were the most important items. Scuds also composed the bulk of the food found in juvenile and adult scaup gizzards taken during the summer in British Columbia (Munro 1941).

Examination of scaup gullets from the Saskatchewan Delta showed that animal items composed 90 percent or more of the food taken in May, June, July, and October. Scuds made up a high proportion of the diet in May, June, and October, and leeches in July. During August and September, when animal life declined to 35 and 6 percent of the foods consumed, yellow water lily seeds predominated, forming 39 percent of the items taken in August and 86 percent in September.

Bartonek and Murdy (1970) examined juvenile and lesser scaup esophagi from the open boreal forest (taiga) north of Great Slave Lake. All birds fed almost exclusively on animal matter. During June, adults fed largely upon scuds, followed by snails, fingernail clams, and leeches, all bottom-dwelling animals. Young juveniles consumed phantom midge larvae and clam shrimp, free-swimming forms. Older juveniles fed upon bottom organisms, predominantly scuds and dragonflies and damselfly nymphs.

Common Eider

Somateria mollissima

There are four races of the common eider in North America, and the nominate race, *Somateria m. mollissima*, is restricted to northern Europe. The four races are: American eider *(Somateria mollissima dresseri)*, northern eider *(Somateria mollissima borealis)*, Hudson Bay eider *(Somateria mollissima sedentaria)*, and Pacific eider *(Somateria mollissima v-nigra)*. The principal differences among the races are size, feathering along the bill, and minor color markings.

VITAL STATISTICS

Age, Sex, and Race	Total Length (inches)	Weight (lb)	Wing (mm)	Culmen (mm)
Adult Males				
dresseri	22.5-26.8	3.9-4.6	263-292	54.0-59.5
Average	24.0(19)	4.38(3)	277.8(15)	56.5(15)
borealis		3.9-4.6	256-289	46.5-56.5
Average		4.12(8)	273.9(16)	50.5(16)
sedentaria		4.9-6.0	284-303	52.0-61.5
Average		5.54(8)	291.3(9)	56.6(9)
v-nigra	21.7-25.0	5.1-6.2	280-315	44.4-54.0
Average	22.7(32)	5.76(9)	303(22)	49.4(25)
Adult Females				
dresseri	21.0-24.4	2.6-3.8	262-284	45.5-55.5
Average	22.8(23)	3.38(8)	270.6(17)	51.2(17)
borealis		3.3-4.6	259-278	44.7-47.2
Average		3.87(12)	267.0(6)	45.8(6)
sedentaria		3.5-6.67	272-305	49.5-55.7
Average		5.23(7)	284.9(24)	52.2(5)
v-nigra	23.0-24.7	4.7-6.4	251-280	44.0-51.5
Average	23.7(5)	5.30(5)	267.7(31)	47.9(30)

Data are from Snyder (1941), Kortright (1942), Brandt (1943), Manning et al. (1956), Macpherson and McLaren (1959), and Freeman (1970*a*). The weights are for summer-collected specimens.

IDENTIFICATION

Field

Common eiders are the largest ducks in North America and in the entire Northern Hemisphere. They are stocky, thick-necked birds that appear ungainly in flight, alternately flapping their wings and sailing, with their heads held below body level. They customarily fly in a line very low over the water, sometimes in the troughs of waves.

The male is a study in black and white—much of the head, neck, chest, and back are white and the breast, belly, sides, rump, tail coverts, and tail are black. The wings of the male in flight resemble white and black triangles—the leading and proximal halves are white and the distal and trailing halves are black. The underwings are similar in pattern but the color tones are muted to gray-white and brownish black. A black cap covers the crown and forehead, and a round white spot occurs on the black flank just forward of the tail.

The head, in both sexes, presents a sloping profile, similar to that of the canvasback. At rest, the head is tilted upwards. Females are russet-brown, heavily barred with dark brown on their backs, chests, breasts, sides, and flanks. Only the females of all four species of eiders are heavily barred. The bars are linear in the common and crescent-shaped in the king eider.

At Hand

The black cap of the adult male is partially cleft by a white line and the sides and back of the head are suffused with pale green. The white chest is tinged with pink. A black "V" marks the white throat of the Pacific race, and, rarely, individuals of other races. The bill of the male is gray-green, turning orange-yellow in the spring. Both sexes have a membranous extension of the bill forming a Y-shaped frontal shield that reaches almost to the eye. The degree to which the tips of this frontal shield are pointed or rounded aids in distinguishing the four races of the common eider. The tips are pointed in the northern and Pacific races and are rounded in the American and Hudson Bay races. Hudson Bay eiders, especially the females, are noticeably paler than the other races.

In adult males the elongated, sickle-shaped tertials and the lesser and middle wing coverts are creamy white; the primaries, secondaries, and greater wing coverts are black. Adult females have black-brown primaries, secondaries, and tertials; the dusky brown middle and lesser wing coverts are margined by chestnut, the central greater coverts are tipped by white, and the others are tipped by russet. The tertials are not as strongly sickle-shaped in females as in males nor in immatures as in adults.

Adult males begin to molt into their eclipse plumage in late June or early July and regain their nuptial plumage by November. The male's eclipse plumage is mostly dusky brown, with the back and chest lightly mottled by white.

Young-of-the-year begin molting from their juvenile plumage in September into an immature plumage that is not complete until April. During this protracted molt, the heads, necks, and chests of the males gradually become whiter and the sides and flanks blacker. In the second fall, immatures largely resemble adults, but the white of their backs is marked by scattered dusky feathers, the lesser wing coverts are brownish, and the white greater coverts are edged with dusky; their breasts and bellies are dull brown-black, presenting a mottled appearance along the borders of their white chests. Immature males assume complete adult plumage after their second eclipse molt at an age of 28 to 30 months (Bent 1925).

POPULATION STATUS

Because of the extensive Arctic range of common eiders, figures on their continent-wide population are lacking. King and Lensink (1971) calculated the summer eider population in Alaska at 105,000. The bulk of this number, possibly 75,000, are common (Pacific race) eiders. Barry (1968) estimated that 1,108,000 king and common eiders migrate east-west along the Beaufort Sea, and that (personal communication) about a fourth of these (275,000) are common eiders.

Ornithological surveys in the high-Arctic, as far east as southern Baffin Island, indicate that king eiders are much more abundant there than common eiders. However, from southwest Baffin Island south along the coasts of Hudson Bay, the Ungava Peninsula, and Labrador to Maine, common eiders are many times more abundant than king eiders. As many as 500,000 American eiders have appeared off the Massachusetts coast (Griscom and Snyder 1955). A consideration of the great abundance of common eiders in the East leads me to speculate that there are 1.5 to 2.0 million of this species in North America.

The common eider in the Arctic and Subarctic has probably maintained a semi-stable population subject to yearly fluctuations caused by aberrant weather. Unusually severe weather during the breeding season no doubt lowers production of young in certain years. Similarly, abnormal freeze-ups in the Arctic ice pack must cause unusually heavy mortality during the years they occur.

However, the south-breeding American race of the common eider has shown an ever upward increase since the early 20th century. The increase has been especially spectacular since the 1930's. Records from the area of Grand Manan Island, New Brunswick, showed increases from a dozen pairs in 1908 to 185 pairs in 1936 to 1,200 nests in the late 1940's (Paynter 1951). Only one pair was known to nest along the Maine coast in 1905 (Gross 1944), but by the early 1940's the population exceeded 2,000 pairs. This number had grown to an incredible 20,000 breeding pairs by 1967 (Mendall 1968). With the establishment of refuges in the St. Lawrence Estuary, nesting eiders increased 37 percent between 1925 and 1935 (Todd 1963).

Sex Ratios

Sex ratios taken of common eiders during spring migration, 1955-56, near Cape Dorset, Baffin Island, revealed a large surplus of drakes (Cooch 1965). Between May 13 and June 3, males outnumbered females 2.24:1 (69 percent) in 1955 and 1:0.28 (78 percent) in 1956. Early arrivals had the largest proportion of males (87 percent to 76 percent); females became more common as May advanced and after June 1 in 1955 and June 5 in 1956, sex ratios were even as birds prepared to nest. Undoubtedly, unmated drakes and nonbreeders moved farther out to sea. On the other hand, in a survey of 8,348 American eiders along the Maine coast in May, Mendall (1968) found 1 male to 0.95 female (51 percent).

Mortality

Hunters take only a small proportion of the common eider population in North America. Eskimos kill perhaps 1 percent of the common eiders at the famed eider pass at Point Barrow, Alaska, and even smaller proportions elsewhere in the state. Perhaps as many as 10,000 are killed along the coasts of Labrador, Quebec, the Maritimes, and New England. However, Salomonsen (1950-51) reported that along the west coast of Greenland, 150,000 were killed; about 30 to 40 percent of those banded at Thule were shot.

DISTRIBUTION

Common eiders are circumpolar in their range, but there

are extensive gaps in their breeding grounds around the rim of the Arctic Ocean. The European race breeds from the islands of Novaya Zemlya, and Vaigach in eastern Russia west along the White Sea coast; around the coasts of Scandinavia to include the Baltic Sea and the northern Jutland Peninsula; in the North Atlantic, the island groups of the Faeroes, the Shetlands, the Orkneys, and the Hebrides; and the coasts of Scotland and Iceland. The Pacific race breeds from Victoria Island, Northwest Territories, Canada, west along the Beaufort Sea and Bering Sea coasts of Alaska and Siberia to include the Aleutians and Karagin Island, and along the Chukot Peninsula as far west as Cape Vankarem and Chaun Bay. The northern race breeds along the coasts of Greenland, Baffin and Southampton islands, and the north coast of Labrador. The American race breeds from southern Labrador to Casco Bay, Maine. The Hudson Bay race is confined to the islands and coasts of Hudson and James bays.

Most races winter amazingly far north, not far from their northern breeding ranges, wherever seas remain open in the Arctic. They migrate only as far south as necessary to find food.

Breeding Range

The Pacific race of the common eider breeds from Sitka and Glacier Bay in southeast Alaska, and from the Alaska Peninsula around the coast to Demarcation Point, then eastward along the Beaufort Sea as far as southeast Victoria Island and the Kent Peninsula. From Victoria Island eastward across the Boothia Peninsula there is a break in continuity between the Pacific and northern races of the eider. The northern race breeds from Cornwallis Island across northern Greenland and south to include Baffin and Southampton islands, Ungava Bay, and the Labrador coast south to Hopedale. From the southern Labrador coast, Newfoundland, and the Gulf of St. Lawrence south into Maine, the American race of the common eider is recognized as the breeding form. A fourth race, the Hudson Bay eider (Snyder 1941), is restricted to the east and west coasts of Hudson and James bays and the islands within these bays.

The Pacific race is by far the most abundant of the four eiders breeding in Alaska. The numbers of eiders breeding in the Aleutian Islands are unknown, but they occur from Unalaska to Attu. On just three islets at the mouth of Constantine Harbor on Amchitka Island, Kenyon (1961) recorded 65 nests. However, the principal breeding ground in Alaska appears to be the coast of the Yukon Peninsula, where King and Lensink (1971) estimate 51,000 eiders, mostly of the Pacific race. The Arctic Slope harbors 47,000 eiders, and James Bartonek estimates from ground surveys that 80 percent are Pacific eiders and the others are king eiders. Most of the 4,900 breeding eiders of the Seward Peninsula and the 1,700 at Bristol Bay are common (Pacific) eiders. Eiders are also known to breed on the islands of Nunivak, St. Matthew, and St. Lawrence in the Bering Sea. Fay (1961) estimated that 3,500 Pacific eiders breed on St. Lawrence Island and, additionally, a smaller nonbreeding population occurs there in summer.

Along the Beaufort Sea in western Arctic Canada, Manning et al. (1956) estimated that there were 500 breeding pairs and 1,500 nonbreeding Pacific eiders on Banks Island, compared with 150,000 king eiders. Smith (1973) reported that common eiders appeared to comprise only 5 percent of the total eider population on western Victoria Island. Parmelee et al. (1967) found the Pacific race breeding on a number of small islands off the southeast coast of Victoria Island. A few eiders assumed to belong to the Pacific race—but no nests or broods—have been seen on King William Island and the Adelaide Peninsula (Fraser 1957). No common eiders have been observed on the Boothia Peninsula, where the king eider is the most abundant duck (Fraser 1957).

To the north on Cornwallis Island, Geale (1971) found the common eider to be a more abundant breeding bird than the king eider. On west-central Ellesmere Island, Parmelee and MacDonald (1960) found no common eiders, but king eiders were fairly numerous. From the Foxe Peninsula along the south coast of Baffin Island, Bray (1943), Soper (1946), and Macpherson and McLaren (1959) have all reported the northern race of the common eider to be the most abundant breeding duck, with few or no king eiders. The northern eiders were particularly abundant on outlying islands. Soper (1946) found them most numerous on the Savage Islands and on the islands west of Big Island off the south coast of Baffin Island. Wynne-Edwards (1952) observed northern eiders at Padloping Island and at several places in Frobisher Bay, Baffin Island. Numerous northern eiders breed on many areas along the coasts of Greenland (Salomonsen 1950-51). The largest breeding colonies are in the Thule District, where the most flourishing colonies, on a number of islets around Etah, harbor more than 10,000 pairs. The northern race is not known to breed farther north than Hall Land on the west coast and Germania Land on the east coast. Bray (1943) reported northern eiders on outlying islands along the northeast coast of the Melville Peninsula southwest of Baffin Island, but nowhere on the peninsula itself. He also found them nesting on the south coast of Southampton Island.

The Hudson Bay form of the common eider is restricted summer and winter to Hudson and James bays, south of the islands of Southampton, Coates, and Mansel (Godfrey 1966). On 1 square mile of Promise Island, near Chesterfield Inlet, Höhn (1968) found 76 pairs of Hudson Bay eiders compared with 1 or 2 pairs of king eiders. Along the east coast of Hudson Bay, Manning (1946) recorded 1,100 common eiders to 10 king eiders. Freeman (1970*b*) found the Hudson Bay eider to be an abundant nesting duck in the Belcher Islands and had a report of king eiders nesting on an island in the North Belcher group. On the east coast of James Bay, Manning and Macpherson (1952) found the common eider nesting on several islands, particularly Solomons Temple. On Gasket Shoal, northwest of Charlton Island in James Bay, Manning and Coates (1952) found 200 nests of the Hudson Bay eider and have an old breeding record of the king eider.

The American race of the common eider breeds from Hamilton Inlet (Labrador) and Newfoundland south through the St. Lawrence Estuary to Casco Bay, Maine. Its center of abundance comprises the offshore islands and islets of the St. Lawrence Estuary. It has greatly increased in breeding numbers since the early 1900's and has steadily extended its range south along the Maine coast. In 1943, the estimated number of breeding pairs in Maine was 2,000 or more (Gross 1944), but by 1967 the estimate had increased to 20,000 pairs (Mendall 1968).

Migration Corridors

Many of the migration courses followed by common eiders are steeped in mystery because they occur over the sea. Seldom are flocks observed migrating offshore, and, complicating the mystery, eiders migrate relatively short distances. The most extensive and best-known migration corridor is the one followed by Pacific eiders between winter grounds in the Bering Sea and breeding grounds along the Beaufort Sea. Both king and Pacific eiders follow this migration corridor, and because king eiders are the more abundant, details of this passage are given in the account of that species.

Cooch (1965) recorded that the northern eiders breeding in southern Baffin Island migrated through Hudson Strait, and, as indicated by band recoveries, some continued as far south as Newfoundland and the St. Lawrence Estuary (Anticosti Island). Todd (1963) also recorded the passage of eiders through Hudson Strait and along the coast of Labrador. Postbreeding birds from the south shore of the St. Lawrence Estuary migrated east along the Gaspé Peninsula between mid-September and late November (Guignion 1967).

Winter Areas

Most Pacific eiders winter in the Bering Sea. However, some have been taken during the winter months as far north as Point Hope (Tigara), Alaska, 125 miles north of the Arctic Circle (Gabrielson and Lincoln 1959). Fay (1961) recorded upwards of 50,000 eiders wintering near St. Lawrence Island, Bering Sea. The majority were king eiders, with smaller numbers of the Pacific race mixed with them. Dement'ev and Gladkov (1967) reported that thousands of Pacific eiders collected in winter near the Diomede Islands in Bering Strait and that many birds congregated in the area of the Commander Islands. There are numerous records of Pacific eiders wintering among islands of the Aleutian Chain. South of Kodiak Island, Pacific eiders are only casual visitors. Godfrey (1966) listed two records for British Columbia, one in the Queen Charlotte Islands and one at Vancouver Island. In the state of Washington, Jewett et al. (1953) cited only a few records of Pacific eiders in Puget Sound, all dating back to the early 1900's. No records are listed for Oregon.

Small numbers of Pacific eiders may winter in the Beaufort Sea as far east as Victoria Island—one was collected off the island's east coast January 9, 1918 (Parmelee et al. 1967). According to Bray (1943), the northern race of the common eider winters as far north as Cape Fullerton, at the northwest corner of Hudson Bay. Soper (1946) reported that a few birds remain through the winter off the southwest coast of Baffin Island. A small number winter in the Thule District of Greenland on the west coast and as far north as Wollaston Forland on the east coast (Salomonsen 1950-51). South of Holsteinsborg, Greenland, the sea remains open all year and that is where most of the northern eiders winter. When the fjords are not frozen, the eiders appear in the evening, spend the night, and depart for the open sea in the morning. The Hudson Bay race winters entirely within the confines of Hudson and James bays, mostly in the vicinity of the Belcher Islands.

Common eiders have been found in winter at Port Burwell (Killinek Island) and Nain (Labrador); specimens taken at Battle Harbour in late fall were of the northern race (Todd 1963). In Newfoundland, Peters and Burleigh (1951) found the northern eider to be a fairly common winter resident that arrives as the breeding population of the American race migrates south. A few specimens of the northern eider have been taken along the Massachusetts coast (Griscom and Snyder 1955).

The American eider is apparently the principal race wintering from the Gulf of St. Lawrence south along the Atlantic Coast to Virginia. Audubon Christmas bird counts in 1972 recorded 1,650 common eiders near St. John's, Newfoundland; 649 in the coastal waters of Nova Scotia; 7,447 in coastal Maine; 655 in New Hampshire; 37,004 in Massachusetts; 234 in Rhode Island and Connecticut; 586 in coastal Long Island; 2 in New Jersey; 1 at Prime Hook National Wildlife Refuge, Delaware, and 1 at Ocean City, Maryland. The large aggregations in Maine occur in the area of Mt. Desert Island and Penobscot Bay, in Massachusetts within the triangle of Cape Cod, Martha's Vineyard, and Nantucket Island. Griscom and Snyder (1955) estimated that the main wintering group in this area increased from 15,000 in 1940 to about 500,000 in 1951. Bull (1964) reported that off Montauk Point, Long Island, the American eider has increased in numbers since 1940.

MIGRATION BEHAVIOR

Migration of common eiders occurs so extensively during daytime that it is doubtful that any appreciable numbers migrate at night. Usually, migrating flocks contain from 10 to 30 birds, but occasionally several hundred form a single flock. Where points of land project into the sea, eiders frequently fly low across them, enabling Eskimos to shoot large numbers. These eider passes have been used since time immemorial and have been reported from widely dispersed regions of the Arctic and Subarctic. One of the greatest and best known eider passes is at Point Barrow,

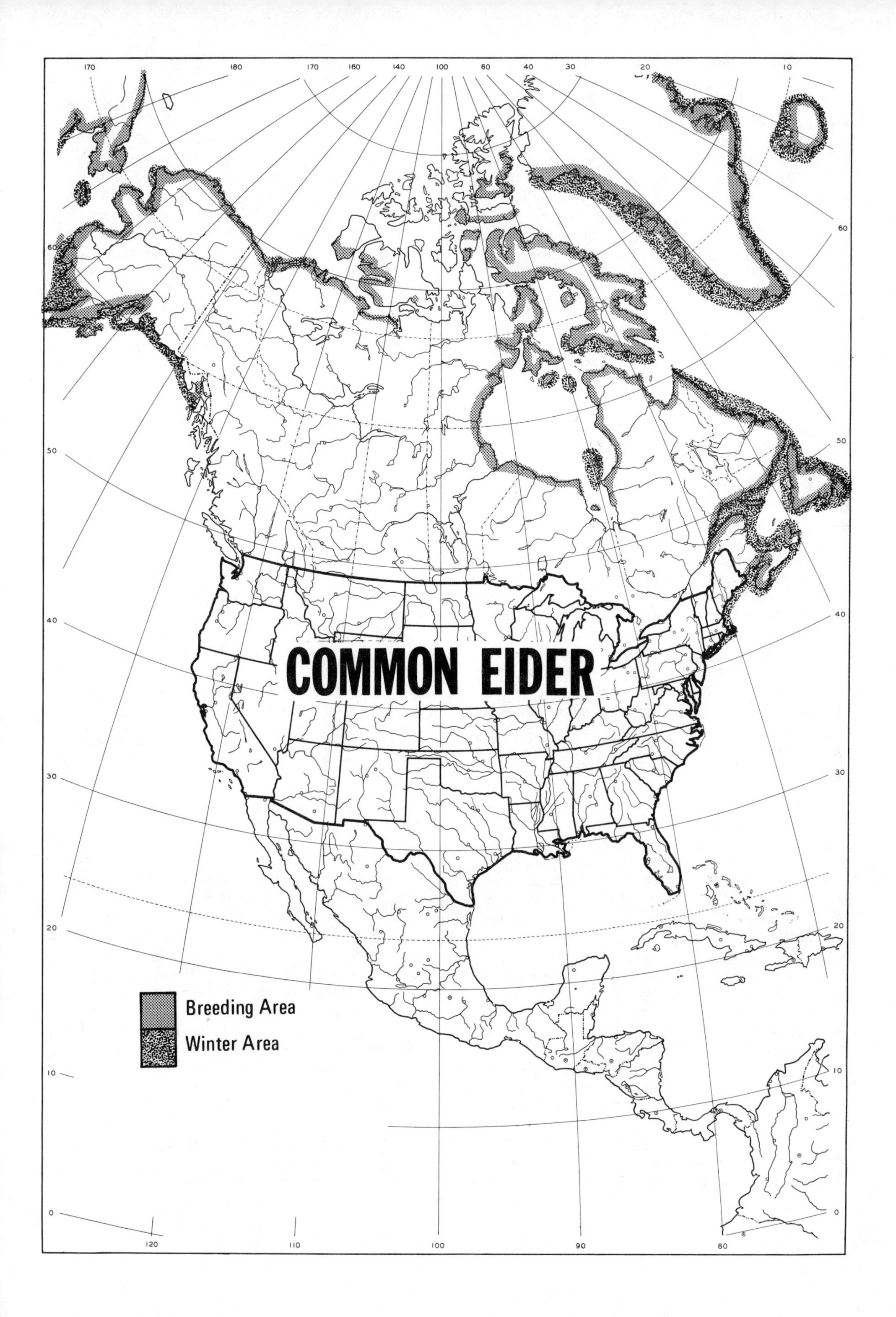
COMMON EIDER
Breeding Area
Winter Area

Alaska, where Pacific and king eiders are abundant. (Thompson and Person 1963).

Chronology

Fall. Although small numbers of eiders remain close to their breeding areas, there is a general exodus during fall, some birds flying laterally out to sea but even more of them heading southward. Pacific and king eiders migrate westward past Point Barrow from early July until late October (Gabrielson and Lincoln 1959, Thompson and Person 1963). The first migrants are adult males, followed by females and young. On western Victoria Island, Smith (1973) saw very few males in August, and all eiders were gone by mid-September. Soper (1946) remarked that males left Baffin Island in early autumn, many weeks before the females and young departed. According to Salomonsen (1950-51), the autumn migration from northern Greenland occurs during September and October, resulting in a large increase in numbers along the southwest coast.

Todd (1963) observed a large passage of American eiders along the southeast coast of Labrador October 9-15. He noted that the sexes were flying in separate flocks. Periodic aerial surveys of sea ducks off the coasts of Maine, New Hampshire, and Massachusetts, 1965-68, revealed these chronological changes in numbers of common eiders (Tice 1970): an increase from 41,900 on October 13 to 119,000 on December 15, 1965 (most of the increase occurred after November 26); a fairly constant increase from 7,300 on September 1, 1966, to 120,000 on January 16, 1967; and a slow but steady increase from 1,300 on September 1, 1967, to 73,900 on January 16, 1968. It should be emphasized that these numbers represent only a sample of the total offshore eider population, which is much larger than is indicated by these figures.

Spring. Tracing early migrants of the Pacific race around the coast of Alaska, Gabrielson and Lincoln (1959) reported their appearance at Hooper Bay on May 4, Icy Cape on May 24, Wainwright on May 23, Barrow on May 16, and Demarcation Point on May 26. Most of the flight of Pacific eiders passed Point Dall, Yukon Delta, between May 7 and May 15, but scattered flocks continued until May 25 (Brandt 1943). Fay (1961) noted that large numbers appeared at St. Lawrence Island about May 15.

Schamel (1974) reports that the availability of open water along the Arctic Slope of Alaska determines the eastward progress of migrating eiders. He noticed the first open water and a pair of eiders near Prudhoe Bay on June 1; 3 days later large flocks of Pacific and king eiders were migrating eastward. As the Kuparuk River opened a large lead in the Beaufort Sea ice, a spectacular increase in Pacific eiders occurred during the period of June 19-22. Earlier, the Eskimos had reported that the first Pacific eiders appeared off Sachs Harbour, Banks Island, about April 10 (Manning et al. 1956). Although small numbers were observed there between May 20 and June 5, they did not appear inland until June 15. Farther east at Dease Strait, Parmelee et al. (1967) noted their arrival about mid-June.

On the opposite side of the continent, the American eider usually leaves Montauk Point, Long Island, by late March (Bull 1964). Near Grand Manan Island, New Brunswick, Paynter (1951) reported arrivals from as early as February 26 to as late as April 7, 1937-48. Peters and Burleigh (1951) believed that the American race is present in Newfoundland from April to October and is then replaced for the winter by the northern race. A record of its arrival at Cape Charles, Labrador, on March 7 dates back to 1771 (Todd 1963)—thousands were flying north there on April 26.

At Churchill, Manitoba, common eiders were not noted until June 5 (Littlefield and Pakulak 1969), but farther north at Chesterfield Inlet they were recorded at sea on May 15, with migration continuing until June 8. Their first appearance on inland tundra ponds occurred at Chesterfield Inlet on June 11. Near the Foxe Peninsula, Baffin Island, Macpherson and McLaren (1959) observed first arrivals May 10-19, 1954-55; pairs and small groups arrived before the large aggregations. On May 15, 1955, they saw 900 in an 8-square-mile opening in the pack ice off the south end of Dorset Island. On remote Cornwallis Island, common eiders did not appear until June 29 (Geale 1971).

BREEDING

Behavior

Age, Pair Bond, and Homing. According to Mendall (1968), American eiders do not breed until they are at least 3 years old. Large numbers of nonbreeding immatures are reported in the vicinity of many breeding grounds.

Guignion (1967) observed that the first eiders returning to nest islands in the St. Lawrence Estuary in mid-April were already paired; subsequently, unpaired birds appeared, resulting in active courtship and pairing throughout May. At Amchitka Island in the Aleutians, Pacific eiders form pair bonds in early May, with many pairs remaining in flocks up to mid-June (Kenyon 1961). Cooch (1965) reported that early migrants to southern Baffin Island are in sex-segregated flocks. He observed courtship at Cape Dorset after their arrival in early May. Earlier in the season, he witnessed more extensive courtship 250 miles east of there, leading him to conclude that pairing occurs during migration as well as on the Cape Dorset breeding grounds. After their arrival on the North Slope of Alaska in June, Schamel (1974) observed little if any courtship, suggesting that pairing had already occurred.

The length of time that male common eiders remain with their mates varies considerably with race. Common eiders in Iceland remain with their females for 2 weeks or more after incubation begins (Munro 1961). In Greenland, drakes remain by the nests during the first period of incubation, then join flocks of other drakes and immatures (Salomonsen 1950-51). At Cape Dorset, Baffin Island, males remain in close association with their mates throughout the egg-laying period and for a few days thereafter, then begin to spend more and more time with other males (Cooch 1965). In early nesting, eiders in Alaska maintain their pair bonds through the first few days of incubation, but in late nesting, the males leave before or during nest initiation (Schamel 1974).

Common eiders exhibit a phenomenal homing ability. Of 26 females banded on their nests at Cape Dorset in 1955, Cooch (1965) found 25 back on their breeding grounds the next year. All but two were retrapped on his study area; one nested on the same islet but outside the study boundaries, the other nested on a nearby islet. Eighteen females nested within 50 feet of their former nest sites, two others within 200 feet. These minor shifts in location probably occurred because lingering snowdrifts covered some of the old sites.

Home Range. Schamel (1974) observed that members of a Pacific eider colony had frequent antagonistic encounters on the nesting grounds. Aggressive displays and physical combat occurred as both mates attacked other pairs for the possession of a nest site. The female of the embattled pair physically attacked other females, biting and push-pulling her opponents whereas the male more frequently resorted to vocalized challenges and bluff charges.

Nesting

Nest Sites. Because the breeding range of the four races of the common eider in North America encompasses such far-flung coasts, their nest sites are quite diverse. Most of their nests are close to the sea, usually on small islands or islets, but sometimes they are located on tundra ponds distant from the coast. Eiders often nest in dense colonies, but many scattered breeders are distributed along hundreds of miles of coastline.

In Maine and the St. Lawrence Estuary, the American eider nests almost entirely on islands. It may nest under shrubs, spruce trees, driftwood, or in grasses and weeds. *Elymus* grass, where present, is often chosen for nest sites. Choate (1967) found that nest densities on two islands in Penobscot Bay, Maine, were 166 and 389 per acre. On 63-acre Brandypot Island (consisting of three islets), Guignion (1967) estimated 1,250 pairs of breeding eiders per 20 acres, and on a 1-acre islet (Little Pot) there were 550 active nests and 700 nest attempts.

Freeman (1970*a*) reported that two breeding eider colonies in the Belcher Islands averaged one nest per 80 square yards (605 per acre). On Promise Island, in Chesterfield Inlet on Hudson Bay, Höhn (1968) found 76 pairs of common eiders in a square mile (0.12 per acre). Cooch (1965) estimated that there were over 100 eider nests on an 8-acre ridge in an islet near Cape Dorset. Pacific eiders appear to nest less densely than the eastern races. No dense colonies have been reported in Alaska. Egg Island, near Prudhoe Bay, was selected for study because of the density of nesting eiders (Schamel 1974). Yet, even there, Pacific eider nests numbered just two per acre.

In Iceland, landowners construct nest scrapes and shelters to increase the number of breeding eiders (Munro 1961). One farmer dug rows of saucer-shaped depressions in hard-packed gravel ridges, where the birds were unable to scrape out nest hollows; most of these scrapes were used by nesting eiders. On another area, three-sided and roofed stalls, constructed of flat rocks, were also adopted as nest sites by eiders. At Cape Dorset, Cooch (1965) noted that eiders preferred nest sites surrounded by rocks or under overhanging rocks, and that many used man-made rock shelters.

Clark et al. (1974) made wood and rock shelters for nesting eiders on three islands in Penobscot Bay, Maine. Wood shelters with an entrance height of 6 to 7 inches were used extensively for early nesting, but as natural vegetation developed, the eiders tended to prefer it for nest sites.

In a study of 486 nest sites of northern eiders in the Cape Dorset area, slightly over half were within 200 feet of water but a few were over 1,000 feet away (Cooch 1965). Where Pacific eiders nested among the tundra ponds on the lower Yukon Delta, the sites were usually on islands in the ponds or on projecting points, but occasionally they were 200 yards from pond edges (Brandt 1943).

Many eiders use old nest sites, which are either in natural cup-shaped hollows or ones formerly scraped out by hens. Six nests of Pacific eiders measured 3 to 6 inches in height, 6 to 9 inches in inside diameter, 9 to 12 inches in outside diameter, and 2 to 4.5 inches in depth (Brandt 1943). On the first visit to an old nest site, the hen churns up the old base material with her bill to permit the contents to dry (Cooch 1965). New nests, however, are constructed the same day that the first egg is laid. Several seasons are required to complete the building of a proper nest base.

What makes eider nests so interesting—and economically important in Iceland and a few other places—is the down that lines the nest bowls. The down is light and cohesive and has the best thermal quality of any natural substance. In Munro's (1961:3) words: "A mass of eiderdown appears brownish-gray, flecked with white. It is marvelously light and soft, and is so compressible that the amount which can be wadded up in a man's fist will, when released, expand to the size of a canteloup." Cooch (1965) found that the amount of down in 748 nests averaged 28.9 grams per nest.

Most of the down feathers in the nest are gradually shed from the breast throughout the nest period (Cooch 1965). When down is lost or renesting is attempted, hens may then pluck down that is shorter and less cohesive than shed down. However, Guignion (1967) observed several females pluck down from their breasts and add it to their nests.

Clutch Size. Neither race nor latitude of nesting seems to account for the slight variations in average clutch sizes of common eiders. American eiders average 3.93 eggs per clutch (2,608); Hudson Bay eiders average 3.67 eggs (120); northern eiders, 3.44 eggs (1,598); and Pacific eiders, 4.25 eggs (97). Clutches of common eiders have ranged from 1 to 14 eggs, but most investigators consider that more than 7 eggs represents laying by more than one female.

Egg loss due to predation, the chronology of the nesting season, and probably the ages and energy levels of breeding eiders cause clutch sizes to vary. At Cape Dorset, the clutch size decreased as the season advanced (Cooch 1965). The earliest layers averaged 6.2 eggs, but for each day that nesting was delayed, clutch size declined 0.27 egg per day. Eiders that started 15 days late averaged only 2.2 eggs per clutch. On Brandypot Island, clutches initiated before May 24 averaged 4.60 eggs, those initiated later averaged 3.99 eggs (Guignion 1967). Pacific eider clutches initiated between June 19 and July 8 declined 0.18 egg per day (Schamel 1974). An eider hen lays one egg a day except when unseasonable weather interrupts laying—sometimes for several days.

Eggs. The pale olive-green eggs of the common eider are ovate in shape, with rough-textured shells. Eggs of the American eider average 76.2 by 51.2 mm (50 by Guignion 1967); eggs of the Hudson Bay eider average 80.6 by 52.7 mm (84 by Freeman 1970*a*); those of the northern eider, 75.4 by 50.4 mm (76 by Bent 1925); and those of the Pacific eider, 75.9 by 50.4 mm (85 by Bent 1925).

Incubation Period. The incubation period of the American eider was first given as 28 days by Gross (1938). In the St. Lawrence Estuary, Guignion (1967) determined that the incubation period averaged 26 days (range, 23 to 30) for 57 nests. Near Prudhoe Bay, Alaska, Schamel (1974) determined that the average incubation period for 11 nests of Pacific eiders lasted 26 days (range 21 to 28). Some confusion concerning the incubation period of the common eider arises because many females begin to incubate prior to the laying of the last egg (Cooch 1965). Some females start their incubation with the laying of the first egg, but most begin incubating after laying their third egg. Both Guignion (1967) and Schamel (1974) used the last egg laid as the basis for determining when incubation began. According to Cooch (1965), female eiders do not visit water areas after the first week of incubation, and Icelanders maintain that the hens do not feed during the entire incubation period (Munro 1961).

Chronology of Nesting. American eiders began nesting in the region of Penobscot Bay, Maine, in late April, with peaks from mid-May to June. Nest initiation usually ceases in late June, but in a late year it has continued to July 6 (Choate 1967, Clark 1968, Bourget 1973). Paynter (1951) reported that at Kent Island, New Brunswick, the dates of first-laid eggs ranged from May 4 to May 12 over a 10-year period. Guignion (1967) found that in the St. Lawrence Estuary, the first eggs were laid in late April. Peak efforts occurred the last 2 weeks of May, and the last nest was begun in late June.

On the Belcher Islands, Hudson Bay, nesting began about June 7 in 1960, and the greatest egg-laying activity occurred a week later (Freeman 1970*a*). Near Chesterfield Inlet, Hudson Bay, egg-laying started June 15 (Höhn 1968). At Cape Dorset, Baffin Island, egg-laying commenced June 19, 1955, and June 23, 1956 (Cooch 1965). More than 70 percent of all nests were started during the first half of the 24 days spanning the period of nest initiation. In high-Arctic Cornwallis Island, Geale (1971) found eight nests of the northern eider on July 7-8. Two nests with no down and only one egg each were probably just started, and a nest with two eggs contained a little down. In the five other nests, containing two to six eggs, there was abundant down.

Pacific eiders nesting on islands off the southeast coast of Victoria Island commence egg-laying in late June and continue into July (Parmelee et al. 1967). Near Prudhoe Bay, Alaska, Schamel (1974) found that nest initiation in 1972 started June 20, peaked June 24-27, and ended July 16. On Amchitka Island in the Aleutian Chain, egg-laying starts June 8-10 and continues into late June (Kenyon 1961).

The span of nest initiation in the races of the common eider varies less with latitude than in most other species of waterfowl. Near the southern terminus of its breeding at Penobscot Bay, Maine, the span for any 1 year is 50 to 60 days. Almost 300 miles due north on the south shore of the St. Lawrence Estuary, the span of nesting is still 50 to 60 days. But 1,100 miles farther north at Cape Dorset, the egg-laying period lasted 25 to 29 days in 1955-56. At Prudhoe Bay, Alaska, 425 additional miles north in latitude, the span of nest initiation embraces 22 days. Compared with other waterfowl nesting at similar Arctic latitudes, the span of nest initiation is longer in the common eider than in other species.

Nest Success. Nest success in the common eider is lowest in the American race, which nests at the southern extremity of the breeding range of the species, and highest in the northern race. American eiders nesting on islands in Penobscot Bay, Maine, have had nest successes that ranged (1964-67) from 15 percent to 40 percent (average for 1,707 nests was 32 percent, Choate 1967 and Clark 1968). Nest success at Kent Island, New Brunswick, was 29 percent for 134 nests (Paynter 1951). On three islets in the St. Lawrence Estuary, nest success was 13 percent on one islet, 29 percent on the second, and 52 percent on the third, an average of 32 percent for 538 nests (Guignion 1967).

Among northern eiders nesting at Cape Dorset, 82 percent of the eggs in 594 nests hatched (Cooch 1965). (Because numerous eggs were lost from successful nests, the actual percentage of success was somewhat higher.) At Prudhoe Bay, Alaska, 64 percent of 48 nests hatched successfully (Schamel 1974). On the Yukon Delta, 85 percent of 13 nests were successful (Olson 1951).

Much of the nest loss and egg destruction occurs prior to incubation. Choate (1967) found that success for nests with complete clutches was 61 percent (585) but for all nests was 38 percent (963). Nests with fewer than four eggs had a success of 51 percent; the success rate for larger clutches was 66 percent.

Nest Failure. Most nest failures and egg losses in common eiders are attributed to predation by herring and black-backed gulls and by ravens. Nesting on islands and islets enables most common eiders to escape destruction of their nests by foxes. Over most of the eiders' range, the destruction of eggs by gulls is the single greatest cause of loss. Losses from gull predation vary considerably among nest colonies, nesting seasons, and years.

Some eider colonies suffer more than others from predation by gulls. The degree of loss may depend upon the availability of overhead nest cover, the density of local gull populations, and weather conditions. As pointed out by Bourget (1973), the breeding chronologies between the herring and black-backed gulls and the common eider vary among years. When the nesting activity of the gulls predates the eider's, the greater aggressiveness of gulls during this period results in heavy losses of eider eggs. Most losses occur during laying and early incubation when nests are left unguarded. Moreover, as their incubation proceeds, female eiders become increasingly aggressive toward gulls, driving them from the vicinity of their nests (Bourget 1973).

At Cape Dorset, Cooch (1965) considered the raven to be the principal predator on eider eggs, with the predation rate remaining relatively constant through June and July. However, the percentage of eggs lost to all predators was highest in late June and early July. Seven days of exceptionally high egg losses in 1955 occurred with bad weather, but in 1956 only 1 of 6 days of heavy losses occurred under adverse weather conditions.

All of the eider nests destroyed on Egg Island, near Prudhoe Bay, Alaska, owed their destruction to glaucous gulls (Schamel 1974). The gulls devoured 42 percent of the 108 eggs laid; 71 percent of these losses occurred during egg-laying and 29 percent after female eiders deserted their nests.

On the Maine coast, 9 percent of 1,147 nests failed to hatch because of desertion (Choate 1967, Clark 1968). Desertion also accounted for 3 percent of 367 unsuccessful nests in the St. Lawrence Estuary. At Cape Dorset, 14 percent of the loss of 320 eggs occurred because of desertion. Human intrusion (including that of the investigator), predator harassment, and adverse weather are all causes of desertion.

Some investigators believe that eiders gain more than they lose by nesting close to breeding gulls. They contend that gulls defending their nests from intruding avian predators (including other gulls) increase the safety of nearly all eider nests in the vicinity. Eider females, in early defenses of their nest sites against adjacent nesting gulls, establish a détente with their neighbors.

Renesting. The common eider renests more than any other sea duck in North America because its breeding season is usually long (for a sea duck) and, physiologically, it is an indeterminate rather than a determinate layer.

Renesting of eiders was evident as far north as Cape Dorset (Cooch 1965). Three banded hens whose nests were destroyed laid eggs 2 days later. One nest lost eggs on two occasions, but because the structure was intact, the female continued to lay 11 eggs in all—4 initially, then 3, then 4. When both the down and the eggs were removed from other nests, the females constructed new nests within a few feet of their original ones. Renesting was successful in 11 of 12 nests experimentally destroyed. Clutches started during the second half of a 24-day period were half the size of clutches in nests initiated earlier (Cooch 1965). Moreover, late clutches contained little down and numerous contour (body) feathers, evidence that the shed down had been deposited in earlier nests.

Rearing of Young

Broods. Young eiders leave their nests as soon as they are dry, usually within 24 hours, but during periods of excessive rain and wind the ducklings may wait 2 days before they depart (Cooch 1965). Cooch believes that eider ducklings require little food during the first 48 hours of life; he observed them feeding a bit during the third day after hatching.

The trek to water is rapid, even though it is often over rocky or boulder-strewn terrain. Usually the mother conveys the young, but sometimes they are joined by an "aunt," a term given to nonbreeding females. Guignion (1967) observed two eider broods, under surveillance by circling gulls, on their way to water. An aunt immediately joined the procession, and as some of the ducklings lagged behind, other aunts joined the group until the two broods were under the escort of a dozen adult eiders. Aunts have been observed on numerous occasions to come to the aid of ducklings under attack by gulls (Guignion 1967). At times several mothers, perhaps aunts, and the young of several broods joined together in large crèches.

Many eider broods at Cape Dorset collect on freshwater ponds on the nest islands before moving on to shallow tidal pools. The longer and more difficult the overland passage to the sea, the longer broods remain on interior ponds. From the tidal pools in the outer islands, the broods move to large tidal pools along the mainland coast, where they remain 4 to 5 weeks before moving among the reefs and islands farther out to sea. Two broods marked by Cooch (1965) were observed 15 and 21 days later, 6 and 11 miles from their nest sites. A banded female with a brood was shot 20 miles away and 43 days later.

Development. Cooch (1965) considered that the preflight period at Cape Dorset lasts at least 8 weeks. He observed the first flying young on September 10 and deduced that most young reached flying stage by October 7.

Survival. Because eider broods move considerable distances at sea during the preflight stage, it is difficult to evaluate brood mortality. This difficulty is further compounded when, as frequently happens, a female (mother or aunt) assumes responsibility for more than one brood. A survey of 100 miles of coastline in the Cape Dorset area on August 19-20, revealed the following declines in crèche size: Class I, 6.1 (136); Class II, 5.5 (74); Class III, 3.9 (46). How much these declines reflect mortality is uncertain because of brood-sharing by breeding hens as well as by aunts. Note that the size of Class I broods was much larger than the average (3.5) clutch size.

Cooch (1965) observed herring and glaucous gulls harrying eider broods on 34 occasions. The greatest losses occurred during the first week of life, before the ducklings were fully capable of diving.

POSTBREEDING SEASON

After deserting their mates early in July, adult males travel varying distances from the breeding grounds to undergo the postnuptial molt. Large numbers of Pacific eiders migrate west along the coast of the Beaufort Sea, past Point Barrow, to undergo the wing molt. However, not all eiders leave the Beaufort Sea prior to molting their wing feathers. On July 25, Smith (1973) observed molting adults near western Victoria Island.

In southwest Baffin Island, Macpherson and McLaren (1959) observed 20 flightless drakes of the northern race on August 14, 1955. Between September 1 and September 12, large rafts of flightless young and adults (probably females) were sighted. In the same general region, Cooch (1965) saw flocks of 200 to 300 male eiders, July 16-30, 1955, but only a few were flightless. He reported that breeding females apparently begin to molt when their broods reach a certain stage of development, so that both young and females begin flying about the same time in the fall. The males and subadults of both sexes are the first to leave the molt areas, followed later by the maternal females and their young (Cooch 1965).

In Greenland, drakes attain their eclipse plumage and become flightless the latter part of July and the first half of August (Salomonsen 1950-51). At this time they inhabit bays and fjords, whereas immatures are prone to remain on the coast.

FOOD HABITS

Near Cape Dorset, northern eiders were observed feeding on bottom organisms in about 22 feet of water, using their wings to aid their dives (Macpherson and McLaren 1959). Cottam (1939) based his discussion of the food habits of the Pacific, northern, and American eiders on an examination of gizzard contents. Animals composed 95 to 99 percent of the gizzard contents in all three races. Mollusks made up 82 percent of the food items in 96 gizzards of the American eider, and 70 and 46 percent of the food items found in the gizzards of the northern and the Pacific eiders. Blue mussels were the single most important food item taken by all eiders—especially the American race. As Cottam (1939) pointed out, no other ducks depend so much upon a single food species. Crustaceans—amphipods, isopods, and crabs—composed 14 percent of the foods consumed by northern eiders, 7 percent by American eiders, and 31 percent by Pacific birds. Horse crabs and box crabs were particularly important to eiders from Alaskan waters.

Only infinitesimal amounts of plant food were found in the gizzards of northern eiders and composed less than 5 percent of the gizzard contents of the other two races. Marine algae, the only plant items of any significance, were restricted to Pacific eiders.

King Eider

Somateria spectabilis

VITAL STATISTICS

Length:	Male, 21.7-25.0 inches, average 22.7 inches (32) Female, 18.5-22.5 inches, average 21.1 inches (27)
Wing:	Adult male, average 10.75 Adult female, average 10.37 inches
Weight:*	Adult male, average 3.68 pounds (41) Adult female, average 3.45 pounds (140)

*From Thompson and Person (1963).

IDENTIFICATION

Field

"Majestic" describes the adult male king eider, one of the larger ducks in North America. Its regal head is characterized by a short orange bill sweeping upward into an orange knoblike frontal shield outlined in black and complemented by a pale blue crest. The forepart of the flying male appears white, and because of the dark linings of the underwings, the body from wings to tail is more densely black than that of the common eider. Large white patches in the forepart of the upper wings are edged in black and are further accentuated by a black hindback. At rest, the king eider appears white in front and black at the rear, with a white patch near the base of the tail. The common eider shows a greater expanse of white because of its all-white back. King eiders fly abreast in long wavering lines, usually only a few feet above the water.

Female and immature king eiders are tawny-brown, barred with dusky brown marks that are similar in color but more crescentic than those in common eiders. The shorter bills of the kings also give their heads a rounder shape. But only in the hand can positive identification be made. In the fall, the immature males appear gray-brown with lighter breasts and dark brown heads. By spring, their chests and forebacks are white, contrasting with the gray-black of backs, sides, and bellies.

At Hand

The side of the male's head is pale green, and a black "V" outlines the throat. The neck, chest, and foreback are cream-white. Black prevails over the lower back, rump, scapulars, tail coverts, breast, belly, and sides, but the tail is brown-black. Except for white middle coverts, the wing is blackish with long curved tertials.

The female can best be separated from the common eider by the feathers on the top of the bill that extend forward to above the nostrils. In the common eider, these top feathers extend only a short distance below the eye, but the feathers along the sides of the bill, which are lacking in the king eider, do extend to the nostrils. Although an unstreaked throat is another characteristic of the king eider, some females share streaked throats with the common eider.

By late July the male begins to enter the eclipse plumage. The frontal knob becomes dull in color and shrunken. The head and body become mottled with brown, and, as the molt progresses in August, become entirely brown. By the middle of the month the male is similar in appearance to the female (Thompson and Person 1963). The adult male regains the nuptial plumage near the end of November.

POPULATION STATUS

There are at least 1 million to 1.5 million king eiders in North America. Barry (1968) calculated that 1.108 million eiders use the Beaufort Sea migration route and estimates (personal letter) that three-fourths are king eiders and one-fourth common eiders. Thompson and Person (1963) estimated that a million adult eiders, both king and common, pass Point Barrow, Alaska, in late summer migration, king eiders being by far the more abundant.

In addition to the estimated population of more than a million king eiders in the central and western Canadian Arctic, there are at least 100,000 in the eastern Arctic and Greenland (Salomonsen 1968) and at most 10,000 along the Arctic Slope of Alaska. James Bartonek believes that about one-fifth of the 47,000 eiders estimated for the Arctic Slope (King and Lensink 1971) are kings.

Sex Ratios

No reliable data exist on the overall sex ratios in the king eider. Between August 4 and August 22, Thompson and Person (1963) checked the sex of 181 birds killed at Point Barrow, Alaska. They found 1 male to each 3.4 females (23 percent). Males greatly predominated in migration flights during August 4-8, but females became increasingly predominant in flocks August 11-22. On the breeding grounds at Perry River, drakes accounted for 61 percent of the 389 eiders checked for sex (Hanson et al. 1956).

Mortality

Barry (1968) estimated that Eskimos kill a maximum of 1 percent of the king eiders that use the Beaufort Sea migration route; this kill occurs largely at Point Barrow and Holman Island, Northwest Territories. However, natural catastrophes occasionally cause enormous losses. During the spring of 1964, Barry (1968) calculated that 100,000 eiders (mostly king) of the Beaufort Sea population died of starvation caused by an unusually late breakup of sea ice. Other records of large losses from starvation or freezeouts have been noted in the journals of early explorers of the Arctic.

The king eider is heavily hunted in southwest Greenland. Band recoveries indicate that 10 percent are shot (Salomonsen 1950-51).

DISTRIBUTION

The king eider's range is circumpolar, occurring throughout the arctic lands of coastal Canada, Alaska, Siberia, Russia, Scandinavia, Spitsbergen, and Greenland. It winters as far north as the seas remain ice-free.

Breeding Range

In North America the kind eider breeds sparingly along the Arctic Coast of Alaska from Point Hope (Tigara) to Demarcation Point. It breeds abundantly in several of the Arctic islands within the District of Franklin, Northwest Territories, and occurs in smaller numbers along the Arctic Coast in the districts of Mackenzie and Keewatin, and along the west coast of Hudson Bay to its juncture with James Bay. There is also evidence of its breeding at Twin Islands (North Twin and South Twin) and near the mouth of the Kogaluk River, close to Povungnituk, Quebec (Todd 1963). It possibly nests in the Belcher Islands (Freeman 1970*b*).

Gabrielson and Lincoln (1959) believed that the center of breeding abundance of the king eider in Alaska was in the vicinity of Point Barrow. Available evidence suggests a maximum summer population of 10,000 king eiders along the Arctic Slope of Alaska. There is evidence that at one time king eiders bred on St. Lawrence Island (Gabrielson and Lincoln 1959), but in later years, Fay (1961) did not find nests or broods. He reported that although 2,000 nonbreeding birds summered offshore, only a few adults remained after the spring migration.

From an aerial survey of the Arctic Coast and the islands of western and central Canada, Barry (1960) estimated the following numbers of king eiders: more than 100,000, Banks Island; 800,000, Victoria Island; and 8,000, Queen Maud Gulf. Macpherson and Manning (1959) estimated 10,000 king eiders on the Adelaide Peninsula but only a few common eiders. They estimated 65,000 eiders on Prince of Wales Island, mostly king (Manning and Macpherson 1961). Tener's (1963) aerial survey of the Queen Elizabeth Islands disclosed a flock of 340 king eiders (in pairs) migrating northward along the east coast of Dundas Island on June 12, 1961. He also saw 45 along the south coast of Cornwallis Island, 7 on Lake Hazen near the north end of Ellesmere Island, and flocks of 18 and 3 on Bathurst Island. On the Perry River, near Queen Maud Gulf, Hanson et al. (1956) considered this species the most abundant breeding duck, composing 76 percent of the ducks seen.

Soper (1946) found king eiders to be abundant breeders near the Foxe Channel in southwest Baffin Island. Bray (1943) reported them as abundant breeders in the northeast region of the Melville Peninsula and also found them nesting on Southampton Island along 20 miles of swampy coast on the north shore of the Bay of Gods Mercy. They were much more abundant than common eiders. On the Fosheim Peninsula of Ellesmere Island, Parmelee and MacDonald (1960) found king eiders widely distributed but not abundant; they found no evidence of common eiders. Fraser's (1957) survey of the Boothia Peninsula, southeast Victoria Island, southern King William Island, and the Adelaide Peninsula revealed that king eiders commonly occurred throughout these areas and were markedly more abundant than common eiders. Geale (1971) reported that king eiders bred on Cornwallis Island, N.W.T., but were less abundant than common eiders.

On the west coast of Greenland, king eiders commonly breed in the Thule District, occur in numbers in Inglefield Land and Washington Land, and have been recorded for Hall Land and Hendrik Island (Salomonsen 1950-51). On the east coast of Greenland, they breed from Scoresby Sound north to Peary Land.

Migration Corridors

One of the most amazing migration corridors in North America is followed by king eiders between winter, breeding, and molt areas. This western corridor stretches along the coast of Alaska from the Aleutian Islands to Demarcation Point and on into Canada, probably as far east as the Adelaide Peninsula. In the East, several corridors extend from Southampton Island on the south, Boothia Peninsula

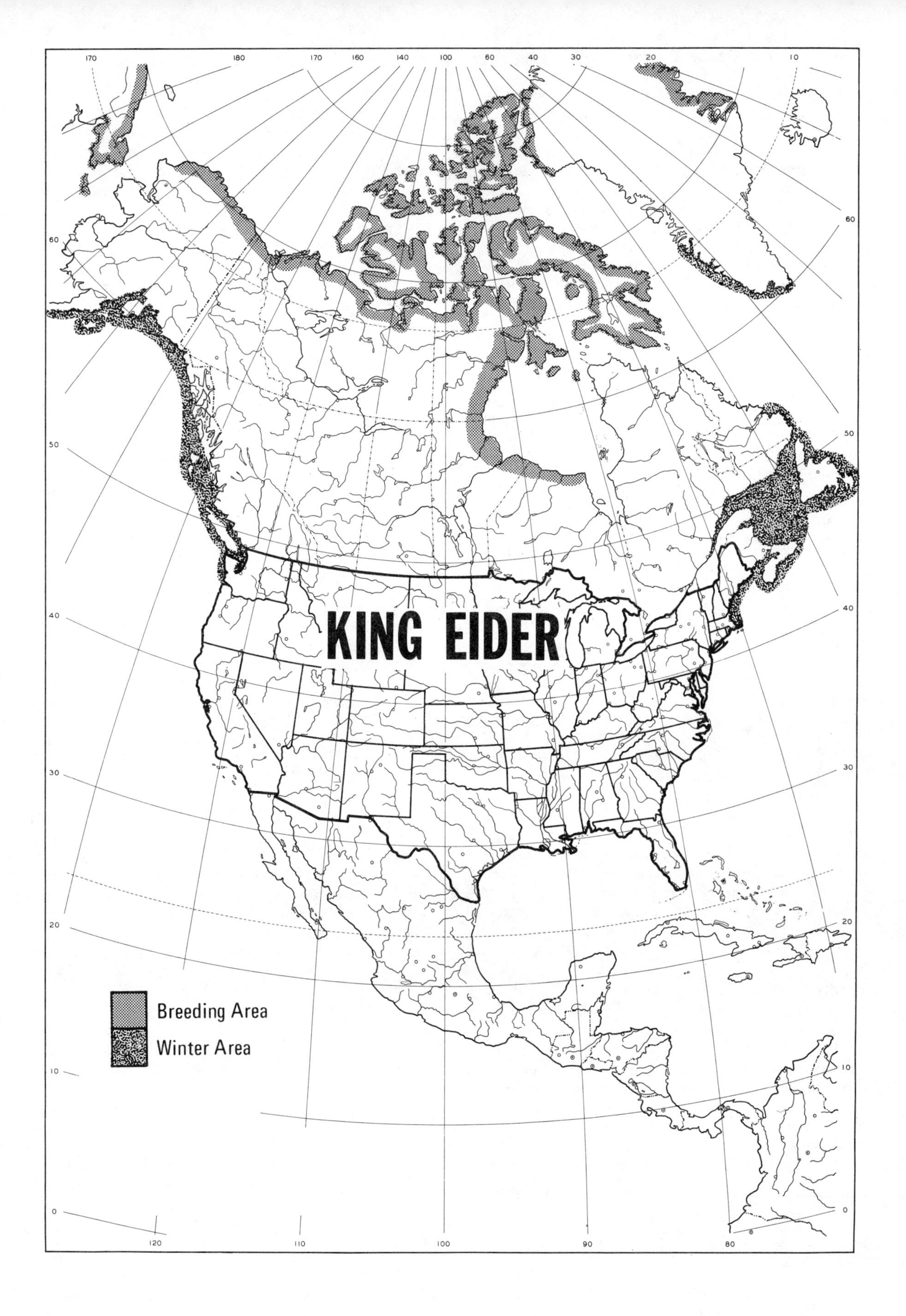
KING EIDER
Breeding Area
Winter Area

in the center, and Ellesmere Island on the north to coastal west-central and southwestern Greenland (Salomonsen 1968).

The Alaskan migration corridor has been documented at several places where the horde of migrants passes close to projecting points of land. At Point Dall, Hooper Bay, and the Yukon Delta, Brandt (1943) viewed part of the spectacular spring passage. During a few hours of each day for 12 days he recorded the passage of 124,900 king eiders! On May 15, he noted 75,000 migrating king eiders. But as the flight started 2 weeks prior to Brandt's first count and small flocks continued to pass for 2 weeks after his last count, the number that passed Point Dall was surely several times the recorded total.

Elsewhere, the spring passage of king eiders has been observed near Nome and Wales on the Seward Peninsula, Cape Lisburne, Wainwright, Barrow, and—almost to the Yukon border—Humphrey Point (Gabrielson and Lincoln 1959). The spring passage has also been observed at Cape Bathurst, 200 miles east of the Mackenzie Delta (Thompson and Person 1963).

The western passage of flocks of king and common eiders at Point Barrow, Alaska, occurs prior to the wing molt (Thompson and Person 1963). Between July 14 and the first of September, 800,000 adult eiders (mostly king) were calculated to pass Point Barrow. Projections for flights prior to and after the observation period yielded an estimate of 1 million adults—observations were concluded before young birds had commenced their westward passage.

As delineated by Salomonsen (1968), migration corridors from the eastern Canadian Archipelago to Greenland pass around the north and south ends of Baffin Island and also lead overland across its middle. Spectacular flights of king eiders across the waist of Baffin Island at the Clyde River and Inlet (latitude 70° N) were observed by Wynne-Edwards (1952) between July 14 and August 17, 1950. The time of passage is similar to the time of arrival of king eiders 400 miles to the east at Disko Bay, Greenland, for some hundred thousand birds collect for the wing molt along the coast from the southern Upernavik District south to the Egedesminde District (Salomonsen 1968). After the wing molt, the eiders migrate farther south along the west coast of Greenland to winter near the ice-free coasts of southwest Greenland (Cape Farewell to Holsteinsborg), Labrador, Newfoundland, and northeastern United States.

Winter Areas

King eiders winter in the seas as far north as open water permits. Upwards of 50,000 eiders winter offshore adjacent to St. Lawrence Island at the north end of the Bering Sea (Fay 1961). Most are king eiders, mixed with smaller numbers of common eiders. One flock of king eiders observed in February contained 15,000 birds. They have also been reported wintering about St. Paul and St. George islands in the Pribilofs (Gabrielson and Lincoln 1959). However, the bulk of the king eiders from the western and central Arctic—and probably as far east as the Adelaide Peninsula—winter at sea along the Alaska Peninsula and Aleutian Islands. Refuge reports indicate that a population of 190,000 to 220,000 winters adjacent to the Aleutian Islands and that 3,000 winter at the Izembek National Wildlife Range. It should be emphasized that sea ducks usually winter far offshore and that reported numbers are but a small fraction of the total numbers actually present.

Apparently few king eiders occur south of the Kenai Peninsula. Gabrielson and Lincoln (1959) cited no records for southeast Alaska, and Audubon Christmas bird counts, 1969-72, do not include the king eider in that region. Christmas bird censuses for the years 1966-72 in the Strait of Georgia, British Columbia, do not record this sea duck. Nor is it recorded on Audubon Christmas bird counts in Washington and Oregon. One king eider was photographed at Monterey Peninsula December 29, 1969, for the only California record during 7 years of Audubon bird censuses.

According to Godfrey (1966), the king eider winters in the Gulf of St. Lawrence, off the coasts of Labrador and Newfoundland, and only rarely along the coasts of Nova Scotia and New Brunswick. From 40 to 90 king eiders are reported along the Atlantic Coast from Nova Scotia to Virginia by participants in Audubon Christmas bird counts. Most are singles or duos except for small flocks usually recorded at Mount Desert Island, Maine, and Montauk Point, Long Island, New York. Only a few are sighted south of Long Island.

King eiders visit the Great Lakes irregularly and casually. In various years, not necessarily the same year, single birds have been recorded at Buffalo, New York; Toronto, Point Pelee, and Hamilton, Ontario; and Cleveland, Ohio. A flock of 5 was observed at Oswego, New York, December 21, 1969, and 18 were sighted in 1970—but none in 1971.

MIGRATION BEHAVIOR

King eiders migrate abreast in long lines, often only a few feet above the sea and the shore ice (Brandt 1943). Flocks range in size from fewer than 10 to as many as 1,100 (Thompson and Person 1963). At Barrow, most flocks contained 25 to 100 birds; 73 percent of the flocks had fewer than 100, and less than 7 percent had over 300. On the Clyde Inlet, Greenland, Wynne-Edwards (1952) observed flocks migrating 20 to 30 feet above the water but climbing to surmount cliffs 1,600 to 2,000 feet high. At Barrow, Thompson and Person (1963) estimated the average height of migrating flocks at 30 to 35 yards.

Chronology

Fall. Shortly after adult males arrive at their most distant breeding grounds, they start the return to their winter grounds, stopping along the way for the wing molt. At Barrow, Alaska, returning males are observed early in July and continue in passage almost daily through August (Thompson and Person 1963). Females appear in considerable numbers by mid-August, and their westward flight continues into September. The young migrate still later—September into October. Near Wainwright, Alaska, females and young were common on inland lagoons through September. They did not appear at St. Lawrence Island until the ice formed in December (Fay 1961) nor at Dutch Harbor in the Aleutians until early December (Cahn 1947).

At Cape Bathurst, Anderson (Thompson and Person 1963) observed the first males migrating westward in late June. Wynne-Edwards (1952) reported migrating flocks of adult males crossing the waist of Baffin Island July 14-August 17. Across Baffin Bay at Disko Bay, Greenland, Salomonsen (1950-51) saw the first adult males on July 16. About July 20 they were common in Upernavik and a week later at Disko Bay. Maximum numbers were reached the first half of August when the adult drakes began the wing molt. After completing the wing molt in the Disko Bay area, adult males migrated farther south in September and October. Females and young departed breeding grounds in northern Greenland in late August and early September. At Cape Dorset, Baffin Island, Soper (1946) observed no males after October 1, but numerous females remained until October 27.

Spring. King eiders begin to leave their winter quarters in late April for a return to their high-Arctic breeding grounds, which some do not reach until mid-June. At Point Dall, Yukon Delta, migrating flocks passed from late April to early June, with the peak on May 15 (Brandt 1943). Early flights are composed predominantly of males, with more balanced sex ratios during the main passage. Gabrielson and Lincoln (1959) reported a large migration near Nome, Alaska, from April 10 to early May; flights at Wales as early as April 6 and for a month thereafter; a heavy passage at Wainwright on May 14; and large flocks, aggregating over 10,000, north of Cape Lisburne on May 14. At Barrow, males begin to arrive by April 3, females by May 1.

Migrants were first observed at Banks Island in 1952 on June 6, with numbers increasing through June 17 (Manning et al. 1956). In 1953, Eskimos reported king eiders on an ice floe opposite Sachs Harbour as early as April 10. At Cape Kellet they did not appear until June 9 and on interior lakes June 7-13, becoming increasingly abundant in the next few days. On southeast Victoria Island, Parmelee et al. (1967) reported first arrivals on June 4, 1960, and June 3, 1962, with peak arrivals in mid-June. First arrivals occurred at Perry River on June 9, 1963, and on June 12, 1964 (Ryder 1967). The first migrants reached the Adelaide Peninsula on June 9 (Macpherson and Manning 1959).

The eastern contingent of king eiders was first observed at Chesterfield Inlet on the northwest coast of Hudson Bay on June 8, and on nearby inland ponds on June 19 (Höhn 1968). Off the southern coast of the Foxe Peninsula, Baffin Island, thousands of males were observed on April 25, 1954, and 4 days later many females were also present (Macpherson and McLaren 1959). On May 15, 1955, some 1,500—the largest number observed on the area that year—were seen feeding in 8 square miles of open water off Cape Dorset. At Bowman Bay, Baffin Island, Soper (1946) first noticed king eiders on June 9, when two flocks passed north; flocks continued to increase in number until June 21. King eiders appeared at Southampton Island on June 4 (Barry 1956). During 4 years of observation, first arrivals on the Fosheim Peninsula of Ellesmere Island occurred June 11-27 (Parmelee and MacDonald 1960).

BREEDING

Behavior

Age, Pair Bond, and Homing. Although yearling male king eiders have an identifiable plumage, none has been found breeding. Males are in full adult plumage as they approach their second summer, and all evidence points to at least a sizable proportion breeding then. Flocks of apparently nonbreeding females observed July 18-20 by Hanson et al. (1956) in the Perry River area were probably yearlings.

Some birds apparently form pair bonds prior to the spring migration, for a male left its own flock and returned to a female that Conover (1926) had shot among migrating birds on May 11. However, courtship activities have been noted in the region of their breeding grounds. On southwest Baffin Island, Macpherson and McLaren (1959) observed pairs and small groups in courtship on June 17-19. At Bylot Island, Drury (1961) saw courting birds when they first arrived on June 24. Males remain only briefly with their mates once incubation has begun. Bray (1943) reported that males remain with females for some time after the eggs are laid. Hanson et al. (1956) believed that males stayed with their spouses during at least the first week of incubation. According to Manning et al. (1956), males leave the females when incubation begins.

Two females were banded on their nests near Cambridge Bay, Victoria Island, by Parmelee et al. (1967). One was taken the next year in June within 5 miles of the former nest site.

Nesting

Nest Sites. King eiders may nest on small islets along the coast or near tundra ponds and lakes inland from the coast, particularly on the large islands of the Canadian Archipelago. On Victoria Island, the favorite nest sites are on dry, often barren slopes overlooking lakes and ponds (Parmelee et al. 1967). Hanson et al. (1956) found isolated nests near small lakes and groups of nests on islands in larger lakes, on the flat coastal tundra 15 to 20 miles inland from Queen Maud Gulf. The king eiders of Banks Island nested beside lakes, on small islands in lakes, in low marshy areas, and occasionally on bare hillsides near the coast, rivers, or lakes (Manning et al. 1956). Schamel (1974) found three king eider nests among 39 common eider nests on Egg Island, a barrier islet on the Beaufort Sea coast near Prudhoe Bay, Alaska.

Home Range. Little is known about the space requirements of breeding king eiders. Unlike the common eiders, which customarily nest in colonies, king eiders usually breed as widely dispersed pairs over tundras dotted with innumerable ponds. However, Hanson et al. (1956) found 19 nests on two islands in Discovery Lake, near the Perry River.

Clutch Size, Eggs, and Incubation. Incubated clutches range in size from 2 to 6 eggs and average 4.92 (53). Omitted from this average because of their abnormal size are clutches of eight and nine reported by Hanson et al. (1956), which probably represent two females laying in the same nest. According to Bent (1925), the smooth-shelled eggs measure 44.7 mm by 67.6 mm (152) and are light to dark olive-buff. The incubation period is 23 to 24 days (Parmelee et al. 1967).

Chronology of Nesting. King eiders begin to nest in the high-Arctic the last half of June, from 2 to 3 weeks after their arrival. Nest initiation extends over a period of approximately 2 weeks. Few nests are started after July 10.

Near Prudhoe Bay, Alaska, Schamel (1974) reported that king eiders began nesting inshore on June 19 and offshore on July 4. Manning et al. (1956) found that nests were begun June 19-21 on Banks Island and that laying and slightly incubated clutches were also in evidence June 28-July 9. A female with an egg in her oviduct was collected on July 8. In the Perry River region, Hanson et al. (1956) discovered a nest scrape on June 29. Eggs candled in 14 nests indicated that incubation had commenced between June 28 and July 4. On Victoria Island, Parmelee et al. (1967) reported that egg-laying started June 12, extended to late June, and ceased by July when the drakes left the region. Parmelee and MacDonald (1960) on the Adelaide Peninsula found nests from June 29 to July 23. On Baffin Island, Soper (1946) found the first unfinished nest on June 26 and reported that all of the many clutches found up to July 8 were fresh.

Nest Success. Most of our information on the king eider is derived from ornithological surveys in the high-Arctic. Because these surveys were taking note of all birds, no attention was paid to nest histories. Consequently, there is a dearth of information on the nest success of the king eider.

Nest Failure. Parmelee et al. (1967) noted that two nests under observation on Victoria Island were destroyed, presumably by jaegers. According to Manning et al. (1956), foxes apparently take a large number of eggs and young, particularly after a crash in the lemming population. Predation by foxes may have caused the scarcity of nesting eiders on Banks Island in 1952.

Renesting. The short span of nesting and the early departure of drakes from the nesting grounds preclude any significant renesting by king eiders. As with other waterfowl nesting in the Arctic, when eggs are destroyed during the course of laying, many hens continue to lay the remaining determinate eggs.

Rearing of Young

Broods. After the hatch, two marked incubating hens moved such a great distance with their broods that they were never seen again (Parmelee et al. 1967). However, other hens with broods moved into the ponds abandoned by the original inhabitants. As the season progressed, certain ponds containing broods one day were not always occupied the next day. Flightless young and escorting females made their way, some via the streams, to the coast.

According to Parmelee et al. (1967), broods of king eiders begin to combine at an early age. Thus, broods may contain from a few to over 100 ducklings and be attended by two or three hens. The largest number of hens observed in attendance on an amalgamated brood was nine.

Development. On the Adelaide Peninsula, MacPherson and Manning (1959) observed the first young king eiders on July 26 and 27; a brood observed on August 23 was almost full-grown. At Victoria Island, Parmelee et al. (1967) first observed newly hatched broods July 14-25. On August 20-21, they observed many flightless young in coastal bays. By August 27-28, young were flying strongly over coastal waters. This evidence indicates that young king eiders have an astoundingly rapid growth rate to reach flying stage in slightly over 1 month. But even so, flightless young were collected by Smith (1973) as late as September 15 in western Victoria Island.

POSTBREEDING SEASON

Many accounts of the king eider in the high-Arctic mention that male king eiders leave the nesting grounds early in July and congregate temporarily at sea before vanishing from the region. Early in August, at least 70 percent of the eiders along the west coast of Banks Island were females, and Manning et al. (1956) questioned the whereabouts of the missing males.

A mass exodus of king eider males from Victoria Island occurred in early July (Parmelee et al. 1967). No drakes were noted inland after July 3. In northern Ellesmere Island, Parmelee and MacDonald (1960) reported that drakes left the nesting ground in early July, and although some remained on nearby fjords until early August, only brown eiders—females, young, or both—were seen after mid-August. Hanson et al. (1956) first observed the postbreeding flocking of males in the Perry River region on July 4, when a flock of 19 was noted. On Southampton and Baffin islands, Bray (1943) observed no male king eiders after July 10.

As recounted in the discussion of fall migration, adult males west of the Adelaide Peninsula migrate west to the Bering Sea, and those east of the Peninsula migrate east to Greenland. Western migrants apparently do not stop for the wing molt until they are 200 miles southwest of Barrow,

Alaska, near Point Lay (Thompson and Person 1963). The eastward passage terminates along the west coast of central Greenland, where the wing molt occurs (Salomonsen 1968). Yearlings, which have summered along the southwest coast of Greenland, join the adults in the region of Disko Bay for the wing molt.

FOOD HABITS

King eiders share with oldsquaws an unmatched reputation for their deep-diving ability. There is a record of one king eider feeding on the bottom in 30 fathoms (180 feet) of water in the Bering Sea (Preble and McAtee 1923). About 95 percent of the food items consumed are animal (Cottam 1939): all mollusks, 46 percent (blue mussels, 20 percent); crustaceans, 19 percent (half are king crabs); echinoderms, 17 percent (sand dollars, 8 percent; sea urchins, 6 percent). Caddis fly larvae and sea anemones make up most of the other animal foods. Eelgrass, widgeon grass, and algae are the plant foods.

Salomonsen (1950-51) reported that during the summer the females and young feed entirely in fresh water, where their food is principally midge larvae and aquatic vegetation. Five gizzards from female eiders in the Perry River area contained mostly vegetable matter: twigs, buds, leaves, and catkins of willow; seeds of water buttercup; stems and leaves of moss; and fly larvae (Hanson et al. 1956).

Spectacled Eider

Somateria fischeri

VITAL STATISTICS*

Length:	Adult male, average 20.8 inches (7) Adult female, average 19.6 inches (13) Subadult female, average 19.8 inches (7)
Wing:	Adult male, average 9.80 inches (48) Adult female, average 9.61 inches (27) Subadult male, average 9.49 inches (5) Subadult female, average 9.41 inches (6)
Weight:	Adult male, average 3.25 pounds (48) Adult female, average 3.22 pounds (40) Subadult female, average 2.75 pounds (13)

*From Dau (1974)

IDENTIFICATION

Field

Only a fortunate few have seen or ever will see the beautiful spectacled eider, for it is restricted to coastal Alaska. Although it is one of our largest ducks, it is slightly smaller than either the common or king eider. A chunky-bodied bird that travels singly, in twos, or in small flocks, the spectacled eider flies low over the sea as do the other eiders.

In flight or at rest, the adult male can be distinguished from other eiders by the black chest and large pale green head with white spectacle-like patches around the eyes. Common and king eiders also have black breasts and bellies, but the black in the spectacled eider extends farther forward, almost to the neck. At close range, the green feathers can be seen to form a "mane" at the back of the head, and the white eye "spectacles" are rimmed with black. The white throat, neck, back and folded wing contrast with the slate-black rump, tail, chest, breast, and belly.

The tawny female spectacled eider is similar to female common and king eiders except for the light brown spectacles that surround the eyes, in contrast to the white spectacles of the male. The basic tawny coloration of the plumage is marked with streaks and discontinuous bars of dark brown.

At Hand

In both sexes of the spectacled eider, the feathers extend down the bill to the nostrils, a characteristic not found in other eiders. The male's bill is bright orange and the female's is gray-blue. The feet in both sexes are yellow-brown. The wing of the adult male is gray-brown with a large cream patch covering the lesser and middle coverts and tertials; the tertials are unusually long and curved. The black of the chest, breast, and sides has a gray cast, differing from the jet-black of the common and king eiders. The iris of the eye is pale blue in all age and sex groups of the spectacled eider (Dau 1972) but is dark brown in the other three eiders.

Immatures are similar in coloring to the female, but males are darker above and females have spotted rather than barred markings on their breasts and bellies. According to Dau (1972), a captive immature male and female assumed full plumage during the winter of their second year.

DISTRIBUTION

Breeding Season

Spectacled eiders nest in a narrow coastal strip of Alaska and in northeastern Siberia. In Alaska, their breeding area extends from the mouth of the Kuskokwim River north along the Bering Sea coast to the Arctic Ocean, and then east to the Colville River delta (Gabrielson and Lincoln 1959). They are most abundant on the Yukon Delta. Dement'ev and Gladkov (1967) reported that in Siberia they breed from Kolyuchin Bay on the Chukot Peninsula as far west as the Lena River. The center of abundance, however, is limited to Chaun Bay east to the area of the Indigirka and Kolyma rivers.

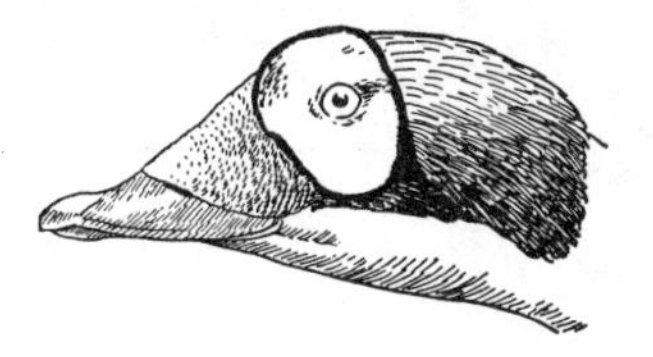

Winter Areas

The spectacled eider disappears from the breeding grounds and apparently into the limbo of the Bering Sea for winter. In a recent review of historical records of wintering spectacled eiders, Dau (1974) lists one at Wales, at the tip of the Seward Peninsula; one at Gambell, St. Lawrence Island; three at St. Paul Island in the Pribilofs; two at Shemya Island in the Aleutians; two at Izembek Lagoon near the tip of the Alaska Peninsula; one at Kodiak Island; and one at Kachemak Bay near the tip of the Kenai Peninsula. Two strays far from their known range have been recorded: one on the California coast (Moffitt 1940) and one off the coast of southern Vancouver Island (Godfrey 1966).

The spectacled eider disappears as mysteriously from its breeding grounds in Alaska as it does from its Siberian ones. Dement'ev and Gladkov (1967) reported that it did not occur in winter on the Siberian coast nor on the Commander Islands; they assumed that it wintered in the Bering Sea at the southern edge of the ice pack. Irving et al. (1970) identified no spectacled eiders during a March 1968 cruise of the Bering Sea that went from Unalaska Island inshore of Nunivak Island almost to St. Matthew Island. However, near the margin of the ice in the central Bering Sea they saw many flocks of flying eiders at a distance that made species identification impossible.

MIGRATION BEHAVIOR

Chronology

Fall. Dau (1974) reports that spectacled eiders leave the Yukon Delta prior to July 1, apparently remaining offshore for up to 2 weeks before migrating to molt areas. Small flocks of mixed subadults and possibly unsuccessful breeding hens leave by mid-August. Adult females and their young remain for about 10 days after fledging before they too move to sea by the second week in September. Departure of spectacled eiders from their Siberian breeding grounds occurs in mid-September (Dement'ev and Gladkov 1967).

Spring. Dau (1974) observed spectacled eiders arrive in the sea off the Yukon Delta during the first week of May. A week or two later they appeared on their nearby nesting grounds. An odd fact was that most flocks arrived from the northwest rather than from the south, the standard direction for other waterfowl. Elsewhere along the Alaskan coast. Gabrielson and Lincoln (1959) gave spring arrival dates as: May 6, St. Michael; May 4, Tigara (Point Hope); May 16, Wales; May 24, Icy Cape; May 28, Wainwright; and May 26, Point Barrow. On the Indigirka Delta, Siberia, first arrivals occurred on June 16 (Dement'ev and Gladkov 1967).

BREEDING

Behavior

Age, Pair Bond, and Homing. Like other eiders, the spectacled eider assumes full breeding plumage the second year and is then presumed to be sexually mature (Dau 1974). Most of them form pair bonds before reaching their breeding grounds and little courtship activity occurs thereafter. However, Mickelson (1973) observed that some pairs formed 1 to 2 weeks prior to nesting. Johnsgard (1964) reported that drakes were still with their mates 1 week into the incubation period in mid-June but that they left the breeding areas shortly thereafter, which suggests that pair bonds last 1 to 2 weeks after incubation begins. Three of six marked adult hens returned the next year to the same nest area. One of 32 young marked females was sighted the next year as a subadult. Dau (1974) saw fewer than five subadult males during the entire period of his study—presumably they remain at sea.

Home Range. Johnsgard (1964) observed no signs of hostility between pairs of spectacled eiders inhabiting the same nest ponds. Pairs often swam within a few feet of each other without provoking an antagonistic response. Sometimes males were accompanied by two or three females. Although spectacled eiders are not colonial nesters, Dau (1974) found seven nests within an area 300 feet in diameter encompassing a network of ponds. The average distance to the nearest neighbor was 122 feet for 33 nests, with a range from 15 to 550 feet. The number of nests per square mile on one study area in the Yukon Delta ranged from 8.0 to 16.7, 1969-73, and on another area from 7.4 to 17.7, 1971-73. Nearby, James King found 22 nests on a 231-acre area, an average of 66 nests per square mile.

Nesting

Nest Sites. Spectacled eiders nest in sedge meadows, peninsulas, and islands adjacent to tundra ponds 5 to 10

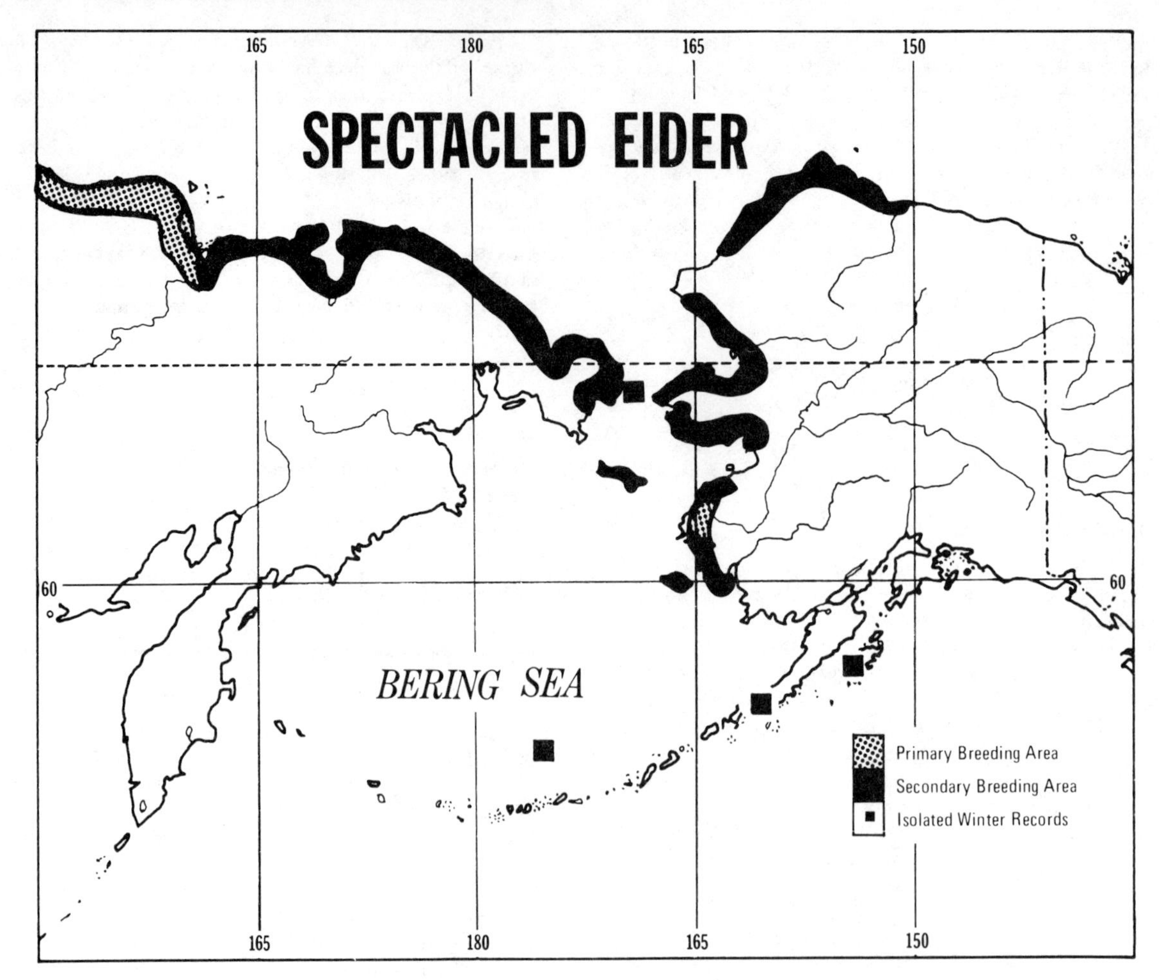

miles from the coast. Dau (1974) found that 41 percent of the nests on his study areas in the Yukon Delta were located on the shores of ponds, 36 percent on islands, and 23 percent on peninsulas. The average distance of 214 nests from water was 7 feet and ranged from 0.5 to 240 feet; only 23 nests were more than 7 feet from water.

In building the nest, the female first creates a depression by making side-to-side movements of the breast and belly against the vegetative cover, then adds a 1-inch-thick layer of sedges and grasses, and finally adds down from her body from the time of the second or third egg through early incubation (Dau 1974). A nest of average dimensions is 2 inches deep and has inside and outside diameters of 5.5 inches and 9.5 inches.

Clutch Size, Eggs, and Incubation. Clutches average 4.5 eggs, with a range from 1 to 8 (Dau 1972). In the late springs of 1969 and 1971, clutches averaged 3.9 and 4.4, respectively; in the normal springs of 1970, 1972, and 1973, clutches averaged 4.7 in 2 years and 5.0 the third. Clutches initiated within the first 5 days of the laying period averaged 5.7 eggs, those started in the second 5-day period averaged 4.9 eggs, and those of the third and fourth periods averaged 4.6 eggs each. One egg is laid about every 24 hours, usually between 12 noon and three in the afternoon.

The olive-green, ovate eggs of the spectacled eider measure 45.3 by 67.9 mm (682), according to Dau (1974); eggs did not vary in size or weight, regardless of clutch size. The incubation of three nests lasted 24 days, and began with the laying of the next to last or last egg (Mickelson 1973).

Chronology of Nesting. For a week or two after the spectacled eiders have arrived on their nesting grounds, the grounds are flooded by the melt from snow and ice (Dau 1974). The earliest record of laying in the Yukon Delta was May 20, the latest June 24. During the period 1969-73, the average dates for the initiation of first and last nests were May 28 and June 15, and the average span of initiation was 19 days (range, 17-24 days).

Nest Success. In Dau's (1974) study of 213 spectacled eider nests on the Yukon Delta, eggs in 73 percent of the nests hatched successfully. Nest success was 78 percent for nests on the margin of tundra ponds, 74 percent for those on peninsulas, and 62 percent for those on islands in the ponds. About 0.3 egg failed to hatch in each successful nest. Seven percent of the known nest destruction occurred during laying, 39 percent early in incubation, and 54 percent late in incubation. Thus, about 4.2 ducklings left each successful nest.

Nest Failure. Most of the nest failures of spectacled eiders on the Yukon Delta were caused by predation. Birds, principally glaucous gulls and parasitic jaegers, caused over two-thirds of the nest losses, and mammals—the Arctic fox and possibly the red fox—somewhat less than a third (Dau 1974). Because spectacled eiders nest on tundra slightly higher than the coastal strip, Dau (1974) believes that storm tides do not inundate their nesting grounds, as occasionally happens in coastal areas occupied by black brant and common eiders. Eskimos are not known to take large numbers of spectacled eider eggs or to kill significant numbers of these ducks.

Renesting. The short span of nest initiation precludes any renesting except for the continued laying of eggs when nest destruction occurs during the period of laying.

Rearing of Young

Broods. Marked spectacled eider broods were reared on fresh to brackish ponds within 1.5 miles of their nest sites (Dau 1974). Although hens with broods are tolerant of each other, they seldom combine broods as do common eiders. Dau (1974) encountered a few crèches, one a group of 7 females and 15 young, Classes I and II; 2 days later this group numbered 13 females (4 were subadults) and 20 young. Another group included six females and eight young.

Development. Dau (1974) determined that young spectacled eiders fledged in about 50 days.

Survival. On the Onumtuk Slough study area, brood sizes declined from 4.2 in Class I (142) to 4.1 in Class II (73) to 3.5 in Class III, an overall reduction of 17 percent from the 4.2 ducklings that departed successful nests (Dau 1974). Broods were smaller elsewhere: 3.7 in Class I (32); 3.9 in Class II (56); and 2.2 in Class III (31), representing a 48 percent loss in the number of ducklings that left successful nests. Dau (1974) considered that avian predation on Class II young was largely responsible for losses within broods but that the inconspicuous coloration of the ducklings and their agility in the water and on the ground enhanced their chances for survival.

POSTBREEDING SEASON

As discussed under fall migration, little is known of the whereabouts of the spectacled eider once it leaves its breeding grounds. Adult drakes leave first, in late June, and adult females and young depart in early September. Nelson (1883) observed the only flock of molting spectacled eiders ever found off North America. On September 15, he discovered a large flock of adult males in eclipse plumage, 25 miles west of Stuart Island in Norton Sound. Dau (1974) did, however, find many primary feathers from adult hens washed ashore, September 9-11, 1972, at Panowat Spit, Igiak Bay (Kokechik Bay). Dement'ev and Gladkov (1967) reported that in northeast Siberia, drakes assembled in large flocks and moved to sea prior to July 1, the latest date that males in nuptial plumage have been seen. Large flocks in femalelike plumage have been observed offshore at the mouths of the Kolyma and Indigirka rivers in mid- and late July.

FOOD HABITS

For diving ducks, spectacled eiders have singular feeding habits. While on the breeding grounds they are largely surface feeders (Dau 1974). They rarely dive for food, and then only the very young and a few females. They usually feed like dabblers, immersing their heads below the water and tipping up in fresh to brackish ponds. Dau (1974) suspected that young ducklings fed upon aquatic invertebrates. The gizzards of older ducklings contained vegetative parts of aquatic plants, pondweed seeds, and caddis flies; those from mature birds contained insect larvae and the vegetative parts and seeds of aquatic plants. From mid-August until their departure, females and their young fed upon crowberries.

Forty-two percent of the food items found in 16 gizzards from adults collected May-July were mollusks, mostly clams; aquatic insects composed 32 percent, pondweeds 7 percent, and other vegetation 15 percent (Cottam and Knappen 1939).

Steller's Eider

Polysticta stelleri

VITAL STATISTICS

Length:	Male, 17.5-18.5 inches, average 18.1 inches (8) Female, 17.1-18.1 inches, average 17.5 inches (9)
Wing:	Male, 8.23-8.54 inches Female, 8.19-8.46 inches
Weight:	Male, 1.87-2.12 pounds, average 1.94 pounds (5) Female, 1.87-2.00 pounds, average 1.94 pounds (5)

IDENTIFICATION

Field

The Steller's eider is the smallest, trimmest, and fastest flying of the four eiders found in North America. Its breeding and winter ranges are so restricted that it is limited to coastal Alaska between Anchorage and Demarcation Point on the Arctic Ocean.

The adult male is strikingly colored. The white head and large white shoulder patch and the chestnut breast and belly contrast with the black throat and yoke that extends arrow-shaped down the back. Although the dark brown female is similar to other eiders, it is more mottled than barred and the wing has a blue speculum bordered on each side by a white stripe, as in the mallard. The wing of the male resembles that of the wigeon but the white shoulder patch is larger and is bordered by a blue rather than a green speculum.

At Hand

The male's coloration is reminiscent of a clown costume. The white head has a black eye spot, and a "roll" of pale green feathers flanked by small black marks protrudes from the back of the head. In front of the eye is a faint green spot, and the black chin and throat merge into a black collar. The moderately long bill and the feet are blue-gray. A tapering band of blue-black extends down the back, margined by white that separates it from the cinnamon chest, breast, and sides marked by a black spot in front of the folded wing. Long scapulars, striped blue-black and white, spray out over the rear of the folded wing like an untidy floral arrangement. Black flanks, rump, lower belly, and tail coverts, and a dark brown wedge-shaped tail complete the bizarre costume.

The hen is garbed almost entirely in dark brown plumage sprinkled with light buff. The yearling female lacks the blue speculum of the adult and is lighter in color (Conover 1926).

In eclipse plumage the adult male replaces the white head and the striking black-white scapulars with dark brown. The collar, except for a remaining trace of black on the hindneck, and the back also become dark brown. The breast and belly change to cinnamon-brown.

DISTRIBUTION

Breeding Range

Steller's eiders have a discontinuous breeding range in coastal Alaska from the Alaska Peninsula along the Arctic Slope to the Yukon border, and perhaps farther eastward. Although they are not known to breed in the western Canadian Arctic, they may do so—for Bartonek (1969) reported flocks migrating along the Arctic Slope to and from Canada, From helicopter surveys, King and Lensink (1971) estimated 47,400 eiders (unadjusted for visual oversight) on the Arctic Slope of Alaska. Even though they may be the least abundant of the four species of eiders, Steller's eiders are common nesters along the Arctic Coast and probably exceed 1,700 in number (Bartonek 1969).

They also nest in Alaska on the Seward Peninsula, Yukon Delta, Alaska Peninsula, St. Lawrence Island, and Nunivak Island (John Bartonek). At the Izembek National Wildlife Range at the tip of the Alaska Peninsula, population reports for May to August, 1967-69, averaged 27,000 Steller's eiders. On the Yukon Delta, King and Lensink

(1971) computed 51,000 eiders of three species: Steller's, spectacled, and common. Their comparative abundance was unknown, but ground observations indicated that the Steller's eider was much less common than the other two species. About 4,900 eiders were estimated during summer on the Seward Peninsula (King and Lensink 1971), but the relative abundance of the four species that nested there was undetermined. Offshore and in the lagoons of St. Lawrence Island, Fay (1961) observed flocks (up to 200 per flock) of immature Steller's and king eiders between mid-June and September. He reported that Steller's eiders occasionally nest on the island but that most of the summer birds were immatures.

In northeastern Siberia, Steller's eiders nest in a narrow zone along the Arctic Coast as far west as Novaya Zemlya (Dement'ev and Gladkov 1967). They are common on the Lena River delta, rare at the mouths of the Indigirka and Kolyma rivers, and again common toward the east in the Chukot Peninsula. South of there, along the coast of the Gulf of Anadyr, they are migrants, but nonbreeders remain through the summer.

Migration Corridors

There is little information on the migration courses taken by Steller's eiders between their winter and summer quarters. From 833 flightless Steller's eiders that Jones (1965) banded in September at Izembek Bay, Alaska Peninsula, he received only 17 recoveries outside the banding area—16 from coastal Siberia, 5 as far west as the Lena River and 1 from Point Barrow, Alaska. The Lena Delta is 3,200 kilometers west of Izembek, which suggests that the bulk of the Izembek Bay population breeds in coastal Siberia. At St. Lawrence Island, Fay (1961) observed large numbers of Steller's eiders arrive about May 15, most of them continuing northward. Brandt (1943) recorded that a small number of Steller's eider flocks passed over Point Dall, Yukon Delta, during a 10-day period. At Old Kashunuk Village,

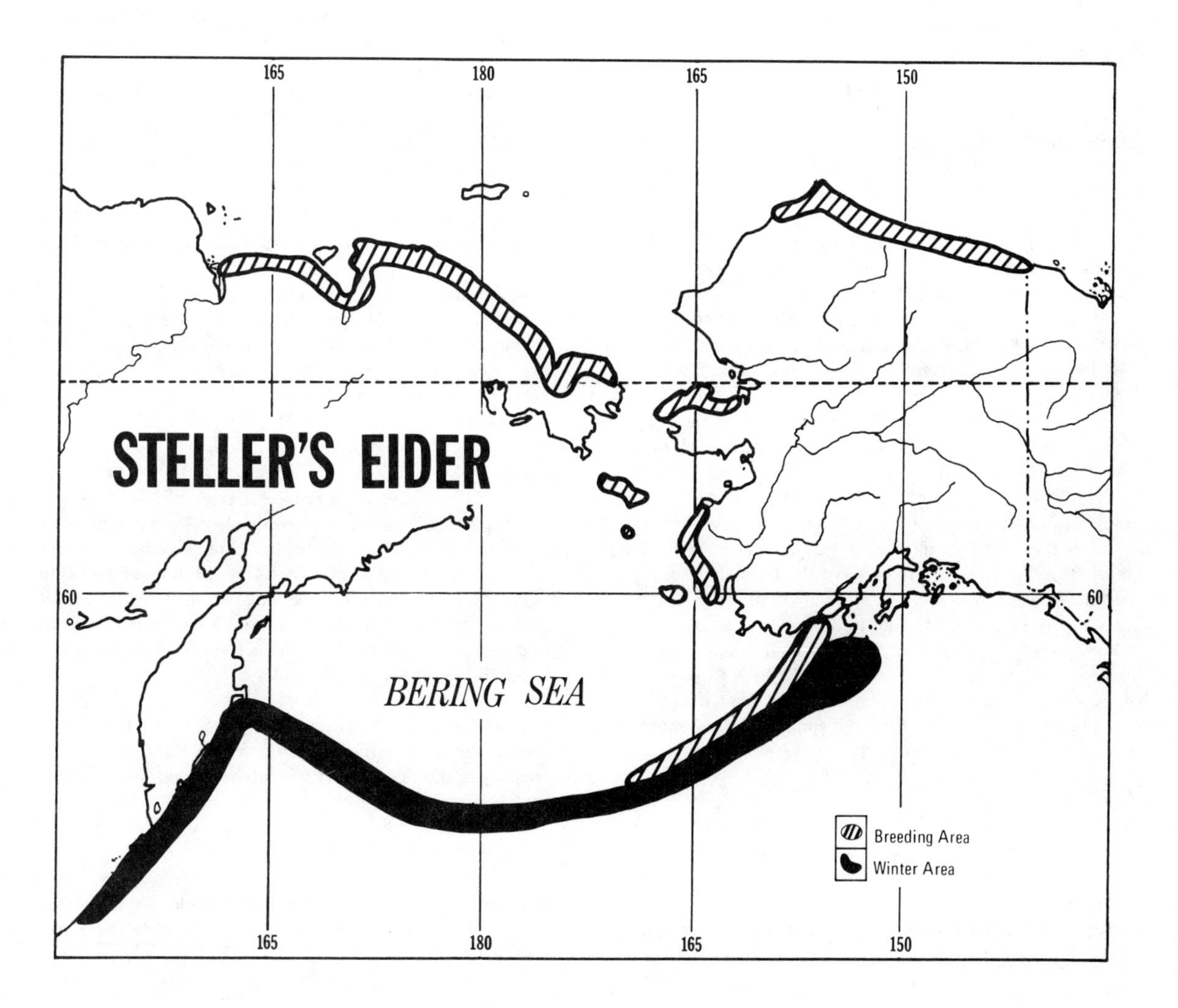

inland a short distance from Point Dall, Dau (1972) observed a flock of three birds, flying northwest. Bailey (1948) reported large flights over Cape Stewart, Bering Strait, between late May and mid-June, and Dement'ev and Gladkov (1967) reported that Steller's eiders passed along the east coast of the Kamchatka Peninsula in May.

Winter Areas

The Steller's eider winters from Kodiak Island west along the south side of the Alaska Peninsula and the eastern Aleutians (Gabrielson and Lincoln 1959). Population estimates (Jones 1965) place about 200,000 Steller's eiders during the winter along the west half of the Alaska Peninsula in Nelson Lagoon and in Izembek and Bechevin bays.

Dement'ev and Gladkov (1967) include the southern Bering Sea at the Commander Islands, the east Kamchatkan coast, and the northern Kurile Islands within the winter range of the Steller's eider.

MIGRATION BEHAVIOR

Chronology

Fall. The adult males are the first to leave their breeding areas in northern Alaska, moving southward in July (Gabrielson and Lincoln 1959). Late fall records cited are October 13, Wainwright; October 15, St. Michael; and October 27, St. Lawrence Island. Dement'ev and Gladkov (1967) reported large flocks moving toward winter quarters from mid-August on, appearing in early September at the Commander Islands and in mid-September at east Kamchatka, becoming abundant in October. Their arrival at Izembek Bay is highly variable (Jones 1965). In some years most, if not all, of the population arrives in August, but in 1964 the population arrived en masse November 6-9.

Spring. At Hooper Bay, Brandt (1943) found the Steller's eider to be the latest spring migrant of the four eiders. It was first seen May 18, when 50 appeared in flocks of 6 to 10 birds, and arrivals continued until May 28. About 25 miles away and almost 50 years later, Mickelson (1973) observed the arrival of this species May 28-June 3, 1970-72. Gabrielson and Lincoln (1959) gave the following spring records: May 12, Wales; May 28, Wainwright; May 25 and June 5, Little Diomede Island; and May 25, Barrow.

Bailey (in Bent 1925) described the main flight of Steller's eiders past Cape Prince of Wales on June 3. Long lines of birds, among them this species, appeared when the wind abated just before a storm from the south. Small numbers had been seen on May 18 and 29.

BREEDING

Behavior

Age, Pair Bond, and Homing. Yearlings do not assume adult plumage until early in their second year. With no information to the contrary, many are assumed to begin breeding late in their second years, as other sea ducks do, the first breeding season after attaining nuptial plumage. Pairs form within flocks in early May and drakes abandon their mates soon after incubation begins. Nothing is known of the homing propensities of Steller's eiders.

Home Range. A chance remark of Conover's (1926) indicates that the size of the home range is limited. He mentioned a tundra pond harboring two pairs of mated adults; the adult drakes drove away two immature drakes whenever these intruders approached the females.

Nesting

What little is known about the nesting of the Steller's eider has been obtained from collections of eggs in museums and from a 1924 study of the birds of the Hooper Bay region, Yukon Delta (Conover 1926, Brandt 1943).

Nest Sites. Brandt (1943) found numerous Steller's eiders nesting on extensive open marshes adjacent to Igiak Bay (Kokechik Bay), about 15 miles north of Hooper Bay. Apparently, they nest in restricted areas near the coast, for recent intensive studies of nesting waterfowl inland from the bay have not discovered them as breeders.

According to Brandt (1943), the Steller's eider nests on a slight rise on a peninsula or along the margin of a tundra pond. A truncated cone of grass 10 inches high may be built as the nest base, or the female may hollow out a depression and line it with grass, adding a layer of down 1 inch thick. Five measured nests had heights of 5.5 to 10 inches, outside diameters of 9 to 20 inches, inside diameters of 5.5 to 6 inches, and cup depths of 3.5 to 4 inches. The down layer is black-brown and forms a thicker mat than is found in the nests of any other ducks except the common and spectacled eiders.

Clutch Size, Eggs, and Incubation. Bent (1925) and Brandt (1943) have each recorded sizes of five clutches, ranging from 6 eggs to 10 and averaging 7.7, a larger number than in the clutches of other eiders. The olive-buff eggs are elliptical ovate and measure 61.4 by 44 mm. There is no accurate information on the incubation period. Brandt thought that incubation lasted about 3 weeks (Gabrielson and Lincoln 1959), but this seems too brief in view of the incubation periods of other eiders.

Chronology of Nesting. On June 19 at Igiak Bay (Kokechik Bay), Brandt (1943) found three nests with fresh eggs and one nest with incubated eggs. Another nest with almost fresh eggs was found on June 20. Pipped eggs were found on July 7, and from then on broods were frequently observed.

Nest Success. Too few data are available to establish the degree of nest success and the causes of nest failure in this species.

REARING OF YOUNG

Brandt (1943) believed that ducklings suffered heavy losses, because broods declined from 7 to 9 ducklings at the start to 3 or 4 young by the time they were half grown.

POSTBREEDING SEASON

Conover (1926) reported that few drakes were seen about the tundra ponds near Hooper Bay after July 10. Apparently, the drakes and later the hens resorted to the seacoast for the wing molt. He collected two drakes on June 4 that differed greatly in their degree of nuptial plumage: one was brown with a mottling of white on the upper breast; the other had a gray head with the tuft of pale green feathers at the back. An adult drake that had started to molt into its eclipse plumage was taken on July 3.

From 1957 to 1962, the population of 200,000 Steller's eiders that winter in Izembek Bay arrived in August and then entered the postnuptial molt, losing their flight feathers (Jones 1965). New flight feathers were regained in the latter half of September. However, in August and early September 1963, only 10,000 eiders appeared for the wing molt. Two eiders banded at Izembek Bay were recovered in mid-September near Cape Vankarem, Siberia, which suggests that these birds, perhaps representing the missing portion of the population, underwent the wing molt somewhere along the east Siberian coast. The missing segment of the population appeared at Izembek Bay later in the fall, having completed the wing molt elsewhere.

Band recoveries indicate that most Steller's eiders that winter at Izembek Bay breed in coastal Siberia as far east as the Lena River. Those that fly to Izembek Bay for the postnuptial molt migrate as far as 2,000 miles.

In northeast Siberia, Dement'ev and Gladkov (1967) reported that adult drakes begin to molt the last third of July and shed their flight feathers in late August. By mid-September they have started the prenuptial molt, first renewing feathers on breast and belly, then on back and tertials, and finally, by mid-October, on head, neck, and long scapulars. Adult males are in full nuptial plumage by early December.

FOOD HABITS

Cottam (1939) cited an 1896 record by Bretherton that Steller's eiders at Kodiak Island, like Harlequins, most often fed in deep water, seldom near shore. Only two stomachs from winter birds have been examined for food items: the one in December had fed almost exclusively on amphipods, and the one in February had consumed mollusks (75 percent) and amphipods (25 percent).

Animal food made up 87 percent and plant food 13 percent in 66 gizzards collected May-July. Crustaceans formed 45 percent of the diet, mollusks 19 percent, insects 13 percent, pondweeds 3 percent, and crowberries 1 percent. Over three-fourths of the crustaceans consumed were amphipods, with isopods and barnacles important items. Bivalves—razor clam, blue mussel, and the Arctic rock borer—were the principal mollusks consumed and midge and caddis fly larvae were the principal insect foods.

Harlequin Duck

Histrionicus histrionicus

VITAL STATISTICS

Length:	Male, 16.0-21.2 inches, average 17.3 inches (16) Female, 14.6-17.2 inches, average 15.8 inches (11)
Wing:	Male, 7.4-8.0 inches, average 7.73 inches Female, 7.0-7.9 inches, average 7.43 inches
Weight:	Male, 1.3-1.6 pounds, average 1.44 pounds (3) Female, 1.1-1.3 pounds, average 1.22 pounds (3)

IDENTIFICATION

Field

The Harlequin duck male is the most bizarrely colored waterfowl, as though a whimsical artist had decorated a deep blue duck with random but precise white-painted markings of various shapes and sizes. The basic body color is a glossy slate-blue, enlivened by a white crescent and dashlike stripes and spots on head, neck, and scapulars. The sides and flanks are chestnut. The female and the immature resemble the female bufflehead but have three white spots on the head rather than one, and the white spot behind the eye is circular rather than oblong. Female and immature Harlequins are also duskier and larger and, in flight, show no white patches on their wings as do buffleheads and white-winged scoters.

At a distance, both sexes of the Harlequin appear black, like scoters. They are not as heavy-bodied or long-billed as the scoters, and, at rest, their longer, more wedge-shaped tails are raised and lowered much like those of ruddy ducks. While swimming, Harlequins often nod their heads in cootlike fashion. Harlequins occur as singles, pairs, and flocks of 3 to rarely more than 10. Scoters usually occur in much larger flocks.

At Hand

Most of the white marks on the glossy slate-blue plumage of the adult male are margined with black. The white marks consist of a perpendicular bulbous white dash between the brown eye and short, blue-gray bill with its yellowish nail. This tapered white dash changes to chestnut over the eye and, at the back of the head, joins with the line from the opposite side. A round white spot is behind the eye, and a perpendicular dash of white extends from behind the eye to the upper neck. A white collar almost encircles the lower neck. Separating the breast from the side is a fingerlike extension of white. The partially white scapulars form a narrow white stripe between the back and folded wing. The white and slate-gray tertials form three broad white stripes near the tip of the folded wing. A small white spot on the flanks near the tail base and a few spots on the greater coverts and secondaries complete the array of white markings. The sides and flanks are a red-brown that increasingly broadens from front to rear. The feet are gray-blue, in harmony with the rest of the Harlequin's costume.

The basic color of the females and immatures is black-brown. Their breasts and upper bellies are a mottled gray that indistinctly margins the darker surrounding plumage. The single round white dots behind the eyes are the most distinct of the three white marks on their heads; the lower one of the three is the least distinct.

Adult males enter the postnuptial molt in late June and remain in eclipse plumage from then until October. During this period they resemble females, but their wings retain the colors of the nuptial plumage.

Immature males, which at first resemble females, undergo their first complete molt in midsummer, but their wings do not yet acquire the glossy purple-blue speculum of the full adult (Dement'ev and Gladkov 1967).

POPULATION STATUS

In a few regions within its range, the Harlequin is an abundant duck, yet most waterfowl hunters and bird watchers will never see one, for it is abundant only in remote areas like the Aleutian Islands, parts of British

Columbia, and Iceland. Within its world range, it is most abundant in the Aleutian Islands. From 600,000 to 1 million Harlequins have been estimated, 1967-69, during the fall and spring on the Aleutian Islands National Wildlife Refuge. Because bad weather and rough seas beset the Aleutians, thereby limiting aerial surveys, this estimate is surely only a crude approximation of its actual abundance. Nevertheless, both the Harlequin and oldsquaw are far more numerous on this 1,100-mile-long refuge than any other waterfowl.

Probably because so much of their range lies within remote regions, Harlequins have suffered little from man's destruction of habitat or from hunting activities. Undoubtedly, their numbers fluctuate from year to year as weather conditions affect their productivity, but these fluctuations have not been measured.

Sex Ratios

Bengtson (1966) has recorded the sex ratios of Harlequin ducks in Iceland for three time periods and for 3 years. During May 20-31, there were 1.56 males to 1.0 female (61 percent); June 10, the ratio of males to females was 1.77:1 (63 percent); and on June 23, 1.26:1 (56 percent).

DISTRIBUTION

The Harlequin's range is divided into two separate and distinct regions: eastern and western. The eastern range embraces Iceland, parts of Greenland, and Labrador, with the winter range extending as far south as New Jersey. The western range includes northeast Siberia west to the Lena River, east to the Kamchatka Peninsula and the Commander Islands and north to the Arctic Circle, then across the Bering Sea to the Aleutian Islands, much of interior Alaska, and south to northwest Wyoming and central California.

Breeding Season

The eastern population breeds in Iceland, Greenland, Baffin Island, and Labrador. It occurs in numerous areas of Iceland, attaining impressive numbers along the Laxá River near Lake Mývatn (Bengston 1966). According to Salomonsen (1950-51) it is a common breeding duck in the greater part of the low-Arctic areas of Greenland, frequenting the Frederikshåb, Godthåb, Sukkertoppen, and northern Julianehåb districts; farther north it is rare.

In eastern Canada, Harlequins breed in sparse numbers over a wide area extending from southeast Baffin Island through Ungava Bay, Quebec, and coastal Labrador to the north shore of the Gulf of St. Lawrence and the Gaspé Peninsula (Godfrey 1966). Soper (1946) found several pairs in the region of Lake Harbour and McKellar Bay, Baffin Island. Harlequins had been found earlier at Cumberland Sound, but not in southwestern Baffin Island. Soper (1946) further concluded from Eskimo reports that Harlequins bred along the coast from about Crooks Inlet to Cumberland Sound.

At the mouth of the Koksoak River on Ungava Bay, Quebec, Gabrielson and Wright (1951) saw five Harlequins on August 22. Murie (Bent 1925) observed several broods on the Swampy Bay River in northeastern Quebec. Although numerous observers had reported seeing Harlequins on the north shore of Labrador from May to July, there was no firm evidence of breeding (Todd 1963). On the Gaspé Peninsula, southeastern Quebec, flightless young were captured and photographed in early August 1959 (Godfrey 1966). Peters and Burleigh reported in 1951 that Harlequins were occasionally found in Newfoundland during the summer but that there were no recent breeding records.

The western population is a hundredfold more abundant than the eastern one. Its main stronghold is Alaska, with the greatest abundance in the Alexander Archipelago, the Alaska Peninsula, and the Aleutian Islands (Gabrielson and Lincoln 1959). Federal refuge reports indicate a summer population of 500 to 1,500 at the Izembek National Wildlife Range, near the tip of the Alaska Peninsula, and 100,000 to 150,000 on the Aleutian Islands Refuge. In the interior of Alaska, the principal breeding areas of the Harlequin lie in the mountain ranges south of Yukon River (James Bartonek). North of the Yukon River it has been found breeding on the Seward Peninsula (Gabrielson and Lincoln 1959) and near Anaktuvuk Pass in the Brooks Range (Irving 1960). Although there are no breeding records, Harlequins have been observed during the summer on the islands of the Bering Sea: Otter, St. Paul, and St. George among the Pribilofs, and the islands of St. Matthew and St. Lawrence (Gabrielson and Lincoln 1959).

According to Soper (1954), Harlequins are sparsely distributed through the Yukon Territory and are probably most numerous in the southern part. Irving (1960) reported a specimen at Old Crow.

South of the Yukon, the Harlequin breeds in estimated numbers of 4,000 to 8,000 throughout British Columbia with the exception of the northeast corner, east of the Rocky Mountains (R. T. Sterling, William Morris, and Ray Halladay). Small numbers lap over, along with the mountains, into southwestern Alberta.

In the conterminous United States, the breeding range of the Harlequin is remarkably similar to that of the Barrow's goldeneye. From northern Washington two fingerlike prongs extend southward: one adheres to the Rocky Mountains, the other to the Cascade and Sierra Nevada ranges as far as central California.

Yocom (1951) reported records of breeding Harlequins in the Okanogan Highlands and Cascade Mountains of Washington and gave summer sightings in the Columbia Basin. Burleigh (1972) considered these ducks uncommon summer residents in the northern panhandle of Idao. The most southerly record was the upper Lochsa River in Idaho County.

The Harlequin occurs on both sides of the Continental Divide through the Rocky Mountains in Montana (Dale Witt). Reports from George Wrakestraw indicate that it breeds in Yellowstone National Park, and as far south as

Lake Alice, northeast of Cokeville, and also that Carl Mueller, former U.S. Game Management Agent, found it breeding in the Bighorn Mountains of north-central Wyoming. In spite of repeated reference to its breeding in Colorado, Bailey and Niedrach (1965:180) concluded that the Harlequin "must be considered as a former extremely rare straggler in the state . . . ."

Chester Kebbe estimates that 100 Harlequins breed in the Cascade and Wallowa mountains of Oregon. They occur sparingly in the Cascade and Sierra Nevada mountains of California as far south as Madera County (Frank Kozlik).

Migration Corridors

For the most part, the fall and spring migrations consist of lateral movements from interior breeding grounds to adjacent seacoasts. However, particularly along the Atlantic Coast, some elements of the Harlequin population move southward from Labrador as far as Long Island. It is apparent that tens of thousands of Harlequins migrate from other areas of Alaska (and perhaps elsewhere) to the Aleutian Islands. The May to August population estimated for the national wildlife refuge encompassing that region is 100,000 to 150,000, but peak numbers from September to April range, as mentioned, from 600,000 to 1 million. Undoubtedly, small numbers migrate south along the coast of British Columbia to favored winter grounds on the Strait of Georgia.

Winter Areas

Harlequins move from interior Iceland to spend the winter in the sea near the coast (Bengtson 1966). Salomonsen (1950-51) considered them year-round residents in Greenland except for the northern part of their breeding range; they winter off the southwest coast as far north as the Sukkertoppen District. In eastern Canada, Harlequins winter from southern Labrador south along the coast of the Maritime Provinces (Godfrey 1966). Peters and Burleigh (1951) classed them as uncommon winter residents in Newfoundland. Along the Nova Scotia coast in winter, they are found infrequently on inshore waters adjacent to rocky shores (Tufts 1961).

Small numbers of Harlequins regularly winter along the northeast coast of the United States as far south as Long Island; strays are occasionally seen as far south as Maryland. Audubon Christmas bird counts, 1965-1972, reported an average of 25 Harlequins from Maine to Cape May, New Jersey. Largest numbers recorded in one area were 44 in York County, Maine, in 1970; 12 there in 1969; and 10 the same year at Martha's Vineyard, Massachusetts. The most southerly records were one at Rehoboth Bay, Delaware, in 1970, and two at Ocean City, Maryland, in 1972.

Occasionally, Harlequins appear in the Great Lakes region. Birders on Christmas censuses have found one or two birds in the following locations in Ontario: Ottawa, Blenheim, Hamilton, Kettle Point, and Toronto; one was recorded at Buffalo, New York, and one at Milwaukee, Wisconsin.

On the west coast of North America, Harlequins winter in greatest numbers in the Aleutian Islands chain. Refuge reports do not make clear whether the entire fall-spring population of 600,000 to 1 million winter there, but they probably do. Cahn (1947) reported them as abundant at Dutch Harbor through the entire winter. Elsewhere in the Aleutians, other observers have also reported them as abundant during the winter months (Gabrielson and Lincoln 1959). According to Gabrielson and Lincoln (1959), they were common to abundant from the Alaska Peninsula through Cook Inlet, Prince William Sound, and the bays and inlets of the Alexander Archipelago.

Nearly 500 Harlequins have been found on Christmas bird censuses in or near the Strait of Georgia, British Columbia; most were recorded close to Comox and Victoria, Vancouver Island. From 25 to 50 have been reported along the Washington and Oregon coasts, principally in the Strait of Juan de Fuca and Tillamook Bay. A few Harlequins have been found scattered along the California coast north of San Francisco Bay.

MIGRATION BEHAVIOR

Harlequins began to arrive in small flocks at Dutch Harbor, Aleutian Islands, Alaska, in mid-September and remained to May (Cahn 1947). Their dates of return to breeding grounds in interior Alaska were given as May 16 at the Beaver Mountains and May 31 for the Brooks Range (Gabrielson and Lincoln 1959).

BREEDING

Behavior

Age, Pair Bond, and Homing. Harlequins are not known to breed until their second year. In Iceland, Bengtson (1966) found only 12 mated pairs among 200 birds observed late in December. There were numerous flocks of 10 to 30 unpaired birds in which 3 to 8 males displayed to a female. Apparently, most adults are paired by the time they leave the sea early in May for their interior breeding grounds. Early in incubation, about the end of June or early July, males abandon their mates and leave the breeding areas. Because well-concealed and uniquely located nest sites were often occupied in consecutive years, Bengtson (1966) concluded that the same hens returned in succeeding years to the same nest sites.

Home Range. Where Harlequins nest in abundance, they maintain very small home ranges and the male appears to defend only that area around the female. However, Bengtson (1966) noted that where numbers were sparse, on the periphery of the breeding area, each pair occupied and defended a small section of the Laxá River.

Nesting

Nest Sites. Harlequins usually nest along rocky shores acjacent to the rapids of turbulent mountain streams. In Iceland, Bengtson (1966) found their nests on the ground

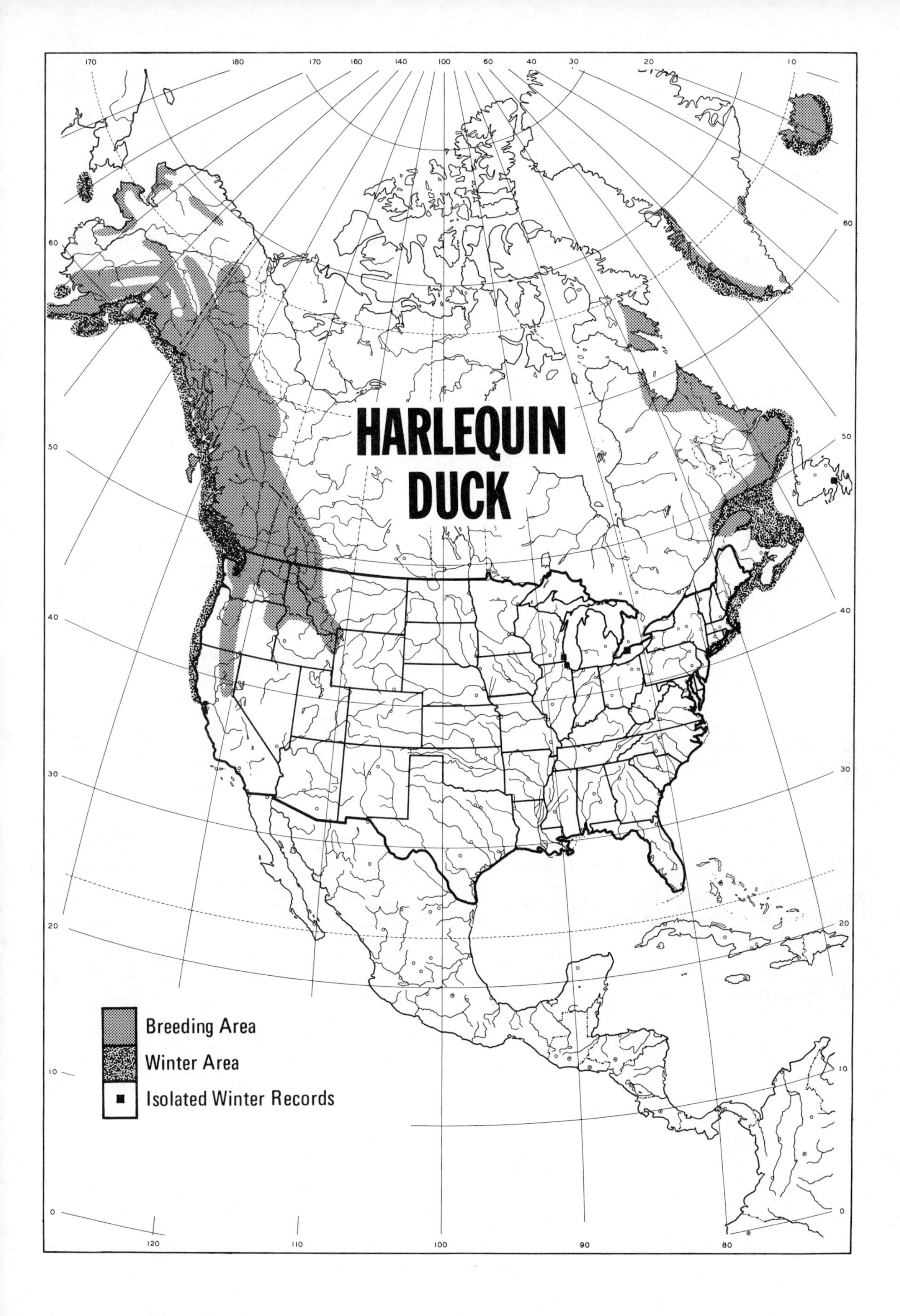
HARLEQUIN DUCK
Breeding Area
Winter Area
Isolated Winter Records

under bushes or among lava blocks, particularly on islands of the Laxá River. Nests are composed of a thin layer of grass, occasionally with a few dry twigs and leaves, and lined with white down in lesser quantities than are found in eider nests. The male follows the female as she searches islands or river banks, walking for an hour or more inspecting crevices in rocks and investigating low shrubbery.

Clutch Size, Eggs, and Incubation. Eggs are laid at intervals of 2 to 4 days (Bengtson 1966). The clutch size in 11 nests found in Iceland ranged from 3 to 7 and averaged 5.5. In captivity, Harlequins lay clutches of 6 to 8 thin-walled, cream-colored eggs that measure 54 by 38 mm (Johnstone 1970). Bengtson (1966) considered the incubation period to be about 28 or 29 days, but Johnstone (1970) reports a 30-day period for eggs hatched in incubators. The female incubates assiduously and takes a rest and feeding break only once every 48 hours (Bengtson 1966). Hens are so intent on their task that visitors have sometimes touched incubating birds.

Chronology of Nesting. For Alaska, Gabrielson and Lincoln (1959) cited records of a brood of Harlequin downy young on July 5, a less than half-grown brood on August 1, a half-grown brood on August 6, and four undesignated-age broods on August 13. These data suggest that in several areas of Alaska, laying begins between May 15 and May 30. Bengtson (1966) observed in Iceland that Harlequins laid eggs from May 10 to July 8, with the greatest activity in early June.

Nest Success. Because only a few nests have been studied, there is no satisfactory information available on nest success, causes of nest failure, and renesting.

Rearing of Young

Broods. On the Laxá River in Iceland, female Harlequins led their broods to secluded sections of the river, where they remained thereafter, with little movement (Bengtson 1966). Several broods often associated amicably and occasionally were joined by hens unsuccessful in breeding.

Development. Bengtson (1966) cited an old record of fledging after 40 days.

Survival. Bengtson (1966) recorded that 24 of 37 ducklings in seven broods survived 1 week (mortality, 35 percent), and 19 survived 2 weeks (mortality, 20 percent).

POSTBREEDING SEASON

After mid-June in Iceland, males desert their mates early in the incubation period and begin to congregate for their postnuptial molt at favorable feeding places (Bengtson 1966). They leave the feeding areas June 20-24 to spend the flightless part of their molt elsewhere, perhaps at sea. Gabrielson and Lincoln (1959) cited a September 5 record of a large flock in eclipse plumage at the mouth of the Savonoski River in Alaska.

FOOD HABITS

Most Harlequins, like torrent ducks in South America, live beside torrential mountain streams during the breeding season. Unlike torrent ducks, however, Harlequins resort to the sea for the remainder of the year. On their breeding ground along the Laxá River in Iceland, Pool (1962) observed Harlequins dive to depths of 3 to 5 feet in swift currents in their search for food and emerge at their points of entry, thus demonstrating a unique ability either to walk on the stream bed or to swim against the formidable current. For about a 5-minute period, they undertook a series of dives, pausing 5 to 10 seconds between each dive, and then briefly rested on the bank before resuming their efforts. At other times they fed by simply immersing their heads or tipping up like dabbling ducks. For much of the day, however, the Harlequins rested on the bank, feeding primarily late in the afternoon (6 P.M.) and secondarily early in the morning (6 A.M.) (Bengtson 1966). Bengtson (1966) recorded the underwater time of seven species of diving ducks and found that Harlequins averaged 16 seconds longer than any other species.

Cottam (1939) found that gizzards from 63 Harlequins collected over 7 months of the year contained almost entirely (98 percent) animal food: crustaceans composed 57 percent, mollusks 25 percent, insects 10 percent, and echinoderms and fishes over 2 percent each. Principal crustaceans were mud crabs (14 percent), hermit crabs (7 percent), and amphipods (14 percent). Over a third of the mollusks were chitons. These mollusks are rarely consumed by other ducks because they are attached to rocks so firmly by suction that prying them loose is difficult, yet Harlequins somehow manage this feat. Other important mollusks were chink shells, periwinkles, top shells, limpets, and blue mussels. Stone flies composed over half of the aquatic insects consumed.

Oldsquaw

Clangula hyemalis

Other Common Names: Long-tailed duck, sea pintail, cockertail, coween kakawi.

VITAL STATISTICS

Length:	Male, 19.0-22.6 inches, average 20.8 inches (35) Female, 14.8-17.2 inches, average 15.6 inches (29)
Wing:	Adult male, 8.7 inches (24) Adult female, 8.3 inches (22) Immature male, 8.2 inches (15) Immature female, 7.8 inches (12)
Weight:*	Adult male, 2.00-2.22 pounds (36) Adult female, 1.65-1.82 pounds (40) Immature male, 1.88-2.07 pounds (31) Immature female, 1.60-1.81 pounds (31)

*From Ellarson (1956). First weights represent birds with dry plumages but with some loss of body moisture; second weights represent birds with wet plumages.

IDENTIFICATION

Field

These sea ducks resemble pintails because of their long pointed tails, but they lack the pintails' long necks. They are, however, the trimmest of the sea ducks, with more tapered bodies than the chunky eiders and scoters possess. They fly swiftly, low over the water, in loose and ever-changing flock formations. Speirs (1945) timed flying oldsquaws at ground speeds of 54 to 73 miles per hour, an average air speed of 51 mph. The wings of oldsquaws in flight are slightly arched, with rapid strokes largely below the body plane, and the tips of the wings appear to move backward as well as downward. Oldsquaws often twist and turn in flight, alternately flashing their white bellies and black-brown backs. When the males are on the water, their long tails sweep upward at a 45-degree angle, and the pattern of black-white-black-white from their backs to the water is unmistakable.

The oldsquaw has the most unusual seasonal plumages of all ducks, mainly white in fall and winter and mostly brown in spring and early summer. The difference in coloration is greater in the male than in the female. From October through March, the drake is about equally black and white: chest, breast, hindback, and wings are black; foreback, sides, flank, belly, scapulars, and lower tail coverts are white; the head is white, with a large brown-black patch extending from the cheek down the side of the neck. By April the male is far along in the acquisition of its summer plumage: the white head, neck, and foreback have become entirely black-brown except for a white cheek patch, and the long white scapulars have become brown with tan margins. The belly, sides, flanks, and undertail coverts remain white.

The female lacks the long central tail feathers of the male. During the fall and winter, the head is white except for a gray-brown dash on the cheek and crown. A gray-brown band separates the white neck from the white chest, breast, and belly; the upper parts are brown. By late spring, the female's head, neck, and chest have become noticeably blacker.

Because of differences in plumage colors between age and sex groups as well as individual variations during stages of the molt, there are many confusing color patterns that occur during the spring. Gabrielson and Lincoln (1959) reported an array of plumages on Alaskan breeding grounds, some ducks appearing in winter plumage, some in summer plumage, and others exhibiting various intermediate patterns. They found birds in summer that still retained vestiges of their winter colors. A June record of an oldsquaw in winter plumage, on Arctic breeding grounds, was reported by Hanson et al. (1956).

Male oldsquaws are among the most garrulous of ducks. Their loud, musical *caloo, caloo* or *ah-ahlowet* carries across the sea to distances almost beyond sight range.

At Hand

The bill is stubby, pink-tipped, and black-based in the male and gray-black in the female. The feet are blue-gray. In the adult male, the two dark brown central tail feathers are 8 to 9 inches long and project 5 to 6 inches beyond the gray-white outer tail feathers; the two brown feathers marginal to the central feathers project about 1.5 inches. The female has a gray-brown tail in which the central feathers are only slightly elongated.

Juveniles are similar to adult hens in appearance, but their heads, necks, and flanks are predominantly gray-brown, with the white restricted to the vicinity of the eyes. From October to March, young males gradually molt toward the adult plumage. However, there is much individual variation in the molt; some birds are still largely in juvenile dress in midwinter. Other juvenile males begin to acquire in November the head and neck coloration of adults. The most advanced juveniles acquire a summer plumage similar to that of adults, but scapulars are shorter, their backs show traces of juvenile plumage, and their chests are less extensively covered by black-brown feathers. The least advanced juveniles acquire little summer plumage. By the second winter, juveniles resemble adult males, but their central tail feathers are shorter.

POPULATION STATUS

An early summer population of 3 to 4 million oldsquaws in North America is the estimate I arrive at on the basis of available data. For the western and central Arctic, the information is based on aerial surveys by the U. S. Fish and Wildlife Service in Alaska and Canada west of Hudson Bay. Barry (1960) surveyed the area extending roughly from the Mackenzie River to the Boothia Peninsula, and Tener's (1963) surveys were confined to the Queen Elizabeth Islands in the more northerly reaches of the Arctic. Manning et al. (1956) supplied data for Banks Island and Macpherson and Manning (1959) for the Adelaide Peninsula. Data from all these sources produce a combined population estimate of 2 million. No data are available for the eastern Canadian Arctic, the region east of the Adelaide Peninsula, including the coasts of Hudson Bay, Baffin and Southampton islands, and the Ungava Peninsula. This region encompasses a tundra breeding ground for oldsquaws over half as large as the region containing the estimated 2 million birds. Therefore, a somewhat arbitrary figure of 1.5 million is assigned to the eastern Canadian Arctic.

Sex Ratios

Ellarson (1956) made a detailed analysis of the sex ratios among 3,451 oldsquaw ducks taken from gill nets set in various regions of Lake Michigan. He found that the adult males wintered the farthest north and west on the lake and the immature females the farthest south and east. Seasonal shifts also occurred among the sex- and age-classes.

In spite of these geographic and seasonal differences in Ellarson's data, the overall sample appears to approximate the sex ratio in the Lake Michigan population: 52.3 percent males (1:0.91) among adults and 48.1 percent males (1:1.08) among immatures. On Lake Ontario, Robert Alison has determined from aerial photographs that 49 percent of the adult oldsquaws were males.

On their breeding grounds near Churchill, Manitoba, arriving flocks of oldsquaws contained a few more females than males (Alison 1972). In the area of the Perry River, Hanson et al. (1956) observed 60.5 percent drakes among the 122 oldsquaws tallied between June 8 and June 16. Based on the data presented here, sex ratios in the oldsquaw are considered to be almost even, an unusual phenomenon among North American ducks.

Mortality

Because man, as yet, has had little effect on the breeding grounds of oldsquaws and because only minor numbers are shot, oldsquaw populations must be as stable as weather conditions permit. A fluoroscopic examination of 643 adult oldsquaws from Lake Michigan revealed that 1.24 percent had shot pellets embedded in their flesh; only 1 among 408 immatures (0.25 percent) had body shot. These birds are targets for Eskimos in the Arctic, Indians and whites in the Subarctic, and hunters along Lake Michigan. In comparison, 36 percent of 3,341 adult drake mallards fluoroscoped in Illinois had shot pellets in their flesh, as did 18 percent of 1,618 immatures (Bellrose 1953).

When winters are unusually cold and ice forms over large areas of the oldsquaws' winter grounds, a catastrophic kill occurs. Ellarson (1956) reported that three large die-offs of oldsquaws in the Great Lakes were caused by starvation. Oldsquaws evidently do not abandon their ancestral winter grounds because of severe ice conditions as readily as many other ducks.

Two decades ago, the number of oldsquaws drowned in gill nets set in Lake Michigan was astounding. From careful surveys and interviews, Ellarson (1956) arrived at a loss of 15,500 from fall to spring, 1951-52, and a loss of 19,600 during a similar period, 1952-53. In recent years this loss has fortunately been greatly reduced because of the decreased intensity of commercial fishing in the lake. Robert Alison reports that oldsquaws are also caught in whitefish nets during November and December on Lake Ontario.

DISTRIBUTION

Oldsquaws nest in greater numbers in the high-Arctic

than any other duck. Their breeding range is circumpolar, extending almost as far north as land occurs and as far south as the tundra persists. In Eurasia they nest north of the Arctic Circle except for a southern extension in the Chukot Peninsula of northeastern Siberia. They breed in Iceland, and along the entire ice-free coasts of Greenland except where high cliffs prevail. Most oldsquaws usually winter along the seacoasts as far south as California, Korea, and northern Japan in the Pacific, northern France and North Carolina in the Atlantic, and the Great Lakes in the interior.

Breeding Range

Unlike the eiders that nest only on or near the coasts, the oldsquaw nests both along the Arctic coasts and inland wherever tundra or tundralike conditions provide the required habitat. In addition to tens of thousands of breeding oldsquaws—the nonbreeding birds, probably mostly yearlings—are found during the summer on lakes south of the tundra in the open and closed boreal forests.

Surveys of summer populations in Alaska by King and Lensink (1971) have led to an estimate of 590,000 oldsquaws. Although Gabrielson and Lincoln (1959) cited a few breeding records for interior Alaska, King and Lensink (1971) considered that most of the 43,600 oldsquaws estimated for areas in interior Alaska were late migrants or nonbreeding birds. The Yukon Delta harbors the largest number of breeding oldsquaws—some 290,000 (11 per square mile). Next in importance is the Arctic Slope with 125,500 (but only 1.2 per square mile). The estimate for Bristol Bay is 53,000 (5.4 per square mile). The 49,000 oldsquaws on the Seward Peninsula have the highest density (12.8 per square mile). Nearby, the breeding grounds at Kotzebue Sound contain 26,000 (4.8 per square mile). The lowest number, 200 (0.09 per square mile), is estimated for the Kenai-Susitna breeding area.

Although oldsquaws nest on the islands of the Bering Sea, their breeding in the Aleutians remains in doubt (Gabrielson and Lincoln 1959). On St. Lawrence Island, Fay (1961) reported that nonbreeders were as numerous as breeders, with flocks of 10 to over 100 frequently seen from June to August.

On the areas of the Old Crow Flats, Mackenzie Delta, and Liverpool Bay, aerial surveys by the U. S. Fish and Wildlife Service yield a population estimate of 208,000 oldsquaws. In an aerial survey of the central and western Canadian Arctic, Barry (1960) found 38,200 oldsquaws: 200 adjacent to Liverpool Bay; 6,000 on Banks Island; 20,000 on southeast Victoria Island and Prince Albert Peninsula; 12,000 on Queen Maud Gulf; and none on the islands of King William, Somerset, Prince Leopold, and Limestone.

On an aerial survey farther north in the Queen Elizabeth Islands, Tener (1963) found only small numbers of oldsquaws: 20 off Cape Phillips on Cornwallis Island, June 14; 2 on Bathurst Island; 40 on Melville Island; 13 on Prince Patrick Island; 10 on Axel Heiberg Island; and 46 at Lake Hazen, Ellesmere Island.

Although Barry (1960) found only 6,000 oldsquaws on the aerial survey of Banks Island, ground reconnaissance by Manning et al. (1956) led them to the conclusion that the population for the island and the surrounding sea was 60,000. Parmelee et al. (1967) considered the oldsquaw the second most abundant waterfowl on Victoria Island, the king eider ranking first. In the Perry River area, the king eider again ranked first and the oldsquaw second, representing 20 percent of all ducks (Hanson et al. 1956). On southern King William Island and northwestern Adelaide Peninsula, also, the oldsquaw and king eider were the two most common ducks (Fraser 1957). Macpherson and Manning (1959) estimated a summer population of 10,000 oldsquaws for the Adelaide Peninsula, about the same number as king eiders. They found densities of 1 to 1.4 per square mile in three tundra zones. On the Boothia Isthmus, Fraser (1957) found the oldsquaw as common as the king eider in early summer. Geale (1971) saw only two oldsquaws on Cornwallis Island, where common eiders were the most abundant duck and king eiders second. Oldsquaws and king eiders are the only ducks that breed as far north as Axel Heiberg Island and the Fosheim Peninsula of Ellesmere Island, and oldsquaws appear the more abundant (Parmelee and MacDonald 1960).

On Bylot Island, Drury (1961) found oldsquaws more abundant than king eiders, the only other breeding duck. Bray (1943) considered the oldsquaw an abundant breeding duck on all the islands surrounding the Foxe Basin, and declared that it is probably one of the few birds inhabiting the far interior of northern islands and the Melville Peninsula. Wynne-Edwards (1952) noted oldsquaws nesting at Clyde Inlet, Baffin Island, and Soper (1946) commonly found them breeding on the Foxe Peninsula, Baffin Island. In the Cape Dorset area of the Foxe Peninsula, Macpherson and McLaren (1959) reported 17 pairs of oldsquaws, 140 pairs of common eiders, and 1 pair of Canada geese.

On the northwest coast of Hudson Bay near Chesterfield Inlet, Höhn (1968) counted 20 pairs of oldsquaws on about 1 square mile. They were second in number to the common eiders, which numbered 76 pairs. Near Churchill, on the west coast of Hudson Bay, Alison (1972) found an average of 44 nesting pairs on a 10-square-mile study area, 1968-71; common eiders were second in abundance with 16 nesting pairs.

At Cape Henrietta Maria, where Hudson and James bays join, Peck (1972) recorded oldsquaws as abundant breeders. On Grey Goose and Bear islands in James Bay, Manning and Coates (1952) observed hens with broods. South Twin Island marks their southernmost breeding record in James Bay (Todd 1963). Although Manning and Macpherson (1952) failed to find any oldsquaws along the east coast of James Bay, they believed that a few nested there. Todd (1963) listed scattered breeding records along the east coast of Hudson Bay from Cape Jones to Povungnituk. A number of oldsquaw nests and broods have been reported from the Belcher Islands, Hudson Bay, by Todd (1963) and Freeman (1970*b*). A short distance north, among the King George Islands and Sleeper Islands, Manning (1946) observed

OLDSQUAW
Breeding Area
Winter Area
Isolated Winter Records

flightless young. Along the east coast of Hudson Bay, he counted 278 oldsquaws, 1,100 common eiders, 185 unknown eiders, and 10 king eiders.

In the interior tundra of the Ungava Peninsula, Eklund (1956) reported that the oldsquaw was the most abundant nesting duck, accounting for 50 percent of all ducks. On a flight around Payne Lake, 37 adults and 15 immatures were noted. Todd (1963) cited breeding records along the south shore of Hudson Strait, around Ungava Bay, and south along the Labrador coast as far as Davis Inlet. Unusual southern nesting records have occurred near Bradore Bay and Kegashka Lake, Quebec, on the north shore of the Gulf of St. Lawrence (Todd 1963). In Newfoundland, the oldsquaw occurs as an occasional nonbreeding summer resident (Peters and Burleigh 1951).

On water areas south and west of the tundra in the open and closed boreal forest associations, aerial surveys by the U. S. Fish and Wildlife Service yield a calculated total of 1.1 million oldsquaws. Most of these are probably nonbreeding birds but probably include some late migrants.

Migration Corridors

Although oldsquaws are not observed as frequently as scoters and eiders migrating offshore, such migration may nevertheless occur but may not be noted because of their greater propensity to migrate nocturnally. Where both breeding and winter areas are near the sea, it is certainly likely that their migration corridors parallel the coasts. At Icy Cape, Alaska, on the Chukchi Sea, Bailey observed a large and extensive southward passage of oldsquaws through September, leading him to believe that large numbers were continually arriving from farther east—the Beaufort Sea (Bailey and Niedrach 1965). Near the tip of the Mackenzie Delta, Porslid (1943) observed oldsquaws migrating eastward daily during the first week of June. Off Depoe Bay, Oregon, Gabrielson and Jewett (1940) reported that 50 oldsquaws were seen migrating northward as singles or in small flocks, the largest numbering 20 birds.

Oldsquaws that winter on the Great Lakes and as stragglers elsewhere in the interior migrate overland. At almost opposite ends of Lake Ontario, at Toronto and Trenton, Robert Alison reports that radar displays indicate a north-south passage of oldsquaws. Large numbers of migrants appear each year on Lake Nipissing, and Alison observed several flocks migrating north near Fort Albany on James Bay, May 25, 1974. This observation suggests that an important corridor extends from James Bay to the west end of Lake Ontario, then probably south-southeast to Chesapeake Bay.

Recoveries of oldsquaws banded by Robert Alison at Churchill, on the west coast of Hudson Bay, indicate that part of this population migrates to Lake Michigan for the winter. Soper (1951) noted large numbers migrating through the Athabasca Delta in spring as well as 200 miles farther north at the Slave River delta. At Old Crow, Yukon Territory, Irving (1960) observed flocks flying eastward over the Porcupine River; he believed that they flew over the Alaska Range from the Gulf of Alaska. Band recoveries have indicated that a large proportion of the oldsquaws in Iceland winter in southwest Greenland (Salomonsen 1950-51).

Winter Areas

On the Pacific Coast, the oldsquaw winters from St. Lawrence Island in the Bering Sea, along the Aleutian Islands chain and the coast of southeast Alaska, and in diminishing numbers to the coasts of British Columbia, Washington, Oregon, and California. A conservative estimate is that 500,000 oldsquaws winter about St. Lawrence Island (Fay 1961). Refuge reports estimate the number of oldsquaws wintering along the Aleutian Chain at 700,000 to 1 million, and 20,000 to 35,000 for the Izembek National Wildlife Range in the Alaska Peninsula. As evinced by the 10,000 oldsquaws observed in the Wrangell Narrows on February 14, large numbers have wintered among the island channels of southeast Alaska (Gabrielson and Lincoln 1959).

Audubon Christmas bird counts in the Strait of Georgia, British Columbia, have yielded an average of 500 oldsquaws. The counts have given 25 to 75 for Puget Sound, Washington, none for the Oregon coast, and 6 or 7 for the California coast, rarely one as far south as San Diego Bay. Jewett et al. (1953) stated that oldsquaws were present in the coastal region of Washington from December through February, in groups of 1 to 4, and, rarely, up to 300. In Oregon, Gabrielson and Jewett (1940) reported it as an irregular winter visitor to the coast. Denson and Bentley (1962) believe that the oldsquaw is a rare but regular visitor at Humboldt Bay in northern California.

On the Atlantic Coast, Audubon Christmas bird counts of the oldsquaw averaged 9,400 during 1966-68 but increased to 18,600 in 1972. The largest concentrations in that year, totaling 8,500, were between Delaware Bay and the lower extremity of Chesapeake Bay. Only 65 were found south of there, mostly in coastal North Carolina. In other winters, a few have been reported from Georgia and the Gulf coasts of Florida, Alabama, and Mississippi.

Coastal New Jersey ranked second in number of oldsquaws in 1972; of the 3,300 found there, 2,300 were in Barnegat Bay. Northward along the coast, there were 1,500 on bays of Long Island Sound; 600 in Massachusetts; 1,900 in New Hampshire and Maine; 300 in New Brunswick; 60 in Prince Edward Island; 1,350 in Nova Scotia; and 80 in coastal Newfoundland.

More oldsquaws winter in the Great Lakes than all other sea ducks combined. Audubon Christmas bird counts, 1966-68, revealed almost 20,000 oldsquaws, 16,000 goldeneyes, and 1,900 other sea ducks. About 12,000 were recorded on Lake Michigan, the bulk of them near Milwaukee, and 6,500 on Lake Ontario, most near Toronto and the Niagara River. For some inexplicable reason, only a small number of oldsquaws were recorded on Lake Erie. Robert Alison also comments on the scarcity there. Although the limited coverage of Lake Huron partially accounts for the few reported, Alison has observed only small numbers along the north shore of the lake. Roberts (1932) termed them common winter visitors to Lake Superior and rare stragglers elsewhere in Minnesota as far south as Iowa.

MIGRATION BEHAVIOR

Large numbers of oldsquaws migrate very short distances between breeding and winter areas, for untold thousands remain at sea in the Far North. Many thousands do, however, migrate southward along the Atlantic Coast, and, apparently, overland into the Great Lakes. An adult female returned to Presqu'Ile Provincial Park on Lake Ontario 1 year after being banded, suggesting homing to specific winter areas (Alison 1974). Two other banded oldsquaws were retrapped at the same site near Toronto in the subsequent winter. A few appear to continue across the interior of the nation to the Gulf of Mexico. Almost every fall we see small numbers of oldsquaws on the Keokuk Pool of the Mississippi River, near Nauvoo, Illinois. On the Pacific Coast, comparatively small numbers migrate south of southeastern Alaska; most winter in the Bering Sea.

Chronology

Fall. Salomonsen (1950-51) reported that oldsquaws leave northern Greenland in early September. Farther south at Scoresby Sound they leave during October, with young birds remaining there up to December, and, rarely, to the end of January. They are observed in the Disko Bay region until mid-November. In Nova Scotia, they are the most common winter duck between October and April (Tufts 1961). According to Robert Alison, oldsquaws leave their breeding grounds at Churchill, Manitoba, about September 1, but remain along the coast of Hudson Bay until late October.

Periodic aerial surveys of oldsquaw populations from Maine to Long Island during the fall reveal pronounced yearly variations in seasonal passage (Tice 1970). The fall of 1965 produced an early migration, commencing with 15 birds on October 13, rising to 365 on October 27, reaching a season's peak of 2,800 on November 10, then declining to 1,300 on December 15. During the fall of 1966, 30 were observed on September 27; 75 on October 11; and a peak of 1,700 on November 15 that declined to 1,500 on December 13. Three surveys in September 1967 and one on October 11 failed to discover any oldsquaws, but almost 2,000, the season's peak, were observed on November 15. Bull (1964) reported that oldsquaws are seen on Long Island every month of the year but are uncommon before late October and after April. Peak numbers of oldsquaws arrive in Chesapeake Bay between November 5 and December 5 (Stewart 1962). At Toronto, immatures arrive from September 18 to October 24, but remain only a short time before continuing their migration. Adult oldsquaws arrive in mid-November and constitute most of the wintering population (Robert Alison). Occasionally, a few appear on Lake Michigan in late September, but most arrive from late October through November (Ellarson 1956). Lowery (1955) reported them as uncommon visitors in Louisiana from November 15 to May 3.

Spring. Most oldsquaws leave Chesapeake Bay for the Arctic between March 15 and April 15 (Stewart 1962). Judging by the seasonal number captured in gill nets on Lake Michigan, the wintering population remains through March and well into April; few are found in May (Ellarson 1956). They depart Newfoundland by March or April, with stragglers remaining until June (Peters and Burleigh 1951). They leave Lake Ontario, April 22-May 15, in two or three waves (Robert Alison).

On the Belcher Islands in Hudson Bay, Freeman (1970*b*) reported that migrating oldsquaws appeared on the adjacent sea by the end of April; a few wintered there. Pairs were observed on interior tundra pools early in May. Near Churchill, the first birds arrived between May 31 and June 4, 1968-71 (Alison 1972). Breeding pairs continued to arrive until June 23, with peak arrivals between June 10 and June 16. Farther north on Hudson Bay, at Chesterfield Inlet, Höhn (1968) saw the first ones on May 30, but they did not appear on inland tundra pools until June 11. Murdy (1964) observed the first oldsquaws at Yellowknife on Great Slave Lake on May 24-25, 1962-64, with major influxes a few days later.

Macpherson and Manning (1959) on the Adelaide Peninsula observed the first oldsquaws on June 16, most in pairs but some in small flocks. At Karrak Lake, near Queen Maud Gulf, Northwest Territories, this species first appeared June 5, 7, and 16, 1966-68 (Ryder 1971*a*). Oldsquaws appeared near Cambridge Bay, Victoria Island, on June 4 and 5, 1960 and 1962, but large numbers did not arrive until June 12 (Parmelee et al. 1967). On the Fosheim Peninsula in the high-Arctic of Ellesmere Island, oldsquaws appeared over several years on June 5, 6, 11, and 16 (Parmelee and MacDonald 1960).

BREEDING

Behavior

Age. Probably most oldsquaws do not breed until they are at least 2 years of age. Many yearlings still retain their juvenile tail feathers on the breeding grounds (Manning et al. 1956), an indication of sexual immaturity. Moreover, Ellarson (1956) found that testes of male oldsquaws in May measured 1.36 mm for juveniles and 11.07 mm for adults, evidence that juvenile males would not breed the first year. He also presented evidence based on oviduct weights that female oldsquaws do not breed until they are at least 2 years of age. Ellarson (1956) compared oviduct weights with age, as indicated by the color of the scapulars, and concluded that more than 2 years are required for adult female oldsquaws to attain full plumage. Alison (1972) reports that sexual maturity is reached in the second winter, but that not all two-year-olds form pairs.

Pair Bond. Pair bonds in oldsquaws are established in winter or during spring migration. Ornithologists throughout the Arctic agree in reporting the arrival of oldsquaws in pairs. Alison (1972) reports that pair formation requires at least 30 days and is very strong. It is apparently reinforced by frequent and vigorous displays, often observed by ornithologists throughout the Arctic. Alison (1972) found that pairs of oldsquaws in captivity resumed their original pair bonds, although other birds were available as mates. At Churchill he captured the same pair on the same lake two consecutive years. The pair bond appears to disintegrate temporarily, early in the incubation period. On Victoria Island, Parmelee et al. (1967) observed males beginning to flock in late June; the last males on interior breeding ponds were observed on July 10, 1960, and July 18, 1962. Hanson et al. (1956) saw the first gathering of drakes on July 8 on the Perry River.

Homing. Salomonsen (1950-51) reported that at Lake Mývatn, Iceland, many banded oldsquaws returned to the same breeding places in subsequent years. Three of 10 banded hens returning to a study area near Churchill, Manitoba, returned to their earlier nest sites, 5 to their previously occupied ponds, and 2 to nearby ponds (Alison 1972). One drake returned the next year to the pond of its original capture, and another returned to the same water area for 3 years after being banded.

Home Range. Oldsquaws are dispersed over the Arctic tundra to a greater extent than other waterfowl. Near the Perry River, Hanson et al. (1956) found a single nesting pair on each tundra pond. At Chesterfield Inlet, Höhn (1968) reported a pair for almost every pool, including those as small as 0.1 acre. Experiments conducted by Alison (1972) explain this dispersion. He placed decoys on a pond occupied by a pair of oldsquaws. The male attacked single adult drake decoys; when a pair of decoys was installed, the female was the aggressor. Subadult oldsquaw decoys were largely ignored and so were decoys of other duck species. When Alison (1972) removed the drakes of 10 mated pairs from their core areas, new pairs moved into these areas and the new drakes defended the same specific areas as their predecessors. The females of the original pairs remained, even though frequently pursued. Alison (1972) concluded that the number of defended home ranges restricted the number of breeding pairs on his study area. However, female oldsquaws frequently nest within the home ranges of other pairs; often their nests are grouped so closely as to approach a colony aggregation.

Nesting

Nest Sites. As usual, the females select the nest sites. Nests are usually placed on islands, either offshore along the coasts or in tundra ponds and lakes. Where ponds dot the tundra landscape, nests are frequently located on nearby upland.

Most nests are located close to the water's edge. On small islands that necessarily restricted the distance to water, Alison (1972) found the average to be 2.3 feet. Nest sites on upland tundra and on marshland areas averaged 27 and 29 feet from water, respectively. The greatest distances of oldsquaw nests from water are reported as 656 feet (Evans 1970), 410 and 150 feet (Alison 1972), 300 feet (Parmelee and MacDonald 1960), and 150 feet (Drury 1961).

In the most intensive study yet made of nesting oldsquaws, Alison (1972) found that near Churchill, Manitoba, 56 of 95 nests (59 percent) were on islands in freshwater tundra ponds or lakes, 24 nests were equally divided between tundra and spruce forests on the mainland, and 9 nests were in marshy areas. In the Belcher Islands, Freeman (1970*b*) found two nests under overhangs of rock, and oldsquaws have been found nesting on rocky sites in the high-Arctic.

Alison (1972) observed two female oldsquaws laying in the same nest and located two active nests that were barely 3 inches apart. In another instance, three active nests were within an area of 3 square feet. Although nest densities were greatest on islands, nests on the mainland were often grouped. All four active nests around one 8-acre lake were on a 40- by 10-foot peninsula, and two nests adjacent to 1- to 1.5-acre ponds were 4.5 and 6 feet apart. The farthest distance between nests around the same body of water was 1,310 feet.

Nests are placed in natural depressions or on former nest sites. Materials at hand—mosses, sedges, grasses—are used as bases. Near Churchill, Alison (1972) found the depressions lined with 1 to 2 inches of dry dwarf willow or dwarf birch leaves. Down is added after the second egg, the amount increasing from the third to the fifth egg. Unlike the interrupted egg-laying schedule of eiders, oldsquaws lay an egg almost every day, averaging about 26 hours apart.

Clutch Size, Eggs, and Incubation. Clutch sizes, as reported from various ornithological surveys in the Arctic, have ranged from 2 to 11, with an average of 7.27 eggs (26). Alison (1972), at Churchill, Manitoba, found that clutches consistently averaged 6.7 to 6.9 eggs during each of 4 years, 1968-71. Judging from several observations of intraspecific parasitism, he considered that a few large clutch sizes may represent more than one hen laying in the same nest. Five marked hens laid identically sized 6- to 8-egg clutches in each of 2 years.

Bent (1925) described oldsquaw eggs as ovate to elongate ovate, averaging 53 mm by 37 mm (139). The surface is smooth but not glossy, and the color ranges from water-green to olive-buff.

Alison (1972) concluded that the incubation period is 26 days, with a range of 24 to 29 days (106 eggs). Eggs under artificial incubation took slightly longer to hatch. Hens do not commence incubation until their clutches are complete. They leave twice daily to rest and feed, between nine and ten in the morning and again between four and six-thirty in the afternoon.

Chronology of Nesting. Near Churchill, Alison (1972)

found that the earliest nest initiation occurred on June 3, the latest on June 28. The average dates for all nests in each of 4 years, 1968-71, were June 12, 23, 11, and 9. The frozen condition of the tundra ponds in 1969 delayed the first nests to June 16, with a resultant extension to June 28. In the year of the earliest nest initiation, 1971, the first nest was started June 3, the last on June 17. During all 4 years, egg-laying lasted 13 to 16 days, brief even for Arctic nesters.

A nest was started June 11 on the Belcher Islands (Freeman 1970*b*). At Chesterfield Inlet, nests with completed clutches were found between June 23 and July 7 (Höhn 1968). On the Foxe Peninsula, Baffin Island, laying in one nest started July 5, and a nest with seven eggs was discovered July 25 (Macpherson and McLaren 1959). Data on the hatch of four nests in the Adelaide Peninsula indicated that they were started between June 20 and July 3. In the Perry River area, oldsquaws started nesting about June 26 (Hanson et al. 1956). A nest on Victoria Island was started about June 12; the first appearance of broods indicated that nesting began on June 16 in 1960 and June 14 in 1962.

Estimated dates of nest initiation in Alaska, as determined by the occurrence of downy young, are June 6, Nunivak Island; July 13, Pribilof Islands; June 25, Point Barrow; June 10, Harrison Bay; June 18, Umiat, Colville River; and June 29, Mount McKinley National Park (Gabrielson and Lincoln 1959). At Hooper Bay on the Yukon Delta, Conover (1926) reported the first eggs on June 5 and the first ducklings on July 2. Near Selawik, the first oldsquaws arrived May 17, the first nesting was estimated as June 10, and the first broods were observed July 18 (Shepherd 1955).

Nest Success. Alison (1972) studied the history of 95 oldsquaw nests near Churchill, Manitoba, 1968-71. Fifty-nine percent of these nests were successful. Nest success was higher on the mainland than on islands. It was high in marshlands and scrublands, slightly lower on the open tundra, and lowest for nests under trees and in the dry upland tundra. Seventy-five of 383 eggs (19.6 percent) in successful oldsquaw nests failed to hatch because of infertility or death of embryos. In an earlier study of oldsquaws in the Churchill area, Evans (1970) found 5 of 28 nests (18 percent) destroyed by predators. He believed that oldsquaws that nested in Arctic tern colonies were protected somewhat from aerial predators, resulting in higher nest success. Alison (1972) found that oldsquaw nests were associated with Arctic tern nests on islands in tundra lakes but not on the mainland. Moreover, he concluded that the presence of Arctic terns made no significant difference in predator losses of oldsquaws breeding on islands but that the two species were merely attracted by the same types of habitat.

Nest Failure. In Alison's (1972) study of 95 nests, losses of the 39 that failed were due to parasitic jaegers (14 nests, 36 percent), unknown birds (5 nests, 13 percent), foxes (6, 15 percent), desertion (10, 26 percent), and unknown reasons (3, 8 percent). Both of the two oldsquaw nests found on Bylot Island were destroyed by jaegers (Drury 1961). The one nest under observation on Ellesmere Island was destroyed, presumably by long-tailed jaegers (Parmelee and MacDonald 1960).

Renesting. Alison (1972) observed no evidence that oldsquaws renested but noted that when partial clutches were destroyed during laying, the females usually returned and deposited several eggs. Certainly the brief period of nest initiation would prevent the establishment of a new nest once incubation had begun.

Rearing of Young

Broods. When the young are dry, about 24 hours after hatching, the females lead them to water. Some females apparently abandon their young soon after the hatch, because broods larger than the egg clutches are frequently observed. The largest "brood" on record was composed of 138 flightless young, with no attendant female, observed on August 21 by Parmelee et al. (1967).

Alison (1972) observed that oldsquaw broods were more unevenly distributed than breeding pairs. Seventy percent of the former home ranges contained no broods, but some tundra ponds within a single previously occupied home range held three or four broods. At Churchill, broods remained on freshwater ponds for 35 to 40 days before flying to the sea. Parmelee et al. (1967) reported that on Victoria Island, adult females and young gradually made their way from interior ponds to the sea. Broods hatched adjacent to freshwater lakes along the coast of Greenland spend at least 2 to 3 weeks there before moving to the sea (Salomonsen 1950-51). When hatched at a distance from the sea, broods are led to the outlets of rivers, where they remain until fledged.

Development. On the basis of the growth of plumages (described by Alison 1972), I judge that oldsquaws are in the downy Class I stage for the first 12 days of life, the intermediate Class II stage from 13 to 28 days, and the fully feathered nonflying stage from 29 to 35 days. Thirty-five days to flight stage is a remarkably short span, compared with the development of prairie-nesting ducks.

POSTBREEDING SEASON

Male oldsquaws leave tundra nesting grounds in late June or early July and move to the sea. Seldom are any found after mid-July. Flocks along the seacoast increase in number and in size from then until departure in late September as they are joined by females, and, still later, the young. A flock of 1,500 was encountered on Sherman Basin, Adelaide Peninsula, by Macpherson and Manning (1959). On Slidre Fiord, Ellesmere Island, Parmelee and MacDonald (1960) found hundreds of molting oldsquaws in August. Flightless adults were observed August 20-26. An adult male and female collected in September had regained their flight feathers. Molting adults were reported on Clyde Inlet, Baffin Island, from July 18 onward by Wynne-Edwards (1952). Salomonsen (1950-51) stated that yearlings and adult males in Greenland lost their flight feathers in late July or in early August and slightly later in the high-Arctic.

FOOD HABITS

Oldsquaws have phenomenal diving ability, probably diving deeper for food than any other duck. Ellarson (1956) obtained records of 37 oldsquaws caught in gill nets set at depths of 144 to 156 feet in Lake Michigan. Most, however, were taken at depths of 72 to 84 feet. Few were found in nets set in water 12 to 60 feet deep. Cottam (1939) cited numerous old records of oldsquaws captured in nets, a few as deep as 180 feet, considered by Ellarson to be the maximum depth reached. However, Robert Alison obtained 85 dead birds reputedly caught in nets set at a depth of 240 feet near Wolfe Island, Lake Ontario, May 1968. He has observed oldsquaws feeding in water 30 to 50 feet deep throughout the winter in the vicinity of Toronto. At Presqu'Ile Park, Lake Ontario, they feed in 4 to 32 feet of water and remain submerged for 20 to 30 seconds.

An examination of 190 gizzards from adults collected mostly in Alaska, Maine, and Manitoba showed that animal items composed 88 percent of the food (Cottam 1939). A variety of crustaceans formed 48 percent of that total, but amphipods and crabs were particularly important. Mollusks made up 16 percent, insects—caddis fly and midge larvae in particular—11 percent, and fishes 10 percent. A variety of plant foods, including domestic grains, formed 12 percent of the diet.

Crustaceans composed 75 percent and other animal life 2 percent of all food taken, according to the contents of 36 gizzards from immatures (Cottam 1939). Most of the crustaceans consumed were shrimps and water fleas.

Ellarson (1956) examined 151 gullets and stomachs from oldsquaw specimens taken from gill nets set in Lake Michigan. Crustaceans made up 82 percent of all food found. Except for the claws of a crayfish, the only crustacean taken was *Pontoporeia affinis*, a shrimplike animal. Fishes and their eggs composed 13 percent, mollusks 3.9 percent, and aquatic insects less than 1 percent of the total food volume. Only trace amounts of plant food were found. Robert Alison reports that from October to May, oldsquaws at Presqu'Ile on Lake Ontario feed almost exclusively upon the crustaceans *Gammarus and Pontoporeia.*

Black Scoter

Melanitta nigra americana

Other Common Names: American scoter, common scoter, coot, black coot, sea coot, black duck

VITAL STATISTICS

Length:	Male, 18.0-20.9 inches, average 19.7 inches (5) Female, 17.0-19.0 inches, average 18.5 inches (6)
Wing:	Adult male, 9.0 inches (69) Adult female, 8.7 inches (30) Immature male, 8.8 inches (34) Immature female, 8.4 inches (30)
Weight:	Male, 2.2-2.8 pounds, average 2.5 pounds (7) Female, 1.9-2.4 pounds, average 2.2 pounds (2)

IDENTIFICATION

Field

The black scoter is aptly named, for the adult male is completely black except for a yellow protuberance at the base of its bill and the gray lower surface of the flight feathers. When the black scoter is in flight, the flashing silver-gray of the underwing tips against the black linings of the wings and the black body aid in distinguishing this species from the surf scoter. Both the female and the immature are black-brown except for the whitish coloration of cheeks, chin, and throat, which contrasts markedly with the dark crown. In this respect they resemble the female ruddy duck, but the scoter is considerably larger. Again like the ruddy, the wedge-shaped tail of the black scoter is sometimes elevated at a 45-degree angle.

Black scoters fly in undulating lines, in irregular groups, or in V-shaped flocks. Off the New Hampshire coast, Stott and Olson (1972) observed that they decoyed as singles 27 percent of the time; as flocks of 2 to 6, 47 percent; as flocks of 6 to 11, 12 percent; and as flocks of 11 to 35, 14 percent. Decoyed white-winged and surf scoters seldom numbered more than six at one time. Dement'ev and Gladkov (1967) claim that the wings of the adult male make a whistling sound in flight.

At Hand

The wedge-shaped tail is longer than those of the other scoters. The feet are dusky in both sexes; the other two species have yellowish or pinkish feet. The black bill, with its yellow protuberance at the base (in the male) is less massive than those of the other two scoters. Both sexes have brown eyes; adult male surfs and whitewings have whitish eyes, but the females are brown-eyed. The inner web of the second primary is deeply emarginated in the adult male but only slightly emarginated in the adult female and the immature.

Immature black scoters are similar to females in appearance, but upper parts are lighter brown and their breasts and bellies are more mottled with white. In midwinter, black feathers begin to appear among the brown feathers of the juvenile males, and they continue to appear through the spring. Some ornithologists consider that the postnuptial molt in scoters does not result in a true eclipse plumage because the color change is so slight. Nevertheless, during this stage, their heads and necks are duller and their flanks and bellies are browner.

POPULATION STATUS

The population status of the black scoter has been discussed under the appropriate heading in the section on the white-winged scoter.

Age Ratios

Black scoter wings submitted by hunters to the U.S. Fish

and Wildlife Service, 1966-73, indicate that there were 1.9 immatures per adult (792). This ratio represents a higher proportion of young than is found in the white-winged and surf scoters, but it probably reflects the greater vulnerability of black scoters to hunting rather than greater productivity. Stott and Olson (1973) found that black scoter females and immatures were more likely to decoy within hunting range than adult males. Moreover, black scoters decoyed more readily than white-winged and surf scoters.

Sex Ratios

Sex ratios of adult black scoters, determined from wing collections, indicate 1.67 males per female (62.5 percent).

DISTRIBUTION

There are two races of the black scoter. The European black scoter breeds across northern Eurasia, from Iceland, Scotland, and Norway east to the Khatanga River, Siberia. From there a large hiatus extends east to the Lena River, Siberia. The American race breeds beyond the Lena River to the Kamchatka Peninsula and the Bering Sea coast of Alaska. The black scoter is the most common one in Eurasia, but it is the least common over most of North America. The European black scoter winters from northern Norway and the Baltic Sea, south along the coasts of Great Britain, the Netherlands, Belgium, France, and Portugal, and out to sea as far as the Azores.

Breeding Range

The breeding distribution of the black scoter is an enigma. Although only about one-third less abundant than surf scoters on the Atlantic Coast, there are few breeding records in Canada. Godfrey (1966) stated that it is widely, though locally, distributed in Canada but he cited few breeding records: three in Newfoundland; one at Leaf Bay, northern Quebec; and one on the Windy River, southern Keewatin District. Manning and Macpherson (1952) counted 226 black—compared with 180 whitewing and 86 surf scoters—along the east side of James Bay in midsummer. It is present during the summer months in the Belcher Islands of Hudson Bay, but it is not known to breed there (Todd 1963, Freeman 1970*b*). Exploring the east shore of Hudson Bay, Manning (1946) observed only one black scoter and no other scoters. Eklund (1956) sighted a flock of 22 black scoters and another flock of 3 in the interior of the Ungava Peninsula, Quebec. In the same region on the False River, Driver (1959) observed flocks of about 50 males on June 6 and July 7, and a few birds at other times.

Harry Lumsden is reasonably certain that large numbers of black scoters nest in the vast muskeg west of James Bay. He has observed scoter broods in aerial flights over this wilderness morass, impenetrable from the ground in summer. Broods of ducks and even Canada geese vanish as if by magic in the dense cover of the muskeg; a few sightings probably represent unseen thousands. Lumsden believes that black scoters breed extensively in this 3-million-acre muskeg because he has observed 30,000 black scoters in July on the adjacent coast of James Bay. At that season they outnumber white-winged and surf scoters by more than 100 to 1. In late June, Lumsden has collected specimens of black scoters off the Albany River. At Cape Henrietta Maria, on the northwest tip of James Bay, Peck (1972) reported many flocks of black scoters.

Moreover, the only scoters George Arthur and Richard Vaught found in surveys of the southwest coast of Hudson Bay were black scoters. On July 4, 1955, they observed several hundred near the mouth of the Shellbrook River and on August 4, 1961, they observed between 2,000 and 3,000 black scoters at the mouth of the Kettle River.

Arthur Hawkins observed black scoters on Hudson Bay near Churchill, Manitoba, in late June. A short time later, on an aerial reconnaissance of tundra ponds and lakes inland from Eskimo Point, he observed dispersed pairs on numerous freshwater areas. About 150 miles southwest of his observations is the Windy River, site of one of the few breeding records given by Godfrey (1966) for all of Canada. Jehl and Smith (1970) record this species as a common summer visitor at Churchill, more abundant than the other two species of scoters.

Hanson et al. (1949) reported large numbers of black scoters on the lower Kenogami River and on the Albany River, near The Forks, Ontario. Hanson considered these birds migrants, for they were gone early in June. Surf scoters were found less commonly and whitewings not at all.

The abundance of the black scoter during summer along the west coast of James Bay and the southwest and west coasts of Hudson Bay strongly suggests a large breeding population in this bog west of James Bay and south of Hudson Bay. The breeding grounds of both the white-winged and surf scoters lie in the boreal forest much closer to James and Hudson bays than the Alaskan breeding grounds of the black scoters. Yet, comparatively few white-winged and surf scoters have been found during the summer on these bays, whereas large numbers of black scoters have been sighted there. If the scoters were non-breeders or were gathering for the wing molt, the most logical species would be whitewings and surfs rather than blacks.

Although its status in Canada is questionable, the black scoter's presence in Alaska during the summer is evident. It breeds along the Bering Sea coast from the Aleutians to Kotzebue Sound. Edgar Bailey reports that black scoters also nest at the Izembek Bay National Wildlife Range near the tip of the Alaska Peninsula and probably at nearby Unimak Island. From there west in the Aleutians, they are rare summer residents, probably nonbreeding yearlings.

Ground observations of breeding scoters along the Bering Sea suggest that the 252,000 found on aerial surveys are largely, if not all, black scoters. The largest number, 157,000, occurs on the Yukon Delta, followed by 75,000 on the breeding grounds adjacent to Bristol Bay and 20,000 on the Seward Peninsula (King and Lensink 1971). Fay (1961) reported black scoters on the sea adjacent to St. Lawrence Island, near Bering Strait, during the summer. However, none was found inland nor was there other evidence of breeding. In the Endicott Mountains of northern Alaska, Irving (1960) observed them in only 1 of 4 years. He considered Eskimo reports of their breeding at Chandler Lake to be reliable. In annual numbers, they fluctuated more widely than any bird species in the region.

Migration Corridors

Because 80 percent of the black scoters that winter outside the Aleutian Islands do so on the Atlantic Coast, a dilemma arises: Do they come from breeding grounds in Alaska, in Canada, or both? If they originate in Alaska, they must make a flight of roughly 5,000 miles to the Maine coast. On the other hand, is the Canadian breeding population sufficiently large to account for the Atlantic Coast population inventoried at 22,000—a population that because of overlooked birds is undoubtedly several times larger than that? Either way, James Bay appears to be intimately connected with the black scoter. Large numbers must either nest in the muskeg west of the bay or else concentrate on the bay during the wing molt and in their fall migration between Alaska and Maine. Harry Lumsden has observed numerous flocks of scoters on James Bay during the fall. One flock near Fort Albany, which numbered several thousand birds, appeared to be entirely black scoters.

The other aspect of the dilemma is that with a population of 250,000 on Alaska breeding grounds, not more than 5,000 can be accounted for wintering along the Pacific Coast south of Anchorage, Alaska. Granted that large numbers have been missed on aerial surveys in the Alexander Archipelago and the west coast of British Columbia, it is difficult to conceive that tens of thousands have been overlooked. However, it may be that the scoters unaccounted for winter along the Alaska Peninsula and the Aleutian Islands. A rough guess by refuge personnel places the wintering black and white-winged scoter populations in this region at 250,000 for each species. If this figure is eventually found to approximate the size of the black scoter population in the Aleutians, then there can be no question that the breeding black scoters of Alaska winter on the Pacific Coast and that the Atlantic Coast birds originate within Canada.

Winter Areas

It is perplexing that so few black scoters winter on the Pacific Coast. In all the Audubon Christmas counts south of the Alaska Peninsula and as far as Mexico, black scoters compose slightly over 3 percent of the total scoter population, whereas on the Atlantic Coast they form 20 percent. Refuge personnel hazard a guess that 250,000 black scoters winter in the Aleutian Islands, but even there they are no more numerous than white-winged scoters, a species eight times more abundant on the Pacific Coast.

Paradoxically, too, unusually large numbers of black scoters winter in the lower portion of the Atlantic Coast—South Carolina and Georgia—whereas in the Pacific Flyway an unusually large proportion winters at the extreme north end, the Aleutian Islands. Stott and Olson (1972) cited a report of 10,000 to 30,000 scoters, all black, frequenting the Georgia coast during the winters of 1968-70. A few have been reported from as far south as Florida on the Audubon Christmas bird counts.

BREEDING

Behavior

Age, Pair Bond, Homing. The European black scoter, according to Dement'ev and Gladkov (1967), breeds at 2 years of age. At Nelson Lagoon on the Alaska Peninsula, McKinney (1959) saw courting parties of black scoters on several occasions, May 10-29. He reported a preponderance of males, and although pairs could be distinguished, most birds were in small flocks that frequently broke up into one or more courting parties consisting of 5 to 8 drakes to 1 hen. At Hooper Bay, Alaska, Conover (1926) observed pairs on ponds as late as July 5, but they were gone a week later, a few days before the first broods appeared. Males were last seen with females at Selawik, Alaska, on July 1. Whether black scoters return to their previous nest areas is unknown.

Nesting

Nest Sites. At Hooper Bay, Alaska, Brandt (1943) found black scoters nesting in the largest clumps of grass on the tundra. However, one nest was found in short grass 300 yards from the sea beach (Conover 1926). A scrape is dug and lined with grass to which large quantities of down are added before egg-laying is completed. Five nests measured 4 to 6 inches in height, 6 to 8 inches in inside diameter, 9 to 11 inches in outside diameter, and 4 to 5 inches in depth.

Black scoters at famed Lake Mývatn, Iceland, preferred to nest among potholes on the mainland rather than on islands, the favorite locations of most species (Bengtson 1970). Most of the nests were placed 10 to 100 feet from the margins of potholes and were dispersed rather than grouped. The scoters preferred potholes surrounded by dense shrubby cover where their nests were well concealed.

Clutch Size, Eggs, and Incubation. According to Brandt (1943), the clutch size of black scoters nesting near Hooper Bay on the Yukon Delta ranged from 5 to 8 eggs, with the larger number the more common. In the British Isles, Witherby et al. (1952) reported the customary clutch size as 5 to 7. At Lake Mývatn, Iceland, Bengtson (1971) found 187 black scoter nests that averaged 8.7 eggs. The smooth-shelled eggs are ovate to elliptical ovate, measure 61.9 by 41.7 mm (58), and are pale pinkish buff (Bent 1925). The

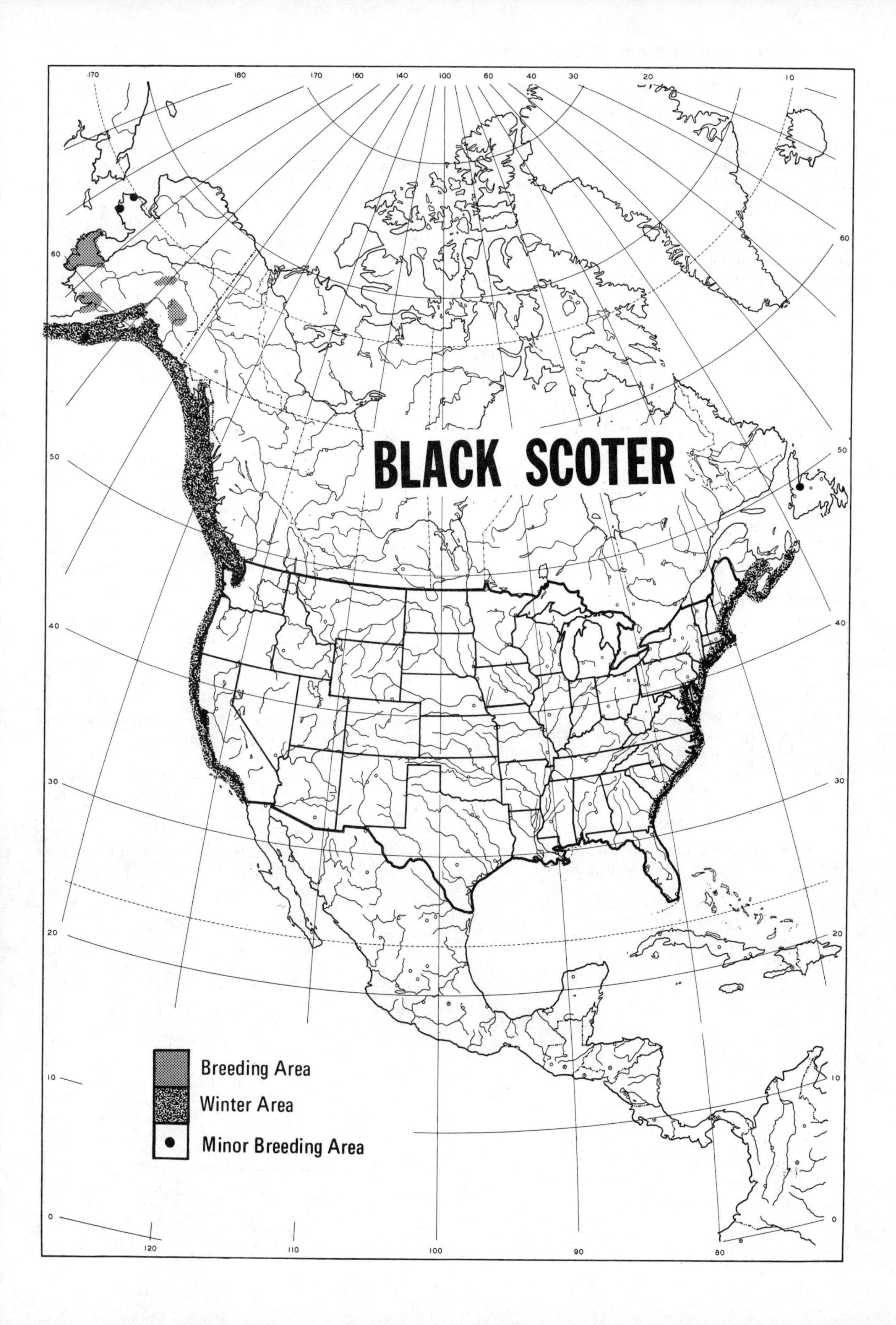
BLACK SCOTER
Breeding Area
Winter Area
Minor Breeding Area

incubation period for confined birds is given as 27 to 28 days (Witherby et al. 1952) and 28 days (Johnstone 1970).

Chronology of Nesting. At Hooper Bay, Alaska, black scoters were first observed on the coast on May 18 and became common by May 20 (Conover 1926). By May 26 they were numerous on tundra ponds, and Conover found the first nest on June 23. In the same region, Dau (1972) found a nest in which the first egg was deposited on June 16. Black scoters are the latest-nesting waterfowl on the Yukon Delta. The first brood observation, on July 16, and a recently hatched brood observed on July 27 indicate the span of nest initiation. At Selawik, Alaska, black scoters arrived May 23-30, 1955, the first nests were started June 15, and the first broods were observed July 23, with the peak of hatch computed as July 25-31 (Shepherd 1955).

Nest Success and Failure. The fate of only one nest is recorded—it was destroyed (Dau 1972).

Renesting. A late-nesting duck in the Arctic, with a short span of nest initiation, probably has no time to renest. As with many species of Arctic waterfowl, black scoters undoubtedly continue egg deposition when eggs are lost during the laying period.

Rearing of Young

Broods. Near to Kotzebue Sound, five broods of young averaging 4.2 were observed, July 11-20 (Gabrielson and Lincoln 1959).

Development. In the British Isles, Witherby et al. (1952) cited a 6- to 7-week period for the young to achieve flight. Dement'ev and Gladkov (1967) reported that in northwest Russia, the first black scoter broods appeared in mid-July and the first flying young during August 10-23.

POSTBREEDING SEASON

A drake black scoter collected on July 5 by Conover (1926) showed no indication of postnuptial molt. But 1 week later, the drakes left the tundra ponds about Hooper Bay, Alaska, presumably for molt areas on the sea. At Selawik, Alaska, molting adults were observed July 18. Dement'ev and Gladkov (1967) reported that the postnuptial molt in the European black scoter began at the end of July and continued through August and September. The flight feathers are shed in the middle of the molt. Drakes molt at sea, gathering in large flocks with nonbreeding yearlings. Females begin to molt when young are able to fly. The prenuptial molt, replacing body and tail feathers, is delayed (as in the ruddy duck) to March and April. Undoubtedly, the 30,000 black scoters that Harry Lumsden observed in July on James Bay had collected for the wing molt. The 1,000 to 3,000 observed by George Arthur and Richard Vaught on August 4 along the southwest coast of Hudson Bay were molters.

FOOD HABITS

The examination of 124 stomachs has shown that ninety percent of the black scoter's food is composed of animal life and 10 percent of plant life (Cottam 1939). Mollusks constitute 65 percent of all food items, the blue mussel alone forming over 24 percent. Short razor clams, oysters, and quahogs are other important foods. (Many of the stomachs examined were from birds that had been collected over commercial shellfish beds.)

On the coast of Washington, the hard rock clam is an outstanding food, composing 17 and 36 percent of the foods in January and February. Crustaceans, mostly sessile and goose barnacles and claw shrimp, formed 17 percent of the food taken. Eelgrass is the only plant food that appears frequently in the stomachs analyzed. Small amounts of muskgrass and other algae and traces of pondweeds and widgeon grass made up other plant items.

McGilvrey (1967) examined the stomachs of 17 black scoters collected between Maine and Long Island. All foods found were animal, blue mussels constituting 54 percent and file yoldia 26 percent. Black scoters along coastal New Hampshire and Massachusetts fed almost exclusively on three clams: Atlantic razor, Arctic wedge, and blue mussel (Stott and Olson 1973).

Surf Scoter

Melanitta perspicillata

Other Common Names: Skunkhead, coot, sea coot

VITAL STATISTICS

Length:	Male, 18.0-20.9 inches, average 19.7 inches (5) Female, 17.0-19.0 inches, average 18.5 inches (6)
Wing:	Adult male, 9.5 inches (46) Adult female, 8.9 inches (40) Immature male, 9.2 inches (40) Immature female, 8.9 inches (55)
Weight:	Male, 1.4-2.5 pounds, average 2.2 pounds (10) Female, 1.5-2.2 pounds, average 2.0 pounds (7)

IDENTIFICATION

Field

Adult male surf scoters are all-black sea ducks except for the white patches on their foreheads and the backs of their heads, which distinguish them from the black scoters, whose heads are entirely black, and from the white-winged scoters with their white "eye hooks." Because of the two white patches on their black heads, many Down East hunters term them "skunkheads." Both surf scoters and black scoters have all-black wings. Surf scoters fly in more irregular flock formations than the line flights frequently associated with white-winged scoters. The whistling sound created by their wings, less sharp than that produced by goldeneye wings, can be heard at a distance of 200 to 400 yards when atmospheric conditions are favorable. Surf scoters are less vocal than the other two species, rarely uttering their low croaking notes.

Adult female surf scoters are dark to black-brown, with two indistinct whitish patches on the cheeks below eye level, and another on the napes of their heads. Except for their dusky brown wings and the indistinct nape patches, female surfs are similar to white-winged scoters, which have distinctive single white wing patches. Female surf scoters have wedge-shaped heads; those of black scoters are rounded and single large gray patches cover the chin, cheek, and neck areas, somewhat as in female ruddy ducks.

At Hand

Surf and black scoters are almost identical in size, about one-fourth smaller than the white-winged scoter. The adult male surf has a "prizefighter's" hump on his large multicolored bill: a round black spot near the base, margined above and at the rear by orange, below and in front by white; the ridge and nostril area are reddish as far down as the yellow bill tip. In the female and the juvenile, the bill is smoother and dark gray, with a darker spot at its base. The male has pale gray eyes and orange-red feet; the female has brown eyes and yellow to brown-red feet.

Juveniles are similar to females in appearance but the two white facial spots are usually more distinct and the whitish nape spot is absent. By early winter, coloration in the sexes begins to differentiate—the male assumes a blackish cast. During spring, the bill of the male becomes parti-colored and the white patch appears on the back of the head.

POPULATION STATUS

Estimates of the continental population of the surf scoter

are so intertwined with deductions made on the basis of the total scoter population that the status of each of the three species is discussed in the section on the white-winged scoter.

Age Ratios

On the basis of wings received from hunters and inspected for the proportion of immatures to adults, there was a ratio of 1.26:1, 1966-73, in a sample of 1,742. The degree to which immatures are more vulnerable to hunting than adults is unknown, but it is reasonable to suppose that they are twice as likely to be killed as adults. If so, the fall populations would contain about 0.6 immature per adult surf scoter.

Sex Ratios

According to data presented by Sorensen et al. (1974), there were 2.2:1 males per female (68.8 percent) in hunters' bags of surf scoters, 1969-73.

DISTRIBUTION

The surf scoter is indigenous to North America—unlike the white-winged and black scoters, there are no races in Eurasia.

Breeding Range

Surf scoters are confined almost entirely to the closed and open boreal forests of Canada and Alaska. East of Saskatchewan, their breeding range is almost exclusively in regions of the open boreal forest. From Saskatchewan west to the Pacific Coast, an increasing proportion of their range lies within the closed boreal forest. Throughout this latter region, the white-winged scoters appear to be several times more abundant than the surfs.

However, surf scoters breed in the open boreal forest of Labrador and eastern Quebec, where whitewings do not breed, and in the region from Great Slave Lake to the Mackenzie Delta, this species is equal to or possibly outnumbers the whitewings. Surf scoters are apparently less abundant than whitewings in the interior valleys of Alaska.

The breeding range of the surf scoter is discontinuous east of James and Hudson bays. It has been found breeding on Sheppard and Charlton islands in James Bay (Todd 1963), but there are few records farther east except for a region embracing east-central Quebec and southwestern Labrador—Petitsikapau Lake and Grand Falls, Labrador, and Otelnuk and Wakuach lakes, Quebec (Todd 1963). Bent (1925) cited a 1903 record of a surf scoter nest on Akpatok Island in Ungava Bay, unusual because this is a tundra habitat considerably to the north of the other breeding records. At Churchill, Manitoba, it is the rarest of the scoters; small numbers have been observed in summer but no evidence of breeding has been found (Jehl and Smith 1970).

Migration Corridors

From their interior breeding grounds surf scoters head for either coast; three to one favor the Pacific over the Atlantic. The numbers of this species that winter along the Alaska Peninsula and eastern Aleutians are too few to alter this ratio significantly. One can visualize their flight over the coastal ranges from their principal breeding grounds in the interior to the Pacific Coast, with flocks dropping off all along the coast at favored feeding grounds as the migration proceeds southward.

The flight of surf scoters across Canada to the Atlantic Coast is more difficult to fathom. The small numbers that appear in migration south of the boreal forest suggest that their migration corridors extend east-southeastward to James Bay, and then on to the northeast Atlantic Coast. I believe that the breeding population of surf scoters in east-central Quebec and southern Labrador is far too small to contribute significantly to the Atlantic Coast population.

Winter Areas

Although the surf scoter is second in numbers to the white-winged scoter on the Atlantic Coast, it is overwhelmingly more abundant on the Pacific Coast. Omitting the Aleutian Islands, about 130,000 surf scoters have been recorded wintering in North America. By way of comparison, averages of 95,000 white-winged scoters and 27,000 black scoters have been inventoried. Unquestionably, however, much larger proportions of all three species are missed on the aerial surveys of the Atlantic Coast, where they are farther offshore, than on the Pacific Coast. Moreover, exceedingly large numbers of both white-winged and black scoters winter offshore of the Aleutian Islands, but few surf scoters do. Thus, because a larger proportion of surfs are observed as a result of winter distribution, their abundance in relation to the other two species is distorted upwards.

On the Atlantic Coast, surf scoters occur in greatest numbers between Barnegat Bay, New Jersey, and Norfolk, Virginia, where they equal or outnumber white-winged scoters. Among the scoters along the Pacific Coast, surf scoters as a general rule increasingly predominate from northern California to Baja California, Mexico. Aerial surveys by the U.S. Fish and Wildlife Service over an 8-year period reveal an average of 1,500 scoters on Laguna San Ignacio and Laguna Scammon in Baja. Most of these are surf scoters except for an occasional whitewing. Leopold (1959) censused unusually large numbers of surf scoters in one of the early aerial surveys of Baja California. In January 1952 he estimated 24,600 surf scoters—11,500 on Laguna San Ignacio; 7,000 on San Quintin Bay; 5,900 on Laguna Scammon; and 185 elsewhere.

In California, the Tomales, Drake's, and San Francisco bays harbor almost half of the surf scoters—San Diego Bay slightly over one-fourth—and the remainder scattered elsewhere along the coast. Farther north, surf scoters are particularly abundant between Vancouver, British Colum-

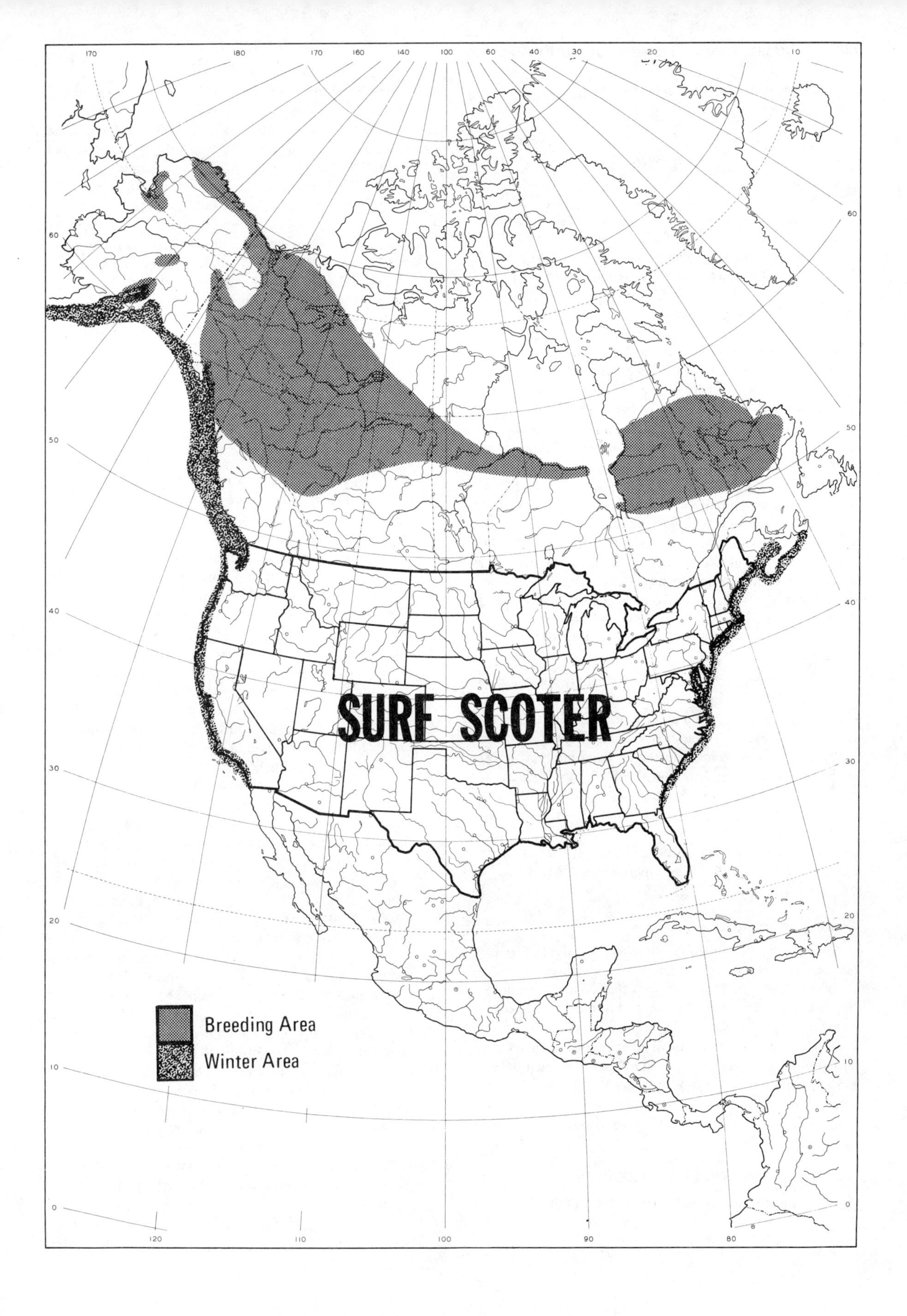
SURF SCOTER
Breeding Area
Winter Area

bia, and Tacoma, Washington, where Audubon Christmas counts, 1969-73, averaged 4,875.

BREEDING

Nesting

Of all the ducks in North America, the surf scoter has the dubious distinction of being the least studied. Very little is known about its breeding habits and other life history activities. It is indeed a blemish on the records of twentieth century ornithologists and wildlife biologists that most of the available information on nesting dates back to the nineteenth century and is only fragmentary.

MacFarlane (1891) has provided much of what little is known on the nesting of surf scoters. He found several nests in the Anderson River area of the Northwest Territories. They resembled those of the white-winged scoter but were flimsier, with fewer grasses and feathers used in construction. In a letter he wrote—excerpted from Bent (1925:145)—nest sites were described as "a considerable distance from open water, and always well concealed underneath the low-spreading branches of a pine or spruce tree. . . ." He gave the clutch size as five to seven eggs, with eight as the maximum. Gabrielson and Lincoln (1959) reported that Urban C. Nelson found a surf scoter nest near Kotzebue Sound, Alaska, on July 12, 1949; it contained six eggs. Todd (1963) concluded from his observation of brood locations in the Labrador Peninsula that nesting surf scoters selected small freshwater ponds, often many miles from the sea.

Bent (1925) described the eggs as unusually shaped from ovate to elliptical ovate but often quite pointed, smooth-shelled but not glossy, and pinkish or buffy white. Thirty-three eggs measured 61.6 mm by 43 mm. The outside dates when 12 clutches were collected in the Anderson River area were June 19 and July 8, with six of these collections occurring between June 25 and July 1.

On a study area near Yellowknife, Northwest Territories, Murdy (1964) observed that 12 pairs of surf scoters produced five broods, a success of 42 percent. These were cumulative figures for a 3-year period, 1962-64.

Rearing of Young

Broods. At Yellowknife, 1961-64, Murdy (1964) observed 16 Class I surf scoter broods that averaged 4.9 ducklings, and one Class II brood that contained 6 ducklings. On his various excursions through the Labrador Peninsula, Todd (1963) recorded the following surf scoter broods: a female with a brood of eight young on August 2; a brood of four downy young with a female, August 6; two hens accompanying a brood of four, July 12 on Charlton Island (James Bay); and a brood of two with a female, August 3, on Sheppard Island (James Bay).

POSTBREEDING SEASON

According to Todd (1963), thousands of all three species of scoters gather at the head of shallow bays and inlets of the Labrador Coast to undergo the wing molt. In August, 1901, he observed two large flocks of flightless scoters near Nain, Labrador. The water was littered with feathers. Todd (1963) reported C.E. Addy's aerial sighting of several thousand scoters along the south shore of Lake Melville at the base of Hamilton Inlet on July 22. Todd refers to these scoters as "this species," and because Addy's sighting is mentioned in his discussion of surf scoters, I assume that these large flocks of molting scoters were surfs.

Porslid (1943), on the Mackenzie Delta, noted that males and nonbreeding female surf scoters were gathered in large flocks, June 26-29. In early August large numbers were observed on the open sea.

FOOD HABITS

Like the other scoters, the surfs concentrate in the bays of the Pacific Coast. However, I have seen a surprising number feeding along miles of the California coastline where no other species appeared—close to the base of the bastionlike cliffs. For some inexplicable reason, the birds faced the cliffs in loose, scattered flocks. As a tumultuous wave approached from the rear, the birds surged upwards on its swelling curve until just before cresting they dove, as if on signal, to reappear after the wave had spent its force against the cliffs. Because their backs were toward the onrushing surf, the scoters did not see the curling crest, yet at the critical moment before it broke, they dove, thereby escaping the battering of the toppling tons of water.

Cottam (1939) reported that 88 percent of the contents of 168 gizzards from adult surf scoters were composed of animal life and 12 percent of plant food. Mollusks made up 61 percent of the animal foods, blue mussels being the most important. Crustaceans (principally barnacles) and crabs made up 10 percent of the contents; aquatic insects—caddis flies, dragonflies, damselflies, diving beetles—also formed 10 percent of all food items. Pondweeds, eelgrass, and widgeon grass were the principal plants consumed.

Fifty-five gizzards from surf scoters collected between Maine and Long Island contained only animal foods (McGilvrey 1967). Yoldias of several species and blue mussels composed 64 percent of the volume.

Stott and Olson (1973) examined 133 gizzards from surf scoters taken along the coasts of New Hampshire and Massachusetts; animal life composed 96 percent of the food volume: Arctic wedge clams, 60 percent; Atlantic razor clams, 24 percent; and blue mussels, 8 percent. In a later paper, Stott and Olson (1974) make a strong case for the association of all three scoters with that part of the northeast coast having a sandy substrate, the site of the important species of clams used as food. They noted also a tendency for scoters to concentrate at the mouths of estuaries because of the greater density of food items. Cottam (1939) cited records of surf scoters diving to depths of 6 to 30 feet and remaining below the surface from 19 to 32 seconds.

White-Winged Scoter

Melanitta fusca deglandi

Other Common Names: Coot, sea coot, whitewing

VITAL STATISTICS

Length:	Male, 20.7-23.0 inches, average 21.6 inches (20) Female, 19.0-23.6 inches, average 20.6 inches (28)
Wing:	Adult male, 11.1 inches (85) Adult female, 10.5 inches (32) Immature male, 10.8 inches (41) Immature female 10.2 inches (39)
Weight:	Male, 3.0-3.9 pounds, average 3.5 pounds (7) Female, 2.1-3.1 pounds, average 2.6 pounds (15)

IDENTIFICATION

Field

An irregular, wavering line of black ducks close to the waves along an inshore seacoast usually denotes scoters. Of the three species inhabiting North America, the white-winged scoter is the easiest to identify because of the large white speculum on its otherwise black wing; in the other two species the wings are entirely dark. At a distance on the water, all three species appear black, but a closer view usually reveals the white speculum as a small patch on the side of the whitewing. It is also helpful to look closely at the head—there, the surf scoter shows the most white, the black scoter none, and the whitewing a small curving white dash below and behind the eye. The bills, too, are different: the whitewing has a black bulbous base on an otherwise orange bill; the surf has a more wedge-shaped head and bill and the bill is massive with a variegated pattern in orange, white, and black; and the black scoter has the smallest bill, black-tipped with a yellow bulbous base, and the most rounded head of the three species.

Female and juvenile white-winged scoters are brown-black with two whitish patches on the sides of their heads, in front of and behind the eye. Vernon Stotts reports that these patches are indistinct in some specimens, but well defined in others. Except for their completely dark wings, surf scoter females and juveniles are practically indistinguishable from whitewings. When white-winged and surf scoters take flight, the motion of their wings makes a whistling sound that can be heard up to 0.5 mile.

At Hand

The white-winged scoter is a chunky bird about as long as a canvasback but even heavier. Among the ducks, only the common and king eiders are larger. Except for the white on wings and head, the black of the male's body is unrelieved except by the black-brown of sides and flanks. Both male and female have pinkish feet. The eyes are pale gray in the male and brown in the female. The black knob at the base of the adult male's orange bill is readily apparent but is less prominent in the dark bill of the female. The bill of the immature male begins to show some color in late winter and spring but lacks the bulbous base of the adult's bill. The immature also shows more mottled white on breast and belly than does the adult female. There is very little color change with the postnuptial molt into the eclipse plumage.

POPULATION STATUS

Aerial surveys of waterfowl populations conducted by the U.S. Fish and Wildlife Service sample a large proportion of the breeding grounds of all three species of scoters. An average yearly summer population of 1.48 million has been computed for the period 1955-73 for Alaska, the open and closed boreal forest region, and the parklands and grasslands of western Canada. Not included in this figure are nonbreeding birds that flock along the seacoasts; birds that breed east of Manitoba or east of the District of Mackenzie; and those that breed in British Columbia.

Judged by the relative abundance of the three species of scoters on winter grounds south of Alaska, the 1.48 million population breaks down as follows: 555,000 whitewings, 765,000 surfs, and 155,000 blacks. However, all the ground explorations indicate that with the possible exception of the open boreal forest north of Great Slave Lake, whitewings outnumber surfs. This discrepancy is apparently due to the large numbers of white-winged and black scoters that winter along the Aleutian Chain. The combined population has been crudely estimated by refuge personnel as 250,000 white-winged and 250,000 black scoters. Adding these figures to those for Canada and the United States results in the following estimates of breeding scoters in North America: 675,000 whitewings, 257,000 surfs, and 543,000 blacks. The breeding black scoter population in Alaska is reasonably well inventoried at 235,000. The unknown number of black scoters breeding in Canada cannot conceivably be as high as 300,000. Therefore, these comparative population figures are also erroneous. The populations of whitewings and blacks are too high, that of surfs too low. Somewhere between the two extremes lie the true breeding populations of the three species.

During three periods of 5 years each, 1957-71, the average scoter population showed these changes—1957-61, 2.02 million; 1962-66, 1.32 million; and 1967-71, 1.35 million. Many changes are inexplicable, as, for example, the steady downward trend of scoters in both coastal and interior Alaska and in the parklands and boreal forest of northern Alberta. The most drastic decline in scoter numbers has occurred in southern Manitoba. The yearly average there was 4,700 for 1957-61; 1,100 for 1962-66; and a mere 500 for 1967-71. Arthur Hawkins told me that a pronounced 20-year decline in numbers of white-winged scoters has occurred at both Delta Marsh and the area south of Riding Mountain National Park, Manitoba.

Age Ratios

The proportion of immature to adult white-winged scoters in hunters' bags in the United States has ranged (1966-73) from 0.27:1.0 in 1972 to 1.69:1.0 in 1969. The 8-year average is 1.01 immature per 1.0 adult in a sample of 1,895 wings. Immature scoters are much more vulnerable to hunting losses than adults, however, thereby considerably reducing their actual proportion in fall populations.

Sex Ratios

Among adult white-winged scoters shot by hunters, there was an average of 2.62 males per 1.0 female or 72.4 percent males, 1969-73 (Sorensen et al. 1974).

DISTRIBUTION

There are three races of white-winged scoters in the Northern Hemisphere. They are not quite circumpolar because of a hiatus from the western Canadian Arctic east to Norway. The European race breeds in northern Europe as far east as the Taymyr Peninsula, Siberia; the Asiatic race breeds south of the tundra, in the forested region of western Siberia as far as, but not including, the Chukot Peninsula; and the American race breeds in northwestern North America.

Breeding Range

The American white-winged scoter breeds from north-central North Dakota northwest across Canada into central Alaska. Although known as a nonbreeding summer resident in Washington (Yocom 1951, Jewett et al. 1953), the only known breeding records in the contiguous 48 states of the United States are from North Dakota. Old breeding records were from the Devils Lake area, but in recent years there have been three nest records on the Upper Souris National Wildlife Refuge and one about 30 miles west of there (Robert Stewart and Harold Kantrud).

Breeding ground surveys in Manitoba by the U.S. Fish and Wildlife Service suggest a summer population of 27,000 scoters, mostly all whitewings. Almost 90 percent occur on lakes in the boreal forest region, with an additional 7 percent in the Saskatchewan Delta. Of the 25,000 scoters in Saskatchewan, 20,000 are found on lakes in the northern two-thirds of the province, an area of closed boreal forest. Ground surveys indicate that the bulk of these scoters are whitewings, with comparatively small numbers of surf scoters. Of the 140,000 scoters in Alberta, 114,000 are found on lakes in the closed boreal forest covering the northern half of the province. Again, ground surveys suggest that the bulk of these scoters are whitewings, with a small admixture of surf scoters.

In the open boreal forest of the Northwest Territories of Canada, between Great Slave Lake and the Arctic Ocean, scoter numbers are at their greatest, with a population of 870,000 and a density of almost 4 per square mile. Both white-winged and surf scoters are abundant, and here, if anywhere, the surf might be more abundant.

Soper (1957) reported that on the Slave River delta, surf scoters were not as abundant as white-winged scoters. But across Great Slave Lake at Yellowknife, Murdy (1964) observed 12 pairs of breeding surf scoters to 2 pairs of whitewings on his study area, 1962-64. Porslid (1943) noted that both white-winged and surf scoters were common on the wooded half of the Mackenzie Delta but that whitewings were more abundant on the tundra half of the delta.

The scoter population on Old Crow Flats, 100 miles west of the Mackenzie Delta, aggregates 52,000. According to Irving (1960), surf scoters were not half as abundant there as whitewings; surfs composed only one-fourth of the scoters during the spring migration. However, in the southeastern region of the Yukon Territory, Soper (1954) reported that white-winged scoters were uncommon summer residents, whereas surf scoters composed one-fifth of all summer ducks, second to greater scaups as breeders. The bulk of the 16,000-20,000 scoters that occur in British Columbia during the summer are whitewings, with minor numbers of surf scoters.

There are 135,000 scoters on interior breeding grounds in Alaska (King and Lensink 1971). According to James King, the majority are whitewings; the others are surf scoters. The largest population (64,000, a density of 4.9 per square mile) is found on the Yukon Flats. The second largest aggregation (35,000, a density of 2.8 per square mile) occurs in the Tanana-Kuskokwim valleys. Breeding grounds along the coast of Alaska from Bristol Bay to Kotzebue Bay appear to be occupied by black scoters. Surf scoters predominate in the Selawik marshes inland from Kotzebue Sound.

During the summer, Fay (1961) observed white-winged scoters offshore of St. Lawrence Island, but none were seen inland where they would breed. According to Irving (1960), whitewings breed fairly commonly on large lakes and on some small ones in the Endicott Mountains of northern Alaska and are known to range north to the Arctic Coast.

Migration Corridors

The white-winged scoter migrates to both the Atlantic and Pacific coasts from its breeding grounds in northwestern Canada and the interior of Alaska. Omitting wintering populations along the Alaska Peninsula and the Aleutian Chain, about 60 percent migrate to the Atlantic Coast and 40 percent to the Pacific. Band recoveries suggest that the farther north and east the whitewings breed, the more likely they are to migrate to the Atlantic Coast, and, conversely, the farther south and west they breed, the more likely that the migration is to the Pacific Coast. All four recoveries from bandings at Yellowknife occurred in the Atlantic Flyway: Maine, one; Vermont, one; and Lake Ontario, New York, two. Of 12 recoveries from bandings in Central Saskatchewan, 67 percent occurred in the Pacific Flyway, 16 percent in the Mississippi Flyway and 16 percent in the Atlantic Flyway. Over 90 percent of 15 recoveries from bandings in east-central Alberta occurred along the Pacific Coast; one recovery was from New Jersey. After arriving at the Atlantic or Pacific coast, the migrating flocks follow the coastline to favored feeding grounds. Peters and Burleigh (1951) reported that migrating flocks of white-winged scoters closely followed the Newfoundland coastline. Bent (1925) related that large flocks of scoters were almost constantly in sight migrating southward along the New England coast before and during northeast storms in October.

Near the New Hampshire coast, Stott and Olson (1972) observed scoters migrating in flocks of 100 to 300 birds at an average distance of 2 to 4 miles offshore. Griscom and Snyder (1955) reported that all three species of scoters were regular transients along the Massachusetts coast. They observed that over 100,000 white-winged scoters sometimes appeared in a single day during fall migration; they saw 25,000 to 40,000 black scoters in November and 33,800 surf scoters over a 4-week period in one fall. Bull (1964) reported that in the New York City area, white-winged scoters regularly migrated inland, although at rare intervals, passing overhead in small flocks.

Vernon Stotts observed migrating scoters on Chesapeake Bay each week for 4 or 5 weeks between late September and mid-October, 1967-69. His observations were conducted 3 hours after sunrise and 3 hours prior to sunset. During this period he observed 9,500 surf, 7,600 black, and 65 white-winged scoters. These scoters passed down the ocean side of the peninsula to the bay's entrance, where they turned and flew back northward up the bay. The small number of white-winged scoters observed suggests that the majority of this species travels overland to reach the bay, entering near the upper end.

On October 31, 1968, John Chattin, Duane Norman, and I observed a migration of white-winged and surf scoters along the Oregon coast, between Coos and Winchester bays. We were flying parallel to the coast at low altitude when 10 flocks—4 of white-winged and 6 of surf scoters—were observed flying south a few feet above the water and about 100 yards offshore. From that point on, many other flocks were seen resting on the open sea. We observed 2,700 additional scoters, 7 percent whitewings, on bays north of Coos Bay. Since only about 900 are found in Oregon during January, the scoter flight that day was impressive.

Apparently, white-winged scoters fly over the Alaska Range from interior breeding grounds to the Gulf of Alaska. In late September and early October, Cahalane (1943) observed that white-winged scoters were the most numerous of all waterfowl around Kodiak Island and that Raspberry Strait was covered with enormous flocks of scoters, almost all whitewings.

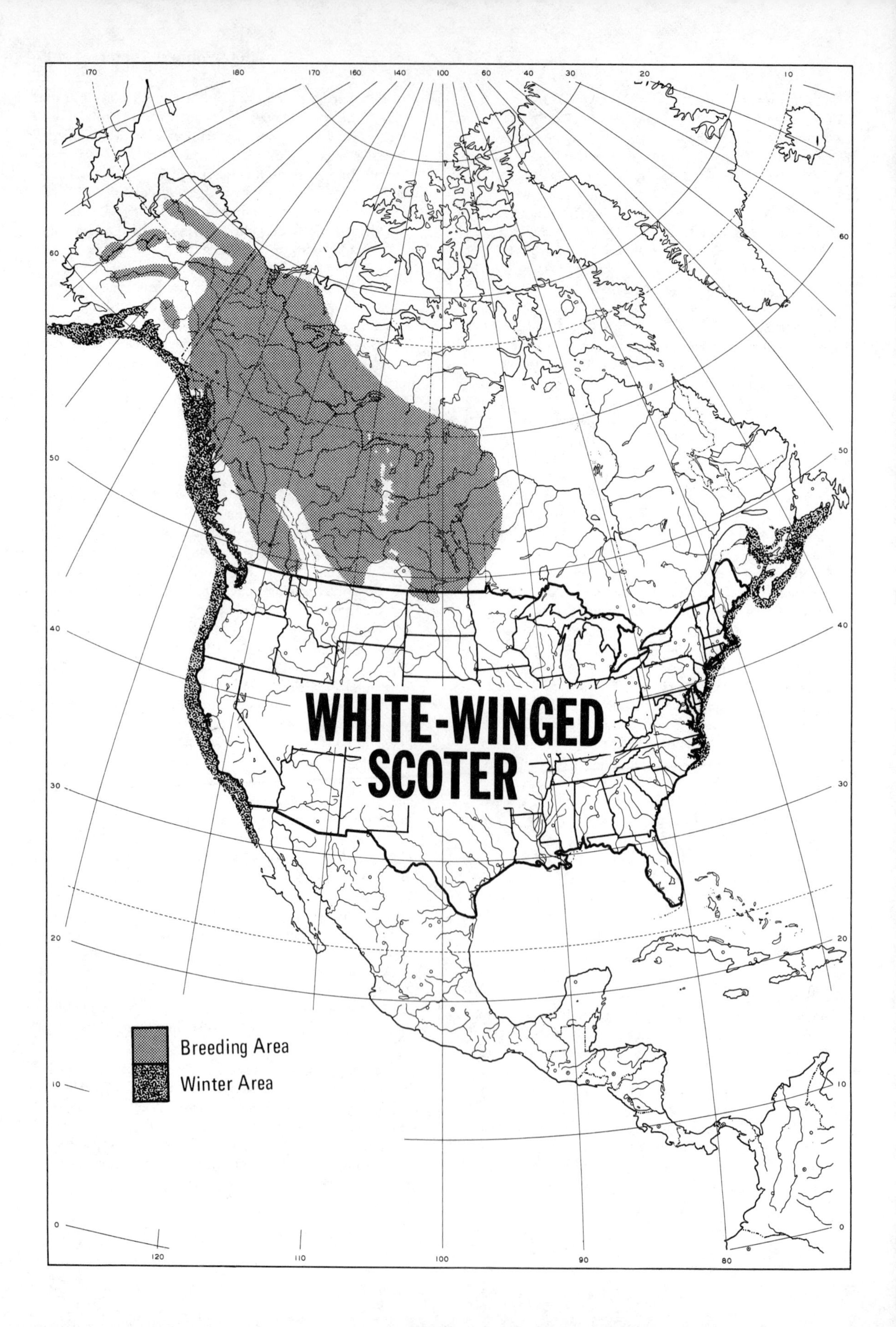
WHITE-WINGED SCOTER
Breeding Area
Winter Area

Winter Areas

Winter inventories of the U.S. Fish and Wildlife Service for 8 years, 1966-73, average 112,000 scoters for the Atlantic Coast. Audubon Christmas counts for 4 years average 34,000. Because the winter inventory figures are not broken down into species of scoters, we have used the Audubon Christmas counts for species composition, state by state, compared with the Fish and Wildlife Service's scoter population for each state.

Of the 112,000 scoters recorded in January along the Atlantic Coast, 56,000 (50 percent) are white-winged scoters, 33,000 (30 percent) are surf scoters, and 22,000 (20 percent) are black scoters. The species composition of these scoter populations are, with few exceptions, remarkably similar. White-winged scoters show a greater predominance over the other two species from Maine to New Jersey; black scoters show a greater predominance over the other two off the South Carolina-Georgia coast; and surf scoters overshadow the others in the lower Chesapeake Bay area. Seventy percent of the entire scoter population along the East Coast winters from Long Island Sound through Chesapeake Bay, with the bay area harboring 30 percent of the total East Coast population.

Bull (1964) termed the whitewing the most numerous of the scoters in the Long Island area although occasionally outnumbered by the surf. He listed 75,000 off Montauk Point on January 1, 1930, and 180,000 on March 16; and 90,000 off Jones Beach on December 7, 1952.

North of Long Island Sound, the largest winter population—some 15,000—is recorded along the coast of Massachusetts. Eighty percent of these are whitewings, with the remainder almost equally divided between black and surf scoters. According to Griscom and Snyder (1955), white-winged scoters winter in flocks of 100,000 to 400,000 on the shoals of Cape Cod and Nantucket, and in smaller numbers (1,000 to 2,000) north along the coast to Essex County. Maine winters 3,000, with distribution among the three scoters similar to that in Massachusetts. Audubon Christmas counts record about 400 in New Brunswick, Nova Scotia, Quebec, and Newfoundland. Peters and Burleigh (1951) cited a record of the white-winged scoter as a common winter resident offshore at Argentia, Newfoundland, where it is the most abundant of the three scoters. Tufts (1961) also called it the most abundant of the scoters in Nova Scotia, common throughout the year along the coast even though they do not breed there.

The numbers of scoters recorded on Audubon Christmas counts, 1969-72, on the Great Lakes have declined each year from a high of 1,235 in 1969 to barely 40 in 1972. About 70 percent were enumerated on Lake Ontario, a large proportion near Rochester. Lake Erie contained 3 percent and Lake Michigan 26 percent of all scoters censused, with additional small numbers recorded on Lakes Huron and Superior. White-winged scoters composed 97 percent, surf 0.4 percent, and black scoters 2.6 percent of the numbers observed on the Great Lakes.

Winter inventory data for the Pacific Coast from southeast Alaska to Baja California, Mexico, indicates 142,000 scoters. Of this number, 39,600 were recorded in southeast Alaska; 8,600 in southwest British Columbia; 63,400 in Washington; 900 in Oregon; 27,800 in California; and 1,450 in Baja California. On the basis of the composition indicated by Audubon Christmas counts, white-winged scoters form 27.6 percent of this population, surf scoters 69.1 percent, and black scoters 3.3 percent. With minor exceptions, the species composition of the wintering scoter population is relatively the same from southeast Alaska into California. The percentage of surf scoters in the population increases in southern California and Baja California, and black scoters are rare south of San Francisco Bay.

White-winged scoters and black scoters appear about equally abundant as wintering species in the Aleutian Islands, but few surf scoters have been found there in winter. A plausible guess by personnel of the Aleutian Islands National Wildlife Refuge is that 500,000 scoters—equally divided between whitewings and blacks—winter in the Aleutians. That these two species are about equally abundant is also suggested by others. At Dutch Harbor, Cahn (1947) recorded both the white-winged and black scoters as common residents from December to February. Farther west at Adak Island, Byrd et al. (1974) found the white-winged and black scoters to be abundant wintering birds but reported only a few surfs. Near the tip of the Aleutians at Amchitka Island, Kenyon (1961) recorded small numbers of white-winged scoters but failed to note any black or surf scoters.

MIGRATION BEHAVIOR

Scoters of all three species usually migrate at higher altitudes along the seacoasts than do eiders, because of their long overland passages prior to reaching the coasts, whereas eiders are wedded to the sea throughout their lives. However, when winds are strong or adverse, scoters usually fly so low that they barely skim the wave crests. Although they customarily fly around projecting points of land rather than over them, Bent (1925) reported a regular crossing of Cape Cod, Massachusetts, at Barnstable Harbor.

A westward departure of white-winged scoters from Nantucket Sound in mid-May is described by Mackay (1891). The flight started between 3 and 5 P.M. and continued into the night, frequently going overland near the coast. The scoters left in large flocks, some of which contained 500 to 600 birds, with as many as 10,000 passing in a single day. Perhaps their late afternoon departure occurred because of their overland migration extending from the southeast Massachusetts coast into the interior. According to MacKay (1891), this phenomenon was a yearly event from 1870 to the time of writing in 1891. When migrant scoters reach the seacoasts, however, their flights appear to be largely diurnal.

Chronology

Fall. The first migrating scoters appear in early September on the New England coast, but it is mid-October before the flights become numerous. They continue until winter. Aerial surveys of all three species of scoters off the Atlantic Coast from Maine to Long Island show the following chronology of abundance in 1966-67 (Tice 1970): September 1, 120; September 13, 4,000; September 27, 8,400; October 11, 20,900; November 15, 35,000; December 13, 30,700; and January 16, 81,500. Along the New Jersey coast, during the same year, the following numbers were found: September 13, 460; September 27, 4,600; October 17, 34,200; October 29, 54,000; November 13, 80,000; December 12, 76,000; January 9, 53,500. These numbers do not represent the total population because many small flocks are not sighted from the air and others may be too far offshore to be seen. Vernon Stotts recorded the passage of the following scoter numbers at Chesapeake Bay, 1967: 60, September 27; 197, October 4; 1,648, October 11; 283, October 18; and 1,327, October 25. His observations ceased before the large flights entered the bay in early November.

Although all three species of scoters appear in flights moving down the seacoast at the same time, their relative numbers vary. Off the New Hampshire coast in 1968, Stott and Olson (1972) found the largest numbers of white-winged scoters on December 1 and 9; in 1969, the largest numbers were observed on November 21, 26, and December 30. The surfs were most numerous on October 10 and 31, and black scoters did not appear in numbers until late—December 17 and 30. At Chesapeake Bay, Vernon Stotts observed that black scoters were the earliest arrivals and that surfs arrived next and whitewings last.

Spring. At Chesapeake Bay, the spring exodus of white-winged scoters starts about March 10 and extends to May 10, with peak departures between March 25 and April 25 (Stewart 1962). Off the Massachusetts coast, spring migration is clearly evident by mid-April, but many scoters remain as late as early June (Griscom and Snyder 1955) and a few nonbreeding birds remain throughout the summer.

Fifty years ago, Bent (1925) observed in New England that the northward passage of scoters commenced in early March, but the principal migration occurred during the first half of May and continued throughout the month. Rawls (1949) noted that the first whitewings arrived at Delta Manitoba, May 4-14, 1939-47. He quoted the observation of Arthur Hawkins that an aerial census of the Delta Marsh on May 16, 1948, revealed that scoters made up 7 percent of the duck population and 20 percent by June 6. On Hudson Bay at Churchill, the first white-winged scoters appeared on May 30, the first surfs on May 24, and the first black scoters on June 5 (Littlefield and Pakulak 1969). At Yellowknife, Northwest Territories, white-winged scoters either arrived at the same time as surfs or no more than 5 days later (Murdy 1964). First arrivals ranged from May 17 to 22, 1962-64, with peak influxes between May 22 and 26. On the Mackenzie Delta, first arrivals occurred on May 25 (Porslid 1943). To the west of the Mackenzie Delta at Old Crow Flats, Irving (1960) observed the earliest white-winged and surf scoters on May 20, with additional flocks each day for the next 10 days. He remarked that scoters migrated later than mallards, pintails, and wigeons.

Gabrielson and Lincoln (1959) noted the difficulty in detecting the northward migration of scoters in southeast Alaska because of the large numbers of nonbreeders that remain through the summer. However, they cited records of white-winged scoters appearing north of their winter areas—in Nushagak Bay, May 7; Akutan Island and Hooper Bay, May 18; and Mountain Village, May 30. At Anaktuvuk Pass in the Brooks Range of northern Alaska, Irving (1960) reports first arrivals of whitewings from May 20 to 31, 1950-54.

BREEDING

Behavior

Age, Pair Bond, and Homing. The large number of nonbreeding white-winged scoters found along the northern seacoasts the entire summer indicate that yearling and probably some 2-year-old birds do not breed. According to Dement'ev and Gladkov (1967), the velvet scoter, a European race of the whitewing, reaches breeding age in its second year of life. The yearlings spend the first summer in flocks at sea, close to winter quarters. Pairing occurs on the winter grounds, so migrating flocks in spring consist of paired birds.

Rawls (1949) reported that at Delta Marsh, Manitoba, the males and females arrived together and appeared paired. He attributed the large decline in scoter numbers that occurred on the Delta Marsh after mid-July to departure of the males. Patrick Brown observed that nearly all females were paired in late May 1976 at Jessie Lake, Alberta. Male white-winged scoters remained with their mates until the first week of incubation. Few males were observed on the lake after July 1.

Home Range. Rawls' (1949) observations on the movements of white-winged scoter pairs on their breeding ground at Delta Marsh convinced him that their home ranges were not fixed. He seldom saw pairs remain on a waiting area for over 3 or 4 days at a time. When a pair frequenting a particular area departed, other pairs might use it. When the first residents returned, the area appeared to be shared by several pairs without conflict. However, Rawls (1949) did see a paired male drive off the male of another pair, and another paired male repulse an immature bird. After studying white-winged scoters for 2 years at Jessie Lake, Alberta, and Redberry Lake, Saskatchewan, Patrick Brown concluded that white-winged scoters had no fixed territory but maintained a defended zone around their mates. The females incited their spouses to attack intruding males, and, more rarely, intruding females.

Nesting

Of all the ducks that nest in North America, less is known

about the nesting of the scoters, including the whitewing, than of any other group of ducks. Considering their abundance and their breeding range, this lack of information is perplexing. But one reason is evident: their nests are extremely difficult to locate. Rawls (1949) spent one entire summer searching for white-winged scoter nests at Delta Marsh, and even with the aid of other observers, he was unable to locate a single nest. Yet whitewings formed about 20 percent of the early-summer duck population there.

Nest Sites. Except on islands, where the distance to water is necessarily limited, many white-winged scoter nests are placed at considerable distances from water. James King says succinctly of the whitewings nesting in Alaska, "Oddly enough they do not orient their nests to water but are usually found hundreds of yards back in the deep woods where when flushed they have trouble flying through the trees."

Rawls (1949) cited a record of a nest 0.5 mile from water and records of others at considerable distances; he also gave records of nests close to water. Near Brooks, Alberta, Keith (1961) found three nests that averaged 300 feet from water. On islands in Lake Newell, located in the grassland of Alberta, Vermeer (1970*b*) found 0.02 whitewing nest per acre on 147 acres. At Miquelon Lakes in the Aspen parkland he found one whitewing nest per acre on islands totaling 11 acres. On Lower Therien Lake in the boreal forest, where islands totaled 1.9 acres, he found 1.05 nests per acre. Rawls (1949) cited several records of whitewing nests close together: Peter Ward found 5 nests in close proximity on a ditch bank through a whitetop meadow; Robert Smith found 20 nests on a willow island of less than 0.5 acre; and William Carrick found 5 nests on a small willow island. Patrick Brown found 97 nests on islands in Redberry Lake, Saskatchewan, and 69 nests on islands in Jessie Lake, Alberta, 1975-76. At Redberry Lake nest density was 0.18 per acre in 1975 and 0.37 per acre in 1976; at Jessie Lake there were 4.2 nests per acre in 1975 and 5.6 in 1976. On islands in Redberry Lake, nests averaged 317 feet from shore, ranging from 91 to 760 feet.

Almost everyone who has found a white-winged scoter nest mentions that it is placed in exceptionally dense cover. Bent (1925) cited records of nests placed under clumps of rosebushes. From personal communication and the literature, Rawls (1949) recorded nests located among rose, raspberry, and gooseberry bushes, willows, and in whitetop meadows. On islands in Miquelon Lakes, Alberta, Vermeer (1968) found that both gadwalls and white-winged scoters nested in denser cover of nettles than lesser scaups and that gadwalls appeared more adept than scoters at returning to their nest sites in dense cover. The 166 nests that Patrick Brown found were located in dense tangles of gooseberry, rose, raspberry, and buckbrush. These nests were in shallow depressions, poorly lined with small twigs and other detritus. The first down was added between the laying of the fourth and the eighth egg.

Clutch Size, Eggs, and Incubation. The clutch sizes in 168 nests of white-winged scoters have been recorded, 12 by Vermeer (1969), 146 by Patrick Brown, and 10 by other investigators. Clutch sizes have ranged from 5 to 17 eggs and have averaged 9.24 eggs. The light pink eggs are elliptical ovate and measure 65.3 by 45.7 mm (Bent 1925). One hundred eggs measured by Vermeer (1969) averaged 67.3 by 46.3 mm; mallard eggs measured at the same location averaged 57.0 by 41.4 mm. Except for eiders' eggs, the eggs of white-winged scoters are the largest of any duck in North America.

Vermeer (1969) observed that 18 eggs were laid in 29 days, an interval of 1.6 days per egg. Patrick Brown noted that eight females laid 37 eggs in 53 days, 1.43 days per egg. Among the eight females, rates of laying varied from 1.3 to 1.5 days per egg.

According to Patrick Brown, the incubation period for 22 white-winged scoter nests ranged from 25 to 31 days and averaged 28 days. Vermeer (1969) observed a clutch that hatched in 25 days.

Chronology of Nesting. The white-winged scoter is one of the last ducks to reach its breeding grounds and one of the last to nest. At Miquelon Lakes, Vermeer (1969) observed that the first scoters arrived on May 6, 1965, and the first egg was laid on June 11, an interval of 36 days. For the combined years 1964-65, Vermeer (1968) determined that 20 nests were initiated between June 6 and July 3, a span of 27 days. Nest initiation occurred at about the same rate throughout this period, 1.4 days per nest. Patrick Brown found that 69 nests were initiated at Jessie and Redberry lakes in 1976, between June 8 and 22, with the average date June 15.

At Delta Marsh, Hochbaum (1944) reported that the late-nesting lesser scaup and ruddy duck do not start until the last week in May. The white-winged scoter is even later—it does not begin to nest until the first and second weeks in June.

Nest Success and Failure. Patrick Brown determined the fate of 143 white-winged scoter nests on islands in Jessie Lake, Alberta, and Redberry Lake, Saskatchewan, 1975-76; 71 percent of these nests hatched. Nest losses resulted almost equally from desertion and from destruction by bird predators. Vermeer (1969) observed that 5 of 10 scoter nests were successful, 4 were destroyed by predators, and 1 was deserted. One of three nests that Keith (1961) found was deserted; the other two were destroyed by mammals. At Yellowknife, Northwest Territories, Murdy (1964) recorded that two breeding pairs of whitewings produced one brood.

Renesting. The late breeding season combined with the short span of nest initiation precludes any significant degree of renesting. Near the southern part of its breeding range, Vermeer (1969) found that nests were initiated over a span of 27 days. Probably like other sea ducks, white-winged scoters continue to lay when eggs are destroyed prior to incubation.

Rearing of Young

Broods. Broods of white-winged scoters, like other sea ducks' broods, often combine to form assemblages of startling size. For example, Rawls (1949) cited records of 1-week-old broods composed of 23, 33, and 50 young each, and a record of 30 young, 1.5 to 2.5 weeks old, with three females. Hochbaum (1944) saw a whitewing brood of 85 young, all under 2 weeks of age. James King reports that white-winged scoter broods in Alaska often amalgamate within a day or two of hatching to form a crèche of 20, 60, or even 100 ducklings with one female attendant, but that flocks of two or more broods are found only on very large lakes. Patrick Brown observed crèches of 30 to 150 ducklings customarily tended by one or two females, but on one occasion seven females were in attendance. About mid-August the last brooding hens deserted their broods, apparently resulting in the breakup of crèches into small mixed-age groups.

Rawls (1949) gave some brood sizes that apparently represented single records. He observed 10 broods under 1 week of age that averaged 4.4 young, 6 broods of 2-week-old ducklings that averaged 5.2 young, and 4 broods 3 weeks of age that averaged 2.7 young.

Development. Hochbaum (1944) estimated that the interval between the first appearance of white-winged scoter broods at Delta Marsh to the first observed flight was 63 to 77 days. First broods appeared about mid-July and first flying young were seen about mid-September. The last broods hatched early in August, and the last broods did not attain flight until mid-October. At Jessie and Redberry lakes, Patrick Brown first observed whitewing broods in mid-July of 1975-76. During the last week of August, most ducklings were in the late Class II or early Class III stage of growth.

POSTBREEDING SEASON

Little is known of the movement of scoters to molt areas. Hochbaum (1944) mentioned the gathering of molting white-winged scoters far out on Lake Manitoba in late July. In eastern Siberia, at the confluence of Aldan and Lena rivers, Dement'ev and Gladkov (1967) observed flocks of drakes congregating as early as June 29, having abandoned their mates. The postnuptial molt of adult males begins as early as late July in the region of the Sea of Okhotsk. On the island of Sakhalin, flightless drakes are obtainable after mid-August. Far south in central Siberia, near Krasnoyarsk, drakes were still able to fly and females were beginning to lose body feathers the first ten days of August. Females molt later, mostly on their nesting grounds.

FOOD HABITS

White-winged scoters feed almost entirely on marine animal life on their winter grounds. Cottam (1939) examined 819 gizzards, 83 percent from whitewings collected along the coasts of Massachusetts and Washington, and found that animal life composed 94 percent and plant material 6 percent of the food contents. Mollusks made up three-fourths of all foods. On the Pacific Coast, the rock clam was eaten by almost all birds; one rock clam swallowed measured 54 by 45 by 29 mm. The blue mussel was the principal food taken by whitewings on the Atlantic Seaboard away from commercial shellfish beds. Birds collected over shellfish beds on both coasts had consumed oysters, scallops, and quahogs, as well as other less valuable mollusks. Crustaceans—rock and mud crabs, crayfish, and barnacles—made up 13 percent of the food, and aquatic insects and fishes 4 percent.

At Humboldt Bay, California, several species of clams formed 80 percent of the volume of 17 white-winged scoter gizzards (Yocom and Keller 1961). Crabs and snails completed the diet.

McGilvrey (1967) examined the gizzards of 124 white-winged scoters collected from Maine to Long Island, 1964-65. In Maine, the Atlantic dogwinkle was the most important food item, appearing in over one-half of the gizzards and composing 55 percent of the total food volume. Off the Massachusetts coast, blue mussels and broad yoldia were the principal foods. In Long Island Sound, sand launce, yellow periwinkle, file yoldia, and New England nassa composed most of the diet.

In further study of scoter food habits along the New Hampshire and Massachusetts coastline, Stott and Olson (1973) found that the Atlantic razor and Arctic wedge clams made up three-fourths of the food contents of 166 gizzards of white-winged scoters. There, all three species of scoters fed most extensively off sandy beaches and least extensively off rocky headlands.

According to Bent (1925), white-winged scoters dive in water up to 40 feet in depth. A male averaged 57.5 seconds under water in six consecutive dives, with rest intervals of 12 seconds on the surface, and a female averaged 60 seconds, with 11-second rest intervals (Roberts 1932).

Bufflehead

Bucephala albeola

Other Common Names: Butterball, dipper

VITAL STATISTICS

Length: Adult male, 14-15.6 inches, average 14.75 inches (11)
Females, 12.7-13.7 inches, average 13.12 inches (11)
Subadult male, 13.9-15.2 inches, average 14.50 inches (14)

Wing: Adult male, 6.68 inches (26)
Adult female, 6.10 inches (12)
Immature male, 6.53 inches (34)
Immature female, 5.96 inches (42)

Weight: Adult male, 1.0-1.4 pounds, average 1.14 pounds (9)
Adult female, 0.8-1.2 pounds, average 0.68 pound (10)
Immature male, 0.9-1.2 pounds, average 1.08 pounds (9)
Immature female, 0.6-1.2 pounds, average 0.75 pound (35)

IDENTIFICATION

Field

The bufflehead is almost a miniature copy of the goldeneyes, a study in black and white. It can be distinguished from the goldeneyes by its smaller size and by the large white wedge-shaped cap extending from below eye level across the top of the male's head, and the white dash on the side of the female's head. The bufflehead, ruddy duck, and green-winged teal vie for the role of the smallest of waterfowl.

Buffleheads commonly appear as pairs and trios, less commonly in flocks of 5 to 10, and rarely in larger flocks. Hooded mergansers, which somewhat resemble buffleheads, also travel in flocks comparably small in size. Buffleheads are among the fastest flying ducks, with one of the most rapid wingbeats. When buffleheads are in flight, the single broad white bands across the wings of the males and the white specula of the females contrast sharply with the dark outer parts of the wings.

On the water, they usually have their heads retracted, so that their necks are invisible. The black lower parts of the drakes' heads are therefore usually merged with the black backs to form islands of black surrounded by white. Females appear entirely gray-black except for the white almond-shaped marks behind the eyes. The white specula in females are often, but not always, visible in birds at rest. Buffleheads have unusually low silhouettes on the water, commonly riding so low that their tails are awash—at times only their heads are readily visible. At close range in April and May, Erskine (1972*b*) considered it possible to distinguish yearling males from females by their larger size, the larger patches of white on their heads, and their whiter sides.

At Hand

The diminutive size and the overall black and white pattern set the bufflehead apart from other species. The puffy head of the male shows purple and green hues and a white wedge-shaped crown patch extending below the eye. The female's head is brown-black with a fingerprint-sized white spot behind the eye. The short blue-gray bill is about half as long as the head, and the eyes are dark brown in contrast to the yellow eyes of the goldeneyes and hooded mergansers. The feet of the male are a pink flesh color, but those of the female are blue-gray.

The tail of the bufflehead is quite long for a diving duck, nearly 20 percent of its total length. By way of comparison, the tail of the lesser scaup is 12 percent of its total length, that of the goldeneye is 18 percent, and those of the hooded merganser and the oldsquaw are 20 percent and 37 percent, respectively. The tail of the male bufflehead is dark gray, that of the female is dusky brown.

The back and rump of the male are jet black; the female has a dusky brown back and a black rump. The lower parts of the bufflehead's body are almost entirely white, sometimes mottled with gray on the lower belly of the male and along the sides and flanks of the female.

The adult male begins to acquire its eclipse plumage in early May when dusky brown feathers appear among the black on the upper throat (Erskine 1972*b*). By mid-June the brownish feathers appear in the white head patch and the white of the lower throat, and by mid-July the entire head is dusky brown, except for the fingerprint-sized white spot behind the eye. The white side, flank, and chest feathers are replaced by gray-brown feathers prior to the wing molt in late July. A few males regain their nuptial plumage by late August, but most do not do so until late September.

The juvenile plumage begins to be replaced by the first winter plumage in late August (Erskine 1972*b*). The heads of the males become darker and the white fingerprint patches are larger than those of the females. They molt into subadult plumage between March and June, but not until the end of September, when they are 15 months old, do they achieve their first nuptial plumage.

Carney (1964) conditionally described sex and age differences in bufflehead wings as follows: The middle coverts over the secondaries are entirely white in adult males but are black or brown-black in the females and immatures. In adult females the tertials are long, slightly drooping, and broadly rounded at the tips. Immatures have short, straight tertials, often with pointed fraying tips showing brownish traces. Wing lengths determine the sexes in immatures—159 mm or less indicate females, 160 mm or more signify males.

POPULATION STATUS

The bufflehead's vast breeding range in forested and often mountainous country, combined with its sparse distribution, makes it difficult to determine its continental status. Based upon breeding ground numbers, 1960-64, Erskine (1972*b*) estimated 500,000. Additional years of breeding ground surveys, plus changes in correction indices for oversight of birds on aerial surveys, have raised this figure.

In the main waterfowl breeding grounds surveyed annually from eastern Manitoba to the Bering Sea, the number of buffleheads during the prebreeding seasons has averaged 585,000 for 1955-73 (Richard Pospahala). The number breeding in Ontario and Quebec is 75,000, based upon 30,000 determined from aerial surveys corrected × 2.5 for oversight. On the bufflehead's British Columbia breeding grounds, there are an estimated 70,000 to 100,000. Thus, the most current estimate of the prebreeding population is about 745,000. Erskine's (1972*b*) calculations, based upon the proportion of band recoveries to hunter kill, indicate a continental population of 600,000 buffleheads.

Populations of buffleheads on breeding grounds surveyed annually have ranged from 360,000 to 930,000, a variation of 38.7 percent. Erskine (1972*b*) cites evidence that in the late 1800's and early 1900's, buffleheads declined over many parts of their range, apparently as a result of overshooting. A summary of Christmas bird counts for 1927-66 reveals a pronounced upward trend in the Northeast, slightly upward trends in the Great Lakes and southeast regions, and a decline in numbers in the Far West (Erskine 1972*b*).

Age Ratios

The proportion of immature to adult buffleheads in hunters' bags in the United States in 1966-73 has averaged 1.35 to 1.0. No information is available on the greater vulnerability of immatures than of adults to hunting losses, but on the probable basis of 1.5:1 to 2.0:1, the average proportion of immatures in fall populations is 0.68 to 0.90 per adult, a lower level of production than in most game ducks. However, such a level may typify ducks that do not breed until their second year.

Sex Ratios

Because yearlings are similar to female buffleheads in appearance, true sex ratios, based on visual observations, are difficult to determine. The apparent sex ratio—that is, the proportionate number of adult males compared with yearlings and females—observed by Erskine (1972*b*) during the fall in British Columbia was 49 males for each 100 female-like ducks (3,335). On the basis of the proportion of immatures in the population Erskine (1972*b*) suggests that the true sex ratio is about 150 males per 100 females.

Mortality

From bandings of buffleheads in British Columbia, Erskine (1972*b*) calculated that adult males suffered an annual mortality of 47 percent, adult females 57 percent, and immatures 72 percent. The recapture of nesting females indicated an annual mortality of 50 percent, probably a more realistic figure than the 57 percent based upon shrinkage in recoveries of birds shot. Because shooting pressure on buffleheads in British Columbia is heavier than elsewhere in their range, Erskine (1972*b*) believes that more representative annual mortality rates are 72 percent the first year and 30 percent each subsequent year.

DISTRIBUTION

Breeding Season

In only a few places within its extensive breeding range is the bufflehead particularly abundant during the breeding season. These are the Cariboo and Chilcotin districts of

British Columbia and the subarctic river deltas—the Saskatchewan, Athabasca, and Slave river parklands.

An aerial survey in the spring of 1955 recorded 18,000 buffleheads in the Cariboo District and 7,900 in the Chilcotin District (Mackay 1955). Adjustments for oversight (× 2.5) result in a population of 45,000 (10.0 per square mile) in the Cariboo District and of 20,000 (3.3 per square mile) in the Chilcotin District. The entire province of British Columbia is estimated to contain 70,000 to 100,000 breeding buffleheads (R. T. Sterling, William Morris, Ray Halladay). The population of 54,000 on the three subarctic river deltas calculates at 2.7 per square mile. Only two aerial surveys have been made of the Yukon Territory east and north of Whitehorse. These surveys yielded a population index of 48,500, which, adjusted for oversight (× 2.5), results in an estimate of 121,000 buffleheads (2.9 per square mile).

Buffleheads number 2.4 per square mile for a total population of 23,000 in the Tanana-Upper Kuskokwim valleys of Alaska. Elsewhere in Alaska, buffleheads are especially numerous on the Nelchina Flats, where there are 1.7 per square mile (population 6,600), and on the Yukon Flats with 1.4 per square mile (population 15,000). Throughout the interior breeding grounds of Alaska, including the above areas, there are 1.6 buffleheads per square mile, a population of 50,000. On the breeding areas of southeastern coastal Alaska, buffleheads number 1,000, a density of 0.4 per square mile. On central coastal areas they number 4,000, a density of 0.09 per square mile. No doubt the buffleheads present on the treeless portions of the coastal areas are nonbreeders.

Over the vast closed boreal forest and the extensive parklands of the Prairie Provinces, the bufflehead density is similar—0.8 per square mile—for a combined population of 423,000. Within these regions, buffleheads are most numerous in Alberta, where a density of 1.5 per square mile occurs in the boreal forest (population 249,000) and of 1.2 (population 33,000) in the parklands.

East of Manitoba, definite breeding records of buffleheads are few, and there are none for vast regions of the boreal forest (Erskine 1972*b*). However, surveys of the U.S. Fish and Wildlife Service record buffleheads scattered across much of the boreal forest of Ontario and Quebec. In the western half of Ontario, 0.1 bufflehead per square mile (total population 30,000) has been recorded. In eastern Ontario and Quebec, an unadjusted average of 25,700 was estimated over a 6-year period (Hansen 1967). Adjusting the estimate for oversight from aircraft (× 2.5) indicates a population of 64,000.

About 34,000 buffleheads (0.2 per square mile) have been recorded in the open boreal forest of Subarctic Canada, but many of these may have been nonbreeding birds. The average number recorded for both the Mackenzie Delta and Old Crow Flats was 460 (0.07 per square mile); these were probably nonbreeding birds, for Erskine (1972*b*) reports there are no known breeding records in the Mackenzie Basin north of Fort Simpson.

South of the parklands on the prairies, nearly 20,000 (0.06 per square mile) have been found in the mixed grass and shortgrass associations. Most of these birds are surely nonbreeders, but sporadic nesting undoubtedly occurs in favorable areas where cottonwoods or aspens have suitable cavities. For example, Robert Stewart and Harold Kantrud have several recent records of buffleheads breeding in the Turtle Mountains and on the Lower Souris National Wildlife Refuge in North Dakota.

A few small breeding colonies of buffleheads occur in the region of the Rocky and Cascade mountains in northwestern United States. Jeffrey and Bowhay (1972) report an average of 340 in Washington, 1963-72. They found 920 in 1972, distributed as follows: 60 in the Cascades, 620 in the Columbia Basin, and 240 in the northeastern highlands. Chester Kebbe estimates that 200 breed in the Cascade Mountains of Oregon. From the air, Frank Kozlik observed 32 breeding pairs in a small colony in Lassen County, California, in 1973. Another area where a limited number of buffleheads occur centers on Yellowstone National Park. George Wrakestraw has found an average of slightly over 100 buffleheads in northwest Wyoming, 1964-72. Currently, Robert Eng has observed numerous pairs in Yellowstone, but no nests or broods. A bufflehead brood reported near Yellowstone Lake by Rosche (1954) indicates that they breed there. Moreover, Erskine (1972*b*) cites recent nest records at Henrys Lake and Red Rock Lakes, short distances to the west of Yellowstone Park, in eastern Idaho.

Migration Corridors

Because most buffleheads are reared in the northwestern part of North America, their migration to coastal winter grounds is short to one coast and long to the other. Distribution of band recoveries, discussed by Erskine (1972*b*), aided in the interpretation of projected migration corridors. Other data used were the fall census figures from various states and refuges and the reported hunter kill in regions of Canada and the United States.

Recoveries of buffleheads banded near Fort Yukon, Alaska, indicated that almost 60 percent migrated down the Pacific Coast, 28 percent to the region of the Alaska Peninsula, 10 percent into Yukon Territory, and 2 percent (1 recovery) to the Kamchatka Peninsula, Siberia. Of 139 buffleheads recovered outside the banding area in southern British Columbia, 94 percent migrated to Washington, Oregon, and northern California, 4 percent to states in the Rocky Mountains, and 1 percent each to the Midwest and New England.

Of 157 recoveries outside the banding area in southern Alberta, 31 percent occurred in British Columbia and Pacific coastal states, 14 percent in Rocky Mountain states and Mexico, 11 percent in the interior, 20 percent in the Great Lakes area, and 24 percent in Atlantic coastal states. Probably most of the recoveries from the Great Lakes area represented buffleheads migrating towards Atlantic Coast winter grounds.

Banding in Saskatchewan resulted in 31 recoveries out-

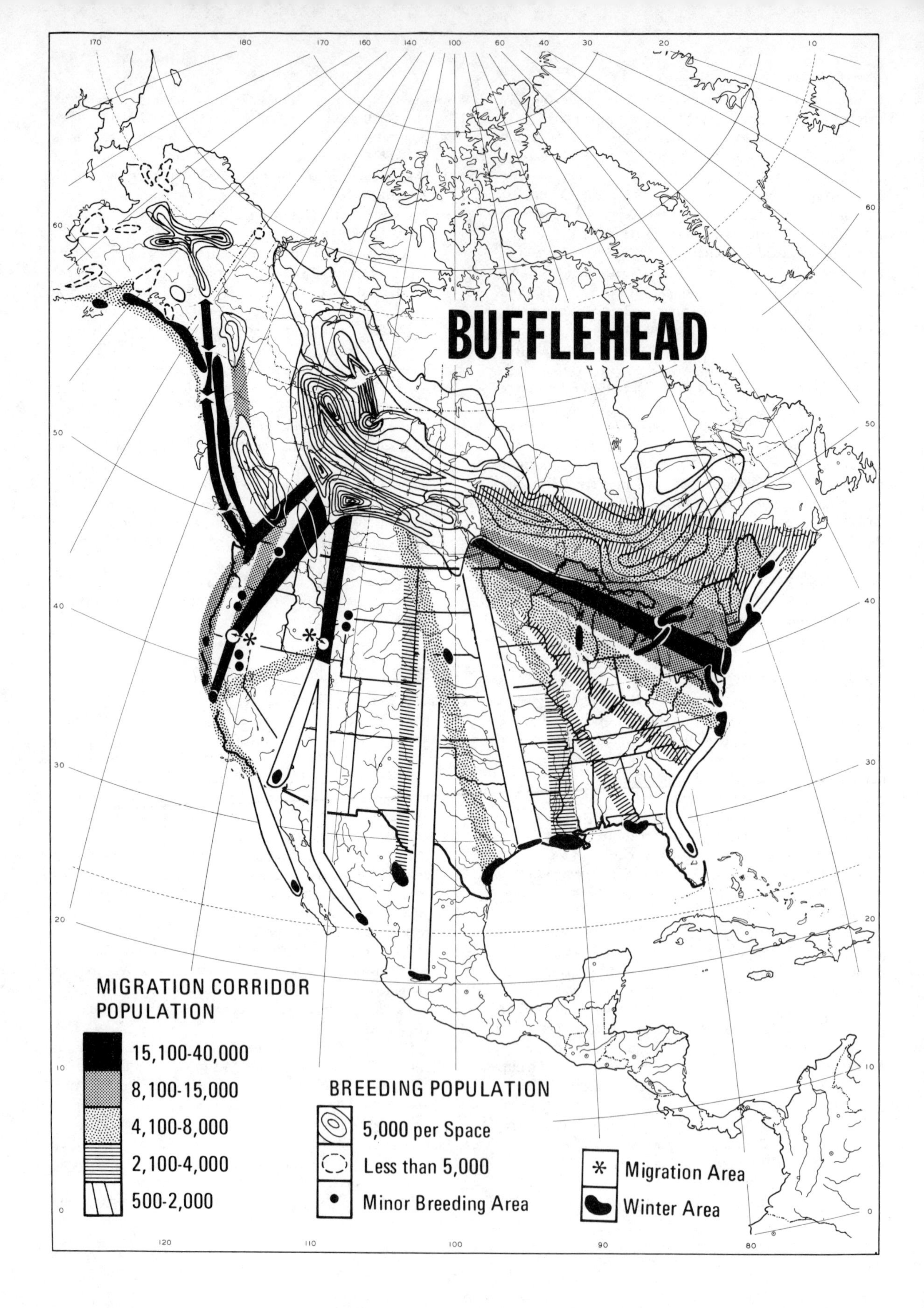
BUFFLEHEAD
MIGRATION CORRIDOR POPULATION
15,100-40,000
8,100-15,000
4,100-8,000
2,100-4,000
500-2,000
BREEDING POPULATION
5,000 per Space
Less than 5,000
Minor Breeding Area
Migration Area
Winter Area

side that province: 74 percent were in the Great Lakes-Atlantic Coast area, 10 percent in the interior, 13 percent in interior Mexico, and 3 percent (1 recovery) in western Montana. Of 13 recoveries outside the banding area in Manitoba, 69 percent were in the Great Lakes-Atlantic Coast area, and 31 percent in the Midwest.

Erskine (1972*b*) calls attention to a major split in migration directions in Alberta. Buffleheads originating west of a line extending diagonally across the province from the northwest corner to the southeast corner migrate largely to the southwest; those to the east migrate largely to the southeast. Buffleheads migrating south originate from a borderline area between the two zones.

Winter Areas

Buffleheads, like goldeneyes, concentrate along both coasts for the winter. They occur along the Atlantic Coast from southern Newfoundland to southern Florida. On the Pacific Coast, buffleheads occur near the tip of the Aleutians along the coast of the Gulf of Alaska, the coasts of British Columbia, Washington, Oregon, California, and the Baja Peninsula, and the west coast of Mexico as far as Mazatlán.

January surveys record an average of 37,000 buffleheads from Maine through Florida. Audubon Christmas bird counts record 29,000 in the same region, and, additionally, 82 in Nova Scotia, 58 in New Brunswick, and 2 in Quebec. Both surveys show about 2,500 in Maine, but Audubon bird censuses found larger numbers as far south as New Jersey: 125 in New Hampshire; 2,150 in Massachusetts; 470 in Rhode Island; 1,300 in Connecticut; and 3,600 in New York. From New Jersey south, January surveys report similar or larger numbers: 9,900 in New Jersey; 1,200 in Delaware; 8,800 in Maryland; 3,700 in Virginia; 7,100 in North Carolina; 350 in South Carolina; 35 in Georgia; and 950 in Florida.

On the Pacific Coast from Adak, Alaska, to Washington, Audubon Christmas censuses for 1970-73 average 3,400 buffleheads, a slightly higher average than for common goldeneyes. Reports from Alaskan refuges indicate that winter populations of buffleheads on the Aleutian Islands National Wildlife Refuge average about 8,500; 2,000 at Izembek; 2,000 at Kodiak; and 300 on the Kenai Moose Range.

From Washington south in the Pacific Flyway there are almost 30,000 buffleheads, according to January surveys. Half of these are found in Washington, over three-fourths on Puget Sound. California surveys reveal 6,800, over 80 percent of which are in coastal areas. Oregon harbors about 3,200, in coastal bays and on Upper Klamath Lake. The lagoons of Baja California support an average of 160 buffleheads and the lagoons of Mexico's west coast have an average of 450. Scarcely 1,500 are found in the states of the Rocky Mountains: 700 in Idaho, 500 in Nevada, and 100 each in Utah and Arizona.

In the interior of the continent, combined data from January surveys and Audubon Christmas bird censuses account for about 10,000 buffleheads, widely dispersed over the entire region from the Great Lakes to the Gulf of Mexico. About 1,200 have been found on the Great Lakes, and all states but Texas report fewer than 1,000. The average recorded for Texas is 4,300 buffleheads, widely distributed in the interior of the state and along the coast. Small numbers winter as far north as Montana, Wyoming, and South Dakota. Fewer than a hundred have been found in the Interior Highlands of Mexico.

MIGRATION BEHAVIOR

Although buffleheads appear in small flocks on many water areas during the fall migration, some favorable areas attract large aggregations. In Washington, Jewett et al. (1953) reported flocks numbering 6 to 2,000. At Alta Lake, British Columbia, Racey (1948) found flocks of 200 and 250 to 300 arriving in November, and, later, Erskine (1972) saw flocks of 80, 90, and 200 there. Other fall flocks cited by Erskine (1972*b*) in the Great Lakes and Atlantic Coast regions number from 500 to 2,000. Large aggregations in migration may travel as *train flocks*, that is, a multitude of small flocks in a line, as suggested by the 500 buffleheads that crashed at Foam Lake, Saskatchewan, between 9:30 P.M. and 2:00 A.M. (Swallow 1941).

As with most other ducks, bufflehead migration occurs largely at night, but under unusually severe weather conditions may occur during daylight. An overnight flight of 12 hours at 50 miles per hour would result in a journey of 600 miles.

Chronology

Fall. Buffleheads generally appear in the conterminous United States later in the fall than the scaups and earlier than the goldeneyes, and do not remain in sizable numbers as late as the goldeneyes. According to Gabrielson and Lincoln (1959), early dates of their arrival on Alaskan winter areas are October 1, Unalaska Island; October 17, Cold Bay; October 5, Craig; and October 7, Wrangell. The last date Soper (1951) observed buffleheads in the Athabasca Delta, northern Alberta, was September 28, but he had reports of stragglers as late as October 10.

Small numbers of buffleheads are present in September in areas south of their breeding grounds, well in advance of the main migration that commences about mid-October. Peak numbers are reached in many northern and central regions at surprisingly similar times in mid-November. Those that winter in southern areas appear from mid-November to December, with numbers increasing through the end of the year. A noted exception is the unusually early arrival of buffleheads in mid-October on the lower coast of Texas.

Spring. Because buffleheads winter in greater numbers farther south than goldeneyes, they are not as numerous in northern areas. It is not surprising, therefore, that buffleheads lag behind goldeneyes in pushing north during

BUFFLEHEAD

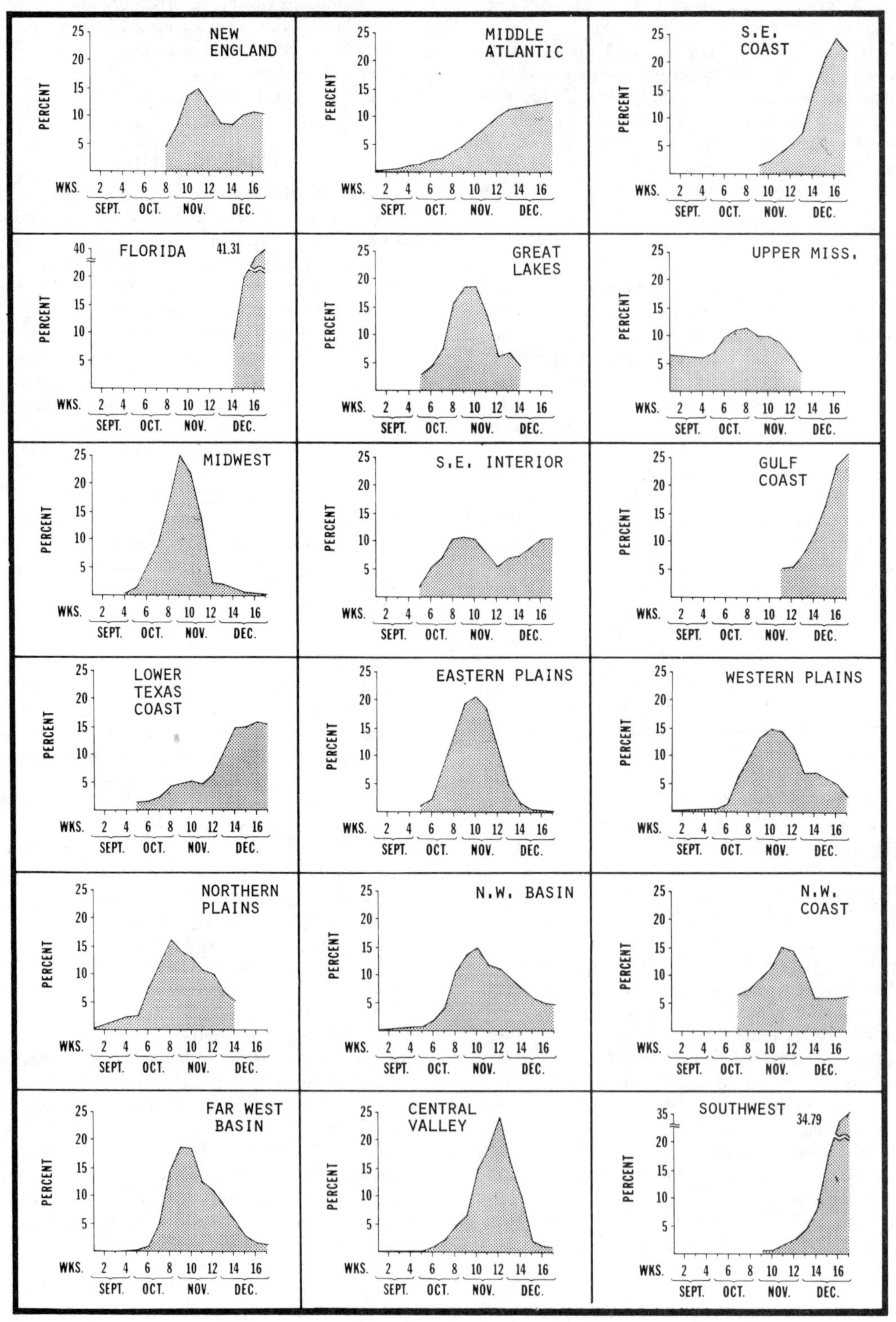

Fall

BUFFLEHEAD

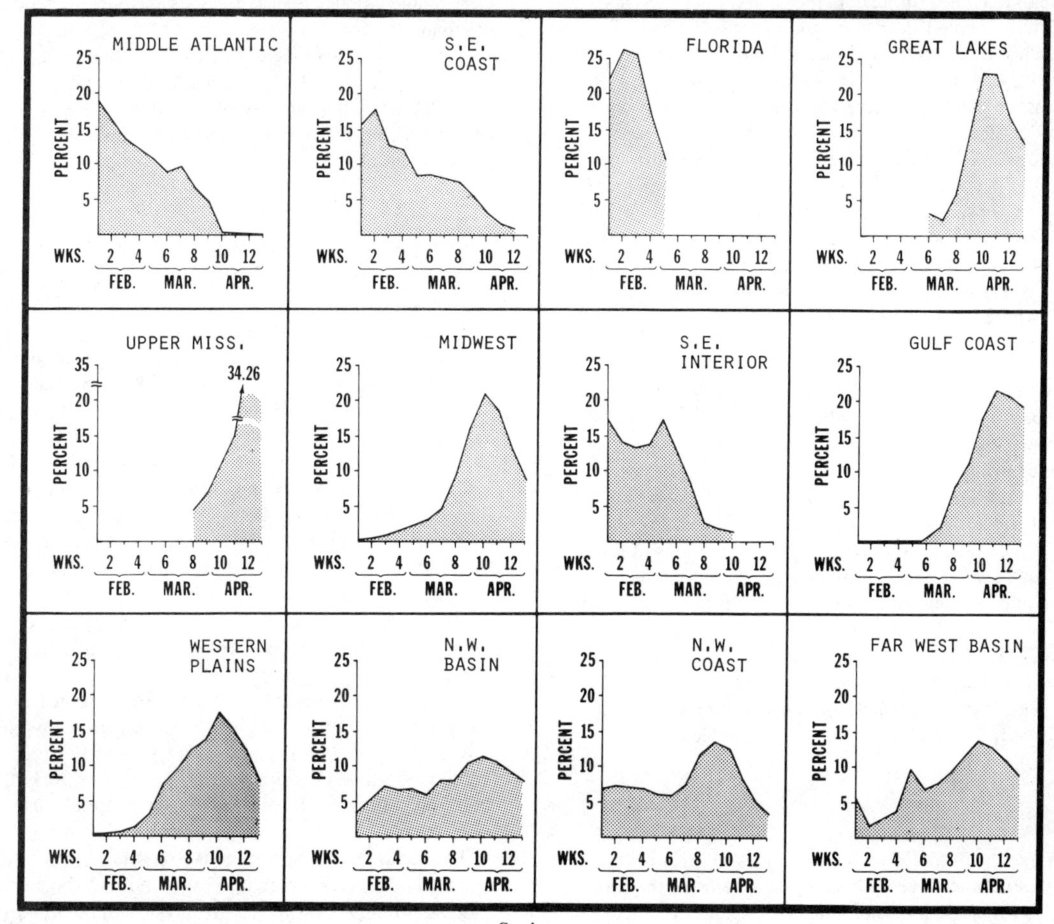

Spring

the spring. Migrant buffleheads begin augmenting winter populations in the Midwest—both in the East and the High Plains—and in the Northwest and Far West basins the last half of February. Numbers in most of these regions continue to increase until the latter part of March, then to steadily decline through April. In the Great Lakes region, bufflehead migrants join winter populations the last half of March, with continued increments for another month before a rapid exodus begins (Jahn and Hunt 1964). They appear in northern areas, between Wisconsin and central Montana, in late March or early April and increase in numbers through the month.

On the Athabasca Delta in northeastern Alberta, buffleheads arrive in late April or early May (Soper 1951). Gabrielson and Lincoln (1959) reported that early dates of arrival on Alaskan breeding grounds were May 5, College; May 6, Fort Chatham; May 8, Chitina Station; and May 12, Tanacross. They noted that late departures from winter grounds in the Alaskan Panhandle extended from May 7 to June 7.

The main bufflehead flight into breeding grounds of interior British Columbia occurs in April (Erskine 1972*b*). Yearlings migrate several weeks later than adults, usually in May except for June stragglers. Where two peaks occur in censuses of spring populations, Erskine (1972*b*) believes that the first represents adults, the second, yearlings.

BREEDING

Behavior

Age, Pair Bond, and Homing. Buffleheads are not known to breed until they are nearly 2 years old (Erskine 1972*b*). Few pairs are formed prior to March; most are formed the first half of April during the time they are actively migrating. Pair formation almost ceases in early

May. Erskine (1972*b*) observed that shortly after the hens began to incubate, drakes commenced to leave their home ranges for brief periods, and soon thereafter most of them completely severed ties with their mates. A few exceptional ones remained throughout the incubation period and, rarely, accompanied their hens and broods.

Buffleheads, like other hole-nesting ducks, demonstrate a remarkable propensity to return in subsequent years to the same nest area. Erskine's (1961) 27 homing records included 20 ducks banded a previous year on their nests, 1 captured with a brood, 1 molting adult, 1 subadult, and 4 young. Eighteen of the 20 hens banded on nests were found nesting in subsequent years at the same lake; one had moved to another lake slightly over 0.25 mile away, and the other to a lake about 4 miles distant. There were 23 instances of the same bird using the same site subsequently and 12 where birds were found at other sites.

Home Range. Erskine (1972*b*) noticed little conflict between pairs, and then only when an adult drake was accompanied by its mate. Nevertheless, spacing occurred among breeding pairs—ponds contained a single pair and pairs on large lakes were well spaced along the shores. The minimal accepted size for isolated ponds was about 2.5 acres. Home ranges were restricted to the shores of large lakes; the central areas provided communal waters for feeding and molting by migrants, yearling residents, and breeding adults. The most frequent distance between nest sites was 110 yards, but Erskine (1972*b*) found three trees that each contained two nests occupied simultaneously. When females were flushed from nests during laying, they flew directly to the areas of the waiting males.

Nesting

Nest Sites. Buffleheads nest in small cavities in trees, usually old flicker holes. Of 11 species of trees that contained cavities used by buffleheads, aspen contained 52 percent, Douglas fir, 2 percent, balsam poplar, 7 percent, ponderosa pine, 6 percent, and other trees, 14 percent (Erskine 1972*b*). Most of the cavities that buffleheads used for nesting were located within 220 yards of the margin of a river, pond, or lake. In British Columbia, about three-quarters were within 25 yards of a water area.

The availability of nest sites is determined by the number of flickers excavating new cavities, the durability of existing ones, and the degree of competition with other species. Occupied cavities measured 2.5 by 2.5 to 3 inches at the entrance, 6 inches in internal diameter, and 10 to 14 inches in depth. Most nests were between 2 and 10 feet above the ground. Many nests were in stubs of aspen and Douglas fir, distributed rather uniformly up to 23 feet in aspen and 49 feet in Douglas fir. At Watson Lake, British Columbia, Erskine (1972*b*) found 79 flicker holes, 22 of which were used by buffleheads, 1958-59. Three others had been used in 1957 and another three were occupied in 1960-62.

Starlings, mountain bluebirds, sparrow hawks, tree swallows, and flickers compete with buffleheads for nest cavities but Erskine (1972*b*) believed that only starlings and flickers were important competitors. Occasionally, buffleheads attempted to nest in cavities that were sufficiently large to admit also Barrow's and common goldeneyes and hooded mergansers, who then proceeded to dominate the incubation.

Small numbers of nest houses have been erected for buffleheads in British Columbia, Alberta, and California. Some houses were occupied in all areas, but intensity of use varied, probably in relation to availability of natural cavities and abundance of breeding birds.

Clutch Size, Eggs, and Incubation. As with the goldeneyes and other sea ducks, buffleheads lay eggs at the rate of about one every 1.5 days. Erskine (1972*b*) found evidence that the rate increased from one egg every other day early in the clutch deposition to one on successive days later in the period. The slowest rate of laying that he observed was 5 eggs in 13 days, and the most rapid was 12 eggs within 14 days and 2 hours. Eggs were laid throughout the morning hours, but particularly between 8 and 10 A.M.

Erskine's (1972*b*) compilation of data on clutch sizes, drawn from his own observations and from the literature, indicate a size range of 5 to 17, with a median of 9 eggs and an average of 8.75 eggs (263 clutches). Clutches of more than 12 eggs probably represented eggs laid by more than one hen. Two unincubated clutches of 20 eggs each were undoubtedly dump nests—two or more hens laying in the same nest.

Eggs of the bufflehead are bluntly ovate to nearly oval, the shells a smooth and slightly glossy ivory-yellow to pale olive-buff (Bent 1925). The average size of 152 eggs measured in the field (Erskine 1972*b*) was 50.9 by 36.4 mm; in museum collections the average egg measured 51.0 by 36.6 mm (105).

The incubation period extends from the laying of the last egg to the hatch. Erskine (1972*b*) found that the period of incubation ranges from 28 to 33 days, with the majority of nests hatching between 29 and 31 days.

After hatching, the young remain in the nest for 24 to 36 hours before jumping to the ground from the entrance hole. In describing this event, Erskine (1972*b*) reported that he heard no calls from the female, but in view of the departure calls by goldeneyes and wood ducks to their young, it is difficult to understand young buffleheads leaving the nest without a release call by their mother. However, in the one departure witnessed by Erskine (1972*b*), the ducklings took 12 minutes to leave the nest cavity, an unusually long time compared with the departures of young goldeneyes and wood ducks.

Chronology of Nesting. The chronology of nest initiation has been calculated from dates of hatch presented by Erskine (1972*b*). Although times of nest initiation vary as much as 25 days from Lassen County, California, to Fort Yukon, Alaska, the time of starting the last nests varies hardly at all. In the southern part of their nest range, buffleheads commence nesting in late April and reach maximum starts May 5-10. Farther north, in the central part of their breeding range, they begin to lay eggs in early May and peak activity occurs about the middle of the month. On the northern fringes of their breeding range, nesting starts about mid-May and reaches maximum starts about May 20. Regardless of location, the time of the initiation of the last nests has ranged only from May 25 to June 8. The span of nest initiation is brief, about 40 to 50 days in the southern regions of their breeding range to 15 to 25 days in the northern regions.

Nest Success. Buffleheads share with goldeneyes an unusually high nest success. Of 193 nests studied by Erskine (1972*b*) in British Columbia, 78.8 percent were successful. Clutch size in successful nests averaged 8.53 eggs of which an average of 0.58 egg failed to hatch. Infertility was responsible for 37 percent of the unhatched eggs and embryonic deaths for 31 percent. Only a few ducklings have been found in nest cavities after broods departed.

Nest Failure. Desertions accounted for most of the nest failures; many resulted from competition for nest cavities by other wildlife. Flying squirrels and tree swallows placed nest material over bufflehead eggs, flickers and starlings punctured eggs, and Barrow's goldeneye females killed four buffleheads on nests. Small mammals and bears destroyed several nests.

Renesting. There is no good evidence that a bufflehead will renest once an incubated nest is destroyed (Erskine (1972*b*). During an intensive study of 75 nests, 1958-59, only 5 were considered as possible renests, and these may have been by birds whose first nests were destroyed during the laying period, causing them to change locations.

Rearing of Young

Broods. Female buffleheads lead their broods to the open water of ponds (2.5 acres or larger) and lakes. When nest sites adjoin ponds too small for brood rearing, females lead their young overland to more suitable habitat. The females establish brood home ranges by the second week (Erskine 1972*b*), and these are maintained for 4 to 6 weeks. Broods move an average of 790 yards the first week, declining to an average of 250 yards by the sixth week. Hens are solicitous of their young until they leave to molt. Then brood bonds appear to disintegrate, and members may mix with molting adults or with broods of other species. Apparently, the maternal drive is stronger in some bufflehead hens than in others, for some young or entire broods may shift from one female to another. Erskine (1972*b*) observed single broods increase from 6 to 24 ducklings, from 11 to 20, and 2 to 13. However, mixing is uncommon where only a few broods are present.

Development. Bufflehead ducklings weigh less than 25 grams at hatch, but increase in weight by 15 to 20 times in 2 months (Erskine 1972*b*). The first body feathers are visible among the down when the young are about 20 days old. Between 20 and 40 days, the males begin to grow noticeably larger than the females. At 40 days, the young are almost completely feathered and are 90 percent as large as adults but only 80 percent as heavy. The first flights occur when the young are 50 to 55 days of age.

Fully grown young have been observed on the following dates: in Lassen County, California, July 22; in British Columbia, July 26 and August 2 and 18 at East Kootenay, July 30 and August 8 in the Cariboo District, and August 2 and 7 at Nechako; in Alberta, August 6 at Ministik Lake, August 8 at Buffalo Lake, and August 11 at Two Hills; and in the Yukon Territory, August 24 at Kluane Lake (Erskine 1972*b*). At Yellowknife, Northwest Territories, the earliest dates of fledging, 1962-64, were August 15 and 30 and September 2 (Murdy 1964).

Survival. Mortality reduces the average of 7.9 ducklings that have left successful nests to 6.4 in Class I (394), 5.7 in Class II (278), and 5.4 in Class III (53) (Erskine 1972*b*). The loss of young from the time of hatch to fledging is 32 percent and is greatest during the first 2 weeks of life.

POSTBREEDING SEASON

Brightly plumaged adult drakes gradually assume their female-like eclipse plumage during June and July as they assemble for the wing molt on favored lakes. In early July, nonbreeding yearlings and females whose nests have been destroyed join the molting males. Next to arrive are hens that have abandoned their half-grown broods. Erskine (1972*b*) reports that the primaries of adult males are shed after mid-July and are replaced by new ones in mid-August. The flightless period of female buffleheads extends from mid-August into early September. Among flightless buffleheads banded in British Columbia, 75 percent of the males, but only 33 percent of the females, were captured before August 10. Drake buffleheads reappear on breeding-ground lakes prior to the fall migration, indicating that they molted close to these areas.

FOOD HABITS

The food habits of the bufflehead, as determined by numerous investigators, have been summarized by Erskine (1972*b*). Throughout the year on fresh to moderately brackish waters, 67 to 84 percent of the food items taken were animal, mostly aquatic insects (dragonfly, damselfly, and mayfly nymphs, caddis fly and midge larvae, and water boatmen). During winter on fresh water, snails formed almost 19 percent of all food items consumed. On salt waters, animal foods, consisting mostly of crustaceans (isopods, amphipods, shrimp) and mollusks, made up 84 percent of the diet in spring and 90 percent during the fall and winter. Fish also became an important article of diet in winter.

The seeds of pondweeds and bulrushes were the most important plant foods taken on freshwater areas. On saltwater areas, pondweeds and widgeon grass were the plants utilized most frequently.

Barrow's Goldeneye

Bucephala islandica

Other Common Names: Whistler, Rocky Mountain whistler

VITAL STATISTICS

Length:	Male, 18.6-19.9 inches, average 19.2 inches (2) Female, 16.2-17.7 inches, average 17.0 inches (1)
Wing:	Adult male, 9.21 inches (9) Adult female, 8.34 inches (5) Immature male, 8.89 inches (11) Immature female, 8.12 inches (14)
Weight:	*Male, 1.5-2.5 pounds, average 2.13 pounds (53) Female, 1.1-1.8 pounds, average 1.31 pounds (14)

*These weights are of flightless birds captured at Ohtig Lake, Alaska (Yocum 1970).

IDENTIFICATION

Field

The restricted range of the Barrow's goldeneye axiomatically relegates this species to comparatively few sightings among the thousands of common goldeneyes observed in the conterminous United States. Unless viewed under the most favorable conditions, it is impossible to distinguish the two species in flight. At a distance on the water, the shape of the adult drake's head is the best distinguishing feature. The crown of the Barrow's is long, low, and evenly rounded, with an abrupt rise in its forehead, and the white mark in front of the eye is crescent-shaped. On the other hand, the head of the common goldeneye is peaked, with a sloping forehead, and the white eye-mark is round. Under favorable light conditions, the black heads show a purplish gloss in the Barrow's and a greenish gloss in the common. The jet-black back of the Barrow's extends farther down the sides and there is a small downward projection like a thumb between the black back and the folded wing.

Griscom (1945) cautions against mistaking common goldeneyes in transitional plumages for Barrow's. As adults change from eclipse to nuptial plumage and as yearling common goldeneyes begin to don nuptial plumage, the developing white spot in front of the eye may appear somewhat crescent-shaped. At this stage, also, the common exhibits a margin of white spots along the gray back. The gray back denotes the common goldeneye—the jet-black back, the Barrow's.

Female and immature Barrow's are such carbon copies of the common goldeneye that they can seldom be separated in the field. The only opportunity occurs between late winter and the breeding season, when the adult female Barrow's has an all-yellow bill whereas her common goldeneye counterpart has only a yellow tip.

At Hand

Barrow's goldeneye, like the common, has a stocky body, short neck, and large head. The adults of both species have yellow eyes; the eyes of yearling females are greenish yellow and those of the young are amber (Munro 1939*b*). The adult drake has a purple-glossed head and a white crescent patch in front of the eye, distinguishing it from all other species. The scapulars are black and white but contain more black than those of the common, therefore forming a series of white spots over the folded wing rather than the fine black hash marks typical of the common.

The wing coverts of the adult male Barrow's have less white than those on the common. The white greater coverts are tipped with black and thus form a black band between the white speculum and the white patch on the greater coverts. In the common goldeneye, the greater coverts are white and merge with the white speculum. According to Carney (1964), the wings of the immature and female Barrow's goldeneyes cannot be distinguished from those of the common.

In the eclipse plumage, adult males resemble females: their heads become brown, the white crescent facial marks indistinct, and the sides brownish. The molt starts in July and ends in late fall. The adult males assume distinctive plumage about mid-October, and from then on the change to complete plumage is rapid (Skinner 1937).

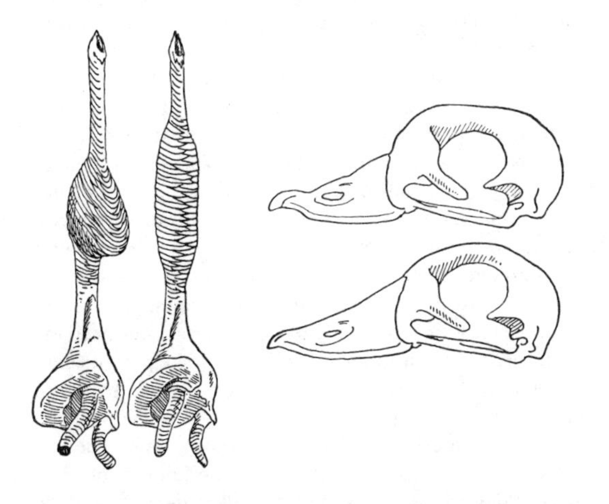

Internally, the Barrow's and common goldeneyes can be distinguished by both the structure of the windpipe and the skull. As the sketches indicate, the common goldeneye has an enlargement in the windpipe midway to the syrinx (voice box) that is lacking in the Barrow's. The skull rises much more abruptly from the bill in the Barrow's than in the common.

POPULATION STATUS

Because of the Barrow's restricted range in isolated regions, little reliable information is available on population size and yearly fluctuations in abundance. Man has little altered its prime habitat. Therefore, in all probability, the Barrow's population is as stable as changes in weather conditions permit. Mary Jackson reported a 40 percent decrease in breeding populations in British Columbia, 1955-57, because the cold, wet weather during the breeding season resulted in lower productivity than prevailed during 1954-55. A crude estimation of the Barrow's prebreeding population, based largely upon the numbers found on its principal range in British Columbia and Alaska, is 125,000 to 150,000.

Sex Ratios

Age ratios are unknown and sex ratios almost so. A tally of 141 Barrow's goldeneyes in interior British Columbia, April 18-21, by Mary Jackson revealed 117 males:100 females (53.9 percent). During January-April, 106 Barrow's on the Snake River, Washington, had a ratio of 121 males to 100 females (Harris et al. 1954). At Lenore Lake, a check of 175 residents during 1950-53 revealed 116 males to 100 females (53.7 percent).

Mortality

Mary Jackson analyzed 400 recoveries of immature Barrow's goldeneyes banded in British Columbia and concluded that their mortality rate the first year was 79 percent. Recoveries of 277 adult females indicated an annual mortality rate of 50 percent. The mortality rate for immatures is slightly lower and the rate for adults slightly higher than those suffered by common goldeneyes banded in Minnesota.

According to Mary Jackson, this mortality rate is too high to maintain the stable population she observed on her study area in British Columbia. She believed that the banding, which was confined to those lakes easily accessible to hunters, resulted in higher kills than were experienced by more remote elements of the population.

DISTRIBUTION

Breeding Season

There are two components to the range of Barrow's goldeneye: a small population associated with the Atlantic Ocean and a comparatively large population associated with northwestern North America. Its breeding in the East is an enigma. Salomonsen (1950-51) concluded that the Barrow's goldeneye bred in western and northern Iceland, and sparsely in southwest Greenland. Yet there is but one record, over 100 years old, of its breeding in Greenland. Salomonsen based his conclusion on the sightings of birds throughout the year, largely in Godthåb and Ameralik fjords.

The Barrow's is also reputed to breed on the northeast coast of Labrador. According to Todd (1963), there are no actual breeding records, but both visual records and specimens of adults and juveniles have been obtained. He quoted L. M. Tuck as collecting Barrow's goldeneyes, including juveniles, at various points along the coast of Labrador, and reported that E. B. Chamberlain observed a raft of 1,500 goldeneyes almost equally divided between the two species at the head of Nain Bay.

In western North America, the breeding range of the Barrow's extends along the mountain ranges from central Alaska to central California. It appears to achieve its greatest abundance in British Columbia, where R. T. Sterling, William Morris, and Ray Halladay estimate a prebreeding population of 70,000 to 100,000. The Cariboo and Chilcotin plateaus appear to support the largest breeding densities in British Columbia.

Of the 90,000 goldeneyes estimated as the prebreeding population in Alaska, about 45,000 are considered to be Barrow's. The breeding range of the Barrow's in Alaska extends from the Yukon Flats southwestward to Bristol Bay and the triangular region lying between there and the coast (John Bartonek). Soper (1954) reported many more common goldeneyes than Barrow's in the southwest Yukon, centering about Whitehorse, but this observation is difficult to reconcile with the range and abundance of Barrow's in Alaska on the one side and British Columbia on the other. Moreover, Swarth (1926) reported that the Barrow's was the most abundant and widely distributed duck in the region of Atlin, British Columbia, just south of the area covered by Soper.

Barrow's goldeneyes inhabit the alpine and subalpine lakes of the Cascade Mountains in Washington, Oregon, and northern California, and the Sierras of central California as far south as Fresno County. About 2,400 breed in Washington (Robert Jeffrey), 300 in Oregon (Chester Kebbe), and a small number in California (Frank Kozlik). In Washington, breeding Barrow's have been reported at numerous locations east of the Cascades (Harris et al. 1954). Most of these were on lakes in wooded mountain areas of Okanogan, Ferry, Stevens, and Spokane counties. It is odd that numerous broods have been found in barren, rocky lands of the Columbia Basin, particularly Lenore Lake. Observations suggested that these birds nested in holes of the surrounding basalt cliffs.

In the Flathead Valley of western Montana, Dale Witt observed broods of both species of goldeneyes. I observed a brood of Barrow's on a subalpine lake on Red Mountain, near Lincoln, Montana, in late July 1968. At Yellowstone National Park, Robert Eng reported that Barrow's outnumbered common by a margin of 9 to 1 during the breeding season; several broods were observed on Yellowstone Lake in 1974. South of Yellowstone in western Wyoming, the Barrow's is a common breeding duck in the drainages of the Snake, Salt, Green, and Bear rivers (George Wrakestraw). In late fall, 600 to 700 Barrow's were captured on the Salt River by nightlighting.

Although Barrow's goldeneyes breeding in southwest Wyoming approach Idaho, Utah, and Colorado, there are few records of them breeding in this conterminous region. Jessop Low observed two broods on the Flaming Gorge Reservoir in northeast Utah in June 1973. They have not been known to nest in Colorado since 1886 (Bailey and Niedrach 1965). In a 2-year study of breeding waterfowl in the Uinta Mountains, Utah, Peterson (1969) failed to record the Barrow's goldeneye in a region that lies adjacent to the Flaming Gorge Reservoir. Of the 4,209 duck broods recorded in Idaho, 1956-65, by the Idaho Fish and Game Department, 31 (0.73 percent) were goldeneye broods and assumed to be Barrow's.

Migration Corridors

The small numbers of Barrow's goldeneyes that winter between the north shore of the Gulf of St. Lawrence and Long Island probably migrate south along the Labrador coast from their assumed breeding grounds in northern Labrador. Apparently, most of the Barrow's in the Northwest and West make a short lateral migration from their breeding grounds in the Rocky Mountain and Coast ranges to the Pacific Ocean.

Of the 475 recoveries from Barrow's goldeneyes banded in east-central Alaska, only 6 were from outside that state: 2 in southwest Yukon Territory and 1 each in Montana, Washington, Oregon, and California. Recoveries within Alaska reveal a migration southwestward from interior breeding grounds to the coast east of the Alaska Peninsula. Most of the recoveries centered around the Kenai Peninsula and Kodiak Island; two came from the Alexander Archipelago.

Recoveries from large numbers of Barrow's goldeneyes banded on breeding areas in the interior of British Columbia reveal a pronounced passage southwestward to the coast, particularly to the vicinity of Vancouver Island. Many move along the coast to Puget Sound, where smaller numbers pass southward through the interior of Oregon and the northern half of California. A somewhat smaller number migrate from central British Columbia eastward or southeastward to Alberta, Idaho, and Montana.

But besides the lateral migration from the interior to the coast, there is an altitudinal migration among part of small elements of the population. These ducks move from the high subalpine and parkland lakes to the lower valleys, where open waters persist throughout the winter. There is probably a minor north-south migration among the Barrow's goldeneyes that winter in the valley and basins of the Rocky Mountains, as shown by their fall and spring appearance at Freezeout Lake, Montana (Dale Witt).

Winter Areas

The regular appearance of small numbers of Barrow's goldeneyes wintering on the northeast coast of North America strengthens the belief that a limited number of this species breeds along the north coast of Labrador. Audubon Christmas bird censuses, 1966, 1967, and 1969 show an average Barrow's goldeneye enumeration of 1 for Quebec, 10 for the coast of Maine, 2 for New Hampshire, 1 for Massachusetts, and 1 for Rhode Island and Connecticut combined. The composition of hunters' bags, 1967-70, as determined by wing collections, shows that Barrow's goldeneyes make up 0.1 percent of the kill in Maine, less than that in Vermont and Massachusetts, and none elsewhere on the Atlantic Coast.

The Barrow's goldeneye was not reported by Peters and Burleigh (1951) at any season in Newfoundland, but since then Godfrey (1966) has reported three records. In Nova Scotia, Tufts (1961) reported it as an uncommon winter resident, late December to early March. Griscom (1945) stated that a few Barrow's appeared on the coast of Massachusetts at Beverly, Newburyport Harbor, and Cape Ann, all north of Boston. According to Bull (1964), there

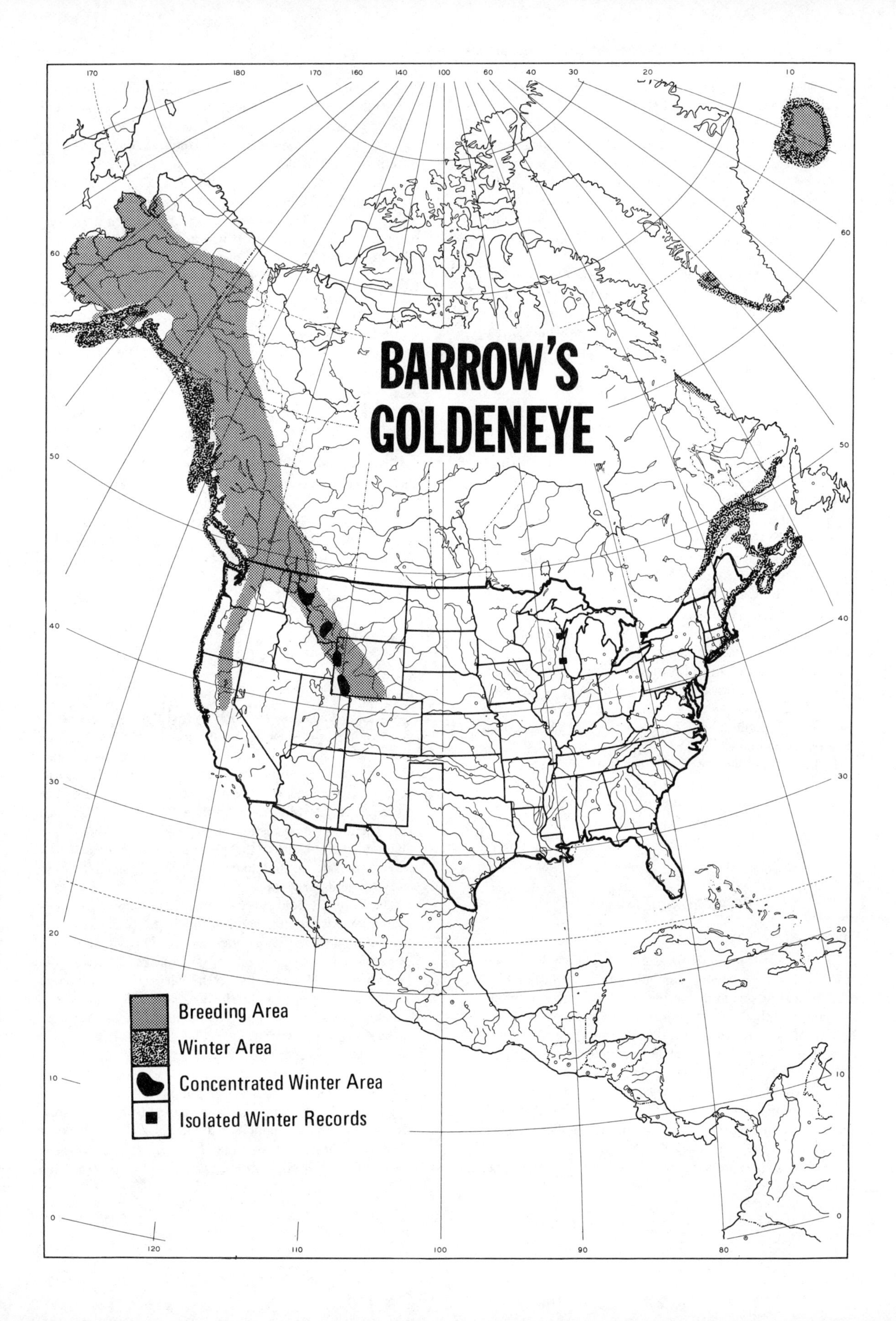
BARROW'S
GOLDENEYE
Breeding Area
Winter Area
Concentrated Winter Area
Isolated Winter Records

have been only five observations of the Barrow's goldeneye off Long Island since 1942.

Small numbers of this species winter at lower elevations in the mountain valleys of the Northwest. At Kleena Kleene, British Columbia, over 100 miles from the coast, several Barrow's have been found in winter (Paul 1959). Dale Witt has observed them in western Montana as far east as Great Falls. In Wyoming, George Wrakestraw reports that small numbers winter west of the Continental Divide almost everywhere that water remains open. They also winter at the lower elevations in Yellowstone National Park. Jessop Low has regularly observed them wintering in the open water of mountain streams in northeast Utah. In Colorado, the Barrow's is considered a rare winter straggler (Bailey and Niedrach 1965). But by far the bulk of the Barrow's goldeneyes winter along the Pacific Coast from the Aleutian Islands to San Francisco Bay. National Wildlife Refuge reports indicate that 400 to 900 winter off the Kenai National Moose Range in southeast Alaska. Audubon Christmas bird censuses reveal that almost half of the 2,410 goldeneyes reported for lower coastal British Columbia are Barrow's. Leach (1972) states that on the lower coast of British Columbia, the Barrow's occurs in larger numbers than the common. Within 15 miles of Vancouver, 3,388 were counted in December 1970, but only 75 Barrow's were reported for the Seattle, Washington, region, and only 1 farther down the coast at San Francisco Bay. Species composition in hunters' bags reveals that Barrow's made up 1.5 percent in Alaska, 0.2 percent each in Washington and Oregon, 0.3 percent in Idaho, 0.4 percent in Montana, 0.5 percent in Wyoming, and trace numbers in Utah and California (Samuel Carney). In contrast, common goldeneyes comprised 2.3 percent of hunters' kills of ducks in Alaska, 1.2 percent in Washington, 0.7 percent in Oregon, and 1.7 percent each in Idaho, Montana, and Wyoming.

If we assume that the proportion of the two species of goldeneyes is the same in January surveys as in hunters' bags, then the number of wintering Barrow's is as follows: Washington, 2,825; Oregon, 495; Idaho, 2,350; Montana, 2,050; and Wyoming, 250.

MIGRATION BEHAVIOR

Chronology

Griscom (1945) found the Barrow's goldeneye in the Northeast to be a late-arriving migrant in the fall and an early-departing one in the spring, surpassing the common goldeneye in this respect. Earliest arrivals in 18 years at Lynn, Massachusetts, included only two dates in November, five the first week in December, and all others later. In 9 of 18 springs, Barrow's left Lynn prior to the last week in March; in 4 springs they left during the last week, and in 5 springs they waited until April. Extreme dates for Barrow's goldeneye on Long Island are December 3 and 31 to March 15 (Bull 1964).

Mary Jackson reports that in British Columbia fall migration to coastal winter areas occurs in late October and early November. First arrivals are observed in the Vancouver area the last week of October. Adult males arrive in large flocks a few days before females and immatures, who arrive in smaller flocks during the next 2 weeks. The latest arrival of immatures in the Okanagan Valley in south-central British Columbia over a 4-year span was October 6-24 (Munro 1939*b*). According to Gabrielson and Lincoln (1959), the first arrivals on winter grounds in southeast coastal Alaska are as follows: Glacier Bay, October 10; Craig, October 11; Wrangell, October 19; and Ketchikan, October 28. Tardy spring migrants have been observed as late as April 20-May 24.

Barrow's leave their coastal winter areas in British Columbia from late February to early April (Mary Jackson). The first to leave are pairs and courting parties, with some yearlings accompanying adults in March and April to breeding grounds in the interior; however, most yearling females arrive in May, and some yearlings linger on coastal areas until late May. In the Okanagan Valley, Munro (1939*b*) recorded their arrival throughout March and as late as April 21. At Yellowstone National Park, Skinner (1937) recorded them making altitudinal movements to winter areas on the Gardiner River, arriving about November 11 and beginning to depart about February 25; males were the first to leave and were followed by females and yearlings.

BREEDING

Behavior

Age, Pair Bond, and Homing. Most Barrow's breed at 2 years of age, but Mary Jackson reports a banded yearling female with a brood and also believes that some individuals may not breed until their third year. Pair formation starts as early as December, and most Barrow's are paired before migrating in late March or April. A few pairs are formed after their arrival on the breeding grounds. Pair bonds are maintained until about the second week of incubation, when drakes desert their mates and gather in small flocks in late May and early June.

The Barrow's goldeneye returns to the same nest cavity year after year if it remains suitable (Mary Jackson). A female banded in 1950 in the Cariboo District of British Columbia was retrapped on the same nest every year from 1952 to 1955. (She was shot in the fall of 1955.) A banded duckling was trapped on the same nest 8 years later. Seventy-five females banded as flightless immatures were recovered a year later as molters; 80 percent were on natal lakes and 13 percent were on nearby larger lakes.

Home Range. The area encompassed by the home range depends upon the size and shape of the water area. On two large lakes inhabited by 38 pairs, Mary Jackson observed that each home range occupied 40 to 60 yards of shoreline. Lower population density resulted in larger and less well defined home ranges. Ponds smaller than 2 acres were usually not occupied; one pond of 3 acres contained two pairs when populations were high but only one pair when populations were low.

Nesting

Nest Sites. Barrow's goldeneyes commonly nest in cavities in trees, in nest boxes, and more rarely in holes in the ground. They have even been recorded as nesting in crow nests in western British Columbia (Edwards 1953). Mary Jackson reports that in British Columbia the goldeneyes often resort to pileated woodpecker and flicker cavities that have been enlarged by weathering. Tree species frequently containing suitable cavities include the quaking aspen, cottonwood, Douglas fir, and ponderosa pine. In Oregon, Chester Kebbe reports that Barrow's often use nest houses placed around lakes at high elevations in the Cascade Mountains. Swarth (1926) found young broods on alpine lakes in northern British Columbia where no tree cavities existed, indicating that nesting occurred on or in the ground. At Lake Mývatn, Iceland, Scott (1952) observed Barrow's nests on the ground, one under a tree, another in thick bushes. In the scablands of the Columbia Basin, Washington, females were observed flying to holes in rock cliffs (Harris et al. 1954).

As others have observed also, Mary Jackson has noted that groups of 2 to 20 adult and yearling female Barrow's make a joint effort to search for future nest sites. This searching occurred during the morning and evening, when the adult hens left their own nests. She reports that the search group may flutter around an unoccupied nest hole for an hour, or even around a stub or telephone pole with no hole. This behavior probably imprints the characteristics and locations of nest sites on the yearlings and influences their future activities.

Nest sites are usually located near relatively shallow lakes and ponds that have extensive beds of submerged aquatic and marsh vegetation. Deep lakes with barren margins support few breeding birds. Nest sites are usually within 100 feet of water, but two have been reported as distant as 400 and 500 yards. In one instance, a newly hatched brood was observed walking toward a lake 3 miles away. Nests consist largely of white down plucked by the hen from her breast during egg-laying.

Clutch Size, Eggs, and Incubation. Like the common, the Barrow's goldeneye deposits her eggs at a slow rate, averaging 1.5 days per egg (Mary Jackson). Intervals between deposition of eggs are as long as 3 to 4 days, especially at the start of laying, but late in the nesting season or when the clutch is near completion, eggs are laid on consecutive days.

The clutch size of 40 nests averaged 9.1 eggs, with a range of 2 to 13 (Mary Jackson, and compiled). Clutches of more than 15 are considered the result of two or more hens laying in the same cavity; as many as 24 eggs have been found in one clutch in Iceland. Eggs of Barrow's have been found with those of hooded and red-breasted mergansers and of a wood duck (Mary Jackson).

The eggs are almost identical to those of the common goldeneye. The shape varies from elliptical ovate to nearly oval, averaging 61.3 by 44 mm (Bent 1925). The color varies from a deep lichen-green to pale grass-green.

Ten clutches observed by Mary Jackson hatched in 32 to 34 days from the date of the last egg. All eggs in a clutch usually hatch over a span of 4 to 6 hours, seldom as long as 24 hours. Although incubation usually starts with the laying of the last egg, occasionally it begins 1 to 3 days earlier or later. Incubation is often premature in late clutches and is delayed, especially by cool weather, in early clutches (Mary Jackson).

Incubating hens leave their nests from one to four times daily for periods of 30 minutes to 6 hours. Most of them leave shortly before sunset and either 2 to 3 hours after sunrise or at midday. The drakes accompany their mates on their return to the nests for the first 7 to 10 days, the time they remain on the home ranges.

Chronology of Nesting. In the Cariboo Parklands, British Columbia, the dates of first eggs in 22 nests averaged May 6 and ranged from April 20 to May 26 (Mary Jackson). In northern British Columbia, near Atlin, nesting began about mid-May, according to an early report by Swarth (1926). Nest initiation embraces a span of 36 days in south-central British Columbia, midway between the 24- to 48-day span of the common goldeneye in the northeast.

Nest Success. Nest success of Barrow's is exceedingly high. In 31 nests with complete histories in British Columbia, Mary Jackson found that 29 hatched (93.5 percent) and further reported that 217 of 240 eggs (91 percent) in 39 nests hatched. Nine eggs were infertile, eight eggs contained dead embryos, one egg was broken, and five failed for unknown reasons. Four ducklings failed to leave the 39 nests.

Renesting. The high nest success and the brief span in which nests are initiated make it doubtful that any significant renesting occurs. Undoubtedly, some of the hens whose nests are destroyed during laying and perhaps in the early stages of incubation lay again. A clutch of a scant two eggs laid June 11-12, an unusually late date, at Williams Lake, British Columbia, was probably a second effort (Mary Jackson).

Rearing of Young

Broods. After hatching, young goldeneyes remain in the nest for 24 to 36 hours (Mary Jackson). When the hen utters a soft *cuc-cuc-cuc-cuc* call from the water or ground, as the case may be, the young respond by climbing the inner nest wall, jumping out, and fluttering to the ground. The female leads the collected brood to a rearing area previously selected.

For several days before the hatch and while the young are in the nest, the hen makes frequent visits to that part of the lake to which the brood is to be led and where they will remain for several weeks (Mary Jackson). Broods are remarkably sedentary for the first 6 weeks, but, when disturbed, they move to a new feeding area. One brood moved an astounding 3 miles overland to another lake. Brood hens vary considerably in attentiveness to their young. Some desert when their broods are only a few days old, others remain until the young can almost fly. By the time most broods reach 6 weeks of age, they are largely on their own.

Development. Ducklings have been observed diving and swimming strongly on their second day of life. At 6 weeks, they weigh about 75 percent as much as adults and at 8 weeks about 90 percent as much (Mary Jackson). When 6 weeks old, males are already 27 percent heavier than females. The young attain flight at 8 weeks of age during the period August 14-31 in the Cariboo District of British Columbia.

Survival. Because young in deserted broods often join other broods, the attrition in brood size cannot be accurately evaluated. Mary Jackson remarks that composite broods of up to 25 ducklings led by one hen are not unusual. These aggregations of ducklings are also indicated by brood sizes: Class I broods average 7.1 ducklings (84), Class II average 6.9 (114), and Class III average 7.2 (30) ducklings. The loss of successfully hatched ducklings from the time of leaving the nest site to attaining Class I age is 10 percent. The loss thereafter appears slight.

POSTBREEDING SEASON

Most adult male Barrow's goldeneyes gather in small flocks soon after deserting their mates and depart in early June for unknown molt lakes. In northwestern British Columbia, Swarth (1926) observed flocks of males flying southward in June, probably to molt lakes. According to Mary Jackson, only 5 percent of adult males remain to molt on breeding grounds, concurrently with flocks of yearling females. The flightless period of adult males and yearlings begins in late July or early August, before that of adult females. Flightless adult males in partial or full eclipse plumage have been trapped in British Columbia between August 7 and September 3. The flightless period of adult females begins August 7-14 and ends in early September. Yocom (1970) captured 53 flightless adult males and 14 flightless adult females on August 10, 44 miles east of Fort Yukon, Alaska.

Adult females breeding on sloughs move to larger but nearby water areas for the molt, whereas those on lakes usually remain there. The longest premolt flight of a banded female recorded by Mary Jackson was 25 miles. During the molt period, adult hens form loose aggregations in association with juveniles, yearling females, and the few yearling and adult males that have elected to remain in the breeding area. They migrate from molt lakes to the coast in late October or early November.

FOOD HABITS

The Barrow's goldeneye is similar to the common in the proportions of animal and plant food eaten. Cottam (1939) reported on the foods in 71 stomachs, collected largely from British Columbia, Quebec, and Alaska. A variety of aquatic insects, the most important being damselfly and dragonfly nymphs, caddis fly larvae, water boatmen, and midge larvae, made up 36 percent of the 78 percent that consisted of animal foods. Mollusks, mostly the blue mussel, made up 19 percent. Crustaceans, particularly amphipods, isopods, and crayfish, composed 18 percent of their diet of animal foods. Fishes contributed 1 percent and miscellaneous items 3 percent. Pondweeds, especially sago, made up 8 of the 22 percent that consisted of plant foods.

In coastal areas of British Columbia, in winter, the bulk of the food consumed by the Barrow's goldeneye consisted of salmon eggs and flesh, caddis fly larvae, and marine algae (Munro 1939*a*). On estuaries, blue mussels, snails, and marine algae were the principal foods. Goldeneyes in the interior fed largely on crayfish, caddis fly larvae, water boatmen, dragonfly and damselfly nymphs, snails, and amphipods. Munro's (1939*a*) detailed study indicated that the plant foods consumed consisted largely of seeds and vegetative parts of sago and other pondweeds, and algae.

Common Goldeneye

Bucephala clangula americana

Other Common Name: Whistler

VITAL STATISTICS

Length:	Male, 17.9-20.2 inches, average 19.2 inches (43) Female, 15.7-19.7 inches, average 17.0 inches (40)
Wing:	Adult male, 8.98 inches (53) Adult female, 8.26 inches (32) Immature male, 8.64 inches (32) Immature female, 7.89 inches (51)
Weight:	Adult male, 2.0-3.2 pounds, average 2.37 pounds (8) Adult female, 1.6-2.8 pounds, average 1.74 pounds (13) Immature male, 1.4-2.7 pounds, average 2.17 pounds (41) Immature female, 1.2-2.6 pounds, average 1.66 pounds (49)

IDENTIFICATION

Field

Often the whistling of the goldeneyes' wings will be heard before the birds are seen. On windless days when the air is dense from low temperatures, the resonant whistling sound produced by their rapidly beating wings may be heard 0.5 mile away and will identify the birds as goldeneyes without the need of visual cues.

Goldeneyes fly in small compact clusters, usually with 6 to 12 members, and, like other diving ducks, they fly very fast. No other duck flies so consistently in such compact formation. Their wing beats are rapid, and the wing arcs are deeper than that of the common merganser, a bird of similar appearance. Their short, thick necks and chunky bodies give the goldeneyes a blocky appearance, unlike the larger, more tapering bodies of common mergansers.

The dark head, white breast and belly, and large white patch on the back of the wing (extending across the secondaries onto the coverts) distinguish the goldeneye from other ducks except the bufflehead and the mergansers. Even in flight, the large puffy head with a round white spot below the level of the eye and top of the bill distinguishes the common goldeneye from the larger common merganser and the diminutive bufflehead.

On the water, the goldeneye rests with its head reclined, so that its white neck is not apparent. The knobby black head of the male seems to merge with the black back, the dark color extending along in a broad band through the tail. The white chest, sides, flank, and partially white scapulars contrast sharply with the black upperparts. Close up, the black-edged white scapulars appear like hash marks bordering the black back.

The females and immatures are similar throughout the fall and winter. Their dull brown heads, more round than the males', provide a degree of contrast to their dapple-gray backs and sides. Usually, the white on the coverts and secondaries of the folded wings gives the appearance of two small white patches on the sides. However, about a third of the goldeneyes I have observed showed no white patches because the gray flank feathers obscured them.

At the approach of danger, goldeneyes are more prone to dive than mergansers but are less likely to dive than ruddies. They take flight with fewer strides across the water than all other diving ducks—three or four strides and they become airborne.

At Hand

At hand, the black head of the drake assumes a greenish cast with a pronounced oval white mark between the eye and the bill. The eyes are a bright amber, and the black bill is about half as long as the head. The black back, rump, and tail contrast boldly with the white neck, breast, belly, and sides. The feet are a yellow-orange in both sexes.

Females are appreciably smaller than males, with brown heads, dapple-gray backs and sides, and white chests, breasts, and bellies. Their bills, a dusky gray, become tipped with yellow in spring. A third of the hens that I observed in mid-February still had all-gray bills. Immatures appear similar to adult hens until the second fall. As noted under vital statistics, immature males tend to be considerably heavier than adult hens whereas immature females tend to be noticeably lighter. In advanced transitional plumage, the brown heads of immature drakes display the oval white spots of the adults.

During the postnuptial molt into the eclipse plumage, the male assumes a coloration similar to that of the female—the head is brown and contains, at most, an obscure mottled white spot between eye and bill. The eclipse plumage starts among early molters in late July and lasts in late molters until early December.

The primaries, tertials, and lesser coverts of the adult drakes' wings are black, and most of the secondaries and the greater and middle coverts (except over the tertials) are white. The black primaries and tertials of the females and of both sexes of immatures have a slight brownish cast, and the lesser coverts are gray-brown. The tips of the white greater coverts of adult females are black and rounded; in immatures, the black tips are less pronounced and are frayed. Adult females have shiny black tertials; immatures have dull black frayed ones. Scapulars with longitudinal white stripes or white centers with dark edges indicate immature males; those without the white stripes but that may have dark centers edged with white indicate immature females (Carney 1964). Among immatures, wing lengths of more than 215 mm denote males, lengths of less than 210 mm identify females, and lengths of 210 to 215 mm indicate that the sex is questionable (Carney 1964).

POPULATION STATUS

Based upon aerial censuses of Alaskan and Canadian breeding grounds by the U. S. Fish and Wildlife Service and upon estimates by state waterfowl biologists, there are roughly 1.25 million goldeneyes during the early summer. Because of the types of habitats occupied by breeding goldeneyes and the limited sampling in their principal breeding range within the boreal forests, this estimate can only be a crude index of their abundance in North America.

Age Ratios

The proportion of immatures to adults in hunters' bags has ranged from 0.80:1 in 1972 to 1.87:1 in 1967, and averaged 1.34:1, 1966-73. Banding data are too few to permit a determination of the relative hunting vulnerability between immatures and adults. On the basis of the comparative vulnerability of age groups in other species, goldeneye immatures are from 1.5 to 2.0 times more readily killed than adults. A correction of the age ratios on this basis suggests that average fall populations contain between 0.7 and 0.9 immature per adult.

Sex Ratios

Perhaps because of the difficulty in distinguishing first-year immature male goldeneyes from females, few sex ratios have been reported. Visual counts of 1,515 goldeneyes in Minnesota during the springs of 1938-40 and 1960-61 revealed that 60.4 percent were males (Moyle et al. 1964). A slightly larger percentage of males, 61.5 (1.6:1) was found by Carter (1958) in spring counts of 2,733 goldeneyes.

Mortality

Little is known about the mortality losses of goldeneyes. The annual mortality rate for 258 banded as flightless young in Minnesota was 82 percent for the first year and 37 percent in subsequent years (Moyle et al. 1964). The imma-

Left, head of male common goldeneye. Right, head of male Barrow's goldeneye.

tures experienced the highest mortality of any duck banded in Minnesota, the older birds the lowest. Fifty-nine percent of the band recoveries from immatures were within a 50-mile radius of the banding station (Johnson 1967).

DISTRIBUTION

The common goldeneye occurs across the Northern Hemisphere with the exceptions of Iceland and Greenland. They breed almost exclusively in the boreal forests of Eurasia, Canada, and Alaska. Goldeneyes winter along the coast of Europe from Norway to Spain, the north coast of the Mediterranean Sea, the coasts of the Black and Caspian seas, and south to Iran. On the Asiatic coast, they winter from the lower Kamchatka Peninsula along the coasts of Korea, Japan, and China south to Taiwan. Although goldeneyes most commonly winter on the bays and estuaries along the coasts, they also frequent large inland bodies of water.

There are two races of common goldeneyes: *Bucephala clangula clangula* inhabits Eurasia and *B. c. americana* is restricted to North America. Two other species, the Barrow's goldeneye *(B. islandica)* and the bufflehead *(B. albeola),* are unique to this continent.

Breeding Range

The common goldeneye breeds across forested areas of southern Canada from Labrador and Newfoundland on the east to British Columbia and the Yukon Territory on the west. From there, a narrow range extends northwestward into central Alaska. Comparatively small numbers breed in Maine, Vermont, and northern New York. Larger numbers breed in northern Michigan and Minnesota.

The centers of abundance for common goldeneyes are the lakes in the boreal forests of Canada. In the eastern boreal forest, Labrador to central Ontario, goldeneyes are almost as abundant in summer as black ducks. Aerial surveys of this region for 7 years between 1955 and 1967 averaged 192,000 goldeneyes and 230,000 black ducks (Hansen 1967). These figures are uncorrected for oversight of ducks censused from aircraft. If goldeneyes and black ducks are overlooked from the air at the same rate (×3), then there are about 575,000 goldeneyes in the region from Labrador to central Ontario during the breeding season.

The western and northern closed boreal forest, extending from western Ontario west to British Columbia and north to Great Slave Lake, harbors an average of 475,000 goldeneyes (1.12 per square mile), 1955-73. The western open boreal forest, lying between the closed boreal forest and the tundra, has about 55,000 goldeneyes (0.20 per square mile). Although the Athabasca and Saskatchewan deltas support greater densities, 19.82 and 2.10 per square mile, respectively, their comparative size limits numbers of goldeneyes to 32,000 and 14,000. The Slave River parklands contain 3,300 (0.28 per square mile), the Mackenzie Delta 11,000 (2.22 per square mile), and Old Crow Flats 12,800 (6.49 per square mile).

Alaska contains a summer population of common and Barrow's goldeneyes combined of almost 90,000. According to James King, the best current estimate is that the two species are about equal in abundance. Gabrielson and Lincoln (1959) reported that the common goldeneye is largely confined to the Yukon and Kuskokwim river valleys. However, in some areas within the range of the common goldeneye, the Barrow's predominates. Reporting on bandings in the Fort Yukon and Tetlin areas, Hansen (1961) listed a total of 3 common goldeneyes and 1,521 Barrow's. All through the mountain ranges and along the coast, the Barrow's appears to be the predominant, if not the exclusive, goldeneye (Gabrielson and Lincoln 1959).

South of the boreal forest in the Prairie Provinces of Canada lie the parklands. About 22,000 common goldeneyes (0.24 per square mile) occur there during May surveys, and 5,000 (0.03 per square mile) are found still further south in the mixed prairie area. Probably the majority are nonbreeding birds, but here and there throughout this region sporadic nesting occurs amid scattered groves of trees. From 20,000 to 30,000 common goldeneyes occur in British Columbia, largely in the Cariboo and Chilcotin districts.

Perhaps 10,000 common goldeneyes breed south of the Canadian border. About 4,000 occur in the Upper Peninsula of Michigan and along Lake Huron south through Presque Isle County (Edward Mikula). They nest in the northeast and north-central regions of Minnesota, where their numbers are estimated at about 1,000 (Robert Jensen). A few have been found breeding in the Turtle Mountain area of North Dakota (Robert Stewart and Harold Kantrud). Montana contains both common and Barrow's goldeneyes as breeding birds; east of the Rocky Mountains probably all of the 1,500 found on surveys are common. Dale Witt has observed broods of both common and Barrow's in the Flathead Valley of west Montana. According to George Wrakestraw, most of the 1,000 goldeneyes that breed in Wyoming are Barrow's. At Yellowstone National Park, Robert Eng reports nine Barrow's to one common goldeneye. Among the 4,209 duck broods that have been recorded in Idaho by the Idaho Fish and Game Department, only 31 were goldeneye broods, all presumed to be Barrow's. The common goldeneye is not known to nest in Washington (Yocom 1951).

Migration Corridors

Band recoveries are too few to determine migration distribution for the common goldeneye. A further complicating factor is the short distance between breeding and winter grounds, thereby mitigating against determining patterns of passage from population distribution.

Fall and winter populations indicate an extensive movement from the interior to both the Atlantic and Pacific coasts. Much of the passage to the coasts must be a lateral one, followed by a limited passage southward down the coasts. Except for the Great Lakes and Mississippi and Snake rivers, there appears to be a light north-south passage across the United States. Almost all refuges report at least small numbers of goldeneyes during the fall. The large numbers of goldeneyes on the Great Lakes and on the Mississippi and Snake rivers suggest that there is some funneling into these waters.

There is also a passage from the interior of Alaska to the coast. Some goldeneyes continue southward down the coast to the Alexander Archipelago and British Columbia; others move out along the Aleutian Chain to its very tip.

Winter Areas

Only a small part of the continental population of common goldeneyes is recorded on January surveys. With a prebreeding season population of probably close to a million birds, only 220,000 goldeneyes of both species have been recorded in January. These figures suggest that several times the number recorded in January have wintered off the Atlantic and Pacific coasts and, to a lesser extent, in the Great Lakes. Because of the costs and dangers involved, only inshore areas are normally surveyed from light aircraft. Ground observations indicate that less than 1 percent of the goldeneyes observed wintering in the conterminous United States are Barrow's.

Slightly less than a third of the common goldeneyes found on January surveys occur along the Atlantic Coast all the way from Newfoundland to Florida. As shown by the 1,100 found in Newfoundland, the 4,400 in the Maritimes, and the 22,000 in New England, goldeneyes are hardy birds. Even so, the main winter ground, embracing some 40,000 goldeneyes, lies between Long Island Sound and North Carolina. Slightly fewer than 1,500 winter south of Virginia, including perhaps 100 that reach balmy Florida.

On the Pacific Coast, as many as 110,000 goldeneyes—half of the continental population—have been observed on winter surveys. The common species winters along the Aleutian Chain to its very tip, and from there south through the bays and inlets of the Gulf of Alaska, the Alexander Archipelago, the coasts of British Columbia, Washington, Oregon, and California, and rarely as far as the northwest coasts of Mexico and Baja California.

One of the larger concentrations of common goldeneyes on the West Coast (at least 12,000) winters in Puget Sound. Elsewhere on the bays of the coast of Washington, goldeneyes winter with 3,000 more on the Columbia and Snake rivers. About four-fifths of the goldeneyes in Washington and 52 percent of 2,400 goldeneyes reported wintering in southern British Columbia are commons. Aerial surveys in January, 1953-57, in southeast Alaska revealed an average of 11,000 goldeneyes. The largest number reported in 1 year (1953) was 32,500; 16,000 of these were in the Ketchikan area. Common goldeneyes make up 60 percent of the goldeneye kill in Alaska (Samuel Carney). Reports from national wildlife refuges in Alaska on waterfowl populations for September-December 1967-69 list the following numbers: 500 to 1,000 Barrow's, Kenai Moose Range; 2,000 to 6,000 goldeneyes (species not given), Kodiak Island; 25,000 common goldeneyes, Izembek; and 20,000 common goldeneyes (Aleutian Islands). Most of these birds are believed to remain through the winter.

In Oregon, almost all of the 1,500 goldeneyes wintering on coastal bays and the 500 wintering inland are of the common species, as are the 3,800 in California. Although goldeneyes winter inland throughout the Pacific Flyway, numbers are in the hundreds except for Idaho, where 15,000 occur. Most of these are on the Snake River, which remains open because of its fast current. A similar situation prevails in western Montana; Dale Witt reports that 500 goldeneyes winter on the Bitterroot River and 1,000 on the Missouri River, near Helena. Elsewhere in the Pacific Flyway, 700 goldeneyes winter in Utah, 300 in Nevada, 200 in Arizona, 400 on the west coast of Mexico, and 150 on the Baja Peninsula.

Next in importance to the coastal areas for wintering common goldeneyes are the St. Lawrence River and the Great Lakes. Although these areas are incompletely surveyed, about 20,000 goldeneyes are found during January surveys and by the Audubon Christmas bird counts. A combination of the two sets of data gives the following distribution: 1,200, St. Lawrence River; 10,000, Lake Ontario and Niagara River; 3,000, Lake Erie; 500, Lake Huron; 500, Lake Superior; and 14,000, Lake Michigan (including nearby inland lakes).

About 8,000 common goldeneyes winter along the Mississippi River from St. Cloud, Minnesota, to Alton, Illinois. Even with subzero temperatures, open water areas usually persist below navigation dams, enabling goldeneyes to winter far north of the customary winter grounds of waterfowl. They seemingly prefer the ice and cold to warmer climates, for in the Mississippi Flyway scarcely 1,000 winter south of the Ohio River and barely a handful reach Louisiana.

Goldeneyes fail to find much suitable habitat on the Great Plains, for only about 11,000 winter there. But even with the frigid winds that blast the Northern Plains, they are more abundant there than on the Southern Plains. In eastern Montana, about a thousand goldeneyes winter along the Yellowstone River, centered on Billings, and another thousand occur on the Bighorn River below Yellowtail Dam. A few winter along the Missouri River in North Dakota and 200 in South Dakota. Of the 5,300 that customarily winter in Nebraska, most are found in the western part of the state along the North Platte and South Platte rivers. Almost 600 winter in eastern Wyoming and 900 in eastern Colorado, but Kansas and Oklahoma each have fewer than 100. Most of the 1,300 that reach Texas winter on the large lakes in the interior, with seldom more than 100 reaching the coast. Reservoirs and the Bitter Lake National Wildlife Refuge attract almost 500 goldeneyes to New Mexico. A few, probably by accidental overflight, appear now and then in the Northern Highlands of Mexico.

MIGRATION BEHAVIOR

Chronology

The common goldeneye is generally regarded as one of

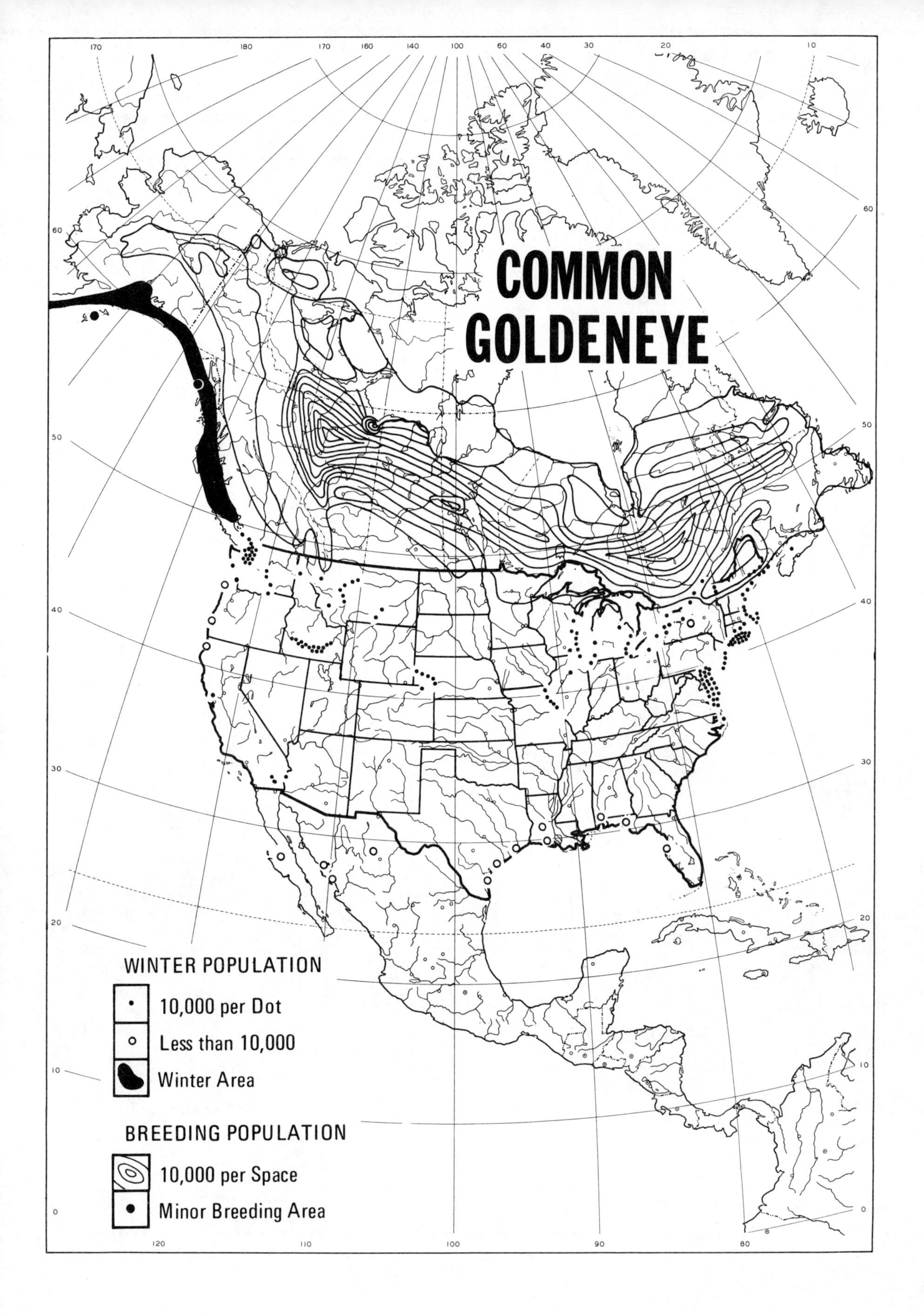
COMMON GOLDENEYE
WINTER POPULATION
10,000 per Dot
Less than 10,000
Winter Area
BREEDING POPULATION
10,000 per Space
Minor Breeding Area

COMMON GOLDENEYE

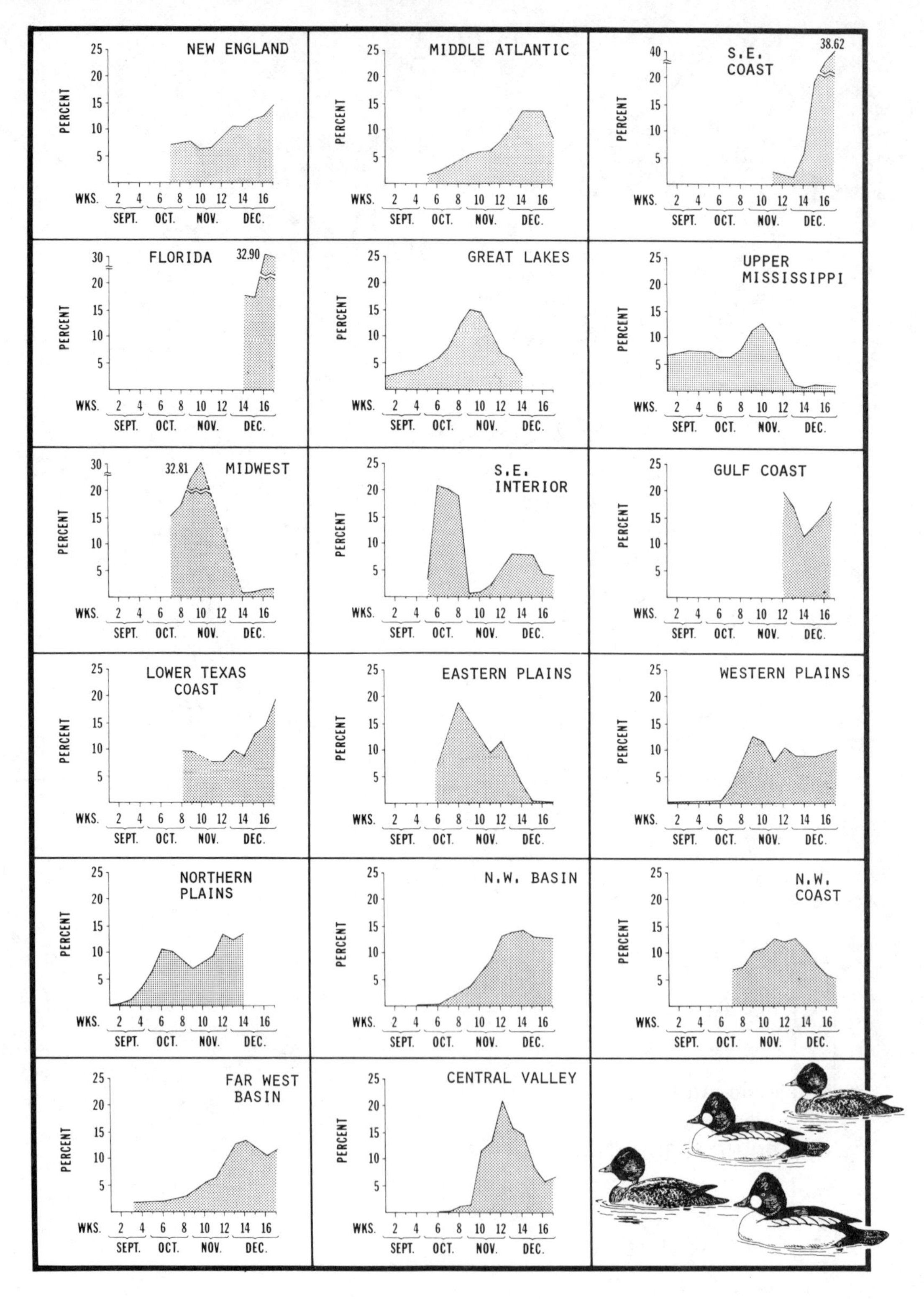

Fall

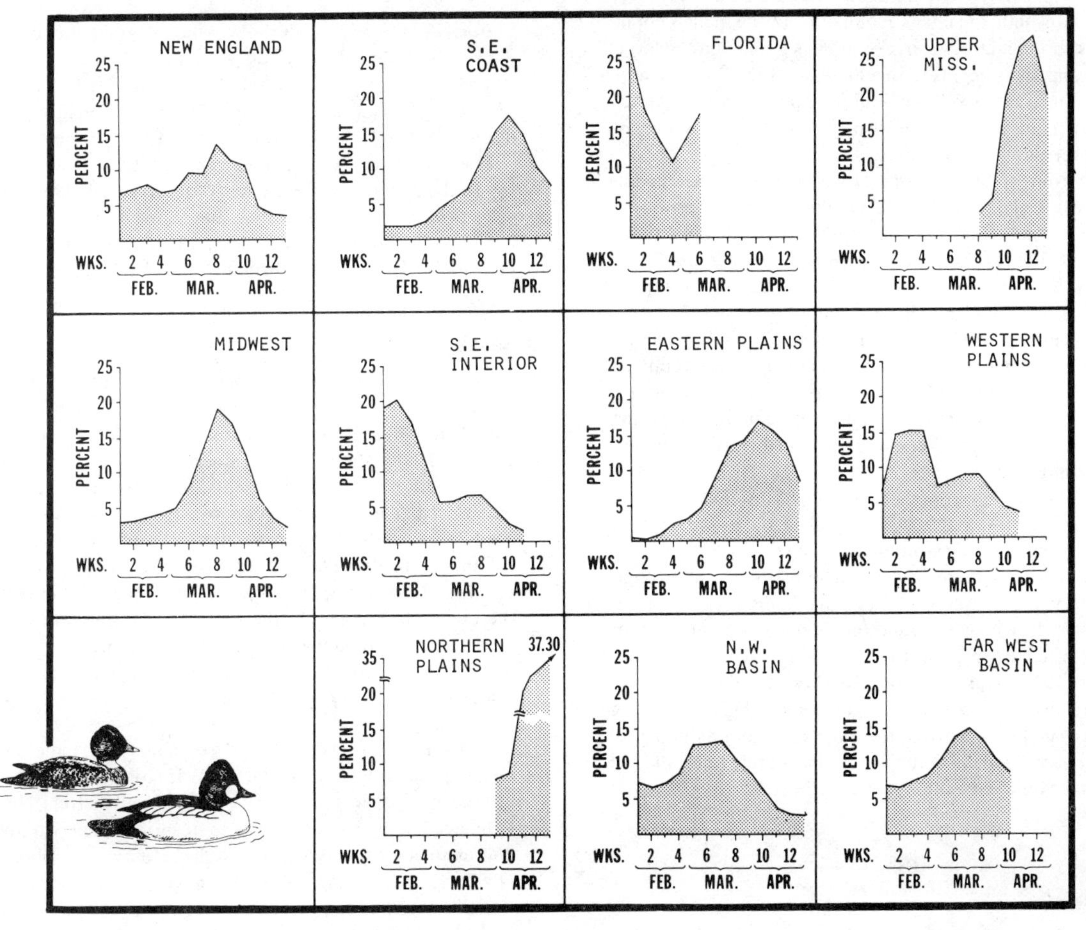

Spring

the last migrants to move south, a harbinger of winter, but small numbers of goldeneyes, especially immatures, appear on northern winter grounds in late October. Populations gradually increase through the remainder of the fall until shortly before freeze-up, when large influxes suddenly occur.

Goldeneyes appear on their winter grounds in coastal Alaska in late September and early October (Gabrielson and Lincoln 1959). They start returning to their breeding grounds in the interior in late April and early May. On the Athabasca Delta, Soper (1951) observed many thousands of goldeneyes in rafts from late September until mid-October; some flocks remained as late as November 6. They returned to this northern breeding area about the third week in April and early May. Soper saw flocks, apparently migrating farther north, along the Slave River, in late May.

In the border region of Nova Scotia and New Brunswick, Boyer (1966) listed the goldeneye as an uncommon migrant, October 10-December 12 and March 14-May 5. Griscom (1945) reported the early arrival of immature and female goldeneyes in Massachusetts coastal waters between mid-October and early November, with adult males arriving later. Along the Atlantic Seaboard from Maine to North Carolina, goldeneyes begin to arrive in late October and remain through the winter. They begin the spring migration in February, and practically all are gone by early April.

Small numbers of common goldeneyes breed in the northern part of the Great Lakes region; immature goldeneyes and perhaps some early migrants appear on censuses in September. Numbers, however, do not increase greatly until mid-October and reach peak levels in mid-November; the reduction to winter populations is completed by mid-December. The first spring migrants appear in mid-March, with a wave of migrants cresting in mid-April.

A few goldeneyes appear in the Midwest in late October, with a large influx in late November resulting in high populations through December. As soon as the ice on the large rivers and lakes begins to recede in late February or early March, migrants swell the wintering populations. The ingress of migrants continues through March, numbers dropping precipitously thereafter.

According to Sutton (1967), the common goldeneye occurs in Oklahoma from late October to mid-April. The northward migration starts in mid-March, with adult males the first to depart. All birds examined between March 25 and April 17 were females or yearling drakes. In the region of the High Plains, goldeneyes begin to arrive in late October, quickly reaching maximum numbers that remain through December. Bailey and Niedrach (1965) reported that the first goldeneyes arrive in the Denver, Colorado, area the last of October and that many remain until spring migration sends numbers of them northward from late April until well into May.

Goldeneyes appear in the mountain basins and valleys of northwest United States in late October; the numbers crest in late November and continue through December. Sizable numbers winter there, but small influxes occur through February and March to produce maximum levels in early April. At Lewistown, Idaho, goldeneyes are found from October to early March (Burleigh 1972). Extreme dates at Rupert, Idaho, are October 30-May 9. Gabrielson and Jewett (1940) stated that in Oregon goldeneyes were among the last ducks to arrive in the fall, November 14 being an early date. Numbers diminished rapidly after March 1, but at times some have remained until May 17.

BREEDING

Behavior

Age, Pair Bond, and Homing. Because yearling goldeneyes are garbed in immature plumage during the breeding season, it has been known for many years that they do not breed. Most young goldeneyes probably breed their second year. In a poll of waterfowl breeders, Ferguson (1966) had two reports that initial breeding occurred the second year, four reports of initial breeding the third year, and one report of a first breeding the fourth year.

At Departure Bay, British Columbia, Munro (1939*b*) observed courtship activity as early as February 11, but it was more intensive during March. In New Brunswick, 62 percent of the goldeneyes were paired when they arrived, March 14-April 7, and 13 percent were lone drakes (Carter 1958). Many unpaired birds were observed in courting groups consisting of six males and three females.

According to Gibbs (1961), male goldeneyes began to leave their nest area at Pierce Pond, Maine, in mid-May; the last ones left June 3. At that time, most nests were in the second week of incubation, indicating that drakes desert their mates soon after incubation begins. Prince (1965) also observed that males on the nesting ground at St. John River, New Brunswick, steadily decreased from the onset of nesting, and most of them had left the area by June 1.

Home Range. As with the wood duck and many diving ducks, the male goldeneye does not defend a general area but rather a small area around his mate (Carter 1958). During egg-laying and the early stage of incubation the drake waits for his mate on a water area near the nest site.

Like wood ducks, goldeneye hens exhibit a strong homing to the same nest areas each year. Johnson (1967) observed in northern Minnesota that 27 of 42 (64 percent) hens returned in the subsequent year to nest on the same lakes—and 50 percent returned to the same nest boxes.

Nesting

Nest Sites. Common goldeneyes nest in natural cavities and nest boxes. On the floodplain of the St. John River, New Brunswick, Prince (1968) found 16 goldeneye nests in cavities, 56 percent of them in silver maples, 38 percent in elms, and 6 percent in butternuts. The trees averaged 26 inches in diameter and 60 years of age. The cavities averaged 23 feet above the ground, with interior dimensions of 8.1 inches in diameter, a depth of 18.2 inches, and an entrance 4.5 by 8.8 inches. Two-thirds of the cavities were the bucket type, open at the top, and one-third were enclosed. Prince noted that goldeneyes were more prone than wood ducks to use cavities of the bucket type, and they selected more open woods, near the edges of fields or marshes.

Goldeneyes, as wood ducks frequently do, sometimes nest in peculiar locations. Carter (1958) told of goldeneyes attempting to nest in chimneys in Fredericton, New Brunswick. One went so far as to nest on a ledge within a church tower. Near Blackduck Lake, Minnesota, Johnson (1967) received reports of 41 goldeneyes, 13 of which died, found trapped in chimneys.

Both in Minnesota and in Finland, nonbreeding yearling goldeneyes have been observed exploring cavities and nest houses as if selecting nest sites for the coming year (Moyle et al. 1964, Grenquist 1968). In Finland, yearlings make these visits near the end of the adult hens' incubation period. As I have observed with wood ducks, yearling goldeneyes may be attracted to nest sites by following incubating hens.

House Use. Over the years 1958-60, Johnson (1967) checked the use of 141 nest boxes of three types for goldeneye occupancy. Two types, made of wood, were 12 inches square and 24 inches deep. One group featured a 4- by 5-inch rectangular entrance and another group a 3.5- by 4.5-inch elliptical entrance. The third group consisted of metal oil drums 12 inches in diameter and 30 inches high with horizontal entrances.

Johnson (1967) found that goldeneyes used 94 percent of the wood houses with rectangular entrances, 45 percent of those with elliptical entrances, and 45 percent of the metal oil drums. Nest boxes placed 18 to 20 feet above the ground were preferred to those at 10 to 12 feet, and those placed in the open along lake shores were used more than those placed at a distance from the shore and partially hidden.

Clutch Size, Eggs, and Incubation. Egg-laying is at a lower rate than by most waterfowl. Prince (1965) reported that on the same area in New Brunswick, goldeneyes laid at half the rate of wood ducks. He noted that one female laid five eggs in 10 days, one laid four eggs in 7 days, and another laid four eggs in 8 days. At Blackduck, Minnesota, Johnson (1967) found that 13 hens laid 66 eggs in 90 days, an average of 1.36 days per egg.

The clutch size of 75 nests in North America averaged 9.21, ranging from 5 to 15. The smallest average clutch of 7.6 eggs (18) was reported by Prince (1965); the largest average clutch was 10.2 eggs (39) in Minnesota (Moyle et al. 1964). Dump nesting occurs occasionally, when more than one female deposits eggs in the same nest, resulting in clutches of up to 19 eggs. In nest houses at Blackduck, Johnson (1967) reported that deserted dump nests accounted for 20 percent of the unsuccessful nests.

The thin-shelled eggs are elliptical ovate, 43.4 by 59.7 mm, with a dull pale green or olive-green luster (Bent 1925). Incubation in 11 nests occurred over periods of 28 to 32 days and averaged 30 days (Moyle et al. 1964), an average also cited by other investigators.

Chronology of Nesting. Gibbs (1961) observed that goldeneyes in Maine started nesting about mid-April and continued to initiate nests until May 8, with peak starts near the end of April. Along the lower St. John River, New Brunswick, Carter (1958) reported that laying extended from about April 7 to May 25. A later study in the same region by Prince (1965) gave April 26-30 as the start, May 11-20 as the peak, and the last nest initiation as May 26-31. Soper (1951) reported that egg-laying on the Athabasca Delta commenced the second or third week of May; downy young were first noted on June 16. The span of nesting in the common goldeneye is of brief duration, 24 to 48 days in the northeast, an unusually short time for nesting at these southerly latitudes.

Nest Success and Failure. There is little information available on nest success, especially that in natural cavities. In the St. John Valley, New Brunswick, Prince (1965) found that 10 of 20 nests hatched successfully. Of the 10 that failed to hatch, 4 were deserted and 6 were destroyed by raccoons.

Johnson (1967) reported that at Blackduck, Minnesota, 62.5 percent of 80 goldeneye nests in houses hatched. Nest success was highest (69 percent) in wood houses with 3.5- by 4.5-inch elliptical entrances, next highest (64 percent) in wood houses with 4- by 5-inch rectangular entrances, and lowest (50 percent) in metal oil drums. Nests were destroyed by raccoons, red squirrels, and starlings, and deserted because of dump nesting and human interference.

Renesting. Probably some renesting occurs when nests are destroyed during the egg-laying period, but because of the brief span of nest initiation, it is doubtful that many hens whose nests are destroyed during incubation have sufficient time to renest.

Rearing of Young

After hatching, ducklings have remained in nest houses 24 to 42 hours prior to leaving (Johnson 1967). Goldeneye ducklings leave their nests in tree cavities in much the same fashion as wood ducks. They jump out and flutter to the ground as the hen calls to them. She collects the brood at the base of the nest tree and then, if water is some distance away, leads them to it—rarely, up to 1 mile.

The broods feed farther away from emergent cover than those of marsh and prairie species. Carter (1958) observed in New Brunswick that 5.5 percent of all downy duckling broods (Class I), 15.5 percent of all intermediate broods (Class II), and 36.7 percent of all feathered broods (Class III) were motherless. Sometimes motherless ducklings combine in large aggregations of 20 or more.

Development. Goldeneye young grow at about the same rate as other large ducks. The ducklings are in the downy stage (Class I) the first 20 days, in the stage where contour feathers gradually replace down (Class II) another 20 days, and fully feathered but unable to fly (Class III) 16 days (Gibbs 1961). In Maine, the young can fly at the age of 56 to 60 days. Flight age was given as 56 days in New Brunswick (Carter 1958).

Survival. For some unknown reason, common goldeneye broods suffer unusually high losses. From an average clutch of 9.2 eggs, Class I broods average 6.3 ducklings (288). Class II broods sustain a 23 percent loss to an average of 4.88 ducklings (155), and the average for Class III broods is 4.71 ducklings (109), a decrease of 26 percent from the original brood size.

POSTBREEDING SEASON

Shortly after female goldeneyes start to incubate in May, males begin to disperse to their molt lakes. Near Fredericton, New Brunswick, Prince (1965) reported that most males had departed by June 1. The majority appear to be in their postnuptial molt in July, when they are flightless for 3 to 4 weeks. Shortly after abandoning their broods between mid-July and early August, some females leave their nest lakes to molt elsewhere.

Banding and population data suggest a general movement northward of both adults and young prior to the fall migration. On favored lakes, large concentrations develop. For example, aerial surveys by personnel of Ducks Unlimited found several thousand at Kazan Lake, east-central Saskatchewan, on August 17, 1951. On September 1, 1964, the number at Kazan Lake was estimated at 2,000 and there were 3,300 on Lake Beaupré. Gabrielson and Wright (1951) counted 116 common goldeneyes on August 24, 1948 near Fort Chimo, Ungava District, a tundra area well north of the goldeneye's breeding range. Near the junction of James and Hudson bays, many flocks of subadult and adult goldeneyes, including flightless ones, were observed on July 16, 1957 (Peck 1972).

FOOD HABITS

An examination of 395 gizzards of common goldeneyes from 26 states and 5 provinces (Cottam 1939) disclosed that 74 percent of the foods consumed were animal and 26 percent vegetable. Of the animal foods, 32 percent were crustaceans (mud crabs and other crabs, crayfishes, amphipods), 28 percent insects (caddis flies, water boatmen, dragonflies, damselflies, and mayflies), 10 percent mollusks (blue and other mussels, and snails), and 3 percent fish. Plant foods comprised pondweed seeds, tubers, and leafy structures, wild celery, and seeds of pond lilies and bulrushes.

On their important Chesapeake Bay winter ground, goldeneyes feed largely on crustaceans (mud crabs, crayfish, amphipods), mollusks (ribbed and bent mussels, little surf clams, snails), small fish, and the seeds, leaves, and rootstocks of sago and other pondweeds and wild celery (Stewart 1962). In coastal Rhode Island, goldeneyes consumed 82 percent animal foods, mostly crustaceans and fish (Cronan and Halla 1968), and 18 percent plant materials.

During late winter and early spring I have frequently watched goldeneyes feeding upon small gizzard shad in lakes of the Illinois River valley. Eighteen dives, timed with a stopwatch, ranged in duration from 11 to 41 seconds and averaged 30 seconds. A hooded merganser diving for gizzard shad at the same time remained underwater only 5 to 10 seconds.

Hooded Merganser

Mergus cucullatus

Other Common Names: Sawbill, fish duck

VITAL STATISTICS

Length:	Male, 17.0-19.2 inches, average 18.1 inches (31) Female, 16.0-18.0 inches, average 17.1 inches (23)
Wing:	Adult male, 7.7 inches (32) Adult female, 7.4 inches (22) Immature male, 7.4 inches (20) Immature female, 7.2 inches (13)
Weight:	Adult male, 1.6 pounds (3) Adult female, 1.5 pounds (2) Immature male, 1.4 pounds (4) Immature female, 1.5 pounds (6)

IDENTIFICATION

Field

Hooded mergansers are wary and retiring ducks, usually found as singles, pairs, and in flocks of 5 to 10 individuals. Although they may be found during migration and may winter on almost any small or moderate-sized body of water, they prefer wooded sloughs, streams, and ponds in swamps.

This medium-sized merganser—about the size of a wood duck—flies low and exceedingly fast over the water, with a rapid wing beat and most of the motion in the wing tips. The wing arc is shallow and below the axis of its body, and, contrary to published reports, the head is held slightly below the plane of the body. Its body is more slender than a wood duck's and its wings are narrower, but it has a similar large tail. Like the wood duck, the hooded merganser appears dark above and white below. A sharp eye can note the black and white markings at the rear of the inner wing despite the rapid movement. The crest, although compressed during flight, lengthens the head and gives it an egg-shaped profile; in the adult drake, the black head shows a white elliptical bar.

The outstanding feature of the adult male on the water is its large white fan-shaped crest bordered by black. Sometimes the crest is compressed, and then only a small triangular patch of white is visible. At other times the crest is frequently raised and lowered, attracting attention as it flashes like a signal light. Behind the head, two black fingers extend from the black back to the water. Usually only narrow portions of the tawny sides and flanks show, because the bird rides so low in the water that little is visible other than the head, back, and folded wings. On the back, in front of the tail, is a series of long narrow white bars that are visible at close range. These bars may be either straight or slightly sickle-shaped and are formed by the exceedingly long black and white tertials of the folded wing. These white markings are sometimes invisible and sometimes visible on the same duck, apparently depending on how tightly the folded wing is held against the body.

The drab females and immatures have russet-brown heads with backward-slanting crests considerably smaller than those of adult males. Their backs are dusky brown, and only parts of their gray chests and sides show because of their low profile in the water. At times, the white-tipped secondaries and white-margined tertials are visible on the folded wings, but at other times, even on the same birds, they are completely hidden.

At Hand

The adult male is a beautiful black and white duck with

tawny-brown sides and flanks. A long, narrow serrated bill identifies it as a merganser. The large white crest, surrounded by black, is its dominant feature. The top of the head, the neck, and the back are all black; the chest, breast, and belly are white. Upon close inspection, wavy black vertical lines can be seen on the tawny sides and flanks. The hindback, rump, and tail are dark brown. The bill is black; the eyes are bright yellow and the feet dull yellow.

Adult females and immatures resemble each other but immatures have smaller crests (or none). Their heads and necks are gray-brown and their crests reddish brown. Gray pervades their necks, chests, sides, and flanks, and brown-black their backs, rumps, and tails. The upper bills are black edged with orange; the lower bills are yellow, the feet are greenish, and the eyes brown.

Wings of adult hooded mergansers have a striking black and white motif crested by exceptionally long black tertials with white center stripes and secondaries that are black on the inner vanes and white on the outer, with basal black bars across the white. The overlying greater coverts are white at the tips, black at the bases. The middle coverts are light gray in adult males and black-brown in adult females. They are either brown or black-brown in immatures, although some males have one or more light gray feathers (Carney 1964). Wings of immatures have a brownish cast—tertials, coverts, and primaries—unlike the black wings of adults. The tertials and the greater and middle coverts are frayed in immatures, smooth and unfrayed in adults.

Adult males begin their postnuptial molt into the eclipse plumage in early summer. This plumage somewhat resembles that of females except that the heads and necks of the males become only partially mottled with brown (Forbush 1925). Adult males usually regain full nuptial plumage in October. Immature males retain their brownish plumage until the second winter, then begin to assume their nuptial plumage and complete it by April (Bent 1923).

POPULATION STATUS

The population of hooded mergansers in North America can be calculated only indirectly and crudely. A population estimate of common and red-breasted mergansers in North America in late spring, based upon aerial surveys of their breeding grounds, is 878,000. These two species make up 92 percent of the total numbers of mergansers found in winter, as derived from Audubon Christmas bird counts and from January surveys of waterfowl numbers reported by the U. S. Fish and Wildlife Service. Employing the summer population as a known quantity (878,000) compared with a ratio of 92:8 (common and red-breasted:hooded), the calculated prebreeding population of hooded mergansers in North America is 76,000.

There is little tangible evidence of the yearly status of the hooded merganser and of present-day numbers compared with those of 50 or more years ago. Most treatises of state bird distribution imply that hooded mergansers are not as abundant as they were earlier in the century. They have suffered from drainage of swamps and river bottomlands, from an increase in turbid waters that reduces their feeding ability, from lumbering practices that remove old hollow trees, and from other human activities.

Age Ratios

There was 1 adult to 1.3 immatures among 2,588 hooded merganser wings submitted by hunters, 1966-73, for age and sex determination. The great vulnerability of immature ducks to hunting suggests that less than half of the fall population is composed of young-of-the-year.

Sex Ratios

Examination of 1,127 wings showed a ratio of 1.85 males per female (64.9 percent) among adult hooded mergansers.

Mortality

Of 18 hooded mergansers banded on their nests in Oregon, 62 percent returned the next year, indicating a maximum mortality of 38 percent (Morse et al. 1969). Of 75 banded in southeast Missouri, 62.5 percent returned in a subsequent year, again pointing to an annual mortality of 38 percent (Hansen et al. 1973). Since some additional birds may have survived without being captured, the mortality rate may actually be lower. Thus, hooded mergansers have both a lower productivity and a lower mortality than wood ducks breeding in the same areas.

DISTRIBUTION

The only merganser that is indigenous solely to North America is the hooded merganser, but a few strays have appeared in Great Britain.

Breeding Range

The hooded merganser's breeding range extends in a discontinuous fashion from southern Nova Scotia west-northwestward across Canada to southeast Alaska. Although there are no definite breeding records for Saskatchewan, Godfrey (1966) believes that they probably breed widely and sparsely in the wooded areas of that province. The breeding records from Alberta are confined to the Rocky Mountains.

Gabrielson and Lincoln (1959) cited several breeding records for southeast Alaska: the Stikine River, near Wrangell, and the Chilkat River, near Haines. An extraordinary record is that of two broods on the Innoko River in west-central Alaska. From 2,000 to 4,000 hooded mergansers are estimated to breed in British Columbia, largely south of the Queen Charlotte Islands and Vanderhoof.

About 2,500 hooded mergansers are calculated to breed in Washington, generally dispersed over all the wooded portions of the state (Jeffrey and Bowhay 1972). Chester Kebbe estimates the breeding population in Oregon at

1,000, largely confined between the Cascade Mountains and the Pacific Ocean. Fifty-five nests were found in wood duck houses in Benton County, Oregon, 1965-68 (Morse et al. 1969). According to Frank Kozlik, hooded mergansers are uncommon breeders in northeast California in the same habitat frequented by buffleheads. They breed along coastal streams north of San Francisco and in the Sierra Nevada Mountains as far south as Yosemite.

Burleigh (1972) believes that the hooded merganser possibly breeds sparingly in both northern and southern Idaho. Waterfowl biologists Dale Witt in Montana and George Wrakestraw in Wyoming know of no recent breeding of this species in their states, but there is an old record for Wyoming. Although a few hooded mergansers have been seen in Colorado during the summer, there is no sound evidence of nesting (Bailey and Niedrach 1965).

There are several breeding records for wooded streams in the eastern Great Plains, and Robert Stewart and Harold Kantrud report old records of hooded mergansers nesting in the Devils Lake region of North Dakota. In recent years, broods have been seen on the J. Clark Salyer and Upper Souris national wildlife refuges, and two broods were observed on the Souris River between these refuges.

Marvin Schwilling reports two nest records of the hooded merganser in eastern Kansas: a brood was seen on May 18, 1966, near St. Paul and a nest was discovered on April 3, 1968, in a wood duck nest box near Pleasanton. Although there are no nest records for Oklahoma, Sutton (1967) believes that the hooded merganser may nest in the wooded sections in the eastern part of the state. It is not known to nest in Texas.

East of the Great Plains in Canada, the hooded merganser breeds in the southern and middle wooded regions of Manitoba; in Ontario as far north as Kenora, Lake Nipigon, and Gogama; in southern Quebec to Montreal, St. Cyrille in L'Islet County, and perhaps to Mistassini Post; in southern New Brunswick; and, rarely, in Nova Scotia (Godfrey 1966). Mowat and Lawrie (1955) found no broods in northern Manitoba but did observe five birds in eclipse plumage at Misty Lake. Although hooded mergansers constituted about 5 percent of the summer ducks along the Pagwa and Kenogami rivers west of James Bay, no broods were observed (Hanson et al. 1949). Limited numbers appear to breed in the Clay Belt south of James Bay in Ontario (Smith 1947), and small numbers apparently breed in southern Quebec. Todd (1963) cited records of breeding hooded mergansers at Lakes St. John and Mistassini as being the normal northward limit in Quebec.

The hooded merganser breeds sparingly all through the states east of the Great Plains as far south as Florida, southern Alabama, Mississippi, and Louisiana. In the New England states, Forbush (1925) reported it a rare summer resident in Maine, New Hampshire, and Vermont, and that it was not known to breed in Massachusetts, Connecticut, or Rhode Island. Miller (1952) found a number of hooded mergansers nesting in houses erected for wood ducks near Milton, Vermont, 1949-51. More recently, Bull (1964) cited four breeding records for Massachusetts, 1936-52; one in Connecticut, 1937; none for Rhode Island and the Catskill area of New York; two in New Jersey, 1949 and 1962; several old records for Pennsylvania; and two for Maryland, 1946 and 1954. Two pairs of hooded mergansers nested in wood duck houses each year, 1961-64, at the Patuxent Research Center, Laurel, Maryland (McGilvrey 1966*a*).

In Wake County, North Carolina, Hester and Dermid (1973) discovered several hooded merganser nests in houses intended for wood ducks. There are but two nest records 100 years apart for South Carolina—the latest, April 6, 1937, at Grays Hill, Beaufort County (Sprunt and Chamberlain 1970). The hooded merganser is listed as a possible summer resident in Chatham County, Georgia, and one has been found nesting in a wood duck house on the Piedmont National Wildlife Refuge in Jones County, Georgia (Odom 1971).

A few hooded mergansers remain to breed in Alabama as far as southern Clarke County (Imhoff 1962), but they are most abundant in the timbered sloughs of the Tennessee Valley impoundments. Strong (1972) reported 25 hooded merganser nests in wood duck houses erected in Lowndes, Madison, and Montgomery counties, Mississippi. At the Noxubee National Wildlife Refuge, Mississippi, Baker (1971) found 31 nests of hooded mergansers in wood duck houses, 1968-69.

A number of hooded mergansers have been found nesting in wood duck houses in Louisiana: one at Concordia Lake, Concordia Parish, 1951; one at Oak Ridge, Morehouse Parish, 1953; one at Black Lake, Natchitoches Parish, 1958; and one at Fletcher's Lake, Concordia Parish, 1961 (Smith 1961*b*). During the early 1970's, Hugh Bateman found a number of hooded merganser nests in wood duck houses each year in Tangipahoa Parish, north of Lake Pontchartrain. They have been found nesting in boxes on the Cross Creeks National Wildlife Refuge, Dover, Tennessee.

As many as 110 hooded merganser nests were found in wood duck houses at the Duck Creek Wildlife Area and the Mingo National Wildlife Refuge, adjacent areas in southeast Missouri (Hansen et al. 1973). In Indiana, Mumford (1954) listed 14 widely distributed breeding records of this merganser. There are seven pre-1900 breeding records for Illinois and a few in recent years. We found a nest in a wood duck house on Lake Chautauqua, near Havana, July 26, 1943. Richard Graber observed a brood of two downy young on Horseshoe Lake, Alexander County, June 18, 1970. David Kennedy has observed at least two broods there every year from 1970 to 1974. At Lake Odessa, near Wapello, Iowa, Dreis and Hendrickson (1952) found three hooded merganser nests in 36 nest houses in 1951.

Karl Bednarik did not find breeding hooded mergansers on Magee Marsh, Ottawa County, Ohio, in 13 years of breeding-season surveys until 1966, when three pairs were recorded. Since then, two to three pairs have nested there each year in wood duck houses.

According to Edward Mikula, the hooded merganser nests occasionally in the southwest corner of Michigan and consistently in moderate numbers in the northern half of the Lower Peninsula and in the entire Upper Peninsula. March et al. (1973) have calculated that 1,400 hooded mergansers breed in Wisconsin. Jahn and Hunt (1964) reported that the northern forested region of Wisconsin is the principal breeding area, with smaller numbers along the Mississippi River and the Kettle Moraine State Forest in the southern part of the state. Moyle et al. (1964) reported that hooded mergansers breed in most parts of Minnesota, but that they are most abundant in the northeastern third of the state.

The numbers of hooded mergansers nesting in wood duck houses in numerous areas of the United States may reflect considerably more abundance than the meager records of broods and of nests in natural cavities indicate. They are shy, retiring ducks, generally sparsely distributed, and are therefore likely to escape notice among the dense wooded cover along streams and in swamps.

Migration Corridors

Because of the extensive overlap between breeding and winter grounds, this species follows no well-defined migration corridors. The meager bandings of hooded mergansers reveal a pattern of migration that appears similar to that of the wood duck. Some of the birds breeding in the south migrate north after the nesting season; birds banded in Alabama have been killed in Michigan, Minnesota, Wisconsin, Illinois, and Tennessee.

Hooded mergansers banded in the Atlantic Flyway appear to migrate largely within that region; recoveries of Maine birds have been received from New Hampshire, Massachusetts, Long Island, Virginia, North Carolina, and Florida. Mergansers banded in Michigan and Wisconsin have been recovered in Tennessee, South Carolina, Alabama, Louisiana, and Texas, as if they had fanned out southward to a broad, ill-defined winter region. Many of the appreciable numbers of hooded mergansers wintering in east Texas must arrive from breeding areas to the northeast.

Small numbers of migrating hooded mergansers sometimes appear at waterfowl refuges on the Great Plains. And George Wrakestraw saw 150 to 200 on the Yellowtail Wildlife Management Area, Big Horn County, Wyoming, early in May, 1973. These observations suggest that they nest in wooded stream and lake areas of the Great Plains of the United States and Canada, for which we have no records. Hooded mergansers banded in the Pacific Northwest appear to make short flights southward to winter areas.

Winter Areas

January inventories of the U. S. Fish and Wildlife Service indicate an average of 235,000 mergansers. Audubon Christmas counts of birds suggest that 8.0 percent of all mergansers are hooded. Therefore, about 18,800 hooded mergansers are calculated as their part of the January merganser populations. Even though many thousands are overlooked, these calculations provide information on the relative winter distribution of the species.

Sixty-one percent of the wintering hooded mergansers occur in the Mississippi Flyway, 22 percent in the Atlantic, 11 percent in the Pacific, and 6 percent in the Central Flyway. In the Mississippi Flyway, hooded mergansers winter all the way from Minnesota, Wisconsin, and southern Ontario to the Gulf of Mexico, but only about 10 percent of these are found north of the Ohio River and the Arkansas border. Most of them winter in Louisiana, Mississippi, Tennessee, and Arkansas.

A few hooded mergansers in the Atlantic Flyway winter as far north as Nova Scotia and Quebec. They are generally distributed from Connecticut south into Florida, 46 percent north of Virginia and 54 percent from there south. The Carolinas and Georgia winter the largest number. Most hooded mergansers along the Atlantic Coast are on fresh and brackish water bays, with only small numbers on salt water.

On the Pacific Coast, several hundred hooded mergansers winter in British Columbia, particularly the Strait of Georgia. About 600 are recorded in the bays of Puget Sound and 150 in the interior of Washington. The 650 found in Oregon are well distributed throughout the water areas of the state, as are the 160 calculated for California. Fewer than 500 hooded mergansers winter in the Rocky Mountains; one of the more important areas is the Snake River of Idaho. Small numbers winter in western Montana, Utah, Nevada, and Arizona.

Over half of the 1,100 hooded mergansers that winter in the Central Flyway are confined to Texas, mostly in the northeastern part of the state, but small numbers reach the coast as far south as Brownsville. Oklahoma and eastern New Mexico winter several hundred hooded mergansers, and a few winter in eastern Colorado and Kansas. There are several records from Mexico (Leopold 1959).

MIGRATION BEHAVIOR

Hooded mergansers frequently migrate singly, in pairs, or in very small flocks. Probably because of this trait they readily decoy to hunters' blocks in spite of their extreme inherent wariness. It is almost a truism among hunters that singles and small flocks decoy more readily than larger flocks.

Chronology

Fall. All mergansers are late migrants, but the hooded is the earliest of the three. The sizable numbers that are present in the New England and Great Lakes states in September and early October indicate resident populations. The resident populations during September in the eastern Great Plains and the mountain basins of the Northwest are smaller.

Migrants begin to appear in the northern states in early November, reach maximum numbers late in the month,

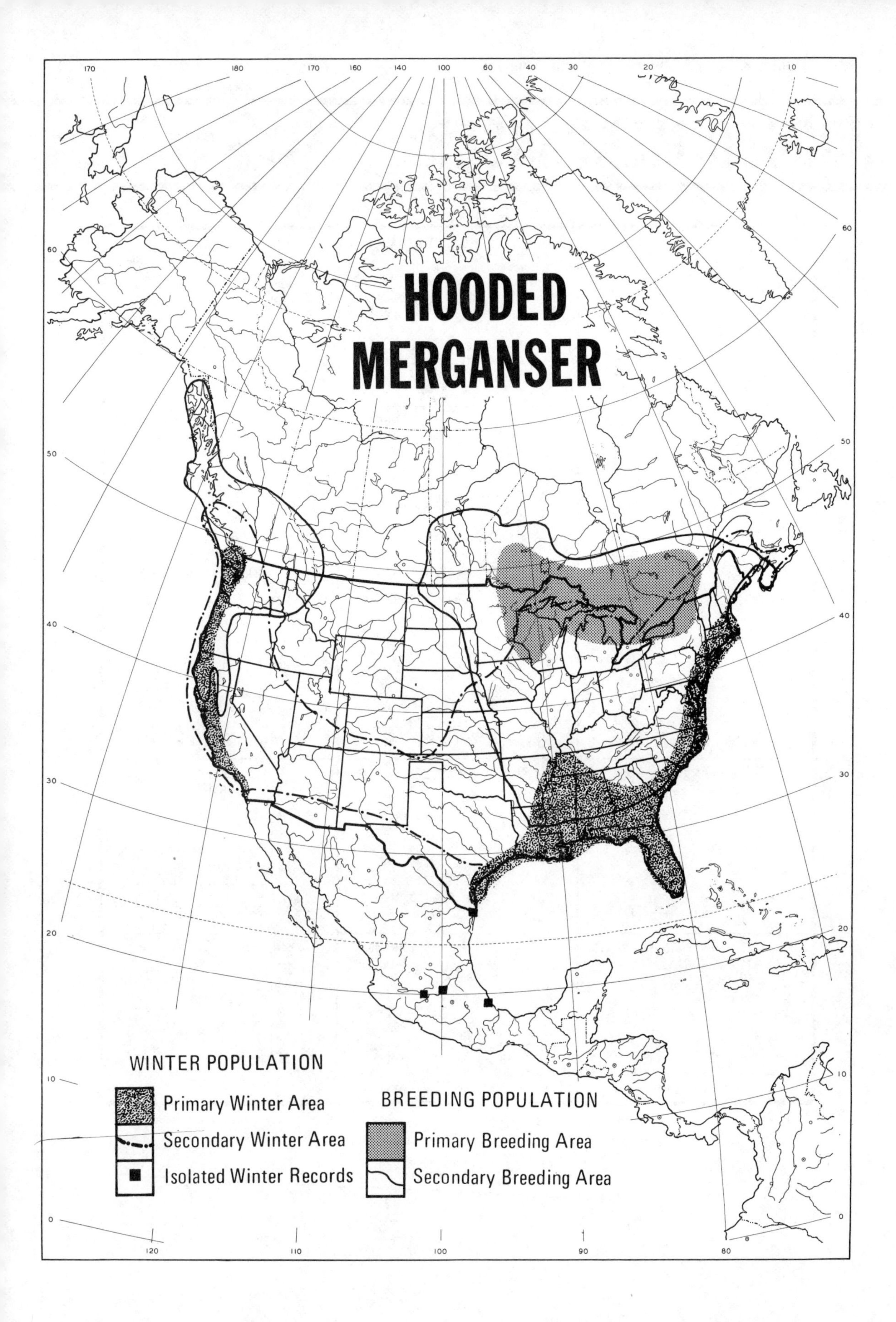
HOODED
MERGANSER
WINTER POPULATION
Primary Winter Area
Secondary Winter Area
Isolated Winter Records
BREEDING POPULATION
Primary Breeding Area
Secondary Breeding Area
170
180
170
160
140
100
60
40
30
20
10
60
50
40
30
20
10
0
120
110
100
90
80

HOODED MERGANSER

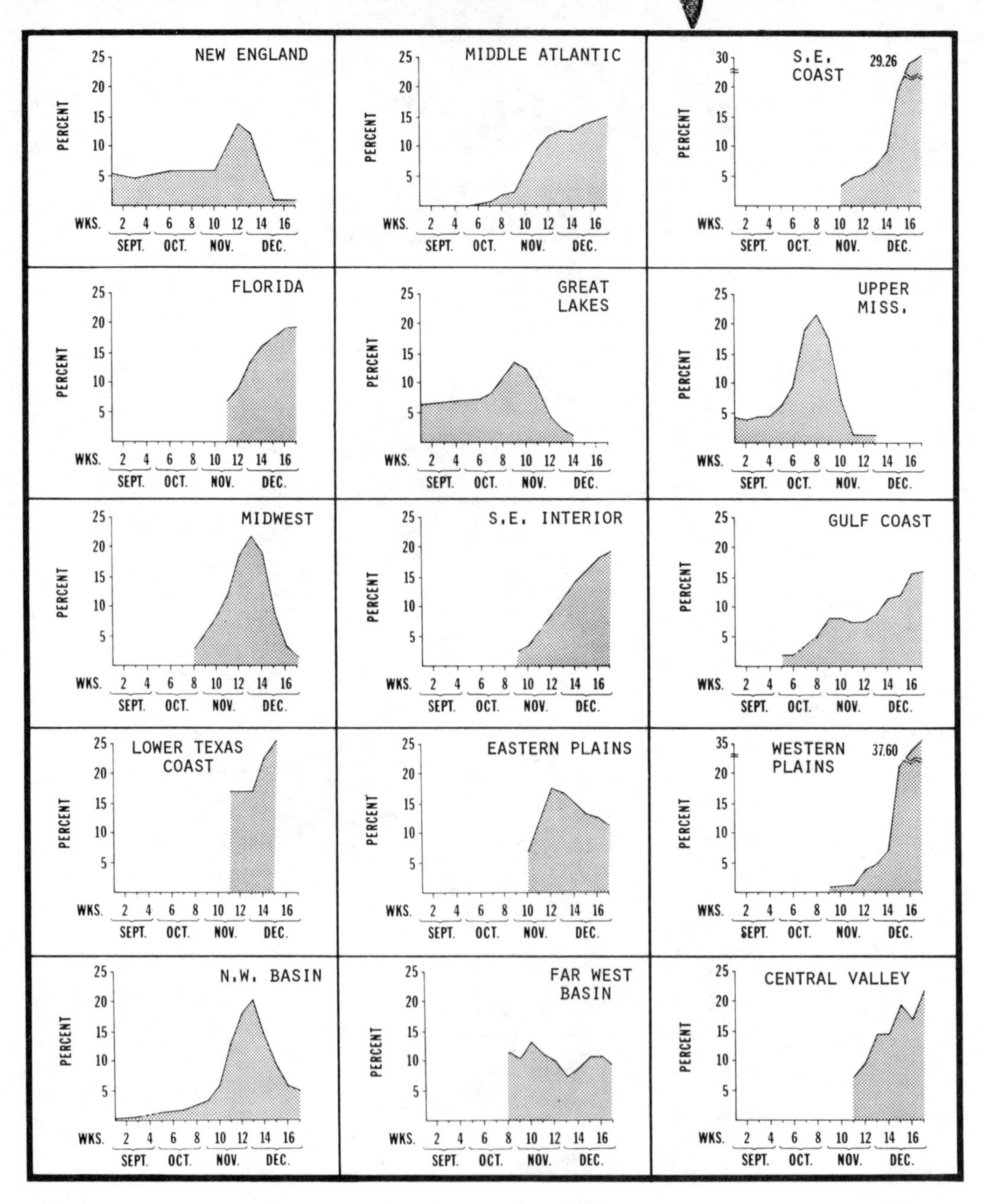

Fall

HOODED MERGANSER

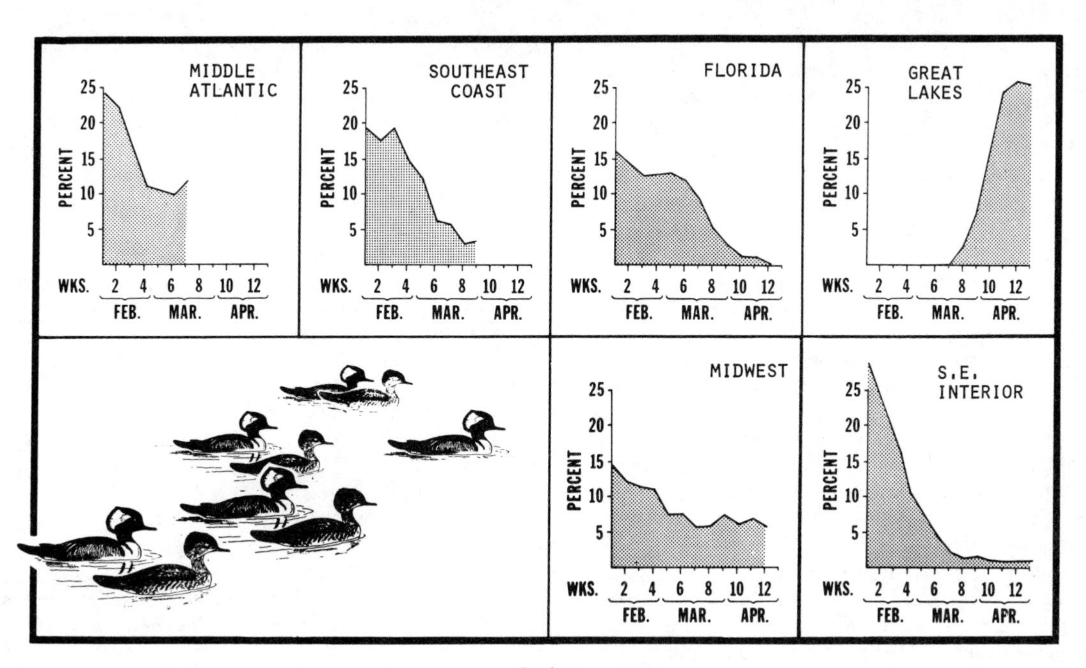

Spring

and decline to small numbers in early December. From New Jersey to Florida, hooded mergansers appear between late October and late November, depending upon the latitude. Migrants continue to arrive steadily, increasing the population through December. In the Midwest, migrants arrive in early November, reach peak numbers the first week of December, and decline to a minimal level by the end of that month. They begin to arrive on their principal winter grounds in the Mississippi Flyway in early November, with additional arrivals through December. Farther west, their arrival on winter areas is slightly later, mid- to late November.

Spring. Hooded mergansers begin to leave their winter grounds in early February, and a gradual exodus continues through March. They arrive in the Great Lakes region in late March, with numbers rapidly increasing to mid-April.

BREEDING

Behavior

Age, Pair Bond, and Homing. No hooded mergansers marked as ducklings have been found nesting as yearlings but have been found nesting as 2-year-olds. Morse et al. (1969) did not find any of 114 web-tagged ducklings nesting as yearlings in Oregon. In southeast Missouri, 10 females marked as day-old ducklings returned to nest, 8 as 2-year-olds and one each at 3 and 4 years of age (Hansen et al. 1973). All male birds accompanying nesting hens were in full adult plumage, indicating that they, too, were at least 2 years old.

The observations of Hansen et al. (1973) suggest that yearling male hooded mergansers display and form loose pair bonds. Most adult birds return to Midwest and more northerly breeding grounds as mated pairs. Males promptly disappear from nest areas when their mates start to incubate (McGilvrey 1966c, Morse et al. 1969, Hansen et al. 1973).

Hooded mergansers demonstrate a strong homing back to their previous nest areas. Along the Willamette River in Oregon, Morse et al. (1969) captured in the same nest areas 61 percent of the hooded mergansers banded in a previous year. Sixty-four percent of those returning nested in the same group of houses used the year before, and 82 percent nested within a mile of their former houses. Hansen et al. (1973) recorded a similar rate of homing in southeast Missouri; 45 of 72 adult females (62.5 percent) were known to return to the same areas. Six hens returned to the same nest houses, and 26 nested less than a mile from their former nest sites. Four birds nested over 3 miles from earlier sites.

The first nest sites of 10 birds marked as ducklings ranged from 0.2 to 5.6 miles (average, 2.8 miles) from their natal sites.

Nesting

Nest Sites. Normally, hooded mergansers nest in tree cavities in southern swamps, river bottomlands, beaver ponds, and along wooded streams and lakes. Both in range and habitat, their requirements are similar to those of the wood duck. One major difference lies in water quality. Hooded mergansers cannot find adequate food in highly turbid waters but wood ducks are less limited. Then, too, hooded mergansers are more retiring than wood ducks and more easily disturbed by man, so they are more prone to shun areas of human activity.

Because of the hooded merganser's acceptance of wood duck houses as nest sites, the natural cavities they select for nesting are probably similar to those chosen by wood ducks. These species are remarkably similar in size. As was pointed out under breeding distribution, numerous hooded merganser nests have been found in boxes intended for wood ducks. Use of artificial nest sites has been reported from many parts of the United States. In southeast Missouri, parts of Mississippi, and the Willamette Valley of Oregon, the hooded merganser's use of wood duck houses has been surprising.

Morse et al. (1969) found that hooded mergansers selected the nest houses that were nearest to the water. Fifty percent of the houses used were adjacent to water. Nest houses painted different colors had no effect upon their selection, so Morse et al. (1969) concluded that relative conspicuousness was not a factor in their use.

Immature birds, presumably females, have been observed inspecting nest houses in early summer (Leigh Fredrickson). This behavior phenomenon has also been noticed among Barrow's goldeneyes, and once in the common merganser.

Clutch Size, Eggs, and Incubation. The clutch size in 191 hooded merganser nests ranged from 4 to 21 and averaged 10.6 eggs; 83 percent of the clutches ranged from 7 to 13 eggs. Morse et al. (1969) considered that clutch size might vary as a result of age: clutch size in birds that had nested previously was 10.8; in those nesting for the first time, 9.4. Moreover, the clutch size decreased as the nesting season advanced. Birds nesting for the first time usually nest later than older birds.

Hooded mergansers frequently lay in wood duck nests and vice versa. The only way of determining which duck initiated the nest is by the species that finally incubates. Hansen et al. (1973) in southeast Missouri found 61 clutches containing eggs of both species; 27 were incubated by hooded mergansers, 32 by wood ducks, and 2 were unincubated. On the Noxubee Refuge, Mississippi, Baker (1971) found nine mixed clutches, four incubated by mergansers and four by wood ducks. He noted that the species laying the majority of the eggs was the one that incubated them. Morse et al. (1969) believed that more than one hooded merganser contributed to several clutches. They considered 1 of 15 nests to be a dump nest in 1967, and 6 of 24 in 1968. Clutch size in dump nests varied from 8 to 36 eggs and averaged 18.2 eggs.

In Oregon, hooded mergansers laid an egg every 2 days in 19 nests. In 11 other nests they deposited eggs in sequences of one each day for 3 days, then every 2 days for each of the other eggs laid in the clutch (Morse et al. 1969). In southeast Missouri, 117 eggs were laid in 205 days, for an average deposition rate of 0.57 egg per day (Hansen et al. 1973), almost identical to the 0.52 rate in Oregon. A small amount of down is added to the nest of decomposed wood after the sixth egg is laid, but most is added with the last two or three eggs.

Bent (1923) described the eggs as pure white unless stained, oval in shape, and measuring 53.5 by 44.9 mm (116). They are larger and more oval than wood duck eggs, so upon close inspection there need be no confusion between the two. Goldeneye eggs are pale green and longer.

Incubating hooded mergansers in Oregon left their nests to rest and feed during three periods—sunrise to about 8 A.M., 10 A.M. to 2 P.M., and 4 P.M. to dark. In Missouri, Hansen et al. (1973) observed that most females were off their nests between 10 and 11 A.M. and 2 and 3 P.M. McGilvrey (1966*c*) observed a hen fly into a nest box at full speed, closing her wings and diving through the entrance without any apparent hesitation.

Morse et al. (1969) determined that the incubation period, from the last eggs laid to the hatch, ranged from 29 to 37 days and averaged 32.6 days (32 nests). The incubation period of 27 clutches in Missouri ranged from 28 to 41 days and averaged 31.8 days (Hansen et al. 1973). One female incubated a clutch of eggs with dead embryos for 70 days (McGilvrey 1966*c*) and another for 74 days (Hansen et al. 1973).

Hooded mergansers and wood ducks have the same incubation period, for eggs of mixed clutches of the two species hatch at the same time regardless of which species does the incubating.

Chronology of Nesting. According to Baker (1971), the hooded mergansers at Noxubee Refuge, Mississippi, began to nest in February and March. Of the 102 dates of nest initiation in southeast Missouri, the earliest was February 9-13, the peak March 6-10, and the latest, April 16-20. Over 72 percent of the nests were initiated between February 24 and March 20 (Hansen et al. 1973). Near Laurel, Maryland, the earliest clutch was started on March 14, 1961, the latest on March 25, 1963 (McGilvrey 1966*c*).

In the Willamette Valley of Oregon, 50 nests over a 4-year-period were initiated at the earliest on February 20, reached peaks during the first and last weeks of March, and underwent a gradual decline through the month of April (Morse et al. 1969). The two peaks were considered to represent two age groups, and possibly, some renesting. Nest initiation over a period of several years covered about 62 days in southeast Missouri and 68 days in northwest Oregon. In any one year the span would be slightly less.

Nest Success. The nest success of hooded mergansers in natural cavities is virtually unknown. Of 222 nests in houses erected for wood ducks, success has averaged 74 percent, almost identical to the nest success among wood ducks utilizing the same groups of houses during the same time period but with slight variations according to locality.

In 148 successful hooded merganser nests containing 10.9 eggs, an average of 10.7 ducklings left each one. The average number of eggs for all nests was 10.6. The eggs hatched at a rate of 90.7 percent. Hansen et al. (1973) found in their study that embryonic deaths accounted for 63 percent of the egg failures, predation on individual eggs 11 percent, infertility 9 percent, and other causes, including freezing, 17 percent.

Nest Failure. One of eight hooded merganser nests in houses at the Patuxent Research Center was destroyed by a raccoon, two were deserted, and one had addled eggs (McGilvrey 1966*c*). In houses in the Willamette Valley, Oregon (Morse et al. 1969), only one nest was destroyed by a predator but 18 percent were deserted, largely because of the investigators' activities. Hansen et al. (1973) in southeast Missouri found the following causes of nest failure (in percentages): desertion, 35; black rat snake, 30; raccoon, 13; starling, 13; and infertility, 9. Two females were killed on their nests, one by a raccoon and the other by a mink.

Renesting. It is doubtful that hooded mergansers renest other than to lay eggs at different sites when their nests are destroyed during the laying period. The early disappearance of males from the breeding areas greatly limits the opportunity for subsequent mating. No marked bird has ever been found incubating a second time.

Rearing of Young

Broods. McGilvrey (1966*c*) observed that hooded merganser ducklings remained in a nest house about 24 hours before departing with their mother. Kitchen and Hunt (1969) studied brood distribution in the Nicolet National Forest, Michigan. They found broods on 5 of 7 river areas and on 1 of 40 lakes and marshes. The highest density of broods, 2.14 per mile, occurred on the Pine River; other streams averaged 0.33 to 0.80 brood per mile. Broods were most common where stream beds were composed of cobbled rocks and had densely wooded banks. These conditions characterized the Pine River, which had 0.75 cavity per acre compared with 0.42 to 0.59 cavity per acre on other streams. A review of other literature disclosed that of 65 brood observations, 71 percent occurred on rivers or river-related habitats, 18 percent on beaver ponds, and 17 percent on various kinds of standing water.

On the Seney National Waterfowl Refuge in Michigan, beaver ponds were used by 67 duck broods of seven species (Beard 1953). Hooded mergansers accounted for 18 percent of the broods. Of 47 duck broods of six species found on 41 beaver ponds in south-central New Brunswick (Renouf 1972), 10.7 percent were those of hooded mergansers.

Development. McGilvrey (1966*c*) records that two young of a hooded merganser brood in the wild reached flight stage at about 71 days, approximately the same as for the common merganser and the wood duck.

Survival. Because hooded mergansers do not appear to combine broods as other mergansers do, the survival of ducklings to flight stage can be determined with a greater degree of accuracy. Class I broods average 7.0 young (21), a reduction of 35 percent from the 10.7 ducklings that leave successful nests. Class II broods average 6.0 ducklings (52), and Class III broods average 5.2 (26), a reduction of 26 percent from Class I brood size and 52 percent from the number hatched. McGilvrey (1966*c*) described the loss of ducklings in two broods at Patuxent, Maryland. One brood of nine ducklings observed May 8-18 numbered seven ducklings 2 days later, and six ducklings on June 10. Another brood numbered eight ducklings at hatch and for the next 2 days, but by the third day only two ducklings were left, and they, too, disappeared by the fifth day.

POSTBREEDING SEASON

After deserting the female merganser at the start of incubation, the male vanishes into limbo. Bent (1923) stated that adult males enter a semi-eclipse plumage in summer and usually assume their full nuptial plumage in October. Males entering their second year do not acquire full nuptial plumage until November or December. Mergansers of both sexes apparently move farther north prior to the fall migration. Certainly, most disappear from southern and midwestern breeding areas until the onset of the fall migration.

FOOD HABITS

The food habits of the hooded merganser are only sketchily known, but they appear more diversified than those of the common merganser. On Patuxent ponds, broods fed in water only 10 to 20 inches deep (McGilvrey 1966*c*). Where broods fed in Michigan streams, the water was also shallow, 14 to 22 inches (Kitchen and Hunt 1969). According to Beard (1964), when ducklings were in the downy stage their dives were shallow and of short duration, but as they grew older their dives increased in depth and time span. We observed an adult hooded merganser and a goldeneye diving for gizzard shad outside our field laboratory. The merganser remained underwater 5 to 10 seconds, the goldeneye 11 to 41 seconds.

Cottam and Uhler (1937) studied the stomach contents of 138 hooded mergansers from various locations in the United States. They reported that fishes of little commercial or game value composed 24.5 percent of the contents, game or pan fishes 15.2 percent, unidentified fish fragments 4.2 percent, and crustaceans and aquatic insects 56.2 percent. The contents of ten stomachs from Michigan birds contained the following foods (Salyer and Lagler 1940): three stomachs, small yellow perch, sunfish, and bass; two stomachs, forage fishes; five stomachs, crayfish; two stomachs, bottom insects; and the contents of one stomach, a frog.

Two gizzards from ducklings 6 to 7 weeks of age contained mostly remains of crayfish, frogs, and dragonfly larvae (Beard 1953). In New Brunswick, White (1957) cited a record of three adults that contained killifish even though they were collected from a well-stocked trout lake. The contents of 10 gizzards from the Chesapeake Bay region consisted of Johnny darters and other small fishes, crustaceans, and insect larvae (Stewart 1962). At Reelfoot Lake, Rawls (1954) found that the contents of 11 gizzards were composed of fishes (81.4 percent), insects (12.6 percent), crustaceans (4.5 percent), and clams (0.5 percent). Hooded merganser gizzards from the Noxubee National Wildlife Refuge, Mississippi, contain large quantities of acorns (Dale Arner).

Red-Breasted Merganser

Mergus serrator

Other Common Names: Sawbill, fish duck

VITAL STATISTICS

Length:	Adult male, 16.1-18.1 inches, average 17.1 inches (4) Adult female, 16.0-16.6 inches, average 16.3 inches (5) Immature male, 17.1-18.3 inches, average 17.5 inches (4) Immature female, 16.2-18.6 inches, average 17.1 inches (3)
Wing:	Adult male, 9.5 inches (51) Adult female, 8.7 inches (8) Immature male, 9.1 inches (15) Immature female, 8.4 inches (7)
Weight:	Adult male, 1.4-1.8 pounds, average 1.56 pounds (4) Adult female, 1.3-1.7 pounds, average 1.52 pounds (5) Immature male, 1.6-1.9 pounds, average 1.76 pounds (4) Immature female, 1.4-1.8 pounds, average 1.63 pounds (3)

IDENTIFICATION

Field

On the sea, the red-breasted merganser is more numerous than the common merganser, but the latter species is much more abundant on freshwater lakes and streams. The red-breasted merganser, like the common, has a rapid, shallow wing beat that propels it at a fast pace. It flies in straight trailing lines, close to the water. Its small head, slender neck, and tapered body give it a streamlined appearance in the air. Large white patches, similar to those in the common merganser and goldeneye, span the inner wing in the male. The female has a smaller white patch at the back of the wing.

On the water, red-breasted mergansers ride low, with their tails awash and the water almost up to their wing tips. The male shows a striking wide band of white that extends almost the full length of the body above the water surface and a dark band across its chest that touches the water's surface. The head is usually drawn back, so that only a small part of the bright white neck shows. The dark green head appears black at a distance and is tufted at the back, unlike the smooth head of the common merganser. The female has a dusky gray back enlivened occasionally by a small white patch forward of the tail. Depending upon the degree that flank feathers cover the folded wing, the white wing patch is exposed or hidden.

Except for their smaller size, female and immature red-breasted mergansers greatly resemble common mergansers. They have cinnamon-brown heads and lightly mottled gray backs and sides. The two species can best be distinguished by noting that the white throats of red-breasted mergansers merge imperceptibly with their brown heads, whereas those of common mergansers are more sharply defined against their more reddish-brown heads.

At Hand

The bills of both sexes are long and narrow with serrated edges, bright red in the male and duller in the female. The male has deep red eyes and feet; those of the female are lighter red. The male's black head is glossed with green and has two tufts of bristlelike feathers protruding from the back of the head. In the female and the immature, the cinnamon-brown head has a slight protrusion of feathers at the back. A white band almost encircles the neck of the adult male except for a streak of black down the hindneck. Between the white neck and breast is a broad band of red-brown with black spots aligned in rows. The back is black, the rump gray-brown with fine black bars. Wavy lines of black bar the white sides and flanks, creating a distinct contrast with the white belly.

Two large white patches separated by two narrow black bars adorn the wings of the adult male. The white patch formed by the white middle coverts on the shoulder is margined at the wing edge by the dusky feathers of the lesser coverts. One black bar is formed by the black base of the white greater coverts and the other by the black base of the white secondaries. The outer secondaries, their coverts, and the inner tertials are black. The outer tertials are white with black margins. The primaries and their coverts are black-brown to black.

Female and immature wings have ash-gray shoulders formed by the lesser and middle coverts. The inner greater coverts are white with black bases, the outer ones entirely black. The speculum has a small white patch formed by the inner white secondaries, with a black base, but the outer secondaries, the tertials, and their coverts are black. The primaries and their coverts are dusky brown.

Adult males assume an eclipse plumage during July and August that resembles the coloration of the females except for the white shoulder patch. They gradually regain the remainder of their nuptial plumage through the fall.

DISTRIBUTION

As a single race, the red-breasted merganser's breeding range encompasses the Northern Hemisphere including the southern tundra and lakes of the boreal forest across Eurasia, Iceland, the southwest coast of Greenland, and, in North America, the area from the Labrador Peninsula northwestward across Canada and Alaska to the Bering Sea. European birds winter from the Baltic and North seas south to the north Mediterranean, Black, Caspian, and Aral seas. Asiatic birds winter from the Kamchatka Peninsula south through the Kurile Islands, Japan, Korea, the east China coast, and Taiwan.

Breeding Range

The breeding grounds of the red-breasted merganser generally extend farther north and not as far south as those of the common merganser. The principal region of overlap of the two species in North America is in southeastern and southern Canada: Newfoundland, the Maritimes, the southern two-thirds of Quebec, and most of Ontario, Manitoba, and Saskatchewan. Again, both species occupy the same breeding range in southeast Alaska and other coastal areas as far north as Kodiak Island. In southeast Alaska, Gabrielson and Lincoln (1959) considered that red-breasted and common mergansers breed in comparable numbers. However, outside the Alexander Archipelago, the red-breasted merganser is, for all practical purposes, the breeding merganser of Alaska. Although it breeds over most of Alaska including the Aleutian Islands, it is most abundant on areas adjacent to the Bering Sea (Gabrielson and Lincoln 1959). Aerial surveys by the U. S. Fish and Wildlife Service show that of the 3,000 mergansers north of the Alaska Peninsula, 840 occur around Bristol Bay. The remaining 2,160 are distributed as follows: 1,300 in the interior, particularly the Yukon Flats and the Tanana and upper Kuskokwim valleys; and 390 on the Yukon Delta, 350 on the Seward Peninsula, and 120 adjacent to Kotzebue Sound.

In eastern Canada, the breeding grounds of the red-breasted merganser extend through the tundra of Labrador and northern Quebec to central Baffin Island. This species also lays sole claim to the tundra along the southern and west coasts of Hudson Bay as far north as Eskimo Point and from there northwestward to Coronation Gulf and south through the tundra and most of the open boreal forest of the Northwest and Yukon territories (Godfrey 1966).

About 95,000 mergansers, almost exclusively red-breasted, have been computed (from aerial surveys by the U. S. Fish and Wildlife Service) on water areas of the tundra and open boreal forest between Alberta and the Beaufort Sea. Porslid (1943) found that the only merganser on the Mackenzie Delta was the red-breasted, which he termed a common summer resident both north and south of the tree line. Hanson et al. (1956) saw three red-breasted mergansers as far east as the Perry River, a short distance south of Queen Maud Gulf. They have been observed as far north as extreme southeastern Victoria Island in the central Canadian Arctic.

At Chesterfield Inlet on the northwest coast of Hudson Bay, Höhn (1968) saw several pairs but did not observe any evidence of breeding. Bray (1943) did not find red-breasted mergansers north of Chesterfield Inlet, including Southampton Island and the Melville Peninsula, but Soper (1946) observed small numbers along the south coast of the Foxe Peninsula, Baffin Island. Later, in the same region, Macpherson and McLaren (1959) saw numerous red-breasted mergansers and two females with nine ducklings.

Across Hudson Strait from Baffin Island, Gabrielson and Wright (1951) saw two broods on Ungava Bay and two broods on the nearby False River. Farther south, in the interior of the Ungava Peninsula, Eklund (1956) reported that the red-breasted was more numerous than the common merganser. He observed a brood on the Payne River and over 100 along the Whale and George rivers. Both species represented 11 percent of all waterfowl seen in the open boreal forest.

About 250,000 mergansers, most of them judged to be red-breasted, were found during aerial surveys of the U. S. Fish and Wildlife Service, 1955-56 and 1963-67, in the open boreal forest and tundra zones of Labrador, Quebec, and eastern Ontario (Hansen 1967).

Far to the south of its breeding grounds in northwestern Canada, there are two breeding areas of the red-breasted merganser: western Montana and western Wyoming. Robert Eng has observed numerous broods—as many as six in 10 miles—on the Missouri River from Three Forks through Canyon Ferry Reservoir, Montana. About 250 miles to the south, George Wrakestraw has observed broods of this species on the

Green River in western Wyoming. Disjunct breeding seems to be a trait of this species. Bull (1964) reported nests and broods on Long Island, New York. And in Russia, Dement'ev and Gladkov (1967) reported two colonies of breeding red-breasted mergansers far south of their normal breeding range—on Lake Sevan in Armenia and at Karkinit Bay of the Black Sea.

South of the arctic and subarctic tundra and open boreal forest, the breeding populations of red-breasted mergansers become so interrelated with those of the common mergansers that they are discussed in the section on the common merganser.

Migration Corridors

The bulk of the red-breasted merganser populations that breed in the interior apparently migrate toward the Atlantic or Pacific coasts prior to reaching their principal winter grounds, although a small proportion evidently migrates into the Great Lakes. Some remain there for the winter, but appreciable numbers continue farther south to winter grounds along the Gulf Coast and probably along the Middle Atlantic coast. I have observed migrating flocks of red-breasted mergansers along the shore of Lake Michigan just north of Chicago. The numbers appearing on water areas south of Lake Michigan in the fall suggest that the lake funnels birds for an overland departure toward the Gulf of Mexico. Between 1,000 and 2,000 appear to fly south from central Canada across the Great Plains to winter along the Texas coast.

Winter Areas

Red-breasted mergansers are predominantly a bird of the Atlantic, Gulf, and Pacific coasts, where they outnumber the common merganser. An average winter population of nearly 60,000 has been computed for the four flyways: 38,000 in the Atlantic; 14,000 in the Mississippi; 6,000 in the Pacific; and 1,100 in the Central.

The largest concentrations along the Atlantic Coast are in the Long Island region (9,000), the Albemarle and Pamlico sounds of North Carolina (11,500), and Florida (6,300). Somewhat smaller concentrations occur in Newfoundland (1,400), the Maritimes (1,500), the bays of the New Jersey coast (1,600), the Chesapeake Bay region (1,700), and the coast of South Carolina (1,800). Fewer than 1,000 winter along the New England coast.

On the Pacific Coast, red-breasted mergansers are distributed as follows: 900, British Columbia; 1,700, Washington; 250, Oregon; 1,000, California; and 1,400, Baja California, Mexico. Unknown but large numbers winter in southeastern Alaska, and small numbers appear as far west as the islands of Adak and Amchitka in the Aleutians (Gabrielson and Lincoln 1959).

A small population of red-breasted mergansers winters in the mountain states: 400 in Nevada, 300 in Utah, and a few in Montana and Idaho. These birds may originate from the breeding populations on the Missouri River in western Montana and the Green River in western Wyoming.

About three-fourths of the 14,000 red-breasted mergansers that winter in the Mississippi Flyway frequent the Gulf Coast from Mobile Bay west to Sabine Lake. Almost 10,000 concentrate on the brackish and saline bays of Louisiana. Although small numbers winter dispersed among reservoirs between the Great Lakes and the Gulf, the Great Lakes, with a wintering population of 1,300, constitute the only other ground of importance. A sprinkling of red-breasted mergansers winter north of the Gulf Coast in the Central Flyway, but about 98 percent of the 1,200 calculated for this flyway are confined to the Texas coast.

MIGRATION BEHAVIOR

Red-breasted mergansers usually migrate in small flocks of 5 to 15. Along the coasts, the migration appears to be diurnal but inland across the country it evidently occurs at night.

Chronology

Fall. On the Middle Atlantic coast, red-breasted mergansers appear in numbers in early November, with continued influxes swelling the population until late in the month. On the southeast coast, winter populations arrive en masse about the third week of November. Even though large numbers arrive in Florida in early December, additional migrants continue to increase the winter population through the month. An abrupt passage occurs through the Great Lakes region the first 2 weeks in November and apparently represents birds bound for the Middle Atlantic coast. In the Midwest, the fall migrants appear in small numbers in mid-November, but the main passage does not occur until December. Red-breasted mergansers begin to arrive in the Deep South in early November, increasing in abundance through December.

In the northern Intermountain valleys, a large part of the migrants, but still relatively small numbers, appear in mid-November. Far to the south in the Imperial Valley region, a flood of migrants appears in early December.

For the New York City area, Bull (1964) listed large numbers for several dates in late November up to March 11. Stewart (1962) reported that in the Chesapeake Bay region, peak fall migration occurs between November 1 and 30 and peak spring migration from March 25 to April 25.

Imhoff (1962) listed dates of migrants in Alabama from as early as October 18 to as late as May 26, with some nonbreeding birds being found in summer. According to Lowery (1955), the red-breasted merganser is moderately common in Louisiana from late October to

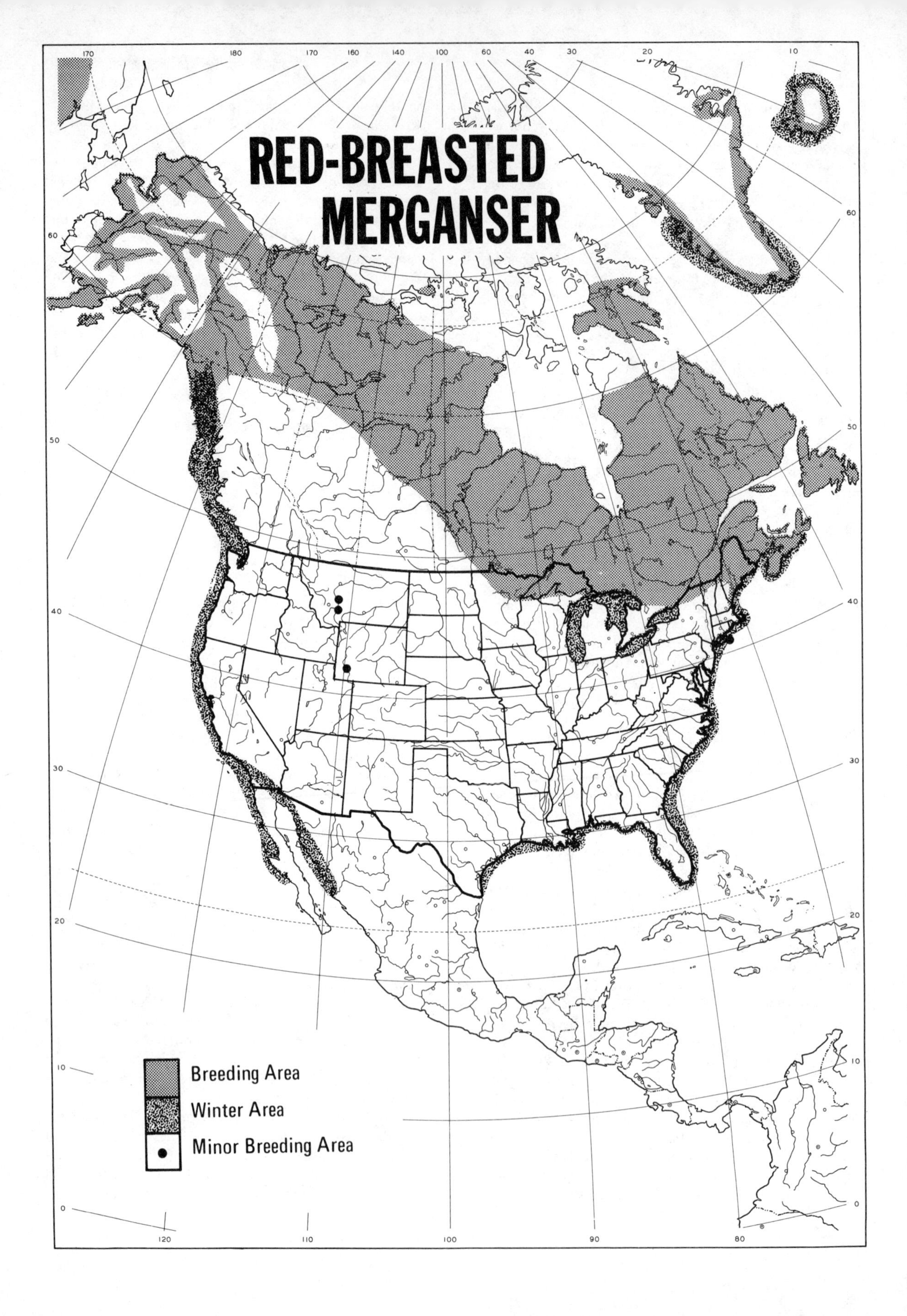
RED-BREASTED
MERGANSER
Breeding Area
Winter Area
Minor Breeding Area

the first of May. Sutton (1967) cited most records for Oklahoma between November 11 and May 31.

Migrating red-breasted mergansers appear in Washington in mid-October (Jewett et al. 1953). Nonbreeding birds have been observed there during the summer. The earliest fall date for Oregon is November 22; the latest spring date, May 23 (Gabrielson and Jewett 1940).

Spring. As some of the dates previously cited indicate, the red-breasted merganser migrates north in late spring—much later than the common merganser. Its later chronology of breeding follows the same pattern. Dates of arrival in Far North breeding grounds are May 24, Churchill, Manitoba; June 4 and 14, Baffin Island; June 9 and July 5, Perry River; May 25-June 10, Mackenzie Delta; May 20, Old Crow, Yukon Territory; May 25, Anaktuvuk Pass, Alaska; and May 11-21, Hooper Bay, Alaska.

BREEDING

Behavior

Age, Pair Bond, and Homing. Red-breasted mergansers are not known to breed before their second year. As yearlings, males still retain much of their immature plumage and do not acquire full nuptial plumage until their second fall. Immatures in Russia migrate north later than adults and do not reach their natal areas in the first year of life (Dement'ev and Gladkov 1967). Mergansers arrive on their Russian nesting grounds in pairs, frequently occupying the same nest sites several years in succession, and apparently desert their mates early in the incubation period. In Nova Scotia, most males have left their breeding areas by mid-June (White 1957).

Nesting

Nest Sites. Unlike the common and hooded mergansers that usually nest in tree cavities, red-breasted mergansers nest on the ground in highly diversified sites. They have been found nesting in marshes, on rocky islets, on vegetated islands in large lakes, in bank recesses, and under piles of driftwood. On the Mirage Islands in Great Slave Lake, Weller et al. (1969) found six nests, all in dense shrubbery—four were among ground-level boughs of spruce, one was under a rock partly hidden by gooseberry bushes, and one was amid Labrador tea shrubs. At Hooper Bay, Alaska, Brandt (1943) found them nesting near tundra ponds screened by long grass and even in an abandoned Eskimoo igloo. Bent (1923) reported large numbers nesting on Seal Island in the Gulf of St. Lawrence. Seal Island is a high island of red sandstone covered by a dense forest of spruce and firs under which the nests were placed. The nests were usually within a few yards of water but sometimes were as far as 50 yards inland. Bent (1923) described one nest as a hollow in the ground, 12 to 14 inches on the outside and 7 to 8 inches on the inside, profusely lined with gray down.

Like many other ducks, red-breasted mergansers lay eggs in nests of other ducks and vice versa. On islands in Lake Michigan, near the Door Peninsula, Pelzl (1971) found one to seven merganser eggs in five nests of other species—mallard, gadwall, and lesser scaup. Weller et al. (1969) found two greater scaup eggs in a red-breasted merganser nest on an island in Great Slave Lake.

Clutch Size, Eggs, and Incubation. Nests reported in North America have held from 5 to 11 eggs and have averaged 7.8 (20). Bengtson (1971) at Lake Mývatn, Iceland, 1961-70, found 158 clutches of red-breasted mergansers that averaged 9.5 eggs. Johnstone (1970) reported clutch sizes of 8 to 10 and an incubation period of 30 days for confined mergansers at Slimbridge, England.

The olive-buff eggs are elliptical ovate to elongate ovate and measure 64.5 by 45 mm (Bent 1923).

Chronology of Nesting. For uniformity, brood chronology has been converted to the date that egg-laying was initiated and combined with nest dates. Forty days were used as the interval from laying of the first egg to the hatch. On the Magdalen Islands, Quebec, nest initiation began June 13 and 14 (Bent 1923); on Cape Breton Island, Nova Scotia, May 24-June 11 (Erskine 1972*c*); on the Labrador Peninsula, Quebec, June 21 (Todd 1963); at Ungava Bay, Quebec, June 20 (Gabrielson and Wright 1951); in southern Keewatin District, June 20-July 1 (Mowat and Lawrie 1955); and in southwestern Yukon Territory, June 28 (Drury 1953). Dates in Alaska range from May 30 to July 20 (Gabrielson and Lincoln 1959).

Red-breasted mergansers nest considerably later than common mergansers. According to Erskine's 1972*c*) calculations, the earliest common merganser nest on Cape Breton Island hatched May 29; the earliest red-breasted merganser nest hatched July 3. Three-fourths of the nests of common mergansers hatched before the first hatch of red-breasted mergansers, but the commons' span of hatching covered a longer period.

Nest Success and Failure. As with so many sea ducks, little is known about the nest success of the red-breasted merganser. On the Mirage Islands in Great Slave Lake, Weller et al. (1969) found shells of red-breasted merganser eggs, suggesting predation by ravens.

Renesting. Because of the late nesting of the red-breasted merganser and its generally Subarctic and Arctic breeding range, it is doubtful that renesting occurs. Nevertheless, records of extremely late broods raise the possibility. On September 3, 1944, a brood of seven downy young was observed on Amchitka Island, Aleutians (Gabrielson and Lincoln 1959). A female and a brood of six almost full-grown young were collected in September 1933 on the Mackenzie Delta (Porslid 1943).

RED-BREASTED MERGANSER

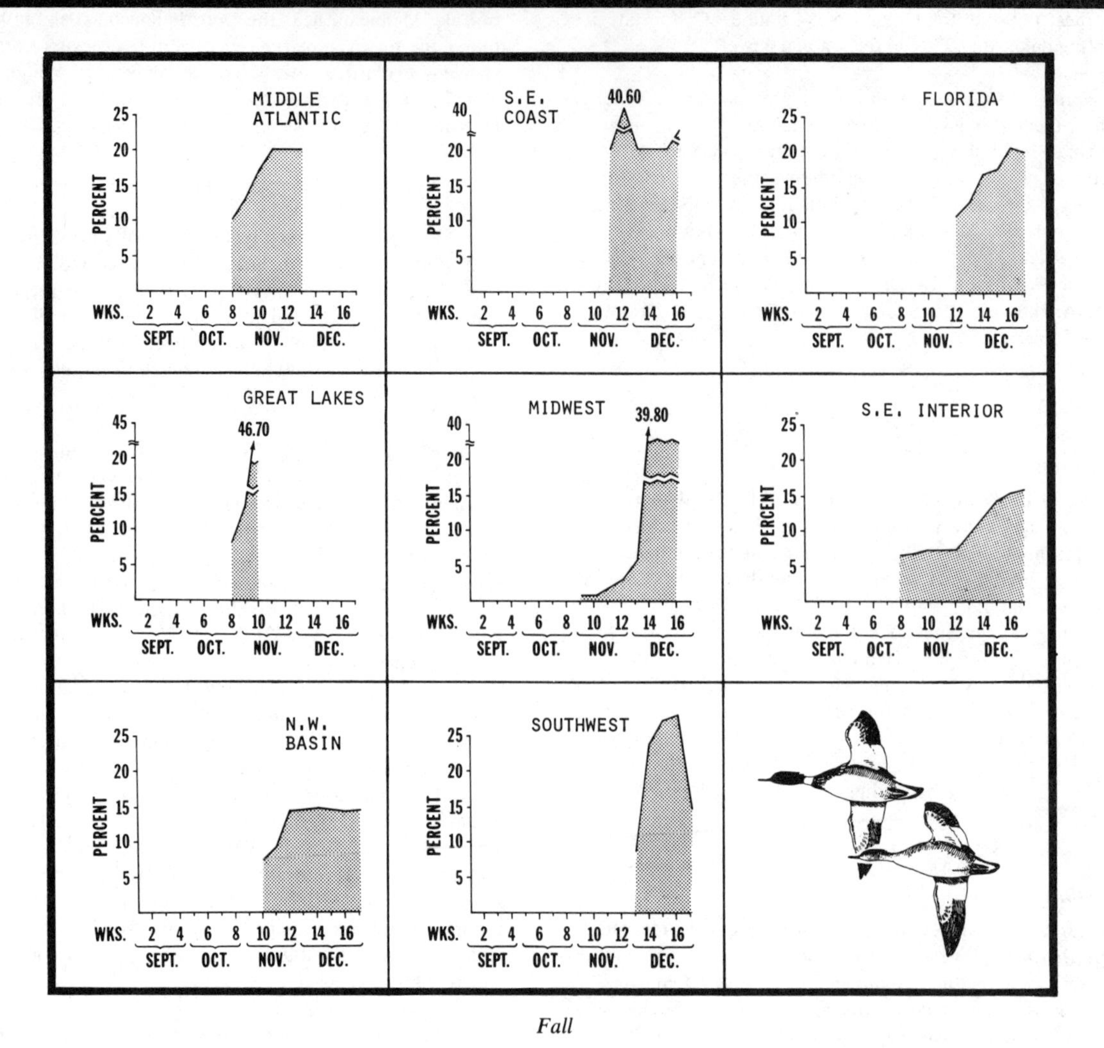

Fall

Rearing of Young

Broods. Some broods combine to form groups of unusual size, often accompanied by a single female. One female was observed with 26 young in southeastern Alaska (Gabrielson and Lincoln 1959). At Cape Breton Island, White (1957) frequently observed a female with 21 small ducklings. Dement'ev and Gladkov (1967) reported that in Russia two to three broods may combine to form pods of 16 to 24 ducklings accompanied by several females. They noted one flock of over 100 ducklings of various sizes in the company of adults.

Individual brood sizes of downy young in North America range from 3 to 13 and average 7.8 (9). In Nova Scotia, White (1957) often noted numerous red-breasted merganser broods numbering 12 to 14, larger than common merganser broods. Because such large clutch sizes appear to be unusual, White probably observed many combined broods.

Development. The time required for this species to reach flight stage is unknown. Presumably it is less than the 65 days or more required by the common merganser, because the red-breasted nests later and most of its breeding range is farther north. If those breeding in the Far North required 65 or more days for fledging, large numbers would be flightless at freeze-up.

POSTBREEDING SEASON

Leaving the breeding grounds in late June, large numbers of males gather in bays and estuarine areas for the wing molt. Flight feathers are shed and regained during July and August. Acquisition of nuptial plumage begins in September and is completed in December. Females molt several weeks later than males.

FOOD HABITS

Munro and Clemens (1939) in British Columbia and White (1957) in Nova Scotia reported that red-breasted and common mergansers have similar food habits when utilizing the same freshwater areas. On rivers and lakes in British Columbia, red-breasted mergansers fed largely on salmon eggs and sculpins. Those feeding in the sea consumed herring and sculpins. At times, attracted by schools of herring, numerous small flocks of mergansers feeding inshore concentrated in large groups. Shrimps and crabs were also found in a few stomachs.

On the river systems in Nova Scotia, White (1957) noted that red-breasted merganser stomachs contained salmon (fry, parr, and smolts), sticklebacks, killifish, golden shiners, suckers, and minnows. Red-breasted mergansers in Rhode Island frequent salt and brackish waters, where they feed on the blueback herring (Cronan and Halla 1968). In Maryland, this species feeds in the coastal bays, in the ocean, and on the brackish estuarine bays of the Choptank and Potomac rivers. A few stomachs examined by Stewart (1962) contained sunfish, minnows, common prawns, and crustaceans.

Munro and Clemens (1939) observed red-breasted mergansers feeding on herring by swimming vigorously, submerging only their heads. Usually they dive for food. During eight dives that Dow (1964) witnessed, this species was underwater from 42 to 48 seconds, with a pause of 24 seconds between dives.

Red-breasted mergansers have been observed coordinating their fish-hunting and pursuit activities to achieve greater capture success (Des Lauriers and Brattstrom 1965, Emlem and Ambrose 1970). Dashing birds drove the fish into shallow water, where they were more readily captured and devoured.

Common Merganser

Mergus merganser americanus

Other Common Names: American merganser, goosander, sawbill, fish duck

VITAL STATISTICS

Length:	Male, 23.5-27.1 inches, average 25.5 inches (42) Female, 21.3-26.6 inches, average 22.9 inches (39)
Wing:	Adult male, 10.5 inches (11) Adult female, 9.8 inches (14) Immature male, 10.3 inches (28) Immature female, 9.5 inches (42)
Weight:*	Adult male, 2.9-4.5 pounds, average 3.64 pounds (19) Adult female, 2.1-3.1 pounds, average 2.73 pounds (30) Immature male, 2.6-4.0 pounds, average 3.23 pounds (62) Immature female, 2.0-3.2 pounds, average 2.59 pounds (75)

*From Erskine (1971), September - February data only.

IDENTIFICATION

Field

Common mergansers are among the largest of the ducks but are less chunky than the eiders and goldeneyes. Like the goldeneyes, the males in flight show a large amount of white and some black on their bodies and wings. They do not fly in the compact clusters characteristic of goldeneyes but in trailing lines a few feet above the water. Although they fly fast, their wing arc is shallow, extending only slightly below the plane of the body. The wing arc of goldeneyes is much deeper. When common mergansers take flight, they patter across the water for several yards to become airborne. Goldeneyes take only a few steps on the water before they are in the air.

Mergansers present a low profile on the water, their bodies appearing more elongated than those of other ducks. The male appears black and white, with a smooth elongated black-green head and black back, set off by a white neck and underparts. The white wing coverts and speculum on the folded wing provide an expanse of white along the side of the body. Female and immature common mergansers have silver-gray backs and sides and tufted red-brown heads. A small white patch, formed by the white speculum and white-dotted greater coverts of the folded wing and divided by a dark line, appears on the side above the flank feathers. Except for their clear white throats sharply outlined by the surrounding red-brown feathers of their heads, female and immature commons are similar to their counterparts among red-breasted mergansers, whose whitish throats are indistinctly margined.

At Hand

The long, narrow bill with edges of sawlike teeth readily distinguishes mergansers from all other ducks. The bills of common and red-breasted mergansers are about the same length, 2.2 inches, but the hooded merganser has a shorter bill, 1.5 inches. The bill of the common merganser is wider and thicker at the base than that of the red-breasted, and the nostrils are closer to the middle of the bill than to the base. In the red-breasted, the nostrils are near the base of the bill. The males of both species have red bills; the bills of females and immatures are slightly duller. Again, the feet of both these species are bright red in the males, duller in the females, and yellow-brown in the immatures. The eyes of the adult male common merganser are dark brown; those of the red-breasted merganser are brilliant red. Females and immatures have brown eyes circled with yellow.

Upon close viewing, it is apparent that the white underparts of the adult males are tinged with pink, the black heads glossed with green. The females and immatures have white underparts margined by silver-gray sides, flanks, and undertail coverts. Their backs, rumps, and tails are also gray, and stiff red-brown feathers protrude untidily from the backs of their heads.

The inner halves of the wings of adult males are largely white, with single transverse black bars formed by the black bases of the white greater coverts. The middle coverts are white, the lesser coverts black on the leading edges of the wings but white next to the middle coverts. The secondaries are largely white, the inner ones narrowly margined by black. The primaries and their coverts are dull black.

Among females and immatures, the "shoulder" of the wing, formed by the lesser and middle coverts, is dusky gray. The greater coverts are black at the base, and the secondaries have broad white spots adjacent to the white speculum. In the immature male, the outer secondary coverts are paler than the others and thus form a light-colored area forward of the speculum (Erskine 1971). The wings of the female lack this pale patch at any season.

Adult male mergansers commence their postnuptial molt in mid-June, and by late summer they are in eclipse plumage and closely resemble females and immatures. In September, they begin the prenuptial body molt that clothes them in full nuptial plumage by late November.

POPULATION STATUS

Aerial surveys by the U. S. Fish and Wildlife Service, made in early summer from Labrador across Canada north to the Beaufort Sea and west across Alaska to the Bering Sea, indicate a population of 850,000 common and red-breasted mergansers. Adding the 28,000 for British Columbia and the United States makes a combined summer population of 878,000 mergansers of these two species.

Audubon Christmas bird censuses indicate that 73 percent of the mergansers on winter grounds are common and 27 percent are red-breasted. Assuming that the composition of summer populations is similar, they include 641,000 common and 237,000 red-breasted mergansers.

Age Ratios

Anderson and Timken (1972) collected 188 common mergansers in South Dakota and Minnesota. They found 1 adult to 0.54 immature in this sample. Of 123 they collected in Oklahoma during January and February, there was 1 adult to 0.33 immature. Wing samples from hunters indicated a ratio of 1:1.63, adults to immatures, 1966-73, but when corrected for vulnerability of immatures—assumed to be twice as high as for adults—there was 1 adult per 0.8 immature.

Sex Ratio

Sex ratios were obtained by Anderson and Timken (1972) simultaneously with age ratios. There was 1 male to 0.54 female (65 percent) in the samples from South Dakota and Minnesota and 1 male to 0.48 female (67 percent) in the samples from Oklahoma.

DISTRIBUTION

The three races of the common merganser breed around the world in the Northern Hemisphere. They occur in a belt that largely embraces the closed boreal forest and montane forest regions of Eurasia and North America. Their ranges generally do not extend as far north as those of the red-breasted merganser but do extend farther south. The European race winters along the coast of Europe from Norway to Spain, the Mediterranean Sea, and Iran. The Asian common merganser winters as far south as central India and southeastern China. The winter quarters of the American race extend along the Atlantic Coast from Newfoundland barely to Florida, in the interior from the Great Lakes to the Gulf of Mexico, and on the Pacific Coast from the Aleutian Islands into Mexico.

Breeding Range

In North America, small numbers of common mergansers breed south of Canada into southern Maine, central New York, the northern one-third of the Lower Peninsula of Michigan, the northern part of Wisconsin, and Minnesota. In the Rocky Mountains, their range extends south through Montana and Wyoming to southern Colorado. Farther west in the Cascade and Sierra Nevada mountains, this species breeds through Washington and Oregon as far south as Tulare County, California. Estimated breeding numbers of common and red-breasted mergansers (almost entirely the former) are 3,600, Michigan; 800, Wisconsin; 500, Minnesota (undoubtedly too low); 1,800, Montana; 7,500, Wyoming; 300, Washington; and 1,200, Oregon. Between 8,000 and 12,000 mergansers, the bulk of which are common, breed in British Columbia.

On the Stikine River in northern British Columbia and southeastern Alaska, all the mergansers that Swarth (1922) identified were common. Both common and red-breasted mergansers were rare in the Atlin Lake region of northern British Columbia (Swarth 1926). According to Soper (1954), common mergansers composed 9.6 percent of the waterfowl population in the southwest Yukon Territory; he noted only a few red-breasted mergansers.

Breeding ground surveys, 1955-74, by the U. S. Fish and Wildlife Service, indicate 3,900 mergansers for the region of the Peace River delta, but ground surveys (Soper 1951) do not clarify the relative abundance of the two species—a few of both were observed. However, 200 miles to the north in the region of the Slave River delta, Soper (1957) did not find common mergansers but noted that red-breasted mergansers were relatively numerous. He observed them most frequently on the Mackenzie River near Big Island and in the northern and eastern parts of Great Slave Lake.

Breeding ground surveys in the closed boreal forest reveal the following numbers of mergansers, believed to be predominantly common: 78,500, Alberta; 98,000, Saskatchewan; 75,000, Manitoba; 98,000, western Ontario; and 155,000 in eastern Ontario, Quebec, and Labrador.

In ground surveys of breeding waterfowl in Quebec, Tener and Lemieux (1952) found 144 common to 38 red-breasted mergansers in 1951-52. According to Todd (1963), the common merganser finds ideal conditions in the lake country northwest of the St. Lawrence River. He reported that this area of high relative abundance continues westward into northern Ontario, southward to include Lakes Nipissing and Temagami, and northward to include the rivers flowing into James Bay. Hanson et al. (1949) did not observe red-breasted mergansers but saw large numbers of common mergansers on waterways both southeast and southwest of James Bay. They reported 19 common mergansers per 100 miles of stream in Ontario between the Pagwa River and Fort Albany and 51 per 100 miles of stream in Quebec, 1947, down to 10.5 per 100 miles in 1948. On a canoe trip in southwestern Quebec, Smith (1947) noted 11 common mergansers per 100 miles of stream. In southwestern Keewatin District, the common merganser appears to be slightly more abundant than the red-breasted (Mowat and Lawrie 1955).

Although the common merganser far outnumbers the red-breasted merganser in the boreal forest, the latter species nonetheless occurs throughout this zone east of Alberta. Todd (1963) cited several breeding grounds of the red-breasted merganser from the interior of the Labrador Peninsula. And along the east coast of James Bay, Manning and Macpherson (1952) found that the red-breasted was probably the more numerous of the two species. However, along the east coast of Hudson Bay, Manning (1946) observed 281 common to 2 red-breasted mergansers. On the west side at Cape Henrietta Maria, Peck (1972) saw both species, but the red-breasted merganser seemed to be more abundant. There is only one record for the common merganser at Churchill, Manitoba, but red-breasted mergansers breed commonly near large lakes along the tree line (Jehl and Smith 1970).

At times, common mergansers have the strange faculty of nesting far south of their normal breeding range. The most extreme case is a downy young collected at Colonio Pacheco, Chihuahua, Mexico, on May 23, 1909 (van Rossem 1929). A female with a brood of five downy young was observed in Chowan County, North Carolina, the last week of May 1938 (Brimley 1941). Several broods of common mergansers were observed, 1953-54, in the Shenandoah River valley of Virginia (Jopson 1956).

Peters and Burleigh (1951) reported that the common merganser was an uncommon resident of Newfoundland, nesting on the larger rivers and lakes of the interior, but that the red-breasted merganser was fairly common and nested throughout the interior. On the Margaree River system of Cape Breton Island, Nova Scotia, Erskine (1972*c*) estimated 51 pairs of common and 8 pairs of red-breasted mergansers, 1960-63.

Migration Corridors

Bandings of common mergansers in the Maritime Provinces of Canada show little migratory movement. Erskine (1972*c*) reports that birds banded on Cape Breton Island winter almost entirely on the Atlantic Coast of Nova Scotia. The passage of a few ducks south to Massachusetts, Rhode Island, and New Jersey occurred with severe cold in December.

Miller (1973) presents additional information on common mergansers banded in New Brunswick, southwest New York, and Oklahoma. Of the 31 recoveries of mergansers banded in New Brunswick, only 4 (12.9 percent) occurred south of the Maritimes in Massachusetts and Rhode Island. Forty recoveries from New York bandings show a migration corridor from northeast Manitoba southwest across Lakes Erie and Ontario to New Jersey and Chesapeake Bay, with one band recovery from coastal Georgia and two from the west coast of Florida. All but 1 of 36 recoveries from bandings in northeast Oklahoma fall in a broad north-south corridor between the banding site and southwestern Ontario and southeastern Manitoba.

In the Mississippi Flyway, common mergansers are most abundant in Lakes Erie and Michigan; the Mississippi River between Keokuk, Iowa, and St. Louis, Missouri; and in the Crab Orchard National Wildlife Refuge in southern Illinois.

Winter Areas

Long-term winter inventories for North America, by the U.S. Fish and Wildlife Service, average almost 235,000 mergansers. Because these figures do not record the three kinds of mergansers, Audubon Christmas counts, 1969-72, are used to determine the species composition. They indicate that about 67 percent are common, 25 percent red-breasted, and 8 percent hooded.

Of the 165,000 common mergansers found on winter grounds, 120,000 (58 percent) occur in the interior of the United States. The largest number—some 70,000—are found in the Central Flyway. Oklahoma is the leading

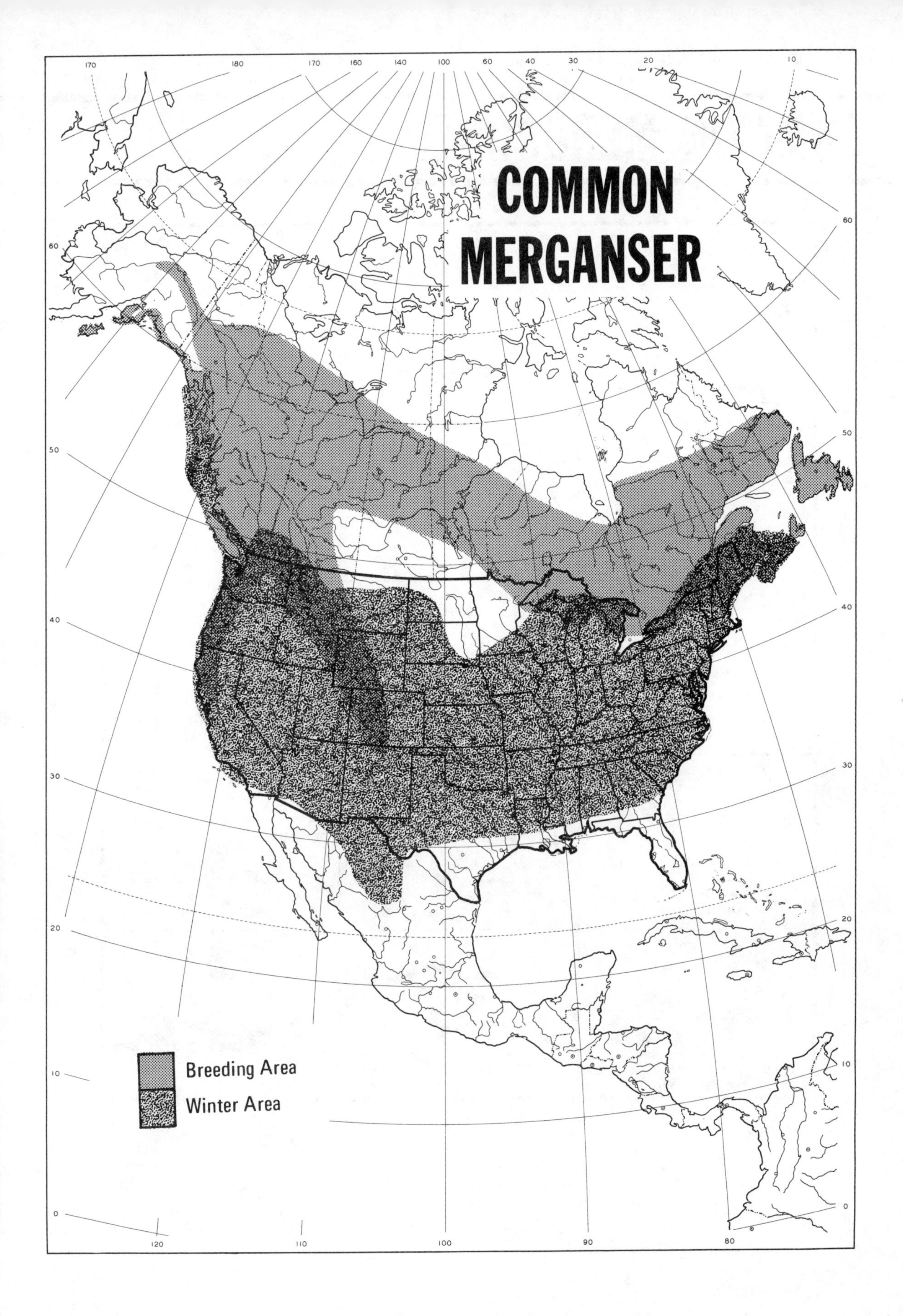

COMMON MERGANSER
Breeding Area
Winter Area

COMMON MERGANSER

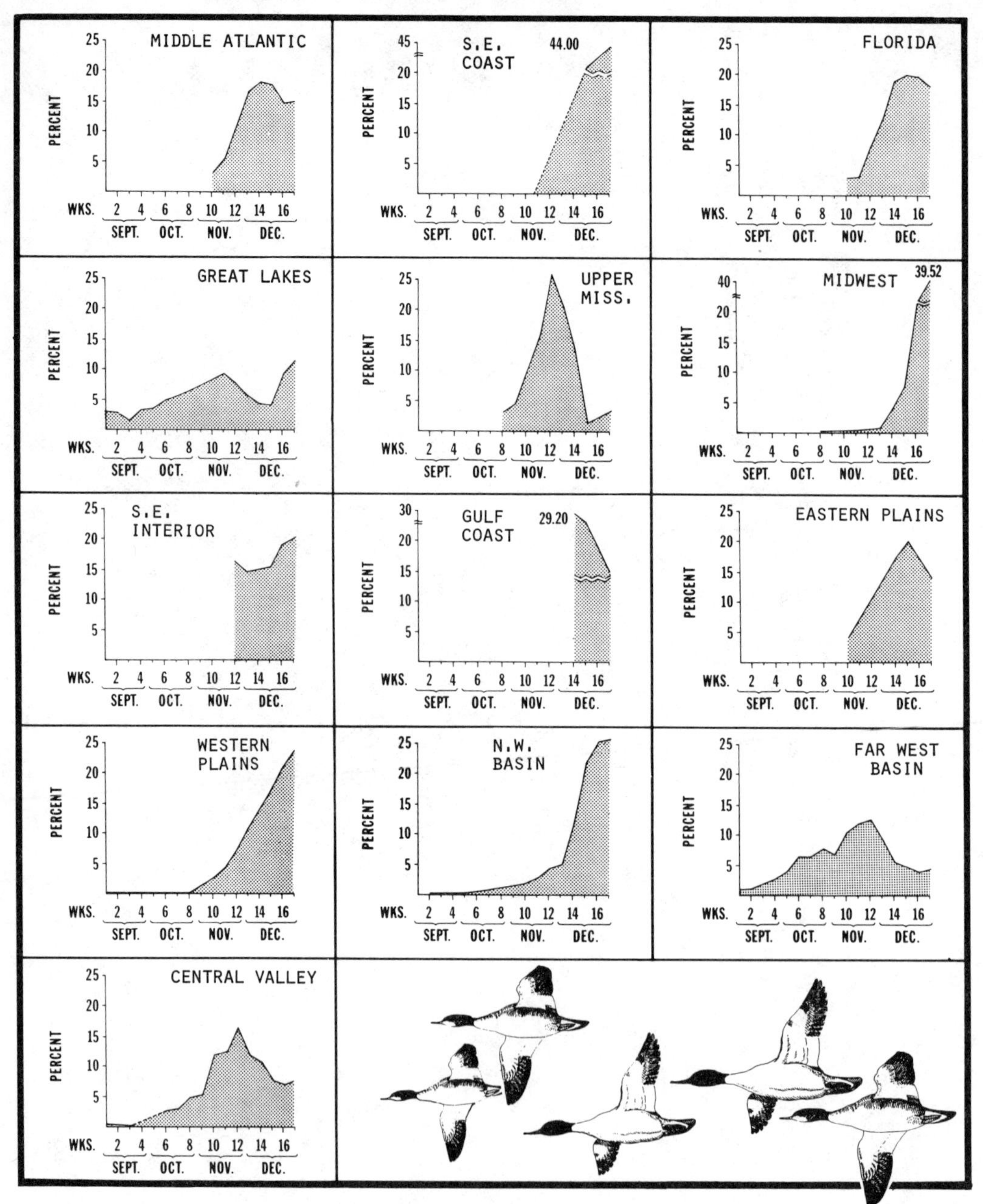

Fall

COMMON MERGANSER

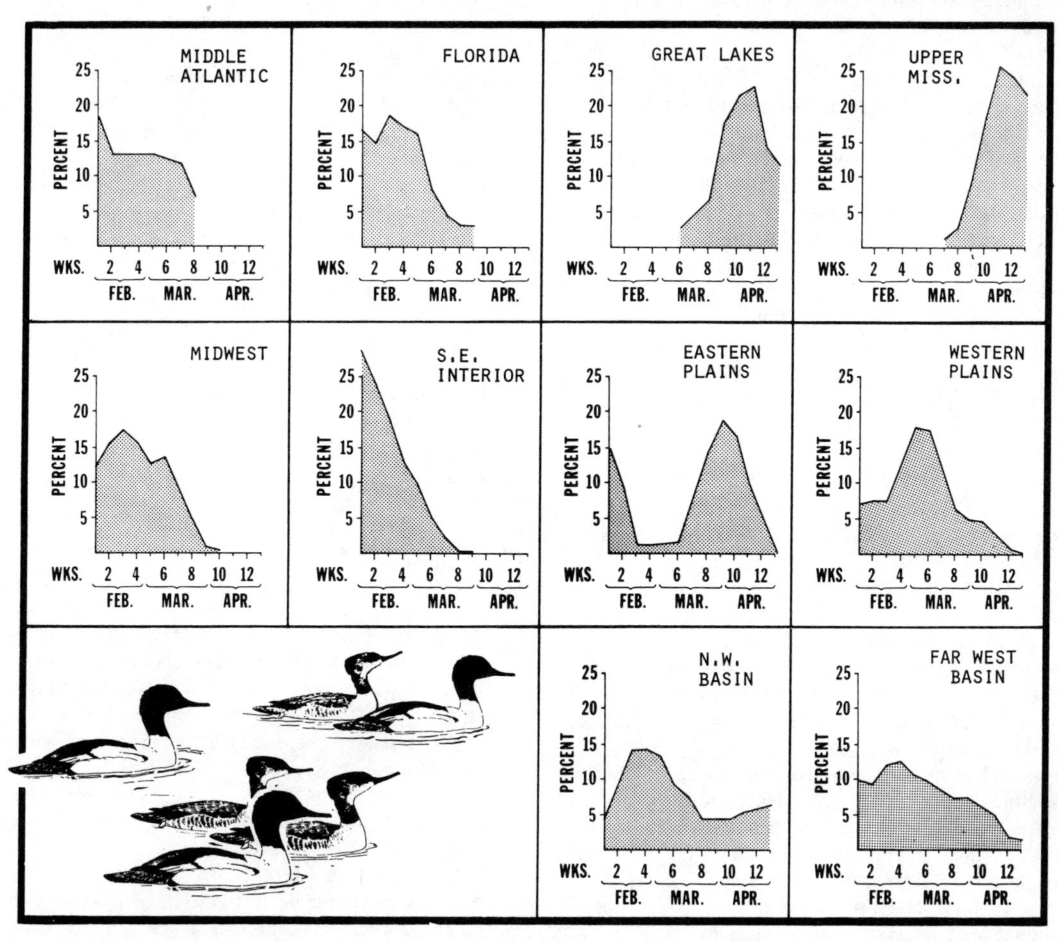

Spring

state with 30,000; eastern New Mexico second with 12,000; followed by Kansas with 10,000; Nebraska with 9,000; South Dakota with 4,000; Texas with 3,000; and eastern Wyoming and Colorado with about 1,000 each. Several hundred winter on reservoirs in the Northern Highlands of Mexico.

Common mergansers have found a bonanza in the artificial reservoirs of the Central Flyway. The large increase in surface water resulting from numerous impoundments has unquestionably caused an increase in the wintering populations throughout the region, particularly in Oklahoma and Kansas.

Almost 50,000 common mergansers winter in the Mississippi Flyway section of the interior. Illinois harbors about 20,000; Ohio, 12,000; Missouri, 5,000; and Michigan, Kentucky, and Tennessee each have 2,000 to 3,000. Although small numbers of common mergansers reach the Gulf of Mexico, fewer than 1,000 winter south of Tennessee and Missouri. Several hundred winter in Wisconsin, Minnesota, and Iowa.

The Pacific Flyway is third in the number of common mergansers—24,000. The large lakes of the panhandle area in the north and the Snake River in the south permit Idaho to winter the most mergansers, about 5,400. The Colorado River supports most of the 3,900 in Arizona and the 1,400 that winter in Nevada. Puget Sound is the principal winter area for the 2,300 common mergansers found in Washington and accounts for one-third of the 1,200 reported for southwestern British Columbia; the others occur in the adjacent Strait of Georgia. California's 2,000 common mergansers are scattered among its numerous reservoirs, with small numbers along the coast. The 1,800 in western Montana are found on Flathead Lake and the Missouri and Yellowstone rivers.

In the Atlantic Flyway, the common merganser is less than a third as abundant as the red-breasted species. Of the 13,000 recorded from Newfoundland to Florida, almost 6,000 occur in upstate New York, particularly Lake Ontario and the Niagara River. Small numbers of common mergansers are found with red-breasted mergansers along the coast of New Jersey, but most of the 1,200 concentrate in reservoirs in the northern part of the state. The 3,500 mergansers in the Chesapeake Bay region of Maryland and Virginia are about equally divided between common and red-breasted. Only a few hundred common mergansers winter between Virginia and Florida, a region dominated by the red-breasted merganser. A surprisingly large number (2,000) of common mergansers winter in Newfoundland and the Maritime Provinces, but fewer than 1,000 winter in New England.

MIGRATION BEHAVIOR

Across country between extensive bodies of water, common mergansers appear to migrate by night. However, along the seacoasts and in places along the Illinois and Mississippi rivers, this species migrates extensively by day, especially when ice encroaches upon the areas where they rest and feed. Large numbers frequent the same water areas fall after fall, suggesting their annual return to places that have proven particularly favorable. For many years I have seen them appear en masse overnight on some lakes, as if their destination were programmed prior to departure from more northerly areas. Nine of 36 mergansers banded in northeast Oklahoma were recovered in subsequent years within a short distance of the banding site, suggesting a homing to winter quarters (Miller 1973). Nonetheless, if ice or a shortage of food develops, they move to new areas. Audubon Christmas counts at many places show pronounced annual variations in the numbers of wintering mergansers.

Chronology

Fall. The common merganser is one of the last ducks to migrate south, vying with the goldeneye for this dubious distinction. In northern states, it seldom appears in numbers before water areas are margined with ice. The chronology of migration along the Atlantic Coast, as shown in the accompanying graphs, is similar from Long Island to Florida. The birds arrive about mid-November and numbers steadily rise until late December.

Because of small breeding populations in the Great Lakes states, small numbers are present at the beginning of fall censuses in September. A continuing influx occurs until the last quarter of November; then populations decline only to rise in late December. On the northeastern Great Plains, mergansers make an abrupt passage. They appear early in November, reach peak numbers near the end of the month, and are largely gone by mid-December. In the Midwest, they quickly reach their peak abundance the last half of December. In the mid-South, wintering birds arrive en masse early in December. The small numbers that winter from Mobile Bay to Galveston Bay arrive in late December.

On the southeastern plains, from northern Nebraska into eastern Texas, common mergansers appear in mid-November, reach their peak in mid-December, and decline in the more northern areas late in the month. On the High Plains, they appear in early November and rapidly increase through December. In the northern Intermountain valleys, small numbers arrive through November, with a great influx in early December. Because of nearby breeding areas, these mergansers appear on Central Basin lakes and streams in September and slowly increase in number to late November, with a decline through December. The Sacramento Valley and the San Francisco Bay area attract common mergansers from early October to late November, when populations partly decline to mid-December.

Spring. Common mergansers depart the mid-Atlantic region abruptly in late March. The small numbers wintering in Florida begin to leave early in March and most are gone by late in the month. They commence leaving mid-South areas early in February and continue to depart steadily through that month and March. Populations in the Midwest increase above winter levels in mid-February as migrants arrive from the mid-South, but numbers decline to low levels in early April. Farther north, in the Great Lakes region, mergansers do not appear until late March but reach peak abundance by mid-April.

In the eastern Great Plains, wintering common merganser populations decline early in February to increase again between mid-March and mid-April. On the High Plains, winter populations increase the first half of March and then numbers decline to the end of April. Populations in Intermountain valleys increase during late February, decline through March, but retain sizable numbers in April. Merganser populations slowly disperse from Northwest Basin areas through March and April.

BREEDING

Behavior

Age, Pair Bond, and Homing. Yearlings, in their identifiable plumage, are not known to breed, and flocks of them are found throughout the breeding season. On breeding grounds in Nova Scotia, White (1957) observed that large flocks of common mergansers arrived as soon as the ice left the rivers. Courtship activities ensued until the flocks broke up into mated pairs that dispersed along the streams. Adult males remained in the vicinity of their nests until females began to incubate, then departed the breeding streams for the sea.

Erskine (1972*c*) reported that young common mergansers banded on Cape Breton Island were shot in subsequent years on the same river. One of five adult females banded was also recovered in a subsequent year on the same river. Where mergansers were eliminated from streams (as part of an experimental program to determine their effect upon Atlantic salmon), breeding populations recovered slowly, indicating that homing is highly precise.

Home Range. Specific information about the distribution of breeding pairs along streams is lacking. However, numerous accounts refer to widely spaced pairs. White (1957) pointed out that the streams must have clear water and sufficient fish of the proper size as food for the ducklings. Mated pairs apparently leave streams that become turbid prior to nesting, for he never found them with broods on these areas during the nesting season or later.

Nesting

Nest Sites. White (1957) reported that in eastern Canada, the common merganser usually nests in hollow trees, the same cavity often being used for several years. Entrances to some cavities are 50 feet or higher above the ground. Where suitable tree cavities are lacking, this species resorts to nesting on the ground, on cliff ledges, and on assorted bizarre sites. Bent (1923) reported finding numerous nests among loose boulders along the shores of islands in Lake Winnipegosis, Manitoba. A few nests were located in dense tangles of gooseberry bushes and nettles on the crests of the islands. Other locations are hollows in stream cutbanks formed by soil washing away from the roots of standing trees, ledges of rocky cliffs, and such strange sites as an abandoned lighthouse tower, amid bales of hay stacked in an abandoned icehouse, and between the floor and top of a stone pier supporting a covered bridge.

Although nest sites are usually close to water, White (1957) observed females leading their broods from woods as distant as 200 yards. He also observed that they sometimes nested far from a large stream and brought their broods to it down a side riverlet.

Griffee (1958) found a common merganser nest containing 11 eggs in a nest box placed along the Wilson River, near Portland, Oregon. They readily occupy nest houses in Finland.

Clutch Size, Eggs, and Incubation. According to Bent (1923), the common merganser lays 6 to 17 eggs, most clutches containing between 9 and 12. Mergansers under confinement at Slimbridge, England, produced clutch sizes of 8 to 12 eggs (Johnstone 1970). Occasionally, two or more females lay simultaneously in the same nest, and large clutches probably represent the efforts of more than a single bird (Erskine 1972*c*). Bent (1923) described the eggs as pale buff or ivory-yellow, with a lack of luster, elliptical ovate to elliptical oval, and averaging 64.3 by 44.9 mm (93). Erskine (1972*c*) considered that mergansers probably lay eggs at intervals greater than 1 day and hypothetically assumed that 15 days are required for the laying of 9 eggs. Eggs from an incomplete clutch were hatched in an incubator in 28 days (Bent 1923). An incubation period of 34 to 35 days is cited by Witherby et al. (1952) for Great Britain. Johnstone (1970) determined a period of 30 days for the mergansers under confinement at Slimbridge.

Chronology of Nesting. To estimate the time of nest initiation I have subtracted 45 days (for egg-laying and incubation) from the estimated days of hatch given by Erskine (1972*c*) for many places in North America. Calculated dates for the start of egg-laying are as follows: From south to north in the Far West, March 29-May 4, California; May 1, Washington; April 8-June 9, British Columbia; May 21, Yukon Territory; and May 2-26, Alaska. In areas in the central interior, April 16-May 29, Michigan; and April 19-June 9, Ontario. On the Atlantic Seaboard area, April 23-May 16, New Brunswick; April 19-May 24, Nova Scotia; and May 1-June 12, Quebec.

Where samples were of modest size, the period of nest initiation spanned the following days: British Columbia, 61; Michigan, 43; Ontario, 51; New Brunswick, 23; Nova Scotia, 35; and Quebec, 42. Considering the short plant-growing season where most of these nest records occurred, the initiation period is unusually protracted.

Nest Success. No one has studied the nest success of the common merganser. However, data presented by Erskine (1972*c*) on the number of breeding pairs of both species of mergansers compared with the number of broods observed, 1960-63, on the Margaree River system indicate the possibility of every nest hatching successfully. During these years, the total estimated breeding population consisted of 51 pairs of common and 8 pairs of red-breasted mergansers. A like number of broods was estimated for the same river system.

Nest Failure. Mergansers nesting in natural cavities have minimal contact with nest predators. Most mergansers nest north of the range of raccoons, fox squirrels, tree-climbing snakes, and starlings that play havoc with wood duck nests. Where raccoons have extended their range into the breeding areas of common mergansers, they no doubt destroy a limited number of nests. Other nest sites used by common mergansers—cliff ledges, overhanging banks, islands—predators find inaccessible.

Renesting. Erskine (1972*c*) does not believe that the common merganser renests, but the prolonged period of nest initiation provides ample time for renesting to occur. Moreover, the production of broods relative to breeding pairs is so high as to suggest some renesting.

Rearing of Young

Broods. A day or two after hatching, ducklings of the common merganser leave their tree nests by jumping out and fluttering to the ground as the female calls from the water or ground near the tree base (Bent 1923). Broods on streams gradually move downstream, sometimes joining other broods to form aggregations of 20 or more by the time they reach estuaries and can fly. At Cape Breton Island, Erskine (1972*c*) found that even by October, few young had moved more than 50 miles from their natal streams. They ranged more widely in November.

Development. According to Erskine (1971), young common mergansers first attain flight at about 65 days, with some probably taking 70 days or more. At the time of initial flight, the primaries are 50 to 70 mm short of their final growth, achieved at an age of 80 to 85 days. Young began to fly to Cape Breton Island in early August when nesting was early, but late-hatched young did not fly until after mid-September.

Survival. White (1957) was greatly impressed with the ability of duckling mergansers to survive in the absence of parental care. He noted instances of downy young reaching maturity on their own. However, because it takes the young so long to reach flight stage, late-hatched broods on the more northern breeding areas probably suffer severe losses when water areas freeze prematurely.

Sixteen broods of common mergansers observed on Owikeno Lake, British Columbia, numbered 4 to 26 and averaged 11.4 ducklings (Stutz 1965). All of these broods were about three-quarters grown, July 13-29, and were accompanied by a single female. One brood of 20 ducklings was without an adult.

POSTBREEDING SEASON

Early in incubation, the adult males leave the breeding areas. According to White (1957), both adult and yearling males begin to leave the streams of the Maritimes in mid-June, a few remaining as late as mid-July. Near the coasts they move to estuaries and inlets for the wing molt; in the interior they congregate on the larger lakes in the boreal forest. On surveys (Ducks Unlimited) of lakes within this region, William Leitch reported 25 mergansers per mile of shoreline on Canoe Lake, August 24, 1950, and hundreds on Kazan Lake, August 24, 1952. By mid-August on Cape Breton Island, White (1957) observed that females deserted well-grown broods for the wing molt.

Adult male specimens from the Hudson Bay region, examined by Erskine (1971), had shed their flight feathers in July, two to four weeks earlier than those at Cape Breton Island. Flight feathers are regained in about a month, by mid-September in the Maritimes. Adult females shed their flight feathers between mid-August and early September and regain flight between mid-September and early October.

FOOD HABITS

At some times and in some places, common mergansers feed on trout and salmon. Because they include these valuable fishes in their diets, the food habits of this species have been researched as thoroughly as those of most valuable game ducks. Mergansers eat a wide variety of fishes, depending upon the geographic areas inhabited relative to the season.

In the Maritime Provinces, the common merganser preys largely on young salmon during the summer months (White 1957). Of all the fish eaten, salmon compose 46 to 91 percent in streams of the Gulf mainland and Cape Breton Island to lows of 5 to 36 percent in drainage systems of the Bay of Fundy and Atlantic Nova Scotia. Other fishes consumed are blacknose dace, common shiners, white suckers, and small eels (pigmented elvers). In the Petitcodiac River system, 64 percent of the fishes eaten are suckers, chubs, and eels. Mergansers in the St. John River made 82 percent of their diet on fallfish, shiners, suckers, and dace.

During prolonged cold winters in Michigan, large numbers of common mergansers have been forced from lakes onto trout streams (Salyer and Lagler 1940). There, 88 percent of the volume of food consumed was made up of trout, with forage fishes accounting for 6.5 percent, crayfishes 2.0 percent, and amphibians 0.8 percent. On bays of the Great Lakes and river-mouth lakes, they found the following volume of foods in merganser stomachs: forage fishes, 49 percent; yellow perch, 20 percent; unidentified fish, 20 percent; and crayfishes, 8.5 percent.

In the Unakwik Inlet area of southeast Alaska, Fritsch and Buss (1958) studied the stomach contents of 40 adult and 15 juvenile common mergansers collected in late summer. They found salmon eggs and fry in so few stomachs that they concluded mergansers had an insignificant effect upon salmon in the area.

Although mergansers make game fishes a varying but sometimes important part of their diet in cold water, in warm water areas their food most often consists of rough and forage fishes. Three-fourths of the fishes found in 110 stomachs from mergansers collected on lakes, on the Carson River, and on irrigation canals of Churchill County,

Nevada, were carp and suckers; perch and catfish largely composed the remainder (Alcorn 1953). Huntington and Roberts (1959) intensively studied the food habits of common mergansers relative to fish populations in reservoirs and in the Rio Grande River in New Mexico. They found that 54 percent of 949 stomachs contained gizzard shad, 9.5 percent carp, 5.2 percent crappie, 3.1 percent sunfish, 3.6 percent other fish, and 17.9 percent were empty. Comparing the composition of the fish population of the several water areas with the proportion of fish species consumed, these investigators concluded that availability largely determined the species taken.

One-third of the 220 common merganser stomachs examined by Timken and Anderson (1969) held food. Most of the samples were collected from the Missouri River bordering South Dakota and Nebraska and from Lake Hendricks on the South Dakota-Minnesota border. Gizzard shad composed 37 percent by weight of fish taken, freshwater drum 26 percent, and white bass 11 percent.

At Lake Carl Blackwell, Oklahoma, Miller (1973) reported on the contents of 65 common merganser stomachs: 84 percent of the volume of all food items consisted of gizzard shad, 6 percent freshwater drum, 5 percent white crappie, 1 percent other fishes, and 4 percent unidentified fishes.

Comparing the fishes consumed with the fish population in the lake indicated some selection of gizzard shad and white crappie. Miller (1973) conducted feeding tests with captive mergansers and reviewed similar investigations by White (1957) and Latta and Sharkey (1966). He concluded that the increased activity of mergansers in the wild would result in about 450 grams of fish being consumed daily, considerably above the 227 grams taken under confinement.

Masked Duck

Oxyura dominica

IDENTIFICATION

The masked duck is seldom found in the United States. An elusive duck, difficult to see, it is in the same size class as the ruddy, bufflehead, and green-winged teal. Its body conformation and basic coloration are similar to those of the ruddy duck, to which it bears a close affinity. But unlike the ruddy, it displays in flight a pronounced white speculum, and the male has an irregularly shaped black facial mask that covers its crown and cheeks and extends to the blue bill. A white spot is visible on the chin, but the remainder of the head, neck, and chest are chestnut-red; the back and sides are a similar shade but are streaked and spotted with black. The lower chest and belly are white. According to Weller (1968), the masked duck takes flight by rising straight off the water, with the body horizontal, and enters a fast ascending flight with rapidly moving wings.

On water, female and immature masked ducks resemble their counterparts in ruddy ducks. The principal difference is that masked ducks have two transverse bars of dark brown across the buff-colored cheeks—one through the eye, the other from the base of the bill to the back of the head. Ruddy females have single transverse bars across their cheeks. The long wedge-shaped tails of masked ducks are spinelike, often bare at the tips, and are frequently erected fanwise over their backs.

DISTRIBUTION

The masked duck is a denizen of the West Indies, Costa Rica, Panama, and South America as far south as Buenos Aires in the east and Lake Titicaca, Peru, in the west. There are scattered records of it in Mexico, including several instances of possible breeding (Leopold 1959). As late as the early 1920's, Bent (1925) listed but four records in the United States, dating from 1905 to as far back as 1857. These records came from such diverse localities as Elkton, Maryland; Malden, Massachusetts; Alburg Springs, Vermont; and Wisconsin. In addition, Fisher (1895) observed several masked ducks near Brownsville, Texas, and collected a female in July 1891.

In the years since the mid-1920's, the number of sightings of this species in the United States has increased, particularly in south Texas and Florida. Johnsgard and Hagemeyer (1969) summarized occurrences of the masked duck through 1968. During the 1950's and 1960's, there were nearly 30 records of singles, pairs, or small flocks—7 records in Florida, 1 in Georgia, 1 in New Jersey, 1 in Iowa, and the rest in Texas. Two breeding records in Texas were cited: a brood of four ducklings and two adults in female plumage at the Anahuac National Wildlife Refuge, near Houston, Texas, October 2, 1967; and a nest with six eggs that hatched successfully near Falfurrias, Brooks County, Texas, during the fall of 1968.

Observers noted a female with eight young on the Anahuac Refuge in Texas, October 26, 1969, and a male and female at Holly Beach, Cameron Parish, Louisiana, May 5, 1970 (Audubon Field Notes 1970). The next year a virtual invasion of masked ducks was reported: one at Dallas, Texas, August 22, 1970; five in female plumage at Anahuac Refuge in October; three in mid-December at the Welder Wildlife Refuge, Sinton, Texas; a female collected at Cameron Parish, Louisiana, January 7, 1971; a female at the Laguna Atascosa National Wildlife Refuge, near Brownsville, Texas, in March; and a male at Loxahatchee National Wildlife Refuge, near Delray Beach, Florida, February 13-March 2, 1971 (American Birds 1971). It is puzzling that only two sightings of masked ducks were listed for the next observation period: a male on March 20, 1972, at Rockport, Texas; two males and one female at Welder Wildlife Refuge, Sinton, Texas, June 8, 1972 (American Birds 1972).

Ruddy Duck

Oxyura jamaicensis rubida

Other Common Names: Butterball, bull-necked teal

VITAL STATISTICS

Length: Male, 14.7-16.0 inches, average 15.4 inches (23)
Female, 14.5-16.2 inches, average 15.1 inches (15)

Wing: Adult male, 5.8 inches (26)
Adult female, 5.5 inches (13)
Immature male, 5.7 inches (24)
Immature female, 5.6 inches (28)

Weight: Adult male, 0.6-1.4 pounds, average 1.2 pounds (13)
Adult female, 1.0-1.4 pounds, average 1.19 pounds (8)
Immature male, 1.0-1.4 pounds, average 1.18 pounds (22)
Immature female, 0.6-1.2 pounds, average 0.76 pound (14)

IDENTIFICATION

Field

Ruddy ducks are seldom observed in flight, preferring to dive to escape danger. When they fly, ruddies skim over the water in small, compact flocks at high speed. Their short-arc wingbeat is rapid and, in combination with their short, stocky bodies, makes them look like large bumblebees.

Through the fall and winter both sexes are in drab gray-brown plumages. The large white cheek of the male, topped by a black cap, is the only distinctive color variation observed at a distance. This color contrast can be detected in flight but is most obvious among birds at rest. A large proportion of the males on the water erect their fan-shaped tails at a 45-degree angle, a feature largely distinctive to this species. During courtship, the tails are erected a full 90 degrees. The cheek of the female ruddy duck is grayish, bisected by a darker line. The crown and back of the head are dark brown.

A few males begin acquiring their red-brown breeding plumage in February, albeit by late March fewer than half have their full plumage. However, from then on the change into nuptial plumage develops rapidly, and by the end of April, about three-fourths of the males are in full color. Helen Hays has observed some ruddy males still in partial nuptial plumage as late as early June on Manitoba breeding grounds. Presumably, these are yearlings, for Joyner (1969) reports captive immature drakes in gray plumage as late as May 28. During the protracted period in which drakes are acquiring their nuptial dress, red-brown patches increasingly appear along their gray backs and sides.

At Hand

The conformation of the small ruddy is distinctive: short, thick neck, chunky body, and a fan-shaped tail of stiff spiny feathers. Except for facial features, the appearance of immatures and adults is similar during the fall and early winter. Their backs, scapulars, and rumps are gray-brown; their breasts and bellies are silver-white, with transverse broken bars of dark gray, the sides and flanks more heavily barred. Their tails are black-brown as are their blue-gray unusually large feet.

The bill of the ruddy duck merits particular attention. It is concave in shape and gray-black during the fall and winter but changes to a bright sky-blue during spring. A few males begin to show bright azure bills in March, and most have attained blue bills by late April or early May (Hays and Habermann 1969), but the somber gray-black hue appears again near the end of July and in August.

Plumage changes in the adult male and the change in bill color occur about the same time. The back, scapulars, rump, neck, chest, sides, and flanks become a rich red-brown in March and April to be replaced in August by the drab gray-brown eclipse plumage.

Joyner (1969) reports that the white cheek patches begin to appear in juvenile males in late December, thus distinguishing them from both immature and adult females. As long as the bare-tipped shafts of the juvenile tail feathers remain, immatures can be readily separated from adults. The juvenile tail feathers are gradually replaced in December and January (Joyner 1969).

The wings of ruddies are dull dark brown; some males have chestnut-tinged coverts, but, for the most part, the sexes cannot be distinguished by wings alone. According to Carney (1964), curved and drooping tertials, round-tipped greater coverts, and rounded and smooth middle coverts characterize adult wings; straight tertials, partly squared greater coverts, and rough middle coverts of trapezoidal shape indicate the wings of immatures.

POPULATION STATUS

An average population of 475,000 ruddy ducks was calculated for their principal prairie breeding grounds, 1955-73. The extremes of 258,000 and 800,000 represent a two-thirds variation in magnitude. In addition to the prairie breeding population, about 120,000 nest elsewhere.

Age Ratios

The ratio of adults to immature ruddy ducks in hunters' bags, 1966-73, has averaged 1:1.72, with a low of 1:1.17 in 1967 and a high of 1:2.42 in 1969. The extent to which immatures are more readily shot than adults cannot be established because of insufficient banding data but is probably between 1.5 and 2.0, suggesting that the average age composition in fall populations approaches 1:1.

Sex Ratios

Visual tallies of sex ratios of ruddy ducks during the spring indicate, as with other diving ducks, an excessive number of males. A compilation of sex ratios from several areas indicated that drakes comprise 62 percent (1.63:1) (Bellrose et al. 1961) of spring populations.

DISTRIBUTION

The ruddy duck belongs to an unusual group of ducks known as the stifftails, genus *Oxyura*. Of the six species in this genus, three are in the Americas, one in Eurasia, one in Africa, and one in Australia (Delacour 1959). The North American ruddy duck has two other races, both indigenous to the Andes of South America.

Breeding Range

The ruddy duck joins the redhead, the gadwall, and the blue-winged-cinnamon teal complex in a similar breeding distribution. Its breeding activities are centered on the northern prairies, with important extensions into the Intermountain basins and valleys of the West. There are a few small outposts in the Subarctic. Small, scattered colonies also breed in the Interior Highlands of Mexico, the freshwater marshes of Baja California (Leopold 1959), and northward through the southern Rocky Mountains and southern Great Plains. In the East, colonies of breeding ruddies occur in southeast Ontario and southwest Quebec (Godfrey 1966); Montezuma Marsh, New York (Cummings 1963); Long Island, New York, and Hackensack Meadows, New Jersey (Bull 1964).

Both the mixed prairie and parklands support ruddy duck breeding populations of similar size—195,000 and 185,000, respectively. However, because of its greater area, the density in the mixed prairie is lower (1.1 per square mile) than in the parklands (1.7 per square mile). The mixed prairie-parkland area in southwestern Manitoba is particularly attractive to ruddy ducks. In that area alone, the average breeding population is calculated at 113,000 (4.1 per square mile). The abundance of ruddies in the prairie-parkland region fluctuates greatly from year to year, depending upon the availability and distribution of ponds needed for nesting.

About 100,000 ruddies nest in the mixed prairie of the Dakotas, for a density of 1.9 per square mile. But the density in the mixed prairie of Saskatchewan declines to 0.5 per square mile (20,000) and in Alberta to 0.6 per square mile (15,000).

The Athabasca and Saskatchewan deltas support similar densities, 1.9 and 1.7 per square mile, but because the Saskatchewan area is larger, it supports 11,400 in contrast to 3,000 on the Athabasca Delta. The vastness of the closed boreal forest results in a population of 95,000 ruddies even though the density is only 0.23 per square mile. A similar density of 0.22 per square mile (30,000) occurs in the relatively dry shortgrass prairie area.

Intermountain marshes maintain a breeding population slightly in excess of 100,000 ruddies. Over half of this number occur in the marshes adjacent to Great Salt Lake, Utah. Almost 12,000 are found in Washington, primarily in the Columbia Basin and secondarily in the Okanogan Highlands. The Cariboo and Chilcotin plateaus of British Columbia are considered to have a population of 15,000. Almost 14,000 ruddies are found throughout California, three-fourths of them in the Klamath Basin. The Harney Basin of Oregon supports about 6,000 ruddies, and about the same number are believed to breed in Idaho. Several hundred breed in the Carson Sink, Nevada, and the Flathead Valley of Montana.

Outside of Minnesota, the Great Lakes states harbor only a few breeding ruddy rucks—perhaps 25,000 in Minnesota, 400 in Wisconsin (March et al. 1973), and nearly 5,000 in the Sandhills of Nebraska.

Migration Corridors

The ruddy duck, like the canvasback, heads for the

coasts from its prairie breeding grounds. Unlike the can, it prefers the Pacific to the Atlantic. En route to central and lower California from Alberta and Saskatchewan, ruddies funnel into three areas, where they concentrate in enormous numbers.

Peak fall populations in the Klamath Basin of northern California may reach 110,000; at the Minidoka National Wildlife Refuge near Rupert, Idaho, 30,000; and 25,000 on the marshes adjacent to Great Salt Lake, Utah. Some years ruddies concentrate more at Minidoka and less in the Great Salt Lake area; in other years the reverse is true. Other important migration concentrations occur at Malheur National Wildlife Refuge, Burns, Oregon, where 2,500 gather, and in the Carson Sink area of Nevada, which frequently harbors 7,500.

From these western focal points, migration corridors of ruddy ducks extend to the San Francisco Bay area, through the San Joaquin Valley to the Imperial Valley of California, and on south along the west coast of Mexico.

The principal migration corridor to the Atlantic Coast extends from North Dakota east-southeastward across Minnesota, Wisconsin, and southeast Michigan to Chesapeake Bay. A migration corridor followed by considerably fewer ruddies extends from southern Manitoba across southeastern Ontario to southern New England.

Ruddy ducks wintering in Florida appear to follow a migration corridor that extends from North Dakota southeastward to the Mississippi River in southern Iowa and northern Missouri. From this focal point, a corridor also extends south along the Mississippi River to northern Louisiana.

Migration corridors used by ruddy ducks in the Central Flyway appear to be simple north-south extensions from the principal breeding areas to the principal winter areas. In migrating across the Great Plains, these large populations of ruddies have been recorded at the following national wildlife refuges: 2,000, Lacreek, South Dakota; 3,000, Valentine, and 1,500, Crescent Lake, Nebraska; 6,000, Washita, Oklahoma; and 1,000, Bitter Lake, New Mexico.

Winter Areas

About 55 percent of the ruddy duck population in North America winters in the Pacific coastal states and along the west coast of Mexico. The Atlantic Coast attracts 25 percent of the population, and the entire interior of the continent only 20 percent. A slightly larger proportion of ruddies winters in the Mississippi Flyway than in the Central Flyway, including the interior and the east coast of Mexico.

California attracts 85 percent—almost 100,000—of the ruddies wintering in the Pacific Coast states. Most congregate in the San Francisco Bay area, followed by the Imperial Valley, and then the San Joaquin Valley and south coastal bays. A few hundred winter in coastal British Columbia near Vancouver; 3,700 in coastal Washington; 9,500 in Oregon; 3,200 in Nevada; and a few hundred each in Idaho, Utah, and Arizona. About 19,000 ruddies winter along the entire west coast of Mexico, 8,000 south of Mazatlán, 9,000 at Laguna Papagayo near Acapulco, and small numbers elsewhere. Small numbers of ruddy ducks also appear in Guatemala as regular winter visitors (Saunders et al. 1950).

On the Atlantic Coast, 70 percent of the 60,000 wintering ruddy ducks concentrate in Chesapeake Bay, and south through Pamlico Sound, North Carolina. In Chesapeake Bay, Stewart (1962) reported that 95 percent frequented brackish estuarine areas. Northward, about 1,000 winter in Delaware; 1,200 in New Jersey; 400 in New York; 50 in Rhode Island; and 80 in Massachusetts. South of North Carolina, 4,000 ruddies winter on the coast of South Carolina, fewer than 100 in Georgia, and 11,000 in Florida. An average of 105 ruddies have been found on winter surveys of the West Indies, in Cuba and in Hispaniola.

Louisiana and Texas host about two-thirds of the 36,000 ruddies found wintering in the interior of the United States. Most of the 13,000 found in Louisiana occur in Oxbow and other lakes associated with the Mississippi River. Similar sites account for most of the 8,000 ruddies wintering in Mississippi and the 3,200 in Arkansas. Over 400 winter along Lake Erie in Ohio, about 75 in southeast Michigan, and a few along Lake Michigan in Wisconsin.

Slightly over half of the 11,000 ruddies that winter in Texas occur along the Gulf Coast; most of the others are found in the Northwest. Of the 5,700 ruddies that winter along the east coast of Mexico, a few manage to reach the Tabasco lagoons. However, over 95 percent remain between the Rio Grande Delta and Tampico. In the interior of Mexico, 2,300 ruddies winter in the Northern Highlands and 1,700 in the Southern Highlands.

MIGRATION BEHAVIOR

Populations of ruddy ducks on migration areas fluctuate widely from year to year, suggesting that elements within the population vary their stopping places and even their migration corridors during some years. We have censused as many as 30,000 ruddy ducks at one time in the Illinois Valley in some years, and in others as few as 300. Populations on the Mississippi River in Illinois have ranged from 200 to 9,000. Perhaps the eccentric distribution of ruddy ducks during migration reflects shifts in distribution on prairie breeding grounds, due to changing water conditions.

Although the ruddy duck appears to migrate almost entirely at night, migrating flocks have been observed crossing northern Iowa during an enormous diurnal mass migration including many species (Bellrose 1957). Migrating flocks of ruddies have also been observed following the Jordan River south to Utah Lake (Joyner 1969). Ruddy ducks usually migrate in small flocks of 5 to 15. When they stop after a night's flight, I have observed them countless times in compact rosette-like clusters.

Chronology

Fall. As a result of local breeding populations, ruddy

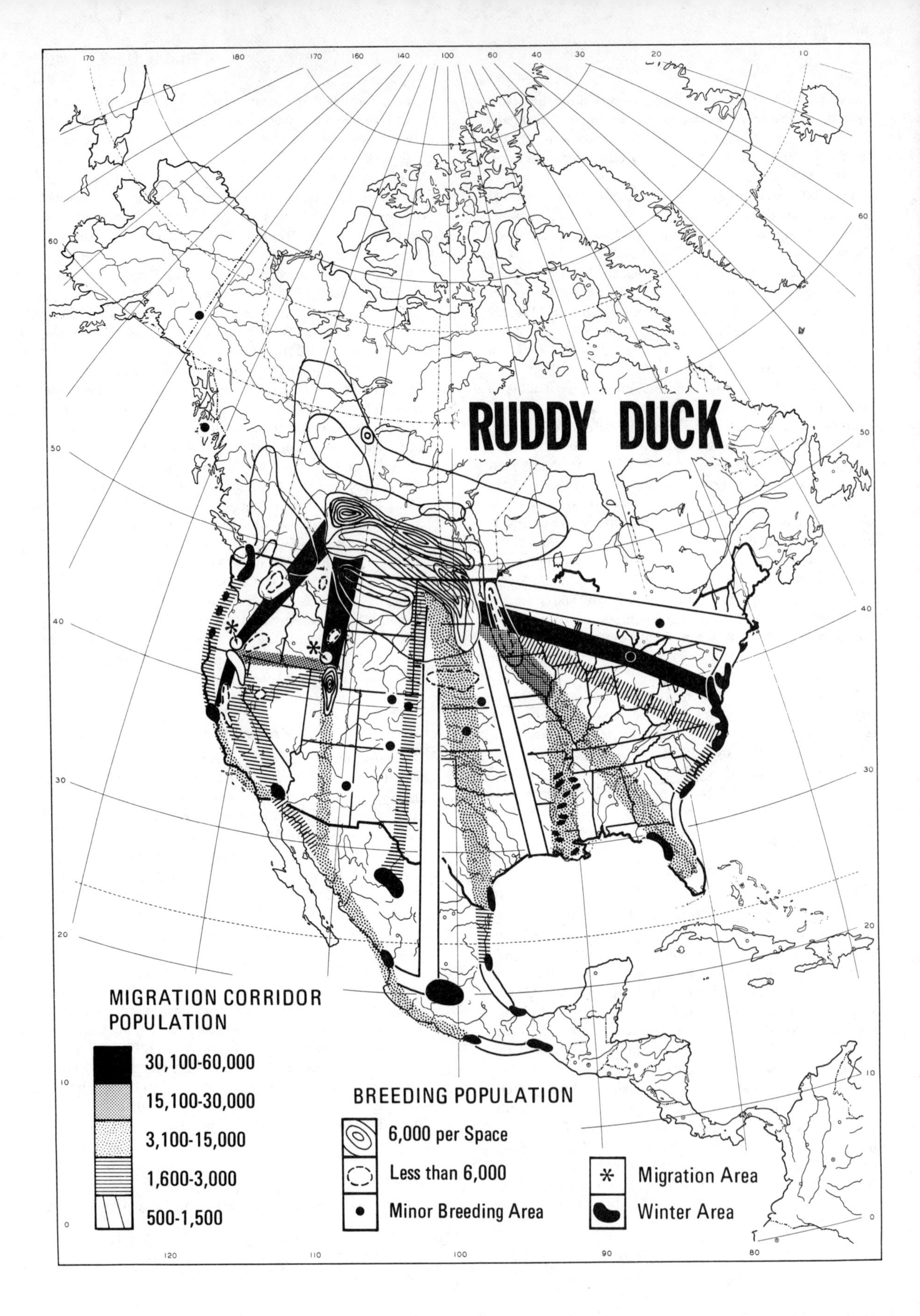
RUDDY DUCK
MIGRATION CORRIDOR POPULATION
30,100-60,000
15,100-30,000
3,100-15,000
1,600-3,000
500-1,500
BREEDING POPULATION
6,000 per Space
Less than 6,000
Minor Breeding Area
Migration Area
Winter Area

ducks, like redheads, are already present in the Northern Plains and Intermountain valleys at the start of their fall migration in September. Their chronology of passage slightly precedes that of other diving ducks, and they depart from migration areas earlier.

They commence migrating from the northern prairies in mid-September and the exodus is virtually complete by the end of October. In September they appear on migration areas (even on some winter areas) and generally move on between mid- and late November. Winter areas in the East show a steady increase in numbers from early fall to early December; in the West the increase continues throughout the month.

Spring. In February, ruddy ducks begin a slow gradual exodus from their winter grounds that continues almost to the end of April. Although a few ruddies appear on migration areas almost as soon as the ice disappears, most arrive later. Peak numbers on migration areas usually occur about mid-April. They arrive on breeding areas in northern United States in early April, with a rapid increase in abundance during the month.

The first ruddy ducks arrived at Delta Marsh, Manitoba, in 14 of 16 years between April 21 and May 6 (Hochbaum 1955). Only the white-winged scoters were later. Near Roseneath, Manitoba, Helen Hays reported that peak arrivals of ruddies occurred the third week in May.

BREEDING

Behavior

Age, Pair Bond, and Homing. Probably not all ruddy duck females nest as yearlings. On a study area near Brooks, Alberta, Keith (1961) found 0.73 nest per pair of ruddies. Two of the game-bird breeders canvassed by Ferguson (1966) reported some first-year layers among their ruddy ducks; two reported only second-year layers, and one recorded no laying until the third year. Apparently, many ruddies do not breed in the wild, for Dwyer (1970) found 21 pairs and no broods. As nest success among ruddy ducks is high, some of these pairs probably made no attempt to nest. The chronology of pair formation in ruddies lacks adequate documentation. I have observed that some were paired upon their arrival in Illinois in early April, and I have also seen extensive courtship displays through May in Utah. Helen Hays observed courtship displays among groups of ruddies when they arrived at Roseneath, Manitoba, in May until many had begun to nest. She reported that peak numbers of single males and females declined on May 23, and by May 30 there were no single females present on the study area.

The duration of the pair bond in ruddy ducks is highly variable. According to Helen Hays, some of the males left their mates when incubation began, but she and other observers have also reported males accompanying broods. Oring (1964) observed three drakes leave their mates at the start of incubation, yet twice saw males accompanying females with broods.

Home Range. Joyner's (1969) observations suggest that, in the ruddy duck, home range is more like a true territory than in any other species of prairie-nesting duck. Territory is usually defined as a defended area. When a pair has selected a nest site, both members defend the area from other ruddies (Joyner 1969). The male begins to lessen his defense of the territory late in the incubation period. The area defended extends only about 10 feet around the nest, but Joyner found that territorial sites were spaced 20 feet to 100 yards apart. Spacing appeared related to the degree of interspersion between marsh vegetation and open water. Where interspersion was favorable, territorial areas were within 20 feet of each other.

Nesting

Nest Sites. Ruddy ducks select both large and small marshes for nesting. Near Roseneath, Manitoba, Helen Hays found them nesting in 11 of 108 potholes in 1955, varying in size from less than an acre to 4 acres. One nest was found in each of eight potholes, two nests in each of two potholes, and five nests in a 4-acre pothole. Low (1941) found greatest nest densities on small 10- to 15-acre marshes and in portions of a 1,200-acre slough near Ruthven, Iowa.

Ruddy ducks nest in the emergent vegetation that is characteristic of the particular marsh or pothole selected. Low (1941) considered that the cover plant growing at the most desirable water depth was more important in the selection of a nest site than the particular qualities of the plant. But he found one nest per 5.5 acres of hardstem bulrush, one nest per 10 acres of lake sedge, and one nest per 11 acres of cattail. All nests were in water 10 to 12 inches deep. At Roseneath, Helen Hays found most of the ruddies nesting in stands of whitetop or a mixture of whitetop and sedge. Keith (1961) reported nests in cattails and juncus rushes in the Brooks, Alberta, area. On the large Delta Marsh, Hochbaum (1944) observed ruddies nesting among hardstem bulrush islands and in bulrush and cattail beds bordering bays and sloughs. In the Bear River marshes, Utah, Williams and Marshall (1938*b*) determined that hardstem bulrush was the primary choice for nesting and sedges were second. Elsewhere in the West, hardstem bulrush beds also appear to be the most important locations for nest sites.

Low (1941) located ruddy nests an average of 32.5 yards from open water (range, 1.1 to 133 yards) and 81.5 yards from shore (range, 6.7 to 210 yards). Helen Hays found nests an average of 26 feet from both open water and the shoreline of small potholes. Some nests were on the very edge of the shore and others 120 yards away, and some were on the edge of marsh vegetation and others 72 yards within it.

Both Low (1941) and Helen Hays reported that nests were built up from the marsh bottom to above the water, and Hays noted that some nests were floating. The nests are meager affairs when the eggs are first laid, but as the clutches near completion, the edges are rapidly built up to

RUDDY DUCK

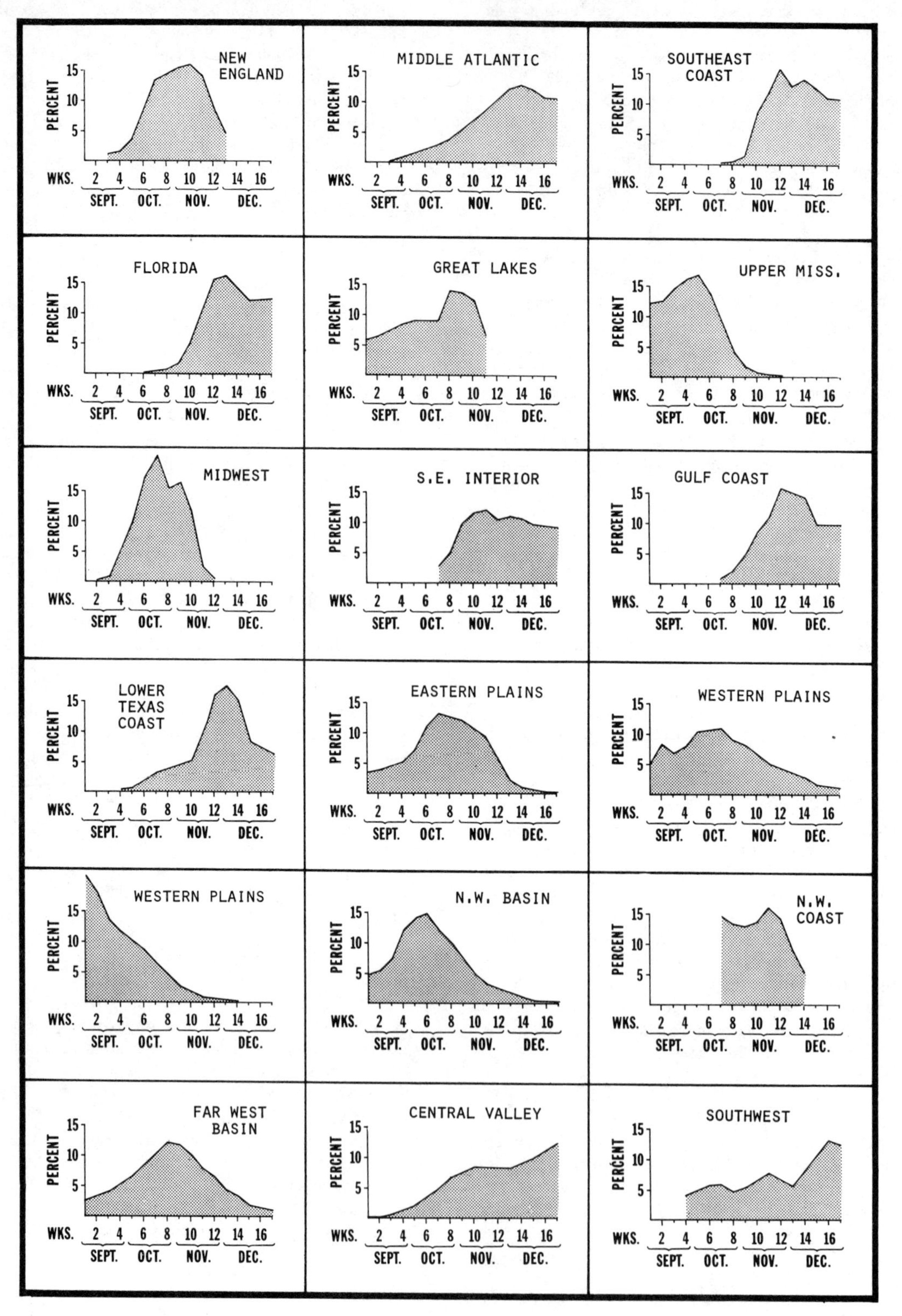

Fall

RUDDY DUCK

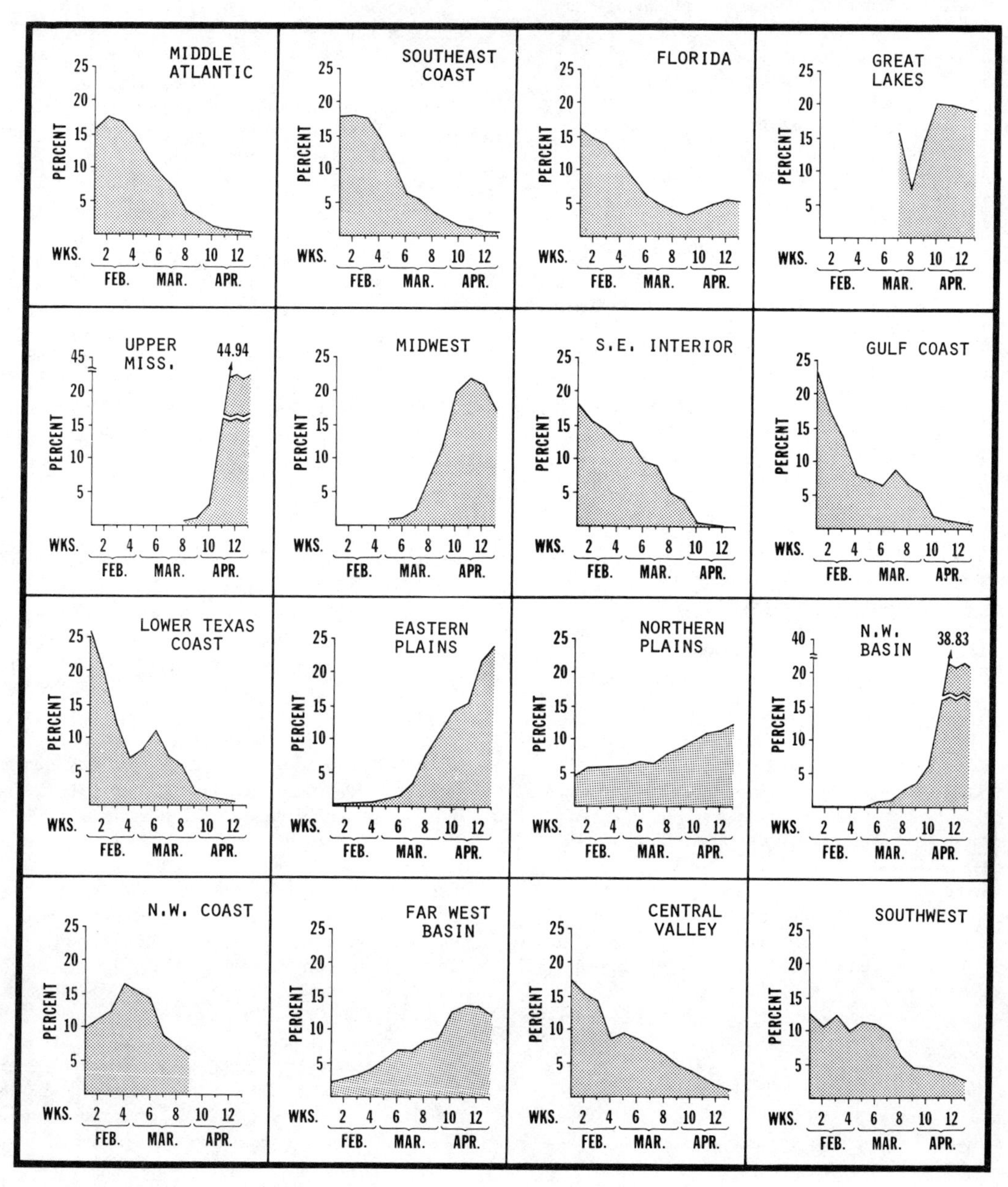

Spring

form bowls measuring 3 inches in depth, with inside and outside diameters of 7 and 12 inches, respectively. Varying numbers of nests have canopies of bent vegetation and ramps of matted vegetation for entering and leaving. The amount of down added to nests varies greatly, from a considerable amount to none at all.

Clutch Size, Eggs, and Incubation. Average clutch size for 312 nests is 8.05 eggs, with a reported range of 5 to 15. Ruddy ducks are noted for their habit of parasitically laying eggs in the nests of other ruddies and other species. At times, several birds have laid 17 to 60 eggs in so-called dump nests that were then neglected by all parties. Weller (1959) listed five species of marsh birds parasitized by the promiscuous laying of ruddy hens and made several references to their intraspecific parasitism. Low (1941) concluded that the degree of parasitic egg-laying by ruddies was proportional to the amount of nest destruction. Considering the ruddy ducks' size, their eggs are astoundingly large, 62.3 by 45.6 mm (Bent 1925). They are as long as canvasback eggs and of greater breadth—more ovate in shape. The eggs are white with a thick, rough, granular shell.

Eggs are usually laid at the rate of one per day. One day was skipped in two of four nests that Helen Hays had under observation for rate of laying. She determined that the incubation period for each of seven ruddy nests was 23 days from the last egg laid. Low (1941) reported that four nests hatched in 25 days and two in 26 days, but he noted that incubation sometimes commenced before laying of the last egg.

Chronology of Nesting. In northwestern Iowa, ruddy ducks began to nest May 8 in 2 years and May 18 a third year (Low 1941). Peak nesting occurred during June 1-15, and the last nest was begun about July 11. At Delta Marsh, Manitoba, ruddies started nesting in late May, reached maximum nesting activity in early June, and started their last nests in late July (Hochbaum 1944). Ruddies began nesting in the Klamath Basin, northern California, in mid-May and continued to initiate nesting into early July (Rienecker and Anderson 1960). The span of nest initiation is between 53 and 63 days and appears to be of similar duration over the entire range.

Nest Success. Ruddy ducks have exceptionally high nest success. Studies of 356 nests in a variety of areas disclosed that 69.6 percent were successful. On areas where the fate of 25 or more nests was determined, success ranged from a low of 55 percent in the Klamath Basin (Rienecker and Anderson 1960) to a high of 88 percent in southwest Manitoba (Helen Hays).

The number of eggs that failed to hatch in 130 successful nests averaged 2.4. Thus, the average successful nest in this group produced 5.7 ducklings. Dead embryos account for over three-fourths of this unusually high proportion of unhatched eggs. The high loss of eggs with embryos is indicative of dump nesting, when intruding hens lay eggs in nests already being incubated by the hosts.

Nest Failure. Of the 86 nest failures reported, 60 percent were caused by desertion, 25 percent by flooding, 5 percent by crows and magpies, and 10 percent unknown. The reasons for the high rate of desertion are unknown, but, in some instances, receding water levels that left nests stranded on dry land were believed responsible. Ruddies attempted to overcome the problem of rising water by building up the bases of their nests, but often the water rose so rapidly that their efforts were doomed.

Renesting. Because of the relatively short span of time in which nesting is initiated, it is doubtful that renesting occurs on a very large scale. Moreover, the high nest success precludes the need for extensive renesting. It is likely that some of the hens whose nests are destroyed during laying or early in incubation do renest. Helen Hays had such an observation. On July 1, she collected a clutch of 10 eggs. Seven days later a new nest was constructed a foot away from the destroyed nest.

Rearing of Young

Broods. Ruddy ducks are unusual among dimorphic ducks in that the drake frequently accompanies the hen and her brood. However, this behavior appears to depend upon the place and season. At Delta Marsh, Helen Hays found that drakes accompanying broods were the exceptions rather than the rule.

On the other hand, at Farmington Bay Refuge, Utah, Joyner (1969) observed that all downy broods were accompanied by both parents up to June 16. During the last half of June he saw both some downy broods and some Class II ducklings escorted only by hens. For example, on June 26, 12 broods were accompanied by both adults, 5 by hens only, and 4 had already been abandoned by both parents. By July 10, only 1 of 22 broods was accompanied by both parents, and 7 broods were without either parent. In Idaho, Oring (1964) reported that three drakes deserted their mates soon after incubation began, and two drakes accompanied their hens and broods until the young were half grown, when both parents deserted and molted. At Minnedosa, Manitoba, Evans et al. (1952) observed 13 percent of Class I broods without hens, 57 percent of Class II broods, and all of Class III broods. Desertion on this scale was almost twice as high as for other diving ducks in the study area. The time when broods are abandoned varies with the age of the brood and the lateness of the season, but most broods are independent by the time they reach Class III.

Helen Hays observed a ruddy brood closely for 4 days. The first 3 days the brood was active 57 percent of the time, but on the fourth day their activity increased to 74 percent. Feeding during the periods of activity also increased from 27 to 42 percent. During this time, the hen brooded her young at night on an old coot nest 100 feet away from her own nest.

According to Evans et al. (1952), marked ruddy broods in the pothole country of southwest Manitoba were more sedentary than other species. Only one of eight broods was known to travel overland. In the same region, Helen Hays saw four female ruddies lead their young overland as far as 674 feet. Indeed, one hen elected to travel 400 feet overland rather than take her brood from a pothole to a large marsh by way of a connecting channel.

In the pothole region of South Dakota, Evans and Black (1956) observed that about a third of the ruddy broods were feeding in deep marshes and two-thirds in open water areas. At Farmington Bay, Utah, Joyner (1969) found that broods congregated along channels leading to ponds surrounded by heavy growths of vegetation.

Development. In southwestern Manitoba, Helen Hays observed that young ruddies could fly when they were 6 to 7 weeks old. She periodically weighed known-aged ducklings in the wild and found that they grew extremely rapidly, reaching 1.45 pounds, an adult weight, in 42 days.

Survival. The average size of Class I broods is 5.69 (962), identical with the number hatching from successful nests, indicating that there is little mortality the first few days of life. An odd fact is that tallies show a decrease of 11 percent in brood size between Class I and Class II (average, 4.96 young in 562 broods) and a further 11 percent decline from Class II to Class III brood size (average, 4.43 young in 164 broods). These losses are a third larger than those for canvasback broods and double those for redheads occupying the same or similar habitats. Perhaps early desertion by the hens causes the mounting losses in ruddy duck broods. Perhaps broods without parental protection suffer unusually large losses from stress, predators, and straying.

POSTBREEDING SEASON

Unlike other prairie ducks, drake ruddies enter the wing molt in midsummer, their nuptial plumage still almost intact (Hochbaum 1944). Helen Hays reports that by the middle of August in southern Manitoba most males have begun their postnuptial molt. She collected three molting males, August 20-23, that showed that wing and tail feathers were lost and renewed first, followed by the more gradual replacement of head and body feathers. One bird had already regained its flight feathers. At Farmington Bay, Utah, Joyner (1969) observed that adult males disappeared in late July, probably for the wing molt.

FOOD HABITS

Ruddy ducks are primarily vegetarians and secondarily consumers of animal life, but their diet varies with age, season, and location. Although they regularly dive for food in water 2 to 10 feet in depth, ruddies occasionally feed on the surface or simply immerse their heads to select bits of aquatic plants. They are more prone to feed in small bodies of water than scaups and canvasbacks, often feeding in ponds excavated for highway fill. In 25 dives, ruddies were recorded below the water surface a minimum of 17 seconds, a maximum of 28, and an average of 20 seconds (Heintzelman and Newberry 1964).

An analysis of the contents of 163 adult ruddy duck gizzards collected in 31 states and 5 provinces showed 72.4 percent plant food and 27.6 percent animal food (Cottam 1939). Pondweed seeds, tubers, and leafy parts comprised a fifth of all food taken, bulrush seeds 16 percent, widgeon grass 5 percent, and muskgrass 4 percent. Midge larvae composed the bulk of the animal foods, with mollusks unusually insignificant for a diving duck. Animal foods were more important for juveniles than for adults; animal life amounted to 63 percent of the juveniles' diet, with midge larvae accounting for over a third of the total contents.

On winter grounds at Currituck Sound, North Carolina, Quay and Critcher (1965) found that widgeon grass made up 37 percent of the contents of ruddy duck gizzards, pondweeds 30 percent, and animal life 6 percent. Similar food habits of ruddy ducks were reported in a study by Sincock (1965) that included Back Bay, Virginia, as well as Currituck Sound. He calculated that during their fall-to-spring stay on these bodies of water, ruddies consumed 75,671 dry weight pounds of vegetation and 8,037 dry weight pounds of animal life. Pondweeds amounted to 30,000 pounds, widgeon grass 28,900 pounds, muskgrass 10,100 pounds, and amphipods 7,900 pounds.

Yocom and Keller (1961) reported that widgeon grass comprised 68 percent of the foods taken by ruddies at Humboldt Bay, California, sago pondweed comprised 19 percent, and shrimp—the only animal food—5 percent. At Swan Lake, British Columbia, Munro (1939*a*) found over half of the ruddy's food consisted of bulrush seeds, 17 percent muskgrass oospores, and 18 percent insects. Rawls (1954) determined that ruddy ducks on Reelfoot Lake, Tennessee, chose insects (45 percent), pondweeds (29 percent), and coontail (11 percent) as their principal foods.

When aquatic plants are lacking or scarce, ruddies turn to animal life. The bulk of the food taken by ruddies in turbid, brackish estuarine areas of Chesapeake Bay consisted of clams and snails (Stewart 1962). But in the fresh estuarine areas, wild celery, sago pondweeds, and widgeon grass were the favored foods. The diet of a small sample of ruddy ducks from Rhode Island consisted almost entirely of bivalve clams (Cronan and Halla 1968). Where ruddies concentrate in large numbers in the Illinois and Mississippi rivers, midge larvae appear to be their principal food.

REFERENCES

Addy, C.E. 1953. Fall migration of the black duck. U.S. Fish & Wildl. Serv. Spec. Sci. Rep.: Wildl. 19. 63 p.

———. 1964. Atlantic Flyway. P. 167-184 in J.P. Linduska (Editor), *Waterfowl tomorrow*. U.S. Gov. Printing Office, Washington, D.C. 770 p.

Addy, C.E., and J.D. Heyland. 1968. Canada goose management in eastern Canada and the Atlantic Flyway. P. 10-23 in R.L. Hine and C. Schoenfeld (Editors), *Canada goose management*. 1st ed. Dembar Educ. Res. Serv., Madison, Wisc. 195 p.

Alaska Game Commission Quarterly Report. 1954. Juneau, Alaska. U.S. Fish & Wildl. Serv. 11 p.

Alcorn, J.R. 1953. Food of the common merganser in Churchill County, Nevada. *Condor* 55:151-152.

Aldrich, J.W. 1946. Speciation in the white-cheeked geese. *Wilson Bull.* 58:94-103.

Aldrich, J.W., and K.P. Baer. 1970. Status and speciation in the Mexican duck *(Anas diazi)*. *Wilson Bull.* 82:63-73.

Aldrich, J.W. et al. 1949. Migration of some North American waterfowl: A progress report on an analysis of banding records. U.S. Fish & Wildl. Serv. Spec. Sci. Rep.: Wildl. 1. 48 p. plus maps.

Alison, R.M. 1972. "The breeding biology of the oldsquaw *(Clangula hyemalis* Linnaeus) at Churchill, Manitoba." Ph.D. Dissertation, Univ. of Toronto, Toronto. 129 p.

———. 1973. Delayed nesting in oldsquaws. *Bird-Banding* 44:61-62.

———. 1974. Oldsquaw homing in winter. *Auk* 91:188.

Almand, J.D. 1965. "A contribution to the management requirements of the wood duck *(Aix sponsa)* in the Piedmont of Georgia." M.S. Thesis, Univ. of Georgia, Athens. 58 p.

Amadon, D. 1966. Avian plumages and molts. *Condor* 68:263-278.

American Birds (incorporating Audubon Field Notes). 1971. The seventy-first Christmas bird count. Natl. Audubon Soc., New York, N.Y. Vol. 25:119-524.

———. 1972. The seventy-second Christmas bird count. Natl. Audubon Soc., New York, N.Y. Vol. 26:135-550.

———. 1973. The seventy-third Christmas bird count. Natl. Audubon Soc., New York, N.Y. Vol. 27:135-558.

American Ornithologists' Union. 1957. *Check-list of North American birds*. Published by the American Ornithologists' Union. The Lord Baltimore Press, Inc., Baltimore, Md. 691 p.

Anderson, B.W., and R.L. Timken. 1972. Sex and age ratios and weights of common mergansers. *J. Wildl. Manage. 36:1127-1133.*

Anderson, D.R., and C.J. Henny. 1972. Population ecology of the mallard. U.S. Fish & Wildl. Serv. Resour. Publ. 105. 166 p.

Anderson, D.R., R.S. Pospahala, H.M. Reeves, J.P. Rogers, and W.F. Crissey. 1970. Estimates of the sex composition of the 1967-69 mallard population. Bur. Sport Fish. & Wildl. Adm. Rep. 182. 4 p. plus tables.

Anderson, H.G. 1959. Food habits of migratory ducks in Illinois. *Ill. Nat. Hist. Surv. Bull.* 27:289-344.

Anderson, J.M. 1974. National Audubon sanctuaries. Letter, 3 March, 1974.

Anderson, W. 1956. A waterfowl nesting study on the grasslands, Merced County, California. *Calif. Fish & Game* 42:117-130.

———. 1957. A waterfowl nesting study in the Sacramento Valley, California, 1955. *Calif. Fish & Game* 43:71-90.

———. 1960. A study of waterfowl nesting in the Suisun Marshes. *Calif. Fish & Game* 46:217-226.

———. 1965. Waterfowl production in the vicinity of gull colonies. *Calif. Fish & Game* 51:5-15.

Arneson, P.D. 1970. "Evaluation of molting areas of Great Basin geese." M.S. Thesis, Utah State Univ., Logan. 71 p.

Arthur, G.C. 1968. Farming for geese. P. 113-115 in R.L. Hine and C. Schoenfeld (Editors), *Canada goose management*. 1st ed. Dembar Educ. Res. Serv., Madison, Wisc. 195 p.

Atwater, M.G. 1959. A study in renesting in Canada geese in Montana. *J. Wildl. Manage.* 23:91-97.

Audubon Field Notes. 1966. Sixty-sixth Christmas bird count. Natl. Audubon Soc., New York, N.Y. Vol. 20:97-388.

———. 1967. Sixty-seventh Christmas bird count. Natl. Audubon Soc., New York, N.Y. Vol. 21:81-388.

———. 1969. Sixty-ninth Christmas bird count. Natl. Audubon Soc., New York, N.Y. Vol. 23:113-436.

———. 1970. Seventieth Christmas bird count. Natl. Audubon Soc., New York, N.Y. Vol. 24:101-472.

Aus, P.B. 1969. What is happening to the wetlands? Trans. 34th North Am. Wildl. & Nat. Resour. Conf.:315-322.

Babcock, K.M. 1973. Study XIII. Evaluation of migration and mortality data of blue/snow and Canada geese associated with the Squaw Creek NWR in Missouri. Completion Rep. Fed. Aid Proj. W-13-R-26. Mo. Dep. Conserv. 26 p.

Bailey, A.M. 1948. *Birds of Arctic Alaska*. Colo. Mus. Nat. Hist. Popular Ser. 8. 317 p.

Bailey, A.M., and R.J. Niedrach. 1965. *Birds of Colorado*. Vol. 1. Denver Mus. Nat. Hist. 454 p.

Baillie, J.L. 1955. On the spring flight of blue and snow geese across northern Ontario. *Can. Field-Nat.* 69:135-139.

Baker, J.L. 1971. "Wood duck *(Aix sponsa)* production from nest boxes and brood studies on the Noxubee National Wildlife Refuge." Ph.D. Thesis, Mississippi State Univ., State College. 48 p.

Banko, W.E. 1960. *The trumpeter swan: its history, habits, and population in the United States*. North Am. Fauna 63, Bur. Sport Fish. & Wildl., Washington, D.C. 214 p.

Barclay, J.S. 1970. "Ecological aspects of defensive behavior in breeding mallards and black ducks." Ph.D. Thesis, The Ohio State Univ., Columbus. 176 p.

Barclay, J., and K.E. Bednarik. 1968. Private waterfowl shooting clubs in the Mississippi Flyway. Trans. 33rd North Am. Wildl. & Nat. Resour. Conf.:130-142.

Barry, T.W. 1956. Observations of a nesting colony of American brant. *Auk* 73:193-202.

———. 1960. Waterfowl reconnaissance in the western Arctic. Arct. Circ. 13:51-58.

———. 1962. Effect of late seasons on Atlantic brant reproduction. *J. Wildl. Manage.* 26:19-26.

———. 1966. "The geese of the Anderson River Delta, Northwest Territories." Ph.D. Thesis, Univ. of Alberta, Edmonton. 181 p.

———. 1968. Observations on natural mortality and native use of eider ducks along the Beaufort Sea coast. *Can. Field-Nat.* 82:140-144.

Barry, T.W., and J.N. Eisenhart. 1958. Ross' geese nesting at Southampton Island, N.W.T., Canada. *Auk* 75:89-90.

Bartonek, J.C. 1969. Build-up of grit in three pochard species in Manitoba. *Wilson Bull.* 81:96-97.

Bartonek, J.C., and J.J. Hickey. 1969. Selective feeding by juvenile diving ducks in summer. *Auk* 86:443-457.

Bartonek, J.C., and H.W. Murdy. 1970. Summer foods of lesser scaup in subarctic taiga. *Arctic* 23:35-44.

Batterson, W. 1968. All about brant. Oreg. State Game Comm. Bull. 23 (11): 3-5.

Beard, E.B. 1953. The importance of beaver in waterfowl management at the Seney National Wildlife Refuge. *J. Wildl. Manage.* 17:398-436.

———. 1964. Duck brood behavior at the Seney National Wildlife Refuge. *J. Wildl. Manage.* 28:492-521.

Beckley, O.E. 1962. Wood duck nesting box program: 10-year summary, 1953-1962. Conn. State Board Fish. & Game Mimeogr. Rep. 36 p.

Beckwith, S.L. and H.J. Hosford. 1956 (1955). The Florida duck in the vicinity of Lake Okeechobee, Glades County, Florida. Proc. 9th Annu. Conf. Southeastern Assoc. Game & Fish Commissioners:188-201.

Bednarik, K.E. 1970. Waterfowl production in the Lake Erie marshes. Completion Rep. Fed. Aid Proj. W-104-R-13. Ohio Dep. Nat. Resour. 13 p.

———. 1974. Local Canada goose production survey. Performance Rep. Fed. Aid Proj. W-104-R-16. Ohio Dep. Nat. Resour. 12 p.

Bednarik, K., J.L. Weeks, and R.A. Warhurst. 1974. Wood duck nest box inventory and utilization, 1974. Ohio Dep. Nat. Resour. Wildl. In-Serv. Note 261. 6 p.

Bell, R.Q., and W.D. Klimstra. 1970. Feeding activities of Canada geese in southern Illinois. Trans. Ill. State Acad. Sci. 63:295-304.

Bellrose, F.C. 1943. Two wood ducks incubating in the same box. *Auk* 60:446-447.

———. 1953. A preliminary evaluation of cripple losses in waterfowl. Trans. 18th North Am. Wildl. Conf.:337-360.

———. 1955. Housing for wood ducks. Ill. Nat. Hist. Surv. Circ. 45 (2nd printing). 48 p. First issued in 1953.

———. 1957. A spectacular waterfowl migration through central North America. Ill. Nat. Hist. Surv. Biol. Notes 36. 24 p.

———. 1958. Celestial orientation by wild mallards. *Bird-Banding* 29:75-90.

———. 1959. Lead poisoning as a mortality factor in waterfowl populations. *Ill. Nat. Hist. Surv. Bull.* 27:235-288.

———. 1963. Orientation behavior of four species of waterfowl. *Auk* 80:257-289.

———. 1964. Radar studies of waterfowl migration. Trans. 29th North Am. Wildl. & Nat. Resour. Conf.:128-142.

———. 1967 (1966). Orientation in waterfowl migration. P. 73-98 in Animal orientation and navigation. *Proc. 27th Annu. Biol. Colloquium.* Oregon State Univ. Press, Corvallis. 134 p.

———. 1968. Waterfowl migration corridors east of the Rocky Mountains in the United States. Ill. Nat. Hist. Surv. Biol. Notes 61. 23 p.

———. 1972. Mallard migration corridors as revealed by population distribution, banding and radar. P. 3-26 in Population ecology of migratory birds. U.S. Fish & Wildl. Serv. Wildl. Res. Rep. 2. 278 p.

———. 1974. The effects of short-term weather on the migration of waterfowl. Fed. Aviation Adm. Final Rep., Washington, D.C. 42 p.

Bellrose, F.C., and E.B. Chase, 1950. Population losses in the mallard, black duck, and blue-winged teal. Ill. Nat. Hist. Surv. Biol. Notes 22. 27 p.

Bellrose, F.C., and R.D. Crompton, 1970. Migration behavior of mallards and black ducks as determined from banding. *Ill. Nat. Hist. Surv. Bull.* 30:167-234.

———. 1972. Nest houses for wood ducks. Ill. Dep. Conserv. & Ill. Nat. Hist. Surv. 4 p.

Bellrose, F.C., and F.B. McGilvrey, 1966. Characteristics and values of artificial nesting cavities. P. 125-131 in J.B. Trefethen (Editor). *Wood duck management and research: a symposium.* Wildl. Manage. Inst., Washington, D.C. 212 p.

Bellrose, F.C. and J.G. Sieh. 1960. Massed waterfowl flights in the Mississippi Flyway, 1956 and 1957. *Wilson Bull.* 72:29-59.

Bellrose, F.C., Jr., H.C. Hanson, and P.D. Beamer, 1945. Aspergillosis in wood ducks. *J. Wildl. Manage.* 9:325-326.

Bellrose, F.C., T.G. Scott, A.S. Hawkins, and J.B. Low. 1961. Sex ratios and age ratios in North American ducks. *Ill. Nat. Hist. Surv. Bull.* 27:391-474.

Bellrose, F.C., K.L. Johnson, and T.U. Meyers. 1964. Relative value of natural cavities and nesting houses for wood ducks. *J. Wildl. Manage.* 28:661-676.

Bengtson, S.-A. 1966. Field studies on the Harlequin duck in Iceland. Wildfowl Trust Annu. Rep. (1964-1965) 17:79-94.

———. 1970. Location of nest-sites of ducks in Lake Mývatn area, north-east Iceland. *Oikos* 21:218-229.

———. 1971. Variations in clutch size of ducks in relation to the food supply. *Ibis* 113:523-526.

Bennett, L.J. 1938. Redheads and ruddy ducks nesting in Iowa. Trans. 3rd North Am. Wildl. Conf.:647-650.

Benning, D.S., and R.K. Martinson. 1971. Trends in duck breeding populations, 1955-1971. Bur. Sport Fish. & Wildl. Adm. Rep. 211. 6 p.

Benson, D., and F.C. Bellrose. 1964. Eastern production areas. P. 89-98 in J.P. Linduska (Editor), *Waterfowl tomorrow*. U.S. Gov. Printing Office, Washington, D.C. 770 p.

Benson, D., and L.W. DeGraff. 1968. Distribution and mortality of redheads banded in New York. *N.Y. Fish & Game J.* 15:52-70.

Benson, D., D.D. Foley, and L.W. DeGraff. 1960. Canvasback abundance in New York. *N.Y. State Fish & Game J.* 7:46-59.

Benson, R.I. 1969. Evaluation of split duck hunting season, 1968. Minn. Dep. Nat. Resour. Q. Prog. Rep. 29:181-192.

———. 1970. Wood duck banding on the Lac qui Parle Wildlife Management Area, 1963-69. Minn. Dep. Conserv. Q. Prog. Rep. 29:251-261.

———. 1973. Experimental Canada goose repopulation studies. Minn. Dep. Nat. Resour. Q. Prog. Rep. 33:71-81.

Bent, A.C. 1923. Life histories of North American wild fowl. Order: Anseres (Part I), U.S. Natl. Mus. Bull. 126. Washington, D.C. 244 p.

———. 1925. Life histories of North American wild fowl. Order: Anseres (Part II). U.S. Natl. Mus. Bull. 130. Washington, D.C. 396 p.

Berg, P.F. 1956. A study of waterfowl broods in eastern Montana with special reference to movements and the relationship of reservoir fencing to production. *J. Wildl. Manage.* 20:253-262.

Berger, A.J. 1972. *Hawaiian birdlife*. Univ. Press, Hawaii. Honolulu. 270 p.

Bergman, R.D. 1973. Use of southern boreal lakes by post-breeding canvasbacks and redheads. *J. Wildl. Manage.* 37:160-170.

Bevill, W.V., Jr. 1970. "Effects of supplemental stocking and habitat development on abundance of Mexican ducks." M.S. Thesis, New Mexico State Univ., Las Cruces. 65 p.

Biaggi, V., Jr., and F.J. Rolle. 1961. Records of two migrant waterfowl for Puerto Rico. *Auk* 78:425.

Biehn, E.R. 1951. Crop damage by wildlife in California. State of Calif. Dep. Fish & Game Bull. 5. 71 p.

Billard, R.S., and P.S. Humphrey. 1972. Molts and plumages in the greater scaup. *J. Wildl. Manage.* 36:765-774.

Bishop, R.A., and R. Barratt. 1970. Use of artificial nest baskets by mallards. *J. Wildl. Manage.* 34:734-738.

Bishop, R.A., and R.G. Howing. 1972. Re-establishment of the giant Canada goose in Iowa. Proc. Iowa Acad. Sci. 79:14-16.

Bolen, E.G. 1967*a*. "The ecology of the black-bellied tree duck in southern Texas." Ph.D. Thesis, Utah State Univ., Logan. 133 p.

———. 1967*b*. Nesting boxes for black-bellied tree ducks. *J. Wildl. Manage.* 31:794-797.

———. 1970. Sex ratios in the black-bellied tree duck. *J. Wildl. Manage.* 34:68-73.

———. 1971. Pair-bond tenure in the black-bellied tree duck. *J. Wildl. Manage.* 35:385-388.

Bolen, E.G., and C. Cottam. 1967. Wood duck nesting record from South Texas. *Southwestern Nat.* 12:198-199.

Bolen, E.G., and B.J. Forsyth. 1967. Foods of the black-bellied tree duck in South Texas. *Wilson Bull.* 79:43-49.

Bolen, E.G., B. McDaniel, and C. Cottam. 1964. Natural history of the black-bellied tree duck *(Dendrocygna autumnalis)* in southern Texas. *Southwestern Nat.* 9:78-88.

Bond, J. 1971. *Birds of the West Indies*. 2nd ed. Houghton Mifflin, Boston. 256 p.

Borden, R., and H.A. Hochbaum. 1966. Gadwall seeding in New England. Trans. 31st North Am. Wildl. & Nat. Resour. Conf.: 79-87.

Bossenmaier, E.F., and W.H. Marshall. 1958. Field-feeding by waterfowl in southwestern Manitoba. Wildl. Monogr. 1. 32 p.

Bourget, A.A. 1973. Relation of eiders and gulls nesting in mixed colonies in Penobscot Bay, Maine. *Auk* 90:809-820.

Boyd, H. 1961. Barnacle geese in Europe in 1959-1960. Wildfowl Trust Annu. Rep. (1959-1960) 12:116-124.

Boyer, G.F. 1966. Birds of the Nova Scotia-New Brunswick border region. Can. Wildl. Serv. Occasional Papers 8. 52 p.

Brakhage, G.K. 1953. Migration and mortality of ducks hand-reared and wild-trapped at Delta, Manitoba. *J. Wildl. Manage.* 17:465-477.

———. 1965. Biology and behavior of tub-nesting Canada geese. *J. Wildl. Manage.* 29:751-771.

———. 1966. Tub nests for Canada geese. *J. Wildl. Manage.* 30:851-853.

Brandt, H. 1943. *Alaska bird trails: an expedition by dog sled to the delta of the Yukon River at Hooper Bay.* The Bird Res. Foundation, Cleveland. 464 p.

Bray, R. 1943. Notes on the birds of Southampton Island, Baffin Island and Melville Peninsula. *Auk* 60:504-536.

Breckenridge, W.J. 1956. Nesting study of wood ducks. *J. Wildl. Manage.* 20:16-21.

Bretherton, B.J. 1896. Kodiak Island. A contribution to the avifauna of Alaska. Oreg. Nat. 3.

Briggs, F.P. 1964. Waterfowl in a changing continent. P. 3-11 in J.P. Linduska (Editor), *Waterfowl tomorrow*.

U.S. Gov. Printing Office, Washington, D.C. 770 p.

Brimley, H.H. 1941. Unusual North Carolina records. *Auk* 58:106-108.

Bromley, R.G. 1973. Observation of greater scaup at Ellice River, Northwest Territories. *Can. Field-Nat.* 87:169.

Brown, B.W. 1973*a* (1972). The Big Lake wood duck: a two-year study of its pre-flight mortality, nest population, growth and migration, 1970-71. Proc. 26th Annu. Conf. Southeastern Assoc. Game & Fish Commissioners: 195-291.

———. 1973*b* (1972). Refinement of a method for calculating wood duck survival. Proc. 26th Annu. Conf. Southeastern Assoc. Game & Fish Commissioners:291-292.

Bryan, P. 1945. Use of wood duck nesting boxes in Wheeler Wildlife Refuge, Alabama. *J. Tenn. Acad. Sci.* 20:35-40.

Bue, I.G., L. Blankenship, and W.H. Marshall. 1952. The relationship of grazing practices to waterfowl breeding populations and production on stock ponds in western South Dakota. Trans. 17th North Am. Wildl. Conf.:396-414.

Bull, J. 1964. *Birds of the New York area*. Harper and Row, N.Y. 540 p.

Buller, R.J. 1964. Central Flyway. P. 209-232 in J.P. Linduska (Editor), *Waterfowl tomorrow*. U.S. Gov. Printing Office, Washington, D.C. 770 p.

Bullis, K.L. 1948. Diseases caused by fungi: aspergillosis. P. 403-408 in H.E. Beister and L.H. Schwarte (Editors), *Diseases of poultry*. 2nd ed. Iowa State Coll. Press, Ames. 1154 p.

Bureau of Sport Fisheries and Wildlife. 1961. Waterfowl production habitat losses related to agricultural drainage. North Dakota, South Dakota, and Minnesota—1954-1958. U.S. Fish & Wildl. Serv., Bur. Sport Fish. & Wildl., North Central Region, Minneapolis, Minn. 39 p.

———. 1962. Managing wetlands for wildlife. IUCN Publ., New Ser. 3:219-231.

———. 1966. Waterfowl production areas. Minnesota. U.S. Fish & Wildl. Serv. 24 p.

———. 1967. Summary of private waterfowl hunting clubs in the United States. U.S. Bur. Sport Fish. & Wildl. Manage. Inst., Washington, D.C. 8 p.

———. 1972. Directory of national wildlife refuges. U.S. Fish & Wildl. Serv. 15 p.

Burgess, H.H., H.H. Prince, and D.L. Trauger. 1965. Blue-winged teal nesting success as related to land use. *J. Wildl. Manage.* 29:89-95.

Burleigh, T.D. 1972. *Birds of Idaho*. Caxton Printers, Ltd., Caldwell, Idaho. 467 p.

Burwell, R.W., and L.G. Sugden. 1964. Potholes—going, going . . . . P. 369-380 in J.P. Linduska (Editor), *Waterfowl tomorrow*. U.S. Gov. Printing Office, Washington, D.C. 770 p.

Byrd, G.V., D.L. Johnson, and D.D. Gibson. 1974. The birds of Adak Island, Alaska. *Condor* 76:288-300.

Byrd, G.V., and P.F. Springer. 1976. Recovery program for the endangered Aleutian Canada goose. Calif.-Nev. Wildl. Trans.:65-73.

Cade, T.J. 1955. Records of the black brant in the Yukon Basin and the question of a spring migration. *J. Wildl. Manage.* 19:321-324.

Cahalane, V.H. 1943. Notes on birds of the Kodiak-Afognak Island group. *Auk* 60:536-541.

Cahn, A.R. 1947. Notes on the birds of the Dutch Harbor area of the Aleutian Islands. *Condor* 49:78-82.

Cain, B.W. 1970. Growth and plumage development of the black-bellied tree duck, *Dendrocygna autumnalis* (Linneaus). *Taius* 3:25-48.

Caldwell, J.R. 1967. Breeding ecology of the Canada goose on the south Saskatchewan River. Final Rep. Dep. Nat. Resour., Regina, Sask. 33 p.

Capen, D.E., W.J. Crenshaw, and M.W. Coulter. 1974. Establishing breeding populations of wood ducks by relocating wild broods. *J. Wildl. Manage.* 38:253-356.

Carney S.M. 1964. Preliminary keys to waterfowl age and sex identification by means of wing plumage. U.S. Fish & Wildl. Serv. Spec. Sci. Rep.: Wildl. 82. 47 p.

———. 1967. Age ratios of some important duck species killed during the 1966-67 hunting season compared with those of prior years. Bur. Sport Fish. & Wildl. Adm. Rep. 135. 11 p.

Carter, B.C. 1958. The American goldeneye in central New Brunswick. Can. Wildl. Serv. Wildl. Manage. Bull. (Ser. 2) 9. 47 p.

Chabreck, R.H. 1960. Coastal marsh impoundments for ducks in Louisiana. Proc. 14th Annu. Conf. Southeastern Assoc. Game & Fish Commissioners: 24-29.

———. 1965. Sarcosporidiosis in ducks in Louisiana. Trans. 30th North Am. Wildl. Conf.:174-184.

———. 1966. Molting gadwall *(Anas strepera)* in Louisiana. *Auk* 83:664.

Chabreck, R.H., and H.H. Dupuie. 1973 (1972). A comparison of nesting in Canada geese used for establishing home-grown flocks. Proc. 26th Annu. Conf. Southeastern Assoc. Game & Fish Commissioners:288-291.

Chamberlain, E.B., Jr. 1960. Florida waterfowl populations, habitats and management. Fla. Game and Fresh Water Fish Comm. Tech. Bull. 7. 62 p.

Chamberlain E.B. 1967 (1966). Progress report: productivity study of whistling swans wintering in Chesapeake Bay. Proc. 20th Annu. Conf. Southeastern Assoc. Game & Fish Commissioners:154-157.

Chapman, C. 1968. Channelization and spoiling in Gulf Coast and South Atlantic estuaries. P. 93-106 in J.D. Newsom (Editor), Proc. Marsh & Estuary Manage. Symp., Louisiana State Univ., Baton Rouge. 250 p.

Chapman, J.A. 1970. Weights and measurements of dusky Canada geese wintering in Oregon. *Murrelet* 51:34-37.

Chapman, J.A., C.J. Henny, and H.M. Wight. 1969. The status, population dynamics, and harvest of the dusky Canada goose. Wildl. Monogr. 18. 48 p.

Chattin, J.E. 1964. Pacific Flyway. P. 233-252 in J.P. Linduska (Editor), *Waterfowl tomorrow*. U.S. Gov. Printing Office, Washington, D.C. 770 p.

Choate, J.S. 1967. Factors influencing nesting success of eiders in Penobscot Bay, Maine. *J. Wildl. Manage.* 31:769-777.

Chura, N.J. 1962. Observation of drakes accompanying hens with brood. *Auk* 79:484.

Clark, S.H. 1968. "The breeding ecology and experimental management of the American eider in Penobscot Bay, Maine." M.S. Thesis, Univ. of Maine, Orono. 169 p.

Clark, S.H., H.L. Mendall, and W. Sarbello. 1974. Use of artificial nest shelters in eider management. Univ. of Maine Agric. Exp. Stn., Res. in Life Sci. 22(2). 15 p.

Collias, N.E., and L.R. Jahn. 1959. Social behavior and breeding success in Canada geese *(Branta canadensis)* confined under semi-natural conditions. *Auk* 76:478-509.

Conover, H.B. 1926. Game birds of the Hooper Bay region, Alaska. *Auk* 43:162-180.

Cooch, F.G. 1958. "The breeding biology and management of the blue goose *(Chen caerulescens)*." Ph.D. Thesis, Cornell Univ., Ithaca, N.Y. 235 p.

———. 1963. Recent changes in distribution of color phases of *Chen c. caerulescens*. Proc. 13th Int. Ornithol. Congr.:1182-1194. Am. Ornithol. Union & Mus. Zool., Louisiana State Univ., Baton Rouge.

———. 1965. The breeding biology and management of the northern eider *(Somateria mollissima borealis)* in the Cape Dorset area, Northwest Territories. Can. Wildl. Serv. Wildl. Manage. Bull. (Ser. 2) 10. 68 p.

———. 1969. Waterfowl-production habitat requirements. P. 5-10 in Saskatoon wetlands seminar. Can. Wildl. Serv. Rep. Ser. 6. 262 p.

Cooch, G. 1954. Ross goose in the eastern arctic. *Condor* 56:307.

———. 1961. Ecological aspects of the blue-snow goose complex. *Auk* 78:72-89.

Cornwell, G.W., and A.B. Cowan. 1963. Helminth populations of the canvasback *(Aythya valisineria)* and host-parasite-environmental interrelationships. Trans. 28th North Am. Wildl. & Nat. Resour. Conf.:173-198.

Cottam, C. 1933. Spring migration of the great blue heron. *Auk* 50:427-428.

———. 1935. Blue and snow geese in eastern United States in the winter of 1934-35—with notes on their food habits. *Auk* 52:432-441.

———. 1939. Food habits of North American diving ducks. U.S. Dep. Agric. Tech. Bull. 643. 140 p.

———. 1968. Research needs in estuarine areas of the Gulf Coast. P. 227-240 in J.D. Newsom (Editor), *Proc. Marsh & Estuary Manage.* Symp., Louisiana State Univ., Baton Rouge. 250 p.

Cottam, C., and W.C. Glazener. 1959. Late nesting of water birds in South Texas. Trans. 24th North Am. Wildl. Conf.:382-394.

Cottam, C., and P. Knappen. 1939. Food of some uncommon North American birds. *Auk* 56:138-169.

Cottam, C., and F.M. Uhler. 1937. Birds in relation to fishes. Bur. Biol. Surv., Wildl. Res. & Manage. Leafl. BS-83. 16 p.

Cottam, C., J.J. Lynch, and A.L. Nelson. 1944. Food habits and management of American sea brant. *J. Wildl. Manage.* 8:36-56.

Coulter, M.W. 1955. Spring food habits of surface-feeding ducks in Maine. *J. Wildl. Manage.* 19:263-267.

Coulter, M.W., and W.R. Miller. 1968. Nesting biology of black ducks and mallards in northern New England. Vt. Fish & Game Dep. Bull. 68-2. 74 p.

Cowardin, L.M., G.E. Cummings, and P.B. Reed, Jr. 1967. Stump and tree nesting by mallards and black ducks. *J. Wildl. Manage.* 31:229-235.

Craighead, F.C. Jr., and J.J. Craighead. 1949. Nesting Canada geese on the upper Snake River. *J. Wildl. Manage.* 13:51-64.

Craighead, J.J., and D.S. Stockstad. 1961. Evaluating the use of aerial nesting platforms by Canada geese. *J. Wildl. Manage.* 25:363-372.

———. 1964. Breeding age of Canada geese. *J. Wildl. Manage.* 28:57-64.

Cringan, A.T. 1971. Status of the wood duck in Ontario. Trans. 36th North Am. Wildl. & Nat. Resour. Conf.:296-311.

Crissey, W.F. 1969. Prairie potholes from a continental viewpoint. P. 161-171 in Saskatoon wetlands seminar. Can. Wildl. Serv. Rep. Ser. 6. 262 p.

Croft, R.L., and S.M. Carney. 1971. Species, age, and sex composition of ducks bagged in the 1970 hunting season in comparison with prior years. Bur. Sport Fish. & Wildl. Adm. Rep. 203. 49 p.

Cronan, J.M. 1957*a*. Effects of predator guards on wood duck box usage. *J. Wildl. Manage.* 21:468.

———. 1957*b*. Food and feeding habits of the scaups in Connecticut waters. *Auk* 74:459-468.

Cronan, J.M., and B.F. Halla. 1968. Fall and winter foods of Rhode Island waterfowl. R.I. Dep. Nat. Resour., Div. Conserv. Wildl. Pam. 7. 40 p.

Cummings, G.E. 1963. Waterfowl nesting and brood production on the Montezuma National Wildlife Refuge, 1961-1963. U.S. Fish & Wildl. Serv. Unpubl. Rep. 9 p.

———. 1973. The Tennessee Valley population of Canada geese. U.S. Fish & Wildl. Serv. Unpubl. Rep. 15 p.

Cunningham, E.R. 1969 (1968). A three year study of the wood duck on the Yazoo National Wildlife Refuge. Proc. 22nd Annu. Conf. Southeastern Assoc. Game & Fish Commissioners:145-155.

Dane, C.W. 1965. "The influence of age on development and reproductive capability of the blue-winged teal *(Anas discors* Linnaeus)." Ph.D. Thesis, Purdue Univ., West Lafayette, Ind. 171 p.

———. 1966. Some aspects of breeding biology of the blue-winged teal. *Auk* 83:389-402.

Dau, C.P. 1972. Observations on the natural history of the spectacled eider *(Lampronetta fischeri)*. Dep. Wildl. & Fish., Univ. of Alaska, College. 96 p. Mimeogr.

———. 1974. "Nesting biology of the spectacled eider *Somateria fischeri* (Brandt) on the Yukon-Kuskokwim Delta, Alaska." M.S. Thesis, Univ. of Alaska, Fairbanks. 72 p.

Decker, E. 1959. A 4-year study of wood ducks on a Pennsylvania marsh. *J. Wildl. Manage.* 23:310-315.

Delacour, J. 1954-1964. *The waterfowl of the world*. Country Life Ltd., London. Vols. 1-4.

Delacour, J., and E. Mayr. 1945. The family Anatidae. *Wilson Bull.* 57:3-55.

Delacour, J., and J.T. Zimmer. 1952. The identity of *Anser nigricans* Lawrence 1846. *Auk* 69:82-84.

Delnicki, D., and E. Bolen. 1976. Renesting in the black-bellied whistling duck. *Auk* 93:535-542.

Dement'ev, G.P., and N.A. Gladkov (Editors). 1967. *Birds of the Soviet Union*. Vol. 2. Translated from Russian by Israel Prog. Sci. Trans., U.S. Dep. Inter. & Natl. Sci. Foundation, Washington, D.C. 683 p.

Denson, E.P., Jr., and W.W. Bentley. 1962. The migration and status of waterfowl at Humboldt Bay, California. *Murrelet* 43:19-28.

Denson, E.P., Jr., and S.L. Murrell. 1962. Black brant populations of Humboldt Bay, California. *J. Wildl. Manage*. 26:257-262.

Des Lauriers, J.R., and B.H. Brattstrom. 1965. Cooperative feeding behavior in red-breasted mergansers. *Auk* 82:639.

de Vos, A. 1964. Observations on the behavior of captive trumpeter swans during the breeding season. *Ardea* 52:166-189.

Dey, N.H. 1966. Canada goose production and population stability, Ogden Bay waterfowl management area, Utah. Utah State Dep. Fish & Game Publ. 66-7. 38 p.

Dickey, C. 1957*a*. Shooting preserve management. Sportsmen's Serv. Bur., New York, N.Y. 32 p.

———. 1957*b*. Shooting preserves in the United States. Trans. 22nd North Am. Wildl. Conf.:396-404.

Dill, H.H., and F.B. Lee (Editors). 1970. *Home grown honkers*. Bur. Sport Fish. & Wildl. 154 p.

Dillon, O.W., Jr. 1959. Food habits of wild mallard ducks in three Louisiana parishes. Trans. 24th North Am. Wildl. Conf.:374-382.

Dimmick, R.W. 1968. Canada geese of Jackson Hole: their ecology and management. Wyoming Game & Fish Comm. Bull. 11. 86 p.

Dirschl, H.J. 1969. Foods of lesser scaup and blue-winged teal in the Saskatchewan River delta. *J. Wildl. Manage*. 33:77-87.

Doty, H.A., and A.D. Kruse. 1972. Techniques for establishing local breeding populations of wood ducks. *J. Wildl. Manage*. 36:428-435.

Dow, D.D. 1964. Diving times of wintering water birds. *Auk* 81:556-558.

Dow, J.S. 1943. A study of nesting Canada geese in Honey Lake Valley, California. *Calif. Fish & Game* 29:3-18.

Dreis, R.E., and G.O. Hendrickson. 1952. Wood duck production from nest-boxes and natural cavities on the Lake Odessa area, Iowa in 1951. *Iowa Bird Life 22:19-22*.

Drewien, R.C., and L.F. Fredrickson. 1970. High density mallard nesting on a South Dakota island. *Wilson Bull.* 82:95-96.

Driver, P.M. 1959. Wildfowl of the Hemiarctic. Wildfowl Trust Annu. Rep. (1957-1958) 10:141-143.

Drury, W.H., Jr. 1953. Birds of the Saint Elias quadrangle in the southwestern Yukon Territory. *Can. Field-Nat.* 67:103-128.

———. 1961. Observations on some breeding water birds of Bylot Island. *Can. Field-Nat.* 75:84-101.

Ducks Unlimited (Canada). 1974. Ducks Unlimited (Canada) 1974 Annu. Rep., Winnipeg. 24 p.

Duebbert, H.F. 1966. Island nesting of the gadwall in North Dakota. *Wilson Bull.* 78:12-25.

———. 1969. High nest density and hatching success of ducks on South Dakota CAP land. Trans. 34th North Am. Wildl. & Nat. Resour. Conf.:218-229.

Durant, A.J. 1956. Impaction and pressure necrosis in Canada geese due to eating dry hulled soybeans. *J. Wildl. Manage*. 20:399-404.

Dwight, J., Jr. 1900. The sequence of plumages and molts of the passerine birds of New York. Ann. N.Y. Acad. Sci. 13:73-360.

Dwyer, T.J. 1970. Waterfowl breeding habitat in agricultural and nonagricultural land in Manitoba. *J. Wildl. Manage*. 34:130-136.

Dzubin, A. 1955. Some evidence of home range in waterfowl. Trans. 20th North Am. Wildl. Conf.:278-298.

———. 1959. Growth and plumage development of wild-trapped juvenile canvasback *(Aythya valisineria). J. Wildl. Manage*. 23:279-290.

———. 1964. Two possible wild hybrids of the white-fronted goose x snow goose. *Blue Jay* 22:106-108.

———. 1965. A study of migrating Ross geese in western Saskatchewan. *Condor* 67:511-534.

Dzubin, A., and J.B. Gollop. 1972 (1969). Aspects of mallard breeding ecology in Canadian parkland and grassland. P. 113-152 in Population ecology of migratory birds. Bur. Sport Fish. & Wildl., Wildl. Res. Rep. 2. 278 p.

Eberhardt, L.L. 1969. Population analysis. P. 457-495 in R.H. Giles, Jr. (Editor), *Wildlife management techniques*. 3rd ed., rev. The Wildlife Society, Washington, D.C. 623 p.

Edwards, R.Y. 1953. Barrow's goldeneye using crow nests in British Columbia. *Wilson Bull.* 65:197-198.

Einarsen, A.S. 1965. *Black brant: sea goose of the Pacific Coast*. Univ. of Washington Press, Seattle. 142 p.

Eisenhauer, D.I., and D.A. Frazer. 1972. Nesting ecology of the emperor goose *(Philacte canagica* Sewastianov) in the Kokechik Bay region, Alaska. Dep. For. Conserv., Purdue Univ., West Lafayette, Ind. 82 p.

Eisenhauer, D.I., C.A. Strang, and C.M. Kirkpatrick. 1971. Nesting ecology of the emperor goose *(Philacte canagica* Sewastianov) in the Kokechik Bay region, Alaska. Dep. For. Conserv., Purdue Univ., West Lafayette, Ind. 66 p.

Eklund, C.R. 1946. Mortality notes on the trumpeter swan. *Auk* 63:89-90.

———. 1956. Bird and mammal notes from the interior Ungava Peninsula. *Can. Field-Nat.* 70:69-76.

Elgas, B. 1970. Breeding populations of tule white-fronted geese in northwestern Canada. *Wilson Bull.* 82:420-426.

Ellarson, R.S. 1956. A study of the oldsquaw duck on Lake Michigan. Ph.D. Thesis, Univ. of Wisconsin, Madison. 231 p.

Ellig, L.J. 1955. Waterfowl relationships to Greenfields Lake, Teton County, Montana. Mont. Fish & Game Comm. Tech. Bull. 1. 35 p.

Emlen, S.T., and H.W. Ambrose III. 1970. Feeding interactions of snowy egrets and red-breasted mergansers. *Auk* 87:164-165.

Erickson, R.C. 1948. "Life history and ecology of the canvas-back, *Nyroca valisineria* (Wilson), in southeastern Oregon." Ph.D. Thesis, Iowa State Coll., Ames. 324 p.

Erskine, A.J. 1961. Nest-site tenacity and homing in the bufflehead. *Auk* 78:389-396.

———. 1971. Growth, and annual cycles in weights, plumages and reproductive organs of goosanders in eastern Canada. *Ibis* 113:42-58.

———. 1972*a*. Postbreeding assemblies of ring-necked ducks in eastern Nova Scotia. *Auk* 89:449-450.

———. 1972*b*. Buffleheads. Can. Wildl. Serv. Monogr. Ser. 4. 240 p.

———. 1972*c*. Populations, movements and seasonal distribution of mergansers in northern Cape Breton Island. Can. Wildl. Serv. Rep. Ser. 17. 36 p.

Evans, C.D., and K.E. Black. 1956. Duck production studies on the prairie potholes of South Dakota. U.S. Fish and Wildl. Serv. Spec. Sci. Rep.:Wildl. 32. 59 p.

Evans, C.D., A.S. Hawkins, and W.H. Marshall. 1952. Movements of waterfowl broods in Manitoba. U.S. Fish & Wildl. Serv. Spec. Sci. Rep.:Wildl. 16. 47 p. plus plates.

Evans, R.D., and C.W. Wolfe, Jr. 1967. Waterfowl production in the rainwater basin area of Nebraska. *J. Wildl. Manage.* 31:788-794.

Evans, R.M. 1970. Oldsquaws nesting in association with Arctic terns at Churchill, Manitoba. *Wilson Bull.* 82:383-390.

Evrard, J.O. 1970. Assessing and improving the ability of hunters to identify flying waterfowl. *J. Wildl. Manage.* 34:114-126.

Ewaschuk, E., and D.A. Boag. 1972. Factors affecting hatching success of densely nesting Canada geese. *J. Wildl. Manage.* 36:1097-1106.

Fallis, A.M., and D.O. Trainer, Jr. 1964. Blood parasites. P. 343-348 in J.P. Linduska (Editor), *Waterfowl tomorrow*. U.S. Fish & Wildl. Serv., Washington, D.C. 770 p.

Farley, F.L. 1932. *Birds of the Battle River region (of central Alberta)*. Inst. of Applied Art, Ltd., Edmonton, Alberta. 85 p.

Fay, F.H. 1961. The distribution of waterfowl to St. Lawrence Island, Alaska. Wildfowl Trust Annu. Rep. (1959-1960) 12:70-80.

Ferguson, W.H. 1966. Will my birds nest this year? *Modern Game Breeding* 2:18-20, 34-35.

Fiedler, D. 1966. Results of wood duck usage of artificial nesting boxes during the 1966 nesting season in the study area in Morrison County, in Central Minnesota—a progress report. Mimeogr. Rep. 12 p.

Fisher, A.K. 1895. The masked duck *(Oxyura dominicus)* in the lower Rio Grande Valley, Texas. *Auk* 12:297.

Fleming, W.B. 1959. Migratory waterfowl in Arizona. Ariz. Game & Fish Dep. Wildl. Bull. 5. 74 p.

Flickinger, E.L. 1975. Incubation by a male fulvous tree duck. *Wilson Bull.* 87:106-107.

Flickinger, E.L., and K. A. King. 1972. Some effects of aldrin-treated rice on Gulf Coast wildlife. *J. Wildl. Manage.* 36:706-727.

Flickinger, E.L., K.A. King, and O. Heyland. 1973. Pen-reared fulvous tree ducks used in movement studies of wild populations. *J. Wildl. Manage.* 37:171-175.

Forbush, E.H. 1925. *Birds of Massachusetts and other New England states*. Part 1. Mass. Dep. Agric. 481 p.

Fraser, J.K. 1957. Birds observed in the central Canadian Arctic, 1953, 1955, 1956. *Can. Field-Nat.* 71:192-199.

Frazer, D.A. 1972. Parental and brood behavior of the emperor goose *(Philacte canagica* Sewastianov) in the Kokechik Bay region, Alaska. Dep. For. Conserv., Purdue Univ., West Lafayette, Ind. 52 p.

Freeman, M.M.R. 1970*a*. Observations on the seasonal behavior of the Hudson Bay eider *(Somateria mollissima sedentaria)*. *Can. Field-Nat.* 84:145-153.

———. 1970*b*. The birds of the Belcher Islands, Northwest Territories, Canada. *Can. Field-Nat.* 84:277-290.

Fritsch, L.E., and I.O. Buss. 1958. Food of the American merganser in Unakwik Inlet, Alaska. *Condor* 60:410-411.

Fuller, R.W. 1953. "Studies in the life history and ecology of the American pintail, *Anas acuta tzitzihoa* (Vieillot), in Utah." M.S. Thesis, Utah State Agric. Coll., Logan. 181 p.

Fuller, R.W., and E.G. Bolen. 1963. Dual wood duck occupancy of a nesting box. *Wilson Bull.* 75:94-95.

Funk, H.D., D. Witt, G.F. Wrakestraw, G.F. Merrill, T. Kuck, D. Timm, T. Logan, and C. D. Stutzenbaker. 1971. Justification of the Central Flyway high plains mallard management unit. Central Flyway Tech. Com. Rep. 48 p.

Gabrielson, I.N. 1946. Trumpeter swans in Alaska. *Auk* 63:102-103.

Gabrielson, I.N., and S.G. Jewett. 1940. *Birds of Oregon. Stud. in Zool. 2.* Oregon State Coll., Corvallis. 650 p.

Gabrielson, I.N., and F.C. Lincoln. 1959. *Birds of Alaska*. The Stackpole Co., Harrisburg, Pa. & Wildl. Manage. Inst., Washington, D.C. 922 p.

Gabrielson, I.N., and B.S. Wright. 1951. Notes on the birds of the Fort Chimo, Ungava District. *Can. Field-Nat.* 65:127-140.

Gates, J.M. 1957. Autumn food habits of the gadwall in northern Utah. Proc. Utah Acad. Sci. 34:69-71.

———. 1962. Breeding biology of the gadwall in northern Utah. *Wilson Bull.* 74:43-67.

———. 1965. Duck nesting and production on Wisconsin farmlands. *J. Wildl. Manage.* 29:515-523.

Gavin, A. 1947. Birds of Perry River district, Northwest Territories. *Wilson Bull.* 59:195-203.

Geale, J. 1971. Birds of Resolute, Cornwallis Island, N.W.T. *Can. Field-Nat.* 85:53-59.

Gehrman, K.H. 1951. "An ecological study of the lesser scaup duck *(Aythya affinis Eyton)* at West Medical Lake, Spokane County, Washington." M.S. Thesis, Washington State Coll., Pullman. 94 p.

Geis, A.D. 1959. Annual and shooting mortality estimates for the canvasback. *J. Wildl. Manage.* 23:253-261.

———. 1971. Breeding and wintering areas of mallards harvested in various states and provinces. U.S. Fish & Wildl. Serv. Spec. Sci. Rep.:Wildl. 144. 59 p.

Geis, A.D., R.I. Smith, and S.V. Goddard. 1963. Blue-winged teal band recovery and annual mortality rates. Bur. Sport Fish. & Wildl. Adm. Rep. 18. 5 p.

Geis, A.D., R.I. Smith, and J.P. Rogers. 1971. Black duck distribution harvest characteristics, and survival. U.S. Fish & Wildl. Serv. Spec. Sci. Rep.:Wildl. 139. 241 p.

Geis, M.B. 1956. Productivity of Canada geese in the Flathead Valley, Montana. *J. Wildl. Manage.* 20:409-419.

Gershman, M., J.F. Witter, H.E. Spencer, Jr., and A. Kalvaitis. 1964. Case report: epizootic of fowl cholera in the common eider duck. *J. Wildl. Manage.* 28:587-589.

Gibbs, R.M. 1961. "Breeding ecology of the common goldeneye, *Bucephala clangula americana,* in Maine." M.S. Thesis, Univ. of Maine, Orono. 113 p.

Gilmer, D.S., T.J. Dwyer, and S.R. Derrickson. 1973. Waterfowl investigators bug ducks. *North Dakota Outdoors* 36:14-17.

Girard, G.L. 1939. Notes on life history of the shoveler. Trans. 4th North Am. Wildl. Conf.:364-371.

———. 1941. The mallard: its management in western Montana. *J. Wildl. Manage.* 5:223-259.

Glasgow, L.L., and J.L. Bardwell. 1965 (1962). Pintail and teal foods in South Louisiana. Proc. 16th Annu. Conf. Southeastern Assoc. Game & Fish Commissioners:175-184.

Glazener, W.C. 1946. Food habits of wild geese on the Gulf Coast of Texas. *J. Wildl. Manage.* 10:322-329.

Glover, F.A. 1956. Nesting and production of the blue-winged teal *(Anas discors* Linnaeus) in northwest Iowa. *J. Wildl. Manage.* 20:28-46.

Glover, F.A., and E.B. Chamberlain. 1960. Winter waterfowl survev (exploratory), Central and South America, January, 1960. P. 35-43 in 1960 winter waterfowl survey, Mexico, Central and South America. Bur. Sport Fish. & Wildl., Washington, D.C. 43 p.

Gochfeld, M. 1968. Notes on the status of the tufted duck *(Aythya fuligula)* in North America with a report of a new observation from Wyoming. *Condor* 70:186-187.

Godfrey, W.E. 1966. The birds of Canada. Natl. Mus. Can. Bull. 203. Ottawa. 428 p.

Gollop, J.B., and W.H. Marshall. 1954. A guide for aging duck broods in the field. Miss. Flyway Counc. Tech. Sect. 14 p.

Greenwood, R.J. 1972. Comparative data on game farm and wild mallard strains. Northern Prairie Wildl. Res. Center Unpubl. MS.

Grenquist, P. 1968. Observations on immature goldeneye *(Bucephala clangula)* yearlings on breeding grounds. *Suomen Riista* 20:112-117. (In Finnish with English summary.)

Grice, D., and J.P. Rogers. 1965. The wood duck in Massachusetts. Final Rep. Proj. No. W-19-12, Mass. Div. Fish & Game. 96 p.

Grieb, J.R. 1968. Canada goose populations of the Central Flyway—their status and future. P. 31-41 in R.L. Hine and C. Schoenfeld (Editors), *Canada goose management.* 1st ed. Dembar Educ. Res. Serv., Madison, Wisc. 195 p.

———. 1970. The shortgrass prairie Canada goose population. Wildl. Monogr. 22. 49 p.

Griffee, W.E. 1958. Notes on Oregon nesting of American merganser and Barrow's golden-eye. *Murrelet* 39:26.

Grinnell, G.B. 1901. *American duck shooting.* For. & Stream Publ. Co., New York. 627 p.

Griscom L. 1945. Barrow's goldeneye in Massachusetts. *Auk* 62:401-405.

Griscom, L., and D.E. Snyder. 1955. *The birds of Massachusetts: an annotated and revised check list.* (MCZ, Harvard U.) Peabody Mus., Salem, Mass. 295 p.

Gross, A.O. 1938. Eider ducks of Kent's Island. *Auk* 55:387-400.

———. 1944. The present status of the American eider on the Maine coast. *Wilson Bull.* 56:15-26.

Guignion, D.L. 1967. "A nesting study of the common eider *(Somateria mollissima dresseri)* in the St. Lawrence Estuary." M.S. Thesis, Laval Univ., Quebec, P.Q. 121 p.

Gulden, N.A., and L.L. Johnson. 1968. History, behavior and management of a flock of giant Canada geese in southeastern Minnesota. P. 59-71 in R.L. Hine and C. Schoenfeld (Editors), *Canada goose management.* 1st ed. Dembar Educ. Res. Serv., Madison, Wisc. 195 p.

Hall, D.L. 1965 (1962). Food utilization by waterfowl in green timber reservoirs at Noxubee National Wildlife Refuge. Proc. 16th Annu. Conf. Southeastern Assoc. Game & Fish Commissioners:184-199.

Hall, L.C., and F.B. McGilvrey. 1971. Nesting by a yearling Canada goose. *J. Wildl. Manage.* 35:835-836.

Handley, C.O., Jr. 1950. The brant of Prince Patrick Island, Northwest Territories. *Wilson Bull.* 62:128-132.

Hankla, D.J., and R.R. Rudolph. 1968 (1967). Changes in the migration and wintering habits of Canada geese in the lower portion of the Atlantic and Mississippi Flyways—with special reference to national wildlife refuges. Proc. 21st Annu. Conf. Southeastern Assoc. Game & Fish Commissioners:133-144.

Hansen, H.A. 1956. Alaska Pacific Flyway report. In John Chattin (Editor), Pacific Waterfowl Flyway Rep. 34.

———. 1960. Changed status of several species of waterfowl in Alaska. *Condor* 62:136-137.

———. 1961. Annual waterfowl report: Alaska—1961. Bur. Sport Fish. & Wildl. 10 p.

———. 1962. Canada geese of coastal Alaska. Trans. 27th North Am. Wildl. & Nat. Resour. Conf.:301-319.

———. 1967. Waterfowl status report 1967. U.S. Fish & Wildl. Serv. Spec. Sci. Rep.:Wildl. 111. 144 p.

———. 1968. Pacific Flyway Canada goose management—federal and state cooperation. P. 43-49 in R.L. Hine and C. Schoenfeld (Editors), *Canada goose management.* 1st ed. Dembar Educ. Res. Serv., Madison, Wisc. 195 p.

———. 1973. Trumpeter swan management. *Wildfowl* 24:27-32.

Hansen, H.A., and D.E. McKnight. 1964. Emigration of drought-displaced ducks to the Arctic. Trans. 29th North Am. Wildl. & Nat. Resour. Conf.:119-126.

Hansen, H.A., and H.K. Nelson. 1964. Honkers large and

small. P. 109-124 in J.P. Linduska (Editor), *Waterfowl tomorrow*. U.S. Fish & Wildl. Serv. 770 p.

Hansen, H.A., and U.C. Nelson. 1957. Brant of the Bering Sea—migration and mortality. Trans. 22nd North Am. Wildl. Conf.:237-254.

Hansen, H.A., C.W. McNeil, and M.D. Priebe. 1957. Mortality of Canada geese and impacted gullets in eastern Washington, 1949-1954. *J. Wildl. Manage.* 21:96-98.

Hansen, H.A., P.E.K. Shepherd, J. King, and W.A. Troyer. 1971. The trumpeter swan in Alaska. Wildl. Monogr. 26. 83 p.

Hansen, H.L. 1966. Silvical characteristics of tree species and decay processes as related to cavity production. P. 65-69 in J. B. Trefethen (Editor), Wood duck management and research: a symposium. Wildl. Manage. Inst., Washington, D.C. 212 p.

Hansen, J.L. 1971. "The role of nest boxes in management of the wood duck on Mingo National Wildlife Refuge." M.A. Thesis, Univ. of Missouri, Columbia. 159 p.

Hansen, J.L., L. Fredrickson, and J.P. Rogers. 1973. Nesting of the hooded merganser in southeastern Missouri. Unpubl. MS. 29 p.

Hanson, H.C. 1949. Methods of determining age in Canada geese and other waterfowl. *J. Wildl. Manage.* 13:177-183.

———. 1965. *The giant Canada goose*. Southern Illinois Univ. Press, Carbondale. 226 p.

Hanson, H.C., and R.H. Smith. 1950. Canada geese of the Mississippi Flyway with special reference to an Illinois flock. Ill. Nat. Hist. Surv. Bull. 25:67-210.

Hanson, H.C., M. Rogers, and E.S. Rogers. 1949. Waterfowl of the forested portions of the Canadian Pre-Cambrian Shield and the Palaeozoic Basin. *Can. Field-Nat.* 63:183-204.

Hanson, H.C., P. Queneau, and P. Scott. 1956. The geography, birds, and mammals of the Perry River region. Arct. Inst. North Am. Spec. Publ. 3. 98 p.

Hanson, H.C., H.G. Lumsden, J.J. Lynch, and H.W. Norton. 1972. Population characteristics of three mainland colonies of blue and lesser snow geese nesting in the southern Hudson Bay region. Ontario Ministry Nat. Resour. Res. Rep. (Wildl.) 92. 38 p.

Hanson, R. 1974. Report on the December, 1973 inventory of Canada geese in the Mississippi Flyway states. U.S. Fish & Wildl. Serv. Rep., Twin Cities, Minn. 13 p.

Hanson, R.C., and A.S. Hawkins. 1975. Counting ducks and duck-ponds in prairie Canada: how and why. *Naturalist* 25:8-11.

Hanson, R.C., and M.M. Smith. 1970. Winter waterfowl survey interior highlands of Mexico. P. 20-32 in Bur. Sport Fish. & Wildl. Rep. 47 p.

Hanson, W.C., and R.L. Browning. 1959. Hanford Reservation nesting geese. *J. Wildl. Manage.* 23:129-137.

Hanson, W.C., and L.L. Eberhardt. 1971. A Columbia River Canada goose population, 1950-1970. Wildl. Monogr. 28. 61 p.

Hardister, J.P., Jr., F.E. Hester, and T.L. Quay. 1965 (1962). Movements of juvenile wood ducks as measured by web-tagging. Proc. 16th Annu. Conf. Southeastern Assoc. Game & Fish Commissioners:70-75.

Harmon, B.G. 1962. Mollusks as food of lesser scaups along the Louisiana Coast. Trans. 27th North Am. Wildl. & Nat. Resour. Conf.:132-138.

Harmon, K.W. 1970. Prairie potholes. *Natl. Parks & Conserv. Mag.* 45:25-28.

Harris, S.W., C.L. Buechele, and C.F. Yocom. 1954. The status of Barrow's golden-eye in eastern Washington. *Murrelet* 35:33-38.

Hartlaub, G. 1852. Descriptions de quelques nouvelles espèces d'oiseaux. Revue et Magasin de Zoologie Pure et Appliquée (2e série) 4:3-7. Paris.

Hartowicz, E. 1965. Evening roosting habits of wood ducks in southeast Missouri. *J. Wildl. Manage.* 29:399-401.

Harvey. J.M. 1971. Factors affecting blue goose nesting success. *Can. J. Zool.* 49:223-234.

Hasbrouck, E.M. 1944. Apparent status of the European widgeon in North America. *Auk* 61:93-104.

Hatter, J. 1960. Baikal teal in British Columbia. *Condor* 62:480.

Hawkins, A.S. 1945. Bird life in the Texas Panhandle. Panhandle Plains Hist. Rev.:110-150.

———. 1964. Mississippi Flyway. P. 185-207 in J.P. Linduska (Editor), *Waterfowl tomorrow*. U.S. Gov. Printing Office, Washington, D.C. 770 p.

Hays, H., and H.M. Habermann. 1969. Note on bill color of the ruddy duck, *Oxyura jamaicensis rubida*. *Auk* 86:765-766.

Headley, P.C. 1967. *Ecology of the emperor goose*. Rep. Alaska Coop. Wildl. Unit, Univ. of Alaska, College. 106 p.

Hein, D., and A. O. Haugen. 1966. Illumination and wood duck roosting flights. *Wilson Bull.* 78:301-308.

Heintzelman, D.S., and C.J. Newberry. 1964. Some waterfowl diving times. *Wilson Bull.* 76:291.

Henny, C.J. 1970. Winter bandings of mallards, black ducks, wood ducks, pintails, canvasbacks, redheads, and scaup in 1967, 1968, and 1969. Bur. Sport Fish. & Wildl. Adm. Rep. 197. 23 p.

———. 1973. Drought displaced movement of North American pintails into Siberia. *J. Wildl. Manage.* 37:23-29.

Henny, C.J., and N.E. Holgersen. 1973. Range expansion and population increase of the gadwall in eastern North America. U.S. Fish & Wildl. Serv. Res. Results and Activities, June 1973.

Herman, C.M., and W.J.L. Sladen. 1958. Aspergillosis in waterfowl. Trans. 23rd North Am. Wildl. Conf.:187-191.

Hester, F.E. 1965 (1962). Survival, renesting, and return of adult wood ducks to previously used nest boxes. Proc. 16th Annu. Conf. Southeastern Assoc. Game & Fish Commissioners: 67-70.

Hester, F.E., and J. Dermid. 1973. *The world of the wood duck*. J.B. Lippincott Co., Philadelphia. 160 p.

Hester, F.E., and T.L. Quay. 1961. A three-year study of the fall migration and roosting-flight habits of the wood duck in east-central North Carolina. Proc. 15th Annu. Conf. Southeastern Assoc. Game & Fish Commissioners: 55-60.

Heusmann, H.W. 1972. Survival of wood duck broods from dump nests. *J. Wildl. Manage.* 36:620-624.

Hewitt, A.H. 1950. Recent studies of blue and lesser snow goose populations in James Bay. Trans. 15th North Am. Wildl. Conf.:304-308.

Heyland, J.D. 1970. Brant breeding on Bylot Island, Northwest Territories. *Can. Field-Nat.* 84:397.

Heyland, J.D., and H. Boyd. 1970. Greater snow geese (*Anser caerulescens atlanticus* Kennard) in northwest Greenland. *Dansk Ornithologisk Forenings Tidsskrift* 64:193-204.

Heyland, J.D., and L. Garrard. 1974. Analyses of band recoveries of Canada geese banded in sub-Arctic Quebec. Unpul. MS. 40 p.

Heyland, J.D., E.B. Chamberlain, C.F. Kimball, and D.H. Baldwin. 1970. Whistling swans breeding on the northwest coast of New Quebec. *Can. Field-Nat.* 84:398-399.

Hickey, J.J. 1952. Survival studies of banded birds. U.S. Fish & Wildl. Serv. Spec. Sci. Rep.: Wildl. 15. 177 p.

Hicks, L.E. 1935. A migration of mute swans. *Auk* 52:301-302

Hinz, T.C. 1974. Factors affecting the fall populations, distribution, and harvest of Canada geese in the Yellowstone River hunting units of southeastern Montana. Final Rep. Fed. Aid Proj. W-120-R-4,5; Mont. Fish & Game Dep. 86 p.

Hochbaum, G.S., and E.F. Bossenmaier. 1972. Response of pintails to improved breeding habitat in southern Manitoba. *Can. Field-Nat.* 86:79-81.

Hochbaum, H.A. 1944. *The canvasback on a prairie marsh*. Am. Wildl. Inst., Washington, D.C. 201 p.

———. 1955. *Travels and traditions of waterfowl*. Univ. of Minnesota Press, Minneapolis. 301 p.

Hocutt, G.E., and R.W. Dimmick. 1971. Summer food habits of juvenile wood ducks in east Tennessee. *J. Wildl. Manage.* 35:286-292.

Hoffman, R. 1927. *Birds of the Pacific States*. Houghton Mifflin Co., Boston. 352 p.

Hoffpauer, C.M. 1968. Burning for coastal marsh management. P. 134-139 in J.D. Newsom (Editor), Proc. Marsh & Estuary Manage. Symp., Louisiana State Univ., Baton Rouge. 250 p.

Höhn, E.O. 1968. The birds of the Chesterfield Inlet District of Keewatin, Northwest Territories, Canada. *Can. Field-Nat.* 82:244-262.

Holder, T.H. 1971. Disappearing wetlands in eastern Arkansas. Arkansas Planning Comm., Little Rock. 72 p.

Hooper, D.C. 1951. Waterfowl nesting at Minto Lakes, Alaska. Proc. 2nd Alaskan Sci. Conf.:318-321.

Howard, J., G. Pospichal, and D. Reid. 1954. Waterfowl breeding ground studies on the Elkhorn area in southwestern Manitoba, 1953. P. 86-93 in U.S. Fish & Wildl. Serv. & Can. Wildl. Serv. Spec. Sci. Rep.:Wildl. 25. 250 p.

Howell, A.H. 1932. *Florida bird life*. Fla. Dep. Game and Fresh Water Fish. 579 p.

Huey, W.R., and J.R. Travis. 1961. Burford Lake, New Mexico, revisited. *Auk* 78:607-626.

Humphrey, P.S., and K.C. Parkes. 1959. An approach to the study of molts and plumages. *Auk* 76:1-31.

Hunt, E.G., and W. Anderson. 1966. Renesting of ducks at Mountain Meadows, Lassen County, California. *Calif. Fish & Game* 52:17-27.

Hunt, E.G., and A. E. Naylor. 1955. Nesting studies of ducks and coots in Honey Lake Valley. *Calif. Fish & Game* 41:295-314.

Hunt, G.S., and A.B. Cowan. 1963. Causes of deaths of waterfowl on the lower Detroit River—winter 1960. Trans. 28th North Am. Wildl. & Nat. Resour. Conf.: 150-163.

Hunt, R.A., and L.R. Jahn. 1966. Canada goose breeding populations in Wisconsin. Wisc. Conserv. Dep. Tech. Bull. 38. 67 p.

Hunt, R.A., L.R. Jahn, R.C. Hopkins, and G.H. Amelong. 1958. An evaluation of artificial mallard propagation in Wisconsin. Wisc. Conserv. Dep. Tech. Wildl. Bull. 16. 79 p.

Hunter, B.F., W.E. Clark, P.J. Perkins, and P.R. Coleman. 1970. Applied botulism research including management recommendations. Calif. Dep. Fish & Game, Wildl. Manage. Prog. Rep. 87 p.

Huntington, E.H., and A.A. Roberts. 1959. Food habits of the merganser in New Mexico. N. Mex. Dep. Game & Fish Bull. 9. 36 p.

Imber, M.J. 1968. Sex ratios in Canada goose populations. *J. Wildl. Manage.* 32:905-920.

Imhoff, T.A. 1962. *Alabama birds*. Univ. of Alabama Press, University. 591 p.

Irving, L. 1960. Birds of Anaktuvuk Pass, Kobuk, and Old Crow. U.S. Natl. Mus. Bull. 217. 409 p.

Irving, L., C.P. McRoy, and J.J. Burns. 1970. Birds observed during a cruise in the ice-covered Bering Sea in March 1968. *Condor* 72:110-112.

Jahn, L.R. 1966. A wildlife organization's views of P.L. 566. Presented at the U.S. Soil Conserv. Serv. Midwest Biol. Workshop, Madison, Wisc., July 25-29, 1966. 24 p. Mimeogr.

———. 1968. Current needs to improve the small watershed program. Presented at the Annu. Meet., Assoc. Midwest Fish & Game Commissioners, Chicago, Ill., July 28-31, 1968. 8 p. Mimeogr.

Jahn, L.R., and R.A. Hunt. 1964. Duck and coot ecology and management in Wisconsin. Wisc. Conserv. Dep. Tech. Bull. 33. 212 p.

Jeffrey, R., and E. Bowhay. 1972. Washington Pacific Flyway report. In John Chattin (Editor), Pacific Waterfowl Flyway Rep. 68.

Jehl, J.R., Jr., and B.A. Smith. 1970. Birds of the Churchill region, Manitoba. Manitoba Mus. Man & Nature Spec. Publ. 1. 87 p.

Jensen, G.H., and J.E. Chattin. 1964. Western production areas. P. 79-88 in J.P. Linduska (Editor), *Waterfowl tomorrow*. U.S. Gov. Printing Office, Washington, D.C. 770 p.

Jensen, W.I., and C.S. Williams. 1964. Botulism and fowl cholera. P. 333-341 in J.P. Linduska (Editor), *Waterfowl tomorrow*. U.S. Gov. Printing Office, Washington, D.C. 770 p.

Jewett, S.G., W.P. Taylor, W.T. Shaw, and J.W. Aldrich. 1953. *Birds of Washington State*. Univ. of Washington Press, Seattle. 767 p.

Johnsgard, P.A. 1960*a*. A quantitative study of sexual behavior of mallards and black ducks. *Wilson Bull.* 72:133-155.

———. 1960*b*. Comparative behaviour of the Anatidae and its evolutionary implication. Wildfowl Trust Annu. Rep. (1958-1959) 11:31-45.

———. 1960*c*. Classification and evolutionary relationships of the sea ducks. *Condor* 62:426-433.

———. 1961. Evolutionary relationships among the North American mallards. *Auk* 78:3-43.

———. 1962. Evolutionary trends in the behaviour and morphology of the Anatidae. Wildfowl Trust Annu. Rep. (1960-1961) 13:130-148.

———. 1964. Observations of the biology of the spectacled eider. Wildfowl Trust Annu. Rep. (1962-1963) 15:104-107.

———. 1965. *Handbook of waterfowl behavior*. Cornell Univ. Press, Ithaca, N.Y. 378 p.

———. 1967. Sympatry changes and hybridization incidence in mallards and black ducks. *Am. Midl. Nat.* 77:51-63.

Johnsgard, P.A., and D. Hagemeyer. 1969. The masked duck in the United States. *Auk* 86:691-695.

Johnson, L.L. 1967. The common goldeneye duck and the role of nesting boxes in its management in north-central Minnesota. *J. Minn. Acad. Sci.* 34:110-113.

———. 1970. A study of the goldeneye, mallard, and other forest species. Minn. P-R Q. 30:129-132.

Johnson, S.R., and C.F. Yocom. 1966. Breeding waterfowl in the Lake Earl-Lake Talawa area, Del Norte County, California. *Murrelet* 47:1-5.

Johnson, T. 1973. The wing molt of the Florida duck. *Wilson Bull.* 85:77.

Johnstone, S.T. 1970. Waterfowl eggs. *Aviculture Mag.* 76:52-55.

Jones, H.L. 1966. The fulvous tree duck in the east: its past and present status. Chat 30:4-7.

Jones, R.D., Jr. 1964. Age group counts of black brant in Izembek Bay, Alaska. Wildfowl Trust Annu. Rep. (1962-1963) 15:147-148.

———. 1965. Returns from Steller's eiders banded in Izembek Bay, Alaska. Wildfowl Trust Annu. Rep. (1963-1964) 16:83-85.

Jones, R.D., Jr., and D.M. Jones. 1966. The process of family disintegration in black brant. Wildfowl Trust Annu. Rep. (1964-1965) 17:75-78.

Jones, R.E., and A.S. Leopold. 1967. Nesting interference in a dense population of wood ducks. *J. Wildl. Manage.* 31:221-228.

Jopson, H.G.M. 1956. Breeding of the American merganser in the Shenandoah Valley of Virginia. *Auk* 73:285.

Jordan, J.S. 1968. Influence of diet in lead poisoning in waterfowl. Trans. Northeastern Sect., Wildl. Soc. 25:143-170.

Jordan, J.S., and F.C. Bellrose. 1951. Lead poisoning in wild waterfowl. Ill. Nat. Hist. Surv. Biol. Notes 26. 27 p.

Joyner, D.E. 1969. "A survey of the ecology and behavior of the ruddy duck *(Oxyura jamaicensis)* in northern Utah." M.S. Thesis, Univ. of Utah, Salt Lake City. 82 p.

Kaczynski, C.F., and E.B. Chamberlain. 1968. Aerial surveys of Canada geese and black ducks in eastern Canada. U.S. Fish & Wildl. Serv. Spec. Sci. Rep.:Wildl. 118. 29 p.

Kalmbach, E.R. 1937. Crow-waterfowl relationships: based on preliminary studies on Canadian breeding grounds. U.S. Dep. Agric. Circ. 433. Washington, D.C. 36 p.

Kalmbach, E.R., and M.F. Gunderson, 1934. Western duck sickness: a form of botulism. U.S. Dep. Agric. Tech. Bull. 411. 82 p.

Keeton, W.T. 1971. Magnets interfere with pigeon homing. Proc. Natl. Acad. Sci. 68:102-106.

———. 1972. Effects of magnets on pigeon homing. P. 579-594 in S. Galler, K. Schmidt-Koening, G. Jacobs, R. Bellville (Editors), Animal orientation and navigation. NASA SP-262, Washington, D.C. 606 p.

Keith, L.B. 1961. A study of waterfowl ecology on small impoundments in southeastern Alberta. Wildl. Monogr. 6. 88 p.

Keith, L.B., and R.P. Stanislawski. 1960. Stomach contents and weights of some flightless adult pintails. *J. Wildl. Manage.* 24:95-96.

Kenyon, K.W. 1961. Birds of Amchitka Island, Alaska. *Auk* 78:305-326.

———. 1963. Further observations of whooper swans in the Aleutian Islands, Alaska. *Auk* 80:540-542.

Kerbes, R. 1975. The nesting population of lesser snow geese in the eastern Arctic: a photographic inventory of June, 1973. Can. Wildl. Serv. Rep. Ser. 35. 47 p.

Kerwin, J.A., and L.G. Webb. 1972 (1971). Food of ducks wintering in coastal South Carolina, 1956-1957. Proc. 25th Annu. Conf. Southeastern Assoc. Game & Fish Commissioners:223-245.

Kiel, W.H., Jr. 1954. Waterfowl breeding population and production in the Newdale-Erickson district of Manitoba—1953. P. 81-85 in U.S. Fish & Wildl. Serv. Spec. Sci. Rep.:Wildl. 25. 250 p.

Kiel, W.H., Jr., A.S. Hawkins, and N.G. Perret. 1972. Waterfowl habitat trends in the aspen parkland of Manitoba. Can. Wildl. Serv. Rep. Ser. 18. 63 p.

Kimball, C.F. 1970. Wood duck band recovery data for 1969 and population trend in the eastern United States and Ontario, 1964-1969. Bur. Sport Fish. & Wildl. Adm. Rep. 188. 8 p.

———. 1971. Wood duck band recovery data for 1970 and population trend in the eastern United States and Ontario, 1965-1970. Bur. Sport Fish. & Wildl. Adm. Rep. 209. 8 p.

———. 1972. Wood duck band recovery data for 1971 and population trend in the eastern United States and Ontario, 1966-1971. Bur. Sport Fish. & Wildl. Adm. Rep. 219. 7 p.

King, J.G. 1970. The swans and geese of Alaska's Arctic Slope. *Wildfowl* 21:11-17.

King, J.G., and C.J. Lensink. 1971. An evaluation of Alaskan habitat for migratory birds. Bur. Sport Fish. & Wildl. Processed Rep. 46 p.

Kirkpatrick, R.G., and J.L. Buckley. 1954. Migratory waterfowl survey, 1954. Prog. Rep. Fed. Aid Proj. W-3-R-9. Alaska Game Comm., Juneau.

Kirsch, L.M. 1969. Waterfowl production in relation to grazing. *J. Wildl. Manage*. 33:821-828.

Kistchinski, A.A. 1971. Biological notes on the emperor goose in north-east Siberia. *Wildfowl* 22:29-34.

———. 1973. Waterfowl in north-east Asia. *Wildfowl* 24:88-102.

Kitchen, D.W., and G.S. Hunt. 1969. Brood habitat of the hooded merganser. *J. Wildl. Manage*. 33:605-609.

Klein, H.G. 1955. Wood duck production and use of nest boxes on some small marshes in New York. *N.Y. Fish & Game J*. 2:68-83.

Klopman, R.B. 1958. The nesting of the Canada goose at Dog Lake, Manitoba. *Wilson Bull*. 70:168-183.

Korschgen, L.J. 1955. Fall foods of waterfowl in Missouri. Mo. Dep. Conserv. P-R Ser. 14. 41 p.

Kortright, F.H. 1942. *The ducks, geese and swans of North America*. The Stackpole Co., Harrisburg, Pa., & Wildl. Manage. Inst., Washington, D.C. 476 p.

Kossack, C.W. 1950. Breeding habits of Canada geese under refuge conditions. *Am. Midl. Nat*. 43:627-649.

Kozicky, E.L., and J. Madson. 1966. *Shooting preserve management: the Nilo system*. Winchester Western Press, East Alton, Ill. 311 p.

Kozlik, F.M. 1972. California Pacific Flyway report, second and third quarters, 1972. In John Chattin (Editor), Pacific Waterfowl Flyway Rep. 68.

Kozlik, F.M., A.W. Miller, and W.C. Rienecker. 1959. Color-marking white geese for determining migration routes. *Calif. Fish & Game* 45:68-82.

Kuyt, E. 1962. Northward dispersion of banded Canada geese. *Can. Field-Nat*. 76:180-181.

———. 1966. Further observations on large Canada geese molting on the Thelon River, Northwest Territories. *Can. Field-Nat*. 80:63-69.

Labisky, R.F. 1957. Relation of hay harvesting to duck nesting under a refuge-permittee system. *J. Wildl. Manage*. 21:194-200.

LaHart, D.E., and G.W. Cornwell. 1971 (1970). Habitat preference and survival of Florida duck broods. Proc. 24th Annu. Conf. Southeastern Assoc. Game & Fish Commissioners: 117-121.

Lane, P.W., G.W. Bond, Jr., and W.H. Julian, Jr. 1969 (1968). Wood duck production and transplants on national wildlife refuges in the South Atlantic states. Proc. 22nd Annu. Conf. Southeastern Assoc. Game & Fish Commissioners: 202-208.

Larche, R. 1970. The waterfowl of Manitoba, 1968-1969. Wildl. Branch, Manitoba Dep. Mines & Nat. Resour. Unpubl. Rep.

Latimer, E. 1968. Jurisdiction and ownership of marshes & estuaries of the South Atlantic and Gulf coasts. P. 33-40 in J.D. Newsom (Editor), Proc. Marsh & Estuary Manage. Symp., Louisiana State Univ., Baton Rouge. 250 p.

Latta, W.C., and R.F. Sharkey. 1966. Feeding behavior of the American merganser in captivity. *J. Wildl. Manage*. 30:17-23.

Lauckhart, J.B. 1956. Calculating mortality rates for waterfowl. *Murrelet* 37:31-34.

Leach, B.A. 1972. The waterfowl of the Fraser delta, British Columbia. *Wildfowl* 23:45-55.

Lee, F.B., and A.D. Kruse. 1973. High survival and homing rate of hand-reared wild-strain mallards. *J. Wildl. Manage*. 37:154-159.

Lee, F.B., and H.K. Nelson. 1966. The role of artificial propagation in wood duck management. P. 140-150 in J.B. Trefethen (Editor), Wood duck management and research: a symposium. Wildl. Manage. Inst., Washington, D.C. 212 p.

Lee, F.B., R.L. Jessen, N.J. Ordal, R.I. Benson, J.P. Lindmeier, and L.L. Johnson. 1964. Waterfowl in Minnesota. Minn. Dep. Conserv. Tech. Bull. 7. 210 p. Edited by J.B. Moyle.

Leibovitz, L. 1969. The comparative pathology of duck plague in wild anseriformes. *J. Wildl. Manage*. 33:294-303.

Lemieux, L. 1959. The breeding biology of the greater snow goose on Bylot Island, Northwest Territories. *Can. Field-Nat*. 73:117-128.

Lensink, C.J. 1954. Waterfowl breeding ground survey, Ft. Yukon Flats, Alaska. Prog. Rep. Fed. Aid Proj. W-3-R-9, Alaska Game Comm., Juneau.

———. 1964. Distribution of recoveries from bandings of ducklings. U.S. Fish & Wildl. Serv. Spec. Sci. Rep.: Wildl. 89. 146 p.

———. 1969. The distribution recoveries from white-fronted geese *(Anser albifrons frontalis)* banded in North America. Preliminary Draft, Bur. Sport Fish. & Wildl., Bethel, Alaska. n.p.

———. 1973. Population structure and productivity of whistling swans on the Yukon Delta, Alaska. *Wildfowl* 24:21-25.

Leopold, A. 1933. *Game management*. Charles Scribner's Sons, N.Y. 481 p.

Leopold, A.S. 1959. *Wildlife of Mexico*. Univ. of California Press, Berkeley. 568 p.

Leopold, A.S., and R.H. Smith. 1953. Numbers and winter distribution of Pacific black brant in North America. *Calif. Fish & Game* 39:95-101.

Leopold, F. 1951. A study of nesting wood ducks in Iowa. *Condor* 53:209-220.

———. 1966. Experiences with home-grown wood ducks. P. 113-123 in J. B. Trefethen (Editor), Wood duck management and research: a symposium. Wildl. Manage. Inst., Washington, D.C. 212 p.

Levine, N.D., and H.C. Hanson. 1953. Blood parasites of the Canada goose, *Branta canadensis interior*. *J. Wildl. Manage*. 17:185-196.

Lewis, H.F. 1933. Banding provides the first certain record of the Eurasian pintail *(Dafila acuta acuta* L.) in North America. *Bird-Banding* 4:112-113.

———. 1937. Migrations of the American brant *(Branta bernicla hrota)*. *Auk* 54:73-95.

Lincoln, F.C. 1943. American pintail on Palmyra Island. *Condor* 45:232.

———. 1950. The American brant—living bird or museum piece. *Audubon Mag.* 52:282-287.

Lindsey, A.A. 1946. The nesting of the New Mexican duck. *Auk* 63:483-492.

Littlefield, C.D., and A. Pakulak. 1969. Arrival dates of birds at Churchill, Manitoba, 1968. *Can. Field-Nat.* 83:397-399.

Lokemoen, J.T. 1966. Breeding ecology of the redhead duck in western Montana. *J. Wildl. Manage.* 30:668-681.

Lokemoen, J.T., and H.F. Duebbert. 1973. An upland nest of the redhead far from water. *Wilson Bull.* 85:468.

Longwell, J.R., and V. Stotts. 1959 (1958). Some observations on the recovery of diving ducks banded in the Maryland portion of Chesapeake Bay. Proc. 12th Annu. Conf. Southeastern Assoc. Game & Fish Commissioners: 285-291.

Louisiana Tech Wildlife Club. 1972. Study of wood duck acceptance of artificial box nests in four North Louisiana habitats. 20 p.

Low, J.B. 1941. Nesting of the ruddy duck in Iowa. *Auk* 58:506-517.

———. 1945. Ecology and management of the redhead, *Nyroca americana*, in Iowa. Ecol. Monogr. 15:35-69.

Low, S.H. 1949. The migration of the pintail. P. 13-16 in U.S. Fish & Wildl. Serv. Spec. Sci. Rep.:Wildl. 1. 48 p.

Lowery, G.H., Jr. 1955. *Louisiana birds.* 1st ed. La. Wild Life & Fish Comm. & Louisiana State Univ., Baton Rouge. 556 p.

Lumsden, H.G. 1969. Kinoje Lake Canada goose nesting study, 1969. Ontario Dep. Lands & For. Unpubl. Prog. Rep. 7 p.

———. 1971. Goose surveys on James Bay, 1971. Ontario Dep. Lands & For. Unpubl. Rep. 31 p.

Lumsden, H.G., and D.G. Raveling. 1968. Kinoje Lake Canada goose nesting study. 1968. Ontario Dep. Lands & For. Unpubl. Prog. Rep. 11 p.

Lynch, G.M. 1968. "Effects of strychnine control on nest predators of dabbling ducks." M.S. Thesis, Univ. of Wisconsin, Madison. 31 p.

Lynch, J. J. 1943. Fulvous tree-duck in Louisiana. *Auk* 60:100-102.

———. 1971. 1970 productivity and mortality and population histories for period 1966-1970 for geese, swans and brant. Bur. Sport Fish. & Wildl. Res. Prog. Rep. 12 p.

———. 1972. Productivity and mortality among geese, swans and brant. Part II. Historical records from productivity appraisals, 1950-1971. Bur. Sport Fish. & Wildl. Res. Prog. Rep. 6 p. plus tables.

Lynch, J.J., and J.F. Voelzer. 1974. 1973 productivity and mortality among geese, swans and brant wintering in North America. U.S. Fish & Wildl. Serv. Unpubl. Rep., Albuquerque, N. Mex. 43 p.

Lynch, J.J., C.D. Evans, and V.C. Conover. 1963. Inventory of waterfowl environments of prairie Canada. Trans. 28th North Am. Wildl. Conf.:93-108.

McBroom, J.T. 1969. Multiple use of the coastal zone. Trans. 34th North Am. Wildl. & Nat. Resour. Conf.:80-86.

McCabe, R.A. 1947. The homing of transplanted young wood ducks. *Wilson Bull.* 59:104-109.

McCartney, R.B. 1963. "The fulvous tree duck in Louisiana." M.S. Thesis, Louisiana State Univ., Baton Rouge. 156 p.

McDougle, H.C., and R.W. Vaught. 1968. An epizootic of aspergillosis in Canada geese. *J. Wildl. Manage.* 32:415-417.

McEwen, E.H. 1958. Observations on the lesser snow goose nesting grounds Egg River, Banks Island. *Can. Field-Nat.* 72:122-127.

McFarland, L.Z., and H. George. 1966. Preference of selected grains by geese. *J. Wildl. Manage.* 30:9-13.

McGilvrey, F.B. 1966*a*. Second nestings of the wood duck. *Auk* 83:303.

———. 1966*b*. Fall food habits of ducks near Santee Refuge, South Carolina. *J. Wildl. Manage.* 30:577-580.

———. 1966*c*. Nesting of hooded mergansers on the Patuxent Wildlife Research Center, Laurel, Maryland. *Auk* 83:477-479.

———. 1967. Food habits of sea ducks from the northeastern United States. Wildfowl Trust Annu. Rep. (1965-1966) 18:142-145.

——— (Compiler). 1968. A guide to wood duck production habitat requirements. Bur. Sport Fish. & Wildl. Resour. Publ. 60. 32 p.

———. 1969. Survival in wood duck broods. *J. Wildl. Manage.* 33:73-76.

———. 1972 (1971). Increasing a wood duck nesting population by releases of pen-reared birds. Proc. 25th Annu. Conf. Southeastern Assoc. Game & Fish Commissioners:202-206.

McGilvrey, F.B., and F.M. Uhler. 1971. A starling-deterrent wood duck nest box. *J. Wildl. Manage.* 35:793-797.

McHenry, M.G. 1971. "Breeding and post-breeding movements of blue-winged teal *(Anas discors)* in southwestern Manitoba." Ph.D. Thesis, Univ. of Oklahoma, Norman. 67 p.

McIlhenny, E.A. 1932. The blue goose in its winter home. *Auk* 49:279-306.

McKay, A.K. 1962. History of the fulvous tree duck in Cove area. Texas Ornithol. Soc. Newsl. 11:7-9.

McKinney, F. 1959. Waterfowl at Cold Bay, Alaska, with notes on the display of the black scoter. Wildfowl Trust Annu. Rep. (1957-1958) 10:133-140.

———. 1965. The displays of the American green-winged teal. *Wilson Bull.* 77:112-121.

———. 1967. Breeding behavior of captive shovelers. Wildfowl Trust Annu. Rep. (1965-1966) 18:108-121.

McKnight, D.E. 1974. Dry-land nesting by redheads and ruddy ducks. *J. Wildl. Manage.* 38:112-119.

McKnight, D.E., and I.O. Buss. 1962. Evidence of breeding in yearling female lesser scaup. *J. Wildl. Manage.* 26:328-329.

McMahan, C.A. 1970. Food habits of ducks wintering on Laguna Madre, Texas. *J. Wildl. Manage.* 34:946-949.

MacFarlane, R. 1891. Notes on and list of birds and eggs collected in Arctic America, 1861-1866. Proc. U.S. Natl. Mus. 14:413-446.

———. 1905. Notes on mammals collected and observed in the northern Mackenzie River District, Northwest Territories of Canada, with remarks on explorers and explorations of the far north. Proc. U.S. Natl. Mus. 28:673-764.

MacInnes, C.D. 1960. "The Canada geese *(Branta canadensis)* of the McConnell River." M.S. Thesis, Cornell Univ., Ithaca, N.Y. 75 p.

———. 1962. Nesting of small Canada geese near Eskimo Point, Northwest Territories. *J. Wildl. Manage.* 26:247-256.

———. 1963. "Interaction of local units within the eastern Arctic population of small Canada geese." Ph.D. Thesis, Cornell Univ., Ithaca, N.Y. 121 p.

———. 1966. Population behavior of eastern Arctic Canada geese. *J. Wildl. Manage.* 30:536-553.

MacInnes, C.D., and F.G. Cooch. 1963. Additional eastern records of Ross' goose *(Chen rossii). Auk* 80:77-79.

MacInnes, C.D., and R.K. Misra. 1972. Predation on Canada goose nests at McConnell River, Northwest Territories. *J. Wildl. Manage.* 36:414-422.

MacInnes, C.D., R.A. Davis, R.N. Jones, B.C. Lieff, and A.J. Pakulak. 1974. Reproductive efficiency of McConnell River small Canada geese. *J. Wildl. Manage.* 38:686-707.

Mabbott, D.C. 1920. Food habits of seven species of American shoal-water ducks. U.S. Dep. Agric. Bull. 862. 67 p.

Mackay, G.H. 1891. The scoters *Oidemia americana, O. deglandi* and *O. perspicillata* in New England. *Auk* 8:279-290.

Mackay, R.H. 1955. Waterfowl production in British Columbia. In John Chattin (Editor), Pacific Waterfowl Flyway Rep. 32.

———. 1957. Movements of trumpeter swans shown by band returns and observations. *Condor* 59:339.

Macpherson, A.H., and I.A. McLaren. 1959. Notes on the birds of southern Foxe Peninsula, Baffin Island, Northwest Territories. *Can. Field-Nat.* 73:63-81.

Macpherson, A.H., and T.H. Manning. 1959. The birds and mammals of Adelaide Peninsula, N.W.T. Natl. Mus. Can. Bull. 161. 63 p.

Maher, W.J. 1960. Another record of the Baikal teal in northwestern Alaska. *Condor* 62:138-139.

Maher, W.J., and D.N. Nettleship. 1968. The pintail *(Anas acuta)* breeding at latitude 82° N on Ellesmere Island, N.W.T., Canada. *Auk* 85:320-321.

Maltby-Prevett, L.S., H. Boyd, and J.D. Heyland. 1975. Observations in Iceland and northwest Europe of brant from the Queen Elizabeth Islands, N.W.T., Canada. *Bird-Banding* 46:155-161.

Manning, T.H. 1942. Blue and lesser snow geese on Southampton and Baffin islands. *Auk* 59:158-175.

———. 1946. Birds and mammal notes from the east side of Hudson Bay. *Can. Field-Nat.* 60:71-85.

Manning, T.H., and D.F. Coates. 1952. Notes on the birds of some James Bay islands. Natl. Mus. Can. Bull. 126:195-227.

Manning, T.H., and A.H. Macpherson. 1952. Birds of the east James Bay coast between Long Point and Cape Jones. *Can. Field-Nat.* 66:1-35.

———. 1961. A biological investigation of Prince of Wales Island, N.W.T. Trans. Can. Inst. 33:116-239.

Manning, T.H., E.O. Höhn, and A.H. Macpherson. 1956. The birds of Banks Island. Natl. Mus. Can. Bull. 143. 144 p.

March, J.R., G.F. Martz, and R.A. Hunt. 1973. Breeding duck populations and habitat in Wisconsin. Wisc. Dep. Nat. Resour. Tech. Bull. 68. 36 p.

Marquardt, R.E. 1962. "Ecology of the migrating and wintering flocks of the small white-cheeked geese within the south-central United States." Ph.D. Thesis, Oklahoma State Univ., Stillwater. 179 p.

Marshall, A.R. 1968. Dredging and filling. P. 107-113 in J.D. Newsom (Editor), Proc. Marsh & Estuary Manage. Symp., Louisiana State Univ., Baton Rouge. 250 p.

Martin, A.C., H.S. Zim, and A.L. Nelson. 1951. *American wildlife and plants.* McGraw-Hill, Inc., N.Y. 500 p.

Martin, F.W. 1960. Analysis of black duck bandings—a progress report. Proc. Annu. Conf. Northeastern Sect., Wildl. Soc. 12 p. Mimeogr.

———. 1964. Behavior and survival of Canada geese in Utah. Utah Dep. Fish & Game Inform. Bull. 64-7. 89 p.

Martinson, R.K. 1965. 1964 summer and pre-hunting season banding and recovery rates of blue-winged teal. Bur. Sport Fish. & Wildl. Adm. Rep. 81. 9 p.

———. 1966. Proportion of recovered duck bands that are reported. *J. Wildl. Manage.* 30:264-268.

Martinson, R.K., and A.S. Hawkins. 1968. Lack of association among duck broodmates during migration and wintering. *Auk* 85:684-686.

Martinson, R.K., and C.J. Henny. 1966. Band recovery data (1965) and preseason population estimates for wood ducks (1960-65). Bur. Sport Fish. & Wildl. Adm. Rep. 114. 16 p.

Martz, G.F. 1967. Effects of nesting cover removal on breeding puddle ducks. *J. Wildl. Manage.* 31:236-247.

Matthews, G.V.T. 1963. The astronomical bases of "nonsense" orientation. Proc. 13th Int. Ornithol. Congr.:415-429. Am. Ornithol. Union & Mus. Zool., Louisiana State Univ., Baton Rouge.

Mayhew, W.W. 1955. Spring rainfall in relationship to mallard production in the Sacramento Valley, California. *J. Wildl. Manage.* 19:36-47.

Meanley, B., and A.G. Meanley. 1958. Postcopulatory display in fulvous and black-bellied tree ducks. *Auk* 75:96.

———. 1959. Observations on the fulvous tree duck in Louisiana. *Wilson Bull.* 71:33-45.

Mendall, H.L. 1949. Food habits in relation to black duck management in Maine. *J. Wildl. Manage.* 13:64-101.

———. 1958. The ring-necked duck in the Northeast. Univ. of Maine Bull. 60 (16). 317 p.

———. 1968. An inventory of Maine's breeding eider ducks. Trans. Northeastern Sect. Wildl. Soc., Fish & Wildl. Conf. 25:95-104.

Mickelson, P.G. 1973. "Breeding biology of cackling geese *(Branta canadensis minima* Ridgway) and associated species on the Yukon-Kuskokwim Delta, Alaska." Ph.D. Thesis, Univ. of Michigan, Ann Arbor. 246 p.

Miller, A.W., and B.D. Collins. 1953. A nesting study of Canada geese on Tule Lake and Lower Klamath National Wildlife Refuges, Siskiyou County, California. *Calif. Fish & Game* 39:385-396.

———. 1954. A nesting study of ducks and coots on Tule Lake and Lower Klamath National Wildlife Refuges. *Calif. Fish & Game* 40:17-37.

Miller, H., and A. Dzubin. 1965. Regrouping of family members of the white-fronted goose *(Anser albifrons)* after individual release. *Bird-Banding* 36:184-191.

Miller, H.W., A. Dzubin, and J.T. Sweet. 1968. Distribution and mortality of Saskatchewan-banded white-fronted geese. Trans. 33rd North Am. Wildl. & Nat. Resour. Conf.:101-118.

Miller, S.M. 1973. "The common merganser: its wintering distribution and predation in a warm water reservoir." M.S. Thesis, Oklahoma State Univ., Stillwater. 90 p.

Miller, W.R. 1952. Aspects of wood duck nesting box management. Proc. 8th Annu. Conf. Northeastern Sect., Wildl. Soc. 6 p. Mimeogr.

Milonski, M. 1958. The significance of farmland for waterfowl nesting and techniques for reducing losses due to agricultural practices. Trans. 23rd North Am. Wildl. Conf.:215-227.

Mississippi Flyway Council. 1965. Wasted waterfowl. Planning Com. Rep. 72 p.

Moffitt, J. 1931. The status of the Canada goose in California. *Calif. Fish & Game* 17:20-26.

———. 1940. An apparently authentic record of the spectacled eider in California. *Condor* 42:309.

———. 1941. Eleventh annual black brant census in California. *Calif. Fish & Game* 27:216-233.

———. 1943. Twelfth annual black brant census in California. *Calif. Fish & Game* 29:19-28.

Moffitt, J., and C. Cottam. 1941. Eelgrass depletion on the Pacific Coast and its effect upon black brant. U.S. Fish & Wildl. Serv. Wildl. Leafl. 204. 26 p.

Moisan, G., R.I. Smith, and R.K. Martinson. 1967. The green-winged teal: its distribution, migration, and population dynamics. U.S. Fish & Wildl. Serv. Spec. Sci. Rep.: Wildl. 100. 248 p.

Monnie, J.B. 1966. Reintroduction of the trumpeter swan to its former prairie breeding range. *J. Wildl. Manage.* 30:691-696.

More Game Birds in America. 1935. The 1935 international wild duck census. New York. 79 p.

Morse, T.E., and H.M. Wight. 1969. Dump nesting and its effect on production in wood ducks. *J. Wildl. Manage.* 33:284-293.

Morse, T.E., J.L. Jakabosky, and V.P. McCrow. 1969. Some aspects of the breeding biology of the hooded merganser. *J. Wildl. Manage.* 33:596-604.

Mowat, F.M., and A.H. Lawrie. 1955. Bird observations from southern Keewatin and the interior of Manitoba. *Can. Field-Nat.* 69:93-116.

Moyle, J.B. (Editor), F.B. Lee, R.L. Jessen, N.J. Ordal, R.I. Benson, J.P. Lindmeier, R.E. Farmes, and M.M. Nelson. 1964. Ducks and land use in Minnesota. Minn. Dep. Conserv. Tech. Bull. 8. 140 p.

Mumford, R.E. 1954. Waterfowl management in Indiana. Indiana Dep. Conserv. P-R Bull. 2. 99 p.

Munro, D.A. 1960. Factors affecting reproduction of the Canada goose *(Branta canadensis).* Proc. 12th Int. Ornithol. Congr.:542-556. Tilgmannin Kirjapaino, Helsinki.

———. 1961. The eider farms of Iceland. Reprinted from: *Can. Geogr. J.*, Aug. 1961. 7 p.

Munro, J.A. 1939*a*. Food of ducks and coots at Swan Lake, British Columbia. *Can. J. Res.* 17:178-186.

———. 1939*b*. Studies of waterfowl in British Columbia: Barrow's golden-eye, American golden-eye. Trans. Royal Can. Inst. 22 (48):259-318.

———. 1941. Studies of waterfowl in British Columbia: greater scaup duck, lesser scaup duck. *Can. J. Res.* 19:113-136.

———. 1943. Studies of waterfowl in British Columbia: mallard. *Can. J. Res.* 21:223-260.

Munro, J.A., and W.A. Clemens. 1939. The food and feeding habits of the red-breasted merganser in British Columbia. *J. Wildl. Manage.* 3:46-53.

Munro, W.T. 1967. Occurrence of the fulvous tree duck in Canada. *Can. Field-Nat.* 81:151-152.

Murdy, H.W. 1964. Population dynamics and breeding biology of waterfowl on the Yellowknife study area, Northwest Territories. U.S. Fish & Wildl. Serv. Prog. Rep. 61 p.

Murray, C. 1948. Fowl cholera. P. 299-310 in H.E. Beister and L.H. Schwarte (Editors), *Diseases of poultry*. 2nd ed. Iowa State Coll. Press, Ames. 1154 p.

Nagel, J. 1965. Field feeding of whistling swans in northern Utah. *Condor* 67:446-447.

Nagel, J.E. 1969. Migration patterns and general habits of the snow goose in Utah. Utah Dep. Nat. Res. Publ. 69-6. 74 p.

National Shooting Sports Foundation, Inc. 1964. 1964-65 national shooting preserve directory. Riverside, Conn. 10 p.

Nature Conservancy, The. 1974. Great Dismal Swamp. The Nat. Conserv. News 24:17.

Naylor, A.E. 1953. Production of the Canada goose on Honey Lake Refuge, Lassen County, California. *Calif. Fish & Game* 39:83-94.

———. 1960. The wood duck in California with special reference to the use of nest boxes. *Calif. Fish & Game* 46:241-269.

Naylor, A.E., and E.G. Hunt. 1954. A nesting study and population survey of Canada geese on the Susan River, Lassen County, California. *Calif. Fish & Game* 40:5-16.

Neff, J.A. 1955. Outbreak of aspergillosis in mallards. *J. Wildl. Manage.* 19:415-416.

Nelson, E.W. 1883. Birds of the Bering Sea and Arctic Ocean. P. 51-118 in: Cruise of the revenue steamer *Corwin* in Alaska and the Northwest Ocean in 1881. Notes and Memoranda: Med., Anthropol., Bot., Ornithol. U.S. Gov. Printing Office, Washington, D.C.

Nelson, H.K. 1972. Wetlands and waterfowl relationships. Water Bank Advisory Board—U.S.D.A. 12 p. Mimeogr.

Nelson, N.F., and A.T. Klett. 1952. Waterfowl breeding ground survey in Utah. P. 159-163 in U.S. Fish & Wildl. Serv. & Can. Wildl. Serv. Spec. Sci. Rep.:Wildlife 21. 303 p.

Nelson, U.C., and H.A. Hansen. 1959. The cackling goose—its migration and management. Trans. 24th North Am. Wildl. Conf.:174-186.

Nichols, M.M., and C.K. Nichols. 1946. White-fronted goose on the coasts of New York and New Jersey. *Auk* 63:598-599.

North American Shooting Preserve Directory. 1974. North American shooting preserve directory: 1974-1975. Reprinted from *Outdoor Life,* Aug. 1974. 4 p.

Odin, C.R. 1957. California gull predation on waterfowl. *Auk* 74:185-202.

Odom, R.R. 1971 (1970). Nest box production and brood survival of wood ducks on the Piedmont National Wildlife Refuge. Proc. 24th Annu. Conf. Southeastern Assoc. Game & Fish Commissioners:108-117.

Oetting, R.B., and J.F. Cassel. 1971. Waterfowl nesting on interstate highway right-of-way in North Dakota. *J. Wildl. Manage.* 35:774-781.

Ohlendorf, H.M., and R.F. Patton. 1971. Nesting record of Mexican duck *(Anas diazi)* in Texas. *Wilson Bull.* 83:97.

Olson, D.P. 1964. "A study of canvasback and redhead breeding populations, nesting habitats and productivity." Ph.D. Thesis, Univ. of Minnesota, Minneapolis. 100 p.

———. 1965. Differential vulnerability of male and female canvasbacks to hunting. Trans. 30th North Am. Wildl. & Nat. Resour. Conf:121-133.

Olson, S. 1951. A study of goose and brant nesting on the Yukon-Kuskokwim Delta. P. 34-61 in Rep. Fed. Aid Proj. 3-R-6, Alaska Game Comm.

Oring, L.W. 1964. Behavior and ecology of certain ducks during the postbreeding period. *J. Wildl. Manage.* 28:223-233.

———. 1968. Growth, molts and plumages of the gadwall. *Auk* 85:355-380.

———. 1969. Summer biology of the gadwall at Delta, Manitoba. *Wilson Bull.* 81:44-54.

Page, C.A., and J.J. Lynch. 1961 (1959). A laboratory study of an Arkansas duck die-off. Proc. 13th Annu. Conf. Southeastern Assoc. Game & Fish Commissioners:161-164.

Page, R.D. [1974.] The ecology of the trumpeter swan on Red Rock Lakes National Wildlife Refuge, Montana. Final Rep., U.S. Fish & Wildl. Serv., Region 1. 131 p.

Page, R.D., and J.F. Cassel. 1971. Waterfowl nesting on a railroad right-of-way in North Dakota. *J. Wildl. Manage.* 35:544-549.

Pakulak, A.J. 1969. "Nesting ecology of Canada geese of the Churchill area, northern Manitoba." M.S. Thesis, Colorado State Univ., Fort Collins. 134 p.

Pakulak, A.J., and C.D. Littlefield. 1968. Breeding status of whistling swans in northern Manitoba. Manitoba Dep. Mines, Resour., and Environ. Manage. Unpubl. MS.

Palmer, R.S. 1972. Patterns of molting. P. 65-102 in D.S. Farner and J.R. King (Editors), *Avian biology.* Vol. 2. Academic Press, N.Y. 612 p.

Parmelee, D.F., and S.D. MacDonald. 1960. The birds of west-central Ellesmere Island and adjacent areas. Natl. Mus. Can. Bull. 169. 103 p.

Parmelee, D.F., H.A. Stephens, and R.H. Schmidt. 1967. The birds of southeastern Victoria Island and adjacent small islands. Natl. Mus. Can. Bull. 222. 229 p.

Parnell, J.F., and T.L. Quay. 1965 (1962). The population, breeding biology and environmental relations of the black duck, gadwall, and blue-winged teal at Pea and Bodie Islands, North Carolina. Proc. 16th Annu. Conf. Southeastern Assoc. Game & Fish Commissioners:53-66.

Paul, W.A.B. 1959. The birds of Kleena Kleene, Chilcotin District, British Columbia, 1947-1958. *Can. Field-Nat.* 73:83-93.

Paynter, R.A., Jr. 1951. Clutch-size and egg mortality of Kent Island eiders. *Ecology* 32:497-507.

Pearson, G.L. 1969. Aspergillosis in wintering mallards. Wildl. Dis. Assoc. Bull. 5:404-405.

Peck, G.K. 1972. Birds of the Cape Henrietta Maria region, Ontario. *Can. Field-Nat.* 86:333-339.

Pelzl, H.W. 1971. Nest parasitism by red-breasted mergansers in Wisconsin. *Auk* 88:184-185.

Penkala, J.M. 1975. Winter food habits and body weight of Atlantic brant. Proc. Annu. Conf. Northeastern Sect., Wildl. Soc.

Penkala, J.M., J.E. Applegate, and L.J. Wolgast. 1975. Management of Atlantic brant: implications of existing data. Trans. 40th North Am. Wildl. & Nat. Resour. Conf.: In press.

Perry, M.C. 1974. Looking out for the canvasback, Part IV. *Ducks Unlimited* 38:21-22, 25-27.

———. 1975. Looking out for the canvasback, Part V. *Ducks Unlimited* 39:14-16, 23.

Peters, H.S., and T.D. Burleigh. 1951. *The birds of Newfoundland.* U.S. Fish & Wildl. Serv. 431 p.

Peterson, S.R. 1969. Ecology of waterfowl in the Uinta Mountains. Utah State Div. Fish & Game Publ. 69-1. 57 p.

Petrides, G.A., and C.R. Bryant. 1951. An analysis of the 1949-50 fowl cholera epizootic in Texas Panhandle waterfowl. Trans. 16th North Am. Wildl. Conf.:193-216.

Phillips, J.C. 1932. Fluctuation in numbers of the eastern brant goose. *Auk* 49:445-453.

Phillips, J.C., and F.C. Lincoln. 1930. *American waterfowl: their present situation and the outlook for their future.* Houghton Mifflin Co., Boston. 312 p.

Pool, W. 1962. Feeding habits of the harlequin duck. Wildlife Trust Annu. Rep. (1960-1961) 13:126-129.

Porslid, A.E. 1943. Birds of the Mackenzie Delta. *Can. Field-Nat.* 57:19-35.

Pospahala, R.S., and D.R. Anderson. 1972. Trends in duck breeding populations, 1955-72. Bur. Sport Fish. & Wildl. Adm. Rep. 221. 8 p.

Pospahala, R.S., D.R. Anderson, and C.J. Henny. 1974. Population ecology of the mallard II: breeding habitat conditions, size of breeding populations, and production indices. Bur. Sport Fish. & Wildl. Resour. Publ. 115. 73 p.

Poston, H.J. 1969. "Home range and breeding biology of the shoveler." M.S. Thesis, Utah State Univ., Logan. 86 p.

Preble, E.A., and W.L. McAtee. 1923. A biological survey of the Pribilof Islands, Alaska. Part I. Birds and mammals. U.S. Dep. Agric. North Am. Fauna 46. 128 p.

Prevett, J.P., and C.D. MacInnes. 1972. The number of Ross' geese in central North America. *Condor* 74:431-438.

Prince, H.H. 1965. "The breeding ecology of wood duck *(Aix sponsa* L.) and common goldeneye *(Bucephala clangula* L.) in central New Brunswick." M.S. Thesis, Univ. of New Brunswick, Fredericton. 109 p.

———. 1968. Nest sites used by wood ducks and common goldeneyes in New Brunswick. *J. Wildl. Manage.* 32:489-500.

Public Health Service. 1963. Report on oil spills affecting the Minnesota and Mississippi rivers: winter of 1962-1963. U.S. Dep. Health, Ed., & Welfare. 40 p.

Quay, T.L., and T.S. Critcher. 1965 (1962). Food habits of waterfowl in Currituck Sound, North Carolina. Proc. 16th Annu. Conf. Southeastern Assoc. Game & Fish Commissioners:200-209.

Racey, K. 1948. Birds of the Alta Lake region, British Columbia. *Auk* 65:383-401.

Raveling, D.G. 1968*a*. Weights of *Branta canadensis interior* during winter. *J. Wildl. Manage.* 412-414.

———. 1968*b*. Can counts of group sizes of Canada geese reveal population structure? P. 87-91 in R.L. Hine and C. Schoenfeld (Editors), *Canada goose management*. 1st ed. Dembar Educ. Res. Serv., Madison Wisc. 195 p.

———. 1969. Social classes of Canada geese in winter. *J. Wildl. Manage.* 33:304-318.

———. 1970. Dominance relationships and agonistic behavior of Canada geese in winter. *Behaviour* 37:291-317.

Raveling, D.G., and H.G. Lumsden. 1967. Progress report: Kinoje Lake Canada goose nesting study, 1967. Ontario Dep. Lands & For. Unpubl. Prog. Rep. 18 p.

Rawls, C.K., Jr. 1949. "An investigation of the life history of the white-winged scoter *(Melanitta fusca deglandi)*." M.S. Thesis, Univ. of Minnesota, Minneapolis. 128 p.

———. 1954. Reelfoot Lake waterfowl research. Tenn. Game & Fish Comm. 80 p.

Reed, A. 1968. Habitat and breeding ecology. Eastern Canada. P. 57-89 in P. Barske (Editor), *The black duck: evaluation, management, and research*. Atlantic Flyway Counc. 193 p.

Reeves, H., M. Lundy, and F. Kreller. 1955. Waterfowl breeding ground survey—Success study area—Saskatchewan, 1955. P. 54-62 in U.S. Fish & Wildl. Serv. & Can. Wildl. Serv. Spec. Sci. Rep.: Wildl. 30. 267 p.

Renouf, R.N. 1972. Waterfowl utilization of beaver ponds in New Brunswick. *J. Wildl. Manage.* 36:740-751.

Rienecker, W.C. 1965. A summary of band returns from lesser snow geese *(Chen hyperborea)* of the Pacific Flyway. *Calif. Fish & Game* 51:132-146.

———. 1968. A summary of band recoveries from redheads *(Aythya americana)* banded in northeastern California. *Calif. Fish & Game* 54:17-26.

———. 1971. Canada goose nest platforms. *Calif. Fish & Game* 57:113-123.

Rienecker, W.C., and W. Anderson. 1960. A waterfowl nesting study on Tule Lake and Lower Klamath National Wildlife Refuges, 1957. *Calif. Fish & Game* 46:481-506.

Roberts, T.S. 1932. *The birds of Minnesota*. Vol. 1. Univ. of Minnesota Press, Minneapolis. 691 p.

Rogers, J.P. 1962. "The ecological effects of drought on reproduction of the lesser scaup, *Aythya affinis* (Eyton)." Ph.D. Thesis, Univ. of Missouri, Columbia. 99 p.

———. 1964. Effect of drought on reproduction of the lesser scaup. *J. Wildl. Manage.* 28:213-222.

———. 1967. Flightless green-winged teal in southeast Missouri. *Wilson Bull.* 79:339.

Rogers, J.P., and L.J. Korschgen. 1966. Foods of lesser scaups on breeding, migration, and wintering areas. *J. Wildl. Manage.* 30:258-264.

Rollin, N. 1957. Incubation by drake wood duck in eclipse plumage. *Condor* 59:263-265.

Rosche, R.C. 1954. Notes on some birds of Yellowstone National Park. *Wilson Bull.* 66:60.

Rosen, M.N. 1971. Avian cholera. P. 59-74 in J.W. Davis, R.C. Anderson, L. Karstad, and D.O. Trainer (Editors), *Infectious and parasitic diseases of wild birds*. The Iowa State Univ. Press, Ames. 344 p.

Rowinski, L.J. 1958. A review of waterfowl investigations and a comparison of aerial and ground censusing of waterfowl at Minto Flats, Alaska. Mimeogr. Rep. 112 p.

Rueter, E. 1955. Waterfowl breeding ground survey, Ft. Yukon Flats, Alaska. Alaska Game Comm. Fed. Aid Rep. W-3-R-10.

Rutherford, W.H. (Editor). 1965. Description of Canada goose populations common to the Central Flyway. Central Flyway Waterfowl Counc. Tech. Com. Rep. 20 p.

———. 1970. The Canada geese of southeastern Colorado. Colo. Div. Game, Fish & Parks Tech. Publ. 26. 65 p.

Ryder, J.P. 1967. The breeding biology of Ross' goose in the Perry River region, Northwest Territories. Can. Wildl. Serv. Rep. Ser. 3. 56 p.

———. 1969. Nesting colonies of Ross' goose. *Auk* 86:282-292.

———. 1970*a*. "Timing and spacing of nests and breeding biology of Ross' goose." Ph.D. Thesis, Univ. of Saskatchewan, Saskatoon. 240 p.

———. 1970*b*. A possible factor in the evolution of clutch size in Ross' goose. *Wilson Bull.* 82:5-13.

———. 1971*a*. Spring bird phenology at Karrak Lake, Northwest Territories. *Can. Field-Nat.* 85:181-183.

———. 1971*b*. Size differences between Ross' and snow goose eggs at Karrak Lake, Northwest Territories in 1968. *Wilson Bull.* 83:438-439.

Rylander, M.K., and E.G. Bolen. 1974*a*. Analysis and comparison of gaits in whistling ducks *(Dendrocygna). Wilson Bull.* 86:237-245.

———. 1974*b*. Feeding adaptations in whistling ducks *(Dendrocygna). Auk* 91:86-94.

Salomonsen, F. 1949. Some notes on the molt of the long-tailed duck *(Clangula hyemalis). Avicultural Mag.* 55:59-62.

———. 1950-1951. *The birds of Greenland.* (In three parts.) Ejnar Munksgaard, Copenhagen. 608 p.

———. 1968. The moult migration. *Wildfowl* 19:5-24.

Salyer, J.C., II, and F.G. Gillett. 1964. Federal refuges. P. 497-508 in J.B. Linduska (Editor), *Waterfowl tomorrow.* U.S. Gov. Printing Office, Washington, D.C. 770 p.

Salyer, J.C., II, and K.F. Lagler. 1940. The food and habits of the American merganser during winter in Michigan, considered in relation to fish management. *J. Wildl. Manage.* 4:186-219.

Salyer, J.W. 1962. Effect of drought and land use on prairie nesting ducks. Trans. 27th North Am. Wildl. & Nat. Resour. Conf.:69-79.

Sanderson, G.C. 1974. Aquatic areas. Proc. Natl. Wildl. Federation 38.

Sanderson, G.C., and F.C. Bellrose. 1969. Wildlife habitat management of wetlands. Suplemento dos An. Acad. Brasil. Ciênc. 41:153-204.

Sargeant, A.B. 1972. Red fox spatial characteristics in relation to waterfowl predation. *J. Wildl. Manage.* 36:225-236.

Saunders, G.B., A.D. Holloway, and C.O. Handley, Jr. 1950. A fish and wildlife survey of Guatemala. U.S. Fish & Wildl. Serv. Spec. Sci. Rep.:Wildl. 5. 162 p.

Schamel, D.L. 1974. "The breeding biology of the Pacific eider *(Somateria mollissima v-nigra* Bonaparte) on a barrier island in the Beaufort Sea, Alaska." M.S. Thesis, Univ. of Alaska, College. 95 p.

Schladweiler, J.L., and J.R. Tester. 1972. Survival and behavior of hand-reared mallards released in the wild. *J. Wildl. Manage.* 36:1118-1127.

Schmidt, R.A. 1966. Needed—a coastwise comprehensive program for development of estuaries. Am. Fish. Soc. Spec. Publ. 3:102-109.

Schneider, K.B. 1965. "Growth and plumage development of ducklings in interior Alaska." M.S. Thesis, Univ. of Alaska, College. 67 p.

Schrader, T.A. 1955. Waterfowl and the potholes of the north central states. U.S. Dep. Agric. Yearb. of Agric. 596-604.

Scott. P. 1952. Mývatn, 1951. Severn Wildfowl Trust Annu. Rep. (1951-1952) 5:125-132.

Scott, R.F. 1948. Waterfowl investigations in the Innoko region of Alaska. P. 107-122 in U.S. Fish & Wildl. Serv. & Dominion Wildl. Serv. Spec. Sci. Rep. 60. 186 p.

Sharp, B. 1972. Eastward migration of blue-winged teal. *J. Wildl. Manage.* 36:1273-1277.

Sheldon, H.P., and F.G. Grimes. 1932. Game laws for the season 1932-33. U.S. Dep. Agric. Misc. Publ. 151. Washington, D.C. 34 p.

Shepherd, P.E.K. 1955. Migratory waterfowl studies nesting and banding, Selawik area. P. 34-52 in Alaska Game Comm. Prog. Rep. Fed. Aid Proj. W-3-R-11.

———. 1963. State of Alaska report on the 1963 black brant production. In John Chattin (Editor), Pacific Waterfowl Flyway Rep. 50.

———. 1964. State of Alaska report on the 1964 black brant production. In John Chattin (Editor), Pacific Waterfowl Flyway Rep. 52.

———. 1965. Waterfowl report. Alaska Game Comm. P-R Q. Rep., Proj. W-6-R-5. Juneau.

Sherwood, G.A. 1960. The whistling swan in the west with particular reference to Great Salt Lake Valley, Utah. *Condor* 62:370-377.

———. 1965. Canada geese of the Seney National Wildlife Refuge. U.S. Fish & Wildl. Serv. Compl. Rep., Wildl. Manage. Stud. 1 & 2, Minneapolis. 222 p.

———. 1967. Behavior of family groups of Canada geese. Trans. 32nd North Am. Wildl. & Nat. Resour. Conf.:340-355.

Siegler, H.R. 1950. Food habits of waterfowl in New Hampshire. N.H. Fish & Game Dep. 7 p.

Sincock, J.L. 1965 (1962). Estimating consumption of food by wintering waterfowl populations. Proc. 16th Annu. Conf. Southeastern Assoc. Game & Fish Comm. 217-221.

Sincock, J.L., M.M. Smith, and J.J. Lynch. 1964. Ducks in Dixie. P. 99-106 in J.P. Linduska (Editor), *Waterfowl tomorrow.* U.S. Gov. Printing Office, Washington, D.C. 770 p.

Singleton, J.R. 1953. Texas coastal waterfowl survey. Texas Game & Fish Comm. FA Rep. Ser. 11. 128 p.

———. 1968. Texas' mistaken mallards. Texas Parks & Wildl. 26:8-11.

Skinner, M.P. 1937. Barrow's golden-eye in the Yellowstone National Park. *Wilson Bull.* 49:3-10.

Sladen, W.J.L. 1966. Additions to the avifauna of the Pribilof Islands, Alaska, including five species new to North America. *Auk* 83:130-135.

———. 1973. A continental study of whistling swans using neck collars. *Wildfowl* 24:8-14.

Smart, G. 1965. Development and maturation of primary feathers of redhead ducklings. *J. Wildl. Manage.* 29:533-536.

Smith, A.G. 1971. Ecological factors affecting waterfowl production in the Alberta parklands. U.S. Fish & Wildl. Serv. Resour. Publ. 98. 49 p.

Smith, A.G., and J.H. Stoudt. 1968. Ecological factors affecting waterfowl production in the Canadian parklands. Bur. Sport Fish. & Wildl. Unpubl. Rep. Jamestown, N.D. 323 p.

Smith, A.G., J.H. Stoudt, and J.B. Gollop. 1964*a*. Prairie potholes and marshes. P. 39-50 in J.P. Linduska (Editor), *Waterfowl tomorrow.* U.S. Gov. Printing Office, Washington, D.C. 770 p.

Smith, I.D., and D.A. Blood. 1972. Native swans wintering on Vancouver Island over the period 1969-71. *Can. Field-Nat.* 86:213-216.

Smith, J.D. 1946. The canvas-back in Minnesota. *Auk* 63:73-81.

Smith, M.M. 1961*a*. Louisiana waterfowl population study, final report June 1949-June 1961. La. Wild Life & Fish. Comm., New Orleans. 49 p.

———. 1961*b*. Louisiana wood duck studies, final report July 1950-June 1961. La. Wild Life & Fish. Comm., New Orleans. [26 p.]

Smith, R.H., and G.H. Jensen. 1970. Black brant on the mainland coast of Mexico. Trans. 35th North Am. Wildl. & Nat. Resour. Conf.:227-241.

Smith, R.H., F. Dufresne, and H.A. Hansen. 1964*b*. Northern watersheds and deltas. P. 51-66 in J.P. Linduska (Editor), *Waterfowl tomorrow*. U.S. Gov. Printing Office, Washington, D.C. 770 p.

Smith, R.I. 1963. Lesser scaup and ring-necked duck shooting pressure and mortality rates. Bur. Sport Fish. & Wildl. Adm. Rep. 20. 6 p.

———. 1965. Recovery rates and relative recovery rates from pre-hunting season bandings of pintails, 1963 and 1964. Bur. Sport Fish. & Wildl. Adm. Rep. 92. 3 p.

———. 1968. The social aspects of reproductive behavior in the pintail. *Auk* 85:381-396.

———. 1970. Response of pintail breeding populations to drought. *J. Wildl. Manage.* 34:943-946.

Smith, T.G. 1973. The birds of the Holman region, western Victoria Island. *Can. Field-Nat.* 87:35-42.

Smith, W.J. 1947. Birds of the clay belt of northern Ontario and Quebec. *Can. Field-Nat.* 71:163-181.

Snyder, L.L. 1941. On the Hudson Bay eider. Royal Ontario Mus. Zool. Occasional Papers 6. 7 p.

Snyder, L.L., and H.G. Lumsden. 1951. Variation in *Anas cyanoptera*. Royal Ontario Mus. Zool. Occasional Papers 10. 18 p.

Soper, J.D. 1942. Life history of the blue goose. Proc. Boston Soc. Nat. Hist. 42:121-225.

———. 1946. Ornithological results of the Baffin Island expeditions of 1928-1929 and 1930-1931, together with more recent records. *Auk* 63:1-24.

———. 1949. Birds observed in the Grande Prairie-Peace River region of northwestern Alberta, Canada, *Auk* 66:233-257.

———. 1951. Waterfowl and related investigations in the Peace-Athabasca delta region of Alberta, 1949. Can. Wildl. Serv. Wildl. Manage. Bull. (Ser. 2) 2. 63 p.

———. 1954. Waterfowl and other ornithological investigations in Yukon Territory, Canada, 1950. Can. Wildl. Serv. Wildl. Manage. Bull. (Ser. 2) 7. 55 p.

———. 1957. Notes on wildfowl of Slave River delta and vicinity, Northwest Territories. *Can. Field-Nat.* 71:74-81.

Sorensen, M.F. 1966. First-hunting-season recovery rates, distribution of the kill, and derivation of the kill for blue-winged teal banded during the summer, 1965. Bur. Sport Fish. & Wildl. Adm. Rep. 117. 15 p.

Sorensen, M.F., and S.M. Carney. 1972. Species, age, and sex composition of ducks bagged in the 1971 hunting season in comparison with prior years. Bur. Sport Fish. & Wildl. Adm. Rep. 218. 49 p.

Sorensen, M.F., C.J. Henny, and R.K. Martinson. 1966. Comparisons of 1964 and 1965 first-hunting-season recovery rates for mallards, black ducks and pintails. Bur. Sport Fish. & Wildl. Adm. Rep. 107. 30 p.

Sorensen, M.F., S.M. Carney, and L.D. Schroeder. 1974. Age and sex composition of ducks and geese harvested in the 1973 hunting season in comparison with prior years. U.S. Fish & Wildl. Serv. Adm. Rep. 40 p.

Southern, W.E. 1971. Gull orientation by magnetic cues: a hypothesis revisited. N.Y. Acad. Sci. 188:295-311.

Soutiere, E.C., H.S. Myrick, and E.G. Bolen. 1972. Chronology and behavior of American widgeon wintering in Texas. *J. Wildl. Manage.* 36:752-758.

Sowls, L.K. 1949. A preliminary report on renesting in waterfowl. Trans. 14th North Am. Wildl. Conf.:260-273.

———. 1955. *Prairie ducks: a study of their behavior, ecology, and management*. The Stackpole Co., Harrisburg, Pa., & Wildl. Manage. Inst., Washington, D.C. 193 p.

Speirs, J.M. 1945. Flight speed of the old-squaw. *Auk* 62:135-136.

Spencer, D.L., U.C. Nelson, and W.A. Elkins. 1951. America's greatest goose-brant nesting area. Trans. 16th North Am. Wildl. Conf.:290-295.

Spencer, H.E., Jr. 1953. "The cinnamon teal, *Anas cyanoptera* (Vieillot): its life history, ecology, and management." M.S. Thesis, Utah State Univ., Logan. 184 p.

Springer, P.F. 1975. Report on observations of Aleutian Canada geese in northern coastal California, spring 1975. U.S. Fish & Wildl. Serv. Migratory Bird Res. Stn., Humboldt State Univ., Arcata, Calif. 19 p. plus tables, figures.

Sprunt, A., Jr., and E.B. Chamberlain. 1970. *South Carolina bird life*. Rev. ed. Univ. of South Carolina Press, Columbia. 655 p.

Steel, P.E., P.D. Dalke, and E.G. Bizeau. 1956. Duck production at Gray's Lake, Idaho, 1949-1951. *J. Wildl. Manage.* 20:279-285.

———. 1957. Canada goose production at Gray's Lake, Idaho, 1949-1951. *J. Wildl. Manage.* 21:38-41.

Stenuphar, C.L. 1974. Artificial nests for mallards. *Pennsylvania Game News* 45:41.

Sterling, R.T. 1966. "Dispersal and mortality of adult drake pintails." M.S. Thesis, Univ. of Saskatchewan, Saskatoon. 57 p.

Sterling, T., and A. Dzubin. 1967. Canada goose molt migrations to the Northwest Territories. Trans. 32nd North Am. Wildl. & Nat. Resour. Conf.:355-373.

Stewart, P.A. 1957. "The wood duck, *Aix sponsa* (Linnaeus), and its management." Ph.D. Thesis, The Ohio State Univ., Columbus. 352 p.

———. 1958. Locomotion of wood ducks. *Wilson Bull.* 70:184-187.

Stewart, R.E. 1962. Waterfowl populations in the upper Chesapeake region. U.S. Fish & Wildl. Serv. Spec. Sci. Rep.:Wildl. 65. 208 p.

Stewart, R.E., and J.W. Aldrich. 1956. Distinction of maritime and prairie populations of blue-winged teal. Proc. Biol. Soc. Wash. 69:29-34.

Stewart, R.E., A.D. Geis, and C.D. Evans. 1958. Distribution of populations and hunting kill of the canvasback. *J. Wildl. Manage.* 22:333-370.

Stieglitz, W.O. 1967 (1966). Utilization of available foods

by diving ducks on Apalachee Bay, Florida. Proc. 20th Annu. Conf. Southeastern Assoc. Game & Fish Commissioners:42-50.

———. 1972. Food habits of the Florida duck. *J. Wildl. Manage.* 36:422-428.

Stieglitz, W.O., and C.T. Wilson. 1968. Breeding biology of the Florida duck. *J. Wildl. Manage.* 32:921-934.

Stirrett, G.M. 1954. Field observations of geese in James Bay, with special reference to the blue goose. Trans. 19th North Am. Wildl. Conf.:211-220.

Stollberg, B.P. 1950. Food habits of shoal-water ducks on Horicon Marsh, Wisconsin. *J. Wildl. Manage.* 14:214-217.

Stott, R.S., and D.P. Olson. 1972. Differential vulnerability patterns among three species of sea ducks. *J. Wildl. Manage.* 36:775-783.

———. 1973. Food-habitat relationship of sea ducks on the New Hampshire coastline. *Ecology* 54:996-1007.

———. 1974. Sea duck populations on the New Hampshire coastline. N.H. Agric. Exp. Stn. Res. Rep. 33. 26 p.

Stotts, V.D. 1968. Habitat and breeding ecology. East central United States. P. 102-112 in P. Barske (Editor), *The black duck: evaluation, management, and research.* Atlantic Flyway Counc. 193 p.

Stotts, V.D., and D.E. Davis. 1960. The black duck in the Chesapeake Bay of Maryland: breeding behavior and biology. Chesapeake Sci. 1:127-154.

Stoudt, J.H. 1949. Waterfowl breeding ground survey in the Dakotas. P. 143-153 in Waterfowl populations and breeding conditions—summer, 1949. U.S. Fish & Wildl. Serv. & Dominion Wildl. Serv. Spec. Sci. Rep.:Wildl. 2. 242 p.

———. 1965. Project report on habitat requirements of the canvasback during the breeding season. U.S. Fish & Wildl. Serv. Proj. A-8. 6 p.

———. 1971. Ecological factors affecting waterfowl production in the Saskatchewan parklands. U.S. Fish & Wildl. Serv. Resour. Publ. 99. 58 p.

———. 1973. Progress report on waterfowl habitat conditions, breeding population, and brood production, on the Louisiana, Redvers, and Minnedosa study areas. U.S. Fish & Wildl. Serv. Unpubl. Rep. 11 p.

Strange, T.H., E.R. Cunningham, and J.W. Goertz. 1971. Use of nest boxes by wood ducks in Mississippi. *J. Wildl. Manage.* 35:786-793.

Strohmeyer, D.L. 1967. "The biology of renesting by the blue-winged teal *(Anas discors)* in northwest Iowa." Ph.D. Thesis, Univ. of Minnesota, Minneapolis. 103 p. Plus appendices.

Strong, L. 1972. Utilization of artificial nesting structures by hooded mergansers in Mississippi. *Miss. Kite* 11:23-24.

———. 1973. Studies of wood duck nesting in artificial structures. Statewide Wildl. Invest. Final Rep.:5-25. Mississippi.

Stutz, S.S. 1965. Size of common merganser broods. *Murrelet* 46:47-48.

Surrendi, D.C. 1970. The mortality, behavior, and homing of transplanted juvenile Canada geese. *J. Wildl. Manage.* 34:719-733.

Sutherland, D.E. 1971. A 1965 waterfowl population model. Bur. Sport Fish. & Wildl., Flyway Habitat Manage. Unit, Proj. Rep. 4. 11 p.

Sutton, G.M. 1967. *Oklahoma birds.* Univ. of Oklahoma Press, Norman. 674 p.

Swainson, W., and J. Richardson. 1832. *Fauna Boreali-Americana. Part 2. The Birds.* London.

Swallow, H.S. 1941. Rain of ducks at Foam Lake, Saskatchewan. *Can. Field-Nat.* 55:130.

Swarth, H.S. 1922. Birds and mammals of the Stikine River region of northern British Columbia and southeastern Alaska. Univ. Calif. Publ. in Zool. 24:125-314.

———. 1926. Report on a collection of birds and mammals from the Atlin region, northern British Columbia. Univ. Calif. Publ. in Zool. 30:51-155.

Swarth, H.S., and H.C. Bryant. 1917. A study of the races of the white-fronted goose *(Anser albifrons)* occurring in California. Univ. Calif. Publ. in Zool. 17:209-222.

Sweet, J.T., and K. Robertson. 1966. Ross' geese in Nebraska. *Nebraska Bird Review* 34:70-71.

Sykes, P.W., Jr. 1961. Old record of Baikal teal in North Carolina. *Auk* 78:441.

Tabberer, D.K., J.D. Newsom, P.E. Schilling, and H.A. Bateman. 1972 (1971). The wood duck roost count as an index to wood duck abundance in Louisiana. Proc. 25th Annu. Conf. Southeastern Assoc. Game & Fish Commissioners:254-261.

Tate, J., Jr., and D.J. Tate. 1966. Additional records of whistling swans feeding in dry fields. *Condor* 68:398-399.

Tener, J.S. 1963. Queen Elizabeth Islands game survey, 1961. Can. Wildl. Serv. Occasional Papers 4. 50 p.

Tener, J.S., and L. Lemieux. 1952. Waterfowl breeding ground survey in the Province of Quebec. P. 92-95 in Waterfowl populations and breeding conditions—summer, 1952. U.S. Fish & Wildl. Serv. & Can. Wildl. Serv. Spec. Sci. Rep.:Wildl. 21. 303 p.

Thompson, D. 1973. Feeding ecology of diving ducks on Keokuk Pool, Mississippi River. *J. Wildl. Manage.* 37:367-381.

Thompson, D.Q., and R.A. Person. 1963. The eider pass at Point Barrow, Alaska. *J. Wildl. Manage.* 27:348-356.

Tice, R.C. 1970. Sea duck migration study, 1965-68. U.S. Fish & Wildl. Serv. Unpubl. Rep., Boston.

Timken, R.L., and B.W. Anderson. 1969. Food habits of common mergansers in Northcentral United States. *J. Wildl. Manage.* 33:87-91.

Timm, D. 1974. Status of lesser Canada geese in Alaska. Pacific Flyway Tech. Com. Rep.:38-50. Alaska Dep. Fish & Game, Juneau.

Todd, W.E.C. 1963. *Birds of the Labrador Peninsula and adjacent areas.* Carnegie Mus. & Univ. of Toronto Press, Toronto. 819 p.

Townsend, G.H. 1966. A study of waterfowl nesting on the Saskatchewan River delta. *Can. Field-Nat.* 80:74-88.

Trainer, C.E. 1959. The 1959 western Canada goose *(Branta canadensis occidentalis)* study on the Copper River Delta, Alaska. In H.A. Hansen (Editor), U.S. Fish & Wildl. Serv. Annu. Waterfowl Rep. 11 p.

———. 1965. A food habits investigation of ducks on the Sauvie Island game management area during the fall and early winter, 1962. Oreg. State Game Comm. Mimeogr. Rep. 17 p.

Trainer, D.O., C.S. Schildt, R.A. Hunt, and L.R. Jahn. 1962. Prevalence of *Leucocytozoon simondi* among some Wisconsin waterfowl. *J. Wildl. Manage.* 26:137-143.

Trauger, D.L. 1971. "Population ecology of lesser scaup *(Aythya affinis)* in Subarctic Taiga." Ph.D. Thesis, Iowa State Univ., Ames. 118 p.

———. 1973. Project report: special canvasback project, 1973. Northern Prairie Wildl. Res. Center, Jamestown, N.D. 3 p. plus table.

———. 1974*a*. Eye color of female lesser scaup in relation to age. *Auk* 91:243-254.

———. 1974*b*. Looking out for the canvasback. Part 1. *Ducks Unlimited* 38:12-15, 30, 36.

Trauger, D.L., and R.M. Bromley. 1975. Greater scaup of the West Mirage Islands, Great Slave Lake, Northwest Territories. Unpubl. MS.

Trauger, D.L., and J.H. Stoudt. 1974. Looking out for the canvasback. Part II. *Ducks Unlimited* 38:30-31, 42, 44, 45, 48, 60.

Trauger, D.L., A. Dzubin, and J.P. Ryder. 1971. White geese intermediate between Ross' geese and lesser snow geese. *Auk* 88:856-875.

Tufts, R.W. 1961. *The birds of Nova Scotia.* Nova Scotia Mus., Halifax, N.S. 481 p.

U.S. Bureau of Biological Survey. 1931. Migratory-bird treaty-act regulations and text of federal laws relating to game and birds. U.S. Dep. Agric. Serv. & Regulatory Announcements. 18 p.

———. 1939. The waterfowl situation: 1938-39. Wildl. Res. & Manage. Leafl. BS-136. 18 p.

U.S. Department of Agriculture. 1969. Duck virus enteritis in the United States, 1967-1969. Agric. Res. Serv.

U.S. Fish and Wildlife Service. 1953. Ducks and drainage in the prairie pothole region. Office of River Basin Stud. 24 p. Mimeogr.

———. 1974. Annual report of lands under control of the U.S. Fish & Wildlife Service as of June 30, 1974. U.S. Dep. Inter. 22 p.

Uspenski, S.M. 1965. The geese of Wrangel Island. Wildfowl Trust Annu. Rep. (1963-1964) 16:126-129.

van Rossem, A.J. 1929. Nesting of the American merganser in Chihuahua. *Auk* 46:380.

Vaught, R.W., and G.C. Arthur. 1965. Migration routes and mortality rates of Canada geese banded in the Hudson Bay lowlands. *J. Wildl. Manage.* 29:244-252.

Vaught, R.W., and L.M. Kirsch. 1966. Canada geese of the eastern prairie population, with special reference to the Swan Lake flock. Mo. Dep. Conserv. Tech. Bull. 3. 91 p.

Vaught, R.W., H.C. McDougle, and H.H. Burgess. 1967. Fowl cholera in waterfowl at Squaw Creek National Wildlife Refuge, Missouri. *J. Wildl. Manage.* 31:248-253.

Vermeer, K. 1968. Ecological aspects of ducks nesting in high densities among larids. *Wilson Bull.* 80:78-83.

———. 1969. Some aspects of the breeding of the white-winged scoter at Miquelon Lake, Alberta. *Blue Jay* 27:72-73.

———. 1970*a*. A study of Canada geese, *Branta canadensis*, nesting on islands in southeastern Alberta. *Can. J. Zool.* 48:235-246.

———. 1970*b*. Some aspects of the nesting of ducks on islands in Lake Newell, Alberta. *J. Wildl. Manage.* 34:126-129.

Vermeer, K., D.R.M. Hatch, and J.A. Windsor. 1972. Greater scaup is common breeder on northern Lake Winnipeg. *Can. Field-Nat.* 86:168.

Walford, L. 1968. Values of the South Atlantic & Gulf Coast marshes and estuaries to sport fishery resources. P. 79-82 in J.D. Newsom (Editor), Proc. Marsh & Estuary Manage. Symp., Louisiana State Univ., Baton Rouge. 250 p.

Ward, P., and B.D.J. Batt. 1973. Propagation of captive waterfowl. Delta Waterfowl Res. Stn., North Am. Wildl. Foundation & Wildl. Manage. Inst. 64 p.

Watson, G.E. 1967. Fulvous tree duck observed in the southern Sargasso Sea. *Auk* 84:424.

Webster, C.G., and F.M. Uhler. 1964. Improved nest structures for wood ducks. U.S. Fish & Wildl. Serv. Wildl. Leafl. 458. 19 p.

Webster, C.G., E.H. Galbreath, and A.E.L. Dierker. 1972 (1971). Propagation, release and harvest of mallards at Remington Farms. Proc. 25th Annu. Conf. Southeastern Assoc. Game & Fish Commissioners:187-190.

Weeks, J.L. 1969. "Breeding behavior of mottled ducks in Louisiana." M.S. Thesis, Louisiana State Univ., Baton Rouge. 79 p.

Weier, R.W. 1966. A survey of wood duck nest sites on Mingo National Wildlife Refuge in southeast Missouri. P. 91-108 in J.B. Trefethen (Editor), *Wood duck management and research.* Wildl. Manage. Inst., Washington, D.C. 212 p.

Weigand, J.P., M.J. Pollok, and G.A. Petrides. 1968. Some aspects of reproduction of captive Canada geese. *J. Wildl. Manage.* 32:894-905.

Wellein, E.G., and H.G. Lumsden. 1964. Northern forests and tundra. P. 67-76 in J.P. Linduska (Editor), *Waterfowl tomorrow.* U.S. Gov. Printing Office, Washington, D.C. 770 p.

Weller, M.W. 1957. Growth, weights, and plumages of the redhead, *Aythya americana. Wilson Bull.* 69:5-38.

———. 1959. Parasitic egg laying in the redhead *(Aythya americana)* and other North American Anatidae. Ecol. Monogr. 29:333-365.

———. 1964. Distribution and migration of the redhead. *J. Wildl. Manage.* 28:64-103.

———. 1965. Chronology of pair formation in some of the Nearctic *Aythya* (Anatidae). *Auk* 82:227-235.

———. 1968. Notes on some Argentine anatids. *Wilson Bull.* 80:189-212.

Weller, M.W., and P. Ward. 1959. Migration and mortality of hand-reared redheads *(Aythya americana). J. Wildl. Manage.* 23:427-433.

Weller, M.W., D.L. Trauger, and G.L. Krapu. 1969. Breeding birds of the West Mirage Islands, Great Slave Lake, N.W.T. *Can. Field-Nat.* 83:344-360.

Wheeler, R.J. 1965. Pioneer of the blue-winged teal in California, Oregon, Washington, and British Columbia. *Murrelet* 46:40-42.

Wheeler, R.J., and S.W. Harris. 1970. Duck nesting and production in the Humboldt Bay area of California. *Calif. Fish & Game* 56:180-187.

White, E.F.G., and H.F. Lewis. 1937. The greater snow goose in Canada. *Auk* 54:440-444.

White, H.C. 1957. Food and natural history of mergansers on salmon waters in the Maritime Provinces of Canada. Fish. Res. Board Can. Bull. 116. Ottawa. 63 p.

Whitesell, D.E. 1970. Wetlands preservation-management in North America. Trans. 35th North Am. Wildl. & Nat. Resour. Conf.:327-334.

Wilbur, S.R. 1966. The tule white-fronted goose *(Anser albifrons gambelli)* in the Sacramento Valley, California. Proc. Annu. Meet. Calif.-Nev. Sect., Wildl. Soc. 7 p.

Wilbur, S.R., and C.F. Yocom. 1972. Unusual geese in the Pacific Coast states. *Murrelet* 52:16-19.

Wilke, F. 1944. Three new bird records for St. Paul Island, Alaska. *Auk* 61:655-656.

Williams, C.S. 1967. *Honker: a discussion of the habits and needs of the largest of our Canada geese.* D. Van Nostrand Co., Princeton, N.J. 179 p.

Williams, C.S., and W.H. Marshall. 1937. Goose nesting studies on Bear River Migratory Waterfowl Refuge. *J. Wildl. Manage.* 1:77-86.

———. 1938*a*. Survival of Canada goose goslings, Bear River Refuge, Utah, 1937. *J. Wildl. Manage.* 2:17-19.

———. 1938*b*. Duck nesting studies, Bear River Migratory Bird Refuge, Utah, 1937. *J. Wildl. Manage.* 2:29-48 plus Plates 1-4.

Williams, C.S., and M.C. Nelson. 1943. Canada goose nests and eggs. *Auk* 60:341-345.

Williams, C.S., and C.A. Sooter. 1940. Canada goose habitats in Utah and Oregon. Trans. 5th North Am. Wildl. Conf.:383-387.

Wilson, R.S. 1948. The summer bird life of Attu. *Condor* 50:124-129.

Wingfield, B.H. 1951. "A waterfowl productivity study in Knudson Marsh, Salt Lake Valley, Utah." M.S. Thesis, Utah State Agric. Coll., Logan. 115 p.

Winthrop, R., and D.A. Poole. 1973. Foreword. P. 5 in P. Ward and B.D.J. Batt, Propagation of captive waterfowl: the Delta Waterfowl Research Station System. North Am. Wildl. Foundation & Wildl. Manage. Inst., Washington, D.C. 64 p.

Witherby, H.F., F.C.R. Jourdain, N.F. Ticehurst, and B.W. Tucker. 1952. *The handbook of British birds.* Vol. 3. H.F. & G. Witherby Ltd., London. 399 p.

Wolf, K. 1955. Some effects of fluctuating and falling water levels on waterfowl production. *J. Wildl. Manage.* 19:13-23.

Wood, J.S. 1965. Some associations of behavior to reproductive development in Canada geese. *J. Wildl. Manage.* 29:237-244.

Wood, R., and W.L. Gelston. 1972. Preliminary report: the mute swans of Michigan's Grand Traverse Bay region. Mich. Dep. Nat. Resour. Rep. 2683. 6 p.

Woolfenden, G.E. 1961. Postcranial osteology of the waterfowl. Fla. State Mus. Bull. 6. 129 p.

Wright, B.S. 1954. *High tide and an east wind: the story of the black duck.* The Stackpole Co., Harrisburg, Pa., & Wildl. Manage. Inst. 162 p.

Wright, T.W. 1961 (1959). Winter foods of mallards in Arkansas. Proc. 13th Annu. Conf. Southeastern Assoc. Game & Fish Commissioners: 291-298.

Wynne-Edwards, V.C. 1952. Zoology of the Baird expedition (1950). 1. The birds observed in central and south-east Baffin Island. *Auk* 69:353-391.

Yelverton, C.S., and T.L. Quay. 1959. Food habits of the Canada goose at Lake Mattamuskeet, North Carolina. N.C. Wildl. Resour. Comm. 44 p.

Yocom, C.F. 1947. Observations on bird life in the Pacific Ocean off the North American shores. *Condor* 49:204-208.

———. 1950. Weather and its effect on hatching of waterfowl in eastern Washington. Trans. 15th North Am. Wildl. Conf.:309-318.

———. 1951. Waterfowl and their food plants in Washington. Univ. of Washington Press, Seattle. 272 p.

———. 1952. Techniques used to increase nesting of Canada geese. *J. Wildl. Manage.* 16:425-428.

———. 1954. American pintail *(Anas acuta tzitzihoa)* on Crater Lake. *Murrelet* 35:9-10.

———. 1964. Waterfowl wintering in the Marshall Islands, southwest Pacific Ocean. *Auk* 81:441-442.

———. 1965. Estimated populations of Great Basin Canada geese over their breeding range in western Canada and western United States. *Murrelet* 46:19-26.

———. 1970. Weights of ten species of ducks captured at Ohtig Lake, Alaska—Aug., 1962. *Murrelet* 51:21.

———. 1972. Weights and measurements of Taverner's and Great Basin Canada geese. *Murrelet* 53:33-34.

Yocom, C.F., and H.A. Hansen. 1960. Population studies of waterfowl in eastern Washington. *J. Wildl. Manage.* 24:237-250.

Yocom, C.F., and M. Keller. 1961. Correlation of food habits and abundance of waterfowl, Humboldt Bay, California. *Calif. Fish & Game* 47:41-53.

Young, C.M. 1967. Overland migration of duck broods in a drought-free area. *Can. J. Zool.* 45:249-251.

Appendix A

List of Names and Geographic Locations

LIST OF COMMON AND SCIENTIFIC NAMES OF PLANTS MENTIONED IN TEXT

Acorns *(Quercus* spp.)
Alder *(Alnus* sp.)
Alfalfa *(Medicago sativa)*
Alkali or prairie bulrush *(Scirpus paludosus)*
Alsike *(Trifolium hybridum)*
American bulrush *(Scirpus americanus)*
American elm *(Ulmus americana)*
American lotus *(Nelumbo lutea)*
American yew *(Taxus canadensis)*
Arrow arum *(Peltandra virginica)*
Aspen *(Populus tremuloides)*
Baccharis bush *(Baccharis halimifolia)*
Bald cypress *(Taxodium distichum)*
Balsam poplar *(Populus balsamifera)*
Baltic rush *(Juncus balticus)*
Barley *(Hordeum vulgare)*
Bassia *(Bassia hyssopifolia)*
Basswood *(Tilia americana)*
Beak rushes *(Rhynchospora* spp.)
Bermuda grass *(Cynodon dactylon)*
Bird's-foot trefoil *(Lotus corniculatus)*
Black ash *(Fraxinus nigra)*
Blackjack oak *(Quercus marilandica)*
Black oak *(Quercus velutina)*
Black willow *(Salix nigra)*
Bladderworts *(Utricularia* spp.)
Blueberry *(Vaccinium* sp.)
Bluegrass *(Poa* spp.)
Brome *(Bromus* sp.)
Broom sedge *(Andropogon virginicus)*
Brownseed paspalum *(Paspalum plicatulum)*
Buckbrush *(Symphoricarpos orbiculatus)*
Buckwheat *(Fagopyrum* sp.)
Bulrushes *(Scirpus* spp.)
Bur oak *(Quercus macrocarpa)*
Bur reeds *(Sparganium* spp.)
Bushy naiad, northern naiad *(Naias flexilis* or *N. guadalupensis)*
Butternut *(Juglans cinerea)*
Buttonbush *(Cephalanthus occidentalis)*
Cattails *(Typha latifolia) (T. angustifolia)*
Chara or muskgrass *(Chara* spp.)
Chufa *(Cyperus esculentus)*
Clasping leaf pondweed *(Potamogeton perfoliatus)*
Coontail *(Ceratophyllum demersum)*
Cordgrass *(Spartina* spp.)
Corn *(Zea mays)*
Cotton grass *(Eriophorum* sp.)
Cottonwood *(Populus deltoides)*
Cow lily, pond lily *(Nuphar luteum)*
Cranberry *(Vaccinium* sp.)
Crowberry *(Empetrum nigrum)*
Curlewberries *(Empetrum* spp.)
Cut-grasses *(Leersia* spp.)
Delta duck potato *(Sagittaria platyphylla)*
Duck potato, swamp potato *(Sagittaria latifolia)*
Douglas fir *(Pseudotsuga menziesii)*
Duck millet, barnyard grass *(Echinochloa crusgalli)*
Duckweed *(Lemna* spp.)
Durum wheat *(Triticum durum)*
Dwarf birch *(Betula nana)*
Dwarf willow *(Salix herbacea)*
Eelgrass *(Zostera marina)*
Elms *(Ulmus* spp.)
Fall panicum *(Panicum dichotomiflorum)*
Firs *(Abies* spp.)

Foxtail millet *(Setaria italica)*
Gooseberry *(Ribes* sp.*)*
Greasewood *(Sarcobatus vermiculatus)*
Hackberry *(Celtis laevigata)*
Hardstem bulrush *(Scirpus acutus)*
Hickories *(Carya* spp.*)*
Horned pondweed *(Zannichellia palustris)*
Hornwort *(Ceratophyllum demersum)*
Horsetails *(Equisetum* spp.*)*
Jungle rice *(Echinochloa colonum)*
Knotgrass *(Polygonum aviculare)*
Labrador tea *(Ledum groenlandicum)*
Lake sedge *(Carex lacustris)*
Leafy pondweed *(Potamogeton foliosus)*
Leatherleaf *(Chamaedaphne calyculata)*
Live oak *(Quercus virginiana)*
Longleaf pondweed *(Potamogeton nodosus)*
Maiden cane *(Panicum hemitomon)*
Mangrove *(Rhizophora mangle)*
Marsh smartweed *(Polygonum coccineum)*
Mesquite *(Prosopis glandulosa)*
Millets *(Echinochloa* spp.*)*
Milo *(Sorghum vulgare)*
Mulberries *(Morus* spp.*)*
Muskgrass *(Chara* spp.*)*
Naiads *(Naias* spp.*)*
Needlerush *(Juncus roemerianus)*
Nettle *(Urtica* spp.*)*
Nutgrasses *(Cyperus* spp.*)*
Oats (cultivated) *(Avena sativa)*
Olney's bulrush *(Scirpus olneyi)*
Orchard grass *(Dactylis glomerata)*
Raspberry *(Rubus* spp.*)*
Red algae (Rhodophyceae)
Red clover *(Trifolium pratense)*
Red fescue-grass *(Festuca rubra)*
Red maple *(Acer rubrum)*
Red oak *(Quercus rubra)*
Redtop, tall redtop *(Agrostis altissima)*
Reed canary grass *(Phalaris arundinacea)*
Rice *(Oryza sativa)*
Rice cut-grass *(Leersia oryzoides)*
River bulrush *(Scirpus fluviatilis)*
Rockgrass *(Phyllospadix)*
Rose *(Rosa* sp.*)*
Rushes *(Juncus* spp.)
Rye *(Secale cereale)*
Safflower *(Carthamus tinctorius)*
Sago pondweed *(Potamogeton pectinatus)*
Salmonberry *(Rubus spectabilis)*
Saltbush, salt brush *(Atriplex argentea)*
Salt grass, salt-marsh grass *(Distichlis spicata)*
Salt-marsh bulrush *(Scirpus maritimus)*
Salt-meadow cordgrass *(Spartina patens)*
Saw grass *(Cladium jamaicense)*
Saw palmetto *(Serenoa repens)*
Sea lettuce *(Ulva* sp.*)*
Sedges *(Carex* spp.*)*
Shoalgrass *(Halodule beaudettei)*
Short sedge *(Carex rariflora)*
Silver maple *(Acer saccharinum)*
Smartweeds *(Polygonum* spp.*)*
Soft-stem bulrush *(Scirpus validus)*
Sorghum *(Sorghum vulgare)*
Sour gum *(Nyssa sylvatica)*
Southern naiad *(Naias guadalupensis)*
Soybeans *(Glycine max)*
Spatterdock *(Nuphar luteum)*
Spike rushes *(Eleocharis* spp.*)*
Spiny naiad *(Naias gracillima)*
Spruce *(Picea* sp.*)*
Strawberry *(Fragaria* sp.*)*
Swamp loosestrife *(Decodon verticillatus)*
Swamp privet *(Forestiera acuminata)*
Swamp smartweed *(Polygonum punctatum)*
Sweet clover *(Melilotus* spp.*)*
Sweet gale *(Myrica gale)*
Sweet gum *(Liquidambar styraciflua)*
Sycamore *(Platanus occidentalis)*
Three-square bulrushes *(Scirpus robustus) (S. olneyi)*
Timothy *(Phleum pratense)*
Tupelo gum *(Nyssa aquatica)*
Walter's millet *(Echinochloa walteri)*
Water buttercups *(Ranunculus* spp.*)*
Water hemp *(Acnida altissima)*
Water lilies *(Nymphaea* spp.*)*
Watermeal *(Wolffia* spp.*)*
Water milfoil *(Myriophyllum* spp.*)*
Water shield *(Brasenia schreberi)*
Water star grass *(Heteranthera dubia)*
Waterweed *(Elodea* spp.*)*
Water willow *(Decodon verticillatus)*
Wax myrtles *(Myrica* spp.*)*
Wheat *(Triticum aestivum)*
Wheat grass *(Agropyron* spp.*)*
White cedar *(Thuja occidentalis)*
White oak *(Quercus alba)*
Whitetop, whitetop grass *(Scolochloa festucacea)*
White water buttercup *(Ranunculus trichophyllus)*
Widgeon grass *(Ruppia maritima)*
Wild celery *(Vallisneria americana)*
Wild grape *(Vitis* spp.*)*
Wild millet *(Echinochloa muricata)*
Wild rye *(Elymus* spp.*)*

LIST OF COMMON AND SCIENTIFIC NAMES OF ANIMALS MENTIONED IN TEXT

ANIMAL LIFE—Invertebrates

Amphipods *(Anonyx* spp.*)*
Ants (Myrmica)
Aquatic beetles (Coleoptera)
Arctic rock borer *(Hiatella arctica)*
Arctic wedge clam *(Mesodesma arctatum)*
Atlantic dogwinkle *(Nucella lapillus) (Thais lapillus)*
Atlantic nautilus *(Nautilus* sp.*)*
Atlantic razor clam *(Ensis siliqua) (Siliqua costata)*
Baltic clam *(Macoma balthica)*
Barnacles (Balanidae)
Bivalve clams (Pelecypoda)
Black flies *(Simulium* spp.*)*
Black mussel, horse mussel *(Modiolus modiolus)*
Blue mussel *(Mytilus edulis)*
Box crab *(Lopholithodes foraminatus)*
Broad yoldia *(Yoldia thraciaeformis)*

Caddis flies (Trichoptera)
Chink shells *(Lacuna* spp.)
Chiton (Polyplacophora)
Clams
(Venus mercenaria) hard or round
(Mya arenaria) soft or long
Clam shrimp *(Conchostraca* spp.)
Claw shrimp *(Limnadia lenticularis)*
Cockles *(Cardium* spp.)
Common prawn *(Penaeus* or *Palaemonetes)*
Copepods (Copepoda)
Crayfish (Cambaridae)
Damselflies *(Enallagma)*
Diving beetles (Dytiscidae)
Dragonflies (Odonata)
Dwarf surf clam, Atlantic surf clam *(Spisula solidissima)*
Eastern mud clam, mud dog whelk *(Nassarius obsoletus)*
File yoldia *(Yoldia limitula)*
Fingernail clam *(Sphaerium transversum)*
Freshwater shrimp *(Lepidurus* spp.)
Freshwater sponges *(Spongilla)*
Goose barnacles *(Lepas* spp.)
Greedy dove shell *(Anachis avara)*
Hard rock clams *(Protothaca* spp.)
Hermit crab *(Pagurus longicarpus)*
Horse crab *(Telmessus cheiragonus) (Erimacrus isenbeckii)*
Isopods *(Mesidotea* spp.) *(Idotea* spp.)
King crabs *(Lopholithodes* spp.)
Leeches *(Glossiphonia* spp.)
Limpets *(Acmaea* spp.)
Mayflies (Ephemeroptera)
Midges (Chironomidae)
Mud crab *(Hemigrapsus* sp.) *(Neopanope texana-sayi)*
New England nassa *(Nassarius trivittatus)*
Ostracod (Ostracoda)
Oyster *(Ostrea lurida)*
Periwinkles *(Littorina* spp.) *(Nassarius* spp.)
Phantom midge larvae (Chaoboridae)
Pond snails *(Physa* spp.)
Quahog clam *(Mercenaria mercenaria)*
Razor clams *(Siliqua* spp.) *(Solen sicarius)*
Ribbed mussel *(Modiolus demissus)*
Rock crab *(Cancer irroratus)*
Rock clam *(Protothaca staminea)*
Sand dollar *(Echinarachnius parma)*
Sand launce *(Ammodytes americanus)*
Sand shrimp *(Crangon septemspinosa)*
Scallop *(Pecten irradians) (P. concentricus)*
Scuds *(Gammarus* spp.)
Sculpin *(Acanthocotlus groenlandicus)*
Sea anemone *(Aulactinia capitata)*
Sea urchin *(Strongylocentrotus drobachiensis)*
Sessile barnacles (Balanidae)
Shellfish (Mollusca)
Short razor shell *(Siliqua costata)*
Shrimp *(Crangon* spp.) *(Crangon vulgaris)*
Soft-shelled clam *(Mya arenaria)*
Stone flies (Plecoptera)
Surf clam *(Mactra solidissima)*
Top shells *(Margarites* spp.)
Variable nassa, variable dog whelk *(Nassarius albus)*
Water boatmen (Corixidae)
Water fleas (Cladocera)
Wedge rangia *(Rangia cuneata)*
Yellow periwinkle *(Littorina obtusata)*
Yoldias *(Yoldia* spp.)

ANIMAL LIFE—Fish

Blacknose dace *(Rhinichthys atratulus)*
Blueback herring *(Alosa aestivalis)*
Carp *(Cyprinus carpio)*
Catfishes *(Ictalurus* spp.)
Chub *(Semotilus atromaculatus)*
Common shiner *(Notropis cornutus)*
Crappie
Black crappie *(Pomoxis nigromaculatus)*
White crappie *(Pomoxis annularis)*
Dace *(Leuciscus leuciscus)*
Eel *(Anguilla rostrata)*
Elvers (Young eels)
Fallfish *(Semotilus corporalis)*
Freshwater drum *(Aplodinotus grunniens)*
Gizzard shad *(Dorosoma cepedianum)*
Golden shiner *(Notemigonus crysoleucas)*
Herring *(Clupea harengus)*
Johnny darter *(Etheostoma nigrum)*
Killifishes *(Fundulus* spp.)
Parr *(Salmo salar)*
Perch *(Perca flavescens)*
Salmon *(Salmo salar)*
Shiners *(Notropis* spp.)
Smolts (young salmon)
Stickleback (Gasterosteidae)
Suckers *(Catostomus* spp.)
Sunfishes *(Lepomis* spp.)
Trouts *(Salmo* spp.)
White bass *(Morone chrysops)*
Whitefish (Coregoninae)
White sucker *(Catostomus commersoni)*
Yellow perch *(Perca flavescens)*

ANIMAL LIFE—Reptiles

Black rat snake *(Elaphe obsoleta obsoleta)*
Bull snake *(Pituophis melanoleucus)*
Cottonmouth, water moccasin *(Agkistrodon piscivorus)*
Gray rat snake *(Elaphe obsoleta spiloides)*
Rat snakes *(Elaphe* spp.)
Texas rat snake *(Elaphe obsoleta lindheimeri)*

ANIMAL LIFE—Birds

American coot *(Fulica americana)*
Arctic tern *(Sterna paradisaea)*
Black-bellied gull *(Larus marinus)*
Brown pelican *(Pelicanus occidentalis)*
California gull *(Larus californicus)*
Crow *(Corvus brachyrhynchos)*
Egret *(Casmerodius albus)*
Fish crow *(Corvus ossifragus)*
Flickers *(Colaptes* spp.)
Glaucous gull *(Larus hyperboreus)*
Golden-fronted woodpecker *(Melanerpes aurifrons)*
Goldfinch *(Spinus tristis)*
Great horned owl *(Bubo v. virginianus)*
Grebes (Podicipedidae)
Gulls *(Larus* spp.)
Heron *(Ardea herodias)*
Herring gull *(Larus argentatus)*

Parasitic jaeger *(Stercorarius parasiticus)*
Long-tailed jaeger *(Stercorarius longicaudis)*
Loons *(Gavia* spp.*)*
Magpie goose *(Anseranas semipalmata)*
Magpie *(Pica pica hudsonia)*
Mountain bluebird *(Sialia currucoides)*
Muscovy duck *(Cairina moschata)*
Osprey *(Pandion haliaetus)*
Pileated woodpecker *(Dryocopus pileatus)*
Raven *(Corvus corax)*
Ring-billed gull *(Larus delawarensis)*
Smew *(Mergus albellus)*
Sparrow hawk *(Falco sparverius)*
Starling *(Sturnus vulgaris)*
Tree swallow *(Irodoprocne bicolor)*

ANIMAL LIFE—Mammals

Arctic fox *(Alopex lagopus)*
Badger *(Taxidea taxus)*
Bears *(Ursus* spp.*)*
Beaver *(Castor canadensis)*
Coyote *(Canis latrans)*
Flying squirrel *(Glaucomys volans)*
Foxes *(Vulpes* spp.*)*
Fox squirrel *(Sciurus niger)*
Gray squirrel *(Sciurus carolinensis)*
Ground squirrels *(Citellus* spp.*)*
Lemmings *(Lemmus* spp.*)*
Mink *(Mustela vison)*
Muskrat *(Ondatra zibethicus)*
Norway rat *(Rattus norvegicus)*
Nutria *(Myocastor coypus)*
Opossum *(Didelphis marsupialis)*
Raccoon *(Procyon lotor)*
Red fox *(Vulpes vulpes)*
Red squirrel *(Tamiasciurus hudsonicus)*
Spotted skunk *(Spilogale putorius)*
Striped skunk *(Mephitis mephitis)*
Weasel *(Mustela erminea)*
White-tailed deer *(Odocoileus virginianus)*
Wolverine *(Gulo gulo luscus)*

GEOGRAPHIC NAMES

A

Aberdeen, South Dakota	45.28 N, 98.29 W
Aberdeen Lake, N.W.T.	64.27 N, 99.00 W
Acadia Parish, Louisiana	30.30 N, 92.50 W
Acapulco de Juárez, Mexico	16.51 N, 99.55 W
Adak, Alaska	51.52 N, 176.39 W
Adak Island, Alaska	51.45 N, 176.40 W
Adelaide Peninsula, N.W.T.	68.09 N, 97.45 W
Agattu Island, Alaska	52.25 N, 173.35 E
Aguascalientes, Mexico	32.18 N, 115.10 W
Akimiski Island, N.W.T.	53.00 N, 81.20 W
Akpatok Island, Quebec	60.25 N, 68.00 W
Akutan Island, Alaska	54.10 N, 165.55 W
Alameda County, California	37.80 N, 122.20 W
Alaska Peninsula, Alaska	57.00 N, 158.00 W
Alaska Range, Alaska	62.30 N, 150.00 W
Albany River, Ontario	52.17 N, 81.31 W
Albemarle Sound, North Carolina	36.03 N, 76.12 W
Alburg Springs, Vermont	44.97 N, 73.30 W
Aldan River, U.S.S.R.	63.28 N, 129.35 E
Alderdale, Washington	45.83 N, 119.92 W
Aleutian Islands National Wildlife Refuge, Alaska	52.00 N, 176.00 W
Alexander Archipelago, Alaska	56.30 N, 134.00 W
Alexander County, Illinois	37.10 N, 89.30 W
Alliance, Nebraska	42.06 N, 102.52 W
Alpine, Texas	30.22 N, 103.40 W
Alsea Bay, Oregon	44.38 N, 123.60 W
Alton, Illinois	38.54 N, 90.10 W
Alvarado lagoons, Mexico	18.46 N, 95.46 W
Amaknak Island, Alaska	53.95 N, 166.65 W
Amarillo, Texas	35.13 N, 101.49 W
Amchitka Island, Alaska	51.30 N, 179.00 W
American Falls, Idaho	42.47 N, 112.51 W
Amguyema Lagoon, U.S.S.R.	66.58 N, 179.16 W
Anacortes, Washington	48.30 N, 122.37 W
Anadyr Bay, U.S.S.R.	64.00 N, 179.00 W
Anahuac National Wildlife Refuge, Texas	29.49 N, 94.68 W
Anaktuvuk Pass, Alaska	68.10 N, 151.50 W
Anchorage, Alaska	61.13 N, 149.53 W
Anderson River delta, N.W.T.	69.90 N, 128.83 W
Angara River, U.S.S.R.	58.06 N, 93.00 E
Anticosti Island, Canada	49.30 N, 63.00 W
Apalachee Bay, Florida	30.00 N, 84.13 W
Aral Sea, U.S.S.R.	45.00 N, 60.00 E
Arctic Slope, Alaska	70.50 N, 154.00 W
Arlone Lake, N.W.T.	67.38 N, 102.14 W
Arrowwood National Wildlife Refuge, North Dakota	47.10 N, 98.77 W
Athabasca River, Alberta	58.40 N, 110.50 W
Atlantic City, New Jersey	39.22 N, 74.26 W
Atlin Lake, British Columbia and Yukon	59.20 N, 133.45 W
Attawapiskat River, Ontario	52.57 N, 82.18 W
Attu Island, Alaska	52.55 N, 173.00 W
Austin, Texas	30.16 N, 97.45 W
Avery Island, Louisiana	29.55 N, 91.55 W
Axel Heiberg Island, N.W.T.	80.00 N, 90.00 W

B

Back Bay National Wildlife Refuge, Virginia	36.64 N, 75.98 W
Baffin Island, N.W.T.	65.00 N, 70.00 W
Baja Peninsula, Mexico	27.00 N, 113.00 W
Ballard County, Kentucky	37.18 N, 89.00 W
Banana River, Florida	28.32 N, 80.64 W
Banks Island, N.W.T.	72.50 N, 120.00 W
Barents Sea	76.06 N, 36.00 E
Barnegat Bay, New Jersey	39.75 N, 74.22 W
Barnstable Harbor, Massachusetts	41.70 N, 70.30 W
Barrow, Alaska	71.38 N, 156.47 W
Bathurst Inlet, N.W.T.	67.00 N, 107.50 W
Bathurst Island, N.W.T.	76.00 N, 100.00 W
Baton Rouge, Louisiana	30.45 N, 91.18 W
Battle Harbour, Labrador	53.32 N, 55.50 W
Bay Fiord, Ellesmere Island, N.W.T.	78.85 N, 84.00 W

Bayhead, New Jersey	40.04 N, 74.03 W
Bay of Fundy, New Brunswick	45.00 N, 66.00 W
Bay of Gods Mercy, Southampton Island, N.W.T.	63.50 N, 86.50 W
Bear Island, James Bay, Canada	54.34 N, 81.00 W
Bear River National Wildlife Refuge, Utah	41.54 N, 112.35 W
Beaufort County, South Carolina	32.55 N, 80.65 W
Beaufort Sea	72.50 N, 143.00 W
Beaver Mountains, Alaska	63.00 N, 157.00 W
Bechevin Bay, Unimak Island, Alaska	55.00 N, 164.30 W
Belanger Lake, Manitoba	53.95 N, 102.00 W
Belcher Islands, Hudson Bay	56.30 N, 79.00 W
Benton County, Oregon	44.50 N, 123.45 W
Bering Glacier, Alaska	60.27 N, 143.50 W
Bering Sea, Alaska	61.50 N, 170.50 W
Bering Strait, Alaska	65.50 N, 169.00 W
Beverly, Massachusetts	42.55 N, 70.88 W
Beverly Lake, N.W.T.	64.50 N, 101.33 W
Big Horn County, Wyoming	44.50 N, 107.50 W
Bighorn River, Montana	46.09 N, 107.28 W
Bighorn River, Wyoming	44.50 N, 108.00 W
Big Island, N.W.T.	62.65 N, 70.62 W
Billings, Montana	45.73 N, 108.53 W
Biloxi, Mississippi	30.40 N, 88.88 W
Bismarck, North Dakota	46.81 N, 100.78 W
Bitter Lake National Wildlife Refuge, New Mexico	33.54 N, 104.40 W
Bitterroot River, Montana	46.50 N, 114.12 W
Blackduck Lake, Minnesota	47.73 N, 94.55 W
Black Hills, South Dakota	44.00 N, 103.70 W
Black Lake, Louisiana	31.74 N, 93.06 W
Blenheim, Ontario	42.44 N, 82.00 W
Bloomington, Texas	28.65 N, 96.91 W
Boas River, Southampton Island, N.W.T.	64.00 N, 85.50 W
Boise, Idaho	43.62 N, 116.22 W
Bolinas Bay, California	38.04 N, 122.88 W
Bombay Hook National Wildlife Refuge, Delaware	39.36 N, 75.45 W
Boonton, New Jersey	40.91 N, 74.41 W
Boothia Peninsula, N.W.T.	71.50 N, 95.00 W
Bosque del Apache National Wildlife Refuge, New Mexico	33.78 N, 106.85 W
Boulder, Colorado	40.00 N, 105.20 W
Boundary Bay, Washington	49.00 N, 122.90 W
Bowman Bay, Baffin Island, N.W.T.	65.70 N, 74.50 W
Bracebridge Inlet, Bathurst Island	75.55 N, 100.10 W
Brandypot Island, Quebec	48.12 N, 69.10 W
Brazoria County, Texas	29.20 N, 95.40 W
Brazos County, Texas	30.60 N, 96.30 W
Bremner River, Alaska	60.51 N, 144.52 W
Brevard County, Florida	28.27 N, 80.83 W
Brigantine National Wildlife Refuge, New Jersey	39.45 N, 74.47 W
Bristol Bay, Alaska	58.00 N, 160.00 W
Brooks, Alberta	51.58 N, 111.95 W
Brooks County, Texas	27.00 N, 98.20 W
Brooks Range, Alaska	68.50 N, 149.00 W
Brown County, Kansas	39.75 N, 95.50 W
Brownsville, Texas	25.91 N, 97.51 W
Brunswick, Missouri	39.49 N, 93.13 W
Buckeye Lake, Ohio	55.83 N, 82.48 W
Buffalo, New York	42.89 N, 78.88 W
Buffalo Lake National Wildlife Refuge, Texas	34.91 N, 102.12 W
Buldir Island, Alaska	52.35 N, 175.93 E
Burford Lake, New Mexico	36.64 N, 106.86 W
Burlington, Iowa	40.82 N, 91.23 W
Burma, Oregon	43.59 N, 96.89 W
Butte County, California	39.10 N, 121.60 W
Butte Creek basin and Butte Sink, California	39.09 N, 121.70 W
Bylot Island, N.W.T.	73.00 N, 77.00 W

C

Calcasieu Pass, Louisiana	29.73 N, 93.31 W
Calgary, Alberta	51.03 N, 114.05 W
Camas National Wildlife Refuge, Idaho	43.96 N, 112.25 W
Cambridge Bay, Victoria Island, N.W.T.	69.10 N, 105.00 W
Cameron Parish, Louisiana	29.91 N, 93.00 W
Campeche, Mexico	19.51 N, 90.32 W
Camrose, Alberta	53.00 N, 112.82 W
Canoe Lake, Saskatchewan	55.20 N, 108.10 W
Canton, Illinois	40.56 N, 90.04 W
Canyon Ferry Reservoir, Montana	46.50 N, 111.50 W
Cape Ann, Massachusetts	42.65 N, 70.63 W
Cape Bathurst, N.W.T.	70.86 N, 125.58 W
Cape Blanco, Oregon	42.82 N, 124.54 W
Cape Breton Island, Nova Scotia	46.50 N, 60.50 W
Cape Canaveral, Florida	28.40 N, 80.60 W
Cape Charles, Labrador	52.26 N, 55.63 W
Cape Churchill, Manitoba	58.72 N, 94.20 W
Cape Cod, Massachusetts	41.90 N, 70.00 W
Cape Dorset, Baffin Island, N.W.T.	64.18 N, 76.62 W
Cape Farewell, Greenland	60.00 N, 44.50 W
Cape Fullerton, Hudson Bay, N.W.T.	63.94 N, 38.68 W
Cape Girardeau, Missouri	37.31 N, 89.53 W
Cape Hatteras, North Carolina	35.40 N, 75.40 W
Cape Henrietta Maria, Ontario	55.05 N, 82.50 W
Cape Jones, Quebec	54.30 N, 79.50 W
Cape Kellett, Banks Island, N.W.T.	72.03 N, 125.50 W
Cape Lisburne, Alaska	68.87 N, 166.20 W
Cape May, New Jersey	38.94 N, 74. 93 W
Cape Prince of Wales, Alaska	65.60 N, 168.00 W
Cape Romain, South Carolina	33.00 N, 79.40 W
Cape Tourmente, Quebec	47.04 N, 70.50 W
Cape Vankarem, U.S.S.R.	66.16 N, 176.00 W
Cariboo District, British Columbia	52.00 N, 121.00 W
Caron Potholes, Saskatchewan	50.28 N, 105.52 W
Carson Sink, Nevada	39.80 N, 118.50 W
Casco Bay, Maine	43.70 N, 70.00 W
Castle Rock, California	41.45 N, 124.16 W
Catahoula Lake, Louisiana	31.50 N, 92.00 W
Cedar Key, Florida	29.10 N, 83.04 W
Centennial Valley, Montana	44.55 N, 111.70 W
Chaleur Bay, New Brunswick	48.00 N, 65.50 W
Chambers County, Texas	29.70 N, 94.50 W
Chandeleur Islands, Louisiana	29.80 N, 88.70 W
Chandler Lake, Alaska	68.25 N, 151.50 W
Charleston, South Carolina	32.82 N, 79.96 W
Charlotte County, Florida	26.90 N, 81.70 W
Charlton Island, James Bay, N.W.T.	52.00 N, 79.20 W
Chatham County, Georgia	32.00 N, 81.10 W

Name	Coordinates
Chaun Bay, U.S.S.R.	70.00 N, 170.00 E
Cheney Reservoir, Kansas	37.70 N, 97.80 W
Chenier au Tigre, Louisiana	29.60 N, 92.40 W
Chesapeake Bay, Maryland	38.50 N, 76.30 W
Chesterfield Inlet, Hudson Bay	63.30 N, 90.65 W
Cheyenne Bottoms Wildlife Area, Kansas	38.45 N, 98.65 W
Chiapas, Mexico	16.30 N, 92.30 W
Chicago, Illinois	41.88 N, 87.63 W
Chihuahua, Mexico	28.38 N, 106.05 W
Chilcotin District, British Columbia	52.50 N, 124.00 W
Chilkat River, Alaska	59.50 N, 136.00 W
Chincoteague Bay, Maryland	38.00 N, 75.25 W
Chitina Station, Alaska	61.54 N, 144.30 W
Choptank River, Maryland	38.63 N, 76.00 W
Chowan County, North Carolina	36.20 N, 76.40 W
Chukchi Sea, U.S. & U.S.S.R.	70.00 N, 167.00 W
Chukot Peninsula, U.S.S.R.	66.50 N, 172.50 W
Chulitna River, Alaska	62.34 N, 154.57 W
Churchill, Manitoba	58.46 N, 94.10 W
Churchill County, Nevada	39.50 N, 118.50 W
Ciudad Obregón, Mexico	27.29 N, 109.56 W
Clarke County, Alabama	31.73 N, 87.91 W
Clay County, Iowa	43.10 N, 95.13 W
Cleveland, Ohio	41.51 N, 81.70 W
Clyde River, Baffin Island, N.W.T.	70.46 N, 68.62 W
Cokeville, Wyoming	42.09 N, 110.96 W
Cold Bay, Alaska	55.18 N, 162.60 W
College, Alaska	64.86 N, 147.81 W
Columbia River basin, Washington	47.00 N, 119.00 W
Columbus, Ohio	39.97 N, 83.00 W
Colville River delta, Alaska	70.45 N, 150.50 W
Commander Islands, U.S.S.R.	55.00 N, 167.00 E
Comox, British Columbia	49.40 N, 124.55 W
Concord, Massachusetts	42.47 N, 71.35 W
Concordia Lake, Louisiana	31.64 N, 91.56 W
Concordia Parish, Louisiana	31.45 N, 91.67 W
Constantine Harbor, Aleutian Islands, Alaska	51.55 N, 179.00 W
Contra Costa County, California	37.82 N, 121.77 W
Cook Inlet, Alaska	60.50 N, 151.50 W
Cooper River, South Carolina	33.05 N, 79.95 W
Coos Bay, Oregon	43.36 N, 124.30 W
Copper Canyon, Alaska	61.50 N, 144.50 W
Copper Center, Alaska	61.96 N, 145.30 W
Copper River delta, Alaska	60.55 N, 144.85 W
Cordova, Alaska	60.55 N, 145.75 W
Cornwallis Island, N.W.T.	75.00 N, 95.00 W
Coronation Gulf, N.W.T.	68.00 N, 112.00 W
Corpus Christi, Texas	27.79 N, 97.41 W
Cosumnes River, California	38.33 N, 120.50 W
Council Grove Reservoir, Kansas	38.69 N, 96.55 W
Crab Orchard National Wildlife Refuge, Illinois	37.72 N, 89.15 W
Craig, Alaska	55.48 N, 133.15 W
Crater Lake, Oregon	42.94 N, 122.11 W
Crescent City, California	41.45 N, 124.15 W
Crescent Lake National Wildlife Refuge, Nebraska	41.72 N, 102.20 W
Crex Meadows, Wisconsin	45.94 N, 92.39 W
Cross Creeks National Wildlife Refuge, Tennessee	36.45 N, 87.75 W
Culiacán, Mexico	24.30 N, 107.42 W
Cumberland Sound, Baffin Island, N.W.T.	65.10 N, 65.30 W
Currituck County, North Carolina	36.45 N, 76.11 W
Currituck Sound, North Carolina	36.42 N, 75.96 W
Cuyahoga Falls, Ohio	41.13 N, 81.46 W
Cuyutlán, Mexico	19.00 N, 104.10 W
Cypress Hills, Alberta and Saskatchewan	49.50 N, 110.00 W

D

Name	Coordinates
Dallas, Texas	32.78 N, 96.82 W
Dauphin, Manitoba	51.09 N, 100.03 W
Davis Inlet, Labrador	56.00 N, 61.00 W
Daytona Beach, Florida	29.23 N, 81.03 W
Dease Strait, N.W.T.	68.75 N, 107.50 W
Decatur, Alabama	34.61 N, 86.99 W
Delaware Bay, Delaware	39.20 N, 75.25 W
Delaware County, Ohio	40.30 N, 83.07 W
Delmarva Peninsula, Delaware, Maryland, and Virginia	39.00 N, 75.50 W
Delray Beach, Florida	26.47 N, 80.07 W
Delta Marsh, Manitoba	50.22 N, 98.31 W
Delta National Wildlife Refuge, Louisiana	29.19 N, 89.18 W
Demarcation Point, Alaska	69.63 N, 141.20 W
Denton, Texas	33.22 N, 97.14 W
Denver, Colorado	39.74 N, 104.99 W
Departure Bay, British Columbia	49.12 N, 123.58 W
Depoe Bay, Oregon	44.82 N, 124.07 W
De Soto National Wildlife Refuge, Nebraska	41.55 N, 96.14 W
Detroit River, Michigan	42.05 N, 83.15 W
Devils Lake, North Dakota	48.03 N, 98.96 W
Devon Island, N.W.T.	75.00 N, 87.00 W
Diomede Islands, Bering Strait, Alaska	65.47 N, 169.00 W
Discovery Lake, N.W.T	67.57 N, 100.86 W
Disko Bay, Greenland	68.50 N, 53.30 W
Dismal Swamp, Virginia	36.74 N, 76.50 W
Dodge County, Wisconsin	43.50 N, 88.60 W
Door Peninsula, Wisconsin	45.00 N, 87.25 W
Dorset Island, N.W.T.	64.10 N, 76.30 W
Dover, Delaware	39.10 N, 75.32 W
Dover, Tennessee	36.29 N, 87.50 W
Dowling Lake, Alberta	51.73 N, 112.00 W
Drake's Bay, California	37.54 N, 122.42 W
Duck Creek Waterfowl Area, Missouri	37.00 N, 89.56 W
Dunnville, Ontario	42.54 N, 79.36 W
Durango, Mexico	23.30 N, 104.45 W
Dutch Harbor, Alaska	53.53 N, 166.32 W

E

Name	Coordinates
East Jordan, Michigan	45.10 N, 85.07 W
East Kootenay, British Columbia	49.15 N, 117.39 W
Eastmain River, Quebec	52.20 N, 78.30 W
Edmonton, Alberta	53.33 N, 113.28 W
Egedesminde District, Greenland	68.42 N, 52.45 W
Egg River, Banks Island, N.W.T.	72.20 N, 125.00 W
Eglinton Island, N.W.T.	118.30 N, 75.70 W
Ekwan Point, James Bay, Ontario	53.26 N, 82.10 W

Name	Coordinates
El Campo, Texas	29.12 N, 96.16 W
Elk City Reservoir, Kansas	37.25 N, 99.25 W
Elkton, Maryland	39.36 N, 75.50 W
Ellef Rignes Island	78.30 N, 104.00 W
Ellesmere Island, N.W.T.	81.00 N, 80.00 W
Ellice River, N.W.T.	68.02 N, 103.26 W
Endicott Mountains, Alaska	67.50 N, 152.00 W
Ensenada del Pabellon	31.52 N, 116.37 W
Eskimo Lakes, N.W.T.	69.15 N, 132.17 W
Eskimo Point, Hudson Bay, N.W.T.	61.07 N, 94.03 W
Essex County, Massachusetts	40.48 N, 74.12 W
Etah, Greenland	78.19 N, 72.38 W
Evangeline Parish, Louisiana	30.75 N, 92.42 W
Everglades, Florida	25.27 N, 80.53 W

F

Name	Coordinates
Fairbanks, Alaska	64.51 N, 147.43 W
Fairfield, California	38.15 N, 122.03 W
Falfurrias, Texas	27.14 N, 98.09 W
Fall River Reservoir, Kansas	37.36 N, 96.02 W
Falmouth, Massachusetts	41.34 N, 70.38 W
Farmington Bay Refuge, Utah	40.59 N, 111.53 W
Feather River, California	39.34 N, 125.26W
Fennville, Michigan	42.36 N, 86.06 W
Finger Lakes District, New York	42.50 N, 76.50 W
Flaming Gorge Reservoir, Wyoming	41.25 N, 109.55 W
Flat, Alaska	62.27 N, 158.01 W
Flathead Lake, Montana	47.52 N, 114.08 W
Flathead River valley, Montana	47.22 N, 114.47 W
Foam Lake, Saskatchewan	51.39 N, 103.33 W
Fort Albany, Ontario	52.15 N, 81.37 W
Fort Bend County, Texas	29.32 N, 95.47 W
Fort Chimo, Ungava Bay, Quebec	58.10 N, 68.30 W
Fort Collins, Colorado	40.35 N, 105.05 W
Fort George, Quebec	53.50 N, 79.00 W
Fort Madison, Iowa	40.38 N, 91.27 W
Fort Randall Dam and Reservoir, South Dakota	42.48 N, 98.35 W
Fort Severn, Ontario	56.00 N, 87.38 W
Fort Simpson, N.W.T.	61.52 N, 121.23 W
Fort Yukon, Alaska	66.34 N, 145.17 W
Fountain Grove Wildlife Area, Missouri	39.35 N, 93.08 W
Foxe Basin, N.W.T.	68.25 N, 77.00 W
Foxe Channel, N.W.T.	64.30 N, 80.00 W
Foxe Peninsula, Baffin Island, N.W.T.	65.00 N, 76.00 W
Franz Josef Land, U.S.S.R.	81.00 N, 55.00 E
Fraser River delta, N.W.T.	49.09 N, 123.12 W
Fraser Valley, British Columbia	52.50 N, 122.50 W
Fredericton, New Brunswick	45.58 N, 66.39 W
Frederikshåb, Greenland	62.00 N, 49.43 W
Freezeout Lake, Montana	47.40 N, 112.03 W
Fresno County, California	36.45 N, 119.45 W
Frobisher Bay, N.W.T.	62.30 N, 66.00 W
Fulshear, Texas	29.41 N, 95.54 W

G

Name	Coordinates
Gambell, Alaska	63.46 N, 171.46 W
Gambill Refuge, Texas	33.40 N, 95.33 W
Garrison Dam, North Dakota	47.22 N, 101.25 W
Garson Lake, Saskatchewan and Alberta	56.19 N, 110.02 W
Gaspé Peninsula, Quebec	48.30 N, 65.00 W
George River, Quebec	58.30 N, 66.00 W
Glacier Bay, Alaska	58.40 N, 136.00 W
Glen Elder Reservoir, Kansas	39.30 N, 98.18 W
Godthåb, Greenland	64.11 N, 51.44 W
Gogama, Ontario	47.40 N, 81.43 W
Golden Gate Park, San Francisco, California	37.46 N, 122.28 W
Gordon Lake, Saskatchewan	55.50 N, 106.26 W
Grande Prairie, Alberta	55.10 N, 118.48 W
Grand Manan Island, New Brunswick	44.40 N, 66.50 W
Grays Harbor, Washington	47.09 N, 123.45 W
Grays Lake National Wildlife Refuge, Idaho	43.04 N, 111.26 W
Great Basin, Utah	40.00 N, 117.00 W
Great Bear Lake, N.W.T.	66.00 N, 120.00 W
Great Falls, Montana	47.30 N, 111.17 W
Great Meadows, Massachusetts	42.29 N, 71.20 W
Great Salt Lake, Utah	41.10 N, 112.30 W
Great Salt Lake marshes, Utah	41.50 N, 112.30 W
Great Slave Lake, N.W.T.	61.30 N, 114.00 W
Green Bay, Wisconsin	45.00 N, 87.30 W
Greenfield Lake, Montana	47.40 N, 112.03 W
Green River, Wyoming	41.30 N, 109.30 W
Gridley, California	39.22 N, 121.42 W
Guadalajara, Mexico	20.40 N, 103.20 W
Guanajuato, Mexico	21.00 N, 101.00 W
Guaymas, Mexico	27.56 N, 110.54 W
Guerrero, Mexico	17.40 N, 100.00 W
Gulf of Alaska	58.00 N, 144.00 W
Gulf of St. Lawrence	48.50 N, 62.00 W
Gulf of Tehuantepec, Mexico	15.50 N, 94.50 W
Gulkana Basin, Alaska	63.00 N, 146.00 W

H

Name	Coordinates
Hackensack Meadows, New Jersey	40.43 N, 74.06 W
Hagerman National Wildlife Refuge, Texas	33.79 N, 96.79 W
Haines, Alaska	59.14 N, 135.27 W
Hall Land, Greenland	80.35 N, 60.00 W
Hamilton, Ontario	43.15 N, 79.51 W
Hamilton Inlet, Labrador	54.05 N, 58.30 W
Hanford, Washington	46.20 N, 119.20 W
Hanna, Alberta	51.38 N, 111.54 W
Harney Basin, Oregon	43.15 N, 120.40 W
Harrison Bay, Alaska	70.30 N, 151.30 W
Harrison Lake, British Columbia	49.31 N, 121.59 W
Hastings, Nebraska	40.56 N, 98.37 W
Havana, Illinois	40.18 N, 90.04 W
Hay Lake, Alberta	58.90 N, 119.04 W
Hay River, Alberta	60.51 N, 115.44 W
Hazelton Reservoir, Kansas	37.09 N, 98.41 W
Hebrides	57.00 N, 6.30 W
Helena, Montana	46.36 N, 112.01 W
Hendry County, Florida	26.36 N, 81.13 W
Henrys Fork, Idaho	43.45 N, 111.56 W
Henrys Lake, Idaho	44.63 N, 111.20 W
Highline Plains, Saskatchewan through Colorado	42.50 N, 105.00 W

Holla Bend National Wildlife Refuge, Arkansas	35.17 N, 93.08 W
Holly Beach, Louisiana	29.77 N, 93.46 W
Holman Island, N.W.T.	70.43 N, 117.43 W
Holsteinsborg, Greenland	66.55 N, 53.40 W
Honey Lake Wildlife Area, California	40.16 N, 120.19 W
Hooper Bay, Alaska	61.30 N, 166.06 W
Hopedale, Labrador	55.50 N, 60.10 W
Hopes Advance Bay, Quebec	59.25 N, 69.40 W
Horicon Marsh, Wisconsin	43.30 N, 88.38 W
Horseshoe Lake Refuge, Illinois	37.09 N, 89.30 W
Houston, Texas	29.46 N, 95.22 W
Hudson River valley, New York	40.42 N, 74.02 W
Hudson Strait, N.W.T.	62.30 N, 72.00 W
Humboldt Bay, California	40.47 N, 124.11 W
Humphrey Point, Alaska	69.97 N, 142.50 W

I

Icy Cape, Alaska	60.00 N, 141.15 W
Iditarod River, Alaska	63.02 N, 158.00 W
Igiak Bay, Alaska	61.38 N, 166.00 W
Illinois River, Illinois	40.50 N, 90.00 W
Imperial County, California	32.60 N, 115.30 W
Imperial Valley, California	32.51 N, 115.34 W
Indian River, Florida	28.40 N, 80.50 W
Indigirka River, U.S.S.R.	70.50 N, 148.50 E
Indigirka River delta, U.S.S.R.	71.30 N, 150.00 E
Inglefield Land, Greenland	78.30 N, 67.50 W
Inner and Outer Hebrides	57.00 N, 6.30 W
Innoko River–Iditarod River breeding grounds, Alaska	63.25 N, 158.45 W
Interlake area, Manitoba	51.50 N, 98.00 W
Iota, Louisiana	30.36 N, 92.50 W
Island Park, Idaho	44.24 N, 111.19 W
Itasca County, Minnesota	47.50 N, 93.50 W
Izembek Bay, Alaska	55.22 N, 162.90 W

J

Jack Miner Bird Sanctuary, Ontario	42.04 N, 82.75 W
Jackson Hole, Wyoming	43.45 N, 110.38 W
Jalisco, Mexico	20.20 N, 103.40 W
James River, North and South Dakota	46.20 N, 98.00 W
Jamestown, North Dakota	46.54 N, 98.42 W
J. Clark Salyer National Wildlife Refuge, North Dakota	48.35 N, 100.44 W
Jefferson County, Texas	29.85 N, 94.10 W
Jefferson Davis Parish, Louisiana	30.40 N, 92.80 W
Jenny Lind Island, N.W.T.	68.70 N, 102.90 W
Jessie Lake, Alberta	54.25 N, 110.75 W
John Redmond Reservoir, Kansas	38.18 N, 95.55 W
Jones Beach, New York	40.35 N, 73.31 W
Jones County, Georgia	33.00 N, 83.58 W
Jordan River, Utah	40.49 N, 112.08 W
Julianehåb, Greenland	60.43 N, 46.01 W
Julimes, Chihuahua, Mexico	28.25 N, 105.27 W
Juneau, Alaska	58.20 N, 134.27 W
Jutland Peninsula, Germany	56.00 N, 9.15 E

K

Kachemak Bay, Alaska	59.35 N, 151.30 W
Kaleet River, Adelaide Peninsula, N.W.T.	67.05 N, 96.88 W
Kamchatka Peninsula, U.S.S.R.	55.00 N, 160.00 E
Kamloops, British Columbia	50.40 N, 120.20 W
Kankakee Marsh, Indiana	41.25 N, 87.00 W
Kantishna, Alaska	63.50 N, 151.00 W
Kantishna River, Alaska	64.40 N, 150.50 W
Karagin Island, Bering Sea, U.S.S.R.	59.30 N, 161.85 E
Karkinit Bay, U.S.S.R.	45.55 N, 33.00 E
Karrak Lake, N.W.T.	67.25 N, 100.25 W
Kasaan Bay, N.W.T.	55.30 N, 132.25 W
Kashunuk River, Alaska	61.35 N, 165.45 W
Kawinaw Lake, Manitoba	52.90 N, 99.60 W
Kazan Lake, Saskatchewan	55.33 N, 108.21 W
Kegashka Lake, Quebec	50.20 N, 61.25 W
Kenai National Moose Range, Alaska	60.50 N, 150.50 W
Kenai Peninsula, Alaska	60.00 N, 150.00 W
Kenai-Susitna breeding grounds, Alaska	61.50 N, 150.00 W
Kendall Island, N.W.T.	79.00 N, 135.06 W
Kennebec River, Maine	44.00 N, 69.50 W
Kenogami River, Ontario	51.06 N, 84.28 W
Kenora, Ontario	49.47 N, 94.29 W
Kent Island, New Brunswick	44.61 N, 66.84 W
Kent Peninsula, N.W.T.	68.30 N, 107.00 W
Kentucky Lake, Kentucky	36.25 N, 88.05 W
Keokuk, Iowa	40.24 N, 91.25 W
Keokuk Pool, Mississippi River, Illinois and Iowa	40.35 N, 91.25 W
Ketchikan, Alaska	55.21 N, 131.35 W
Kettle Moraine State Forest, Wisconsin	43.00 N, 88.45 W
Kettle Point, Ontario	43.21 N, 82.00 W
Kettle River, Manitoba	56.73 N, 89.40 W
Khatanga River, U.S.S.R.	72.00 N, 102.50 E
Killinek Island, Quebec	60.30 N, 65.00 W
Kindersley, Saskatchewan	51.27 N, 109.10 W
King George Islands, James Bay, Quebec	57.20 N, 78.25 W
King Ranch, Texas	27.25 N, 97.55 W
Kings River, California	36.03 N, 119.49 W
Kingston, Ontario	44.14 N, 76.30 W
Kingsville, Ontario	42.02 N, 82.45 W
King William Island, N.W.T.	69.00 N, 97.30 W
Kinoje Lake, Ontario	51.55 N, 81.80 W
Kinoje River, Ontario	51.60 N, 81.80 W
Kirwin National Wildlife Refuge, Kansas	39.39 N, 99.50 W
Kivalina, Alaska	67.59 N, 164.33 W
Klamath Basin, Oregon	42.55 N, 121.45 W
Kleena Kleene, British Columbia	51.58 N, 124.59 W
Kluane Lake, Yukon	61.15 N, 138.40 W
Knoxville, Tennessee	35.58 N, 83.56 W
Knudson's Marsh, Utah	41.31 N, 112.10 W
Kobuk, Alaska	66.54 N, 156.52 W
Kobuk River, Alaska	66.45 N, 161.00 W
Kobuk River delta, Alaska	66.55 N, 161.50 W
Kodiak Island, Alaska	57.30 N, 153.30 W
Kogaluk River, Quebec	59.35 N, 77.30 W
Kokechik Bay, Alaska	61.66 N, 166.00 W
Koksoak River, Quebec	58.30 N, 68.10 W
Kolomak River, Alaska	59.00 N, 159.85 W
Kolyma River, U.S.S.R.	69.30 N, 161.00 E
Kolyuchin Bay, U.S.S.R.	66.86 N, 175.00 W

Kootenay Lake, British Columbia	49.35 N, 116.50 W
Kotzebue Bay and Sound, Alaska	66.20 N, 163.00 W
Koukdjuak River, Baffin Island, N.W.T.	66.45 N, 73.09 W
Kovik Bay, Quebec	60.54 N, 76.75 W
Koyukuk, Alaska	64.53 N, 157.43 W
Koyukuk River, Alaska	64.55 N, 161.12 W
Krasnoyarsk, U.S.S.R.	56.00 N, 92.50 E
Kuparuk River, Alaska	70.25 N, 148.55 W
Kurile Islands, U.S.S.R.	46.10 N, 152.00 E
Kuskokwim Bay, Alaska	59.45 N, 162.25 W
Kuskokwim River, Alaska	60.17 N, 162.27 W
Kutawagan, Saskatchewan	51.20 N, 104.20 W
Kvichak River, Alaska	59.21 N, 156.50 W

L

Lacassine National Wildlife Refuge, Louisiana	29.90 N, 92.52 W
Lac qui Parle Lake, Minnesota	45.07 N, 96.00 W
Lacreek National Wildlife Refuge, South Dakota	43.10 N, 101.44 W
La Crosse, Wisconsin	43.49 N, 91.15 W
Lac Saint-Jean, Quebec	48.35 N, 72.00 W
Ladner, British Columbia	49.05 N, 123.05 W
Lafayette, Louisiana	30.14 N, 92.01 W
Lago de Chapala, Jalisco, Mexico	20.27 N, 103.00 W
Lago de Managua, Nicaragua	12.30 N, 86.30 W
Lago de Maracaibo, Venezuela	10.00 N, 71.80 W
Lago de Nicaragua, Nicaragua	11.50 N, 85.50 W
Laguna Atacosa National Wildlife Refuge, Texas	26.27 N, 97.40 W
Laguna Bustillos, Chihuahua, Mexico	28.32 N, 106.39 W
Laguna de Agua Brava, Mexico	22.10 N, 104.75 W
Laguna de Babicora, Mexico	26.62 N, 106.91 W
Laguna de la Joya, Chiapas, Mexico	15.95 N, 92.85 W
Laguna del Caimanero, Mexico	22.47 N, 106.02 W
Laguna del Carmen, Mexico	18.18 N, 92.88 W
Laguna de los Mexicanos, Mexico	28.08 N, 106.48 W
Laguna de Santiaguillo, Mexico	24.40 N, 104.75 W
Laguna Madre, Texas and Mexico	26.50 N, 97.40 W
Laguna Papagayo, Guerrero, Mexico	16.27 N, 98.83 W
Laguna San Ignacio, Baja California, Mexico	26.45 N, 112.60 W
Laguna Scammon, Baja California, Mexico	26.86 N, 114.10 W
Lake Alice, Wyoming	42.05 N, 110.90 W
Lake Andes, South Dakota	43.09 N, 98.32 W
Lake Apopka, Florida	28.60 N, 81.64 W
Lake Arthur, Louisiana	30.05 N, 92.41 W
Lake Ashtabula, North Dakota	47.08 N, 98.00 W
Lake Baikal, U.S.S.R.	107.00 N, 53.00 E
Lake Beaupré, Saskatchewan	54.55 N, 107.05 W
Lake Borgne, Louisiana	30.05 N, 89.40 W
Lake Carl Blackwell, Oklahoma	36.16 N, 97.23 W
Lake Cayuga, New York	42.45 N, 76.45 W
Lake Champlain, New York–Vermont	46.27 N, 72.17 W
Lake Chautauqua, Illinois	40.37 N, 90.00 W
Lake Christina, Minnesota	46.02 N, 95.82 W
Lake Claire, Alberta	58.30 N, 112.00 W
Lake Corpus Christi, Texas	28.10 N, 97.53 W
Lake Earl, California	41.83 N, 124.19 W
Lake Erie marshes, Ohio	41.65 N, 83.20 W
Lake Harbour, Baffin Island, N.W.T.	62.51 N, 69.53 W
Lake Hazen, Ellesmere Island, N.W.T.	81.94 N, 70.70 W
Lake Hendricks, Minnesota	44.50 N, 96.45 W
Lake Huron, Michigan	44.50 N, 82.50 W
Lakehurst, New Jersey	40.01 N, 74.19 W
Lake Istokpoga, Florida	27.36 N, 81.30 W
Lake Kissimmee, Florida	27.55 N, 81.16 W
Lake Manitoba, Manitoba	50.50 N, 98.30 W
Lake Mathis, Texas	28.08 N, 97.82 W
Lake Mattamuskeet, North Carolina	35.30 N, 76.11 W
Lake Melville, Labrador	53.45 N, 59.30 W
Lake Merritt, California	37.48 N, 122.16 W
Lake Mývatn, Iceland	65.37 N, 16.58 W
Lake Newell, Alberta	50.25 N, 111.56 W
Lake Nipigon, Ontario	49.50 N, 88.30 W
Lake Nipissing, Ontario	46.17 N, 80.00 W
Lake Odessa, Iowa	41.20 N, 91.10 W
Lake Okeechobee, Florida	26.55 N, 80.45 W
Lake Pátzcuaro, Mexico	19.35 N, 101.35 W
Lake Petén, Guatemala	16.58 N, 89.50 W
Lake Pontchartrain, Louisiana	30.10 N, 90.10 W
Lake St. Clair, Michigan and Ontario	42.25 N, 82.41 W
Lake St. Francis, Quebec	45.08 N, 74.25 W
Lake St. Joseph, Ontario	51.05 N, 90.35 W
Lake St. Peter, Quebec	46.20 N, 72.75 W
Lake Sardis, Mississippi	34.27 N, 89.43 W
Lake Sevan, U.S.S.R.	40.20 N, 45.20 E
Lake Temagami, Ontario	47.00 N, 80.05 W
Lake Texoma, Texas and Oklahoma	33.55 N, 96.37 W
Lake Titicaca, Peru and Bolivia	15.50 S, 69.20 W
Lake Winnipeg, Manitoba	52.00 N, 97.00 W
Lake Winnipegosis, Manitoba	52.30 N, 100.00 W
Lake Yuriria, Mexico	20.15 N, 101.06 W
Lane County, Oregon	44.00 W, 123.00 W
La Pérouse Bay, Manitoba	58.78 N, 93.44 W
Laramie, Wyoming	41.19 N, 105.35 W
Lassen County, California	40.50 N, 120.50 W
Last Mountain Lake, Saskatchewan	51.05 N, 105.10 W
Laurel, Maryland	39.06 N, 76.51 W
Laxá River, Iceland	65.78 N, 17.12 W
Leaf Bay, Quebec	58.78 N, 70.00 W
Lee County, Florida	26.60 N, 81.70 W
Lena River, U.S.S.R.	72.25 N, 126.40 E
Lenore Lake, Washington	52.30 N, 105.00 W
Lenox, Massachusetts	42.22 N, 73.17 W
Lerdo de Tejada, Mexico	18.37 N, 95.31 W
Lethbridge, Alberta	49.42 N, 110.50 W
Lewellen, Nebraska	41.20 N, 102.09 W
Lewiston, Idaho	46.25 N, 117.01 W
Lexington, Virginia	37.47 N, 79.27 W
Liard River, N.W.T.	61.50 N, 121.20 W
Lima, Peru	12.00 S, 76.35 W
Lincoln, Montana	46.58 N, 112.41 W
Linn County, Oregon	44.50 N, 122.50 W
Little Clarke Lake, Saskatchewan	54.42 N, 106.97 W
Little Diomede Island, Bering Strait, Alaska	65.45 N, 168.57 W
Little George Island, Manitoba	52.87 N, 97.78 W
Liverpool Bay, N.W.T.	70.00 N, 130.00 W
Lochsa River, Idaho	46.08 N, 115.36 W
Lonesome Lake, British Columbia	52.26 N, 125.65 W
Long Island, New York	40.50 N, 73.00 W
Long Island Sound, New York and Connecticut	41.05 N, 72.58 W
Long Point, Ontario	42.57 N, 80.25 W

Los Angeles County, California	34.25 N, 118.15 W
Los Banos, California	37.04 N, 120.51 W
Los Mochis, Sinaloa, Mexico	25.45 N, 108.57 W
Lousana, Alberta	52.14 N, 113.15 W
Lovewell Reservoir, Kansas	39.88 N, 98.02 W
Lower Cummins Lake, Saskatchewan	55.56 N, 108.83 W
Lower Klamath Lake and National Wildlife Refuge, California	41.55 N, 121.42 W
Lower Souris National Wildlife Refuge, North Dakota	48.35 N, 100.44 W
Lowndes County, Mississippi	33.50 N, 88.50 W
Loxahatchee National Wildlife Refuge, Florida	26.49 N, 80.13 W
Luther Marsh, Ontario	43.95 N, 80.45 W
Lynn, Massachusetts	42.28 N, 70.57 W

Mc–Mac

McAllen, Texas	26.12 N, 98.15 W
McConnell River and delta, N.W.T.	60.87 N, 94.41 W
MacCormick Bay, Greenland	76.57 N, 68.44 W
McGrath, Alaska	62.58 N, 155.38 W
McKellar Bay, Baffin Island, N.W.T.	62.35 N, 70.00 W

M

Macallum Lake, Saskatchewan	55.02 N, 108.39 W
Machichi River, Manitoba	57.03 N, 92.06 W
Mackenzie River, N.W.T.	69.15 N, 134.08 W
Mackenzie River delta, N.W.T.	69.35 N, 135.08 W
Macklin, Saskatchewan	52.20 N, 109.56 W
Madera County, California	36.64 N, 118.73 W
Madison County, Mississippi	32.66 N, 90.00 W
Madison River, Montana	45.56 N, 111.30 W
Magdalena River and delta, Colombia	11.06 N, 74.51 W
Magdalen Islands, Quebec	47.50 N, 61.75 W
Magee Marsh, Ohio	41.60 N, 83.11 W
Maguse River, N.W.T.	61.40 N, 95.10 W
Makkovik Bay, Labrador	55.01 N, 59.09 W
Malden, Massachusetts	42.26 N, 71.04 W
Malheur Basin, Lake, and National Wildlife Refuge, Oregon	43.22 N, 118.81 W
Malta, Montana	48.21 N, 107.52 W
Manikuagan River, Quebec	51.00 N, 68.59 W
Mansel Island, Hudson Bay	62.00 N, 79.50 W
Manzanillo, Mexico	19.03 N, 104.20 W
Maracaibo, Venezuela	10.40 N, 71.37 W
Maravatío de Ocampo, Mexico	19.54 N, 100.27 W
Margaree River, Cape Breton Island, N.S.	46.24 N, 61.05 W
Marion Reservoir, Kansas	38.21 N, 97.01 W
Mark Twain National Wildlife Refuge, Missouri and Illinois	39.56 N, 91.23 W
Marshall Islands	9.00 N, 168.00 E
Marsh Island, Louisiana	29.35 N, 91.53 W
Martha's Vineyard, Massachusetts	41.25 N, 70.40 W
Marysville, California	39.09 N, 121.35 W
Mason County, Illinois	40.18 N, 90.00 W
Mason Neck, Fairfax County, Virginia	38.63 N, 77.16 W
Matagorda Bay, Texas	28.35 N, 96.20 W
Matapedia River, Quebec	48.33 N, 67.32 W
Mattamuskeet National Wildlife Refuge, North Carolina	35.30 N, 76.11 W
Mazatlán, Mexico	23.13 N, 106.25 W
Meighen Island, N.W.T.	80.00 N, 99.50 W
Melville Island, N.W.T.	75.15 N, 110.00 W
Melville Peninsula, N.W.T.	68.00 N, 84.00 W
Mendota, California	36.45 N, 120.23 W
Merced County, California	37.18 N, 120.29 W
Merced National Wildlife Refuge, California	37.10 N, 120.71 W
Merced River, California	37.21 N, 120.58 W
Merritt Island, Florida	28.33 N, 80.40 W
Methy Lake, Saskatchewan	56.47 N, 109.67 W
Mexico City, Mexico	19.24 N, 99.09 W
Michoacán, Mexico	19.10 N, 101.50 W
Milford Reservoir, Kansas	39.15 N, 97.00 W
Milton, Vermont	44.38 N, 73.07 W
Milwaukee, Wisconsin	43.02 N, 87.55 W
Mingo National Wildlife Refuge & Swamp, Missouri	36.95 N, 90.15 W
Minidoka National Wildlife Refuge, Idaho	42.75 N, 113.60 W
Ministik Lake, Alberta	53.40 N, 113.00 W
Minneapolis, Minnesota	44.59 N, 93.13 W
Minnedosa, Manitoba	50.14 N, 99.51 W
Minto Lakes, Alaska	64.95 N, 148.90 W
Miquelon Lake, Alberta	53.25 N, 112.95 W
Mirage Islands, Great Slave Lake, N.W.T.	62.03 N, 113.20 W
Mississippi Lake, Ontario	45.05 N, 76.12 W
Mississippi River delta, Louisiana	29.10 N, 89.15 W
Missouri Coteau, South Dakota, North Dakota, Saskatchewan	46.00 N, 99.30 W
Mistassini Post, Quebec	50.37 N, 73.80 W
Misty Lake, Manitoba	59.95 N, 100.00 W
Mitla Lagoon, Mexico	17.03 N, 100.25 W
Moar Bay, James Bay, Quebec	52.90 N, 78.80 W
Mobile Bay, Alabama	30.25 N, 88.00 W
Mohave County, Arizona	34.50 N, 114.25 W
Mokelumne River, California	38.13 N, 121.28 W
Moline, Illinois	41.30 N, 90.31 W
Monida, Montana	44.33 N, 112.18 W
Monomoy National Wildlife Refuge, Massachusetts	41.35 N, 70.02 W
Montauk Point, New York	41.04 N, 71.52 W
Monterey Peninsula, California	36.35 N, 121.51 W
Montezuma Marsh and National Wildlife Refuge, New York	43.00 N, 76.75 W
Montgomery County, Mississippi	33.50 N, 89.65 W
Montreal, Quebec	45.31 N, 73.34 W
Montrose Waterfowl Area, Missouri	38.25 N, 94.00 W
Moosonee, Ontario	51.17 N, 80.39 W
Morehouse Parish, Louisiana	32.75 N, 91.60 W
Morgan City, Louisiana	29.42 N, 91.12 W
Morrison County, Minnesota	46.00 N, 94.25 W
Morro Bay, California	35.20 N, 120.51 W
Mountain Village, Alaska	62.05 N, 163.44 W
Mount Desert Island, Maine	44.20 N, 68.20 W
Mount McKinley National Park, Alaska	63.30 N, 150.00 W
Mount Vernon, Washington	48.25 N, 122.20 W
Mud Lake, Ontario	51.50 N, 90.15 W
Muleshoe National Wildlife Refuge, Texas	33.95 N, 102.43 W
Murray Bay, Quebec	47.39 N, 70.10 W
Muscatine, Iowa	41.25 N, 91.03 W

N

Nags Head, North Carolina	35.95 N, 75.62 W
Nain Bay, Labrador	57.00 N, 61.40 W
Nantucket Island, Massachusetts	41.16 N, 70.03 W
Nantucket Sound, Massachusetts	41.30 N, 70.15 W
Natchitoches Parish, Louisiana	31.46 N, 93.05 W
National Antelope Refuge, Nevada	41.75 N, 119.75 W
National Elk Refuge, Wyoming	43.30 N, 110.37 W
Nauvoo, Illinois	40.33 N, 91.23 W
Nebraska Sandhills	42.00 N, 102.00 W
Nechako Plateau, British Columbia	54.00 N, 124.30 W
Nechako River, British Columbia	53.56 N, 122.42 W
Nelchina Flats, Alaska	62.50 N, 146.50 W
Nelson Island, Alaska	60.35 N, 164.45 W
Nelson Lagoon, Alaska	55.60 N, 160.45 W
Netarts Bay, Oregon	45.24 N, 123.56 W
Nett Lake, Minnesota	48.06 N, 93.10 W
Newburyport Harbor, Massachusetts	42.49 N, 70.53 W
New Cumberland, West Virginia	40.30 N, 80.36 W
New London, Connecticut	41.21 N, 72.07 W
New York City	40.40 N, 74.00 W
Nexpa Lagoon, Mexico	18.05 N, 102.46 W
Nicolet National Forest, Wisconsin and Michigan	46.00 N, 89.00 W
Niska Lake, Saskatchewan	55.35 N, 108.38 W
Nizhnyaya Tunguska River, U.S.S.R.	65.48 N, 88.04 E
Noatak River, Alaska	67.00 N, 162.30 W
Nome, Alaska	64.30 N, 165.24 W
Norfolk, Virginia	38.40 N, 76.14 W
Normal Wells, N.W.T.	65.17 N, 126.51 W
North Bay, Ontario	45.04 N, 79.35 W
North Belcher group, Hudson Bay	56.20 N, 79.30 W
North Park, Colorado	40.44 N, 106.17 W
North Platte River, Nebraska	41.15 N, 100.45 W
North Platte River, Wyoming	42.80 N, 106.00 W
Northumberland Strait	46.00 N, 63.50 W
Northway, Alaska	62.59 N, 141.43 W
Norton Sound, Alaska	63.50 N, 164.00 W
Nottawasaga River, Ontario	44.32 N, 80.01 W
Novaya Zemlya, U.S.S.R.	74.00 N, 57.00 E
Noxubee National Wildlife Refuge, Mississippi	33.25 N, 82.92 W
Nueces River, Texas	27.50 N, 97.30 W
Nunivak Island, Bering Sea, Alaska	60.00 N, 166.30 W
Nushagak Bay, Alaska	58.40 N, 158.40 W
Nushagak River, Alaska	59.00 N, 158.30 W

O

Oakdale, Long Island, New York	40.44 N, 73.07 W
Oak Grove, Louisiana	32.52 N, 91.23 W
Oak Lake, Manitoba	49.70 N, 100.68 W
Oakland, California	37.47 N, 122.13 W
Oak Point, Manitoba	50.30 N, 98.00 W
Oak Ridge, Louisiana	32.62 N, 91.77 W
Ocean City, Maryland	38.20 N, 75.05 W
Ogallala, Nebraska	41.08 N, 101.43 W
Ogden Bay Waterfowl Area, Utah	41.20 N, 111.60 W
Ogden River, Utah	41.14 N, 111.58 W
Ohtig Lake, Alaska	66.30 N, 145.20 W
Okanagan River Valley, British Columbia	49.50 N, 119.43 W
Okanogan County and Okanogan Highlands, Washington	48.50 N, 119.50 W
Okefenokee Swamp, Georgia	30.42 N, 82.20 W
Okse Bay, Ellesmere Island	77.26 N, 87.50 W
Old Crow, Yukon	67.35 N, 139.50 W
Old Crow Flats, Yukon	68.00 N, 140.00 W
Old Kashunuk Village, Alaska	61.35 N, 166.00 W
Omaha, Nebraska	41.16 N, 95.57 W
Onumtuk Slough, Alaska	61.35 N, 165.45 W
Orange, Texas	30.01 N, 93.44 W
Orkneys, Scotland	59.00 N, 3.00 W
Osceola County, Florida	28.00 N, 81.30 W
Ossining, New York	41.10 N, 73.52 W
Oswego, New York	43.27 N, 76.31 W
Otelnuk Lake, Labrador	56.00 N, 68.00 W
Ottawa, Ontario	45.25 N, 75.42 W
Ottawa County, Ohio	41.31 N, 82.56 W
Ottawa National Wildlife Refuge, Ohio	41.39 N, 83.32 W
Ottawa River, Ontario	45.20 N, 73.58 W
Otter Island, Pribilof Islands, Alaska	57.05 N, 170.40 W
Outer Hebrides, Scotland	57.50 N, 7.32 W
Owikeno Lake, British Columbia	51.41 N, 127.00 W

P

Padilla Bay, Oregon	48.35 N, 122.32 W
Padloping Island, N.W.T.	67.07 N, 62.35 W
Padre Island, Texas	27.00 N, 97.15 W
Pagwa River, Ontario	50.00 N, 85.23 W
Palmyra Island	5.52 N, 162.06 W
Palo Alto, California	37.27 N, 122.09 W
Palo Alto County, Iowa	43.00 N, 94.75 W
Pamlico Sound, North Carolina	35.20 N, 75.55 W
Panowat Spit, Alaska	61.30 N, 166.06 W
Paris, Tennessee	36.19 N, 88.20 W
Paris, Texas	33.40 N, 95.33 W
Patuxent Wildlife Research Center, Maryland	39.05 N, 76.75 W
Payne Lake, Quebec	59.30 N, 74.00 W
Payne River, Quebec	45.14 N, 75.08 W
Peace River, Alberta	59.00 N, 111.25 W
Peace River delta, Alberta	58.80 N, 111.50 W
Pea Island National Wildlife Refuge, North Carolina	35.70 N, 75.50 W
Pearl River, Mississippi	30.11 N, 89.49 W
Peary Land, Greenland	83.50 N, 30.00 W
Pecan Island, Louisiana	29.65 N, 92.40 W
Pelican Island National Wildlife Refuge, Florida	27.79 N, 80.44 W
Pel Lake and Marsh, Saskatchewan	51.70 N, 104.60 W
Penobscot Bay, Maine	44.15 N, 68.52 W
Peoria Lake, Illinois	40.42 N, 89.36 W
Perry River, N.W.T.	67.38 N, 102.00 W
Perry River delta, N.W.T.	67.66 N, 102.05 W
Petersburg, Alaska	56.49 N, 132.57 W
Petitcodiac River, New Brunswick	45.50 N, 64.33 W
Petitsikapau Lake, Labrador	54.45 N, 66.25 W
Phillips County, Montana	48.30 N, 107.70 W
Pickle Crow, Ontario	51.30 N, 90.04 W
Piedmont National Wildlife Refuge, Georgia	33.14 N, 83.72 W
Pine River, Wisconsin	46.00 N, 88.90 W

Platte River, Nebraska	41.00 N, 95.50 W
Pleasanton, Kansas	38.11 N, 94.43 W
Plumas County, California	40.00 N, 120.50 W
Point Barrow, Alaska	71.23 N, 156.30 W
Point Dall, Alaska	61.50 N, 166.06 W
Pointe au Huard, Quebec	53.00 N, 79.00 W
Point Hope, Alaska	68.21 N, 166.80 W
Point Lay, Alaska	69.70 N, 163.05 W
Point Pelee, Ontario	41.54 N, 82.30 W
Polk County, Oregon	45.00 N, 123.23 W
Porcupine River, Yukon	66.35 N, 145.15 W
Portage Plains, Manitoba	49.57 N, 98.25 W
Port Burwell, Quebec	60.35 N, 64.80 W
Port Clinton, Ohio	41.31 N, 82.56 W
Port Harrison, Quebec	58.30 N, 78.15 W
Portland, Oregon	45.33 N, 122.36 W
Port Moller, Alaska	55.59 N, 160.34 W
Port Nelson, Manitoba	57.03 N, 92.36 W
Potomac River, Maryland	38.00 N, 76.18 W
Povungnituk, Quebec	59.12 N, 77.51 W
Pozo de Agua, Costa Rica	10.00 N, 85.33 W
Presque Isle County, Michigan	45.35 N, 84.00 W
Presqu'Ile Provincial Park, Ontario	44.00 N, 77.42 W
Pribilof Islands	57.00 N, 170.00 W
Prime Hook National Wildlife Refuge, Delaware	38.86 N, 75.28 W
Prince Albert Peninsula, N.W.T.	72.50 N, 118.00 W
Prince Edward Island, Canada	46.30 N, 63.00 W
Prince Edward Sound, Canada	43.57 N, 76.57 W
Prince George region, British Columbia	54.20 N, 130.11 W
Prince Leopold Island, N.W.T.	74.02 N, 90.00 W
Prince of Wales Island, N.W.T.	72.40 N, 99.00 W
Prince Patrick Island, N.W.T.	76.45 N, 119.30 W
Prince William Sound	60.40 N, 147.00 W
Promise Island, N.W.T.	63.25 N, 90.45 W
Prudhoe Bay, Alaska	70.43 N, 148.30 W
Puebla, Mexico	18.45 N, 97.50 W
Puget Sound, Washington	47.50 N, 122.30 W
Puxico, Missouri	36.57 N, 90.10 W
Pyasina River, U.S.S.R.	71.50 N, 82.40 E
Pymatuning Lake, Pennsylvania	41.37 N, 80.30 W

Q

Quebec City, Quebec	46.49 N, 71.13 W
Queen Charlotte Islands, British Columbia	51.30 N, 129.00 W
Queen Elizabeth Islands, N.W.T.	78.00 N, 105.00 W
Queen Maud Gulf, N.W.T.	68.25 N, 102.30 W
Quiver Creek, Illinois	40.15 N, 90.00 W
Quivira National Wildlife Refuge, Kansas	38.15 N, 98.50 W

R

Rae, N.W.T.	62.50 N, 116.03 W
Rainwater Basin, Nebraska	40.50 N, 98.00 W
Raleigh, North Carolina	35.47 N, 78.39 W
Raritan Bay, New Jersey	40.28 N, 74.12 W
Raspberry Strait, Alaska	58.00 N, 153.00 W
Rat Rapids, Ontario	51.18 N, 90.25 W
Rebecca Lake, Quebec	53.00 N, 79.00 W
Redberry Lake, Saskatchewan	52.72 N, 107.13 W
Redmond Lake, Kansas	38.18 N, 95.55 W
Red Mountain, Montana	47.07 N, 112.44 W
Red Rock Lakes National Wildlife Refuge, Montana	44.64 N, 111.40 W
Redvers, Saskatchewan	49.33 N, 101.39 W
Reelfoot Lake and National Wildlife Refuge, Tennessee	36.25 N, 89.22 W
Refugio County, Texas	28.30 N, 97.25 W
Regina, Saskatchewan	50.25 N, 104.39 W
Rehoboth Bay, Delaware	38.40 N, 75.06 W
Remington Farms, Maryland	39.22 N, 76.10 W
Rice Lake National Wildlife Refuge, Minnesota	46.50 N, 93.39 W
Riding Mountain National Park, Manitoba	50.55 N, 100.25 W
Rio Grande delta, Texas	25.57 N, 97.09 W
Rio Yaqui, Sonora, Mexico	27.37 N, 110.00 W
Rivière du Loup, Quebec	47.50 N, 69.32 W
Robertson Bay, Greenland	76.35 N, 68.50 W
Rochester, Minnesota	44.02 N, 92.29 W
Rochester, New York	43.10 N, 77.36 W
Rockefeller Refuge, Louisiana	29.63 N, 93.00 W
Rockport, Texas	28.01 N, 97.04 W
Rodeo, New Mexico	31.50 N, 109.02 W
Roggan River, Quebec	54.10 N, 78.00 W
Romanzof Cape, Alaska	61.73 N, 166.10 W
Roosevelt Lake, Arizona	33.42 N, 111.07 W
Roseneath, Manitoba	52.00 N, 100.20 W
Ruby Lake National Wildlife Refuge, Nevada	40.10 N, 115.30 W
Ruby Mountains, Nevada	40.25 N, 115.35 W
Rupert, Idaho	42.37 N, 113.41 W
Rupert House, Quebec	51.29 N, 78.45 W
Ruthven, Iowa	43.08 N, 94.54 W

S

Sabine Lake, Texas & Louisiana	29.50 N, 93.50 W
Sabine River, Texas & Louisiana	30.00 N, 93.45 W
Sachs Harbour, Banks Island, N.W.T.	72.00 N, 125.00 W
Sackville, New Brunswick	45.85 N, 64.38 W
Sacramento and Delta Marshes, California	38.10 N, 121.80 W
Sacramento National Wildlife Refuge, California	39.42 N, 122.20 W
Sacramento River valley, California	39.00 N, 121.75 W
Saginaw, Michigan	43.25 N, 83.58 W
Saginaw Bay, Michigan	43.50 N, 83.40 W
Saint Cloud, Minnesota	45.33 N, 94.10 W
Saint Cyrille, Quebec	45.92 N, 72.42 W
Saint George Island, Bering Sea, Alaska	56.35 N, 169.35 W
Saint John River, New Brunswick	45.50 N, 66.10 W
Saint John's Newfoundland	47.34 N, 52.43 W
Saint Joseph, Missouri	39.46 N, 94.51 W
Saint Lawrence Island, Bering Sea, Alaska	63.30 N, 170.30 W
Saint Lawrence River estuary	49.00 N, 68.00 W
Saint Louis, Missouri	38.38 N, 90.11 W
Saint Matthew Island, Bering Sea, Alaska	60.30 N, 172.45 W

Name	Coordinates
Saint Michael, Alaska	63.29 N, 162.20 W
Saint Paul, Kansas	37.50 N, 95.17 W
Saint Paul Island, Bering Sea, Alaska	57.10 N, 170.15 W
Saint Vincent Island, Florida	29.65 N, 85.17 W
Sakhalin Island, U.S.S.R.	51.00 N, 143.00 E
Salt Lake marshes, Utah	41.15 N, 112.25 W
Salt Marshes, Kansas	38.15 N, 98.50 W
Salton Sea, California	33.19 N, 115.50 W
Salton Sea National Wildlife Refuge, California	33.10 N, 115.65 W
Salt Plains National Wildlife Refuge, Oklahoma	36.78 N, 98.22 W
Salt River Range, Wyoming	43.00 N, 111.00 W
Salt River valley, Arizona	32.23 N, 142.18 W
Samish Bay, Washington	48.36 N, 122.28 W
San Antonio Bay, Texas	28.20 N, 96.75 W
Sandhills of Nebraska	42.00 N, 102.00 W
San Diego Bay	32.37 N, 117.07 W
Sand Lake National Wildlife Refuge, South Dakota	45.75 N, 98.25 W
Sandusky Bay, Ohio	41.27 N, 82.52 W
San Francisco, California	37.48 N, 122.24 W
San Francisco Bay, California	37.43 N, 122.17 W
Sanibel Island, Florida	26.27 N, 82.06 W
San Ignacio Bay, Mexico	26.50 N, 113.11 W
San Joaquin River, California	37.50 N, 121.00 W
San Juan, Puerto Rico	18.28 N, 66.07 W
San Luis Potosí, Mexico	22.09 N, 100.59 W
San Luis Valley, Colorado	37.45 N, 105.70 W
San Marcos, Mexico	21.00 N, 105.35 W
San Quintin Bay, Mexico	30.18 N, 115.53 W
San Simon Marsh, Arizona	32.27 N, 109.23 W
Santa Ana National Wildlife Refuge, Texas	26.09 N, 98.15 W
Santa Maria Bay, Mexico	25.05 N, 108.15 W
Santee River, South Carolina	33.14 N, 79.28 W
Saskatchewan River, Saskatchewan	53.12 N, 99.16 W
Saskatchewan River delta, Manitoba	53.50 N, 101.15 W
Sault Sainte Marie, Michigan	46.30 N, 84.21 W
Sauvie Island, Oregon	45.41 N, 122.49 W
Savage Islands, N.W.T.	61.90 N, 66.00 W
Savonoski River, Alaska	58.50 N, 155.35 W
Schell-Osage Waterfowl Area, Missouri	38.00 N, 94.00 W
Scioto River, Ohio	38.44 N, 83.01 W
Scoresby Sound, Greenland	70.50 N, 23.00 W
Scottsboro Wildlife Management Area, Alabama	34.40 N, 86.02 W
Sea Island, British Columbia	49.12 N, 123.10 W
Seal River, Manitoba	59.04 N, 94.48 W
Sea of Okhotsk, U.S.S.R.	53.00 N, 150.00 E
Seattle, Washington	47.36 N, 122.20 W
Selawik, Alaska	66.37 N, 160.00 W
Selawik Marshes, Alaska	66.54 N, 159.00 W
Selawik River, Alaska	66.30 N, 160.20 W
Seney National Wildlife Refuge, Michigan	46.25 N, 86.00 W
Sesecapa Marshes, Mexico	14.65 N, 92.40 W
Seven Islands, Quebec	50.12 N, 66.23 W
Severn River, Ontario	56.02 N, 87.36 W
Seward Peninsula, Alaska	65.00 N, 164.00 W
Shagamu River, Ontario	55.65 N, 87.00 W
Shasta County, California	40.75 N, 121.80 W
Shellbrook River, Ontario	55.60 N, 87.39 W
Shemya Island, Alaska	52.43 N, 174.05 E
Shenandoah River valley, Virginia	39.19 N, 77.44 W
Sheppard Island, James Bay, Canada	51.72 N, 79.28 W
Sherman Basin, N.W.T.	67.50 N, 97.45 W
Sherman Inlet, N.W.T.	68.08 N, 98.50 W
Shetland Islands, Great Britain	60.30 N, 1.30 W
Shiawassee National Wildlife Refuge, Michigan	43.30 N, 84.10 W
Shismaref, Alaska	66.14 N, 166.09 W
Silver Lake, Minnesota	44.54 N, 94.12 W
Sinton, Texas	29.41 N, 95.58 W
Sioux City, Iowa	42.30 N, 96.23 W
Sitka, Alaska	57.03 N, 135.14 W
Six Mile Lake, Louisiana	29.75 N, 91.20 W
Skagit Bay and Flats, Washington	48.19 N, 122.24 W
Skykomish Pass, Washington	47.50 N, 122.03 W
Slave River, N.W.T.	61.18 N, 133.39 W
Slave River delta, N.W.T.	61.10 N, 133.40 W
Sleeper Islands, Hudson Bay, Canada	57.20 N, 78.25 W
Slidre Fiord, N.W.T.	80.00 N, 85.80 W
Slimbridge, England	51.60 N, 2.57 W
Snake River valley, Idaho	42.54 N, 114.00 W
Soap Lake, Washington	47.23 N, 119.29 W
Socorro, New Mexico	34.04 N, 106.54 W
Socorro County, New Mexico	34.00 N, 106.70 W
Soda Springs, Idaho	42.39 N, 111.36 W
Solano County, California	38.20 N, 121.70 W
Solomans Temple Island	52.89 N, 79.00 W
Solway Firth, Scotland	54.50 N, 3.35 W
Somerset Island, N.W.T.	73.00 N, 94.00 W
Sonora, Mexico	32.27 N, 115.10 W
Souris River, North Dakota	49.39 N, 99.34 W
Southampton Island, N.W.T.	64.20 N, 84.40 W
South Fiord, Axel Heiberg Island, N.W.T.	79.36 N, 94.20 W
South Platte River, Colorado	40.80 N, 103.00 W
South Saskatchewan River, Saskatchewan	53.15 N, 105.05 W
Spitsbergen Archipelago	78.00 N, 19.00 E
Spokane County, Washington	47.70 N, 117.50 W
Springview, Nebraska	42.49 N, 99.45 W
Spruce River, Ontario	51.55 N, 90.00 W
Squaw Creek National Wildlife Refuge, Missouri	40.09 N, 95.25 W
Squaw Lake, Minnesota	47.50 N, 93.30 W
Staked Plains, Texas	33.30 N, 102.40 W
Starkville, Mississippi	33.28 N, 88.48 W
Stevens County, Washington	48.50 N, 117.75 W
Stikine River, British Columbia	56.40 N, 132.30 W
Stikine River delta, British Columbia	56.70 N, 132.33 W
Stillwater National Wildlife Refuge, Nevada	39.52 N, 118.50 W
Stockton, California	37.57 N, 121.17 W
Strait of Georgia, British Columbia	49.20 N, 124.00 W
Strait of Juan de Fuca, British Columbia & Washington	48.18 N, 124.00 W
Stuart Island, Alaska	63.35 N, 162.30 W
Stutsman County, North Dakota	47.00 N, 99.00 W
Stuttgart, Arkansas	34.30 N, 91.33 W
Sudbury, Ontario	46.30 N, 81.00 W
Suisun marshes, California	38.15 N, 122.00 W
Sukkertoppen, Greenland	65.25 N, 52.53 W
Sullivan Lake, Alberta	52.00 N, 112.00 W
Summer Lake, Oregon	42.50 N, 120.45 W
Surprise Fiord, Axel Heiberg Island, N.W.T.	78.25 N, 90.30 W

Susitna River basin, Alaska	61.50 N, 150.03 W
Susitna River delta, Alaska	61.33 N, 150.50 W
Sutter County, California	39.08 N, 121.37 W
Swan Creek marsh, Michigan	42.32 N, 85.53 W
Swan Lake, Manitoba	52.30 N, 100.45 W
Swan Lake National Wildlife Refuge, Missouri	39.61 N, 93.19 W
Swift Current, Saskatchewan	50.17 N, 107.50 W

T

Tabasco, Mexico	18.25 N, 93.00 W
Tacoma, Washington	47.15 N, 122.27 W
Tallahassee, Florida	30.25 N, 84.16 W
Tamaulipas, Mexico	24.00 N, 98.50 W
Tamaulipas Lagoon, Mexico	24.00 N, 97.30 W
Tamiahua Lagoon, Veracruz, Mexico	21.35 N, 97.35 W
Tampa Bay, Florida	27.45 N, 82.35 W
Tampico and Tampico Lagoon, Mexico	22.13 N, 97.51 W
Tanacross, Alaska	63.23 N, 143.21 W
Tanana River valley, Alaska	65.09 N, 151.55 W
Tangipahoa Parish, Louisiana	30.20 N, 90.18 W
Taymyr Peninsula, U.S.S.R.	76.00 N, 104.00 E
Tehachapi Mountains, California	34.56 N, 118.40 W
Tehuantepec, Mexico	16.20 N, 94.50 W
Tempisque River basin, Costa Rica	10.12 N, 85.14 W
Tennessee National Wildlife Refuge, Tennessee	36.40 N, 88.20 W
Tennessee River valley, Tennessee	36.00 N, 88.00 W
Tepatitlán, Jalisco, Mexico	20.49 N, 102.44 W
Tetlin, Alaska	63.08 N, 142.31 W
Tha-Anne River, N.W.T.	60.31 N, 94.39 W
Thelon River, N.W.T.	64.16 N, 96.05 W
The Pas, Manitoba	53.50 N, 101.15 W
Three Forks, Montana	45.54 N, 111.33 W
Thule, Greenland	76.34 N, 68.47 W
Thule District, Greenland	76.30 N, 68.50 W
Tierra del Fuego, Argentina	54.30 S, 67.00 W
Tigara, Alaska	68.21 N, 166.50 W
Tillamook Bay, Oregon	45.30 N, 123.53 W
Tlaxcala, Mexico	19.25 N, 98.10 W
Toledo, Ohio	41.39 N, 83.32 W
Tomales Bay, California	38.18 N, 122.90 W
Topolobampo Bay, Mexico	25.50 N, 109.05 W
Toronto, Ontario	43.39 N, 79.23 W
Toronto Reservoir, Kansas	37.46 N, 95.57 W
Tracy Arm River, Alaska	57.90 N, 133.50 W
Traverse Bay, Michigan	44.46 N, 85.37 W
Trimble, Missouri	39.47 N, 94.57 W
Troy, Oregon	45.94 N, 117.36 W
Troy Meadows, New Jersey	40.50 N, 74.22 W
Tuktoyaktuk, N.W.T.	69.27 N, 133.02 W
Tulare County, California	36.20 N, 119.18 W
Tule Lake National Wildlife Refuge, California	41.50 N, 121.35 W
Tundovaya River valley, Wrangell Island, U.S.S.R.	71.30 N, 180.00
Tuolumne River, California	37.36 N, 121.10 W
Turbid Lake, Wyoming	44.55 N, 110.35 W
Turnbull National Wildlife Refuge, Washington	47.50 N, 117.60 W
Turtle Mountains, North Dakota and Manitoba	49.00 N, 100.25 W
Tuxpan, Veracruz, Mexico	21.00 N, 97.20 W
Tweedsmuir Provincial Park, British Columbia	52.55 N, 126.05 W
Twin Cities, Minnesota	44.58 N, 93.10 W
Twin Falls, Idaho	42.34 N, 114.28 W
Twin Islands, James Bay, Canada	53.27 N, 80.00 W
Two Buttes and Two Buttes Reservoir, Colorado	37.64 N, 102.50 W
Two Hills, Alberta	53.43 N, 111.45 W

U

Ugashik Lakes, Alaska	57.50 N, 156.90 W
Uinta Mountains, Utah	40.45 N, 110.05 W
Umiat, Alaska	69.22 N, 152.08 W
Unakwik Inlet, Alaska	56.10 N, 131.16 W
Unalaska Island, Alaska	53.45 N, 166.45 W
Ungava Bay, Quebec	59.30 N, 67.30 W
Ungava District, Quebec	60.00 N, 73.00 W
Ungava Peninsula, Quebec	60.00 N, 74.00 W
Unimak Island, Alaska	54.50 N, 164.00 W
Union, New Jersey	40.42 N, 74.16 W
Upernavik District, Greenland	72.47 N, 56.10 W
Upper Cummins Lakes, Saskatchewan	55.50 N, 108.83 W
Upper Darby, Pennsylvania	39.58 N, 75.16 W
Upper Klamath Basin, Oregon	42.50 N, 121.44 W
Upper Klamath Lake, Oregon	42.25 N, 122.00 W
Upper Kuskokwim Valley, Alaska	63.50 N, 153.00 W
Upper Mississippi Wildlife and Fish Refuge, Minnesota and Wisconsin	44.00 N, 91.50 W
Upper Souris National Wildlife Refuge, North Dakota	48.70 N, 100.80 W
Utah Lake, Utah	40.15 N, 111.75 W

V

Vaigach Island, U.S.S.R.	70.00 N, 60.00 E
Valentine, Nebraska	42.91 N, 100.33 W
Valentine National Wildlife Refuge, Nebraska	42.50 N, 100.35 W
Vancouver, British Columbia	49.16 N, 123.07 W
Vancouver Island, British Columbia	49.50 N, 126.00 W
Vanderhoof, British Columbia	54.01 N, 124.01 W
Veracruz, Mexico	19.11 N, 96.23 W
Vermilion Parish, Louisiana	29.90 N, 92.41 W
Vermilion River, Louisiana	29.91 N, 92.12 W
Vernon, Texas	34.09 N, 99.17 W
Victoria, Texas	28.80 N, 97.00 W
Victoria Island, N.W.T.	71.00 N, 110.00 W

W

Wabash River, Illinois and Indiana	37.46 N, 88.02 W
Wainwright, Alaska	70.38 N, 160.01 W
Wake County, North Carolina	35.80 N, 78.70 W
Wakuach Lake, Quebec	55.60 N, 67.80 W
Wales, Alaska	65.36 N, 168.05 W
Wallowa Mountains, Oregon	45.10 N, 117.30 W
Wapello, Iowa	41.11 N, 91.11 W
Washington, D.C.	38.54 N, 77.01 W
Washington Island, Wisconsin	45.23 N, 86.55 W

Washington Land, Greenland 82.00 N, 65.00 W
Washita National Wildlife Refuge, Oklahoma 35.64 N, 99.28 W
Waterhen Lake, Manitoba 52.15 N, 99.40 W
Watson Lake, British Columbia 60.07 N, 128.48 W
Waubay Hills, South Dakota 45.50 N, 97.35 W
Wax Lake, Louisiana 29.64 N, 91.42 W
Webster Reservoir, Kansas 39.45 N, 99.50 W
Welder Wildlife Foundation Refuge, Texas 28.13 N, 97.40 W
Wells River, Vermont 44.16 N, 72.11 W
Whale River, Quebec 58.00 N, 67.50 W
Wharton County, Texas 29.17 N, 96.13 W
Wheeler National Wildlife Refuge, Alabama 34.62 N, 86.80 W
Whitehorse, Yukon 60.43 N, 135.03 W
White Mountains, Arizona 33.45 N, 109.40 W
White Mountains, New Hampshire 44.10 N, 71.35 W
Whitewater Lake, Manitoba 49.26 N, 100.32 W
Wichita, Kansas 37.41 N, 97.20 W
Wichita Falls, Texas 33.54 N, 98.30 W
Willamette River, Oregon 45.00 N, 123.00 W
Willapa Bay, Washington 46.60 N, 124.00 W
Williams Lake, British Columbia 52.08 N, 122.09 W
Willows, California 39.31 N, 122.12 W
Wilson Reservoir, Kansas 38.57 N, 98.40 W
Wilson River, Oregon 45.28 N, 123.53 W
Winchester, New Hampshire 42.46 N, 72.23 W
Winchester Bay, Oregon 43.71 N, 124.02 W
Windy River, N.W.T. 60.23 N, 100.50 W
Winisk, Ontario 55.15 N, 85.12 W
Winisk River, Ontario 55.17 N, 85.05 W
Winnipeg, Manitoba 49.53 N, 97.09 W
Winous Point, Ohio 41.50 N, 82.96 W
Wolfe Island, Lake Ontario 44.12 N, 76.36 W
Wollaston Forland, Greenland 73.73 N, 20.00 W
Wood Buffalo Park, Alberta 58.50 N, 112.00 W
Wrangel Island, U.S.S.R. 71.00 N, 179.30 W
Wrangell, Alaska 56.55 N, 132.43 W
Wrangell Island, Alaska 56.15 N, 132.10 W
Wrangell Narrows, Alaska 56.45 N, 132.10 W

Y

Yakima, Washington 46.36 N, 120.31 W
Yakutat Bay, Alaska 59.45 N, 140.45 W
Yamhill County, Oregon 45.15 N, 123.20 W
Yampa River, Colorado 40.32 N, 108.59 W
Yaquina Bay, Oregon 44.63 N, 124.00 W
Yazoo National Wildlife Refuge, Mississippi 33.10 N, 91.00 W
Yellowknife, N.W.T. 62.27 N, 114.21 W
Yellowstone Lake, Wyoming 44.25 N, 110.22 W
Yellowstone National Park, Wyoming 44.30 N, 110.35 W
Yellowstone River, Montana 46.50 N, 105.50 W
Yellowtail Dam, Montana 45.12 N, 107.57 W
Yellowtail Wildlife Management Area, Wyoming 44.90 N, 108.25 W
Yenisei River, U.S.S.R. 71.50 N, 82.40 E
Yoder, Wyoming 40.56 N, 85.11 W
York County, Maine 43.50 N, 70.50 W
York Factory, Hudson Bay, Manitoba 57.00 N, 92.18 W
Yorkton, Saskatchewan 51.13 N, 102.28 W
Yosemite National Park, California 37.51 N, 119.33 W
Yuba County, California 39.16 N, 121.17 W
Yukon Delta, Alaska 61.00 N, 164.00 W
Yukon Flats, Alaska 66.50 N, 146.00 W
Yukon River, Alaska 62.33 N, 163.59 W

Z

Zacatecas, Mexico 22.47 N, 102.35 W

Appendix B — TABLES

Aquatic habitats of substantial benefits to waterfowl
(tables 1-8)

Table 1. National wildlife refuges in the United States of substantial benefits to waterfowl, June 30, 1974 (U.S. Fish and Wildlife Service 1974); not including Alaska (see Table 8).

State and Unit *a*	Total Acres
ATLANTIC FLYWAY	
CONNECTICUT	
Salt Meadow	177.5
DELAWARE	
Bombay Hook-2	15,110.8
Prime Hook-3	6,953.8
Total	22,064.6
FLORIDA	
Chassahowitzka-4	30,072.1
J. N. "Ding" Darling-5	4,787.7
Lake Woodruff-6	18,416.8
Loxahatchee-7	145,635.4
Merritt Island-8	140,393.0
Okefenokee-9	3,668.1
St. Johns-10	2,395.8
St. Marks-11	64,073.6
St. Vincent-12	12,489.9
Total	421,932.4
GEORGIA	
Blackbeard Island-13	5,617.6
Eufaula-14	3,231.0
Harris Neck-15	2,686.9
Okefenokee-9	373,860.0
Piedmont-16	34,678.5
Savannah-17	5,555.2
Wassaw-18	10,064.9
Wolf Island-19	5,125.8
Total	440,819.9
MAINE	
Franklin Island	11.9
Moosehorn-21	22,665.6
Pond Island	10.0
Rachel Carson-23	1,587.3
Seal Island	65.0
Total	24,339.8
MARYLAND	
Blackwater-25	11,627.2

State and Unit *a*	Total Acres
Chincoteague-26	417.8
Eastern Neck-27	2,286.4
Martin-28	4,423.4
Susquehanna	3.8
Total	18,758.6
MASSACHUSETTS	
Great Meadows-30	2,717.2
Monomoy-31	2,697.9
Nantucket	39.8
Oxbow	622.0
Parker River-34	4,649.9
Thacher Island	22.0
Total	10,748.8
NEW HAMPSHIRE	
Wapack	738.0
NEW JERSEY	
Barnegat-37	3,577.5
Brigantine-38	20,229.6
Great Swamp-39	5,886.1
Supawna Meadows	658.4
Total	30,351.6
NEW YORK	
Amagansett	35.8
Conscience Point	60.4
Elizabeth A. Morton	187.3
Iroquois-45	10,818.1
Montezuma-46	6,432.3
Oyster Bay-47	3,117.0
Target Rock	80.1
Wertheim	148.9
Total	20,879.9
NORTH CAROLINA	
Cedar Island-50	12,526.0
Mackay Island-51	6,181.7
Mattamuskeet-52	50,179.8
Pea Island-53	5,915.0
Pee Dee-54	7,439.0
Pungo-55	12,350.4
Swanquarter-56	15,500.8
Total	110,092.7
PENNSYLVANIA	
Erie-57	7,993.8
RHODE ISLAND	
Block Island	28.7
Ninigret	27.5
Sachuest	71.0
Total	127.2

State and Unit *a*	Total Acres
SOUTH CAROLINA	
Cape Romain-61	34,218.3
Carolina Sandhills-62	45,591.4
Santee-63	74,353.1
Savannah-17	7,617.8
Total	161,780.6
VERMONT	
Missisquoi-64	4,794.0
VIRGINIA	
Back Bay-65	4,588.8
Chincoteague-26	9,021.0
Mackay Island	842.3
Plum Tree Island-66	3,275.6
Presquile-67	1,328.9
Total	19,056.6
WEST VIRGINIA	0.0
Subtotal - ATLANTIC FLYWAY	1,294,656.0
MISSISSIPPI FLYWAY	
ALABAMA	
Choctaw-68	4,218.0
Eufaula-14	7,929.0
Wheeler-69	34,184.7
Total	46,331.7
ARKANSAS	
Big Lake-70	11,022.9 *b*
Holla Bend-71	4,082.7
Wapanocca-72	5,484.2
White River-73	112,399.0 *b*
Total	132,988.8
ILLINOIS	
Chautauqua-74	5,124.9
Crab Orchard-75	43,017.4
Mark Twain-76	14,680.5
Meredosia-77	1,849.8
Upper Mississippi River Wildlife and Fish Refuge-78	23,260.9
Total	87,933.5
INDIANA	
Muscatatuck-79	7,724.0
IOWA	
De Soto-80	3,496.2
Mark Twain-76	10,375.5
Upper Mississippi River Wildlife and Fish Refuge-78	50,639.2

State and Unit *a*	Total Acres
Union Slough-81	2,155.6
Total	66,666.5
KENTUCKY	
Reelfoot-82	2,039.6
LOUISIANA	
Breton-83	9,047.0
Catahoula-84	5,308.5
Delta-85	48,799.1
Lacassine-86	31,776.3
Sabine-87	142,845.6
Total	237,776.5
MICHIGAN	
Seney-88	95,455.2
Shiawassee-89	8,857.2
Wyandotte	304.5 *b*
Total	104,616.9
MINNESOTA	
Agassiz-91	61,487.1 *b*
Minnesota Valley	123.0
Rice Lake-93	16,515.5
Sherburne-94	28,858.1
Tamarac-95	42,484.7 *b*
Upper Mississippi River Wildlife and Fish Refuge-78	33,004.5
Total	182,472.9
MISSISSIPPI	
Noxubee-96	45,845.2
Yazoo-97	12,470.9
Total	58,316.1
MISSOURI	
Clarence Cannon-98	3,735.5
Mingo-99	21,672.5
Squaw Creek-100	6,886.6
Swan Lake-101	10,669.5
Total	42,964.1
OHIO	
Cedar Point-102	2,245.4
Ottawa-103	5,627.9
Total	7,873.3
TENNESSEE	
Cross Creeks-104	8,861.5
Hatchie-105	11,220.3
Lake Isom-106	1,845.9
Reelfoot-82	8,101.6
Tennessee-107	51,346.7
Total	81,376.0

State and Unit *a*	Total Acres
WISCONSIN	
Horicon-108	20,976.4
Necedah-109	39,549.0
Trempealeau	706.9
Upper Mississippi Wildlife and Fish Refuge-78	88,044.2
Total	149,276.5
Subtotal - MISSISSIPPI FLYWAY	1,208,356.4
CENTRAL FLYWAY	
COLORADO	
Alamosa-111	10,353.5
Arapahoe-112	11,330.9
Browns Park-113	13,690.8
Monte Vista-114	13,547.7
Total	48,922.9
KANSAS	
Flint Hills-115	18,463.2
Kirwin-116	10,777.8
Quivira-117	21,820.1
Total	51,061.1
MONTANA	
Benton Lake-118	12,382.5
Black Coulee-119	1,480.0
Bowdoin-120	15,436.7 *b*
Creedman Coulee-121	2,728.0
Hailstone-122	2,240.0
Halfbreed Lake-123	3,096.8
Hewitt Lake-124	1,680.9
Lake Mason-125	18,692.3
Lake Thibadeau-126	3,868.5
Lamesteer	800.0
Medicine Lake-128	31,457.4 *b*
Ninepipe-129	2,022.0
Pablo-130	2,542.0
Ravalli-131	2,628.1
Red Rock Lakes-132	40,223.5 *b*
Swan River	399.2
UL Bend-134	46,303.9
War Horse-135	3,192.2
Total	191,174.0
NEBRASKA	
Crescent Lake-136	45,818.0
De Soto-80	4,324.2
North Platte-137	5,047.0
Valentine-138	71,515.6 *b*
Total	126,704.8
NEW MEXICO	
Bitter Lake-139	23,269.4
Bosque del Apache-140	57,191.1

State and Unit *a*	Total Acres
Grulla-141	3,230.6
Las Vegas-142	8,238.7
Maxwell-143	3,454.1
Total	95,383.9
NORTH DAKOTA	
Appert Lake *c*	1,160.7
Ardoch-144	2,690.9
Arrowwood-145	15,934.4 *b*
Audubon-146	14,775.6
Bone Hill	640.0
Brumba	1,977.5
Buffalo Lake-147	2,096.3
Camp Lake	584.7
Canfield Lake	313.2
Chase Lake-149	4,384.6 *b*
Cottonwood	1,013.5
Dakota Lake	2,756.0
Des Lacs-150	18,881.0 *b*
Flickertail	640.0
Florence Lake-151	1,888.2 *b*
Half-way Lake	160.0
Hiddenwood	568.4
Hobart Lake-152	2,077.2
Hutchinson Lake	478.9
J. Clark Salyer-153	58,693.5
Johnson Lake-154	2,007.9
Kellys Slough-155	1,620.0
Lake Alice-156	9,571.8
Lake Elsie	634.7
Lake George-157	3,118.8
Lake Ilo-158	4,031.1
Lake Nettie-159	2,894.9
Lake Otis	640.0
Lake Zahl-161	3,823.2 *b*
Lambs Lake	1,206.7
Little Goose	359.0
Long Lake-162	22,310.1
Lords Lake-163	1,915.3
Lost Lake	960.2
Lostwood-164	26,747.5 *b*
Maple River	712.0
McLean	760.0
Pleasant Lake	897.8
Pretty Rock	800.0
Rabb Lake	260.8
Rock Lake	5,506.6
Rose Lake	836.3
School Section Lake	680.0
Shell Lake-167	1,835.1
Sheyenne Lake	797.3
Sibley Lake	1,077.4
Silver Lake	3,347.6
Slade-168	3,000.2
Snyder Lake	1,550.2
Springwater	640.0
Stewart Lake-169	2,230.4
Stoney Slough	1,100.0
Storm Lake	685.9
Sunburst Lake	327.5
Tewaukon-171	8,156.5
Tomahawk	440.0
Upper Souris-172	32,092.5
White Lake-173	1,040.0
Wild Rice Lake	778.8
Willow Lake-174	2,620.4
Wintering River	239.3
Wood Lake	280.0
Total	286,248.4
OKLAHOMA	
Salt Plains-175	32,008.9
Sequoyah-176	20,800.0
Tishomingo-177	16,464.2
Washita-178	8,083.9
Total	77,357.0
SOUTH DAKOTA	
Bear Butte	374.2
Lacreek-180	16,147.2
Lake Andes	939.4
Pocassee-182	2,540.0
Sand Lake-183	21,451.6 *b*
Waubay-184	4,649.7 *b*
Total	46,102.1
TEXAS	
Anahuac-185	9,836.6
Aransas-186	90,069.1
Brazoria-187	9,625.4
Buffalo Lake-188	7,663.9
Hagerman-189	11,319.8
Laguna Atascosa-190	45,204.4
Muleshoe-191	5,809.1
San Bernard-192	15,413.8
Santa Ana-193	1,980.5
Total	196,922.6
WYOMING	
Bamforth-194	1,166.0
Hutton Lake-195	1,968.3 *b*
National Elk Refuge *d*	300.0
Pathfinder-197	16,806.9
Seedskadee-198	13,403.4
Total	33,644.6
Subtotal - CENTRAL FLYWAY	1,153,521.4
PACIFIC FLYWAY	
ARIZONA	
Cibola-199	8,208.0
Havasu Lake-200	33,747.5
Imperial-201	17,806.2
Total	59,761.7
CALIFORNIA	
Cibola-199	1,255.0

State and Unit *a*	Total Acres
Clear Lake-202	33,439.6 *b*
Colusa-203	4,039.7
Delevan-204	5,633.5
Havasu Lake-200	7,747.3 *b*
Humboldt Bay	76.3
Imperial-201	7,958.2
Kern-206	10,618.2
Kesterson-207	5,900.0
Lower Klamath-208	20,122.1
Merced-209	2,561.5
Modoc-210	6,355.1
Pixley-211	4,131.0
Sacramento-212	10,783.3
Salton Sea-213	35,483.3
San Luis-214	7,430.4
San Pablo Bay	185.0
Sutter-216	2,590.9
Tule Lake-217	37,616.7
Total	203,927.1
IDAHO	
Bear Lake-218	16,977.6 *b*
Camas-219	10,656.3
Deer Flat-220	11,423.5
Grays Lake-221	13,735.1
Kootenai-222	2,762.0
Minidoka-223	25,629.8
Total	81,184.3
NEVADA	
Fallon-224	17,901.9
Pahranagat-225	5,381.6 *b*
Ruby Lake-226	37,631.3
Stillwater-227	24,203.4
Total	85,118.2
OREGON	
Ankeny-228	2,796.3
Baskett Slough-229	2,492.3
Cold Springs-230	3,116.9
Deer Flat-220	162.4
Hart Mountain National Antelope Refuge	731.1
Klamath Forest-232	15,426.8
Lewis and Clark-233	5,403.4
Lower Klamath-208	1,336.6
Malheur-234	181,967.1
McKay Creek-235	1,836.5
Umatilla-236	8,879.8
Upper Klamath-237	12,456.9
William L. Finley-238	5,325.0
Total	241,931.1
UTAH	
Bear River-239	64,895.0
Fish Springs-240	17,992.2
Ouray-241	11,362.8
Total	94,250.0
WASHINGTON	
Columbia-242	28,951.6
Conboy Lake-243	6,725.8
Dungeness	756.1
Little Pend Oreille-245	2,251.3
McNary-246	3,630.7
Nisqually-247	1,295.0
Ridgefield-248	3,016.7
Smith Island	65.0
Toppenish-250	1,762.8
Turnbull-251	15,564.8
Umatilla-236	13,335.8
Willapa-252	9,608.2 *b*
Total	86,963.8
Subtotal - PACIFIC FLYWAY	853,136.3
GRAND TOTAL	4,509,670.0

a Unless otherwise designated, add "National Wildlife Refuge" to the name of each area. Numbers after names refer to locations of areas of 1,000 acres or more shown in Figure 5-1.

b Including "meandered area" that was not included in the listings in 1974. The Fish and Wildlife Service reports that the former meandered acreages will probably be reflected in the 1975 report but under a different category.

c Areas in North Dakota of 1,000 acres or more and not followed by numbers are under lease or easement only and are not shown in Figure 5-1.

d Only about 300 acres of this refuge have substantial values for waterfowl.

Table 2. Waterfowl production areas, U.S. Fish and Wildlife Service, June 30, 1974 (U.S. Fish and Wildlife Service 1974).

State and Unit	Acres Acquired by the U.S. Government *a*	Total Acres
ATLANTIC FLYWAY		
MAINE		
Carlton Pond	1,068.2	1,068.2
Subtotal - ATLANTIC FLYWAY	1,068.2	1,068.2
MISSISSIPPI FLYWAY		
MINNESOTA		
Becker	7,089.7	7,512.7
Big Stone	8,130.3	12,553.3
Clay	5,801.5	7,098.1
Cottonwood	930.5	930.5
Douglas	6,734.4	10,091.4
Grant	6,583.9	7,917.9
Jackson	1,877.8	1,877.8
Kandiyohi	8,147.9	11,134.9
Lac qui Parle	2,297.7	2,438.7
Mahnomen	3,800.3	8,062.3
Otter Tail	11,084.5	16,018.0
Polk	6,698.3	7,370.3
Pope	8,784.4	14,162.9
Ramsey	152.0	159.4
Stearns	6,111.7	6,601.7
Stevens	6,023.1	6,618.1
Swift	5,418.9	5,817.9
Traverse	2,034.5	2,937.5
Wilkin	1,072.9	1,239.9
Yellow Medicine	70.0	87.0
Subtotal - MISSISSIPPI FLYWAY	98,844.3	130,630.3
CENTRAL FLYWAY		
MONTANA		
Blaine	2,250.5	2,250.5
Daniels	646.4	646.4
Flathead	3,241.5	3,241.5
Roosevelt	179.2	179.2
Sheridan	5,871.6	10,406.4
Total	12,189.2	16,724.0
NEBRASKA		
Clay	4,437.8	4,437.8
Fillmore	2,365.7	2,365.7
Franklin	1,542.1	1,542.1
Gosper	1,451.5	1,451.5
Kearney	2,714.4	2,714.4
Phelps	1,526.0	1,526.0
York	559.2	559.2
Total	14,596.7	14,596.7
NORTH DAKOTA		
Barnes	4,552.8	18,506.1
Benson	6,402.2	37,719.1
Bottineau	1,841.7	24,616.1
Burke	3,158.1	25,993.1
Burleigh	1,621.9	23,507.4
Cass	2,848.7	4,237.7
Cavalier	9,460.8	23,611.8
Dickey	5,365.8	28,348.4
Divide	8,861.3	41,035.4
Eddy	3,345.5	14,334.9
Emmons	2,892.1	13,646.1
Foster	1,326.1	7,770.1
Grand Forks	3,297.6	4,182.9
Griggs	1,871.4	15,869.5
Kidder	3,789.2	59,893.0
LaMoure	3,669.1	16,199.7
Logan	6,861.0	39,658.1
McHenry	3,456.3	25,487.2
McIntosh	14,446.4	40,648.2
McLean	2,655.9	16,361.9
Mountrail	6,049.6	31,141.5
Nelson	3,053.2	37,625.4
Pembina	2,141.6	2,280.6
Pierce	4,410.7	38,596.7
Ramsey	7,500.0	35,343.1
Ransom	2,643.5	18,176.5
Renville	203.9	11,455.9
Richland	4,162.9	4,578.9
Rolette	3,697.6	22,953.6
Sargent	3,531.4	14,456.4
Sheridan	6,438.3	27,876.5
Steele	2,060.6	5,331.6
Stutsman	20,719.4	60,014.1
Towner	1,654.2	25,766.2
Traill	703.1	942.1
Walsh	1,322.9	10,151.8
Ward	4,751.7	35,671.5
Wells	5,068.3	15,031.3
Williams	3,755.5	10,457.5
Total	175,592.3	889,477.9
SOUTH DAKOTA		
Aurora	1,952.2	8,875.2
Beadle	2,875.0	14,081.0
Bon Homme	641.7	846.7
Brookings	3,190.7	4,767.7
Brown	2,133.5	6,967.2
Brule	1,073.6	9,525.6
Buffalo	0.0	837.0
Campbell	1,073.1	2,822.1
Charles Mix	576.9	4,625.9
Clark	2,454.1	21,820.8
Clay	40.0	47.0
Codington	1,843.6	5,133.8
Davison	224.5	342.5
Day	5,370.7	22,197.5

State and Unit	Acres Acquired by the U.S. Government *a*	Total Acres
Deuel	2,298.6	3,967.6
Douglas	1,352.8	3,688.8
Edmunds	1,853.4	28,575.4
Faulk	678.8	27,722.8
Grant	2,198.7	5,275.7
Hamlin	518.4	1,571.4
Hand	1,078.3	15,013.3
Hanson	708.6	2,915.6
Hughes	0.0	257.0
Hutchinson	246.2	865.2
Hyde	0.0	7,302.0
Jerauld	630.4	3,976.4
Kingsbury	2,158.0	11,914.0
Lake	3,626.6	5,536.6
Lincoln	177.2	177.2
Marshall	2,734.1	11,699.3
McCook	2,465.8	5,416.8
McPherson	5,036.0	30,895.0
Miner	1,301.7	6,895.7
Minnehaha	3,162.4	3,327.4
Moody	1,286.3	1,401.7
Potter	409.3	4,288.3
Roberts	3,955.8	14,244.8
Sanborn	93.0	8,597.0
Spink	1,003.2	5,616.2
Sully	266.5	478.5
Turner	218.3	311.3
Union	96.0	96.0
Walworth	229.0	3,207.5
Yankton	21.6	144.6
Total	63,254.6	318,269.1
Subtotal - CENTRAL FLYWAY	265,632.8	1,239,067.7
GRAND TOTAL	365,545.3	1,370,766.2

a Open to hunting unless designated closed. On lands controlled under agreement, easement, or lease, hunting is controlled by the individual landowners.

Table 3. Waterfowl habitat under state control in each flyway, as of January 1, 1975. Areas are state owned unless indicated otherwise, and the numbers after the names indicate the locations of areas of 1,000 acres or more as shown in figure 5-2.

State and Unit	Acres Open to Hunting	Total Acres
ATLANTIC FLYWAY		
CONNECTICUT		
Assekonk Swamp	300	300
Barn Island	500	500
Bride Lake Sanctuary	0	2
Chas. E. Wheeler, Milford, Stratford	812	812
Charter Marsh	0	240
Cromwell Meadows	486	486
Durham Meadows	571	571
East Haven River Marsh	33	33
East Swamp, Bethel	82	82
Farmington Shade Swamp	0	560
Guilford-Madison East River	142	142
Guilford Great Harbor	270	270
Haddam Meadows	0	175
Haddam Neck, Haddam, East Haddam	94	94
Higganum Meadows	56	56
Lords Cover, Lyme, Old Lyme	340	340
Milford Refuge	0	290
Milford Sanctuary	0	15
Mystic River Sanctuary	0	190
Niantic River Sanctuary	0	162
Old Lyme Great Island	504	504
Old Saybrook Ferry Point Marsh	24	24
Plum Bank, Old Saybrook	217	217
Poquetonuck Cove	0	187
Ragged Rock, Old Saybrook	202	202
Roy Swamp	40	40
Salmon R. Cove	94	94
Shade Swamp Sanctuary	0	560
Smith Cove	0	40
Tolland Charter Marsh	0	240
Wangunk Meadows	100	100
Total	4,867	7,528
DELAWARE		
Appoquinimink	40	40
Assawoman	500	800
Augustine-1	1,000	1,000
Blackiston	30	30
Canal-2	1,000	1,000
Delaware Seashore State Park	800	800
Gordons Pond	500	800
Little Creek-3	2,500	2,800
Milford Neck	540	540
Nanticoke	100	100

State and Unit	Acres Open to Hunting	Total Acres
Petersburg	50	50
Prime Hook	525	525
Woodland Beach-4	2,500	3,000
Total	10,085	11,485
FLORIDA		
Arbuckle-5	0	3,200 *a*
Paynes Prairie-6	0	13,000
Apalachee-7	6,000	6,000 *a*
Charlotte Harbor-8	103,300	103,300 *b*
Everglades Management Area-9	725,000	725,000 *b*
Lake Iamonia-10	5,300	5,300 *b*
Lake Istopoga-11	28,100	28,100 *b*
Lake Jackson-12	3,520	3,520 *b*
Lake Kissimmee-13	41,400	41,400 *b*
Lake Miccosukee-14	7,000	7,000 *b*
Lake Okeechobee-15	467,000	467,000 *b*
Lake Talguin-16	6,700	6,700 *b*
Tampa Bay-17	185,200	185,200 *b*
Total	1,578,520	1,594,720
GEORGIA		
Altamaha River Waterfowl Area-18	30,000	35,000
Bainbridge-Lake Seminole-19	6,000	6,000
Total	36,000	41,000
MAINE		
Brownfield-20	2,739	2,739
Chesterville	466	466
Fahi Pond	297	297
Great Works	640	640
Hodgdon-21	1,049	1,049
Howard L. Mendell	242	242
Jonesborough	716	716
Lt. Gordon Manuel	472	472
Madasaska	295	295
Mercer Bog	95	95
Merrymeeting Bay WMA *c*	50	50 *d*
Muddy River	160	160
N.W. River	47	47
Oakes Lot	433	433
Old Farm Pond	600	600
Orange River	588	588
Pennamaquan	293	293
Pleasant River Salt Marsh	24	24
Pond Farm-22	1,232	1,232
Powell Lot	200	200
R. Lyle Frost-23	1,818	1,818
Ruffingham	610	610
Sandy Point	540	540
Scarboro-24	2,866	2,866
St. Albans	542	542
Steve Powell-25	515	1,753
Weskeag	533	533
Total	18,062	19,300

State and Unit	Acres Open to Hunting	Total Acres
MARYLAND		
C & D Canal Lands-26	2,400	2,400
Cedar Island-27	2,880	2,880
Deal Island-28	8,787	10,287
Diersson	0	40
E. A. Vaughn-29	1,326	1,326
Earlville	190	190
Ellis Bay-30	1,924	1,924
Fairmount-31	2,346	2,446
Fishing Bay-32	12,749	12,749
Le Compte	0	458
McKee-Beshers-33	1,275	1,475
Merkle-34	110	1,223
Myrtle Grove	300	754
Pocomoke River	505	505
Pocomoke Sound	922	922
Sinepuxent Bay	25	25
St. Clements Island	0	61
Taylor's Island	973	973
Total	36,712	40,638
MASSACHUSETTS		
Barnstable-35	2,800	2,800 *e*
Becket WMA	50	50 *f*
Delaney WMA	110	190 *f*
Fairhaven Marshes	23	23
Hockomock Swamp-36	2,500	2,500 *g*
Hodges Village	873	873 *a*
Marquand Estate, Parker River	467	467
Mill Creek Marshes	700	700
North Shore Marshes	146	146
Pantry Brook WMA	393	393
Parker River	704	704
Quaboag WMA	100	100 *f*
Stafford Hill WMA	100	100
West Hill Dam	757	757 *h*
West Meadows WMA	221	221
Total	9,944	10,024
NEW HAMPSHIRE		
Airport Marsh	25	25 *e*
Ballard Marsh	77	77 *i*
Bellamy River Access	17	17
Burnham's Marsh	25	25
Carpenter's Marsh	256	256
Casalis Marsh	10	10
Cascade Marsh	250	250 *i*
Dole's Marsh	30	30
Elm Brook Marsh	150	150 *a*
Eva's Marsh	77	77
Great Bay Access	39	39
Hall Mountain Marsh	21	21
Hampton Salt Marshes	225	225
Hayes Marsh	60	60
Hoit Road Marsh	191	191
Knights Meadow Marsh	100	100
McDaniels Marsh	300	300 *i*

State and Unit	Acres Open to Hunting	Total Acres
Merrymeeting Marsh	722	722
Perkins Pond	307	307
Reed's Marsh	64	64
Sand Brook Marsh	188	188
Stark Pond	60	60 *j*
Stumpfield Marsh	95	95 *a*
West Peterboro Marsh-37	1,271	1,271 *a*
Wilder Management Area	40	40
Woodman Marsh	20	20
Total	4,620	4,620
NEW JERSEY		
Absecon	639	639
Cape May Wetlands-38	4,180	4,180
Corson-39	1,032	1,032
Dennis Creek-40	5,110	5,110
Dix-41	1,760	1,760
Egg Island-Berrytown-42	6,892	6,892
Fortescue	894	894
Great Bay-43	4,450	4,450
Heislerville-44	2,813	2,813
Mad Horse Creek-45	5,555	5,555
Manahawkin	965	965
Marmora-46	4,100	4,100
Nantuxent	916	916
Osborne	183	183
Port Republic	755	755
Swan Bay	818	818
Tuckahoe-Corbin City-47	12,438	12,438
Total	53,500	53,500
NEW YORK		
Ausable	640	640
Connetquot River	286	286
Fish Creek-48	2,545	2,545
French Creek-49	1,160	1,160
High Tor-50	1,000	1,000 *f*
Howland Island-51	800	3,200
Indian River-52	1,160	1,160
Lake Shore Marshes-53	2,640	2,640
Lake View Marshes-54	3,340	3,340
Oak Orchard-55	2,260	2,560
Perch River-56	3,650	7,150
Rogers Island	270	270
Three Mile Bay-57	1,640	1,640
Three Rivers	0	800 *f*
Tonawanda-58	3,500	5,500
Upper Lower Lakes-59	7,620	7,620
Vischers Ferry	810	810
Wickam Marsh	270	270
Wilson Hill-60	1,210	3,410
Total	34,801	46,001
NORTH CAROLINA		
Cowan's Ford Waterfowl Refuge	0	150 *i*
Goose Creek Game Lands-61	2,200	2,200
Gull Rock Game Lands-62	3,850	3,850
Jarrett Bay Game Land	300	300 *i*
Northwest River Marsh	500	500
Orton Waterfowl Refuge-63	0	1,500 *i*
Pamlico Point Waterfowl Area-64	1,200	1,200
Sutton Game Lands	1,300	1,300 *i*
White Oak Game Lands	100	100 *i*
Total	9,450	11,100
PENNSYLVANIA		
Akley Swamp	350	350
Alder Marsh	600	600
Allegheny National Forest Ponds	400	580 *a*
Blue Marsh-66	2,510	2,630
Bradford County (N-3)	430	430
Buzzard Swamp	400	400 *a*
Clemson Island	216	364
Conneaut Marsh-67	3,630	4,180
Crawford County (C-3)-68	4,269	4,369
Crawford County (B-2)	585	585
Crawford County (C-2)	805	895
Erie County (C-2)-69	1,032	1,072
Erie County	1,638	1,638
Hoovers Island	106	381
Middlecreek-71	3,000	3,325
Moraine State Park-72	1,000	1,450 *d*
Pymatuning-73	6,100	9,600
Sandy Creek-74	1,300	1,300
Shenango Reservoir-75	1,750	2,000 *a*
Shohola-76	2,000	2,480
Sweigerts Island	171	330
The Glades-77	1,328	1,328
Total	33,620	40,287
RHODE ISLAND		
Belding Marsh	34	34
Charlestown Breachway	49	49
Dutch Island	80	80
Galilie Bird Sanctuary	0	128
Great Swamp Management Area	180	180
Haffenreffer Marsh	0	19
Hundred Acre Cove Management Area	21	21
Jerusalem Marsh	100	100
Kerney Land	0	5
May C. Donovan Marsh	17	17
Newton Marsh	111	111
Ninigret Salt Marsh	302	302
Rock Island	12	12
Rumstick Point	35*k*	35
Sapowet Marsh	180	180
Total	1,121	1,273
SOUTH CAROLINA		
Bear Island-78	2,000	7,500

State and Unit	Acres Open to Hunting	Total Acres	
Hatchery Pool-79	2,454	2,454	
Pee Dee-80	900	1,275	
Santee Coastal Reserve-81	0	24,000	
Santee Cooper-82	200	1,275	
Santee Delta-83	1,500	1,500	
Turkey Creek-84	0	2,000	
Total	7,054	40,004	
VERMONT			
Black Creek	158	158	
Buezek Marsh	96	96	
Cornwall Swamp	150	150	
Dead Creek-85	2,245	2,445	
East Creek	378	398	
Little Otter Creek-86	1,083	1,183	
Love's Marsh	100	100	
Lower Otter Creek	298	298	
Marsh Pond	90	90	
McCuen Sland	53	53	
McQuam Bay	409	409	
Mud Creek-87	1,050	1,050	
Sandbar-88	800	1,650	
South Bay	646	646	
South Hero	19	19	
South Stream	130	130	
Fairfield Swamp-89	1,196	1,196	
Richville Dam	154	154	
Total	9,055	10,225	
VIRGINIA			
Barbours Hill-90	1,600	1,800	
Chickahominy	500	500	*f*
Elm Hill	0	1,000	
Game Farm Marsh	429	429	
Hog Island-91	3,163	3,163	
Kittewan Waterfowl Refuge	0	250	
Lands End	0	430	
Mockhorn Island-92	6,110	9,110	
Pocahontas Trojan-93	1,142	1,142	
Saxis Island-94	2,636	5,158	*f*
Total	15,580	22,982	
WEST VIRGINIA			
McClintic Wildlife Station-95	1,776	2,451	*m*
Subtotal-ATLANTIC FLYWAY	1,864,767	1,957,138	

MISSISSIPPI FLYWAY

State and Unit	Acres Open to Hunting	Total Acres	
ALABAMA			
Crow Creek-96	2,161	2,161	*a*
Crow Creek-96	0	2,395	*a*
Mallard-Fox Creeks-98	2,560	2,560	*a*
Mobile Delta-99	30,000	30,000	
Mud Creek-100	8,193	8,193	*a*
North Sauty Creek-101	0	5,400	*a*
Raccoon Creek-102	7,080	7,080	*a*
Seven Mile Island-103	4,701	4,701	*a*
Swan Creek-104	6,242	6,242	*a*
Total	60,937	68,732	
ARKANSAS			
Bayou DeView-105	4,254	4,254	
Bayou Meto-106	33,701	33,701	
Big Lake-107	12,161	12,161	
Black River-108	20,805	20,805	
Black Swamp-109	3,888	3,888	
Bois D'Arc-110	5,523	5,523	
Cut-off Creek-111	8,612	8,612	
Dagmar-112	7,959	7,959	
Galla Creek-113	2,204	2,204	
Harris Brake-114	2,844	2,844	
Hurricane Lake-115	16,191	16,191	
Nimrod-116	3,364	3,634	
Petit Jean-117	14,534	14,534	
Shirley Bay-Rainey Brake-118	10,528	10,528	
St. Francis Sunken Lands-119	16,791	16,791	
Sulphur River-120	15,955	15,955	
Trusten Holder-121	4,321	4,321	*h*
Total	183,905	183,905	
ILLINOIS			
Anderson Lake-122	1,364	1,364	
Banner Strip Mine	0	228	
Barkhausen-123	0	1,163	
Burnham Island	0	779	
Carlyle Reservoir-124	18,000	19,252	*a*
Calhoun County-125	1,232	1,232	
Chain O' Lakes-126	55	2,655	
Diamond Access Area	65	65	
Eckert Woods-127	1,185	1,185	
Horseshoe Lake-128	1,946	7,901	
Lake DePue	0	524	
Marshall Co. Management Area-129	2,557	2,557	
Mermet Lake Wildlife Area-130	800	2,577	
Mississippi River Management Areas-131	10,599	10,599	*a*
Nauvoo Flat Wildlife Sanctuary	0	700	
Pekin Lake	0	548	
Pike Station Access Area	0	263	
Quincy Bay Access Area	542	542	
Rend Lake-132	5,000	20,198	*a*
Rice Lake-133	1,383	2,618	
Sanganois-134	1,550	7,450	
Shelbyville Lake-135	7,000	11,505	*a*
Sparland Management Area-136	1,281	1,281	
Spring Branch-137	0	1,100	
Spring Lake-138	885	1,285	
Titus Hollow Access Area	51	51	

State and Unit	Acres Open to Hunting	Total Acres
Union Co. Wildlife Area-139	850	6,202
Woodford Co. Management Area	2,700	3,000
Total	59,045	108,824
INDIANA		
Glendale-140	700	7,000
Hovey Lake-141	300	4,200
Jasper-Pulaski-142	0	7,785
Kankakee-143	1,400	2,300
LaSalle-144	600	3,100
Mallard Roost-145	1,200	1,200
Pigeon River-146	800	10,605
Willow Slough-147	2,400	9,200
Total	7,400	45,390
IOWA		
Allen Green Refuge	0	152
Badger Lake	444	444
Barringer Slough-148	1,071	1,071
Bays Branch	592	797
Big Creek-149	850	2,010 *a*
Big Marsh-150	2,263	2,813
Big Wall Lake	978	978
Blackbird Bend	625	625
Black Hawk Lake	114	957
Black Hawk Marsh	206	206
Blue Lake	987	987
Blue Wing Marsh	160	160
Browns Lake	784	784
Buffalo Creek	380	380
Burt Lake	40	40
Cardinal Marsh	862	862
Center Lake	329	329
Cheever Lake	359	359
Christopherson Slough	535	535
Clear Lake-151	247	3,643
Clear Lake Pond	42	42
Colfax Area	350	350
Colyn Area	600	770
Cone Marsh	701	701
Cory Marsh	38	38
Crystal Lake	283	283
Cunningham Slough	362	362
Dan Green Slough	311	311
Deweys Pasture	401	401
Diamond Lake	563	563
Dudgeon Lake-152	1,257	1,257
Dunbar Slough	307	507
Eagle Lake	919	919
Eagle Lake	277	277
East Okoboji-153	304	1,873
East Twin Lake	493	493
Elk Creek Marsh-154	1,623	1,623
Elk Lake	261	261
Elm Lake	466	466
Fallow Marsh	105	105
Finn Pond	60	60
Five Island Lake-155	710	1,110
Forney Lake-156	1,071	1,071
Four Mile Lake	0	243
Garlock Slough	222	222
Goose Lake	224	224
Goose Lake	456	456
Goose Lake	887	887
Green Bay	228	228
Green Island-157	2,722	2,722 *a*
Hale's Slough	85	85
Harmon Lake	483	483
Hawkeye Wildlife Area-158	11,078	13,078 *a*
Hendrickson Marsh	601	601
High Lake	82	683
Hottes Lake	378	378
Ingham Lake-159	120	1,002
Iowa Lake	116	116
Iowa Lake	526	526
Iowa Lake Marsh	126	126
Jemmerson Slough	343	343
Kettleson Hogsback	262	262
Klum Lake	650	650
Lake Manawa	110	919
Lake Odessa-160	3,800	3,800 *a*
Lakin Slough	300	300
Lekwa Marsh	36	36
Little Clear Lake	187	187
Little Spirit	214	214
Little Wall Lake	273	273
Lizard Lake	348	348
Lost Island-161	151	1,260
Lower Gar Lake	33	273
Marble Lake	183	183
McCord Pond	0	112
Meadow Lake	320	320
Minnewashta Lake	13	126
Miami Lake	601	601
Morse Lake	172	172
Mt. Ayr Game Area	65	65
Muskrat Slough	366	366
Myre Slough	430	430
Louisville Bend	50	900
Nobles Lake	289	289
North Twin Lake	118	569
Opedahl Area	184	184
Otter Creek Marsh-162	2,810	3,360
Otteson Potholes	106	106
Perkins Marsh	25	25
Peterson Pothole Area	45	45
Pleasant Lake	84	84
Prairie Lake	109	109
Princeton Area-163	1,178	1,178 *a*
Rathbun Wildlife Area-164	12,529	13,729 *a*
Red Rock Area-165	8,188	16,235 *a*
Rice Lake-166	1,600	1,831
Riverton Area-167	2,000	2,000
Rock Creek Marsh	435	435
Round Lake	0	430
Round Lake	393	393
Rush Lake	331	331
Rush Lake	522	522
Sabula Access	498	498
Schwob Marsh	265	265

State and Unit	Acres Open to Hunting	Total Acres
Silver Lake-168	132	1,103
Silver Lake	82	684
Silver Lake	338	338
Silver Lake Marsh	109	109
Smiths Slough	291	291
Snake Creek Marsh	240	240
Snyder Bend	0	500
Soldier Bend	350	350
South Twin Lake	150	400
Spirit Lake-169	682	5,684
Spring Run	753	753
State Line Marsh	147	147
Storm Lake-170	250	3,097
Sunken Grove	371	371
Sunken Lake	62	62
Swan Lake	44	44
Swan Lake	380	380
Sweet Marsh-171	1,625	1,925
Tomahawk Marsh	40	40
Troy Mills	277	277
Trumbull Lake-172	1,224	1,224
Tuttle Lake	118	981
Tuttle Lake Marsh	160	160
Twelvemile Lake	290	290
Upper Gar Lake	5	43
Ventura Marsh	752	752
Virgin Lake	25	225
Wapti Marsh	80	80
Weise Slough-173	1,550	1,550
West Okoboji-174	473	3,939
West Swan Lake-175	1,043	1,043
West Twin Lake	0	109
Willow Slough	599	599
Yager Slough	56	56
Total	94,978	136,639
KENTUCKY		
Ballard County-176	6,873	8,373
Barkley Lake-177	1,923	5,429 *a*
Barren River (Goose Island)	0	67 *a*
Henderson Sloughs-178	1,109	2,555
Kentucky Lake-179	3,274	3,274 *a*
Peal Tract-180	1,821	1,821
West Kentucky, area 6-181	1,200	1,200 *a*
Winford	237	237
Total	16,437	22,956
LOUISIANA		
Biloxi-182	39,583	39,583 *a*
Bohemia-183	33,000	33,000 *a*
Catahoula Lake-184	0	1,010
Marsh Island-185	0	78,000
Pass-a-Loutre-186	66,000	66,000
Pearl River-187	2,008	2,008
Point-au-Chien-188	28,243	28,243
Rockefeller-189	0	82,000
Salvador-190	27,498	27,498
State Wildlife-191	0	13,000
St. Tammany-192	0	1,300
Wisner-193	21,621	21,621 *a*
Total	217,953	393,263
MICHIGAN		
Au Train-194	4,985	4,985
Allegan-195	3,102	6,026
Baraga Plains-196	5,456	5,456
Baraga Plains-197	0	1,500
Betsie River	698	698
Crow Island-198	0	1,157
Erie-199	1,795	1,795
Fish Point-200	2,023	3,035
Grand Haven	913	913
Haymarsh-201	6,299	6,299
Lapeer-202	6,736	6,736
Leidy Lake	0	107
Little Bay De Noc	0	730
Long Lake	0	810
Manistee River-203	3,641	3,641
Maple River-204	5,880	5,880
Martiny Lake-205	3,467	3,467
Munuscong Bay-206	7,035	7,500
Muskegon-207	6,700	6,700
Nayanguing Point	678	882
Pentwater River	506	506
Pere Marquette	33	33
Pointe Mouillee-208	2,362	2,727
Quanicassee	217	217
Rush Lake	471	471
Shiawassee River-209	8,000	8,000
St. Clair Flats-210	6,614	6,614
Sturgeon River Sloughs-211	7,720	7,720
Tobico-212	704	1,694
Wigwam Bay	140	140
Wildfowl Bay-213	1,500	2,500
Total	87,675	98,939
MINNESOTA		
Carlos-Avery-214	18,750	22,750
Hubbel Pond-215	1,576	2,156
Lac qui Parle-216	16,016	27,074
Roseau River-217	52,913	61,333
Talcot Lake-218	2,879	3,279
Thief Lake-219	28,331	33,772
County *n*		
Aitkin-220	35,590	35,590
Anoka	360	360
Becker-221	3,140	3,104
Beltrami-222	1,164	1,164
Benton	990	990
Big Stone-223	2,085	2,203
Blue Earth	710	710
Brown-224	1,541	1,541
Carlton-225	1,480	1,480
Carver	270	270
Cass-226	18,611	18,611
Chippewa-227	1,464	1,464
Clay-228	4,213	4,213

State and Unit	Acres Open to Hunting	Total Acres
Clearwater-229	3,357	3,357
Cottonwood-230	1,941	1,941
Crow Wing-231	2,471	2,471
Dakota-232	1,966	1,966
Dodge	80	80
Douglas-233	3,672	3,672
Faribault-234	1,817	1,817
Freeborn	224	224
Goodhue-235	4,256	4,256
Grant-236	1,957	1,957
Hennepin	51	51
Hubbard	725	725
Isanti-237	3,360	3,360
Itasca-238	4,960	4,960
Jackson-239	2,731	2,731
Kanabec-240	3,421	3,421
Kandiyohi-241	2,737	2,737
Kittson-242	28,878	28,878
Lac qui Parle-243	5,430	5,430
Lake of the Woods	681	681
Le Sueur-244	1,970	1,970
Lincoln-245	4,647	4,647
Lyon-246	6,922	6,922
McLeod-247	1,572	1,572
Mahnomen-248	9,132	9,132
Marshall-249	32,531	32,531
Martin-250	1,255	1,255
Meeker-251	1,180	1,180
Mille Lacs-252	2,152	2,152
Morrison-253	3,394	3,394
Mower	553	553
Murray-254	5,530	5,530
Nicollet	113	113
Nobles-255	1,418	1,418
Norman-256	4,537	4,537
Olmstead	741	741
Ottertail-257	8,020	8,850
Pennington-258	1,259	1,259
Pine-259	2,109	2,109
Pipestone-260	1,411	1,411
Polk-261	11,095	11,095
Pope-262	2,664	2,664
Red Lake	505	505
Redwood-263	2,900	2,900
Renville	177	177
Rice	995	995
Roseau	354	354
St. Louis-264	1,940	1,940
Scott	482	482
Sherburne	988	988
Sibley	510	510
Stearns-265	1,629	1,629
Steele	798	798
Stevens-266	1,928	1,928
Swift-267	3,599	3,599
Todd-268	5,434	5,434
Traverse-269	1,056	1,056
Wabasha-270	1,219	1,219
Wadena-271	1,077	1,077
Waseca-272	1,613	1,613
Watonwan	880	880
Wilkin-273	3,472	3,512
Wright-274	3,199	3,199
Yellow Medicine-275	3,433	3,433
Total	409,155	440,042 *o*
MISSISSIPPI		
Arkabutla-276	0	2,200 *a*
Grenada-277	0	2,750 *a*
Indian Bayou	500	500 *d*
Leflore	350	350 *d*
Malmaison	750	850
Okatibbee	500	600 *a*
O'Keefe-278	1,050	1,050 *d*
Pearl River-279	500	1,700 *d*
Sardis-280	0	1,800 *a*
Sunflower-281	1,700	1,700 *a*
Yellow Creek	0	250 *a*
Total	5,350	13,750
MISSOURI		
Ben Cash	982	982
Bradyville	287	287
Duck Creek-282	2,453	6,034
Fountain Grove-283	1,870	5,451
Missouri River Refuge-284	0	1,000
Montrose-285	850	3,060 *a*
Rhineland-Morrison Refuge-286	0	1,600
Schell-Osage-287	1,600	8,633
Ted Shanks-288	3,000	6,123
Ted Shanks-288	0	2,300 *a*
Thurnau	366	366
Trimble-289	797	1,197
Upper Mississippi-290	8,784	11,311 *a*
Voelkerding Refuge	0	800
Total	20,989	49,144
OHIO		
Killdeer Plains Wildlife Area-291	6,350	8,162
Little Portage	0	357
Magee Marsh-292	0	2,132
Metzger Marsh	0	558
Mosquito Creek-293	0	5,814
Total	6,350	17,023
TENNESSEE		
Barkley-294	3,609	3,609 *a*
Cheatham Reservoir-295	2,100	2,900 *a*
Chickamauga Reservoir-296	5,163	8,163 *a*
Douglas Reservoir-297	578	1,263 *a*
Gooch-298	6,180	6,480
Kentucky Lake-299	7,605	7,605 *a*
Moss Island-300	1,400	3,400
Old Hickory Reservoir-301	3,425	3,925 *a*
Reelfoot-302	13,900	13,900
Tigrett-303	3,900	3,900

State and Unit	Acres Open to Hunting	Total Acres
Watts Bar Reservoir-304	141	2,391 *a*
Woods Reservoir-305	3,395	4,395 *a*
Total	51,396	61,931
WISCONSIN		
Amsterdam Slough-306	5,140	5,140
Avoca-307	3,615	3,615
Bakkens Pond-308	1,930	1,930
Bayfield County-309	1,267	1,267
Bear Lake	262	262
Big Island	960	960
Blue River-310	4,003	4,003
Bog Brook	266	266
Bong-311	4,568	4,568
Brillion-312	4,099	4,099
Brown County	403	553
Charles Pond	108	108
Clam Lake	26	26
Collins Marsh-314	3,935	3,935
Columbia County-315	1,464	1,464
Crex Meadows-316	24,023	26,323
Dane County-317	1,384	1,384
Dewey Marsh-318	4,200	4,200
Dunn County	764	764
Dunnville-319	2,067	2,067
Eldorado-320	4,968	5,968
Fish Lake-321	12,961	12,961
French Creek-322	2,725	2,725
Gardener Swamp	992	992
Germania Marsh-323	2,331	2,331
Grand River Marsh-324	3,675	7,075
Grant County-325	1,813	1,813
Horicon Marsh-326	8,762	10,962
Jackson Marsh-327	1,449	1,449
Jefferson County-328	1,433	1,433
Kiel Marsh	808	808
Kiezer Lake-329	1,352	1,352
Killsnake Creek-330	2,740	2,740
Knapp Creek-331	1,855	1,855
Lake Noquebay-332	1,300	1,300
Liberty Creek	505	505
Little Rice-333	1,757	1,757
Lone Rock	867	867
Loon Lake-334	1,774	1,774
Mazomanie-335	2,751	2,751
McMillan Marsh-336	4,032	4,032
McMillan Marsh-336	942	1,642 *e*
Mead-338	25,043	26,948
Meadow Valley-339	40	40
Meadow Valley-339	55,440	56,440 *a*
Mud Lake (Columbia County)-340	1,846	1,846
Mud Lake (Dodge County)-341	4,244	4,244
Mud Lake (Door County)-342	1,680	1,680
Mukwa-343	1,291	1,291
Mullet Creek-344	1,474	1,774
Navarino Marsh-345	12,672	13,172
New Auburn-346	1,028	1,028
North Bend	906	906
Outagamie County	590	690
Parker Creek	219	219
Peat Lake	171	171
Pensaukee Marsh	365	365
Pershing-347	6,672	7,072
Peshtigo Harbor-348	2,718	3,318
Pierce County Islands	453	453
Pine Island-349	3,304	4,504
Powell Marsh-350	4,096	4,096
Poygan Marsh-351	2,110	2,260
Price County-352	1,076	1,076
Princess Point-353	1,281	1,281
Quadered Creek	350	350
Rat River-354	2,934	2,934
Richland-355	1,395	1,395
Richwood-356	1,192	1,192
Rome Pond-357	1,938	1,938
Rusk County-358	1,753	1,753
Sandhill-359	9,455	9,455
Sawyer County	873	873
Seagull Bar	90	90
Shaw Marsh	738	738
Sheboygan Marsh-360	0	1,740
Sheboygan Marsh-360	0	160 *e*
Spoehr's Marsh	307	307
St. Croix Islands	815	815
Storr's Lake	632	632
Swan Lake-361	1,319	1,319
Sweeny Pond Creek	281	281
Theresa-362	2,953	5,283
Thunder Lake-363	2,070	2,070
Tichigan-364	1,207	1,207
Tiffany-365	10,197	10,197
Totagatic River-366	2,719	2,719
Turtle Creek	963	963
Van Loon-367	3,173	3,173
Vernon-368	3,122	3,122
Wauzeka-369	2,391	2,391
Westford	462	462
White River Marsh-370	10,105	10,105
Wolf River-371	4,224	4,424
Wood County	959	959
Wood County-372	18,344	18,344 *e*
Woods Flowage-373	1,152	1,152
Total	343,108	363,443
Subtotal - MISSISSIPPI FLYWAY	1,564,678	2,003,981
CENTRAL FLYWAY		
COLORADO		
Atwood Property	806	806
Baller Property	160	160
Banner Lakes Management	934	934
Empire Reservoir	538	538
Ft. Lyon Property	563	563
Holyoke	160	160

State and Unit	Acres Open to Hunting	Total Acres
Isolated BLM tracts	436	436
Lamar Management Area-374	1,175	1,175
Lowery Exchange	96	96
Means Recreation Area	69	69
Murphy Property	15	15
North Sterling Reservoir	230	230
Poley Management Area	5	5
Rio Grande Management Area	935	935
Sand Draw	209	209
Sedgwick Bar	157	157
Smith Property	642	642
South Platte Easement-375	5,788	5,788
South Republican Management	952	952
State School Land	640	640
Tamarack Ranch-376	10,527	10,527
Two Buttes Management Area-377	4,962	4,962
Wellington Management Area-378	1,340	1,340
1-Lo (Lennartz)	10	10
1-MO (Boyd)	177	177
1-We (Brower)	20	20
2-Lo (Skaggs)	11	11
2-We (Mitani)	14	14
Total	31,571	31,571
KANSAS		
Cheyenne Bottoms-379	12,090	19,840
Jamestown-380	1,626	2,728
Marais des Cygnes-381	4,838	7,110
Neosho-382	2,016	2,976
Total	20,570	32,654
MONTANA		
Canyon Ferry-383	5,000	5,000 *a*
Clark Canyon-384	1,200	1,200 *a*
Fox Lake-385	1,362	1,362
Freezeout Lake-386	8,500	11,506
Helena Valley Reservoir	0	518
Milk River-387	2,047	2,047
Ninepipe-388	2,755	2,755
Pablo	387	387
Tiber Reservoir-389	19,485	19,485 *a*
Total	40,736	44,260
NEBRASKA		
American Game Assoc. Marsh	160	160
Ballards Marsh-390	1,560	1,560
Bazile Creek-391	4,500	4,500 *a*
Big Alkali	890	890
Branched Oak Reservoir-392	5,000	5,600 *a*
Burchard Lake	0	560
Clear Creek	3,500	6,000
Conestoga Lake-393	0	716 *h*
Enders Reservoir-394	2,300	4,177 *a*
Hedgefield Lake	115	115
Killdeer Lake	90	90
Minatare Lake-395	0	2,970
Northeast Sacramento	40	40
Ogallala Strip	294	294
Plattsmouth Game Management Area-396	500	1,310
Sacramento-Wilcox-397	1,583	2,313
Smartweed Marsh	80	80
Smith Lake	640	640
South Levin Lake	160	160
Southeast Sacramento	175	175
South Sacramento	167	167
Stagecoach Lake	600	600 *h*
Twin Lakes-398	0	1,270 *h*
Wagontrain Lake-399	1,035	1,035 *h*
Walgren Lake	0	130
West Sacramento	320	320
Total	23,709	35,872
NEW MEXICO		
Artesia	0	480
Belen	230	230
Bernardo-400	600	1,600
Clayton Lake	403	403
Jackson Lake-401	500	1,240 *p*
La Joya-402	2,500	3,531
Miller Mesa-403	0	1,034
San Simon	0	40
Wagon Mound	735	735
Total	4,968	9,293
NORTH DAKOTA		
Arena	800	800
Ashley	80	80
Audubon (Snake Creek)-404	11,285	11,285 *a*
Black Swan	855	855
Blue Lake	13	13
Blue Ridge	240	240
Buffalo Lake	856	856 *h*
Bunker Lake	161	161
Camp Lake	799	799
Cedar Lake	178	818
Charles C. Cook	324	324
Chase Lake	116	116
Crary	315	315
Crete Slough	151	151
de Trobriand-405	1,229	1,229 *a*
Englevale Slough	0	160
Frettim Township	80	80
Fullers Lake	720	720
Golden Lake	579	579
Grant Township	160	160
Green Lake	101	101
Heffner Lake	277	277
Hyatt Slough-406	1,354	1,354
Karl T. Frederick	400	400
Kisselberry	120	120
Knox Slough	518	518
Koldak	214	214
Lake Legreid	200	200
Lake Patricia	0	631

State and Unit	Acres Open to Hunting	Total Acres
Lake Washington	910	910
Leaf Mountain	160	160
Lehr	611	611
Logan County	598	598
McIntosh County	80	80
McKenzie Slough	682	682
McPhail	170	170
McVille	244	244
Meszaros Slough	598	598
Minnewaukan	160	160
Mud Lake	351	351
North Salt Lake	95	95
Overbeck Slough	320	320
Palermo	40	40
Pelican Township	60	60
Rab Lake	22	22
Ray Holland	201	201
Rice Lake	976	976 *e*
Rusten Slough	160	160
Seth Gordon Marsh	482	482
Sibley Lake	103	103
Stack Slough	597	597
Taayer Lake	80	80
Tewaukon-407	1,208	1,208
Upham	78	78
Valley City	200	799 *h*
Wakopa-408	5,228	5,228
Wild Rice-409	2,089	2,089
Wolf Creek-410	4,180	4,180 *a*
Total	42,808	44,838
OKLAHOMA		
Fort Gibson	17,465	21,465 *a*
Hulah	8,778	10,578 *a*
Lake Carl Etling	0	440
Oolagah	10,441	12,941 *a*
Wister	15,996	17,996 *a*
Total	52,680	63,420
SOUTH DAKOTA *q*		
(County/Area Name)		
Aurora	1,812	1,812
Beadle	1,317	1,317
Bon Homme	152	152
Brookings	1,600	1,600
Brown	2,875	2,875
Brown-Renziehausen Slough	1,160	1,160
Brown-Zabraska	1,120	1,120
Brule	107	107
Brule-Boyer Area	1,392	1,392
Brule-Brule Bottom	1,700	1,700
Butte	800	800
Campbell	1,415	1,415
Charles Mix	2,797	2,797
Charles Mix-Gray Area	1,973	1,973
Clark	4,582	4,582
Clark-Dry Lake #2	3,459	3,459
Clark-Swan Lake	1,078	1,078
Clay	90	90
Codington	4,908	4,908

State and Unit	Acres Open to Hunting	Total Acres
Codington-Goose Lake	1,206	1,206
Davison	170	170
Day	5,661	5,661
Day-Bitter Lake	2,748	2,748
Day-Mydland Pass	1,470	1,470
Deuel	3,143	3,143
Deuel-Round and Bullhead Lakes	1,082	1,082
Dewey	720	720
Dewey-Moreau Refuge	3,040	3,040
Edmunds	787	787
Fall River	713	713
Faulk	2,233	2,233
Grant	996	996
Gregory-Buryanek	3,639	3,639
Hamlin	3,510	3,510
Hamlin-Sioux Poinsett	1,805	1,805
Hand	2,819	2,819
Hand-Lake Louise	1,280	1,280
Hanson	232	232
Hughes	557	557
Hutchingson	379	379
Hyde	516	516
Jerauld-443	1,256	1,256
Kingsbury-444	1,166	1,166
Lake-445	2,683	2,683
Lawrence-446	1,080	1,080
Lincoln	122	122
Lyman	528	528
Lyman-Carpenter Area-447	1,209	1,209
Lyman-Kiowa-448	1,810	1,810
McCook-449	1,003	1,003
McCook-East Vermillion Lake-450	1,713	1,713
McPherson-451	3,044	3,044
Marshall-452	5,346	5,346
Marshall-Bonham Area-453	1,040	1,040
Marshall-Cattail-454	1,490	1,490
Marshall-Four Mile Lake-455	1,280	1,280
Marshall-West Roy Lake-456	2,035	2,035
Meade	600	600
Miner-457	2,233	2,233
Minnehaha-458	1,906	1,906
Moody	350	350
Pennington	200	200
Potter	40	40
Roberts-459	2,782	2,782
Roberts-White Rock-460	1,828	1,828
Sanborn	570	570
Sanborn-Rifle-Calahan Lake-461	1,536	1,536
Spink-462	2,010	2,010
Stanley	107	107
Sully-463	2,258	2,258
Tripp-464	1,158	1,158
Turner	892	892
Walworth-465	1,360	1,360
Yankton-466	1,137	1,137
Total	120,815	120,815

State and Unit	Acres Open to Hunting	Total Acres
TEXAS		
Angelina-Neches Scientific Area Number One-467	4,042	4,042
Gambill	0	674 *e*
Pat Mayse-468	1,500	8,925 *a*
J.D. Murphree-469	4,000	8,408
Sheldon-470	0	2,503
Toledo Bend Reservoir-471	0	3,600 *r*
Total	9,542	28,152
WYOMING		
Ocean Lake-472	13,093	13,093
Springer-473	1,571	1,571
Table Mountain-474	1,736	1,736
Yellowtail-475	19,424	19,424
Total	35,824	35,824
Subtotal - CENTRAL FLYWAY	383,223	446,699
PACIFIC FLYWAY		
ARIZONA		
Arlington	160	160
Chevelon	428	668
Cibola-476	1,287	1,287
Robbins Butte	320	320
Topock	320	320
Wilcox Playa	120	440
Total	2,635	3,195
CALIFORNIA		
Honey Lake-477	4,800	4,981
Gray Lodge-478	6,000	8,375
Imperial-479	6,700	7,826
Joice and Grizzly Islands-480	6,800	10,487
Los Banos-481	2,700	3,208
Lower Sherman Island-482	3,100	3,100
Mendota-483	7,900	9,444
Napa Marshes-484	5,000	5,000 *a*
Volta-485	2,200	2,700 *a*
Total	45,200	55,121
IDAHO		
Boundary County-486	900	1,211
Carey Lake	751	751
C.J. Strike-487	7,216	7,216
Coeur d'Alene River-488	4,694	4,694
Ft. Boise-489	1,389	1,389
Hagerman-490	752	1,152
Market Lake-491	5,763	6,168
Mud Lake-492	8,571	8,571
Sterling-493	1,797	1,797
Total	31,833	32,949

State and Unit	Acres Open to Hunting	Total Acres
NEVADA		
Alkali Lake-494	3,448	3,448 *h*
Fernley-495	13,645	13,645 *s*
Humboldt-496	36,235	36,235 *i*
Key Pittman-497	1,332	1,332
Mason Valley-498	12,031	12,031
Overton-499	11,527	12,727 *h*
Railroad Valley-500	14,720	14,720 *h*
Scripps-501	2,674	2,674
Stillwater-502	119,663	143,866 *h*
Wayne E. Kirch-503	13,956	15,456 *h*
Total	229,231	256,134
OREGON		
Camas Swale-504	2,522	2,522
Fern Ridge-505	3,973	3,973
Irrigon	505	505 *a*
Klamath-506	6,448	6,458
Ladd Marsh-507	2,098	2,418
Sauvie Island-508	7,861	11,434
Summer Lake-509	8,783	18,065
Willow Creek-510	1,151	1,151 *a*
Total	33,341	46,526
UTAH		
Bicknell-511	1,200	1,200
Browns Park-512	1,774	1,814
Clear Lake-513	6,075	6,150
Desert Lake-514	2,411	2,621
Farmington Bay-515	8,095	8,725
Harold Crane-516	5,100	5,100
Howard Slough-517	2,820	2,820
Locomotive-518	12,000	12,000
Ogden Bay-519	15,780	16,680
Olsen Slough	25	25
Powell Slough	631	631
Public Shooting Grounds-520	11,300	11,755
Rock Island	2	2
Salt Creek-521	2,785	2,850
Salt Creek (Chambers Addition)-522	1,734	1,734
Stewart Lake	635	635
Timpie Springs-523	1,440	1,440
Topaz	700	700
Total	74,507	76,902
WASHINGTON		
Banks Lake-524	44,702	44,702
Crab Creek-525	17,005	17,005
Desert-526	26,840	26,840
Gloyd Seeps-527	7,107	7,107
Johns River-528	1,230	1,230
Lake Terrell-529	1,051	1,051
Lenore Lake-530	8,941	8,941
McNary-531	9,497	9,497
Nisqually	651	651

State and Unit	Acres Open to Hunting	Total Acres
Oyhut	682	682
Potholes-532	38,588	38,588
Priest Rapids-533	2,501	2,501
Quincy-534	12,759	12,759
Scatter Creek	852	852
Shillapoo (Vancouver Lake)-535	1,456	1,456
Long Lake (Stratford)-536	6,020	6,020
Skagit-537	12,751	12,751
Stillwater	433	433
Sunnyside-538	1,684	1,684
Winchester Wasteway-539	1,920	1,920
Wahluke Slope-540	57,838	57,838
Total	254,508	254,508
Subtotal - PACIFIC FLYWAY	671,255	725,335
GRAND TOTAL - CONTIGUOUS STATES	4,483,923	5,133,153

a Owned by the federal government and managed for waterfowl by the state under a lease or agreement.

b State-owned and private areas used for waterfowl hunting but not managed for waterfowl.

c WMA—wildlife management area.

d Owned by a state agency other than the department primarily concerned with natural resources and leased to the natural resources agency for waterfowl management.

e Owned by a local unit of government and managed for waterfowl by the state under a lease or agreement.

f Acres of waterfowl habitat; there are additional acres in the total area.

g Total area will eventually exceed 5,000 acres.

h Area under joint state and federal ownership and managed for waterfowl by the state under a lease or agreement.

i Area under joint state and private ownership and managed for waterfowl by the state under a lease or agreement.

j Owned by a local unit of government and the federal government and managed for waterfowl by the state under a lease or agreement.

k Part of area closed to hunting.

m Area under joint federal and private ownership and managed for waterfowl by the state under a lease or agreement.

n Total acres in each county.

o A total of 7,644 acres included in this total are licensed from the federal government.

p Land not owned by the natural resources department is owned by another state agency and leased to the natural resources department for waterfowl management.

q Only areas of 1,000 acres or more are listed separately for South Dakota. There are 268 state-owned waterfowl areas in South Dakota managed primarily for waterfowl and 128 secondary areas for waterfowl.

r Area leased or licensed by the state in cooperation with a nonstate agency.

s Under joint state, federal, and private ownership and managed for waterfowl by the state under a lease or agreement.

Table 4. Areas of substantial benefits to waterfowl in Canada and the continental United States that are under provincial, state, or federal ownership or control, or both, as of June 30, 1974. ***a***

Category of Unit and Country	Total Number of Units	Total Acres
UNITED STATES		
Federal		
National Wildlife Refuges	282 *b*	4,509,670.1
Waterfowl Production Areas	116	1,370,766.2
State *c*	2,022 *d*	5,130,153
Subtotal	2,420	11,010,589.3
Alaska		
Federal	8	6,854,700
State *e*	5	657,958
Subtotal	13	7,512,658
Total - United States	2,433	18,523,247.3

Category of Unit and Country	Total Number of Units	Total Acres
CANADA		
Federal	21	47,902 *f*
Provincial	128	2,701,239
Total - Canada	149	2,749,141

a Summary of Tables 1-3 and 5-8.

b Includes one national antelope refuge, one national elk refuge, one migratory bird refuge, and one fish and wildlife refuge.

c Excluding Alaska.

d Only the major areas and total acres for each county are listed for Minnesota and South Dakota.

e Excluding tidelands; see Table 8.

f Excluding more than 27 million acres of federal Crown lands in the Northwest Territories established as migratory bird sanctuaries (Table 5).

Table 5. National wildlife areas in Canada acquired primarily to conserve waterfowl habitat, acquired or under negotiation January 1, 1975. (Data courtesy of the Canadian Wildlife Service.)

Province and Unit	Total Acres *a*
ALBERTA	
Blue Quills *b*	240
BRITISH COLUMBIA	
Alaksen	669
Vaseux-Bighorn-255	2,800
Wilmer Marsh	933
Total	4,402
MANITOBA	
Pope Reservoir	77
NOVA SCOTIA	
Chignecto-258	2,500
Sand Pond-259	1,289
Wallace Bay-260	1,500
Total	5,289
NEW BRUNSWICK	
Portage Island-261	1,114
Shepody-262	1,500
Tintamarre Marsh-263	3,800
Total	6,414
ONTARIO	
Big Creek-264	1,450 *c*
Dover Marsh	620
Hahn Marsh	402
Mississippi Lake	580 *c*
Total	3,052
QUEBEC	
Cap Tourmente-268	5,256
Iles de la Paix	300 *c*
Lac St. Francois-270	5,471
Total	11,027
SASKATCHEWAN	
Last Mountain Lake-271	14,000 *d*
Stalwart-272	2,520
Tway Lake	881
Total	17,401
GRAND TOTAL	47,902

a Not included in this table are approximately 27,400,000 acres of land and water in migratory bird sanctuaries established on Crown lands, mostly in the Northwest Territories but small acreages in Quebec and Ontario.

b Numbers indicate locations of areas of 1,000 acres or more shown in figure 5-1.

c Area closed to hunting.

d Area partially closed to hunting.

Table 6. Waterfowl habitat under provincial ownership and management as of January 1, 1975, Canada.

Province and Unit	Acres Open to Hunting	Total Acres
BRITISH COLUMBIA		
Bearskin Bay	700	700
Boundary Bay-275	20,000	20,000
Columbia River Floodlands-276	60,000	60,000
Creston Valley WMA-[a] 277	16,000	16,000
Duck and Barber Islands	600	600
Cecil Lake	80	80
Elizabeth Lake	227	227
George C. Reifel Waterfowl Refuge-281	0	3,500
Goose Island Group-282	3,000	3,000
Green River	42	42
Haden Harbour	800	800
Hansen Lagoon	700	700
Hominka River-285	35,000	35,000
Horse Lake	640	640
Kutzey Mateen Inlet	640	640
Ladner Marsh	90	90
Lanz and Cox Islands-288	0	2,560
Larsen and Alkali Lakes	300	300
Little White Lake	640	640
Loch Lomond	0	225
McGillivray Creek Reserve	320	320
Moberly Marsh	0	30
Nikomekl River	200	200
Oyster River	73	73
Pitt Polder	660	660
Roberts Bank-299	27,200	27,200
Robert W. Starratt Wildlife Sanctuary	0	500
Salmon Arm Foreshore	140	140
Salmon Arm Sanctuary	0	50
Sea Otter Cove	240	240
Serpentine River	200	200
Serpentine WMA	0	240
St. Mary's, Reed, McGinty, and Saugum Lakes-306	1,400	1,400
Stum (Pelican) Lake	250	250
Stum Lake Pelican Sanctuary-308	4,800	4,800
Sturgeon Bank-309	30,000	30,000
Swan Lake-310	0	1,000
Tofino-311	8,700	8,700
Tunkwa Lake Island	0	10
Wasa Lake	0	80
Watun River Foreshore	40	40
Westham Island Foreshore-315	1,000	1,000
Woodward Island	350	350
Subtotal	215,032	223,227
QUEBEC		
Boucherville-317	200	200
Thurso-318	260	260
Subtotal	460	460

Province and Unit	Acres Open to Hunting	Total Acres
MANITOBA		
Alfred Hole Goose Sanctuary-319	0	2,560
Big Grass Marsh GBR-[b] 320	0	1,600
Big Point PSG [c]-321	8,392	8,392
Cape Tatnam WMA-322	1,290,000	1,290,000
Delta PSG-323	19,200	19,200
Delta GBR-324	0	2,535
Dog Lake Islands GBR-325	0	1,440
Dog Lake WMA-326	80,000	80,000
Fort Whyte GBR-327	0	2,304
Grant's Lake GBR-328	0	900
Gypsumville WMA-329	6,400	6,400
Jackfish Lake GBR-330	0	3,120
Langruth WMA-331	4,400	4,400
Lee Lake GBR-332	0	3,840
Lee Lake WMA-333	12,800	12,800
Lynch Point GBR-334	0	640
Maple Lake PSG-335	160	160
Marshy Point PSG-336	5,590	5,590
Marshy Point GBR-337	0	960
Marshy Point Goose Refuge-338	0	6,344
Minnedosa Lake Wildlife Refuge-339	0	1,280
Netley PSG-340	44,140	44,140
Netley Marsh GBR-341	0	2,650
Oak Hammock WMA-342	0	8,136
Oak Lake PSG-343	3,158	3,158
Oak Lake GBR-344	0	5,500
Oak Lake Special Canada Goose Refuge-345	0	15,334
Pelican Lake PSG-346	6,150	6,150
Point du Bois GBR-347	0	960
Red Deer Point GBR-348	0	22,270
Reykjavik GBR-349	0	4,960
Rock Lake GBR-350	0	4,550
Sleeve Lake GBR-351	0	9,060
Spruce Woods Wildlife Refuge-352	0	21,410
St. Ambroise GBR-353	0	885
Swan Lake GBR-354	0	23,040
Tom Lamb WMA-355	538,360	538,360
Waterhen PSG-356	35,700	35,700
West Shoal Lake GBR-357	0	19,420
Whiteshell GBR-358	0	159,365
Whitewater PSG-359	4,182	4,182
Whitewater WMA-360	22,182	22,182
Subtotal	2,080,814	2,405,877
NEW BRUNSWICK	0	0
NEWFOUNDLAND AND LABRADOR	0	0
NORTHWEST TERRITORIES	0	0

Province and Unit	Acres Open to Hunting	Total Acres
NOVA SCOTIA		
Antigonish Harbour-361	0	150
Beaver Dam Meadows-362	171	171
Blanford-363	0	550
Brule Point-364	0	200
Chebogue Meadows-365	182	182
Debert-366	0	665
Hacmatac Lake-367	0	85
Maccan Marshes-368	82	82
Martinique Beach-369	0	760
Melbourne Lake-370	0	60
Missaquash Marsh-371	6,000	6,000
Round Lake-372	0	240
St. Andrews-373	0	300
Subtotal	6,435	9,445
ONTARIO		
Aylmer Airport-374	0	455
Aylmer Pond-375	106	106
Calton Swamp-376	60	60
Camden Lake-377	490	1,700
Darlington-378	100	100
Fingal-379	680	780
Holiday Beach-380	250	489
Holland Marsh-381	1,300	1,300
Hullett Marsh-382	4,600	4,600
Long Point-383	1,450	1,750
Luther Marsh-384	8,500	11,000
Macgregor Point-385	500	500
Nonquon-386	2,650	2,650
Presqu'ile-387	1,170	2,170
Rankin-388	3,600	3,800
Rondeau-389	9,000	9,200
Tiny Marsh-390	1,900	2,300
Winchester-391	3,600	3,600
Wye Marsh-392	1,700	2,400
Subtotal	41,656	48,960
PRINCE EDWARD ISLAND		
Dromore-393	500	500
Forest Hill-394	700	700
Indian River-395	0	74
Orwell Cove WMA-396	0	1,900
Subtotal	1,200	3,174
SASKATCHEWAN		
Eyebrow-397	0	320
Flat Lake-398	416	416
Nisku-399	5,760	5,760
Scentgrass and Moore Lake-400	1,200	3,000
Skinner's Marsh-401	600	600
Subtotal	7,976	10,096
YUKON TERRITORY	0	0
GRAND TOTAL	2,353,573	2,701,239

Note: In many provinces and territories much land is publicly owned. For example, more than 80 percent of Quebec is owned by the province; however, this table attempts to list only those areas acquired and managed for the benefit of waterfowl.

a WMA—wildlife management area.

b GBR—game bird refuge.

c PSG—public shooting grounds.

Table 7. Areas of substantial benefits to waterfowl under state or federal ownership or control in each flyway in the United States, as of June 30, 1974.

Flyway and Unit of Government	Acres Open to Hunting *a*	Total Acres
ATLANTIC		
Federal		
National Wildlife Refuges		1,294,656.0
Waterfowl Production Areas	1,068.2	1,068.2
State	1,864,767.0	1,957,138.0
Subtotal - ATLANTIC FLYWAY	1,865,835.2	3,252,862.2
MISSISSIPPI		
Federal		
National Wildlife Refuges		1,208,356.4
Waterfowl Production Areas	98,844.3	130,630.3
State	1,561,978.0	2,000,981.0
Subtotal - MISSISSIPPI FLYWAY	1,660,822.3	3,339,967.7

Flyway and Unit of Government	Acres Open to Hunting *a*	Total Acres
CENTRAL		
Federal		
National Wildlife Refuges		1,153,521.4
Waterfowl Production Areas	265,632.8	1,239.067.7
State	383,223.0	446,699.0
Subtotal - CENTRAL FLYWAY	648,855.8	2,839,288.1
PACIFIC		
Federal		
National Wildlife Refuges		853,136.3
State	671,255.0	725,335.0
Subtotal - PACIFIC FLYWAY	671,255.0	1,578,471.3
GRAND TOTAL	4,846,768.3	11,010,589.3

a Not including areas on National Wildlife Refuges.

Table 8. Areas in Alaska of substantial benefits to waterfowl that are under state or federal ownership or control.

Control and Name	Acres Open to Hunting	Total Acres
STATE *a, b*		
Copper River Delta-402 *c*	330,000	330,000
Creamers Dairy-403	1,768	1,768
Potters Marsh-404	3,800	4,200
Susitna Flats-405	304,890	304,890
Stikine River Delta-406	17,100	17,100
Subtotal	657,558	657,958
FEDERAL *d, e*		
Aleutian Islands National Wildlife Refuge-407	272,000	272,000 (10) *f*
Arctic National Wildlife Range-408	2,668,000	2,668,000 (30)
Clarence Rhode National Wildlife Range-409	2,887,000	2,887,000 (100)
Hazen Bay National Wildlife Refuge-410	6,800	6,800 (100)
Izembek National Wildlife Range-411	160,400	160,400 (50)
Kenai National Moose Range-412	346,000	346,000 (20)
Kodiak National Wildlife Refuge-413	181,500	181,500 (10)
Nunivak National Wildlife Refuge-414	333,000	333,000 (10)
Subtotal	6,854,700	6,854,700
GRAND TOTAL	7,512,258 *b*	7,512,658 *b*

a Information from the Alaska Department of Fish and Game. January 1975.

b There are also approximately 1,000,000 acres of tidelands—critical habitat areas designated to protect waterfowl values. Any use, lease or other disposal of these lands must be approved by the commissioner of the Department of Fish and Game. These state-owned lands are all open to hunting and are not managed.

c Numbers refer to locations in Figure 5-1.

d From U.S. Fish and Wildlife Service (1974).

e For these areas, only the acreages judged to be significant waterfowl habitat are listed.

f Number in parentheses is the approximate percentage of each area that is significant waterfowl habitat.

Index

C

Index

N

O

P

R

S